The Double Bond

The Double Bond

PRIMO LEVI • A BIOGRAPHY

Carole Angier

FARRAR, STRAUS AND GIROUX

NEW YORK

Farrar, Straus and Giroux
19 Union Square West, New York 10003

Copyright © 2002 by Carole Angier
All rights reserved
Distributed in Canada by Douglas & McIntyre Ltd.
Printed in the United States of America
Originally published in 2002 by the Viking Press, Great Britain
Published in the United States by Farrar, Straus and Giroux
First American edition, 2002

Illustration credits appear on pp. xi–xii.

ISBN: 0-374-11315-7
Library of Congress Control Number: 2002104433

www.fsgbooks.com

1 3 5 7 9 10 8 6 4 2

Contents

PART THREE

List of Illustrations

Illustration Acknowledgements

Frontispiece by permission of Giovanna Borgese; pages xxiii and 517, photo by the author; family tree (abridged) courtesy of Giovanni Levi; pages 1 and 37 courtesy of Silvio Ortona; page 5 courtesy of Silvio Ortona; page 8 courtesy of Gisella; page 25, photo by the author; page 56 courtesy of Vera Gay Marconi; page 68 courtesy of Pierluigi Olivetti (apart from Primo Levi and Mario Piacenza, identified on the page, Olivetti is the first on the left in the middle row, Vittorio Daneo fourth from left and Giorgio Lattes third from right in the same row, Ennio Artom third from left in the front row); page 106 by permission of Guido Salvini; page 112 courtesy of Emma Vita Levi; page 132, from the *Chronache di Milano*, 1943, by permission of Eugenio Gentili Tedeschi; page 138 courtesy of Ester Valabrega; page 151 courtesy of Nico Dallaporta; page 161, photo by the author; page 167 courtesy of Signora Mariotti; page 184 courtesy of Signora Mariotti; page 193, photo by Silvio Ortona (an occasion on which they were not turned away from the mountain, see pages 200–202); page 195 by permission of Eugenio Gentili Tedeschi; all drawings in Chapter 6 from the *Chronache di Milano*, 1943, and the *Libri segreti*, 1942 (Mussolini), by permission of Eugenio Gentili Tedeschi; all photographs in Chapter 6 by permission of Silvio Ortona; pages 203 and 214 also by Silvio Ortona; page 224 courtesy of Gabriella Garda Aliverti; page 230 from *Resistenza*, May 1963; page 237, photo by the author; page 247 courtesy of Carla Maestro and Luciana Nissim; page 262 by permission of the Museo Monumento al Deportato, Carpi; page 266 courtesy of Ulda Sacerdoti; page 271 courtesy of Paolo Dalla Volta; page 323 by permission of CDEC (the Fondazione Centro Documentazione Ebraica Contemporanea), Milan; page 324 courtesy of Emma Bard; page 328 courtesy of Jean Samuel; page 356 courtesy of Charles Conreau; page 368 by permission of Michael Joseph, London; page 386 courtesy of Lello Perugia; page 417 by permission of Stefano Levi Della Torre and the Holocaust Education Centre, Vancouver, Canada (from a photograph by Sergio Pancaldi, 1982); page 419, *If This is a Man* flyer issued by De Silva, 1947 (it reads: 'PRIMO LEVI has written this calm and dazzling account of the most tragic experience a man could have. / Is he still a man who, hour by hour and trial by trial, is stripped of the physical appearance of a man, and destroyed in his moral being? / That is the question which, amazed and bitter, PRIMO LEVI asks himself and the world: IF THIS IS A

MAN'); page 433, photo by the author; page 473 courtesy of Carla Maestro; page 476, from *Gente*, 20 September 1963; page 484 courtesy of Paola Accati; page 489, from *Gente*, 20 September 1963; page 506 courtesy of Gisella Vita Finzi; page 529 by permission of Jerry Bauer; page 535, photo by the author; page 553 courtesy of Orsola Azzario Ferrero (apart from Primo, Orsolina and Renato Portesi, identified on the page, the others are, from the left: *Back row*, Giuseppe Venezia, Aldo Nani, Andrea Carlino, Giuseppe Gilardi, Adolfo Arri; *Front row*, Giuseppe Cordua, Massimo Palazzoni); page 556, photo by the author; page 585, photo by the author; page 591 by permission of Rizzoli Corriere della Sera Periodici; page 633, photo by Silvio Ortona; page 635 courtesy of Elio Vitale; page 651 by permission of Graziano Arici; page 657 by permission of Corbis UK; page 671 courtesy of Philip Roth; page 675, photo by Silvio Ortona; page 697, *Ulysses' Return* by Giorgio De Chirico by permission of Galleria Nazionale d'Arte Moderna, Rome, and of the Ministero per i Beni e le Attivita Culturali and the Design and Artists Copyright Society Ltd; page 721, photo by the author.

Acknowledgements

I would have liked to thank all my interviewees by name, but that is impossible. Instead I thank them all collectively, but most sincerely, here.

Many others I thank in my Notes for their help in particular areas.

That still leaves many people to whom I owe a special debt of gratitude for helping me through the eight years of researching and writing this book.

First, for encouraging me and showing me the way, my friends and masters in biography, Michael Holroyd and Hilary Spurling, and my agent Gill Coleridge. For welcoming me into the world of Primo Levi readers, Paul Bailey, Robert Gordon, David Mendel and Anthony Rudolf. For financial support, the Winston Churchill Memorial Trust, for the Travelling Fellowship which took me to Turin; the Authors' Foundation and the Arts Council, for Writer's Grants; and the Royal Literary Fund, for my last three years as a Fellow and Associate Fellow at the University of Warwick. For typing the chapters I couldn't, starting with the ninth, Jane Bolton. For teaching me Italian, Isabella Hepton. For housing me, feeding me, and helping me to cope with life in Italy, Giuliana Tedeschi, Elena Vita Finzi, Carlo and Maria Lorenza Bertola, Stefania Bertetto and Michele Di Mauro, and Laura Fracchia of the Banca CRT, all in Turin; Antonio and Diana Chiesara in Milan; and Jane Armstrong in Rome.

For reading the book as I wrote it, and again when it was done, and for rescuing me from many stylistic quicksands, my first editor and friend Diana Athill, and Sue Steinberg, linguist, lexicographer and friend.

For editing my book with great skill and dedication, my editor at Viking, Mary Mount. For precious editorial support, Juliet Annan at Viking and Jonathan Galassi at Farrar, Straus and Giroux. And for saying that this book was the only one he could read in the weeks after September 11, Jonathan's fellow editor Lorin Stein.

Most importantly of all, my thanks go to those in Italy and elsewhere without whose extra help and support this book could not have been written.

Amongst the many libraries and institutions I consulted:

CDEC, Milan; the Centro Studi Piero Gobetti and the Istituto Storico della Resistenza in Piemonte, Turin, especially Carla Gobetti; the Einaudi Archive, especially Fulvio Barbarino; the Istituto Storico della Resistenza in Valle D'Aosta, especially Dr Paolo Momigliano; the Ginnasio-Liceo

Massimo D'Azeglio, especially its Headmaster, Professor Giovanni Ramella; the Registry Offices of Bene Vagienna, Fossano, Mondovì and Turin, especially Signora Maria Cristina Pittia of Bene and Dr Alessandro Bracco of Mondovì; the *La Stampa* Archive, especially Professor Italo Longhina; and the University of Turin Archive, especially Dottoressa Luisa Schiavone.

Amongst Primo Levi's friends and relations:

First and foremost, for their trust and friendship, Gisella, and Primo Levi's other two secret sharers, Gabriella Garda and Lilith.

Next, for everything, Primo Levi's oldest friends, Silvio Ortona and Eugenio Gentili Tedeschi, and Silvio's wife, Primo's cousin Ada Luzzati Ortona; Bianca Guidetti Serra; Alberto Salmoni; and Luciana Nissim, who sadly died in 1998.

Primo Levi's scholars and previous biographers, Alberto Cavaglion, Gabriella Poli and Giovanni Tesio; especially Gabriella Poli, for everything.

Primo Levi's past and present editors, Ernesto Ferrero and Marco Belpoliti; especially Ernesto Ferrero, for his friendship and support from the start.

And last but far from least:

Luciana, Luisa and Paola Accati, and Paola's secretary Ornella Tabone, for everything; Giorgina Arian Levi, for introducing me to Gabriella Garda and Jole Segre; Guido Bonfiglioli, for trying to save me from chemical errors; Edith Bruck, for her conversation and friendship; Maria Giulia Cardini, for introducing me to everyone in Orta; Giulia Colombo Diena, for her endless patience and friendship; Nico Dallaporta, for his conversation and friendship; Dr Michelangelo Fessia, for showing me around Bene; Dr Renata Gaddini, for her help in psychiatric matters, and for a holiday in Capri; Giovanni Levi, for his ideas and for his mother's family tree; Stefano Levi Della Torre, for his ideas and his painting; Felice Malgaroli, Ferruccio Maruffi and Renato Portesi, for their insights into Primo and their friendship; Jean Samuel, for everything; Vittorio Segre, for his conversation, and for lending me his De Silva edition of *If This is a Man*; Giuliana Tedeschi, for her insights and her friendship; Bruno Vasari, for his help and friendship; and Stuart Woolf, for his.

Also, and finally: Lucy Luck, for copying the whole book twice; and Valeria and Simonetta Steri of Turin, whom I have never met, but who found and returned my first taped interview, and so stopped me from giving up before I'd begun.

Preface

Primo Levi's most characteristic and unvarying trait was his reserve. It is in his books: in that just, detached narrative voice, whose most unbuttoned mood is quiet irony; in the narrator himself, on the rare occasions he appears, as confidant, adviser, assistant, peacemaker. We feel we know him – and love him – because we know every movement of his gentle, rigorous, open mind. But it is only his mind we know. He very rarely betrays his feelings, and almost never his negative feelings – that is the first and most important thing everyone notices in his great books about the Shoah. Except in *The Periodic Table*, he rarely tells us about himself at all. His great portraits are all of other people; even (and in this he was unique) in his reports from Auschwitz. When he came, rather late, to write about Jews, in *If Not Now, When?* (*If This is a Man* is not about Jews in particular, but about human beings), he chose Eastern European Ashkenazim, whom he had to study, rather than Western European Sephardim, of whom he was one. He explored himself through others, rather than others through himself – making him the opposite of most writers.

In life this great reserve of his was equally striking. Everyone spoke of it to me, from the merest acquaintance to the closest relative (or the closest relative who would speak to me). And most of them also shared it. Everyone in Turin does – if this is a stereotype, it's their own. 'Of course, we're not real Italians,' they say – and remind you of their French kings, their Protestant minority, their cold, wet, positively English weather. The rest of the country agrees, calling Turin '*il frigorifero d'Italia*', the refrigerator of Italy, and the Turinese '*pesci morti*', dead fish – like the 'cold fish' the English, again, are traditionally meant to be.

This was the first thing I learned about Primo Levi and his world – which was not very encouraging to a biographer. Italy in general is not very encouraging to a biographer. There is a high conception of intellectual endeavour, according to which an interest in the mere facts of someone's life is uncivilized, typical of a nation of shopkeepers. There is also a high concept of personal and family honour: confessions are for the confessional, and it is always a moral duty (not, at least sometimes, a moral failure) to cover up, to keep up appearances. But to this cultural and Catholic base the Turinese add their own puritan, their almost Victorian, reserve. Many things that even English people nowadays consider quite normal subjects of conversation – their health, for instance, or their safer and more distant family history – still seem to the Turinese vulgar gossip and invasion of privacy. It really is possible in polite Turin society to be reduced to talking about the weather.

Primo Levi was a Jew; so were – naturally – all his relatives, and many of his friends. But as one of them (a Jew) said to me, when Jews assimilate they become 110 per cent like their neighbours. And this being Italy, that doesn't mean like their fellow Italians, but like their fellow Romans, or Milanese, or Turinese. Roman Jews are more like Roman non-Jews than like other, non-Roman Jews; and the same is true of the Turinese. It is even truer of the Turinese, because Jews have played a bigger and prouder part in the history of Turin than of any other Italian city. In that great reserve of his, therefore – as in several other things – Primo Levi was being a typical, a conventional Turinese. And so were his friends and family.

Primo Levi himself almost never wrote or spoke publicly about his family. (There are a few allusions to his wife in his poetry and in *The Periodic Table*; almost none to his children in his writing, only one or two in interviews. About his father there are a few paragraphs in *The Periodic Table*, singling out some of his odder habits to celebrate amongst the ancestral eccentricities of 'Argon'; about his mother Levi never wrote a word, giving as his reason that she was still alive.)

In Turin I discovered that he almost never spoke about them either. And they, in turn, were extremely reserved about him to everyone, including me. His closest family – his wife Lucia, his sister and his children – did not speak to me at all.

There were many reasons for this, some of which I knew from the beginning. There was that high wall of reserve and family privacy, even higher in Turin than elsewhere. There was the tragedy of his death. There were too many inquirers – students, journalists, other biographers. Lucia Levi shut the door on all of us. She literally shut the door of Primo's study, deciding not to release his papers for many years. And she wrote to me, courteously but firmly, that she did not want to stop any book about her husband, but did not wish to contribute herself.

I realized from the start, of course, that this would be a very great obstacle: not just directly, closing to me the immediate family, and much of Levi's correspondence and unpublished papers; but also further afield, when people knew how his widow felt. What I didn't know was how powerful an obstacle it would be, in the small, tight, well-behaved world of Turin. And because of that, for a long time I also didn't know all its reasons.

There are others who remain silent too, but only as they do in all biographies: the dead. The most important witnesses are almost always dead long before the historians arrive – grandparents, parents, uncles and aunts; and several others almost always die just before. Two of Primo Levi's oldest friends, for instance, Giorgio Lattes and Livio Norzi, died before I could speak to them – Livio Norzi when I was already in Turin, in 1994.

But though a few important people have remained silent, others have spoken, and some of them only to me. A few of these have asked for anonymity. Others told me things in indirect ways – through novels they'd written, for example; or through encounters I had with them, beyond our ordinary interviews. Where I can, I tell Primo Levi's story straight. Where I cannot – because I cannot betray my sources, or because I have felt and imagined the past from a story, or from an encounter – I simply give you the story, or the encounter.

That is why this book is on two levels: a rationally tested, known or knowable one; and the other. Perhaps I needn't say that the felt and imagined level seems to me equally true, and even more important. But I would have liked to say so to Primo Levi. For these two, the rational and the irrational, were also his own two sides; but he chose to live in only one of them. And though this was the key to his achievement, it was also the key to his suffering. That is one of the main things I want to say: that Primo Levi chose to live in only the rational half of himself, and closed the door on the other. This was his armour, but also the gap in it.

In his own terms, he chose inorganic over organic chemistry for his emotional economy, very early on. Now the molecules of inorganic matter (I have learned from him) attach to each other at one point only, making long but stable chains. Organic molecules, by contrast, have a double bond: they attach to each other at two or even more points, making possible richer but also less stable combinations. In the last year of his life Primo Levi was trying to write a book to which he gave the title *The Double Bond*: a book, that is, which would fill the gap left by that long-ago decision. He didn't succeed. But that is the gap that my felt and imagined chapters try to inhabit. That is one reason why I have taken over his own title, like a torch from a previous runner.

Often, indeed, my irrational chapters seem to me *more* true than the rational ones, because they contain more of the truth about remembering and reconstructing the past (which was, of course, a central subject of Primo Levi's). The sense that there are thicker and thicker layers of time between ourselves and the person we want to remember, that it is harder and harder to reach him – this is one of the most poignant truths about any act of remembering, but one that biographies and histories exist to abolish. The more successful they are, the more they abolish it; which means (and not only here) that there may be more truth in failure.

The biographer, then, does not belong in a wholly rational biography. But I could belong in this one, in the irrational, imagined failures of it. That is another reason why I took Primo Levi's title: because this book is two biographies of him; it has two biographical bonds with him, a single, stable one, and the other.

★   ★

I have been suggesting that only the second, unstable biography is a failure, but of course both are. All biographies depend on who happens to be still alive and willing to speak, on who kept diaries, who burnt letters and who wrote them. All biographies are like archaeology, constructing whole civilizations on a few shards of pottery, changing millions of years of prehistory with every new skull or jawbone. And the first of my biographies, the stable one, is the more misleading here, because however certain I am that the line of enough evidence has been crossed, I may be wrong.

But you know all this. There are other books about Primo Levi, there will be many more books about Primo Levi; you can read them all, and read *him*, and make up your own mind. After all, learning about people from books is not very different from getting to know them in life. They tell you, and show you, about themselves, and you hear about them from family and friends and friends' friends, until you have a picture of them. This picture changes more or less slowly over the years, sometimes not at all – but sometimes suddenly, when you realize you were completely wrong, some vital piece of evidence was missing, and you never knew them at all. Getting to know someone from his biography is as provisional and unpredictable as that. But no more than that. Fortunately there is no precise and guaranteed way to know another person.

★   ★

In Italian, *Il doppio legame* has a double meaning: the double bond of organic chemistry, but also the 'double bind' of psychology. That is: a crippling conflict between contradictory or unfulfillable requirements, which you can neither escape nor win. Both these meanings are at the heart of this book. It aims, that is – like Levi's own last book – to be primarily personal and inward. To look at relatively private sides of him, such as his life in chemistry; and at very private sides of him, such as the hidden life of his psyche.

That came about for two reasons. First, because reserve intrigues, and extreme reserve intrigues extremely: his and everyone else's silence about his personal life only showed how important it must have been. And because, in the end, I did find witnesses to the secret side of him. They are secret witnesses — that is part of the problem I have already described. But what they told me was important; indeed it seemed to me a key to everything, his life, his writing and his death. Despite all my own double binds, therefore, I knew I had either to make it the heart of this book, or not write the book at all.

But that was the question — should I write the book at all? I had set out to write about Primo Levi, the great witness of *If This is a Man*, the great philosopher of *The Drowned and the Saved*: a rare and precious hakam or wise man of our disastrous age, admired and beloved by his readers, including me. Was it right to tear out of the shadows the man behind the hakam, behind the secular saint? Do we not need secular saints? Was it right towards his readers, was it right towards him?

The story I had to tell wasn't easy. It upset some of the clearer ideas of good and evil, some of the higher hopes of human nature that he'd helped us to hang on to, despite everything. It showed that his gentleness, justice and detachment were not so much moral or literary choices as his own psychological imperatives, modes of survival he'd chosen long before Auschwitz (though he'd often told us that himself). It showed something it seemed blasphemous to say — that though the experience of Auschwitz had hurt him in all its inhuman ways, it had also helped and strengthened him (but he had bravely said that too). It showed that he could never accept the dark, unconscious and animal sides of humanity or of himself; that he could only sustain his faith in life if he could believe in its rational correctability. This he did (on the whole) for many years; and it continued to produce great writing. But as he grew older it became less and less possible, both in the outer world of Cambodia, of Sabra and Chatila, of historical revisionism, and in the inner world of his own psyche. There, he had never resolved the hidden torment of his youth, in which the 'double bond' of life was also the 'double bind' of irresolvable conflict. The attempts he had made to resolve it had only, in the end, made it worse. At slowly diminishing intervals it rose up, and dragged him under.

If this was the story, should I tell it?

Since this is the preface to a book, you know that I answered yes. Because, of course, I think it's true. Because I think it illuminates his work and explains his death. Because his death had already suggested that everything was not what it seemed — and the interpretations that some people put on this were worse than the truth. Auschwitz did not 'kill him in the end'. His message to Alex the Kapo and his successors, that they failed to destroy him, is not affected by the manner of his death. They should not imagine they have that satisfaction.

I answered yes towards Primo Levi himself, despite his huge reserve, because his reserve was part of the problem. Because it was one of the prisons from which I wanted to release him; and *because he wanted to be released from them too*. From the prison of 'Holocaust writer', for example. If he were just a writer, the true story would seem less shocking; many writers are bad at life, it's part of what makes them good at writing. And Primo Levi wanted to be a writer, free from the impossible moral burdens of the hakam, the secular saint, the guru: 'I am not a guru,' he repeated many times in the last years of his life, 'I have no answers.'

He wanted to be free from the prison of his double bind too – above all from that one. In his last years he wrote *The Drowned and the Saved*, in which he entered the 'grey zone' of human nature he had only sketched in *If This is a Man*; in interviews he talked about not being the *uomo equilibrato*, the serene and balanced man he seemed, of having troubles, of having depressions. And in his final work, *Il doppio legame*, he tried at last to explore and to heal his divisions. It was too late; the fears of a lifetime were too strong. But what he himself began it cannot be wrong to continue.

Finally, I also answered yes towards his readers. Because we can and should have a truer view of his whole humanity, and still love and admire him for the hakam he was. For of course I don't want to show in this Life that Primo Levi was *not* a hakam. He was. He gave us a true picture of the best of human nature, through his writing (until *The Drowned and the Saved*) and in himself (always); and we need to remember it, especially today. But I do want to show what being a hakam cost him: what he had already had to pay by the age of twenty-four, to be able to write his first great book, and what he went on paying after. *Not* mostly (as I've said) because of Auschwitz: Auschwitz caused him guilt and shame, and torment about human evil; but he contained these in decades of writing and talking, and with the knowledge that he had done everything he could to right them. What we suffer from most in the end is our own private condition. It was his own private condition that killed Primo Levi, and I wanted his readers to know it.

Because – and this really is my last reason – he wanted his readers to know it. He was writing *Il doppio legame* for publication. It wasn't ready for publication when he became too ill to go on with it; it is locked in his study with his other papers, and may never be published now. But from the beginning to the end of his writing life Primo Levi's greatest desire was to communicate to his reader. One of the first things he ever dreamed of writing was also one of the greatest: 'Carbon', in *The Periodic Table*. And 'Carbon' is one of the most extraordinary acts of communication between writer and reader ever written: bringing his act of writing and our act of reading together in a single instant, as his hand makes, and our eyes read, 'this dot, here, this one'.

In this story, in this ending, through all the layers of time Primo Levi comes as close as I sometimes felt him in Turin, almost close enough to touch us. Closeness was part of his double bind, and the best solution he ever found to it was writing. It seems the best solution to me too.

Introduction

Corso Re Umberto 75

Corso Re Umberto 75 is a quiet, solid house, very like all the other houses built in the good middle-class areas of Turin around the turn of the century. Its façade is dark grey stone at the bottom, then dusty red brick, broken by four tiers of grey stone balconies in front of tall windows. Long slatted shutters cover the windows, drawn from top to bottom like eyelids.

The doorway is like all the doorways in Turin, even in the poorest quarters: wide and high, in solid burnished wood. Inside, the stone passage is dark and cool. The wrought-iron door at the end leads into the inner courtyard, the private heart every Turin house hides behind its blank and stony face. It's locked; only the tenants have the key. On the right there's a glass-paned door to the hallway, and this one is open. But inside the stairs curve up to four floors of front doors. There are three on every landing, all in heavy, dark wood, and all closed.

The house is neither large nor beautiful, but self-sufficient and resistant to change. Its thick walls muffle the noise of the street outside. In the still air you can sniff the faint, musty odour of old Turin. Primo Levi, whose house this is, identified it: it's the smell of saltpetre, potassium nitrate, and comes from the marriage of the city's particular damp with the particular stone and plaster of its buildings.

Except for one year in Milan and one in Auschwitz, Primo Levi lived here for all his sixty-seven years. He was born here, on 31 July 1919, behind the last tall door on the third floor, in the room which later became his study. The exact spot varied in family legend: it was where he later sat reading in his favourite armchair, or where he sat at his desk, writing.

His mother's family lived all around them in Crocetta, Turin's best bourgeois neighbourhood (the really rich lived, as they still do, on the *collina*, the hill overlooking the city from the other side of the Po). His grandparents lived on the corner of Corso Re Umberto and Corso Vittorio Emanuele II, nine or ten streets away; his uncles, aunts and cousins in the streets and avenues between.

A year and a half later his sister Anna Maria was born behind the same door. Here he waited impatiently for her to grow up, so that he could talk to her. Here, when he was seven and she was five, he sat her down beside their cousin Giulia, who was also five, and taught them how to form the letters he had just learned at school. Here, as brother and sister grew older, they grew closer, until they seemed to be able to communicate without speaking. They invented a private language which not even their parents could understand; and thought and spoke so quickly, like typewriters, that they were hard to follow even in Italian.

Their parents both came from Jewish families who had been observant up to a generation or two before. Their grandparents still kept the High Holidays, and they and their cousins were taken there for Passover Seders, and for Friday night suppers as well. But this weekly ritual had lost its religious meaning, remaining a family gathering only. Even so their father always arrived late, to show, perhaps to himself, that he wasn't following a religious duty. Their mother was if anything still less religious. They were like most Italian Jews, loyal to the Enlightenment ideas that had first freed them; the same ideas that allowed Jews to live freely had also freed them of their Judaism.

But not wholly: their Jewishness was still there in the air, like the smell of saltpetre. It was there in their father's memories of idle schoolboy persecution in his long-ago boyhood. Primo met it more directly, but still painfully, when he was thirteen, and had his bar mitzvah. After that it dropped out of his life, until a new and far from idle persecution. But during his bar mitzvah studies he had briefly become intensely involved, and very serious. He *was* serious, especially about anything that involved principle, and especially as a child. Later on people would often see the small boy in the grown man; now they saw the grown man in the small boy.

That is, at least, how people saw him outside that tall front door: a pale, shy child, dressed in a sailor suit with a stiff white collar. Behind it he was rather different. Anna Maria was livelier, bossier; the two mostly did what she wanted. But Primo was creative, and quietly subversive. Once he built a complex trap of ball and string over a door, so that people opening it would tug the string, and bring the ball bouncing down on their heads. Mostly, however, he built vast constructions in Meccano, for which his father brought him the pieces. When his cousins came to visit on Sundays they would find him engrossed for hours, with fabulous but unstable results. He was too eager to pursue his grand visions, and didn't tighten the bolts enough, as his engineer father never ceased to tell him.

Later he would do chemistry experiments in his room, and peer through a microscope at dead flies, salt crystals, and the stagnant water from a vase of his mother's flowers. This, he discovered, was full of breath-taking movement, both violent and delicate, quite unlike the orderly, geometric growth of crystals. He saw that even the most sedentary microscopic creatures occasionally pulled up their anchors, and set off on voyages of adventure; and he imagined them to be animals like us, moved by hunger, fear, boredom, or even love.

His father, Cesare, was an omnivorous and undiscriminating reader, who read not in the subjects he already knew, but in those he didn't, and who found new subjects to study until he died. Cesare Levi never read fewer than three books at a time, and never passed a second-hand bookstall on the Via Po or the Via Cernaia without buying a sample at random, plus several for his son. In this way the house filled up with strange and unseen life, like the water from the vase of flowers; and in this secret, teeming sea of knowledge and adventure Primo swam from the start as boldly as his father. As a boy he read (for instance) all Jules Verne and Jack London; and hundreds of scientific books, from all of Camille Flammarion to *Man the Unknown* by Carrell, and a book called *An Introduction to the History of Human Stupidity*.

★　　★

How many times in his boyhood alone must he have gone in and out this closed door, up and down these circling stairs? He went down these stairs to the Rignon School, around the corner in the Via Massena. He went down them the day he met his gentle teacher, Signorina Glauda, in the street, and was so overcome by shyness that he blushed a deep red and hid behind his mother. Up these stairs came the baskets of dirty clothes from the poor children of the Rignon, lice-infested and full of holes; his mother would wash, disinfect and mend them, and tell him not to touch them. Down them went the three great wicker baskets of their own clothes, bedlinen, pots and pans, as every summer the family left the sweltering city for the mountains.

They would follow the baskets down, and out on to the Corso Re Umberto. The side avenues were still cobble-stoned, the horse-chestnuts newly planted, and the city ended in green fields only a few hundred yards to the south. They would take the train to Torre Pellice or Bardonecchia, seventy miles away; there to remeet uncles, aunts, cousins and friends, and rebuild Crocetta around them.

The mountains start so near Turin that on clear days they suddenly appear at the bottom of the streets, like ships in a port city; they give you the same sensation of the world sailing into town, or a piece of the town sailing away. These mountains would come to mean as much as Turin itself to Primo Levi, as they do to all Turinese. They would come to mean both adventure and home; both escaping himself, and finding out who he really was.

But to him as a boy they meant plants and birds and insects, and tadpoles to catch and watch as they transformed; and Meccano for hours every day, like three months of Sundays. In the summer he turned eleven he fell in love with Lidia, who was nine; but she preferred Carlo, who was bigger and stronger than him. Now, Carlo was his Meccano friend; they had little else in common, but as builders they complemented each other perfectly – he was the head and Carlo the hands. He devised his most ambitious creation yet: a clock, and one that would run not on a manufactured Meccano motor, but on a pendulum and weights, all calculated and designed with great effort and ingenuity by himself. This clock he and Carlo would build, and present to Lidia on her saint's day. She would surely understand who the inventor was, and who the mere bolt-tightener. She would understand that this was his secret offering: the reaching out to her he did not dare to do with his hand. It was as though the Meccano clock was his first book, and Lidia his first reader.

PART ONE

Primo and Anna Maria Levi, date unknown

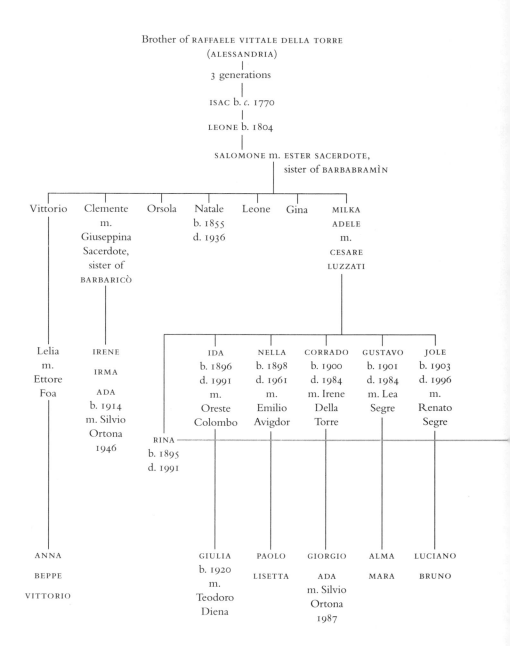

Brother of RAFFAELE VITTALE DELLA TORRE
(ALESSANDRIA)

3 generations

ISAC b. *c.* 1770

LEONE b. 1804

SALOMONE m. ESTER SACERDOTE,
sister of BARBABRAMÌN

Vittorio   Clemente   Orsola   Natale   Leone   Gina   MILKA
            m.   b. 1855   ADELE
            Giuseppina   d. 1936   m.
            Sacerdote,   CESARE
            sister of   LUZZATI
            BARBARICÒ

Lelia   IRENE   IDA   NELLA   CORRADO   GUSTAVO   JOLE
m.   IRMA   b. 1896   b. 1898   b. 1900   b. 1901   b. 1903
Ettore   ADA   d. 1991   d. 1961   d. 1984   d. 1984   d. 1996
Foa   b. 1914   m.   m.   m. Irene m. Lea   m.
            m. Silvio   Oreste   Emilio   Della   Segre   Renato
            Ortona   Colombo   Avigdor   Torre   Segre
            1946   RINA
                        b. 1895
                        d. 1991

ANNA   GIULIA   PAOLO   GIORGIO   ALMA   LUCIANO
                        b. 1920
BEPPE   m.   LISETTA   ADA   MARA   BRUNO
                        Teodoro   m. Silvio
VITTORIO   Diena   Ortona
                                            1987

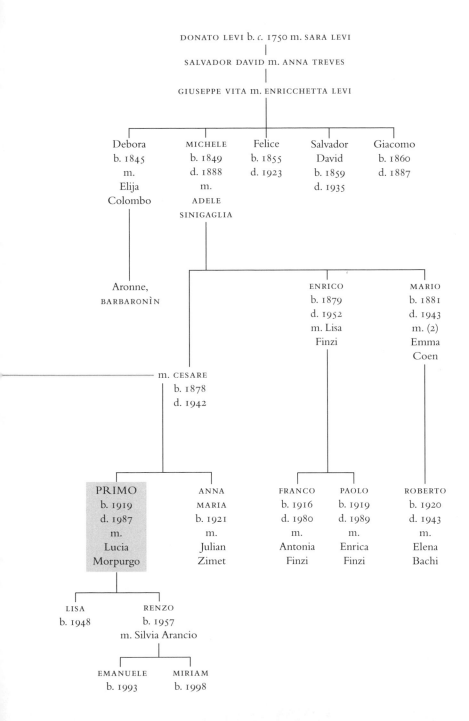

DONATO LEVI b. *c.* 1750 m. SARA LEVI

SALVADOR DAVID m. ANNA TREVES

GIUSEPPE VITA m. ENRICCHETTA LEVI

Debora
b. 1845
m.
Elija
Colombo

MICHELE
b. 1849
d. 1888
m.
ADELE
SINIGAGLIA

Felice
b. 1855
d. 1923

Salvador
David
b. 1859
d. 1935

Giacomo
b. 1860
d. 1887

Aronne,
BARBARONÌN

ENRICO
b. 1879
d. 1952
m. Lisa
Finzi

MARIO
b. 1881
d. 1943
m. (2)
Emma
Coen

m. CESARE
b. 1878
d. 1942

PRIMO
b. 1919
d. 1987
m.
Lucia
Morpurgo

ANNA
MARIA
b. 1921
m.
Julian
Zimet

FRANCO
b. 1916
d. 1980
m.
Antonia
Finzi

PAOLO
b. 1919
d. 1989
m.
Enrica
Finzi

ROBERTO
b. 1920
d. 1943
m.
Elena
Bachi

LISA
b. 1948

RENZO
b. 1957
m. Silvia Arancio

EMANUELE
b. 1993

MIRIAM
b. 1998

1. Paradiso

Nonna Pina and Barbaricô, Turin, 1952

Italy is the oldest home of Jews in Europe, and Jews are among the oldest continuous inhabitants of Italy. There were Jews in Rome two centuries before Christ: neither Ashkenazim (German and East European Jews) nor Sephardim (Spanish and Portuguese Jews), since neither of these two main families of European Jewry yet existed, but still earlier exiles direct from Palestine, Egypt and Babylonia.

The next wave of Jewish immigration into Italy came much later: from France and Germany in the fourteenth century, from Spain and Portugal in the late fifteenth, after their various expulsions and persecutions. Those who settled in Sicily and southern Italy were expelled once again, when much of the south fell under Spanish domination in the sixteenth century. But several princes in the north were relatively liberal, and absolutely in need of money; and after 1497 (the date of the expulsion from Portugal) the only centres of

Jewish life in Western Europe for over 100 years were in northern Italy. The Princes of Acaia, for instance, began to let Jews into Piedmont in the early 1400s, where they remained more or less undisturbed ever after. By contrast, Jews were only readmitted into England (expulsion: 1290) and France (expulsion: 1394) in the seventeenth and eighteenth centuries. Primo Levi, therefore, was born into the only part of Western Europe, apart from a few German cities, where Jews had been living uninterruptedly for at least 500 years.

His ancestors, he always said, had probably come from Spain via Provence around 1500, like most Piedmontese Jews; but his origins 'lay hidden in darkness', and he didn't even know if he was Ashkenazi or Sephardic. In fact he was almost certainly mostly Sephardic; but among his ancestors on each side there was at least one Ashkenazi name – Luzzati on his mother's, Treves on his father's.★ 'Italian Jewry is neither,' he said. Clearly he thought, with some justification, that after well over 2,000 years Italian Jews had become a branch on their own. And after 500 years in settled, endogamous communities, so, in particular, had Piedmontese ones.

When his ancestors had first entered Piedmont they were given 'less than a warm welcome in Turin'. Emanuele Filiberto of Savoy allowed only a few Jews to live in his capital; instead he spread them throughout Piedmont, in small groups of ten to twenty families. Thus they settled in small agricultural centres, always a tiny minority, provincial, and mostly poor. No doubt because of this modesty and relative invisibility, they were, in Primo's own words, 'never very much loved or very much hated; stories of unusual persecution have not been handed down'.

From the start the Jews of Piedmont were restricted to living in certain areas. But in 1555 Pope Paul IV emitted the punitive papal bull which confined Jews to walled ghettos, and deprived them of the right to practise almost all trades except the sale and repair of old clothes. In Turin the first small ghetto formed on the Via San Tommaso. The Dukes of Savoy, however, defied the Vatican, and went on relying on their Jewish bankers; they held out for over a century, and only enclosed the Jews of Turin in a proper walled ghetto (between the Via San Francesco da Paola, the Via Maria Vittoria and the Via Bogino) in 1679. Slowly, ghettos also came to the small towns where Primo's ancestors lived: Alessandria, Casale Monferrato, Mondovì. But here they arrived even later – in Mondovì in 1720, in Casale in 1724; and here they remained less efficient, even ignored, in the Italian fashion. Like their neighbours, therefore, Primo's ancestors stayed where they were. In the eighteenth century the silk trade was opened to Jews, and

★ Luzzati comes from Lausitz, Treves from Trier.

became, after money-lending, their second traditional route to slightly greater wealth and security. In the latter years of that century legal restraints on them eased still further, especially in Piedmont. By the time of the French Revolution Italian Jews in general, and Piedmontese Jews in particular, were better integrated into their communities than anywhere else in Europe.

As the ghettos of Piedmont had been the last to be enclosed, so they were the first to be opened: in 1848, as part of the Risorgimento, the great movement towards Italian independence and unification, which began in Turin. And finally, from all the towns and villages of Piedmont the freed Jews began to flow into the city. The provincial centres of Jewish life for so many generations emptied; and by the end of the nineteenth century Turin's Jewish population had doubled, to around 4,000. Among them were Primo Levi's maternal grandmother, from Alessandria, and his maternal grandfather, from Casale.

It is a classic Jewish joke (which is of course quite serious) to ask of every possible event, large and small, 'Is it good for the Jews?' The Risorgimento was good for the Jews. It was a liberal, secular, enlightened movement, all three of whose great leaders, Mazzini, Garibaldi and Cavour, were philosemites; and it had already freed them. Not surprisingly, therefore, Jews were among the most passionate supporters of a united Italy; and none more so than the Jews of Piedmont, where the Risorgimento was based and began. Among Garibaldi's famous *Mille* (One Thousand) were eight Jews, when the Jewish population of Italy was less than one per 1,000; the Piedmontese Cavour, architect of unification, had a Piedmontese Jewish secretary, Isacco Artom.

In 1861 the Kingdom of Italy was proclaimed under Vittorio Emanuele of Savoy, with its capital and Parliament in Turin. After three short years history moved on, the capital was moved to Florence, and finally, with full unification in 1870, to Rome. But the Turinese – who, some say, have never got over their loss of the capital – to this day feel a special pride as the founders of modern Italy; and this pride, and perhaps also this sense of loss, is deeply shared by Turin Jews. Arnaldo Momigliano, the great Turinese Jewish historian, remembers that his grandmother was so intensely patriotic that she cried every time she heard the anthem of the Italian monarchy (even though, he adds, the music is so awful that 'if you can cry at that, you can cry at anything').

It is, therefore, also unsurprising that from 1861 – indeed, from 1848 – there was an extraordinary flowering of Jewish participation in Italian culture. The great Jewish gift which history has always acknowledged, Primo said ('Perhaps the only one'), is literacy, for it is a duty for every Jew to be able to read the Bible. In the second half of the nineteenth century the great

Letter from Garibaldi to the first Primo Levi. The text reads:
'Electors! To demonstrate the affection and respect which our fellow
citizen PRIMO LEVI inspired in the most illustrious of all Italians,
we reproduce below, in his own hand, the letter which the Hero of
two worlds sent to him, in a solemn moment for himself and his
family: *My dear Levi, By fighting so generously for my cause and that of my
family, you have earned all our lifelong gratitude. G. Garibaldi.* Primo Levi,
Director, *La Riforma.*'

majority of Italians were still illiterate; and this gave their newly-born fellow citizens their chance. Within one or two generations Italian Jews had transformed themselves from small provincial traders, moneylenders and rabbis to metropolitan professionals, particularly in the professions of writing and the Word: government service, the law, the universities, journalism. Turinese Jews distinguished themselves most of all in the University, especially in the sciences. Until 1938 the whole of Italy was famous for the numbers of Jews who reached the highest positions in the land: in government, where there were nineteen Jewish senators by 1920, and two Jewish prime ministers (though one, Sidney Sonnino, had become a Protestant); in the army, where Jews could even become generals, and several Piedmontese Jews did; in the navy, which after the racial laws of 1938 found itself having to expel its two top commanders. One of the most eminent newspapermen in newly united Italy was a Jew called Primo Levi, who had been such a tireless supporter of the Risorgimento that Garibaldi sent him his own personal thanks. On the wall of his study in Turin the second Italian Jewish writer called Primo Levi hung a copy of Garibaldi's letter to the first – lightly expressing, in the pun on his name, his own Jewish pride in liberal, enlightened Italy.

★　　★

Piedmontese Jews were the most Italian of all Italian Jews: but not the most assimilated. In Mantua, for example, the Jewish community was already losing members to intermarriage before the turn of the century. In Turin numbers held steady, at around 4,000, right up to 1938. Endogamy remained unbreached up to the First World War, and beyond: the second Primo Levi himself still married 'in' after the Second.

He wrote about this in 1984, for an exhibition of Jewish life in Turin. If every country gets the Jews it deserves, he said, Piedmont deserved its loyal Jewish citizens, having accepted them with 'fundamental tolerance' for 500 years. In return, of all the integrated Jews of Italy Turinese Jews were among the most integrated. Uniformly middle-class and educated, they played the largest role in their city's intelligentsia of all the Jews of Italy. Nonetheless, they lived in a very special balance. They were integrated, but not assimilated; accepted, but apart. Anywhere else this may have seemed the special and suspicious exclusiveness of Jews. But here it was not unusual. Turin is a city made up of many small circles of people, coming together in their public and working lives, but spending their private and social lives apart. Into this mixture, which is not a solution, the Jews could fit. Their 'age-old reserve' matched 'the famous reserve of the Piedmontese'; and neither took the other's personally. Turinese Jews lived in peace: but with a 'double inheritance of reserve'.

The Famous Reserve of the Piedmontese

In 1797, high in the mountains between Piedmont and France, ten battalions of Piedmontese soldiers were given the command '*Bugia nèn*': Do not move; do not yield. And they didn't. The French grenadiers were turned back, and the Piedmontese had acquired their name.

The typical Piedmontese is a *bugia nèn*. He comes (even if not personally) from a military and monarchical tradition: spartan, conservative and hierarchical, based on values of hard work, discipline and duty. He is patient and stubborn; he never abandons what he has begun. He does not yield or complain, but endures. Although fortunately he need no longer obey it, he quotes the old proverb with admiration: *Fa il tuo dovere e crepa*, Do your duty and die. But he is no slave: there is a long tradition of *bugia nèn* rebels, who, having decided, after long and careful thought, to dissent, did that patiently and stubbornly too.

The *bugia nèn* is a hard worker, but here again he is no slave. His work is his own personal dignity: *il lavoro ben fatto*, the job well done, is his personal pride, whether he is (or more likely was) an old-fashioned Turinese craftsman in a small workshop, or a modern worker on the factory floor. Either way, the original Turinese working class was its own self-contained élite, bearer of a proud Jacobin tradition. Even after the mass immigration of workers from the South in the 1960s, that tradition has never quite disappeared.

The *bugia nèn* is orderly, honest and moral; he lacks the normal Italian taste for chaos, and for doing a deal. In fact the *bugia nèn* is more than moral, he is positively puritan. He is serious and sober, and doesn't often laugh out loud. He is, in fact, a bit of a misery. He combines peasant realism with aristocratic aplomb, and ends up with something very like English understatement. Another of his key phrases is *esageroma nèn*: let's not exaggerate.

Above all, perhaps, the *bugia nèn* is careful and cautious. He does not abandon old roads for new ones. He has two other favourite proverbs, which he still obeys: *Chi va piano va sano e va lontano*, Slow and steady wins the race; and *Non fare il passo più lunga della gamba*, Do not step longer than your leg. This is the wisdom, and the fear, of his peasant ancestors. His famous reserve is the protective lack-of-colouring of anyone whose rights fell short of his obligations for hundreds of years. Like, indeed, the Jew's: who has, in Primo's words, been 'accustomed since time immemorial to live in silence and suspicion, to listen much and say little, and to keep his head down, because "you never know"'.

The *bugia nèn* hides his wealth, and he hides his feelings: as Primo Levi told the world, in Piedmontese there is no verb 'to love'. This makes other

Italians suspect a cover-up – but curiously enough, only about the money. They think the Piedmontese cold and calculating, like their city. They cannot believe the rational French abstraction of Turin's right-angled streets; there's nothing like it anywhere else in Italy. They stand on the viewing gallery of the Mole, the tallest building in Turin, and clamour like birds: how could anyone live in a city like this? It would be like living in a cage, like living in a prison. It would drive them crazy.

They don't notice that what they are standing on itself is hardly rational, and hardly austere or cautious either. The Mole Antonelliana was begun in 1863 by the Jewish community of Turin to be their synagogue, and the expression in stone of their gratitude for emancipation in 1848. That gratitude was immense; and so, perhaps, was their desire to display their new-found wealth and security. At any rate the Mole, the international symbol of Turin, is the exact opposite of everything Turin stands for. It is a mad excess, a huge, grand, literally empty gesture. It never became a synagogue; the Jewish community had stepped far longer than their leg, and had to abandon the building. The city fathers completed it, but had no idea what to do with it, and left it empty for 100 years.*

Nor is the Mole the only anomaly in Turin's sensible geography. There is the fake medieval castle of the Valentino, stage set for some of the first films ever made; and the vast basilica of Superga, on the top of a hill, which was unreachable for two centuries. There is the most sensuous and sinuous art nouveau building I have ever seen, like a tree that has grown in stone. And these are only the ones you can see. The real fantasies and follies of Turin are hidden. They are hidden in the green courtyards behind the grey fronts of the houses, in the strange decorations of their pediments and fountains. They are hidden in the myth of Turin as one of the three 'magic cities' of Europe, like Prague and Lyons, at the confluence of three rivers: a myth mocked by her rationalists, touted by her tourist board, and deeply rooted in her ordinary citizens, who have a secret passion for psychics and clairvoyants.

It is not only other Italians who can feel imprisoned by Turin's unforgiving grid of streets, or the deliberate dullness of her character. A *torinesissimo torinese* (a most Turinese Turinese) says: 'Turin is pleasant to live in, splendid to work in, and beautiful to see, but not fun.' Indeed, it is not only other Italians who can be driven mad by Turin. This is the special privilege of the Turinese. Their outer phlegm breeds inner restlessness. Their mathematical correctness breeds fear and longing, in equal measure, for transgression. Their grey stone, their smoky mists, their cold climate, breed melancholy. Their city *is* pleasant to live in, splendid to work in, and beautiful to see;

---

* In 1997 it finally became the National Museum of Cinema.

but they have to get away from it occasionally to stay sane. The *bugia nèn* must, occasionally, move.

The Piedmontese are border people, living on an edge, closer in character to their ancestral enemies over the Alps than to the nation they created. They are natural outsiders, proud and melancholy. Piedmontese Jews are outsiders within outsiders, border people within border people; doubly proud and doubly melancholy. They are, typically, *torinesissimi torinesi*; Jewish *bugia nèn*.

The Age-old Reserve of the Jews

One of the great Jewish commandments is *Yizkor*: Remember. When Primo Levi, secular and un-Jewish as he was, came back from Auschwitz, he was galvanized to remember. First and foremost, of course, the millions who had been murdered. But others as well. The Jewish communities of several countries had been wiped out; his own had not, but it had been a narrow escape. And he himself had nearly been stopped from remembering them forever. In 1946, alongside *If This is a Man*, he wrote two other things: 'I mnemagoghi', a short story about memory; and the sketch of an essay about his ancestors.

When he returned to it more than twenty-five years later, the darkness and urgency had gone, but the vow to remember remained. The sketch became the first chapter of his chemist's autobiography, *The Periodic Table*. It was, he said, an '*opera di pietà*', '*almost an ex voto*': a work of family piety, the fulfilment of a vow. He wrote it with love, but also with irony. The irony is a form of self-mockery, since any Jew who tells a Jewish joke is laughing at himself. The first chapter of *The Periodic Table* is a Piedmontese Jewish joke. This is what Primo said about it, running together Piedmont, Piedmontese Jews, his ancestors and himself:

The chapter on . . . my Piedmontese Jewish forebears in *The Periodic Table* is written with love . . . I'm perfectly aware of the defects in the Piedmontese character, because they're my own defects.

The Periodic Table is a subtle, teasing book in which the chemical element which is the title of each chapter is a metaphor for its subject. Primo's metaphor for his ancestors is the noble gas Argon. The noble gases, he tells us, are also called 'inert' and 'rare' – though it is not absolutely certain that all noble gases are rare, or all rare gases noble. 'Argon' means 'the Inactive'; the other noble gases are Krypton, the Hidden, Xenon, the Alien, and Neon, the New.

All these names beautifully and comically sum up the Jews of Piedmont, most obviously, perhaps, 'alien', 'new' and 'rare'. But Primo picks especially 'inert', and (with Argon) 'inactive'. Not materially inert, he explains, since of course they had to earn a living. But 'inert' and 'inactive' in the chemical sense: 'that they do not take part in any chemical reaction, they do not combine with any other element'. In 1962, he notes, a chemist managed to make the Alien, Xenon, combine fleetingly with fluorine; 'and the feat seemed so extraordinary he was given a Nobel Prize'.

Why are the Alien, the Inactive and the others so uncombining? Primo's first explanation, ostensibly about the gases, contains a hint of Jewish self-blame: because they are 'so satisfied with their condition'. When he moves to the human beings themselves he is more even-handed. On the one side, though those stories of persecution had not been handed down, 'a wall of suspicion, of undefined mockery and hostility' was raised against the new, the rare and alien Jews. And on the other, the Jews 'erected a symmetrical barrier against all of Christianity'; and though they became less Jewish and more Piedmontese with every generation, they still proudly called themselves ''l popol d'Israel', the people of Israel.

In 'Argon' the great image of the wall, both impermeable and yet curiously permeable, is the language of the Piedmontese people of Israel: *giudeo piemontese* or *piemontese ebraico*, Piedmontese Jewish or Piedmontese Hebrew. The Venetian people of Israel, the Anconan, Ferraran and Roman peoples of Israel – all the Italian peoples of Israel had similar languages: small, exclusive, doubly secret combinations of Hebrew and the local dialect, which like their neighbours they spoke well into the twentieth century in preference to Italian.

The Italian–Hebrew languages were equivalent to Yiddish, the Ashkenazi combination of Hebrew and German. But not very equivalent. Each group of speakers was so small, and separated from every other group: from their neighbours by the Hebrew roots of their words, which they shared with other Jews; from other Jews by the dialect endings and inflexions, which they shared instead with their neighbours. Piedmontese Hebrew, for instance, 'was never spoken by more than a few thousand people', as Primo says; it never gave birth to a literature, or made more than the most fleeting and secret marks upon the world. And yet, as he also says, 'its human interest is great, like that of all languages on a frontier and in transition'.

Its first function was secrecy and self-defence, the maintenance of that wall against the majority and their rule. It was in this way an underground language, a code, like criminal jargon; and indeed the ordinary Italian criminal classes have borrowed quite liberally from it, most famously the word for prison: *tafùs*. Its origins in oppression and powerlessness show in its most common words: *davàr*, silence, nothing; *lachtì*, flee or hide; *manôd*, money; *pàhad*, fear. In this defensive (and aggressive) part of the wall was the sub-jargon used by Jewish shopkeepers in the fabric trade, which in Italy, as in America and elsewhere, was largely in Jewish hands. There were code names for prices, so that they could be decided on the spot, according to the wealth and attractiveness of the client: 100 lire was *'na gamba*, a leg, 1,000 *un corp*, a body. Even more useful were words for conveying secret warnings to one another: a *Missià*, Primo tells us, was a boring customer; a *tërdes-un* (a 'thirteen-one') was the worst kind, who made you take down every bolt of cloth in the shop, and then bought nothing.* Most useful (and enjoyable) of all were the secret insults and curses, such as *mamzer*, bastard: '*Duman arivu i mamzer*' meant that the next day the tax inspectors would arrive. A polka-dot dress was ''*na vesta a kinim*', *kinim* being the Hebrew for lice, one of the ten plagues of Egypt. In the fullness of time many non-Jewish salesmen became owners in their turn; some of them still use this and other old expressions, and are 'quite surprised', Primo says, to learn they are speaking Hebrew.

But the language was not only a barrier. Some things, such as these, seeped through. And by nature it was as much a transition as a frontier. For though so many individual words were Hebrew, the language itself was essentially Piedmontese. As Primo noted, such hybrid languages do not arise where the gap between majority and minority is too large: 'There has never been a Polish-Jewish dialect, for example, nor any Italian-German hybrid languages in the Alto Adige' (what the Austrians call South Tyrol, since even the name – especially the name – cannot be the same in the two languages). The existence itself of *ebraico piemontese* is proof that the wall was permeable; it was defence, but also passage.

From childhood, Primo wrote, he had been 'intrigued, and also moved' by the improbable combination of two such different languages into one: the sacred and solemn flight of biblical Hebrew, and the rough, laconic, earthy speech of Piedmont. It was a symbol to him of other, larger conflicts and improbable resolutions. The contrast between the two elements of his ancestral tongue, he wrote,

reflects another, the essential conflict of Diaspora Jews, dispersed among the gentiles, the *goyim*, torn between their divine vocation and the daily misery of their exile.

---

* So called because the superstitious often refrained from buying on a 13th, and January, just after Christmas, was the leanest month of the year. The code came in handy during Fascism, when there was a quiverful of secret names for the Duce: from *ghevìr*, boss, through *chelèv*, dog, to *mamzer* (see above), in the liberating but safe phrase *cul mamzer*, 'that bastard'.

And this in turn reflects yet another, still more general conflict, one which is inherent in the human condition, since man is a centaur, a tangle of flesh and mind, of divine inspiration and dust.

★ ★

The permeable wall of mutual self-defence is the historical meaning of the metaphor of 'Argon'. But there is also a personal one. His ancestors, Primo wrote, 'were inert in their inner spirits'. They were more inclined to 'gratuitous discussion' and 'disinterested speculation' than to getting and spending; their characters and deeds, in the stories that have come down about them,

have in common a touch of the static, an attitude of dignified abstention, of voluntary (or accepted) relegation to the margins of the great river of life.

'Gratuitous discussion' is a peculiarly Jewish passion; it was, in particular, one of Primo's own. And it is true that there was a strain of unworldliness on both sides of his family. But both sides had their fair share of worldly ambition as well, as we shall see. The truth is that in 'Argon', as in all his writing, Primo is choosing carefully what to tell. The stories of 'Argon' are all true; but so were many others. The picture of Primo Levi's ancestors in 'Argon' tells us as much about him as about them. He is like Krypton, the Hidden – and not only in 'Argon': he hardly describes himself at all, only others; yet in what he tells us about them, we see him after all.

He knew this, of course, and sometimes it worried him. But not here. Two years before it was published he showed a first draft of 'Argon' to much of Jewish Turin, asking for their corrections and contributions. On it he had written *Quem legis, ut noris*: 'That you may know whom you read.'★ This has disappeared from the published version, perhaps because he had second thoughts, more likely simply to bring 'Argon' in line with the other chapters, none of which had its own *envoi*. But he had kept it right up to the last moment; it is still on the final typescript, scored through with a neat line.

So what does he pick out to tell? First of all, that element of 'inertness': stasis; abstention; the inability, or unwillingness, to combine. But second, and just as important – the bizarre, the eccentric and entertaining. 'Naturally,' he said,

★ This is a quotation from Ovid's *Tristia* (*Sorrows*), elegies for his homeland written from exile. The full quotation is: *Ille ego qui fuerim, tenerorum lusor amorum, quem legis, ut noris, accipe posteritas*: 'That you may know who I was, the singer of tender loves whom you read, hearken to me, O you who follow.'

there were also . . . some dim, dull and pale [characters]. But those I put aside. They left no trace. It was the strange and curious ones who left a trace, who passed into family history, sometimes for a single phrase.

Once again, this is true: the dull leave little trace. But worse than that, they're *dull*. Primo trawled not only his extended family, but the collective memory of the Jews of Turin, to find the proud, mild, unforgettable *barba* (uncles) and *magne* (aunts) of 'Argon'. He hinted at this in 'Argon' itself ('I should warn the reader straight away that ["uncle"] must be understood in a very broad sense'), and happily admitted it later: many of his ancestors were 'borrowed'. After *The Periodic Table* was published, he said, friends frequently remarked to him: 'It's odd, but my grandfather said exactly the same thing as yours.' The reason was, of course, that it was their grandfather.

Thus, Primo's *zia* (Aunt) Jole – the oldest surviving member of the family, with a *memoria di ferro*, a memory of iron – could not remember either 'Nona Bimba', the beautiful baroness, or 'Nona Fina', who had a 'slight indisposition' at sixty-eight, and spent her last twenty years in her room. I never did find out whose grandmother Nona Bimba was. But Nona Fina was Primo's friend Silvio Ortona's: she was called Delfina Jona, and lived in Trino Vercellese. Then there were the *barba* and *magne* who were neither Primo's own relations nor any of his friends', but the subjects of stories handed down for generations in the ghettos of Casale, Alessandria or Acqui. According to *zia* Jole, the story of Aunt Regina and Uncle David in the Caffè Fiorio in Turin was one of these; and indeed in Primo's first draft they are walking down the main street of Trino Vercellese when Aunt Regina says her famous line: '*Davidìn, bat la cana, c'as sentô nèn le rôkhòd*': 'David, thump your cane, so they don't hear my winds.' (The real Aunt Regina, *zia* Jole* says, had something wrong with her intestine.)

The most distant ancestors are *figés dans une attitude*: caught in a single phrase or act of their lives, in which they are preserved like amber. Young women are tenderly treated, remembered like Nona Bimba for her beauty. Older women are absurd and touching, like Aunt Regina; or like Aunt Allegra, who when she sees her son on the stage shouts out, '*Rônin, co't fai! Posa côl sàber!*': 'Aronne, what are you doing! Put that sword down!' (These were, in fact, real and not so very distant relations: Primo's paternal great-aunt Debora, and her son Aronne Colombo, who would later play an indirect but important role in Primo's own life.)

It is the men, the *barba*, who are the real eccentrics, and the real bearers

---

* *Zia* Jole died at the age of ninety-three in 1996, two years after I first met her. She kept her *memoria di ferro* to the end.

of the tradition of 'inertness' and double reserve. Deep in the amber of the past lie Barbamoisìn, Uncle Moses, who had his two lower incisors removed to make room for his pipe; and *nonno* Leonin, who had flat feet, and was remembered for his joy when the good burghers of Casale replaced the cobblestones on his street: ''*Na brakha a côi goyim c'a l'an fàit i lòsi!*' he cried – 'A blessing on the *goyim* who made these paving stones!' Barbaraflìn, Uncle Raphael, when well past his prime fell in love with a beautiful young woman, but did not dare to declare himself; he wrote her love letters which he never posted, then wrote himself her passionate replies.

There are two *barba* in particular whom Primo remembers in 'Argon', and whom he brings closest to us in the detail and vividness of their stories. In reality both were linked to the family only by marriage. Their closeness was neither in blood nor in time (one was the same generation as Barbaraflìn, the other the remotest of all). Rather, it was to the model of the *barba*; or – which is the same thing – to the metaphor of the inert, rare and noble gases.

The first is Barbaricô, whom the metaphor, Primo says, 'fits like a glove'. His name was Riccardo Sacerdote, and he was born in Casale Monferrato around 1860, only a dozen years or so after the opening of the ghettos. His sister Giuseppina – *nonna* Pina – married Clemente Della Torre, so that Primo 'borrowed' him from his Della Torre cousins.

Barbaricô, Primo recounts, studied medicine, but 'did not like the world'. That is, 'he liked men, and especially women', but no form whatsoever of activity. He would have liked to escape Casale, but was too inert to do so; in the end he escaped by an exercise of inertia itself, which you can find in 'Argon'.

After that he settled in Turin, where he continued to avoid both marriage (with several women) and the regular exercise of his profession. When Primo met him in the 1930s he was a timid, shrivelled little old man who lived in a filthy room in the Borgo Vanchiglia, then one of the poorest districts of Turin. He had never in his life sought any patients, but read all day, and remembered everything he read. Nonetheless the poor people of the Borgo all came to him, since he never asked to be paid; and so indeed did other people, including his family, because as Primo says he was 'a fine doctor, full of human wisdom and diagnostic intuition'.

In the last many years of his long life Barbaricô lived with a big, vulgar *goyà*, whom he occasionally and feebly attempted to escape, and whom he called ''*na gran beèma*', a great beast – with, however (Primo notes), 'a vein of inexplicable tenderness'. This *goyà* was given, by Barbaricô's family, the 'ironic and cruel' name of Magna 'Môrfina': ironic because an unmarried and childless *goyà* could never be a *magna*; and cruel because 'Môrfina' 'contained an allusion, probably false and in any case pitiless, to a certain exploitation on her part of Barbaricô's prescription forms'. Thus Primo hints at a darker side of families in general, and Jewish families in particular. But he stops short, in this gentle elegy, of describing poor Magna Môrfina's end: she committed suicide. Instead he ends Barbaricô's story with his own perfectly inert and noble death: 'He ate almost nothing, and in general had no needs; he died at over ninety, discreetly and with dignity.'

Most inert of all, however, 'portentously inert, wrapped in a thick shroud of legend and the incredible, fossilized in every fibre of his being as an uncle', was Barbabramìn. His story was famous throughout the Della Torre clan; Primo's cousin Ada Della Torre used to tell it too, with great gusto.

Barbabramìn was the brother of Primo's great-grandmother Ester Sacerdote. Like Barbaricô, therefore, he too was a Sacerdote: Abramino Sacerdote, born in Chieri, near Turin, in the early years of the nineteenth century. As a young man he must have been active enough, since he acquired several farms in the fertile plains between Chieri and Asti, and became very rich. His inertia was of a different kind.

His mother seems to have guessed at his weakness, and refused to have any female servants in the house. But one day she fell ill; and though she resisted as long as she could, in the end she was forced to hire a maid. 'Punctually,' Primo wrote, Barbabramìn was smitten with love for this maid: 'probably the first less than saintly female he had ever had the chance to meet'.

She was, of course, a *havertà*, in the full sense of that Piedmontese Hebrew word: a *goyà*, an illiterate peasant girl who went about barefoot and was insolent to her employers. She was also, however, an excellent cook, and above all very beautiful. Barbabramìn fell in love with her beauty, her naked ankles, her delicious dishes, and her insolence. He told his parents he intended to marry her. They went wild with rage and forbade it. And now came Barbabramìn's mythically inert reply: he went to bed, and stayed there for twenty-two years.

All day, like Barbaricô, he lay in bed and read; so that eventually he came to be considered wise and just, regularly received delegations of Chieri notables, and settled disputes from his bed. At night, it is said, he slipped down to the café below to play billiards. 'It is also said,' Primo wrote, 'that the path to the aforementioned bed was not unknown to the aforementioned *havertà*'; and when Barbabramìn's parents finally died he married her. He had passively resisted for nearly a quarter of a century, and by now his legs were so weak he could no longer stand. But this hardly mattered; he simply took her into his bed for good. 'He died poor,' Primo concludes, 'but rich in years and fame, and in the peace of the spirit, in 1883.'

For the final version of 'Argon' Primo would write a last section, adding himself to the story as a young boy. The first draft ends here, with Barbabra-mìn: the original Jewish *bugia nèn*, fabulously patient and stubborn, slipping out at night for twenty-two years while he waits to achieve his desire.

The Della Torres and Luzzatis

Only one branch of the family was sufficiently distinguished to have left a clearly traceable history: Primo's mother's mother's family, the Della Torres.★

The earliest Della Torre who may have been an ancestor was a Manuele de Turre, who combined the offices of banker and doctor in Carignano in 1535. But the first known head of the family appears 200 years later: Raffaele Vittale Della Torre, who in 1735 was 'first among the Jews of Alessandria', according to the city's Catholic bishop.

There had been Vitales in Alessandria since the late 1400s. By the late 1500s a few had already been rich enough to escape the Spanish expulsions of the period (their exile was postponed until their loan to the Court of Madrid was repaid – which never happened). To this branch of the Vitales the Vittale Della Torres belonged; and by the mid-eighteenth century 'Raffaele Vittale Della Torre & Bros.' was the richest Jewish company in Alessandria.

One of Raffaele's brothers was the founder of the modern family. His son Israele (born 1692) was a representative of the Jewish community to their secular masters. One of *his* sons, Leone (born 1734), became a cloth merchant; and Leone's grandson, also Leone, born in 1804, became a rich landowner, and the oldest ancestor in living memory: Primo's great-great-grandfather.

From now on, therefore, the history becomes oral, and closer to the mythology of 'Argon'. In the next generation (which finally dropped the 'Vitale') Primo's great-grandfather Salomone married Ester Sacerdote, sister of the famous Barbabramìn. Salomone, who seems to have owned a tannery, was an extremely handsome man; whether because of this, or because (as *zia* Jole says) he had a competition with a friend, his wife had twenty-four or twenty-five pregnancies. Of these, five miscarried; but that still means

---

★ Much of what follows summarizes the researches of Silvio Ortona, who was not only Primo's close friend, but twice married into his family: first to Ada Della Torre, Primo's mother's first cousin, and secondly to Ada Luzzati, Primo's own first cousin. (See the family tree on pages 2–3.) Silvio Ortona undertook his research after Primo's death (*Ortona, Della Torre, Casale Monferrato etc.*, privately printed in 1993). I'd like to thank him for it here.

that Ester, who was minute and apparently frail, gave birth to nineteen or twenty children. Only seven survived childhood; at least one died in infancy (Primo claims, and *zia* Jole confirms), 'devoured in his cradle by a pig'.

Of the seven survivors the eldest was Vittorio, who became the great-grandfather of Primo's cousins Anna, Beppe and Vittorio Foa; the youngest was Clemente, grandfather of Primo's close friend and cousin Ada Della Torre. Primo's grandmother Adele was the youngest daughter. Two other daughters and a son found spouses in such faraway places as Genoa, and their families grew distant from the Turin line. But most distant of all was the third surviving child of Ester and Salomone, Natale, born in 1855. His story was probably the best known of all the Della Torre family legends; but for reasons which will soon become obvious, Primo did not put it into 'Argon'.

Zio Natale was not unlike Barbaricô in extreme intelligence, and – from the family's point of view – extreme eccentricity. But while Barbaricô was famously inert, *zio* Natale was famously active. (And that was the obvious reason.) He had attended the Brera Academy of Fine Arts in Milan, and was recognized as a promising young painter. Perhaps this was already bad enough; but he was also a revolutionary. A police report of 1879 called him 'the notorious Della Torre Natale', leader of the new 'socialist and internationalist' movement in the province of Alessandria. He was arrested several times. Finally he published, as its only founder, director and editor, the only issue of Alessandria's only socialist newspaper, *La Miseria* (*Poverty*). This issue, dated 6 November 1881, was immediately seized, and Natale charged with crimes against the state. On the same day he put on worker's clothes and fled to France. He returned only once, secretly, to see his family, and to take the poorest foundling in Alessandria as his wife. He worked first as a labourer in Nice and Menton, later as an engraver in Paris. In the end he became a saintly figure with a long white beard, known and loved throughout his *quartier* as Père Noel. He made his elder son a French citizen, his younger one an Italian. The French son became a poet, and a socialist journalist like his father, before dying in the First World War. The Italian son, though he lived in France all his life, had himself entered on the electoral roll in Alessandria, and voted Communist in memory of his father.

On one side of the family the legend of *zio* Natale was entirely positive. His niece Lelia Foa, herself a natural iconoclast, told her children stirring tales of his idealism: of the day, for instance, when he had at last been persuaded by his parents to wear a smart coat with a fur collar, but returned the same evening without it, having given it away to the first stranger. Lelia's son Vittorio later became one of Turin's bravest antifascists; in prison in the 30s he wondered, 'with a touch of vanity', if *zio* Natale ever knew the influence he had had on him.

Primo's branch of the family was more ambivalent. They called *zio* Natale an 'anarchist', not a 'socialist' – that is, someone who sought not a new order, but no order at all; and this is the word Primo repeats when he briefly mentions Natale in his writings. His side of the family was slightly shocked, as well as secretly admiring; they kept *zio* Natale a family secret, until enough time had passed to make him a family legend.

Clearly, if Vittorio Foa had written 'Argon' it would have been very different. But Vittorio, and Natale, were exceptions among the Della Torres, as they would be in most families. Primo's elimination of *zio* Natale from 'Argon' was a choice, but it was not a distortion. As far as I know, no one else in any branch of Primo Levi's family travelled so far, in mind or body, from the place where they were born; not until the dislocations of his own time.

There is unlikely to have been any *zio* Natale among the Luzzatis. They were at the opposite end of the social scale: an extremely poor and humble family, from Casale Monferrato. They had probably been in Casale for generations (though one version of the family history says that Primo's *bisnonna* – great-grandmother – Luzzati came from Moncalvo, a village nearby). Primo's *bisnonno* Luzzati – possibly the flat-footed Leonin – was most likely a pattern-maker. Like everyone else, he and his wife had a large number of children, many of whom did not survive childhood. All those who did came to Turin. As well as Primo's *nonno*, Cesare, there was at least one other son, and many daughters. The daughters all married very humbly; but the sons prospered, and helped their sisters generously throughout their lives. By the next generation, many Luzzatis had completed the leap from rural working class to urban professionals; by Primo's generation the family bristled with chemists, biologists, engineers, doctors, professors.*

Cesare Luzzati, say his grateful descendants, was an excellent businessman and an extremely hard worker. When he arrived in Turin in the last decade of the nineteenth century he had nothing. But somehow – perhaps with the help of his Della Torre father-in-law – he set out in the cloth trade. By 1903, when his last child was born, he had his own shop, even if it was only two rooms on the Via Cernaia, with the family living above. When the First World War began they were still there. But he must have been carefully

---

* For example, Mario Luzzati, son of a brother of Cesare's, became a professor of history. In the next generation, in Cesare's family alone, Primo was of course a chemist; Corrado's daughter Ada also became a chemist, and his son Giorgio a doctor. Nella's son Paolo is an engineer, Gustavo's daughter Alma is a biologist, and Jole's son Luciano another professor. The only profession missing, this being Turin, is psychoanalysis.

planning his next move, and accumulating the capital for it. Some time before the war he had met a man whom we have already seen in his youth, brandishing a sword upon the stage. This was Aronne Colombo, who had since become the wealthy owner of a large wholesale fabric depot. During the Great War Cesare Luzzati and Aronne Colombo became partners. Together they bought a large and well-established draper's shop on the Via Roma, the best shopping street in Turin. Cesare moved his family to a new home on the nearby Corso Vittorio Emanuele, and began to flourish.

He went on working as hard as ever, spending all day in the shop, walking the last few hundred yards of the Via Roma to the Corso Vittorio and back four times a day.★ He seems to have had few relaxations apart from food (he was an excellent cook, and an even better eater). His relaxation was business. He never missed a silkworm market anywhere in Piedmont; and he never missed the opportunity to do a deal, in his own trade or outside it. When the war was over, for instance, he bought up a large number of military trucks and resold them, no doubt at a handsome profit. At much the same time his two elder daughters reached marriageable age. He was able to provide both of them with generous dowries, possibly (though possibly not, he was already solidly established) with the help of the trucks.

Cesare's shop, the main source of his fortune, was at No. 37 in the old Via Roma. It was called Ugotti, after its founder and long-time owner, from whom he and his partner had bought it. Over the next twenty-five years he made it into one of the most successful and elegant drapers in Turin. He had excellent relations with his neighbours, with whom he made mutually profitable arrangements to scoop up the innocent provincial customers pouring off the trains at nearby Porta Nuova. With his competitors, the other drapers of the Via Roma, his relations were naturally more complicated. They made, Primo said, 'friendly visits to each other's shops, which were also missions of industrial espionage'; and called each other 'Signor Thief' and 'Signor Swindler'. Cesare's more public name was also not his real one. All his customers and acquaintances – indeed everyone, according to Primo – called him Monsù Ugotti, after his store. The name passed to his sons, who took over from him; and by extension, to his whole family. 'For several years after the war,' Primo wrote, 'even I was called Monsù Ugotti

---

★ This last is a detail preserved by Primo in 'My grandfather's store' (in *Other People's Trades*, 1985). Cesare, of course, went home for a long lunch. (The practice may be declining now in big cities like Rome and Milan, but it is still a cherished right and duty in Turin.) Later the family moved once more, up the Corso Vittorio to the corner of Corso Re Umberto. This very slightly increased Cesare's daily walk, though not enough to affect his bulk, which grew with every year.

on the Via Roma.' He was clearly amused by this link to the past, and to his canny, hard-working, self-made grandfather. I think he was also very pleased.

The Levis and Sinigaglias

The ancestors of 'Argon', when they *were* part of Primo's own family, were almost all on the Della Torre side. There are not even any definite Luzzatis; and there are almost no Levis. There is Barbaronìn; but he was a rather special Levi, being *nonno* Luzzati's partner as well. In the final version Cesare Levi, Primo's father, and Cesare's mother Nona Malia arrive in the last few pages. But that is in the present. There do not appear to be any Levis – or, apart from Nona Malia herself, any Sinigaglias either – among the ancestral gases.

Nor do any appear in any other work of Primo's. In the Introduction to his 'personal anthology' of favourite books, *La ricerca delle radici*,* he mentions his father's two brothers; but describes them, like himself, only in relation to books. All three brothers, he says, 'one engineer, one doctor, and one stockbroker', were avid and undiscriminating readers. 'They were very fond of each other, but stole books from each other's libraries at every possible opportunity.'

Of this generation of Levis, at least, there are some accounts in the family, and they agree with Primo's. His father, Cesare, was the engineer; Mario was the doctor (an eye specialist), and Enrico the stockbroker. In fact both Mario and Enrico would have fitted extremely well into 'Argon'. Mario was intelligent, cultured, and detached; he was more interested in books than in his patients, and at home allowed his wife to command, while he sat silent, reading. Enrico was more active, but not more practical. He loved collecting things – anything, but especially books, of which he had enormous numbers on every subject under the sun, many in languages he couldn't understand.

Primo did, however, make a few allusions, *en passant*, to one Levi ancestor. In a long conversation-interview with the physicist Tullio Regge† he referred briefly to his paternal grandfather, saying that he was 'a small landowner' from a 'well-to-do family', and adding: 'It seems he had a bank, which later failed.' In 'Argon' he makes an even briefer reference to this grandfather, which is also shocking and enigmatic. His grandmother Nona

---

* *The Search for Roots* (Einaudi, 1981). The last of Primo Levi's books to be translated into English (by the Penguin Press, in 2001).
† Published in English as *Dialogo*, Princeton University Press, 1989.

Malia, he says, 'was known in her youth as "*La Strassacoeur*", "The Heart-breaker": she was left a widow very early, and the rumour spread that my grandfather had killed himself in despair over her infidelities.'

If this was true, perhaps it was not surprising that Primo hesitated to explore his Levi heritage. Was it true? The family is no keener to talk about it than he, or his father before him. Cesare never talked about his father, *zia* Jole says, but only told funny stories about his family: there was one, for example, about a Levi who had become a monk. Nonetheless, she *had* heard that Cesare's father had committed suicide. So had Primo's closest cousin, Giulia. No, Giulia did not know if it was because of his wife, or because of the bank that had failed. Nor had Primo known. Years after that glancing reference in 'Argon', in the middle of a conversation he had suddenly turned to an older Levi relation and asked: 'Tell me, why *did* my grandfather kill himself?' But she hadn't known either.

Paradise Lost

Paradiso

Bene Vagienna is a small, tranquil town on the rich plains of Southern
Piedmont. Nearby lie the ruins of its first, Roman incarnation: Augusta
Bagiennorum, named after the Vagienni, the original settlers of the land
between the Po and the Tanaro. The new town which grew up in succeeding
ages Italianized its name to Bene, then in 1862 sonorously reattached the
Roman form as well, as though in double invocation of its ancestors.

The Levis came to Bene from Mondovì, a dozen miles away. Mondovì
consists of two parts, Mondovì Breo, which hugs the foot of a hill, and
Mondovì Piazza, which perches on top of it. Mondovì Piazza is narrow,
steep and beautiful. From the sixteenth to the nineteenth centuries it was
the home of a flourishing Jewish community, whose relations with their
Catholic neighbours were as good as any in Italy, and probably better. At its
height they called Mondovì (though not in front of the neighbours, even
so) 'the little Jerusalem'.

The first head of the family whom records show was a certain Donato
Levi, born around the middle of the eighteenth century. He married a Sara
Levi – Levi was by far the most common family name in little Jerusalem.
Their son Salvador David managed to marry a Treves; but all their children

(at least the ones I found) married Levis. One of these, Giuseppe Vita Levi, married *'La Damigella'* ('Mistress') Enricchetta Levi in 1844, when he was twenty-four and she just twenty. Soon after that – perhaps when the ghetto was opened in 1848 – they moved to Bene.

I too arrived in Bene from Mondovì. I'd followed them through the archives there, as they rushed from birth to marriage to death, and I had the reader's double feeling about them. I knew them better than I knew anyone around me – much better, in fact, since I'd only been here a year, and my relationships with the living were still at the stage of formal politeness. Yet at the same time they belonged to another, different world, made of faded paper and ancient illegible writing, that had no possible connection to this one.

I knew that Mistress Ricchetta, who had signed her marriage certificate in such a bold and childish hand, had since lost three children of her own, all around the age of two. But I knew too that five children had eventually survived; and with the unfair advantage of the biographer, who has done nothing but be born later, I also knew what had happened to them. I knew, for example, that the eldest, Debora, would become Zia Allegra of 'Argon', the mother of Barbaronìn. In particular I knew that the next, Michele, born in 1849, would become the father of Cesare, Enrico and Mario, and the grandfather of Primo Levi; and that he would commit suicide.

In Bene Ricchetta's husband Giuseppe had combined the traditional Jewish roles of cloth merchant and moneylender, and added to them a trade in jewellery and real estate. He had prospered; so much so that both Michele and another son, Salvador David, had made the great leap to the professional classes a generation before the Luzzatis, Michele becoming an engineer, Salvador David a doctor. Nor had Giuseppe himself remained a mere merchant-moneylender: he had become a banker. His bank was called *'Giuseppe Levi e figli'*, Giuseppe Levi & Sons; presumably his other two sons, Felice and Giacomo, were the *figli*. Indeed – I remembered – Michele the engineer must have been one too, if this was the bank that failed.

Mondovì Piazza had been exciting, its houses red and grey, tall and thin, all huddled together to keep from falling off the edge. Bene was solid, low and ochre-gold in the sun. Peaceful; beautiful. I passed two baroque churches, one after the other, like pubs in England; and walked under that most Piedmontese invention, the *portici*, or arcades: pillars and fan vaulting, which make the street half like a church, and half like an umbrella.

Even before the churches, I had caught the glint of glass, set into a wall, behind which some treasure was clearly preserved. It was a door, not to be entered but only to be marvelled at: tall and fabulously carved, like wooden lace. Cut into it were the words *O PARADISO*. It was called (the note beside it said) the *Portico Desideri*, the Door of Desires, because when Napoleon had famously dined in Bene in 1796 he had desired to carry it off with him. Plainly the people of Bene had desired equally fervently to keep it; and they had won.

Bene is so small that in under ten minutes I was in the centre. At a more ordinary but still rather handsome door I stopped and rang the bell. I had an appointment with the Amici di Bene, the group of proud citizens who had preserved the Door of Desires, and all the other ancient glories of their town. The door opened on to a stone passage. At the end I glimpsed the green of an inner garden: and then I was in the Secretary's office.

On the telephone from Turin Dr Michelangelo Fessia had been rather cool. He was very busy, and my questions would require some research (with little hope of success, I'd heard in his precise, reproving tone). But now he received me with old-fashioned courtesy, making a little bow over my hand. He was short, plump and smiling; if he'd been born a little earlier, I thought he might have been a priest instead of a civil servant.

His smile warmed from politeness to quiet pride. He had done the research, he said, and he had good news for me: he'd learned a great deal about the Levis. It was true that they had been bankers; and it was also true that their bank had failed. It was quite a story, he said, shaking his head. They had lost everything, and disappeared. After the turn of the century there was no trace of the family left in Bene.

He had planned my day carefully. First he would take me to see the Levis' house, or rather houses. Then I could visit the Registry Office, while he went home for an early lunch. (His smile grew apologetic: family duty could not be shirked, even for history.) In the afternoon we would go somewhere else. I must see, I thought he said, *Paradiso*: Paradise.

Leaving the office ('The internal garden is a great feature of Bene'), we turn towards the main square, with its *duomo* and *Municipio*,* both of which we can see from the Amici di Bene's front door. The Levis, Dr Fessia begins, were well-off from the beginning. Their first house in Bene was on the main square itself: that was already, of course, a very good address. But soon they began to grow decidedly rich. In 1850 the anticlerical government of Piedmont passed a famous, or infamous, law (he clearly means infamous, crossing himself gravely as we pass the *duomo*).

'As you know,' he says politely, 'the *legge Siccardi* seriously curbed the powers of the Catholic Church, including its right to own land, so that a great deal of church property had to be sold. Good Catholics hesitated to buy it; which opened the door to Piedmont's newly liberated Jews. The

---

* Cathedral and Town Hall.

Levis began to buy large amounts of property in and around Bene. They owned houses on both sides of the Via Roma, near mine; and many others all over the town, including two on the Via XX Settembre, which was called the *contrà dei nobili*, the nobles' quarter. They themselves moved to a beautiful house next door to the Marchesi di Villar. The bank was on the ground floor. This was their last home in Bene: that one, there.'

He's pointing at a large, whitewashed house on the corner of the Piazza: Via Costanzo Gazzera No. 1. It too has a lovely garden, half-hidden behind tall wrought-iron railings. He points out the letter *T* entwined among the leaves and scrolls of a green wrought-iron balcony: ' "T" for "Tabuglio",' he says, 'the family who owned it after the Levis. After them came the Ravera family, who still own it today.' '*Only two owners* since Giuseppe Levi?' I ask. Now Dr Fessia's smile is one of pity for my city-dweller's surprise. 'Please call me Michelangelo,' he says, with one of his little bows.

We walk up to the house and stand gazing at it for a long time, as though the Levis themselves might emerge. Michelangelo points to the tall foundation stones that make a pleasing pattern at the foot of the walls. 'It was called "La Ca' d'le Pere" because of those,' he says. *Pere* is Piedmontese for *pietre*, stones; so this means 'The House of Stones'. 'There is another word, *zoccoli*, which means foundation stones. People around here say, "If it all goes on the *zoccoli*, there's nothing left for the walls." They mean, if you live too high, you'll have nothing left for a rainy day. That's what they said of the Levis, when the crash came.'

Was it true? I wondered. Or just the envy of their Catholic neighbours, chafing under the *legge Siccardi*? Either was possible (think of the Mole Antonelliana, beggaring the Jews of Turin in the same heady years). But Michelangelo is waiting. He's standing, hands folded, in front of a large, green-painted double door. 'This was the entrance to the bank,' he says. 'In there, in a small room – perhaps a toilet – one of the Levis hanged himself.'

I don't know why I haven't foreseen this: what more natural place to kill yourself than at home? But I haven't. Suddenly the past seems very close – not just two owners away, but right there, as though poor Michele might be hanging now behind those high green doors.

'How do you know?' I ask Michelangelo. It hadn't sounded like historian's knowledge, from maps and deeds, like his account of the Levis' houses. And it wasn't; it was memory. The last Ravera to live in the house had told her daughter, who owned it now, and she had told Michelangelo. The old lady had probably remembered much more; but alas she died last year. Those who remember most have always just died last year; and what remains of their memories is always the worst – violent death, adultery, the loss of children. Our memories are not stronger than our imaginations; both need shocks, like mine on the Via Gazzera, to come alive.

★   ★

I knew that nothing before unification in 1861 would be in the Registry Office in Bene, or anywhere else in Italy.★ The Registrar, Maria Cristina Pittia, had told me that on the phone. But since Michele was only twelve in 1861, I had always hoped his death might be registered in Bene. Now that I knew it had happened here, I was sure it would be.

Signora Cristina took out a special bunch of keys from a cupboard and led me upstairs. Registers were moved out of the working offices after only a few decades, she explained; even in a town as small as Bene, the paperwork soon overflows. The oldest Registers, from the last century, were naturally moved the furthest: right up into the attic.

When she opened the door there was a shocked pause; then a tremendous scurrying: clearly the mice hadn't been disturbed for decades. And when she turned on the light my heart sank to the dusty floor. Piles of antique paper tied with leather thongs stared from every shelf, eaten away like sad leprous faces. Could anything have survived? Signora Cristina explained cheerfully that these were the very oldest records of all, dating from the fifteenth and sixteenth centuries; they didn't concern us. Guiltily, I felt relieved.

It took a while to find the Registers for the last decades of the nineteenth century. But when we did my hopes revived: they had good solid hard covers, and only a few frustrated nibbles out of the edges of their pages. Signora Cristina checked the Index for 1866–1875: no Levis. But that would surely have been too early – Michele was only twenty-six in 1875. 1876–1885 was more likely. I checked the Index myself; no. Signora Cristina had 1886–1895. 'Yes!' she cried. In 1887. We had found him.

We turned to page nineteen, 26 September 1887. No. 70 was a son of Giuseppe Levi, Banker, and his wife Enricchetta, but it wasn't Michele. It was Giacomo.

I stared at the page in disbelief. It was *Giacomo* who had hanged himself in his father's bank. When I had felt Michele's anguish just behind the double door it wasn't Michele's at all, but Giacomo's. When I had *imagined* Michele's anguish. Remember that.

★ Before that, records of births, marriages and deaths were kept by the church for Catholics, and by the synagogue for Jews. The ancient tomes through which I had pursued the Levis until Giacomo's birth in 1860 were all synagogue records, preserved now in the main Registry Office in Mondovì.

Poor Signora Cristina couldn't understand my dismay. I hadn't said I was looking for Michele Levi's death, just a Levi death – it had never occurred to me there might be more than one. And then there it was as well. *Levi Michele*, No. 1139, 1888.

Michele's entry was in a different form, completely handwritten. Signora Cristina said, 'This certificate does not come from Bene. It's been copied in by hand.' Slowly, she puzzled out the words. Levi Michele, engineer, had died on 26 July 1888 in the San Giovanni Hospital in Turin.

Permission had to be formally sought, and granted, for photocopies; this could take a week or two (read three, I thought). Signora Cristina would send them on to me. In the meantime I could copy out the contents of the two certificates by hand, if I liked. As I copied out Giacomo's I noticed something else I would have to ask Michelangelo.

At the Maggi café everyone was hailing Michelangelo as though he'd just come back from America instead of lunch. 'Micol!' they cried. '*Bon dì!*' He unbent in their warmth, and plied me gaily with coffee and cakes. This was a lucky development, since my question might be delicate.

Primo had written in 'Argon' that his grandmother raised her sons alone; then 'at an advanced age gave in and married an old Christian doctor'. The doctor's name, I knew from *zia* Jole (indeed from everyone, he was a memorable man), was Rebaudengo. What I had seen on Giacomo's death certificate was two signatures: his brother Felice's; and a doctor's, resident in Bene, called Rebaudengo. *So Adele Levi must have known him at least a year before her husband died.* Surely she *had* committed those 'infidelities', and with him. But why had they waited until old age before they married? Perhaps he was already married, and his descendants were still in Bene . . . I began cautiously, though as it turned out I needn't have bothered.

'Do you know the name Rebaudengo?'

'Ah,' said Michelangelo. 'So you know that already.'

'Know what?'

He looked positively roguish. 'That *Madama* Levi married *il dottor* Rebaudengo before her husband was a week in his grave.'

'She *did?*'

'So you didn't know?' He was pleased.

'I knew she married him, but I thought it was years later, when they were old.'

'No, no, it was straight away, within a week. It was quite a scandal, as you may imagine.'

Scandal no longer said how long the affair had been going on; that had died with Signora Ravera, if not before. But this remained, 100 years later:

a week after Michele Levi died his wife married the doctor, and left Bene for ever. I would have to disturb the mice again to look for their marriage.

★   ★

We were going to Paradiso.

Michelangelo had explained, as usual. On the hills outside Bene there were three very beautiful villas, and the first of these was Paradiso. It had been built in the eighteenth century by the Marchesi di Villar, who still owned it when the Levis arrived a century later. But the Marchese of the day was a terrible gambler, who lost a large part of his patrimony, including Paradiso. Perhaps it came to the bank to pay for a loan, or perhaps they simply bought it: in any case, until they in their turn lost everything, the Levis owned Paradiso.

We caught sight of it for a moment, a flash of pink on top of the hill. It was tremendously overgrown, Michelangelo said; he hoped I didn't mind creepers and thorns. There was a whole forest of chestnuts, and every other tree imaginable – even a pomegranate, the only one in Piedmont. And Paradiso had another very rare and beautiful feature: in spring one side of the hill below it was covered in tulips. Because of this, he said, even though they cannot have owned it for long, the family was called *i Levi dei tulipani*, the Levis of the tulips.

We walked the last few hundred yards through creepers and thorns, as Michelangelo had warned me. And there was the house: calm and serene in the wilderness, its walls still coloured a deep, strong rose. It too had only had two owners since the Levis, Michelangelo said. First the Colombos, who were also Jews, and who had kept it right up to the Second World War; in fact they had lived there during the war, and no one in Bene gave them away. And now the Beltrandis; but neither they nor anyone else had lived in it for many years.

We fought our way around to the front. I could just make out the cracked stone terrace beneath our feet, and the remains of two small round towers which had once pretended to be the gates to Paradise. Carefully we climbed the ruined steps, and Michelangelo pushed open the door.

Inside it was very still. The rooms were empty, everything stripped and stolen, including the floorboards. Only in one room was the floor intact – perfect medieval tiles, which no one had been able to budge. On the walls there were still patches of colour – blue, green, ochre and rose. We stopped at a window. From here, Michelangelo said, you would see thousands of bright red tulips, if it were May. But it was November, and growing cold.

He had one more thing to show me, he said. He led the way to a small room that still had faint traces of a floral design on the walls. I was about to admire them, but he pointed up at the ceiling instead. There was the same design, complete and beautiful; and in the centre, enclosed by curling sterns and leaves, a painting of Paradiso in its heyday, with one of its little round towers at the side.

The cold disappeared. I clambered around, trying to find a good position for a photograph. Just as I took the first, there was an extraordinary sound. Something – surely a motorcycle – was roaring and coughing through the trees. I took a second. Yes, definitely a motorcycle – now it was pulling up with a great fanfare of noise, like a whole gang of teenagers. 'Who on earth –?' I asked. Michelangelo shook his head, and his smile became inscrutable. 'It's Fulvio,' he said. 'He always knows when anyone comes to Paradiso.'

Quickly I took a few more photographs. When I looked round, there was Fulvio, in shiny black leather and a purple helmet. He tore the helmet off his head, seized first Michelangelo's hand, then mine. Michelangelo explained my interest in Paradiso; and for the next half hour no one spoke but Fulvio.

By the time he waved us goodbye I knew his whole life story. But the important part of it, he said, was this. When he was a small boy his grandfather used to take him to a garden to play. Its wild trees, its rose-coloured ruin, were unlike anything he'd ever seen, and he couldn't understand where he was until he heard its name: Paradiso. Then of course he knew he was in heaven. He decided that when he grew up he would buy the rose-coloured house, and live in it for ever. Now he knows that this will never happen. But he still comes to Paradiso every day, because he feels so happy there; and he still plans and schemes to buy it. It's been his dream all his life. His black eyes still shone with calculation, but he gave a fatalistic shrug. 'Of course,' he said, '*i sogni non si realizzano*, dreams don't come true. That's the point of them.'

★   ★

There was no certificate of marriage between Adele Levi, née Sinigaglia, and Dr Felice Rebaudengo in Bene. Nor in Turin, nor in Vicoforte where Dr Rebaudengo was born, nor in any of the other towns of Southern Piedmont either. So I could not confirm the 100-year-old rumour that they had 'married within a week' of Michele's death. Certainly, though, they had known each other before; and certainly too they had married not long after. For Dr Rebaudengo had brought up Cesare, Enrico and Mario from boyhood. This I learned from *zia* Jole, when I told her of my discoveries in Bene. (Of course she had volunteered nothing before.) He had been a good, if strict, father to the boys, she said, and they had liked and respected him.

Indeed he was very *simpatico*, and a good doctor; she had even gone to him herself.

Clearly the rather sinister eccentricity which Primo describes in the Doctor and his wife in 'Argon' only overtook them later. (It did overtake them, *zia* Jole agreed.) I do not know why Primo thought – or at any rate wrote – that Adele had raised the boys alone, and 'in a Spartan manner', since neither was true. Perhaps he just imagined that she had always been as mean as she was when he knew her. But even without Dr Rebaudengo Adele Levi and her sons would not have starved. Her own family, the Sinigaglias, were rich; and six months after Michele's death she won her case against his creditors, and was freed from all liability for his debts. With a highly respectable doctor for their stepfather, Cesare, Enrico and Mario must have had a perfectly ordinary bourgeois upbringing. It was what had happened before that was not ordinary: the suicide of their father when they were only nine, eight and seven years old.

Both explanations of that suicide which Primo had hinted at in 'Argon' were surely true. Adele Levi had almost certainly been unfaithful to her first husband with her second; and the slow collapse of Giuseppe Levi's bank had already cost the life of one of his sons. Now that I knew the date of Michele's death I could find the traces that it, and the events leading up to it, had left in newspaper and court records. As far as these sources can establish, this is what happened.

Michele Levi married Adele Sinigaglia in 1877. The last really healthy balance of Giuseppe Levi & Sons appeared in May 1879, when Michele was thirty, Cesare an infant of seven months, and Adele two months pregnant with Enrico. From then on the bank's liquidity steadily declined. When Mario was born in 1881 the account books were beginning to show holes. By 1883 they were almost completely unreliable; in 1885 they stopped altogether. From April 1885 the bank was really in debt, kept going from day to day in the hope of restoring its fortunes before its creditors suspected that anything was wrong.

After two years of this, Giacomo hanged himself. Perhaps, like Michele, he had other troubles as well; but the terrors of that losing game must surely have been the main reason. He did it at half past six on a Sunday evening, when the bank was closed. He had, therefore, deliberately gone there to die. Perhaps the house was full of his family. Still, it is hard not to see a message in the place where he left his body to be found.*

---

* One of the mysteries of the story is what Giuseppe Levi was doing while his sons took his affairs so much to heart. He survived both of them (he was only sixty-eight in 1888), though I don't know for how long. I looked in all the obvious places – Bene itself, Mondovì,

By then – late September 1887 – the end was approaching. The economy of Southern Piedmont depended on agriculture, and agriculture was in crisis. In 1888 the price of livestock was derisory, and a hailstorm devastated the crops around Bene. The summer was so rainy that whatever had survived became mildewed. Several other banks began to fail – in Savigliano, in Carmagnola, in Genoa. Somehow Giuseppe Levi & Sons had still managed to preserve its reputation, both for honesty and for stability. It was believed to own over half a million lire in property alone. And it was the only bank in Bene, with the entire population of the area, from richest to poorest, as its depositors. But just this, which had made its fortune, was now the cause of its downfall.

On 21 July, a Saturday, a rumour suddenly spread that the Bank of Fossano was refusing to renew several large loans to Giuseppe Levi & Sons. Some clients became worried; and one, a priest called Canon Dompé, went straight to the bank and demanded to withdraw his entire account, about 11,000 lire. When this was refused, he went mad. 'He shouted, he stormed and raged,' the papers reported: in short, he made such a scene that the news spread like wildfire. The poor peasant farmers of Bene, of Trinità and Carrù, were already facing bankruptcy. Even though the next day was a Sunday, over 200 of them poured into town and fell upon Via Gazzera No. 1. They surged around the entrance to the bank, baying threats and demanding their money. Finally the police arrived and rebarred the double doors.

Over the next few days Giuseppe and his remaining sons Michele and Felice must have discussed feverishly where to turn.* They had surely exhausted all the possibilities already. In the end only one remained: Adele Levi's rich family, the Sinigaglias. We cannot know if this was Michele's own idea, or someone else's; in any case it was surely a last desperate and reluctant throw. On Wednesday the 25th he was in Turin, at the Sinigaglias' house at No. 18, Via San Francesco da Paola. Perhaps they knew that Adele's marriage was already shaky; or perhaps the sum he had asked for was just too big. In any case, they must have refused. There was nowhere else to turn; and perhaps Michele could not bear to return to his family empty-handed. At two o'clock in the morning of the 26th he threw himself out of a second-floor window of the Sinigaglias' apartment into the courtyard below. He did not

---

Fossano, Turin – but I never found a death certificate for him, or for poor Mistress Ricchetta either.

* The third son, Salvador David, never appears in any of the documents to do with the case brought against Giuseppe Levi & Sons. Unlike Michele, he practised his profession (*medico chirurgo*, doctor and surgeon); and judging by her name, Anna Tanzi, he married a Catholic. Most probably he had completely separated from the family.

die instantly. He was carried to a bed, and a doctor was called. The doctor immediately had him sent to hospital; but Michele died on the way. His death was registered with the notation *Suicide: Fall from a height.*

For days after, Bene was in a fever of anger and uncertainty. Giuseppe Levi fled to a house in the countryside. A few nights later a furious crowd broke down its door ('certainly not in order to caress him', said the paper which reported the incident); but he had disappeared. Probably he got as far away from Bene as he could.

In those first days rumour put Giuseppe Levi & Sons' debt as high as a million lire. But even then cooler heads said something very different. The investigators registered a difference of only 81,000 lire between the bank's credits and debits. It seems that the Levis really were getting their house back in order. If they had just had a bit more time, or if there hadn't been that sudden run on the bank, their tragedy, and the tragedy of many of their customers, might never have happened. In 1897 one of the founders of a new bank in Bene was that same Canon Dompé who had led the panic rush against Giuseppe Levi & Sons in 1888. We cannot be certain that what he did that day was personally self-serving. But the Catholic Church had a historical hatred of Jewish usury; and since the *legge Siccardi* still more reason to resent Jews like Giuseppe Levi. Even the reports of the time implied that Canon Dompé deliberately manoeuvred to bring the Levis down. It looks very much as though one of the forces behind Michele Levi's suicide was antisemitism after all: even though, as his son Cesare would tell his grandson Primo, it had been mild and 'without malice' among the schoolboys of Bene.

★   ★

Although Cesare Levi never talked about his father, he called his son after him: Primo Michele. I do not know whether Primo ever thought of this as a fateful link. But at the end of his life he thought more than once of his grandfather. Several times he spoke of a 'hereditary taint' of suicide in his family. What he did not know was that it had come out not once but twice in his grandfather's generation. And he did not know that Michele had thrown himself to his death 'from a height', as he himself would do ninety-nine years later. Michele had even leapt into a small inner courtyard, as he would leap into a stairwell. A 'taint' cannot (surely) be so specific. But there are qualities of mind and character which can bind people who never knew each other. When we come to consider Primo Levi's own death, we must remember the mystery of that bond.

Long after my visit to Bene, I found an interesting book, which will appear again in these pages. It was by Enrico's son Paolo, who like his cousin Primo became a writer. Paolo, however, was a novelist; and *Il filo della memoria* (*The Thread of Memory*) is a novel about his family. In it the Levis of Bene Vagienna become the 'Sacerdotes of Chiusa di Pesio'; Michele Levi becomes 'Ettore Sacerdote', his wife Adele 'Serena', and their son Enrico 'Edoardo'. Edoardo never talks to his children about his father either: indeed 'the whole history of this branch of the Family is shrouded in darkness, as though they were a nocturnal race whom the light of the sun might damage'. Nonetheless the story has come down to all the descendants of *nonno* Ettore that he committed suicide. There are several conflicting accounts of both how and why. According to Edoardo's son Renzo it was a lovers' suicide pact, *nonno* Ettore having fallen madly in love with a noblewoman of the highest rank; she swallowed poison, and he drove his carriage into the Po. According to Renzo's cousin Giovanna (who, transposing the relationships to reality, is Anna Maria), the unfaithful partner was rather *nonna* Serena, who was disturbingly beautiful and had many lovers. In this version, 'Giovanna's father was in reality the son of a cavalry officer, or possibly of a Russian baron'; and *nonno* Ettore shot himself in the heart in grief and shame.

In both these romantic versions, a story of financial ruin is put about to cover the scandalous or humiliating truth. In the last version, which is Edoardo's wife's, the financial motive is the true one. Ettore had lost all the money entrusted to him in 'a small bank', she says; and 'on the verge of bankruptcy, and just as the police were arriving to arrest him, he threw himself into the stairwell'.

Il filo della memoria was published three years before Primo died. In this story about his grandfather's death I cannot help seeing the uncanny accuracy, even the prescience, of a novelist's imagination.

2. Botticelli Angels:
1919–30

Primo and Anna Maria

Primo's cousin Vittorio Foa was in prison in Rome when he heard of the death of Cesare Levi. He was nine years older than Primo, and one of the leaders of the antifascist resistance in Turin in the 30s. In 1942 he was in the seventh year of his sentence for activities against the state. His letters home were usually about his political passions, and his hopes and fears for the future. But now he thought of his cousins, whom he cannot have seen since 1935 or even earlier, when they were still little more than children. He wrote to his parents:

I remember my Botticelli cousins, little angels without wings, uncertainly poised between angels and nonentities. Anna Maria could have become either – an incredibly dull person, or a very rare and spiritually original one. The first seemed more likely then, but in fact she's become the second. The boy was excessively shy; but it was so long ago.

★   ★

Primo was excessively shy. He blushed, he hid – as on the day he met Signorina Glauda outside school; in photographs he always seemed to be turned aside, about to run away. He was extremely sensitive, and cried inconsolably at tragic stories in the news: the death of the explorer Nobile at the Pole; or the crew of a sinking submarine, borne down to the depths still alive, beating their fists against the walls. He was small, pale, extremely thin; by fifteen he still weighed only seven stone, which put him in the bottom 3 per cent of boys. As a small child he looked particularly weak and delicate. Sergio Valvassori, who knew him especially well in these early years, thinks that this was the source of Primo's shyness. '*Io ero timido di timidezza*,' he says: 'I was shy out of shyness.' But '*Primo era timido di fragilità*': Primo was shy because he was so small and thin.

Behind the closed doors of Corso Re Umberto 75, with his sister, younger cousins, closest friends, he could emerge from his shell. Then he was lively, curious, knew everything and could explain it to you better than any adult. 'If I ever wanted to know anything at all,' says his cousin Giulia, 'all I had to do was ask Primo.' Sometimes their games even seemed wild to Giulia, who was an only child. But in these games Anna Maria was the leader. Almost always, even among family and friends, Primo was the quiet one, reserved, never naughty. At school he rarely spoke or smiled; he was serious, unsporty and solitary. He seemed like a grown-up among children, responsible, already formed. Though he was clearly of a different order of intelligence from the rest, he never showed off or gave himself airs. Even with his sister and cousins he never imposed his own will, his own ideas; at most he would make suggestions for things to do or games to play, which were always, Giulia says, 'a cut above, civilized'. He got on with everyone, says a childhood friend, and he wanted everyone to get on; he wanted, she says, peace.

He liked to build and to explore. Apart from his favourite, Meccano, he briefly messed around with fretwork, which he'd learned at school. Later, as we know, he gazed through his microscope at salt crystals, at his own hair and skin, at the unsuspected life in his mother's vases; and up at the stars, through a small telescope his father bought him one summer holiday in Bardonecchia. He read as voraciously as his father: science books from the second-hand stalls of Turin; once a whole cellar-full, including Voltaire and the famous Flammarion, bought on that same Bardonecchia holiday. Like his father, too, he read everywhere: most famously, in family legend, up a tree.

His father was responsible for the high proportion of science in Primo's early reading, and for its high intellectual level. Jack London and Jules Verne were encouraged; but Emilio Salgari, for example, was forbidden. Salgari wrote hugely popular, highly coloured tales of adventure among savages and buccaneers. Cesare Levi was a famously liberal reader, who even supplied frowned-upon French authors – Stendhal, Romain Rolland – to Primo's cousin Anna, sister of Vittorio. But in approving Verne and banning Salgari he was typical of the Jewish parents of his generation, in love with the scientific enlightenment which had freed them, and transformed them from provincial pedlars to urban professors and engineers. Almost certainly, like them, he thought Salgari's romances unreal, corrupting, uneducational.

As a child Primo wrote little poems, which once again suggest a connection between his father and the Word: the one Giulia remembers began '*Caro Babbo*', 'Dear Daddy'. He gave this up after nine or ten, and didn't begin again until he was twenty-four, and the war was closing in on his first hopes of love and freedom. During his earliest years he also drew; but this too he gave up after primary school, as though both poetry and drawing had to be put away — as he would later say about the consolations of religion — among childish things. But he drew well, Giulia remembers; and when towards the end of his life he bought a computer, he admitted that 'I had to force myself to leave the drawing programme, and return to writing.'

There was one other thing Primo gave up as he grew older. It was connected in his mind to poetry, and most closely of all to his father: music. Cesare Levi was passionately musical. He had studied the piano, quite seriously; he had lived in Austria and Hungary, countries saturated with music; he was himself, Primo said, saturated with music. He was knowledgeable, and also adventurous, enjoying even moderns like Wagner; he went to every concert in Turin; and he filled all his spare moments with music. When he shaved in the morning he sang, when he came home in the evening he played the piano, almost always Beethoven. Primo does not record how well or badly his father sang. But he is very clear how he played — and the family agrees: loudly, joyously, and very badly. 'He assassinated Beethoven,' Primo used to say. And this put him off for life. His father killed music for him, as he'd killed Beethoven; that was Primo's picture, and the family's.

He had a good ear; as a young man he loved the songs of the Piedmontese mountains, and taught them to his friends. When he left Turin for the first time, at twenty-three, the only things he took with him, besides books, his bike, and his climbing equipment, were his slide rule and his recorder. But as he grew older he felt he had to choose; and he did not choose music. In his sixties he would say that his relationship to music was aborted, a thing of the past; that his life now was 'almost without music'. And in fact his relationship to music, or at least to the piano, was troubled from the start. His piano lessons at the age of six were not a success. It was not that he couldn't learn to play: he learned perfectly well, but unhappily. He cried and made scenes, he saw off two teachers, until finally the lessons were stopped. The only reason he gave for this later was that the hand position — wrists down, fingers up — had bothered him; it had seemed to him 'unnatural'.

At around the same time, however, he had his first experience of being deeply touched by music. This experience too was connected to his father. Cesare Levi (Primo told an interviewer in 1984) had bought one of the first wireless radios, to which the children were allowed to listen when he wasn't home. One afternoon when he was six years old, Primo said, he sat in an armchair, the earphones clamped to his head, and listened for hours. Suddenly he heard an extraordinarily beautiful sound: a piece of music which moved him deeply. He listened carefully for the title; and when his father came home he said, 'They played something very beautiful. It's called "Carni".' 'My father explained,' he tells the interviewer, 'that I had heard *Carmen*.' '*Carmen is* rather carnal,' the interviewer jokes. Primo gives one of his short explosive laughs. 'Very carnal,' he agrees.

He had many very clear childhood memories; but he wrote (and spoke, at least publicly) of very few. The things which drove him to write, he said, happened later. Either, then – despite his intense shyness and sensitivity – those childhood memories were not of the sort that needed exorcizing; or he did not want to exorcize them in this way. He spoke only once to an interviewer – who was not a journalist, but a student at the University of Turin – of an unhappy memory of early childhood. At around the age of eight someone had told him he was not good-looking. From eight till twelve, he said, he had worried about this, had even been 'quite tormented' by it. From then on he had known he was not physically attractive; and though he implies that after a few years the torment stopped, even he admits that his childish despair at not being good-looking 'must have counted very much'.

He does not write of fear of the dark, nor of that attic or cellar or cupboard under the stairs that everyone has. He did write of his paternal grandmother's dark and dusty flat, of her husband the Doctor's sinister instruments, of the mouldy chocolates she gave him, week after week, from the same box. He did not want to meet the Doctor, he says, who (he'd heard) treated stammering children by cutting the skin under their tongues; he did not want to eat those chocolates, which 'with great embarrassment' he would slip into his pocket. He makes it all sound absurd, farcical, comic-grotesque. In truth he was terrified of this grandmother: of her flat, of her husband, above all of her chocolates.

Only one childhood fear did he write of openly, probably because it lasted all his life. When he was about nine years old, on holiday in the country, he slept in a room in which the wallpaper was hanging off the walls, magnifying any noise that came from behind them. Just as he was drifting off to sleep, a loud ticking woke him. He switched on the light, and the monster was there. All legs, it descended towards my night-table, with the unpredictable and inexorable tread of Death.

He called the maid, who squashed the spider '(a harmless Tegenaria)' with 'visible satisfaction'. He does not say whether he too felt satisfaction. Rather he tries to understand why, to this day, he should feel such irrational horror and disgust, exclusively for spiders ('I would touch a toad, a worm, a mouse, a cockroach, a slug'). He is sceptical about popular explanations (their cruelty, their hairiness), and even more sceptical about psycho-sexual ones ('Who can stop psychologists of the subconscious from exercising their trade?'). Instead he suggests explanations in terms of mindless instinct, and silent, insidious movement; or in terms of the symbolism of cobwebs, 'signals of abandonment, absence, decay, oblivion'.

But for the birth of his own 'slight phobia' he returns to a particular event of his childhood. When he was a small boy, he says, he 'collided with' the illustration of Arachne by Gustave Doré, in the Twelfth Canto of *Purgatorio*. The young girl who had challenged Minerva in the art of spinning was turning into a spider before his eyes, six knotty, hairy spider's legs sprouting from her back, beside them her human arms still waving desperately. Dante (Primo notes) 'seems to be gazing at her groin, half revolted, half voyeur'.

Is this not rather close to the sexual fear of the psychologists' account, which Primo has just presented with an ironic smile? . . . Well, irony is ambiguous, that is the point of it. An ironic claim leaves room for its opposite – but also for itself, since (especially in these areas) without irony one could easily seem to protest too much. Perhaps Primo *is* both telling us something, and at the same time denying it. But 'Primo' is also ambiguous. He is both the man remembering, and the small boy remembered. Perhaps the small boy put himself in Dante's position, or perhaps only the man put him there. But in either case at six years old he is closer to another of the man's explanations:

The spider's technique of capture – tying up the prey caught in its web with its silken thread – would make it a symbol of maternity. The spider is the Mother-Enemy who enfolds and engulfs us, who wants to make us re-enter the womb from which we have come; to bind us tightly, so that we return to the impotence of infancy, and she can take us back into her power.

School

Throughout his childhood (and later too) Primo's health was thought to be very delicate. In his first year of primary school, when he was six, he stayed at home for almost half the year. In the second and third years he seemed to be better, though he still missed a month or so of each year, and remained one of the poorer attenders. In the fourth year his absences leapt up to nearly two months; and in the fifth and last year, when he was ten, he stayed at home altogether, and was prepared privately for the move to secondary school.

All of this was put down by the family, and later on by Primo himself, to his 'weak' or 'delicate' constitution. It is not clear that he was ever actually ill. But he was, and remained, small and extremely thin. The idea of physical weakness stuck; so that when he was deported, at the age of twenty-four, almost no one thought he could possibly survive. And yet he did. Long before that, in fact, he had proved to himself and to his closest friends that his thinness, his pallor, his apparent fragility were misleading. They hid not only an iron will, but an iron constitution. Even starved and enslaved he did not fall ill, when all around him the strongest men were dying. That did not happen suddenly, miraculously, to a fragile and delicate boy: like everything else that happened to him then, it did not reverse the rest of his life, but was a part of it, a product of it. He *was* delicate and fragile, especially as a child; but the impression of fragility did not really come from his body.

Its real source was shyness, his 'extreme introversion'. Primo Levi – at six, eight, ten – was an unusually intelligent, and an unusually quiet, solitary, insecure child. He was so intelligent that even after missing half the first year he still got '1°' – 'primo', or 'first', the top mark – in most of his subjects; so intelligent that Sergio Valvassori, reporting his friend's achievement to his family, said week after week in every year, 'Primo Levi primo.' He always seemed composed, answering questions in class with calm assurance, and he always knew the answer. And yet he wrote more than once later of the 'terror', the 'intense anguish' of the young, as they wait to be interrogated, tested, reproved or exposed by their teachers.

He and Sergio, whose fathers were friends, played at each other's houses, and were sent to school together (with an escort, Sergio remembers, in the protective practice of the time). But Primo did not seem to mix with the other children, or to have any particular friends. He never mentioned any later; and wrote only of one Rignon classmate, a boy called Giovanni Comi, whom he re-met about ten years later in farcical circumstances. By then Comi had acquired the nickname 'Schifùs', which means 'dirty' or 'disgusting' in Piedmontese; and this reminds Primo that already at school he had 'worked hard at being disgusting: he was the only one in the class who could lick the soles of his shoes, without taking them off, of course'. Already as a small child Primo was more observer than partaker, his cousin Giulia remembers; and already, it's clear, he particularly noticed the comic and bizarre.

What this quizzical, lonely, almost morbidly sensitive child needed could not come from other children. But at the Rignon, to his great good fortune, he found it. *Maestra* Glauda was a grey-haired spinster in a long black dress, still under fifty, but looking much older; old-fashioned, upright and virginal. Like all her pupils, Primo was in awe of her; when they met that day on the street he was even frightened. But he soon discovered the truth. Emilia Glauda was the soul of gentleness and kindness. She loved and understood small children, and she was particularly fond of him. She often used homely Piedmontese instead of formal Italian. She was never angry, she never shouted, but always spoke sweetly, especially to the little ones. She was, quite simply, good. Looking back, Primo called her 'an angelic person'; he remembered her with affection, even devotion.

Alas, this good fortune did not last. In the fourth year his all-male class had to leave *Maestra* Glauda and graduate to a *Maestro*, a male teacher. The idea, clearly, was that nine-year-old boys should no longer be mothered, but made to move on into the harsher, realer world of men. And that is exactly what happened. Ferruccio Introna, who had adored *Maestra* Glauda as much as Primo did ('I said I would marry her when I grew up'), remembers that '*Maestro* Spagnolo was a shock'. He was, he says, 'an ordinary teacher', which was quite bad enough after *Maestra* Glauda; he was also badly crippled, which (though Ferruccio Introna does not say this) must have made him even more frightening than the authorities intended. When Primo spoke of the Rignon at the end of his life, he did not mention the 'shock' of *Maestro* Spagnolo, nor his withered arm and leg. But he said, with feeling, that after *Maestra* Glauda he had had '*un maestro sciocco e noioso*', 'a stupid and boring teacher'. Of his last year of primary school he remembered only 'great boredom', and a hatred for history (though he did very well in it anyway). He seems to have taken refuge in numbers, which he loved: 'I noticed that if you added any number, of any length, to its inverse, the answer would be a multiple of nine.' Later he would write of geometry that it could be a child's first revelation of 'the austere power of reason'; and 'a joyful proof, for a young person, of his mental musculature'.

It is very likely that Primo's absences from primary school, especially for half his first year and all his final one, were not caused by 'delicate health' at all. He may no longer have 'cried and made scenes' at ten, as he had at six;

but I suspect that he saw off *Maestro* Spagnolo nonetheless, as he'd seen off the two piano teachers before him. I think that the prospect of another year of *Maestro* Spagnolo made him ill with dread; and that his parents, who knew by now how unusually clever their son was, and how unusually vulnerable, decided not to force him to return.

In fact it wasn't unusual for clever children to 'skip' the last year of elementary school; or to do two years in one privately, as in effect Primo did, after which he entered *ginnasio* in the second year. There was no real reason for any explanation at all; and yet one was always given. Probably it was plain that *something* was going on, beyond mere academic ambition. The truth is, I think, that the 'delicate' part of Primo's health was never really the physical one, but already then the emotional one, as it would remain. This was not (and still isn't) an easy thing to admit in Turin; it was easier – and in Primo's case quite plausible – to suggest a physical weakness instead. But the likelihood is that he was allowed to study at home for a year not for physical, but for emotional reasons. It would allow him to avoid *Maestro* Spagnolo – though this, it's true, is only a guess. It would also allow him to avoid other children: and this is more than a guess. For several of the family say that, as a small child, Primo had great difficulty relating to other children; and that this was the real reason for his year and a half away from school.

If this *was* the plan, it worked. The tutor who was found for him was Marisa Zini, daughter of one of the great antifascist teachers of Turin, the philosopher Zino Zini. Perhaps she had an independence of mind which appealed to him, or a feminine gentleness, or both; certainly she was cultured, learned, and a good teacher. After his year with her Primo passed easily into the second year of *ginnasio*; he remembered her always with respect and – he even said – affection.

And once he was in secondary school the worst of his social difficulties seem to have been over. His absences fell again; until by *liceo* (the last three years) they were, as far as I can tell, perfectly normal. He began to have friends (though also, as we shall see, enemies). Whatever was going on inside him, he was increasingly able to control it, and when necessary to hide it. But something *was* going on. There was about him (as he would one day write about a boy in a story) a severity, a seriousness, the sense of an invisible weight on his thin shoulders which was at once pathetic, absurd and impressive. All this comes out in the first description of him ever published. In 1932, when he was thirteen, his school magazine did a page of spoof '*Interviste ginnasiali*', 'Interviews with the Lower School'. The first thing you notice about his is its content. But the second is its position: first, and longest.

Sono andato per il primo
a trovare LEVI PRIMO.
Ch'era là, solo soletto,
serio e triste nell'aspetto.
L'intervista cominciai
e gli chiesi 'Come stai?'
Ei pensòvvi e dopo un po'
mi rispose: 'Non lo so.'

Down I went to see the babies,
The first I chose was PRIMO LEVI.
Alone and lonely in that place,
A sad and serious little face.
Starting the interview anew,
I inquired, 'How are you?'
He thought it over, rather slow.
At last he answered, 'I don't know.'

Anna Maria

In all this Primo had one great ally: his sister Anna Maria.

Anna Maria, a year and a half younger, was also extremely intelligent, strong-willed and reserved. But otherwise her character was very different from Primo's. Though she was reserved she was not timid. Instead she was confident, outgoing, attractive. She did not hesitate to impose her will, to argue. She had very different interests, artistic rather than scientific, and was bored by Primo's researches; also, occasionally, disturbed by them – saving an ant, for instance, as it was about to fall to its death under his objective gaze. He was older, and his intellect and knowledge superior. But if either was the leader, it was Anna Maria; if either was the protector of the other, it was not Primo of Anna Maria, but the other way around.

On the deepest level, however, they were equals: each was the other's closest confidant, partner and spiritual ally. They understood each other without speaking; or else they spoke in a language of their own, that no one but their cousin Giulia could understand – as fast as typewriters, and packed with abbreviations (like turning 'the Symphonie Pathétique by Tchaikovsky' into 'the Pachovsky'). Everyone in the family, from Giulia who grew up with them to their most distant relations, remembers how specially close they were, how specially attuned to one another. Primo himself remembered, and continued to feel it, all his life. His first biographer summed it up like this, from his own words:

It would not be accurate to call this merely affection between brother and sister. The bond which grew between the two children, and which has existed ever since, was certainly something more: a spiritual affinity, which expressed itself in solidarity and profound understanding. Levi does not hesitate to call the emotional bond between himself and his sister fundamental for his development as a human being: the bond which, in more ways than one, helped him to overcome the obstacles of his extreme introversion.

★   ★

Where did his timidity come from? His sister did not have it, neither of his parents had it. He lived in the midst of a large and stable extended family of the *media borghesia*, the comfortable, unspectacular middle middle class. True, this solidity was all on one side. Cesare Levi and his brothers were (according to Primo) fond of one another, but their families were not close. Enrico, the stockbroker, lived in Genoa, with his wife Lisa and his two sons Franco and Paolo; Primo's contact with these cousins, therefore, was friendly but rare. Mario lived in Turin; indeed his oculist's studio was in his mother's house on the Via Po. But Mario was a strange, detached man, with an elegant and worldly wife who permanently, openly, and with his apparent compliance deceived him. This was quite outside Primo's mother's world; and though Mario's son Roberto was almost exactly Primo's age, there was almost no contact between their families.

At the heart of this forbidden side of the family there was, of course, his paternal grandmother Adele Levi, whom his father called 'Maman'. Though Primo can have known nothing, as a child, of the dramas and tragedies of her life, this was the grandmother of whom he was afraid. She was tiny and wrinkled, but still living on her capital as a *femme fatale*. In her second marriage too she had taken a lover (or at any rate a devoted admirer), a certain Dr Sibaldi. She and her husband were a famous sight in the Via Po, as they proceeded every evening from their house to the Café Nazionale: he so tall and she so small, covered in a long fur coat and all her jewellery, but with her slippers forgotten on her feet. She died when Primo was twelve, leaving behind mountains of the beautiful and solid possessions of the rich, almost unused, and equal mountains of pointless and revolting rubbish, which she had hoarded for years. He remembered her as short-tempered, fabulously deaf, and more than half mad; completely uninterested in her son and grandson, letting them in with visible reluctance when they came to call, and always offering him, like a not very efficient witch, those same mouldy chocolates. 'Even now, inexplicably,' he wrote in middle age, the relics of this grandmother would resurface from his cupboards: 'as though, after almost fifty years, her restless spirit still visited our house'.

The contrast, the solidity, stability and normality, were provided by his mother's side: by the wealth and extended family of his maternal grandfather Cesare Luzzati. Throughout his and Anna Maria's childhood their Luzzati grandparents lived ten streets away, on the corner of the Corso Vittorio Emanuele II and the Corso Re Umberto. Their aunt Ida, mother of Giulia, lived almost next door, on the Via Lamarmora, and every day the three cousins would go to their *nonna* Adele's for tea. Their other aunts Nella and Jole, and their uncles Corrado and Gustavo, all lived within walking distance in the solid *palazzi* of Crocetta, with Primo's younger cousins. The family was close, meeting every Friday night at *nonno* Luzzati's in town; in summer holidays and High Holidays at Saccarello, his villa just outside Turin, or at his house in Piossasco, ten miles away in the Val Sangone.

Nonno Luzzati was the undisputed head of the family, who dominated his sons and spoiled his daughters, especially the youngest, Jole. This he did even more after she had lost her husband at only twenty-five, and had to bring up her sons Luciano and Bruno alone. These two, as a result, were perhaps his closest grandchildren. Otherwise he tended to be more indulgent towards the girls than the boys, as he had been with his own children. Nella regularly called on him to discipline her son Paolo, who not surprisingly was afraid of him. To Corrado's son Giorgio he seemed *chiuso*, 'closed'; affable, but impossible to understand. Primo too remembered a mysterious, impressive personality: the *nonno*, he wrote, 'never laughed, and spoke very little, with spare and carefully measured phrases heavy with meaning, often ironic, and always full of quiet authority'.

That was the key. The *nonno*, self-made man, supporter of many children and several sisters, was the classic patriarch: very generous, and very, very authoritarian. Huge and fat, he dominated his tiny fragile wife, who was never allowed to leave the house alone, except to go to the *pasticceria* on the ground floor of their own building. 'I don't think he ever read a book in his life,' Primo wrote; while she was cultured and precise, a true Della Torre. Since he was diabetic, she tried hard to control his diet; but he paid no attention, ate hugely, and indulged in forbidden treats in forbidden cafés. She was the traditional 'queen of the household', but only of the household; and this both exalted and exhausted her. 'Her face had the regal look of the mother of many children,' Primo wrote; but at the same time 'the rapt and timeless expression of ancestral portraits in their enormous frames'.

As well as running his flourishing shop, with its fabrics designed and supplied from as far away as Finland, the *nonno* was a partner for a time in one of the first cinema societies in Italy, the Pittaluga. This company owned half a dozen cinemas in Turin, including the grand and beautiful Ghersi, in the Via Roma almost opposite the shop. Primo's father and Giulia's were associates too, and when they were small all the older cousins could go to the Ghersi and the others free. Sadly, this adventure ended in the mid-1920s, when the company collapsed.

Apart from his major enterprises, the *nonno* also dealt in the silk trade, and in buying and selling houses, and the contents of shops which had gone out of business. He owned a farm which was let out to tenants; and on his land at Saccarello and Piossasco he kept at least a dozen cows, and made his own wine from his own vineyards.

The *nonno*'s shop played a great part in his grandchildren's lives. Throughout Primo's childhood and youth it was on the Via Roma: still Turin's smartest shopping street, in those days narrow and teeming, paved with wooden blocks to stop the horses from slipping, and bisected by the tracks of the electric tram. Its front door and a single window gave on to the street; coming in you stepped down into the long, narrow, dark shop, stuffed with bright rolls of silk and cotton. On the floor above were the offices, and the darker, heavier materials for men's suits. This floor had a balcony over the Via Roma, from which the grandchildren were allowed to watch the Carnival procession every year. The *nonno* would give Anna Maria and Giulia samples and remnants for their dolls; 'Tell your friends,' he said, and troops of little girls would bear away the brightly coloured pieces.

The business was a big one, with up to thirty employees. Primo, of course, delighted in the strangest ones: Monsù Ghiandone, for instance, 'who rolled his r's and wore a wig', and who worked at nights as a make-up artist in a theatre; or the legendary cashier, Tota Savina ('Tota' is 'Signorina' in Piedmontese), whom Primo calls Tota Gina in 'Il fondaco del nonno', 'My Grandfather's Store': 'She made one continuous mass with her cash register and the high dais on which it reposed. From below you could see her majestic bosom, which covered the whole desk, and overflowed at the edges like homemade pasta.' Oddly enough, he did not memorialize the *nonno*'s minute chauffeur, Carletto Tagliavacca, who must have been new to the job, since he once ran out of petrol and had no idea what was wrong; or Emilio, who lived over the shop, but was so deaf that he never heard when anyone rang. To all these employees the *nonno* was expansively generous on Sunday outings to the famous Boringhieri pub; but the instant they were over the threshold of his shop, Primo wrote, 'their subjection was absolute'.

Most absolute of all, however, was the subjection of his sons, Primo's uncles Corrado and Gustavo. The two had been born within a year of each other, and would die within months. Corrado, the elder, was the striking one, whom all the children of the family loved and admired. He had never studied, but spoke several languages (badly), and played several instruments;

according to family legend he had played the piano in the cinemas of Rome during his military service. He'd worked on the other side of the screen as well, in the infant film industry, building models and special effects, and even, when required, acting. He was a daring climber, and also conducted the most adventurous, even dangerous, expeditions in his car, in the days when few decent roads existed. (His nephew Paolo, who spent the war there, says that Corrado would have made a good pioneer in Brazil.) He could repair absolutely anything; and built marvellous mechanical toys, including an electric train and a pedal car for his son. During many years he built a real car: one that didn't need petrol, which was impossible to find, but ran instead on clockwork. Unfortunately it was extremely slow, he had constantly to climb out and rewind it, and it was lost or stolen almost immediately. Still, he had invented and built it *ex nihilo*. Both the brilliance and the absurdity of this would have appealed to Primo. He always said Corrado was *un uomo notevole*, a remarkable man, and his favourite uncle.

Gustavo was quieter and less brilliant. In his bachelor days he too went on voyages, but of a more conventional kind: ocean cruises to exotic places, which he assiduously filmed to show to the assembled family at home. He too was mechanically gifted, especially in minute precision work, so that the family called him *l'orologiaio*, the watchmaker. Gustavo was the timid one; and the one who had the detached, ironic Della Torre smile.

Both uncles would probably have preferred a life beyond their father's store: especially Corrado. At one stage friends of his were setting up the very first Italian company to make radios, and wanted him to join them. This would have suited Corrado perfectly; and later on that company became the largest manufacturer of radios in the country. But the *nonno* would not permit it. Corrado had to stay in the shop, however much he hated it. And he did hate it; all except the customers (or some customers), who in return loved him, and told him all their troubles. But he had to obey. If anyone wanted a reduction, both brothers had to ask their father's permission until they were nearly forty years old.

When, around 1970, Primo wrote a gloomy (and funny) story about a man summoned by death, he used this side of Corrado, or of both his uncles. 'Giuseppe was tired,' he wrote. 'Tired of being on his feet, tired *in* his feet, tired of saying "Yes ma'am", tired of selling fabrics, tired of being Giuseppe, tired of being tired.' He didn't give Giuseppe a rather demanding, dominating wife; which, each in his own way, both uncles also had. (He avoided the issue, and didn't give Giuseppe a wife at all.)

Perhaps the habit of submission had been bred into the Luzzati sons. And the daughters? Not the two younger, Nella and Jole: they were famously lively and dominant, Jole managing feistily as a widow for most of her life,

Nella single-handedly moving her husband and children out of Italy in 1939. The two elder were quieter. Ida's daughter Giulia is clear that, in her family, her father ruled. In Primo's it was, I think, more complicated.

Rina

Ester Luzzati was the first of Cesare and Adele's six surviving children (a seventh had been stillborn). At some stage 'Ester' must have become 'Esterina', and then 'Rina'; she was always known as Rina in the family.

Rina was the quietest and most serious, and accepted her responsibilities as the eldest. Once, when her mother had to go away for treatment (she suffered from chronic headaches), she left Rina in charge of the family. To Jole, the youngest, Rina seemed like a second mother.

In educating his children Cesare followed family tradition and (mostly) his own inclinations. After school and military service the two boys went straight into the serious business of the shop, resigning all their other skills to the level of hobbies. The four girls, however, were encouraged to become as cultured as their mother while they waited to marry. Rina and Ida, the old-fashioned ones, went together to the Istituto Maria Letizia, where young ladies were taught languages, calligraphy and pianoforte as well as sewing, embroidery and the domestic arts. Nella and Jole were not only more headstrong but more artistic. Jole studied the piano; Nella even attended the Academy of Fine Arts for a year, until her father decided that that was going too far, and hired a well-known artist to teach her at home.

By her early twenties, therefore, Rina was a cultured and competent young woman. She was dark-haired and dark-eyed, not beautiful, but sweet-faced; quiet, reserved, and very intelligent. She spoke French fluently, and was an avid reader. She too played the piano, though she did not love music as much as her brothers and sisters did, or as her husband would. She was married to Cesare Levi on 7 October 1918, when she was twenty-three and he was forty.

Her husband was chosen for her by her father. The connection was almost certainly Aronne Colombo, Cesare Levi's first cousin and Cesare Luzzati's partner, who was thus indirectly responsible for Primo Levi's being born. In 1918 marriages were no longer formally arranged between Jewish families, with brokers and contracts, over the heads of their children. Nonetheless, the only men respectable young women could meet would be presented to them by their parents. Not only Rina's marriage was arranged. So, in short order, was Ida's, to Oreste Colombo (though they fell in love immediately, according to family lore); and probably Nella's and Gustavo's as well. The only one who definitely chose his own partner was Corrado, who fell madly in love with his cousin Irene Della Torre.

Rina and her new husband had almost no time alone together. Primo was born forty-two weeks after their wedding day: in other words, he was conceived in the second week of their marriage. Anna Maria followed eighteen months later. For the rest of her life Rina was known, both in the family and outside it, as a *regina della casa*: a queen of the household, like her own mother, and like most Jewish women of her generation; a quiet, private woman entirely dedicated to her family.

Perhaps she was not as completely absorbed and fulfilled by this role, however, as her sister Ida was. Throughout her marriage she had a servant called 'Cia' (Primo's childhood version of 'Silvia'); Rina much preferred reading to cooking and sewing, and left most of the domestic work to Cia. But this was, of course, only what most middle-class ladies of her day could do, and did not detract from her being the *regina della casa*; on the contrary. She was a very private person, not as outgoing as Nella, nor as wilful as Jole; but not as retiring as Ida either. She was quiet and refined, like her mother; but she was also strong-willed and dominating, like her father. She was used to leading from an early age, and she expected to be obeyed. In fact she *was* the *regina della casa*: the *nonno* had given the flat to her as a wedding present – not to her and her husband together, but to her alone, as long as she lived. In those days, when a woman's property would otherwise pass wholly to her husband, this was a common way for rich fathers to protect at least part of their daughters' dowries against any unforeseen marital disaster. Corso Re Umberto 75 was, from the start, Rina's castle: she was the house, and the house was her.

She was not only the house, she was Turin. Later the novelist Philip Roth would say, with amazement and irony, that Primo had never lived anywhere else, except for a year in Auschwitz. Primo himself would write that his was 'an extreme case of sedentariness'; like that of certain molluscs, who after a brief youth 'attach themselves to a cliff, grow a shell, and never move again for the rest of their lives'. But he, at least, would have that brief youth, in which he lived for a year in Milan; later he would also travel for his company (mostly, ironically, to Germany, but as far as Russia as well). The true, the original, the genuinely *bugia nèn* case of sedentariness was his mother. Few people moved very far from Turin in her day, especially women. But she was the most immobile, the most limpet-like of her immobile family. Only *zio* Natale had, famously, got right away in the past; only Nella would get right away in the future, when the habit of moving would have been a precious legacy. Rina especially did not have it. In all her life she did not travel further from Turin than the mountains and coast of Piedmont: twice a year on holiday, and for a year and a half of war. Even Ida, who was a stay-at-home like her, at least went to Rome on her honeymoon. But Rina had married during the great flu epidemic, so had stayed home even on her wedding night.

'Mother' means home to all young Italians, perhaps to all Italians. But it especially meant home to Primo Levi. Almost the only time he ever mentioned his mother in his writing was in 'The Canto of Ulysses' in *If This is a Man*, when amid the agony of Auschwitz he could, for a rare moment, think of home. Together with Jean, the Pikolo of his Kommando, he wrote, 'We spoke of our houses, of Strasbourg and Turin, of the books we had read, of what we had studied, of our mothers.'

His mother too had scolded him for never knowing how much money he had in his pocket; his mother too would have been amazed if she had known that he had found his feet, that day by day he was finding his feet.

This is about Jean's mother as well, but really it is only true of Primo's. *His* mother, not Jean's, had kept him home for half his first year of school, at the age of six; his mother, not Jean's, had feared he was not strong enough to do his *servizio pre-militare* at eighteen. His mother would certainly not expect him to find his feet in Auschwitz; or anywhere away from Corso Re Umberto 75, and her.

Cesare

Cesare Levi was exactly the opposite. From the start he had shown a rare nomadic instinct for a bourgeois Italian of his generation, and especially for a bourgeois Turinese. After his mysterious childhood and youth, about which he told his children so little, he had specialized as an engineer in Liège, and worked for a long time in France, Austria and Hungary. For several years before the First World War he worked in Budapest for a company called Ganz; he spoke German, which was the company language, and even a little Hungarian. This was a happy time in his life, about which he told his son more, though no doubt not everything: memories of much eating and drinking, and many friends; of a careless bachelor life in one of the most elegant and sophisticated capitals of Europe.

This lasted until 1914. When the First World War broke out, Cesare Levi finally had to go home. But by now he was thirty-six, and almost as much Austro-Hungarian as Italian. He stayed with Ganz, and continued to return to Hungary even after his marriage. Primo remembered, for example, that his father had been in Budapest during Béla Kun's Communist revolution;

since this lasted from March to November 1919, Cesare must have been in Hungary just before, during or after Primo's own birth. He thought that Cesare stopped travelling two years after his marriage, and settled down as Ganz's representative in Piedmont and Liguria. But it was probably several years later: at least three or four.

By then Cesare had spent half his life abroad. This made him very rare in Turin, and unique in his new family: apart from the legendary *zio* Natale, he was the only family member who had left Italy and travelled the world.

He had also spent the last part of his life in a glittering, rotten empire that had collapsed just before his son was born. Traces of this exotic past remain in what Primo and the rest of the family would say of him, half a century and three quarters of a century later. He was a *bon vivant*, even a dandy, with his bamboo cane for weekdays and special silver-handled one for Sundays, and with a cigarillo always in the corner of his mouth. He was worldly, even perhaps a bit of a snob; the only sport he approved of was tennis, the game of the upper classes. Unlike Rina, *regina della casa*, he loved life outside the house, in the elegant streets and cafés of Turin. Unlike her, he loved social life, even high life, regularly disappearing to play cards in the *salons* of rich and noble ladies, whom he probably met through his brother Mario, or rather through Mario's pretty, wicked wife. He was, in fact (the family says with a nervous smile), a *man of the world*, a bit wicked himself, though definitely not pretty. On the contrary, he was frankly ugly: short and squat, with poor sight and thick glasses. But his great intelligence, his wit, charm and *joie de vivre* made him fascinating and attractive, especially to women. He was, Primo said (right at the end of his own life), 'a bit of a womanizer', and flirted with his wife's friends by quoting Schopenhauer to them, 'with little success'.

He had none of the Della Torre irony, precision or reserve. Instead he was a cheerful extrovert, a great talker, and a great teller of jokes and stories. He was full of unguarded and unashamed passions – for music, his greatest love, for mathematics and philosophy, for science and literature. All of these (except music) he taught himself, on vast, eager and undisciplined voyages of reading. He loved the bizarre and eccentric, and was quite happy to be eccentric himself. So (Primo wrote, and Giulia remembers) he had his jackets made with enormous pockets, each wide and deep enough to hold one of the many volumes he was reading, and walked around bulging with books. He was wholly urban, with 'a savage hatred of the countryside' (Primo again); on the rare occasions he consented to go for a walk in the country he stopped as soon as possible, sat down ('on a newspaper, so as not to dirty his suit'), and blocked off the view with a book. He hated any form of violent exercise, and claimed never to have done any, even in his youth.

His entertainments were entirely intellectual and sedentary: chess and music, card games and crossword puzzles, detective novels, the cinema. He didn't mind behaving badly, and shocked the children by using (very mild) bad language.

All this worldliness, this openness and frivolity were, of course, very un-Turinese. Cesare Levi was also very open-minded intellectually; which was less un-Turinese in general, but still uncommon in Crocetta. He was a passionate believer in science and reason, who had known the famous positivist scientists of Turin in his youth, and had dreamed of becoming a scientist himself. And he was extremely liberal, even scandalous, in his reading. He secretly gave forbidden French novels to young ladies, as we know; he even bought *Lady Chatterley's Lover* in the 30s, and let his teenage children read it.

He tended to criticize everything, but only superficially, without taking it seriously; really he was a 'lover of life', Primo said, who dealt with troubles and dangers by ignoring them. He did this, for example, with Fascism: first with the mere troubles it caused, and later also with its dangers. He was apolitical; if anything he was more afraid of Communism, after having witnessed Kun's Communist coup in Hungary. He was scornful of Fascism, of the buffoonery and vulgarity of the parades, the uniforms, the salutes and speeches; but his disapproval was not one of principle, only one of taste and style. However reluctantly, he joined the Fascist Party, and put on his black shirt when he had to. Like all the cousins, his children joined the Fascist children's organizations as a matter of course, Primo becoming first a *balilla*, then an *avanguardista*, until the racial laws released him from this particular bondage. He had very much disliked it; but only, at this stage, for his father's reasons: because the uniform was ugly and uncomfortable; because the meetings and marches bored him, quite literally, to tears.

Cesare Levi was proud of his son's intelligence and scholastic triumphs, and did helpful fatherly things for him when they were needed. But he was not a fatherly man; and Primo was not a childish child. They were too far apart in age and nature, and there was little understanding between them. Their only communication was through the intellect, and especially, of course, through science: through the microscope, the telescope, and the books of chemistry, physics and astronomy that Cesare bought him.

Primo saw his father's charm, but it was not directed at him. Cesare had married too late. His love of life was a love of bachelor, not family, life; it was grown-ups he liked, and who liked him. He did not alter his tastes and habits for children, never tossed a ball to a child, never took one for a walk or – Heaven forbid! – a picnic. Towards his own he was affectionate, but in a curious, almost entirely physical way, Primo thought, 'as one would be with kittens'. He caressed them, but didn't bother much with them. In Primo's ironic phrase, 'He had no aptitude for the career of fatherhood'; he left their upbringing and education to their mother. On holidays he stayed indoors and read; at home he sat alone for hours, reading, playing the piano, or working on chess problems out of a book. He was, in sum, a distant, even an absent father. When his children were small he was often away; and his last illness began while they were still in their teens. From the outside, the family seemed to consist of three people rather than four. Friends and neighbours rarely saw Cesare Levi; at least one of Primo's friends was convinced his mother was a widow.

Like any boy, Primo wanted his father's approval. But he had only part of it. Cesare Levi, lover of life, 'a bit of a womanizer', would have liked a precocious son, or at least a normal one, who showed desire for something other than a microscope at the age of fifteen. And Primo knew it. 'He advised me to drink, smoke, go with girls,' he said. 'But I didn't smoke, I didn't drink, I had no girls.' His father was not at ease with him, and he was not at ease with his father. Sometimes he was even afraid of him; and sometimes it was the other way around. Cesare Levi no longer believed in his religion, but it still had a superstitious hold on him. When he yielded to temptation, as he often did, and bought *prosciutto*, he would glance at his son out of the corner of his eye: 'As if he feared my judgement,' Primo wrote. Or hoped that for once it might be suspended.

The Hare and the Tortoise

Anna Maria, Giulia and Primo, Bardonecchia, 1935

'You must remember,' says the family friend, 'the extraordinarily puritan atmosphere of those days.' You can't forget it, it's still here. Puritanism rubbed off on to the Piedmontese from their Protestant minority years ago; or was already there in their bones, chilled by their cold climate and stiffened by their military kings. It's what makes them so reserved, so cautious, so un-Italian. Honest and hard-working, say the Turinese – straitlaced and dull, says the rest of Italy; polite and principled, say the Turinese – *falsi e cortesi*, says the rest of Italy: courteous and false, in other words hypocrites. It's what's behind the jokes about *pesci morti* and *il frigorifero d'Italia*; which like all jokes are not entirely jokes, even now.

But when Primo was growing up in the 1920s and 30s the puritan repressiveness of good Turin society was unchanged from Victorian times. Girls were never allowed to associate with boys outside their immediate family, or go anywhere alone: Primo's cousin Anna Foa had to repeat a whole year of school because the next year's schedule didn't fit with her brothers', and it was more important that they should continue to escort her. As for the boys, even Primo's more relaxed friends did not speak to a girl without blushing until long after school, or even university. Many of them, like him, were neurotically shy and awkward, as underdeveloped socially as they were advanced intellectually; strange uneven creatures, like hothouse plants bred for only half their purpose.

But before that, during his mother's girlhood, the containment was still more complete. Even in Italy, even today, sex is not an easy subject, and must be barricaded with punishments in this life and the next. But in respectable, bourgeois, puritan Turin in the first part of the twentieth century it was an impossible one. It was never mentioned in decent families, and only men and the lower classes were meant to do it. As in Victorian England, women were either whores or angels; with wives, of course, on the side of the angels. And assimilated Jewish families were much like Catholic ones, in this as in other things: young men's sexuality was admitted, even tolerated; but young women remained firmly enclosed within their families and religions, and suffered sex only in order to have children. If a respectable wife with a respectable number of children became pregnant much after her early thirties, eyebrows were raised: this looked too much like pleasure.

From sex, suspicion spread until it covered feeling in general. And this affected the men more than the women. Women were not supposed to have sex, but they did have children; they could not be stopped, therefore, from having feelings. But this whole sphere was left to them, and kept strictly behind closed doors. As a result, even women might have little practice in their intimate emotions; little chance to think and talk about them outside the narrowest circles, with mothers and sisters as inexperienced and inhibited as themselves. But men had still less. The smallest mention of their private lives or feelings outside those closed doors, to all but their closest friends, was taboo, *un'indiscrezione intollerabile*. And the taboo was passed down, hardly diluted, to Primo's generation.

The family friend looks at me as she says this, and falls silent.

★   ★

Perhaps this taboo is the beginning of an explanation for one of Primo's central silences: the silence about his mother. Later he would also be silent about his wife and children; that too was part of the Turinese ban on the private. But in his silence about her, his mother stands out from the rest of his first family.

Apart from the memory evoked in *If This is a Man*, I recall only two images of her from his writing about his childhood: receiving important guests in her 'best room' twice or three times a year; and knitting in the shade of a willow as he explores a river-bank (guarding him, I imagine, from afar). And he never spoke about her publicly at all: except towards the end, to explain that it was her illness that made it increasingly impossible for him to leave Turin, the flat, and her.

By contrast, in 'Argon' he wrote of all the most distant members of her family he could, and in 'Il fondaco del nonno' of his Luzzati grandparents; of these grandparents, and of his Luzzati aunts and uncles, he spoke a good deal, for example to his authorized biographer, Giovanni Tesio. Of his sister there are only brief glimpses in his childhood – helping him with his tadpoles, refusing to help when he wanted a blood sample to examine; but there is a charming, admiring portrait of her at twenty in 'Il mitra sotto il letto' ('The Tommy-Gun under the Bed'). Of his father he wrote quite a bit, in 'Argon' and elsewhere; and talked about him too, always with the same ironic affection, and the same detachment. In his writing especially, but also in interviews, it seemed to me that he had turned his father into one of his best characters: eccentric, self-sufficient, absurd but rather admirable – or admirable, but rather absurd.

The reason he gave for not writing or speaking about his mother was that she was still alive: while by the time he began to write, his father, for instance, was long dead. There was clearly much truth in this explanation. He was (after one or two early experiences) very alert to how painful people could find even positive portraits of themselves; and 'Argon' clearly shows that, like any writer with a conscience, he wrote more freely about people when they'd been long dead.

And yet, surely this wasn't the whole story. Primo's mother was *always there*, throughout his life; it was really quite strange that so little of her had crept into his work. Certainly, he was capable of iron self-discipline; but why should he have applied it, if all was well between them? This was an unworthy thought, however, which I hesitated to express in Turin. There (and not only there) only someone completely beyond the pale would openly query a good moral reason; so of course nobody does. Not, at least, until they know you a little better.

One day I ask someone again why Primo was so silent about his mother, and again he quotes Primo's answer: 'Because she was still alive.' But this time he raises his eyebrows, and just for a second his fingers sketch a series of dot-dot-dots in the air.

Not long after that Nella's son Paolo Avigdor remarks that 'Cesare Levi was a man of the world'. I'm startled. No one in Turin is a man of the world, it's a very dubious thing to be. Paolo has a rather Primo-like twinkle in his eye; but he is also as shy as Primo, and never quite looks at me. He hadn't wanted to meet me in the first place; pursuing him, and now talking to him, feels like chasing a small animal, or a runaway child. There *is* something childlike about Paolo, just as there'd been about Primo. I remember when I first met him – when I first cornered him, in *zia* Jole's room in the Jewish old people's home. Jole was unhappy there; it was like a prison, she said, and she often longed to get out. Paolo said he'd just seen *Escape from Alcatraz* on the television, in which the prisoners escape through the central heating system. He looked up at the grille on her wall, then down at the old lady, and let out a brief, delighted laugh.

I try to probe Giulia, who has already told me how different from the other uncles Cesare was, so outgoing and sociable, a 'difficult character', 'a terrible man'. Yes, she says, he was a great charmer – yes, of women too. But no – not a seducer (her word, not mine). She can't judge – she was only a child. She tells me, not for the first time, one of Primo's famous stories of his father as amiable eccentric; probably the one about having special pockets sewn into his jackets for the three books he was simultaneously reading. I find another, more distant cousin, who is very entertained by her memories of Cesare, but does not share them with me. She smiles mysteriously and says, 'He was *un amante della vita*, a lover of life.' Still smiling, she adds something in Piedmontese, which she knows I don't understand.

At last, I find two books: the one by Paolo Levi, *Il filo della memoria*; and one by Luisa Accati, the eldest daughter of Federico Accati, Primo's employer and close friend from 1947. They are both novels; but they tell a very similar tale.

Il filo della memoria

Half-way through the chapter on 'the Sacerdotes of Chiusa di Pesio', Paolo moves from his fictional account of his (and Primo's) grandparents to their three sons: Edoardo, Lodovico and Arnaldo. These are gently ironic portraits of, respectively, his father Enrico, Primo's father Cesare, and their brother Mario.

Lodovico Sacerdote is 'ugly and *simpatico*, with eyes of a slightly disturbing, light blue-grey. He was always smiling, as though he was about to burst into roars of laughter on the smallest provocation.' He is warm, generous and unpredictable. He becomes a mechanical engineer, and spends a good deal of time in Czechoslovakia on business. There, according to family rumour, he has had an illegitimate child. 'I'm convinced,' says the narrator (Edoardo's daughter Sandra), 'that when Uncle Lodovico conceived her, he did so with the best of intentions.'

In fact, it was Paolo Levi's own father, Enrico, who had had an illegitimate child (though of course Cesare may have had one too). But if Paolo removed Enrico's love-child from Edoardo, he added something else. In the novel,

Edoardo's wife Lydia ('She insisted on the *y*') has been denied a starring role in life by merely average looks, and by a deeply puritan mentality. All that is left to her (says Sandra) is to suffer. Edoardo constantly betrays her; she knows it, and punishes him with long, thunderous silences, which regularly break in storms of argument. Their children take opposite sides, Renzo his father's and Sandra her mother's. But forty years later, when Sandra becomes our narrator, she's no longer so sure. 'Years of practice had sharpened Mama's nose,' she says; but at the same time Edoardo was childishly easy to catch, leaving his pockets full of addresses and love letters. Sandra concludes that though Edoardo won, since he always denied everything and went on to the next affair, Lydia did not lose, since she criticized his every move, and made his life a misery.

Il matrimonio di Raffaele Albanese

Luisa Accati is an historian at the University of Trieste, and has spent years interviewing women about their lives, going back to the 1910s and 20s. *The Marriage of Raffaele Albanese*, her first novel, is subtle and accomplished. It is as much about competing stories, and the possibility (or impossibility) of truth, as it is about the lives of women in her mother's and grandmother's generations.

There are two families in the novel, the Albanese and the Rinaldi. The first half is about the Albanese, and the marriage of the title. The second half is about the Rinaldi: Maria and Giulio, and their sons Emilio and Piero.

The first story about the Rinaldi is told by Anna Albanese, contemporary of Maria and Giulio. They married, she says, when Maria was a shy and reserved girl of twenty-five, and Giulio twelve years older. Maria's father chose Giulio for her because he was a respected engineer, well-off and from a good family. But the marriage is a disaster. Giulio is a chronic libertine; he betrays Maria openly and repeatedly from the start, and she is profoundly unhappy all her life. But she adores her sons, especially Piero; and for their sakes she puts up with everything.

The next narrator is Anna's daughter Emma, who has married Emilio Rinaldi. She describes Maria's campaign against Giulio: no open war, but a permanent rain of small blows, to which his only response is a black silence. Maria enlists both her sons on her side – impatient, independent Emilio to join in harrying his father; gentle, timid Piero to console and comfort her.

This description of the Rinaldi sons is confirmed in the next story, told by the family maid, Angela. Piero is the delicate, sensitive one from the start.

One day, when they are very young, their mother tells them not to go near their father's office when his secretary is there, 'out of respect for me, because she is your father's mistress'. Emilio flies into a passion of anger; but Piero goes silent, and very pale. Later they remain the same. Emilio tells his mother to leave his father, and leaves home himself as soon as he can. Piero refuses to judge his father, saying, 'He is unhappy'; and dedicates himself to the consolation of his mother, sticking to her side like a shadow.

Angela changes one very important part of the story, however. According to Anna Albanese, Giulio Rinaldi was a hardened libertine long before Maria ever met him; however cruel she may have become, the first cruelty was his. As Angela tells it, Giulio fell deeply in love with Maria. But 'their wedding night was a tragedy, and so were all their other nights'. Maria runs home to her parents from her honeymoon, horrified by the disgusting things her husband has asked of her. Her father makes her return. But Maria is deeply, neurotically frigid; she suffers Giulio's attentions only until her two sons are born, after which she locks him out of her bedroom for ever. Giulio tries everything to win her over, but she is hard and unreachable. Finally his infidelities begin: at least at first, Angela says, 'out of desperation'.

This version is repeated by the last narrator, Dr W., friend and contemporary of Giulio Rinaldi. Maria's and Giulio's story, he says, was not unusual in their generation. Maria had come to him on the morning of their return from honeymoon, saying she 'was not a normal woman', and begging him to ask Giulio to release her from their marriage. This had not happened; and the marriage had continued in the way the other narrators had described. But this was the true reason behind its failure. If Giulio was a more flagrantly unfaithful husband every year, it was because he had been rejected by his frigid and punishing wife.

★   ★

Surely the similarities between 'Lydia and Edoardo Sacerdote' and 'Maria and Giulio Rinaldi' are more than coincidental? And what other connection was there between Paolo Levi and Luisa Accati apart from Primo? If, for the purposes of fiction, Paolo Levi gave Cesare Enrico's illegitimate daughter, did he also give Enrico Cesare's marriage? And *were* 'Maria and Giulio Rinaldi' based on Luisa Accati's knowledge of Rina and Cesare Levi – and 'Piero and Emilio' on Primo and Anna Maria?

Paolo Levi, alas, died two years after Primo. But his widow and sister-in-law are still very much alive. They are happy to talk about Enrico, their own father-in-law; but not about Cesare, whom they say they hardly knew. Very well: were Enrico and his wife Lisa at all like 'Edoardo and Lydia' in *Filo*? Enrico's and Lisa's marriage was arranged, they agree, not a love match;

Enrico *was* rather a womanizer, and had that illegitimate child; and Lisa did grumble about him – but more about his eccentric way with money than about his women. No: Lisa Levi was a normal, agreeable person, she was not at all the professional punisher of *Filo*.

Luisa Accati is not only alive, but willing to answer my questions. She wrinkles her forehead and tries to remember. The trouble is, she's a novelist. Maria and Giulio seem realler to her now than Rina and Cesare; she'd rather talk about them, and perhaps she does.

But this is what she tells me. She has grounded her imagination on three foundations: her historical research; her own family; and Primo's. Yes, Piero and Emilio *are* based on Primo and Anna Maria; and yes, Maria and Giulio *are* based on what she has heard about Rina and Cesare. Dozens of women in her survey had similar tales to tell, and some of what went into Maria came from them. But the main inspiration for the drama of Maria and Giulio Rinaldi came from the story told in the Turin Jewish community about Rina and Cesare Levi. The story said that Rina had run away from Cesare on their honeymoon; that she remained the epitome of the rejecting puritan wife throughout their marriage; and that he betrayed her openly and always, even bringing his 'secretaries' to his office in Corso Re Umberto 75.

A few weeks later, confirmations arrive. One old lady says that she heard the story of Rina's and Cesare's wedding night from her own mother. According to her, Cesare did not have endless affairs, like Giulio Rinaldi and Edoardo Sacerdote: rather, he had one endless affair, with his secretary. But he did, for a time, have his office in Corso Re Umberto 75; and during that time he did bring his secretary into his wife's house. Once (she says) Rina and Anna Maria heard him making love to her there.

In this old lady's picture, after the initial disaster the suffering was all on Rina's side; and Primo, like Piero Rinaldi, would spend the rest of his life trying to console his mother, 'to be the husband she never had'. But the second old lady disagrees. Rina did not suffer, she says: she despised her husband for his sexual appetites, and took it for granted that he would try to satisfy them elsewhere. This, at least, is what *she* had always heard. If Primo was enslaved to his mother – and he was – it was for different reasons. It was because she was *una madre tremenda*, a terrible mother: controlling, dominating, a complete egotist. She was not the only mother who tried to bind her son to her for life – her own husband (says the old lady) had such a mother, and so, for instance, had Primo's friend Livio Norzi. The difference was (and here her eyes flash) that Primo's and Livio's succeeded.

But this old lady, who is not really so old, only knew Primo and his mother after the war, not when he was a child. Of those early days I have had only two brief glimpses outside fiction (and outside the family): Primo as a small boy, showing his mother 'reverence'; and Rina with her children in their early teens, having 'natural authority' over them.

Now, however, I meet a last old lady, who is the oldest of the three. She *did* know Primo when he was a child. And she is not a novelist. At last, therefore, she can give me an independent, non-fictional picture of the mother of Primo's childhood.

It is the only one I have, and a single picture is not proof. But this is what she says. Her family did not have much to do with Primo's, because Rina was an '*orsa dura*', an extremely unsociable person. And she was – she uses the same phrase – a *madre tremenda*. In what way? I ask. '*Era particolarmente severa*,' she replies: 'She was especially strict, and very distant'; and she makes a gesture of pushing someone – everyone – away. 'I used to wonder,' she says, 'if Primo had ever once been hugged by his mother.'

Dr W. in *The Marriage of Raffaele Albanese* diagnoses Piero's trouble. Since his mother did not love his father, he says (he's very discreet), his father was driven into a loveless pursuit of sensuality; so that Piero was left without *un educazione sentimentale*, an emotional education. That is: he had no example of how to love a woman, except a bad one.

Now I think I can add something else: that Primo's mother did not love him either. How could she? He was the fruit of the first terrible days of her marriage, and he was male. Or rather: she did love him, but possessively, controllingly, and only as long as he was in her own image, and not his father's. So that it was not only in loving that he had no education, but also in being loved. And what Dr W. says of Piero, therefore, was even truer of Primo: he was 'left defenceless in the face of all emotion'. Only his alliance with his sister showed him what love and trust could be. No wonder they forged that extraordinary bond; no wonder they invented a language their parents couldn't understand. And no wonder that his childhood alliance with someone more open, more daring and independent than he became a model for Primo for many (perhaps the best) of his friendships and loves.

*　　*

And could he, then, really love his mother? Did he really take her side, even as a boy, and condemn his father? Cesare Levi surely feared that he did; that is the meaning of his glance, as he yields to temptation and buys the *prosciutto*.

In the end I found the answer to that question, and to the others as well, when I found the secret sharers of Primo's later life. I gave them the novels, and they all said: Yes. Something very like this was Primo's story. He did not tell them the reasons, or his mother's response, but he knew about his father's mistress. Perhaps that was why he devoted his life to his mother, they agreed; but he did not love her. That is nature's revenge: if you make your child unable to love anyone but you, he will not be able to love you either. One remembered something terrible he said, which answered the last old lady: 'I do not think my mother ever hugged me.'

No, he did not choose his mother over his father. But he did choose her example over his. He chose Rina's suffering and endurance over Cesare's indulgence of his appetites – but utterly rejected her revenge. And he chose Rina's stasis and self-imprisonment over Cesare's insistence on his freedom. The only legacy he acknowledged from his father was his love of reason: though he had picked this up, he said, secretly and unconsciously. This was, I think, a kind of double joke. Cesare Levi stood much more for irrationality than for rationality in his son's life. And to the extent that Primo did learn his 'love of reason' from his father, it did not have to be unconsciously. On the contrary: scientific rationalism was the one thing he could consciously accept from him. Everything else Cesare stood for he had to reject – emotion and aggression, sex and betrayal, adventure and escape. *These* were his unconscious legacies from his father.

He never left his mother's house, so that in the long battle between Rina and Cesare she seemed to have won. But in truth Primo brought his escape inside. He hid Cesare's legacies deep inside him, where even he couldn't enter: like his father's office in his mother's house, when his father's secretary was inside it. This was the last closed door. It only opened much later, in his writing; and on a few other, darker occasions.

★   ★

I'd gone to see Paolo Levi's widow Enrica, and his brother Franco's widow Antonia, hoping to learn more about Rina and Cesare. As it turned out, I learned almost nothing about them. Enrica and Antonia hadn't known them, and if they knew anything about them they weren't telling. The Levi dedication to personal privacy is immovable; and not only with someone who might write it all down in a book. When I asked one of Antonia's daughters when her parents had married, she said she didn't know, because 'No one asks such questions in the family.'

Instead, however, I learned something else. It wasn't about Rina and Cesare, but about Primo and Paolo; and about writing things down in books, which of course they both did as well.

The cousins were born only days apart, Enrica Levi said: Paolo eleven days before Primo, on 20 July 1919. Unlike Primo, Paolo had always had *la passione della scrittura*: since he was a small boy, he'd never wanted to do anything but write.

This was a handicap from the start. When they became engaged, Enrica's father, who was an engineer, asked Paolo if he was really serious about this writing business. Paolo said he was. Despite this, however, they were allowed to marry.

Paolo began as a playwright for the theatre, but he had one or two flops, and cannot have made very much money. True Levis are not interested in money, Antonia says; but Paolo had two young sons to bring up. He turned to writing television plays, short stories and thrillers. He stuck to his childhood dream, and never did anything but write. But a lot of it was hack-work; and though several of the thrillers are better than that, he was never very successful.

In the meantime almost the opposite was happening to Primo. He told everyone, especially in the family, that he had never meant to be a writer. He was a chemist, who happened to be caught up in one of the great tragedies of the twentieth century, and reported on it. After that he went on writing; but only in his spare time. He did not admit to being 'a real writer' until his first novel came out in 1982. By then he was already famous. He had won all the top literary prizes; and his first book was a classic, read by every schoolchild in Italy.

This was a painful contrast for Paolo. But what made it worse was that they had the same name: not only Levi, but *P.* Levi. And with one 'P. Levi' so famous, the other didn't just live in his shadow; he ceased to exist altogether. If Paolo ever wrote anything that attracted attention, people would assume it was by Primo. This happened with a short story of his, for example. Although it was slightly racy and risqué – which was often Paolo's style, but never Primo's – it was Primo the journalist wanted to interview; and when he realized the story wasn't by Primo Levi after all, he lost interest.

It's still going on, I thought: it's going on right now, with me. Here I am interviewing Paolo's widow – about Primo. I hoped she wasn't thinking this too. And I didn't tell her something that had happened the week before, as I was working my way through a huge pile of television programmes on Primo Levi, in the Cineteca of the RAI* in Rome. One of them was about film thrillers, and it did just cross my mind that this was an unusual subject for Primo. But there it was in black and white on the computer print-out: PRIMO LEVI. I put the cassette on, and waited for Primo to appear. One of the people taking part was a handsome, dapper man with dark hair and a dark moustache, who reminded me of Clark Gable. Suddenly his name flashed up on the screen: PAOLO LEVI.

I told one of the secretaries in the office before I left. She gave me the usual weary look. If Paolo ever wrests his identity back from Primo, it won't be in the Cineteca of the RAI in Rome.

---

* Italian state radio and television.

Il filo della memoria, however, was different. It's not a thriller, but a serious novel – or rather, a funny novel – about family, memory, and being Jewish in Italy. Just reading it I could tell that Paolo Levi had put more of himself than usual into this book. And that is what I learned – though needless to say, only from hints; from sentences that trailed off into silence. *Il filo della memoria* was Paolo's bid for immortality, his attempt to wrest back his identity from Primo. He knew it was his best book, and hoped it was a good one. On the television he looked a sanguine and pugnacious man; I think he thought it *was* good. He sent not just one copy but three to Antonia (Franco had died four years before). And waited for her response, and for the reviews.

All that Enrica will say about what happened is that it was a great disappointment. But I think of Paolo and Primo, and it seems to me a tragedy. *Il filo della memoria* had lukewarm reviews, and disappeared. And the family wasn't impressed either. On the contrary – they were outraged. There were all their secrets on the page, 'in the square', as the Italians say: Franco's alcoholism, Enrico's (or was it Cesare's?) infidelities, Cesare's (or was it Enrico's?) illegitimate daughter . . . I don't know if Primo said anything to Paolo; but I'm sure he did, and that it was kind. Anna Maria was upset and angry. And angriest of all was Antonia.

After Franco's death, she says, *Il filo della memoria* was the worst thing that ever happened to her. Paolo, his own brother, had exposed him to the world as a charming, intelligent, but hopelessly weak-willed alcoholic. And he had portrayed her as a wonderfully doughty fighter, who sets about her husband's alcoholism with every weapon fair and foul, and finally destroys it – but not without destroying him in the process.

The sad and funny thing is that this was all true, and not only about Franco. Antonia *is* a wonderful, passionate fighter; and now she turned the full fire of her anger on Paolo. She refused to speak to him ever again, or to Enrica either, though they are first cousins. (She has relented about that now, and they speak to each other often; but never about *Filo*.) Later she refused to go to Paolo's funeral. But her first action was the most direct. She took an axe, and chopped all three of her copies of *Il filo della memoria* into little pieces.

When I think of this, half of me wants to burst into laughter, and the other half wants to burst into tears. Paolo had longed for his family to like and admire his book, to recognize the truth of its insights as only they could do; and all they saw was a personal betrayal.

Of course he should have known that this would happen. Writers put books first, but nobody else does, especially if they think they've been used for one without even being asked. The truth is that *Il filo della memoria* is a good novel. It is a tender, funny story of a Jewish family, and an intimate and moving portrait of an alcoholic. But you can see why the alcoholic's wife mightn't like it. It was extraordinarily dense of Paolo, who had drawn his lioness of a sister-in-law so well in his book, not to realize that she would be the same outside it. But perhaps he was just being a typical writer, so used to moving people about in his imagination that he forgot that real ones may not be so docile. Perhaps that is the sin for which he was being punished. He died five years later, never having written another book.

He outlived Primo by two years, so at least in one way he won the race. Though even that only meant watching Primo's posthumous reputation grow . . . I don't know if they saw their relationship as a race. But I think of Primo's crippling timidity, his denial that he was even trying to be a writer for so many years, his extraordinary and unexpected triumph. And I remember Paolo's Clark Gable looks, the worldly ease of his writing, the confidence with which he proclaimed himself a writer from childhood. And I see a very ancient and dramatic race, in which the loser has always expected to win and the winner to lose; the race between the hare and the tortoise.

3. Primo Levi Primo:
1930–37

First year *liceo*, 1934–5. Primo Levi is in the back row, fourth from
left; Mario Piacenza is in the same row, third from right

Ginnasio Liceo Massimo D'Azeglio

Italian grammar schools are divided into two categories, Classical and Scientific. Even in pragmatic Turin, traditional classical culture has always had a firm hold on prejudice; and no *bien pensant* family with a clever son would consider anything but Liceo Classico for him – even if, like the Levis, they'd been engineers for two generations.

The Ginnasio Liceo Massimo D'Azeglio is one of the top Classical Liceos of Turin, together with the Cavour, Alfieri and Gioberti. The early decades of the twentieth century were its Golden Age, which made it a legend throughout Italy: more a university than a school, as famous for its independence – that is, for its antifascism – as for its learning; the home of great antifascist teachers like the philosopher Zino Zini and the literature teachers Umberto Cosmo and Augusto Monti; and of great antifascist students, like the writers Leone Ginzburg and Cesare Pavese (who tried, however, to remain 'apolitical'), the publisher Giulio Einaudi, the philosopher Norberto Bobbio, the music critic Massimo Mila, the writer and politician (and Primo's cousin) Vittorio Foa.

By the 1930s, however, the second decade of Fascist rule, open resistance to Fascism was a thing of the past, even here. Cosmo, Zini and Monti were all retired, in prison, or sent to the *confino* (that is, to house arrest in various distant and isolated parts of Italy; the most famous account of this was by the 'other' Levi, Carlo, in *Christ Stopped at Eboli*). Ginzburg, Foa and the rest of the younger generation had been driven underground; soon they too were arrested and imprisoned. The journalist Carlo Casalegno – a near contemporary, and later a friend of Primo's – remembered that, despite the heavy hand of the regime both inside and outside the school, it still retained 'a certain spirit, a certain freedom'. Primo agreed, to some extent: the opposition to rhetoric and the critical vigilance which, for example, their famous Italian teacher Azelia Arici still managed to convey 'were, in effect, an act of resistance'. But even she could only resist silently, by example; and these and other silences, he said, he understood only afterwards.

Still, the school's high academic standards remained. So did its social prestige. It was set in, and served, the good bourgeois district of Crocetta; and since this was, of course, Primo's own district, it was also nearby. All this made it a natural decision, hardly a decision at all: at eleven, he would enter the Ginnasio Liceo Massimo D'Azeglio.

Throughout his D'Azeglio education he was a model student. I have not seen the records of his first two years, in *ginnasio inferiore*; but he was almost certainly more diligent and better-behaved the younger he was. For the two years of *ginnasio superiore*, from thirteen to fourteen, and the three of *liceo*, from fifteen to seventeen, his mark for Conduct (the first on the list) only once dropped below nine out of ten, and was usually ten. His lowest mark was almost always for *Educazione fisica*: usually six, once as low as four. In all academic subjects he kept to eights and even nines in *ginnasio* (except in Italian, as we'll see); in *liceo* to sevens and eights, with a very occasional six; and one lone five, again in Italian.

These marks put him at the top of his class: usually first, second or third, never lower than fifth. (The two he competed with at the top were Ennio Artom, who was a near genius; and Maurizio Panetti, who was an extremely hard worker, and usually number one.) But Primo was so quiet, so self-effacing, that the true quality of his mind was noted mostly by his peers.[*] The more ordinary clever boys hardly noticed him; the *briganti* – the rogues and rascals – noticed, but despised him. The girls didn't notice him at all.

---

[*] For example, by Alfredo Fedele, who became a professor of law; and by Fernanda Pivano, who became a famous critic and translator of American literature. I tell her story of Primo in Pavese's Italian class below; in chemistry class, she says, 'He was extraordinary, he became a hero, he soared.'

Many of the teachers, of course, both noticed and admired him. Giorgina Pangella, the Natural Sciences teacher, was 'wide-eyed and worshipful', according to his *ginnasio* classmate Fernanda Pivano. (According to Primo himself, she was more embarrassed than pleased, since 'I knew more chemistry than she did, and asked her questions she couldn't answer.') Anna Borgogno, who taught him Italian in *ginnasio inferiore*, said in front of the whole class: 'One day a plaque will be put up in this classroom: *Primo Levi studied here.*' This time, of course, it was Primo who was embarrassed.

But one teacher, at least, failed to distinguish him from the ordinary clever boys, or the hard workers like Panetti. Amazingly, it was Azelia Arici, who taught him Italian in *liceo*: so far from ordinary herself, a big, heavy woman who was a brilliant, intuitive teacher. Arici was the one he remembered, as did all the students she ever taught, male and female, good, bad and indifferent. Her dedication to Dante gave him the love and knowledge which inform his whole work, and the memory which is the central moment of his first great book. When she read it, ten years later, she knew that it was he of all her pupils who had been able to transmute her teaching of great literature into great literature of his own. But she had not foreseen this at all; he had not seemed to her exceptional. He had been *chiuso fin in fondo*: utterly closed, incapable of communication. She had never imagined he would be capable of the ultimate communication of this book.

He was, he said himself, 'a diligent and decorous student' – but not a genius, and not a *violino* – the current slang for swot. At around thirteen or fourteen he began his life-long love affair with the mountains that rise up, and go on rising, behind Turin. He certainly did not shine in the gymnasium. But his response to this was not the traditional intellectual's response of despising physical activity, and never setting foot in field or arena again. On the contrary (as we'll see), he set himself to compete with the best in the class, like a certain knight who sought out windmills.

As he got older he relaxed a little, and even joined in some mild schoolboy mischief. This explains his one eight out of ten in Conduct, which he got in the first term of his last year. A group of them had put a firework in the school's mailbox, and waited agog for it to explode. Unfortunately it did so just as the august mother of one of the girls was passing. She was too deaf to hear their warning shouts, but not too deaf to be shocked out of her skin; and for a while it looked as though they would not be allowed to take their final exams in the summer. Secretly, this may have confirmed Primo's fears about bad behaviour; on the surface he remained unapologetic.

At seventeen, therefore, he was much as he had been at seven: so quiet and shy he could easily be overlooked in a crowd; except for the stubborn quality of his quietness. He kept his own counsel, and went his own way.

He took part if *he* decided to, but not otherwise. In sport, yes, even in japes; but not, for example, in dancing. Many boys went to the dance-halls every weekend, to the Sala Castellino, the Sala Gay, the Sala Debenedetti. But not Primo; never.

Unsurprisingly, his entertainments were more cultural. The cinema (especially French cinema), the theatre, the concerts to which his family subscribed. And, of course, he read and read and read. The books on science, and especially chemistry, which allowed him to embarrass poor Pangella: at thirteen, Darwin's *Origin of Species*; at sixteen, the whole Mondadori popular science series, bought for him by his father. But not only science. He read the great French classics, especially Flaubert, de Maupassant, Victor Hugo; the great Russians; Conrad and Huxley, Kafka and Mann, Faulkner and Dos Passos. And these were only the classics; he probably read a similar number of modern and popular Italian novels, which he promptly forgot. Only one made a deep impression on him: Moravia's *Gli indifferenti*, a savage satire of the corrupt Italian bourgeoisie in the first decade of Fascism.

And what of his ambitions? Is it possible that such a gifted writer did not dream, did not even think of writing, from the start? Primo always insisted that he did not. He always insisted that science was his whole aim and dream as a boy; that he had never thought of writing, before Auschwitz – except 'maybe scholarly articles about chemistry'. Once, at the very end of his life, he said that he'd had the idea of writing 'Carbon' as far back as *liceo*: but perhaps (he didn't make it clear) only as a scholarly article. His family believed that he had never thought of writing before Auschwitz. His friends at school, and later at university, saw only his huge interest and gift for science – except for one, who was among the closest. Livio Norzi remembered how Primo had introduced him to Conrad, Huxley and Lawrence when they were sixteen; and he at least never doubted that Primo would have become a writer, even without the imperative of Auschwitz.

This is one of the great questions about Primo Levi; one of the almost unique mysteries about him, since as a practising scientist he was almost unique among great writers.* The mystery of his true ambitions as a writer will recur at every stage of his life: when he writes his first stories, his first

---

* There are, famously, a good many doctors – for example, Keats, Rabelais, Sir Thomas Browne, Chekhov – but very few 'hard' scientists. Interestingly, several are Italian: Carlo Emilio Gadda, who was an engineer, and Italo Calvino, son of science teachers and himself fascinated by pure science. Two other important writers of the twentieth century actually ran paint factories: Italo Svevo in Italy and Sherwood Anderson in the United States (Primo discussed this with Philip Roth in their 1986 interview). But Primo Levi was unique among all these, because so much of his greatest writing was *about* science.

great book, his second; when he finally retires as a chemist; when he writes his tenth book and first novel in his sixties. It is connected to his sense of being split into two halves, which do not meet, which do not even communicate. (But only to the conscious part of it.) And it is connected to his *piemontesità*, his being Piedmontese; perhaps the most extreme example of how far he took it.

The mystery may, I hope, become clearer at each stage. At the start it was at its darkest, especially to him. But one thing he said, sixty years later, may be a clue: 'When I was at school, I had a polemical relationship to literature. Later it became clear that it was love, resisted like all great loves.'

At first, in *ginnasio inferiore*, when the work in Italian lessons was 'writing original, creative compositions', he did very well. Sometimes he even got ten out of ten from Anna Borgogno ('*Primo Levi studied here*'). And from someone else too. According to Fernanda Pivano, who would also become a writer, for a few months in their first year they were taught literature by the young Cesare Pavese. And, she says, 'Pavese gave us both wonderful marks, and above all wonderful comments.' But at the time he was at the height of his passion for '*la donna della voce rauca*', his hoarse-voiced lady (Pivano remembers him constantly rushing off to telephone her). Since she was deeply involved in the antifascist resistance, soon so was he; though more out of love than political commitment. His motives were a matter of indifference to the OVRA, the secret police, and in May 1935 he was arrested.★ If this story is true, Primo's high marks in Italian, and just possibly his last chance to love literature sooner and less painfully, were over.

What is certainly true is that his main teacher of Italian throughout *liceo* was Azelia Arici; and that she did not manage to give him the chance. On the contrary: the gap between science and the arts, between the two cultures in Italy in general and in Primo Levi in particular, became unbridgeable for him while he was her student. Their relationship was 'excellent', he said; he did the work, even well; but inwardly they clashed.

Arici was an inspiring teacher, but a severe one. She was passionate about literature, and wanted you to be; but if you weren't, she could destroy you with a phrase. She hated time-servers, who were (she would say) like Dante's Slothful, the *ignavi*: people incapable of passion or commitment, who don't even merit Hell, but spend eternity in its Vestibule. Arici's *ignavi* were the lazy, and those who worked only for marks. No one could ever think Primo

★ At the same moment as other great *dazegliani* – that is, alumni of D'Azeglio: for example, Monti, Mila, Einaudi, Foa, Bobbio; also Franco Antonicelli, who'd been Monti's teaching assistant, and who would later publish *If This is a Man*. Unlike the others, Pavese was released after a few months.

lazy; but if she thought he worked only for marks in her class, she wasn't entirely wrong.

For his part, he had already decided that science, not literature, would be his key to the universe: that the analysis of matter, not poetry, was the way to unlock its secrets. This opposition is perennial, and to some extent unavoidable. Even in the empirical Anglo-Saxon world there is the same gap between the 'two cultures' (the phenomenon was first described, of course, by an Englishman). But in 1930s Italy the gap was a chasm. The humanities were dominant, and dominated by a high Crocean idealism, which dismissed the sciences as mere utilitarian 'pseudoconcepts' which did not yield true understanding of the world. And Azelia Arici was a Crocean. She told her class, not once but often, that 'literature is formative, science merely informative'. 'My hair stood on end,' Primo said.

He was polite, pacific, and '*chiuso fin in fondo*', as Arici said. I am sure that he did not defend his choice to her; that he did not even mention it. That would be his way of defending it. She either did not know of the special way he 'soared' in chemistry class, or more likely did not count it. She had a special gift for 'seeing inside' the shy and sensitive child; but she did not see inside Primo. She judged him *un allievo normale*, an ordinary student. In other words, she did what he wanted, on one level (but only on one level): she didn't notice him. And she scorned his beloved science. In turn he felt 'a certain aversion', he said, 'for the teaching of Italian'. Not for the teacher of Italian: he would never say that, and perhaps he wouldn't feel it. But somewhere there was an aversion.

Nonetheless, she *was* an extraordinary teacher; and he was a very good student. Like the great Augusto Monti whom she succeeded, she was a wonderful, dramatic reader, who made especially Dante alive, real, easy to understand. Even the poetry he liked less stuck in his mind. But Dante, Leopardi, Manzoni he loved; especially Dante. That passion Arici did plant in him, or help to flower. Later, when he needed great literature as much as he needed food – more – he found it was there inside him: a richness unwillingly acquired, but still alive, and able to keep him alive, like a garden.

Chemistry

This is how Massimo Mila summed up the Liceo Classico of the late 20s and 30s, dominated by philosophical idealism and Fascist rhetoric: 'Aesthetic analysis, much Spirit and little reading, great discoursing of "the world of poetry" and don't worry if you don't know the exact date of Ariosto's birth, you can always go and look it up in some encyclopedia.' This was exactly calculated to infuriate the young Primo Levi. 'It was enervating, nauseating, to listen to lectures on the problem of being and knowing, when everything around us was a mystery pressing to be revealed,' he wrote. He had the sensation that school was a 'monstrous conspiracy', a plot to keep something hidden from him – to keep everything hidden from him, or everything important. 'In school they loaded me with tons of notions which I diligently digested, but which did not warm the blood in my veins,' he wrote in *The Periodic Table*:

I would watch the buds swell in spring, the mica glint in granite, my own hands, and I would say to myself: 'I will understand this too, I will understand everything, but not the way *they* want me to. I will find a short-cut, I will pick the lock, I will force open the doors.'

And his short-cut, his lock-pick, his battering-ram, would be science. In *ginnasio* he dreamed of becoming a philologist; in *liceo* a physicist, a mathematician, an astronomer. But at fourteen, or fifteen, or sixteen – at different times he settled for slightly different ages – he decided, consciously and without hesitation: he would be a chemist.

He chose chemistry because – he would say with a grin – it smelled clean. Because it was 'inherently antifascist' (here he would grin again, and admit, 'We had famous chemists who were Fascists'). Philosophy, history, literature were all subjects which could be, and were, distorted by ideology, by rhetoric and lies. It was not so easy to distort chemistry – or physics, or mathematics. Here there was experiment, demonstration, proof. And here there was clarity, and responsibility: something was the case or not the case, you were right or you were wrong, and there was no getting out of it with fine phrases. This was something absolutely new to a boy brought up under Fascism. From his first day of school to his last, he said, he had never felt as autonomous, and as responsible, as in a lab: 'a man confronting matter, a boy confronting matter'. Fascism openly discouraged independent thought. Fascist history books, Fascist philosophy books pullulated with discouragements of independent thought. Chemistry was 'an island of reason', a rare piece of free and solid ground on which to walk.

He chose chemistry, then, for clean, hard, Piedmontese reasons. And for exactly the opposite ones as well – for wildly romantic, philosophical, almost religious reasons. He didn't reject the great questions of philosophy as unanswerable – he just thought chemistry could answer them instead. Chemistry seemed to him 'magical', the key to 'the secrets of heaven and earth', 'one of man's greatest powers': with it he 'hoped to go very far, to the point of possessing the universe, to understanding the why of things'. *This* was his goal, from the start – to understand the why of things, to 'dredge the bowels of the mystery'. Later chemistry disappointed him, and later still he said, 'Now I know it doesn't exist, the why of things.' But then, and for a long time afterwards, he did believe in it, and hoped to find it; and not only in chemistry. His voice when he pursues the 'why' of recent human history is so calm, so controlled, that perhaps we forget how high a goal that also was. It comes out in this voice, which we also tend to forget, because he uses it so rarely – the young, free, exultant voice in which he writes about chemistry, and the way he chose it at fourteen, fifteen or sixteen:

For me chemistry represented an indefinite cloud of future powers, which enveloped my life to come in black coils riven by flashes of fire, like the cloud which hid Mount Sinai. Like Moses, from that cloud I awaited my law: the order in me, around me, and in the world.

His desire for this order was exuberant, confident – and also, he told his first biographer, Flora Vincenti, pressing. He did not tell her why. But he did say this, much later: Scientists, who are used to foreseeing physical events,

are a bit shocked and annoyed at not being able to foresee anything about themselves, or their closest colleagues. And yet it happens, it happens all the time – we're unable to predict not only what Germany or Japan or the USSR will do in the next five years, but even what our sister, our brother, our wife will do in the next five minutes. It's outrageous, but it's true.

When he looked back later at his choice of vocation as a boy he never said this in so many words: that he had preferred the orderliness and predictability of chemistry to the unfathomable chaos of human affairs. Nor did he stick to this division, or to one side of it: the whole triumph of his writing would be to cross from one to the other, in a 'double leap, up and down, between two levels of energy'. But we can guess that he made that decision, and chose that side, now; and at least partly for that reason. Only later would he discover that he'd opened up a gap it was harder and harder to cross; that it would be possible to make the double leap in writing, but only in writing; and therefore more and more necessary to make it there.

But of course he couldn't give such a serious reason, even to himself. The few remarks he made on the subject were meant to amuse. For instance: chemistry, at the time, had been unfashionable, looked down on, 'almost prohibited' – which made it all the more fun to choose. Really (he said) his decision had had more to do with such small, personal pleasures than with grand and rational reasons. For example, with the fact that he had always been fascinated by smells.

I have often suspected that, deep down, the motives for my boyhood choice of chemistry were different from the ones I rationalized and repeatedly declared. I became a chemist not (or not only) from a need to understand the world around me; not in reaction to the cloudy dogmas of Fascism; and not in the hope of riches or scientific glory; but to find, or create, an opportunity to exercise my nose.

Bar Mitzvah

Religion made only a brief appearance in Primo's early life. So at least he believed, or wanted to believe, later.

There was, as we know, little religion left in the family. Rina followed the basic traditions. She bought unleavened bread at Passover, and took the children to her father's house for Passover, Purim and Rosh Hashanah; but she herself was entirely secular and agnostic. Cesare was less consistent. He was a scientist, a positivist and a man of the world; and yet, Primo said, he was 'religious in his own peculiar way'. He didn't consent to the laws, but suffered and swore under them; having to fast, or deprive himself of pork, just because God said so maddened him. But he obeyed, just in case. When — as in the famous episode of the *prosciutto* — the temptation became too great, he 'abandoned himself, growling, to transgression'. Often he didn't manage to fast at Yom Kippur for more than a few hours. He went to synagogue then, but only because it was *bon ton* among the Jewish bourgeoisie.

Primo never went to synagogue, and hardly felt Jewish at all. It was no more than a small, light-hearted difference from his Christian friends: 'like having a crooked nose, or freckles', he would write in *The Periodic Table*. He remembered light-hearted things about it, and things that bridged the difference: like the little Catholic peasant girl who was invited to their table at Rosh Hashanah, and who 'held a goose on her lap throughout the meal'. A Jew, he wrote, looking back on this time, is just someone 'who at Christmas does not have a tree'.

But he *didn't* have a tree, he *was* different. When he was around eleven he began Hebrew lessons. One day he learned the Hebrew word for house or home: *bait*. But that must be where the Piedmontese *baita* came from! He felt (he wrote, fifty-four years later) 'a puerile pride'. The Romans might have defeated the Jews and destroyed Jerusalem — but at least one Hebrew word had ousted a Latin one! This was fighting talk (or thought) for an Italian Jewish boy; for the Romans and their language were both, of course, Italian.

Then, in his thirteenth year, he began to prepare for his bar mitzvah. Though Cesare wasn't properly religious, it had clearly never occurred to him not to have his son make the ritual passage into his faith, like all the good Jewish boys and girls of Turin. This had, in the end, an expanding, enriching effect on Primo Levi the writer, adding the stories and rhythms of the Old Testament to his literary resources. But it had the opposite effect on his attitude to religion. Or perhaps this attitude was already formed; more cause than effect of what happened. Either way, there was certainly a passage, but not in the planned direction.

When the writer described it later, he used mild, defusing Turinese terms – it had been a period of 'uncertainty', of 'worry', of 'suffering a little, as everyone does'. But not everyone suffers during religious instruction. (Primo often suggested that he thought and felt just like everyone else, and it was rarely true.) Why did he suffer?

One interviewer asked him: did he enter the community of believers without believing? Primo answered: for months, that was a worry. And he *did* seek contact with God, for several months after the ceremony he even believed; this happens to many, perhaps even most, Jewish boys ('I dare say,' he says, 'out of fear'). But when he'd sought that contact, he'd found nothing. His teacher ('who was probably not a very good one') presented him with a tyrannical, punishing God, a *Dio Padrone* who did not appeal to him. She described an unknown, an unknowable, to whom nonetheless he was asked to pay homage, and in whom he must believe. '*Mi sembrava una violenza*,' he says: it seemed to him an act of violence. Slowly his other interests – his interest in the natural world, his reading of Darwin – helped him to break away. After the brief time of 'uncertainty' he withdrew from God completely, and put Him away among childish things.

I have taken this account from two interviews: the only times I know of (apart from the one below) when he spoke in such detail of his religious experiences at the age of thirteen. I put his answers in chronological order; but I changed none of them, and left none of them out. And they seem to me to show that what he said in his sixties was true: that his attitude to religion hadn't changed since his teens. The friends who saw the fully formed man in the boy weren't wrong: to certain things his responses were always the same.

He was painfully honest and honourable: others might sail through their passage without believing a word, but the inconsistency would hurt him; if he said he believed he would have to believe, if he didn't believe he would have to say so. He had to say he believed; so for a time he did. That was his way: he bent his will on himself, not on the world. This might seem submissive, it might *be* submissive; but it was submitting only to himself. He could never inwardly give himself up to anyone else: not even to God. Especially not God – that obscure, invisible, arbitrary tyrant. The demand to give up his own judgement, the threat of punishment and the reward of privilege – nothing could be more distasteful to him, at sixty-five, or twenty-five, or thirteen. Later he would often say he envied the happiness of those who could give their burdens to a loving Father. But this would not change either: he could not do it.

At the end of his life he gave one more interview on Jewish themes, for a book called *Essere ebrei in Italia*, *Being a Jew in Italy*. This time he suggested that the period of 'worry', of the struggle to believe, or perhaps not to believe, but in any case to be what the Turinese call 'coherent', *coerente* – that this period had lasted more than a few months. He had been 'emotionally involved', he says, 'for a couple of years': the year of preparation, evidently, and the year after. He had even made a vow to wear the *tefillin*, the phylacteries, for that year after . . . He does not say outright that, in fact, he carried out his vow; that therefore he wore the *tefillin* for two whole years.

We cannot be surprised that, in later life, he minimized this religious episode, certainly in what he publicly said, probably also in what he privately thought. It did not fit; and we all prefer our memories to fit – perhaps especially the most rational among us. Though Primo was as a rule unsparingly honest about himself, he was supremely rational. That was why he was almost bound to reject religious belief; this episode was an aberration and a surprise. It didn't connect to anything before or after it, and would naturally come to seem shorter than it was. He would also, perhaps, prefer not to remember that he was ever tempted by the irrational, even at thirteen; or that he had briefly been as 'peculiar' in that way, as *non*-coherent, as his scientific but superstitious father. I think this was, in fact, a painful and humiliating memory, which he covered in a self-mocking (but not only self-mocking) irony. The real reason he'd made the vow, he said, was because he wanted a bicycle. 'And in the end the bicycle did arrive; but I don't think it had much to do with the *tefillin*.'

Love

It was not only his boundless dreams of chemistry that he hid behind a cool exterior. He did the same with anything important; the more important, the more he hid it. And the most important, and most boundless, of all were his feelings.

He seemed so calm, so quiet, so preternaturally mature. But inside he was an adolescent like the others – only more than the others. 'I was extraordinarily shy,' he said, 'I hung back, I blushed.' He was hypersensitive, terribly vulnerable; he swung between extremes of exaltation and abasement, vaulting confidence and utter despair. He hid it then, and almost never talked or wrote about it later. But his close friends knew. In *The Periodic Table*, contrasting himself to his sensible friend Enrico, he fleetingly refers to his 'tormented oscillation', at the age of fifteen:

. . . between the heaven (of a school or sports success, a new friendship, a rudimentary and fleeting love) and the hell (of a failing grade, a remorse, a brutal revelation of an inferiority which each time seemed eternal, definitive).

Perhaps this was an exaggeration, for dramatic effect? I asked the real Enrico. His answer was clear: 'I think the self-portrait of Levi at [fifteen] is very close to the truth.'

Of course the most boundless and secret feelings of all – not only for adolescents, and not only for Primo Levi – are about sex and love. About these above all he almost never spoke or wrote. Here in *The Periodic Table* there is the mention of 'the heaven of a rudimentary and fleeting love'; but more often he hinted at hell. There was his torment over his looks, which had lasted 'from eight to twelve' the first time he mentioned it, but later spread to 'his years at school': every time he looked in the mirror, 'the image reflected back at him . . . was short, ugly, weak'. There was his inability to use bad language, however hard he tried. There was that habit of blushing which overtook him now, especially at any mention – or even thought – of sex. And there was his refusal to go dancing.

As late as seventeen or eighteen, he seemed to have no interest in girls at all. Now, even in England or Germany this would be bad enough; but in Italy it is scandalous, an insult to the whole culture of male and female pride. It attracted unwelcome attention from his father, as we know; and also from the other boys. 'You really don't like women, do you?' they mocked, and implied it was because he was a Jew. One even told him, quite seriously, that circumcision was castration: 'Not for everyone, maybe, but for you.' This sentence, Primo wrote, 'weighed on me like a paralysis for years'.

For his lack of interest in girls was a cover-up: perhaps his greatest cover-up of all. He *was* interested, intensely interested. But, he wrote – just once, reluctantly, and very late – 'It was not easy for me.' Then he pushed himself further: '*Anzi, è stato difficile e doloroso*': 'On the contrary, it was difficult and full of pain.'

In fact, he fell in love with every girl who spoke to him, and even more with those who didn't. But somewhere there was a block, a gap, an uncrossable chasm. He could not make himself approach them. He was afraid to talk to them, afraid to touch them, afraid most of all that they would touch him. Instead he fell in love from afar. He would follow his objects of desire on the street, keeping 'at a safe distance', ready to run off at any moment, if by chance they should turn around. 'I would shadow them as far as their houses, and then spend hours beneath their lighted windows, trying to interpret the rare shadows I caught sight of; determined to make no move, yet jealous to the point of madness.'

But even this was not the worst. The worst was that even when he was sitting with a girl, talking to her, the chasm was still there: no longer between them, but inside him.

What was this? Can anyone ever say? He could not; not even in his writing. He did write about it later, once or twice in his autobiography, indirectly in a few stories. But it was one thing he did not try to understand. He talked about it even less, of course: a glancing allusion, here and there, to his 'complexes' or 'inhibitions'. Until the end. At the beginning of 1986, for instance, he gave an interview to his friend Giovanni Tesio's daughter for a school project. He was among friends, he liked the young, and it was already on his mind. When Silvia asks if there is 'anything he's never told anyone else' – 'She wants a scoop,' Tesio laughs – Primo says, 'All right, I'll give you a scoop.' Before the great divide of Auschwitz, he says, he had been a *timido*, a *nevrotico* – a timid, neurotic person. Afterwards, this was gone. (Of course, it was really more complicated than that.) 'Why?' he says. 'I don't know.'

A year later he was giving his last interviews to Tesio himself, and telling him too about his 'inhibitions'. At the end he said, 'These are things that should not be told.' But he meant: told by Tesio. For he had already written them himself, to the Signora of *The Double Bond*, and given the chapter to his publisher. He was trying to tell them: to himself, to the Lady, to us. This was the last dark room in his familiar house, the one room he had not dared to enter.

Primo wrote Chapter 3 of *The Double Bond* in the week of 15–22 October 1986. In it he speaks openly – 'shamelessly', he calls it – of his torment over sex and love for perhaps only the second or third time in his life.

He'd picked up his first notions of sex, he says, at school. He was 'head of the class', and kept out of such things by the other boys; but he listened, and felt on the edge of a world that was forbidden, dirty, and above all strange. Was there really such a strange instinct in every man? He could find no trace of it in himself.

At this point he made a characteristically severe decision, which he describes to the Signora with characteristic self-satire. Either he was fit to propagate the species or he wasn't. If he was, all he had to do was wait, and the instinct would arrive. If he was not, he would have to resign himself to his unfitness, in order not to pass on this hereditary taint. It was his duty not to interfere with natural selection; and not to cheat, therefore, by digging up out of books a knowledge which ought to arise naturally, as it did in animals. Hadn't he seen dogs and chickens doing it? Who had taught them? Nobody. Then nobody should have to teach him either.

Smile, he says to the Signora; he is smiling too, in retrospect. But he didn't smile then. Instead he swung back and forth between periods of desolation, and periods of repression and forgetting. This went on from his 'Darwinian' thirteenth year right up to the great divide of Auschwitz in his twenty-fourth. He soon gave up his quixotic ban on information; but still the long-awaited instinct did not arrive. He fell in love constantly; but chastely, sexlessly, 'so to speak from the waist up'. They were all, therefore, hopeless and solitary loves. Never once did the spark leap, which he came to know only much later. He racked his brains to understand why, in vain. Now, of course, he knows why: because they saw his own doubt and his own anguish in his eyes.

In this dark maze he wandered entirely alone, because he did not dare to speak to anyone. Not to his mother, that 'austere and Victorian being', whom he could see was even more ignorant and inhibited than he. Not to friends, or a doctor, because he was afraid they would confirm his worst fears: that his case was hopeless. And not to his father either. Nonetheless, when he was about seventeen, his father must have realized that all was not well with this son of his, who was otherwise perfectly healthy, and not particularly ugly – though I thought I was, Primo says, in order to explain the girls' reactions – but dedicated only to the mountains, his microscope, his bike and his books. The fact that he had no girlfriend irritated Cesare, rather than worried him; he made jokes about it, as the boys at school were also beginning to do. Then one day, without warning or explanation, he gave Primo *The Physiology of Love* by Paolo Mantegazza. That done, he seems to have felt his paternal duty discharged.

But it only made Primo's depression worse. This book was for the others, he felt, the normal ones: not for him. His case would not be in it; his case did not exist.

And yet he kept falling in love. The list of his loves included the baker's girl he met every morning on the way to school, the blonde daughter of the tenants on his *nonno*'s farm, and a little girl as shy as he, whom the teacher put beside him in the third year. Most memorably of all, it included the girl who did the ironing in the house across the road. About this girl he decides to tell the Lady in more detail.

He was about fifteen, he says, the girl two or three years older. She worked at her ironing board in front of the window directly across from his, where he sat at his desk and studied. He watched her, at first distractedly, then more intensely. There she was, 'flesh and blood beneath my eyes', across the canyon of the Via Vico: brown-haired, red-cheeked, her forearms bare. Then one day she came right up to the glass of her window and smiled at him. She made a gesture, as if to say 'Wait'; and then bared one of her breasts.

This so disturbed him that he told his parents he was ill; and soon he really was, with a sore throat and cough, and stayed away from school for three days. Surely he should have signalled to her to meet him in the street? – but he completely lacked the courage. What would he have said or done? 'From that day on I kept the curtains over that window carefully closed.'

Friendship

He had shut himself in. But he couldn't 'stoically resign himself', as he had so bravely planned. His tell-tale blushing gave that away; so did the depth of his anguish, which would increase rather than diminish in the following years.

What he did now perfectly expressed, or perhaps formed, his deepest character. Was he to be allowed no girls in his life – except at a distance, watching their shadows behind lit windows? Very well. But he would not retreat into Greek verb endings and Newtonian binomials; he would not leave the world of 'normal, happy' boys, who had the instinct, who went dancing. He couldn't join them, but he wouldn't withdraw from them either. He certainly didn't despise them, indeed he envied them, he was interested in them; perhaps he could learn to be more like them, to find the missing piece of himself in them. Instead of looking for himself in Leopardi, his *semblable*, his *frère*, he would look for himself in his opposite: in them.

His nature, and his life, were cut across by divides, like the great divide of Auschwitz: by frontiers, gaps, blocks, between himself and others, between himself and other parts of himself. Some of these divides were impossible to cross, and that impossibility gave him the greatest pain. The main longing of his life was to cross frontiers, to bridge gaps, to heal divisions. If he couldn't always, or even often, do it in life, he could and did do it in writing. If there is one way to describe the whole of his work, it is this: it seeks out his opposite, even his enemy – human, animal and material – in order to cross the gap between them, to explore and understand them, to find a connection.

This is not how it looked from the outside. As a boy he stuck close to his family, as close as all children had to stick in those days, or closer; in his sixties he admitted, 'I haven't left it even now.' The closest friends of his youth, Giorgio Lattes and Livio Norzi, were not his opposites, but from very similar backgrounds: well-brought-up, over-protected Jewish boys from good Turinese families. Livio especially was another *semblable*: highly intelligent (Primo said he was the most intelligent person he'd ever known); brilliantly gifted in mathematics and physics; but reserved, solitary, difficult, and later at least given to melancholy. Giorgio and Livio both remained among his three or four closest friends throughout his life. ('I am faithful in friendship,' he said; and he was.)

But they were not his only friends at school, and perhaps not the most important. They were familiar, they were his home. But he did not only want a home. He also wanted something different, something opposite. And many of his friends at school were both. They were, for example, Christians (he once said that most of his friends at school were Christians); and they were also less shy, less well-behaved, less protected. It was these friendships that he wrote about later: not the closed, inward-turned ones, in which no one could change; but the more open, outward-turned ones, in which – just possibly – someone might. Not the safe, predictable friendships, in other words, but the complicated, unpredictable ones; not the chemist's friendships, but the writer's.

It may be that these friendships only seem important now because he wrote about them. But it may be – and I think it is – the other way around. He wrote about them because they were important: because they contained that hope, and also fear, of change which still lie behind his poem 'To My Friends', written when he was sixty-six years old.

> . . . O no one, or someone, or perhaps one alone,
> Or you who read me: remember the time
> Before the wax began to harden,
> When each of us was like a seal.
> Each of us bears the imprint
> Of the friend met along the way;
> In each the trace of each.
> For good or for evil,
> In wisdom or in folly,
> Each marked by each for ever.

Enrico

The first friendship in Primo's autobiography is with a boy he calls Enrico, at the age of fifteen.* It is, in fact, the very first thing he tells us about himself: between his fond and comic account of his ancestors and this friendship he leaves his own family, and the first fifteen years of his life, in silence.

'Enrico' borrowed a few details from elsewhere, mostly from Primo's imagination; but essentially he was based on one real boy: Mario Piacenza.

Mario, like Enrico, was an honest, likeable, ordinary boy. He and Primo had been classmates since *ginnasio*. He too chose chemistry; and the two became friends in much the way Primo describes. They did simple experiments together at Primo's house; they talked with adolescent enthusiasm of the great researchers of the nineteenth century, and of how they too would become researchers, and thus find the short-cut to truth that school denied them. Primo gave Mario the chemistry books he was reading (Mario still remembers *The Microbe Hunters* today); and several times the friends went together to the laboratory that belonged to Mario's older brother.

The laboratory was in an attic, rather than at the back of a courtyard; but otherwise the story of 'Hydrogen' is essentially true. The lab was primitive, dusty and cold. Mario was the host, Primo the planner and theoretician. But both were sorcerer's apprentices without the sorcerer. They did the electrolysis experiment, which ended with an explosion, as Primo describes. It was, Mario says, 'minimal'.

This friendship, and the work together in the lab, may be the first events in Primo's autobiography; but they sound familiar. Enrico has a 'slow, pedestrian imagination', he is 'not very active', and not very clever; Primo is indisputably the leader in their adventure, even the teacher, writing the electrolysis equation on the blackboard, and explaining to Enrico that this mere theory 'was actually taking place'. At the same time, he is fascinated by Enrico. Enrico is brave, and never lies; he is good at sports, but doesn't boast about it; he doesn't join in show-off theorizing. He has down-to-earth, attainable goals, he works for them patiently, and he achieves them: now a passing grade, or a microscope; later 'the money to live quietly', 'a certain woman'.

What this reminds us of is Carlo: Carlo, who was merely Primo's bolt-tightener, but whose pedestrian gift ('a series of stamps from Nicaragua') won him Lidia, whom Primo had secretly loved. The story of Carlo was

---

* In 'Hydrogen', Chapter 2 of *The Periodic Table*. Primo says that he was sixteen, but he was probably out a year.

only one story. Now, four or five years later, there's another; soon there will be more. There is a pattern in this carpet. It's the pattern of the Opposite, the Other: the friend, or enemy, whom Primo both admires and does not admire, against whom he measures himself, and with whom he tests what will become the question of his life: *What is a man?*

'Hydrogen' begins with Enrico as a model Piedmontese man – which is not very different from a model Englishman: brave, modest and honourable, unwaveringly calm. True, without much intellect or imagination; but these absences are virtues as well, in the ideal Piedmontese (and in the ideal Englishman). By comparison, Primo's 'tormented oscillation' of emotional highs and lows is lightweight, immature, almost feminine.

As soon as they are in the lab, however, they become equals, at least in ignorance. And when Primo conducts the electrolysis experiment, and writes the equation on the board, *he* becomes the man to Enrico's boy. The writer, looking back, makes fun of himself in this role: he gave himself, he says, 'as much importance as I could'. But it is a real seizure of power, and Enrico resists it: 'Who says it's really hydrogen and oxygen?' he demands. 'What if there's chlorine? Didn't you put in salt?'

The objection struck me as insulting: how dared Enrico doubt a statement of mine? I and I alone was the theorist. He was the owner of the lab (though only to a certain extent, and at second hand); but precisely because he was in no position to boast of anything else, he should have abstained from criticism.

The small, weak, wavering adolescent is gone. Here Primo is the scientist, the chemist, who knows the secrets of the universe, who wields the almost magic power of the formulas which the elements obey. 'Let's see who's right,' he says.

I carefully lifted out the cathode jar, and holding it with its open end down, lit a match and brought it near. There was an explosion – small, but sharp and angry – the jar burst into splinters (luckily, I was holding it level with my chest and not higher), and there remained in my hand, like a sarcastic symbol, the glass ring of the bottom.

He was right; it *was* hydrogen. His honour is saved, his superiority proved. If the important thing about a man is his capacity for knowledge, the power of his mind to comprehend the world, then he is a man; he is more of a man than Enrico.

And yet, of course, that is only half the story. They have had a lucky escape, afterwards his legs shake in retrospective fear; and he is left with that 'sarcastic symbol' in his hand. What does it sarcastically symbolize? He doesn't say; but I think we can guess.

It symbolizes the opposite answer to his question: the answer which says that Enrico is the man, and he is not. For he was right this time, but he might not have been, he might have failed. Perhaps this ambition of his – to comprehend the world with the power of his mind – is too high, too hubristic, too much like a god, in fact, and not a man. Perhaps that is why all their experiments have ended in a punishment – to teach them a lesson; to teach *him* a lesson, since patient, unpretentious Enrico does not need one. He has even hinted at this, when their first, glass-blowing experiment also ended in an explosion:

In a sense, this was a just punishment. Glass is glass, and should not be expected to behave like soapy water. Forcing the terms a bit, one could even draw an Aesopian moral from the story.

Once again, he does not spell out what the moral is. But surely it is this: that if *he* tries to behave like something he is not, he too may be justly punished. If he tries to behave like a god, or like one of the great researchers of the nineteenth century, will he too not shatter like a glass bubble?

In fact the whole of 'Hydrogen' is a comic catalogue of small failures, after the grand vision with which it began ('We would be chemists, Enrico and I. We would dredge the bowels of the mystery with our strength, our talent: we would grab Proteus by the throat . . . [and] make him speak'). Their second failure, trying to make nitrous oxide, could have been far from small. In fact they stop, when the lab fills with a choking fog: 'Luckily for us,' Primo says, 'because we did not know what can happen when this explosive salt is heated less than cautiously.' This time, instead of a small glass tube or jar, the whole lab could have blown up, with them inside it.

This possibility of explosion hangs over many of Primo's stories of chemistry. It is perfectly realistic, and also perfectly symbolic. It represents the fear of failure, and shows how dramatic that fear was to him: 'a brutal revelation of an inferiority which each time seemed eternal, definitive'. Throughout his writing life he repeated that the two great adult experiences were (as Pavese had said) success and failure, killing the white whale or failing to kill him. He went out to meet these experiences half-way, in chemistry and in the mountains; he talked of chemistry and of climbing as ultimate tests of maturity and responsibility, in which you could stake your life on a single move. This extreme vision of adulthood thrilled him, and frightened him – thrilled him *because* it frightened him; because it was such a triumph to him when he did – only rarely in the mountains, but regularly in chemistry, and in writing – face and overcome his fear of failure.

Why was failure so extremely frightening to him? 'Hydrogen' suggests an answer: *because he aimed so high.* That is the difference between him and

Enrico. Enrico's goals 'were always attainable', he 'knew his limitations'. Primo, by contrast, does not know his own limitations at all; his future is that 'indefinite cloud of future powers'. And if he does not know his powers he may exceed them. That is, indeed, what happens, over and over again, in the story. Their experiments all fail, because their means – their knowledge, the lab's equipment – are absurdly inadequate to their goals.

Primo's picture in 'Hydrogen' of his choice of chemistry, indeed of this whole time in his life, turns on contrast and oscillation. There is the heaven of success and the hell of failure, and his 'tormented oscillation' between them. There is the central contrast between himself and Enrico, and the oscillation between his sense of inferiority, and of superiority, to him. But this is the main and overarching one: the contrast between his grand, godlike ideal of chemistry, and the dusty, puny reality of two ignorant boys; the oscillation between the vast ambition of the boy looking forward, and the wry realism of the man looking back. And in this gap between end and means, vision and knowledge, past and future, lies the fear.

Looking back, there is the same oscillation at the very beginning of the story. Primo has pledged to seize the 'key to the highest truths' on his own, despite his school and his society – to pick the lock, to force the doors. *And that is just what he and Enrico have done*, since they have 'borrowed' the key to Enrico's brother's lab without his permission. This may be an image of independence and triumph – but it may also be one of doubt and fear. Enrico's brother is older, 'a mysterious and choleric personage': and chemistry too is owned by older, mysterious and possibly angry men. This key they have appropriated is not theirs. Will chemistry, perhaps, remain like this – at least for him, who asks so much of it? A key which is *not his*, and not even properly acquired?

In this story, everything oscillates. First the answer to the question, which of these two boys is more a man: the one who aspires to know the world, or the one who is content to know himself. But also, the question itself. On one level it is about man in the sense of *human*. But in another it is about man in the sense of *male*.

It may already have struck you that chemistry in Primo's description is a very masculine activity. It's fact and proof; it's adventure, risk and war. But in 'Hydrogen' it is also masculine in another way, which leaves them both embarrassed. This embarrassment is 'deep' and 'essential', 'tied to an ancient atrophy . . . of our caste'; specifically of its males.

What were we able to do with our hands? Nothing, or almost nothing. The women, yes – our mothers and grandmothers had quick, agile hands, they could cook and sew, some even played the piano, painted watercolours, embroidered, braided their hair. But we, and our fathers?

Our hands were at once clumsy and weak, backward, insensitive: the least well-trained parts of our bodies. After the first basic experiences of play, they'd learned to write, and that was all . . . [T]hey knew nothing of the solemn, balanced weight of a hammer, or the concentrated power of a blade, which had been too cautiously forbidden us; nothing of the wise texture of wood, or the similar and different pliabilities of iron, copper and lead. If man is a maker, we were not men; we knew this and suffered from it.

It is curious that, just at this point, Primo should drop his motif of contrast. From the start Enrico's character has been particularly masculine – strong and silent; good at sports; given to deeds, not words. We can believe that his hands are as untrained in the lab as Primo's; but they certainly know, for example, the 'balanced weight' of his pole-vaulter's pole. The sudden identity of the two, especially here, seems odd and out of tune.

I suspect that this is a point at which the real Primo Levi and Mario Piacenza have resisted literary shaping into the emblematic opposites of 'Hydrogen'. For Mario was a good friend of Primo's, both then and later. Carlo before him was a rival, Guido after him would be an enemy. Mario was closer to Sandro of 'Iron', or Emilio of 'Tin': both great opposites, but great friends. In the history, both real and literary, of Primo's *alter egos*, friends help and ease his male self-doubts, while enemies increase them. Mario Piacenza was somewhere in between; and so therefore is Enrico. He cannot be a threat to Primo's masculinity, because that would make him an enemy, which Mario wasn't. And yet he *is* really a bit of a threat . . . The only refuge is that moment of confusion, in which the ideally manly Enrico joins Primo in uncertainty about his manhood.

In order to make emblematic Enrico out of Mario, Primo also changed his future. 'Later,' he wrote, 'he wanted a certain woman and he got her; he wanted the money to live quietly, and obtained it after ten years of boring, prosaic work.' In fact, Mario's work was the opposite of boring – he emigrated to Peru, and founded his own chemical company; and he made far more than 'the money to live quietly' – he became decidedly rich. On the other hand, he says, 'Perhaps I wanted that certain woman, but I did not get her.' In other words, *this* oscillation, between reality and literature, is a complete inversion. It proves, I think, that Enrico represented male success to Primo after all; and it betrays his idea of what male success was: not money, which hardly mattered to him; but getting the woman you wanted.

★

I remember the boy who keeps a closed window between himself and the girl he wants; and I am afraid 'Hydrogen' is right – he has unattainable goals. But 'Hydrogen' doesn't say only this, it also says the opposite; it too oscillates, between pride and fear, between exaltation and self-doubt. And right at the end it thrillingly joins them.

We left, discussing what had happened. My legs were shaking a bit; I felt a retrospective fear, and at the same time a kind of foolish pride, at having confirmed a hypothesis and unleashed a force of nature. It had really been hydrogen, therefore: the same that burns in the sun and stars, and from whose condensation the universes form in eternal silence.

A Long Duel

There is a latent fascism in all boys, a tendency to despise the weak and worship the strong. When political Fascism takes over this tendency is no longer controlled, like the dangerous animal it is, but let out, its coat brushed to a glossy sheen. The bullies are encouraged, the victims left more defenceless than ever; and altogether the situation of a small, skinny, clever Jewish boy becomes unenviable, even in an academic, ex-antifascist school.

In later life Primo was always firmly on the side of those who say, especially about antisemitism, '*italiani brava gente*': that the Italians are not racists, and could not be moved to real antisemitism even by Mussolini. And this is certainly true, as the historical record clearly shows.★

At school, however, he did not escape some trampling by the glossy animal of Fascism. In his happier moods, he remembered living 'reasonably well in an ex-antifascist school, almost without incident'. But the only event he told his authorized biographer, Tesio, in detail was a (mildly) antisemitic one. 'We were talking about avarice, about a miser. Someone at the back of the class said, "A Jew, in other words."' Primo, at the front, blushed red, but didn't speak. The teacher, Anna Borgogno, did speak. She 'was violently angry, and said: "Decent people don't say such things."'

To the Catholic journalist Ferdinando Camon Primo admitted: 'As a Jew, I was made fun of by my schoolmates: not beaten up, or insulted, but made fun of, yes.' He had admitted it to Fiora Vincenti too, and half alluded to the fact that some of the 'fun' was sexual. Only once, to two interviewers in 1984, was he quite open. One of them later quoted his examples – *You*

★ For further discussion of this, see Chapter 4.

really don't like women, do you? and *Circumcision is castration*; and his wry remark that, 'without admitting it', he'd half believed this.

He did not write any more openly than he spoke about these adolescent humiliations. But he did write about them indirectly, in a few stories.

The first was 'Retirement Fund', published in *Storie Naturali* in 1966; one of his strange and prescient science fiction fables. In it he imagines a device called a Torec: a helmet which, when you put it on, gives you a perfect and powerful version of today's 'virtual reality' experiences. One of the 'virtual' experiences the narrator finds himself having is that of a boy being racially taunted. His feelings are ambivalent, painfully real; the writer has clearly known some version of this situation. But the boy in this story-within-a-story is a Catholic Italian.

I was nineteen, I was strong and stocky, and I was indeed a Wop [as his tormentors have called him]; the son of Italian immigrants. I was deeply ashamed of this, and at the same time proud. My persecutors were authentic ones, my neighbours and enemies since childhood: blond Anglo-Saxon Protestants. I detested them, and at the same time I admired them a little.

The WASPs' taunts are at once racial and sexual, as the worst ones aimed at Primo had been. 'Wassa matta, Momma's boy?' one of them says, and blows him a kiss. Whereupon the 'Wop' hurls his glass at the sneering blond face, and watches the blood flow 'with a fierce exultation'. The narrator feels this exultation as though it were his own. Then immediately he feels the terrible blows, given and received, of the boys' fight, until the 'Wop' loses consciousness under the cruel battering of his enemies.

In this story Primo was doing many of the things he needed to do in writing. One of them was this: to remember his earliest encounters with prejudice, persecution and violence. These are things he cannot accept – yet they're things he has spent the rest of his life trying to understand. The Torec is a brilliant metaphor for this dilemma, and a brilliant solution to it. When the narrator puts the helmet on his head, he feels anger, hate, revenge – he fights, he feels and inflicts pain. But it is not *his* anger, *his* hate, *his* fighting and pain. While he wears the Torec he feels them – but he can take it off, he can return to innocence and safety. *The story itself is Primo's Torec*: in writing he can allow hatred and violence inside himself just far enough to (perhaps) understand it, and no further. Indeed the story is even better than the Torec, because if the Torec is a fiction to the narrator, the story is a fiction about a fiction to Primo – and both are invented, and controlled, by him.

The Torec is, therefore, like literature – it is indeed a metaphor for literature. It is cathartic to the narrator as literature is cathartic to the reader, allowing him to experience in imagination things he is afraid to experience in life. But literature is even more cathartic to the writer, since it does not only happen in his own imagination – he also makes it happen in his readers'. Writing this story, Primo not only feels he's turning the tables on his old enemies, he really does so. For the story, unlike the Torec, is real; other people will read it; perhaps even his old enemies themselves. And at least while they read, while they wear his Torec, they will have to remember that – as he will write in *If Not Now, When?* – 'Everybody is somebody's Jew.' They will have to remember that they too have been despised, as they despised him; they will have to feel, while they wear his Torec, the shame, the fear, the impotent anger of Jews.

There is, therefore, a kind of revenge for Primo in writing this story. But there is also the opposite. For he not only makes his old enemies in the story (and perhaps the real ones, reading it) 'somebody's Jew', he recognizes that they were: that as immigrants in America, boys like his tormentors were tormented in their turn. And more: the story is about their sufferings, not his. In it his surrogate, the narrator, does not re-experience his own Jewish suffering, as he could easily have done, but theirs. This is, on the one hand, an extreme kind of distancing – when he first writes about this most painful adolescent experience he makes it someone else's, even his old enemy's. But it is also an extreme kind of closeness. What has happened between these enemies has gone much further than the wax-and-seal exchange between friends: they have – in imagination, in literature – exchanged identities.

'Retirement Fund' is not a particularly important story. And yet it contains the deepest level of Primo Levi's urge to understand. He would always want most to understand what was furthest from himself. And at the same time, this was how he tried to understand himself; he would never want, or be able, to do it more directly. That is why his most characteristic move in writing is the 'double leap between two levels of energy' – in which he joins what is nearest to what is furthest away, like the vast universe to the two small boys at the end of 'Hydrogen'. And that is why his most characteristic writing itself takes what is furthest away, and draws it near: finding himself, and us, in our enemies, in plants and animals, in insects, bacteria, elements, atoms.

Guido

In the story Primo wrote about Guido, he can only describe their relationship in long, tense sentences, which reveal, step by step, pairs of balanced opposites. It was a 'strange bond, which was perhaps not friendship, which both united and divided us'; it was 'a curious, rough, exclusive, polemical friendship, never affectionate, not always loyal, which involved a continual competition, a battle to the bitter end, which in effect made us inseparable'. He never calls it an enmity, or Guido and himself enemies. They are 'adversaries', they are 'rivals', they are in 'competitive tension'. The best word for this does not appear in the story, but in its title: 'Un lungo duello'. It is a duel, governed – at least at the start – by strict and chivalrous rules.

At first the duellists are surrounded by others – the forty-one boys of their first year *liceo* class, the five or six of their little 'clan', their self-proclaimed élite. The others are unnamed, however, and soon drop away; leaving Primo and Guido alone to begin their duel.

Immediately they take up tense, balanced, ritual positions. Guido is 'a young barbarian with the body of a statue', who envies Primo's scholastic success; 'symmetrically', Primo envies 'his muscles, his height, his beauty and his precocious lusts'. Primo is mind and Guido body, Primo brain and Guido brawn. Right at the start the story predicts who will win: for Primo's superiority is vulnerable in a way that Guido's isn't. Guido is 'intelligent and ambitious', he borrows all Primo's books and doesn't return them, so that he quickly catches up to his opponent's culture. But Primo cannot make himself tall, handsome and strong.

Nonetheless, he tries. He is determined to compete with Guido on Guido's own territory. So their competitions begin. First, a breath-holding competition, both comic and dangerous ('We both held out stubbornly, to the brink of passing out'). They give this up by mutual agreement.

The next one is even odder, and more violent. It is, Primo says, Guido's idea: a slapping competition, in which the aim is to catch your opponent by surprise, and hit him in the face as hard as you can. Like the previous one, however, this competition is governed by chivalrous rules. You are allowed to distract your opponent, even to hit him from behind; but it is against the rules to hit him again, while he is still dazed; it is dishonourable to protest or complain. With this game the rest of the world disappears, and the obsession of mutual hostility comes very close to its opposite: the obsession of friendship, even of love. The duellists must watch each other like hawks ('We became very skilful at reading on each other's faces the imperceptible contraction that preceded a slap'); when the other isn't there, they must wonder where he is, when he may suddenly appear.

'Against all expectations,' Primo says, he was the winner of this competition, 'on points'. One draw, then, and one to Primo. But immediately Guido takes revenge. He invents a competition for the whole class, which he knows he will win: a striptease, to be performed during a lesson, and all the way. Of course he is right. 'I could not overcome my modesty,' Primo wrote. 'I competed only once, and stopped at my shoes.' A few of the others get as far as baring their chests, four get down to their underpants; but only Guido manages to strip naked from head to toe.

On some pretext he'd had himself moved from the second to the last row, he'd trained himself to get his clothes back on quickly, and he'd waited till the day after he'd been called on in class. Finally, while the teacher was giving a lesson on the school skeleton, naming its parts with a pointer, he not only stripped completely, but entirely nude stepped first on to his seat and then up on to his desk, while the whole class held its breath, suspended between shock and admiration. Thus he remained for a long moment.

The body has won, at least in beauty and daring. But now we come to the last and most serious competition: sport. The 'prince of sports' among the clan is athletics, and many of their afternoons are spent in the old Stadium not far from the school. This Stadium, built in 1915, in 1934 is already abandoned and falling down, its track full of holes, trees growing on its stands. It is also officially closed, and they have to sneak in through the bar, the only part of the structure still in use.

Perhaps this means that Primo will have to force his entrance to sport, just as much as his entrance to science. *But he will.* They choose their favourite Olympic sport, running. 'It was soon clear,' Primo says, 'that Guido would win hands down in all events but one: the 800 metres. So of course it was precisely in the 800 metres that he wanted to beat me, to make his athletic supremacy complete.'

For weeks they run, first against each other, then against the clock, tearing their feet on the pot-holed track, 'hating each other . . . with the unconfessed hatred of athletes', terrifying each other with their refusal to give up. They are more inseparable than ever; as each drives himself along the track the other follows on his bike, shouting out the times. Guido abandons chivalry and shouts out dirty jokes instead. But he needn't bother, and they both know it. At the end of the school year there is an abyss of at least five seconds between them. Guido's superiority is public, proven. He has won.

But has he? The duel is not quite over; and Primo claims a victory after all. A 'meagre' one, though;* a rueful, self-mocking one; perhaps only a joke. By now the bar in the Stadium had closed too, and the only way in was right at the top, where someone had forgotten to close a gap. This meant a long climb up the buttresses, which the others, including Guido, had to make.

---

* In Italian 'meagre', *magro*, is the same word as 'thin'. This is, of course, part of the self-mockery.

Now I noticed that the railings which barred the entrance at ground level had sixteen-centimetre openings, which my skull just squeezed through. But at the time I was so skinny that if my skull could squeeze through, the rest of me would easily follow.

Of this particular feat, I alone was capable. Well: wasn't it a specialty too? A gift of nature, like Guido's quadriceps and deltoids? Forcing the terms a bit, like the Sophists, it might even be called an athletic event, details to be determined by the appropriate regulations. Perhaps a new category could be added to Horace's list . . . : the *passatori di cancellate*, those who can slip through locked gates.

It *is* a joke — and yet I'm sure it isn't. This image, or ones like it, come up so often in Primo's stories of his adolescence, the time when he was poised to enter the adult world. First in 'Hydrogen': the images of lock-picking, of the forced door, the stolen key — which are partly celebrations of independence, and partly self-doubt, the ignorant boy playing with vast forces which explode in his hand. Then in 'Un lungo duello', the image of entering the closed Stadium through the bar, as though the adult world of sport is equally closed, and here too he must steal or force his entry. And now this image of his lone, ironic achievement — being skinny enough to slip through the railings, while Guido and the others have to climb . . . It *is* at least half a victory. He has squeezed into the world of sport, which has been locked against him, just as he squeezed into chemistry. And he has done it by turning handicap into advantage, defeat into victory: he has made his skinny body itself into his key.

'I have lost track of Guido, and so I do not know which of us has won the long-distance race of life,' Primo wrote in the concluding paragraph of 'Un lungo duello'. If Guido was a real boy, the second part of this sentence at least could not be true. If Guido had become as successful as Primo himself, he would have known. He was being modest, as usual, in the Turinese way, according to which it is neither seemly nor Christian to crow.

The whole story is modest in the Turinese way. The long duel ends with his defeat — and an inner victory, hidden inside a joke about his weakling's body. And now 'Un lungo duello' ends the same way: with a public image of defeat, and a secret inner victory. For this is how that concluding paragraph ends:

[Guido's] image has remained fixed in my memory like a photograph: standing naked on his absurd desk in *liceo*, symmetrical to the obscene skeleton which the teacher was describing; provocative, Dionysian, obscene in the opposite direction, ephemeral monument of earthly vigour and of insolence.

That is our final image of Guido: naked, daring, insolent. And that is his victory, the victory of the body. But where at the start Primo had been 'symmetrical' to him, now the skeleton is: now his opponent in the duel is the skeleton, and to the skeleton he must inevitably lose. The skeleton reminds us that the victory of the body is – as Primo says – ephemeral; that the insolence of the body ends in death. Unlike the victory of the mind, which can outlive death, for example in books; for example, in this book of Primo Levi's, which we are now reading. Primo doesn't say *that*. But it's there, in the skeleton, in the word 'ephemeral'. This is like one of the slaps in the game of the story – disguised in friendly talk, delivered without warning, perhaps from behind. And just as Primo won that game in the story, so he now wins the game of the story: secretly, silently, by sleight of hand, or word. This is as close as a Turinese can come to crowing.

Man-made

Apart from 'Hydrogen' and 'Un lungo duello', Primo wrote one other story of boys at school. This one is more fantastical. But it exposes the self-doubts and struggles of a twelve-year-old boy called Mario with surgical accuracy, as though he were Eliot's patient etherized upon a table: 'waiting', in Primo's own later words, 'for the surgeon to cut him open, or rather in the act of doing it myself'.

The story is called 'I sintetici', and has never been translated into English. We could call it, literally, 'The Synthetics'; or possibly 'Man-made'.

When we meet Mario he is whispering an answer in a class test to his neighbour, Renato. They leave school together, and are joined by another boy, Giorgio. Renato likes sport, Giorgio likes stamps, Mario likes science. Mario is serious, bookish; Renato taunts him for being a swot and a teacher's pet. Giorgio is a kind, biddable boy, who feels sorry for Mario, but is helpless against Renato's certainty: that *Mario is different*. Mario protests – 'I'm the same as everyone else'; but the narration notes that he has been 'touched on the raw'. 'It was true, that was one of his dominating thoughts, which he only escaped by repeating to himself that everyone was different. But he felt "more different", though hopefully better; and from this he suffered often.'

Renato lays out his evidence, culminating in the most telling: in the gymnasium Mario always undresses facing the wall. 'You know why?' Renato demands. 'Because Mario has no navel.'

Mario blushes violently, his knees shake with anger and fear, and he says, 'I'm exactly the same as all of you, just a bit thinner.' When he has bolted into his house, Renato explains his theory to Giorgio. Mario is a test-tube baby, born of an incubator, not of woman. That is why he has no navel. Renato has always suspected it, but now he's certain – Mario's own reaction has proved it. And Giorgio had better not be too sympathetic. Hasn't he noticed how different Mario is? How strange his freckles are, his fingernails, his way of speaking? How he can't swim, has only now learned to ride a bike, never takes part in fights, even for fun? *Of course* he's so brilliant at school . . . What do you mean? asks Giorgio. I mean, Renato says, that he has a computer memory. Have you never noticed that his eyes shine at night, like the dial of a clock?

The next time Mario is asked a question in class he says he doesn't know the answer; he has forgotten it, he never knew it. The teacher calls him aside. Mario won't talk; his voice emerges as though 'through a crack in a visor'. But the teacher is sympathetic, and guesses the truth. Renato often speaks to you, and you look away, she says. Is he trying to humiliate you? Telling you some nonsense? Mario pales, and says wearily, It's not nonsense. I'm different from the others. Different? the teacher says. In what way? If anything, you're better. What's so terrible about that? No, Mario says. I was born in a different way. I'm man-made.

The teacher takes him to the headmaster. How can a logical, rational boy like you listen to such nonsense? the headmaster says; but it's quite hopeless ('even the best headmaster has crossed a certain threshold, and only understands certain things').

When we next see Mario he is in the school playground, amid rowdy groups of boys playing basketball. He stands in a corner, speaking to a small crowd.

Now we are few, he says, but soon we shall be many, and rule the world. Then there will be no more war, no more famine, and no more differences between people. Everyone will be equal. And everyone will be born like me. Not by chance, but by choice. I'm one of the first, and maybe they haven't got it quite right yet. But they will. People will be born to order: as tall, strong and intelligent, as good, brave and just as you like. There will be order and justice, and everyone will be happy.

I'm not alone, he continues. Right here at school there's another of us: Miss Scotti. I realized that the other day, when she called me in to see her. But I'd already suspected it, from her way of speaking, from the fact that she never gets angry, and never raises her voice. Never getting angry means you've gained control. When it's complete you can even stop breathing, stop feeling pain, stop your heart beating . . .

Suddenly Renato appears, his arms raised, 'full of anger, and an obscure fear'. 'Shut up, you fool!' he shouts. 'Scotti's just an old witch!' Mario replies, in a voice so loud and strong the whole playground turns to listen:

'She is not a witch. She is one of us. Yesterday she gave me the sign.' 'What sign?' Renato scoffs. Mario stares at him; and suddenly something inside him goes out like a flame. In a voice so low it's barely audible he says: 'Go away, Renato. You've made me speak. I've spoken, and now I'm like everyone again; like Renato, like one of you. Go away, all of you, leave me alone.' Soon afterwards Giorgio finds him in a corner of the gymnasium, sitting on the ground with his head in his hands, sobbing.

'Man-made' is about the battle between mind and body, just like 'Un lungo duello'. But this battle is much more deadly. For Renato is not content to show that the superior body is the superior human being: he wants to show that the superior body is the *only* human being. Mario is not just too clever, physically ungifted, and so ashamed of his body he cannot undress in front of his classmates, like the narrator of 'Duello'. On the basis of this, and of some half-assimilated biological science, Renato constructs a classical racist theory: Mario is different; therefore he is not human.

This is the element of racism which was missing from the story of Guido. It is brilliantly infused with Primo's later understanding of racist ideas, particularly of course of Nazism, with its pseudo-science, its paranoia, its crude worship of a physical ideal. But we know that antisemitism *was* part of his experience at school. Primo has abstracted from antisemitism to prejudice against 'difference' in general, no doubt because he wanted his story to be universal, like the great book he had written just over twenty years before. And he made Renato's accusation against Mario more extreme than the real taunts against him had been – I don't suppose the real Renatos went so far as to call him non-human, or that he went so far as to feel it. This too comes out of his later knowledge of where branding someone 'different' could lead. But that does not mean that Renato was not a portrait of a real kind of boy; or that Mario was not a portrait of himself, and of a struggle he waged against himself when he was young.

'Un lungo duello', however, was a genuine duel, in which we saw and knew as much of Guido as of Primo. In 'Man-made' Renato is not much more than the cause of the drama, a voice which expresses what is already Mario's own self-doubt. From then on, though the story is told from outside Mario, it really takes place inside him, in the battle between two sets of feelings about himself.

The first set is the one he starts with: the fear that he is different, that he is not like the others. And that does mean: that he is not quite human. Renato's picture of this – that Mario is a computer, a kind of puny Franken-stein's monster – is of course absurd; but the story shows that it is not without foundation. Mario is undeniably a one-sided, entirely intellectual and rational boy; and under stress he briefly becomes an out-and-out monster of reason. His speech is clearly meant to remind us of Huxley's *Brave New World*, with its ultra-rationalist vision of planned, made-to-order people. Mario still imagines that justice and equality will prevail in his Brave New World; but we all know what happened in Huxley's. And Primo counted on our knowing. Thus he silently implies that the danger for Mario *is* a kind of inhumanity; that his great rationality, taken to extremes, is politically, and even personally, dangerous ('When [control] is complete, you can even stop breathing . . .').

Primo himself certainly shared some of this first set of feelings. He had 'tried not to be different' from his schoolmates, he said (in 1966). He had rejected the whole idea of difference, he said nearly twenty years later: he hadn't wanted to be identified as anything in particular, 'neither Italian nor Jewish, but just a person', just himself. ('I know now that that is impossible,' he says in this recorded interview, and coughs convulsively.)

Then there is the second set. From the start Mario has hoped that 'different' may mean 'better'. His teacher and his headmaster both tell him that it does. He does not seem to believe them. But he goes away; and comes back with his fantasy of world domination.

While he is filled with this vision, he briefly becomes as strong as Renato, Renato's rival for the others' attention and admiration. But when Renato appears, it's suddenly over. Why? Renato doesn't himself win their struggle for power. His question – 'What sign?' – hands the initiative to Mario. All he has to do now is what any twelve-year-old would do – refuse to tell; and for the moment at least he could keep his advantage. But he doesn't. Rather: as soon as he realizes this is a struggle for power, he gives it up.

Is it because he is afraid to fight, afraid to lose? That would be a fair guess. But it is not what the story says. What the story says is that he is *ashamed*. 'You have made me speak,' he says to Renato, 'and now I'm like you.'

In other words: You have made me boast about my superiority, as you do; you have made me try to use it to gain power and prestige, as you use yours. That is why he is sobbing so desperately when Giorgio finds him: not because he has lost to Renato, but because he has betrayed himself. He has descended to Renato's level.

This is a strange shame, exactly opposite to the fear with which he started. He had been afraid of being different; now he is ashamed of *not* being different. But why had he been afraid of being different? Because being like the others – being human – was so excellent? No. There is nothing excellent about Renato; nor about the other boys, playing basketball 'with scant attention to the rules'. Even Giorgio is kind but weak. No:

Mario was afraid of being different in the way that people, especially children, really are: because he was afraid of being alone. What changed, in that moment of exaltation, was not that he believed he was superior, since he'd often suspected that; but that, for once, the thought didn't make him suffer.

Being human, in 'Man-made', is not noble. It is seeking power and prestige, if you're Renato, and being their dupes if you're the others; it is dehumanizing anyone different if you're Renato, and believing him if you're the others. In his moment of madness, Mario himself becomes all those things – drunk with power, dividing the world into 'them' and 'us', rulers and ruled. His vision is inhuman; but his desire to impose it on everyone else is all too human. He may not be aware of the first part, though the writer is; but he is very much aware of the second. His shame at the end of the story is shame at being human.

If he is ashamed of being inhuman, and ashamed of being human, what is his solution? There is only one: to be alone after all, as Mario finally asks to be, and is. For he *is* different, and that is the consequence. His difference may be a superiority; but to take advantage of that, even speak of it, is despicable, and a destruction of that superiority itself. That is the lesson of this story. The only solution, therefore, is silence. He has seemed strongest when he spoke most loudly, weakest now when he is alone and sobbing. But that is in the eyes of the world, in the eyes of – for instance – Renato. True strength is this: to bear his difference alone, in silence. To snuff out in himself the need to seem stronger than Renato, to *be* stronger than Renato. To refuse to betray his difference, merely in order not to be alone.

★　　★

Did Primo Levi really make a decision like this at twelve years old – or fourteen, or sixteen? Well, the boy who was capable of his theory of Darwinian self-sacrifice was capable of this too. In any case he was groping his way towards it, as Mario does. One rational level of 'Man-made''s connection between 'different' and 'non-human' came from later experience; so did one emotional level of its shame at being human. But I think both began now. He *was* taunted at school for being different – both a Jew, and not a real man. These two *were* first connected then, for at least one other boy, and secretly for him. He *was* so pathologically shy that he really did undress with his back to the other boys. And he *was* at the top of the class – but never tried to impress, or to use his superior knowledge to any advantage at all – except to talk to girls, and embarrass Pangella. He simply shared it, as Mario does with Renato; or hid it in silence.

But he couldn't always hide it, and his silence wasn't always interpreted as modesty. There was at least one boy in his *liceo* class who thought it was something else entirely. He thought it was contempt.

Sixty years later, he tells me so. The Jews keep to themselves, he says. They are the Chosen People, and they think we Aryans are nothing. Primo kept completely to himself. He never spoke, certainly not to me. If you said something that suited him, he would reply; if it didn't suit him, he turned away. He never gave anything away; he wanted to know, but not to tell. He was head of the class, and I was a Bad Boy. Once I sat behind him in a Greek lesson, and since he knew everything and I knew nothing, I asked him for help. But he refused.

This is a very different story from most, but I do not disbelieve it. The Bad Boy – he is an old man now, but still thinks and even looks like a boy – is so openly, so aggrievedly antisemitic, even now when it's no longer in fashion; what on earth was he like then? Perhaps Primo did refuse to help him, or even talk to him, and who could blame him? At the same time, this is not the only person who felt, locked inside Primo's reserve, not a sense of inferiority, but the opposite. They usually had their own reasons; but they may still have been right. For he struggled against both feelings, but against this one hardest. The others who felt that struggle in him came later. This boy, though I'm sorry to have met him, confirms that it was already there at school; along with the solution of lonely silence.

At the end of our interview the Bad Boy says, 'If you want an image of Primo Levi it's this: *un treno con respingenti*, a train with buffers'; and he shoots out both his hands, palms forward. He holds the pose for a moment: hands out, feet apart, a solid wall. But his eyes are frightened. I'm not sure whether these are Primo's eyes in his memory or his own.

Numero Unico

By his last year of school Primo had, I think, reached a certain equilibrium. He was still unable to cross the gap to girls: that paralysis and that solitude would only grow. But with the boys he had made a settlement, if only in his own mind. He had made real friendships with several Christian boys – with Mario Piacenza in *ginnasio*, with Vittorio Daneo and Alfredo Fedele in *liceo*. He had even partaken in some minor horseplay. Of course, he remained too small, too thin, too clever and too Jewish to be really accepted. And internally, I'm certain, his equilibrium was a permanent tension, like 'Hydrogen''s and 'Man-made''s: between the fear of inferiority and failure, and a secret self-belief held back in irony and silence.

There'd always been a paradoxical sense of maturity about him, a sense of responsibility, of self-control. When he was a child it came from other burdens. From now on it also came from this genuine, but tense and unstable equilibrium.

It shows in something he did now, in his last year of *liceo*. When he'd first arrived, in 1930, there was one sign that D'Azeglio still retained some of its freedom and spirit: a satirical student magazine, called *Numero Unico*, or *Single Issue* – no doubt to tease the authorities further, since it was a whole series. It was in the 1932 edition, called *Vecchio D'Azeglio*, that he had been described at thirteen – '*solo soletto, serio e triste nell'aspetto*'. The next issue was the last, because the Headmaster of the day banned it. The ban remained in force for Primo's first two years of *liceo*. But in his own final year *Numero Unico* reappeared, under the title *D'Azeglio Sotto Spirito*, *D'Azeglio Preserved* (or literally, *D'Azeglio in Alcohol*, again perhaps a mildly daring joke). And he was one of the editors.

It remained under careful surveillance: about a dozen lines were blacked out by official censorship. In fact this was unnecessary; self-censorship had already done the job ('We could only joke, and stick to the surface,' one contributor said). Nonetheless it showed a good deal of spirit in all the editors to have overturned the ban and written anything at all; especially perhaps in the two Jewish ones, Aldo Sorani and Primo Levi.

And the portrait of him that emerges confirms that tense equilibrium. He was still being teased. In the list of 'Books Not Received', for example, there appears: 'LEVI PRIMO, *Lo sviluppo*, Ed. Mingherlini (esaurito)' – '*Growth* by Primo Levi, pub. Frail, [stocks] exhausted.' And the 'School Code', which lists cruel punishments for strict teachers, stuck-up girls and swots, includes 'Article 7896':

Any student who, in order to demonstrate his zeal, performs chemistry experiments at home, shall be duly punished by: the breaking of all his test tubes; having poured over him an unidentified mixture which causes a terrible smell of rotten eggs; and, since he shall be unable to get rid of said smell, by being avoided by all as a public menace.

However, he was not Top Swot. That position was still occupied in his class (indeed in the whole *liceo*, after a girl called Dolza) by Panetti. And Primo's sister Anna Maria was also in *liceo* now, which reflected some glory on him. For Anna Maria was not only lively and clever, but extremely attractive, and most of his friends were in love with her. Some of this comes out in *D'Azeglio Sotto Spirito*: for example, in a very seductive drawing of Anna Maria by Giorgio Lattes. He also drew, opposite and apparently gazing at her, Alfredo Fedele.

But Primo also displays his own glories, some of them unsuspected. He too produces drawings of people: eight altogether. Apart from one of Pavese and one of the chemistry caretaker, they are all of Christian classmates. And he publishes his first poem.

The portraits are rather good, the poem rather bad. Its idea is that science should not be studied out of books, but – literally, in the case of botany – on the ground, and *by you*: '*Make your own herbarium.*' This was his great idea at school: that he would have to find his own way, to science but also in it, since his teacher knew less chemistry than he did, and knew it only from books ('She had never in her life touched a crystal or a solution'). But the serious idea is immediately mocked by reality. This marriage of ambitious idea and tripping-up, falling-off reality would always be Primo Levi's adult idea of chemistry, and perhaps of life; and here it is already, at the age of seventeen. At seventeen, of course, he was also protecting himself against mockery by mocking himself first. But perhaps that too would always be part of what he was doing.

YOU DON'T KNOW HOW TO STUDY!

Do not study Botany from books,
(Not even texts Vaccarian):
But freely roam the fertile fields
And make your own herbarium.

One day (the forest murmured,
Bluebottles flew the flow'ry roads),
Fired by a swot's ambition,
I set my bike upon the road.

Fast I pedalled towards the fields
Where the sea-borne mistrals blow:
Oh, to plunge in the cormophytes' green,
Where tubers and receptacles grow!

. . .

So I mused: and lo, the 'chafers
Flew thick around my head:
A shrub stuck out into my chain,
And off I tumbled, face all red.

I swore, remounted: but good Linnaeus
Placed a thorn amid my path:
It pierced, I fell, and when I rose
My nose was broken, my eye was black.

Worn out, white-haired, I returned:
But what awaited in the city?
An evil-hearted youth pursued me,
Spewing forth an obscene ditty.

Back at home the horrid servant
Threw out my samples, dear accrued;
Next day, I made a mess of science:
BIOLOGY, GO THOU POOR AND NUDE.

La guerra di Spagna

The Primo Levi who approached his final exams, in the summer of 1937, was closer to being confident than he'd ever been. Not completely confident: that was not his nature, and in any case it wasn't possible. The *maturità* in his day was (he said later) a game of chance, more a test of nerves than of knowledge. Students were examined on the work of all three years of *liceo*, rather than, as now, on the last year only: and since not even Primo Levi could commit to memory three years' work in ten subjects, like all the others he had to guess what to prepare, and hope against hope that his guesses would come up. Students down the ages will know the consequence: fear.

Primo certainly felt this fear, though he would only call it 'agitation'. He was also exhausted; and in the end fatalistic, because so much was out of his hands. But he had his extraordinary memory; he had the coolness that came out in him when he faced a challenge. And he had, at last, that hard-won equilibrium, in which he kept his sense of intellectual superiority suppressed, but also protected. Where could it emerge more freely, where could it course through his veins more electrifyingly, than in the silent, private communion between his pen and paper?

And then it happened. Primo Levi, who had never failed an academic subject in his life, whose most regular mark throughout school was eight out of ten, failed Italian, and had to retake all his examinations in October.

The family was astounded, the school was astounded. What had happened? Primo did not tell Fernanda Pivano, as they stared together at the lists, on which she had received the same mark as he: three out of ten — stark, flat failure. Her failure was almost more shocking — she was a top student on the literary side. However, hers was explicable. She had written a boldly, a romantically antifascist and antiwar essay, in which flowers had grown from the barrels of guns. Primo had picked the same subject:

La guerra di Spagna, The Spanish Civil War. Had he done the same? she asked him, as they stood there. 'Are you mad?' he replied. 'You know I'm Jewish.'

Fernanda tried to put on a brave front, but collapsed in tears as soon as she got home. Primo, of course, was calm and ironic in front of her; and at home too, we can be sure. But inwardly he was devastated. His name in that column of failures seemed to him 'like a life sentence'; as, in 'Hydrogen', each failure had seemed 'eternal, definitive'.

Over the years he very rarely spoke of that essay on the *guerra di Spagna*. And each time he said something different — that it had been drearily obsequious, or absurdly thin, or even that he hadn't written anything at all, and had handed in a blank page. But he always said that it had fully deserved that three; and gave the same account of why it had happened.

The Italian written paper was the first exam. Just two days before, a summons had arrived from the War Ministry: Levi, Primo was to present himself on the next day to the local office of the Naval Draft Board. He did so, mystified and full of foreboding. And indeed what happened now was like a nightmare.

There was one other boy there, who was also called Levi; and an apoplectic lunatic in Fascist uniform. Of all Turin, the lunatic said, these two Levis had been selected to do their military service in the Royal Navy. They had been sent their call-up papers: *But*, he thundered, *neither had replied*. It does not seem to have occurred to him that if the only two naval recruits in the city both claimed not to have received their papers, they might possibly be telling the truth. Instead, 'scarlet-faced', 'in a paroxysm of fury', he hurled insults at them — Primo only lists 'cowards', but we might guess at others, given their names — and shouted that they were guilty of attempted desertion, which carried a sentence of twenty-four months' imprisonment, and they needn't think they would escape.

'At the time,' Primo says, 'I couldn't even swim.' He went home in a state of abject terror. And the next day he had to face his first exam. The wonder is that he managed to get through the others.

When I picture that scene, both Levis are very small, and the Fascist lunatic has Mussolini's face. It is only just over a year away from the first racial laws. Primo's father is already ill with the cancer that will kill him five years later. Nonetheless he does the rounds of all the authorities who may be able to help, until he discovers a bizarre solution: Primo can be excused from military service if he immediately enrols in the Milizia Volontaria per la Sicurezza Nazionale: the Fascist Militia. That is why, every Saturday afternoon during his first year of University, Primo will march up and down the courtyard on the Via Po in Fascist uniform. After a year they will kick him out anyway, because he is a Jew.

This was not the only irony in the final chapter of his schooling. Neither he nor Fernanda Pivano could resist pointing out that the Literature examiner of 1937 – possibly a certain Professor Pasero of Brescia – with 'brilliant critical insight' (Pivano) had managed to find the two D'Azeglio students of the year who would become writers, and fail them.

In October Primo retook his exams, and of course passed with flying colours. (So did Fernanda.) He got an eight in chemistry, and a seven in Italian. The nightmare was over; and despite other nightmares, the next few years would be happier.

But his 'immaculate school career' had been spoiled at the last minute, and a shadow cast back over it for the rest of his life. It had ended with the two experiences he feared most: anger and failure. Suddenly, out of the blue, he had been subjected to insults and threats over something he had not done. And this had so upset him that he had failed the one thing he had never expected to fail: an examination. He had, it seemed, snatched failure from the jaws of success. However, he had maintained his calm irony, and he had survived.

The Hare and the Tortoise II

Was Guido a real boy?

In Fiora Vincenti's biography there is a friendship which sounds very like the one in 'Un lungo duello'. The only difference is that Vincenti puts it in *ginnasio*, not *liceo*; and that she describes not one boy, but two.

In these early school years, she wrote, Primo had his first encounter with arrogance and bullying.

Despite his weak constitution . . . Levi's intellectual achievement had put him at the head of his class. This brought out the competitive instinct in his school-mates, especially in those who were physically the best endowed, and the least willing to accept his academic successes with good grace. With two of these in particular Levi formed a singular friendship, based precisely on this underlying conflict. The two boys . . . challenged him to athletic duels, such as boxing matches and races, which they could easily win. And Levi did not decline. Remember that these were years in which he was already becoming aware, though confusedly, of his Jewishness. In his classmates' repeated challenges, he sensed more than simple adolescent competition to prove the superiority of physical endowments over intellectual ones.

All this Primo must have told her. And it included an important element which he had left out of the story: the racial charge in the duel, like the one in the imagined fistfight of 'Retirement Fund'. So there *was* a model – or two models – for Guido, and I knew at least one thing about them: they were not Jews.

Almost everyone in the school photograph was taller and better-looking than Primo; several were decidedly handsome, more than possible candidates for Guido. Was he – were both of them – there? I pored over those faces of sixty years ago as though they could tell me. No one else was likely to. The role of the first bullies of Primo Levi, the forerunners of Auschwitz, was an important one; but I couldn't expect anyone to claim it.

Several in the photograph had died, many had vanished. But slowly most of the faces were named, as I found at least some of their owners. Each time I asked about that famous striptease. Primo's friend Guido Bonfiglioli remembered a spectacular one, on one of those athletic afternoons: a naked boy descending like a god from the top row of the Stadium to the bottom, watched not only by the other boys, but by two of the D'Azeglio girls. I looked for him, but he had disappeared.

Then one day I traced one of Primo's Christian school-friends, now a distinguished, rather lonely old gentleman. When I mentioned the striptease his courtly formality broke like a cloud, and he gave a sudden, adolescent grin. Yes, he remembered it well. Not one but two of the *mascalzoni*, the tearaways, did it together, right there in the classroom, during a lesson. They'd done similar things before, showing off their precocity; once they'd even brought a tart into the school . . . It wasn't really a striptease. Simply, for a long moment they danced, completely naked, behind the high benches at the back of the room. 'I was so innocent,' he said, 'I never forgot it.'

Which were they? I asked, holding out the photograph. Yes, two of the handsome ones. One was a very good sportsman, my informant said; the other could have been as well, but he was too lazy. The lazy one had also disappeared. But the sportsman I found straight away; he'd never left Turin.

When I asked to meet him he was reluctant, but he didn't refuse outright. I heard in his voice the Turinese desire not to offend – and also, surely, a flicker of interest? You mustn't give up in Turin; people often try to put you off at first, but don't really expect to succeed, perhaps don't even want to. I tried again. And this time he said, 'Very well, Signora, I would be happy to meet you.' Then he added: 'But there is something I must tell you. I made the *scelta sbagliata*, the wrong choice: I was on the other side.'

One of the great differences between England and the rest of Europe is that in Europe the war is not forgotten, indeed is not over. There was only one thing he could have meant: he'd been a Fascist. Of course Guido would have become a Fascist! But would he have admitted it like that?

He was ill; it was weeks before he could fit me in between visits to his doctors. In the meantime I asked the others I'd found among the athletes of those long-ago afternoons: could the Sportsman be Guido, or half of him? He could be, they said. But no one would say he was; perhaps because they really didn't know.

When he met me at the door I saw two things at the same time, as though they'd been superimposed on one another: a skeleton, and the handsome boy of sixty years before. I remarked only on the second, of course, saying that he had hardly changed since the school photograph. He bowed his head with the grace of one used to accepting compliments. But when he lifted it I caught a mocking look in his eye, meant either for himself or for me. No, no, he knew what he'd become. But yes, he *had* once been . . . Laughingly he admits that years ago, when he saw Primo's story in *La Stampa*, it did occur to him he might have been a model for Guido.

Inside his wife greets me effusively, but I hardly hear what she is saying, I'm so amazed – is he going to admit to being Guido just like that, without a fight, as he admitted to being a Fascist? We sit down, he moves aside his worn *Stampa* copy of Primo's story to make room for the coffee. He starts to tell me his memories of the Olympic afternoons: and immediately it is clear that the *lungo duello* is not forgotten, is not over.

His event was the javelin, he says. He was very serious about it, and his trainer had great ambitions for him. Levi, on the other hand, was no sportsman at all, as he admits in his story. 'But he was no *mostro* either, Signora, no monster, pale and deformed by study; like, for instance, Ennio Artom. He was more *uomo*, more man than that. He came to the Stadium with us, Signora: with the others, the Aryans, the sportsmen. And he raced with me, just as he describes. Well, not *just* as he describes. He says 800 metres: but he could never have beaten me at that. We did 100 metres, perhaps even 50; the sprints. That is why he won, once or twice: because the thin, nervous runner *can* sometimes overtake the real athlete, for very short distances. Especially in those conditions – in tennis shoes, on a track full of holes, where strength and technique don't have the time to prevail. Piacenza would get angry and say it wasn't fair – not because he favoured me, Signora, but on principle, because we aimed at true, objective sport. But the truth is' (he smiles ruefully) 'that in those circumstances the non-sportsman did sometimes win.'

'We were friends for many years,' he says. 'I went to his house often. At first his mother was very guarded with me, very suspicious, because I was an *ariano*, Signora, a *goy*, isn't that what you say? But I must have passed the test, because I went back many times. We weren't antisemitic, we didn't tease the Jewish boys – or only harmlessly, maybe we did the *orecchie di maiale*★ once or twice . . . It was they who stayed apart. They all belonged to the same class, and they kept themselves to themselves. But Levi less than the others. I remember once when we were walking to school, and he said to me – not in these exact words, but it's what he meant: "*Mi sento integrato,*" "I feel I belong." And he did belong, Signora; he came with us, with the sportsmen, as I told you.'

Yes, I think, he did. He accepted your distinction between *uomo* and *mostro*: between the real man and the pale, intellectual Jew. He was determined to become a real man, and he did: at the Stadium, in the mountains, in the place where Jews were ultimately non-men. But – except there – he did it on your terms. Your distinction entered him; he measured himself against you, and sometimes, he even won. But since it was on your terms, was it really a victory?

The Sportsman has moved on to university. They were still friends – even after the racial laws. Another memory: one day he stops and chats to Primo in the corridor; and Primo says, 'So you are still friendly to me.' He wants me to hear the respect and gratitude in Primo's voice; but I also hear surprise.

Of course he hasn't admitted to being Guido after all; with the memories he has selected, he's denied it. Shall I challenge him? Shall I ask straight out – did you bully Primo Levi for being more monster than man? It would be more honest, but could it possibly work? I must try to make him betray himself instead. So I stick to writing, and ask about the other competitions in 'Un lungo duello'. The breath-holding competition, carried to the very edge of unconsciousness; the face-slapping competition, with its strict rules of catching the opponent by surprise, then striking as hard as you could; above all, the famous striptease competition. Does he remember any of these?

He stares at me in amazement. He's never heard of them; they're not in the *Stampa* edition of the story. *They're not?* It had never occurred to me to check. I put my copy of *L'Altrui mestiere* beside his creased newsprint, and we compare. He's right. The entire central section of the story, recounting all three competitions, is missing in *La Stampa*. And so is the final image of Guido poised naked on his desk, 'ephemeral monument of earthly vigour and of insolence'.

As the Sportsman reads the full version of the story, I drink another cup of coffee. It's my third; I can feel my heart beating. When he looks up his

---

★ 'The pig's ear'. This was a traditional gesture of mockery of Jews, no doubt based on the Kosher rule against pork: mockers would gather the corners of their jackets in their fists like pigs' ears, and chant: 'Pig's ear, donkey's ear, give 'em to the Jew that's here.' (See 'Argon', p. 5.)

face is dark. 'I don't understand, Signora,' he says. 'This is all completely untrue, and completely impossible. Primo Levi strike someone in the face? Never! And as for striking back . . . If I had hit Primo Levi as hard as I could, Signora, I'd have killed him. This game is outrageous, it's unsportsmanlike, it's utterly dishonourable. And Levi says I invented it! According to him, Guido also tried to make him lose their races by telling him dirty jokes . . . And you, Signora, thought that *I* might have behaved like this? *No one did.* Levi invented the whole thing – though I cannot imagine why, and I would not have thought him capable of such baseness.'

I can imagine why: to strike back, if only in imagination, against that taunting, bullying, beautiful boy. But I still can't say it, I can't accuse him to his face. Instead I say: 'What about the striptease? That's not dishonourable – it's a dare, and an image of Guido's beauty; and someone remembers you doing something like it.' He listens to my story, then shakes his head. No, no, they were all far too shy, far too backward, he'd never have done a thing like that; perhaps he took his *jacket* off once, or a tiny bit more, but that's all. 'Besides, Signora,' he says, 'that skeleton . . .' He holds up my book and reads from the last paragraph: Guido's nakedness blazing across the room, opposite the skeleton on which the teacher's pointer is ticking off the bones. '*Symmetrical to the skeleton*,' the Sportsman reads out, and his voice shakes with anger. 'That means: at a certain moment, all Guido's beauty will be dust.'

He's right of course. But Primo was right too; and the certain moment has arrived.

As we say our farewells, I suddenly realize why, in the confusion of my arrival, the hallway had seemed to shine: its walls are lined with glass cabinets. Smiling again, he shows me his collection of tortoises: tortoises of glass, of gold, of stone, of clay; tortoises of every shape and size, of every colour, collected from dozens of countries over dozens of years. And in the middle of the centre cabinet he has placed a large red glass hare. '*Per ricordare la favola*,' his wife explains: in memory of the fable.

If he's been remembering the fable all these years, his *lungo duello* has been carrying on long before I reminded him of Primo Levi. With whom? I think of the things he's let drop about his life since the war – his pedestrian job, his hint that the good ones all went to the winners. His duel, and his race, are surely with the antifascists, of whom Primo was only one. Is that why his hare is red? And does *his* imagery mean that in the end his fascist tortoises will still win?

*   *

At home, I looked again at 'Un lungo duello', trying to imagine Primo writing it, and remembering the Sportsman reading it, in its complete version, for the first time. It was like their 'strange friendship' itself: both an act of friendship, and the opposite. It was an act of friendship because it joined Guido on his own athletic ground, and admitted his victory there. Its image of Primo himself was the *passatore di cancellate* – and he was that, all his life, a slipper-through of gates, a crosser of barriers. Barriers not only between science and literature, Italians and Jews; but between men of the body like Guido, and men of the mind like himself.

But it was also an act of revenge. Its slaps were as disguised as the ones in the story, but just as accurate. I think of the Sportsman's fury at that image of the skeleton, and of the real skeleton daily devouring his beauty. He had lost, and he knew it.

It seems to me then that he is also a little right to be angry. Wasn't there something cruel in that image of what all Guido's superiority would come to? And wasn't it a bit underhanded, too – to hide the cruelty in an image, and to hide the image in a book which Guido would very likely never read? Wasn't that – from Guido's point of view – pretty unfair, a way of striking back at him when he wasn't looking, and couldn't defend himself – just as in the slapping game, except that this time he hadn't agreed to play?

Primo Levi cruel, and unfair? . . . Yes, and I think he knew it. That is shown by the slapping game, which the Sportsman says Primo invented. I believe him about that, at least, because the slapping game is a secret image of the whole long duel. It began with Guido's cruelty and unfairness, when he taunted and bullied a weaker boy. And it ends now with Primo's own cruelty and unfairness, as he sneaks back a final slap in Guido's face, in the way that he writes and publishes the story.

★   ★

As it turned out, even that concession was probably wrong. There *was* a slapping game, as well as the races. Primo told one of his secret sharers so; and eventually – several years after my encounter with the Sportsman – she repeated it to me. Primo also told her that 'Guido' was one real boy after all, not two; and the name he gave her was the Sportsman's.

If Primo's story was cruel, so is mine. I should, therefore, add this. The Sportsman was a bully, and on the bullies' side. Nonetheless, his claim to have remained friendly to Primo even after the racial laws was true. Years later, again, I learned that only one of Primo's Christian school-friends had dropped him then: and it was the lonely, distinguished old gentleman who told me of the naked dancers.

4. Chemistry:
1937–41

Chemistry class, February 1940
The girls are, from the left: Ester Valabrega, Emma Vita Levi, Vanna
Rava, Lilia Beer, Clara Moschino

'Night lay beyond the walls of the Chemical Institute,' Primo would write
about his second year at university: and already in the first it was gathering.
But within the walls of the Chemical Institute everything opposite blazed:
youth, friendship, freedom.

Freedom was the prize. The young people who entered the University
of Turin in 1937 had lived under a triple unquestionable authority all their
lives: their family, their Church and their Fascist school had controlled
everything, and above all everyone, they knew. Now for the first time they
spent long days away from home, thrown together with other unknown,
eager young people from many different backgrounds and places – some
not even from Turin! For two years at least – until the work got too hard,
and the war too near – most seized their freedom in both hands. They sang,
they danced, they saw plays, they went to cinemas and cafés. They played
sports, and travelled to GUF★ competitions and displays all over Italy. They
smoked, they behaved badly, they even flirted. Between lectures in the

★ Gioventù Universitaria Fascista, the Fascist university students' organization.

mornings boys and girls strolled together in the Valentino, the great park along the River Po, just across the road from the Chemical Institute; or sat together on the benches, studying. During the long afternoons in the laboratory they gathered around the sink to chat; at five o'clock the girls would make tea on the Bunsen burners, and serve it with pastries from a nearby shop, or even with tiny, starchy biscuits they'd baked in the small oven used for drying precipitates.

Primo was still far too shy to join in. He belonged to no group; he remained apart, separate and serious. He didn't sing silly songs in the streets, he didn't stroll in the park, or sit in the café, with a girl. He was in a different world, whether he wanted to be or not. But very few now felt that suppressed sense of superiority in him – or at least the need to prove it. Almost everyone consulted him at one time or another, even the cleverest; and all who did found his answers clearer, but also kinder, than most of their teachers'. Though he had few friends, he was always friendly; he made people think less of superiority than of sadness. A few girls, especially, worried about him.

He was too kind, too gentle, too sensitive for his own good, they thought. One, who saw herself as an ordinary, carefree girl, was divided. She was afraid of him, 'because I thought him so superior to me'. At the same time she was afraid for him: because 'for such a person, life could only have suffering in store'.

But during these years he suffered less than before. He was finding a way to live with his isolation, and even to share it. As reality became more openly hostile, he became better able to endure it. It made his choices easier, it stirred him to a stubborn pride, and it brought him a group of friends who were similarly outcast. These were, of course, his fellow Jews. But from the beginning he had happy, if not close, relationships with the others as well. They were all Fascists, naturally – but so, at the start, was he. Being a Fascist was simply normal, like being Italian, or white. The University of Turin was not a Fascist university – it was even, so far as it dared be, an antifascist university; and most professors, so far as they dared, were the same.*

Not a single one of Primo's companions in chemistry ever offered him a hostile look or word. They too were threatened by war; and they too were seizing their day, their moment of freedom between the prison of childhood and the prison of adulthood. They were learning the same trade, they were fighting the same battles against blank matter, gruelling study, and the long,

---

* Only three had refused to take the oath of loyalty to the regime, in 1931 – but since only twelve had refused in the whole of Italy, Turin had provided a full quarter of the total. The three who refused (and lost their jobs, of course) were the art historian Lionello Venturi, and two professors of law, Francesco Ruffini and Mario Carrara.

painstaking hours in the lab. The lab especially was a crucible for friendship, a place of solidarity and camaraderie. In all this Primo partook quietly but deeply, and with a pleasure he never forgot. He saw only a few of his classmates outside the lab; even fewer of them in later life. But the bonds he had made with them then remained. He kept in touch with many. When, after thirty years, they began to hold reunions, he never failed to attend. He remembered his university laboratory, and his whole university life, with warmth and nostalgia. 'Despite everything,' he wrote to one classmate forty-three years later, 'the years we spent together were wonderful ones: objectively, and not only in memory.' All the others I found felt the same.

In 1937 the University of Turin was a very different place from today. Like all Italian universities, after the economic boom and the political agitations of the 60s it has opened its doors to all, built more buildings and employed more teachers (but never enough), and has became a huge, democratic, but anonymous and overcrowded institution. In the 1930s the University was still the province of an élite: restricted, with very few exceptions, to the educated middle classes. As Europe shuffled towards war, however, the Chemistry Faculty was expanding. Even five years before Primo arrived it had had only a handful of entrants; without the unemployed seeking shelter from the streets, the lecture halls of the Chemical Institute would have been almost empty. But in Primo's year around eighty students entered the Faculty of *Chimica Pura*: a tiny figure compared to today, but a proud one for 1937.

After the first few months, which consisted entirely of theoretical lectures on General and Inorganic Chemistry by the terrifying head of the Faculty, Professor Giacomo Ponzio, an oral examination reduced the eighty to around fifty. The fifty survivors were at last permitted to don white coats (or black or grey ones), and enter the portals of the Preparations laboratory. Here they were taught to use the still arcane tools of their trade – the acids and bases, the flasks and tubes, the scales, kilns and burners. Or rather, they learned to use them by themselves, since Professor Ponzio was a cynical man, who trusted to the harsh process of natural selection. At the end of each year examinations culled them still further. In Year Two they graduated to the Qualitative Analysis laboratory: Professor De Paolini handed each apprentice alchemist a gram of powder, whose components they had the next five hours to divine, 'hesitations not allowed'. In the third year came the most testing laboratory, Quantitative Analysis: here an element in solution had to be precipitated, washed, dried, calcinated, left to cool, and finally, carefully, weighed: an infinitely demanding, dull and mechanical process, which modern chemists leave almost entirely to machines.

The day started at eight, with the first lecture. Another followed at ten, or eleven, or both, with the café or the Valentino in between. Most lectures were given in the Aula Magna, the great hall of the Chemical Institute: rising tiers of wooden benches, and at the front, suspended over the Professor's head like a crown, a huge framed Periodic Table. For mathematics Primo and the others walked or took a tram to Via Po 17, the heart of the University (to whose courtyard he returned every Saturday of his first year, to march up and down with Schifùs and the others). For Industrial Chemistry they went to the Polytechnic, which was also in the centre in those days; for physics they returned to the Institute of Physics, next door to Chemistry in the Corso D'Azeglio. And after the long mornings of lectures, the long afternoons in the lab: starting at two, ending finally at seven.

No wonder they were ready for tea and sympathy at five; no wonder that if Panetti refused to share his knowledge, or Gennari the difficult solution he was so good at making, they ganged up on them like schoolchildren, and syphoned off Gennari's solution when he wasn't looking. Not Primo, however; from this and all similar punishments, however deserved, he quietly withdrew. Nor, even now, did he ever swear – not even when the work of hours was lost, through some minor mishap or miscalculation. He tells of a strange practice which grew up for the venting of frustration: for a few *lire* you could buy damaged laboratory glassware, and 'publicly, with the greatest possible noise and violence', hurl it against a wall. He doesn't say whether he ever indulged in this public catharsis himself; but we can surely guess.

During their four years he and the others learned to weigh and measure, to test and distinguish, to filter and distil. And during those years the same things were being done to them. Chemistry weighed and tested them; it distinguished the adapted from the unadapted; and it distilled them down from eighty, to fifty, to thirty, who finally graduated. Those who survived all the tests were not always the ones you would have expected. The best at theory were not always the best at the hard, slogging work of the lab; and chemistry, like genius, is 90 per cent hard work. Here, Primo said, you needed other virtues: humility, patience and method; endurance, both mental and physical; resilience in the face of failure. Amongst those who had been broken early to these virtues were many of the girls, who grew from a quarter of the first year to a third of the graduates; and perhaps also the Jews, who grew from just over a fifth to just over a quarter. And amongst them was certainly Primo Levi, who had found in himself all the humble virtues he enumerates, and many less humble ones, which he does not. He graduated with *100/100 e lode*, which is to say with full marks, and *summa cum laude*. Later he would claim that the *lode* reflected his professors' anti-fascism more than his own merit; this is possible, but not likely, and in any case the 100/100 was entirely his own. Unlike his school career, his university career was not spoiled by its end. It had difficulties that most students today – most people today – can hardly imagine; but he overcame them. His university years were what university years should be, the first stage of growing up. And unlike many young people, especially young men, he liked growing up. The dependence of childhood did not suit him; and nor did the larger dependence of Fascism. Fascism did everything in its power not to give you any choice, or any responsibility. Chemistry gave you both. From the moment you accepted your first consignment of glass, he wrote, 'you were responsible, for the first time in your scholastic career, indeed in your life, for something not yours', and 'if you broke it, you paid'; every day in your laboratory reports you had to choose, yes or no, this answer or that. This thrilled him – especially since, as most of his marks show, at this early stage it was still possible to get the answers 100 per cent right. And another thing thrilled him too. He turned out to be good not only at book-learning, which he already knew, but at something he had been much more doubtful about, even tormented. 'Every evening,' he wrote, 'and even more intensely at the end of the course, one left with the feeling of having learned *how to do* something: which, as life teaches us, is very different from having learned *about* it.' Learning *about* you could do with your brain only; learning *how* required your hands, your eyes, your nose, your whole body. It was a return to humanity's origins, he thought: to an earlier, wholer way of knowing. This was something he would always celebrate and seek, and he glimpsed it first now.

Year One: The Racial Laws

His university years meant two battles joined and won for Primo: one with chemistry, and the other with the racial laws against the Jews.

When he arrived at the Chemical Institute in the autumn of 1937, the laws themselves were still half a year away. Nonetheless antisemitism was in the air; indeed the clouds had been massing while he was still at school. Looking back, he (and other historians) put the turning point in 1934. In March of that year came the first arrests of Giustizia e Libertà★ members in Turin: and eleven of the seventeen arrested were Jews. The most virulently right-wing Fascist newspaper, *Il Tevere*, immediately pointed this out; and so did the rest of the papers, including *La Stampa*. Until then it had been perfectly natural to be both Jewish and a Fascist: especially in Turin, with its particular tradition of Jewish patriotism. But now the two began to pull

★ The antifascist party founded in exile in Paris in 1929 by Carlo Rosselli and others.

apart, like diverging paths. You had either to become less Fascist, or more. Most began, inwardly, to become less; but many became more. Prominent Jews throughout Italy sent letters to newspapers and telegrams to Mussolini protesting their loyalty; several Jewish communities, including Turin's, sent specially generous donations to the Party. In Turin the patriots took over the running of the community, and founded a Jewish Fascist newspaper, *La Nostra Bandiera* (*Our Flag*), which would try more and more desperately over the next four years to bridge a gap that inexorably widened.

From 1934 to 1937 it widened, for most Jews, only slowly. Mussolini, ever the opportunist, made pro- or antisemitic statements according to his momentary calculations; you could find whatever you wanted in his speeches. In this, as in everything, he was the Italian populace writ large, and worse: never a biological racist, like the Nazis (in any case Italians might not come out on the right side of this divide, at least from the German point of view); but perfectly ready to desert the Jews for his own ends whenever it suited him. Throughout the mid-30s he maintained this indelicate balance: publicly mocking Hitler's racist theories, and giving refuge to thousands of Jewish refugees; but at the same time allowing his right wing to build several small Nazi bridgeheads, in case he should ever want to use them.

In 1937 he decided that he did. Where once he had championed the Zionist cause, he now had himself proclaimed Protector of Islam. In April the Fascist publicist Paolo Orano published *The Jews in Italy*, a book of antisemitic propaganda disguised as scholarship. Attacks on Jews grew in the Italian press, led by Mussolini's own *Popolo d'Italia*; *La Stampa*'s were particularly virulent. In August Mussolini announced the Rome–Berlin axis, which came into effect in October. In the same month, Primo Levi entered the University of Turin.

This was the atmosphere of his first year. Nothing was encoded in law. Nonetheless accusations had been made, and everyone knew they were official: you are different, you are dirty, you are dangerous. If anyone wanted to take them up, they could. No one did. But public life was already tainted, even at university. In Primo's first year, for example, the GUF put on a play which was openly antisemitic.

In March 1938 Mussolini announced that he was not contemplating any racial or religious discrimination against the Jews. By July Jewish families, on holiday in the mountains or at the seaside, were opening their newspapers on the 'Manifesto of the Racial Scientists'. This document, commissioned by Mussolini, consisted of ten pronouncements, of which the sixth was *There is a pure Italian race* and the ninth *Jews do not belong to the Italian race.*

The government rushed to defend the Italian race from the Jewish one. The first racial laws appeared in early September: expelling foreign Jews from Italy, depriving Italian Jews of the right to attend any public school, as either pupils or teachers. In October came the 'Declaration on Race', which laid down the guidelines for detailed legislation. This followed in November. It stripped Italian Jews of their basic civil rights, and the means to keep themselves alive. They could no longer hold any public service job, or serve in the armed forces; they could not own any business or property above a certain value; they could not marry non-Jews, or employ any. These first laws still protected their right to practise their religion, and allowed them to establish their own schools; they also exempted the so-called *discriminati*, the families of those who had died, or otherwise distinguished themselves, in the service of Italy or of Fascism. But further and harsher laws quickly followed. The definition of Jewishness was extended, the category of *discriminati* reduced to vanishing point. Jews could no longer possess radios, set foot in holiday resorts, or go anywhere near Italy's borders. Finally, in June 1939 the professions were closed to them as well: Jewish doctors and lawyers, architects and engineers, journalists and accountants, were no longer permitted to practise. The gates of the new ghetto banged shut.

The racial laws shocked and devastated the unsuspecting Jews, who had never believed such a thing could happen in Italy. Secretly, they shocked everyone. Ordinary Italians knew perfectly well this was a *volte face* by the Duce, which had more to do with Hitler than with Italian Jews. Why should they suddenly hate and fear the Jews, who were far too few to be a danger to anybody? Many people had never even met one; those who had knew they were almost all good Fascists like themselves. The racial laws were a turning point for almost everyone, not only Jews: a moment of dissent, embarrassment, recoil. The story goes that Victor Emanuel III himself, as he was about to sign the first acts, stopped and said, '*Qualcuno allontani il generale Levi*': 'Someone please take General Levi away.'

Nonetheless, no one resisted. Italians do not resist laws they dislike, they just ignore them; and this many would do, from the beginning. Catholics continued to marry Jews, if they could find a willing priest: at least three of Primo's classmates tried to marry across the divide, and two succeeded. Catholics who bought Jewish businesses promised to return them after the war, and many did. Jews themselves broke the laws as long as they could. For example, the law against employing Christian servants, which many had done for so long that they had become part of the family – like the Levis' own Cia. 'It was forbidden to have a Christian maid,' Primo said, 'but everybody had one. When the doorbell rang, you just told her to go upstairs.'

Of course it was really much more serious than this. Primo's uncle Oreste Colombo – his cousin Giulia's father – was a bank manager: he went to work as usual one day, and an hour later came home again. Primo's own father was less directly affected, since he was an independent businessman, employed by a foreign company. The *nonno* began to be ill now, and would die in 1941; but he managed things as cleverly as usual, and the shop would return to his sons after the war. Until 1943 they continued to work in it; so did Oreste Colombo, who during his period of enforced leisure became their book-keeper. Not for the first time, the *fondaco del nonno* came to the family's aid.

As a result the racial laws did not destroy Primo's family, as they destroyed many others. Nor did they destroy his university career. With typically arbitrary mercy, they decreed that in universities, unlike schools, Jewish students who had begun their courses could finish them. This concession was immediately surrounded by fierce restrictions, in order to show the Jews – or perhaps the law-makers themselves – that they had not weakened. Jewish students could not change courses, or extend them, but only complete the one begun, in the time officially allotted – which meant that they could not afford to fail even a single subject. Luckily this last qualification did not affect Primo (though the other would). Thanks to his family, and the good fortune of his birth date, he managed to escape the practical effects of the racial laws. So did his seven other Jewish classmates. The main effect on them all was psychological.

In the first moments, like the others he was shocked and humiliated. The absurd and trumped-up accusations, the base and baseless injustice of it all, deeply offended him. And it was an ironic twist of his own fate that the gates should swing shut now, just when they had begun to open for him. If the Jews of Italy had had only ninety years of freedom, Primo Levi had had barely one. He liked his new Christian classmates; with them he had tasted the possibility of comradeship, and even friendship. But immediately the possibility receded. They still seemed to like him; they dismissed the racial laws as ridiculous. And yet – how could he be sure? Didn't some people believe some pretty strange things about Jews already? Hadn't he himself half believed them? The racial propaganda pushed him back towards his own worst self-doubts. Despite their protestations, he thought he could feel his new friends withdraw; and so, 'following an ancient pattern', he withdrew as well. But all those I found told me they really had thought the racial laws beneath contempt, and hadn't withdrawn at all; and I believe them. *He* withdrew, out of fear of their withdrawal. 'Every look between me and them,' he wrote, 'was accompanied by a minute but perceptible flash of mistrust and suspicion. *What do you think of me? Am I still the same person I seemed to you six months ago . . . ?*' Nothing had changed; but everything had.

On this level the racial laws were a special blow to him, reopening private wounds that had hardly begun to heal. Fiora Vincenti, always alert to this level, calls them 'an unprecedented trauma'. But on another level they were a liberation. They worked 'like a reagent' on all Italians, Primo wrote, waking consciences that had slept for fifteen Fascist years. He included his own. For him the racial laws were a final proof of the impossibility of Fascism, of its stupidity, criminality and danger. They stripped away the last traces of his childhood, and of his political passivity. 'The racial laws gave me back my free will,' he said.

He did not admit to any humiliation. On the contrary. Now that his will was free to act on his Jewishness, it did what his will always would: it made the best of a bad job, it went against the tide, and out of humiliation it made pride. If he was no longer allowed to feel Italian, very well: for the first time, he felt Jewish. His father had rejected the safety route of baptism for himself, but tried to persuade his children to take it. Together, they refused. Jews were impure, outcast, unwanted? Then Primo Levi was proud to be a Jew.

By the end of the second year, the Jews were marked out from the other students: they were forbidden to wear the regulation *camicia nera*, the Fascist black shirt, to examinations. 'Pay no attention,' the others said, embarrassed, 'it's just a rule'; and 'You're so lucky you don't have to wear these stupid things!' But in June 1939 the three Jewish students waiting to take the Mineralogy exam stood out palely from the rest: Primo; Emma Vita Levi – who was only half-Jewish, but that was enough; and Primo's friend Guido Bonfiglioli, who was at the Institute of Physics.

The racial laws were nearly a year old; and the Professor of Mineralogy, Fenoglio, was one of the few who had the reputation of being a willing Fascist. Still no one was prepared for what happened. Guido, the first of the three in alphabetical order, got ready for his turn. But when it came, Fenoglio called the name after his instead. A mistake, Guido thought; but each time Fenoglio returned he called the next name, and the next. Finally Guido got up and entered the examination room. When the student who was being examined had finished, he stood up and said, 'Excuse me, *Professore*, you have forgotten me.' Fenoglio waved him away, saying, 'In a moment.' Guido returned to his seat. Many moments later Fenoglio reappeared at the door, his face flushed, and announced: 'Bonfiglioli, Levi and Vita Levi will take their examinations last.'

He did not need to say more; everyone understood. At that moment Guido decided that he was no longer Italian. Primo remained impassive. But Emma started to weep. As each student was called she wept more, and could not be consoled. When Guido's turn came at last she was still weeping. At the end of Guido's examination Fenoglio said '*30/30 e lode*.' He showed Guido a university order, and said, 'Try to forgive me.' Guido returned to Primo and Emma and told them. Next was Primo. He disliked Fenoglio, and had not worked as hard as usual; he got a 26. At last it was Emma's turn. She had touched the bottom of despair; but she was twenty-one years old. She left the examination room with a streaked and swollen face, and 30/30.

Zinc

Primo's story of his first year at university is one of the lightest, but also one of the darkest, in *The Periodic Table*. It's like the year itself, for himself and Emma and the others: the most hopeful and free they'd ever known, and then the least. It's about night outside and the blaze of youth within; it's about making light out of darkness – or trying to.

The first event prefigures the whole. 'Professor P.''s lectures instantly deflate Primo's romantic dream of chemistry, and replace it with a smelly, dangerous, difficult reality. Is he daunted, is he disappointed? On the contrary – he's excited. He likes P. He likes his irony, his scepticism, his disillusion. He likes these qualities because they make P. antifascist; but he also likes them because they make him free. P.'s cynicism gives Primo his first glimpse of the real subject of this story, which is a new possibility of daring, and of freedom.

'Professor P.' was, of course, Professor Ponzio; and he really was much as Primo describes him. He *was* antifascist, or as antifascist as his cynicism allowed: not for reasons of conscience, but because he would tolerate no interference. He really did wear a little black dicky instead of a proper black shirt, to show his minimum compliance, and maximum contempt; he refused to put the Fascist year on his famous books of organic and inorganic chemistry;* and he treated all his students equally, the Fascists just as badly as the others. He was, as Primo says, ferociously cold and outrageously prejudiced: especially against women students, who were all terrified of him, and whom he regularly failed; but also against nuns, priests, and anyone in uniform – indeed against anyone at all, for any reason at all, including being too clever. He was also fabulously mean, as Primo describes, and really did turn down the flame on every Bunsen burner he passed, and make the students prepare silver nitrate from the 5-lire coins in their own pockets.

Whether Ponzio really did preserve every rag and filter paper, and carry out a ritual burning every year, after which he would sift the ashes with insane patience for any valuable which, phoenix-like, remained – whether any of this was true is less clear. But true or not it is Primo's image of

---

* Like the leaders of the French Revolution, Mussolini instituted a new calendar from the start of his regime – 1938 was Year XVI of the Fascist Era.

chemistry, and of the metaphorical chemistry of this year: 'a foul and secret orgy of salvage', in which the poisons of chemistry and racial prejudice are calcinated into knowledge and pride.

Still, if this was Professor Ponzio, how could Primo like him? He may have been antifascist, and a rigorous and devoted chemist. But how could Primo Levi admire a tyrant, whose books were 'saturated with his surly contempt for humanity'? Because, precisely, he was so far from anything that Primo himself could be: unkind, contemptuous, cynical, proud. He was, in fact, another great opposite. Primo's admiration for him in 'Zinc' is genuine – and was shared, at least by the other boys. But it is partial, and playful. He had to forget his kind, responsible self in order to celebrate this savage hunter he had more than half invented, who abandons his students to sink or swim in the hellish brews of the lab. That is what 'Professor P.' is in 'Zinc', despite his reality: a fictional creation; an image of a kind of ascetic irresponsibility which thrilled and amused the young student, and the middle-aged writer, but which was quite beyond both of them – except in writing.

P., however, is only the introduction to the new possibilities of this year. The main one is much more genuine. It comes in the shape not of a half-legendary old man, but of a real live girl, working with him in the crucible of the lab.

Primo is now nineteen, and for years girls have been his trouble. They mark the point at which racial slurs have already bonded with his own self-doubts, and doubled them. Now the racial campaign is gathering speed. Approaching a girl, especially a Christian girl, must surely be more impossible than ever. *Yet that is exactly what he will do.* It's as though his will has been restored even here.

All this meets in the metaphor of zinc, and its transformation into zinc sulphate: which was, Primo says, his first task in the Preparations lab. Zinc, he tells us, is a grey metal, modestly useful ('they make tubs out of it for laundry'), but neither glamorous nor attractive. In this it is not unlike himself, as he felt at the time. It is also not unlike the girl, Rita: who is pale, thin, and modestly dressed; capable, but silent and sad, 'nobody's friend'. Primo does not yet draw out these personal meanings, but moves straight to the philosophical: the preparation of zinc sulphate as an image of his encounter with Fascist propaganda.

Ponzio's instructions, he says, contained a detail which had at first escaped him: that the transformation will not take place if the zinc is very pure. Only if an impurity is introduced will it respond to sulphuric acid, loosen its bonds, and recombine. 'One could draw from this two conflicting philosophical conclusions,' he writes:

the praise of purity, which protects from evil like a coat of mail; and the praise of impurity, which gives rise to change, in other words to life. I discarded the first, disgustingly moralistic, and lingered in the second, which I found more congenial. In order for the wheel to turn, for life to live, impurities are needed, and impurities of impurities: in the soil too, as we know, if it is to be fertile. Dissension, diversity, the grain of salt or mustard are needed. Fascism does not want them, it forbids them, and that's why you're not a Fascist; it wants everyone to be the same, and you're not the same.

This is the young, strong Primo Levi, who chose dissent and diversity in principle, and in his friends. He was partly the zinc itself, roused to this change by the acid of the racial campaign. But he was also the impurity that would make the zinc change, when the zinc was Rita – with all Italian Jewry symbolized by him, and Italy itself by Rita. That is his own version of the metaphor, at the peak of his hope and pride in 'Zinc': '*I am the impurity that makes the zinc react, I am the grain of salt or mustard.*'

'So take the solution of copper sulphate from the shelf of reagents,' he says,

add a drop of it to your sulphuric acid, and you'll see the reaction begin: the zinc wakes up, it is covered with a white fur of hydrogen bubbles, and there we are, the enchantment has taken place, you can leave it to its fate and take a stroll around the lab, see what's up and what the others are doing.

With that image of 'enchantment' in his mind (and ours), he sets off. He goes over to Rita, and sees that she has been given the same preparation: zinc sulphate. For weeks he has been hovering around her, preparing 'brilliant conversational openings' he has been too shy to utter. But now suddenly there is a 'small zinc bridge' between them; and a paper one too, because he sees that she is reading *The Magic Mountain*, his own passion at that time. He asks her about it; and the enchantment happens, she responds.

They talk so long, in fact, that Primo's zinc sulphate spoils. He abandons it, and asks if he can walk her home. By now we know that Rita is one of those opposites to whom he is most drawn: the daughter of a poor shop-keeper, dignified, hardworking and brave. She lives a long way from the Chemical Institute. He hesitates, he trembles, he no longer knows what he's saying; but finally he slips his arm through hers. This time she does not respond, but nor does she pull away; and for the first time he feels the warmth of a woman's body next to his. When we thought he might give in to despair, he produced pride. Now, in the midst of exhilaration, he reminds us of his despair. 'It seemed to me,' he writes, 'that I had won a small but decisive battle against the darkness, the emptiness, and the hostile years that lay ahead.'

★   ★

In the original version of 'Zinc', Rita had been called Carla. This turned out to be the best clue to who she really was.

For a long time no one could tell me; they weren't sure she had existed at all. If Primo really had been stirred, like the zinc, to a new daring, if he really had asked to walk a girl home, and done so – nobody had noticed.

But when I saw how 'Carla' had been scratched out each time, and replaced with 'Rita' in Primo's neat hand, I thought that there *must* have been a real girl called Carla. The only trouble was that there was no Carla in the class. But there was a Clara: Clara Moschino, who had graduated with 90/100, and whom I had not yet met because she lived the furthest away, on the Lago di Garda.

As soon as I suggested Clara Moschino to the others, they agreed: yes, she did fit at least some of Rita's description. Now they thought of it, she *was* the daughter of a shop-keeper, and clearly came from a poorer family than most. But she was a sweet, kind, sociable girl, not the silent and sad outsider of Primo's story. But then they thought back to the beginning. And one or two began to say – it's true, she was a bit shy at first, perhaps because she came from a different background, and wasn't sure how we would react. She was certainly serious, and studious; even Bassignana, the handsomest boy in the class, didn't quite dare to flirt with her. And yes, perhaps there was even something a little sad. A sense that she had already faced hardships, that she was facing hardships then, that we knew nothing of. Still no one remembered a special friendship; and when they did I was no longer sure they weren't reading back from the story.

When I met her, I tried to resist, but Clara Moschino seemed to me just like Rita. She had Rita's self-possession and steady gaze. She was friendly and welcoming, but very reserved. And though she was no longer poor, she still had many hardships, which she bore with particular courage. If you *are* Rita, I thought, Primo made a splendid choice. That made it easy to ask; and she answered with equal ease. 'Oh yes,' she said, 'I'm Rita.' Primo had described her family, her difficulties, her shyness and apartness, which she had felt very much, and which he had seen.

So was it really true – had the racial campaign really woken Primo, like the zinc, to a new pride and daring? Certainly to pride; as I already knew. But less, perhaps, to daring. They were great friends, Clara says, they studied together, and she liked him enormously – his deep sympathy, his sense of humour, his extraordinary clarity. A great friendship, then, which would continue: but she did not know, until she read the story, that he had had any special feeling for her. She does not remember the zinc bridge, or *The Magic Mountain*. In particular, she does not remember that night walk, alone together, across the city: his moving near, his taking her arm. Perhaps, I say, he did do it, on another occasion; but as it didn't mean as much to her, naturally she has forgotten . . . She is a very clear person, but also a kind one, and she can see that I would like at least this to be true. So she says firmly but gently that she does not think so. He may have wanted to do it, or dreamed of doing it, but he did not. Not then, and not later either. They saw each other several times over the years, and exchanged several letters; he sent her several of his books. But he did not send her *The Periodic Table*; and they never mentioned 'Zinc'. The zinc bridge was never crossed.

There are so many reasons why people lie: to themselves, to each other, especially, alas, to me. But when I look into Clara Moschino's steady sad brown eyes, I see that she is utterly honest. The conversation in the lab, or something like it, may have happened, and been forgotten. But not the night walk; and probably no other moment either. 'Rita', like 'Professor P.', is partly a fiction. Or rather, in Rita's story the narrator himself is a fiction. Primo did not make his first move towards a woman now, emboldened by his new, paradoxical pride. His self-portrait in 'Zinc' is like his portrait of Rita: more faithful to inner than outer truth, which is why at first people didn't recognize Clara Moschino. The outer truth had not changed. This is betrayed by the last line: the darkness that has not been banished, but still lies ahead. The truth remained what it was before the fictional Primo stepped on to the zinc bridge:

I was desperate, and not for the first time. In fact in that period I thought myself condemned to a perpetual masculine solitude, denied a woman's smile forever, which yet I needed as much as air.

★   ★

The real Primo won all the battles of his university years but this one. Two years after *The Periodic Table*, he published a story in *La Stampa*, in which a young poet is driven by his despair to consult a doctor. What he describes is depression.

. . . the universe (which nonetheless he had studied diligently, and with love) felt to him like an immense and useless machine, a mill which eternally ground nothingness to no purpose at all; not mute, indeed eloquent, but blind and deaf and impervious to human pain. Every instant of his waking life was filled with this pain, which was his only certainty; his only joys were negative ones, the brief cessations of his suffering.

Delicately the doctor inquires about his personal relationships. He blushes, and says that his human contacts are few. In *La Stampa*, that is all; but when the story appeared in *Lilit* in 1981 it contained a fuller reply.

He hesitated, then added that his relationships with women had always been troubled. He fell in love often and intensely, but lacked the courage to declare his love, because he was conscious of how unattractive he was. As a result his loves were solitary. When he sat at his studies, or walked in the fields, he carried with him a purified, ideal and perfect image of the woman he loved; while instead he adored that of the flesh and blood woman, to which he hardly dared raise his eyes. From this split he suffered atrociously ... He had to admit that love had always been a source of torment to him, instead of joy; and without love, what was the point of living?

In the young poet's description of his metaphysical despair, Italian readers instantly recognized Leopardi, the great nineteenth-century poet of pessimism and melancholy. That was, of course, Primo's intention, and where he wished his readers to stop, even in *Lilit*. But when he was young (he told the Signora in *The Double Bond*), he'd read Leopardi 'as perhaps no one else has ever read him, trying to see myself in him, to draw comfort from his despair'. He also told her that even before university, his anguish at being 'a condemned man, a reject' in affairs of the heart had reached such depths that he had several times contemplated suicide.

Even without *The Double Bond*, it would be hard not to think that in 'Dialogue of a poet and a doctor' Primo is once again seeing his young self in Leopardi. Since we have *The Double Bond*, it is impossible. Indeed, at a certain point I knew more: he was holding out the image of Leopardi like a shield, but the flesh and blood young poet was himself. Certainly before his marriage, and perhaps as early as university, he went to a doctor for the first time.

Year Two

In his second year Primo took six courses, and entered the Qualitative Analysis lab. This was, he said, 'a vast, dark and smoky room', in which a permanent cloud of ammonium chloride was regularly rent by fires and explosions. Here things started to get serious. Everyone strained not to miss a single element in their gram of powder, and even more not to 'invent' one ('In the former case you might be merely distracted, or myopic, but in the latter you could only be a fool'). From a dream, chemistry had become a duel: on one side 'the unfledged, unarmed chemist', on the other 'Matter, the Spirit's antagonist', hostile, secretive and sly.

Luckily the presiding spirit of Analytical Chemistry was Professor De Paolini, one of the best teachers in the Institute, and certainly the kindest. This was not difficult, given the competition; but De Paolini was particularly kind, especially to the Jews. Like Fenoglio, he had fought in the Great War, and that may have marked them both. Fenoglio had been badly wounded, and left with a limp; he was a lonely, unpopular figure, who seemed to take pleasure in failing as many people as he could. De Paolini was reserved, even melancholy, but with a gift of sympathy. He was ascetic and religious; rumour had it that as a young man he had wanted to be a priest. Fenoglio taught until 1962, became Professor Emeritus, and died at the ripe age of seventy-eight. De Paolini died young, less than a decade after Primo's class had graduated. They heard that he had committed suicide.

There was another suicide, this very year. A boy called Agostino Neri was found dead one morning on the floor of the Qualitative Analysis lab. He had gone in while the rest of the class was at a lecture, and drunk a whole glass of sulphuric acid. Caselli, the caretaker of the Chemical Institute, found him, and came to tell them. Caselli was just as Primo describes him in *The Periodic Table*: a grim and taciturn old man, Ponzio's loyal servant and shadow for over thirty years. Hirsute, smelling of acid, he must have appeared in the lecture hall like Charon the ferryman, bearing his baleful message from the underworld. There were cries of horror, people clutched at each other, some of the girls were in tears. But Primo sat still and expressionless, not responding at all. Some of his classmates were shocked by that. But poor Agostino Neri had been not unlike himself: highly intelligent, introverted and shy. And though no one knew why he had done it, there was a rumour that it was for love. Primo was surely frozen by shock, and by long habit in the face of emotion. And perhaps also by terror, thinking: *there but for the grace of God go I.*

The Jewish Group

When the racial laws came out, Primo Levi was not the only young Jew in Turin who suddenly felt more Jewish. Almost all had been as assimilated as he, some of them even more. But now, slowly and reluctantly, but instinctively and inevitably, they began to seek out their Christian friends less, and each other more.

When Vittore Veneziani, Jewish conductor of the La Scala choir, lost his job, he came to the newly opened *scuola ebraica* (Jewish School) in Turin, and started a wonderful choir there: this was Giulia Colombo's main new Jewish activity, for instance, and also that of a young man called Alberto

Salmoni. On Wednesdays many young people would meet in the School's library, ostensibly to exchange books, but really to exchange news, and new antifascist ideas. And in the evenings, or on Sunday afternoons, the most serious returned to special courses on the Bible and on Jewish history: and here too their quest was partly, secretly, political.

Primo took part in all these activities, except the choir; and in the process made some of the most important and enduring friendships of his life.

He would already have noticed Alberto Salmoni at the University – everyone did. Alberto was tall, athletic and very handsome, with wavy black hair and a dreamy, romantic air. He was extremely musical, rather lazy, and did surprising and elegant things: on winter mornings, for instance, when the paths of the Valentino were covered in ice, he would glide to lectures on a pair of skates.

He too was studying chemistry, almost as enthusiastically as Primo. Later, Primo was noted for an unorthodox and dangerous addition to analytic method: he would pick up a few grains of powder on a moistened fingertip, and taste them. Another Jewish classmate, Leo Gallico, remembered his already doing this at university – or was it, he suddenly wondered, Alberto? I am sure it was both; and that the idea had come from Alberto.

He was the youngest of three brothers born in Egypt to Italian parents. Their father was also Egyptian-born: an open-minded, adventurous man, who spoke English, French and Arabic as well as Italian, and was a merchant of many things, primarily lumber. He was even more handsome, and even more restless and impulsive, than Alberto. When he decided to bring his family back to Italy he spread a map on the table, dipped his pen into ink, and held it high over his unknown homeland; the ink spattered on to Naples, so to Naples they came.

In 1936 they moved once more, to Turin. In 1938, therefore, Alberto was still a newcomer, who had had only one year of *liceo* and one of university in Turin. Even today it takes years for most people to be fully accepted by the Turinese. Not Alberto. When he had arrived from Naples he was a good swimmer and sailor, but had hardly ever seen a mountain. His classmates took him into their mountains immediately; and soon he was an excellent, classically Piedmontese climber – casual and proudly amateur; loving the mountains not just for their challenge but for themselves. Alberto Salmoni was happy everywhere; especially in his own skin.

Primo would have seen Alberto at lectures and in the lab. Then one day he also saw him at the end of a long day's climb. Tired, content, they were all waiting in the piazza of a small mountain village for the bus home. Suddenly someone began to sing arias at the top of his voice: Alberto. The bus appeared, and slowed; long before it had stopped, he leapt on to the front step. It circled the entire piazza, Alberto hanging on with one hand and waving with the other, calling 'Farewell, friends!' in his musical tenor. Primo had met his greatest opposite of all. It was the start of a lifelong friendship.

Naturally Alberto had a girlfriend. He never said she was his girlfriend, and no one ever asked; if the taboo against doing such things was strong, the taboo against mentioning them was stronger. But nothing needed to be said about Alberto and girls. It was clear that he fell for them, and they for him, as naturally as rivers fall to the sea.

Alberto's girlfriend was called Bianca Guidetti Serra. She was an extraordinary girl, quite different from Alberto, and from everyone else as well. First of all, she wasn't Jewish. She was witty and lively, and threw herself happily into their weekend outings. But underneath she was more mature, more serious, and more politically aware than most of the friends – especially Alberto. Her father, a lawyer, had died that very year. And her mother had come from a very different kind of family. She had started work at ten, and had been a top dressmaker by eighteen. Once she had married Bianca's father she no longer needed to earn a living. But she did not forget her past; and nor did her daughter.

From the age of seventeen Bianca had taken small jobs in lawyers' offices. Now she was studying law, and at the same time working as an *assistente sociale*, helping factory workers with their legal and welfare problems. Even her desire to spend her free time with Alberto's friends had a political element: she was outraged by the racial laws, and wanted to express her solidarity with Jewish Italians. She and Primo immediately became friends. They were not unlike in their idealism, their reserve, and their self-discipline. In fact they had more in common with each other than either had with Alberto – which is no doubt why they both loved him.

Bianca would remain one of Primo's closest lifelong friends. So would two others: Silvio Ortona and Eugenio Gentili Tedeschi.

Silvio Ortona we have already met, since he was to marry not just once but twice into Primo's family. He was three years older, and had finished both his law degree and his officer's training course in 1937. The next year the racial laws expelled him from the Army. He then spent six months in London, learning English and looking for work. In August 1939 a British firm finally offered him a job, the only disadvantage of which was that it was in the Belgian Congo. He went home briefly to say goodbye to his family. On 3 September Britain declared war on Germany, and the company wrote to say that Axis employees were no longer wanted. Silvio was spared the Belgian Congo.

Instead he met Primo and the others, in the late summer of 1939; though their real friendship did not begin until a few years later. For the moment Silvio was still spending most of his time with his old, largely non-Jewish friends, and only came occasionally to the *scuola ebraica*. Perhaps because he was older, he was a few steps ahead on the road to political engagement; and it may be (he is too polite to say so, even now) that he found some of their discussions a bit naïve. Primo did so himself. That was one of the things they would share later: a sharp, ironic critical intelligence, which they wouldn't hesitate to turn on themselves.

Eugenio Gentili Tedeschi was also on the edge of the group: not because he was politically engaged, but because he would not spare a moment from his work. Euge (as he was always called) was a student of architecture, and a fanatic for two things in life: architecture and the mountains. He was the most serious and accomplished climber of the group, and a passionate skier. Euge was perhaps the most favoured by fate of them all. He was handsome and athletic, like Alberto, intellectually powerful like Silvio, both gifted and disciplined like Primo.

He says, ruefully, that his maniacal dedication to work and to the mountains in those years was the same as Primo's: a compensation for sexual repression. But there was a difference. Like Primo's, his dedication to the mountains would help him to survive the war; and his dedication to work would earn him a brilliant career after it. But by the time the two cemented their friendship, just before the war, Euge would have sloughed off his sexual repression.

Franco Momigliano had been Euge's best friend since boyhood. The two were a bit older than Primo (both born in 1916, like Silvio), practically inseparable, and way ahead of the others on the mountains. Franco was the possessor of yet another brilliantly powerful mind. His official subject was law; but his passion was for politics and economics, which he also managed to study, under the famous economist Luigi Einaudi.* In one important way he was different from Euge. Euge's family was musical (his father was Professor of Music at the University); Franco's was political. And so, therefore, was he. That is common in totalitarian times: only those who have thought before are armed. Most early antifascists, like Vittorio Foa, came from antifascist families; it took those from apolitical families, like Primo's or Euge's, longer to find their way. So now, while the others were only beginning to imagine the possibility of political resistance, Franco already belonged to the Partito d'Azione (the political expression of Giustizia

---

* Professor of Economics at the University of Turin until 1943; later Finance minister and first President of the Republic (1948–55). Father of Giulio Einaudi, founder of the famous publishing house and (eventually) Primo Levi's publisher.

e Libertà). He came to the *scuola ebraica* more often than Euge, to take part in the political discussions. He could not openly incite anyone to resistance, or let on that he had already joined it. But he could and did try to make everyone think of it for themselves.

Luciana Nissim was a natural resister. When she arrived at the University in 1937 her first friends were antifascist and non-Jewish. Then came the racial laws: and like Primo and the others, she felt Jewish for the first time. She went straight to the *scuola ebraica*, and there made the central friendships of her life. She met Primo and Vanda Maestro, with whom she would be arrested and deported only five years later. And she met Franco, whom she would marry.

Luciana had chosen medicine, because, she says, it was such a long course no one would expect her to come home for years (her family lived in Biella); and such a tough, masculine one no one would ever expect her to play the little woman. Not that anyone ever would; Luciana is a kind of female Alberto, a *forza della natura*, as the Italians say – a force of nature, like an ocean wave. Alberto does not like to remember; he would never describe the friends of the Jewish group in any detail. Silvio and Euge are both, in their different ways, abstract and cautious men; they tell funny stories against themselves, but won't say much about the others. Franco died a year after Primo; but in any case he was a tall, gloomy intellectual, who would always peer over the heads of a crowd. Luciana, however, became a psychoanalyst. The core members of the Jewish group, she says with a grin, were all *piccoli geni*, little geniuses: physically small, ugly and repressed, mentally towering giants.

Of course this wasn't always true. Giorgio Segre was a brilliant, dashing young man, his friend Guglielmo Piperno a climber and a *bon vivant*. Guido Bonfiglioli and his cousin Franco Tedeschi were both intelligent and cultured, but also attractive – Vanda was in love with Guido, until she fell in love with Giorgio Segre instead; and Anna Maria Levi, who could have her pick, would choose Franco Tedeschi. Giorgio Lattes was big, gentle and slow-spoken, intelligent but not intellectual. The brothers Italo and Leo Diena were both great talkers, with Leo the more brilliant of the two; certainly Euge's caricature of Italo suggests no great beauty (see next page).

No: by the *piccoli geni* Luciana really meant the three or four most intelligent, and most physically repressed and unattractive, of the group. She meant, alas, Primo. She also meant Livio Norzi, who was a mathematical genius, and at least as repressed as Primo. And above all she meant the two founders and leaders of the most intellectual side of the *scuola ebraica* meetings: the brothers Ennio and Emanuele Artom. Ennio was even more intelligent than Emanuele, Emanuele even more unattractive than Ennio; but both were more intelligent, and more unattractive, than anyone else.

Italo Diena

We have met Ennio before, as the extreme intellectual monster of Primo's D'Azeglio class. He was a classical prodigy: giving lectures at the *scuola ebraica* from the age of thirteen, writing the entries on Judaism for the UTET encyclopedia at fifteen, writing and translating for Einaudi while he was still an undergraduate. He read half a dozen modern languages, was expert in Latin and Greek, knew Hebrew and Aramaic. In 1940, a year early, he would take a brilliant degree. Only a few months later, on holiday in the mountains, he slipped and fell, hit his head on a rock, and died.

This absurd accident would leave Emanuele with inconsolable parents, and with the task of carrying on the pursuit of excellence alone. That is exactly what he did – though not, in the end, in the way for which nature had prepared him. Emanuele was also an outstanding scholar. He had studied under the great Augusto Monti at D'Azeglio, and had taken a brilliant degree in literature in 1937. He too taught at the *scuola ebraica*, contributed to the UTET encyclopedia, and published articles, translations, and a book on Jewish history for schools. But he had only lately begun to concentrate on Jewish subjects. The Artoms were a religious family: and yet at the same time completely Italian, with that special combination of gratitude and pride which made Italian Jews (as one scholar puts it) 'doubly Italian'. Despite the daily practice of his religion, therefore, Emanuele only began to seek a Jewish identity for himself at the same time as his secular friends: when his Italian identity was stripped from him by the racial laws. That was when he, Ennio and Giorgio Segre, who had been put in charge of the library by the rabbi, began to organize the courses and classes on Judaism to which Primo and the others came.

After Ennio's death Emanuele turned even more intensely inward, on study and teaching. And yet not entirely inward. Despite being *piccoli geni*, the Artoms had edged their classes from the start in a political direction. The group of friends studied the Bible, Primo said, to prove to themselves that justice and liberty – *giustizia e libertà*, which even the most ignorant would recognize – were fundamental Jewish values, so that a Jew had no choice but to be an antifascist. Emanuele's father Emilio was already antifascist, one of the very few teachers in Turin who had refused to join the party. And now Emanuele moved early towards political action. By the spring of 1943 he was working for the Partito d'Azione. The Germans entered Italy on 8 September; on the 9th the smallest of the small geniuses joined the partisans of Giustizia e Libertà.

He was sent to the Val Pellice, to become political commissar to the first partisan groups trying to organize themselves there. 'Partisans', in those early days, meant soldiers deserting from the collapsing Italian Army, and young men from the valleys who had avoided joining it in the first place, none of them remotely interested in political education. 'Political commissar', accordingly, meant giving talks to which no one listened, delivering heavy bundles of antifascist newspapers which no one read, and generally providing less education than entertainment. But Emanuele had courage equal to Primo's. For six winter months he tramped the Waldensian valleys, going from band to band, joining in long marches and dangerous raids. One day, in the railway station at Barge, he saw a recruiting poster for the Fascist Militia, which included in its list of requirements 'Unexceptionable morality'. He went up and wrote beside it, 'In that case, do not join.' You could be shot for less.

In March 1944 the Germans began a series of offensives against the partisans in the area. A group which included not only Emanuele but also Franco Momigliano, Giorgio Segre, and another, younger member of the *scuola ebraica* classes, Ugo Sacerdote, left Prali in the afternoon of 23 March, heading for the Val Pellice. On the 25th, just as they reached the Col Giulian, an SS patrol caught up with them. Franco, Giorgio, Ugo and the others managed to escape. But Emanuele was too weak, and too exhausted. He and another young Jewish partisan from Turin, Ruggero Levi, were both captured. Levi was not recognized as a Jew; but Emanuele was. (When Ada Gobetti, one of the founders of Giustizia e Libertà, heard that he had been arrested, she despaired. 'I thought with terror,' she wrote in her diary, 'of his face, his eyes . . .') He was also recognized as a political commissar, someone who knew all the G. & L. groups, their leaders, their plans. For five days he was tortured, but did not reveal a single name. Finally he was transferred to the Nuove Prison in Turin; where a week later, on 7 April, he was found dead in his cell. Two of his companions were forced to bury him hurriedly at night, in Stupinigi on the edge of the city. Though great efforts were made at the end of the war, his body was never found.

In Primo's second year at university the war with Germany began; in his third France and the Low Countries fell, the whole of Europe was German or (nominally) neutral, and Italy joined the winning side. By his fourth and last year, he and his friends had met many French, Polish and Yugoslav refugees, and had read an English book on Nazi atrocities. The refugees did not know the worst, and they only half believed the book; 'but that was enough', Primo wrote. 'Only a voluntarily deaf and blind man could have any doubts about the fate reserved for the Jews in a German Europe.' And yet they still could not imagine such a fate for themselves. Not *here*: not in Italy, not in Piedmont and Turin.

What we know now makes it hard to imagine how they could have remained 'voluntarily deaf and blind' for so long. But then even their small move towards political resistance was unusually enterprising, and also brave. Their talk may have been naïve, but it was undeniably subversive. They criticized the government's propaganda and policies, not only against themselves. They talked about the war, and hoped that Italy would lose. They discussed whether they should be liberals, socialists or communists: that is, not whether to become enemies of the state, but which kind. They invited their Christian friends to the formal lectures and classes – and many even came, intrigued by the first hint of a challenge to Fascism they'd ever heard. It all happened in a thoroughly Italian way. Though some of those who came to listen were Fascists, and understood the challenge perfectly well, no one ever denounced them to the authorities, and the meetings were never stopped. Indeed, they were approved by the security police, as all public meetings had to be. At every lecture, Primo recalled, there was a poor, bored policeman who smoked his pipe, read his newspaper, and finally fell asleep.

Iron

Whenever people mention Alberto Salmoni, they smile. The smile contains several elements, which vary from person to person: amazement, amusement, shock; but mostly pleasure. Alberto, says his cousin Anna Cases with that smile, is mad. Giulia Colombo remembers that during the war his father worked in an abattoir, baking the blood into a kind of cake, which people bought eagerly in those lean years. The abattoir gave Alberto an idea. He caught several of its well-nourished mice, and took them home to his mother to cook. She was used to him, and cooked them; but when it came to eating them, even Alberto's courage failed.

Above all, Anna says, you couldn't go anywhere with him, it was far too dangerous. Again Giulia remembers something. In the summer of 1940 she and Alberto were both in Cogne, visiting Primo. Since they were returning to Turin at the same time, they left together. Cogne is high in the mountains of Gran Paradiso, a dozen miles above Aosta if you are a bird, many more by twisting mountain path or road. Nowadays no one would dream of making the journey in either direction except by bus, or car; and it was not much more common then. But the young in general, and Alberto in particular, were not afraid of a bit of exercise. He faced Aosta, and plunged down the mountainside, Giulia following. He was a confident, enthusiastic guide; with only one disadvantage, that he had no sense of direction at all. They wandered in the steep forests, completely lost, for hours. Alberto treated the whole thing as a glorious adventure, so that Giulia never worried – though she says now that they probably had a narrow escape, and if she had been with anyone else she would have died. Then, when they finally trailed into Aosta, utterly exhausted, Alberto insisted on visiting the castle.

Primo felt the same as Giulia; and despite the danger, or because of it, he went everywhere with Alberto. Together they cycled hundreds of miles – in one summer holiday, all the way to Trieste and back in twenty-two days, via the Dolomites, Cortina and Venice. To Trieste they went alone – with Primo, I imagine, navigating. But on most of their expeditions, especially in the mountains, there was a third.

Primo had started climbing at thirteen or fourteen, on holidays in Cogne, Bardonecchia and Torre Pellice. This was not – he would explain – *alpinismo*, proper mountaineering, at real heights and exposed to real dangers. Rather, he said, 'there was a tradition in my family' of mountain walking and (mild) climbing, for health, strength and contact with nature. Not on his father's side, but on his mother's – in his uncle Corrado, for example; and in general amongst the progressive, self-improving, often Jewish middle classes. Even big, clumsy Giorgio Lattes loved the mountains; and even Livio Norzi, who was completely obsessed by maths and science, was a keen climber. So too were the monster geniuses, the Artoms, whose parents had a house in Courmayeur. It was this family feeling for the mountains that would make the move from urban intellectual to mountain fighter possible for so many.

At around eighteen or nineteen, Primo moved on to real mountaineering. This was, of course, less common. But it was the ideal choice of most young Piedmontese sportsmen: and Primo Levi, therefore, chose it too.

That he did so is deeply revealing of both his culture and his own nature, and of how closely the two were related. The *alpinista* is the perfect type – the peak, we might say – of Piedmontese values. He is strong and silent: never telling his triumphs, but only his failures, in a mocking tone which makes up for the immodesty of talking about himself at all. He is simple, tough and self-reliant, using his hands, an old rope, a few nails, and his best but oldest boots. He *never* buys new equipment, but spends hours keeping the old in perfect condition. He is always an individualist, and often an outsider: the proportion of Jews, and of Waldensian Protestants, amongst Piedmontese mountaineers was much higher than the proportion of either in the population. This would also be true of Jews and Protestants in the Piedmontese resistance: not unnaturally, since quite often they were the same people.

One reason why Primo turned to *alpinismo* now was specific to the time: to the racial campaign, and then the laws, of 1937 and '38. In the words of Silvio Ortona (an *alpinista* himself), it was 'a revenge for humiliation'. As Primo put it: 'You Fascists pick me out, isolate me, tell me I am a person of lesser value, inferior, *unterer*: well, I'll show you you're wrong.' It was also – obscurely, instinctively – a rehearsal and a preparation for the looming future. On the mountains you learned (Primo said) patience, persistence and endurance; how to cope with hunger, fatigue and pain; how to survive on what you could find. You gained in confidence, and in toughness. In the same spirit, Franco Tedeschi and Guido Bonfiglioli took up boxing.

But essentially Primo climbed mountains because it answered to his nature. He would have been a writer without Auschwitz; and he would have been a climber without the racial laws. Of all physical adventures, mountain-climbing is closest to a spiritual one: recognizing the danger of the world, and yet embracing it; celebrating your youth and life with every move – and with every move remembering your weakness, the power of death, the beauty of creation. For Primo climbing was, like chemistry, *la libertà di sbagliare*, the freedom to err – which he deliberately chose. It was overcoming his greatest weakness: fear of failure, fear of risk, fear of fear.

Like chemistry, too, it was a battle between Mind and Spirit: between the light of the mind and the darkness of matter, *materia nemica*, our hostile mother. And like chemistry, but even more, climbing was a glimpse of something beyond this enmity, which could be its resolution. This is how Massimo Mila, himself a great *alpinista*, describes it:

There is a way of knowing which is purely mental, a matter of using your intelligence; and there is a way of knowing with your muscles, your flesh, your own experience . . . To know the Matterhorn doesn't mean seeing it from Breuil, and reading Guido Rey's book: it means inching your way up [its] *cheminée*, leaving pieces of your clothing and your skin on [its] rocks.

This physical way of knowing, and the triumph over fear, were Primo's most personal goals and desires, the healing of his own divisions. Yet at the same time he shared them with every other mountaineer. What one of his first fictional creations, the old doctor of 'I mnemagoghi', says of the smell of sun on rock surely expressed Primo's own feeling: it means, he says, *pace raggiunta*, peace achieved.

All mountaineering careers, however, start with failure: that, as Primo might say, is how one learns. His first failure came at fourteen, in Bardonecchia. He and two friends set off with sublime carelessness at two in the afternoon, without having eaten, without supplies, and in short trousers. When they reached the peak it was almost dark; and the mountain refuge where they'd planned a brief and condescending call was 600 metres down a crumbling escarpment. They sat on the edge and shouted for hours. Finally, at about midnight, there was an answering signal from the refuge; and slowly, stopping to drink and curse, a squad of rescuers toiled up towards them. When they arrived two hours later they destroyed what remained of the boys' dignity by bellowing downwards: 'It's just a bunch of kids!' Then they lashed them up like salamis, and lowered them down without another word.

But this was only the beginning. The real *libertà di sbagliare* came later, when Primo had graduated to serious climbing, and when he had met the third member of most of his expeditions. The third was really the first, since as a climber he was in a different class altogether from Primo and Alberto. His name was Sandro Delmastro; he too was studying chemistry; and in Primo's personal periodic table, he was Iron.

To Primo, Sandro was in a class of his own, both as a climber and as a man. He was Primo's greatest *alter ego* of all, the one who stands as a symbol for all the others: the hero, pure and simple. He took the craziest risks of all, but he could meet them. With Alberto you were safe because you felt safe; with Sandro you felt safe because you were. Of Primo and Alberto Anna Cases says: 'Together they made one normal man.' Together with Sandro, they made an ideal one. Clara Moschino – Rita of 'Zinc' – remembers the three of them as though they *were* one ideal man. 'Levi was the brain,' she says, 'Salmoni the poetry, and Delmastro the power.'

★

Sandro

Sandro was born in 1917, which made him a year older than Alberto and two older than Primo. He was the youngest of four children of a builder, Enrico Delmastro. Enrico had begun as a foreman, then risen to found his own company. He died young, when Sandro was still a child; but left the family reasonably well off, living in a house he had built himself, on the Via Madama Cristina.

Like his brother and sisters, Sandro had been born in Turin; he had gone to the Liceo Alfieri, D'Azeglio's rival for the title of top Classical Liceo. In other words, his own life had been urban and middle-class from the start. But his roots were in the provinces, and in poverty; and they were very near. Enrico Delmastro came from the village of Zubiena, between Ivrea and Biella; his wife's family from Ala di Stura in the Val di Lanzo. They had made the journey into the city, and into the middle classes, just as Primo's own family had done, but a generation or two later. And they were still mountain people: taciturn, proud and independent. Enrico, who had risen from the ranks, had been a socialist. Under Fascism – that is, during the whole of Sandro's life – the family was politically passive; but deeply, instinctively, liberal and antifascist.

Sandro's brother Giuseppe was a mythical climber and skier, even stronger and more silent than Sandro. But he was ten years older, and already working; and apart from his private *alpinismo* he lived a normal city life. It was Sandro, the youngest, to whom the family's mountain roots meant most. He was a *montanaro* through and through – a man born and bred in the mountains, though he had been born and bred in Turin.

He was of medium height, thin but extremely strong, with a bony face and short black hair growing low on his forehead. He was not handsome, and he was gruff and unsociable to girls; yet he was very attractive, because of his strength, and his plain, peasant masculinity. This he expressed in his clothes: always wearing old, worn corduroy breeches and kneesocks of homespun wool; never an overcoat, but only a short jacket, or sometimes a short black cape. He walked or cycled everywhere, never took a bus or tram. Everyone remembers his walk – though slightly differently. Primo said it was a long, slow, peasant stride. Clara Moschino makes it sound more energetic: he marched *pom-pom*, she says, and you could see his muscles move. Ester Valabrega, who was also in the chemistry class, became his girlfriend in their second year. They called him *gobbo*, hunchback, she says, because he leaned forward as he walked, as though he were always going uphill.

Sandro was a loner, an introvert. He had the *montanaro*'s extreme reserve, through which, Primo said, almost nothing of his inner world was allowed to show. He was very intelligent, got *30 e lode* in most of his classes, and ended with 95. I do not know if he was as uninterested at school, and flowered as suddenly at university, as 'Iron' describes; or whether this was more a trait of Primo's dramatized *alter ego*, an echo, for instance, of Guido at *liceo*. But certainly the heart of Sandro's life was not learning, as it was of Primo's. The heart of his life was the mountains. This was the true *montanaro* core of him, for Primo the city boy, the bourgeois intellectual. Sandro, he wrote in 'Iron',

did not belong to that race of people who do things in order to talk about them (like me). He didn't like big words; he didn't like words at all. It seemed that in speaking, as in mountain climbing, no one had taught him; he spoke as no one speaks, saying only the heart of things.

He spent every Sunday, and many other days, in the mountains. In winter he skied, tying his skis on his rusty bike and cycling to the snow. He led Primo and Alberto along invisible tracks 'he seemed to intuit like a savage'. Since they were too poor to buy the sealskin strips you bound around your skis for the ascents, he taught them to use rough hemp cloths instead – 'Spartan devices which absorb the water and freeze like codfish,' Primo said; then down you skied with these lumps of ice tied round your waist.

And in the summer he climbed. If necessary (Primo wrote) he carried a thirty-kilo pack; but usually he went without it. He could walk for two days without eating, or eat three meals all together and then leave. He would put some lettuce in his pocket, a piece of bread, a pocket knife, and a length of wire for emergency repairs. He might also take the CAI (Club Alpino Italiano) guide, but only to mock and vilify: nothing pleased him more than to show Primo and Alberto that it was wrong, even at their own expense. He climbed less by technique than by instinct. He climbed not to prove anything to them, or to the mountain. He climbed, Primo said, to test and improve himself: to know his limitations, and then extend them. He 'seemed to be made of iron'; and he was 'bound to iron by an ancient kinship', since his father's fathers, he told them, had been *magnin* (tinkers) and *frè* (blacksmiths). As he climbed he saluted, ironically, the silicon, calcium and magnesium he had learned to recognize in Mineralogy; and less ironically, perhaps, the red traces in the rock of his kinsman, iron. The mountains, Primo wrote, were Sandro's place, what he was made for. In the mountains 'he became happy, with a silent, infectious happiness, like a light that is switched on'. And Primo caught that infection: the mark that Sandro left on him was happiness. Sandro 'aroused a new communion with earth and sky', he wrote: openly meaning *in me*. And 'To see Sandro in the mountains reconciled one to the world': secretly meaning *reconciled me*.

Most of the time they didn't have to go far: only two or three hours' bike ride away lay the 'rock gymnasia', in which generations of Turinese have practised: the Picchi del Pigliaio (Straw Stack Pinnacles) and Denti di Cumiana (Teeth of Cumiana); the Roca Patanüa, which means Naked Rock, and the Sbarüa, which means, roughly, the Terrifier ('it is split from base to summit by a fissure that gets narrower as it rises, finally forcing the climber out on to the rock face itself, where, precisely, he is terrified'). But occasionally, when they had time, they went further afield. It was on one of these more ambitious expeditions that Primo had his first encounter with the true *libertà di sbagliare*, miles from any hope of rescue. There were others, later, though not many. But this one remained the model and symbol for him of *alpinismo*, as Sandro was the model and symbol of *alpinisti*.

'*Dôma, neh?*' Sandro said to Primo and Alberto one Saturday in February: tomorrow they would put into action one of their plans, the winter climb of the Uja di Mondrone, a 3,000-metre peak in the Val di Ala, near his mother's family's home. They left that night, slept in an inn, and set off 'at some indeterminate hour' (Sandro did not like watches, Primo notes). Around midday they stepped out of the fog into the sunlight of a great peak: and saw it was the wrong one.

Alberto, who was used to such misadventures, suggested that they return to the point where they'd gone wrong, and take the right route to the right peak from there; Primo, in his own words 'the weakest and most prudent', suggested that they be satisfied with the wrong one. But Sandro, 'in splendid bad faith', said that they could reach the Tooth of Mondrone in half an hour from where they were, via what the CAI guide called 'the easy north-west ridge'; and what was the point of being twenty if you couldn't permit yourself the luxury of taking the wrong route now and again? They would have plenty of time when they were forty to look at the scenery.

The 'easy north-west ridge' was easy in the summer, but it wasn't summer. On the side facing the sun the rock was wet, on the shady side covered in ice. In between the outcrops there were large pockets of soft, melting snow into which they sank up to their waists at every step.

By the time they reached the top it was twilight; and Primo and Alberto were at their last gasp. But Sandro, Primo wrote, 'was seized with a sinister hilarity'. When they asked, 'And how do we get down?' he just said, 'We'll see. At the very worst we'll taste *la carne dell'orso*, bear meat.' They'd no idea what he meant; but they were about to find out.

With the help of their rope (or rather the hindrance – it had frozen solid), they inched downwards until darkness fell. Then they ate the little they had left, built a useless wall of stones against the wind, and lay down on the frozen ground. Every hour or two they changed places; only the man in the middle slept. Whenever they did so, 'it was as though time itself had frozen': the same wind, the same strip of moon, across which the same torn clouds were racing. When dawn came at last their limbs were numb, their eyes glittering, and their boots frozen so hard they rang like bells. But they got down to the valley; and when the innkeeper asked with a leer how things had gone, they said they had had a very pleasant outing.

That, Primo said, was Sandro's bear meat:

And now that many years have passed, I regret that I have eaten so little of it. For of all the good things life has given me, nothing has had, even distantly, the taste of that meat, which is the taste of being strong and free: free to err as well, and be master of one's own destiny.

This rare adventure really happened, and almost exactly as Primo described. But not quite. First of all, in 'Iron' he left out Alberto. He did so because 'Iron' is the story of Sandro; if he had not needed an observer and a foil, he might have left himself out as well. But secondly, he did of course dramatize Sandro. Sandro was quite as unusual and striking as Primo describes, quite as strong and forceful, quite as reserved, taciturn and *montanaro*. But he was also more ordinary. He went on more ordinary mountain outings as well – even in groups, and even with girls; for example, with Ester. And he was not quite so poor.

This difference caused Primo a good deal of trouble. People are often proudest of their peasant origins when they are furthest from them; in this as in other things Sandro was an exception. He was not born in the Serra d'Ivrea, as Primo says in 'Iron', but in Turin; he was not the son of a mason, and did not 'spend his summers working as a shepherd' (perhaps he joined the flocks once or twice on holiday, Ester says, for pleasure, when he was a boy). Above all, his family were not such 'simple, poor people' that 'they had decided to make him study, so that he would bring money home'. This line in particular stung Sandro's proud and prickly family, when *The Periodic Table* was published in 1975. First through Ester, then by letter, they required Primo to change it, even at one stage threatening to go to law. But Primo stood firm, as he always did on matters of principle, and of writing. 'I will not change a word,' he said. And didn't.

He knew himself that the portrait of Sandro contained inaccuracies: 'some intended, some involuntary', as he put it to Ester. He wanted to remember Sandro as truthfully as possible – and their friends agree that he did. But he knew that it would, inevitably, be *his* Sandro that would emerge: the Sandro of his memory, his recounting. And that is really the point of the story.

There is a way of looking at some of Primo's writing as though he and it were *alter egos*, just as he and Sandro were, or he and Alberto. In this way of looking at it – which is a good one, and one that several of those who knew him best believe in – Primo put into books like *The Truce, The Wrench, If Not Now, When?* everything he himself wasn't, all the adventure and action he himself never had (except briefly, and by *force majeure*). 'Iron' is the acme of this writing-as-*alter-ego*, writing-as-compensation: a homage, as he says himself, to everything he missed in life; to everything he wasn't, and Sandro Delmastro was.

Now this is certainly true. 'Iron' is the acme of that exchange which Primo celebrated among the friends of his youth: the mark which each left upon each, 'before the wax hardened'. He and Sandro were 'rich in exchangeable goods', he wrote: his being words and ideas, Sandro's deeds and things, especially the rocks and ice of the mountains. And certainly 'Iron' is the homage of the man of words to the man of deeds: of those who 'do things in order to talk about them (like me)' to those who do them purely, for their own sake, like Sandro.

And yet it was not completely true; not in reality, and not even in the story. For first of all, Sandro was not so purely and simply a man of deeds as Primo paints him: this was the real dramatization, the real meaning of the 'inaccuracies' about Sandro's poverty. And perhaps it wasn't he who introduced it, but Sandro. Sandro was as sophisticated as Primo himself; he lived as much in ideas as any other educated, intelligent young person. In fact he lived in ideals: believing passionately in democracy and social justice, for example, and preparing himself quite consciously for the war with Fascism soon to come. But most of all he lived an ideal of himself. He chose to be a *montanaro*, rather than finding himself one; and he played the role to the hilt. I do not mean that he was play-acting, in the sense of pretending to be what he wasn't. He was pretending to be what he was. His walk, his voice, his clothes were all expressions not of what he just happened to be, but of what he was glad to be, and wanted to be more. Primo even hints at this in 'Iron', when he says that Sandro's black cape 'made me think of the Tuscan poet Renato Fucini'. Sandro was the power, and Alberto the poetry; but Sandro was poetry too.

And Primo was not only a brain. 'Iron' is not a simple contrast between words and deeds, and a simple tribute from the one to the other. It is more complicated than that, just as 'Hydrogen' was, and 'Un lungo duello'. There is, in fact, a bridge between words and deeds in 'Iron': books. Their chemistry textbook, by Autenrieth, is a 'bridge, a missing link, between the world of words and the world of things'; the CAI guide is another. Sandro (at least the Sandro of 'Iron') despises the guide, precisely for being such a mixture of words and things: 'a bastard creature, a detestable cross of rock and snow with paper'. But Primo is always drawn to bridges; if he calls something a bridge, it must be praise. And so it is here, I think. Though he loved and admired Sandro almost more than anyone, though he eagerly learned all he could from him, he did not in the end, or even then, put the mountains at the heart of his life, as Sandro did. What *he* wanted to be was much more an Autenrieth, or the writer of the CAI guide. He wanted to write (science then, literature by the time he wrote the story) like an Autenrieth, or like the guide: putting rock and snow – reality itself – on paper. What he admired in Sandro, as much as his deeds, were *his* words: how he 'spoke as no one speaks, saying only the heart of things'. This is what he wanted to do as a writer, when he wrote 'Iron': and he did. He wanted to be a bridge between words and deeds; and he was.

The end of 'Iron' is as elegiac, and as ambivalent, as the end of 'Duello':

Today I know that it is a hopeless task to try to dress a man in words, to make him live again on the page, especially a man like Sandro . . . : he lived completely in his deeds, and when they were over, nothing of him remained – nothing but words, precisely.

Words may be poor things, but they remain: just as a thin body is a poor thing, but can squeeze through the gate. It may be a hopeless task to make a man live again on the page; but it is the only place where he can live again at all.

Sandro was the first of Primo's friends to die, a few days before Emanuele.

As soon as he had graduated he had to join the Italian forces at war. He chose the Navy, because it was slightly less Fascist than the other services. He and Ester tried to marry before he left for the Naval Academy in Livorno. But Ester was half-Jewish, and the local priest refused to marry them. They did not get another chance.

In 1942 Sandro went to La Spezia, then to Aqui Terme, working as a chemist in a Navy lab (much as Primo would soon work too, in rather different circumstances). On 8 September 1943, when Italy surrendered to the Allies in the south and Germany invaded in the north, he immediately went home to Piedmont to join Giustizia e Libertà.

Primo, who had hoped to find him, didn't; Alberto did instead, and another friend of Sandro's called Gianni Aliberti. Together the three of them tried to establish a partisan band in the Val di Lanzo. In the first days of chaos and confusion they could find no one to join them. Soon, however, they contacted, or were contacted by, the leadership of G. & L.: and together with several others were sent to Pra del Torno in the Val Pellice. Here they established the *gruppo del Sap*, the Sap group, named after the tiny spot above Pra which was their base. Aliberti, a fierce antifascist who had already been arrested three times, was the band's political commissar; Sandro was its first leader, and Alberto its second.

The early *gruppo del Sap* was a glorious, and impossible, mixture. Apart from Sandro, Alberto and Gianni Aliberti there were, for example, four eager young Turinese Jews: Ugo Sacerdote, an engineering student, whom we already know; Sergio Diena, who was an agricultural scientist, and his cousins Giorgio, an engineer, and Paolo, who was still a medical student. And then there were, for example, a barber, a tram driver, and three young toughs from Turin's criminal classes; plus one Australian and two British ex-POWs, one of these a miner and the other a farm worker. The bourgeois quickly became the leaders, the others the workers – and the class war that ensued threatened to overtake the one against the Germans. Sandro, with his powerful personality and his *montanaro* toughness, managed to keep order. But in late October he returned to Turin to join G. & L.'s Military Command. Easy-going Alberto did not manage so well, and soon moved on to other adventures.*

---

* Sergio Diena became the first partisan to die in the Waldensian valleys; in June 1944 Paolo Diena followed. Ugo Sacerdote and Giorgio Diena both survived. Gianni Aliberti returned

Back in Turin Sandro was put in charge of all G. & L. activities in the city. At least now he and Ester were together again; and for five months they worked together in the Resistance. Then it all ended. On the last day of March 1944 Ester was waiting for him in a restaurant when a friend ran in and told her the news: the entire Military Command had been arrested. Ester sat on, refusing to give up hope. And half an hour later Sandro arrived. Somehow he'd escaped the arrests. They ate quickly. He hadn't decided yet what to do; he'd let her know. They said goodbye at a tram stop on the Via Garibaldi; and Ester returned to her family in Ivrea.

She waited, but no word came. A few days later, as she was about to take the train to Turin, a young man stopped her. He led her to another man, who told her that Sandro had been killed.

Giorgio Agosti, one of the leaders of G. & L., told her what had happened. It was his fault, he said. Sandro, who knew every inch of the city by now, had wanted to stay there; but the leadership had been convinced that Turin was too dangerous. Instead they sent him back into the mountains, into the Valle Roja beyond Cuneo. And on his way there he was arrested.

He was taken to the Fascist headquarters on the Corso IV Novembre in Cuneo. They must have left him unguarded for a moment; and Sandro being Sandro, he tried to escape. He had heavy mountain boots on, which held him back; but still he ran so fast that his light raincoat flew out on either side of him like wings. He was only a few yards from the corner when two shots rang out, then two more. He lifted his arms, and fell.

A young boy in Fascist uniform – 'one of those wretched murderers of fifteen whom the Repubblica di Salò recruited in the reformatories', Primo would write – ran up, picked up Sandro's cap where it had fallen, and tossed it contemptuously on to his face. Sandro's body lay on the pavement for half an hour, then was tipped on to a rubbish cart. It was 3 April. Two days later, eight other members of the Military Command were shot in Turin.

So Sandro died in his beloved mountains after all, though not in the way he would have imagined. It is a great irony that he of all people chose the city – and that if he had stayed there, he might just possibly have survived. But the likely reason for his choice is a greater irony still. By the time he became a partisan, Sandro's legendary strength was much reduced. During his naval training he had had a severe attack of rheumatoid arthritis, which had affected his heart. He joked to Ester that he might die of a heart attack

---

to Turin with Sandro, was arrested almost immediately, and was on the first Italian transport to Mauthausen. Much of the literature of the camps lists him among the dead, as indeed he should have been; but he managed to survive Mauthausen and Flossenberg, fought with Czech partisans in 1945, and finally came home in January 1946. He died in 1985.

at any moment. Ironically again, this may even have been true: if he had not died as he did at twenty-seven, Sandro of all people may still have died young. And the greatest irony of all is that he may have brought this possibility of early death upon himself, as he brought the real one, by his daring. Ester, at any rate, believes so: that Sandro's enlarged heart was as much the result of all the bear meat he'd tasted as of the rheumatoid arthritis; and even that the rheumatoid arthritis itself was the result of his having tasted so much (too much?) *carne dell'orso*.

After the war Sandro was reburied in Zubiena. He was awarded a Silver Medal for gallantry; and a plaque was put up to him in Cuneo, on the spot where he died, which gets the date of his death slightly wrong.

So the man of deeds died, and the man of words was left to mourn and admire him: this was Primo's first taste of survivor's guilt, and observer's shame.

'Every time I try to speak of him . . . I feel a great sadness,' says the elderly narrator of the first version of the story. And when Primo spoke of Sandro thirty years after he had last seen him, he could not hide his emotion.

Years Three and Four

In the last two years of Chemistry everything closed down. Europe had gone to war in 1939; in 1940 Italy joined what Mussolini thought would be the winning side. Christian friends began to disappear into the forces and further, into death; others began to attend classes in military uniform. Primo, Sandro and Alberto continued to push the future 'into the limbo of things not perceived, or immediately forgotten', throwing themselves into the clean trials of the mountains. And work became still harder: especially for the Jews, who could not afford to fail a single examination.

In his third year Primo took eight courses, including the maniacally exact Quantitative Analysis under Professor Ponzio; and the most theoretically difficult course, Physical Chemistry, which took both of the last two years. The difficulty of Physical Chemistry was not helped by the fact that its Professor was Mario Milone. Milone was an ambitious mediocrity, more interested in his career than in his students, and in consequence a poor teacher. Primo disliked him intensely. Milone was, perhaps, no more convinced a Fascist than Fenoglio. But he happily obeyed the regime's orders about Jews – refusing Emma's thesis with alacrity, giving Ester a low mark in his course, and even lowering her over-all mark on graduation, when she persisted, despite his best efforts, in graduating. Primo would have known about both events, and probably others. All his university teachers, he said forty years later, were decent men, 'with one exception'. He meant Milone. Nonetheless, he typically did a minor thesis under him. (And typically too, Milone soon rose to become Director of the Institute.)

In *The Periodic Table* Primo dates an important decision to his fourth year: chemistry did not, after all, answer his needs. Was there real precision in chemistry? – Were there chemical axioms, logical deductions from self-evident truths? No, for that you had to go further back: 'to the origins, to mathematics and physics'.

And so he would. As once he had determined to be a chemist despite the opposition of the world, he now determined to be a physicist: though he would have to do it without a degree, since 'Hitler and Mussolini forbade it'.

As usual, I think, he was slightly dramatizing. He did not encounter physics for the first time in the fourth year, as he implies in *The Periodic Table*, but had been taking it all along. The decision did not so much explode in him as strengthen over the years. Physics was his passion throughout university, and he never got less than 30/30 in it. If it had not been for the ludicrous racial laws he would certainly have changed from chemistry to physics; if it had not been for the war, and after it the need to earn a living, he could have continued in physics as a graduate. If it had not been for all these things, he would surely have become a research scientist – possibly an astrophysicist (like the hero, as we shall see, of his last year). That was what he wanted; and he was more than capable of it. The racial laws and the war – Mussolini and Hitler – deprived us of a pure scientist: that seems to me as certain as such things can be.

Except, perhaps, that we must add his own name to Hitler's and Mussolini's. Even war, even Auschwitz, do not have to stop a man doing what he wants to do, if he is willing to take certain risks. Primo was not willing, or not able; and I do not mean only the risk of not being able to afford the wife and children he longed for. I do not think it would have been enough for him to be an ordinary scientist, even a good scientist; he would have wanted to be a great one. I remember the explosions, the fires, the fear of failure at the end of every experiment in *The Periodic Table*; and I think he secretly welcomed not being put to that test. 'I did want to become a scientist,' he told Philip Roth, 'but war and the camp prevented me. I had to limit myself to being a technician all my professional life.' The truth is that limiting himself suited him. Primo Levi himself deprived us of a scientist, and gave us a writer instead, partly because he could tell the world, and himself, that this was not his real job at all. Being a chemical technician was the shield he hid behind. First physics, then writing, were his real adult dreams: the first unlived, the second lived only secretly, behind the shield of chemistry, until his last years.

And what of that last dream? Had it stirred in him yet? No one thinks so. His fellow students, even his friends, saw only the scientist; that is what they were sure he would become. And yet the seed was there. Bianca, for instance, remembers that he already had *la mania di raccontare* – a great love of telling stories, and a great ability too. He'd always been good at explaining scientific questions and answers. Now, in their hunger for knowledge the friends would recount the books they were reading to each other, so that each could 'read' them all; and Primo's accounts were always wonderful – well-shaped, dramatic stories in themselves. And he was already inventing his own. He told his friends 'I mnemagoghi' – the first story of his first collection, not published until 1966 – now, at university. 'And I think,' Bianca says, 'that he wrote it down as well.'

In those last two, most difficult years Primo seems to have overflowed with interest and energy – however sublimated from his various repressions. He crammed all the exams he could (seven of them) into the third-year session, so as to leave his final year free to write not just one but three theses. Then he took an extra course anyway, out of sheer interest – organic preparations, which was so fiendishly difficult that even he called it 'high acrobatics'. For the final year's exams, he prepared Physics with Nereo Pezza, and Physical Chemistry with Clara Moschino; both say it was thanks to him that they passed. Then he helped Edith Weisz with her thesis, saying it was so fascinating he wished he could write it himself.

The explosion of energy in his own three theses was the result of external repression as well: that of the racial laws. Jewish students were officially barred from doing a higher, 'experimental' thesis, which involved original laboratory work. They were restricted to the inferior 'compilatory' kind: a purely theoretical exercise, collating and analysing the history of a chemical problem from the literature. It is not hard to guess which Primo wanted to do; nor that, despite official policy, he still hoped to do it. As he said later, his professors were decent men (with that one exception, or perhaps two); and no one could have been better qualified than he.★ But everyone turned him down: some openly and 'snidely' invoking the racial laws, some making other transparent excuses. Even Ponzio reluctantly said that he could not break the law. Primo grew desperate.

He did finally find someone to take him on: that is the story of 'Potassium', which we shall turn to in a moment. 'Potassium' is a warm and lively story. It hides (as usual) the real frustration of this time for Primo. He wanted to

---

★ No doubt this was also why he took all his exams in the third year – to prove his ability to do an experimental thesis in the fourth.

do an experimental thesis, and couldn't. He wanted to do physics, and couldn't. He told himself that the compilatory thesis in chemistry, officially his main one, wasn't really, and devoted only twenty pages to it; that his 'real' thesis was the subthesis in physics which he eventually managed to do, and which grew to 100 pages and 500 measures and calculations. But he cannot really have been satisfied with either. Both involved enormous amounts of painstaking labour. And in the end the 100 pages offered to his unrequited love, physics, yielded only a few conclusions, and was not superior; while the twenty pages of chemistry, which he had hoped to leave behind, explored a problem which – like so many chemical problems – grew into a metaphor in his mind, and stayed with him to the end of his life.

With his *100/100 e lode*, Primo came equal first with Panetti and Gennari. The other Jewish students also did very well. Emma Vita Levi and Leo Gallico, together with Emma's friend Vanna Rava and a boy called Cesare Dalmasso, came equal second, with 98; Lilia Beer came equal fourth (Sandro was third, with 95). Edith Weisz got 84; but as Fenoglio failed her in the final Mineralogy exam ('I saw his malicious smile,' she says), she was denied her degree until after the war. Ester was pushed back by Milone to 78, which she shared with Franco Momigliano.* Alberto, relaxed as ever, came last of the Jewish students, with 75 – still comfortably ahead of the lowest mark in the class, 65.

So – except for poor, furious Edith – they had their degrees: but what good was a degree to a Jew in 1941, even a *100/100 e lode*? None at all, Primo feared. But he was wrong. This was Italy; as all the legally employable chemists were going off to war, companies simply employed illegal ones. Five months after graduating he was in his first job; and there would be a second before the curtain fell on 8 September 1943. It was the same for the others. Alberto found a job immediately, in a fertilizer factory in Turin. Both Leo and Ester were taken on by nearby companies (Leo in Biella, Ester in Vercelli) to which they would return after the war, and where they would spend their working lives. Emma also found a job in a small factory in Turin; but she had already secretly married her Catholic fiancé, and soon left to join him. Edith, despite the lack of a piece of parchment, found work in Milan, which she kept even beyond 8 September – right up to January 1944.

By then, of course, everything had changed. In January 1944 Primo was in the first circle of hell, with much deeper yet to fall. Alberto was high in the mountains, tasting fear for the first time in his life, face to face with a

---

* Another Franco Momigliano, Lilia Beer's cousin.

German officer on a narrow mountain path. Ester was working with Sandro in Turin, and he had only a few more months to live. Leo was with his family in Biella; a certain partisan leader called Silvio Ortona came looking for him, but missed him, and Leo remained in hiding. Emma was in hiding too, with her new baby daughter; she had just heard, after months of fear, that her husband was in a prisoner-of-war camp in the United States. And soon Edith was living in great luxury and great terror, working for the publishing firm of Hoepli under a false name, and fearing discovery at any moment. But she was bold, and – as the bold so often are – lucky. That had already emerged in their last days at the Institute of Chemistry. Jewish students could graduate, but not be seen to graduate: consequently, they could not be in the graduating class photograph. Edith was the only Jewish student who had not, in fact, graduated; but she alone marched into the photographer's room with the others. So there she is in the photograph, the only Jewish graduate of 1941. If, later, she *had* been caught, and sent to a hell like Primo's, I think she might have survived.

Potassium

In the late 70s or early 80s, on a ferry to Portofino, the theoretical physicist Tullio Regge caught sight of a fellow physicist, Professor Nico Dallaporta of Padua. He'd always wondered, ever since reading *The Periodic Table*. He shouted out: 'Are you Potassium?' Across the deck, Dallaporta smiled. 'In a word,' he called back, 'yes.'

In 1941 Nico Dallaporta was a thirty-year-old teaching assistant in physics at the University of Turin. Some of his teachers, Primo said, were 'barons', for whom their subject was a power base, a route to personal prestige. (Here he no doubt included Milone, Fenoglio, and probably Ponzio.) Others were wholly dedicated scientists (I expect he meant De Paolini, and once again Ponzio). But Dallaporta was neither. He was detached, ironic, almost playful. His 'embarrassed and nobly ironic smile', Primo wrote, seemed to take their side; it seemed to say 'I know you can't do much with this ancient and clapped-out equipment, and anyway these are marginal futilities, and knowledge lives elsewhere; but this is a trade you must work at, and so must I – so please try not to do too much damage, and learn as much as you can.' In short, Primo concluded, 'all the girls on the course fell in love with him'.

Dallaporta was a cosmopolitan, at home in the world. His parents were Greek, he was born in Trieste and grew up in France. As well as Italian he spoke French, Greek, German and English. He was tall, thin, and slightly

Nico Dallaporta, 1941

stooped, and walked with an inimitably long, slow stride. He'd begun as a plain physicist, but had moved towards astrophysics; and had begun, too, as a positivist, but had long since become dissatisfied. He had a new wife and son, to whom he was devoted; but in other ways the real world did not much interest him. He accepted Fascism with a shrug, since at least it kept a kind of order, but he paid it no attention at all. On the contrary, he was automatically tempted to the opposite of whatever it enjoined: especially to a sympathy for its outcasts, such as the Jews. He was quiet, shy, and a very good listener, with an extraordinarily sweet smile. In other words, he was more of a natural aristocrat, and also more of a natural democrat, than anyone Primo had ever met; and quite simply a delightful person.

By January of his last year Primo had approached all his professors about an experimental thesis, and been turned away. One chill evening – so he tells us in 'Potassium' – he was cycling hopelessly home, after the fourth or fifth rejection. In the mist and dark he glimpsed a tall, thin figure, slightly stooped, walking with a long, slow stride. He passed him; he went back, and passed him again. Finally he thought that 'I risked nothing but another rejection', and asked Dallaporta if he would accept him for experimental work in his school. 'He looked at me, surprised and amused,' Primo wrote. Then, 'in his quiet, well-bred voice', he 'replied with two words from the Gospel: "*Viemmi retro*", "Follow me."'

At the time, Dallaporta was working on (among other things) electric dipole movements: that is to say, on the behaviour of polar molecules, which orient themselves in an electric field in a magnet-like way. They would, or might, behave differently, according to whether they were in diluted or in pure solutions. Dallaporta was not a chemist, and did not know how to purify the required solutions; he was also (in Primo's words) 'nobly lazy'; and last but not least he was glad to help a brilliant student defy a cruel and stupid law. So it was that Primo found himself painstakingly distilling benzene (and chlorobenzene, and chlorophenols, and many other liquids); then painstakingly making the 500 calculations of his subthesis in physics, *Dielectrical Behaviour of the Ternary System Benzene-Chlorobenzene-Chloroform.*

'Potassium' describes this work, and at the same time a great new friendship – with the one as an image and metaphor for the other, in the chemical crossover which is Primo Levi's special invention.

This time it was not a friendship of opposites. Despite the differences in age and experience of the world, and despite the fact that one was a physicist, the other a chemist, what both first noticed were their great similarities. They both loved science, especially physics; they both loved literature, especially Huxley, Conrad, and Primo's great companion Thomas Mann. They were both antifascist – passive for so long, but united now in open opposition. Both had a calm, detached, quietly ironic manner; behind which both were intensely serious, and obsessed with understanding nothing less than the universe as a whole.

They had endless enthusiastic conversations, and hugely admired each other. To this day Dallaporta says that Primo Levi was one of the two most intelligent people he has ever known. He was amazed at his precocious intellect, at his extraordinary perfectionism and self-control; and he pitied the isolation they brought him. In return Primo almost hero-worshipped the young Assistant. He was an astrophysicist ('in flesh and blood!') and a linguist; beneath his humorous resignation he was a visionary, a dreamer, and – as Primo's own request had revealed – a brave, uncorrupted man. Not even of Sandro had he written, as he wrote of Dallaporta in 'Potassium': 'To be the Assistant's disciple was a constant enjoyment for me, a bond never before experienced, without a shadow, made more intense by the certainty that the relationship was mutual.' Sandro, Alberto and his other opposites were ideals he longed to approach, but knew he could never become. Dallaporta was like an ideal version of himself, which he *could*, perhaps, become: the scientist and observer, detached from the world, but at peace with it. Outwardly there were differences: but inwardly and essentially Dallaporta was like an older, more perfect twin.

Even inwardly, however, there was one great, invisible difference between the Assistant and his assistant. It was what lay behind Dallaporta's detachment, behind his suspicion 'of every activity that set itself a goal'. Yes, he too loved physics, especially astrophysics, and he too was 'diligent and eager'. And yet he soon confirmed what Primo had already guessed: that for him even astrophysics was a 'marginal futility', and knowledge lived elsewhere. Science deciphered only the world of appearances; 'Truth lay beyond, inaccessible to our telescopes.' Dallaporta's real quest, and the real centre of his life, was not science but religion.

And in his religion too he was a visionary, original and unconfined. He was neither Catholic nor Orthodox, as he had been born. He agreed with René Guénon, whose works he had recently discovered: all the great religions expressed one and the same Truth, at different metaphysical levels. According to Guénon, the most profound way of approaching God and understanding the world was through the Hindu Vedanta. Dallaporta had become deeply convinced of this: he was a new and passionate adept of Hindu philosophy.

This became the heart of their conversations. Dallaporta did his best 'to harpoon my last hippogriff', as Primo put it in 'Potassium' – to prove to him that his new choice, physics, was no better than his old; that western science in general – that is to say, Primo's whole world view – was a wrong road. It was the key to the domination of the planet, even of the universe. But what did that matter, if there was an infinite number of universes, and if the point of the soul's journey through them was only to escape them, and so find eternal bliss? This was the true road of understanding, which he was travelling 'with effort, wonder and profound joy'. Would Primo not follow him?

Dallaporta was Primo's ideal; and his God was not the Father of Judaeo-Christianity, but a rational, impersonal principle. If Primo Levi could ever have accepted a religion, it might have been this one. Perhaps he was even tempted: 'It was a terrifying request,' he says, and one is only terrified by what one can imagine. But he did not accept. 'Potassium' is the point in Primo's young manhood when he finally rejected religion, and decided, for good, for material reality and for science.

It is clear even from the surface of the story that this is its heart – though the point is ironically made, as ever. 'I did not mount the new gigantic hippogriff the Assistant offered me,' Primo wrote.

During those months the Germans destroyed Belgrade, broke the Greek resistance, invaded Crete from the air: that was the Truth, that was Reality. There were no escape routes, or not for me. Better to remain on the Earth, playing with the dipoles for lack of anything better, purify benzene, and prepare for an unknown but imminent and certainly tragic future.

The closer one looks, however, the clearer it becomes that the essence of this encounter is religion. The Assistant calls Primo not his student, or his assistant, but his disciple; and this description Primo accepts and repeats. But the clearest sign is the very first one. When Primo asks if the Assistant would accept him for experimental work, he replies with those two words from the Gospel: Christ's own words, 'Follow me.' From the start, that is, the discipleship he offers is not scientific, but religious. 'I was much too shy at the time to affirm myself in such an absolute way,' Dallaporta says; and he is almost certain that he did not really speak those words. Indeed, though they are beautifully appropriate to the story – perhaps its most beautiful moment of all – they are, if we stop to think of it, not at all appropriate to the well-bred, ironic Assistant, who is as far from solemnity and self-importance as it is possible to be. In fact, we can be certain, they are one of Primo's literary inventions, artfully placed to signal the inner meaning of the story.

Nico Dallaporta may never have quoted Christ: but he and Primo did have those eager conversations; he did try to persuade Primo to share his new religious passion; and Primo did refuse. He refused, no doubt, for many closely argued reasons; but Dallaporta remembers one in particular.

He told Primo the Hindu theory of death and rebirth: that souls pass through an infinite number of existences, in the infinite number of universes; with the ultimate aim of reaching such a high degree of spirituality that they escape from the infinite chain of death and rebirth altogether. Each time, Dallaporta explained, the soul is reborn into its new world at a level dictated by the degree of spirituality it reached in the last one; so that higher and lower levels of being, inequalities determined ineluctably from birth, are inseparable from existence itself, and part of the nature of God, as it manifests itself in any possible world.

This picture Primo rejected violently. It seemed to him, Dallaporta remembers, the 'utmost injustice' that men should not be born equal. 'And I think that is the main reason why he refused to climb on my "hippogriff".'

The rejection of injustice is one of Primo Levi's greatest themes, in both life and work. He had a passion for equality; it was the one point on which he allowed himself to feel – and speak, and write – almost violently. Equality of respect, the equal right to dignity of all creatures (which incidentally is also a Hindu idea), was his highest personal principle, and the single greatest motor of all his writing. It does not make it any less a moral principle that it came out of his most personal battles: against others, when they treated him as an inferior; against himself, when he was tempted on the contrary to feel superior. These struggles of his early life – between his senses of inferiority and superiority, between the need to win, and the need not to win – thus lie behind 'Potassium', as they lay behind 'Hydrogen'. They led him to his passion for equality; and his passion for equality led him, for all his liking and admiration, to refuse to follow Dallaporta. Dallaporta was a natural democrat, as I've said, making friends among his students – with Alberto, for instance, as well as Primo – and willing to look for distinction anywhere. But he looked, precisely, for distinction. 'To me,' he says, 'inequality is strongly inherent in existence itself; whether I like it or not, I cannot but accept it as a matter of fact.' This Primo would always refuse to do; and that was the deepest difference between them.

It led to many others. Nico Dallaporta is humane, disengaged, pessimistic, and fundamentally conservative. He has lived without guilt, on the contrary with delight to himself and others, a highly civilized life, dedicated to his twin abstract passions, astrophysics and Hindu philosophy. Primo toiled in the lower reaches of industrial chemistry, lived plainly, even austerely, and, resisting deep instincts to the contrary, strove always towards optimistic engagement in human affairs. Dallaporta is still deeply religious. For Primo the question occasionally recurred, as we shall see; but ever since the decision of 'Potassium' (or even before), that road was closed to him. Primo, finally, was a genius, while Dallaporta is only an extremely gifted man. Even these are certainly not all the reasons. But fifteen years after his student's death, at over ninety the Assistant is still alive and writing.

★   ★

Primo spares us the measures and calculations of the dipole experiment. What he describes is the first stage of his task: the distillation (or rather the rectifying, which is the distillation by fractions) of benzene.

After two days of careful cooking he has a fraction of reasonable purity. Now he has to distil a second time, in the presence of sodium. In the basement of the Institute of Physics he finds hundreds of ampoules and phials, untouched for generations; but no sodium. Finally he finds a small phial of potassium. 'Potassium is sodium's twin,' he tells us; it will do.

He puts a tiny pea of potassium in his flask of benzene, and begins again. Though potassium is sodium's twin, 'it reacts with air and water with even greater energy': on contact with water it even ignites. He treats it, therefore, with the utmost respect. When the operation is over he delicately removes the pea of potassium, wraps it in a piece of filter paper, and buries the corpse in the courtyard.

He stores his first small treasure of pure benzene, and cleans his apparatus. He puts the empty flask under the tap, and turns on the water. There is a thump, a flash leaps from the throat of the flask, and the curtains next to the washbasin catch fire. By the time he manages to put out the flames the room is full of smoke, and the shutters permanently blistered.

When he checks later, he finds a tiny white spot on one of the pieces of the flask. A minute particle of potassium had stuck there: which had been enough to react with the water, and set fire to the benzene vapours. And now comes the crossover, the Primo Levi leap from the laboratory to life, from chemistry to us. In the ironic eyes of the Assistant he reads his conclusion: 'Better not to do than do, better meditate than act': better his cool and godlike astrophysics than Primo's kitchen chemistry, as messy and dangerous as life itself. But he, Primo, thinks of another moral, 'more earthly and concrete': 'that one must distrust the almost-the-same . . . , the practically identical . . . all surrogates and all patchwork.' For 'sodium is potassium's twin, but with sodium nothing would have happened'. He himself was the surrogate, the practically identical, in this experiment: if the Assistant had done it himself, perhaps nothing would have happened.

This, with its stubborn trace of self-doubt, is part of what Primo meant, I think, in his moral to the story. And more. 'The differences can be small, but they can lead to radically different consequences, like railway switch points,' he wrote: and I think he had in mind the differences between himself and Dallaporta. Not necessarily all the same ones that struck me; but certainly the main one, the religious difference at the heart of 'Potassium'. By 1973 (the date of the typescript), the consolations of religion, and the requirement not to accept them, were subjects he had written about more than once. He could not have foreseen the ultimate consequences of his stoic refusal of this, or any other, consolation. But he had already experienced some. And an older, less voluntary religious difference – the fact that he was a Jew, and Dallaporta was not – had long ago led to a fairly radical difference in their lives.

'The chemist's trade,' Primo concluded in 'Potassium', 'consists in good part of being aware of these differences, of knowing them from close up, and foreseeing their effects. And not only the chemist's trade.' He meant, of course, the trade of understanding life; and especially the distilled version of it which is writing.

There is a striking passage in 'Potassium', which recalls another passage so closely as to be its twin. Distilling is beautiful, Primo wrote, because it involves a metamorphosis: from liquid to vapour (invisible), and back again; in this double journey, up and down, purity is attained, an ambiguous and fascinating condition, which starts with chemistry and goes very far.

The twin passage comes at the end of 'Carbon'. In it the carbon atom enters a cell of Primo's brain, the very cell which decides the next mark he will make upon the page:

a double leap, up and down, between two levels of energy, guides this hand of mine to make this dot upon the page: this one.

Thus are writing and chemistry once more brought together, through the same vision of a double movement, 'up and down', between two states or levels of energy. The aim of distilling is to boil down and purify: *to clarify*, as cooks say, who are chemists' older sisters. There is no better word for the act of the writer; at least of the writer Primo Levi. And the aim of writing, for him, was to meet another human being in that dot on the page. Writing was his own double leap, in which he transformed chemistry into communication and back again. In writing he moved between the two levels of his own being, his rational need for understanding, and his emotional need for contact and communication. In 'Potassium' he calls distilling 'almost a religious act', in which from 'imperfect material' you obtain the essence and the spirit. In 'Carbon' he recognizes once again the imperfection of his material of words – 'the trade of clothing facts in words is bound by its very nature to fail'. Yet the ravishing paragraph which follows – and the whole of 'Carbon', which it concludes – is a celebration of life as profound and beautiful as a prayer. It *is* a prayer; a chemist's prayer. Writing 'Carbon', I want to say, was 'almost a religious act' for Primo Levi. And not only 'Carbon'. All his writing, his double leap between chemistry and communication, was his form of religious devotion; his surrogate, his almost-the-same.

Walden's Inversion

For the first months after graduating in 1941 Primo had no job, and no prospect, he thought, of getting one. He was also still without love, and without prospects there either. But he had an idea.

It was, he tells the Signora in *The Double Bond*, a compensatory idea. Very well, he was alone, and a Jew: but he would show them what he could do. At twenty-two, he would make a fundamental contribution to chemistry. He would carry out an *experimentum crucis*, alone and unaided; alone and unaided he would demonstrate a theory which had come to him out of the inferior work he'd been forced to do for his main dissertation.

In fact, he did the experiment, but not alone and unaided: that was his first simplification for the sake of the story. He did it with his friend Guido Bonfiglioli; and when I tell Guido what Primo wrote about it forty-five years later, he says that there are many more. The science is oversimplified, he says, to the point of distortion. I expect that is true; Primo was looking for metaphors, as always, not for scientific accuracy. With apologies to science, therefore, let us follow him.

Walden's Inversion was a hot scientific topic in 1941, Primo says. It was where the revolution in physics was beginning to reach chemistry (well, beginning to reach Italy, Guido says). Fifty years or so before, a German professor called Walden had done something which could not be done, if the molecule was the solid little package that chemists had once imagined. There were more than twenty current theories on how it had been possible, all involving the new, non-solid ideas of physics − ideas of waves, for instance, and of the vibration and rotation of atoms. In the conclusion to his dissertation, Primo had named the theory which seemed to him the best. Now he would test and prove it.

What Walden had done was to take a compound containing a carbon atom, and derive from it other compounds, which behaved in ways they should not have done. The details of this rogue behaviour are complex, but they amount to this. From each kind of compound it should be possible to derive only compounds of the same kind; but Walden's derivatives were of both. And here is where Primo found his metaphorical significance. For the carbon atom in the compounds was of a particular kind, which is called asymmetric. And though not all asymmetric substances are living, all living substances are asymmetric. Moreover, of the two possible kinds of asymmetry, left and right, all living organisms on earth, with very few and marginal exceptions, are of the left kind. What Walden had done was to derive left compounds from right ones and vice versa. In other words, he had derived substances with a key quality of living organisms from ones without it, and vice versa.

Primo explains to the Signora the theory he thought the correct one. Picture the asymmetrical carbon atom as a pyramid with a triangular base, he says, with each of its four vertices attached to a different atom. At certain temperatures, with certain reagents, and with certain atoms, the atom attached to the apex is replaced by another; and when this happens, it is as though the structure becomes unstable. It begins to oscillate; and its base turns over and back again repeatedly, like an umbrella blown inside-out and back again by the wind. Now, therefore, the atom that was at the left vertex of the base is repeatedly on the right, and vice versa; and if the oscillation stops at the appropriate phase, the impossible has happened: an inversion has occurred. In other words, in a pictorial representation of what has happened, you have got a left atom from a right one, and vice versa.

This theory was, it turns out, the right one; and today Walden's Inversion is part of a well-known problem in chemistry called 'double oscillation'. But to prove it right was another matter altogether: especially since Primo had added another idea of his own. Some researchers had claimed that the inversion occurred when the base atoms were very light, ceased to occur when their atomic weight increased, but occurred again when it increased still further. Primo's idea was that the phenomenon of inversion might be periodic: that it might appear and disappear regularly, as the weight of the base atoms increased.

Confident of his own powers of patience and rigour, at least, he determined to produce the required atoms of increasing weight himself. Or rather, of decreasing weight, since for this operation there was a method to hand. It was called 'the degradation of Hofmann'; and it would enable him to reduce the number of atoms in a fatty acid one by one. He assembled several such acids; and began his degradations.

On the text-book page it had all looked easy. But the book did not tell you how much effort, how much cost and risk, would be required to translate each short line into reality. Every step of Hofmann's degradation meant, in hard fact, four. Much glassware was broken; and with it, the last of Primo's childhood illusions. Finally another disaster happened – not fire this time but flood, when one of the fatty acids overheated, and filled the room with foam. 'I was forced to stop, my inferiority made manifest, in the middle of the second step,' Primo told the Lady. So much for showing them what he could do; so much for making a fundamental contribution to chemistry at twenty-two.

Thus, from his first (and only) attempt at pure scientific research he came away defeated. His intellectual life, throughout his boyhood and youth, had itself been a Walden's Inversion – an oscillation between confidence in his abilities, and fear they were not enough for what he wanted to do. Now, his first adult battle with 'real-life chemistry' left him in the negative phase. In his defeat he saw a general lesson, as ever: *Woe to him who works with inadequate means, woe to him who presumes upon his powers.* This was the moral with which he set out on life: the moral, we might call it, of the Tortoise.

And perhaps we may see a second crossover in this chemical inversion. Since life on earth is (as he put it) built on the left model, when the atom oscillates between left and right, it is oscillating between the model of life and the model of not-life. Perhaps Walden's Inversion caught Primo Levi's imagination at twenty-two because it hinted at two models for himself, one of not-life and one of life: the lonely theorist in the lab, and the living, loving, acting man. Walden had managed to transform the one into the other; but he, Primo, had failed. He would mostly continue to fail. Only a very few times in his life would he become sufficiently unstable to flip over, like the carbon atom of *The Double Bond*, into his impossible, longed-for opposite.

Alberto

Alberto

When I opened the door to Alberto Salmoni I couldn't believe my eyes. He was seventy-five years old, he belonged to the past, and I had rarely seen such a handsome man. He was tall, slim and very upright. People had talked of his beautiful black hair: it was grey-white now, and short, but as thick and vigorous as ever, as though his irrepressible vitality were bursting out of his head. His skin was tanned, and his tawny eyes set close together; when he smiled – as he was doing now – he looked like a fox. He was dressed casually in a soft grey polo shirt, black trousers, and an old overcoat which hung elegantly from his shoulders.

He didn't want to wait for the lift, though I lived on the top floor. By the time we reached my flat I was convinced we'd changed places, and it was I who was seventy-five. As I made coffee, he chatted and joked as though we'd known each other for years. He was putting me at my ease, I realized, rather than I him; but then I needed it more than he did. How dared he be so handsome, so straight and loose-limbed? Didn't he realize he wasn't twenty any more? No, he didn't; and neither could I.

We sat down, and I switched on the tape recorder. People sometimes balk at being recorded, but Alberto didn't seem to mind that. It was sitting still he found hard. He kept jumping up and down, taking our coffee cups to the sink, fetching me a pen from my desk, then a map to show me how far it is to Trieste, where he and Primo had cycled in around (he is vague about dates) 1939.

As we go on he gets interested, and when he is interested he is very acute. But when we go on still further he's restless again. He doesn't like to remember, it makes him sad; he lives in the present more than anyone over the age of seven I've ever known. And he doesn't like to put things into words. 'I'm not an intellectual,' he says – though I know he can answer the kind of question I've just asked if he wants to, since he's already done so several times. But he only did it to please me. Questions displease him; as though he'd brought me a bouquet of flowers, and all I'd done was ask how much they cost.

The only sign of age in him is deafness: and when I press him he doesn't seem to hear. Perhaps, though, this isn't deafness: perhaps he was always like this, shutting out what he didn't want to hear. (And now things are taking their revenge, and even what he wants to hear is disappearing.) Instead he slips off, smiling, into a private dream. Yes, he was always like this, I'm sure. People have said so – Alberto the dreamer, they say, *nelle nuvole* – 'head in the clouds', shaking their heads in fond despair. He was a wonderful climber, they say – but as often as not on the wrong mountain; he was clever and full of ideas, but he never settled down. I gather, I say now, that he did many jobs in his life? But he has clearly heard the same accusations I have, and denies them hotly: no, no, only a few jobs, and most of them in chemistry. But it's true (his smile returns) that he would have liked to be many things besides a chemist: an actor, for example, or a singer. I can easily imagine Alberto as a singer, but I can't imagine him as a chemist at all. I don't suppose anyone could, even when he was one. That is his secret: you pick up Alberto's dream life, not his real one; and he picks up yours.

Now, he says, he will show me Turin: that will tell me more about Primo than anything he could say. And after that, if I still have legs (he casts a dark look at my desk), we will go for a walk, or even a climb: that will teach me even more. And he sets off down my five flights of stone stairs without a backward glance, never doubting I will follow.

We had lunch first, which is serious business for Alberto, so we didn't get beyond Turin that day. And while we were eating, a thick December fog closed in, as though to keep Primo safely hidden. Alberto insisted we get into his car anyway. We crossed the river, and began to climb the *collina*.

Here the fog was even denser, hiding not only Primo and Turin, but also the road. Alberto did not slow down; indeed it seemed to me he drove even faster. But I felt his foxy glance on my face, and stayed silent. 'Soon,' he said, 'we'll be above the fog, and there'll be bright sunshine.' 'I don't believe you,' I replied, and the next moment it happened. He laughed with pleasure; then shook his head in mock concern. 'You're worse than Primo,' he said.

★ ★

A few weeks later he rang: the weather had turned, it was time for my next lesson. He would take me to Musinè, a small mountain – no more than a hill – where Primo had often gone for Sunday walks with his friends, right up to the end.

Musinè soon appeared, looking strangely smooth and bare in the distance. It *was* bare, Alberto said. Although it was so low, above a certain level nothing would grow on it; botanists came from around the world, but no one could explain why. He parked beside a football field, and we started to climb. At first the path was wide and laid with stones, almost like a cobbled road, with a small chapel at every corner. But soon both cobbles and chapels ended, and it was a narrow dirt track the rest of the way.

The track became steep; and once again Alberto and I performed that impossible change of places, like the left and right sides of Primo's atom. He moved steadily, easily, as though he were indeed on a Sunday stroll; I fell behind, and felt my legs, and breathed like a train. He waited for me, but not for long: I could see him poised like a cat, and as soon as I was close enough to hear his even breathing, he leapt off again. I didn't let myself stop, and tried not to show my fatigue; and suddenly I realized it had gone. We settled to a steady pace, Alberto lengthening the gap between us, I closing it up again. I started to match my stride to his, placing my feet in the marks he'd made. He turned his left foot out, I noticed, as though he were always about to turn left. Now I was sad: that was the sort of small, living detail I would never know about Primo.

Alberto was waiting by some sharp, snaggle-toothed rocks. These, he said gravely, belonged to the witches who'd cast the spell of barrenness on the mountain. He stayed beside me then as we entered a wood. The trees were small and thin, and strangely bent in different directions, as though scattered by an alarm. Blue sky showed through them; but it was darker here, and still. 'This is our *selva selvaggia*,' Alberto whispered. When I looked bewildered he shook his head at my ignorance. 'Dante,' he said. 'I'll tell you.' We sat down under one of the trees, and he began to recite, as naturally as he'd breathed.

'Nel mezzo del cammin di nostra vita
mi ritrovai per una selva oscura
che la diritta via era smarrita.

Quanto a dir qual era è cosa dura
questa selva selvaggia e aspre e forte
che nel pensier rinova la paura . . .'

'In the middle of our life's journey
I found myself in a dark wood,
having lost my way.

I cannot tell how hard it was,
that cruel wood, so bitter and strong
that at the thought alone my fear returns . . .'

I kept quite still, afraid he might stop; but he went on, following Dante in his half-sleep or swoon, through the valley of terror to the bottom of the hill. Now Alberto raised his eyes and gazed at a distant mountain.

'Guardai in alto e vidi le sue spalle
vestite già de' raggi del pianeta – '

'I raised my eyes and saw its form
clothed in the rays of the sun . . .'

Here he did stop: he couldn't remember the next line. He tried for a moment, as Primo had tried to remember another of Dante's lines, in a true cruel wood, long ago. Primo had sought the words through their rhyme, Alberto sought them through their rhythm. But they wouldn't come. Never mind, let them go. He loved these best, anyway; and he repeated them softly: '*Guardai in alto e vidi le sue spalle, vestite già de' raggi del pianeta . . .*' Of course, I thought – his beloved mountains. *Their* beloved mountains, that Primo could not bear to think of, in that wood: '*my mountains, that appeared brown in the evening when I came home by train from Milan to Turin . . .*' Yes – 'brown', because clothed in the rays of the sun . . .

It was almost evening now too, and there was no need to go any higher. We turned downwards. Down is easy; but once more I couldn't keep pace with Alberto. He ran, weaving from side to side to control his speed, like the partisans I'd seen in films. Or like a dancer spinning across a stage. I remembered Clara Moschino telling me about Sandro's walk, *pom-pom*; and Alberto's, more graceful ('like everything he did'): '*Come se ballasse,*' she'd said: as though he were dancing.

Watching him disappear, I thought: it's terrible, but he still has the same effect on women he always did. He's seventy-five years old, and I'm half in love with Alberto Salmoni. When I rejoined him at last I couldn't look at him. Instead, I looked at our shadows, cast on the hillside by the late afternoon sun. As we walked, I realized that that was what I was in love with: Alberto's shadow, the shadow of his young self, just behind him; and behind that, the shadows of two other young men as well.

What shadow did he see? Suddenly he took my hand. For a moment I left it in his warm hand; but then I withdrew it. Alberto looked crestfallen, like a little boy. 'It's impossible,' I said. 'Why?' he asked, and I saw he really didn't know. I thought of the greatest impossibility of Primo's life, the shadow of this one. 'What would Primo say?' I asked him. '*Davvero!*' he replied – 'Truly.' He took my hand again, kissed it, and let it go.

⋆   ⋆

When I'm next in Turin, Alberto says, 'You must climb a real mountain now.' When I hesitate, he turns his tawny gaze on me and smiles. 'Don't worry,' he says; and I don't.

The only danger is his driving. Alberto drives as he does everything – elegantly and casually, with one hand. We leave Turin so fast he misses our turning, and blithely does a U-turn in the middle of a furious, fist-shaking road. Then we begin to climb; and he takes the hairpin bends at such speed I wonder if I shall die with Alberto Salmoni. With an innocent grin he tells me the story of a local girl who leapt off this very mountain to escape a seducer, and who, for her chastity, was saved in mid-air by an angel. But then her heart was touched with pride, and she bragged to her friends of the miracle that had saved her; until they challenged her to leap again, and she did, and died.

We stop near some low, weather-stained houses. A pair of goats is tethered on the hillside above the last house; there is a moment, as we walk towards it, when they look exactly as though they are standing on the roof. An old man greets us effusively in Italian. Alberto replies in Piedmontese; and I wait for a while in polite incomprehension. Then the old man gives me a stump-toothed smile, and asks if we would like to buy one of his goats – or both, if we desire. Thank you, we say, not just at the moment. 'Well, if you know anyone,' he says. As we set off he calls after us again: 'If you know anyone . . .'

It's about two o'clock, a cool, bright March day. For the first hour or so of our climb I keep up well with Alberto. It's getting colder, but I'm exhilarated. Then, as the trees grow thinner, patches of snow appear. Soon they are no longer patches, but a field; and the field slowly deepens. We've only city shoes on, which are soon soaked through. The bottoms of my jeans quickly follow; so, I see, do the bottoms of Alberto's beautiful grey trousers. He throws me a hilarious, challenging look, and climbs faster.

Half an hour later we are sinking in to our knees, and Alberto tells me to step into the holes he's made. Now my left foot turns out as well. When the snow covers our knees he has to shorten his stride, or I can't reach his next foothole. Briefly we try it with me leading; but after half a dozen steps I'm exhausted, and when Alberto steps into my footholes he sinks in up to his thighs.

He takes the lead again. Perhaps an hour passes, perhaps more, I can't tell. I hang on to the sound of Alberto's laboured breathing like a rope; until I remember that he *is*, in fact, seventy-five and I may die with him after all. But his long back still has a spring in the shoulders, and whenever he turns to give me an encouraging glance he looks irritatingly happy. I've just worked out that it's fifty-four years since Giulia Colombo nearly died with him in Cogne, when we emerge from the last windblown trees on to a rocky promontory. It's not the peak; but to my great relief Alberto strides to the edge and beckons me to sit down. We sit there, surrounded by sky, our breath still cutting our lungs like knives. Suddenly I feel extraordinarily alive. Alberto turns from the sky to me, and there is a strangely familiar glitter in his eyes.

Somehow we got down; and though I shivered for hours after, I wasn't cold, and I didn't catch cold either. In fact, I'd never felt better in my life. I too had learned something by doing it – and Primo was right, it was the best learning I'd ever done. I'd tasted danger, and therefore safety; safety unrisked is safety unnoticed, and unloved. Alberto had taught me this, as he and Sandro had taught it to Primo; and in the same outrageous way. As we were parting he told me, with his foxy grin, that the old man had warned him there was still snow on the mountain. He was clearly hoping this would make me furious, but instead it made me even happier. I burst out laughing, Alberto joined in, and in our laughter I clearly heard not only two young voices, but four.

5. Nickel:
1941–2

Ennio Mariotti, on left

Though Primo was so ready to grow up, several things held him back. One was his own self-distrust ('Woe to him who presumes upon his powers'); another was his mother. Now a new oscillation began in him: a duel between his desire to go and his desire to stay; between his father in him, and his mother.

When Primo was only sixteen, and he himself only fifty-seven, Cesare had had an operation for bowel cancer. After that even he tried to take more exercise, and live a healthier life; but it was too late. By 1937, though he still managed to save his son from the consequences of involuntary draft-dodging, he was already gravely ill. During Primo's last university years he could do no more than sit, play Tarot, and listen to music.

I do not know what happened, in this period, to his secretary-lover of so many years; or what went on between him and Rina. But I think we can imagine. Outside Corso Re Umberto 75 – genuinely now, not only in her mind – were persecution and danger. Inside it was the man she had been punishing for his abandonment of her for twenty years, and who was about to abandon her for ever. I imagine that she devoted herself scrupulously to his care; and that her every move was a reproach, and an expression of victory. His lover was surely banned, and her husband what he should always have been – hers alone. Even the fact that he was dying was, perhaps, a bitter victory, as well as a defeat. For day by day death was extinguishing her enemy in him: his appetite, his lust, his *joie de vivre*.

Clara Moschino remembers that Primo was very depressed by his father's illness. He himself said that he 'suffered from it, but at the same time rejected it', because he was too young to understand the significance of death. That was possibly true; at least, it would be true of most sixteen- to twenty-two-year-olds. But Primo Levi was not most sixteen- to twenty-two-year-olds, and already then had more than a nodding acquaintance with the idea of death. What he suffered from, and at the same time rejected, was more likely to have been the last struggle between his parents. That struggle would have gone on in him as well, since he more than half admired his father's *joie de vivre*, and yet in their battle to the death took his mother's side. Cesare Levi's last illness was the second great suffering which Primo repressed in those years, and which drove him to his compensatory excesses in chemistry and the mountains. Its strange, deceptive shape – punishment by care, revenge through sacrifice – would reappear in his life; and also in Rina's.

Then, as though a dying husband were not enough, her oldest and truest support also began to weaken. In 1938 her father was nearly seventy, and having to twist and turn to save his beloved shop. He did save it; but the extra effort may have killed him. In around that year his diabetes worsened. He became so enormous that a special chair had to be built for him. He grew blind; his legs were covered in sores, and in the end partly amputated. On 12 June 1941 Primo graduated; two weeks later his grandfather was dead. It must have seemed to his mother, and perhaps to him, that death could hardly wait for him to be fledged before pushing him into the front line of defence for his family.

A few months later there was a sudden flurry of antisemitic activity in Turin. An amateurish effort was made to set fire to the great door of the synagogue; leaflets howling *Death to the Jews* were thrown into the courtyard of the *scuola ebraica*, and stuck on to neighbourhood walls. All this was organized by the German consulate; with their usual distaste for their allies, Fascist city officials removed them. But the group of friends at the *scuola ebraica* decided to do something for themselves as well, and took turns standing guard at the school gates. Primo took part 'at least once', as he put it, in this new, more active form of self-defence.

Shortly afterwards the attack escalated: posters attacking the Jews, along with other 'enemies of Italy', were put up in the Via Roma, in the heart of the city. Now their response grew too. Franco Momigliano mobilized the friends: Euge, who was home from Milan for the weekend; Alberto, who arrived wearing a windbreaker and 'a stern and determined air'; Bianca, of course, and many others. For several evenings in a row they set off, in pairs – one boy, one girl – for the Piazza Carlo Felice. From there they calmly proceeded down the Via Roma, stopping at each fat Fascist column, and ceremoniously stripping it of its poster.

Euge says that no one said anything, or even appeared to notice. Primo, as usual, makes the event sound faintly comic, noting that each couple carried a plastic bucket (no doubt to put the posters in: defying the state was one thing, littering the streets was another). But in fact, of course, what they were doing was more than mildly dangerous. When their parents heard of it they were furious. What on earth did they think they were doing? – It was perfectly pointless, and only fed the antisemites' fire; the thing to do was to keep one's head down, give them no excuses, and let it all blow over . . . The young did not agree. This, Euge says, was the moment when the group of friends finally rejected the age-old Jewish tradition of endurance, and chose action. It was also the first public demonstration against Fascism in Turin by any group, Jewish or non-Jewish.

But though he knew all about it, Primo was not there. Now, this was quite strange. He was a central member of the group of friends, and had partaken in everything up to now. It was so strange that Euge, for instance, was perfectly certain that he'd partaken in this too. But Primo could not pretend to a distinction he did not deserve – he found it hard enough to admit to the ones he did. When Euge reminisced about those heady nights in Turin's Jewish newsletter, *Ha Keillah*, in 1978, Primo wrote to put the record straight, in the next issue but one: '*Io non c'ero*': 'I was not there.'

He explained why, on several occasions: because he was working away from Turin, and because his father was dying. The second was true; but the first almost certainly wasn't. He began his first job in December (unless he was romancing, on the day Japan attacked Pearl Harbor, and America entered the war: 7 December). The poster nights were in mid-October. Primo was still in Turin.

Why, then, did he not take up his plastic bucket, and march into battle with his friends? Surely because the second reason was enough. His father was dying, his grandfather was already dead; he was his mother's only defence against the world. She would have let him know this, and he would have felt it. Perhaps she heard of the plan, and begged him not to go; perhaps she said that it was too dangerous, that the worry would kill his father before the cancer did, and what would she do with a husband dead, and a son in prison? – Perhaps, in other words, she made him a classic Jewish mother's scene. Or perhaps she didn't even have to. Perhaps Primo knew every word she'd say before she said it; and perhaps he decided himself not to go. Because of the past, because of the present, his first adult responsibility was to his mother. His first adult responsibility, therefore, was to remain the good, safe, obedient boy.*

Primo Levi, then, did not take part in the first public act of resistance in Turin. Nonetheless he recalled its details better than most of its participants. Euge, for instance, remembered that the passers-by, determined to enjoy their evening stroll, had simply ignored the acts of sabotage going on under their noses. But Primo, who had clearly questioned everyone eagerly – perhaps enviously – reported that several of the reactions had been still more tolerant. 'Don't you realize this is *dangerous*?' a few strollers had said, kindly, to the saboteurs. 'You could end up in jail!' The saboteurs thanked them, and moved on to the next column.

For the first few nights (Primo wrote) nothing else happened. Only on the last night did the police make a reluctant appearance. They were no more on the side of the posters than the public were; and these saboteurs were all well-behaved, well-dressed young *dottori* and *dottoresse*.† The poor policemen were caught between fear for their jobs, and fear of having to do them. The first won, but only just. They asked for everyone's papers, and told them all to go home; but with 'visible fear', Primo wrote, 'of possible complications'.

The scene was a perfect one for his descriptive talents, balanced between farce and fear, comedy and terror. This atmosphere was intensified, he wrote, by one of the friends, Guido Foa.

. . . Guido, who was blond and over six feet tall, did not look very Jewish; nor did he share the fatal Jewish tendency to intellectuality. He would have liked to become a comic actor, and indeed I think had already appeared on stage, in several sketches written by himself. Towering over the crowd, he too began to demand '*Your doguments*', in a strong southern accent – even of the police themselves, who were in civilian clothes; and then to bawl nonsensical orders at them, still in his southern

---

* And why did he lie about the reason? Surely because there was a limit even to *his* honesty. He would not take credit for an act of courage he didn't commit; but nor would he want people to know that the only reason he didn't commit it was that, at twenty-two, he still had to obey his mother.

† All university graduates in Italy are called 'Doctor'.

accent, until the confusion was extreme.* It is almost unbearable to recall that fantastic and hilarious appearance of his now, for only a few years later Guido, like so many of our friends of that time, was destined to die in Auschwitz.

This was Primo's position at the end of 1941: his father was dying. He had no love, no work, and his 'fundamental contribution to chemistry' had failed. The Germans had poured through Poland, Norway, Holland, France, Greece, Yugoslavia and the Russian steppes like a flood; and he could not even tear down a few posters on the Via Roma. In the oscillation of his life, it can be no exaggeration to say that this was a negative phase.

What happened now? Something at once ordinary and miraculous, like the hydrogen he'd made in a jar at fifteen, but which at the same time burned in the sun and stars. The doorbell rang.

The doorbell rang. It was a tall, thin young man, in the uniform of a Lieutenant of the Italian Army: and I immediately recognized in him the figure of the Messenger, the Mercury who guides souls, or if you like, the Annunciating Angel. In short, the person for whom everyone waits, whether he knows it or not, and who brings the message from heaven that changes your life, for good or ill – you don't know which until he opens his mouth.

When the Messenger opened his mouth out came a Tuscan accent, and the offer of a job. He told Primo his name, and who had sent him: Caselli, the caretaker of the Chemical Institute ('another Mercury', Primo says, but without recalling Caselli's first, deathly message). He also told Primo a bit – but only a bit – about the job. 'Somewhere', not very far away, there was a mine, which produced 2 per cent of something useful (he didn't say what), and 98 per cent of something useless. In this useless material, however, there was something valuable: nickel. Very little of it; but in wartime even a very little might be enough to make its recovery worthwhile. He had lots of ideas, but no time. He needed a lieutenant, a substitute: someone to test his ideas in the lab, and help develop them. This would mean, of course, living and working at the mine. Unfortunately – Primo would understand – until he'd accepted, he could tell him no more. They would both need secrecy. He, in order to protect his ideas; and Primo in order to protect himself, since the mine was under contract to the army, and no Jew was allowed anywhere near. If he accepted he would have to work under a false name.

* The police – like the army, the post office, the whole of public service – is still full of people from the poverty-stricken South of Italy, drawn by the promise of security. '*I dogumende*' is Guido's rendering of a Southern accent.

No one could be permitted to know (as Primo put it, with bitter irony) 'my abominable origin'.

He sensed a similar bitter playfulness in the Lieutenant. It might be a clever move to hire a Jew, whose own secret would ensure that he kept his employer's; but he could see that it also pleased the Lieutenant to break the racial laws. He could see that he wore his uniform with revulsion. He had liked him instantly; now he liked him even more. He had not the slightest doubt: this message was for good, and he could hardly wait to begin. The only trouble was his parents.

But for once they were no trouble at all. He was the main prop of the family now, and money was urgently needed. His mother had to let him go.

Nickel

The Messenger-Lieutenant was called Ennio Mariotti. He was a chemist and a Florentine. In 1941 he was twenty-seven years old, tall and thin as Primo says, his hair already beginning to recede. He was an officer in the Chemical Service of the army, working with explosives: testing Italian bombs in the lab, and defusing enemy ones in the field. And he was, as Primo saw, contemptuously antifascist. His father was a Socialist senator who had been sent to the *confino* for his pains. The Lieutenant himself had been an active antifascist at university; but after his father's experience he had restricted himself to the 'sinister gaiety' (in Primo's words) 'of a whole generation of Italians'. He was the least passive person imaginable, and must have been an undefused bomb himself throughout the war. With his height and his blue eyes he was often mistaken for a German, which angered him even more. I think he must have enjoyed his visit to Dr Levi, whose liking he immediately returned.

When Primo accepted, he wasted no time. The very next day they took a train to Balangero in the Val di Lanzo, about twenty-five miles north of Turin. Then they climbed another few miles up the side of the valley, through a forest sparkling with frost. And there was the mine: the *Cave San Vittore*.

It was, Primo thought, exactly like Dante's picture of Inferno. In a squat, rocky hill was sunk an enormous cone-shaped crater, 400 yards across the top. All day along the crater's sides explosions dislodged the rock, which rolled down the circling, narrowing tiers to the bottom. Here, 'in Lucifer's place', was a pit, covered by a shutter. The pit led to a long horizontal tunnel, through which an armoured train carried the rock from the centre of the hill to the open air, and tipped it into the great crusher below. Here, with an unceasing, hellish roar, and amid clouds of dust, the rock was shattered and crushed until it became gravel, then dried out and sifted for its '2 per cent of something valuable'. Primo learned now what that was: asbestos.

All the rest, thousands of tons a day, was dumped into the valley below. This second pit, even vaster than the first, was Primo's. This was the 98 per cent of detritus, of dust and gravel made grey and slightly sticky by the asbestos that was still in it, from which he was meant to conjure nickel, the silver gold. As a Jew he was himself detritus, according to the laws of his land; yet in this very Jewishness the Lieutenant had found his value. Now he had to perform the same alchemical transformation on the dust and gravel torn out, stripped, and dumped from the mountain.

It would not be easy. His analyses showed that the percentage of nickel in the rock was low indeed: only two parts in a thousand. Nonetheless he tried out all the Lieutenant's ideas for enriching and separating it. Nothing worked. At first he had been happy just to work, to put what he had learned in the long hours of Quantitative Analysis to real use, at which point it suddenly came alive. But day after day, week after week, the proportions remained the same: 0.2 per cent nickel, 8 per cent iron. He grew discouraged. The rock came to seem his enemy, 'pure hostile passivity', 'a massive fortress' he had to tear down stone by stone.

But he pulled himself together; or the energetic, optimistic Lieutenant did. 'One must not surrender to incomprehensible matter,' Primo wrote of their efforts, thirty years later. 'One must never feel unarmed: nature is immense and complex, but not impermeable to intelligence.' Their weekly consultations 'sounded like war plans'.

And with tenacity came the breakthrough. One day Primo saw a note by an earlier chemist of the mine, observing that at very high temperatures the asbestos became 'fragile'. The mine's rock, serpentine, was 'the father of asbestos', he reasoned: if asbestos breaks its bonds at 800 degrees Centigrade, serpentine should too.

'Nothing is more vivifying than a hypothesis.' He set to work immediately, though it was already late afternoon. He heated the powdered serpentine, passed hydrogen through it, cooled it, and dispersed it in water. By now it was dark, and everyone had gone home. For hours he passed a magnet through the water, and put aside the milligram of brown powder it brought out. By midnight he had a gram. He couldn't wait any longer; he stopped, and began the analysis. By three in the morning the result was 'written in letters of fire' on his slide rule: 6 per cent of nickel. *Victory.*

He wanted to wake the Director and telephone the Lieutenant; he wanted to 'roll around on the dark fields, which were dripping wet with dew'. 'I was thinking many foolish things,' he wrote, 'and I was not thinking anything sensible and sad.' He was thinking of 'having opened a door with a key', which this time was his alone, not 'borrowed' from anyone's older brother; of 'having the key to many doors – perhaps to all of them', as though his boyhood dream of chemistry had come true. And he was thinking that he had, at last, had his revenge 'on those who had declared me biologically inferior'. He was not thinking (he wrote) that any nickel he produced would go straight to his enemies, Hitler and Mussolini, who would use it to murder his friends. He was not thinking that perhaps no magnetic selector of an adequate size and scale existed (it didn't). And he did not know that in any case his idea was largely mistaken, as the Lieutenant pointed out as soon as he told him.

This classically self-mocking tale is all, alas, true. Primo and Ennio Mariotti did find a small amount of nickel in the slag-heaps of the San Vittore mine; but none of their methods for developing it were industrially or commercially viable, and after nearly a year the project was dropped. But their dream went beyond industry and commerce, which is why Primo tells it in *The Periodic Table*.

The dream of finding something precious in waste, diamonds in ashes, 'sets fire to the imagination', as Primo says, and never goes away. It was the alchemists' dream of transforming base metal into gold; it was Ponzio's dream in his yearly ritual of salvage. It continued to be the dream, Primo tells us, of the people of that valley, who for years went at night to the slag-heaps, and boiled up the gravel with ever new reagents, hoping to release the nickel. It continued to be his own dream of chemistry, when after the war, for example, he tried to produce an expensive element of lipstick from chicken shit: 'gold from dung', he said with a grin, '*aurum de stercore*'. Above all, it was his dream in writing, and his achievement. What better description could there be of *If This is a Man*, of the wealth of human understanding it salvaged from the ashes of Auschwitz, than *aurum de stercore*? And the same is true of all his books, in one way or another. From the lives, and deaths, of humble, forgotten people, in the first two great books, in *The Wrench*, in *If Not Now, When?*, in *The Drowned and the Saved*; and from the stinks of despised science in his stories, he conjured literature. And that began now.

Perhaps, as Bianca believes, he had already written 'I mnemagoghi', with the compensatory energy of his university years. But here both the need to compensate and the time to do it in had grown. He was more isolated than ever. After the first few weeks he realized that all his co-workers knew his name, but were as careful as he not to use it, in order to avoid trouble for themselves, and also for him. They were friendly, they even gave him clear signs of solidarity; but he could not relax with them nor they with him, since everyone had to pretend. And since he knew no one else for miles around, his evenings were interminable. He went back to the lab, or shut himself up in his 'monastic cell' with Thomas Mann; or went for long solitary walks on the mountainside, which was silent at last, apart from 'the distant howls of dogs' down in the valley. And on some of those long nights he also sat down in his cell and wrote two stories, the first he publicly admitted to.

The mine at Balangero was thus where Primo Levi began as a chemist – and as a writer, at the same time. He always spoke as though the one came long after the other; but in 'Nickel' he tells us himself that they came together. Of course, chemistry was his job, and his only public identity; while writing was his private, even secret, activity. *That* is what came only long after: the writer-tortoise catching up with the chemist-hare.

But 'Nickel' follows the first steps of the writer just as much as those of the chemist. Exactly as much, in fact. After the first five pages, which introduce the Lieutenant and the mine, the rest is equally divided. The last five describe the chemist's search for nickel. But the five in the middle are not about science: instead they are the personal and private – mostly very private – stories of the inhabitants of the mine. Despite the tensions of his anonymity, people told these stories to him: their own and one another's, openly and in great detail. 'It is not clear,' he wrote, why they did so, 'particularly to me, who on the contrary could tell nothing to anyone, not even my own name.' It is simply, he suggests, his 'fate': 'I am someone to whom many things are told.'

But this is the 'fate' – the character, the gift – of a writer: of someone as attentive to mankind as a scientist to matter. And Primo was. From the start he was as amazed by people as by rock, and as eager to understand them; that is why he remembered them better than anyone else, from Comi Schifùs to Guido Foa. And people are not like rock: they need attention, as plants need water. If the attention is as unjudging, as compassionate as Primo's, they open. The stories he attracted, almost without trying, at Balangero in 1942 were a rehearsal for those he would deliberately, even desperately, collect two years later. He was not preparing himself for that, of course, since he had no idea it would happen. But when it happened, he was prepared. He already knew he was 'someone to whom many things are told': that he had only to ask, and people would tell him their stories.

What *is* remarkable is the sort of story they told him. At Balangero he was, of necessity, particularly anonymous and silent. And he was always mild-mannered, neutral, visibly repressed. Yet all the stories he was told –

at least all the ones he passes on to us – were exactly the opposite. They were wild, transgressive, full of chaos, disorder and sin. The first tells, symbolically, of a flood which had swept down from the pit and destroyed the mine years before. Then come stories of shooting (chickens), stealing (turkeys), and sex. Especially sex. From what he could gather, Primo wrote, 'all fifty of the mine's inhabitants had reacted with all the others, two by two, as in combinatorial analysis: I mean everyone with everyone else, and especially every man with all the women, married or single, and every woman with all the men'.

There was even a legend, like the legend of the flood, about the destruction of the mine by sex. In a remote time, long before any of the other stories, the plant had been a veritable Gomorrah.

. . . During that legendary season, every evening when the 5.30 siren sounded, no one went home. At that signal bottles and mattresses appeared between the desks, and an orgy erupted which embraced everything and everyone, from young pubescent secretaries to balding accountants, from the director of the day right down to the disabled doormen. The sad cycle of paperwork gave way, every evening, to a boundless, classless fornication, public, and variously combined.

From this fabulous orgy there were, not unnaturally, no survivors, since it produced 'a series of disastrous balance sheets', and everyone was fired. Except one, Primo notes: Signora Bortolasso.

With Signora Bortolasso, therefore, he brings the seething sexuality of the mine down to the present. And that means – to its disappearance. True, the current inhabitants of the mine have also 'variously combined', every man with every woman; but we see none of this. We see only Signora Bortolasso, whose sexuality, and indeed humanity, are equally confined to the past.

Around fifteen years before, at the age of nineteen, Gina delle Benne had fallen in love with a young, slim, redheaded miner. But her parents forbade her to marry him; and the redhead would not wait for her. She had had to watch him court two other women, and marry a third. At that moment she forbade herself marriage forever, 'in a refined and merciless manner, that is, by getting married'. She had married Bortolasso, the idiot of the mine, on condition that he never lay a hand on her. He had agreed; and every night since then had tried to violate her, without success. Signora Bortolasso remained a virgin.

By the time he had arrived at Balangero, Primo wrote, these nightly battles 'had become the talk of the mine, and one of its few attractions'. Weather permitting, people would go and stand under the Bortolassos' window, and listen to the (faded) Beauty fend off the Beast. One night they invited Primo to come along; but he refused.

At this point in the story he switches to the search for nickel. A young girl works with him in the lab: Alida, who is lazy and cunning, and physically 'raw-boned' (which probably means larger than Primo). But she is eighteen, a *liceo* graduate, and her presence is 'not unpleasant'; she also has 'fiery red hair, and green, slanting, mischievous, inquisitive eyes'. Perhaps we are meant to glimpse in her Gina delle Benne's young redheaded miner; in any case we wonder, we even hope – will wicked Alida give Primo his first taste of a woman's warmth, a woman's smile?

But no: she only gives him her story, which is that she is in love with one man at the plant, and engaged to another. Sex is for the other fifty inhabitants of the mine, in various combinations; but not for him. It is as though it is already in his past – though he is only twenty-two.

Primo Levi wrote 'Nickel' more than thirty years later, and (as we shall see) it reflects the time of writing. But he had told these events and stories very soon, probably straight away; perhaps, like 'I mnemagoghi', he'd even written them down. 'Nickel' does also, therefore, reflect something of him at the time. We already know – from 'Zinc', from *The Double Bond* – how he longed then for sexual love; how without it he felt an outcast, a freak, and deeply alone. And we know that he also felt a block, a chasm he could not cross, and could not fathom either. He'd 'racked his brains' to understand it, he says in *The Double Bond*, but he could not. Only in the writing, in 1986, did the answer come clear to him. No spark had lit in the girls he loved, he wrote, because they saw his own doubt, his own anguish: so that 'they felt ill at ease with me, even in danger; and not without reason'.

It's true – self-doubt and fear kill the spark, and make women (and men, and other animals) feel uneasy. But why *in danger*, and *not without reason*? There is no answer to that in *The Double Bond*; even in 1986 Primo did not openly ask himself that question. Nonetheless there may be an unopen answer to it somewhere: and surely there is, in 'Nickel'.

For the feeling about sex that lurks beneath its surface is not just fear, but horror. Sex in 'Nickel' is not personal, private and to do with love. It is a promiscuous, anarchic flood, which mates each to all indiscriminately, from young to old – the young *to* the old, the pubescent secretaries to the ageing accountants – and from director to doormen – perhaps the director *to* the doormen as well, since it is only 'especially' every man with all the women, and every woman with all the men. It sweeps away the mine, just as the real flood did; and that one, we recall, came from the pit, from 'Lucifer's place'. Sex is destruction, not creation: breathe a sigh of relief, not regret, that it is mostly past.

What remains of it is almost worse: an idiot, 'dirty as a pig', trying every night to violate the faded icy Beauty, who once chose this perverse way to punish love, or perhaps herself, and now can hardly keep the Beast at bay in nightly battles . . . No wonder Primo refused to listen to them. No wonder that the closest he could let sex come was other people's stories.

Primo Levi was not a cold or sexless young man. On the contrary, he longed intensely for sex – and probably indiscriminately too, like most young men. For this Primo Levi, the sex stories of 'Nickel' were a compensation: an *alter-ego* imagining of all he could not be or do. But then there was the other Primo Levi: the son of his betraying father and punishing mother; the self-denying, self-punishing ascetic. This one – like his mother, *for* his mother – was revolted and terrified by sex. He preferred to think himself a freak, without the instinct at all, rather than face his own lust. And if he ever got an inkling of it, his self-loathing was so strong it threatened to spill over on to the girls. That, I think, is why they were in danger. Not physical danger – he was incapable of hurting anyone, except himself. But mental danger. If he lusted after a girl, he – or his mother in him – loathed her.

But how could this be true? He hated no one – hate was as evil as lust, more evil. He hated her least of all – this girl, these girls; on the contrary, he loved them. And he did. That was the truth too; that was the double bind. It stopped him in his tracks like a wall, it fixed him to the spot like the Gorgon's stare: unable either to love or to hate, to pursue or to flee. It castrated him more effectively than anything his old enemy in *liceo* had imagined. And it left him as the inhabitants of the mine, spinning in and out of their various combinations, saw: separate, and still. Sympathetic, and wise beyond his years, but more than virginal: inert, neutral, uncombining.

And that, of course, is why they told him their stories, so openly, without fear of judgement or betrayal. Primo Levi was like a priest, who knows and understands everything about the world, but does not belong to it. He was the perfect listener to the sexual secrets of men – and women – precisely because he was not, quite, a man. Soon he would be the perfect listener to their torture, humiliation and death secrets for the same reason. His greatest book, in other words, came out of the ashes not only of Auschwitz, but of his own life. And not only his greatest book, but all of them. *Aurum de stercore* describes all Primo Levi's art in this sense too; in this sense most of all.

'Lead' and 'Mercury'

His first two stories came out of this double bind: the love-hate for women that kept him transfixed and apart, amid the fevered couplings of a tiny, isolated community. He said that they came out of a double bond instead: the love-hate that he felt for rock. Both were true. Transposed from women to rock, from life to work, what was a bind for the man was a bond for the writer: still dangerously unstable, but creative now instead of destructive, as always when Primo Levi brought to bear his transforming will.

Both lead and mercury, in their respective stories, are deeply ambivalent. The gift of divining lead in rock makes Rodmund rich, but it also makes him die young. Lead is more important to him than love, which he does not seem to feel; he takes girls only to 'make merry' with 'for a night or a month', and a wife, in the end, only to produce the next Rodmund. Lead is, indeed, more important to him than life, since he knows perfectly well that it will kill him. For the simpler, more earthy Corporal Abrahams of 'Mercury', it is the other way around. He needs women, and dislikes cold, uncanny mercury; but when he finds a cave full of it, he needs it too – if only to buy himself another woman.

At this early stage there was, perhaps, more bind than bond. Both stories deal in rather adolescent fashion with the problem of women: Rodmund scorns them, Corporal Abrahams finds them ready for the taking. And as stories, they are not particularly good. Of course, they are juvenilia, so perhaps that is not surprising.* What is surprising is the sort of not-particularly-good they are. Most juvenilia is like the later work, but worse: the same writer, practising. These stories are not like Primo Levi at all. There are glimpses of him, family resemblances, so to speak. The fascination with the distant past, with distant lands, for example, would remain; so would their formal correlative, the device of the alien narrator, who sees our world with a naïve, revealing eye. But the essence of these stories is the exact opposite of the later Primo Levi. To start with, they are fiction; and not only fiction but fantasy fiction, which, as a substitute for the discipline of reality, uses the discipline of genre and convention instead: in this case, the genre of the adventure fable, like *Gulliver's Travels*, or *Robinson Crusoe*. In other words: these early stories by the great master of non-fiction, and of the plain, realistic, non-literary style, are entirely literary, and hardly realistic at all. It seems that, at twenty-two, Primo Levi still divided literature off from science, as he had been taught to do in *liceo*. He did do both, from the start; but not together. The unique Primo Levi, who writes literature like a

---

* Until Primo Levi's papers are opened to scholars, we cannot know whether, or how much, he reworked them later. The typescripts in the Einaudi archive are dated in the 1970s; but it is of course possible that he simply retyped the battered originals ('they have suffered bombings and escapes, I had given them up for lost'), without changing a word. Possible, but not likely. As we shall see, he never reworked the next story he wrote – but never published it either. I think he probably did smooth and tidy up these two; but didn't substantially change them.

laboratory report, is not here. That crossover, that breaking down of barriers, was the breakthrough; but there is no sign of it yet. 'Lead' and 'Mercury' show that one of the most persistent ideas about Primo Levi, that *he was not a writer before Auschwitz*, is not true. It is the opposite of the truth. Auschwitz did not 'make him a writer', since he was writing already. What it did was stop him being an ordinary, conventional, literary writer, and force him to become Primo Levi.

'Lead' and 'Mercury' are like false signposts for Primo's writing, pointing to a road he did not take. But they are accurate signposts for the solutions he would attempt to his double bind, his problem about women. 'Mercury' points to the direction he would take in life, 'Lead' to the one in work.

In 'Mercury' Corporal Abrahams and his wife Maggie live on 'Desolation Island', 'the loneliest island in the world'. Recently they have been joined by four other men. Maggie takes up with two of them, leaving the other three tormented by jealousy and desire. Then one day the island's volcano erupts, and Maggie's favourite cave fills with mercury. Hendrik, her lover, knows how to distil it. Corporal Abrahams organizes the production of forty jars of purified mercury, which he gives to the captain of a ship which calls once a year. Six months later the ship deposits four women on the beach. Each man takes one: including the Corporal, who leaves Maggie to Hendrik, and takes for himself young, grey-eyed Rebecca Johnson, who 'brought to mind the idea of catching her on the wing, like a butterfly'.

This story seethes with sex – again betraying something very different beneath the wry, detached tone of 'Nickel'. It explodes with sex, in the volcano; it drips with it, in the mercury itself ('the female principle'); in any case, it quite openly has sex as its theme. That would not happen again in Primo's work, until *If Not Now, When?*, in 1982, and *The Double Bond*, right at the end.* Nor do I mean to say, alas, that it happened in his life. But the heart of it did. Unlike Rodmund, he never left home. But the long-awaited instinct did struggle to the surface, if not to freedom. And when a woman finally appeared, he took her, as Corporal Abrahams did, and brought her into his own Desolation Island, Corso Re Umberto 75.

Rodmund, by contrast, the descendant of six generations of lead diviners, sets out to walk across the known world in search of new deposits. He is a hunter and traveller, a man of the mountains, proud, free and alone. He leaves home to seek what he wants; and what he wants is lead – work, the exercise of his skill, the gaining of knowledge and respect. He does not want

---

* Except (as we'll see) in the occasional short story: e.g. 'La bella addormentata nel frigo' in *Storie naturali*, 'Lumini rossi' in *Vizio di forma*, or 'Disfilassi' in *Lilit*. Of course, 'Mercury' is itself a short story. In prose, Primo only let his subconscious (slightly) off the leash in stories.

women, or men either, except for occasional company, or for skills he does not himself possess: glass-blowing, for instance, in a man, the ability to bear the next Rodmund in a woman. Rodmund, in other words, is the archetype of Primo's adventurer hero: who will begin – in involuntary, comic mode – with himself in *The Truce*, and will reach his peak in Faussone of *The Wrench*. If Corporal Abrahams's open sexuality echoes one real *alter-ego* friend – Alberto – Rodmund more than echoes the other: Sandro.

But Rodmund moves still further away from Primo himself. For his name sounds German; and his native land is clearly Germany. Primo's own encounter with Germans still lay ahead: but he knew all too well that Germany was the enemy, that it was Germans who threatened the little freedom he had left. And yet he made the hero of his first 'dream of escape' an ancient German. Later, in 'Retirement Fund', he would imagine his persecutor as his enemy's as well. His capacity to imagine his opposite he shares with all great imaginative writers. But his capacity – or perhaps his need – to imagine his enemy is unique. Think of it: in 1942, in Europe, a Jew makes a German the hero of a story. 'Lead' is not a great work, like *If This is a Man*; but it is almost as surprising.

★   ★

On the morning of 24 March 1942 Primo was called to the telephone. His father was suddenly much worse, he must come home immediately. He rushed down the hill and on to a train. At the station in Turin Giorgio Lattes was waiting for him. He was too late; his father was already dead.

It was the end of his childhood, and the end of a long nightmare. But that does not mean, of course, that he felt either relieved or free. Whatever he had felt for his father, it was not simple, and he went on feeling it for part of himself: horror, but also pity; and somewhere deep down, transferred to opposites like Alberto, admiration, and a longing to cross over to his side. It is easier, or at least less complicated, to mourn someone you have simply loved. Primo suffered over the death of his father; and he never forgot that awful journey, which was too late anyway. I wonder whether Rina called him too late half deliberately, because she could bear no reconciliation between her enemy and her ally; not even a hurried goodbye. Perhaps Primo wondered too. But whether he understood it or not, his father's death did not end that long war. It would not free him from his mother, or not for long. On the contrary.

★   ★

He returned to the mine; but that was not for long either. By June, he and Ennio Mariotti recognized that they were never going to find a practical solution to the problem of nickel. Primo was going to have to find another job.

He started looking, but once again a Message came to him, this time by telephone. A Milanese voice instructed him to come the next day to the Hotel Suisse in Turin. Primo's alert ear noted the 'Hotel': a loyal Fascist would have used the pure Italian 'Albergo'. He went.

After the dust and din of the mine the Hotel Suisse, with its draperies and shadows, must have seemed to him impossibly quiet, rich and absurd. The owner of the voice was waiting. He was, Primo learned, a *Commendatore*;* his name was Molina (Primo changed this to 'Martini' in *The Periodic Table*); and he had a factory on the outskirts of Milan. The factory was Swiss; indeed, the *Commendatore* said briskly, he himself was Swiss, so there would be no problem for him in hiring Dr Levi. Primo found this explanation, belied by the thick Milanese accent, deeply comic, but perfectly justifiable. Italians could help Jews, or mutually help them; but it was not advisable to show too much humanity, 'so as not to be forced later to offer understanding or compassion'.

The *Commendatore* was in general evasive, and Primo's many questions remained unanswered. Nonetheless, the key points were clear. The factory, which was called Wander, produced health drinks, tonics and medicines. Primo's job would be to research into a cure for diabetes, about which the *Commendatore* – like Ennio Mariotti about nickel – had some pet ideas. His starting salary would be – and the *Commendatore* named a sum Primo would never have dared to ask for. His laboratory would be modern, well-equipped and spacious. And it also contained – here the *Commendatore* made his final move, 'like a magician pulling a rabbit from his tall silk hat' – a classmate of Primo's from university, who had, in fact, been the one to recommend him: a girl whom Primo calls Giulia Vineis, and whose real name was Gabriella Garda.

He had two weeks to decide, but he didn't need them. 'The very next day', he says in *The Periodic Table*, he quit the mine and moved to Milan. Perhaps 'the very next day' is an exaggeration: but not the sense of determination, of audacity, of a prospect opening before him. Two summers later he would remember Ulysses' mad flight, eagerly he would explain to his friend Pikolo why Dante did not write *I set out* but *I set forth* – 'because it is much stronger and more audacious, it is a chain which has been broken, it is throwing oneself over the barrier, we know the impulse well'. That is what he did now. He did not escape his family: in that time, in those times, perhaps no young Jew could or would. In Milan he would live with his

---

* This is the Italian equivalent of a knighthood.

cousin Ada Della Torre. In Turin his mother kept a bed made up for him, not only at Corso Re Umberto 75, but also at her father's house near Superga, where the whole family moved later that year, when the bombing started. It was inconceivable that he should not return to one of his mother's houses every weekend; and he did. Nonetheless, for him, perhaps even more for her, this was his breaking of the chain, his throwing himself over the barrier. It was his moment of flight. Perhaps he remembered that line of Dante's best of all later, because he said it to himself now:

Ma misi me per l'alto mare aperto.

'So I set forth upon the open sea.'

Burning

Firebombs over Turin, 1942

The Lieutenant ended the war as an explosives expert, with many *coups* (if that is the right word) to his credit: the greatest, for which he received a letter of recognition from the Ministry of War, being the dismantling and copying of a delayed-action fuse from an unexploded Allied bomb. Italy lay in ruins, he had a new young wife, and a family soon to come. But like Alberto, the Lieutenant did not like working for other people; like Sandro, he was a risk-taker supreme. He set up his own Studio, with laboratory attached, on the Via San Secondo in Turin; and became one of the first independent chemist-consultants in Italy, ready to work on any chemical problem, anywhere.

He was an excellent chemist, a volcano of energy, and he loved the excitement of solving a new problem every month and moving on. The Studio Chimico Ennio Mariotti flourished. When I ask, fifty years later, it is no longer clear exactly how soon. When Primo arrived home, in October 1945, he looked for work everywhere; and surely he would have thought of the Lieutenant too. No one remembers now if he came to him or not. Perhaps he did, and the Studio was not yet busy enough to take on another chemist. Or perhaps he didn't. He was full of admiration for the Lieutenant's pioneering daring; but entrusting it with his own fate was another question. In any case, he took a job in a factory. He and Ennio Mariotti never did work together again – though many years later, when Primo had retired, they talked about it eagerly.

Their friendship was that constant move of Primo's life, the reaching out to his opposite. And the Lieutenant reached back. If Primo admired his daring, he admired Primo's fortitude: the quiet dignity with which he spoke, and wrote, of his terrible experiences. The Lieutenant was a writer himself, publishing articles and art criticism in a Florentine newspaper. If Primo would have liked to be the kind of chemist he was – free, independent, non-routine – he would have liked to be the kind of writer Primo was. His daughter Vanna says that their friendship was 'a reciprocal dream': each dreamed of changing places with the other. And the funny thing was, she says, that it seemed as though they had. For it was Primo who had *il temperamento del chimico*, the temperament of a chemist, and her father who had *il temperamento dell'artista*, the temperament of an artist. He was romantic and bold, he didn't care about money or security, he loved food and jokes and fun. While Primo was quiet and cautious, supremely reserved, concerned about safety in life and work. He came to her father as a chemist might come to an artist, or a bourgeois to a bohemian: to talk about everything – science and religion, language and literature, Auschwitz, his private troubles; but most of all to relax. He came to their house, she says, for its warmth. Her father filled it with animals: cats, geese, tortoises, even a hedgehog, which was allowed into his bed. Primo didn't touch them, not even the cats. But he liked to be there. He came regularly, almost every fortnight until the Lieutenant died.

That happened in 1982. Ennio Mariotti had become an expert in many fields, including the biochemistry of wine, and the ecological improvement of the Italian chemical industry, which had grown unchecked for years. But his main interest and expertise remained what it had been during the war: explosives, and fire. During the *anni di piombo*, the terrorist years of the 1970s, he was called in regularly to deal with firebomb attacks, at Fiat, at Pirelli. Then, for many years, he worked on a new and better method of fire extinction, which he patented in 1979.

The research and testing of this idea was, of course, extremely dangerous. The Lieutenant was literally playing with fire. His courage saw him through; and also his metaphysical imagination, which he shared with Primo. What sustained him, he wrote, was 'the knowledge of having won a battle against the obscure forces of destruction'.

He won, but at a cost. A container of the nitrate solution used in his new system was kept in a corner of the lab. One day when he picked it up he saw that it was smoking, and knew it was about to explode. Instinctively he threw it to his left, in order to save his right hand. He did save three fingers of that hand, but the other was blown away entirely. For the rest of his life he worked, wrote, drove, and in general carried on just as before, with double the energy and optimism, and half of one hand.

But the terrific impact of the explosion did not stop at his hands. It caused an aneurysm in one of the arteries leading to his heart, for which he refused to have an operation. Four years later, at the age of sixty-eight, he dropped dead of a heart attack, in the middle of giving expert evidence at a trial. No one doubts that the aneurysm killed him. He had spent much of his life fighting explosions and fire; and he chose, in effect, to die by them.

Acids, caustics, fires and explosions are the great perils of the chemical trade, and the greatest of these are fires and explosions. Ennio Mariotti feared them, as any chemist must; but the fear brought him out fighting. That is what Primo so envied and admired. When he became the director of a chemical company, he worried so intensely about accidents, and felt so responsible for the few that occurred, that it drove him to depression. Fear of fire and explosions made the Lieutenant an explosives expert and a firefighter. It made Primo want to resign.

But like all his failures, it also made him write. In *The Periodic Table*, 'Hydrogen' ends in an explosion, 'Potassium' in a fire. His first factory story, 'Sulphur', written as early as 1950, was already about explosion and fire: a workman, Lanza, narrowly saves a boiler from exploding, then hands it over to the next shift without a word. The second chapter of *The Wrench* describes, in the laconic tones of its hero Faussone, one of Primo's worst moments: when it became clear that he'd made a 'king-sized mistake' in the design of the drying tower of his factory, and the whole vast structure – so high you could see it from the Turin–Milan motorway – threatened to explode. In *Other People's Trades* he describes several similar moments. He had also designed, for example, some tanks for storing solvents. Since people often had to draw off small amounts from one, he'd added a longish pipe and spigot. For years all was well. Then one hot summer a worker went up to the pipe, opened the spigot, and the solvent shot out in flames. Within seconds a stream of burning solvent was heading for the production section. Fortunately, the department head ('a brave and experienced man') managed to squeeze between flames and tank and close the spigot, and the situation was saved. Later Primo read that some liquids can become electrified by the friction of flowing through a pipe: there was the sun's heat, perhaps a spark between solvent and spigot, when the latter was turned – and instant, furious fire.

A second event also involved fire, or the fear of fire. One 31 December, when the factory was closed, a petrol tanker overturned on the road outside, and began to spill its petrol into the adjoining field. When Primo arrived ('bracing myself for an unusual New Year's Eve'), he found the cold air saturated with gas vapour. It would be very dangerous, he warned, to lift the tanker with a crane: the grip of iron on iron could produce sparks. The fire brigade agreed, and covered everything – tanker, road and field – with white foam. Then Primo had another thought. As the petrol ran out, the tanker filled up with air: again an explosive mixture would form, this time inside. He suggested they fill the interior with carbon dioxide from the factory's fire extinguishers; which they did. At last the crane arrived – and with it midnight, and a bottle of champagne. The tanker was lifted; everyone drank heartily to the New Year, and to danger overcome. Only later did Primo realize how great it had been. In an obscure book, he read that carbon dioxide extinguishers are excellent for putting out fires, but must *never* be used for preventative purposes, near flammable solvents. The carbon dioxide condenses into dry-ice 'needles', which can themselves generate sparks. 'The book,' Primo concludes, 'described a ruinous fire and explosion which took place in Holland': it had been caused in just this way, and dozens of people had died.

The third and last story is one of Primo's most beautiful. It is called 'Stable/Unstable', and it is about wood. Or rather, it begins with wood. Wood is the most extraordinary material, he reminds us: strong, light and lovely, with so many uses throughout history that 'in some languages "material" and "wood" were the same word'. But its great mechanical strength is accompanied by chemical weakness. Like all organic substances, it is only apparently stable. In truth, it is only waiting for the slightest encouragement to become unstable. 'Wood is anxious to oxidize', in Primo's words: that is, most commonly, to burn.

He then recalls a third incident from his many years at the factory. The sawdust for cleaning the floors was not kept indoors, because 'we knew it was a substance which should not be trusted'. So it was kept outdoors, but uncovered. One day a foreman came to Primo to say that smoke was coming from one of the barrels. He went to look – and it was already half burnt away. If they *had* kept it inside, or any closer, 'the entire factory could have gone up in flames'.

But why had only one barrel ignited, and not the others? Primo put the question to the head of the local fire brigade. He was 'a solid and practical man', and rejected talk of spontaneous combustion. And yet he had seen several cases like this before, in which an inert and stable mass suddenly became unstable, for no reason anyone could discover.

There did not have to be a reason. All living substances, Primo tells us, all organic substances, natural and synthetic, and many other substances as well, have the same 'fragile stability' as wood. Chemists call it 'metastability'; and it is tempting, he says, to stretch its application further:

. . . to our social behaviour, our tensions, to all of mankind today, condemned and accustomed to living in a world which seems stable and is not, in which awesome energies (and I am not speaking only of nuclear arsenals) sleep a light sleep.

His fear of fire was much more than physical. How could he have changed places with Ennio Mariotti, the professional firefighter, who kept the most flammable solution he knew unprotected in his lab? His own experience had been too hostile: the bitter struggle between his parents, his mother's cold possessiveness, the racial laws, the camp, the war – all by the time he was twenty-five. How could he not – it seems, looking back – how could he not have been obsessed with safety? How could he not have wanted to avoid the fires of life, when they had burnt him so badly from the start? But he couldn't. Life *is* fire; if you run home and close the door you only shut it inside. Like the Lieutenant's nitrate solution, after all.

★   ★

In late 1996, the Studio Chimico Ennio Mariotti was moving out of the Via San Secondo. The Lieutenant's letter from the Ministry of War was still on the wall; so was a photograph of him standing silently in his lab, as a Fascist official shows off its achievements to Giuseppe Bottai, one of the fiercest antisemites in Mussolini's cabinet. But everything else was being dismantled and packed up, or tossed into corners to be thrown away. Over half a century of chemical dust hung in the air, stirring furiously and settling again every time Signora Mariotti's little dog rushed to bark and snap at some imaginary intruder. The Lieutenant's widow was tired and despairing, the atmosphere melancholy, and I cursed myself for having arrived so late. I didn't want to see this sad end to Ennio Mariotti's life work; and surely Signora Mariotti didn't want me to see it either.

But I was wrong. For one thing, the main part of the Studio had already been on the Corso Regina Margherita, with her daughter and son-in-law, for years; and she wasn't closing her part down, but only moving it to smaller premises. It was the end of an era, but not the end of the Studio. And as we talked about the past, her eyes stopped darting miserably from side to side, as though they could not bear to remain on a single one of these dusty, uprooted objects. Slowly they stilled, and grew deeper. She scratched the little dog's ears reflectively, and it grew quiet too. She took documents out of a drawer to show me – photographs of Ennio, his patents, articles about his achievements, for instance in *il caso Scarlino*, one of the first and most famous cases of environmental pollution in Italy. She laughed, she blinked away tears; her pale cheeks became very slightly pink. I asked if I could have a copy of one of the photographs: the one of the Lieutenant in his despised uniform, defusing a bomb. She pressed her own copy on me, saying that both her daughters had one, and she was sure there were plenty more. But I couldn't take it; not after watching her change as she remembered him. No, I said, I never accepted originals, because people often regretted parting with them afterwards. Please would she find one of the others, or make a new copy for me – I'd pay, of course – and I'd come back in a week or two to fetch it.

This is also a way of ensuring a second meeting; which we had. But this time the magic of memory did not work. Moving day was nearer. The piles of dismembered objects were higher, the little dog never stopped barking. Signora Mariotti told me the same story twice, and her eyes slid about hopelessly. I said I would go. She pulled herself up, saying she had prepared something for me. Good! – she'd remembered the photograph. But when she returned she had two bulging plastic bags in each hand, and an ancient cracked briefcase under one arm. 'It's everything I showed you,' she said. It was – the photographs, the patents, the articles; and much, much more. There were photographs I'd never seen – parts of bombs neatly labelled, fire-bombs lacing the sky; there were patents going back to 1946, with elaborate stamps and franking and curlicued writing. There were letters requesting Ennio Mariotti's services as a consultant, there were his replies, his reports, his proposals. The cracked lid of the briefcase wouldn't open; when it did it cracked entirely, and hung down like the lid of a winking eye. Inside were thousands of newspaper clippings: every article in which the Lieutenant's name had ever appeared.

'Take it,' she said. No, no! I protested, I couldn't possibly, it was hers. 'Maybe something will be useful,' she said. 'If not, burn it.' I stared at her in horror, but she stared back quite calmly. 'If you won't, I will,' she said. '*Ormai non serve*': 'It's no use any more.'

I thought she had probably forgotten me as soon as she'd closed the door, but still I staggered up the Via San Secondo until I was out of sight of her windows. Then I stopped and sat down, right there on the pavement; with my plastic bags and broken briefcase, no one was surprised. Legs scissored past, the traffic swirled, and I thought: this is all that's left of Ennio Mariotti. Words on paper. As Primo said of Sandro: just words.

And she had said, 'Burn it.' *It's no use any more.* It wasn't that she hadn't loved him; I'd seen that faint glow on her tired face. It was the opposite. For her their love, their life, was enough. It was all there was, and when it was over there was nothing left. Just words.

★   ★

My friend the Biographer told me an experience he had never forgotten. One day a friend of his, an ageing writer, had invited him to his house in the country. The roads were narrow and winding, and the Biographer had a good deal of trouble finding the way. When he finally arrived, the ageing writer revealed the reason for his invitation: he wished to appoint him his literary executor. The Biographer felt a frisson of foreboding; but he agreed.

A few years later, the writer died. The Biographer did not want to intrude immediately upon his widow. He waited for several weeks before he made his appointment; then he set off once more down the winding lanes. This time he couldn't find the house at all. Peering through the window of his car for some sign, he saw, a mile or two off, a white plume of smoke rising into the sky. He had had his sign. He found the writer's widow in the garden, throwing the last of her husband's correspondence into the flames.

Standing there – 'as if at a second death', he said – he thought back over many previous conflagrations: Samuel Johnson burning his mother's letters, then bursting into tears; Dickens, Hardy, Henry James all making bonfires of their papers; Freud, the greatest arsonist of all, making the first of several fires at only twenty-nine. Somehow the Biographer managed to scoop up one unconsumed packet of letters, hide it behind his back, and bear it away.

I am very much afraid that Primo's widow will burn *his* letters, and other papers too; if she hasn't already. She has refused to deposit them anywhere, not even in the main Jewish library of Italy, the Centro di Documentazione Ebraica Contemporanea in Milan. Fifteen years after his death they are still in his study, which she guards like Cerberus.

I know we have all the words he left safely in his published books, but he wrote these words as well. I want to read every mark he left on paper; and every mark he left on people. But these, too, many of them burn away, like the wax to which he compared them: some involuntarily, by forgetting, changing, dying; but some deliberately, because they owe him a duty of privacy. That is what I am up against, in his widow too: the duty they all owe him, and the right he and she both have, to privacy.

But are there no other rights? As I gathered up the bags with Ennio Mariotti's life inside, I thought of his Studio disappearing from the Via San Secondo as though it had never been. I thought that even as I arrived in Turin, Primo's factory had stopped making the most important of the products he had developed, nearly fifty years before; that a year later the great tower he had designed – the one you could see from the Turin–Milan motorway – was no longer needed, and had been pulled down. *Change and decay in all around I see.* It seemed to me terrible enough that death had destroyed the men: how could people destroy the few traces they had left behind? The Studio, the tower – they were business, even I could see that. But letters, papers, truths, memories – how could people not hand them on, how could they burn them, how could they take them with them, as one friend swore she would, to the grave? It was like having to watch a second death, as the Biographer said. It reminded me of Alberto Levi's joke, the one that Primo's fellow survivor Luciana Nissim told me. Alberto Levi★ was famous for his outrageous jokes; everyone had their favourite. Luciana had once remarked to him that she had decided to be cremated. 'What?' Alberto had said. 'You miss the biggest opportunity of the century, and now you want to pay for it yourself?'

It is a duty of Primo's family and friends to protect his privacy. But there are other duties too. Those who deny this believe that burning is right. I cannot say it isn't. All I can say, with the Biographer, is that the need to keep death in its place lies deep in human nature. That is why biography has a duty too, to sift the ashes of their fires, and recover as many precious objects as it can.

★ Elder brother of Natalia Ginzburg, son of the brilliant and eccentric Professor of Anatomy at the University of Turin, Giuseppe Levi. Until his early death, Alberto Levi was friend and doctor not only to Primo, but to most of Jewish Turin.

PART TWO

Primo on Disgrazia, August 1942

6. Milan:
July 1942 – 8 September 1943

Primo, by Eugenio Gentili Tedeschi, 23 September 1942

In 1933 Primo's great-uncle Clemente Della Torre and his wife *nonna* Pina, sister of Barbaricô, moved from Alessandria to Milan. In May 1942 Clemente died. *Nonna* Pina, left on her own, went to live with her elder daughter Irma in Ivrea, leaving Ada in possession of the family flat on the Via San Martino. It was rather empty, since Pina had taken some of the furniture with her. But it was Ada's, alone and undisturbed. It looked out on to the garden, green and rather wild in wartime. In its courtyard stood a statue of the Greek philosopher Diogenes: he who had taught the reduction of desires, and who had had the temerity to tell Alexander the Great to get out of his sun.

Then as now Milan was a bigger, brasher and more open city than Turin, and one in which it was easier for Jews to find work. Euge, for instance, despite having come top in the postgraduate exam of 1940, could find no Turinese practice willing to take him; instead he taught architecture at the Jewish *liceo scientifico* for a year. But in early 1941 Giò Ponti, one of the best and most famous architects in Italy, offered him a place in his Milan studio. Euge seized his chance – and would never again live in Turin. Later that year, Anna Maria introduced him to Ada; and the first bond in the Milan group of Primo's friends was formed.

The next to arrive was Silvio Ortona. Since his return to Turin from England he too had been unable to find a job. But Otello Bonzano, the owner of a small Milanese shipping company, happily winked at the racial laws, and took Silvio, with his good English, into the foreign department – where he dealt mostly with Germany and Romania. Silvio too was immediately drawn to the Via San Martino. There was the Della Torres' flat, where you could think anything, and say anything, without fear; and there were the friends to do it with: Euge, the revolutionary young architect, who said that if it were up to him, he would rebuild Milan from scratch; and wonderfully witty, intelligent Ada, who talked even faster than Primo and Anna Maria, and had two degrees instead of only one, so that Silvio called her 'double-doctor', *bidottore*. Ada worked at a publishing house called Corbaccio, or Crow – which explains the drawing Euge made of the three founding members of the Milan group of friends.

SEBBENE SEMBRI STRANO
CIASCUN DEI TRE A MILANO
STANNO PER CONTO LORO
E FANNO IL SUO LAVORO:

COSTRUZIONI
GELONI
SPEDIZIONI
ESTRAPOLAZIONI
EDIZIONI.

Euge is, modestly, in the top corner, overseeing a building site; Silvio –
who was indeed very tall, and whom Euge always drew as a gangling giant
– pushes one of Bonzano's freight cars single-handed; and Ada corrects a
Corbaccio manuscript, with the Crow himself perched on her finger. The
verse below describes their days: Euge's *costruizioni e geloni*, buildings and
chilblains, in the cold winter of 1941–2; Silvio's *spedizioni e estrapolazioni*,
shipments and extrapolations – which was a pun on a book he was writing,
as we shall see; and Ada's *edizioni*, publishing. Ada's description is the most
modest now, because she wrote it. The page comes from a book called *Le
Cronache di Milano*, *The Milan Chronicles*, which the two wrote – 'Text by
Ada Della Torre, Drawings by Eugenio Gentili Tedeschi' – shortly after the
break-up of the group of friends in 1943. It is a wonderful record of the
crucial year (or two, for the founders) they spent together.

The next to appear in it is Emilio Diena, a young engineer with Olivetti,
who kept the group supplied with cigarettes, and rarely appears in the
Chronicles without one in his hand. Then, in the spring, a bunch of gossips
gather: '*Ed ecco che si mormora in città,*' Ada wrote, '*Che forse un giorno Primo
arriverà*' – 'A buzz fills the city like a hive, One day soon Primo may arrive!'
And in July, he did.

When Primo arrived at Crescenzago, Wander's home on the edge of
Milan, everything the *Commendatore* had promised him was waiting: a
wonderfully well-equipped lab ('a palace compared to the mine's'), and
Gabriella Garda. Gabriella was not working; instead she was calmly darning
her stockings. She greeted him affectionately, but with 'a meaningful grim-
ace'. She'd vaguely heard he was looking for work, and she was fed up being
alone in the lab: what better solution could there be? But she didn't think
much of the work at Wander: she should tell him that straight away. Gabriella
never hid her thoughts and feelings from anyone; she was quick and sure in
her judgements, impossible to fool, and absolutely direct. Her solution was
simple, and she recommended it to him: not to work at all. She didn't want
to boast, but she'd hardly done a thing all year, apart from setting up the
apparatus in the morning and taking it down at night, and making up an
entirely fictional report. What she was really doing was preparing for her
marriage, which was approaching: putting the finishing touches to her
trousseau, writing (Primo said) 'torrential letters' to her fiancé in his distant
barracks, and practising cooking, which she proposed to do on Primo. It
made him slightly uneasy when she did it in the lab. But rationing was strict,
good restaurants were few, and Gabriella was lively and attractive, as well as
an increasingly expert cook. Soon the whole group of friends was delighted
to let her practise on them, though they thought they ought to warn her.
'We're Jews, you know,' they said to her. 'If we're arrested, you'll be taken

too.' She just shrugged and smiled, in her warm, impatient way. '*Pazienza*,' she said – 'No problem.'

And so the time of flight, of breaking the chains, began, not just for Primo, but for all the friends. At first their political chains were not included: they still had some growing up to do for that. They were still ignorant, still the prisoners of severely limited and distorted information. At least they knew now that this was so: despite the dangers, like most Italians they listened in secret to the BBC, and read Swiss newspapers, which slipped across the border. They met soldiers home from Russia, Greece and Croatia, who told terrible tales of slaughters and deportations; they met Jewish refugees from Croatia and Poland, who said it was all true. And yet they still only half believed it. It was too horrible, it was surely exaggerated, it couldn't happen here. They knew what happened here: the racial laws, which were bad enough, but which you could bend, break, and certainly bear. No one had been slaughtered or deported from Italy, and no one ever would be. The Germans were invincible, but so were the Americans. The war would go on for years, far away from Italy, and far beyond the power of all Italians, never mind Italian Jews. What did these 'stupid and cruel Aryan games' have to do with them? For years they had been told they weren't even Italian. Good – then they needn't care what happened to Italy. They raised the cynical gaiety of all Italians by several bitter Jewish degrees, and threw themselves into having a good time. To do this they would have to forget, to deny the danger, to be ignorant. And so they did, and were – for a few more months, at least. 'Our ignorance allowed us to live,' Primo wrote, 'as when you are in the mountains, and your rope is frayed and about to break, but you don't know it, and feel safe.'

Politics excepted, they thought about everything, they talked about everything, they grew in everything. 'It was the single most formative period of all our lives,' says Silvio; and Primo agreed. They were, at last, truly independent; they were in a new, wide-open city; and they were among the closest and cleverest of friends. They read everything – Primo and Silvio especially never stopped reading. They went to concerts, to the cinema and theatre, they thrilled to O'Neill's *Mourning Becomes Electra* and Wilder's *Our Town* – daring modern plays, unlike anything they'd ever seen. They invented intellectual games, they even went to a spiritualist session ('in vain'), and discussed theosophy with friends. Euge did four or five drawings every night, until they all joined in, sitting around a table and scribbling in black ink on an old red tablecloth of Ada's. They sang folk songs – dialect songs from Lombardy and Piedmont, Waldensian songs Silvio had learned in the mountains; in one, about a man who chopped his wife to pieces, it was Primo's job to illustrate the chorus.

E LA TAGLIARONO · IN DODICI PESSI
E IL PIÚ LUNGO · ERA LUNGO COSÍ

'They cut her in a dozen bits
The biggest was like THIS'

But most of all, they talked. They talked about Primo's passions, which were not only for science: strange legends and traditions, Piedmontese, Rabelais; and the classic mountaineering books he was reading, like Lammer's *Fountain of Youth*. They talked about Euge's revolutionary plans for reducing the infant mortality rate ('and the senile birth rate') through architecture; and about other, no less revolutionary ideas of his, such as a closet for small children, with built-in steps so that they could reach everything themselves. They talked about their experiences of work, which were pushing them all rapidly to the left: especially Silvio, who decided that if a good and decent man like Bonzano was practically a bandit in business, it must be the fault of the system. They talked openly about everything, when you were meant to talk about almost nothing; they even talked, occasionally, about the war. They capped each other, they challenged each other, they sparked each other into great fireworks of arguments and ideas. Especially the very cleverest ones: Primo, Silvio, Euge and Ada. The rest gathered round, fascinated, attracted, slightly intimidated: Emilio the silent one, and shy Anna Cases, whom they often visited; Gabriella, more amused than intimidated; and others later, as we shall see.

In all this Primo took part eagerly. He did not stop being shy; he spoke rarely, quietly, and always with his ingrained, ineradicable modesty. Nor did he stop being serious. There remained something different about him, 'something better', Anna says: something unusually gentle, and unusually pure. But in this company he was not separate. He was relaxed, open, at ease; and brimming with his subtle, ironic humour. In fact, he was happy. I don't think he ever found a group of friends with whom he was happier; when he was happy in a similar group later, it would have at its heart some of the same people.

There were only two things as important as talk. One was climbing mountains.

Euge, Silvio and Primo were all equally keen. They went regularly to La Grigna near Lecco, a 'rock gymnasium' like the ones near Turin; and occasionally further afield. One of the most ambitious of their goals was Monte Disgrazia: 3,676 metres of rock and ice in the Valtellina. Silvio climbed it twice, once with Euge and once with Primo. In fact he and Primo had already tried to climb it the month before, and failed. This was the attempt that Primo chose to record: partly because of why they failed; and partly, I think, for another reason.

They set off one sunny morning in July 1942. Euge drew them, thus:

PRIMO E SILVIO AL DISGRAZIA SE NE VANNO
CON TRISTO ANNUNZIO DI FUTURO DANNO.

'Disgrazia' means, appropriately, 'mishap', 'bad luck'; so underneath Ada wrote (loosely translated):

> Mishap is the goal of our bold friends
> Which could be a clue to how they'll end.

They took the train to Sondrio, then the bus to Chiesa, in the Val Malenco: a long day's journey, especially in wartime, and by the time they arrived night was falling. They chose a modest inn, the Albergo Amilcar; handed in their documents, ate their supper, and went straight to bed, ready for an early start the next day. But almost immediately there came a nervous knock at their door: Please to come down, the police are here.

Downstairs they found a Marshal of the *carabinieri* talking excitedly to the innkeeper, and waving a copy of the *Official Gazette* in the air. He greeted them with a beaming smile. They were, he announced, in contravention of the law: Italian citizens of the Jewish race were not permitted to reside within ten kilometres of the country's borders – and Chiesa, gentlemen, is 9.9 kilometres from the Swiss border, as the crow flies, he'd measured it himself on the map. His red face shone with pride and perspiration; he expected praise, even from them. Was he drunk? Primo and Silvio wondered. Yes, Primo wrote,* but not with wine: 'with "the exercise of his powers", which as we know is a drug that exalts and intoxicates at least as much as alcohol'.

To the Marshal's surprise, the two young Italian citizens of the Jewish race were not impressed by his zeal. Instead, one was a lawyer and the other an ironist, and a game of cat and mouse ensued. There were no more buses at that time of night, Silvio pointed out, would he have them walk? The Marshal thanked him for his kind offer, but he had no spare men for an escort: how could he be sure they would walk in the right direction? They had the greatest respect for the law, Primo said, but they didn't know it; only he did, and only he, therefore, could decide what to do. It would have to be the police cells, then, the Marshal said. But now the innkeeper objected. These were his clients, 'race or no race', and anyone could see they were respectable people – they'd even paid in advance. Well then, said the Marshal, perhaps the innkeeper would take them as prisoners on consignment for the night, and one of his men would escort them to the first bus in the morning. In that case, however, Silvio said, their room at the

---

* In the story of this adventure, 'Weekend', in *Lilit*. All the quotations that follow are from this story.

inn was, in law, equivalent to a prison cell, and its cost should be borne by the police; perhaps, in law, even their meal the night before . . . The Marshal was no longer amused. They would have to apply to the District, he said, or even the Region, for that; the process would no doubt take a month or two. The innkeeper said he had a simpler solution, and gave them back their money then and there. The Marshal recognized defeat, and everyone retired to bed.

The prisoners woke the next morning, Primo wrote, 'rested and refreshed'. They'd made a long and difficult journey in vain, and had failed to climb Disgrazia; they were being expelled from a part of their own country, in which, as Jews, they were not merely outcasts but criminals. But this is a Primo Levi story: and what they'd salvaged from defeat was not little. Primo names only the smallest, most ironic part of it: 'the fact of having slept at the State's expense'. But he has shown us much more. He has shown us, in fact, why he and Silvio still loved their country. He has shown us Italy before 8 September 1943: a kind innkeeper; an absurd, officious, but human policeman.

He also shows us how near this Italy is to its end. Of their adventure, he says, only two photographs remain, taken just before their bus left at eleven in the morning. One shows Silvio gazing out of their window at the forbidden peaks, and at the clock on the church tower, which stands at half past ten. The other shows himself, washing his face at the basin: and 'you can see the same time on my wristwatch, which I am holding out to the camera'. Silvio still has both photographs, of which he has given me the copies opposite. He points out that Primo changed a detail in his description of the first: you cannot see the mountains, as he implies, but only fog. In fact, Silvio says, when they woke in the morning the weather was terrible, and 'We should probably have missed Disgrazia anyway, even if the State had not forbidden us to go.' It's easy to guess why Primo changed this detail: because his point was their defeat by the racial laws, not by the weather. But in his description of the second photograph there is a bigger change: he did not really hold out his wristwatch to the camera. Why did he invent that? Why did he repeat the time, twice, at the end of the story, as though he were holding out his watch to us as well? In order, perhaps, to signal that time was running out: that for him, for Silvio, for all the Jews of Italy, it was literally the eleventh hour.

★

Primo, the youngest member of the group, was twenty-three in 1942; the eldest, Ada, was twenty-eight. Their other major activity, therefore, was falling in love.

Primo even says so himself: between 'climbing' and 'inventing intellectual games' he puts 'falling a little in love with each other'. Who fell in love with whom? – he doesn't tell us that, of course. Even fifty years later the survivors are still reluctant to say. But in the distance something can still be seen. Ada was deeply in love with Silvio; but Silvio was in love with Anna Maria, who wasn't there. And shy Anna Cases was a little in love with Primo.

Anna was small, plain, gentle, and very intelligent, though she didn't think so. She didn't think she could attract anyone, least of all Primo, who, she saw clearly, was the most extraordinary person in this group of extraordinary people. But she did attract him, since more than anything Primo needed to be loved. Anna's parents watched over her so well that she had never seen or even spoken to him alone. But one day he happened to telephone when she was alone at home, and for one unguarded moment her voice was eager and warm. Immediately he asked, 'Why don't we meet somewhere tomorrow?' and she agreed. Perhaps he had been wanting to say this, had been practising saying it for weeks, as he had done with Clara Moschino. And perhaps she had been hoping, or not daring to hope, that he would.

But when they actually met the next day it was a hopeless failure. It was pouring with rain, and they had forgotten their umbrellas. Primo suggested they go into a cinema, but Anna didn't dare. Primo couldn't change her mind; probably he didn't try. When he thought he felt someone withdraw, he withdrew: this too had happened before. Very soon Anna made her excuses and fled. She was even more frightened than he was. She was so like him, she could have understood him almost better than anyone. But that is just why she couldn't help him; neither then nor later.

There was only one kind of girl who could have helped Primo Levi, who could have swept away the layers of reserve, self-doubt and sexual fear which bound him, and released the warm, longing man beneath. That was a girl who was the opposite of Anna: who was the opposite of himself, like Sandro and Alberto. He needed an opposite in love, as well as in friendship. And there was one, here in Milan, beside him in the lab, in the Via San Martino. Primo had been strangling his instincts at birth for twenty-three years, and had almost succeeded. But he had not lost the instinct to save himself from himself. He had tried to do it before – with Lidia, with the little daughter of his grandfather's tenants, with sweet, strong Clara Moschino. Now he did it again, most daringly of all. He fell in love with Gabriella Garda.

Phosphorus

In the story he wrote about her in *The Periodic Table* he called her 'Giulia Vineis'. Giulia, he wrote, was a slim dark girl, with elegantly arched eyebrows in a smooth, pointed face. She was Catholic 'without rigidity'. She was 'more open to practice than theory', 'generous and slapdash', 'full of human warmth and thirst for life'. All true, says Gabriella. She was 'an ordinary girl', intelligent, but with her greatest gifts in her hands. And she was lively, happy, optimistic – *too* lively and optimistic, she wore people out. She would always want to do new things – change jobs, move houses; later she would only have to say 'I have an idea' for her husband to groan, 'Oh no, not again!'

In 1942 she was already engaged to him. So yes, she admitted to Primo, she *had* engineered his job at Wander, and was very glad of his company; but he shouldn't get any ideas. She was very much engaged, very much in love. What about him? No? That was bad. No wonder he was wasting his time on work. The *Commendatore*'s ideas were quite mad, he did realize that? His cornflower petals were very pretty, but quite useless – and indeed the *Commendatore* soon decided this himself, and told Primo to move on to his second plan. But this one was even madder, according to Gabriella; and Primo agreed. Since phosphoric acid is crucial to the metabolism of carbohydrates, and diabetes is a disorder of this metabolism, all the diabetic needed was a little phosphorus. Just find out which plants are highest in phosphorus, extract it, inject it into rabbits, and measure their glycemia. So poor Primo did. Every night dozens of plants were left on his bench: 'onion, garlic, carrot, burdock, blueberry, yarrow, willow, sage, rosemary, dog rose, juniper'. And every day he tested their phosphorus content, feeling 'like a donkey tied to a pump . . . because to do work in which one does not believe is a great affliction'. In the next room Gabriella sang, and cooked, and every so often came to glance at his labours, 'provocative and mocking'.

Just as in Balangero, Primo very quickly knew all the gossip: that the *Commendatore* was sleeping with his secretary, Signora Loredana, that Signor Grasso was also after her, that Michela was probably a Fascist spy. (Gabriella no longer remembers Signor Grasso or Michela, but confirms that 'Signora Loredana' was the *Commendatore*'s mistress. Although they are both long dead, she consequently declines to tell me Loredana's real name.) This time Primo gathered his stories not by talking to everyone, but by talking only to Gabriella, who knew them all. 'Giulia was one of those people,' he says in 'Phosphorus', 'who, apparently without asking questions or going to any trouble, immediately knew everything about everybody, which never happens, God knows why, to me.' He had to ask, or he wouldn't know what people might do, or why; whereas Gabriella only had to look inside herself to find most human possibilities, good and bad.

This was fortunate, in the circumstances, since the *Commendatore* was obsessed with security, and actually prohibited conversation among his employees; to this end, for example, each had to arrive, and leave, at a different time. Primo always had difficulty breaking regulations, even ones as absurd as these; whereas Gabriella had no difficulty at all, and talked to everyone all the time. Without her he would have been even more isolated at Wander than he'd been at Balangero. She not only brought him the love story at the heart of 'Phosphorus', but all its other stories as well.

Primo told Gabriella that he not only had no girlfriend now, he had never had one. She was shocked. It was truly a pity, she told him, that she wasn't available herself, 'because she realized the sort of person I was, one of those who do not take the initiative, indeed run away, and must be led by the hand, solving all their little conflicts one by one'. But she had a cousin in Milan, who was also a bit shy; she would introduce them as soon as possible. In the meantime, he should get busy himself, it was ridiculous to throw away his best years on rabbits. 'This Giulia,' Primo wrote, 'was a bit of a witch: she read palms, consulted mediums, and had clairvoyant dreams. I have sometimes allowed myself to think that that haste of hers to free me from an old anguish, to procure for me immediately a modest share of joy, came from an obscure intuition of what fate held for me, and was unconsciously aimed at deflecting it.'

It's quite possible that Gabriella had such an intuition. Later, when she heard that Primo had been arrested and deported, she dreamt about him every night for months, 'terrible dreams about him suffering'. But now she was absorbed in her own passionate *Sturm und Drang* of love. Primo did not want to meet her cousin, and she did not insist. Nor did she try to find him someone else. Instead – egotistically, she says, because she loved his company – she let him do what he clearly wanted to do: spend all his time with her.

In 'Phosphorus' Primo describes a visit to the cinema with 'Giulia Vineis', to see *Port of Shadows*, a romantic love story with Michèle Morgan and Jean Gabin. When Giulia confesses that she identifies with lovely Michèle Morgan, Primo says that *he* identifies with dashing Jean Gabin – which is ridiculous, of course, and no, of course they're not in love with each other, like those two . . . But he *is* in love with her, and Giulia knows it. When the film is over, she announces that he must take her home. He can't, he says, he has a dentist's appointment. 'If you don't,' Giulia says, 'I'll yell *Giù le mani, porco!* – "Get your hands off me, you pig!"' Primo tries to argue, but Giulia opens her mouth and begins: '*Giù –*' Primo phones the dentist and takes her home.

This is the only part of 'Phosphorus', Gabriella says, which is not true – not even she would have dared to behave like that in 1942. When Primo sent her the story, just before it was published, she asked him to remove this episode. But he said that it showed her nature better than anything that really happened; and he refused. That showed *his* nature, I think – a ruthless writer, even with the woman he'd loved for thirty years. But he was right about hers. 'Giulia was a lioness,' he wrote; and Gabriella was.

But at the same time she had strange feminine fears. Once she called him to remove a spider from her workbench; and again he felt his desire for her tempted. Finally one day the tension between them came to a head. There was a furious thunderstorm, and Gabriella was afraid of thunder. Somehow she withstood the first two gigantic claps; but at the third she ran to him in terror. 'I felt the warmth of her body against mine,' Primo wrote,

dizzying and new, familiar from dreams; but I did not return her embrace. If I had, perhaps her destiny and mine would have gone crashing off their rails, towards a common, completely unpredictable future.

The chains of his double bind would not release him, even with Gabriella.

Primo describes one more encounter between them. Gabriella appeared one afternoon, eyes flashing, saying she needed him. She had important business right on the other side of Milan, there was no time to waste, would he take her on his bicycle? Primo, who according to the *Commendatore*'s crazy schedule had to leave twelve minutes before her, waited around the corner. Then he settled her on his crossbar, and began to pedal.

Gabriella was a restless person at the best of times, but that day she was like a volcano. She jerked the handlebars, she tossed her head, she gestured wildly; it was a miracle they stayed upright. At first she tried to stick to generalities; but 'Giulia was not the type to bottle up her secrets,' Primo wrote. Soon the truth was out: *his* parents had said no. Well, they wouldn't say no for long – she'd show them!

Primo listened, and tried to understand. How could anyone not want this glorious girl for their son? And where was *he*, why wasn't he rushing to defend her? As Gabriella continued to writhe between his arms, 'dishevelled and splendid in her anger', he felt 'an absurd hatred' growing inside him for this unknown rival, and 'a nauseating sense of emptiness'. *So this is what it meant to be different.* This is what it meant to be a Jew, an outcast, a grain of mustard: 'To carry on your crossbar a girl you desire, and to be so far from her you cannot even fall in love with her: to carry her on your crossbar along the Viale Gorizia to help her belong to someone else, and vanish from my life.'

As Primo waited outside his rival's parents' house, he thought that for the rest of his life he would regret that there had been nothing between himself and Gabriella but a few memories.

He thought that perhaps she would fail, and emerge in tears, and he could console her; and then he thought that these were wicked, mean hopes, and banished them. Finally he fell back on 'my dominant thought during those years': that the fiancé, the racial laws, were only excuses, and the real impediment was in himself; 'that my inability to approach a woman was a sentence without appeal, which would accompany me to my death'.

When at last Gabriella emerged – not in tears, of course, but shining with victory – he was ready, and in control. He congratulated her as believably as he could. And perhaps anyone else would have believed him. 'But,' he wrote, 'it is impossible to make Giulia believe things you don't really think, or to hide from her things you do.' 'What were you thinking about?' she asked. 'Phosphorus,' he replied.

In fact he did manage to hide a great deal from Gabriella. She did not realize the depth of his feeling for her until much later. And she did not realize the depth of his inhibition. How could she? She was young and vital, in love with love: she sensed his difficulties, but how could she imagine his real paralysis, his real despair? He hid them from everyone; and most of all, in hope and shame, from her. But even with her they were there. Therefore they are in her image, phosphorus, as well; and when he answered that he'd been thinking of phosphorus, it wasn't quite a lie.

Phosphorus is 'not an emotionally neutral element', he writes, but a deeply seductive one. Its beautiful name means 'bringer of light'. It is essential to both brain and blood, and to the growth of plants. But it is also in the tips of matches, which 'girls driven desperate by love ate . . . to commit suicide'. And it is in will-o'-the-wisps, the phosphorescent flames which dance above marshes, promising light where there is only mud. Phosphorus thus connects beauty and treachery, love and death. And phosphorus is not only Gabriella. In a poem he wrote much later, about another woman he desired – or perhaps any woman he desired – he used the same image. He called her Lilith, after the great seductress of men, Adam's first wife. 'It is written in the great book,' he wrote,

> That she is a beautiful woman down to the waist.
> The rest is will-o'-the-wisp and pale light.

★

Gabriella married her fiancé, Ercole Aliverti, on Christmas Day, 1942. By the autumn she had already left Milan, and Primo was left alone. He felt, he wrote, 'a widower and an orphan'. His life sentence of solitude had been confirmed. He must have been deep in gloom.

Did the group of friends notice? I doubt it. He was extremely skilled by now at disguising his elations and – especially – despairs; at presenting, even to his friends, a calm and even temper. Besides, they did not know how much in love he'd been. He would not tell anyone; or, if he did confide in one person – Ada perhaps, or Silvio – they would never tell anyone else. Anna had guessed, because she loved him. The others had probably guessed that he had a *tendresse*; but they had no idea how serious it was until they read *The Periodic Table* in 1975. After all, as Gabriella says, 'Neither had I'; though she wouldn't have to wait quite that long.

★   ★

Carla Consonni was Euge's girlfriend. They had met in Ponti's Studio, where she worked as a secretary for several years. From there she'd moved to an art gallery, which Allied bombing soon closed. Now she was managing another gallery: in Varese, near Milan, where both paintings and clients were safer. But Carla liked Euge's friends as much as they liked her; and every evening, despite the bombs, she returned. Most people were doing the opposite – still working in the city during the day, but leaving it at night. Carla thus found herself in splendid isolation on suburban trains, as her fellow citizens crowded together on the other platform. Where on earth, the evening commuters may have wondered, was this mad young woman going? She couldn't tell them the truth: 'In the opposite direction, gentlemen. To join a group of Jews.'

Carla was, and is, much too modest to think anything like this. But in fact her family had always taken the opposite direction. Her father, Paolo, was passionately antifascist, her brother's wife was Jewish, and she herself would eventually marry a Jew – whom she would meet, in fact, through the group of friends. Very soon, too, she would be more than brave, and take great risks to help Euge. But she is determined that she was not in any way unusual, and certainly not brave. She did not seek out Jewish friends on principle, she says. When she met them, through Euge, she simply enjoyed their company, she had the best time of her life with them. I try to say that it was not so simple, to have the best time of your life then, with Jews. But then I see that it was, for her. She enjoyed them quite simply, because they were clever, adventurous and exciting, and she was young, and like them free and independent for the first time. And that was why they enjoyed her. She was neither Turinese nor Jewish, neither repressed nor oppressed, all of which they still were. She was more normal, more ordinary – and not intimidated at all. Like Gabriella before her, she was a breath of fresh air.

When no one was looking (except Anna), Primo would gaze longingly at Euge and Carla. He was surely longing for his own Carla, cursing himself for having lost Gabriella, for never even having tried to win her. And then another girl joined the group. She would soon become very important to Primo. But he made no move towards her now: because of his 'sentence without appeal'; because he was mourning Gabriella; and perhaps also for another reason.

Vanda Maestro was exactly Primo's age. Like him, she was small and thin, and seemed frail; she *was* physically frailer than he, but her real fragility, like his, was inner. In Milan in 1943 she was lonely and unhappy. She'd come to join her family; which meant separation from her lover, Giorgio Segre. She was in a permanent state of restless dissatisfaction, because she was trying and failing to do what she'd always wanted to do: study medicine. In the formidable group of friends she was silent and shy, and very frightened during bombardments. In other words, she was weaker than Primo, instead of stronger. Perhaps that was the main reason he did not turn to her now.

She hadn't always been like this. Vanda's Italian Jewish family was very similar to Primo's. Her mother's family had been Piedmontese for generations, like Rina's. Her maternal grandparents had also come to Turin from the provinces around the turn of the century; and her maternal grandfather, Bonaiuto Colombo, was in the textile trade, like Cesare Luzzati. But here the resemblances ended. Vanda's father was not Turinese, or even Piedmontese, but from Padua. Her parents each had one sibling who became a teacher and academic; but her own family was less educated and intellectual than Primo's. In Primo's case it was his grandfather who owned a fabric shop; in Vanda's it was her parents. Rina had taken care of her younger brothers and sisters, but she had never worked a day in her life. Clelia Maestro ran a lace shop with her sisters before she married; then she and her husband worked together in their shop on the Via Lagrange. The Maestros were practical, conventional, money-oriented *petit bourgeois*. Vanda, who was intelligent, and gifted at mathematics, was the family intellectual. But neither she nor her parents had the seriousness, or the Turinese high-mindedness, of Primo and his family. They were simpler, warmer people. Vanda had inherited no crippling inhibitions; on the other hand, her mother had stopped her from entering medicine.

Her mother was the dominating force in Vanda's family, and probably in her life. Her father, Cesare, was a big, handsome but passive man, who left the running of both his shop and his family to his wife. Clelia was an excellent businesswoman, and an ambitious mother. Aldo, Vanda's elder brother, was probably less intelligent than Vanda, rather anxious and unambitious, like his father; but he was the son, and Clelia pushed him to study. He ended up with a degree in accountancy, entirely due to her persistence. She encouraged Vanda too, though not into medicine: first into mathematics, and when that did not suit her, into chemistry, like Primo. But other things were more important for girls. Vanda was not conventionally pretty, but her conversation was lively and curious, and she was at ease with and attracted to the opposite sex, dreaming of marriage from her early teens. And they were attracted to her. She had black eyes and black wavy hair, and she was full of spirit, despite her fears: she reminded Primo's cousin Giulia of Edith Piaf, the street singer, the sparrow. But Clelia prodded and pushed her daughter too. Vanda's physical frailty was not very serious, but it was real, and potentially deforming: she had a curvature of the spine, for which she had to wear a corset for most of her childhood. This made her clumsy; and it made her mother afraid that she might not appear healthy or attractive enough for marriage. So as she harangued Aldo to study, she harangued Vanda to wear her *bustino*: *he* had to be as brainy as possible, and *she* as beautiful.

Vanda wanted to be beautiful as much as any young girl, probably more. Her great friend Renata Debenedetti was very beautiful, and healthy and athletic as well; no doubt this was one reason why Vanda chose her. And Renata remembers that there was something obsessive, even desperate, in Vanda's dream of adulthood and marriage, as though she was afraid it might never happen. But this is Renata's only memory of strain in her friend. Her own rich, eccentric Jewish father had married a Catholic girl, who never got used to her grand new life; so that no one in Renata's family ever seemed to belong together, or to this world. By contrast not only Vanda's family but Vanda herself seemed to Renata wonderfully rooted and real. Many of their boldest ideas came from her – the idea of skipping their last year of *liceo*, for example, and entering university a year early. Vanda needed affection and reassurance from Renata, and perhaps the reflected glow of her beauty. But in turn she gave Renata her gift of attachment to reality. Theirs was a friendship of equals, Renata says; and within the limits of their families and times, one between two normal, happy girls.

Later, something changed. Probably it was reality itself: to which it is nourishing to be open in normal times, but dangerous in nasty ones. In 1938, when Vanda was nineteen, came the racial laws. At around the same time she wanted to change from mathematics to chemistry; Ponzio, happy to reject a female student, invoked the law, and she had to go the University of Genoa instead. Her brother had already moved to Milan in search of work: the family was beginning to break up. Then in 1939 its mainstay, Clelia, died. She had been ill for some time before; and it was during her decline and death that Vanda seemed to change. Before that it was her own health that was weak, yet she had not seemed to worry about it. True, there was her peculiarly intense longing to grow up; and once she had said to Renata, 'Who knows if we shall live past sixteen?' But otherwise she seemed to feel as immortal as the young always do.

Until her mother fell ill and died. After that – her first boyfriend, Guido Bonfiglioli, remembers – she became fearful about her health: 'She would have a sore throat, and be convinced she was dying of cancer.'

Perhaps that was natural enough. But Vanda – the Vanda people remember after 1939 or 1940 – was not only afraid of illness. She was afraid of all pain and suffering. And she was particularly afraid of bombardments. In Genoa in 1940 and '41 there were few; but there were many alarms, and each one sent her into paroxysms of terror. The same thing happened later in Milan, in the Via San Martino. Whenever there was a raid, the friends would ignore it; but Vanda would be terrified, and desperate to run and hide in the cellar.

Unlike her, Primo had iron control, and hid his fears. But he was like her in all of them – in the fear of pain and suffering and death; in the inability to block out the knowledge that they would come. Later, at the worst moment of their lives, he would learn this about her, and love her for it. Later still he would describe it: her 'terrible clairvoyance'; her inability to deploy 'those manoeuvres, those mists, those deliberate forgettings and illusions which are our best defences against the attacks of the world'. He could have been writing about himself.

The new version of the group of friends carried on as before, 'in an atmosphere of theoretical pessimism and actual pleasure', as Silvio puts it, 'living a happy life under the bombs'. With their new sense of themselves as Jews, they celebrated Passover in the Via San Martino. On New Year's Eve 1943 they partied so wildly at Saccarello, Primo's family house near Superga, that Ada echoed Dante, as Primo would do later, in darker key: 'Many things happened then, which shall best be left in silence.' They continued to talk and read to excess; and to write to excess too.

Everyone was writing – except, probably, Vanda, and also Emilio, 'who said it was undignified for an engineer'. Ada was writing poetry, Carla stories and 'novellas'. Silvio was writing 'a philosophical treatise' (Primo said), and Euge a novel. Silvio's treatise was called *Extrapolation* – hence his 'shipments and extrapolations'; it consisted of 'notes for a work on social ethics', written on hundreds of tiny pieces of onion-skin. Euge's *Twenty-four Hours* was an 'anti-novel', razing the traditional novel to the ground, like Milan: following a set of characters linked only by accidental encounters, telling the story through dialogue and external description alone. Despite this – or because of it – it drew a horribly convincing picture of a fragmented, alienated society.

On top of all this, Ada, Silvio, Euge and Primo also wrote two little books together, in late 1942 and early 1943. They called them *Libri segreti, Secret Books* – which indeed they had to be. They were hilarious, and thoroughly dangerous – full of jibes at Fascism, and jokes about rationing, censorship, the racial laws, prison ('The honest are in it, the thieves are outside'), and all the myriad pleasures and privileges of their lives. This, for example, is Euge's drawing of Mussolini:

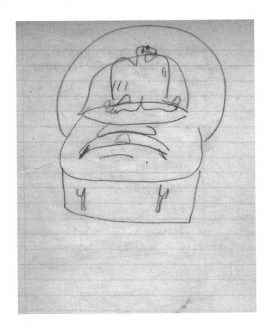

And Primo himself? He was writing too. And what he was writing, and what he said about it, are both very interesting.

'I . . . fantasized about writing the saga of an atom of carbon,' he says in *The Periodic Table.* Even this may not have been the first time he had had the idea. But by now it had become, at least in plan, a complete Primo Levi story – a cross between literature and science, in which he wanted to convey 'the solemn poetry . . . of chlorophyll photosynthesis'. But he would not write 'Carbon' for nearly twenty years. Instead he wrote poetry, like Ada, and like Silvio too; and a story, which had been meant to be a short novel.

Only one of these early poems has survived, at least in Primo's published opus. It is dated February 1943, and is called 'Crescenzago', after the Milan suburb where he went to work every day. 'Crescenzago' is a poem of suburban hopelessness and industrial misery, full of the horrified sympathy with workers which Silvio remembers from that time.

'Perhaps you've never thought of it,' Primo began. 'But the sun rises even in Crescenzago.' It shines sadly, finding no forest, no hill, but only smokestacks emitting smoke 'so black and poisoned / The wind is afraid its breath will be cut off.' Children's faces are the colour of dust, 'the women never sing'. A girl sits at a window sewing, never stopping until closing time; then 'She sighs and weeps, and that is her life.' Men rise at dawn to feed the 'grim black stonecrusher' (shades of Balangero!), or to watch the hand creep round a dial all day. The poem ends: 'They make love Saturday nights in the ditch / By the crossing keeper's cottage.' And that – we hear the echo – is their life.

These hopeless industrial lives were very far from Primo's. But we know by now that the further away from himself a subject was, the more he could explore himself in it. The real hopelessness in this poem is Primo's; left alone with work he despised, 'widowed and orphaned' by Gabriella. Many years later he told Silvio that the fact that he had written a depressed poem did not mean he was depressed – not in general, and not even at the time. It was a passing moment: he wrote it down, and it was gone. Perhaps he wanted to reassure his friend, or himself; and when he was young, it was mostly true. The moment did pass. But in early 1943 I think it came often, or lasted long. In that same month of February Silvio photographed the young poet at Saccarello, among the evening shadows; and the darkest shadow, not only literally, is on his face.

*

Primo recognized that his Milan poems were 'sad, crepuscular' – but so, he said, were everyone else's. He only wrote in Milan, he claimed, because everyone was writing. And it may be true. Perhaps he only wrote his sad Milan poems because Ada and Silvio were writing theirs. But what about his prose? What about that story?

He himself made no distinction. He did not write that story seriously either, he said. Besides, it was terribly bad – '*proprio molto brutto*'; it was unpublished, and would remain so; 'I could even throw it away perfectly happily and with a light heart.' But he had, in fact, worked on it very seriously. He often spoke as though it was the first story he'd ever written, forgetting 'Lead' and 'Mercury'. And he didn't throw it away.

'Uomo'

For forty years after Auschwitz Primo Levi asked the same question: What is a man? Now we know that he'd asked it even before. For this 'first' story by the author of *If This is a Man* was called 'Uomo': 'Man'.

'Uomo' asks the same question – but gives the opposite answer. This is the great debate of Primo's life, and it goes back even beyond 'Uomo'. It goes back to his boyhood – to the bullies, from Hitler and Mussolini down, who said that Jews were not fully human; and to his secret fear that they were right, at least about him. We might say that Primo Levi's life falls into three parts, according to the answer he gives to his question, *What is it to be fully human?*, and to its corollary, *Am I fully human?* His first answer appears when he – or his surrogate, Mario of 'I sintetici' – is twelve years old: human beings are physical, tribal and cruel; Mario is rational, and perhaps better; but he is, therefore, not human. This makes him very lonely and unhappy, but he resolves to bear his difference in silence. 'Uomo' comes at the end of this first part. It gives a similar answer to Primo's question, and its corollary; but it suggests a new and different resolution.

'Uomo' is a very strange tale, though none of the group's survivors seem to remember that now. Presumably, beside Silvio's philosophical abstractions and Euge's experiment in alienation, it did not stand out as peculiar. Nonetheless, it *is* peculiar, and disquieting.

It is cast in the form of a philosophical fable. L'Uomo, the Man, lives on the edge of nothingness, in a 'desert' where space and time have not yet begun. We shall call him 'Man', Primo wrote, only because there is no other name for him; but clearly this being outside space and time is not – or not yet – a man. In fact he sounds more like God: for the only thing we know about him, apart from his name, is that 'he understands everything', infinitely and perfectly, as we understand 'a mechanism we have built ourselves'.

It is impossible to conceive a beginning to space and time, for what can be outside space but another space, what can be before a moment but another moment? Primo recognizes this ancient philosophical problem by saying that what happened now, in this realm where there was no *happening* and no *now*, 'must perhaps be called a miracle'. 'Before' and 'after' began to 'oscillate', he wrote – rather like the atoms in Walden's Inversion! – until they separated enough for time to begin, and for decision and action to become possible. At that point, the Man decided to enter the world.

As the Man walks towards the world, for the first time the stars move, night follows day, the desert gives way to shrubs which live and die. He hears his first animal, far away, and sees his first birds. So far he is only on the edge of the living world: the land is poor, there are no trees, animal life has only reached the stage of 'spiders, snakes and beetles'. But the Man feels great joy as his mind enters this new communion, and his understanding extends easily to this new, changing reality. He is particularly drawn to the mountains, which appear for the first time now on the horizon, and which share something of the eternal with him; and he bends his steps towards them.

All is well until he finds himself high on a peak, in a long, cold night during which he cannot sleep. 'Then,' Primo wrote, 'it came to pass that the Man thought of himself.'

Now this has never happened to him before – though, Primo noted, it rarely happens to us either. We are so distracted by daily life and all its mysteries that we forget 'what is perhaps the one true mystery – our existence as thinking beings', 'the miracle of the human mind'. This too sounds like a step on a philosophical journey. But it soon becomes something rather different. To the Man, with his clear, undistracted mind, the thought of himself is like an abyss, in which he soon realizes that he could become caught and lost for ever.

He understands that this is a terrible and dangerous mistake: 'he, who understood everything, saw that there are limits to understanding'; and drew back from the brink.

At first light he rises and continues his journey, and for several pages Primo wrote about climbing – the ache of your limbs, the beat of your heart in your ears, the hot dry smell of rock, about which he would write (or had already written) in 'I mnemagoghi' that it meant 'peace achieved'. This climb is the end of the Man's journey, or as far as Primo got in telling it. He pulls himself up one last step, and he is on top. A new world lies beneath him: the world of life. Far below, at the bottom of a cliff so steep 'it took the strength from your heart', he sees the shining ribbon of a river, and beyond it a forest of firs, as 'dark and forbidding' as Dante's wood.

Primo was right – 'Uomo' isn't very good. It is so abstract it's hardly a story at all; its only character is so abstract he's hardly a character at all. The narrative voice is a recognizable ancestor of the Primo Levi voice we know – measured, detached, with Biblical echoes. But later this will give readers just the distance we need, in the face of too much reality. Here there isn't any reality. We feel like the Man peering into the abyss of himself, our ears 'ringing with emptiness'.

The story is a philosophical fable, and the Man is not a self-portrait. But Mario of 'I sintetici' *is* a self-portrait, though Primo never admitted it. And the Man is like a grown-up Mario. He is completely rational, and 'understands everything'. As long as he only proceeds towards the world of life, but is not yet in it, his thoughts retain the godlike certainty and completeness which is available to humans only in mathematics and logic. He is, Primo says, 'simple and healthy': because he does not know pain, his mind has not been 'tested and worn by the desperate complications of human affairs'; he does not know human beings – or rather he only has 'complete and geometric knowledge of them, cut off from human affections'. And these human experiences – pain, complication, affection – Primo wrote, 'are capable of blocking the cool and lucid mechanism of his faculty of understanding'.

The world of humanity, of life, in other words, is just as dangerous and threatening to the Man as it is to Mario. All both want to do is understand, and to that understanding, the complications of human feeling are opposed. This *does* connect to Primo Levi: to the Primo Levi who, a few years later, would refuse to hate, but only try to understand. And it must also connect to the Primo Levi who, a few months before, still did not dare to love; and who in this story itself retreated into a desert of abstraction.

But even the world of humanity is not the most frightening thing that the Man encounters, and the most dangerous to his faculty of understanding. That thing is himself. The night on the mountain during which he makes this discovery is the most disturbing episode of all, and the most prophetic. When the Man looks into himself Primo uses words like *vertigo*, and *dark tangle*, and *procession of shadows*, as in Dante's Hell. Here, long before the 'desperate complications of human affairs', he recognizes a block and limit to the understanding; and 'draws back sharply'. And 'the memory of that night did not leave him':

. . . every so often it suddenly seized him, making his heart beat faster. And he knew that this recent experience had changed him: a narrow crack ran from top to bottom of the solid structure of his mind.

The journey from before space and time to the world was convincingly philosophical; even the idea that reality disturbs the mathematical mind had some philosophy left in it. But now philosophy disappears. We are left with a mystery, even a pathology. What *is* the Man so afraid of in himself that it cracks his mind in two? What was the young author thinking of, and how did he know? The story does not tell us. But later on, split and division will become Primo Levi's most common images for himself, and for all of us – 'Man is a centaur; a tangle of flesh and mind, of divine inspiration and dust'. It would be no coincidence that he became – that he already was – the great builder of bridges, the great crosser of barriers – between people, between races, between species – if there was a barrier inside himself that he could never cross. I think there was; and that he knew that now, and put it in the story.

Of course I think that the Man was Primo himself in other ways as well, not least in his fear of the world he is about to enter. And when we consider the world Primo was about to enter, 'Uomo' suddenly seems frighteningly prescient: as though, despite its hyper-rationality, in writing it he had glimpsed not only his own darkness, but the future's.

That future now came closer. In November 1942 the Allies landed in North Africa, in early 1943 came the Russian victory at Stalingrad. The tide of war had finally turned; and suddenly its end seemed possible. 'In the space of a few weeks,' Primo wrote, 'each of us matured more than we had done in the previous twenty years.'

Some time before, someone – possibly Italo Diena – had introduced the friends to a young man called Camillo Treves. Treves, at thirty, was a few years older than them, a committed socialist and an active antifascist. Together with two older friends, he took part in whatever few and modest subversions he could – printing socialist posters, for example, and distributing underground newspapers. He saw the group often, and introduced them to one of his friends, Luigi Bissi, who was fifteen years older, and a Communist. But for a long time Treves dismissed the group politically. Their political discussions were as theoretical as ever; they knew that he was an activist, but never asked what he was doing. Primo struck him as particularly immature and politically uninterested.

Around the end of 1942 all this changed. Euge, who had in fact been deeply impressed by Treves, sought him out, saying that he was tired of words. Treves found him a contact; and Euge began using his visits home to bring antifascist underground papers from Turin to Milan. Silvio, who was moving to the left of Treves, sought out his Communist friend Luigi Bissi instead. Several times he and Primo went to Bissi for 'catechism' in Communism, and to be taught a secret history they knew nothing about – one which included names like Gramsci, Gobetti and the Rosselli brothers.

They too began small subversive activities – tearing down Fascist posters and putting up antifascist ones at night; writing *Viva la pace*, 'Long live peace', on banknotes – especially on the ten-lire ones, which (Silvio says) had large white spaces. And Ada too was finally 'cured', as she put it, of the 'drawing-room antifascism' of Milanese intellectuals. One evening a friend, Dino Luzzatto, who belonged to the Partito d'Azione, asked if he could meet another friend in her house. That friend was Mario Andreis, who later became one of the party's leaders. From that night on, Ada had joined the Partito d'Azione – typing for them, carrying their posters and newspapers to Novara and Turin.

But their preparation for what was to come was all too brief – and did not include, Primo said, 'how to make bombs or shoot a rifle'. In early March – only a few weeks after he had written 'Crescenzago' – came the first signs that Fascism was losing control: factory strikes broke out in Turin, and spread to many northern cities.* On 10 July the Allies landed in Sicily. On the 24th the Fascist Grand Council passed a vote critical of Mussolini; and on the 25th the King asked for his resignation. The Duce tottered out on to the steps of the Villa Savoia, unbelieving. Twenty-one years of Fascism were over.

The streets and squares of Italy filled with singing, dancing crowds, Fascist headquarters were burned, Fascist slogans and insignia were torn down. But though Mussolini had (temporarily) gone, his most faithful – or most compromised – followers were still there; and so was the new military dictatorship under Marshal Badoglio. In the middle of the wild celebrations, Ada and her Partito d'Azione friends found themselves being shot at by Fascist snipers, and then arrested. They were released the next day; but as they were being dragged away the crowd, thinking they were Fascists, yelled, 'It's all over, you bastards!' 'These words gave us immense pleasure,' Ada said.

* Primo even witnessed some of these. Bianca (who was a Communist by now, before Silvio) went to several striking factories, in solidarity with the workers, and took her Milan friends along on their weekends home.

The friends knew it wasn't over, but just starting; and Primo now approached the Partito d'Azione as well. But he didn't know that he would have only forty-five days to turn himself into a man of action. His new, practical teachers had argued that Badoglio was no fool – he would hold the Germans at the Brenner while he made a secret peace with the Allies, who could then reach the Alps within days. The reality was not so tidy. While the government hesitated throughout August, German troops poured over the border. By the time the peace was signed, northern Italy was already occupied.

For Primo and the others, as unaware as all Italians, life went on as normally as possible. In June he and Euge took a short holiday in Rome. In August the bombing of Milan intensified, and Ada was summoned to safety in Ivrea. On the 14th, after one of the worst bombardments of all, Primo and Silvio went to Cogne for the August holidays, to join Alberto and Bianca, Anna Maria and Franco Tedeschi, and other old Turinese friends. Afterwards it seemed extraordinary to them that they should simply have gone off on holiday as usual, in those final weeks 'so pregnant with tragedy'. But they still thought it was armies who would finish the war. So did everyone; Cogne was full.

By 8 September, when Badoglio announced the armistice on the radio, everyone except Ada was back in Milan. When Primo remembered that fateful day forty years later, he spoke for all of them.

. . . The news of the armistice [he wrote] filled us with stupid joy. Peace was coming – and with it the return to justice, equality and fraternity. The war would soon be over – and with it Fascism, Nazism, discrimination, humiliation and slavery. We felt like our ancestors after the flight from Egypt, when the waters of the Red Sea closed over the Pharaoh's chariots.

But Silvio was more political than he, and Euge more practical; and in fact neither was with him. After the August bombings Silvio's mother had insisted that he move out of the city, and live with relatives in Meda, about an hour away. And on 8 September Euge was also outside the city, visiting his sister. That first wildly idealistic, optimistic moment was Primo's alone. And so was this forlorn hope, of which we can guess the meaning – 'Now we could go back to our interrupted studies; we could enter professions that had been ruled out . . .'

But even for Primo that first instant of joy was very quickly over. The King and Badoglio fled to Brindisi to set up a 'Kingdom of the South', abandoning the northern half of Italy to the Germans. They left the Army with no clear instructions, except to stop fighting the Allies; and leaderless, demoralized, under-equipped, and for many on the wrong side, it collapsed like a house of cards. For days and weeks Italy teemed with men in ill-fitting civilian clothes, trying to get home before the Germans could stop them. Over half a million would be captured and deported to Germany.

At that moment of decision almost all the friends were separate from each other, and on their own. But their time together had set them on the same road. For a long time they had known who their enemies were, but not how to fight them. Until 8 September 1943 Nazis were nowhere, Fascists were everywhere, and the cells of resistance secret and small. Now the Nazis were about to knock on their doors. The nation was dividing between those who remained loyal to their allies even now they were invaders, and those who did not – who soon became the vast majority, even if only a few would take up arms. The decision was easy now: they would fight.

But in those first terrible days after 8 September there was no army to fight with – there never would be, they would have to invent their own. In the meantime, Italy was a Nazi-occupied country, and they knew enough about what happened to Jews in Nazi-occupied countries. Everyone had one overriding idea: to get back to their families, to make sure mothers and fathers, sisters and brothers, were safe, to decide together what to do.

Ada was already with her mother in Ivrea. Emilio went home to Ivrea too, and Euge joined his parents near Courmayeur. Silvio stayed with his uncle in Meda. Carla invited Vanda to her mother's house in Boffalora, a small village outside Milan, where she was sure she would be safe; but this was still too close to the bombing for Vanda. Instead she and her brother Aldo planned to escape to Switzerland.

Primo watched 'the grey-green serpent' of German troops enter Milan on the 8th. On the same day he resigned from Wander and went home. He left Milan so quickly that he may not even have managed to take all his books with him. His recorder was left behind in Carla's house, and lost later in a bombardment.

★   ★

Soon after they all left, the Via San Martino house was hit as well. Someone told Ada that it had been completely destroyed; or perhaps she simply heard the news that way. For that 'splendid season' of their lives, before the war engulfed them, was truly destroyed, as though it had never been. So Ada wrote an epitaph for their youth; and Euge drew the Via San Martino as a smoking ruin.

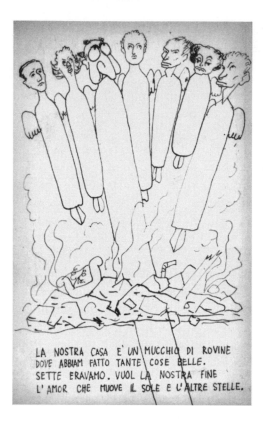

LA NOSTRA CASA E' UN MUCCHIO DI ROVINE
DOVE ABBIAM FATTO TANTE COSE BELLE.
SETTE ERAVAMO. VUOL LA NOSTRA FINE
L' AMOR CHE MUOVE IL SOLE E L'ALTRE STELLE.

From left to right: Euge, Carla, Silvio, Ada, Primo, Vanda, Emilio

> Ada's epitaph reads:
> 'A heap of ruins is our home
> Where we lived as happy friends.
> Seven were we. The love which moves
> Sun and stars wills our end.'

In fact, the house survived the war. Diogenes still stands, the garden is still green, and the building itself is rather more elegant and serene today than it was then. The survivors of the group of friends discovered this from one of Primo's biographers exactly fifty years later. But neither Primo himself, nor Ada, ever knew it.

★   ★

No one had any intuitions about what would happen, except perhaps Gabriella. Vanda had had that dark adolescent moment, when she suddenly felt she might not live beyond sixteen; but she'd probably just quarrelled with her mother. And yet this *was* a kind of intuition – not into her future, but into her nature. Unlike most of us, she could not instinctively and irrationally believe that nothing bad would happen to her. Nor could Primo. In a way he too had had an intuition, and not only in writing 'Uomo'. It had happened some months before, on a climb. He had been inching up a rock face after Euge. Suddenly the rope between them dislodged a stone, which plummeted directly on to his head. It was not a large stone, and the wound was superficial; but it bled profusely, and they had to give up their climb and go home. Primo told Euge what had happened when he looked up, and saw a small dark object falling down on him. He was only twenty-three years old; but he had instantly thought, '*Sono morto*': 'I'm dead.'

Gabriella

Gabriella

'I am not a fit person to be seen,' Gabriella said. She was still mourning her beloved younger son, who had died two years before. She spoke to very few people, and no new ones. She was also afraid (she said later) of losing Primo for a second time, by talking about him. As long as her memories of him were locked up in her mind they were hers. If she shared them they would fade.

Even though she was saying no, her voice was not cold, only sad. I could feel the sadness on the telephone line all the way from Milan. I did not ring again for many months; and this time she sounded better. 'Do you think so?' she said hopefully. All right – we'd try.

When she opened the door, for one moment I saw a young girl. Then she smiled; and her face was soft and lined and old, but the elegantly arched eyebrows Primo had described were still there. She led me to the sofa, and straight away poured the tea she'd prepared for me, because I was English, and had had a long journey.

We began to talk about all the people we now knew in common – the chemistry graduates of 1941, the friends of 1942. Gabriella was as eager for their latest news as I to hear about them over fifty years before, and it seemed as though we couldn't talk fast enough. Intense, contradictory impressions filled me. One moment she was like a mother, telling me I worked too hard, pouring more tea; the next she was like a child, wanting praise for some long-ago decision. One moment she was so sad I felt my own heart crack; the next we were giggling like girls over some gossip she shouldn't have told me, and made me promise to forget. She talked about her grandchildren, whom she loved dearly – 'but it's not the same as your own children. For my children I had a *consuming passion.*' She talked about them: her sons Gabriele and Valerio, her daughter Beatrice. She talked about her husband, Ercole. And she talked about Primo.

I think she told me everything that day; all our conversations since then, and all our letters, have only drawn out and deepened what she told me the very first time we met. She couldn't bear to talk about Primo, she hadn't wanted to talk about anything for a long time. Then suddenly, and for good, she changed her mind. She did not so much tell me her memories as fill me with them, so that I sat there shaken by storms, and could hardly totter to my feet at the end. She affected me, she changed me; and she made me wonder how much she had changed Primo, and whether she could have changed him still more.

The next time we met downtown. The street where she picked me up was a cul-de-sac, with cars parked so thickly on either side that only the narrowest passage was left between. But Gabriella backed down it with absolute aplomb. When we got to the café she'd chosen, there was nowhere to park as far as the eye could see. So she pulled up on a zebra crossing, and left the car there. She was in lioness mood today.

She was simply and beautifully dressed, in a white blouse and a grey skirt and jacket. Every time I saw her she was very beautifully dressed, in warm browns or cool greys. It was very important to her to be elegant and attractive, she admitted; perhaps too important. She quoted her grandmother to me: *Una giovane deve piacere, una vecchia non deve dispiacere*, A young girl should please, an old woman should not displease. She teased me about my shapeless sweater, my innocence of make-up. 'It's too late to learn now,' I said. She was shocked. 'It's *never* too late,' she said.

What happened, I asked, after her marriage to Ercole, on Christmas Day 1942? She followed him on his various postings around the country, she said. Once he was about to be sent to Africa, but in the last minute the order was cancelled. Then after 8 September he did not want to fight for the

Republic of Salò.* Like so many others, he tore off his uniform and went home: so Gabriella returned to Milan just as Primo left it. But with a young husband of military age, she too had to live in hiding. The only work Ercole could get was illegal and underpaid. And then, in May 1944, Gabriele was born. In the autumn, still nursing him, Gabriella went back to Wander.

But the long hours of lab work were not easy to combine with a family. So after the war Gabriella left what Primo would call 'militant chemistry', and became a chemistry teacher for the next thirty-two years. She loved teaching. Not the chemistry itself, which at *liceo* level is not very exciting; but (she smiled) the relationships with her students. She loved them, and they loved her. Once a young man in a flower shop pressed a bouquet of roses in her hand, saying, '*Per la mia professoressa*', 'For my teacher' – he was an ex-student, who still remembered her after more than ten years.

She had remained a lioness. During the student protests of 1968 – Italian students were among the first to catch the Parisian fever – she had arrived at school one day to find a picket line. 'What's this?' she'd asked. 'We're protesting,' the students answered. 'Well, I'm going in,' she said, and did. She no longer read palms, or went to mediums. But in her inconsolable grief for her son Valerio she had turned to spiritualism, and it had helped her. She has no faith, she explained, she cannot believe in the Christian afterlife – but the thought that Valerio did not exist any more, that he was simply wiped out, was intolerable to her. At last someone suggested this solution, and she tried it, and was comforted. One day she had had such a strong sense that he was beside her that she had spoken to him; and felt, if not heard, his reply. Ever since then she has known that he is somewhere, even if it is not with her. 'Oh, I know what people think,' she said, 'and besides I think it too, *Where will it all end?*' She tapped her forehead; and suddenly we were laughing again.

She was seventy-six years old when I met her, but I'd never known anyone so mercurial and contradictory: so normal and so strange, so weak and so strong, so loving and so in need of love. But always brave. Once when she asked me how I was, I grimaced – I had some minor ailment. 'You must say, "Fine, thank you",' she said. 'Just "Fine, thank you", no matter what. A friend taught me that, long ago.' In the years that have passed since then she has had many serious ailments. I always know when she is lowest, because she ends her letter '*Io sto bene*', 'I am fine.'

When you are with Gabriella, you keep forgetting an important thing about her, even now that she is old and can no longer disguise it. When she was

---

* The puppet Fascist government the Nazis set up under Mussolini, whom they snatched from prison on 12 September.

young you hardly noticed it at all, because she was so determined to overcome it. But it was even more important then, at least to her. She had been born with a small bone missing in one leg. Today this could be put right; but she was born too early. In her first six or seven years she had at least half a dozen operations, which didn't really work; she had to wear braces and calipers throughout her childhood. Later she did everything a normal girl would do, and more – from hiking, to swimming, to carrying her children everywhere. In 1942 Primo particularly noted her 'lively and precise way of moving', her capacity to '[travel] for ten hours standing up in a train . . . to spend two hours with her man'. But though she overcame it, and disguised it, Gabriella could never use her right leg normally. And of course she couldn't wholly disguise it. Everyone knew there was something wrong.

Until she lost Valerio, this was the dominating tragedy of Gabriella's life. As a young girl she was convinced she could never have a normal life, a husband and children. So of course she hid this too, and defied it. She came top in all her classes, to show how normal she was; she affected a tremendous confidence and gaiety. And all the time, underneath, '*mi vergognavo tremende-mente*': she was terribly ashamed.

On top of all this, she was the only child of a difficult marriage. Her father was a career army officer who retired at forty, immediately after the First World War, and never worked again. He never loved her mother, Gabriella says, he blamed her for everything, and made great neurotic scenes, in which he threatened to kill himself with his Army revolver. And perhaps he was right, Gabriella adds, for her mother was a cold woman. He was very severe to her too, and yet she knew he loved her. But her mother never gave her the affection she craved, because she was not a boy, and because she was not perfect.

And yet – she was Gabriella. The more unhappy she was at home, the more she simply determined to find happiness elsewhere. As a child she was extremely sociable, always outside with her friends; if her mother tried to keep her home she simply climbed out the ground floor window. She was afraid of nothing, except her father's revolver. But already she had visions which came to her aid. In one of these she saw a woman rider, whom she knew to be herself. She heard a shot, and the woman fell from the horse. After this vision of her own death by shooting she wasn't afraid of the revolver any more.

When she was sixteen a strange thing happened. One day after school a boy asked if he could carry her books for her. Every day after that he asked her again. Finally she asked him why, and he told her that he loved her. She couldn't believe it – she thought she would explode or fly or die, that someone could love her after all. This was the happiest moment of her life, and it became her happiest year.

Then one day he came to her and said that they couldn't go on, he couldn't tell her why. But his sister did: and of course it was her leg. He wasn't sure he could bear it, that he could cope with her disability. Her love changed into the most intense loathing. For days she wanted to die, and thought only about how to kill herself. But the *liceo* examinations were coming, and she thought: I'll do those first, and kill myself after. By then, naturally, the impulse had passed. But whenever she saw him she felt so sick that she went to a different school just to avoid him.

Not long afterwards he came back, saying that he'd been wrong, he couldn't live without her. But she said she never wanted to see him again; and she didn't. Though it broke her heart, whenever she saw him the sickness returned. He volunteered as soon as he could, out of youthful despair, and died in Greece at twenty-one.

Gabriella never forgot this boy, whose name was Nando. But by the time Primo met her she had found her way back to happiness, as she always would. At university she had many eager suitors, and her fear of spinsterhood began to fade. By their next meeting, in Milan, it was gone – Ercole loved her, he wanted to marry her, she could have a husband and children after all. As she did.

⋆   ⋆

So all along, Gabriella had been close to Primo inside. She too had felt a freak, condemned to solitude. For her too life meant the constant overcoming of a hidden flaw. But Primo endured, and compensated. Gabriella refused to endure anything. She is selfish and bad, she says – but also kind, and generous. She was his opposite, but also his twin. She was everything.

After he had been married for twenty-seven years, and Gabriella for thirty-two, Primo wrote this about her, in the last lines of 'Phosphorus':

. . . we have remained friends, we see each other every so often in Milan, and talk about chemistry and other sensible things. We are not dissatisfied with our choices and with what life has given us. But when we meet we both have the curious and not unpleasant impression (which we have described to each other several times) that a veil, a breath, a throw of the dice, deflected us on to two divergent paths which were not ours.

Is this true? I wonder. Could Gabriella have saved Primo from himself, could she have made him happy?

She doesn't hesitate – yes, she says, yes. They saw each other always, until the end. She loved him, she was never happier than when she saw him, when she was talking to him. And he loved her. When they were old he asked her: 'If one day both our spouses were dead, would you marry me?' She answered 'Yes.' 'And I think,' she says, 'it would have been a very happy marriage.'

There would only have been one problem, which, honest as ever, she admits to me. But it wouldn't have mattered, she says, when they were old. They were never lovers. She was never in love with him that way; nothing had changed since 'Phosphorus'. And he knew it. She loved him, but did not want him; and he settled for that, and never tried to change it.

I look at Gabriella, and I think, sadly: no. It wouldn't have worked. Primo needed sexual love, and she felt none for him. He needed unconditional love; but she wasn't his mother, and couldn't give him that either. She thought he told her everything, but he didn't. When she'd talked to him about her childhood shame, about her unhappy parents, locked in battle – why had he never said *Me too*, that is just what happened to me? He never did. He never mentioned his childhood at all, and he never mentioned his depressions. He told her his troubles, but not his weaknesses. That was his instinct; and I think it was the right one. Gabriella was a passionate, primitive woman, a lioness who needed a lion. His sense of his own unloveability had already stopped her from desiring him. If he had shown her its true depths, perhaps she couldn't have loved him at all.

And it wouldn't have worked for her either. She needed passion and devotion, and Primo spent his life in his study. She thinks now that loving kindness would have been enough, especially when she was old. But she's wrong. She needs as much now as she ever did, perhaps more. Now and then she allows herself to believe it would have worked, because it comforts her, as it comforted him. But really she knows it is an illusion. And she doesn't really need it: 'I know,' she says, '*io sto bene*'. And she smiles.

7. Amay and Aosta:
September 1943 – January 1944

Primo as a partisan

When Primo arrived at Saccarello he found not only his mother and sister, but most of the Luzzati clan. The only one who definitely wasn't there was Rina's second sister, Nella Avigdor, and her family. In July 1939, when Paolo was fourteen and Lisetta three, they had boarded an almost empty ship, and set sail for Brazil.

Of the Turin Jewish community of 4,000 or so, only 1,500 managed to leave Italy before the storm. That the Avigdors should have been among them was almost entirely due to Nella, the one member of the family who turned out not to be a *bugia nèn*.

In fact, she'd never been one. People didn't change their peacetime character in war; they lived, or died, by the one they'd always had. Nella had never liked the narrow, inward-looking atmosphere of Turin; when she married she moved away, and didn't return. Then – and this is the element of luck that was always needed – her husband Emilio had an uncle in Brazil. Emilio *was* a *bugia nèn*, and would never have thought of leaving. But like all Jews he had lost his job in 1938. When his uncle offered him work, and visas for the family, Nella said they must go; and Emilio reluctantly agreed. On arrival he discovered that there was no work waiting for him after all: it had been a ruse devised by Nella and his uncle to make him go.★

In order to pick up and go, these were what you needed – a daring and decisive nature (or wife), luck and help, and preferably money. The rest of the family had either none, or not enough, of these. Since the autumn of 1942, when the worst bombing had begun, they had abandoned the city; but only for Saccarello, four or five miles away.

Everyone was doing this: by the summer of 1943 half the population had left Turin, at least at night. Fifteen minutes away down the hill, for example, was one of the villas owned by Renata Debenedetti's father. Many of her friends would join her here. That summer one of those friends was Luciana Nissim, who had just taken her degree in medicine in July. One evening Luciana arrived in an even greater rush than usual: it was 8 September, and she had just heard the announcement of the armistice on the radio.

The next day, and the days after, were 'dead days', Renata says, days of silence and confusion. There were no newspapers, the radio was silent, no one knew what was happening, or what they ought to do. Somehow she and Luciana knew that Primo and Anna Maria were at Saccarello. 'Let's see what they're going to do,' Luciana said. The two climbed up the hill – through the woods, so as not to be seen. They found Primo, Anna Maria and Rina together; Renata doesn't remember anyone else. The occasion was hurried and anxious – and yet, compared to what was to come, still innocent and hopeful. Probably Primo was already thinking of the Val D'Aosta; perhaps he said so, so that Luciana, when she herself went there, knew he was nearby. Luciana doesn't remember; she doesn't remember the meeting at all. But Renata doesn't think so. The Levis were as undecided as they were, she remembers. They didn't know what to do either. But one thing struck her very clearly: when she saw Primo that night, on the eve of decision, 'I felt that his bond with his mother was very strong.'

For the next few days the debate continued, still in the dark. But finally the first decisions were made. Luciana went to join her family in Pistoia;

★ After a few months he found work as an electrical engineer. Nella flourished in São Paolo, first as an interior decorator, later as the founder of a small knitwear company, with two other (non-Jewish) Turin ladies. The family settled happily in Brazil for over twenty years. Emilio died there in 1957. Nella, Paolo and Lisetta only returned to Turin by chance, when on a visit home in 1961 Nella was found to have cancer, and soon after died there.

from there they went together to Brusson in the Val d'Ayas, about twenty miles from Aosta. Renata decided to return to Rome, where she'd been living, and where she hoped her fiancé would come looking for her (he did). And Primo, Rina and Anna Maria went together to the Val D'Aosta, at first (Primo wrote) to stay with friends.

Giulia Colombo remembers them leaving. But she and her parents stayed on at Saccarello; so did her cousins Giorgio and Ada and theirs. Until one day Franco Momigliano came and told them it was too dangerous: everyone knew them, and their address was on the 1938 census of 'Italian citizens of the Jewish race'. So finally, on 8 October – exactly a month after the occupation began – the last of the Luzzatis left Saccarello. Giulia's family went to Murazzano in the Langhe, Giorgio's and Ada's to Santena, about twelve miles from Turin. Later the Colombos would end up near Santena as well. The *nonna*, Cesare Luzzati's widow, lived with Corrado, Irene, Giorgio and Ada in their single freezing room in Santena. Her other son, Gustavo, remained hidden in Turin; his wife and daughters moved from convent to convent in and around the city. Jole and her two young sons went to Val della Torre, also about a dozen miles away. The whole Luzzati family would survive in hiding; only Primo was deported, and no one died. Even the *nonna* lived to see Italy liberated, and – apart from Primo – the family reunited, before dying in the midst of the celebrations, in late April 1945.

In the Val D'Aosta the Levis found terrible scenes: soldiers streaming home from France, tired, hungry and demoralized, avoiding the roads, 'marching interminably along the high mountain paths, from hamlet to hamlet, like a flock without a shepherd'. After a month or so Rina and Anna Maria left. Both would have rather a brave war. Rina was constantly on the move, living mostly near Ivrea, but regularly visiting her mother in Santena and her daughter in Turin; often staying, when she was there, with the Guidetti Serras. Anna Maria became a *staffetta*, a courier, for the Partito d'Azione in the city – liaising between groups, distributing news-sheets, helping and even treating wounded partisans. She slept in ruined houses, or with friends, some of whom took her in willingly, some less; later she and Ada Della Torre found rooms together in the Corso Re Umberto, and stayed there till the end. She was a good *staffetta*, Primo wrote, because she was so strongly motivated, not only politically but personally: for 'both her fiancé and I had been deported, and to all intents and purposes had vanished from the face of the earth'. Franco Tedeschi did vanish from the face of the earth. He was captured, together with his father, in the spring of 1944, as they were trying to escape to Switzerland. He was deported, first to Sosnowitz, and then to Mauthausen, where he survived almost to the end. But in March 1945 he died in Mauthausen, probably of fever.

Primo's movements now are unclear. Probably in late September, he, Rina and Anna Maria came to a tiny hamlet called Amay, above St Vincent, which is at one end of a high and winding pass called the Col di Joux, at the other end of which lies Brusson. Perhaps he promised his mother, before she left, that he would only hide there. And in truth he still hesitated. He must fight – but with whom, and how? And *could* he fight? Could he overcome his horror of violence, could he overcome – he admitted to himself – his fear? 'I felt indecisive, and unprepared,' he wrote, 'and the prospect of combat terrified me.' Several more days passed in agonizing indecision.

Perhaps the most dangerous moments of all were these very first ones. Italy was like someone stunned: defenceless, disorganized, still ignorant of her enemy's real nature. Some of the cruellest and most cowardly events of the next twenty months happened now, not far from where Primo was struggling with himself; and caught up in them were members of his own family.

All three Levi brothers, Cesare, Enrico and Mario, had drifted away from their religion and community. But of the three, Enrico still kept up the most connection: he and his wife Lisa went to synagogue on Saturdays, and met and helped Jewish refugees in Genoa. He was, therefore, very likely the best informed; and also the richest. Perhaps for these reasons, he was the only one to act. In 1939 he sent his sons Franco and Paolo abroad – to Brazil, like the Avigdors. Unlike Nella and Emilio Avigdor, however, he and Lisa did not go themselves. Perhaps Enrico – hard hit, like all Jews, by the racial laws – could no longer afford four passages, and chose to save the children. In any case, he and Lisa had a difficult war. They spent most of it hidden by a priest in the Langhe, where their problems were mostly hunger and fear. But at one stage even this refuge became too dangerous, and they had to leave. Enrico and Lisa would never speak of this time afterwards. Nonetheless, they survived it. When Franco and Paolo returned from Brazil, complete with new wives, Enrico was poor, and ill with diabetes, but still alive. He died of heart failure in 1952; Lisa survived him for another fourteen years.

It was Mario, the youngest brother, who stumbled into one of the very first anti-Jewish atrocities in Italy.

Mario was the oculist whose wicked worldly wife, Emma, had put his family beyond the pale for Rina. All Turin knew that Emma had a lover – her cousin, Rodolfo Segre; and all Turin knew (or said) that Mario accepted the situation with detachment. He was also detached from his religion; and he, Emma and their son Roberto had all been baptized into the Catholic Church, probably at the time of the racial laws. As a result, Roberto had been able to enter university in 1938. Nonetheless he suffered from his exclusion as a Jew (he was still called Levi, and no one was fooled); and from a sense of futility about preparing for the future. He failed his exams, and threw himself into bridge, parties and love instead.

A year or two before, he had met a pretty, lively girl called Elena Bachi, with whom he had fallen violently in love. Elena too had suffered very much from being that '*bestia rara*', that rare animal, a Jew; and she too had converted to Catholicism after the final insult of the racial laws. (In her case this was not just an externally protective move: her parents converted with her, and all three remained fervent Catholics for the rest of their lives.) At first both families were opposed to the match – Roberto was too young, and too unqualified. But the power of his love bowled everyone over, including Elena herself. In February 1943, when he was not yet quite twenty-three, they married. A month later they joined Mario and Emma in Orta, on the Lago d'Orta, one of the loveliest places in the world. The Levis had rented summer lodgings there for years; and like many others now, they'd taken refuge in their holiday home from the bombing in the cities.

On 8 September they were still there. Over the next weeks and months the area around the Lago Maggiore and the Lago d'Orta would fill with Jews trying to flee to Switzerland. But the Levis were not part of that. They were only *sfollati*, evacuees from the bombing; the young couple in particular had spent the last six months forgetting the war, forgetting everything but their new life together. Roberto and his parents felt perfectly safe in Orta; even after 8 September they never thought of leaving.

But Elena did. Perhaps the pain of exclusion, which had gone very deep in her, had left her permanently on the alert to danger; perhaps, simply, she felt less at home in Orta. In any case, she said straight away that she no longer felt safe in Italy, and they should leave. The Levis looked at her pityingly; but of course Roberto said that he would go wherever she wanted. So it was decided: the young ones would go to Switzerland; Mario and Emma would wait out the war in Orta.

Mario went to his friend, *Avvocato* (Lawyer) Gabriele Galli, who was the mayor of Orta. Galli knew exactly what to do: he contacted the priest of Omegna, at the northern tip of the lake, Don Giuseppe Annichini. The date was fixed for Wednesday, 15 September. *Avvocato* Galli would bring Roberto and Elena to Omegna; from there Don Giuseppe would take over. Then Galli suggested the next day would be better: Thursday was market day in Omegna, he could meet his clients, it would look more natural. That one day's delay – so sensible, so innocent – was fatal.

On 11 September the First Battalion of the Second Regiment of the *Leibstandarte* Adolf Hitler, stationed at Chivasso near Turin, dispatched two *Sonderkommandos* to the area around the Lago Maggiore. *Sonderkommando* means 'Special Commando'; 'special' being the Nazi euphemism for murder, in particular the murder of Jews. They arrived a day or two later. By the time they left at the end of September fifty Jews had been killed: fifteen at Meina, fourteen at Baveno, ten at Arona, four at Stresa, three at Mergozzo, two at Pian Nava, and 'two', say the history books, 'at Orta'.

Between four and five in the afternoon of the 15th Roberto and Elena were sitting in the café on the main square of Orta when a small lorry arrived. Several SS got out and went into the *Municipio*, the town hall. No one had heard of round-ups of Jews yet; but round-ups of young men of military age were common. Roberto had better not be seen. The young couple hurried home.

The SS summoned Mayor Galli and his deputy to the town hall, and told them that all Jews living in Orta were to be handed over. Galli said that there were no Jews living in Orta. Whereupon the SS officer in charge showed him a list, which had on it the Levi family's name and address. Galli stood his ground, saying that the Levis were baptized Catholics. The SS officer turned to the head of the *carabinieri* and ordered him to direct them to the address on the list: Via Olina 50.

Mario, who must have seen or heard what was happening, ran to Galli's house. Galli, returning, met him there, and urged him to come away with him straight away.

In the meantime, at the Via Olina Roberto and Elena heard the SS arrive. Not knowing where to hide, and not, of course, suspecting the worst, they presented themselves as required. They found two young SS, one slightly older and in charge, the other 'a good-natured boy' (Elena remembers) of eighteen or nineteen. They had an interpreter with them. Questions were put – were they Jews? What were they doing in Orta? – but extremely courteously. The Germans offered cigarettes, the Levis offered coffee; it was more like a polite tea party than an interrogation. At the end of it the SS said they would have to escort them elsewhere for further questioning; and they would need to speak to Professor Mario Levi as well. Roberto was sent to look for his father, but returned alone, saying he hadn't found him. In fact he *had* found him, at *Avvocato* Galli's; but Galli had told him to deny it.

By now Emma had returned. The conversation continued, and again the SS asked Roberto to look for his father. They were as polite as ever; but they spoke more insistently this time, and Roberto clearly sensed a menace. He returned to Galli's and told his father that Emma and Elena were in danger, he must come. Galli tried to persuade the two Levis to save themselves, but they refused. They returned to the house together.

At one stage the older SS, a tall, distinguished-looking young man, told Elena that she too would be required. But when she had fetched a sweater

and handbag he looked at her again and said, 'No, you can stay.' He cannot
have been more than twenty-five years old, but he held the power of life
and death. Elena has never known why he changed his mind. But 'That was
my luck,' she says. 'That is why I am here.'

The Germans then put Mario and Roberto between them and left, telling
the women not to follow. They followed nonetheless, and saw that the SS
were less polite now: they marched the two men rapidly towards the square,
shoving passers-by out of the way. When they reached the lorry they
bundled them on. Then there was a pause: a long pause, it seemed to Elena.
They were waiting, she thinks, for darkness. The square filled with *ortesi*;
mostly women, since all the men between fifteen and fifty took care not to
appear. The SS did not let Emma and Elena approach their husbands.
Finally, when the sun had gone down, they drove off. Elena remembers
that Roberto leaned down and said to a friend: 'Take care of my wife.'
Gianna Travaglini, who was a young girl in 1943, thinks that Mario had his
cane in one hand. With the other, she says, he gave a little wave, and tried
to smile.

For the next few days Emma and Elena went from one German headquarters to another, in Pallanza, in Baveno, in Stresa. 'Our name is Levi,'
they said, 'we are looking for our husbands.' No one knew anything, of
course; but each time they were politely received, and allowed to go. A
week later, bodies began to surface in the Lago Maggiore, with their hands
bound and bullet-holes in the backs of their necks. Mario's and Roberto's
were not among them. They included women and children (the youngest,
Blanchette Fernandez Diaz from Salonika, was twelve years old). It was
never clear why Emma and Elena were spared, or exactly what had happened
to their husbands. It seems certain that they were killed immediately by the
distinguished-looking young officer and his good-natured teenage soldier.

Emma and Rodolfo Segre survived the war hidden in a nursing home
near Turin, and married in 1950. *Avvocato* Galli and Don Giuseppe helped
Elena to flee to Switzerland, but she was turned back at the border. She
made her way back to Omegna, where her parents joined her; and here they
spent the rest of the war, as Don Giuseppe's 'cousins' – as he told everyone,
including his elderly father ('they had so many relatives the old man couldn't
remember them all'). During all this time Elena was quite fearless, because
she didn't care if she lived or died. She too finally remarried and remade her
life. But it has been an unending anguish not to know what happened: like
having a book torn from your hands, she says, and never knowing how it
ended. She had hoped the pain would fade as she grew older; but on the
contrary it has deepened.

Don Giuseppe Annichini, who had helped many other Jews as well, was officially thanked by the Jewish Communities of Italy after the war. SS Captain Hans Walter Krüger and SS Lieutenant Karl Heinz Schnelle, the heads of the *Sonderkommandos* responsible for the murders of September 1943, were given life sentences in 1968. It is not clear which of the two was the well-bred young officer Elena remembers, or whether he was someone else altogether. Perhaps it doesn't matter: both were released in 1970, having served less than two years. The German Army officer in charge of the area after the SS reign of terror was a Captain Stamm, who secretly cooperated with Don Giuseppe to save several Jewish lives. He, by contrast, killed himself at the end of the war. If you had any moral feeling left, it seems, whatever you did didn't seem enough; the only solution was not to have any at all.

The Levis were the only Jews to come to Orta, the most beautiful place in the world, to die. After the war the town put up a plaque to them on Via Olina 50.

'The victims of barbaric violence, Dr Mario Levi and his son Roberto were taken from this hospitable house, torn from their family's affections. They live on in our unending grief and remembrance. 15 September 1943.'

True to their 'Argon' ancestors, none of Primo's family would have made eager martyrs. But it is particularly ironic that the only ones to die for their Jewishness were the two least Jewish of all.

*   *

While Primo hesitated, what were his friends doing?

Ada had worked for the Partito d'Azione, but she had never heard the word 'partisan'. Now she heard it. 'If the Germans come, I'm joining the partisans,' a friend said, and told her what they were. But when the Germans came, Ada couldn't join anything. She was with her mother, Pina, her sister

Irma, and Irma's three small children; her first duty was to them. They went into hiding: she and Pina with a Signora Riva in Borgofranco, just north of Ivrea,* Irma and the children deep in the mountains, at Issime;† then all together even deeper in the mountains, at Gaby in the Val di Gressoney. During this time of enforced idleness, Ada sat down and wrote the verses of the *Chronache di Milano*, and sent them to Euge for illustration. He was as eager as she to remember their good times, and fired off all seventy-eight drawings in short order. Then he brought them back to her himself, making a rash trip to Ivrea for the purpose.

In October, at Gaby, Ada began to carry messages between the first groups of partisans: but at this stage (she wrote later) more out of friendship and a sense of adventure than any settled resolve. In November the family found permanent rooms in two houses in Torrazzo, on the Serra d'Ivrea. In one the landlord knew they were Jews, but pretended not to; in the other they had to do all the pretending themselves. Irma's family had false papers in the name of Cardone, which the children were carefully taught was now theirs. But there is more in a name than Juliet imagined. Once, when the eldest boy was asked to write his full name, he wrote '*Andrea e basta*', 'Just Andrew', with visible emotion. The youngest, Stefano, had the opposite problem: when he was told after the war that his real name was Levi, he at first refused to abandon Cardone.‡

Once her mother and sister were settled, Ada could begin to 'join the partisans' in earnest. She was not alone in the family. Irma's husband Riccardo was a brother of Carlo Levi, author of *Christ Stopped at Eboli*, one of the most famous antifascists of all. Riccardo himself had belonged to Giustizia e Libertà since his youth, and had been imprisoned for it in 1934; on 8 September he'd gone to Turin, where he became a political organizer for the Partito d'Azione in the factories. Riccardo's sister Luisa, who lived with the family in Torrazzo, was a doctor; she soon offered her services to the partisans as well. But it was not easy for the activists. Whenever Riccardo returned from Turin, Ada from Turin or Ivrea, Pina and Irma would greet them with joy – but also with reproaches. They were being selfish; they were having a splendid time, but what would it cost, and who would pay?

---

* Later, Primo's mother probably rented the same room.

† On 7 December, a week before Primo was captured, another Turinese Jew, Remo Jona, his wife and two children were arrested at Issime. They were eventually deported to Auschwitz on the same transport as Primo. Of the family only Remo returned.

‡ Today he is Stefano Levi Della Torre (he added the Della Torre in honour of his mother). Andrea is a physicist, Giovanni a historian, and Stefano an artist and writer. Their sister, Anna Lisa, born after the war, is a teacher.

So families have always said, to idealists of every kind. And they are not wrong. Their arguments weighed on Ada, and she held back from complete commitment a little longer.

Silvio, by contrast, was not with his mother and sister (his father had died in 1940), but with his uncle in Meda. This uncle was a timber merchant, who dealt with woodcutters near Biella. A very few days after 8 September he heard from them that *ribelli*, rebels, were gathering in the Biellese, the forests and mountains around Biella; and he was incautious enough to mention this at home. There were four young men there: his son, Silvio's cousin Giacomo; two of Giacomo's friends, a pair of brothers from Fiume called Mattei; and Silvio. Immediately all four set off to look for the *ribelli*. And found them, already being organized by the local Communists: a group which would become the Second Brigade of *garibaldini* in the Biellese. This brigade would soon have seven units, of which the first was called the 'Fratelli Bandiera'. Silvio and his companions were invited to join the Bandiera. And now the family factor was decisive. Silvio and the Mattei brothers, who were away from theirs, joined; Giacomo did not, because his father insisted he flee with the rest of the family to Switzerland.

Silvio had been one of Primo's most politically aware friends from the beginning. And now, no more than a week after 8 September, he was already a partisan. His *nom de guerre* was 'Lungo' (for obvious reasons); he would be vice-commandant of the Bandiera, then Commandant and ultimately Chief of the General Staff of the whole Second Brigade. He would, in fact, have an extremely brave and distinguished war, about which he never breathed a word to me.

Alberto and Bianca also threw themselves from the start into the partisan war. Bianca became a Communist organizer in the factories, and occasionally a *staffetta* in the mountains as well. She, her mother and her sister Carla opened their house to partisans, to resistance workers of all kinds, to Jews.

Alberto went to her immediately on 8 September. Just as quickly he decided what to do: he would go into the mountains of the Val di Lanzo, where he'd heard (like Silvio about the Biellese) that groups of partisans were forming. Neither he nor Bianca knew any more than that; Alberto had no contacts, no papers, and little more than the clothes on his back. But he would go, and she would help him. They hatched a plan of escape from the city: they'd ride out on their bicycles, and he would simply carry on. Bianca went ahead; she had not only her genuine identity card, but her work permit as a Social Assistant, which provided a perfect excuse for travel, even towards the mountains. They needed a signal, in case Bianca saw policemen or soldiers approaching. Since she couldn't suddenly burst into song without arousing suspicion, they decided, it would have to be the other way around: she would have to sing loudly all the way, and *stop* if she saw any danger. Which is what they did.

Bianca sang for an hour or two, they met no one, and Alberto disappeared into the mountains. But this first, sublimely hopeful effort ended in failure. Silvio must have had more accurate information; Alberto trusted to luck, as always, and this time it let him down. He wandered the Val di Lanzo for several days without finding a single partisan. Only when he met Sandro did his hopes take on practical shape. Alberto needed an opposite too. He needed someone to tie him down to reality, as much as Primo needed someone to release him from it.

Together, Sandro, Alberto and Gianni Aliberti now set out to form a band, instead of find one, under the aegis of Giustizia e Libertà. And already by mid- to late September they were beginning to succeed, with the *gruppo del Sap* in the Val Pellice. Sandro, as we know, was its first commander, Alberto its second. Sandro then returned to Turin, and his five months of organizing the G. & L. squads in the city. Alberto soon moved on to other formations. Until the spring of 1944 he fought in the Val Germanasca; finally, from the summer of 1944 on, he commanded a (very independent) unit of the Fourth G. & L. Division in the Val di Susa: the 'Franco Dusi'. He was as brave and daring as we would guess; or more, as we shall see.

Primo's two oldest friends, Giorgio Lattes and Livio Norzi, made different choices, or had different things happen to them. Livio, who was an only child, and completely apolitical, spent the war in hiding with his parents in the Biellese. Giorgio stayed in Turin. After 8 September he joined the Partito d'Azione; and for the next twenty months he worked in the city, distributing the news-sheets which were the lifeblood of information and communication among resisters. Gentle Giorgio was as improbable an activist as Emanuele, or Primo, and his friends could not resist teasing him in his new heroic role. One of the rooms in which he kept his newspapers was near the Porta Palazzo – the heart of poor, criminal Turin, as far from the innocent calm of Crocetta as you could get. One day a prostitute was murdered in Giorgio's building; and he couldn't go back, in case a police investigation blew his cover. His friends pretended to think there was another reason. A euphemism for prostitute in those days was '*ballerina*'; and for months afterwards Giorgio was known to all as '*l'assassino della ballerina*'.

And what was happening to Vanda and Luciana? Vanda's fearfulness made her like Elena Levi, Roberto's young wife: alert to danger, quick to respond. Immediately after 8 September she too decided to try for Switzerland. Her father, Cesare, stayed in Milan: too old to move, or still passive, and preferring to hide. Vanda and her brother Aldo went together to Valtournen-che in the Val D'Aosta, due north of Primo in Amay: a place they almost certainly knew from skiing holidays. Soon they were part of a small group of hopeful fugitives, with a guide and a date arranged. But the very night they were meant to leave the guide called off the attempt: the conditions were not right, it was too dangerous. They waited for a new date. Days passed, and none came. Aldo, who was always impatient, gave up and returned to Milan. Vanda waited a little longer, but she must have been afraid. No one wanted to be alone in those days (though in fact it was probably safer); Vanda couldn't bear it. She must have known that Luciana and her family had gone to Brusson. She went to join them.

Luciana's family consisted of her parents, Davide and Cesira, and her sisters Lea and Fernanda, known as Dindi, who was only sixteen. Luciana had decided from the start that she must do something, and her father didn't try to stop her. Perhaps he was impressed by her dedication: she, who had so passionately rejected the traditional female role, now sat patiently knitting winter socks for the men and boys gathering in the mountains. When Vanda arrived they knitted together, and fervently discussed what else they could do. At least, Luciana would have fervently discussed it. Vanda would have listened, and worried, and admired; she would have remembered the impassioned talk in the Via San Martino; and slowly and reluctantly, but profoundly, she would have agreed.

As October passed, and November, the men in the mountains were forming into bands; and women were joining them, as messengers, doctors, spies. Surely they could do the same. Perhaps they thought of asking to join the boys whose socks they were knitting. But then they heard that another group was forming, over the Col di Joux in Amay; and in it were some of their own friends from Turin, including Primo. Their problem was solved. 'We had no doubts at all,' Luciana says; and nor did her father. He had heard of a local priest, Don Giuseppe Péaquin of Challand St Anselme, who was helping Jews, and who was willing to take in the whole family. At the beginning of December Davide Nissim moved his wife and younger daughters to Challand, and said to his eldest daughter: 'Go.'

★   ★

The Val D'Aosta after 8 September was in a state of indescribable confusion, worse perhaps than anywhere else in occupied Italy. Hiding in it, fleeing through it, was 'a veritable multitude', Riccardo Levi wrote, 'of different kinds, in different clothes, speaking different languages'. There were British, Australian and New Zealander prisoners of war, who had escaped from a camp in the Vercellese and were heading for the Swiss border. There was the Fourth Regiment of *alpini* who'd been based in Aosta, and the tattered remnants of the Italian Army in France whom Primo had seen; men from the rest of Italy streamed out of the Valley, *valdostani* who'd been elsewhere streamed in. There were antifascists old and new, and fascists who'd seen the writing on the wall; there were boys evading the call-up, evacuees, and many, many Jews. The soldiers wore borrowed clothing, the Jews had borrowed names; almost every fugitive had false papers, or no papers at all. You had to decide quickly – whether to hide someone or hide from him, help him or ask him for help, enrol him in your band or send him packing; and soon – very soon – whether or not to shoot him, whether or not to kill.

The confusion was mirrored in Primo's mind. And not only in Primo's. Even Franco Momigliano would find it difficult to adapt to life as a partisan, when he arrived in the Val Pellice in February. Not because of the hardships and dangers, said Ada Della Torre,

but because this was war, this was killing. Many of our friends, who were used to political work in the cities, but who now had to face death and the possibility of torture every day, could not completely accept the necessity of killing.

Primo could not accept it at all. That was the heart of his torment. And yet, he would fight. Once again he would resist his instincts, and make a moral choice which went against the whole of his nature: to accept the necessity of killing. He would never get over it. He would spend his brief career as a partisan tormented by it. Afterwards he would hardly ever talk about this period in his life. He would call it 'tragic', 'stupid', 'without doubt the most obscure of my career'. When we think of what followed it, that may seem extraordinary. But there is nothing more characteristic of him than this: that he could bear a whole year under the threat of an inhuman death better than a few short weeks in which he might himself have to kill.

His hesitation ended when he met two other young men in Amay. He gives them their real names in 'Gold'★: Guido and Aldo.

Guido Bachi was ten years older than Primo, Jewish, and a G. & L. member from the start. His father, Donato, was a socialist, and so outspoken in his antifascism that he was sent to the *confino* at the age of seventy-five. Guido himself was invited to police headquarters once or twice, but never charged.

Guido had a degree in Economics and Commerce, and worked in insurance with his father. But his real interest in life was music. He was a wonderful pianist. As director of the University orchestra in the early 30s he

★ The tenth chapter of *The Periodic Table*.

brought artists from all over the world to stir up Fascist Turin. He was a charming, sociable man, well-off and well-connected.

All this changed, of course, in 1938: but without affecting Guido's spirit. By 1943 he was staying with his friends the Segres in their villa outside Turin. On 8 September a group of officers and men of the Italian Fourth Army billetted themselves in the villa. The next morning all the officers had gone. Guido looked at the bewildered soldiers milling around, and immediately made up his mind.

He contacted a friend, the *Avvocato* Camillo Reynaud, who agreed to help. Then he took two of the soldiers with him and went to St Vincent, and from there to Brusson, which he knew well. By 9 September he was already looking for a base for a partisan band. Soon he found some isolated huts for the men at Frumy, above Amay; and another for himself, fifteen minutes away on the Col di Joux. Ten days later *Avvocato* Reynaud brought up several more of the ex-soldiers. The core of the band was established.

'Aldo' was Aldo Piacenza. Despite his surname, he was not Jewish;* unlike Guido (and Primo), therefore, he had been in the army. When Italy joined the war in 1940 he was a nineteen-year-old law student in his first year; he had immediately volunteered. By 1943 he was a Second Lieutenant, recently returned from Russia. On 8 September his unit was in Beinasco on the outskirts of Turin. In the chaos and confusion his first idea, like most others', was to disappear, to avoid capture, to think what to do. One of his men came from St Vincent. He suggested to Aldo and to two other officers, Captain Lo Bue and Lieutenant Rota, that he take them there. He knew the Albergo Ristoro at Amay: a quiet, isolated spot. That is how Aldo arrived at the same small hotel as Primo, at much the same time, or a little earlier: around the middle of September.

After a while Lo Bue and Rota left, to try to make their separate ways home. But Aldo didn't. Perhaps he was more mature, and freer of his family than most twenty-two-year-olds: he'd lost his parents in childhood, and he'd already been in the army for three years. Perhaps, too, he was already thinking of resistance. In any case, he stayed.

And now the smallness of Turin enters the story. When Primo met Guido and Aldo in Amay, he already knew both of them. Not well: Guido was too much older, and Aldo younger. But all the Jews of Turin knew each other; and Anna Maria had known Aldo at D'Azeglio.

At some point during his days of indecision Primo learned what Guido was doing: either from Guido himself, or from the hotel owners, the Pages, who would help the group a great deal. As far as Guido remembers, he did

---

* Jews often took place names as their surnames, in Italy as elsewhere (see Chapter 1 above).

not recruit Primo himself. Primo came and asked if he could help. Then he must have said that he knew Aldo. Cautiously, the two sounded him out; and Aldo immediately agreed to join. As the only one with military experience, he was made military head of the group, in charge of the soldiers up at Frumy, and second in command to Guido. Primo became an 'officer', with the rank of Lieutenant. He took the *nom de guerre* of Ferrero: which was both practical and symbolic, since Ferrero is as Piedmontese as Faussone.

It was now, probably, the first or second week of October.

The extra confusion in the Val D'Aosta affected resistance there throughout. Its people speak French as much as Italian, and feel closer to France and Switzerland than to Rome. Resistance to Fascism came naturally to many, but in many conflicting forms – separatist, federalist, Catholic, Communist. On top of these local dissonances came others: between groups of fugitives, like Primo's, all of different political colours; between groups of ex-soldiers and draft-dodgers, who often became partisans more for reasons of survival and self-defence than of political conviction. Later their efforts would be further divided by fears – or hopes – of annexation by France. Already now, at the beginning, they were divided enough to be even slower than elsewhere to communicate and organize.

But groups were starting up in all the small settlements near Primo – at Issogne, a traditional centre of antifascism, at Champdepraz, at Fénis, at St Vincent, and high in the Upper Valley, at Valgrisenche and Valsavarenche. Already on 13 September a small group carried off cases of mortar shells and ammunition from the fortress at Bard, perhaps ten miles from Amay. And across the Col di Joux, at Arcésaz near Brusson, the first large and well-armed group in the Valley was forming. It would play an important part in what was about to happen.

The Arcésaz group was an outsiders' one, like Primo's: founded by, and mostly containing, men from Casale Monferrato. Its leaders were two brothers from Casale, Francesco and Italo Rossi. They seem to have arrived in October, or very early November. They brought with them a third brother, Bruno; and a thoroughly mixed group of men, from old socialists to veterans of the last war to young ex-army officers. Some young *valdostani* from Verrès joined them, and a number of British POWs. In the end they numbered around 100 men, based in the old, half-ruined castle of Graines, on the mountainside above Arcésaz.

The founding Committee in Casale provided funds and supplies; supplemented by the band's own raids, which for the sake of good relations with the local population were carried out some distance away – whenever possible, which was probably not always. At first, before the Fascists began to get organized, most raids were on the barracks and armouries so recently abandoned by the army. Here the band stole food, clothes, arms, transport. On army lorries that had once taken them to internment camps they now drove Allied prisoners of war to the Swiss border. Once a group from Graines arrived in Ivrea on an army lorry, dressed in army uniforms; smartly saluted the Germans guarding a barracks; and marched out with whatever they wanted.

At just about this time – early November 1943 – Primo's group was also beginning to act. Throughout October they'd just managed to survive. The ten or so soldiers were too few, and had only a few pistols between them; despite Bachi's and Reynaud's efforts, there was no money yet, and no contacts, to increase them. But starting in October the Comitato di Liberazione Nazionale in Turin began to send representatives to the Val D'Aosta, to help organize resistance there.* Apparently by a lucky chance, Bachi met one of them: Aurelio Peccei, a young FIAT director, and member of Giustizia e Libertà. And things started to move. Peccei sent two officers from the Military Command in Turin to Brusson to meet Bachi: Captains Edmondo De Ambrosi and Enrico De Valle. They gave him advice, instructions, and money. In the meantime Reynaud may have managed to raise some money himself. In any case, the group's first funds materialized in November; which allowed Reynaud to bring up more men to join the group at Frumy.

At the same time, Guido began to hear about the band at Arcésaz. His brother Emilio, who was living in Brusson, went to contact them. When De Ambrosi and De Valle arrived, Guido took them to meet the Rossis; he also immediately shared the Turin funds with the other band. Since they were already being funded from Casale, this was generous; but also, perhaps, deliberate. The Arcésaz group was very much bigger, stronger and richer, and very much more unruly. By enlisting them under the Turin Military Command, Guido may have hoped to introduce some order and discipline into his nearest allies. If so, however, he would fail.

His own band was also growing. The Pages spread the word that a partisan group was based in Amay, and several *valdostani* joined them. During November the number of men in the huts above grew to fifteen or more. And the band began to carry out its first, preparatory actions: searches for arms and supplies, sorties to spy out Fascist positions. Guido remembers raiding a tax office in Chatillon with the leader of another band, a Turinese aristocrat: the two gentlemen made off with two or three thousand *lire*. Aldo

---

* In fact it would take until the end of the year before a stable link was established between the CLN in Turin and the Valley.

remembers long reconnaissance missions with his men; and one arms-gathering mission with Primo.

'It was typical of Primo,' Aldo says. They'd heard of a cache of arms somewhere above Chambave, beyond Chatillon. They'd walked for a long cold night through the mountains, snatching an hour or two of sleep propped up against a wall. And, miraculously, they found the weapons. They loaded them on to their backs – hand grenades, rifles, revolvers – and walked all the way back again. Aldo was jubilant; and Primo was pleased as well. But at the same time – 'and this is what was so typical' – he was not pleased. He thought, he told Aldo: *How sad that a man must seek weapons to use against other men.* And he felt it. Bearing their prizes home in triumph, he was profoundly sad.

But even Aldo does not know how sad he was. At least, I hope he doesn't. Primo spoke so rarely of his time as a partisan that Aldo may never have heard what he said. Sometimes it was: 'I hadn't done any military service. I didn't know the first thing about guns, I had one but didn't know how to use it . . .' But sometimes it spread to: 'None of us had military experience . . . none of us had a gun, or would have known how to use it . . .' This was not true. Aldo had had three years of military experience, and knew how to use a gun perfectly well; so did the ex-soldiers under his command. If he ever did hear Primo say this, he must have minded. Certainly he read 'Gold': 'we were the most unarmed partisans in Piedmont, and probably also the most unprepared'. He defended the band to me – he said they were no more unprepared than everyone else at that moment, he saw no justification for Primo's extreme negativity. But he understood it: he understood Primo's deep incapacity for violence, his metaphysical despair. Aldo did not seem to me an easy-going man, but he expressed no anger or blame. On the contrary, he seemed to blame himself for what happened later to Primo, Vanda and Luciana; though it was certainly not his fault, even if what he remembered was true. People do often blame themselves for events beyond their control, because they prefer any explanation to none at all, and even guilt is better than powerlessness. But fifty years later Aldo still seemed almost as troubled as Primo. I couldn't yet guess why.

Primo also remembered the arms trip with Aldo. He even described it once, in 1983; and his description shows the depth of his trouble. It was, he said, his one and only action as a partisan: which is very unlikely to have been true. The destination he remembered was different: a barn above Nus, which was a good deal further away than Chambave. And the result he remembered was different too.

... We went on foot, of course, at night, we walked all those miles between the Col di Joux and Nus, and from Nus up to the barn, we took all the hay out on to the snow – which was a back-breaking job. And we found one rifle, the kind that fires wooden bullets, and is used for exercises. One. And being decent people, we put all the hay back again before leaving.

I do not think this was true either. About the facts, I trust Aldo. But Primo could not bear the facts then, or therefore remember them after: that he himself had sought, and found, weapons to use against other men.

★   ★

If Primo had barely a month and a half as a partisan, Vanda and Luciana didn't even have two weeks.

Vanda and Luciana

Women were very rarely fighters. They were kept on the edges of the
bands, as liaison between them, or with their organizing committees; as
couriers, information gatherers, distributors of Resistance newspapers. The
exceptions were doctors, like Irma's sister-in-law Luisa Levi in Torazzo.
Luciana, of course, was just such an exception; and in the first official
account of the band after the war she is listed as its doctor. Vanda, who was
an ordinary *staffetta*, isn't listed at all. Despite this, and despite Luciana's
great strength and energy, it is Vanda whom Aldo, for instance, especially
remembers.

In ten or twelve days they did not have time to do much. They went
into St Vincent to dance and chat with German officers, and extract information. Then the CLN in Turin asked for intelligence about a waterworks
near Valtournenche; and perhaps because Vanda had been there, she chose,
or was chosen, to go. This is what Aldo remembers: and that it was
particularly brave of her, because, like Emanuele Artom's, her face gave her
Jewishness away.

It is unlikely Vanda would have gone alone. Perhaps Luciana went with
her – she remembers very little of that time, its traces swept away by what
came after. Perhaps, in those early days, the *staffetta* did do more, while the
doctor's work had not yet begun. Or perhaps people remembered Vanda
precisely because she was an unlikely heroine. But like Aldo, they did
remember her. So her anonymous biographer wrote, in *Piedmontese Women
in the War of Liberation*:

No one who saw her in those days, climbing up the snow-covered paths, can ever
forget her tiny, gentle face, marked by the physical effort, and also by a deeper
tension: because for her, as for the best of that time, and in that position, the choice
had not been easy, or joyous, or free from doubt.

This anonymous biographer, I am certain, was Primo. Every word he
wrote about Vanda is filled with the profound understanding of one fearful
person for another, because only he knows how much her courage cost her.
In writing about Vanda, Primo could praise his own values and choices,
without praising himself. In writing about her, he *is* writing about himself
– but a self, since it is not himself, whom he could pity and love.

. . . Vanda was dominated, and often defeated, by an extreme sensitivity. . . No one
was more open to suffering; for suffering she had an almost unlimited capacity. You
sensed in her a constant underlying sorrow, conscious, accepted, but powerfully
silenced; and this won her the immediate respect of all.

She was not naturally strong: she was afraid of death, and more than of death,
of physical suffering. The strength which she showed in those days was one which

had grown inch by inch; the fruit of a resolution constantly renewed with every minute.

★   ★

From the very beginning Primo had been warned that Amay was not the best place for a partisan band.

The first warning came from his friend from university days, Guido Bonfiglioli. Guido and his family had come to the same part of the Val D'Aosta immediately after 8 September: not far from Brusson either, but much higher in the mountains, at Fiéry. Once again it was a spot Guido knew well, from climbing holidays; and it was very near the Swiss border. Here he could pause and make up his mind: if there was anyone to fight with, he would stay and fight; if not, he would take his family to Switzerland.

Very soon he heard that Fascist forces were reforming in these Swiss border regions first of all, for obvious reasons. They should go now, quickly. But in reality his plan was hopeless: his parents might just manage the long and perilous trek through the snow, at over 3,000 metres; but he had already had to carry his grandmother the last stretch to Fiéry. As he was hesitating, a friend of his, Vittorio Finzi, arrived. Vittorio told him that a partisan group was forming at the Col di Joux; and probably also that Primo was in it. That could be his answer, Guido thought: if he could join this group, he would stay.

He met Primo and half a dozen others above Amay, almost certainly in the soldiers' huts at Frumy. Aldo was there, he thinks, and Captain Lo Bue. He also remembers Vanda and Luciana, but that must be a mistake. It was early October at the latest, and Vanda and Luciana did not arrive until December. But what he remembers very clearly is his impression, and the argument.

He instantly thought that Amay was not a good base for a band. It was near not only one road but two: the one up from St Vincent, and the one over the Col di Joux from Brusson. Both, in those days, were only unpaved tracks: but wide enough for vehicles, or a large column of men. The Albergo Ristoro could be reached too easily from both directions, Guido said. Then it could be easily escaped in both directions, said Captain Lo Bue. Aldo agreed with Lo Bue. Guido does not remember what Primo said; but in the end, he says, 'He had more faith in the military expert than in common sense.' That is Primo all over, and certainly true. Guido said that the whole side of the Val D'Aosta towards Switzerland was dangerous, and the Col di Joux most dangerous of all; he would not stay, and nor should they.

He returned to Fiéry, put his grandmother in the care of the hotel owners, whom he trusted, and went with his parents to Champorcher, away from the border area. Perhaps it was common sense, perhaps it was more: Guido is one of those alert to danger, and quick to see evil intention. But he was right. He joined Giustizia e Libertà in Champorcher; and the next eighteen months were not without incident for him or his family. But all of them – even his grandmother – survived.

The second warning came from Euge. He was still with his parents in La Salle, on the other side of Aosta. Perhaps through Ada, Primo knew he was there. In early December, as soon as the girls had joined the band, Vanda was sent to ask Euge to join. She described Amay to him, and the group, in great detail; and Euge's reaction was the same as Guido Bonfiglioli's. He refused to come to Amay, and told Vanda urgently to recommend to Primo and the others that they leave. He too said that it was too easily reached from the valleys on both sides. And he added something else. They were, he thought, too trusting of the people around them, and of those who wanted to join. Did they really know who they were, what their history was, whether they had the necessary experience? War was a terrible thing, but you had to wage it properly: with utmost caution, and utmost ruthlessness.

Was Amay a dangerous place? Aldo still rejects the arguments about the roads (or tracks), pointing out that the Langhe and the Monferrato, which were soon packed with partisans, had more and better ones. You could also disappear over the peaks behind Amay, far from any track, he says; and this is undoubtedly true. Perhaps the issue of the roads must remain open – though certainly the Fascists who fell upon them so quickly and silently one early morning used them.

But Amay was dangerous for other reasons as well. It was a village – a tiny, isolated one, but still a village. There were houses nearby from which the Albergo Ristoro could be watched, and the movements of its residents reported. Silvio, for example, knew two bands based in villages in the Biellese, both of whom were told to move to the mountains, and both of whom were caught before they could go; one of the first things he did was to persuade the Bandiera to move from *their* village into the mountains. And he echoes Euge's other argument too. Primo's group were outsiders in the Val D'Aosta. Both Guido and Primo knew the area well from holidays; they had the support of the Pages; and some local men were beginning to join them. But this was not enough. The safest bands were – like Silvio's own – made up mainly of locals, with a few careful additions; only when people had known one another all their lives could the risk of spies and traitors be kept to a minimum. And finally, Amay *was* in the border region, where the Fascists reorganized first, and which they would continue to patrol most heavily. Euge would note this too, and would join a group well away from the border: in Cogne, not far from Guido Bonfiglioli.

Some of this is hindsight. (Guido Bonfiglioli says, 'Only believe a quarter of people's war stories, including mine.') Bianca, for instance, is convinced that Primo's group was no more naïve or mistaken than others, but only more unlucky. If it had not been for bad luck at the very beginning, she says, before their group – or any group – was properly organized, they would have been no more likely to be captured than anyone else. Aldo and Guido (Bachi) would certainly agree. And on the whole I agree as well. They *were* particularly exposed in those early days, but so were many others. If they had had time, surely Primo and Aldo, and perhaps the two girls as well, would have left the Albergo and moved up to Frumy, or even further into the mountains. There was bad luck, and bad judgement as well, as we shall see; but it was not their own. This much is certain: Primo's particularly dark judgement of the group does not reflect reality. It reflects his own deep horror of violence, and his guilt at accepting it; guilt which was about to become intolerable.

It was now the first week in December. Some *garibaldini** turned up and asked to join them, but Bachi refused: this was a G. & L. band, or about to be. He gave his men strict orders: sit tight, prepare, await orders from Turin. But not everyone wanted to obey.

There was – especially in these first chaotic days – an acute and general problem of discipline. It was vital for the partisans to gain, and keep, people's confidence. They needed to convince the local population that they were soldiers fighting the Fascists, not a lawless rabble. They needed to convince their backers of the same thing; and also that they were backing the right side, that they would win.

This was not easy to do. Into the vacuum of power had poured not only the politically motivated of every kind, but every kind of opportunist, delinquent and crook. Many of these, calling themselves partisans, roamed around 'requisitioning' everything people owned and reselling it on the black market. Others joined genuine bands, but only for the chance to loot and steal. This situation had to be brought under control quickly; and there was only one way to do it.

This is how a partisan from Giaveno, near Turin, put it:

It was indispensable for us, and for the people, to eliminate those responsible for thefts as soon as they occurred. Unfortunately the only possible method was physical elimination, which was also a deterrent . . . We had to act immediately, or we would have lost credibility.

*

---

* Communist partisans.

On 7 January two men were shot outside Giaveno. The next day a notice was put up in the town, signed by the local partisan commander: this would be the fate of all those who committed acts of theft and looting while falsely claiming to be partisans. Over the next weeks they were as good as their word; and a rough order was restored.

In the Amay band there were two such fake partisans. No one remembers, or wants to remember, very much about them. One came – Bachi thinks – from Genoa. They were stealing and extorting – or threatening to steal and extort – from local people. Bachi and others were trying to restrain them. They were – probably – refusing to obey orders, threatening to leave the band and even to betray it, if they were not allowed to carry on. They may have threatened to 'top' Bachi – so he remembers Piacenza telling him. He said he would talk to them. But some time on 8 or 9 December they were shot, and their bodies dumped in a ditch. No one remembers or wants to remember where.

Bachi and Piacenza try to spread the responsibility. Piacenza says that the order may have come from the Arcésaz group – and that the two men had come from there as well. Bachi also said, in 1945, that the suggestion had come from Arcésaz, from an officer who turned out to be a spy. Today he says that he had nothing to do with the killings, had no idea they were planned, and only heard about them afterwards. Piacenza rang me specially to say that Bachi would not have known about the shootings. But he remembered nothing about them himself, he said, and was probably away at the time. In a deposition in 1946 he said that he had spent the night of 8 December in Brusson. While he was away his second-in-command, Sergeant Major Giovanni Bertolini, known as Berto, killed the two men outside the huts at Frumy.

The problem, and the solution, were common, as both Bachi and Piacenza must know now. Still they do not bear the burden lightly. Almost certainly – as both insist – cautious, law-abiding Bachi was not involved. Piacenza was the soldier, and the younger, more impulsive man. And as the band's military commander, he might be expected to take the lead, and not leave the dirty work to his men.

It may well be that he no longer remembers what happened. That is how memory works – to protect us, and allow us to go on living. But it may be this (or partly this) that underlies the trouble I felt in Aldo Piacenza. He saw little of Primo after the war. Primo never sent him a letter like the one he sent to Guido with *The Periodic Table*, saying: *In friendship, and hoping you will forgive the telling of a part of our past.* I wonder if Aldo doesn't think that Primo blamed him for the killings – I wonder if Primo *did* blame him. And I wonder if Aldo doesn't accept this blame – secretly, unconsciously. Maybe that is why he blames himself for something he didn't do instead.

Guido is quite certain that Primo did not take part in the decision about the killings, or in carrying them out. Yet he wrote about them as though he had; and with a horror that blasts the page. I think we can only understand this if we understand the depth of his revulsion at the necessity of killing. And the very first time he had to face it, it was turned not against the enemy, but against his own side. Fate could not have devised a crueller way of destroying his will to fight as soon as it was born. And that is what it did. So he wrote, in 'Gold':

. . . amongst us, in each of our minds, there weighed an ugly secret: a secret which had exposed us to capture, because it had extinguished in us, a few days before, all will to resist, even to live. Our consciences had forced us to execute a sentence, and we had executed it; but we had come out of it destroyed, destitute, wanting everything to end, and to end ourselves.

I do not believe that the killings destroyed Aldo, after three years of war, or Guido, who had had nothing to do with them. The one they destroyed was Primo. He had already spent weeks near despair. On 9 December he crossed over into it: *wanting everything to end, and to end ourselves*. Perhaps this is literary dramatization, as so often in *The Periodic Table*. But I do not think so. I think it is the opposite – one of the rare moments when his real despair broke through Primo Levi's literary, moral and private containment. I think he was in this state of despair when he was arrested. That was the starting point from which he faced prison, Fossoli, and Auschwitz.

It was really the Arcésaz band the Fascists were after. Primo and the others were captured because of their link to the bigger, more dangerous band, like tiny fish caught with a whale.

Towards the end of November an ex-*alpino* called Edilio Cagni offered his services as a spy to the new Fascist head of the province, Cesare Augusto Carnazzi. Carnazzi immediately sent him, together with two aides and assistants, to the Val d'Ayas.

By 5 December Cagni had managed to meet some of the Arcésaz men in Verrès. On the 6th they took him to Arcésaz itself, where he met a group which included Piacenza and Berto. On the 7th he reached the Arcésaz leaders: the Rossis, and several representatives of the Committee in Casale. Cagni was clever and subtle; unfortunately the *casalesi* were neither. He realized immediately that there was trouble amongst them which he could exploit.

The Committee was worried about interference from Turin, about the Rossis' poor accounting for funds and supplies from Casale, and about the general disorganization and lawlessness of the band in those early days. Cagni attacked the Rossis' leadership on all these points, and refused to join. He focused especially on one of the Committee's representatives, Giuseppe Barbesino. Barbesino was a fifty-year-old farmer, station-master and ex-*carabiniere*, a simple, old-fashioned, but – Cagni noted – opinionated man. It worked. Barbesino was impressed by Cagni's 'seriousness and culture'. Led by him, the Committee men removed the Rossis from the group's command, and gave it to Cagni.

By 7 December, therefore, the Arcésaz band was not only infiltrated but actually led by a Fascist spy. Together with his two assistants, Cagni immediately set about exhausting the men and using up the ammunition in a series of 'military' exercises. He also immediately discovered that there was another band of 'about 15 *ribelli*' at Amay.

On Friday the 10th the two groups met in Brusson. There appear to have been nine men present: two from Turin, two from Amay, and five from Arcésaz. The two from Amay were Bachi and Piacenza. One of the CLN representatives from Turin was De Ambrosi, who called himself 'Della Torre'. The other called himself 'Rossi', and was variously thought to be an engineer, a lawyer, a Colonel, or simply an 'unknown'. He was either De Valle or Aurelio Peccei. The five from Arcésaz were three senior *casalesi*, plus their new leader, Cagni, and one of his assistants, Domenico De Ceglie. Cagni called himself 'Renato Redi', De Ceglie 'Mario Meoli'. (Since the third spy, Alberto Bianchi, had also taken an alliterative name – 'Carlo Cerri' – you would think, in hindsight, that someone might have wondered. But no one did.)

The CLN delegates gave instructions and handed out funds. Cagni was confirmed as leader of the Arcésaz band – though only provisionally, the delegates saying they would seek final approval from Turin. Bachi gave a full account of his band's activities and plans, with names and places. He reported the loss of two men, and asked for replacements. 'Meoli' volunteered, and 'Redi' agreed. In a few short hours Cagni had learned all he needed to know about the Amay band, and equipped it with its own personal spy. The next meeting was fixed for Sunday the 12th at 4 p.m. in Bard.

Cagni may have thought – rightly – that the CLN would check on him more carefully than the Casale Committee had. In any case events now rushed to their conclusion like a stone falling. Piacenza took 'Meoli' up to Amay that same day and introduced him to 'Signorina Nissim (*ebrea*), Signorina Maestro (*ebrea*) and Signor Levi (*ebreo*)'. Bachi showed him around the 'camp' – that is, the hotel, and probably his own hut as well – and told him exactly where the soldiers were, twenty minutes above them in Frumy. In the early hours of Saturday 11th De Ceglie met Cagni in Arcésaz. That afternoon, on the pretence of going to survey German positions in Valpelline, he went to Aosta instead, and reported to Carnazzi. Early Sunday morning he brought Carnazzi's instructions back to Cagni.

On Sunday morning Bachi and *'Ingegnere* (Engineer) Rossi' – who may or may not have been Peccei – failed to persuade Barbesino and others to restore Francesco Rossi to the leadership of the Arcésaz band. At four, Piacenza arrived at the Albergo in Bard where the second meeting had been arranged. Several Arcésaz men were there – but not Cagni. It is hard to say exactly what happened now, because the only accounts are Piacenza's, and they conflict.* But this much seems certain. One of the CLN delegates who was meant to attend (whether as *'Ingegnere* Rossi' or not) was Peccei. And part of Carnazzi's instructions to Cagni was to ambush the meeting, and arrest everyone, especially Peccei. But either Peccei never turned up, or something else went wrong. No one was arrested – yet.

Piacenza was tempted not to return to Amay that night, through the dark and the snow. Why not spend the night at Bard, and go back the next day? But he wanted to report to Bachi. He got as far as St Vincent on his bicycle, then struggled up on foot the rest of the way. Having escaped the first half of Carnazzi's trap, he had just walked into the second.

On Sunday evening De Ceglie joined Cagni and Bianchi at Graines, and the three spies threw a party for the Arcésaz men, with dancing, food and flowing wine. But it seems the band had its own spies. At 9.30, long before the men were drunk and snoring as Cagni had intended, two local men brought a message: the Fascists were planning a raid at dawn. Cagni gave useless orders, and threw as many rifles as he could into the river. Then he and the others melted away to join the other side.

In the skirmish at dawn the first *casalese*, nineteen-year-old Giuseppe Carrera, was killed, two others were wounded, and over forty captured. The band was destroyed. It reformed later, under the Rossis, but never fought again in the Val d'Ayas.†

Amay had no warning at all. Aldo must have fallen into bed as soon as he'd made his report to Guido. The last thing Luciana remembered was Primo talking about Lippizaner horses: they can't really count, he said, they're just following their riders' signals. All night she heard dogs barking.

---

* One – given in gaol in Aosta in 1944 – was certainly meant to mislead. This may have confused Piacenza himself later, when he tried to recall the truth.

† Two of the three Rossi brothers, Italo and Bruno, were later killed. Francesco Rossi named the reformed band after Italo: the 'Divisione Italo Rossi', which belonged (after the summer of 1944) to the Matteotti (i.e. Socialist) Brigades. Since the Amay band was never reconstituted, it was to this Division that Primo and the others were later said to belong.

Then, in the 'spectral snowy dawn' – Primo's words in *If This is a Man* –
the silence of the sleeping Albergo was broken. There were shots, shouts,
the clank of heavy guns being mounted. Aldo opened a window and leapt
out, and one was pointing straight at him.

Fifty militiamen surrounded the hotel. They were four, two of them
women; they had no chance at all. Primo quickly hid his revolver in the
ashes of the stove: if you were found armed, you were shot immediately.
Luciana ran to flush some G. & L. leaflets she had in her pocket down the
toilet, but it was too late. The militia burst in. They pushed Marie Varisellaz,
the wife of Eleuterio Page the hotel owner, against a wall, and threatened
to shoot her. One hit Primo so hard he still had the marks of a hand on his
face hours later. Their commander yelled: 'You think *you* are the saviours
of Italy? *We* are!' It was all over. The whole thing cannot have taken half an
hour.

Ferro, the commander, now divided his men in two. A small group
guarded the captives; the rest moved up to Frumy. But a local man who had
heard the fracas at the hotel ran up and warned the soldiers, who all escaped.
That part of the plan, at least, had failed.

Four prisoners taken without a fight was not very impressive. (This
evidently struck Carnazzi painfully, since he invented 'six killed and several
wounded' to add to his report.) But the militiamen determined to make the
most of things. They 'promised to question us in a certain very convincing
way of theirs', Primo wrote, 'and shoot us immediately after'. They separated
the four, put them at intervals in the middle of their column, and began to
march them down the Col di Joux to Brusson.

By now it was early morning, and Bachi was making his way up to Amay
as usual. He rounded a bend in the track, and walked straight into them. He
saw Primo, Aldo, Vanda, Luciana, all surrounded by militiamen. They
pretended not to recognize each other, and Bachi presented his false identity
card. But Ferro knew who he was, and knew he was carrying a revolver.
He drew up a firing squad to shoot Bachi on the spot – and only called them
off at the last minute. Again it was only show, to induce fear and obedience;
but it did. Bachi was placed in the column with the others, and the march
continued.

It took several hours. The Frumy men followed, weaving through the
woods. But they were too few for battle, and a bullet from the side might
have caught one of their own. They did not shoot. The militiamen did
instead – 'firing at hares with their tommy guns', Primo said, 'and flinging
grenades into streams to kill the trout'.

He did two things on the way down. Pretending to stumble, he slipped
a notebook of addresses into the snow; and he got rid of his false identity

card. Not only was it too new, and obviously forged; but 'Ferrero' – i.e. himself – was meant to come from Eboli, and so did the militiaman who had hit him. He tore the card into small pieces, and, bit by torn bit, ate it.

The militiamen marched, singing, into Brusson, brandishing their rifles, showing off their prisoners like animals killed in a hunt. Cagni was waiting for them – and Bachi realized the truth, and gave up pretending not to know the others. In the main square in Brusson that morning there was a young man who knew them well: Paolo Spriano, later a distinguished historian, now a G. & L. partisan. He saw them, but could do nothing; only tell Luciana's family as soon as possible. Months later, when he was himself in prison, he met several of the Arcésaz men: and together, he wrote, 'we recalled, with renewed bitterness, the impotence of that day'.

The five were pushed into a waiting bus, each still separated from the others by a circle of militiamen. Right in front of Primo, hanging from the belt of one of the men, was a hand grenade. 'I could easily have lifted the safety pin, pulled the cord, and done away with myself and several of them,' he wrote in 'Gold', 'but I didn't have the courage.' One of the early stories he wrote after the war was about a man who did have the courage. Primo described every stage of the act; and being Primo, tried to imagine not the man's courage, but his fear.*

Meanwhile, Ferro had kept Luciana in his own circle. He had, of course, found the G.& L. leaflets in her pocket. As they approached Aosta, he leaned towards her and said: 'If they ask you about those leaflets, say they're advertisements for medicines.'

In Aosta they were taken to the militia's barracks, the Caserma Cesare Battisti. Primo, Aldo and Guido were put into cells in the basement. The girls were probably in another part of the barracks; they don't remember seeing each other.

For the men there were rations once a day, an hour of exercise, and endless interrogations. These were conducted either by Ferro or by Cagni, and varied accordingly. Ferro was a soldier, stupid but decent; he 'questioned me', Primo wrote, 'to indoctrinate me and give himself importance, but without any serious inquisitorial intent'. Cagni was a sadist, a clever, criminal,

---

* At the last moment, 'in depths he had never explored, in some recess of his body – that rebellious animal body that finds it so hard to die – something was born, and grew huge, something dark and ancient and unknowable . . . [He] understood, though not straight away, that this was fear; and knew that in a moment it would be too late. He filled his lungs with air . . . and pulled the cord as hard as he could.' He dies, of course, but takes four Germans – in the story they are Germans – with him.

natural torturer and spy. His interrogations lasted for hours. He did not beat
them; in this they were lucky they'd been caught so early, since later on that
came too. But he did everything to terrorize them, in the classical manner.
He placed his Luger prominently on his desk, he threatened them with
torture and the firing squad, he 'alternated moments of simulated cordiality
with equally simulated explosions of rage'. But they said nothing. Guido
insisted – untruthfully – that Cagni already knew everything, having
attended the meeting on the 10th. Primo and Aldo fortunately knew very
little, having left the organization to Guido; the few names Primo did know
he kept to himself. The only thing he did admit, in the end, was that he was
a Jew.

It is this move for which Aldo takes the blame. It was, he says, a collective
decision; and as one of the leaders of the band, 'I took, and take, responsibility
for it.'

Everyone thought then – and for a long time after – that it was far less
dangerous to be recognized as a Jew than as a partisan. As a partisan you
were sent for trial to the Tribunale Speciale, which meant almost certain
death; as a Jew you just went to the new camp they'd set up at the beginning
of December, at Carpi near Modena. And there you would be kept until
the war was over: '*We don't hand anyone over to the Germans,*' the militia said,
and it was true. At least it had been true, until the Germans were there, and
had ways of insisting. But this had only just begun. The militiaman from
Eboli who arrested Primo still believed it. Ferro believed it, even Carnazzi
probably believed it. Guido didn't, having known about the German concentration camps since the 30s; and Primo didn't either. But Luciana did,
and so did Aldo. Guido declared himself a Jew as well, but as head of the
band he could not escape the Tribunale Speciale, along with Aldo. Just
possibly, however, Primo, Vanda and Luciana could. They all decided
together, Aldo says, to seize that chance; to say that Primo and the two girls
were just Jews in hiding, and nothing to do with any partisan band.

It's almost certainly not true. Aldo – I've guessed – has transferred his
sense of guilt to this point from another. Neither Luciana nor Guido
remembers this shared decision, though Guido remembers coordinating
other answers to their interrogators with Primo and Aldo. (They exchanged
the books they were allowed to read, he says, marking letters in them to
spell out messages.) And in all the dozen or so times Primo wrote or spoke
publicly of this moment, he always said he made the decision alone.

Why *did* he make it – especially if, as he said, he knew that the Germans
were taking over everywhere, and it would not necessarily keep him out of
their hands? Afterwards he gave three reasons. The practical one, that
between certain death (on the spot, or from the Tribunale Speciale) and

possible death (the camp at Carpi) he chose possible death. An impractical – a perverse, an even 'stupid' one: that he felt 'an irrational digging in of pride'; he wanted to show his interrogators that Jews were partisans as well. And finally, perhaps the deepest one: 'because I was tired'. I think this was his way of admitting, without describing, his state of despair; the result of the violent events of only a few days before.

If Ferro was decent to the men, he was more than that, and also less, to the women.

Immediately after 13 December, the great success of 'operations against partisans and Jews' in the Val D'Aosta was trumpeted on the radio. Aldo Maestro, listening in Milan, knew or guessed that his sister was among them. He went to Carla Consonni to ask if she had any news: Carla didn't, but that was how they met. Aldo quickly fabricated a fake identity card and went up to Aosta. He presented himself at the Caserma Cesare Battisti as Aldo Martini, a friend of the prisoner Maestro's brother. Ferro looked at his forgery, and at his face. 'Vanda's brother has come to see her,' he told Bachi, and let him in. Aldo gave her books, cigarettes, promises to do what he could; but he could do very little. They had a brief, hurried meeting; probably they didn't even dare to embrace. Then Ferro let him out again.

Luciana's family knew immediately that she'd been taken: first of all she didn't come down to Challand that day, as they'd planned; and then Paolo Spriano told them. Her father, Davide, came to the *caserma* the very next day; she saw him walking round and round it, hoping to catch a glimpse of her. Then her younger sister Dindi arrived. Ferro recognized her, as he had recognized Vanda's brother. 'He should have arrested Dindi, and tortured her, to make her tell him where our parents were,' Luciana says. 'But he didn't.' Instead he told her that she and her family should leave Italy as soon as possible. Which they did: in February, with the help of Don Péaquin, the Nissims escaped to Switzerland.

Of course, Ferro had fallen for Luciana. He made advances to her; he said that if she was nice to him, he'd get her out of there. They'd escape together. What did she say? Luciana didn't hesitate. 'With a Fascist?' she demanded. 'Never!'

Three months after 8 September, Ada was struggling with her last doubts about joining the partisan war. The arrest of Primo, Vanda and Luciana decided her. As soon as she heard the news she wrote to Silvio, saying they must do something. Silvio came straight to Ivrea. He suggested a plan: they should take a Fascist hostage, and propose an exchange.

Not without difficulty, Ada chose their target. She went back and forth several times between Ivrea and Biella, coordinating the plan. On her last trip one of Silvio's men asked: 'Do we bring him here first, or do we top him straight away?' 'You can't kill a hostage!' Ada cried. But they just looked at her.

At this point, Primo, Vanda and Luciana were removed from Aosta. It was too late; the plan to rescue them had failed.

But this was not the end of the disaster. The plan was set, and Ada did not have the power to stop it. She went through a terrible day and night. How could she let a man be killed – for nothing? But how could she warn him, and by saving him betray her own side? 'I felt I couldn't go on with it,' she said. Like Primo, like Franco, she couldn't kill. And yet, in the course of that night, she decided it was her duty to go on.

Luckily, it all fell through. Somehow Silvio and his men failed to meet the local partisan who was meant to guide them. The latter then determined to kidnap the Fascist himself – but couldn't, because that morning the man did not leave home alone, but was accompanied by two friends. Ada was profoundly relieved. But this was the turning point for her. The Fascist was alive, but Primo was gone. This was no longer an adventure, but a deadly war.

'Gold' is coldly accurate about Cagni's interrogations – and gives his real name. But most of Primo's story of this desolate time is truer (again) about what it meant than how it was. Fighting was for men; he could not fight; therefore he was not a man. *That* is what it meant. So he leaves the girls out altogether – because fighting is for men. And so he makes Aldo say, 'Too bad for my chromosomes', as he 'stoically lit a cigarette' – because fighting is for brave, hard men.★ Amongst these men Primo is like a woman, with a tiny ladies' revolver he doesn't know how to use. Or like another opposite of a man: the mouse who kept him company in his cell. 'I felt,' Primo wrote, 'more of a mouse than he.'

That is one of the meanings of 'Gold'. The other is what makes him feel a mouse and not a man: the life he has not lived, the freedom and adventure he has not seized. The two come together at the end of the story.

One evening a new prisoner appears. He is thin, with a lipless mouth and shifty eyes, and he has been arrested for smuggling. Yet he turns out to be one of Primo's heroes of freedom and adventure, like Sandro or Rodmund – Sandro or Rodmund in minor, sardonic key. He has an ancient trade, he

---

★ Perhaps Aldo did say this, or something like it. But he was not a doctor, as Primo says: which makes me think that Primo invented this masculine detail, then gave Aldo the background to support it.

tells Primo, which he cannot practise in winter, when the River Dora freezes over. The Dora, he says, carries gold, which it brings down from the mountain, and buries in its sand. There is never very much, but it is constantly renewed, like the grass in the fields. He will never be rich; but like his father and grandfather and all his great-grandfathers before him, he is free.

Back in his cell, Primo listens to the Dora flowing by outside his window like the life, and the chance to live it like a man, which he has lost, perhaps for ever. He feels a painful envy for his crooked companion, 'who would soon return to his precarious but monstrously free life, to his inexhaustible trickle of gold, and to an endless succession of days'.

8. Fossoli:
February 1944

Fossoli

On or about 26 January, Primo, Vanda and Luciana were taken from their
cells and put on a train for the concentration camp of Fossoli. Towards
evening they passed through the station of Chivasso, a few miles from Turin.
The sky was cloudy and dark, but in the distance Primo could make out the
Mole. That was the moment of farewell. He watched it disappear like life
itself, like all he knew.

The next day the train rolled through the Po Valley towards Carpi. It was
an ordinary train, lightly guarded. They walked up and down their carriage,
as though that might answer their question, or change their destination.
Once Primo and Luciana found themselves alone beside the rear door,
staring out at the open plain. They looked at each other. 'Shall we?' they
said. But maybe Fossoli really was in Italian hands, and would remain so.
The plain was vast and empty; where could they run, surely they'd be seen?
Above all, they could not leave Vanda. They did not jump.

Fossoli is a northern suburb of Carpi. In July 1942 Prisoner of War
Camp No. 73 was opened there for British POWs captured in North Africa.
No one escaped from Fossoli on 8 September 1943: the Germans took it
over that very night. During the next few weeks all the POWs – around

5,000 of them – were deported to concentration camps in the Third Reich.

On 30 November Police Order No. 5 was issued by Minister of the Interior Buffarini Guidi: all Jews were to be collected and held in provincial centres, until special concentration camps were available. Prisoner of War Camp No. 73 was chosen for that role: it was ready, empty, and on the main railway line between central Italy and the Brenner Pass. It was opened on 5 December. By the end of 1943 it held just under 100 Jews. When Primo, Vanda and Luciana arrived on 27 January 1944 there were around 200. And they *were* still in the hands of Italians.

All along, in fact, Buffarini Guidi had tried to keep the fate of the Jews under Italian control – or at least to seem to. On 10 December he had exempted the old, the ill, and the children of mixed marriages from internment. On 20 January he declared his firm intention that the Jews should remain in camps in Italy, and not be handed over to the Germans. It is hard to say whether he was deceiving himself in this, or only the Jews. But it is perfectly clear that neither he nor anyone else had the slightest chance of achieving his aims. One of the early Italian Commandants of Fossoli told the prisoners repeatedly that he would dismantle the camp and send them all home, rather than hand them over to the Germans. When the day came, the opposite happened: everyone was handed over immediately, including the old, the ill, and the children of mixed marriages.

But at the time none of this was clear. From the start the word went round that Fossoli was not at all a bad place to be – *much* better than the local prisons in which people were held for weeks or months before their transfer here. Even later, when the SS had taken over the camp and put the inmates to forced labour, the Jews in San Vittore Prison in Milan still looked forward almost eagerly to the transfer to Fossoli: as long as you worked there, they heard, you were left alone. A number of half-Jews in Ferrara, afraid that their exemption would not last, *asked* to be sent to Fossoli: at least there they'd be in the countryside, and safe from the bombing. In Aosta, when Vanda allowed herself to hope, it was for Fossoli.

It was largely, of course, Buffarini Guidi's empty promises that had created this illusion. Those, and the long meanness of the racial laws, which had accustomed people to humiliation and suffering, but also to the notion that this, too, could be survived. Jews have traditionally made a bargain with their hosts – or thought they did: we will be good and loyal citizens, and you will treat us as such. In Italy even now that bargain seemed sound. As long as Italians remained in charge, as Buffarini Guidi said they would, nothing really bad would happen. In Ferrara again, when the prison was bombed one day the Jews escaped in the confusion – but reported back afterwards, to show their good will. Thereafter the guards let them go every time there was a raid; and every time, with very few exceptions, they returned.

Three weeks after Primo arrived, a new group of Jews was being brought to Fossoli from prison in Treviso. Among them was a young Yugoslav Jew called Silvio Barabas, whom Primo would come to know in Auschwitz. As they were changing trains in Verona there was an air-raid warning, and Silvio suddenly found himself alone. For an instant he thought of escape. But their police guards were young men like himself, they'd been friendly and kind, if he disappeared they'd be severely punished . . . He went looking for them, and was as relieved as they were when he found them.

Throughout their journey the guards reassured Silvio and the others that Fossoli was in Italian hands. In the city hall in Carpi, where they spent the night, a local man confirmed it. After that they slept better than they had for many weeks. The next morning they went out to look for breakfast. The police made no attempt to follow them; but they all returned. Why run away, they asked each other, if the camp is run by Italians?

In fact, for the last day or two it no longer had been. Neither the police guards nor the local man would have known it, but the real bosses of the camp were already the SS. Still the deception, and self-deception, continued. For the next six days, at the end of which all the Jews in the camp were deported, the transports poured in. Most of these prisoners were women and children, who arrived with the same hope, and wept bitterly when they saw the Germans.

For earlier arrivals the disillusionment had been slower. True, this was undeniably a concentration camp, and they were undeniably prisoners. They were enclosed by a high double fence, part electrified (but the electricity didn't always work), studded with watch-towers, and floodlit at night. They lived in long brick barracks with communal washrooms, and slept on wooden, two-tier bunks, a dozen or so to a 'room' (each room had walls but no ceiling, so that in reality you slept with the whole barrack, hearing their quarrels, their conversations, the noises they made in their sleep). At night the men were separated from their wives and children, though they could see them every day. Thrown in with them, in a different part of the camp, were other rejects of society: antifascists and out-of-favour Fascists; fellow 'racial inferiors', such as Slavs; common criminals. And over them all hung fear: fear of the future, fear that they would be surrendered to the Germans after all, despite all their captors' vows 'on their Fascist faith' to the contrary.

But Fossoli lived up to its reputation. In hindsight, for the early arrivals at least it was a paradise. They were treated with a good deal of humanity – *all'italiano*, as Primo said. You could write letters and receive packages, and they all did: Vanda asked her family for clothes and shoes, soap and towels, especially cigarettes. Rations were reasonable; as long as there was no forced labour, you could survive on them for a long time.★ But for Italians, of course, food is much more than survival. Most of the prisoners had a bit of money, especially after their first letters had been answered. So vans, carts, vendors on foot lined up outside the barbed wire, or were even allowed into the camp; and people would buy as much as they could afford – bread, cakes and sweets, fruit and vegetables. In those early, still human days, they pooled the vegetables. The women would add them to the basic rations of rice or pasta; and twice a day cooked good and tasty meals for everyone. When Primo remembered Fossoli in Auschwitz, he remembered food: 'dancing before my eyes I see the spaghetti we had just cooked, Vanda, Luciana, Franco and I . . . when we suddenly heard the news that we would be leaving for here the following day; and we were eating it (it was so good, yellow, filling), and we stopped, fools that we were – if only we had known . . .'

While Primo was at Fossoli there was no forced labour, no visible brutality, and no shootings (all of which would come later). There was no uniform. You did not have to get up or go to bed at any particular hour. You could have visits, though they were not officially allowed: friends and relations walked up and down the road outside the camp while you walked up and down inside it, talking through the barbed wire. If you were rich or persuasive enough, you could even leave the camp occasionally. Primo remembered 'some of the girls who were with me' – almost certainly Vanda and Luciana themselves – getting permission from the Italian Commandant to go into Carpi with him. They had a bath in the public baths; they even went to the hairdresser.

This 'Italian' atmosphere held to the end of Primo's stay. Silvio Barabas remembers going for a walk around the camp on 16 February, his first day. It was midday, warm and sunny. Young people were 'parading, chatting and laughing as if they were in Rome or Milan'; older ones sat in front of their barracks, enjoying the spectacle. When a van arrived from Carpi they rushed to buy provisions, and especially newspapers. Groups of men stood around reading, commenting loudly to each other, as though they were still on their own street corners. Silvio felt, with them: *If only we can stay in Fossoli.*

★   ★

★ It has been calculated from bakers' bills, for example, that each prisoner received 225 grams (nearly half a pound) of bread a day, even after the Germans had taken over.

What would young people do, in a place like Fossoli in those early days? When they are locked up and deprived of their freedom – but this isn't new, if anything they are slightly freer than before. When they are afraid, but also hopeful – perhaps they'll be here for months or years, perhaps this is the worst that's going to happen? When there's nothing they can do, and nothing *to* do, except be afraid and hopeful together? The barbed wire, the watch-towers filled my mind, and I didn't guess until Luciana told me. They fell in love. '*Vanda, Luciana, Franco and I*,' Primo wrote, remembering Fossoli. Luciana fell in love with Franco; and Primo fell in love with Vanda.

Franco

Franco Sacerdoti was something new in Luciana's experience. She was used to brilliant and rather silent intellectuals, like the *piccoli geni*, like Franco Momigliano. She had fallen in love with Franco, she would say, because he knew ancient Greek. Luciana loved where she admired, and she did not admire ordinary bourgeois businessmen. Perhaps she felt a little contempt for them, if she thought of them at all. Franco Sacerdoti swept all that away.

He was called *il più bello ebreo di Torino*, the best-looking Jew in Turin; and – apart from Alberto Salmoni – it was probably true:

Franco

Like the best things in many places, he came from elsewhere. He was born in Naples, and came to Turin even later than Alberto. He was the seventh of eleven children of Guido Sacerdoti, the very successful owner of a paper factory. His two eldest brothers had to go into the business; but the others were allowed to strike out further. At twenty, Franco was sent to Turin to work in his uncle's textile firm.*

For three years he enjoyed to the full his reputation as *il più bello ebreo di Torino*. Then, in September 1942, he married Nuccia Treves, whose family had owned a large furniture factory in Turin. Franco's charmed life seemed to be assured: Nuccia was delightful, beautiful and still rich, and they were very much in love. But their idyll only lasted a year. They were entirely apolitical; but not even they could escape the stresses of the time. Perhaps because of these, by the time 8 September 1943 came they were quarrelling. When Franco left Turin for the safety of the country Nuccia did not go with him, but stayed hidden in the city.

What happened next is unclear, and so has given rise to several stories, some improbable, some bitter. One is that Franco gave in to the most common, and most dangerous, impulse: he returned to his and Nuccia's house to save some of their belongings, and was caught on the spot. (Even on the roof, in one dramatic version, about to escape like a cat over the tiles of Turin.) This was Luciana's impression, and what she has always believed. Franco may have let her believe it, out of delicacy; but it wasn't true. One thing we do know is that he wasn't arrested in Turin, but in the Val di Lanzo where he was hiding.

Franco's family remember this: that Nuccia's father Ettore was arrested and imprisoned in Turin. He was a rich man, and not one to resign himself to his fate: he soon found someone who, for enough money, was willing to help him escape. The money had to be raised, and Ettore (or someone else) seems to have decided that he must raise it himself. Someone had to take his place: to be a hostage for him. Nuccia sent a message to Franco in the country, begging him to be that hostage – it would only be for a very few days . . . Perhaps, as his family believe, Franco was still in love with her, and wanted to make up their quarrel. Or perhaps he was simply being his kind and gallant self: his nickname in the family was *il principe*, the prince, for the beauty of his character as well as his face. In any case, he agreed. And before

---

* This uncle was called Elio Mordo, and came from Greece (he'd married one of Guido Sacerdoti's sisters). I imagine he was also a canny businessman, and that Franco entertained his friends in Fossoli with his exploits: thus providing Primo with part of the name for his Greek god of trade in *The Truce*, Mordo Nahum.

Ettore Treves returned, he and all the other Jews in the prison were sent to Fossoli.

This story has a similar problem: Franco was arrested in Lanzo, not in Turin. But he may have given himself up there, knowing he would be sent to Turin, as indeed he was.

More seriously, the story also has several versions, or several explanations. Like Vanda, Franco would not return. His family and his young wife would never meet or speak again, after the war; no doubt they couldn't bear to. So the Sacerdotis never asked her what really happened. Time has softened their grief; they remember now how she adored Franco. It was, they say, a tragic accident of timing: when Ettore returned with the money, Franco was gone. But this is not what they believed for many years; what some of them may still secretly believe. That is, that Ettore did not return, and never meant to. Perhaps even that he and Nuccia had known the move to Fossoli was coming. That either way, Nuccia had deliberately sacrificed her husband for her father.

Nuccia Treves is dead, and no one can ask her now. Perhaps it was true – Italian families are close, Italian Jewish ones even closer, and anything is possible in war and fear. But more probably it was an accident. The story doesn't tell us, for certain, what happened; it tells us the consequences when people do not know what happened in terrible times.

Of one thing we can be certain: Franco himself did not think he had been grossly betrayed by his wife. The man who survived Auschwitz until the end, in the ways we shall see, did not suffer from such a deep wound. Nor did Luciana's lover. It's tempting to think that if he loved Luciana, he can't have loved Nuccia – that he might indeed have hated her, and wanted to punish her. But a man who hates a woman and wants to punish her cannot love another one. Not the way that Franco loved Luciana.

He loved her with a warmth and tenderness she hadn't known before, she hadn't known existed. He loved her so that she was happy in Fossoli, happy even (she had to say this, because it was true) in the transport to Auschwitz, because he was there. He was so handsome, so quick to understand, so generous. He taught her that goodness was the most important thing, far more important than brains. He gave her happiness, and the experience of goodness, to take into hell with her. It was not the least reason she survived.

Vanda

Vanda's first feeling in Fossoli was relief. She'd hoped to come here all the time they'd been in Aosta, and she'd been right. There was plenty of food, she was even putting on weight. She could write to her father and brother (carefully, via a cousin), and they could write to her: her father was lazy about this, as usual, but Aldo wrote regularly, and sent her everything she asked for – even brand new clothes, which was unnecessary, and made her feel guilty. On 4 February, a week after their arrival, she told her cousin Nella that there were 'very few difficult moments'; the mood in the camp was excellent, she was fine, and so was Primo – if Nella saw Anna Maria, please would she tell her so. Of course letters from Fossoli were censored, and above all self-censored, since everyone was trying to reassure their families. But at the end of the first week Vanda could still write light-heartedly, even jokingly: 'The Jewish company here is very boring, the non-Jewish company really good.' In his own letters home, Primo had a characteristic explanation for this: the company was dull because the *furbi*, the clever ones, hadn't been caught.

Primo didn't distinguish between the Jewish and non-Jewish company, and I wondered how Vanda could. The Jews were in their own separate part of the camp: what non-Jews could she meet? Then I remembered what Primo himself had said, about the Italian Commandant who'd taken the girls into Carpi, to the public baths, to the hairdresser . . . Could this be an oblique reference to him, and perhaps to other friendly Italian guards as well? This seemed the most likely answer; and probably the right one, as we shall see.

Vanda's relief did not last long. By the end of the third week in Fossoli she was beginning to despair. She tried not to show it – 'I'm fine,' she insisted to Nella – but she couldn't help it. She dreamed constantly of her loved ones, and who knew if she would ever see them again? The thought saddened her dreadfully. She begged them to write, she begged them not to think badly of her. 'I do not think,' she wrote, 'that I shall trouble you much longer.'

Had something happened, or was it just her natural fearfulness and darkness emerging? Two days later she was more cheerful, because she'd had a letter. But a few days after that her despair had returned. It was only a day or two before the end (the date on her letter isn't clear), and she probably already knew. Her last words try once more to be brave and reassuring – 'We're a group of young people, so we're mostly quite calm' – but the real message is at the beginning. 'Please,' she asks Nella, 'if you're sending me a package, put in two tubes of Veronal, a good amount of that tranquillizer Aunt Ida took . . . I'll be eternally grateful. It would be a great help to me, as you will understand.'

Probably Nella did understand; certainly Aldo did. Their Aunt Ida had had a near-fatal accident, which left her in permanent pain. She had borne it as long as she could; until finally she had committed suicide, by taking Veronal. Vanda was asking her family to help her take the same way out, if and when the worst happened.

And during all this time, she and Primo were drawing closer. It may have begun even earlier, in Amay. But in a place like Fossoli, full of need and dread, friendship quickly became love; and so it did for Primo and Vanda. They loved each other as best they could; but for them love did not banish fear, as it did for Luciana and Franco. It is painfully clear from Vanda's letters that Primo's love did not stop her from falling into despair. And we may guess that it was the same for him, who remained in the grip of his double bind until after his return. Luciana's love affair in Fossoli made her more zestful, more in love with life than ever. Primo's did the opposite. He would have to find some other reason to survive.

★   ★

Friendship, for Primo, was the opposite of love. Here he had no secret block, waiting like a reef to wreck him. Here he had what he lacked in love – confidence, trust and luck. All his life he was as lucky in friendship as he was unlucky in love. And never more so than now. In Fossoli he made two of the friends who would literally save his life over the next terrible year.

Alberto Dalla Volta was only twenty-one years old, three and a half years younger than Primo. He was in Fossoli with his father, Guido: a charming and dignified man who soon became *capo*, or head, of their barracks. *Capo* at Fossoli had none of the sinister implications of the Auschwitz *Kapo*: it meant someone whom everyone liked and trusted, a natural leader. (Luciana, for example, was a *capo* too.) Alberto possessed all these qualities of his father's, and more. Soon, when youth and resilience were all, they would leap up in him like a light, and he would save his father for as long as he could. But here, where life was still semi-normal, it was Guido who was the leader. Alberto, always modest and quiet, did not stand out. Silvio Barabas remembers him as silent, even withdrawn. I think that Primo, suffering over Vanda, was the same. His friendship with Alberto seems to have been born at the last minute, in the cattle car to Auschwitz. But they would have seen each other for the first time now, in the long days of waiting at Fossoli.

Primo's friends had always been his *alter egos*, the other halves of his ideal Platonic whole. Alberto Dalla Volta was the perfect one, the one whom Primo himself called his *alter ego*. He was not just Primo's opposite, like Sandro, or the first Alberto, but his completion.

Alberto

They were, Primo would write, of the same age, build, temperament, profession. In Auschwitz they would be inseparable, interchangeable, 'the two Italians', whom foreigners wouldn't bother to distinguish. People would just yell 'Primo!' or 'Alberto!' – whichever came to mind; and whichever of the two was closer would reply.

They *were* alike – but not as alike as that. Alberto was younger, as we know. He was slight, but not as small and thin as Primo; he was profoundly intelligent and serious, but neither a genius nor a depressive. He was much closer to Sandro and the first Alberto in his taste for freedom and risk. One of Primo's greatest stories of Alberto would turn on a small difference between them, which would lead to an incommensurable difference in their fates: for Alberto, like Franco, would not return.* But it was also the small

* The story, 'Small Causes', is in *Moments of Reprieve*. We will return to this book later (see page 353 below).

differences between them which made Alberto, as Primo said, his 'ideal symbiont'. Alberto *was* like himself – but himself freed from his bonds: without the isolation of his genius and his double bind, and with the security of loving parents.

Alberto was also a first-born son. He had been a genuinely delicate child, catching every possible childhood ailment, and nearly dying of several. He grew into a thoughtful, intellectual boy, passionate about science, literature, music. Like Primo he chose chemistry as his special route to knowledge early on. He was more gregarious than Primo, more at ease with people, simply happier. But by the time he lost his freedom at twenty he had found no girlfriend either. He was devoted to his work, and to his parents; especially to one of them. His brother Paolo, the sportsman and the devil, was the apple of his father's eye. Alberto was the gentle, cultured, intellectual son, closest to his mother. 'I don't mean to say that she would rather have lost me than my brother,' Paolo says, and his voice trails away.

Until Alberto's early teens they lived in Mantua, where Guido Dalla Volta worked with his six brothers in the textile trade. Guido was a democrat, and a determined antifascist; when his sons had to wear the black shirt at school they felt ashamed. He was also an immensely energetic, popular and active man, joining large numbers of clubs and associations, and becoming head of most of them. All his posts were of course taken away from him in 1938; including his reluctant membership of the Fascist Party, which was, Paolo says, 'the one kind thing they did'.

In 1936 the family had moved away from Mantua, partly because Guido's wife Emma complained that he was always working. He left the shop to his brothers and took over a medical supplies business in Brescia; and for the next six years he went on overworking there. When the curtain finally came down in 1943 he was as well known in Brescia as he'd been in Mantua; and rather richer, with a house on the Lago di Garda as well as in town, and two cars. When the war was over all this had been lost, together with the business. That had had to be signed over, as usual, to a Catholic 'partner'; who turned out not to be one of the decent ones.

After 1938, then, the Dalla Voltas lost control over their business – though only officially and temporarily, they would have hoped; Guido lost his honorary jobs, and his officer's commission in the Army. But on the whole they remained remarkably untouched by the racial laws; even more untouched than the Levis. Like the Levis, they were still attached to their Jewish culture, but profoundly secular and Italian. In Mantua they had lived in the last reaches of their Jewish history, in a family house near the synagogue, in what had once been the ghetto. But in Brescia there was no

Jewish history, and hardly any Jews: only the Sinigaglias from Turin, and perhaps one or two other families. With no Jews, there was no Jewish problem; people barely knew what Jews were. Guido went on working after 1938 just as he'd done before; and the boys went on with their schooling. At first they'd been expelled, as the law required; but since they were the only Jewish students in the school, an arrangement was soon made. Where, in the new column headed *razza*, they were supposed to write *ebraica*, they would write *italiana* instead. After a few days they returned, and all went on as before.

On the strength of this ruse, Alberto entered the University of Modena in 1941, three years after the racial laws should have banned him. By the autumn of 1943 he had done two full years of Industrial Chemistry, and was starting his third. He was also working hard in the business, running the branch in Modena, and visiting clients between Modena and Brescia.

After 8 September, Guido had prepared for escape: not to Switzerland, but to a village in the mountains, where he had taken a small apartment and filled it with supplies. But now the family's luck ran out. In the early days of occupation the Germans had unleashed the first *Judenaktionen* themselves – around the Lago Maggiore, as we know, in Rome (the infamous round-up and deportation of the entire ghetto on 16 October 1943), in Milan, Florence, and other cities of the north. With Police Order No. 5 the Republic of Salò took over the dirty work: and nowhere faster than in the Dalla Voltas' homeland.* The very first round-up of Jews by Italians was probably the one in Mantua, in the early afternoon of 1 December. And on the night of 2–3 December there was one in Brescia. It netted only two victims: Guido and Alberto.

It would have netted Emma and Paolo too, but some humanity still remained in those very early days. Fifteen-year-old Paolo was dying of typhus, and his mother was left to stay with him until he died. Miraculously, he didn't die; equally miraculously they escaped from their guarded house into the mountains, and both – Paolo in a group of *garibaldini* – survived the war. Guido and Alberto would never know this: on top of their own fears, they must have dreaded every day that Emma would arrive at Fossoli, and Paolo would be dead.

In prison in Brescia Guido had not been idle. With the help of friends, he had arranged – that is, paid for – their escape: in the first air-raid, or bombardment, he and Alberto would slip away. But no air-raid or

---

* The first fellow prisoner Primo names in *If This is a Man*, the interpreter Flesch, was arrested by Italians near Brescia on 30 November, the very day Police Order No. 5 was issued.

bombardment came; and after a few weeks the chance was lost. By the time Primo arrived Alberto had already spent two months in Fossoli.

Leonardo

About Leonardo De Benedetti Primo would write: 'We met in the transit camp at Fossoli, we were deported together, and from that moment on, until we arrived back in Italy in October 1945, we were never parted.'

In 1944 Leonardo was forty-five years old: old enough to be Primo's father. Perhaps there *was* a father–son element in their relationship: Leonardo was a doctor, and kindness and care were his whole nature. On the other hand he always had an innocent, childlike side; so that Primo, bowed down by his determined realism, alone and unconsoled, may have seemed the older one.

If Leonardo was like a father to him, it was in a different way. There was something in Leonardo's presence that lifted people up, that made his patients feel better as soon as they saw him; something in his 'childlike smile', Primo said, 'that eased the heart'. Primo didn't name it, perhaps because he didn't know it: it was affection. Leonardo had a huge gift of natural sympathy and affection for his fellow human beings. This was unlike Primo's own father; and unlike Primo himself, whose feelings for the human race were more complicated, and more considered. In Auschwitz his closest bond would be to Alberto, since Leonardo's age and profession would put him on a slightly different course. But for the long months of their return Primo and Leonardo were never apart; after it they were only separated by a few blocks of the Corso Re Umberto until Leonardo died.

In fact Primo did have a name for that quality of Leonardo's, which Alberto shared, and which made each of them a light in the darkness, not only for him: goodness. This was the most extraordinary thing about him, and the reason why he is most loved: that from the pit of Auschwitz he brought back not only the truth about human evil, but these – and other – proofs of human goodness. That is the meditated, moral greatness of Primo Levi the writer and scientist. But the first, natural greatness was that of Primo Levi the man – really not much more than a boy – who, already in the first circle of hell, chose and was chosen by such friends.

Leonardo was born and bred in Turin. When he was five years old his father died; and it would have gone hard with the family if his mother had not been a Segre. Her brothers, Dino and Emanuele, were rich and generous, especially to her. They helped, for example, to pay for Leonardo's education in medicine; which would become his whole life, and which in Auschwitz would repeatedly save it.★

Leonardo's background and experience were close to Primo's, even though he was almost a generation older. His mother had kept up the Jewish traditions in the family, but he himself was a firm unbeliever. As a boy he had been undisposed towards religion; later he read and reasoned his way to atheism. Like all instinctively liberal and realistic Jews, he was antifascist; but he'd been still less politically active than Primo. Education and hard work were the great values in his family: his sister Ester took not just one but two university degrees, a generation before Ada Della Torre. And he himself worked hard all the way through university, and after it: his life was medicine, and there was little time for anything else.

As a medical student during the First World War he did his military service in the Medical Corps, working in hospitals. In mid-1918 he took part in a strange adventure: an Allied expeditionary force† to Murmansk, north of the Arctic Circle. Its aim was to hold the Germans in the east, which soon proved unnecessary; and to topple their new Bolshevik allies, which soon proved impossible. Leonardo's unit never fought. He narrowly escaped dying of Spanish flu instead, had an entertaining time, and came home six months later. It was almost like a rehearsal for his adventures with Primo in *The Truce*: a dangerous, chaotic, improbably enjoyable disaster.

In 1923 he graduated. He did two years of hospital work in Turin; and then settled down to his life of the next thirteen years, as *medico condotto* – national health service doctor – in nearby Rivoli. He was completely dedicated, and worked every hour of the day and night. His gift of sympathy made him instinctively a treater of people, not just of bodies, and an inspired diagnostician. For dozens of his patients he was more than a doctor: he was 'the doctor friend of the family'. For forty years and more after he left Rivoli his patients there still talked of him; at least one wrote to his family when he died.

Once he was settled in his career, a bride was found for him: Jolanda

---

★ They were apparently less generous to Leonardo's first cousin Dino Segre, Dino's illegitimate half-Catholic son, who would become the notorious novelist, scandalmonger and spy Pitigrilli. It was Pitigrilli who, as friend and relation to many of them, betrayed the Turinese Jewish antifascists of the 30s to the OVRA, the secret police: including Vittorio Foa, who owed his eight years in jail entirely to him. Pitigrilli seems to have been motivated at least partly by revenge on his father's rich and clannish Jewish family, who did not, he felt, help *him*.

† Italy had joined the Allies in 1915 – the opposite choice to the one she would make in 1940.

Debenedetti, who despite her name was no relation. Jolanda was born in Alba in 1901 and grew up in Asti, the eldest daughter of a prosperous, gifted and very close family. She was gentle, quiet, reserved. She'd been presented with several suitors before Leonardo, and turned them all down. This time, however, she accepted. In around 1928, when she was twenty-seven and he thirty, she and Leonardo were married.

They had no children, which was a great sadness to him, and probably also to her. Instead they devoted themselves to each other, and to their work: Leonardo to his patients, Jolanda to ADEI, the Associazione Donne Ebree d'Italia.★ Then, in 1938, their lives in Rivoli ended. Since Leonardo was a state employee, he could be one no longer.

For the next five years they would live with Jolanda's family in Turin. Leonardo continued to work privately, as much as he could; Jolanda became the last pre-war President of the Turin ADEI. And from its founding in 1940, they both worked hard for DELASEM.

DELASEM† was an extraordinary organization, one of the main reasons why so many Italian Jews, and Jewish refugees in Italy, survived the war. It was founded – with the full cooperation, even collaboration, of the government – by the Union of Italian Jewish Communities, with financial backing from Jewish aid organizations abroad, especially the American Joint Distribution Committee, the 'Joint'. It functioned right up to 1943 and even beyond, helping around 5,000 people in all to leave Italy, and tens of thousands to survive inside it. Leonardo's and Jolanda's work was with refugees, finding them food, clothing and homes; occasionally with Jolanda's own siblings, who temporarily took in several Yugoslav children. Through this work, Leonardo heard many terrible stories. He found the worst ones hard to believe, like everyone else – or even harder, since he was constitutionally incapable of suspicion. Nonetheless, he heard them; and the experience made him better prepared for the near future.

When the Allied bombing intensified in the autumn of 1942, the Debenedettis began to think of leaving the cities, like everyone else. Jolanda's brother Arturo and his family were also in Turin; so was her next sister, Nella, and hers. The youngest sister, Elsa, and her family were in Milan. Then the parents' house was hit. Beniamino, their father, made up his mind: they must all withdraw to the safety of Asti. It made sense; and the patriarch must be obeyed. Around October, the brothers and sisters all left their homes and returned to their father's.

★ Association of Jewish Women of Italy, which was part of WIZO, the Women's International Zionist Organization.
† Delegazione Assistenza Emigranti Ebrei, or Delegation for Aid to Jewish Emigrants.

For the next year, apart from brief periods they all lived there together. They were nineteen people, including nine children. The children had a glorious time – surrounded by cousins, let loose in the countryside, free of school for a whole year. But for their parents it was less easy. The men continued to go into the cities for work; but as time went on there was less and less of it. Leonardo had some patients in Asti and Alessandria, and continued to work with DELASEM in Asti. But for much of the time he went for bicycle rides, or did crosswords. Jolanda and her sisters struggled to keep the children from going wild; to keep house together, when each had had her own; and to keep the peace with their mother, Emma, who was as autocratic as their father. Yet this was their last moment of normal happiness; or of normal unhappiness, which would come to seem just as precious.

When Mussolini fell on 25 July 1943, there was celebration in the villa. The men in particular were jubilant: at last they could be useful again – active, loyal, normal Italians. It was Leonardo who reminded them: Fascism was still in power, and they were still Jews. Nothing had changed.

On 8 September, of course, the change came. Beniamino was certain that no one in Asti would ever betray them to the invaders, but this time his children overruled him. Each moved to one of his small properties nearby, and made their plans.

Elsa and her family decided to stay in Italy. They moved to a village near Voghera, closer to Milan; and there, by great good luck, they would survive.

The first family to leave was Arturo's. It was still so early that they were able to take an easy route into Switzerland, from Chiasso near Como. Shortly afterwards this route, and all other obvious ones, were closed. By the time the others were ready to go only the higher mountain passes were left; which may have made them hesitate still further.

Once again it was probably Leonardo who urged them on. Amongst the Yugoslav refugees he'd met in Asti was a family of four, parents in their sixties, a son and daughter-in-law in their twenties. Immediately after 8 September the son went to the Val D'Aosta and found a guide to take them over the Monte Rosa into Switzerland. Leonardo had been appalled. How could they think of crossing one of the highest mountains in the Alps, in winter, with two elderly people? 'You're crazy,' he'd said. 'You'll all die on the Monte Rosa.' 'Better to die on the Monte Rosa,' the boy had said, 'than in one of Hitler's gas chambers.' Whatever Leonardo had been able to believe, he did not forget that. Beniamino was over eighty, Emma nearly seventy, and Leonardo's own mother seventy-two. Nonetheless, by the beginning of December they had all gathered in Elsa's empty house in Milan, together with Nella and Pino Fubini and their three young children. The decision had been made. They too would go over the mountains: not as high as the Monte Rosa, but high enough, from Lanzo d'Intelvi north of Como.

Leonardo's sister Ester had been with their mother since soon after 8 September, when her husband Silvio and their fifteen-year-old son had crossed to Switzerland. At first Silvio had thought it would be less dangerous for the women to hide in Italy than to attempt escape; but now he too had changed his mind. The group that left from Lanzo d'Intelvi on 3 December, therefore, consisted of eleven people: the five Fubinis, Beniamino and Emma, Jolanda and Leonardo, and Leonardo's mother and sister.

They set off at night; it was very cold. Along the route they met other groups of fugitives: Yugoslav refugees, with whom they went on more or less together. At one point the guides called a halt, and when they looked around they were alone. After a while the guides returned. They'd thought they heard German soldiers approaching; but it was a false alarm. Beniamino, the oldest, was extraordinarily strong. But at one stage Emma could not go on, and had to be carried by a guide; at another stage it was Sandra Fubini, who was only five. She, at least, had no idea of the danger they were in; unlike her brothers, who were ten and thirteen.

They made it. That is, they made it as far as the border. There they were stopped by Swiss border guards. They gave their names, ages, particulars. Leonardo said, truthfully, that he and Jolanda had no children; he also said, untruthfully, that he was in perfect health (he had had an ulcer for years), and so was she. Later they were told that only the old, the ill and the parents of young children would be admitted: but by then it was too late. (Today Sandra believes that her mother tried to pass one of them off as Leonardo's; but this is almost certainly a wish that has grown into a memory over the years.) They would all be kept in the militia's barracks overnight; but the next day only the old people and the family with children would be allowed to proceed.

That night, Leonardo's mother had a stroke. In the morning he tried desperately to be allowed to stay with her: he was her son, he was a doctor, she needed him. But the Swiss were unmoved: she had her daughter with her, that was enough. He and his wife had to return. Leonardo's knowledge had saved, or helped to save, his parents-in-law, his mother and sister, the five Fubinis; but not himself, and not Jolanda.

The next day they went back the same way they had come. The Yugoslav refugees – fifteen or sixteen of them, all young – were sent back with them. It snowed heavily the whole way. By the time they arrived back in Lanzo d'Intelvi it was late evening. They took a room for the night. And there it all ended, in the shape of two polite and friendly Italian militiamen, who requested that they come 'to answer a few questions'.

They spent two nights in the militia's barracks in Lanzo, and two weeks in prison, first in Como, then in Modena. Throughout, the Italians holding them insisted they would not be handed over to the Germans: they were Italian prisoners, and so they would remain, that was the law. The Marshal of the border militia was as happy as they were when he could tell them that. Leonardo believed he was in good faith, and very likely he was. But it was just this need to go on believing in good faith, and in the law, that undid him, as it would so many others. They were not heavily guarded on their journeys between prisons, or even in the prisons themselves. Like Primo and Luciana, they could have escaped. One of the Yugoslavs with them probably did. But Leonardo was trusting, law-abiding, mild; and Jolanda was resigned and pessimistic, not someone to take her fate into her hands. They did not try. On 21 December they were delivered to Fossoli.

★   ★

At first, like Vanda, like everyone, they were relieved. They had no money, and only the clothes they stood up in; but since they'd put those on to cross a mountain, at least they were warm. They wrote to a secretary of Beniamino's in Asti, to Elsa, to Jolanda's uncle Giorgio Jarach; and soon they were very adequately resupplied. Unlike Primo and Vanda, they were not tempted to joke about the Jewish company. It was almost like being in a big family, Jolanda told Elsa: everyone seemed to be a friend of a friend, or a relative of a relative. They kept busy on the cooking and cleaning corvées; Leonardo even did some doctoring. They made friends, they ate well, they read a lot. And once again the decency of the Italian way was a snare and a delusion. Giorgio Jarach, who had himself escaped from a POW camp in the First World War, bribed someone in Fossoli to let them out. But in the end they wouldn't take the risk. Perhaps the regime was already hardening, perhaps Jolanda was too afraid. But most likely life still seemed safer inside Fossoli than out of it.

Around 15 February, this changed. On the 15th Vanda's mood plummeted. On the 16th Jolanda warned her family of '*nuove disposizioni*', new arrangements, under which, for example, prisoners could only write two letters a week; she and Leonardo were 'no longer as calm and confident as before'. On the 16th, as Silvio Barabas and his companions were registering with the Italian *capo campo*, the *capo*'s voice suddenly froze, and his eyes fixed on the door. There stood an SS sergeant. The *capo campo* fell over himself to cede his chair; until the German waved him to carry on. 'At that point,' says Silvio, 'we all knew who was in charge.'

They were right. The real commandants of Fossoli were now SS Lt Karl Titho and his deputy, Sgt Hans Haage. For a week the illusion was maintained. Prisoners continued to deal only with the Italian administration, and on the whole their humane treatment continued. When a transport arrived from Trento on the 17th, their spirits rose. Why on earth would the Germans – the sensible, efficient Germans – ship hundreds of people south, if they were planning to ship them north again? On the 20th their spirits rose still higher. The SS inspected the camp, and loudly, publicly, reprimanded the Italian 'commandant' for its failings. The kitchen service must be improved, more wood must be collected for heating, an infirmary would soon be opened. The very next day came the announcement. On the following morning all the Jews, without exception, would be leaving for an unknown destination.

This was the moment Primo, Vanda, Franco and Luciana were eating spaghetti, and stopped. Leonardo and Jolanda wrote to Beniamino's secretary and asked him to tell the family. In Silvio's barrack people thronged the corridor, begging each other for information. At last Guido Dalla Volta appeared. 'I have been ordered to inform you,' he said, 'that tomorrow we shall be leaving. My task is to say a few encouraging words. However, to be frank with you, I have no hopes. We shall be travelling in cattle-cars. That is all I can tell you.'

'Only a few ingenuous and deluded souls continued to hope,' Primo wrote. The rest knew that this was a sentence of death, though they did not know, and could not have imagined, how and where it would be carried out. The most ordinary things are the most precious, when you are about to lose them; and about this moment Primo Levi became the poet of the ordinary. The corvées for cooking and cleaning went on as usual, he wrote, the teachers of the little school went on teaching. And the mothers went on being mothers. Even for *that* journey, they packed the food 'with tender care,

and washed their children and packed the luggage, and at dawn the barbed wire was full of children's washing hung out in the wind to dry . . . Would you not do the same? If you and your child were going to be killed tomorrow, would you not give him to eat today?

That night, 'everyone took leave of life in the manner that most suited him'. Some prayed: like the Gattegno family, who sat in a circle all night saying the *Kaddish*, the prayer for the dead, for themselves. Some abandoned themselves: to drink, to 'futile rebellion', to resignation, fear or despair. These Primo reports, but does not describe, as he described the mothers, and the Gattegnos; and this combining of dedication to truth with dedication to human dignity will be the key to all his testimony.

There was a last way of taking leave of life, which he also reports. It was probably the most common, and certainly the most natural, as the coming years of horror and suffering would show. The closer people came to death, the more it surrounded and threatened them, the more they longed to defy it, in the most direct way possible. As long as they had an ounce of strength left, they made love – wherever they could, at the side of the road, next to piles of dead bodies. And so it was in Fossoli that night. For the lucky ones, like Franco and Luciana, it was a last night of love. For others it might be only fear, blind need, oblivion.

Primo reports it: that is his dedication to truth. But there is also his dedication to dignity; and beyond that, his double bind. 'Some,' he wrote, 'intoxicated themselves with a last, iniquitous passion.' Even on the threshold of death, he seems still in the grip of sexual horror.

But what, then, about Vanda, whom he himself loved? The truth is that he is thinking here of Vanda. And he is thinking of her again in the last line he wrote about Fossoli: *Many things were said and done among us then; but of these it is better that there remain no memory.*

Vanda was more afraid than she had ever been, and the Veronal had not arrived. That night, she went to the Italian Commandant. Perhaps she had resisted his advances before; perhaps she hadn't. Whenever she first gave in to him, it was in the hope of saving her life. That was the agonized choice of many thousands of women – and not only women – in those terrible years. But that did not help Primo. During that last night he not only looked into the abyss of death, but into the abyss of what he knew that Vanda was doing, and why. Writing about it, even two years later, he could not keep out that word *iniquitous*. And yet, in the last few dreadful days they had left together, he would go on loving her, he would love her more. He had to believe in the human capacity for nobility; but he could love a weak and frightened human being. That made him the harsh and tender witness he would be.

9. Auschwitz:
22 February 1944 – 27 January 1945

Inferno, Canto III, engraving by Gustave Doré

There are some days on which the sun ought never to rise; but of course it does. The dawn of Tuesday, 22 February 1944 was a moment of intolerable consciousness for the 650 Jews in the camp of Fossoli: like the long moment before a car crashes, a hurtling body hits the ground. In it, wrote Primo Levi the man of reason, 'all reason dissolved'. In it Vanda Maestro realized there would be no escape for her, and slashed her wrists in despair. But she did not do the job well enough, or well at all. One wrist was roughly bandaged, and she was sent to the roll-call with the rest.

Some, perhaps not the most fortunate, would become very familiar with this Nazi roll-call. Afterwards, Primo wrote, it would stay in their dreams as 'the very emblem of the Lager': of its insane order, its gratuitous cruelty, its reduction of human beings to numbers. '*Wieviel Stück?*' the SS officer asked now – 'How many pieces?' '*Sechshundert-fünfzig Stück,*' the corporal replied. Only a few of the Jews would have understood the words; but the tone was unmistakable. With this first roll-call, still at Fossoli, they had entered the Lager world.

We know what it would hold; they did not. They had heard of concentration camps, of work camps, of harsh conditions. But no one had heard of Auschwitz and what happened there – or if they had, like Leonardo, they did not believe it. The first touch of the Lager had already cut their ties to the normal, responsive world, had left them alone and uncertain. They had children to calm, old people to help, belongings to keep an eye on. That was enough for the moment. They climbed on to the buses for Carpi without protest.

Primo's was one of the first buses. When they arrived at Carpi station an SS guard ordered him to unload the luggage from the roof. Primo did not understand, and received his first blows.

At the station the train was waiting. Twelve goods wagons for 650 people – that meant over fifty people per wagon. Surely that was not possible? (But in the last transports it was often 100, even 120.) The escort was waiting too; more SS. They gave orders in German: *Line up in alphabetical order.* When people did not understand they repeated the same words loudly, then bellowing. Still people hesitated; now they were afraid as well. Once again the blows fell. Primo was kicked and hit with the butt of an SS rifle; near him someone's face was smashed open against the side of the train. This was so new, and so shocking, Primo wrote, that they felt no pain: 'Only a profound amazement'. Near him stood an Italian gendarme, guarding the train. 'Remember this,' Primo told him, 'and remember that you took part.' 'But what else can I do?' the man said, stricken. 'Be a thief, it's more honest,' Primo replied.

Amid the chaos, not even the SS could achieve the mad perfection of alphabetical order. Primo, Vanda, Luciana and Franco remained together; Alberto and Guido Dalla Volta joined them, and probably Leonardo and Jolanda as well. There were forty-five people in their small wagon. Among them were two young mothers with infants, and many elderly people, including the whole Jewish Old People's Home of Venice. As soon as they were inside the doors were closed, although the train would not leave until the evening. They had time to think now – too much time. So it was true after all, what they had never quite believed: cattle-cars crammed with human beings, which vanish God knows where, and never return. Only this time, Primo wrote, 'it is we who are inside'.

The Transport

Almost always, Primo would write, the train is the first memory, and not only for chronological reasons. The roll-call was the shadow the Lager threw before it; in the train you had entered the shadow, and it was already too late.

You had been torn away from Fossoli, you were being torn away from Italy, you had no idea where you were going except that it was to Germany, the worst place on earth for a Jew. You had been told only that the journey would be long, it would end in work in a cold country. The SS had given the 'self-interested and ironic' advice to take along your furs, your gold and jewels; apart from that, almost nothing. They provided minimal rations, once a day, of bread, jam and cheese; but nothing to drink, no blankets, no latrines or even buckets, no straw to cover the floor. Since — though you did not know it — you were about to die anyway, what was the point of feeding you, of keeping you warm, or sane, or even alive?

The mothers had packed food, and the *capo campo* had thought to procure more. But he had not thought about water, which costs nothing, and would surely be supplied. Thirst and cold became their torments. Hunger exhausts, Primo wrote, but thirst enrages. Once a day when the doors were opened they could slake their thirst with snow; for the rest of the twenty-four hours their only relief was to lick the rusty pipes that ran near the ceiling, where their own breath had risen, condensed, and frozen into ice. The infants screamed without ceasing because their mothers' milk had dried up; the poor young mothers begged for water night and day.

The train was already the Lager in its suffering, in its imprisonment. It was already the Lager in its crowding, made worse by all the useless trunks and bundles; so that there was no room to lie down, and even if the cold and thirst had let them, no one could sleep. But above all it was already the Lager in its essence: in the contempt of the perpetrators, and the degradation of the victims.

Worse than the crowding and the cold, worse even than the thirst, was what Primo would call 'the cruelty of violated modesty'. In the Lager it would flower in many forms; here it began with one. Parents and children, friends and strangers, men and women had to urinate and defecate in front of one another, beside one another, in closed cars, on to the floor. In Primo's car, by sheer chance there was a single chamber pot, brought along by one of the young mothers. Two days into the journey they found some nails in the wooden sides of the wagon. They prised out two, strung a blanket between them in one corner, and placed the chamber pot behind. It was no more than symbolic. But what happened in cars that had not even an infant's chamber pot, Primo wrote, 'is difficult to imagine'.

Once every twenty-four hours the train halted and the doors were opened, for the people to relieve themselves outside. But this too was in plain view; not only of each other now, but of the SS, who grimaced with disgust, and amused themselves by taking photographs of humiliated men and women squatting in the snow.

'Few men know how to go to their deaths with dignity,' Primo wrote; in such circumstances, even fewer. Maddened by thirst, by humiliation, by fear, they kicked and cursed and fought each other for a breath of air, an inch of space. Some went mad altogether. The journey took four nights and four days. Long before it was over the true offence of the Lager had already begun to take place: not death itself, of however unimaginably many; but the destruction of dignity, of the human personality: what Primo Levi would call *the demolition of a man*.

This did not happen to Primo and his friends. They had no old parents or small children with them to break their hearts. They had youth and strength; above all they had each other. Luciana, in particular, spent the four days and four nights in Franco's arms, and feared nothing. As the train left the last Italian cities behind – Verona, Trento, Bolzano – they threw letters to their families and friends out through the small slit in the wagon wall. Most of the transports from Italy followed the same route; along it there must have lived many heroes, who regularly picked up and posted the last words of the condemned. Certainly Primo's and Luciana's messages all reached their destinations. Luciana's were typically sanguine, ending (she smiles self-mockingly now) *Viva la libertà*. So was the card they sent together to Bianca Guidetti Serra:

Cara Bianca, tutti in viaggio alla maniera classica. Saluta tutti. A voi la fiaccola. Ciao, Bianca, ti vogliamo bene.

Dear Bianca, we are travelling in the classic manner. Greetings to all. The torch passes to you. Goodbye, Bianca, we send our love.

Primo, Luciana, Vanda.

At midday of the second day they crossed the Brenner Pass. Everyone stood up, Primo wrote, in silence. Luciana remembered it differently, or remembered the moment before, as they passed through the station. Through the slit they saw people staring back at them. 'See?' they shouted out. 'We're women and children, old people, sick people. That's what the Nazis are deporting!'

Then they were in Austria, and free people were skiing. 'Are people still free?' Luciana asked, amazed. After Vienna they saw camps surrounded by barbed wire: grey huts, grey people bent over spades, surrounded by guards. 'Germany must be one enormous prison,' Primo said.

All Jews must die: 'that was a postulate,' Primo wrote. Nothing was left to chance. In his convoy there were thirty-one young children and 118 old people. Two men were over eighty, two women were ninety, or very nearly. There was a quadriplegic, and a man who had suffered a stroke just before leaving. One of the ninety-year-old women and three of the men over seventy died on the journey. One of these, a Viennese living in Genoa, died in Primo's car. Would it not have been simpler and more economical, Primo would ask in *The Drowned and the Saved*, to let them die in their beds, instead of adding their agony to the agony of the transport? But no. 'The enemy must not only die, but die in torment.'

There was a second death in Primo's car, which was still more of a torment, and not only to the victim. To Primo it was such a torment that he would never speak or write of it afterwards; when he was asked point-blank, he denied that it had happened.

The man who died was sixty-seven years old. He would certainly have been killed on arrival; so his too was a gratuitous death. But his killers did not know that. That was one important difference between them and the SS, who had pushed the crippled, sick and dying on to the train.

The man's name was Arturo Foà. He was – absurd as it sounds, in a cattle-car to Auschwitz – a poet. He was also a Jew, and not originally a Fascist. But from the moment Mussolini came to power he became his fanatical admirer, and self-appointed poet laureate to the regime. Until 1938 he poured out volume after volume of hyperbolic praise. After 1938 he poured out equal numbers of letters to the Duce, pleading for *discriminazione*, and for the chance to continue his exaltations, under any name or none. His pleas were ignored. But his passion for the Duce did not dim; nor for himself, as the exception to every rule, still secretly loved in return. Even after 8 September he did not hide; and in early February he was arrested, walking openly in the Piazza San Carlo in Turin.

In Fossoli he did not hide either, but defended his Fascist faith as loudly, as foolishly as he had always done. He was not the only Jewish Fascist, even now; very likely the others met the same fate. In Fossoli dimly, with horrible clarity in the cattle car, his fellow-prisoners knew that they had been betrayed; and he was one of the betrayers. In the crush and horror of the transports it was easy to die, if you were no longer young, if no one spared you a helping hand, a drop of water, an inch of room. Perhaps it was like this, perhaps it was worse. But when the convoy reached Auschwitz, Arturo Foà was dead.

Primo never told this story, out of loyalty to his companions, and because he could not bear to think that all men could feel the need for violence and revenge. That is, of course, part of his great question, and part of what was intolerable to him in his ultimate answer. It was so intolerable to him that when he was asked about Arturo Foà, on the occasion I have mentioned, he turned his head away and wept. Yet in his last book he forced himself to look at the grey zone between victims and perpetrators, saying that it was necessary, 'if we wish to know the human species'. The story of Arturo Foà belongs there.

Neither this nor anything else broke Primo Levi, now or later. But it came near. For the last five years his human rights, his life's ambitions, his hopes of love had all been thwarted. His bid to fight back, to turn himself into a man of arms, had failed, and been the wrong road. His first experience of killing had been against his own side; now the second was as well. It was as though violence hated him as much as he hated it: as though the moment he brought himself to touch it, it turned inward, like a sword that cut him instead of his enemy as soon as he picked it up.

During those four days and nights he felt innumerable contradictory things. Perfect unhappiness was as impossible as perfect happiness: that was the first lesson of the Lager. He wrote *A voi la fiaccola* with Luciana, he drank in Leonardo's calm, he found his perfect friend in Alberto Dalla Volta. But his main companion on this journey was Vanda: poor terrified Vanda, who knew so well she would not survive that she had tried to escape her agony before it began. Primo was not like Luciana, and not like Alberto. He would be like Leonardo – gentle, indomitable, enduring; but no one could guess that now. At this moment, and up to this moment, the person he was most like was Vanda. He too was afraid, without illusion about his strength, defeated by the last few months of mistakes and humiliations. He was not perfectly unhappy, but he was as unhappy as it is possible to be; and though his unhappiness might be relieved, it would also be deepened by sharing it with Vanda, who was as unhappy as he.

That is what he mostly did, on this journey to nothingness: he shared with Vanda the deepest fears of their lives, and of their deaths. I think that is what he meant when he wrote *Now, in the hour of decision, we said to each other things that are never said among the living*. I think that for the first time in his life he told someone his darkest secrets. And she told him hers. After that, they were both ready to die.

The Arrival

The train reached Auschwitz on the night of Saturday, 26 February. It stopped outside the station. On either side were rows of red and white lights, as far as the eye could see; beyond them, a vast dark plain. Searchlights showed a line of lorries, and in the distance a camp, surrounded by barbed wire. So there *was* a camp – perhaps they would work after all. They waited, in silence.

Then the doors were opened with a crash, and the next stage had begun. Shouts, lights, SS men with dogs and truncheons, orders barked in angry, incomprehensible German. Someone translated: get down with your baggage, leave it on the platform. Primo, Vanda, Luciana and Franco had planned to say they were relatives, so they could stay together. But immediately they were separated, Primo and Franco pushed to one side, Vanda and Luciana to the other. Jolanda was torn from Leonardo's arm. No time for a single word; within seconds they were gone.

No one understands what is happening. Next to Luciana in the women's group is an Austrian refugee, who translates: the tired, the ill, the old, the mothers with children may take the trucks, the others must walk. What would you have done? Luciana wants to walk, after all those days in the train. Vanda's arm hurts, she should take the truck, by all means. But Vanda refuses. 'You are all I have left in the world,' she says. 'We must stay together.' She locks her good arm through Luciana's, and will not let go.

The SS pass along the line, looking sharply at each of the remaining women. They point most to the left, a few to the right. What are they looking for? Some strong and healthy girls are sent to the left, with the old, the sick, the pregnant, the mothers with small children. Vanda has her arm in a sling, she and Luciana are both small. Was it Luciana's beauty, her strength, her luck? They are sent to the right together. When the SS have finished, only twenty-nine women will still walk. All the others are added to the lorries.

Among them, Primo would write, was Emilia, daughter of Aldo Levi of Milan, 'a curious, ambitious, cheerful, intelligent child', her mother and her brother. The family had been betrayed by the person who had offered to help them escape to Switzerland. Emilia was beautiful and full of character; everyone indulged her, even the German engineer of their train, who had allowed her parents to draw water from the engine for her bath. All that ended here. Emilia was five years old, her brother Italo twelve.

Among them, too, was Jolanda.

★

It was the same for the men. An SS officer, or perhaps several, looked at each of them, asked some their age, and whether they were well or ill; then divided them to left and right. Primo and Franco may still have been together, or perhaps they had lost each other. Primo found himself, he said, next to another man from his wagon, older, and in poor health. Primo said he would declare himself fit for work. 'You must do as you like,' the man said. 'Nothing can help me any more.' He said he was ill, and Primo never saw him again. His name was probably Paolo Shaul Levi, and he was only forty.

In less than ten minutes this first selection was over. Ninety-six men had been chosen for work. Among them, from Primo's wagon, were Primo, Franco and Leonardo, Silvio Barabas, and Alberto and Guido Dalla Volta.

That may have been all that happened. Or there may have been more. The rest was told to me by Paolo Dalla Volta, who says that Primo told it to him and his mother as soon as he came home.

Of all the shock, paralysis, incomprehension that would engulf all who entered this infernal world, the worst was at the moment of entry. No one understood what those two lines of people meant. But they knew that they were 'on the other side', beyond all aid, all mercy: 'on the threshold', Primo would write, 'of the darkness and terror of an unearthly space'.

At that barest, most bereft moment, Luciana wanted to walk: to move of her own free will. That was what the SS man saw in her face. Vanda wanted to stay with the one strong person she knew; and that, for the moment, saved her too.

Once they were inside – Primo would write – of all the Italians Alberto was the one to react most quickly and most intelligently. According to Paolo, that began now. When the SS man reached him Alberto said, in German, that he was an experienced industrial chemist, and the SS pointed to the left. Alberto spoke again. That man in the other line, he said, is my assistant: and the SS moved Guido Dalla Volta from right to left. And *that* man, Alberto said, is also a chemist, he works in a large factory. And Primo too was moved from the line of the dead to the line of the living.

So Primo Levi nearly disappeared into Hitler's gas chambers at the very beginning, and owed his salvation to Alberto Dalla Volta? Yes, says Paolo. Primo told them so, many times: '*Alberto mi ha salvato la vita*', 'Alberto saved my life.' That was the base and beginning of their friendship, and of his lifelong love and gratitude to Alberto.

But if Primo had said he was twenty-four and fit, surely he was already in the line for work? No, says Paolo. He was small, pale, extremely thin; he would have looked no use a labourer. That is true. He weighed only 49 kilos.* He would indeed be little use as a labourer; and soon one of the most acute observers in Auschwitz would dismiss his chances of survival.

But this was not the reason Primo himself gave, Paolo says. What Primo said was that he had arrived at Auschwitz utterly exhausted, beaten down by the sufferings of the transport, of Fossoli, of before: in a state, says Paolo, of *absolute depression*. Now, this also rings true – all too true; and I do not know where Paolo can have learned it, if not, as he says, from Primo.

Might the whole story, then, be true? With time all our memories become more beautiful, and kinder to ourselves and those we love. The Dalla Voltas loved each other very much; according to Primo himself they were all inclined to believe what they longed to believe about each other. I am certain that Alberto saved Primo's life many times over the next weeks and months. That may be what Primo meant; and this is only Paolo's fond embellishment.

Yet it *may* be true. *If This is a Man* says nothing at all about how Primo himself entered Auschwitz. He tells his own story only as far as it is necessary, and universal. Nearly dying straight away because of your own depression was not universal. It was also, perhaps, too painful to remember. But if it was not universal, it was nonetheless full of meaning. Apart from careless, mad and completely arbitrary decisions, which were legion, people's souls were bared in that moment. Perhaps Jolanda's resigned and gentle soul had been thus bared. It would not have mattered what Primo said to the SS man, if the self-doubt of a lifetime, and the defeats of the last months and years, were in his eyes. Not Auschwitz, but his own private depression killed him in the end. It may be that, if it had not been for Alberto Dalla Volta, it would already have killed him there.

The Italian transports were among the smallest, and contained some of the most innocent, most *bon bourgeois* Jews of Europe. With them the SS used less violence than usual. After the first tumult of shouting, everything was as silent, Primo wrote, as a dream. The SS divided them quietly, like policemen doing their duty; until someone took too long to obey. Then they knocked him to the ground.

It was incomprehensible, mad, unreal. And who were these strange creatures in striped clothes, who suddenly appeared in the light of the lamps, and began to remove their luggage, still in silence? But that they did understand. This is what awaited them. These creatures would be themselves.

---

* 108 pounds, the weight of a slender girl.

The Entry

They were loaded on to trucks and driven at speed through the darkness. After twenty minutes they saw a gate, with a sign above it. It should have said, like the gate of Hell in the *Inferno*: *Lasciate ogni speranza, voi ch'entrate*: *Abandon all hope, ye that enter*. What it actually said, with boundless and profane irony, was the Auschwitz motto: *Arbeit Macht Frei, Work Frees*.

They are made to undress, and everything is taken away. They are completely shaven: head hair, beards, pubic hair. Their mouths and anuses are searched for hidden objects. Naked, shocked and sheared, they are locked in a shower room all night, asking each other if they will ever see their women again, if water or gas will come out of these showerheads, for some have heard a rumour. At dawn they are doused with disinfectant; then finally the showerheads open, and it is water, boiling hot water, five minutes of bliss. But immediately they are pushed into a freezing room, striped rags and wooden clogs are thrust into their hands, and they have to run naked through the icy dawn to another hut. Here they are at last allowed to cover themselves. Striped suit and coat, a shirt, a pair each of underpants and foot-rags, both often made, contemptuously, from the material of a prayer-shawl, a *tallith*. No one's rags fit, no one's clogs match their feet, or each other. Guido Dalla Volta, the perfect elegant Italian, is bald, with livid marks under his eyes, in filthy patched prison stripes and wooden shoes. He looks at the others, then down at himself, in disbelief.

This being a German camp, they are taken to register: nationality – but Jews have no nationality, the countries they live in are not theirs; age; distinguishing features (here they must list gold teeth, bridges and crowns); profession. If you put 'lawyer', 'professor', 'businessman', like the majority of Primo's transport, you will be assigned to the worst Kommandos. Primo puts *chemist*, and will be assigned to a bad one anyway.

In the census each has received a number, which is now tattooed on his left forearm. Alberto's number is 174488, Primo's is 174517. Their clothes, their shoes, their hair have all gone; now their names have gone too, and they are only numbers.

Finally they are sent for a medical examination. This is in fact a second selection, though they do not understand that, any more than they understood the first. It is carried out by prisoner doctors, who try to pass everyone, and encourage them all to work. Leonardo is forty-five; Guido Dalla Volta is fifty, and so is Aldo Levi, Emilia's and Italo's father; Flesch the interpreter, and Glücksmann, whom Primo will call Steinlauf, are over fifty, and so are at least a dozen others. But the doctors pass them all. Hell awaits, as it is described on Dante's gate:

> *Per me si va nella città dolente,*
> *Per me si va nell'etterno dolore,*
> *Per me si va tra la perduta gente.*

> Through me you enter the Woeful City,
> Through me you enter eternal pain,
> Through me you go among the lost people.

Luciana is not afraid. Instead she is excited. 'At last we'll see one of these camps with our own eyes,' she says to Vanda. They too pass under a gate which says *Arbeit Macht Frei*. They walk for half an hour, through one camp and into another. They do not know it yet, but this one is called Birkenau.

Everything happens as it happened to the men: with the same inexorability, the same stupefaction; no thought or will possible, as though they are animals, or objects, or already dead. The stripping of everything they still possess, the tattooing of their numbers on their arms. Perhaps even worse for women, the shaving of their hair: bare skulls, bare pudenda. Luciana asks a German refugee how to say *I am a doctor* in German; you never know, it might help. When her turn comes she says it loud and clear: '*Ich bin eine Ärztin.*' And it does help; in fact it will save her life. Already she is treated differently. She will be a prisoner, but also a doctor, and her status must be marked. Her hair is roughly cut, but not shaved.

The disinfection, the shower, the handing over of torn, ill-fitting rags: a vest, a pair of pants – sometimes male, as the men's were sometimes female – striped trousers, jacket and coat, and the same unmatched, ill-fitting clogs. Often no socks or foot-rags; and nothing to cover their heads, which felt so cold.

They too spent the first night locked in the shower room. Vanda was deathly tired, her arm ached; she laid her naked head on Luciana's lap. The next day they registered: name, age, profession. While they were filling in the forms a young Italian woman came in. She had long hair, a blue coat, good shoes: a prisoner doctor, like Luciana. She runs from one to the other, asking after family and friends – were they on your transport, God forbid? Her name is Bianca Morpurgo, and she has already been here for three weeks. Her parents and two sisters were deported with her, but they disappeared on the platform at Auschwitz, and she has never seen them again. *Never seen them again?* the new arrivals ask in horror, thinking of their own mothers, their own sisters. Bianca cries, she is afraid they are dead.

There are such terrible rumours – that all the people on the trucks are taken straight to the gas chambers . . . No one believes her, she must be crazy. They are relieved when she goes away.

They are lined up in groups of five and marched to the Quarantine Block. A thousand women are crammed into two tiers of sleeping platforms, six or even eight and ten to each small space. They hardly look up as the new ones enter; if they look, it is with anger, hostility, envy of those who have only just arrived. Vanda and Luciana understand nothing, they are beyond despair.

The Initiation

The worst was not death itself, but the destruction of personality: the 'demolition of a man'. That is one of the main things that Primo Levi has to tell us.

This happened straight away; it was the aim and intention that it should happen straight away. That was the reason for the symbolic contempt of the cattle-car, for the terrifying ritual of arrival – the screamed commands, the kicks and punches, the nakedness, shaving and violation of the body, the dressing in rags, the tattooing. All went beyond the merely practical: your number already had to be sewn on your jacket, coat and trousers, for example; was that not enough? No, Primo answered, it was not enough. It was not enough to suffer and die; first you had to be demolished. You had to be demolished so that you would not resist, or attract help; so that not only your oppressors, but you yourself would accept that your suffering and death were just, that you deserved no more.

In the first few hours, almost everything has already gone: home and family, past and future; clothes, shoes, hair, name, the smallest personal possession. You were already a 'hollow man', Primo said: light, empty, ready to fall.

It might seem you had nothing left to lose; but you did. The 'excremental' violation increased, not only because the latrines were public, and access limited, but because you soon had chronic diarrhoea and a swollen bladder from the watery soup, so that you soiled and wet yourself frequently. Many women's periods stopped immediately, and everyone's after a short time; but until then you had nothing, not even a rag, to put between your legs, and the blood ran down with everything else. The violation of nudity increased, because you were reshaven every week, and were submitted to innumerable harsh strippings every day: morning wash, lice checks, flea checks, scabies checks; not to mention the selections, soon to come. You were not given a spoon, so that you had to lap your soup like a dog; often from the same bowl as others, which you, or they, had also had to use for other functions. After a week, at most two, depending on your size and habits, you had the chronic Lager hunger, 'which makes you dream at night', Primo wrote, 'and settles in all the limbs of your body'. Soon you could think of nothing else, you wanted to scream, you wanted to steal.

These were only the first physical assaults on human dignity. The mental ones were immediately complete. The desire to make sense of one's surroundings, and as far as possible to predict events, is a universal human need, as deep as hunger. This was instantly impossible. You could not understand anything – the orders, the signs, the whole point of the place; you didn't even know where you were.

The moment you stepped off the train it was as though you had entered a madhouse. You instantly lost all capacity for logical thought, not only because your brain was stunned by fear, but because you had no model, and no information to go on. If you did get information you couldn't believe it. On the first night, a thin man in glasses slipped into the shower room, and spoke in bad Italian to Primo and the others. He was a Hungarian who had studied in Italy; he would explain things to them, he said, though it was against the rules, because he liked Italians, and 'had a little heart'. Yes, their women were well, and they would see them again soon; but immediately he changed the subject and would say no more. Instead he told them other things. On Sundays there were concerts and football matches. If you were a good boxer you could become a cook. He himself was a doctor and a criminal, but here he was a dentist. Yes, there were a few other Italians in the camp; but again he quickly changed the subject. Then a bell rang and he hurried off.

The next day they were locked in a hut until evening. Still tormented by thirst, Primo leaned out of a window and broke off an icicle. Instantly a guard snatched it away. '*Warum?*' Primo asked, in his basic German. '*Hier ist kein Warum,*' the guard said, pushing him back inside.★

Hier ist kein Warum: that was the essence of the Lager, especially for Jews. They were here, not because of anything they had done, but simply because they existed. After that, how could there be any logic, any explanation? Everything was forbidden, not for any particular reason, but because that was why the Lager was created: to forbid them everything, ending with life itself.

For the Italians, and also for Greeks, Yugoslavs and Hungarians, there was an extra barrier to understanding: the language of the Lager. That language was primarily German, secondarily Polish, and among Jewish prisoners themselves, Yiddish. Only those Italians from Trieste or the South

★ 'Why?' 'Here there is no why.'

Tyrol had any German; none had either of the others. That meant, first of all, that they did not understand orders; and orders had to be understood. They were repeated once, if you were lucky; after that came only beatings. And it meant that they could not learn from other, more experienced prisoners. The Italians were always late, always last, because they did not understand. The majority, both men and women, died in the first ten to twenty days: ninety-four out of 125 of Primo's transport, according to one historian. They died, Primo wrote, 'at first sight of hunger, cold, fatigue, disease; on closer examination, of insufficient information'. They died, in fact, of not understanding.

There is always a tendency to treat people without a recognizable language as less than human. For Germans brought up under Nazism, people without German were hardly human at all. And the prisoners soon felt less than human themselves. If you find no one to talk to, Primo wrote, 'your tongue dries up in a few days, and your thought with it'. But the Italians were so few – perhaps one in 100, in Primo's Lager – and soon dispersed throughout the camp. The men of his transport decided to meet every Sunday evening, for this essential human contact. But they stopped almost at once, because it took up too much energy; and it was too painful to be reminded of their past, and to watch their number fall.

There was a last blow which fell immediately. It was perhaps the least expected, and the most lethal. 'One entered hoping at least,' Primo wrote, 'for the solidarity of one's companions'; but it was not there. On the contrary, the new arrival was treated more harshly now than he would be later, if he managed to survive. As Vanda and Luciana also saw, he or she aroused only irritation, hostility, envy. He was useless, even dangerous in his ignorance; he was an extra mouth to feed, an extra body to make room for. He was ridiculous, Primo said, 'because he was fat, he was inept, he understood nothing'; and 'with the cruelty of schools and barracks' he was despised, cheated and derided. You could tell him that leather shoes were being distributed, he should run to get some, and leave his soup with you. You could point out a *Kartoffelschalenkommando*, a Potato-Peeling Commando, and he would run to one of the cruellest Kapos of all and ask if he could join. This happened to Primo.

'The worst – that is, the fittest – survived,' Primo wrote in his last book. 'The best all died.'

By 'best' he did not mean the bravest: those, like Alberto and Leonardo, who fought without contamination by the evil around them, who 'had courage to spare', and gave it to others. He meant, I think, the most civilized: those who literally could not live without decency, privacy and dignity, without the ability to trust and rationally communicate with other people. The 'best' in this sense were the most delicate, the most innocent: often, though not only, the educated *bourgeoisie*. They could not bear to see degradation and bestiality everywhere, to lie and steal, to pick lice off their bodies and split them between their fingernails. Many died straight away, because they could not adapt to this infernal world. They looked around, and down at themselves, and died of horror.

Who was more civilized than Primo Levi? Was there anyone more likely to die of horror at nakedness, at bestiality? Was there anyone who needed rationality and predictability more, and faith in man, and the hope of communication? All rules were reversed in this world. Being small and thin unfitted him for work, but fitted him for starvation, since he required fewer calories than most men. Before, his body had been his burden, his mind his salvation. Here it could be the other way around.

It very nearly was the other way around, especially in these first traumatic days. It was his principle (and need) not to speak about himself, but about others, about everyone. But once or twice he made an exception. In his interview for the Piedmont Archive of Deportation, for example, he said: 'I myself was in great danger in the early days.'

How did he survive them? His own answer was: through friendships, especially, 'from the very first day', with Alberto. Alberto, he wrote, 'understood before any of us that this life is war'; he 'lost no time complaining and commiserating with himself and others, but entered the battle from the beginning'. And from the beginning he fought with a sure instinct, with great astuteness and great daring. He would always have more of these than Primo. Later, Primo would contribute his extraordinary intelligence, his moral courage, and – Alberto would say – his luck. But not yet. After what had happened at Amay, and on the transport, how could he accept after all that 'this life is war'; that he had to find some way to fight it? It must have taken him many days, perhaps weeks. In the meantime, Alberto helped to keep him alive: with encouragement, no doubt, with information, with his mere presence and example. 'In him,' Primo said, 'I found a saviour.'

But it was only later that they were together all the time, in the same Kommando, Block and bunk: to have a friend beside you night and day was a priceless advantage, which you already needed many Lager skills to achieve. For the first four months Primo and Alberto can only have met in the evenings, on Sundays, in the breaks between work. But in the battle of each against each there were other exceptions; and Primo found other helping hands.

There was Schlome, a young Polish Jewish boy, no more than sixteen years old, who called out to him on the first evening, and asked him where he came from. During their brief and halting German exchange Schlome gave this strange new arrival excellent advice: his profession, chemist, was good; drinking the water was bad. There was Chaim, one of his first bed companions: a religious Jew from Kraków, who despite the language barrier 'explained to me, the foreigner', Primo wrote, 'the essential rules for survival during the first crucial days'. And there was Reznik, to whom Primo dedicated a chapter in *If This is a Man*.

Reznik was a Polish Jew who had lived in France for twenty years, and who therefore spoke French, though very badly. He had been in the Lager for a year. He had narrowly survived his own initiation, and became *Block Schneider*, tailor to his Block, which gained him extra rations, and the chance of gifts. By the time Primo met him he was, in Lager terms, strong, healthy and relatively secure, as Jews could only be if they possessed a marketable skill. Schlome and Chaim had been the same: Schlome a metalworker, Chaim a watchmaker. Only those who were relatively secure could help anyone else: 'on the way down' (as Primo's companion 'Henri' puts it), you had nothing to spare.

But of course not everyone who could help did; and Reznik did. Primo first noticed him when they became bed partners. Primo was always given tall bed partners, because he was small, and even in that place it was recognized that two tall men could not share the same narrow space, and both sleep. This way at least the tall one slept, or slept more; as Primo had already discovered. But he noticed at once that Reznik was different. He was quiet and courteous. In the morning he offered to make their bed, a dangerous job at which the smallest failure was severely punished; and he did it quickly and well.* When Primo saw that Reznik was also in the same Kommando, he felt a vague stirring of pleasure: as much as a man could feel in his first weeks in Auschwitz.

Theirs was Number 85, a hard outdoor Kommando. Reznik noticed Primo's physical fragility straight away; without help, he thought, he could not survive. Their job that day, as on many other days, was '*Bohlen holen*': carrying railway sleepers to make a path through the deep, clinging mud. The sleepers weighed up to 175 pounds each, they were dripping with mud and snow, they had sharp edges and even sharper metal plates. After only one journey Primo was deaf and blind from the effort. He could ask to go to the latrine, he could try to hide; or he could ask to work with Reznik, who was so much taller he would take most of the weight. Of course Reznik would refuse; but he could try.

---

* Reznik had learned this valuable art in the French Foreign Legion.

Reznik did not refuse. He lifted the sleeper and placed Primo's end on his shoulder as gently as he could; then he shouldered his end, taking almost all the weight. They made several trips like this that day, and perhaps other days as well: Reznik always gentle, always bearing the main weight. We may understand how extraordinary the help was. But the gentleness was even more extraordinary. Gentleness in Auschwitz was rarer than gold.

Maurice Reznik survived Auschwitz, he survived the death march after it, and finally returned to Paris and his wife. He may well have helped others apart from Primo, but he has not said so. Primo, he says, was special. 'He was very reserved, shy and nice. In such a violent place, he attracted sympathy. I remember that people liked him.'

He remembered something else as well: 'When he talked to me, he smiled with kindness.' That was as rare in Auschwitz as Reznik's own gentleness; and it may explain why so many people held out a helping hand to Primo Levi.

But he was not only helped; he helped himself. He had no physical courage, he said, and especially no courage in the face of aggression. But he had plenty of other kinds.

He had, above all, fortitude. Consciously he needed to believe in human goodness; but emotionally he expected little for himself, and was used to doing without it. Like Vanda he suffered very much from fear, because secretly he always expected the worst; but unlike Vanda, when the worst happened it roused in him a stubborn, combative side, which refused to be defeated by the forces of darkness. This had happened with chemistry, and with the racial laws; it happened again now.

Despite the trauma of arrival, it happened straight away. Before his transport had been assigned to their various Kommandos, they were sent together to widen a large trench. 'They handed me a shovel,' Primo wrote, 'and immediately it was a disaster.' The trench was more than six feet deep, the earth had to be thrown up over the edge without falling back on your head; and hardly anyone in his group of urban Italians had ever held a spade. They tried to explain this to their foreman, who was not amused. Work was the only point of their existence; if they didn't know how to do it, they'd better learn. Some objected, Primo said, and received their first blows. One of these – Baruch, a docker from Livorno – hit back, as though he was still in the normal world; and was murdered on the spot by three Kapos. Some gave up then, on their very first day. But others, and 'I among them', Primo wrote, despite their horror 'confusedly perceived that there was no way out, and that the only solution was to learn'.

That had always been his solution, and it still was. Auschwitz was like the rock that had nearly defeated him in Balangero: hostile, dark, incomprehensible. He had not surrendered to incomprehension then, and he would not now. He would learn how to hold a spade, how to endure pain, how to stop before exhaustion, because 'blows . . . are not usually fatal, but collapse is'. After a few days his hands were covered with suppurating blisters, and he went at dawn to KB★ to have them bandaged. He took the shortest route, which he already knew; and was given the first serious blow of his career, because of something he did not yet know: this road was banned to ordinary prisoners, because it passed the camp bordello.

This too he learned. He learned all the infinite rules and prohibitions of the camp: not to go near the barbed wire; to put on and snatch off his beret at the orders '*Mützen auf – Mützen ab!*'; not to sleep in his jacket, or leave the hut with it unbuttoned; to scrape the mud off it, though it was already irretrievably filthy. To make his bed perfectly flat and smooth in a few minutes, to go for his shower on the prescribed day and not on any other; to present himself for shaving, for the control of lice, of skin disease, of the buttons on his jacket, which had to be exactly five. He learned never to ask questions, but always to pretend to understand. He learned to scan the ground as he walked, and pick up and pocket anything he saw – a battered spoon, a piece of string, a button. He learned to wait at the end of the queue, despite the clamourings of his stomach, so as to get the thicker soup near the bottom of the vat; he learned to scrape his bowl, and hold it under his chin as he ate his bread, so as not to lose a crumb. He learned to wrap a rag he had found around his feet, one day the left foot, next day the right; to tie up his shoes, and the loose buttons on his jacket, with wire. He learned to carry everything he owned – spoon, bowl, wooden shoes – everywhere, even in the shower and in the latrine, or they would be stolen; for the same reason he learned to wrap them in his jacket at night, and sleep with his head on the bundle. From Chaim, from French prisoners, from an Alsatian whom he paid in bread for 'private lessons', he learned to decipher the primitive, obscene barracks-German of the Lager, so that he could understand his number when it was called, the barked orders, the cynical mottoes on the walls and beams: *Eine Laus, dein Tod; So bist du rein, So gehst du ein*, beside pictures of a good prisoner washing, and a bad one balking at the trough like a horse.†

It took time. Some things, like learning to steal, took several months; some he may never have learned at all, like blowing his nose into his fingers, or urinating while he ran to save time. But by the end of the first fortnight

★ The *Krankenbau*, or infirmary.
† 'A louse is your death'; 'Like this you're clean, like this you'll soon go down.'

he had learned enough to have passed the first danger. Even before that, after a week or ten days, the doctors could pick out those who would succumb. Primo Levi was not one.

And being Primo Levi, he did not just learn in order to survive. On the contrary: he survived in order to learn. That was his great and rare resolve; and one of the main reasons he did, against all the odds, return.

To understand, he said, remained a universal need, even in Auschwitz. Its rules were insane, its aims beyond imagination, its prisoners brutalized and dying; they could not understand how it worked, or why. Yet all who continued to live tried. And all had the same aim, if they were lucky enough to survive: to tell the world what had happened.

But the quality of Primo Levi's desire to understand, and to tell, was different from the norm. He shared it with very few: with doctors like Robert Waitz, from his own sub-camp, and Ella Lingens Reiner, from Birkenau; with political prisoners turned historians, like Hermann Langbein in Auschwitz main camp. But both doctors and political prisoners had a level of life far above Primo's. Characteristically, he himself tells of another ordinary prisoner he knew, who perhaps came close: Robert, a professor from the Sorbonne, who 'wore himself out recording everything in his prodigious memory, and had he lived would have answered the questions I cannot answer'.

Most people shielded themselves from taking in too much – if possible, from taking in anything at all. They knew their own terrible stories, and their families', and they burned to tell those to the world, in an overwhelming need for recognition and revenge, as a memorial to the dead, and in the hope of preventing a repetition. Primo shared all these natural hopes and needs. But some of them, like the desire for revenge, he suppressed, as he suppressed so many of his natural desires. As always, he did not want to tell us his own story, or to be understood. His will to understand and to tell looked outward: it was objective, scientific and philosophical. He did not want to accuse or to judge, and he did not want to lament. He wanted to record, and to analyse. He wanted – he says almost shockingly, in the Preface to *If This is a Man*, written in 1946 – 'to furnish documentation for a quiet study of certain aspects of the human mind'.

Primo Levi saw Auschwitz as an unimaginably cruel, but therefore unimaginably excellent, laboratory. He said so often, never more clearly than in *If This is a Man* itself: '*the Lager was pre-eminently a gigantic biological and sociological experiment*'.

Thousands of individuals, of different ages, conditions, origins, languages, cultures and customs, are enclosed within barbed wire. There a regime of life is imposed on them which is constant, controlled, identical for all and inadequate to all needs:

more rigorous conditions than any experimenter could have set up to establish what is essential and what adventitious in the conduct of the human animal in the struggle for survival.

Finding himself there, he knew what he had to do: study this blasphemous experiment as mercilessly as it was conducted; record every detail of it in his memory, as prodigious as Robert's; and if he survived, report it to the world with all the clarity and objectivity of his scientific training.

It may be that he had to cross the frontier of arrival as everyone did, struggling in the first days simply to survive; that only after that did he have the strength and balance to look around, and make his extraordinary decision. But it may have been the other way around. His first instinct in any trouble was to turn to his best weapon: his rationality. On the very first night, hearing a German mock a man who wore a truss, he may have made his decision quite instinctively: to turn into objects for his study those who sought to turn them into objects for their use and whim. It may have been his extraordinary decision, made immediately, that enabled him to survive the trauma of arrival.

Whether it was immediate or soon, whether from instinct or professional training, there is no doubt at all that he conceived his plan then and there, in the Lager, and carried it out, despite extreme suffering and danger, every day. Already there, he wrote afterwards, 'I was conscious of living the fundamental experience of my life.' '[T]he idea of *having* to survive in order to tell what I had seen obsessed me night and day':

I never stopped recording the world and the people around me . . . I had an intense wish to understand, I was constantly pervaded by curiosity . . . the curiosity of the naturalist who finds himself transplanted into an environment that is monstrous but new, monstrously new.

He lived his entire year in Auschwitz in a state of exceptional attention, of heightened sensibility; so much so that names and faces, sounds and scenes remained fixed in his memory in pathological detail, and more and more kept returning over the years, as though he were Borges' *Funes el Memorioso*, or the recording angel of the Lord.

It is hard to exaggerate how rare that was, and how difficult. This was a world where unlimited power was bent on snuffing out every trace of individual thought; where even those few with the skill and determination to survive had to husband every ounce of energy, rarely spoke to anyone unless it served their struggle, rarely knew anyone's name or even number, apart from a few close allies', almost always of their own country and language. And this was a man who was by nature cautious, obedient and not brave; who was slowly starving, and for ten months of the twelve living at the limit of his physical powers. Yet this man, in this place, not only noted and remembered every detail of the Lager regime, and penetrated its deepest aims and meanings. He also spoke to scores of people, the vast majority of them not Italian; and knew their names, their histories, their camp stories – here where no one spoke willingly of the present or the past, because it would only drive you mad.

Only someone whose whole life had prepared him for this moment could have done it: someone whose instinct to dominate experience through understanding was stronger than any other instinct, even to survive; who combined scientific training with passionate human interest; who possessed huge gifts of memory, intellect and will, and who inspired people to entrust him with their stories. Primo fiercely rejected the idea that Providence might have chosen him among millions to survive, because he was uniquely fitted to speak for them: it was intolerable to him to think that anyone might have died in his place, or that any book was worth more than a life. Most of us will agree with him that it was ultimately chance, not Providence, that was responsible for his survival. But in that case, and despite his protests, we must be as grateful to chance as ever the world was to Providence.

Deliberately he set out to gather all the information he could, and to remember it. Towards the end, in the relative peace of the laboratory, he even began to write it down – perhaps twenty lines, fragmentary and obscure, which he destroyed as soon as they were written, because anyone caught writing was immediately hanged as a spy. But he had written many things down; and what you write down you remember.

His task was therefore dangerous, as well as difficult. It was a huge drain on his energy, it had worn down Robert, and it must have worn him down as well. Yet at the same time it bore him up. If Luciana survived for life, Primo survived to testify. Those with faith, he would tell us – religious, political, any kind whatsoever – endured better, and survived in greater numbers. *He* had a faith: in knowledge, and in man to make use of it; and the task he had set himself, to bring this new knowledge to the world, carried him through. It enabled him to remain an active subject, rather than a passive object: to resist dehumanization, which killed more surely than starvation. In the Lager, as after it in life, he made himself a researcher, a student of humanity, an anthropological scientist. In his life after, this would save him for many years; in the Lager it saved him altogether.

★   ★

Primo's camp was called Monowitz, or Auschwitz III (Auschwitz I was the main camp, Auschwitz II Birkenau, where the women were). Auschwitz had forty or fifty sub-camps altogether, all supplying slave labour to the industries which had grown up around it for that purpose. Monowitz became the biggest. It was the *Arbeitslager*, the labour camp, for the Buna factory: the first and largest of these industries, established by the German chemical giant I. G. Farben. Buna was a vast plant, 'as big as a city', Primo said, covering an area of about twelve square miles, and employing about 40,000 foreign workers in all, speaking fifteen to twenty different languages. Its main product was to be the synthetic rubber called Buna, after which it was named; plus several by-products such as methanol, which the starving prisoners often died of drinking. In fact, as a result of local sabotage and then of Allied bombing, the production process never properly began; and despite the unimaginable sufferings and deaths of thousands of slave labourers, not an ounce of synthetic rubber ever emerged.

Among the foreign workers were English prisoners of war, and French, Italian, Polish, Ukrainian and other civilians from German-occupied countries, more or less forcibly enrolled by the Todt Organization for work in the Third Reich. Each of these groups had their own camps close by. Monowitz – '*Judenlager, Vernichtungslager, Kazett*',★ as Primo wrote – provided 'the slaves of the slaves': 10–12,000 prisoners, or *Häftlinge*, almost all Jews. It was near the Buna factory – though the site was so big you might still have to march up to four miles to work.

The camp was set in a grey, desolate plain across which the cold Polish wind blew without mercy. It consisted of sixty wooden huts set in a rectangle about 600 yards long, surrounded by the obligatory double barbed-wire fence, the inner one electrified. Eight of the huts were set aside for KB, the infirmary; half a dozen for *Reichsdeutsche*,† Kapos, and other camp aristocrats; and one for the brothel. The rest were the ordinary living Blocks, each of which contained 148 bunks on three levels ('like the cells of a beehive', Primo wrote), divided by three narrow corridors. In these all the *Häftlinge* had to live: 200–250 to a hut, two to almost every bunk.

The bunks were wooden platforms, each covered with a thin straw sack, two stained blankets and a straw pillow. In the morning the 'mattress' had to be fluffed up, and so it remained all day; but as soon as you lay down on it at night it flattened to nothing, and you slept on wood.

Primo dedicated a whole chapter of *If This is a Man* to this so-called sleep, which was really a struggle not to wake. It was a struggle against appalling nightmares, which continued the nightmare of the day; so that you woke

---

★ 'Jews' camp, extermination camp, concentration camp'. ('*Kazett*' came from the German letters K and Z, acronym for *Konzentrazionszentrum*.)
† Aryan Germans, either political prisoners or criminals.

constantly, 'frozen with terror, shaking in every limb', hearing another incomprehensible order, expecting another vicious blow. It was a struggle against the fleas and bedbugs that infested the wood of the bunks and the sawdust and straw of the mattress. And it was a struggle against the need to get rid of all the water you had ingested in the so-called soup during the day. This battle you inevitably lost every two to three hours; then not only did you have to join the shivering procession to the bucket, but when it was full – and it was always full – you had to carry it to the latrine, through the dark and the snow, knocking 'disgustingly warm' against your calves, and spilling its contents on your feet.

It was a struggle, finally, against desolating dreams, which everyone shared. The dream of eating, or rather not eating – the food is at your lips, you smell its glorious smell, but as soon as you open your mouth it disappears. Even worse, the dream of speaking and not being heard. You are at home, among friends and family, as you have longed to be for months and years, and you are telling them your story. The pleasure is intense: 'physical, inexpressible'. But then you notice that they are not listening. In Primo's dream there was, above all, Anna Maria. 'My sister looks at me, gets up and goes away without a word.'

And behind the dreams, the nightmares and the trips to the bucket lay the knowledge that day was coming, the anguish of the word that was approaching: 'Get up', '*Aufstehen*', or more often, in Polish, '*Wstawàch*'. Then even the illusion of rest, of a truce, dissolved. You seemed to sleep, Primo wrote, on a road, on a bridge, on a threshold; and inexorably you were pushed over.

The *Wstawàch* came before dawn. Instantly the whole Block was on its feet: they had been waiting. The hut shook, the air filled with dust and curses as 200 men tried to make their beds, to dress, to run to the latrines and washrooms, all in five minutes, so as to be ready for the distribution of bread: the small, 'sacred grey square', as Primo said, which was life, money, everything. Then the hut-sweepers rushed in, and drove them out with shouts and blows.

Still in pitch darkness, all 10,000 had to assemble in the *Appellplatz* in the centre of the Lager to be counted. These were the infamous *Zählappelle*, the counting roll-calls, which lasted at least an hour, two or three if the numbers did not match, in rain and wind, in ice and snow. In the evenings after work they could last much longer, as punishment or warning: twenty-four hours or even more, if an escape was suspected. Many prisoners died during the *Appelle*.

When the counting was finally over, the march to work began. This is one of the best known and most grotesque images of the Nazi Lagers: the striped emaciated figures in their lines of five, marching like puppets to German military music, or to a popular and sentimental song like *Rosamunda*: caps off, eyes left as they pass the officers at the gate.

By now the sky was lightening. All the hours of daylight were working hours: 8 – 4 in winter, 6.30 – 6 in summer, Primo said (but some remembered them even longer). The 10,000 prisoners were divided into about 200 Kommandos, 15 to 150 men each. There were good Kommandos and bad Kommandos. The good ones were the skilled Kommandos, for electricians, mechanics, bricklayers, welders and other craftsmen, attached to particular departments in the Buna, and led by civilian foremen. The bad ones were the transport Kommandos: left with all the manual labour, almost always outside, and commanded by prisoner Kapos, usually common criminals. But the 'skilled' Kommandos had no more than 300–400 members, many of those skilled only at corruption. The vast majority of prisoners, therefore, dug trenches, laid roads, loaded and unloaded wagons, carried bricks, rails and pipes, sacks of cement, sand and coal – even if they were, in fact, mechanics or electricians. The very worst Kommandos of all, the *Todeskommandos* (Death Commandos) such as the *Kabelkommando*, the *Eisenknupferkommando*, and the *Konkretträgerkommando*,★ were reserved for the 'High Numbers', the new arrivals; and for the '*Akademiker*' or '*Intelligenten*':† the middle-class professionals, whom the SS and the criminal Kapos particularly despised.

At midday each *Häftling* was allowed a litre of soup, that is to say a few scraps of cabbage or turnip in hot water. In the evening, the same, a little thicker; occasionally with bits of rotten potato or swede, a few chick-peas or peas. Dr Waitz, reporting on the soup at Monowitz, judged it 'frequently inedible'; but Primo, like all the ordinary prisoners, was too near starving to care. The bread distributed in the morning came to about 350 grams each; with it were served (irregularly and decreasingly) a few grams of margarine, jam or salami, and a half litre of coffee substitute, sweetened only on Sundays. Another half litre of 'coffee' followed the soup in the evening. The ordinary tap water, as Schlome had warned Primo, was undrinkable. All this amounted to about 1,600 or 1,700 calories a day, in theory; in practice to a good deal less, given thefts, the need to keep back part of your rations for trade, and the fact that the bread was stretched with all sorts of inedible additions, including sawdust. Dr Waitz estimated that the number of calories a prisoner in Monowitz actually received was no more than 1,000–1,100 per day; and all of it was entirely deficient in proteins, fats and vitamins. A healthy man,

★ The cable-laying, track-laying and concrete-carrying commandos.
† 'Academics', 'intellectuals'.

Primo noted, can just about survive on 2,000 well-balanced calories a day, provided he is no larger than average, and stays in bed and doesn't move. The Monowitz *Häftling* received half of this, and did hard labour for eight to twelve hours a day. In these conditions his death from starvation, if nothing else, was guaranteed in a maximum of three months.

But of course there was a great deal else to die from: cold, terror, beatings, disease. Prisoners regularly died directly of cold and exposure, and of the diseases caused by them – bronchitis and pneumonia, frostbite and gangrene. They died of infectious diseases like scarlet fever, diphtheria, tuberculosis and (towards the end) typhus. They died, most of all, of the diseases of starvation: especially diarrhoea, and infections and dropsies of the soft tissue and skin – boils and abscesses, oedemas and phlegmons, which are vast, spreading, suppurating inflammations. These almost always began on the legs, and were caused by marching for hours in the ill-fitting wooden clogs: blisters and sores would open, and rapidly become infected; your feet would swell, you would start to walk with a strange stiff gait, like a puppet, and soon you could not walk at all. Primo had these suppurating sores immediately – but 'miraculously', he said, they healed by themselves, and did not return.

This was, indeed, one of the most important examples of his good health and good luck. After diarrhoea, such infections were the most common cause of decline and death. What you needed most, therefore, after a grasp of the Lager language, was a matched and reasonably fitting pair of shoes. Death came from so many things – starvation, cold, fatigue, disease; it took Primo Levi to point out that two of the main ones were not understanding, and shoes.

'Dying was easy,' he said. It was the aim of the system, the purpose for which it was designed, and all you had to do to achieve it was obey: carry out all the orders you were given, eat only the food and wear only the clothes you were allowed. To live was much more difficult and dangerous. You had to defy the rules, despite the risk of punishment – to avoid the hardest work, to stuff waste paper under your jacket against the cold, to steal and scheme for extra food and clothes. You had to resist eating rotten and filthy scraps of food, even though you were starving; you had to resist dwelling on your cold and hunger, on your fears for your family and yourself. If you did not, you were immediately overwhelmed and lost. Despite this, Primo said, they did all talk incessantly of food: it was impossible not to, they were obsessed; and though they knew it weakened them, almost no one could resist the temptation. But of death they did not speak, though it was all around them: even less of the gas chambers, or of the 'Chimney', once they'd begun to understand (and it took a long time) that such things really existed. Or rather: if you wanted to survive another day, you did not allow yourself to think of such things. If someone talked incessantly of death and of the gas chambers; if he complained and lamented, if he talked of his family, and of what he used to eat at home: then you knew he would not last; soon he would be a *Musulmann*.

No one really knows why the term '*Musulmann*'* – which appeared in all the Lagers – arose: possibly because the stooped figure draped in a blanket looked like an Arab in a hooded *djellaba*. But we all know him, or her. The *Musulmann* was the main product of the Lager: manufactured with great efficiency, in his hundreds of thousands, unlike the synthetic rubber of the Buna. The *Musulmänner* were the starved and dying, the skeletons we have seen in their slag-heaps, or just still standing, just still alive. Grown men and women weighed as little as fifty pounds, their muscles and fat had been consumed as energy, their bones had begun to decalcify. Every ounce of strength had been squeezed out of them for the Third Reich, and they were ready to be thrown away. They were empty shells, 'like the slough of certain insects', Primo wrote, 'which you find on the banks of ponds, attached to stones by a single thread, and shaken in the wind'. They hardly moved any more, they hardly reacted; they had too little energy left even to suffer. 'One hesitates to call them living,' Primo wrote, 'one hesitates to call their deaths death, in the face of which they have no fear, as they are too tired to understand.'

For the *Musulmann* there awaited the last form of death in the Lager: its own special death, in Hitler's gas chambers. The route to this special death began in selections, like the first one that had happened so long ago, on the platform at Auschwitz.

Selections took place regularly in KB: at least once a month, and more often in winter, when it quickly filled to overflowing. With typical Lager logic, therefore, the more the hospital was needed, the more people would try to avoid going there; in Birkenau, where there were 70–80,000 prisoners instead of 10,000, and the constant danger of experiments as well as selections, the women avoided the hospital like the plague, and went there only when they were already dying. In Monowitz there were also selections every three or four months in the camp as a whole (many more, again, in Birkenau): Primo probably went through two. This experience, unique to the Nazi Lagers, in which thousands of starving men and women had a few seconds each to run naked past an SS doctor, and convince him at one rapid indifferent glance to let them live – of all Lager experiences this was the one that burned most deeply into their stunned and disbelieving minds; and into ours whenever we learn of it, in each succeeding generation. When Primo

---

* i.e. 'Muslim'.

Levi wrote his great book, he first told its episodes not in chronological order, but in order of 'urgency' – and one of the earliest was the selection.

If you managed to survive the work, the march, the evening *Appell* for one more day, you could return to your Block for the distribution of the soup. Then strip once more, for the lice control, for the inspection of clothes and shoes. If your shoes are still not matched, or finally collapsing, run to the shoe exchange and grab a new one; for this too you have only a few seconds, and only one choice. Run to meet your friends or protectors, if you have any, or to trade whatever you have saved or stolen. At last, at nine o'clock, climb into your bunk, struggle for your share of space; lay your head on your shoes, and your body instantly on the wood; and if you do not die in the night, you will soon hear the *Wstawàch*.

March – April 1944

It was my good fortune to be deported to Auschwitz only in 1944.

These are the opening words of *If This is a Man*. They are the first shock: *It was my good fortune . . .* Instantly we know we are in the presence of an irony and detachment beyond the ordinary.

Yet, like every other word in this book, these were also true. Towards the end of 1943 conditions in Auschwitz did very slightly improve. With every able-bodied German needed for the war machine, even slave labourers became more valuable: the Reich itself needed them to live, or to live longer. The hospital at Monowitz opened only a few months before Primo's arrival: before that there had been no chance of medical treatment at all. The camp regime improved; and Kapos were no longer allowed to beat prisoners to death, or past the point at which they could, eventually, return to work. In fact the Kapos' violence was so ingrained, and their power in practice so unlimited, that most carried on as before; but the rule was there, and it was sometimes obeyed.

For the first few days Primo was moved from hut to hut and from Kommando to Kommando. Finally he was assigned to Block 30, which was relatively new, and so slightly cleaner and less infested than many. This too was a small piece of luck to start with. His Kommando, Number 85, was less lucky; but not one of the worst, not a *Todeskommando*. He nearly did die in the very first days, but not from the work, or the cold, or despair. He nearly died of his one and only attempt at retaliation.

In Block 30, or even before, he met a camp phenomenon: Number

141565, Elias Lindzin. Later Primo would study him as an extreme example of the 'saved': 'the human type most suited to this way of living'.

Elias was a dwarf, with a muscular body like a miniature Hercules, and a huge, bulging, low-browed head. He was as strong as a god, and as crazy as a devil. Outside the Lager he would be in a prison or a lunatic asylum; inside it he was a king. He could carry four sacks of cement at a run, he could climb like a monkey in his wooden shoes, he could eat twenty pints of soup without getting diarrhoea. His fame as a worker spread so that even the SS came to admire him; and 'by the absurd law of the Lager', Primo wrote, 'from then on he practically ceased to work'. He could not carry on a normal conversation; but he shouted and cursed, sang Polish and Yiddish songs, and made long, insane, capering speeches to enthusiastic audiences. He stole with the cunning of a fox; he fought like a bear, like a ram, like a spider, clinging on to his victim with his arms and legs, butting him in the stomach with his huge stone head. 'I never saw him quiet or still,' Primo wrote, 'I never saw him injured or ill.' He was like a beetle, or a machine: something perfectly adapted to its primitive purpose, without conscience or mind. In the Lager, Primo said, 'as far as the phrase can have meaning', Elias was 'probably a happy person'.

One day very soon after Primo's arrival, Elias seized him by the wrist and pushed him up against a wall, bawling insults into his face. Suddenly – as in the distant days of the racial laws – Primo felt a surge of pride. 'Conscious of betraying myself', he wrote, 'and of transgressing a norm handed down to me by innumerable ancestors alien to violence', he hit back: he kicked Elias on the shin with his clog. In a flash he was on the ground, with all Elias's gross weight upon him.

Then he gripped my throat, attentively watching my face with eyes that I remember very well, a few inches from mine, fixed, a pale porcelain blue. He squeezed until he saw the signs of loss of consciousness begin; then, without a word, he let go and walked away.

It was like a terrible picture of the essence of Auschwitz: a lunatic dwarf, with the power to snuff out your life at the smallest sign of resistance. From that moment on, Primo said with his customary self-mockery, his natural pacifism was confirmed. He never 'returned the blow' again, in Auschwitz or after.

Soon after that he had another symbolic encounter. This one pointed in the opposite direction: towards a model of resistance he could, perhaps, follow.

The washroom was cold and dark, the water stank, the floor was covered in mud. 'I must admit,' Primo wrote, 'after only one week of prison the instinct of cleanliness [had] disappeared in me.' Why should he wash? Would he live a day, an hour longer? On the contrary, he would live less long, because washing was a waste of warmth and energy. But in the washroom was 'Steinlauf', as Primo called him in *If This is a Man*: Eugenio Glücksmann, a Hungarian from Milan, ex-sergeant in the Austro-Hungarian Army, fifty-three years old. Glücksmann was scrubbing himself vigorously, though he had no soap, the basin was filthy, and he would have to dry himself in his jacket, which he would have to put on wet in the freezing air. Quietly he delivered a lesson to Primo. Precisely because the Lager was bent on reducing them to beasts, they must not become beasts, he said.

. . . We are slaves, deprived of every right, exposed to every insult, condemned to almost certain death; but we still possess one power, and we must defend it with all our strength, because it is the last: the power to refuse our consent. So we must certainly wash our faces in dirty water, and dry ourselves on our jackets . . . We must walk upright, without dragging our feet, not in homage to Prussian discipline, but to stay alive, not to begin to die.

These values, of dignity, autonomy and civilization, are the values of *If This is a Man*. Or almost. In that dark washroom, at the end of his first week in Auschwitz, Primo had glimpsed his own road, but not yet found it. 'No,' he wrote, 'the wisdom and virtue of Steinlauf, certainly good for him, are not enough for me.' Glücksmann's was the virtue of the soldier: cleanliness, polish, a straight back. This was the dignity of the body. Primo Levi's would be the dignity of the mind.

Now came the worst time. Two months: March and April, still deep winter in Silesia. Not even Primo Levi can tell how each day passed, and each moment. 'Pain', 'cold', 'hunger', 'exhaustion' are just words. We fill them in with our own experiences; we literally cannot imagine, therefore, what they meant to them. If the Lager had lasted longer, Primo wrote, 'a new, harsh language would have been born; and only this language could express what it means to toil the whole day in the wind, with the temperature below freezing, in . . . a cloth jacket and trousers, and inside only weakness, hunger, and knowledge of the end drawing near'.

When they returned, they soon forgot this language themselves; perhaps it could never really have existed. There could be no words for this suffering; it went beyond expression, beyond experience. When you were 'hungry', 'cold', 'tired' in this language you could no longer say so, no longer clearly know it. The days were endlessly long, and all alike; you thought each one would never end, then as soon as it did you couldn't remember it, only the next one loomed ahead of you, 'invincible and eternal'. While you worked, or marched, or haggled, you had no time to think of anything else. When you had a moment's respite, the thoughts began; then they went in a circle, like the days – would the war ever end? would you ever see your home again? was your family still alive? – until the recall to mindless work was almost welcome.

We can only guess how Primo survived these first two months, even when he told us in that language. I have guessed that he survived them because of friends: because of Alberto and Leonardo, whom he went on meeting in the evenings, after most of his transport had died or fallen away; because of Chaim, and Resnik, and others as well, whose names he never knew. And – I have guessed – because he decided from the beginning or very near it to observe, understand, and remember every detail of this world. That he was already doing so in March and April emerges from a memory of Resnik's, his bed-companion at the time. It is as clear as Primo's memory of himself pinned to the ground, his consciousness being squeezed out by Elias; but opposed to it, like the panels of a diptych. 'I used to call Primo Levi "Rodin's Thinker",' Resnik says, 'because very often, in the evening, he would sit for a long moment, reflecting, his head leaning on his hand.'

★   ★

Leonardo was even less likely to survive the first crucial months than Primo. He was twenty years older, his wife had been torn from his side and vanished, he was physically weak, and unused to any physical labour or exercise. He spoke no German. Even being a doctor did not help, since in that place where the majority was dying, there were many more doctors than patients. The moment patients numbered more than 500–600 there was a selection. But the single largest group of people admitted to Monowitz were doctors and medical students: out of 10,000–12,000 prisoners, by Leonardo's own reckoning as many as 2,000 were doctors. At the very most twenty of these could work in the hospital at any time; and no one ever willingly surrendered the best and safest job a *Häftling* could find. Leonardo never managed to become a doctor in Monowitz.

So he laboured in the mud and cold like everyone else, shovelling and digging, loading and unloading coal, cement, gravel. Almost immediately his feet were torn to shreds, his legs swelled, his circulation was affected, and he had to go to the hospital. He spent forty days there, most of March and well into April; and this was only the first of many times.

At least he was warm, and not working. But it was extremely dangerous to spend so much time in KB. He left as soon as he could, and went back to his Kommando. But each time the swelling in his legs returned; his weight fell until it was below 100 pounds; and each time he was a more obvious candidate for selection.

Leonardo himself did not really know how he survived until afterwards. He knew that he was lucky: apart from the trouble with his legs, he was never ill; starvation was good for his ulcer, and even the stomach pain he'd had for years disappeared. He knew his medical knowledge had helped, and the strength to use it: despite his hunger he had never eaten rotten or tainted food, and never begun the fatal decline into diarrhoea. Above all, he knew that he owed his life to another doctor: an Alsatian (he thought) called Klotz, whom he met in the very first days, and who was to him what Chaim was to Primo. Klotz explained to him all the myriad camp rules, what to do and especially what not to do, in order to have at least a chance of survival. Most important of all, he told Leonardo, 'If they want to transfer you to another camp, saying the work is easier there, *don't go.*' Tell them you are a doctor, Klotz said; then they'll let you stay.

What Klotz was arming him against – gently, cautiously – was the selections. They were always presented in just such disguises, which terrified people often believed. In KB Leonardo went through no less than four selections. But each time, following Klotz's advice, he shouted out to the examining doctor: '*Ich bin ein Italiener Arzt*', 'I am an Italian doctor.' And each time, against all expectations, he ended up in the group of the saved.

After liberation he learned that it was not only Klotz he had to thank for his salvation, but also other prisoner-doctors: they put his name in the list of the saved themselves, and moved it there whenever an SS doctor had put it in the other.

That was why Leonardo survived: because he was lucky, and attracted help, like Primo. But it was not just their luck that attracted help; it was their courage, and their goodness. Leonardo never learned to steal and scavenge and trade, like Primo, helped by Alberto. But he found his own courage and his own cunning. He often managed to hide, and avoid work, at the cost of many beatings; once he managed to speak to two Italian soldiers, and get food from them, by daring to ask for permission. He even performed small acts of sabotage: when they were replanting cabbages he tore off their roots, and put them back in the ground useless; when they had to fill boxes of bolts and screws he put the bolts in the screw boxes and the screws in the bolt boxes, so that work would grind to a halt for a few minutes or hours. For each of these small rebellions he could have been hanged; but they filled him with euphoria. He remained unchanged, undestroyed by the ferocious life of the Lager: mild and serene, Primo said, 'a friend to everyone, incapable of rancour, without anguish or fear'. Later he *was* anguished and afraid; but not then. Perhaps, he said – trying to explain to his family afterwards – because he was so certain he was going to die. He did what he could to avoid his fate; but what he could not avoid he bore, without despair and without complaint. And so he spread patience and hope around him, like Alberto, like Engineer Levi, Emilia's and Italo's father. Though he was not a doctor in Monowitz, he helped all who knew him there as he had helped his patients.

Of Franco Sacerdoti's course through Monowitz we have only a few glimpses.

The first one comes, almost certainly, right at the beginning. Before each set of new arrivals entered the camp, they faced a second selection: a medical examination by prisoner-doctors. The doctors did their best to pass everyone; but if their examination showed up a chronic illness, or any other serious impediment to work, it was dangerous to themselves, and useless to the prisoner, to postpone his death by a few agonizing days. One of the key points of the examination was the feet: especially in Buna-Monowitz, where most Kommandos had to march several miles to work each day. Anything that meant a prisoner could not march normally ruled him out from the start. And Franco could not. His beautiful body had only one defect: on one foot, a hammer toe.

Men died for less every day. But Franco was particularly strong and healthy; and he very much wanted to live. Perhaps the doctor suggested it, or perhaps Franco fought for it himself: his toe was amputated, and after a few weeks he could march with the rest.

Primo saw him a few times after that, and so did Silvio Barabas. He worked for a long time in the hardest Kommandos, carrying railway sleepers, and stones for the railbed. Then at some stage he managed to be moved to a factory; which, like Primo's laboratory, saw him through to the end.

There are two other brief glimpses of him. One from Luciana, in Birkenau: someone told her that a boy in Monowitz had asked after her, and sent her his greetings. And the other from Silvio afterwards, who told the Sacerdotis that Franco had somehow managed to keep a minute photograph of Nuccia, which he would take out every night, and touch gently before he slept. He had not forgotten either of his loves.

Silvio also told the Sacerdotis that Franco was always 'dignified, and full of altruism towards his companions in misfortune'. In such reports of the dead there is always a measure of decorum. But of gallant, loving Franco we can believe it was true.

Vanda and Luciana spent a month in the Quarantine Block in Birkenau. There they were introduced to their first faithful companions of the coming months: cold, hunger, beatings, the endless hours of *Appell*. Even before the deadly work began, people began to decline: several of their transport, Luciana noticed, were already very thin, some were already ill.

From the start she was better off. No one was spared the horror of the present, the fear of the future. But she was strong; and she was better treated than the rest, because she was a doctor, whom everyone might need one day.

Because she was strong and better off she asked questions, and weighed the answers. Soon she understood what had happened on the platform at Auschwitz, what happened regularly in the Lager, and often in the Revier;* what those flames were, and that smell. The others refused to believe her; she was a cynic, she was a bore, didn't she realize the war was nearly over? And so her ambiguous life in the Lager began: a life of privilege, but also of loneliness, unable to help, or to help enough, burdened with a knowledge she could do nothing about, and could only rarely share.

Her fate and Vanda's were drawing apart. At the end of March they were separated: Luciana went to the Revier; Vanda to Lager B, and the more or less rapid death of the ordinary *Häftling*.

Luciana worked in the worst parts of the hospital: in Block 24, the Diarrhoea Block, where everyone was dying; in Block 12, for Jewish prisoners only, where the selections took place, and where, therefore, almost everyone would die as well. She worked without medicine and without hope, with a constant, almost physical pain around her heart. And yet she knew she was immeasurably fortunate. She slept in a room with only five others, and in her own bed; she could find a moment to herself every day, or to sit and talk to Bianca Morpurgo. She was doing her own work, however badly; and if people hadn't given up, or gone too far, she could even help them.

But for Vanda the nightmare began, and it was beyond even her dark imaginings. The women worked like the men, like beasts: digging, carrying, pulling wagons, breaking stones; marching, being beaten, marching again. The most fortunate, clever or desperate at least worked indoors, in the factories, the workshops, the brothel. But Vanda was not among them. From the first days her feet were torn and swollen; from the first weeks diarrhoea tightened its hold on her. Luciana went to see her almost every evening after work. She watched Vanda's face grow smaller, her poor arms thinner, her legs more swollen; she encouraged her, reproached her, told her not to come to the hospital – anything but the hospital. Vanda was so small, and so helpless, many people tried to help her. And week after week she hung on. But every day she was weaker. She clung to false hopes, she cried at a harsh word; and every day she was more afraid.

Now it was Luciana's turn to run to the showers whenever an Italian

---

* The hospital, Birkenau's equivalent to KB.

transport arrived: to search each face, terrified it might be her mother's, her sisters', to ask if they had news of her family, of Franco Momigliano, of Anna Maria; to try to prepare them for this hell; to look away when they asked where the others were, and when they would arrive.

In the second week of April Giuliana Tedeschi of Turin was in one such transport. She saw Luciana the night she arrived; and again a few days later, walking easily in her good shoes, her long hair falling to her neck in black waves. She came over to ask how they were: were they getting used to it? She spoke quickly, the corners of her mouth twitched. 'What's wrong?' Giuliana asked. 'Nothing,' Luciana said. 'Tell me,' Giuliana insisted. Luciana's eyes filled with tears, her voice choked. 'Selection at the hospital,' she whispered into Giuliana's ear. 'This morning. Almost everyone.' Giuliana's heart stopped, and she had to ask the next question. 'The mothers with babies, and the old people,' she said, 'who took the trucks when we arrived . . . them too?' Suddenly Luciana was ruthless. 'Every trainload is decimated on arrival,' she said harshly. Then she turned and fled.

Three days later – there was always a cruel delay – around 300 women went to the gas chambers, among them twenty Italians.

*   *

It was as well they did not know what was happening at home, in that cursed spring of 1944. In late March, Alberto Salmoni and his group of partisans, outnumbered and out-equipped by the Germans, had to cede their territory in the Val Germanasca and retreat to the next valley. Both Euge Gentili Tedeschi and Franco Momigliano were arrested and imprisoned. And in the first week of April, first Sandro and then Emanuele died.

May 1944

By the end of the first two months, of the ninety-six men of Primo's transport only forty were left alive.

For days Kommando 85 had been moving cast-iron rail supports from a railway to a store. Primo was weak with exhaustion; naturally, therefore, he was paired with Null Achtzehn, the *Musulmann* of the Kommando, a young boy more dead than alive. In the afternoon, in the middle of one of their infinite, agonizing journeys, Primo could go no further. He shouted a warning, his companion fell, and the heavy iron support sliced across the back of Primo's foot. That night, despite the danger, he would have to go to KB.

He was examined, and admitted for twenty days. Once again he was lucky: his wound healed; he did not catch dysentery from the dysentery patients; though there were many rapid, casual selections he was always spared. He rested, he slept, he was not beaten. When he came out it was almost summer. Those twenty days in KB were among the chances that saved his life. But they were also among his lowest moments.

After the initiation, and two months of hard labour in the dead of winter, he was at his lowest point physically. When he entered KB a Polish nurse pointed him out to another Pole, as if he were a corpse in an anatomy class: his ribs that already showed, his swollen cheeks and belly, his stick-thin neck and limbs. When the nurse pressed his skin with a thumb the dent remained, as though he were made of wax instead of flesh. He was becoming a *Musulmann*. So the nurse calmly informed him: '*Du Jude, kaputt. Du schnell Krematorium fertig*': 'Jew, you finished. You soon ready crematorium.'

Almost more important, KB was a low point mentally. It was in KB that Primo was brought face to face with the reality and meaning of selections. At first he was still not sure. Schmulek, in the next bunk, undertook his education. He pointed to Primo's number: he was the 174,517th entrant to Auschwitz, and by no means the last, in a numbering process which had begun only eighteen months before. There were 10,000 of them at Mono-witz, perhaps another 30,000 in Auschwitz and Birkenau:★ '*Wo sind die Anderen?* — Where are the others?' 'Transferred to other camps?' Primo suggested. '*Er will nix verstayen*,' Schmulek said, in Yiddish: *He does not want to understand*. That evening Schmulek himself was selected; and Primo understood.

Understanding was the torment of KB. It could only happen there, where there was time and energy to think, and therefore to suffer. In KB they could hear the music of the marches morning and evening, and understand what it was doing: driving human beings like dead souls, a symbol of the monstrous victory of Auschwitz over the human will. KB was a brief truce in the daily war, when dreams and memories started up like forgotten sorrows; a foretaste of the longer truce to come, in the life after, for all who would survive. When you were reduced to a dead soul, your deadness protected you: you no longer felt or knew you were dead; you no longer felt or knew anything. It was in these moments of truce that your fears and regrets awoke, and your knowledge of what you had become: then your conscience awoke as well, and 'the old ferocious suffering', Primo wrote, 'of feeling myself a man again'. It was in KB that you understood what a man was, and that you were no longer a man. In KB you understood how fragile the human personality is, how much easier to destroy than the human body. That was the real lesson of the Lager. If from inside it, Primo wrote,

★ This was an underestimate; but Schmulek's argument was in principle all too accurate.

'a message could have seeped out to free men, it would have been this: take care not to suffer in your own homes what is inflicted on us here'.

★   ★

The other great disadvantage of KB was that you had to leave it – almost always to a new Block and Kommando, needing to find new clothes and shoes, a new knife and spoon. In other words, you had to go through a new initiation: with more experience this time, but almost always with your illness not quite cured, your wound not quite healed.

This was Primo's case, sometime in the second half of May. He felt 'ejected into the dark and cold of sidereal space', 'as helpless and vulnerable as a new born babe'. He had to start again from zero; and there was no reason to think it would go better, or even as well, this time.

But at this point he was lucky once again. He was not sent to a new Kommando; and though he *was* sent to a new Block, by sheer chance it was Alberto's. From now on they could see each other every evening without effort; and from now on their great cooperation began to flourish. The re-initiation which Primo had so feared turned out to be the turning point of his Auschwitz career. He did not know it, of course, and it need not have been true – at any moment, for any of a million reasons, the Lager could have prevailed, and he could have sunk back down for ever. But it did not happen. From now on he would rise slowly into the ranks of the saved.

One morning after his return from KB the sun rose unclouded and almost warm above the mud. For the first time they saw green instead of grey; for the first time they saw each other in sunlight. Someone even smiled. Primo quotes Ziegler, in his Kommando: '*Das Schlimmste ist vorüber*' – 'The worst is over.'

From the beginning, Primo's account leaves out one element in his symbiosis with Alberto: the presence of a third, Alberto's father Guido.

There were, no doubt, several reasons for this. Primo's private need was for twos, not threes: for the completion of himself in another. Thus, too, he would leave the first Alberto out of his story of Sandro, when he came to write it. But the main reason (in both cases, I think) was literary. He wanted to focus on the key relationships in each story, and its key meaning. So here, in *If This is a Man*, he also leaves out Leonardo, though in reality they remained in touch, at least occasionally: because Leonardo's importance in the story was in their return to life together, not here. So, too, he removed Rappoport, Bandi and the other 'moments of reprieve' from *If This is a Man* to *Lilit*, published a quarter of a century later: so as not to dilute his first and most urgent witness, to the destruction of the human soul. Alberto was his ally against this destruction: that was the point of their story. Guido was with them, and supported by them: that was true, but did not add to the essential meaning. So Primo did not tell it. Instead he reserved Guido for a different meaning.

He may also have left out the third presence because it did not last long. The family has always believed that Guido lived right to the end, and died only on the death march, in January 1945. But this is almost certainly wrong. Silvio Barabas saw Alberto on the march, but not Guido, though they would certainly have been together; nor did Alberto mention his father to Silvio, or show distress, as he would surely have done had his father just collapsed or been killed at his side. Primo said and wrote many times that Guido Dalla Volta had died in a selection. He dated it only once, to the last great selection in Auschwitz, in October 1944. This is quite possible, especially given Guido's support by the two younger men; and in Paolo Dalla Volta's memory, Guido figures in many of the episodes Primo recounted to the family, including some which probably happened after the summer. On the other hand, Primo's dating may have been wrong: after forty years even he might not be immune to the 'bunching' effect of memory, in which everything we recall seems to collect around a few definite dates, like space debris around the stars. Silvio Barabas – who had liked and admired Guido Dalla Volta since Fossoli, and looked out for him in Monowitz – saw and spoke to him several times before the summer, but never afterwards. He is convinced that Guido died no later than May or June: when Primo's and Alberto's cooperation had only just begun.

Since the official record of the fate of both Dalla Voltas is unreliable, we cannot be sure. In what follows, I have told Primo's and Alberto's story as though Guido had already gone by June: because Primo does so, in *If This is a Man*, and Silvio confirms it. But this may be wrong. Guido may still have been there until October, thanks to his son and his son's friend, and to his own attachment to life, which was very strong. Perhaps readers will add his name themselves, now and again, in his memory.

The meaning for which Primo used Guido Dalla Volta was a painful one. Alberto, he wrote, was unusually brave and clear-sighted; together they resisted the comforting illusions people offered each other, and criticized those who eagerly accepted them. But when Guido was selected, 'in the space of a few hours Alberto changed'. Suddenly he believed everything he had scoffed at a moment before – the Russians were near, the Germans wouldn't go on with their murders now; this selection was not for the gas, but for the convalescent camp at Jaworzno . . . So, Primo noted, not even Alberto could remain clear-sighted to the end. When the horror touched someone he loved, he told himself lies like everyone else. In other words, even Alberto was weak: even Alberto was human.

Primo was alone in Auschwitz. No one he loved was with him, except Alberto himself, whose death he did not have to face until after. He was not put to this test, therefore. *His* test – which he would not fail – would involve himself alone. Perhaps that was what allowed him to retain his almost superhuman detachment; which could seem almost inhuman as well. It seemed so to Emma and Paolo Dalla Volta. It may also seem so to us, when in *The Drowned and the Saved* Primo uses his friend as an example of human weakness, and shakes his head in his regretful, rational way.

Lorenzo

On 7 June 1944, the day after the D–Day landings, the English prisoners of war marched to work with a different step, and gave V–signs to the ordinary *Häftlinge*. A great wave of hope rushed through the camp; and again at the news of the Russian offensive, and the assassination attempt against Hitler in July. But each time it withdrew like a tide, leaving them emptier than before. It was better not to hope at all; and each day it was harder to feel anything but hunger. As soon as their worst enemy, the cold, had gone, hunger rushed in to take its place. 'The Lager *is* hunger,' Primo wrote. 'We ourselves are hunger, living hunger.'

Then one day in June, Primo met Lorenzo. Primo and Alberto were holding each other up, like two drowning men; Lorenzo would save both of them. He would abolish, if not their hunger, at least their danger of starvation; and not only physically.

It happened completely by chance. That day Primo was sent to work with two civilian masons. Suddenly the older one spoke – and he was Italian. Not only that: unless Primo was dreaming, he had a strong Piedmontese accent.

It was a crime for a *Häftling* and a civilian worker to speak to one another; and Lorenzo – as Primo would discover – rarely spoke at all. But they exchanged a few words: enough to learn that Primo was from Turin, and that Lorenzo was from Fossano, thirty miles away, and knew Primo's Colombo relatives by name.

Primo didn't ask Lorenzo for help, because he didn't know that he could give it. But though Lorenzo did not speak, Primo wrote, he understood. A few days after their first meeting he brought Primo his army mess tin full of soup. From then on, although they only met a few more times, and although Lorenzo risked being sent as a prisoner to Auschwitz himself if he were caught, every day for six months he left two quarts of soup in an agreed hiding place for Primo, and sometimes a few slices of bread as well. For two months the soup was full of strange objects – 'plum pits, salami peel, once even the wing of a sparrow' – because Lorenzo had collected it from his fellow-workers, who added their own scavengings to the ration. For the last four months it was more normal, and more nourishing, because he got up at three every morning, slipped into his camp kitchen, and took what was left in the vats. But even the sparrow-wing soup, shared with Alberto, meant an extra quart each:* another four to five hundred calories a day, enough to make the difference between life and death.

Lorenzo also gave Primo a vest of his own, full of patches, and wrote several letters for him, even though he had left school at ten years old, and wrote with effort. He would take nothing in return, not even money for his family in Italy. He accepted only two forms of help in kind: Primo had his shoes repaired by the Monowitz shoemakers; and once, when Lorenzo ripped open a leg on barbed wire, Primo gave him medicine for the wound – perhaps scrounged or stolen by Leonardo in KB, or begged from one of the prisoner-doctors.

Primo and Alberto told no one about Lorenzo, so as not to endanger him, or have to share his bounty. But together they talked about him often. They were amazed by him, Primo wrote; they could hardly believe he existed. In Auschwitz, 'a man helping other men out of pure altruism was incomprehensible, alien, like a saviour come from heaven'. And he was such a strange saviour. He was a Catholic, but not a believer. He was only a little better off than they were, and he did not seem gentle or good-natured; he was silent, morose, and often smelt of wine. Yet he risked his life to help a stranger: an Italian, even a Piedmontese, but an *ebreu*† from the city, someone he would never know at home.

Only after his return did Primo learn Lorenzo's story – and not mostly from Lorenzo. In 1944 he was forty years old: grey-haired, tall and slightly stooped, with a long, slow, countryman's stride, like Sandro's. He had grown up in rural poverty such as Primo had never seen, and we can no longer even imagine. His father, Giuseppe, collected and sold scrap metal and rags; his mother, Giovanna, sold the rags. There were six children, four boys and two girls. The family lived at Via Michelini 4, in the heart of the Borgo Vecchio, the poorest quarter of Fossano: three rooms for eight people, plus one for the metal and rags, and one for the mule and cart.

The Perones were far from the poorest family in Fossano; but for everyone in the Borgo Vecchio life was a daily battle for survival. Hunger was never far away; life was constant labour, twelve to fourteen hours a day. The

---

* i.e. an extra two pints each; or an extra 1⅓ pints each, if Guido was still alive.
† Piedmontese for *ebreo*, Jew.

children's clothes were made by their mothers; their shoes were wooden clogs, not unlike the prisoners' at Auschwitz. None had more than primary schooling. In the Borgo Vecchio before the second War there was little knowledge of the outside world, little conversation beyond the practical, or occasionally the political – the masons and bricklayers, especially, were all famous Communists. There was no comfort or entertainment, except the church for the women, the tavern for the men. The masons and bricklayers were also famous drunks.

In this closed, hard world violence and brutality found a natural home; and also a deep-rooted instinct to help one another, almost always in silence. So it was in the Via Michelini. Giuseppe was a classic *padre padrone*: harsh and tyrannical, often drunk, and when drunk quarrelsome and violent. He was also withdrawn, and given to dark depressions; and secretly devoted to his children. All these characteristics he passed on to them, especially to his sons. In the Borgo Vecchio, where everyone had a nickname, the whole family was known as *Tacca* instead of *Perone*: which may have come from many things, but most of all from '*attacca-briga*' – a fighter, a chronically quarrelsome person.

Lorenzo was the second son, and 100 per cent Piedmontese, 100 per cent Perone. Like his father, he was silent and withdrawn, given to drink and fighting. Although he was tall and handsome, like his elder brother and his next sister he never married. And like them too, behind his roughness, his obstinate, sore-headed isolation, he was absolutely upright, generous and kind.

Like his sister, and like their mother, he was a tireless and perfectionist worker – even in Auschwitz. He hated the Germans, Primo said, 'their food, their language, their war; but when they set him to build walls, he built them straight and solid, not out of obedience, but out of professional pride'. He never lasted long with any employer, because he was too proud: if anyone made the smallest remark about his work, 'he put on his hat and left'. For several years before the war, because work was scarce in Piedmont, and because he did not want to be called up, he followed his brother to France: crossing the border on smugglers' paths, moving from job to job, always on foot, always alone.

That is where the war found him. When Italy invaded France in June 1940 he was interned, like all Italians. What happened next is not clear; but when France surrendered soon after, he probably went back to work in his normal anarchic way. Then in early 1942 the Germans arrived in his area. They were looking for labour, as usual; and especially for construction workers, to work on the three synthetic rubber plants that I. G. Farben was building in Upper Silesia. Altogether 7,000 Italians were recruited for the three sites: Blechhammer, Heydebreck and Auschwitz. Boetti, the company for which Lorenzo was working, was offered, or allocated, Auschwitz. Like all 7,000 Italians, Lorenzo would have had little choice. But even if he *was* given the choice, he would have gone: for he had certainly never heard of Auschwitz, and all his life he'd taken whatever work he could find. He arrived at Buna on 17 April 1942; two years before Primo.

The Italian workers' camp was on a hill between Buna-Monowitz and Birkenau. Every day for nearly three years they looked down on the smoking chimneys of Birkenau on one side, and the living dead of Monowitz on the other. They understood exactly what was happening; and suffered accordingly. Some protected themselves, most protected each other, many did more. By the time Lorenzo began to help Primo, in the summer of 1944, he had already risked his life several times before: for a Frenchman, a Pole, and at least one other.

One day in late June Primo found himself alone for an hour or two, stacking cardboard tubes in a cellar. Some time before he had bought or stolen a piece of paper and a stub of pencil; now at last he could draft a letter for Lorenzo to copy and send for him. Writing belonged to a lost world – could he do it here, would he remember how? He was concentrating so hard that he didn't hear Eddy the Vice-Kapo come down the stairs. Before he knew what had happened Eddy had snatched the paper, and slapped him to the ground.

Primo knew that he was in very great danger. Writing was a hanging offence; he had put his life in danger, and Lorenzo's, and Eddy's as well, as the Kapo responsible. Eddy was not a brute; but what would he do?

What he did was disappear, for a very long hour. When he returned he made a strange speech. He had given Primo's letter, he said, to two prisoners to translate, warning them that if the translations were different in any way he would denounce not only Primo, but them as well. Luckily for Primo, the two translations were the same, and not compromising. Primo was crazy, but he would not denounce him this time. He could not say why: perhaps just because he *was* crazy.

By 'crazy' Eddy meant: valuing the connection to your human past more than your life. That was the ultimate craziness in Auschwitz, the ultimate rejection of Auschwitz logic. It should have killed Primo, but it did the opposite. He had been lucky again: lucky that it was Eddy who had caught him writing, and none of the other Kapos. But the episode of the letter shows more than Primo Levi's luck. It shows that it was harder than the architects of Auschwitz hoped, and than we might sometimes fear, to destroy the instinctive respect for other people's humanity, even in a simple German street thief like Eddy.

The next time Primo saw Lorenzo he could give him nothing to copy.

Instead he must have hurriedly told him the message he wanted to send to his mother and sister, and the name and address of the friend, as brave as Lorenzo himself, who would take it to them. This is what Lorenzo wrote:

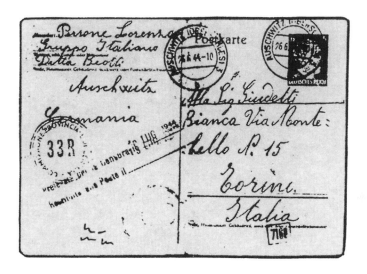

25.6.44

Carissima signorina Bianca, o visto ieri primo sta bene, lavora e forse le scrivera è un po dimagrito e attende di rivederla o almeno le tue notizie. Qui ce niente di nuovo molti ringraziamenti da parte sua e tanti saluti Lo Pe ce sono il suo amico Perrone Lorenzo spero di ricevere un suo scritto addio

Perrone Lorenzo Gruppo Italiano Ditta Beotti Auschwitz – Germania

Dearest Miss Bianca, yesterday i saw primo he is well, he is working and perhaps he will write to you, he is a bit thinner, he hopes to see you or at least to hear from you. There are no news here, many thanks from him and his best regards. Lo Pe this is his friend Perrone Lorenzo i hope to have a letter from you goodbye

Perrone Lorenzo Italian Group, Beotti Co. Auschwitz Germany

'I believe that it is really owing to Lorenzo that I am alive today,' Primo wrote, back home in Turin in 1946. And not only, or even mostly, for the material help which had saved his life; but for another kind of help, which we can see in the letters.

The characters in these pages [Primo wrote] are not men. Their humanity is buried, or they themselves have buried it, under an offence received or inflicted . . .

But Lorenzo was a man; his humanity was pure and uncontaminated, he was outside this world of negation. Thanks to Lorenzo, I managed not to forget that I myself was a man.

Lorenzo

The Chemical Kommando

Sometime in June or July, in anticipation of the Buna entering production, a new specialist Kommando was formed: the Chemical Kommando, for chemists and pharmacists. Primo and Alberto saw their chance, and applied.

On the day of its official formation fifteen *Häftlinge* assembled in the roll-call square. There were a few each of French, Dutch, Poles and Germans; several Hungarians – during May and June vast numbers of Hungarians had been pouring into Auschwitz; a Czech rabbi called Mendi, Silvio Barabas, and Primo and Alberto.

It had happened – they had made it to a specialist Kommando. But straight away they were reminded not to relax, not to hope, they were still in the Lager. The Labour Service, Primo wrote, 'had not thought it necessary for the Kapo of the Chemical Kommando to be a chemist'. Instead he was a 'green triangle': a common criminal, like most Kapos, who were thieves and murderers dredged up from the prison cells of Germany. 'As a rule', Primo said roundly, 'they were scum'; and this one was no exception.

His real name was Oscar; but Primo called him Alex in *If This is a Man*, and it is hard to think of him as anything but Alex. He was small and not particularly strong, but stupid and violent like most Kapos; full of boastful pride in his pure German blood, servile to his Buna bosses and the SS, sneeringly contemptuous of his starving, ragged charges. Just because they were intellectuals, he told them, they needn't think they could make a fool of *him*. Whoever had lied about his qualifications would be found out, since there would be a chemistry examination very soon. And until production began, Kommando 98 was an ordinary transport Kommando, attached to the magnesium chloride warehouse. In either case, transport Kommando or chemical Kommando, he, Alex, was the boss.

Five of the fifteen immediately admitted they knew nothing about chemistry, and asked to go back to their previous Kommandos. For some reason, or no reason, they were allowed to remain as ordinary labourers. It made no difference, anyway; they were all ordinary labourers, as Alex had said. Three days after the Kommando was formed, when no one believed in the chemistry examination any more, it actually happened; but that made no difference either. Throughout that hot summer they loaded and unloaded wagons, shifted earth and bricks, scraped and cleaned the tanks and pipes of the Buna, just as they had done before. In August, at the height of the heat, they worked with 125-pound sacks of phenylbeta.* When the air-raids began they carried the sacks out of the warehouse, when the air-raids stopped they carried them back in, when the warehouse was hit they carried them out again. The phenylbeta powder seeped through their clothes and chafed their bodies like leprosy; it stuck to their sweating hands and faces and burned their skin off in large patches, leaving the sensitive under-layers to sting and burn still deeper. This lasted for twenty days, during which they were never given anything to protect their skin, and not even the worst affected was allowed into KB.

Nonetheless it was a good Kommando. Many people *were* chemists, or else physicists, doctors, engineers, mathematicians. Since it was a specialist Kommando, once people entered they usually stayed, and not many new ones could enter; so that the squad was relatively stable, it had a certain *esprit de corps*, and even, Primo said, a certain rough friendship. In the grey dawn they greeted each other with mock formality: 'Good morning Herr Doktor,

---

* Betaphenylnaphthalene, a caustic derivative of benzene.

good day Signor Lawyer, how was your night Mr President? Did you enjoy your breakfast?' Some made real friendships in the Kommando; including Primo. When he got home he made a list of everyone in it he could remember. At its height it reached about sixty members; he remembered just under fifty, not counting himself and Alberto. The majority of people in his Lager memoirs were in the Chemical Kommando: not only the ones we meet as members, like Elias, Iss Clausner, and Jean the Pikolo in *If This is a Man*, or Eddy in *Moments of Reprieve*; but others as well: Mendi, 'Henri', 'Alfred L.' and Sómogyi in *If This is a Man*, for example; and almost all the other heroes and anti-heroes of *Moments of Reprieve* – 'Rappoport', Bandi, Tischler, Wolf and 'Ezra'. Primo Levi's memories reflect Auschwitz, and indeed the Nazi Lager in general; but they were drawn specifically from Buna–Monowitz, and most of all from the Chemical Kommando.

The Chemistry Examination

When the day of the examination came, Primo knew that he had a chance to save himself. He was half-starved, a convict and a slave; but if he became a specialist, he might just possibly survive.

He tells the story in *If This is a Man*; and it is one of the most quietly devastating moments in the book, in which the great achievement of Nazi Germany, the reduction of human beings to things, is displayed not in numbing rows of corpses, but in the acts of two living men, or what they have become.

In the middle of the Buna, a vast pit of mud and death, were the offices of the Polymerization Department, hushed and clean, with brass plates on their doors, like offices anywhere. ('Today,' Primo wrote two years later, 'at this very moment as I sit writing at a table, I myself am not convinced that these things really happened.') Alex led his applicants for salvation from one world into the other like a reverse Charon; Primo twice, because there was only time for six candidates in the morning, and he was the seventh. Both times Alex looked at him with particular disgust, roughly straightened his collar, took out his beret and slapped it on his head. Nothing that looked like *this* could be a chemist; it must be another Jewish trick, another *Häftling's* lie.

Then Primo was standing in front of Doktor Ingenieur Pannwitz, who was a notorious Nazi, tall and blond, with 'eyes, hair and nose as all Germans are supposed to have them'. When he finished writing he raised his eyes and looked at Primo, standing like a stain in the midst of all this order. That look, Primo wrote, was not a look between two human beings; if he could have explained it, 'I would also have explained the essence of the great insanity of the third Germany.'

Then the examination began: and despite his months of starvation, despite the immeasurable distance that separated him from his life of less than a year ago, it went well. His brain still worked, his examination nerves still held, which his friends had so envied; and luck was still with him – Pannwitz seemed particularly interested in 'my poor old. . . "Dielectrical Constants"'', his first university sub-thesis.

As suddenly as it had begun, it was over, and Alex was leading him back to his real life, which had not changed, and would not change for many weeks and months more. And now it was Alex's turn to stand for the third Germany, not as he imagined but as he deserved, in the mind of this contemptible slave, and in the minds of the slave's readers as long as books are read. As they clambered over a heap of iron, Alex grasped at a cable, smearing his hand with thick black grease. And without meaning to mock, as you would an enemy, but quite naturally, he wiped his hand clean on his prisoner's shoulder, as though he were a rag. 'He would be amazed,' the prisoner wrote,

that poor brute Alex, if someone told him that today, for that action I judge him and Pannwitz and innumerable others like him, great and small, in Auschwitz and everywhere.

Pikolo

Primo always said that he wrote *If This is a Man* under the pressure of an overwhelming need to tell, without any conscious literary aim apart from clarity.* But under that pressure his mind also fixed on certain distilling, dramatizing images, which neither he nor we could ever afterwards forget. The images of Pannwitz's look, and the wiping of Alex's hand, are two of them. And immediately after there is another: for the next time we see Primo he has literally sunk back into the underworld. He is inside an underground petrol tank, with five others of his squad; and his two Gorgon encounters with inhumanity are about to be balanced by one of the opposite sign.

By this time the Chemical Kommando had been in existence for some weeks, and Jean Samuel had become its Pikolo. The Pikolo was an important

---

* Well, almost always: forty years later he began to admit that, like every writer, he had inevitably had to shape and order his material. See Chapter 10.

and privileged member of each Kommando. He was almost always the youngest, often still in his teens; and he was the personal assistant of the Kapo, responsible for the washing and sewing of the Kapo's clothes, for the cleaning of the Kommando's headquarters, for keeping the register, and making out the daily work report. For these services he was excused much of the heavy labour, and – privilege breeding privilege, as always in the Lager – had the right not only to the soup at the bottom of the vat, but to an extra half-ration as well. Usually he also had to supply sexual services to the Kapo; but 'either I was not attractive enough', Jean says today, with a grin, or Alex was not that way inclined. If he had been, Jean does not know what he would have done. But he was lucky, and did not have to decide.

The Kommando was lucky too, because Jean was an exceptional Pikolo. He was twenty-two years old, an Alsatian, with the inestimable advantage, therefore, of knowing German. He had won his position by daring – volunteering to iron Alex's trousers when he had no idea how, and risked a whipping if he burned or spoiled them; and by careful manoeuvring, slowly taking over the paperwork without ever showing Alex that he – and everyone else – knew it was beyond him. And as Pikolo he never abused his power, as most people did, if only to retain it. On the contrary: he was gentle, modest and friendly; and he had already saved more than one fellow-prisoner from punishment or denunciation by a single, well-placed word.

Jean (on the left), his brother Pierrot and their parents,
Dausse, Lot et Garonne, 1944

He had arrived at the end of March, a month after Primo, with his whole family: mother, father, younger brother, three uncles and a girl cousin. His eldest uncle, Arthur, had vanished straight away. The rest of the family entered Auschwitz: the two women to Birkenau, Jean's father to Auschwitz main camp, Jean and the other men to Buna-Monowitz. From then on he had lost sight of his father, mother and cousin; only the women would survive.

In Monowitz Jean registered as a chemist, his brother and uncles as gardeners. To start with theirs was the luckier choice: they did relatively light work, while he struggled through the first months in a lethal transport Kommando. Then, as always in the Lager, things suddenly and unpredictably changed. Jean, who had only just managed to survive, slipped into the Chemical Kommando. In August his eighteen-year-old brother Pierrot, who was taller, stronger and at this stage healthier, was chosen for the notorious quarry at Jawischowitz, near Auschwitz; some time later his uncle Prosper was sent to another camp, Janina. Neither would survive. Jean was left alone in Buna-Monowitz with his last uncle, René, who was still working as a gardener. Jean and René were as close as Primo and Alberto; in the autumn Jean would get René into the Chemical Kommando.

Primo would have known some of this already – Jean's cleverness and kindness, and his close bond to his uncle, which kept his moral and emotional life alive. And he would have known something else: Jean was keeping his mind alive as well. For several weeks before Primo, Jean had been Alberto's bed companion, and he had asked Alberto for Italian lessons. Italian was no use at all in the camp; it was sheer exercise. And Jean already had a favourite, passionate exercise: mathematics. Together with four or five others he formed a little group around Jacques Feldbau, a brilliant mathematician from the University of Toulouse, whom he had met in KB. They talked maths on the march to work and maths on the march back; they gave bread to a German civilian worker to buy them books on logarithmic equations; Jacques filled a fifty-page exercise book with a course on topology for Jean, which he kept through thick and thin, until it was destroyed with all his other possessions in Buchenwald in 1945. Never again in his life, Jean says, did he have the grasp of mathematics he had in Auschwitz: never again did he have such a capacity – such a *need* – to concentrate on pure numbers, not to think of the past or the future, not to think, above all, of the present. Without mathematics, he says, he would never have returned to France: it was they that lifted him above the cold and hunger, the pain and fear.

Primo and Jean had two extraordinary meetings in Buna-Monowitz in the summer of 1944. The first, which was more personal, more emotional, mattered most to Jean; he never had another like it in the camp, and still remembers it today with profound emotion. The second, which was more universal and more intellectual, mattered most to Primo: brought him closest to his immense goal, to the answer to his question. That was the difference between Jean Samuel and Primo Levi. But it was Primo who helped Jean to talk and remember, Jean who helped Primo to understand.

Their first meeting came not long after the Chemical Kommando was formed. There was an air-raid – not the first, but the experience was not yet routine. The Germans scattered to their bunkers; and the two prisoners found themselves alone.

This almost never happened. To be alone, in less than a vast crowd smelling of starvation, without shouts or blows, without spies, Kapos, SS – it was like a miracle, like something out of the most distant memory or dream. It was a glorious sunny day, they were in an almost empty part of the Buna. They took shelter in a small hut; and for twenty minutes – or thirty, or even more – they talked. They talked about things they had almost forgotten: their homes, their families, their friends; their studies – maths, science, chemistry; Jean's family pharmacy in the small town of Wasselonne, Primo's beloved mountains.

At last the all-clear siren sounded. The return to reality was worse than if they had never left it, and it took several days to recover, to reharden themselves, to forget again. But from now on they were friends. For the next week or two they could only smile briefly in the washroom, on the *Appellplatz*, in the few moments between work and sleep. But Jean was the Pikolo; and soon he saw the chance of another meeting. This was the one that would be so important to Primo, and to us. He put it at the heart of his great book; into it he put his most personal, most universal and most urgent message. If one day there is a new Holocaust, and we can save only one chapter of one book from the twentieth century, it should be this one: Chapter 11 of *If This is a Man*, 'The Canto of Ulysses', in which a twenty-four-year-old Italian tries to remember, recite and explain Canto XXVI of Dante's *Inferno* to a twenty-two-year-old Frenchman in Auschwitz.

'The Canto of Ulysses'

Every day before noon Pikolo and one other fetched the Kommando's soup from the kitchens, carrying the pot on wooden poles slung on their shoulders. On the way back the soup was heavy, and you couldn't talk, separated by the length of the poles; but on the way there you were free, you could talk, you had a right to be walking in the sun. People waited to be chosen by

Pikolo. Silvio Barabas did it once, but though his legs were tireless his arms were weak, and the hundredweight of soup was too much for him. Most recently it had been Stern, a Hungarian who had been in Palestine; very likely Jean had been learning bits of Hebrew from him. But now Stern had had twenty-five lashes for stealing some brooms, and wouldn't be walking anywhere for some time. Jean clambered down into the cold and rusty darkness of the underground tank and pointed at Primo. '*Aujourd'hui c'est Primo qui vient avec moi chercher la soupe*,' he said.

They climbed out into the sunshine. Pikolo gave Primo one of the poles, and they walked along as slowly as they dared. Pikolo had worked out the longest possible route; they would have a whole hour together. They picked up where they had left off – Strasbourg and Turin, the books they'd read, their mothers. Then Pikolo said he would like to learn more Italian: he'd never managed to stay awake for more than a few minutes in his evening lessons with Alberto. Primo felt suddenly light-hearted and strong. Of course he could teach Pikolo Italian, today he could teach him anything, everything – did they not have a whole hour?

It was natural that Primo the marvellous teacher should leap at the request for a lesson, natural that Primo the marvellous student should choose Dante. But he himself had no idea why the Canto of Ulysses came into his mind. It was an intuition, Jean says. An intuition, an instinct – that mysterious thing that Primo Levi never allowed himself to have – is at the heart of his great book. An intuition that the Canto of Ulysses held a lesson that was not just about Italian, and not just for Pikolo: that it had a message for both of them, for all of them, above all for himself. So he began to recite.

Ulysses' voice speaks to Dante and Virgil from a flame, the image of death and torment that hung over their own lives. He tells the tale of his end; and it comes not from the *Odyssey*, but from Dante's own imagination.

After leaving Circe, Ulysses does not return to Ithaca. Instead, not even 'reverence/For my old father, nor the debt of love/I owed Penelope' – Primo remembered these lines – could conquer his burning desire 'to know the world and have experience/Of all human vices, and human worth'. So – and now we will remember the lines as well – '*Misi me per l'alto mare aperto*': 'I set forth upon the open sea'.

His ship sails for months, until it reaches the ends of the earth: *quella foce stretta*, that narrow strait beyond which men should not venture – '*Acciò che l'uom più oltre non si metta*', Primo remembered this line too, and 'it was worth stopping for'. But now Ulysses exhorts his crew to break this last barrier as well, in words which burst on Primo 'like the blast of a trumpet, like the voice of God':

Considerate la vostra semenza:
Fatti non foste a viver come bruti,
Ma per seguir virtute e conoscenza.

Consider your seed:
You were not made to live like brutes,
But to follow virtue and knowledge.

'Pikolo begs me for a repetition,' Primo wrote – 'How good Pikolo is', perhaps he has understood! Ulysses' message to his crew was *their* answer to the Kapos, the SS, the whole infernal system around them, it was a clarion call to them, and he and Pikolo were obeying it, they were fulfilling it at that very moment, together. 'My companions I made so eager / With these brief words,' he went on – and his own companion *was* so eager; but suddenly there was a blank. It was dreadful, he had forgotten at least four tercets. '*Ça ne fait rien, vas-y tout de même,*' Pikolo said. 'At last a mountain appeared, dim / With distance' – 'Oh Pikolo, Pikolo,' Primo wrote, 'do not let me think of my mountains . . .' He would give today's soup if only he could connect the mountain tercet to the end. But it was no good, they had reached the kitchens, he must finish:

> Three times it whirled us round with all the water,
> The fourth time raised the poop up high
> And plunged the prow below, as pleased Another.

Primo held Pikolo back, it was absolutely vital that he understand this 'as pleased Another', and something else as well – 'Something gigantic that I myself have only just seen, in a flash of intuition, perhaps the reason for our fate, for our being here today . . .'

But he could not seize it; or else there was no time to tell it to Pikolo. Instead there came a different announcement: the soup today was cabbage and turnips. '*Kraut und Rüben. Choux et navets. Kaposzta és répak.*' And Primo remembered the last line of the Canto:

> *Infin che'l mar fu sopra noi rinchiuso.*

> Until the sea closed over us again.

Today Jean profoundly understands the first great message of the Canto of Ulysses, and its special significance in that place. Then he only sensed it. He did not know the story of Ulysses, or the story of the Divine Comedy; he did not understand the antique Italian words, or most of Primo's hurried translations and explanations. 'I did not understand Dante,' he says. 'But I understood Primo.' He understood that Primo's remembering Ulysses' exhortation, his huge effort to seize its meaning for them and pass it on, was a salvation: an extraordinary act of resistance, as Jean's mathematics were for him. He understood, above all, that Primo was deeply moved; and this moved him. He could not share Primo's thought, but he shared his emotion: 'Which is often more important,' he says, 'in the camp and everywhere.'

But Primo would not have told Jean his private sufferings, before their great shared one. There was a private part of his emotion, therefore, which Jean could not have guessed. *The characters in these pages are not men*, he would write. But what was a man? That had been his question for a long time; and so far his answers had been painful ones to him. A man was strong and brave, at home in the world, capable of war – like Sandro, like both Albertos; but not like him. So far, in his own answers to his question, he was not a man. But now came Ulysses' answer – 'like the blast of a trumpet, like the voice of God'. A man was *made to pursue virtue and knowledge* – he was mind and will, ideal and reason. This was his essence, that the Lager meant to destroy, that in retrieving the Canto of Ulysses he himself was saving, was *being*. In Ulysses' answer to his question, Primo Levi was a man.

And then there was that other 'gigantic' intuition: 'perhaps the reason for our fate, for our being here today . . .' He did not tell this to Pikolo either, or to us; '*C'est un peu dommage, hein?*' Jean says. But perhaps he didn't tell us because it too was private; and because it bore the opposite, negative sign.

Dante had reinvented Ulysses' story, as Primo the classical student would know. And Primo the classical student would also know why: to celebrate a new vision of human knowledge, at the dawn of the Renaissance. Ulysses' clarion call to man to pursue virtue and knowledge, beyond all previous limits, beyond where *l'uom più oltre non si metta* – that call was Dante's, to his readers and himself. 'No one of his age was more deeply moved than Dante by the passion to know all that is knowable,' Croce said, 'and nowhere else has he given such noble expression to that noble passion as in the great figure of Ulysses.'

Ulysses is great and glorious – but also damned, and burning in the fires of hell. The reason for his fate is contained in that 'as pleased Another' which Primo so wanted Pikolo to understand. The Other is God; and He is punishing Ulysses for his presumption. Ulysses has aspired to a knowledge of all creation, including a knowledge of good and evil ('all human vices, and human worth'), which belongs to God alone. To a secular, rationalist thinker he is a great man; but to a religious thinker he is also a great sinner – a fallen angel like Lucifer; like Icarus punished for his pride.

Dante, caught between medieval theology and the first stirrings of secularity, was torn between these two conflicting visions. So, I think, was Primo

– and not only in relation to Ulysses, but in relation to himself. For if Dante had looked into Ulysses as into a mirror, so in turn did Primo. Croce might have been speaking of him: no one of *his* age was more deeply moved than Primo Levi by the passion to know. His was no longer a religious age, and he was not a religious thinker. Yet like his father he retained an atavistic dread. He had always feared punishment for presumption, even in his ordinary scientific ambition. And now his ambition was far from ordinary. It was – as he told Pikolo then, many times – to record and report Auschwitz to the world. Auschwitz is further beyond the limits of human knowledge of good and evil than even Ulysses had gone. But Primo Levi determined to be the new Dante of this new earthly Inferno; as in fact he would become. Perhaps that was what he had glimpsed: the gigantic risk of his own *folle volo*, his own mad flight.

August – September 1944

In August things took a turn for the worse. This was the time of the phenylbeta, and their skin searing off in the sun. Then Alex disappeared; and though he was a brute, they feared change, which was almost always for the worse. For Jean it was worse immediately, because he lost his post as Pikolo. For the rest of the Kommando it was soon worse as well. At first Eddy the Vice-Kapo took over, and was as roughly decent as he'd been to Primo; but that lasted only briefly, in Jean's memory a few days. Then their third and final Kapo arrived. He was not a criminal, and not German; in fact he was a Dutch musician. Even so their fears were realized; for Jup Lessing was a Jew. That was one of the hardest lessons of the Lager: that those you had to fear the most were those who had most to fear. Jup was a cellist in the camp orchestra; in the logic of the camp this privilege entitled him to others, so he became a Kapo. Now a *Reichsdeutscher* Kapo could be as vicious as he liked; but a Jewish Kapo had to be as vicious as he could, in order to keep his job. Jup was not naturally violent, and he was far from the worst. Mendi, who was one of those whom the corruption of the camp did not touch, thought Jup a nice man. But he was very glad to profit from his privileges, which included a decent diet, and an almost clean striped suit, of which (Primo noted) he was stupidly proud. In his record and report Primo concentrated on Alex, who represented the crucial offence underlying all the others, the treatment of another human being as a thing. It wasn't until *The Drowned and the Saved* that he entered the grey zone inhabited by such as Jup Lessing; and then he didn't mention his name. But Jean does; saying, 'I felt safer with [Alex], who wasn't afraid of the SS.'

The wider situation also worsened. In August 1944 the Allies began regular, concentrated bombing of the industries of Upper Silesia. Not of the railway line, the prisoners of Auschwitz noticed: that continued to deliver its human fuel to the Buna and the other factories, and not least to the crematorium, with uninterrupted efficiency. Only the factories themselves were targeted – and carefully, so as to damage but not destroy them, and leave them intact for use after the war. It worked.* The production of synthetic rubber was postponed, and postponed again; the Buna could not be finished, only constantly repaired. The prisoners knew the planes were on their side, and welcomed the destruction; but they suffered from it as much as everyone else. They were not allowed into the shelters, but had to press their rags of bodies into the earth, as the smoke and dust rose around them; when they returned to camp in the evening they found no water, no soup, no light. And worst of all, as always, were the Germans. The bombs were rousing them, Primo wrote, 'from a long dream of domination'; suddenly they could see the end, and it was not the end they had imagined. All of them – the SS and the political prisoners, the criminals of Monowitz and the civilians of Buna – drew together in shock and fear. In their slaves they saw enemies again – and enemies who were glimpsing revenge. Any laxness that had crept in disappeared; their savagery redoubled.

Despite all this, Primo was winning his own war. After six months he was 'bone-weary, with an ancient, incarnate weariness I thought irrevocable'. But he was an old *Häftling* now. He knew how to protect himself, physically and above all mentally. He had Lorenzo, and he had Alberto. By now 'the two Italians' were inseparable: marching, working, eating, sleeping, organizing. And they were very good organizers: especially Alberto, but Primo as well. By September he had his own secret hiding place from the bombs; he and Alberto even slipped into KB now and again to rest, with the help of an Italian prisoner-doctor. Their pact was absolute, they shared everything, and it showed. Every morning Lonzana, from their transport, complimented Primo on his health. To Silvio Barabas he seemed on a different plane altogether.

Silvio had squeezed into the Chemical Kommando by saying he was a chemistry student – which he wasn't, yet. He was one of those who had failed the examination, but had been allowed to stay on as assistants. Silvio spent his whole Auschwitz year at the lowest level of the camp, one of the grey army of ants swarming on the bottom. He never learned to work the

* In its post-war plan as well, at least as far as the Buna was concerned. 'Today,' Primo wrote in 1984, 'it is Poland's largest synthetic rubber factory.' When I visited it in 1995 it was still a huge and active chemical complex; and I believe still remains so.

system, but only to endure it. He survived by shutting off all thought, all feeling; by retreating into a shell that contained only himself and his one inseparable friend, Jakov, from Radom in Poland. He did not even 'organize', he says, but survived on the ration: the *Bunasuppe*, sawdust bread and so-called coffee. This was not, in theory, possible; but in Auschwitz the impossible happened all the time. In any case, by great good fortune Silvio did survive (and so did Jakov): and he still cannot believe how rich Primo seemed to him, over half a century ago in Auschwitz. Most of the images engraved on his memory come from the end, after Primo had entered the laboratory: his new, clean, tailor-made uniform, his huge *menaschka* of soup, containing *three or four litres* . . . But it was like this always, Silvio says, or as far back as he can remember: Primo seemed to him unimaginably rich, like a king to a pauper.

It was this great wealth that allowed Primo to talk, observe and remember, Silvio says; apart from his bond to Jakov, and a few isolated memories, he could do none of these things. He had closed down to the lowest level of being; he was glad if he could go on breathing. Whereas Primo was almost more alive than he had ever been before, or would ever be again: more open to experience, to thought, to memory. Silvio is as amazed as Jean whenever he thinks of this. *If This is a Man* was a revelation to him, he says; he, who was there, learned almost as much as we.

His wealth also kept Primo alive, or half-alive, in other ways. The ordinary *Häftling* hardly ever saw a woman, or even dreamt of one. If he did, he felt nothing – certainly not desire, not even interest; he was too far gone. But for Primo, after the turning point of the summer this was no longer true. He was a filthy, half-starved convict, covered in fleas; and the penalty for talking to a civilian was death. The impossibility of ever approaching a woman was lifted out of himself and made real, like the barbed-wire fence all around him. Despite this – or because of it – he remained a man in Auschwitz, or even became a man in Auschwitz, in this sense too. One day – it was 31 July, he tells us, his twenty-fifth birthday – he saw a young woman, hiding from the rain in a section of iron pipe opposite the one in which he and a companion were doing the same. She had a broad red face, and was bundled up in a thick jacket: a 'voluntary' worker, probably Ukrainian. She looked at them and laughed; scratched herself provocatively under her jacket, undid her hair and began, slowly, combing it. Primo stared at her, as once he'd stared at the laundry-girl across the Via Vico: but this time he did not turn away. Instead Tischler, his companion, stared with him. It was his twenty-fifth birthday too, Primo wrote: 'We were twins.' Perhaps this was true; in any case it is an extraordinary image, Primo's shy gaze not just doubled but twinned, as though both gazes were his own. And just before they see the woman, Tischler gives Primo a present for their birthday: a slice of apple. Perhaps that too was true; but Primo surely means us to remember another woman, and another apple. Tischler then goes on to tell Primo the story of Lilith, Adam's wife before Eve, whose defiance of God was even greater: she became a she-devil, and has shared men's sexual sins, and even God's, ever after. 'Lilith' will become Primo's name for the woman, or women, with whom he himself will be tempted to sin; looking back, he would put his first encounter with her here, in Auschwitz.

Together with Alberto, his other twin, he also met another woman; and they both fell half in love. Flora (but her real name was probably Maria) was Italian. She was a small-time prostitute, who had also ended up with the Todt Organization; in Buna she swept the cellar floors. She was small and plain, but to Alberto and Primo she seemed 'beautiful, mysterious, incorporeal'. Filled with shame, they asked her for bread; which she brought them, her eyes filling with tears. Alberto found a comb and gave it to Flora, and they dreamt of her at night. When they realized that, perhaps out of habit, she kept on with her old trade, they felt deep jealousy and disillusion, and her bread tasted bitter. Still they went on eating it, Primo said; and probably they went on dreaming.

In August, Primo's riches were doubled and trebled. On the 20th Lorenzo sent a second card to Bianca for him, saying that he was in good health, and his German was improving, 'which is a great advantage in the work' (they would know, then, that he was working). '*O saputo poco fa,*' Lorenzo wrote, 'I 'eard a while ago that Luciana is working not far from here.' '*Abbi come me tanto coraggio e tanta speranza e ricevi un cordiale saluto e un forte abbraccio di chi sempre ti ricorda, tuo Lorenzo*': 'Be very strong and very hopeful, like me, my best regards and a big hug from someone who will never forget you, your Lorenzo.'

Soon after, something even more miraculous: Lorenzo brought Primo an answer from his mother. It was brief, and careful to give nothing away to the censor. Even so, and though it was more precious to him than anything he had ever owned, or could own, Primo knew he would have to destroy it before evening, and the inspection at the camp gates. He knew too that it was more than his life was worth to tell anyone; and yet he had to. That day he was working with a young Hungarian called Endre Szanto, known as Bandi. Bandi was a new arrival, one of the thousands of Hungarians who had poured into the camp that summer. He was friendly, brave, and absolutely honest; for weeks Primo had been trying, without success, to teach him to steal. He read his precious letter out to Bandi, translating it into German. 'German was neither my language nor his,' Primo wrote;

Bandi can have understood very little. But if he did not understand the words, like Pikolo he understood Primo. When the hasty reading was over he took a radish from his pocket and gave it to Primo, blushing. Primo had stolen this small piece of paper from the 'black universe' around them. Now Bandi's radish was a gift in kind, another twin: it was the first thing he had stolen.

★   ★

Luciana was still working in Birkenau, as Primo had heard. On one of her hurried visits to new Italian arrivals she found a distant cousin, who at last gave her news of her family: with the help of Don Péaquin, they had escaped to Switzerland. From then on Luciana knew she was not alone. She could, she must survive.

She worked with renewed energy, especially for her fellow-Italians, so much the weakest and worst off. That summer for instance, she cured Giuliana Tedeschi of influenza in the Revier, then hurried her out before the next selection. Giuliana would survive: through her own grit, and her invincible will to return to her children; and through Luciana's help at that key moment.

But she could not do the same for Vanda. By late summer Vanda was barely hanging on. Her legs and feet were terribly swollen. Yet she was still avoiding the Revier; instead she had managed to enter the *Schonungsblock*, the rest hut, for less serious cases. At the end of August Luciana went to see her there, with an aching heart. She had to tell her she was leaving.

Luciana had always sworn she would never leave Vanda; but she knew now that she could not save her, and must save herself. She found Vanda sitting on the ground, in the heat and dust of that stifling August, her poor legs stretched out in front of her. Somehow she managed to tell her: she had been offered another hospital job, in a labour camp in Germany. Luciana gives only the bare facts now; she hurries the story to its close. Vanda said, 'But of course you must go, that's absolutely right.' Then she said: 'If I die, and you have a baby girl one day, will you call her Vanda?' Luciana promised.

Three years later, married to Franco Momigliano, she did have a baby girl, and called her Vanda. But 'I was crazy,' she says: she'd thrown herself back into work without a pause, and had never been treated for any of her Auschwitz ills. Vanda was stillborn. And when Luciana and Franco had another child, thirteen years later, it was a boy.

October 1944

'We fought with all our strength to prevent the arrival of winter,' Primo wrote. At the beginning of October there were only twenty-nine of their transport left; and winter meant that seven out of ten of them would die. By the next April only eight would be left . . . In fact, double that number would survive; but only because the end came half-way through the winter. Their calculations were exact.

It was the last act now. It did not seem possible for people to be more desperate; but in October 1944 they were.

Perhaps the most desperate of all were the prisoners of the *Sonderkommandos*, the Special Squads who manned the gas chambers and crematoria: who ushered living people – fellow Jews, sometimes relatives – into the gas chambers, and pulled out their corpses; who cut their hair, extracted the gold from their mouths, transported them to the ovens, removed their ashes, and spread them on the Auschwitz roads. The *Sonderkommandos* of Birkenau contained up to 1,000 men; they were kept isolated, well fed, and sodden with alcohol. Every few months they were themselves murdered and replaced; and each new squad burned the corpses of the one before.

By the end of the summer 400,000 Hungarian Jews had been exterminated, plus the 67,000 Polish Jews of Łódź, the largest surviving ghetto. The number of transports began to decline. At the same time the Russians were approaching. The rumour spread that the gas chambers would soon be closed and their traces obliterated. On 24 September 200 *Sonderkommando* men were told that they were going to work elsewhere, then taken to Auschwitz main camp and murdered. The last *Sonderkommandos* knew they were doomed; and plotted the only mass revolt in the history of Auschwitz.

What happened was secret and confused, and there are several fragmentary, conflicting versions. The Germans uncovered the plan. On Saturday 7 October the senior *Sonderkommando* man was told to list 300 men for 'evacuation'. He refused; and at the subsequent roll-call the revolt began before it was ready. One Kommando attacked the SS with axes, crowbars and stones, and set fire to their barracks, which spread to the roof of their crematorium. A second Kommando saw the flames, launched their own attack, and escaped. Another Kommando was surrounded. At the end of the day one crematorium had been blown up, three or four SS had been killed and a dozen wounded. But all the rebels would be caught and killed: not a single one survived. Altogether about 450 *Sonderkommando* prisoners died; plus all those who helped them, including four women who had smuggled explosives from their factory into Birkenau.

Nonetheless, for the others a tiny crack had opened in the black universe of the camp: 'a few hundred men', Primo wrote, 'helpless and exhausted slaves like ourselves, had found in themselves the strength to act'. And then, of course, it closed back down again, tighter than before.

One evening when they returned from work the gallows were up in the *Appellplatz*. This was nothing new: they were regularly made to watch the punishments for theft, sabotage, attempts to escape. In their nine months in the camp Primo's transport had already witnessed thirteen hangings. But this one was different. The man who was being led out in the glare of the searchlights was one of those who had helped the rebels of the *Sonderkom-mandos*. Two or three others in Monowitz had already been caught and hanged. Now the Germans had rooted him out as well, and chosen him for their ruthless demonstration. But at the last minute he turned the demonstration against them. '*Kameraden, ich bin der Letzte!*' he called out, into the dark and snowy air: *Comrades, I am the last one.*

Primo made this a rare moment of celebration in *If This is a Man*, and one he always wanted remembered: because it showed how doomed resistance was, and yet it happened. 'Perhaps the Germans do not understand,' he wrote, 'that this solitary death, this human death which they have reserved for [this man], brings him not infamy but glory.'

But being Primo Levi, he made it even more a moment of hard truth, and of darkness. One man – a few hundred men and women, a few thousand – did manage, despite the certainty of torture and death, to resist. But all the rest – many thousands, many millions, almost all the prisoners of the Lagers, almost all the citizens of Germany and Austria, of all occupied Europe – all the rest did not. And can we judge them? Primo would judge no one, except himself. *Der Letzte* is a double image for him: of pride, but also of its opposite. This too – daring pain and death, and bearing them bravely when they came – was being a man. And on this measure, Primo Levi was not a man. 'Alberto and I went back into the hut,' he wrote, 'and we could not look each other in the face.'

. . . Because we too are broken, conquered: even if we know how to adapt, even if we have finally learned how to find food, how to resist the cold and fatigue, even if we return home.

We lifted the *menaschka* on to the bunk and divided it, we satisfied the daily ragings of hunger, and now we are oppressed by shame.

By late October even the rulers of Auschwitz knew the end was near. The *Sonderkommando* revolt had been a warning; and when the wind was in the east they could hear the rumble of the front, like an avalanche approaching. The machinery of death would have to be destroyed, as the rebels had foreseen. So the Germans prepared to use it one last time.

If it was to be the last time, it must be especially efficient. The selection of October 1944 was carried out not just in the hospitals but in the Blocks of the whole Lager, Auschwitz I, II and III. In Monowitz alone 850 men were sent to the gas chambers, including eight from Primo's transport.

The prisoners knew for many days that a selection was coming. Those few who were in the least danger already could bribe their way to safety. The others could only wait: and hope, or despair. Most should have despaired. But in fact, Primo tells us, almost everyone hoped. They reassured each other – You'll be all right, you're no *Musulmann*; and besides it's not a selection for the gas chambers but for the convalescent camp at Jaworzno, haven't you heard? 'The young tell the young that all the old will be chosen, the healthy tell the healthy that only the ill will be chosen . . .' Work went on as usual, cold and hunger went on as usual, they could not think very long about anything, even this. So even these days, Primo wrote, 'which in the telling seem as if they ought to have passed every limit of human torment, went by not very differently from the others'.

It happened on a Sunday. Just as the distribution of the midday soup was starting, the bell rang: *Blocksperre*, everyone to be locked in the huts. Undress and wait. After an hour it is the turn of Block 48. They are driven into a small office at one end of the hut: 250 bodies in a room seven yards by four. The doors are closed, all except one, leading to the outside. An SS officer stands there, flanked by the officers of the Block. Each man must run past him, hand him his card, and re-enter the hut through the dormitory door. It is a few steps, a few seconds. In three or four minutes the life or death of 250 men is decided.

Like everyone else, when it was his turn Primo ran as athletically as he could, his head high, his chest out, his muscles tightened. When he glanced back he thought he saw his card being put on the right. But which was the *schlechte Seite*, the bad side – the left or the right?

It was the left, and Primo's card *was* put on the right. He would never be absolutely certain why: probably because it said *Facharbeiter*, Specialist; but possibly just by mistake. Mistakes were made all the time – how could they not be, with everything happening so fast, so carelessly? The man ahead of him was young and strong, yet he was selected. Perhaps, Primo thought, their cards had been confused, and the other had gone in his place.

It is very unlikely: 'Specialists' were usually spared, and he said himself that his card seemed to land on the right. He was, as he once said, 'saved by my trade'. What was tormenting him was his passionate hatred of inequality. That hatred, if it did not begin in Auschwitz, became incandescent there, then set in him for ever, like steel in a forge. What else was at the heart of Fascism but the lust for inequality, what else was brought to its extreme fulfilment here? This lust was the one thing he allowed himself to hate and to fight, not only in his enemies, but even more in himself and his own side. Many years later, when someone asked Primo about the *Untermenschen* of Auschwitz, he replied fiercely, 'We were all *Untermenschen* there.' He famously dissented from Jean Améry's exaltation of the intellectual and his special sufferings in the Lager. We know how furiously he rejected Nico Dallaporta's notion that Providence had chosen him out of many millions to survive, because he could write and testify. He had a horror of any human being's being chosen over any other. That is what lies behind his irrational fear that he might have been saved at the expense of the unknown young man: even by mistake, and one that he had not influenced, or even desired.

And what if you do desire, and try to influence, the choice of yourself over another human being? That is Primo's view of prayer; or was his view there. And it inspired his most violent rejection.

He himself was tempted to it during the selection. In that tiny room groaning with bodies he looked death in the face; and for an instant he longed to ask for help and protection. But he did not. 'You do not change the rules of the game at the end of the match,' he wrote, 'nor when you are losing.'

. . . A prayer under these conditions would have been not only absurd (what rights could I claim? And from whom?) but blasphemous, obscene, laden with the greatest impiety of which a non-believer is capable. I rejected that temptation: I knew that otherwise, if I survived, I would have to be ashamed.

This is a peak moment of Primo Levi's humanist faith. During that ultimate test he remained true to his vision of man in the Canto of Ulysses: rational, responsible for himself. It is also, as such tests are, a peak moment of self-revelation; and one that shows his secret paradox. He thought himself the opposite of courageous – but this refusal to give in to mortal fear was extremely, almost unimaginably courageous. And he thought himself, and strove always to be, ordinary, unspecial, equal to every other man. But this refusal to indulge his own ordinary weakness was surely also an act of great and special pride. He told the story once to a young Catholic, who remarked that turning to God in fear and need was 'very human'. 'But not very brave,' Primo replied. In truth, he wanted to be brave even more than he wanted to be human; he wanted to share humanity's strengths, but not its weaknesses.

Or rather: that was his feeling when he despaired of humanity, but he did not often allow himself to despair. Mostly he wanted the whole of humanity to be brave, more than he wanted it to be human: he wanted the whole of humanity to shed its weaknesses. Given his experience, he thought it was a matter of life and death; and perhaps he was right.

This may explain one of the strangest moments in *If This is a Man*. The selection is over. First, Primo picks out Ziegler: the one who'd said, when spring came, 'The worst is over.' Ziegler has been selected. In Monowitz there was an absurd rule (or a clever, controlling one): in the day or two, or even more, between selection and death, those who were about to die received an extra ration of soup at every meal. When he is refused, Ziegler insists: his card was on the left, everyone saw it, he is entitled to a double ration. At last he's given it, and 'goes quietly to his bunk to eat'.

This is a classic piece of Levi observation, and Levi writing: painfully true, no judgement imposed, heart-rending. But now comes the strange moment. From his top bunk Primo sees an old man, Kuhn, praying. 'Kuhn is thanking God he has not been chosen.' And suddenly he judges, very harshly.

Kuhn is out of his mind. Does he not see Beppo the Greek in the bunk next to him, Beppo who is twenty years old and is going to the gas chamber the day after tomorrow and knows it, and lies there looking fixedly at the light without saying anything, and without even thinking any more? . . .

If I were God, I would spit on Kuhn's prayer.

Is this the same writer, the same book? How can Primo Levi, who will express no anger against the oppressors, express such contemptuous anger against one of the oppressed? Of course his whole book is an act of anger against the oppressors, all the harsher for its restraint. But here he lets that restraint go. Why? Partly because he rarely saw his real oppressors – and the few whom he knew (Pannwitz, Alex the Kapo) do also receive the icy blast of his anger. And partly because Kuhn represents his most bitter disillusion. Yes, he wanted the whole of humanity to shed its weaknesses; but he had given up on the Nazis long ago. Unless and until they repented, he placed them firmly outside the boundaries of the human. But when he entered the camp he still hoped that his fellow victims would remain inside those boundaries, despite everything that was done to them. And they did not. That was why he was so bitterly angry at Kuhn. He judged him as harshly as he would have judged himself, if he had prayed. Which shows the same paradox: how very high was his conception of man, of Kuhn, and of himself.

*   *

The last selection in Auschwitz took Vanda. With fifty others she waited in the Death Block at the end of the Revier. She had managed to be brave for Luciana – or perhaps Luciana could not bear to remember. But now death had come for her, as she had always known it would. She was so small and thin, she looked like a child again. And like a child she flung herself on Bianca Morpurgo, sobbing, begging Bianca to save her – 'I don't want to die. I'm going mad, I'm going mad!' She locked her emaciated arms around Bianca's neck and would not let go.

Bianca had not eaten or slept since the selection began; she was more than half mad herself by now. She went to a medicine cabinet and stole a tube of pills. That night she crept out of the hospital and felt her way along its walls until she came to the Death Block. At the level of the bunk Vanda shared with Laura, another Italian, she called their names, and put the tube into the thin hand that reached out through the bars. 'Take these, they're strong sleeping-pills,' she whispered. The Veronal had come at last: so, perhaps, Vanda believed. So her brother Aldo certainly believed, when Bianca came and told him the story after the war. It helped him, and perhaps it helped Vanda; for that slim hope Bianca had risked her life. But in fact the sleeping-pills cannot have been real; no real medicines of any sort had been left in the Revier for a long time. Perhaps they were aspirins, or placebos left over from some terrible experiment. It is very likely that they did not work. According to the reports that reached Primo and her other friends, Vanda went to the gas chambers at the end of October '*in piena lucidità*', in full consciousness.

November and December

With the blind arbitrariness of time, those same days brought Primo the opposite of Vanda's suffering and death. When he told the story, he made it sound as though it happened rather later: perhaps partly for literary reasons, but perhaps also because he could not bear to remember the cruel contrast between his fate and Vanda's.

On 1 November Lorenzo sent Primo's third and last message home. His health was holding up, he wrote, despite the beginnings of winter. 'I dream of you all night and of our house and of our life as it used to be, and let us hope will be again . . .' 'Please tell the Dalla Volta family of Brescia,' he says, but that cryptic message never got through. The rest is cryptic too – perhaps a plea to Bianca about Rina and Anna Maria: 'Please do all you can, because I have so much faith in you.' But right at the start is the reference to what had happened in the days of Vanda's agony. '*Abbiamo finalmente ricevuto quanto da tempo attendevo*': 'What we've waited for for so long has finally arrived.' A package had come all the way from Italy, and been brought to him by Lorenzo.

This was truly what Primo would later call it – a miracle. Jews were not allowed to receive packages – 'Anyway, from whom could [they] have received them?' If their families were not already dead they were dying, in the last surviving ghettos, in hiding, in other camps, starving like themselves. But not in Italy. Rina had sent ersatz chocolate, biscuits and powdered milk

– things beyond price, beyond memory, in Auschwitz. With their *menaschka* of soup from Lorenzo, Primo and Alberto were already among the saved. With their package from Italy they were, for a time, among the fabulously rich, members of the camp royalty.

To describe the real value of that package, Primo wrote, 'is beyond the powers of ordinary language'. It was impossible, other-worldly, 'like a meteorite, a heavenly object charged with symbols': a link to the past, and to the future. It was also dangerous. If they ate everything at once, as every cell in their bodies demanded, they would be ill, or worse. But if they hoarded it they would attract envy, attack and theft. In the end they gave most of the biscuits to the Kapo and *Blockälteste*,★ as an investment; the rest they divided into small daily rations and hid in their pockets, and in special secret pockets they sewed into the backs of their jackets. But despite their best efforts, the whole camp was soon eyeing them with envy and desire. And one day, when he was in the shower, Primo's jacket was stolen, with everything in it. Almost half their miraculous gift was gone. Immediately they divided what was left in Alberto's jacket, and ate it. Alberto refused to despair. They had eaten more than half, he said, and the other half was not wasted – some other starving wretch had had a good Christmas.† Best of all, this would be their last Christmas in Auschwitz. He was right, as usual.

The Chemical Kommando was going up in the world. It had fifty to sixty members now – and therefore its own latrine: a '*Zweiplatziges Kommando-scheisshaus*', Primo solemnly recorded in the camp language, a two-seater shithouse, for their use alone. 'We are not unaware of this mark of distinction'; but it will remove one of their best chances to meet civilians. ' "*Noblesse oblige*," says "Henri", who has other strings to his bow.'

We have already heard of 'Henri'. He joined the Chemical Kommando late, from a second (or perhaps a first) Chemical Kommando, from which he was expelled, he recalls, for not knowing the formula for benzene.‡ With his arrival Primo's examples of the saved were complete.

★ The Head of the Block, literally the Block Elder.
† This was, I've guessed, Primo's literary touch, which meant making the event two months later than it really was. By Christmas Auschwitz was only three weeks from evacuation, and no package could get through. Indeed, Rina sent a second package, which almost certainly did not arrive.
‡ I have not been able to confirm the existence of another Chemical Kommando. But 'Henri''s memory of moving from one to the other is clear; and I can see no reason why he would want, consciously or unconsciously, to invent or distort it. In fact there were very few Germans in Kommando 98, according to Primo's list, and only one professional German, or rather Austrian, scientist (Gerhard Goldbaum, a sound engineer, to whom Primo would

Already now, in Auschwitz itself and on his return, he began his research into the 'grey zone' of human behaviour, the compromise with evil. And already now he saw that it was inescapable: that in extremity many compromise entirely, and almost all to some extent, apart only from 'a very few superior individuals, made of the stuff of martyrs and saints'. He counted Leonardo among them, and Alberto. But even Alberto – and he himself, though he would not say so; but he too stole no one's bread, and no one died in his place – even they were not wholly innocent, since they helped only each other, and hardened themselves to pity. But many, even most survivors were very much more compromised. Though he would not write a whole book about this for many years, already in *If This is a Man* he wrote a chapter – the one, as we know, of the same name. In it he considers several examples. One is Elias Lindzin; who is, however, a limiting case, since he is insane. He does not compromise with evil, he is evil already; in Auschwitz the world has compromised with him, and all who adapt to it completely become like him: insane.

Another is 'Alfred L.', whose real name was Alfred Fisch. Fisch had been a Prominent in the normal world, the director of an important chemical company; and he determined to become one here. He knew (Primo wrote) that there is only a short step between seeming powerful and being so. In order to become a Prominent, therefore, he made himself look like one: clean, well-shaven, prosperous. It cost him a great proportion of his bread and energy, and might well have cost him his life. But he stuck to his plan with rigid self-discipline; and it worked. When the Chemical Kommando was formed it was clear to the *Arbeitsdienst* who was the Prominent. The post of *Technische Leiter*, Technical Head, was created for Fisch, and he became an analyst in the laboratory of the Styrene Department. Later, Primo said, he was appointed to examine all the new candidates for the Kommando: 'which he always did with extreme severity, especially towards those in whom he scented possible rivals'.

Fisch was not insane, he was not violent, he did not steal. But he adapted to evil, and made it his own; he played the Nazi game by Nazi rules, with no sign of regret, at least to Primo. His real crime, though, goes even deeper;

---

dedicate the story 'Un giallo del Lager'; see Chapter 15). The three chemists chosen from among them were, as Primo points out, 'three "*Franzosen*"', a Pole from Belgium, a Romanian from France, and an Italian. But there must have been many chemists and other scientists among the German Jewish prisoners; and it would make sense if another Chemical Kommando (or even more than one) had been formed earlier, containing people who were not only chemists but German, or German-speaking. This was true of 'Henri' himself, who had been born in Berlin.

and brings him close to 'Henri'. What it is, I think, emerges from a comparison to the hero of one of Primo's 'moments of reprieve': 'Rappoport', whose real name was probably Leon Treistmann.

Rappoport 'lived in the camp like a tiger in the jungle', Primo says: he was shrewd and violent, he corrupted the strong and preyed on the weak. Yet Primo does not condemn him. Why? Because Rappoport has a plan too, or rather a theory, of survival; but a very different one from Fisch. While he could, he tells Primo, he ate, drank and made love; he studied and travelled the world. So he accumulated a treasure of good things; they balance the horror around him, and no one can take them away. He has an instinctive, animal vitality, and even here he is 'happy', 'like the adventurers of long ago'. That word 'happy' is very important: unless it was perverse and twisted, like Elias's, happiness was a virtue to Primo Levi. Fisch, by contrast, is 'joyless'. Rappoport is like one of Primo's opposites gone wrong; Fisch is like himself gone wrong. Rappoport is open, Fisch is closed. Rappoport is bad, but Fisch is inhuman. Rappoport loves life; Fisch loves only himself. That is his real crime – an absolute egotism, calculating and cold.*

'Henri' is somewhere between the two, and therefore the most complex and interesting of all. Fisch was like the dark, dour side of Primo gone wrong – his pride and isolation, his strenuous and self-sufficient will. 'Henri' was something still more worrying: Primo's escape route gone wrong, his whole project in Auschwitz and in life – his fascinated, dedicated interest in other people.

'Henri''s real name was Paul Steinberg. When he was arrested, at not quite seventeen, he was much older in experience than Primo. His family was well-to-do, and he was highly gifted and intelligent. He lived in the XVIe Arrondissement in Paris, he went to a top *lycée*, and he could have lived the life of a brilliant, cosseted student. But he had begun with loss. He had been exiled from his first home in Germany; and his mother had died giving birth to him, as his father never let him forget. Paul found his own way from the start. He preferred the racetrack to school, and was a clever, daring gambler. He refused to wear a yellow star. When he was arrested he was alone.

---

* The case of Fisch is extremely interesting, not only about survivors, but about Primo. For it shows, he says, *'how vain is the myth of equality among men'*. But this myth is his own. It is the founding myth of his humanist faith – that all human beings deserve equal respect, and if not equal, at least not grossly unequal treatment, simply because they are human. The case of Fisch shows how much support there is in reality for the other and easier path. And that Primo Levi recognized this from the start of his writing life: that his commitment to equality, as to much else, was a moral one, in the face of a reality he always knew to be different.

At Drancy he met Philippe Hagenauer, who was six months older. They entered Buna-Monowitz together on 10 October, four months before Primo, and remained together until Philippe died. Everyone thought Paul and Philippe were brothers, including Primo. After Philippe's death Paul reverted to the isolation he was used to; and fought to live with all his many and great resources. He spoke perfect German, with the best Berlin accent, perfect French, good English and Russian. He was young and attractive, with deep, dark eyes. He had an excellent education, and a gambler's cool nerves. Above all, he had his powerful mind. And like Fisch, he made a plan.

He did not often talk – and never, of course, about the details of his operations or the identity of his protectors. But he and Primo did occasionally speak on the way to and from the Buna; and one day Paul explained to Primo in detail the method he had worked out for his survival.

Like everyone else, he stole and organized – only better than everyone else. He had a monopoly of the English products in the camp, extracted from the British prisoners of war with his excellent English: and with a single English cigarette, Primo noted, you could make enough not to starve for a day. Steinberg regularly acquired an extra three to seven litres of soup daily, which, like a rich uncle, he dispensed to a small group of French friends.

But his own invention, his special skill, was pity. Pity was, in Primo's words, 'his instrument of penetration'. He had discovered that even the brutish rulers of Auschwitz could feel pity – perhaps they especially needed to feel it, from time to time. You just needed to find '*leur point faible*', their weak point; and to know how to appeal to it. Nobody was better at this than Paul. 'Psychologically,' he says, 'I practised all the arts of the circus: lion tamer, tightrope walker, not to say conjuror . . .' He disarmed one *Reichsdeutsche* by asking him about his son at the front, another by showing him the scars on his legs. To Pannwitz he displayed a passion for science; to Elias a human interest. His protectors were legion – English soldiers, French civilian workers, German political prisoners; at least four *Blockältester*, and the *Lagerälteste* himself – the head prisoner of the whole camp, who was a notorious murderer; a cook, an SS man, and several of the prisoner doctors in KB, who took him in whenever he wanted.

All this Primo records with sober wonder; but also with dismay. Part of his dismay is sexual: he clearly suspects that Paul used his body as well as his mind to win favours. But it is not only sex. What Primo sees in Paul is the deepest form of deceit. He appeals precisely to the humanity in people – only to exploit it, cheat it, and not return it. Of course no one would expect him to return any real human feeling to the *Lagerälteste*, to Pannwitz or Elias. But what about the prisoner-doctors, what about *someone*, beyond perhaps that one 'brother', lost many months ago? Paul shows no human feeling for anyone. Sometimes he seems 'warm and near', Primo says: 'communication, even affection, seems possible.' But a moment later the human being is gone, leaving only the hunter: 'hard and distant, enclosed in armour, the enemy of all, inhumanly cunning and incomprehensible like the serpent in Genesis'.

It is a harsh verdict – as harsh as the verdict on Kuhn. Is it fair? Steinberg did not steal from his companions; he didn't need to. He was not violent: he even remembers with shame the one time he lifted a hand against someone, though Primo would not have known that. Paul himself accepts Primo's description of him as a merciless manipulator. But he is less willing to accept Primo's judgement. Primo wrote in *If This is a Man* that he did not want to see 'Henri' again. He changed his mind later, but in fact they never re-met. If they had, what would Paul have said in his defence? 'I would have said that I had no choice,' he replies. He clung to life in the best way he could, using the best gifts he had. 'Is it,' he asks, 'so wrong to survive?'

Well, there were better and worse ways of surviving, and Paul Steinberg's was not one of the worst. He was absolutely and exclusively selfish: but so were most people who survived (and many who didn't as well). If you were not selfish you died – though that rule was broken too, for example by Primo himself, with Alberto. There were very few men in Auschwitz, on either side. But in *If This is a Man* Primo was more disappointed in the victims than the oppressors, because he had still had hopes for them. Those hopes were, perhaps, illusory; in any case they tell us more about Primo Levi than about humanity. I do not think he would have judged Steinberg so harshly later, when he came to accept the size of the 'grey zone'; and when he insisted on an absolute distinction between victims and oppressors, on Steinberg's own grounds: because the latter still had a choice, while the former had none.

But *If This is a Man* was his testament to a higher requirement on all men. And Steinberg failed that requirement at the most fundamental level, because he treated other people as things. That was the original sin that led to the Lager; and Primo could not forgive it.

Perhaps, too, there was a private element in his dismay. In all their talks, he wrote in *If This is a Man*, he felt 'an instrument in ["Henri"'s] hands'. And not only would Steinberg use him as he pleased, *he would know exactly how to.*

. . . I felt penetrated, subjugated, almost drugged – I felt he knew everything about me, and about everyone. I felt diminished by him; I don't often feel I'm being X-rayed . . . That is why I didn't want to see him again.

Even in Auschwitz – especially in Auschwitz – Primo Levi wanted to be the X-rayer, not the X-rayed. He wanted to study Steinberg, not have

Steinberg study him. There was a great difference: he studied Steinberg in order to understand Auschwitz, and the human race; whereas Steinberg studied him for use, for his next meal. (In fact he found nothing to use, and more or less dismissed Primo from his mind.) Nonetheless, Primo did also use Steinberg, and treat him as an object: as a bad example in his book. It was almost like the revenge he would take, in another book, on the Sportsman. Auschwitz could not change the deepest needs and habits of a lifetime: not in Paul Steinberg, who remains a brilliant, charming calculator; nor in Primo Levi either.

By November the snow was deep on the ground, and huge blue icicles hung from the pipes of the Buna. The Germans changed to their winter clothing; even the outside Kommandos got their heavier canvas jackets and their striped overcoats. But Kommando 98 were 'Specialists', who in theory worked indoors; they were left in their thin summer uniforms.

'So far,' Primo wrote, 'the advantages of the Chemical Kommando have been limited to the following: the others have received overcoats, while we have not; the others carry 100-pound sacks of cement, while we carry 125-pound sacks of phenylbeta.' All summer there had been rumours that the Polymerization laboratory would choose its analysts from among them; but they didn't believe it any more. The Buna was silent; much of it lay in ruins, including half of *Bau*★ 939, the home of the Polymerization Department. Auschwitz could not last much longer, but neither could they.

And then it happened. One icy dawn the rest of the Kommando marched off to their jobs, leaving only the phenylbeta workers, including Primo. Dully they waited for the order to move; when Jupp the Kapo said instead: 'Dr Pannwitz has communicated to the *Arbeitsdienst* that three *Häftlinge* have been chosen for the laboratory: 169509, Brackier; 175633, Kandel; and 174517, Levi.'

'For an instant,' Primo wrote, 'my ears ring and the Buna whirls around me.' Men are not equal, their fates are not equal, and at that moment he could not desire it. *He has been chosen.* There is no water or electricity, the ration has been reduced still further, there is scarlet fever, diphtheria and typhus in the camp. But the Russians are fifty miles away. The French civilian workers walk upright, the British prisoners of war are giving the *Häftlinge* V-signs again. He will be indoors, no one will beat him, there will be fabulous new things to steal. If he weren't such an old camp hand by now, he might even begin to hope.

★

★ Building.

When Primo first entered the laboratory the smell hit him 'like a whip', and he was back home again, in his fourth year at university, in 'the mild air of May in Italy'. Then the vision was gone, and he was still in Auschwitz.

The work was both easy and not easy. It was easy because it never really began: most of their time was spent dismantling the apparatus when the air-raid siren sounded, and setting it up again at the all-clear. It was not easy because they had few raw materials left; once when Primo was told to prepare a reagent the water stopped, and he used grey snow from the windowsills instead, to Pannwitz's scowling suspicion. It was not easy because they were still slaves, and all the dirtiest jobs fell to them. And it was not easy just because it was, after all, so very easy. Each day, Primo wrote, as he stepped out of the murderous wind into the shelter of the laboratory, instead of joy he felt 'the pain of remembering, the old ferocious suffering of feeling a man again, which attacks me like a dog the moment my conscience emerges from the dark'. Just because he was safer, he felt responsible again, and guilty; for being safer than the others, for being chosen.

But that was in the moments of truce. Most of the time the battle continued, even here, because he knew that at the first error, at the first serious scowl from Pannwitz, it could all be over, and he could be thrown back into the snow and wind. And it was so wonderful here! When the heating was on it was 65° in the laboratory; even when it failed, as it often did, he was still inside thick walls. He sat still for much of the day. He had a new shirt, new underpants, a new and better-fitting striped suit; he was shaved once a week, and later twice; he may even have had a pair of leather shoes. He was given his own drawer, a notebook and pencil, even a book on analytic method to refresh his memory. When he wanted to go to the lavatory he only had to ask; the head of the laboratory, Herr Stawinoga, never said no, and never asked questions, even if he was away for a very long time. The reason for that, of course, was the best part of all: the chance to meet civilians, and to steal. Primo stole soap, petrol and alcohol, cotton, acid and glycerin. He stole brooms, sawed them into pieces, and carried them into the camp strapped to his thighs; there he put them together again with tin-plate, hammer and nails, also stolen. He stole a cork-borer, with which Alberto cut out small circles from the coloured labels he was fitting to pipes, and sold them as shower tickets to the bureaucratic *Blockältester*. He stole the cerium rods out of which he and Alberto fashioned their flints, which alone bought them two months of life each. And he stole the pipettes which saved his life but not Alberto's, because the payment was a bowl of soup infected with scarlet fever.

In the laboratory there were eight or ten women workers, German, Polish and Ukrainian. So this suffering returned to Primo too. 'We know what we look like,' he wrote. And he was filthy and covered in fleas, and he smelled of death. The girls were healthy and clean, they wore beautiful clothes, their long blonde hair was carefully waved. They filed their nails, they sang, they talked about home. And at best they ignored the three chemist-slaves. They never spoke to them; when they heard the clatter of their clogs on the shining floor they looked away. When they swept, they swept over their feet as if they were not there. The worst of the German girls was a sullen adolescent called Fräulein Drechsel, who wore a swastika badge, and whose dull eyes, when they were forced to rest on them, filled with hostility, revulsion and fear. Fräulein Liczba, the Polish storekeeper, was worse still: when Primo asked her a question she turned away angrily, and said something which contained the word *Stinkjude*. Only one of the Ukrainian girls was different, and spoke normally, even kindly, to the three Jews. Her name was Sina Rasinko; Primo tried to find out what happened to her after the war, but without success.

With the Germans who ran the laboratory his experiences were at least sometimes different. Pannwitz we already know, and so did Primo; he did not change. But there was, for example, a civilian chemist who came several times to inspect their work. He was a tall, heavy man in his late thirties, whose name, Primo would say, was Dr Müller. In fact his name was Meyer; and he had just arrived at Auschwitz, in mid-November. He spoke to Primo three times: each time 'with a shyness rare in that place, as if he were ashamed of something'. The first time was about work. The second time he asked Primo why he was unshaven; to which Primo replied that none of them had a razor, or any other personal possession, and that they were shaved by order once a week. The third time Meyer gave Primo a note authorizing him to be shaved twice a week, and to be issued with a pair of leather shoes: that is how Primo came by these two privileges. Then, using the formal *Sie*, Meyer asked, 'Why do you look so worried?' At the time Primo merely thought, in the harsh camp slang, '*Der Mann hat keine Ahnung*': 'This guy hasn't got a clue.' No one could be so ignorant unless he chose to be; despite the shoes, Meyer was still an enemy. But later he thought that there was in Meyer's ignorance at least an effort to escape it, like a bird trying to break out of a cage. He never forgot Dr Meyer. Many years later he would come across him again, in an extraordinary reckoning between master and slave. We will see what happened then, and whether the bird ever wholly escaped its cage.

Then there was Herr Stawinoga, the head of the laboratory, a German Pole. He was a doctor not of chemistry but of philology – '*ne pas chercher à comprendre*', Primo said, quoting the reminder Iss Clausner had scratched in the bottom of his bowl. Stawinoga was still young, but he looked sad and tired, as though 'suffering in his flesh for the ruin that surrounds him'. He spoke to the Jews rarely but courteously, even calling them 'Monsieur'; he let them leave whenever they liked; after the incident with Fräulein Liczba he told Primo to deal only with him. Then one day the air-raid warning sounded, and they all ran down the stairs as usual: the civilians to the bunkers, the three prisoners to whatever fold they could find in the freezing ground. Outside the bombers were already visible – hundreds of them, this was going to be a tremendous raid. And suddenly Stawinoga stopped them. 'You three come with me,' he said. Astonished, they obeyed. At the entrance to the bunker the guard barred their way. 'You can go in,' he told Stawinoga, 'the others beat it.' 'They're with me,' Stawinoga said, 'it's all of us or none', and tried to push inside. The guard resisted, and he and Stawinoga actually began to fight. Stawinoga would certainly have had the worst of it, Primo noted; but the all-clear sounded, the planes had flown on, the raid was not for Auschwitz. – Now that, Primo would write to Meyer more than twenty years later, was an act of real courage. He asked what had become of Stawinoga; but Meyer did not know. He did not remember him.

Finally, there was a young German woman: Frau Mayer. In *If This is a Man* Primo says she was the secretary; in *Moments of Reprieve*, the laboratory technician. Already in *If This is a Man* we sense that she was an exception to the rule among the girls: Primo dreams of explaining himself to her, of telling her that he too was once a free man. In *Moments of Reprieve* it is confirmed. Like Sina Rasinko, like Herr Stawinoga, Frau Mayer never showed contempt to him, or hostility. Then one day there was a particularly dirty job to do, which according to the rules should have fallen to her; Primo, who was already filthy, did it instead. When he got up off the floor she came close to him. Since his hands were already dirty, she whispered, could he repair the puncture on her bicycle? Naturally, she would pay him for his trouble.

Now this request, Primo wrote, which seems so ordinary, was in that place and time as rare as any act of resistance, which in fact it was. Frau Mayer had broken the law, by speaking to him about something other than work; she had made a contract with him, 'and a contract is made between equals'; she had said 'please'. It was extremely dangerous, but Primo agreed. He made the repair; and Frau Mayer, in great secrecy, gave him a most generous reward – a hard-boiled egg, like 'Henri''s, and four lumps of sugar. As she slipped him the package, she whispered to him again. Primo thought for a long time about what she had said: '*Christmas will soon be here.*' What could that mean, to a prisoner and a Jew? Not the compliments of the season. It meant something hardly any Germans dared to say then, even to themselves; and Frau Mayer had said it to him.

*   *

At the end of December Primo saw Lorenzo for the last time. In this final period Lorenzo was working near *Bau* 939, and Primo could take the soup once more from his own hands. On that day Lorenzo appeared as usual through the snow, walking with his long, patient stride. But when he handed over the mess tin Primo saw that it was dented, and the soup full of grit and sand. He was sorry the soup was dirty, Lorenzo said. Primo asked why; but Lorenzo just shook his head, and didn't reply. Then he left; and a few days later, on 1 January, he set off home for Italy.

It was only when Primo himself reached home that he learned what had happened. That morning the Italian workers' camp had been hit in a raid; a bomb had fallen close to Lorenzo, burying the mess tin, and bursting one of his eardrums. 'But he had the soup to deliver,' Primo wrote, 'and had come to work anyway.' Very likely those were Lorenzo's own words.

A week or so later, looking for something to steal, Primo found the fatal pipettes in a drawer. He slipped a dozen into the secret pocket in his jacket and took them back to the camp. After roll-call he ran to KB and offered them to a Pole he knew, who worked in the Infectious Diseases Ward. The Pole said it was too late, he had no bread left, all he could offer was a bit of soup: that is, it was too late for Primo to approach anyone else, he would have to take what he could get. Primo agreed.

The Pole disappeared, and came back with a curious object: a bowl half full of soup, not horizontally but vertically. It was so cold the soup had frozen, and half of it had been eaten from the side, like a cake. But who could have left half a cake of soup, in that hell of starvation? 'Almost certainly someone who had died halfway through the meal,' Primo answered himself. And in that ward, almost certainly someone who had died of a terrible disease: diphtheria, probably, or scarlet fever, both of which were raging through the camp.

Now, Primo and Alberto were still alive, thanks to their extra rations; but they too were starving. Such niceties as fear of infection had dropped out of their calculations long ago; besides, it had never happened. Primo bore the cake of soup back to the barrack in triumph, and he and Alberto devoured it.

A few days later Alberto was still quite normal. But Primo had a high fever, his throat was on fire, he could hardly swallow. Dozens of others had the same symptoms; they knew perfectly well what it was. Primo had scarlet fever. Alberto, who had had it in childhood, did not. Between 'the two Italians', the twins who had shared everything, a small difference had finally appeared.

You were only allowed to report sick in the evenings; so that morning Primo went to work as usual, reeling with fever. And that day of all days, he was given a special task: to teach Fräulein Drechsel a new analytic method. The Russians were at the gate, now he might die before they came, and he had to hand on his knowledge to a Nazi. The analytical method involved a pipette – a twin of those which had brought this difference upon him. 'I believe,' he wrote, telling the story, 'this was the only time I have deliberately done someone wrong.' He put the pipette between his lips, to show how it was done; then he handed it to Fräulein Drechsel, only pretending to wipe it clean. 'In short, I did everything I could to infect her.'

Whether or not he succeeded he never knew. That evening he himself entered the Infectious Ward of KB. It was 11 January 1945.

Ten Days

11–16 January: Infectious Ward

He was such an old hand by now that he managed to enter KB with all his belongings: a wire belt, a spoon, needle and thread, five buttons, and eighteen of the cerium rods he and Alberto had been working on. He also got an upper bunk to himself, and the sulpha drugs he needed. He felt strong enough, and rich enough, to survive the scarlet fever; and also the selections, which he did not know no longer happened. He was anxious only not to lose his place in the laboratory. The Russians might be near, but you could count on nothing. He set himself to rest and recover.

The Infectious Ward was divided into several rooms, roughly by diseases: one for dysentery, one for TB, and so on. Primo's was Room 8. It was very small – nine feet by fifteen – and already contained twelve other patients, at various stages of typhus, diphtheria, scarlet fever. Five of these were 'high numbers': French non-Jews, only recently arrived. Two of these, Arthur Ducarne and Charles Conreau, had scarlet fever like Primo.

Charles and Arthur were the least ill, still so close to the normal world that Primo thought they had only entered the camp a few days before. In fact it was a few weeks; but they had spent the first two in quarantine, and the rest in KB. Arthur was a small, thin man in his forties, a peasant farmer, and a courier in the Resistance. Charles was, as Primo says in *If This is a Man*, a thirty-two-year-old schoolmaster. After Lorenzo, Alberto and Pikolo, he would become Primo's last image in Auschwitz of a man.

Charles Conreau came from the small village of Lusse near Provenchères. He was tall, big-nosed, very gentle. Instead of a shirt, Primo noted, he had been given 'a summer vest, ridiculously short'. Though this was certainly

Charles

true, it also instantly conjures up Charles's presence: innocent, out of place in this hell, but bigger and stronger than he knew.

Though he was so gentle, he too had joined the Resistance. He had been arrested along with nine others of his group, including two of his own pupils; plus thirty ordinary citizens of Provenchères and the surrounding villages. Only five of them would return; from among the Maquis only Charles.

When they had arrived in mid-December, the Alsatian Dr Waitz had ordered his fellow-Frenchmen into quarantine. Then, towards the end of the two-week period – just in time, like Primo – Charles had fallen ill. He was transferred to KB with a dangerous sinus infection and scarlet fever. Dr Waitz remembered the tall young schoolmaster, and arranged for him to be operated on immediately. Dr Coënca from Salonika did the operation in a crowded corridor. This, together with his providential scarlet fever, saved Charles's life. He arrived in *Stube* 8 of the Infectious Ward weak and already very thin, but ready to recover. There he met Arthur, whom he remembered from the Quarantine Block. They were both French, they were both recovering, their bonds to life had never been broken. In that world of the dead and dying they instinctively joined forces, and took a bunk together.

In the bunk above them Primo lay for four or five days, too sick to eat, rarely speaking. One day Charles and Arthur heard him say something in French to one of the others, and tried to talk to him. He was still obeying the rules of survival: trust no one, speak only if it is useful. These two were 200,000s, no use at all. He didn't reply. But no one could doubt Charles's simple honesty for long. As soon as Primo had any energy to spare he began to exchange a few words with the two Frenchmen.

16 January: Samuelidis

On the fifth day the barber of KB came to shave them. His name, Primo tells us in *If This is a Man*, was Askenazi, and he was a Greek from Salonika. Before he came into their room he talked for a long time with a fellow Greek, Dr Samuelidis. From his top bunk Primo saw them, and knew something was afoot. He must find out what it was. Though he was still very weak, he made himself climb down and take his turn to be shaved. Was there any news? he asked Askenazi. Askenazi winked, and pointed out the window, to the west. '*Morgen, alle Kameraden weg,*' he said: 'Tomorrow, everybody leave.'

Primo looked around at his fellow patients. They were all too far gone; they would not care. Even he could not care properly, but only distantly, in the manner of the Lager. If he were normal, he knew, this would be a very moving moment. He turned to the two normal ones, and told them.

That afternoon Samuelidis came and told all of them. He was an intelligent and cultured man, Primo said, but selfish and calculating. 'He added,' Primo told Jean, in his first letter after the war, 'that it was not in our interest to stay in KB, in the hands of the SS.' Very likely he delivered this piece of advice sardonically, since it was perfectly plain that no one in the room was capable of walking much further than the door.[*] But the two Hungarian boys immediately began to talk feverishly. One went out, and returned with an armful of rags and two pairs of broken-down shoes. Primo tried to tell them that, however dangerous it was to stay, in their state it was even more dangerous to go. But they did not listen, the eyes they turned on him were wild with fear. For a moment he even thought they might be right; and if he had not been so weak he might have gone with them. That night they climbed out of the window and disappeared. He learned later that, unable to keep up, they had been shot by the SS in the first hours of the march.

Finally, very late, Samuelidis returned. He was well-equipped, with a rucksack and a woollen balaclava. He tossed a book on to Primo's bed.

---

[*] In *If This is a Man* the 'Greek doctor' says that probably the Germans would leave them to their fate, and not kill them — but without any effort 'to hide the fact that he thought otherwise'. Perhaps Primo was uncertain which had been Samuelidis's apparent message; but the real one was clear.

'Keep it, Italian,' he said. 'You can give it back to me when we meet again.' Why did he say that? Primo wondered. For the last time his deep anger was kindled by a fellow prisoner, who should have shown solidarity, and did not. He did not name Samuelidis in *If This is a Man*, as he did not name 'Henri', or (probably) 'Kuhn'. But 'Even today,' he wrote, 'I hate him for those words. He knew that we were doomed.'

17 January: Alberto

And finally Alberto came, to say goodbye through the window. He could not come in: *Eintritt Verboten* it said on the door, and with good reason. As always, Alberto was cheerful, confident, full of resource; somewhere he had found a good strong pair of leather shoes. As always, too, his courage and confidence passed like a spark to Primo. 'We did not think we would be separated for long,' he wrote. No one knew what would happen, anything was possible; Alberto had his health and his shoes, but Primo had his luck, his intelligence, his flints. They had survived against all the odds together, and they could survive apart. It must have been something like this that they thought, looking at each other through the window. Primo does not spell it out. But they said very little; they did not need to. They said goodbye.

18 January: The March

The prisoners of Monowitz thought they would be leaving on 17 January, but nothing happened that day. At dawn on the 18th they were given their ration of bitter 'coffee', 250 grams of grey bread, and a piece of so-called sausage. In the later afternoon they were assembled on the *Appellplatz*. March in fives, anyone who falls out of line will be shot. Five hundred grams of bread and a bit of margarine for each man. The count came to just over 10,200, including 110 Italians. As night fell, they marched out of the camp for the last time.

They joined perhaps 10,000 more from other Auschwitz camps: altogether between 50,000 and 60,000 Auschwitz prisoners would soon be on the roads. They marched all night through the snow, in temperatures of more than 20 degrees below freezing, and the crucifying Polish wind. At six in the morning, after almost fifty kilometres, they stopped for a few hours in a place called Nikolai. They marched on again all day, until they reached the camp of Gleiwitz, at around ten o'clock on the night of the 19th. They had walked nearly seventy kilometres, over forty miles, in just over twenty-four hours. It is impossible to say how many thousands fell by the wayside, were shot and died, already in this first stage.

But Alberto and Franco Sacerdoti were still alive. Silvio Barabas saw them both at Nikolai, in an abandoned brick factory where all three had taken refuge. He had fully expected to see Primo too. When Alberto told him that Primo had remained in KB, Silvio was certain, like Samuelidis, that he was doomed. Probably he was already dead.

The camp of Gleiwitz was built for 500 internees, and already contained thousands. Many Monowitz *Häftlinge* failed to squeeze into the huts. In the morning those inside could not open the doors, because the ones nearest them had frozen to death; when at last they emerged they found hundreds of corpses outside.

Still Alberto and Franco survived. The prisoners spent two days at Gleiwitz. Nothing to eat until the afternoon of the second day, Sunday the 21st; then the usual dark block of bread and slice of fake sausage. That day they were funnelled down a narrow corridor, in a last selection. Outside there stood a train. A hundred and ten carriages, not cattle-cars this time but coal wagons, open to the skies.

The Russians were so close they could hear their artillery fire. Most of them tried not to be forced on to that train; to stay at Gleiwitz and be liberated by the Russians. Reznik, Jean Samuel, Mendi the rabbi, Silvio Barabas all failed. For the next five days and five nights they underwent an experience so terrible that for Jean, for example, it has blocked out and buried everything that went before. A hundred, 120, even 140 men were packed into a space that could hold at most fifty. You could not sit, you could hardly stand; if you fell, you were instantly trampled. They were fed only twice in five days; for water they drank the snow that fell on them. Perhaps a third died; at first the corpses were removed, but for the last two days they were left where they were, and the living stood on them in the day and slept on them at night. 'We were,' Jean says, 'three-quarters insane.' But somehow he, and the others too, survived.

Alberto and Franco must have managed not to be pushed on to that dreadful train. They were young, and in good condition; they would surely have survived the transport. But when it arrived in Buchenwald Silvio looked for them, and did not find them. They had disappeared. Then, not long after the liberation, he heard what he still believes to be the explanation. In Gleiwitz the Nazis took all the prisoners who remained behind into a forest, and shot them.

Primo also heard this story, or a similar one. Another version said that during an air-raid some thousands of Monowitz marchers scattered in a forest, then tried to stay there, in hiding; but the SS surrounded them and opened fire, killing all but 100.

Whichever version was true, this much seems clear: sometime on or soon after 21 January 1945, in a forest near Gleiwitz, the Germans shot most of the Monowitz prisoners whom they had not managed to force on to the transport for Buchenwald. Both Alberto and Franco were still alive on that day; after it neither was seen again by anyone who knew him. There would be many stories and rumours about Alberto, all eagerly investigated by his family, and one, as we shall see, believed. For most of that year Primo also continued to hope that Alberto might have survived. But by the time he came to write the story of the 'Ten Days', in late 1945, he had already accepted that the hope was vain. That was his Vanda-like surrender to reality, his inability to delude himself in the normal way. But he was right, for neither Alberto nor Franco ever returned. Having been strong enough to avoid the transport, they were almost certainly killed in the Gleiwitz forest that day.

18–19 January: 'Remorques'

Primo may not have known it yet, but Leonardo was also in KB. Exactly a month before, on 18 December, he and his friend Aldo Moscati had at last been taken on as nurses, just in time to save their lives. Now Leonardo had stayed behind, his legs too swollen to walk; together with Aldo, who had been ordered to remain as a doctor, and put in charge of two Blocks full of the sick and dying.

For a day or two the camp continued. The central heating plant was abandoned, and the temperature in the huts dropped by the hour. But the rations of soup and bread continued to appear, and the watch-towers were still manned, the SS were still there. They patrolled the empty camp, their submachine guns at the ready. Then they made a tour of KB. They appointed a Kapo from among the non-Jews in each Block; and ordered a list of all patients to be drawn up immediately, divided into Jews and non-Jews.

Everyone knew what that meant. The order had certainly been given to leave no witnesses, and in particular no Jews. 'In the evening we wondered why they hadn't killed us during the day,' Leonardo said. 'In the morning we wondered why they hadn't killed us during the night.' Primo decided that since they were going to die anyway, they might as well die warm, and fetched blankets for them from the Dysentery Ward. He was not afraid; or only in the detached manner of the Lager, as though it were happening to someone else.

On the afternoon of the 19th he picked up the book Samuelidis had thrown at him like a challenge. It was, he saw, a French novel: *Remorques*, by Roger Vercel. He had never heard of it, nor of Vercel. But as soon as he began to read he forgot Samuelidis, the SS and their death list, even his hunger. *Remorques* was a strangely perfect book for him. It told the adventures of a salvage vessel on the high seas, its rescue missions, its own brushes with death and disaster: men saving themselves and others, with their ingenuity and their bare hands. One day it would provide a model for his own technological hero, Libertino Faussone. Then and there, perhaps, it provided a model for him.

All that night, 'the Germans hesitated between killing us and running away'; and all that night he read. Until about eleven he could see an armed SS man in one corner. Then suddenly there was the roar of planes, and a huge explosion, very near. The windows broke, the walls shook, the lights went out, and he could see no more. Three bombs had fallen directly on the camp. Many of the huts were burning. Dozens of patients came begging for shelter, but they had no room; they barricaded the door. 'They dragged themselves elsewhere,' Primo wrote, 'lit by the flames', their bandages streaming behind them. The next morning there was no SS man in the corner. They stumbled outside, into the snow and the smouldering ruins. The Germans had made their choice: the towers were empty.

No one will ever know for certain why, against all logic, the SS left over 800 prisoners alive in Monowitz, the largest number in any camp. Hitler had ordered their extermination; Baer, the last Commandant of Auschwitz, had repeated it; in other camps, including other sub-camps of Auschwitz, many thousands who could not walk were killed. Himmler may have given conflicting orders; but these probably concerned only the Jews of Theresienstadt, whom he was hoping to use in a secret deal with the Red Cross. If any countermanding orders *were* given in Buna-Monowitz, they probably came from the SS doctor Wirths, who had increasingly been helping prisoners, and who would soon hang himself.

The most likely explanation is the oldest – chaos, confusion, fear. The Russian advance was extremely rapid, and from an unexpected quarter; only a day after the others had gone came the terror and destruction of that air-raid. There was no electricity, no heating, no water; there was nothing left. In such circumstances even the orderly German soldier – especially the orderly German soldier – may crack.

20 January: Heat

It was extremely cold. They would need a stove, coal, wood, food. Primo, Charles and Arthur formed their own salvage team.

The scene outside was black, grey, blasted. The snow of Auschwitz had always been grey, from the smoke and soot of the factories; with the ash from the fires it was greyer still. The doors and windows of the huts gaped open. Ragged, skeletal survivors ransacked them for food and wood, smashed the comfortable lairs of the *Blockältester*, roasted potatoes in the embers of the fires, glaring at anyone who came near.

In the ruins of the Prominents' Block Primo and Charles found what they had been looking for: a cast-iron stove, still usable. Primo staggered back to their hut with the heavy stove on a wheelbarrow. When he was halfway there a lone SS man roared into the camp on a motorcycle. Primo froze with terror; but still his luck held. The SS did not see him; he wheeled round behind a hut, and roared off again.

By the time he reached KB, black spots were dancing in front of Primo's eyes. Arthur had passed out in the snow and cold; Charles found him and carried him home. But despite their exhaustion they could not stop now. For hours they worked, mending the windows, setting up the stove. The flue was blocked; with infinite care, they prodded sticks of wood through it until a passage was cleared. At last it was ready. They lit the stove; and slowly, slowly, the blessed heat spread through the room.

At that moment something happened. Towarowski, who was twenty-three and dying of typhus, proposed that everyone give a piece of the bread they had left to the three workers; and they all agreed. It was not only gratitude; they were afraid that the three might abandon them, and save only themselves. But it was a human gesture: the recognition of their dependence, and the offer of a bond. It meant, Primo wrote, that they were becoming men again. It meant that the Lager was dead.

Primo, Charles and Arthur accepted the bond. They stayed in *Stube* 8, even though it was crawling with disease, and extremely dangerous. That night, exhausted, at peace, they sat and began to talk. His own return from *Häftling* to man was not slow, as Primo wrote. It was quick, irresistible, almost immediate.

21 January: Light

Since his brush with death in the snow, Arthur preferred to stay indoors. He took on the cooking, cleaning and care of the patients; Charles and Primo remained the hunter-gatherers.

On their second day of freedom they found two large frozen piles of cabbages and turnips, and with immense effort hacked off about 100 pounds with an axe. Charles found a large can of water, also frozen; for a day or two they could cook in good clean water, instead of the grey melted snow.

In the afternoon they explored the surgery. It had already been looted; not a bottle or basin remained. But then Primo saw something the looters had missed: a truck battery. He touched the poles with his knife – a spark. That evening they had light as well as heat in their room.

22 January: Soup and Speeches

The Primo Levi whom Charles, Arthur and the others saw during the last ten days of Auschwitz was stripped down to the essence of himself. His body, which had always been so small and thin, was so thin now it hardly existed. But his mind and will were huge. At first you did not realize it, because he was so frail, and so quiet; he seemed, Charles says, like any other half-dead *Häftling*. But then, to your surprise you began to see his immense intelligence and resource. He organized everything. He was the rock on which they all rested.

Except for Charles. Here Charles was his Alberto, the symbiont he always needed. Charles was new; he was more shocked and afraid than Primo, and he suffered more from the deprivations. But he had a natural energy, a love of life that had never been broken. Primo had only will, and that *could* sometimes be broken. Then Charles would say '*Vas-y, Primo*' and smile his shy smile, and light the stove; and Primo would want to live again.

Today they would make soup from the cabbages and turnips. Everyone who could hold a knife helped to peel the turnips; though it could have killed him, Towarowski wolfed down several of them raw. Primo and Charles looked for a place to light a fire. It wasn't easy: the latrines were unusable, and everyone had diarrhoea; every corner of KB, inside and out, was fouled. Finally they found a spot in a corner of what had once been the laundry. They disinfected their hands in snow mixed with chloramine, which Primo had found and identified – using the first Alberto's method, tasting things and spitting them out. They lit their fire, and began to cook the precious soup.

Soon half the camp was clamouring at the door. But once again they could not save everyone. Charles made a 'short, vigorous speech' – in French, but everyone understood. Only Maxime, a Parisian tailor, stood his ground. For two pints of soup, he said, he would make them new suits out of blankets. Charles already had a good Kapo's uniform, which he'd found in the store, but Primo agreed. Maxime got his soup; and the next day Primo had a new jacket and trousers, rough but warm.

That night, after the soup, he definitely wanted to live again. He wanted them all to live. So he made a speech, first in French, then in German. It would be a great pity to die in the last moment, he said. They must try to recover from their own illnesses, and not catch anyone else's. Everyone should keep his own bowl and spoon; Arthur should not wash them, for fear of confusing them. If they wanted anything they should ask one of the workers; otherwise they should stay in bed, and conserve their energy. They could now – they must now – think of going home.

23 January: The Finest Hour

That morning Primo and Charles left the Lager for the first time.

The SS camp lay just outside the gate, with its sign *Arbeit Macht Frei*. The two friends simply (simply!) walked through it, and into the SS quarters.

They may have been the first who dared. On the tables they found plates still half full of frozen soup, which they gleefully devoured. In the dormitories they found many wonderful things – a bottle of vodka, medicines, newspapers and magazines, four sumptuous eiderdowns. Hilarious with triumph, they bore it all back under *Arbeit Macht Frei* to KB. Perhaps only a half an hour later an SS patrol returned briefly to their barracks, found eighteen French survivors sitting at their table, and shot them all.

That evening, Primo took another step out of the Lager. Next door in the Dysentery Ward, he knew, were two Italians. He could hear them talking through the wooden wall, inches from his head. But since he spoke only French, they did not guess there was a fellow Italian in that paradise next door, where there was heat, and light, and fabulous sounds of cooking and eating. Until that day, when Charles called out his name. Since then their voices had never stopped begging him through the wall – for help, for food, for a drop of water.

When work was over he felt his way along the dark, freezing corridor to their door, carrying a bowl of water and the remainder of the day's soup. The Dysentery Ward was a hell of darkness and death. At least half the patients were already dead, their corpses frozen in their bunks. The others were cursing, groaning, dying. They cried out to him as he passed, clutching at his clothes and face. The stink of death and excrement choked him. But at last he reached the end wall, and the two Italians.

He recognized them both. One, whom he calls Marcello, was from Cannaregio, the old ghetto of Venice. His real name was Raffaele Grassini. He had been on Primo's transport with his whole family, including his parents, wife and child. They had all been killed on arrival. Raffaele had lasted to the end; but for him help had come too late. He died a month later in the hospital in Auschwitz.

The other Italian was Lello Perugia. Lello would become one of the great companions of Primo's return to life: in his story of it he would call him Cesare.

Lello was starved and ill, but if he had dysentery at all he had caught it in the ward. He had entered KB on a gamble and a trick. Inside, he thought, it was very possible he would die; but outside it was absolutely certain. So a week or two before – just in time, in fact – he had played his trick. In the best traditions of magic and conjuring, its precise mechanics remain mysterious. To be admitted to KB for dysentery, patients had to produce the evidence in a chamber-pot on demand. In one version of the story, Lello lined up behind a real sufferer, offered him payment in soup or bread, and at the key moment switched pots with him. (We needn't worry about the poor sufferer, who would have no difficulty producing another sample for himself.) In the other version, Lello put a few drops of water into his pot, and armed himself with a handful of the dark ochre sand used for dousing fires. When it was his turn to squat, he dropped the sand between his legs, gave it a moment to mix with the water – and hey presto.

However he had done it, the trick had worked. It had saved him from the death march – but only to condemn him to the hell-hole of the Dysentery Ward. He and Grassini clung together for warmth; they had not eaten or drunk for days. Primo gave them the water and the soup. For the next four nights and days fifty dying men unceasingly called his name. Every evening he fought his tiredness, his disgust, his despair that he could not help them all; and doggedly bore his two small bowls through the reeking, shrieking air.

That night the young Dutchman, Lakmaker, could no longer move. He fouled his bed; then threw himself out of it, crying and groaning, covered in excrement.

They had hardly any water, and no straw mattresses or blankets to spare. Whilst Primo held the lamp, Charles cut the dirtiest patches from Lakmaker's mattress and blankets. He cleaned him as best he could with straw, and lifted him gently back on to his bed. Then he scraped the typhus-laden filth off the floor, and spread disinfectant over everything, including himself.

True, hundreds were dying all around them, in abject misery. But they were helping nine – eleven, including the two Italians – to survive a little longer. They were reinventing everything – heat, light, food, medicine; above all, decency. For the rest of their lives, Primo said, both felt 'those ten days were our "finest hour"'.

24 January: 'On est dehors'

Somewhere near the camp the Germans had stored tons of potatoes underground. That day, someone found them.

Primo and Charles saw the hole torn in the fence, and lines of prisoners going in and out, laden with potatoes. No one would starve any more. They pushed through the hole themselves, and stood on the open plain. '*Dis donc, Primo,*' Charles said. '*On est dehors!*'

It was true. For the first time in over a year he was free.

But though they were free they could not go anywhere. And though they would not starve, they would not recover either. After months and years in the Lager, Primo wrote, you need more than potatoes for that. During the Ten Days about one quarter of the survivors died. And over the still living hung an agonizing fear: what if the SS should return, and kill them all in the last minute?

25 January: Sómogyi

Sómogyi had not spoken for many days. Today he spoke just once. There was a ration of bread under his mattress, he said. 'Divide it amongst the three of you. I shall not be eating any more.'

That evening he became delirious. All that night and the next day he raved. Endlessly he repeated the word of his slavery: *Jawohl*: Yes sir, yes sir. 'I never understood until then,' Primo wrote, 'how laborious is the death of a man.'

26 January: Charles

In the evenings Primo, Charles and Arthur sat around the stove and talked of home. Arthur remembered Sundays in his village, Charles his busy days in the schoolroom. Primo talked about his mountains, and about the desperate adventures of his small Resistance band, which had ended in betrayal. In their bunks the others listened eagerly – even those, Primo wrote, who did not understand a word of French. He loved Arthur's account of Sunday in the Vosges; Charles was so moved by Primo's story of his capture that he almost cried.

They had returned. They had resisted the death the Nazis had planned for them, which was less for their bodies than for their souls. Whoever waits for his neighbour to die to take his bread, Primo wrote, is guiltless, because he is not responsible for his own destruction. Nonetheless, he is no longer human. To be human is to know that others are human as well: which even the sadist knows, or he wouldn't bother. A sadist does not kick a stone. The Nazis treated their victims like stones, like things; that is why *they* were not human. And they tried to make their victims treat each other like things, to prove that they were right about them. They succeeded with many starved, tormented millions. But with a few who were strong and lucky, they failed. They failed with Alberto, Leonardo and Jean, and they failed with Primo, Arthur and Charles. Primo's friendships with all of them were more than friendships, they were monuments to what friendship means. Charles was as *bugia nèn* as Primo; they met only twice after the war, and wrote only rarely, as busy people do. But their friendship lasted to Primo's death, and beyond. When Charles talks of Primo today, he still almost cries.

In the middle of the night Primo woke: Sómogyi had stopped. With his last breath he threw himself out of his bed. Primo heard the dreadful thud as his knees, his hips, his head hit the ground.

27 January: Burial

In the morning they could not move the body until they had cooked and eaten, emptied the bucket and cleaned the room: there was only water to wash once, if at all. So it was noon before Primo and Charles carried Sómogyi out on a stretcher, and lowered him on to the grey snow. Charles took off his beret; they stood for a moment. When they looked up the Russians had arrived.

10. The Truce:
27 January – 19 October 1945

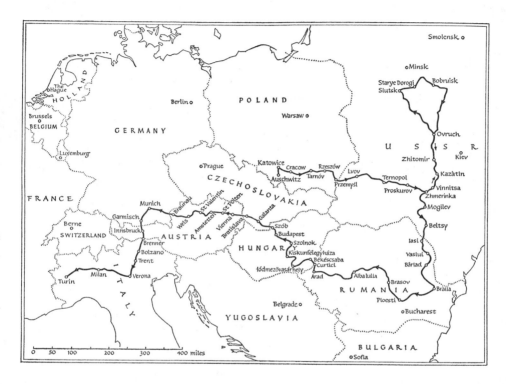

Primo's journey, March–October 1945

Liberation came to Primo Levi and his companions in the shape of four young Russian soldiers, all in white, on enormous white horses, moving slowly towards them against the vast grey sky.

It should have been a moment of intense joy. But it could not be, Primo tells us; or not only. For a few there could be joy – for those who had suffered only briefly, in whom the poison had not had time to work; for those who had fought, and saw their victory achieved. But for those, like Lello Perugia, who were almost dead, there was nothing: when he understood it was over, he felt nothing at all. And for those like Primo and Charles, like Leonardo and Aldo, there was more anguish than joy. There was their old anguish: the awareness of their degradation, which they felt only when it lifted. And there was a new anguish, which they would always feel now: the awareness that this degradation, which should never have happened, did happen, and could never be cleansed: not from themselves, not from those who had inflicted it on them, not from anyone who ever came to know it had existed. This is what Primo called, both then and later, shame.

Again there were those who did not feel it: Jean Samuel, for example, has never felt shame. He is right, and Primo thought so: rationally, there is no reason to feel ashamed of having been an innocent victim. Nonetheless Primo did feel shame, and so do many survivors. As he made Francine say (the Auschwitz survivor in *If Not Now, When?*): 'It's stupid, but I feel it.' He felt shame for having been safe in the lab, for being alive, when so many were dead. And he felt shame for being human: for belonging to the same species as those who had, shamelessly, committed these crimes; for having seen them, and not died.

At the moment of liberation, that is what he saw in the eyes of the four young horsemen who moved so warily towards the barbed wire, 'throwing strangely embarrassed glances at the sprawling bodies, at the battered huts, and at us few still alive'. It was the same shame other young soldiers would soon feel at the gates of other camps; the same shame we feel, when we see the films the accompanying journalists made. We think, *Could human beings have done this?*; and we still can't believe it.

That anguish and shame is what Primo Levi felt, after a year of Auschwitz. 'Not "pleasure the son of misery"', he told his hero Leopardi harshly, in his last book: 'misery the son of misery'. That was liberation.

Now came the thaw, and it was the same. They were released from the cold – but so were putrefaction and disease, and the stink of death all around them. The Russians marched into the town of Auschwitz and roughly recruited everyone they found. Against their will, Polish men and women began the work of removing the corpses; Polish girls, 'pale with disgust and pity', cleaned the patients and dressed their sores.

The dying did not end, but on the contrary increased. Those who were sickest could not be rescued; many who were less sick died of their rescue, their starved stomachs collapsing under the shock of a sudden abundance. And some, drowned in the flood of awareness released by the thaw, killed themselves precisely now, at or soon after the moment of liberation.

For Primo, the release of liberation meant the collapse, finally, of the strength he had maintained by sheer will. He fell into a series of strange ailments: ones 'unknown to civilized society', he wrote, since a year in Auschwitz deformed human illnesses as much as everything else.

For three days he remained in Monowitz, 'semi-conscious, tended fraternally by Charles'. On the third day Charles and Arthur lifted him on to the cart that was slowly transferring the survivors of Monowitz and Birkenau to the main camp of Auschwitz. There they were washed and dressed, and for the last time their heads were shaved. The gigantic Russian barber did his job ungently, hissing at Primo '*Italiano Mussolini*', and at the two Frenchmen '*Fransé Laval*': 'from which', Primo remarks, 'one sees how little general ideas help the understanding of individual cases'.

After that they were separated. Primo was sent to the infirmary, and from there to a new Infectious Ward. Charles and Arthur were put in a Block of healthy Frenchmen. They visited Primo whenever they could, and saw him slowly recover. Then one day he was gone. The war and its aftermath kept the French waiting for many months; but at last they could leave. On 27 July Charles and Arthur were home.

Hurbinek's Word

Primo spent his first night in free Auschwitz in a huge dormitory of the dying: in the morning dozens of the 'patients' were corpses. It was as though this vast and unattended place – there was only one doctor, Primo said, and not a single nurse – was a test, like a reverse of Charon's boat, or of the gate to hell itself, allowing only the still living to pass through. Seeing that Primo was one of these, the next day the doctor transferred him to a small ward of about twenty people who might possibly survive.

For the first few days he remained in his Monowitz state, hardly conscious, with a raging fever. But on the fifth day the fever disappeared. He stayed in bed for a month, as other Auschwitz ailments worked their way through his body. But the worst was over. He felt 'as light as a cloud', which in fact he was; but his head was clear, his senses 'as though purified'. And what he saw and remembered – or saw and told – has the vividness of symbols. There were four such symbols of his return from hell: sex, children, love and death.

In the shadow of death people think of sex as someone dying of thirst thinks of water. We have seen this before: during the last night at Fossoli, for example. Primo has never recorded this effect of war – or only obscurely, and with anguish. But now he does; and finally the anguish has gone.

He shows us one member of either sex. The girl, Jadzia, is one of their Polish nurses: pale, timid and silent, but attracted to every man she meets like (Primo says) iron to a magnet. She follows them like a sleepwalker, like someone bewitched, like an amoeba enfolding its prey: hardly images of freedom and joy, but not of horror either. What Primo seems to see in a woman's hunger for sex in these circumstances is what was probably there: a deep, unconscious, biological compulsion.

It's when we come to the man that we see the great change. Noah sets the tone for *The Truce*; he foreshadows all its ambiguous heroes, great and small, and that other ambiguous hero of the Lager, Rappoport, whom Primo will celebrate a few years later. Noah is the 'Scheissminister of free Auschwitz, Minister of latrines and cesspits': he drives around all day on his cart, collecting ordure. But the lowness of this role dismays no one, least of all Primo. Noah leaves the dirty work to his men, while he himself descends on the female dormitories like a shower of gold, and seduces all the women. *And now this does not dismay Primo either.* Instead it makes him want to laugh and cheer. 'The deluge was over,' he wrote, 'in the black sky of Auschwitz, Noah saw the rainbow shine out, and the world was his, to repopulate.'

Now that he has looked death in the eye, Primo Levi is no longer afraid of the springs of life. He has always loved the physical courage and gaiety he did not have; now he loves physical appetite as well. The great suppressor of instinct has become the great champion of instinct – at least on paper. For he had made not just one but two discoveries in Auschwitz. First, that without thought or conscience man is merely an animal, and an empty shell: that gave him his first great answer to the question, *What is a man?* But second, that the instinctive attachment to life is the best defence against death: and that gave him his second. In *If This is a Man* he celebrates one half of man, which he supremely shared; in *The Truce* he celebrates the other half, which he shared as much as he ever would in the months (and years) after his liberation.

If Noah's unborn children are symbols of hope, the symbols of despair are also children. There were very few of them in free Auschwitz, since there had been few in Auschwitz-Birkenau, and hardly any survived. Those who did were the world's innocence destroyed.

The least destroyed is Henek, the first of the ambiguous heroes of *La tregua*, whom we meet even before Noah. Henek is a fifteen-year-old Hungarian boy, whose real name was as apt as Noah's: König, which means King. Henek is affectionate and kind to everyone in the ward, especially the weakest; but in the Lager he was a King of instinct, and would surely be so again, the moment it was required. His whole family had been killed on arrival. He had said he was eighteen, and so had entered Birkenau; once there he announced his real age, fourteen, and was sent to the Children's Block instead of to work. The children of Birkenau, Primo wrote, 'were like birds of passage': they never lasted more than a few days, after which they went to the Experiment Block, or straight to the gas chambers. But Henek was 'shrewd [and] ferocious': he became the children's Kapo, and made the selections himself. Did he feel no remorse? Primo asked. No, he replied. Why should he? Was there any other way to survive?

It was Steinberg's answer, for deeds more incomprehensible than Steinberg's. But Henek is a child, and a good boy, and Primo is the new champion of instinct. He accepts Henek's answer without judgement; and so should we. But we must also fear for him: that he will condemn himself one day; or if he does not, that he will become a monster instead. Instinct alone is no more the answer than reason alone. The damage done to Henek does not yet show; but it is surely there.

There was a small pack of younger children, who had been hidden, or protected by some Prominent, or who had arrived in the Children's Block in the last weeks of the Lager. 'They were wild and judicious little animals,' Primo said; and the one he describes is like a tiny version of Henek. His name was Peter Pavel, he was no older than five, and he was absolutely self-sufficient. 'Peter Pavel spoke to no one and had need of no one,' Primo wrote; he was intelligent, strong and beautiful, and surely lost to the world.

In the last two children the destruction is not hidden or postponed, but present and heavy. One, Kleine Kiepura, at twelve years old had been the catamite of the Lager-Kapo of Monowitz, the Kapo of all the Kapos. Kleine Kiepura must once have been especially beautiful, for the Lager-Kapo to have snatched him away from death and preserved him; indeed, Primo notes that the traces of his 'infantile grace' could still be seen in his pale features. But in Auschwitz he had grown deformed. First physically, with long thin arms and legs sprouting from his child's body, like Arachne's; now mentally as well, huddled in his bunk, singing the Buna marches and screaming at imaginary prisoners, aping his Kapo. The other patients tried to reach him in his delirium: but reluctantly, as the boy-soldiers had shot their troubled glances through the barbed wire. And, Primo wrote, in vain. Kleine Kiepura left their ward unchanged.

I have left the first child to the last, because he is the most terrible of the child-symbols, and one of the most unforgettable of all Primo's images of the Lager. His five short paragraphs on Hurbinek the child of Auschwitz show once again that he is not just a great witness but a great artist; and the first because the second.

Hurbinek looked only about three years old, and had perhaps been born in Auschwitz. Like Kleine Kiepura, he was a living image of the ferocious deformation of the Lager: paralysed from the waist down, with atrophied legs, unable to move. And mentally too he was deformed, and utterly devastated – but not like Kleine Kiepura. For Hurbinek embodies not only the worst destruction of the human spirit, but its most noble resistance. He had never known anything but Auschwitz; and he could not speak. That is the key to humanity, for Primo Levi and for everyone: without language, knowledge and virtue are impossible, and we are dumb animals. No one had ever taught Hurbinek to speak, perhaps no one had ever spoken to him. *But all Hurbinek desired was to speak.* His eyes stared out of his wasted face, Primo wrote, 'full of demand', 'of the will to break free, to shatter the tomb of his dumbness', and speak.

No one could bear the anguish of that demand for long: except Henek. Henek washed and fed Hurbinek with maternal care; and sat beside him for hours on end, speaking to him slowly and patiently in Hungarian. After a week, Primo wrote, Henek announced that Hurbinek ' "could say a word" '. What word? Henek didn't know; it was not Hungarian. The others came to listen: yes, Hurbinek was trying to say something, perhaps a name, perhaps *his* name – they had called him Hurbinek, no one knew his real name, or if he had one. They listened for many days, Primo wrote, 'and among us were speakers of all the languages of Europe; but Hurbinek's word remained a secret'. He fought to his last breath to 'gain his entry into the world of men'; but died in the first week of March, without having been understood.

Which should we remember more, Hurbinek's victory, which is his will to speak, or his defeat? And what *was* his word? Did it mean 'bread' or 'meat', as some of his companions thought, was it indeed his name, or perhaps his mother's? Or was it, instead, an infernal word, an Auschwitz word: one that meant something unspeakable in any human language? Primo does not choose. Hurbinek, his first portrait after liberation, remains an image equally of hope and horror, of the grandeur and the fragility of the human.

Love and death came together. In free Auschwitz Primo met Olga, who had befriended the girls of his transport in Birkenau.

In the middle of one night she came and told him about Vanda.

In the published version of *The Truce*, Primo maintains his reserve, and relates Vanda's death austerely, without comment. But in the first writing, for once he had been unable to keep himself out of the story. 'At the time,' he had written,

I did not suffer at this news, because I felt distant, cut off, able to remember my previous life only occasionally and vaguely; but I knew with extreme clarity that I should have to suffer later.

The Greek

By early March Primo was not yet well. Nonetheless, he decided, the Infectious Ward had done what it could for him: if he stayed in bed any longer he would grow weaker instead of stronger. He gathered up several striped jackets and pairs of trousers, and said goodbye to Henek. The doctor warned him to avoid the cold; and he walked out into the snow.

His plan was to make a new base – perhaps with Charles and Arthur, or with Leonardo, if he could find them – and slowly rebuild his strength for the return home. But he was too weak to go far that first day. There was a warm Block; he went in. They gave him soup, and a bunk, he would go on the next day. But he had chosen the wrong Block. The next day the Russians evacuated it; and his involuntary adventure had begun.

Before dawn ('this is a story interwoven with freezing dawns', Primo wrote), he and a dozen others were loaded on to a cart, and unloaded again by a broken railway line. There they waited for hours in the vast empty plain, standing and sometimes lying in the snow. At last a thin string of goods wagons arrived on one half of the line, and they climbed on. But their relief was short-lived. They were heading east, towards Kraków, the passengers said: but Kraków was full to overflowing, and the Russians were sending all ex-prisoners to Katowice now – to the west, on the other half of the broken line. They were going the wrong way.

This first disaster pictures the whole disaster to come, which will consist of going entirely and endlessly the wrong way – east instead of west, north instead of south, towards primeval chaos and freedom, instead of towards home. And in this chaos, Primo meets the first master of his new life: the Greek, Mordo Nahum.

'He was a great Greek,' Primo wrote – and the 'great' contains all the celebration, and all the ambiguity, of that time. Mordo Nahum was a Jew from Salonika: a member of the most united and most ruthlessly cunning group in Monowitz, who had dominated the Lager market, the main means of staying alive. And that is the heart of the matter. Wherever there is a spark of life left – or wherever it rises again from the ashes, as it was doing now in Kraków, in Poland, in all of ravaged Europe – there is a market. Now, trade is harsh; at worst unscrupulous, at best unequal. But *trade is life*: that is the great equation of *The Truce* – and of *If This is a Man* too, which had dedicated a whole chapter, and by no means the shortest, to the Monowitz market. Mordo Nahum the Greek, and soon Cesare the Roman, are masters of trade: therefore masters of life, and masters to Primo Levi.

As we know, Primo invented 'Mordo Nahum'. The true name of his great Greek was Leon Levi. Like all the surviving Greeks, Leon Levi had spent two years in the Lager; but of this he never spoke. He was, Primo thought, about forty. He was tall and stooped, with red hair and skin, large pale eyes, and a large curved nose like a beak; he looked, Primo wrote, 'like a night bird surprised by the light'. In fact he was no more impressive than Primo himself: neither realized what he had found in the other. They drew together for the old Auschwitz reason: they were the only Mediterraneans in their group, and they had French in common. Besides, the Greek was a Greek, which was a guarantee of exceptional survival skills to anyone who had known Auschwitz; and this particular Greek had a large and bulging sack on his back, and a truly amazing pair of leather shoes on his feet. When their train broke down, on the second freezing evening of their journey, Leon Levi turned to him and said: '*On y va?*' And Primo Levi, who knew how to stay, but not how to go – and when he did go, into the mountains, or out of the Infectious Ward, look what happened – Primo Levi said, '*On y va.*' And the adventure of his lifetime began.

It wasn't just an adventure – it was an education. Primo had entered Auschwitz a sheltered boy, with two brief jobs behind him, and a failed attempt to turn himself into a fighter. His return would be into manhood. *The Truce* is not just a great picaresque adventure, like *Don Quixote* or *Tom Jones*; it is also (like both of these) a comic-ironic *Bildungsroman*: the story of the education of an innocent in the ways of the world. That began straight away.

Primo would carry the sack, the Greek announced. 'But it's yours!' Primo protested. 'Exactly,' the Greek replied. '*Because* it's mine. I organized it, you carry it. That's division of labour.' So Primo shouldered the heavy bundle, and they set off towards the spires of Kraków, red in the setting sun.

After only twenty minutes a problem arose: Primo's shoes. They were of very soft leather, like moccasins; perfect for the Infectious Ward, less so for the road. One had already lost its sole completely, and the other was starting to follow. Krakow was still four or five miles away; but Primo could go no further.

Leon Levi came back to where he was sitting at the side of the road. 'How old are you?' he asked. 'Twenty-five,' Primo replied. 'What do you do?' 'I'm a chemist.' 'Then you're a fool,' the Greek said. 'A man who has no shoes is a fool.'

Shoes are more important than food, because with shoes one can search for food, but not vice versa: that was Lesson Number One. The Greek gave Primo two strong pieces of cloth from his sack, and showed him how to bind his useless shoes to his feet. Then he turned and stalked off to Kraków, with Primo hobbling behind.

★

That is how it will be from now on. In youth Primo Levi's *alter egos* represented the youthful gifts he did not have – physical courage, dash and ease. In adulthood they will represent the adult gifts he did not have – realism and practicality, ruthlessness and guile. His attitude to his new *alter egos* will always be what it was now to the Greek: fascination and sympathy, tempered by a double mockery, as much of himself as of them. He is an eager pupil, but not a good one; he will remain unworldly, and never quite learn their lessons. Because, somewhere beneath his apprentice's enthusiasm, he doesn't really want to.

It is his key question again, *What is a man?* – on the personal level this time. When he was young he had secretly answered: a man is handsome, brave and irresistible to girls, like Alberto Salmoni. Now he is an adult he answers: a man is clever, strong and ruthless, like Leon Levi. But he could never be Alberto; and he could never be Leon Levi either.

In fact Leon Levi was an extreme and eccentric case, and Primo did not really want to be like him. But he was intensely fascinated by him. He would have liked to write a whole book about him, he once said; and it's a shame he never did. That unwritten book is the missing twin to *The Wrench*, which is Primo Levi's last word on his ideal, independent, self-sufficient man.

The problem with Leon Levi is that he was *too* independent and self-sufficient. He was selfish and cold, and Primo did not admire that outside Auschwitz any more than in it. But he was amazed and intrigued by the Greek's moral code, which was rigid and singular. It was based, like that of the hero of *The Wrench*, on one supreme value: work. But for Faussone – as for Lorenzo, and for Primo himself – the point of work was to do it well, and thus satisfy both one's own pride, and the purpose for which it was done. While for the Greek the point of work was 'to bring profit without limiting liberty'. *Le travail d'homme*, the work of a real man, he explained, was individual enterprise of any kind. It included certain activities which were not commonly counted as honest work, such as smuggling, theft and fraud; and utterly excluded others which *were* commonly counted – which were indeed the only kind the common herd knew: any form of employment, no matter how well paid.

Creative work can only rarely have entered his world, and it must have been Primo who raised it. But when he did, the Greek's ideas were clear. It was permissible to produce creative work for profit, even – or best, since most cunning – false creative work, such as fake paintings, or literary trash; but absolutely reprehensible to waste time on an unprofitable ideal. On the other hand, someone who withdrew into meditation and the pursuit of wisdom *could* be a 'real man', so long as he did not expect the world to keep him for nothing: 'for wisdom was also merchandise, which could and should be exchanged'.

Can Primo Levi really admire this extreme ethic (or anti-ethic), this Darwinian vision of the survival of the hardest bargainer? On the one hand – no, of course not; his own ideal of man could not be more different, and the Greek is in fact his 'ideological opponent'. And on the other – he is Primo Levi, whom nothing interests more than what is furthest from himself. He may not really want to learn from the Greek, but part of him knows that he should. He has just escaped from Auschwitz, which has immensely strengthened his own ideal; but has also taught him that where there is no law the Greek is right, and much more likely to survive. Besides, there is that fanatic dedication to freedom, which he has always admired, and always will – in Sandro Delmastro, in Alberto Dalla Volta, in Lorenzo, in Faussone. His admiration for his 'great Greek' is partly playful, but mostly genuine: a nod of respect from one opponent to the other.

And there was something else. It was part of the Greek's iron ethic that all the tender pleasures of life were strictly secondary, to be indulged only when work was done. But on their very first night in Kraków Primo saw a human warmth in him which, in all their months together, he had never once surprised in Fisch, for example, or in Paul Steinberg.

When they had finally arrived, they were rewarded: someone told them where to find an Italian barracks. At first, Primo relates, all his pleas to the guard were in vain. Yes, he was Italian, but not a soldier; and not only was his companion not Italian, he was Greek, and the soldiers inside were veterans of the Greek campaign; did he want to start another war? Then the Greek pushed him aside, and held out the result of the search he'd been making in the sack on Primo's back: 'a dazzling tin of pork'. They were in.

And instead of war, there was celebration. The Italians, 'veterans of the most compassionate military occupation that history records', welcomed the Greek like one of themselves: he had fought in the same campaign, 'on the other side of the front, naturally, but this detail at the moment seemed trifling to everyone'. Perhaps they would have welcomed any Greek just then; but there was something special about Leon Levi. He was a 'super-Greek': he spoke a little Italian, he told extraordinary stories of the war, he was an expert on wine, women and song. He, who was 'so laconic with me', Primo wrote, 'quickly became the centre of the evening': and not only out of calculation. Like a cactus in the sun, in the warmth of fellowship he blossomed, and to his astonishment Primo glimpsed the hidden humanity in him, 'singular but genuine, rich with promise'.

It did not last long. At dawn the next day he roused Primo: it was time for work. What for? Primo demanded. He was happy where he was, he was still tired and ill, and he was no use at all in a market. '*C'est pas des raisons d'homme*,' Leon Levi barked – 'Those are not a man's reasons.' And still in his hopeless shoes, with the sack once more on his back, Primo followed the Greek to the first market of his freedom.

For the next few hours they played out a comedy which would be repeated, with variations, throughout the months that followed. The Greek, frowning and pitiless, planned the campaign and gave the orders; Primo carried them out. And despite his cold and hunger, curiosity began to stir in him, and delight in this spectacle, and in his new, inexhaustible freedom. The best items in his sack, the Greek decided, were three shirts, stolen with his usual foresight from the Auschwitz store. Primo knew German, did he not? Very well. Primo should discover the going rate for shirts; then they would sell one, eat at the soup-kitchen, and invest the remainder in eggs.

Primo hobbled around, the Greek's eye following him like a hawk. Shirts were selling for 50 to 100 *zloty*, he reported; 'shirt' in Polish was something like '*koshoola*'; and the right way to address one's customers seemed to be '*Panovye*' – which must be the plural vocative of *Pan*, 'gentleman', a term he remembered well from *The Brothers Karamazov* . . . The Greek paid no attention to this last piece of information, and did not comment on the rest; but he was not displeased. As for Primo, he was filled with a 'foolish and puerile joy' at his philological discoveries – which was not foolish at all, because it was joy at the return of life, and of the things he loved. Until once again the tall hard businessman called the small hilarious scholar to order, instructing him to hold up the shirt, and call out the strange new words he had learned. Then he pushed him aside, closed the deal, and slid the 70 *zloty* firmly into his own pocket.

Now for the soup-kitchen, behind the Cathedral – and once more the scholar could serve. Which of the many beautiful churches of Kraków was the Cathedral? That young priest would know. But the young priest spoke neither French nor German, nor any of the Greek's other languages (Spanish, Turkish, Bulgarian, Albanian). So Primo approached, in his striped suit, and his bandaged feet like a Chinese lady, or an Eskimo. '*Pater optime*,' he said, '*ubi est mensa pauperorum?*' And for a few mad moments the ex-prisoner and the priest stood in the ruined heart of Europe speaking Latin, as though not merely six years but six centuries had fallen away.

The Greek stopped that too, as soon as he realized the essential information had been obtained. At the soup-kitchen he ordered two bowls of soup, but only one plate of beans and lard: Primo must be punished for his idling. But after his soup, the Greek began to relent. Once again a fugitive warmth grew in him; and patiently he tried to explain to this boy the error of his ways. Time is money, business is business, especially in war. 'But the war is over,' Primo objected. Then the Greek delivered himself of a pronouncement which Primo would never forget. 'There is always war,' Leon Levi said.

That was the difference between them.

The Lager had happened to both of us: I had felt it as a loathsome anomaly in my history and in the history of the world; he, as sad confirmation of things well known. 'There is always war', man is wolf to man: an old story.

At that moment of hope and renewal it was the difference between them; but it remained so only by the force of Primo's will. In the darker meanings of this book, and in its title, he *has* learned the Greek's lesson. There may not be war now, but it will return.

Primo and his Greek spent one more night in Kraków, then several days travelling back along the broken line to Katowice. At Katowice they went their separate ways, Leon Levi to join his fellow Greeks, Primo Levi to join the Italians. At the moment of parting, all Primo's contradictory feelings towards the Greek ran through him: 'gratitude, contempt, respect, animosity, curiosity'; and 'one solitary surge of friendship'.

He would see him only twice more: once in May, leading the Greeks out of Katowice, when he stopped and gave Primo a pair of trousers; and once in July, when he offered Primo one of his latest pieces of merchandise, a woman. After the war Primo wrote twice to the Jewish Community of Salonika, looking for him; but was told that there were many Levis in Salonika, of whom at least seven were called Leon. *His* Leon Levi never replied. It is extremely unlikely that the Greek ever read *The Truce*, or *If This is a Man* either; or that he ever knew, therefore, who his young assistant really was, and what a famous character he had made of him.

The Messenger

On the way to Katowice the train stopped at a small place called Trzebinia, and Primo climbed down. Perhaps he was the first ex-*Häftling* to appear there, though Auschwitz was nearby. He was immediately surrounded by a small crowd, all peering at his striped suit, and plying him with questions in Polish.

As he tried to reply in his halting German, a man stepped forward: a lawyer, with a kind and courteous air. And suddenly Primo knew that he had met a Messenger, someone who would pass on his ghastly tale, which he had been waiting so long and so furiously to tell. So now, for the first time, he did what he would do over and over again for the next year and more: he turned to a perfect stranger, and began to pour out his story at dizzying speed.

He spoke in French, the Messenger translated, no one moved. Then Primo noticed something. He did not know Polish, but he knew the words for 'Jew' and for 'political': the Messenger was telling the people that he was a political prisoner, not a Jew. He stopped him and asked him why. '*C'est mieux pour vous,*' the Messenger said, embarrassed. '*La guerre n'est pas finie.*' It is better for you. The war is not over.

The words of the Greek, Primo thought. 'I felt myself suddenly old, lifeless, tired beyond human measure.' His listeners drifted away, as they did in his dream. The Messenger too prepared to leave. 'Good luck,' he said to Primo, and then he advised him not to speak German. 'Why not?' Primo asked; but he did not explain.

Soon someone did explain: 'Tonight all Germans kaputt,' he said cheerfully, and sliced his fingers across his throat from ear to ear. The next day their train passed a long line of cattle-cars going east: and this time Germans were inside. Primo could not exult; but perhaps he could not fail to exult either. The sight aroused in him, he wrote, 'confused and contradictory feelings, which even today I have difficulty in disentangling'. Later, he and his fellow survivors would see a dozen starved and half-mad German prisoners, who begged them for bread. Luciano, who had lost his entire family of eighteen members in Auschwitz, would throw his bread on the ground, and tell the Germans to crawl for it; 'which they did, docilely', Primo wrote. This time he did not even attempt to describe his feelings.

Katowice

The transit camp of Katowice was built on a low hill in the suburb of Bogucice, next to a frozen pond. Until a few weeks before it had been a German Lager for Russian prisoners, who worked as slave labourers in a nearby coal mine. Now it held about 500 ex-prisoners of the Nazis, liberated by the Red Army: French, Dutch, Belgians, Yugoslavs, Greeks, Italians, Czechs, Romanians, Hungarians, Austrians; civilian workers, prisoners of war and *Häftlinge*, including about 100 women. It consisted of a dozen long low brick huts, each containing around twenty rooms, on either side of a long corridor. One such hut belonged to the Italians. Primo was directed there; and the next stage of his adventure began.

What interested Primo most in his freedom, as in his imprisonment, was human beings. He was amazed by Russia, and by the wreck of Europe; but most of all he was amazed by the wild variety of human types thrown up by the war, like the crowds of improbable creatures he'd once seen in the water from his mother's vase. Now he met the first of these, after the Greek: Colonel Rovi, the head of the Italians in Katowice.

He almost certainly changed Rovi's name, as he would change the names of almost all living people in his work. But otherwise he seems not to have changed, invented, or even exaggerated anything about him; it wasn't necessary. 'Colonel' Rovi wasn't a colonel; he wasn't a soldier at all. He was a Milanese accountant, and his real name was probably Riva. *Ragioniere* Riva had not been elected to his office by the Italians, nor assigned to it by the Russians; he had simply appointed himself. Now, Primo sees that this wasn't simple at all, but a 'highly complex', 'mysterious' and fascinating process. For Riva was not particularly intelligent, or outstanding in any way; in fact, Primo says, 'he was basically foolish'. What he possessed was the instinct for power; and that is all he needed. He acquired a desk, official forms, rubber stamps, and a large placard reading 'Italian Command'. He created a uniform out of a pair of Soviet boots, a Polish railwayman's cap, and what had probably been a Republic of Salò jacket and trousers. He surrounded himself with a small court of interpreters, messengers and spies, most of them ex-criminals from the prison of San Vittore in Milan, and ('as always happens', Primo wrote) far worse than himself. Thus equipped, he presented himself to the Soviet *Kommandantur*, and as naturally as Fisch with the *Arbeitsdienst* of Auschwitz, was immediately confirmed in office.

But Riva was no Fisch. He 'was not a tyrant, and not even a bad administrator', Primo recalled: he ran Italian affairs with surprising efficiency, given the surrounding chaos; and he kept the abuses of his followers within reasonable limits. His will to power was not pathological, but on as human a scale as the rest of him. Years later Primo would study the pathological will to power, in the character of Chaim Rumkowski, King of the Łódź ghetto. 'Colonel Rovi' is a decent, comic version of Rumkowski, as 'Cesare' will be a decent, comic version of the Greek; that is, of the will to profit. It is no coincidence that it is now, at the moment of liberation, that Primo can take such a tolerant view of the most selfish human instincts – like the instinct of Noah, too, to repopulate the world.

In the Italian barracks Primo found several of his Monowitz companions waiting for him. There was Luciano Mariani from Venice, the one who had lost his whole extended family; Eugenio Ravenna of Ferrara, who had lost his parents, brother and sister; and Remo Jona from Turin, who had been arrested in the Val D'Aosta, like Primo himself, and who had lost his wife and both young sons. All three men were 'feeding on grief', as Primo would say of Mariani; especially poor Remo Jona, whose hair had turned white, and who wandered the camp like the ghost of a Chagall painting, in a long flapping kaftan, and a pair of glasses with only one lens. But at Katowice Primo also found Leonardo.

Leonardo had been delivered to Auschwitz main camp a few days after the liberation. Still emaciated, his legs still swollen, he told the Soviet Command he was a doctor, and was appointed to a surgical ward. There were no drugs, no medicines; all he could do was record his patients' histories, and watch them die. Still he stayed for over a month, slowly regaining strength. And as he regained his strength, he lost his resignation. He had come so close to death, so many times; could Jolanda possibly have escaped it? He wrote to her family, repeating over and over again his longing for her, his belief that she might still be alive. Almost certainly he did believe it, because he had to. But his fear did not cease.

The worst of these struggles he faced on his own, as one by one his friends left for Katowice and (they were told) repatriation. Together with the other doctors, he stayed on with his patients. Then one day he suddenly realized that he was the only healthy Italian left in Auschwitz. That was too much, even for Leonardo. He could do no good here; and in the meantime, perhaps, his friends were on their way home. He walked out of that gate, and took a train to Katowice.

There he found Mariani, Ravenna and the others, still as far from repatriation as ever. As he would remember it, Primo too had arrived a few days before. As Primo would remember – or as he told it – Leonardo had got there before him.* In any case, they both arrived in Katowice around the middle of March, no more than a week or so apart. And from then on, as Primo would write, they would not be parted again.

Leonardo, of course, immediately offered his services as a doctor to a second Soviet Command. This Katowice *Kommandantur* consisted of half a dozen officers, a dozen Territorial soldiers, a few doctors, a nurse, and a group of girls who did all the work, in the kitchens, the laundry, the offices, and (Primo adds) in the hearts and beds of their comrades. Their nominal head was Captain Egorov, a small, sad man whom the Italians rarely saw; if anyone was in charge of them it was the quartermaster, who seemed to have more authority, or perhaps simply more energy, than the other officers. Altogether the command structure of the *Kommandantur* was obscure, or rather entirely absent: they lived together, Primo wrote, like a big family, or a group of gypsies, and like gypsies they had moved around the front together for many years. In their disorder, their somnolence, and their

---

* This often happens: loneliness, separation from one's group, is the hardest to bear, and each person's experience of it seems longer to him than anyone else's. For the same reason, it makes a dramatic part of a story; and Primo may have told it that way round for that reason.

passion for red tape ('of which, however', Primo wrote, 'they wholly missed the ultimate rational significance'), they distilled the nature of the whole Soviet Army, and the whole Soviet people, on whom his fate, and the fate of millions of Europeans, now depended. He had few illusions about the dangers of this gigantic new (or very old) power: 'suspicious, negligent, stupid, contradictory and in effect as blind as the forces of nature'. Yet the contrast to the rigid, murderous, servile discipline of the Germans could not be greater, nor more in favour of the anarchic, melancholy Russians. Primo laughed at them, and loved them; if he ever allowed himself an unguarded sentimental feeling, it was for his liberators – 'these loveable, sympathetic, dear dear Russians', as Leonardo said.

The *Kommandantur* accepted Leonardo's offer with alacrity. Of their own doctors, one was very young, and did nothing but drink, smoke and court the girls; he appeared only once a day, early in the morning, for a rapid inspection, and already then he was drunk 'and full of happiness'. Another, a woman, Primo notes at the start, and then never mentions again: perhaps she worked conscientiously, and did not amuse him; or perhaps she never worked at all. In any case, since treatment was free, they were overwhelmed with patients: not only the inmates of the camp, but soldiers, civilians, beggars – anyone passing through Katowice – could, and often did, end up in the Bogucice surgery. At least here there were medicines: Leonardo could do some proper doctoring at last.

The medicines were procured by the *Kommandantur*'s nurse, Marya Fyodorovna Prima.* Indeed, Marya Fyodorovna had created the whole infirmary single-handed, according to Primo: thus confirming the rule that the real work of the Command was done by the women. Marya Fyodorovna was about forty. She came from Siberia, and had slanting green eyes, a flat Mongol nose, and 'the agile, silent movements of a forest cat'. She was 'energetic, stormy and disorderly', and she got results any way she could. Some of Leonardo's drugs came through proper Soviet military channels; but most were the fruit of Marya Fyodorovna's black market dealings, and of raids on abandoned German stores. As a result, the drugs poured in; and this gave Primo an idea. He went to Marya Fyodorovna and proposed himself as her pharmacist.

Marya Fyodorovna did not speak German, but somewhere on her mysterious travels she had learned a little Yiddish; thus she managed to understand Primo's proposal. At first she was sceptical. Was he a *doktor*? she asked,

---

* This was very likely her real name, though it may possibly have been 'Natalie' instead, as we shall see. Primo's practice with the Russians varied: he kept Egorov's name unchanged, but changed 'Danchenko''s (the happy young seducer's) slightly, probably from 'Klimchenko'.

and looked as unconvinced as Alex the Kapo. But then he wrote down his name for her, and everything changed. He was *Primo*? – but she was *Prima*, they were practically related! So Primo Levi got his first post-war job.

Soon after, he added a second one, as assistant to Leonardo in the surgery. He was, Leonardo wrote to his family, 'extremely intelligent and willing', and rapidly learned everything Leonardo could teach him. By now Marya Fyodorovna had also noticed how very clever and hard-working this strange new relative of hers was. When she received orders to keep a detailed register in the surgery, she knew where to turn. Primo took on a third job.

But now a problem arose. The register must be kept in Russian, naturally; and the one unaccountable failing of her prodigy was that he knew no Russian. For a moment it looked as though her plan might fail. But Marya Fyodorovna did not give up so easily. 'Galina!' she said. Galina was one of the fleet of girls attached to the *Kommandantur*, she was Russian, but she knew German. Beaming, Marya Fyodorovna sent for Galina. Her register was saved.

For Primo, however, the first crack in his strange suspended peace was about to appear, the first of his old sufferings to return. The girls of the *Kommandantur* were Valkyries, 'as solid as oaks', with shoulders, hands and feet the size of men's. Except for Galina. Galina was seventeen or eighteen years old, small and graceful; she dressed elegantly, was a bit of a flirt, and had a different soldier in love with her every week. And now, evening after evening, Primo was alone with her, with the shadow of Auschwitz still upon him: and suddenly he was conscious once again of his weakness, his illness, his absurd and hideous convict's clothes; and of Galina's glance, in which he saw compassion, but also repulsion, and perhaps he was right.

For the next few weeks they worked together every evening and saw each other every day, and between the lines of his story Primo's bittersweet longing grows – not only for love, but for youth and laughter and freedom. Galina is all of these to him. He racks his brains for the German words for their patients' ailments, and if, occasionally, he knows one, Galina doesn't; they fall back on gestures and charades, and Galina collapses in gales of laughter. She assures him that Marya Fyodorovna doesn't care what they write in the register, so long as they write something; while Dr Klimchenko is as interested as in 'last year's snow', being otherwise occupied (and she proceeds to tell him, in great detail, how). They work less and less, and laugh more and more; Primo falls deeper and deeper, and never says a word.

This sounds, suddenly, familiar: and in fact Galina is a kind of archetype of everything Primo has always sought in women, of the difference from himself he has always loved in light-hearted, singing girls. And especially in Gabriella. Galina is so like Gabriella, it is as though he has carried an image of Gabriella with him, and played it on to Galina, as on to a screen. Very likely that was part of it: certainly he carried the image of Gabriella with him, always. But Galina was real, and very much herself as well. She was a country girl from the Ukraine, and shared the unselfconscious dignity Primo noticed in all Russians at that time. In the morning she carried her washing on her head, 'singing like a thrush'; in the afternoon she hammered at a typewriter, her feet bare; at night she leaned dreamily on her balcony, while a ragged survivor, madly in love, serenaded her on a guitar. In the middle of May, a few days after the end of the war, she came to say goodbye to Primo: she was going home. She disappeared, he wrote, 'along the paths of her endless country, leaving behind her a sharp scent of earth, of youth and of joy'.

Who was Galina? Did she still feel repulsion for Primo, after all their laughter? – had she really felt repulsion for him at all? It would be wonderful (but also terrible) if he were wrong. We shall never know. But he was strangely bloated in those days, because he could not stop eating; and he had grown a beard. Years later, an Italian woman survivor remembered him in the surgery at Katowice. 'How old are you?' he had asked her. 'Twenty-four,' she'd said, 'and you?' 'Twenty-five,' he had replied. She was appalled: he looked sixty.

Cesare

Cesare and the Greek are the twin heroes of *The Truce*. Both are masters of trade: that is, of trickery, of life. But the Greek is the dark master, and Cesare the bright one. For the Greek trade was deadly serious, proud and cold: a lone, eternal war. Primo's most recent experience told him this was intolerable but true, and he had better learn it. But then he met Cesare, the 'main partner' of his journey, and the presiding comic genius of his book. For Cesare trade was as essential, as natural, and as close to trickery as for the Greek. But there the similarities ended. Where the Greek was cold, mean and 'a slave to himself', Primo wrote, Cesare was warm, prodigal and above all free. For him trade was not a war, but a game. He wanted to eat, of course; but he also wanted to entertain and be entertained, to be the centre of attention, to exercise his wit, cunning, audacity, imagination. Cesare liked trickery, as he liked life, for its own sake, for sheer enjoyment. And later, as Primo would learn, he liked story-telling too, as much as Primo himself; and their stories would not always agree. This would cause a good deal of pain (and some mystery); but it would not break the bond between them. Cesare let Primo's stories stand for over fifty years; he still says he does

not want to challenge them now, and it is half true. For his part, Primo
made Cesare the great hero of his return to life, saying that his friend's
escapades 'reconciled me to the world, and once more lit in me the joy of
living Auschwitz had extinguished'. And indirectly in *The Truce*, and later
openly, he made Cesare a twin not only to the Greek, but to himself: since
they are both inventors, that is to say tricksters, in their own ways.

Cesare, we know, was Lello Perugia, whom we last saw in the freezing
hell of the Monowitz Dysentery Ward. But who was Lello Perugia, and
how had he got there?

Lello Perugia, five months after liberation

Lello came from Rome: not from the ghetto, but from San Lorenzo, a
working-class district famous for its anarchist traditions. He was born in
October 1919, the seventh of the nine surviving children of Israele Perugia
and Emma Dell'Ariccia. From the start the whole family was free-thinking,
politically active, and deeply antifascist. His father owned a series of shops,
ending, in the best Jewish tradition, as a wholesale rag merchant; he was a
socialist and a Freemason. Lello's mother also owned a shop, together with
one of her sisters; she was the most *engagée* of all – a dedicated Communist,
a founding member of the Union of Italian Women, and after the war one

of the Roman delegates to the Paris Peace Conference. Like Primo's, the family's Jewish culture was still strong, though they were no longer religious. But at thirteen, in a first, characteristic act of his manhood, Lello refused to have a bar mitzvah, on the grounds that he was an atheist ('as I still am today', he says roundly). A few years later he joined the anarchists of San Lorenzo. In 1942 his father died; and in 1943 he moved from the anarchists to the Communists, like his mother. In the meantime he had trained as a book-keeper. As a Communist, however, he declined to contribute to the profits of capitalist commerce; instead he worked for a friend, in the administration of a jointly-owned block of flats. By 8 September there were few young men in Rome more theoretically prepared, or more naturally ready and willing to fight than Lello Perugia.

And fight he did. When the Germans entered Rome he joined the armed resistance that fought hard for two days, then continued as snipers and saboteurs when the battle was lost. At the end of September, when the Nazis made their infamous demand for fifty kilograms of gold from the Roman Jewish Community, if it wished to stop the deportation of 200 of its members, Lello was not fooled. We know what Germans do to Jews, he said. There is only one answer to this demand: the Resistance. But most of the Jews of Rome, like most Jews everywhere, were more hopeful, and less able to conceive the inconceivable. Thousands of them, including Lello's mother, contributed their wedding rings, their jewellery, their gold coins. By 28 September nearly eighty kilos had been collected, and the Roman Community breathed a sigh of relief. The very next day the Germans began the rape of the synagogue and offices, carrying off 2 million *lire*, all the archives and registers, and the entire contents of one of Rome's most precious libraries. Finally, on 16 October, the SS surrounded the ghetto, and rounded up and deported to Auschwitz not 200 but over 1,000 people, most of them women and children. Eight hundred were gassed on arrival; only around fifteen would return. After the war the box of Roman gold was found in the office of Ernst Kaltenbrunner, last head of Reich Security, unopened.

In November Lello and his brothers joined an international band of left-wing partisans called 'Liberty': and the whole family – mother, five brothers and four sisters – moved together to the mountains of the Abruzzi.

After several months of fighting – during which Lello became the leader of his small sub-group of partisans – on 14 April he and all his brothers were captured by the Gestapo. For two weeks or so they were held in a local prison near Aquila, where they were interrogated and ('naturally', says Lello) beaten. That was followed by a day or two of more sophisticated tortures, at the infamous Via Tasso in Rome; then Regina Coeli prison, and Fossoli. On 26 June it was their turn for the cattle-cars.

They arrived four days later, on 30 June. The two elder brothers, Giovanni and Mario, never entered Auschwitz. Giovanni was only forty, Mario thirty, and both were strong and healthy. But the Lager was full; and when there was no room, even thirty was old. Settimio, Lello and Angelo were all in their twenties; and though Lello was small, he had blond hair and blue eyes. These saved him, he says; and it may well be true. He was sent to Birkenau.

At first he believed – as new arrivals always did – that Giovanni and Mario had been sent to another camp. But then he asked a Pole, an older prisoner, where they could have gone: and – as older prisoners always did – the Pole pointed to the chimney of the crematorium. Once again Lello showed that capacity of his to accept the worst: quickly, without illusion, but without allowing it to destroy him. 'I understood straight away,' he says. It is a rarer capacity than he knows, and not the least of those that saved him.

In Birkenau he and Angelo managed to stay together for four months, though always in the hardest Kommandos. Then one day towards the end of October he was bundled on to a truck and driven away – as it turned out, to Buna-Monowitz. From then on, none of the surviving brothers knew what had happened to the others. Angelo thought that Lello had been sent to the gas chambers that day; Lello, looking back on Birkenau, thought that Angelo could not survive. In fact, they did both survive; and so did Settimio, right up to liberation. But only till then. Settimio was one of those who died shortly after: his frostbitten legs became gangrenous, and the doctors could not save him. He was still only twenty-eight years old.

Buna-Monowitz was better than Birkenau. But by January Lello's weight had fallen to below forty kilos, and he was still in a brutal outside Kommando; he knew he could not last the winter. So he made his decision. Perhaps only days before the camp was evacuated, he entered the Dysentery Ward, using the mysterious trick we have already admired. That is where Primo found him, a week or so later: clinging to his dying companion, and burning with fever.

Lello's sickness was not really physical. He too had badly frozen feet; and by the time Primo reached him with his soup he was in the last stages of starvation. But he probably did not have dysentery, and he certainly had no other disease. What he had was despair. After seven months of Birkenau, the loss of his brothers, and the final horror of the Dysentery Ward, even Lello Perugia no longer wanted to live.

But the Russians did not ask if you wanted to live, any more than the Germans had asked if you wanted to die. Lello was carted off to the hospital at Auschwitz like the others. And there, being Lello, he almost immediately recovered. He was probably among the first to reach Katowice: 'not only restored,' Primo wrote, 'but little less than flourishing, and as lively as a grasshopper.'

A little too flourishing, in fact. For the Germans had mounted a final counter-offensive, and the Russians suddenly needed extra manpower, to dig anti-tank trenches across the Oder Valley from Gleiwitz. One day in early March they descended on the camp at Bogucice, armed to the teeth, and ordered all the inmates to assemble on the main square. In a strange parody of a German selection, they divided the able-bodied from the ill: and let the ill go, and prepared to take the able-bodied off to Gleiwitz.

Before long everyone realized what was going on, and dozens tried to slip away and hide. Soon the Russians were chasing people all over the camp, like a giant game of tag, or hide-and-seek – except that the hunters had Sten guns, and the penalty for being caught was hard labour. Lello had smelled a rat from the start; instead of the *Appellplatz* he had gone straight to the woodshed, and hidden under a pile of logs. It nearly worked. But in the last minute another inmate dived into the woodshed, with a Russian in hot pursuit; and in the ensuing scramble Lello was uncovered.

He did his best – he shook like a leaf, as though with fever, he limped and dragged a leg; no one in the whole camp looked sicker or more useless. But the Russians just waited until he'd finished, then sent him to Gleiwitz with the others.

There it was like being back in the Lager: they had far too little to eat, and slept in a barn; and they dug trenches for sixteen hours a day, under the brooding eye of an armed guard. Lello had been right: this was no place for him. This time he had better be ill for real. For several days he saved his bread; when he had enough, he exchanged it for two cigars. One he soaked in water and held in his armpit all night; the other he ate. The next day he was as sick as a dog. He was dizzy, he had a high fever, he vomited ceaselessly. The Russians put him to bed, and watched the strength drain from his limbs. Clearly this one was no use to them any more. They sent him back to Katowice; and even before he arrived Lello had miraculously recovered.

At Katowice, he found that Primo had recently arrived. The two had not seen each other since the last apocalyptic days in Monowitz; they re-met with profound emotion. 'I managed to settle him in my room,' Primo wrote, 'and we remained inseparable until the return journey.'

Now, this real Cesare is not quite the Cesare Primo portrays. He knew it very well; it was part of what he meant by the new 'literariness' of *The Truce*. '[The] words and adventures I've given Cesare have been freely re-created and interpreted, and in parts invented,' he wrote – to 'Cesare' himself, when

La tregua was published. In fact, he'd hesitated for many weeks before sending Lello a copy: he was afraid he might mind some of those interpretations, some of those inventions. You'll judge for yourself, he said to Lello: but please remember that 'for some reason', everyone seems to find this Cesare 'a pretty sympathetic character'.

Lello did judge for himself, of course – and Primo's fears were more than justified. Lello minded very much, and he still does. Primo saved his life, they went through the most important time of their lives together, they were friends in a way few can ever be friends; and Lello will not breathe a word against him. But underneath he is very angry. He is angry at everyone, at life – at the fact that Auschwitz existed, and that other Auschwitzes have existed since, as he had always known they would. That realism of his – that quickness to believe the worst – has aged into bitterness: a sparky, pugnacious, Lello-like bitterness, but a bitterness still. And some of it, though he will not say so, is for Primo. For Primo betrayed him too, in his way; and like the grasshopper to which Primo so brilliantly compared him, Lello is hopping mad.

How did Primo betray him? He made Cesare into one of his archetypal *alter egos* – just as he would do with Sandro, and in similar ways. He made him rougher, poorer and simpler than he was. Cesare comes from the ghetto; he has been a street trader all his life, a barrow-boy, who 'kept a stall at the Porta Portese'. Lello was outraged. He was a book-keeper, not a barrow-boy – and he was a *Communist*, for heaven's sake, who despised commerce and the profit motive, whose parents had kept shops because they had to, but who had sworn that he himself would never in his whole life stoop to trade (and he never has). It is true, he says, that he did all the 'organizing' for the group, and very much as Primo describes: well, someone had to, and only he could; Primo and Leonardo were quite hopeless. But that was the point – he did it for the group. Not for himself, as many did, but for his friends, his companions, his fellow survivors.

Well, Primo was creating a character, and a more amusing (and believable) one than that. Anyway, Cesare *does* organize for the whole group; if he makes sure to do well for himself as well, it is not out of selfishness, but in order to preserve his reputation. As for turning the Communist book-keeper into a barrow-boy, that is undeniably true. But as I have said, Primo was creating a character: and that character is not as far from Lello as he imagines. He was – and is – a Communist; he has worked all his life in government service; and only in that extraordinary time and place did he bargain and cheat and deal. But (unlike Primo, as he says himself) he could and did; it came naturally to him. That particularly Italian gift for ignoring the rules, for dealing and fixing, for corruption mixed with charm, warmth and *joie de vivre* – that very Italian mixture is what Cesare embodies; and so does Lello. Even fifty years on it's still strong in him, as he sneaks a third illicit cigarette, and flaps his newspaper at the smoke, so that his wife won't try to stop him dying of cancer; grinning and winking at me throughout with impish delight. Now I have betrayed him too. But he knows very well in life – though he was shocked to see it on the page – that people love him for his wicked ways, and for how he enjoys them: especially Primo. For Primo wickedness was freedom, but freedom was therefore wicked: he admired and envied people who were both wicked and free, but couldn't himself be either. That is why Cesare is the picaresque hero of *La tregua*, while the narrator is his timid, law-abiding stooge, always one step behind him. If *The Truce* exaggerated some embarrassing truths about Lello Perugia, it did the same to Primo Levi.

Spring blossomed, and the Katowice market grew from 'a fair of human miseries' to a feast of riches, as the peasants' carts rolled in from the country-side laden with cheese and chickens, fruit, eggs, sugar, butter, lard. Like dozens of others, Lello regularly slipped out to Katowice to supplement his and his companions' diet.

Strictly speaking, they were not meant to leave the camp, and the entrance was permanently guarded. But there was only one guard: a huge old Mongolian, with fierce Stalin moustaches and a Sten gun, who was as unpredictable as all the Russians. Sometimes he let no one pass, sometimes everyone; sometimes he asked for your *propusk*, your permit, sometimes only for tobacco. Opposite the entrance there was a hole in the fence, so large you could get out without even bending down; the Mongolian never paid it the slightest attention, though it was in full view. But that way was muddier, and perhaps a few hundred yards longer; and Lello disdained it. Primo had a *propusk*, because he worked in the infirmary (the infirmary, canteen and washrooms all lay just outside the boundary fence); and Primo had said he would like to see the market. Well, then? For a long time, Primo says, he could not overcome his inertia. But at last, one glorious spring day in April, he was ready to be free.

This is what they did: Primo went first. He gave his name to the Mongolian, and showed him his *propusk*: yes, the names corresponded. Primo turned the corner, and passed the *propusk* to Lello through the barbed wire. Now Lello gave his name: 'Primo Levi'. Again the Mongolian checked the *propusk* – and yes, again the names corresponded. Lello walked out 'in a wholly legal manner', and without a spot of mud on his shoes.

This happened; Lello confirms it. He claims it was rather more practical, less purely a *jeu d'esprit* than Primo makes it; but it happened. Like the episode of the Canto of Ulysses, however, which also happened, it carries a charge of buried meaning; and that is why, consciously or unconsciously, Primo tells it. In his first adventure with 'Cesare', *they swap identities.* Lello becomes Primo, and so behaves in a 'wholly legal manner' – except, of course, that the whole thing is a scam, so that really Primo becomes Lello, or like Lello, and behaves, for once, in a wholly illegal one. And what is he doing? He is escaping, leaving somewhere he is not supposed to leave: becoming free. Freedom is wickedness, and wickedness freedom. To seize them Primo must lose his identity; must substitute it, like a magic trick, for Lello/Cesare's.

And so he did. Several times in April he went with Lello to the Katowice market, very likely using the *propusk* trick every time. He went to learn, to interpret, to carry things; but mostly he went to watch, and to enjoy the 'live and fortifying spectacle' of Lello's cunning, innocent, irresistible charm.

It worked like this. Lello had found a professional partner, a wily old jailbird called Giacomo Pavoncello (Primo calls him Giacomantonio in *The Truce*). Giacomo bought cheap: from Russian soldiers, for example, returning from Germany laden with booty. Then Lello sold high, and they divided the profits between them. One day, Giacomo brought Lello a pile of goods, including a fountain pen that didn't write and a woollen shirt with a hole under the collar. Lello and Primo set off to the market. There Lello let the pen go to the first bidder, without bargaining, and immediately a little crowd formed, like bees scenting honey. Now Lello held the shirt up in the sun, his fingers just happening to cover the hole. He sang its praises 'with torrential eloquence' – in Italian, of course, or rather in Roman dialect, but this only made his performance more intriguing. He fixed his blue eyes on each person in turn, addressing them with his own safely incomprehensible nicknames – Booby, Buttocks, The Bearded Lady, Frankenstein. He kissed the shirt lingeringly, as though he could not bear to part with it; then stiffened his back and swivelled his eyes on to his victim. 'You, Big Belly,' he said, 'how much will you give me for this little *koshoola* of mine?'

Big Belly was struck with fear and desire. Shyly he mumbled a sum: '*Pinjee-shi zlotych*', fifty *zloty*. Lello clutched the shirt to his breast, horrified. '*What did he say?*' he demanded, and Primo translated. 'You're crazy,' Lello said, twirling his finger at his temple; then, leaning forward, '*Du meschuge*'* – and the crowd burst into mocking laughter. He had won. '*Sto zlotych*,' Big Belly said, red with embarrassment. From now on it was just a question of time. Primo and the crowd willed Lello on as he coaxed, harangued and shamed Big

---

* *Meschuge* is the Yiddish word for 'crazy'; as Primo says, it was universally understood in Central and Eastern Europe.

Belly up to *sto pinjeeshi*, 150 *zloty*. Finally the goal was reached, and money and shirt changed hands. But immediately, Primo wrote, 'Cesare tore me from my ecstatic admiration.' 'Let's scarper,' he hissed, 'before he sticks his finger through the hole.' So they gathered up their goods with smiling regret, and walked slowly to the nearest corner. Then they exchanged a triumphant glance – and Primo Levi from Crocetta, *dottore in chimica* from the University of Turin, scarpered. No wonder he loved Lello Perugia.

Towards the end of April Lello disappeared for several days. When he finally reappeared, very early one morning, everyone was still half asleep. 'Leave me alone,' he demanded, though no one had said a word. He threw himself on to his bunk 'with an air', Primo wrote, 'of extreme exhaustion'. Still no one spoke; and after a few minutes he could bear it no longer. He got up and went over to Primo. He had bags under his eyes, Primo saw, but 'they still shone with a proud light'. 'I've made it at last,' he announced. 'I've got a *panienca*.' He had found himself a girl.

They'd met in Katowice. She'd invited him home for a meal; then it had got late, and she had offered him a bed. Not hers, to start with, which she shared with her two-year-old child; but near it, in her one small room. When Lello was sure the child was asleep he approached her, saying, '*Ich kalt*', 'Me cold', even though it was a warm and balmy night. She asked if he was ill. No, he said, he was from Auschwitz. Then she said, '*Komm*,' and he got in beside her. Soon they made love, twice, while the baby slept peacefully beside them.

When Lello tells me this story I'm touched by the girl's kindness, by her desire to comfort an Auschwitz survivor. But that is not what struck either Primo or Lello. Primo did not report what the girl said at all, but made the episode into one of Cesare's roguish adventures, from which he returns bursting with masculine pride. But that is not how it was, Lello says, still aggrieved. This too he did not do for himself alone, but for all of them. I must look a little surprised; he hastens to explain. As Auschwitz had taken away the women's periods, so it had made the men impotent: the Germans had put something in the water (though Leonardo said it was just the starvation and disease). In any case, that had been his idea, when he found himself alone with the girl – to test himself, for everyone's sake. And *that* is what he told Primo, with such joy, on his return: don't worry, we are normal men once more!

I think I know why Primo wouldn't tell it that way. But was it true? Was Lello's group of friends really thinking, at that moment, about impotence – Leonardo, the grieving Mariani? Or Primo? No, Lello admits cheerfully, he was the only one. Perhaps because he was the only rover, as he was the only organizer, he says, with a touch of pride . . . He does not seem to notice any inconsistency. But about the story of the *panienca*, perhaps I believe Primo slightly more.

Lello's affair coincided with the last dramatic days of the war. Primo watched the headlines of the Polish papers swell with victory; day after day he puzzled out their key words: Vienna – Koblenz – Rhine – Bologna . . . Then, 'with emotion and joy', *Turin* and *Milan*; and finally, in red letters covering half the page: BERLIN UPADL!

During the first week of May Lello vanished again. On 1 May the Mongolian guard vanished, and the *Kommandantur* offices emptied: everyone was drunk, or asleep, or making 'mysterious and feverish preparations' in the gymnasium (the Command's HQ was in an abandoned school). On 3 May there was a Polish holiday; and on 8 May the war ended. The camp – and Bogucice, Katowice, the whole of Poland, the entire Red Army, Primo wrote – exploded. The Russians embraced each other and everyone else, they drank oceans of vodka, they sang and danced and shouted; they fired shots in the air, 'and not always in the air'. A young parachutist, still beardless, with 'eyes as virgin as the sea', was brought into the surgery with an entrance wound in his stomach and an exit wound in his back: by some miracle the bullet had missed his vital organs. He stayed in bed for three days, as good as gold; on the third he jumped out of bed 'fully dressed, in his uniform and boots', Primo wrote, and 'like the good parachutist he was', leapt out of the first-floor window and disappeared.

On one of these wild days of celebration Lello returned, black-browed and haggard: his *panienca* had dumped him for a Russian. But he could not sulk for long. The war was over, the other nationalities had already left, any day now the Italians too could surely *go home*. And in the meantime the mystery of the 'feverish preparations' was solved: they were invited, as honoured guests, to the Russians' Victory Day gala performance.

The whole *Kommandantur* took part. Captain Egorov was the compère: blind drunk, he was more lugubrious than ever, and presented each new act sobbing and weeping. There were patriotic songs, comic acts, recitations. Above all, there was dancing. Dr Klimchenko and the Mongolian guard did an extraordinary Cossack dance, crouched down and spinning around like dervishes, kicking out their legs, somehow managing to keep together and not fall over, though they too were full to the brim with vodka. And then there was Galina. She danced alone, Primo says, dressed in a Circassian costume and high boots. No one had known – certainly he had not known – that she was a wonderful dancer; the audience roared and stormed with applause, and she thanked them, overwhelmed, 'her face red as a tomato and her eyes glittering with tears'. A few days later she was gone.

The End of Katowice

'This time,' Leonardo wrote to his family on 11 May, 'it seems we're really going': but still they didn't go. Why was it only they, the Italians, who were left behind? Because they had been allies of Germany? But so had the Austrians, the Hungarians and Romanians, and they had all gone. The war was over, there was no longer any reason to keep them; from now on every day they were still there was unjust, unbearable, much worse than before. More and more people began to slip away, and to try to make their own way home, via Vienna. Even Primo and Leonardo, the endurers, the cautious ones, thought of doing the same: of crossing Europe without papers, without permission, without money. At least so they told their friends, and probably themselves. But then something happened that took the decision out of their hands: Primo fell ill.

He had gone to a football match between the Katowice team and the Italians. It was a long walk back to the camp; as soon as they started it began to pour, and they arrived home soaked to the skin. Primo had endured long months in the rain and snow, labouring and starving, without even catching a cold: but that extraordinary resistance, like a soldier's in battle, deserted him now. The next day he could not breathe properly; soon he could hardly breathe at all. For days he lay in his bunk, terrified, unable to move, taking only short, shallow breaths like 'a panting dog'.

Now Leonardo showed his special qualities, both as a doctor and as a friend. With no equipment apart from one elderly stethoscope, he diagnosed the problem: pleurisy. Then, with Lello's help, he turned himself into 'a black market trader and drug smuggler'. Together, Primo's two oddly matched, desperately worried friends scoured the back streets of Katowice for the necessary drugs. If they found them they could not afford them; not even Lello's best tricks could raise such sums. But they found something better, Primo tells us: they found Dr Gottlieb.

'Gottlieb''s real name was Einhorn: Dr Adolfo Einhorn. They knew that; but that was all they knew. Everything about him, Primo wrote, was wrapped in a fog of mystery. He came from Fiume (probably), and spoke perfect Italian; but he also spoke perfect German, Polish, Hungarian and Russian, and came equally from Vienna and Zagreb. He had been in Auschwitz; but how he had entered and survived was mysterious. He had one arm crippled by arthritis (according to Primo), or one lame leg (according to Lello): it is typical of Gottlieb/Einhorn that even the nature of his handicap should be unclear. He was a doctor, it's true, and had no doubt told the SS so on arrival; but normally even that wouldn't help, since cripples were almost as bad as Jews in Nazi eyes. Dr Einhorn, however, was not normal. That must have been what saved him; as it saved Primo now.

'Intelligence and cunning emanated from him like energy from radium,' Primo wrote, in a 'silent and penetrating' stream. He had high intellect, boundless self-assurance, and a magic ability to turn 'enemies into friends', 'no into yes'. Not only had he survived Auschwitz, together with his brother and brother-in-law; but a few months after liberation he was a rich and respected doctor in Katowice.

Now he came once to examine Primo, then several times to treat him, bringing syringes full of mysterious (and no doubt illegal) liquids. As rapidly as Primo's breathing had shut down to almost nothing it freed itself again; the stabbing pain in his lungs eased; he could turn over by himself, and sit up, and read. One day Einhorn gave him a final injection; after which he said (at least 'Dr Gottlieb' said), 'Rise up and walk.' 'I felt very weak,' Primo wrote, 'but I got up, and I could walk.' It was as though a hand had reached out from the darkness of the Dysentery Ward and briefly clutched him; but it had been forced to let go. He had taken one more step away from Auschwitz.

It was now late May, or early June. Tantalizing smells of new grass, of moss and mushrooms from the nearby wood, drifted into his room through the open window; and here he was, still inside. But this time they were not lost, like the sounds of the Dora eighteen months before. They were waiting for him, they were offering him a second chance – or even, now, a third one.

For several weeks he read and recovered. Perhaps (as Leonardo said about himself) he could even have been happy, if it had not been for the constant anxiety about everyone at home. It was four months now since he had seen the young Russians on their horses, and knew that he had survived. But his mother and sister still did not know it, and he did not know what had happened to them; nor to Sandro, to Alberto and Bianca, to Guido Bachi and Aldo Piacenza, whom he'd last seen in the barracks in Aosta, to all his friends. Leonardo doggedly wrote letters, and posted them into the void; but neither he nor anyone else ever had a reply, and no one believed the Polish post was working. When, therefore, another Turinese decided to break for home in early June, Primo gave him a letter – holding his breath, and suppressing a prayer – for Rina and Anna Maria.

The messenger was well chosen, from one point of view: he was one of the ex-convicts from San Vittore, 'an accomplished rogue', as Primo says, used to living outside the law. He had no difficulty slipping through dozens of checkpoints and borders without documents; it took him only a month to reach Turin. He also managed to find Rina and Anna Maria, even though they were not yet back in the flat in Corso Re Umberto, which had been impounded under the racial laws. Thus, in July 1945, Primo's family knew at last that he had survived, and was still alive.

But now Cravero's★ talents stopped being useful to anyone but himself. Yes, he said, the Lord be praised, Primo was still alive: but only just. Naturally he hadn't said so in his letter, but in fact he was ill, alone, and generally in a very bad way. But he, Cravero, was ready to come to the rescue. If Signora Levi could give him, say, 200,000 *lire*, he would immediately return to Poland, and bring her sick son home.

After twenty months of war, Rina and Anna Maria had learned caution: they didn't have such a sum in the house, they said, Cravero should come back in a few days' time. But after a lifetime of villainy, Cravero knew when he had failed. He didn't bother to return; instead he stole Anna Maria's bicycle in compensation. 'Two years later, at Christmas,' Primo wrote, 'he sent me an affectionate card from prison in Turin.'

In Katowice, on the contrary, Primo was getting better. He left his bed, and his room; and for a week or so he wandered around the edges of the city: '[taking] possession of my body again', he wrote, accepting the offer of the trees and grass, and of 'the heavy brown soil, in which one could feel the seeds trembling'.

Perhaps he and Leonardo began to talk again of leaving under their own steam. But abruptly, without warning, it was no longer necessary. At the end of June Captain Egorov made an announcement: the order for repatriation had finally come. Their route would be via Odessa, the Black Sea and Constantinople to Bari. The Italians were going home.

The whole camp exploded. People ran up and down the corridors yelling '*A casa! a casa!*' – 'We're going home! We're going home!' They rushed to Katowice, to buy provisions, to celebrate, to say goodbye to their girls. Primo and Leonardo went to the surgery to say goodbye to Marya Fyodorovna and Dr Klimchenko. The doctor had brought a bottle of vodka, from which they all drank a farewell toast. He had also brought two mysterious pieces of paper. These turned out to be declarations of thanks for their humane treatment at Katowice, which Klimchenko asked them to sign: making sure to mention his name explicitly, and to add 'Doctor of Medicine' to theirs. Primo hesitated, pointing out that in his case it was not true; but he soon repented and signed ('Who was I to deprive him of a little help in his career?').

Dr Klimchenko then brought out two more pieces of paper, which he

---

★ Primo calls him Cravero not only in *The Truce* but in 'Il mitra sotto il letto', published in *La Stampa* in 1986. The repetition of the name so many years later suggests (though of course it doesn't prove) that it was real.

presented to them with a flourish. Leonardo's testimonial said, in a fine flowing hand and with several repetitions, that Dr Leonardo De Benedetti had been of the greatest assistance to the 125th Russian Command, saving the lives of many of its allies, and showing his patients much understanding. It was signed 'Natalie' – which was possibly, therefore, Marya Fyodorovna's real name; and something illegible, which must have been Klimchenko's.

Primo's (he wrote) said: 'Primo Levi, Doctor of Medicine, of Turin, has given able and assiduous assistance to the Surgery of this Command for four months, and in this manner has earned the gratitude of all the workers of the world.'

Well, it probably said something closer to the rambling, simple sincerity of Leonardo's. But Primo could not resist a good story; and not only about Lello Perugia.

To Zhmerinka

By the end there were well over 1,000 Italians in Katowice, including whole families with children. Several different convoys left on several different days, amid wild cheering and forests of waving red and red-white-and-green flags. The train taking the women and children seems to have got furthest, perhaps only a few miles from Odessa.* But they would all end up in the same place as Primo.

His train left Katowice on 1 July. There was no escort, indeed not a single Russian on board; instead their unofficial officer-in-charge was Dr Einhorn. This was just as well, since the *Kommandantur* had made no arrangements whatever for this frail ship of hope: they had pointed each convoy in the direction of Odessa, and that was all. No one knew they were coming, where they were going, or what to do with them in the meantime; and if it had not been for Einhorn they would probably have starved, or have been left on a siding for months instead of hours. But Einhorn was there, 'as sharp as a knife', Primo wrote; and his assurance, his inventiveness, his sheer effrontery cut through the bureaucracy that bound them, like Houdini dissolving his chains. When one station-master required a travel warrant Einhorn quickly fabricated one, in incomprehensible jargon and smothered with stamps and seals; when another said he had no authority to feed 800 Italians, Einhorn told him, with a confidential smile, that it was by personal order of Stalin – and they were fed.

---

* The women included several survivors of Birkenau who would return to Turin: Elena Levi, Elsa Levi, Emma Pacifici, Miranda Avigdor, for instance; and perhaps others as well.

For a week their train rolled through endless fields of wheat and corn, through tall dark forests like tunnels, past ruined villages and towns; to stick fast in the knots of the stations until Einhorn freed them, and they rolled on again. At Lvov it poured, and the roof of their wagon leaked; Primo and his friends could find nowhere to sleep but the station underpass. At Proskurov they squeezed into a corner of the waiting-room; and here Einhorn performed his last miracle.

Although Primo's pleurisy was cured, he wasn't; but this time neither Leonardo nor Einhorn knew what was wrong. Every night he was invaded by a mysterious fever, so high he would lose consciousness. The next morning he would be half delirious, and crippled with pain; during the day he would recover, but promptly at night the fever would return. By now even Einhorn had run out of drugs; but at Proskurov he found something else: half a litre of raw vodka, bought from some peasants. It tasted, Primo said, of 'must, vinegar and fire'. Einhorn told him to drink it all, it would do him good. He passed out; and when he woke he felt as though he were under a huge, heavy weight. He *was* under a huge, heavy weight: dozens more people had pushed into the waiting-room during the night and, finding not an inch of floor left, had simply lain down and slept on those who were already there. And when their weight lifted, Primo discovered that the pain was gone, the delirium was over, his eyes were once more clear. The animal heat of so many bodies, combined with the fiery vodka, had driven out the poison in pints of sweat. In a triumphant reversal of the piles of corpses he had left behind, a pile of living bodies had cured him, at least physically, of his last Auschwitz disease.

A few hours after it left Proskurov the train arrived in Zhmerinka, where it stopped. This was not unusual, of course. What was unusual was that Einhorn could not make it move again. No one was more surprised and disturbed than he. We have to get off the train, he told them, it's not going any further. *What?* they asked. Why? Then how would they get to Odessa? But Einhorn – Einhorn! – didn't know. They got off the train and spent the night in the station. The next morning Einhorn, his brother and brother-in-law had disappeared.

He seems to have got home barely a month later, more than two months before the rest of the Italians, and it is true that he took none of them with him. Nonetheless he performed a last good deed. He reported to the Red Cross that he 'had left Dr Leonardo De Benedetti in good health in Zhmerinka, on 8 July 1945'. Very likely he did this for others too, including Primo. Despite everything, Leonardo's family had received at least some of his letters. But anything could happen, and every sighting of a survivor was precious, like every glimpse of someone's head still above water after a shipwreck. The Debenedettis cherished Dr Einhorn's Red Cross report; and it was still among Leonardo's papers when he died.

The Wrong Way

They stayed at Zhmerinka for several days, in a torment of anxiety. It soon became clear that they would not be going to Odessa after all. Why was less clear, though they never stopped asking; and rumours rushed in to fill the void. They were going to be sent to the Far East instead, to work for the Allies in the war against Japan. Or: the Allies had already fallen out, and they were being held as hostages for a new war about to begin. Or (more practically): Odessa was full, there was no room for them, and they would have to wait until there was. Or (most likely): it was the chaos of war. No one had any plans for them, for good or for ill; they were simply forgotten, and would grow old in the station at Zhmerinka.

Instead, on or about 10 July, they did move; but the wrong way. No one could tell them their destination, but they could see for themselves that they were heading northwards: 'away from the sea, away from Italy, towards exile, solitude, gloom, winter'. But there was nothing to be done; even Lello had climbed aboard with the rest, grumbling furiously. They were given no provisions at all this time, not even the skeletal amounts of bread and margarine the Katowice *Kommandantur* had supplied. Primo the optimist said this meant that the journey would be short; Lello the pessimist said it meant that the Russians, like the Germans, wanted them to starve.

For once Primo turned out to be more or less right. The journey was not short, but it was fast. For two days and a night they raced northwards, hardly ever stopping. During one brief halt, on the first evening, he and Lello got out to stretch their legs. At the head of the train they saw an empty hospital car. Lello's eyes lit up. 'Why don't we get in there?' he hissed. 'But it's not allowed,' Primo said, in instinctive alarm, and immediately felt ashamed. In they scrambled; and spent a glorious night in proper bunks, with clean sheets and blankets, while Leonardo and the others lay awake on the floor of their freight car, worrying themselves sick over their lost companions.

The next night they arrived at their destination: the assembly camp at Slutsk, about sixty miles south of Minsk. Slutsk had been a Soviet military camp. It stood, unfenced, in a vast grassy plain between the railway line and a row of small distant hills. In the middle of the camp the grass reappeared: a huge square of it, which had once been the parade ground, and was now a football pitch, campsite and general meeting place for 10,000 ex-POWs and displaced persons from all over the world, many of them Italians. Around the square stood crumbling barracks, stripped and plundered by the retreating Germans. All that was left was the walls, and the 10,000 prisoners slept on the floors. But it was hot, there was plenty of food, and they were free to do as they pleased, if there had been anything to do; even to go where they pleased, if there had been anywhere to go. Once Primo and his friends ventured out on to the plain, to look for herbs; but very soon they seemed to be in the middle of the sea, lost and dizzy, overcome by the 'immense, heroic space of Russia'.

It was here, on the plain outside the camp of Slutsk, that Primo re-met the Greek, and was offered one of his huge blonde girls, all lying in the grass around him, like a herd of sleepy cows. Amazed to see the Greek again, and shocked (he says 'dumbfounded') by his proposal, Primo turned it down. But the Greek's appearance at Slutsk wasn't as unusual as Primo makes it seem. When he and his friends had arrived, they discovered that all those they had so envied, as they watched them leave for home in May and June, had got no further than they had. Not only Leon Levi, but all the Greeks of Katowice – and French, and Hungarians, and Romanians – had fetched up at Slutsk as well, a month or two before them. They had probably been better off at Katowice.

Slutsk, however, was not to be their final destination either. After several slow, hot, empty days, as hard to measure as the Russian plain – Leonardo says five, Primo says ten – a rumour suddenly erupted: the Italians would be moving to a special Italian camp. It was called Starye Dorogi, it was forty-five miles away, and they would be walking.

That was all. 'The Germans', Primo said, 'would have covered the walls with bilingual notices', announcing the date and hour of departure, 'and threatening deserters with the death penalty'. The Russians just let the news spread, and the march organize itself. Some decided not to go; others managed to slip on to the train which (it turned out) ran between Slutsk and Starye Dorogi. The rest assembled themselves on the central square, around 20 July. There were several false starts. Finally, about noon, hundreds of Italians – soldiers, civilians, ex-*Häftlinge*, ex-criminals – set off to cross the Pripet Marshes, under the endless Russian sky.

There was a road: a wide, straight road, so straight that in all the forty-five miles between Slutsk and Starye Dorogi there was, Primo wrote, 'only one curve, barely visible'. There were no villages, no houses, no people; only the occasional hawk or crow. They walked for hours, and still seemed to be in the same place; as though time and space had expanded to infinity, or didn't exist at all. It was, in fact, remarkably like the journey *l'Uomo*, the Man, had made in Primo's long-ago story, on his way to enter the living world.

At first they all kept together, in a brave pretence of order. But soon some began to flag, and the column began to thin and straggle. By dusk, Primo and his group were almost alone.

There were six of them: Primo, Leonardo, Lello, and Luciano Mariani; plus two *triestini* who had almost certainly been in their dormitory in Katowice, and who had attached themselves to Primo's group ever since (or to Lello's group, as he would have called it; and probably they did as well). One was much older: a 'mild, touchy little old man' whose survival of Auschwitz was as mysterious as Einhorn's, and whom Primo calls 'Mr Unverdorben', which means 'unspoilt'. He was the sort of character Primo would find more and more fascinating, and whom he met in great numbers in this strange, dreamlike time: a fantasist, who constructs 'the past that suits him best', who invents his own story. 'Mr Unverdorben''s story was that he was a musician, 'a great misunderstood musician', who had composed a lyric opera hailed by Toscanini; but whose enemies had accused him of plagiarism, and forced him (he would say with tragic dignity) to abandon art for ever.

'Mr Unverdorben' and his friend now partook in one of the more improbable adventures of Primo's return, which Lello modestly confirms was entirely true: the adventure of the *kuritsa*, the little hen.

By the side of the road there was, miraculously, a tumble-down hut; and behind it, even more miraculously, a well. Why not stop, and spend the night here? Their feet were aching, it was warm and dry, no one would notice if they arrived a day late in Starye Dorogi. So it was decided. They hid in a wood until the last stragglers had passed; then they spread their blankets on the ground, pooled their resources, and began to prepare a meagre supper: bread and water, some millet *kasha*, and a tin of peas. Except for Lello. 'To hell with your peas,' he said. 'I'm going to have roast chicken.'

'Cesare is an untameable man,' Primo wrote. It was useless to point out to Lello that they had no money, no Russian, and no idea where to find a chicken in the middle of the Pripet Marshes. And he, Primo, was intrigued: how would Lello pull this one off? He offered to accompany him. The others reluctantly handed over their earthenware plates as barter; and with the six plates under their arms, Lello and Primo strode off into the gathering dusk.

Now, Lello was untameable, but not crazy: he had seen a path leading from the hut northwards through the wood. Where there was a path, he announced, there was a village; and where there was a village, there were chickens. He was right. They hadn't gone far when they saw a light shining between the trees. They went on with a will now, calling out at intervals. There was no reply, until they were close enough to see five or six wooden houses. Then the reply came: not a voice but a bullet, whistling past their ears. Primo dropped to the ground; but not Lello. 'We're friends!' he yelled.

'Not Deutschski, Italianski! We only want a chicken!' And on he went, still shouting, with Primo behind him, ready to hug the ground again at any moment.

Nothing happened; and when they entered the village the entire population was waiting for them, murmuring and staring with curiosity. 'Now it's your turn,' Lello said. He had done the hard part: as soldier and strategist, he had got them in. Now it was up to the scholar and linguist to finish the job. But this was not as easy as he imagined. Primo's Russian vocabulary was very limited, most of it remembered from nineteenth-century novels; it did not contain any words that might conceivably be useful here, and it certainly did not include 'chicken'. He tried to say 'chicken', 'hen' and 'bird' in every language he could think of, to no avail.

Meanwhile, Lello was getting angry. Could it really be so hard to understand 'chicken'? He was an excellent mimic; but this wasn't his job, so he did it badly. He squatted on his haunches and pecked; then he laid an egg, making obscene gestures with one hand, and shouting insults at his audience at the same time. Primo saw that they were rapidly losing all the good will they had won. Perhaps the danger inspired him. He led one of the men to a window, where a lamp threw a pool of light outside; with a stick he carefully drew a hen in the earth, 'complete with all its attributes, including an egg'. He pointed to the man, and to the plates, lined up on the ground; then to himself and the hen. 'You, plates,' he said. 'We, eat.' There was a brief whispered conference; then an old woman stepped forward, 'her eyes alight', Primo wrote, 'with joy and comprehension'. '*Kura,*' she cried. '*Kuritsa!*' '*Kuritsa, kuritsa!*' everyone echoed, laughing and clapping.

The mystery was solved. A little hen was triumphantly produced; and Lello and Primo bore it back even more triumphantly to their companions. We relit the fire and cooked it, Primo wrote, 'and ate it with our fingers, because we no longer had any plates'.

Starye Dorogi

They arrived at Starye Dorogi the next night in style, on a wagon driven by an old man from the village.

Starye Dorogi, Primo wrote, was not a village: or rather there was a village, but they were not in it. The Italian camp was a single, vast building, standing alone on the edge of the forest. There was a Russian Command, who lived in a wooden hut nearby; but the Italians were not fenced in, or guarded or watched in any way. Their fence was the endless Russian plain all around them, like the seas around Devil's Island.

Their building was a village in itself, with a theatre, a surgery, a gymnasium, and a series of lecture rooms and classrooms, as well as the dormitories, kitchens and washrooms of a normal barracks, which it had probably been. On to its central three-storey block other wings and extensions had stuck like fungi, or spilled out like (Primo says) a volcanic flow: 'it was hard to tell if it was the work of many quarrelling architects, or of a single one who was mad'. All over it, inside and out, were staircases, trying to connect the disparate parts. One climbed fifty feet up a façade and ended in nowhere, as though its builder had given up in despair. The whole pile was empty, everything movable having been stripped and carried away, as at Slutsk; in all the maze of staircases, not even the steepest retained a banister. And all of it, inside and out, was painted red; which gave the place its name, *Krasny Dom*, the Red House.

This is a description of hell. No doubt it was so – the flame-coloured walls, the disconnected rooms, the staircases going nowhere; but by telling these details and no others, Primo makes the house itself express the dislocation, the maddening entrapment of its tenants. For two long months, from around 20 July to 15 September, they waited in the Red House for the Russians to decide their fate. They did not have to work, or be counted, or obey any rules. They ate Russian military rations of dark rye bread and *kasha*; they slept on Russian military cots, wooden planks covered with straw sacks, two feet wide. Compared to what they had just survived, life was comfortable and easy – 'and full, therefore', Primo wrote, 'of a piercing longing for home'. Homesickness, he wrote, 'is a clear, clean pain, but demanding: it permeates every minute of the day, leaves no room for other thoughts, and insists on escape'. But how could they escape? The whole of Russia was like the Red House: an endless jumble of spaces and dead ends. Many tried; some got as far as Odessa or Moscow; but very few managed to cross the borders to the West, which were still firmly closed. Most returned, after a few weeks, to Starye Dorogi and their companions.

What did Primo do? He went with Lello and watched him bargain with the peasant women of Starye Dorogi. He went for walks in the wood and got lost, and thought he would never get home after all. He went to film shows, and watched the audience. He went to theatre shows, and saw reflected in them 'the impotence and nullity of our life, and of life itself' – which may make us wonder if the depression of the past did not sometimes creep back over him here.

He worked in the surgery with Leonardo; but it was summer, people were eating, and they had hardly any patients. Here in the surgery, however, he had an encounter with the past. A small dark girl came in one day; and there stirred in him distant memories of desire, fear, and unvarying anguish.

At last he realized who she was – the girl he called Flora, whom he and Alberto had met in the Buna cellars, and who had lit up their dreams a year, a lifetime, ago. Now here she was, still exactly the same: humble, submissive, beaten by her current lover, a cobbler from Bergamo. And he, Primo, was burdened by memory and waiting, but alive and full of hope; and Alberto was possibly – no, probably – dead.

He did not identify himself to Flora, to spare her, and also himself. Unlike Flora, he felt intensely changed, 'like a butterfly beside a caterpillar', he said. But he should have said: 'like a chrysalis beside a caterpillar'. He had not yet changed, at least in this. He still did not find it easy to speak to a woman of love or desire; not even when it was safely past, and the woman as humble as Flora.

Now that life had returned almost to normal, everyone's thoughts had turned to love. The only guard in the Red House stood at the door to the women's quarters; not that that deterred anyone, Russian or Italian. Those few women who were not already married soon chose their partners; together they would go to the sailor Cantarella, who made pots and pans out of empty tins; and with Cantarella's pots and pans they set up house, and were 'married'. The hundreds of men who were left single talked obsessively of women: but not, it seems – any more than his schoolmates long ago – in front of Primo. He was the last one, he says, to know about 'the girls in the wood'.

'The girls in the wood' were two young German women left behind by their army. They had built themselves an extraordinary hut of tree trunks and branches, half underground, with an earth floor and beds of hay; here they had lived on small thefts and occasional prostitution, until 'the arrival of the Italians', Primo said, 'brought them prosperity and safety'. Untold numbers went to them regularly; and not just out of necessity. Their hut in the wood was romantic and wild, like something out of a fairy-tale. The girls themselves had grown half-savage; and at the same time they were poor, dependent, and in need of protection. All this Primo noted. Probably he did not go to 'the girls in the wood' himself; but he understood their attraction very well.

These were some of the things he did (and failed to do) in the long days of waiting at Starye Dorogi. But what he mostly did was observe. Observation had always been his natural habit and his professional training. In the last year and a half it had become his duty, and his dedication; now it also became his joy. He had observed the Greek, and Lello, and Einhorn; and the pleasure and amazement they gave him had begun to cure his mind, as the raw vodka of Proskurov had cured his body. He had observed his companions in the dormitory at Katowice – especially the most eccentric and individual ones: mild little 'Mr Unverdorben', for example; and his opposite, the huge old Moor of Verona, who never stopped cursing; but whose insane rage was redeemed (Primo wrote) by 'a barbaric dignity', and by dedication to his sick daughter at home, for whom alone he went on living.

At Starye Dorogi too it was the eccentrics and self-inventors who most caught Primo's imagination. Cantarella the hermit, for example, who married people with his pots and pans; or the Velletrano,★ who also withdrew into the forest, and our ancestral past. Barefoot, half-naked, he hunted small animals with stones and traps, and slept on the bare ground. 'But as he too was born of man,' Primo wrote, 'in his own way he pursued virtue and knowledge': he made a knife, then a spear, then an axe, 'and had he had the time, no doubt he would have rediscovered agriculture and pasturage'.

More than anyone, however, 'Cesare' remained the focus of Primo's observation and entertainment. He watched as Lello bargained with Irina, who milked her cow directly into her clients' pails. Lello wants his full, Irina offers half. Lello holds his fish under Irina's nose, and closes his eyes, as though swooning at its smell. Quick as a flash Irina grabs the fish, and bites off its head; then she offers him three-quarters of a pail of milk. For once Lello is defeated; he accepts, and leaves Irina the fish, 'which she devours on the spot'.

Once, after several days of rain, the mushrooms and berries sprang up in such abundance that everyone took to the wood to collect them. Most of the mushrooms were small, brown and familiar; but some were larger, and a different shade, and no one was certain they were edible. As usual, Lello took over. He boiled up a potful of the strange mushrooms with vodka and garlic, which (he explained) 'kill all poisons'. Then he gave a few dozen people a small amount of the stew each, and ate the same amount himself. The next day he sought out his subjects; and never, Primo said, had he been so polite, so solicitous. 'How are you?' he asked each one. 'Did you sleep well? Did you have a good night?' 'And all the while,' Primo noted, 'he examined their faces with a clinical eye.' Everyone was well; the mushrooms could be eaten.

Today Lello nods and grins happily at these stories. But there is one story of Cesare at Starye Dorogi with which he is less happy. Primo invented it, he says; or at least changed it beyond recognition.

Three or four times a week, Primo recounts in *La tregua*, the Russians added fish to the daily distribution of black bread and *kasha*: a raw, unsalted

---

★ Not his real (nick)name, Primo notes; that may have been 'the Marinese', i.e. from Marino. Very likely 'Cantarella' wasn't Cantarella's real name either.

fish, not very fresh, which they called *ryba*. Even well cooked the *ryba* was not to the Italians' taste; and they soon decided that its best use was for trade in the village. Enter 'Cesare'.

On the morning of fish days he collected all his friends' and acquaintances' *ryba* on a piece of wire, 'slung the stinking garland round his shoulders', and disappeared. In the evening he returned and divided the spoils – chickens, eggs, cheese – 'to everyone's advantage, and above all his own'. With the profits he bought a pair of scales; and began to sell the *ryba* by weight, with a minute precision that much enhanced his professional reputation.

Then one day he came to Primo in the surgery and asked to borrow a syringe. He wouldn't say what it was for; a good friend, he said sharply, wouldn't inquire. Primo stopped inquiring and handed over the syringe. In the next few days Cesare was seen doing mysterious things with the *ryba* and a bucket of water in the woods. Finally he was back in the village with them; and instead of the limp, scrawny creatures they'd been given, he was weighing beautiful, firm, fat fish on his scales.

Primo is hugely amused, and tells us in convincing detail how Cesare found the best place to inject the *ryba* with water (the swimming bladder), and the best customers to gull (Russian soldiers passing through). But all of it, Lello says, is untrue. It happened only once, according to him, when the *ryba* of the day stank even more than usual. When he opened his bag (a bag, not that memorable garland), the peasants fell back, gagging, and refused to buy. So he took the *ryba* back to the Red House; and together he, Primo and Leonardo washed them in soap and water, until – at least for an hour or two – they stopped smelling. That was the extent of it – one day's laundering, not a regular cheating on weight; with not only Primo himself, but also the irreproachable Leonardo, as accessories.

Well, Primo may well have made it up; or perhaps he heard the story elsewhere, and couldn't resist attributing it to Cesare. Or perhaps it happened, and Lello denies it because it no longer suits his role as respectable citizen. Something else matters more. Whether the story was true or not, Primo knew that Lello would mind if he told it – and one or two of his other Cesare stories as well. He never mentioned Lello's name in public, and did all he could to keep Cesare's real identity secret: short of simply not telling those stories. Later, we know, he would not change or withdraw anything about other people he loved: not about Sandro, not even about Gabriella. That started now. He loved Lello; but he loved the stories more.

His version of the *ryba* story does not end here, however. One day, he says, Cesare returned empty-handed, without either the fish, or anything to show for them. He said that they had been stolen – torn from his hands by an angry client. For two days, Primo wrote, he brooded over his defeat, 'as bristly as a porcupine'. But much later he admitted the truth to his friend. On his way to Starye Dorogi he had passed an isolated hut, with a thin woman and three pale children sitting on the threshold. He stopped and offered the woman the *ryba*. Her face grew thinner still with desire; but with gestures of her skinny hands she explained that she had nothing to give him in exchange, that she had had nothing to give anyone for several days. At that point 'the children had looked at him with such eyes' that Cesare couldn't bear it. Don't tell a soul, he begged Primo, or his reputation would be ruined: but *he had given the fish away*.

This ending may be as true or untrue as the rest, but what it shows is profoundly true: that under all his layers – rogue, cynic, civil servant – Lello Perugia has a tender heart; and that despite his enchantment with Lello's wicked side, Primo wanted to tell that too.

★   ★

Around the middle of August a few timid signs of hope began to appear. One night they were rudely woken, made to queue for hours, and handed a wad of roubles each, without explanation. A unit of young soldiers arrived, saying that they had been sent to escort a group of foreigners, they didn't know when or where. And for the first time the Command issued shoes to all who needed them.

Each person responded to these signs according to his nature. Some were immediately convinced that the day of repatriation had arrived, others that on the contrary they were about to be transferred to yet another camp – or deported, for ever, to Siberia. The rationalists, like Primo, tried to suspend judgement, and wait and see. But then September came, and the air turned cold and damp: winter was near, and they were the furthest north they had ever been. Gloom and despondency settled back on the Red House; especially on those who had hoped the most.

'But finally the announcement came,' Primo wrote – 'the announcement of our return, of our salvation, of the conclusion to our long wanderings'. It came in two ways, he said; and though once again he picks out the strangest and most symbolic details, probably both were essentially true.

The first announcement came in the theatre: during one of their favourite sketches, in which a hoary castaway at long last spies a sail. Suddenly the cannibal chief tumbled on to the stage, tore off his crown of feathers and yelled: '*Domani si parte!*' – 'Tomorrow we leave!' And the next day, though they did not leave quite yet, the second messenger arrived. He was a Soviet General – perhaps, as Primo says, Marshal Timoshenko in person, the hero of Stalingrad; and he came to tell them and their Command that they were going home. He is, in Primo's account, an extraordinary apparition: a conquering hero borne towards them in a tiny Fiat Topolino smaller than himself; an angel of salvation dressed in a great black cloak like Death. He is at once grand and absurd, glorious and sinister: like a vision of the life awaiting them, which he announces; or rather, like Primo Levi's vision of it, at once deeply longed for and deeply feared. Ambivalent, too, is the last image of their deliverance that Primo leaves us with, if we think back to the start of their journey: in the station at Starye Dorogi, Timoshenko tells them, the train is waiting.

Thirty-five Days

On 15 September 1945 the Italians of Starye Dorogi left the Red House at last. In the station the train *was* waiting: sixty battered freight cars, and a magnificent engine, 'like a monument of itself'. They were, Primo says, about 1,400 people — which meant only twenty to twenty-five per car; luxury. Half the cars went to the 'Romanians' — officials from the Italian Legation at Bucharest, with their wives and children. Four or five went to couples, whether married legally or by Cantarella, and two to families with children. With home approaching, many women were once again single, and the San Vittore criminals were returning to their separate underworld; each of these groups had several cars to themselves. The rest went to the many hundreds of single men: soldiers, civilians, survivors. One of these contained the theatre company, and was called the orchestra car; and one, since it contained Leonardo and his stethoscope, was called the hospital car, though not a single patient ever appeared. Primo, of course, was in that car; so were Lello, Luciano Mariani, the Moor, 'Mr Unverdorben', Giacomo Pavoncello, and the Velletrano (or Marinese); plus a dozen or more soldiers.

They were on the train: but they did not leave. That would have been too much to hope for. No one slept very well that night. But in the morning the engine was smoking; it only had to reach the right pressure. And at last it did. It shook, it roared, it poured out clouds of black smoke; and it began to move. 'We looked at each other, almost bewildered,' Primo wrote. After the year of Auschwitz, the illness of Katowice, 'the idleness and bitter nostalgia of Starye Dorogi', they were moving at last.

'We had resisted after all: we had won.'

Of course the final victory was still many weeks, and many thousands of miles away; and the 'happy journey' was, in most of its lived moments, far from happy. The cars were in terrible condition, the track in worse; their top speed was thirty miles per hour, and they spent hours in sidings;

sometimes they covered no more than a few dozen miles in twenty-four hours. Once again the Russians had planned and provided for their journey with sublime carelessness, if at all. Rations were a lottery: for days only carrots, or gherkins, or nothing; then bread and sausage, 'and everybody breathed again'; then only grain, 'for a week on end, as though we were chickens'. But they were old hands at fending for themselves, and stripped the countryside of wood and water, and whatever could be bought or stolen – milk, maize, bread, unguarded poultry. Once, when they were left standing for seven whole days in the village of Curtici, on the Hungarian border, they wreaked havoc of biblical proportions: 'the scourge of our passage', Primo wrote, 'doubtless became a local legend, and will be talked of round the fire for generations, as elsewhere they still talk of Attila the Hun, or Tamburlaine'.

At first they retraced their steps of two months before, back to Zhmerinka. On the second day, already furious with boredom, Lello devised an entertainment for himself – and, as usual, for Primo.

He acquired a brass ring from one of their companions, and polished it until it shone like gold. When the train stopped at a small country station, he climbed down and flashed it at a group of peasants, hissing '*Zèloto, tovarisch!*' – 'Gold, comrade!' Much haggling followed, in which Lello performed all his favourite tricks, like a great athlete, for pure enjoyment. When the whistle blew he pocketed the best offer (50 roubles, says Primo; 100, says Lello), and leapt on to the train, which was already moving.

Now Primo's and Lello's accounts begin to differ once more, in the usual ways. All was well, says Lello proudly; and at the next stop he spent all 100 roubles, as was his wont, for his group of survivors. All was *not* well, says Primo. After a few yards the train screeched to a halt, panting like a dog. Already the buyer had discovered the fraud, and he and his friends were racing towards Cesare's car. Cesare fled to a dark corner, and made Primo and the others hide him under a mass of blankets and jackets; from which there rose, Primo wrote, the faint and muffled sounds of prayer. The peasants were already battering at the doors when the train jerked, and moved, and Cesare was saved. He emerged as white as a sheet, but as cocky as ever. 'Let 'em look for me now!' he said.

Well, Lello denies it. You decide.

Before the train left Russia, Primo had his own adventure. On the morning of (probably) 19 September, the train stopped at the station of Kazàtin, just before Zhmerinka. And there on the platform stood Galina from Katowice, whom he hadn't seen since May: the translator, typist, laundry-girl, dancer! He jumped down, full of joy, to greet her.

She had not changed much, he saw: less than he, like Flora. 'We exchanged a few hurried and embarrassed words,' he wrote; she wished him a happy return. Then the train began to move, and they parted. Primo breathed in the last traces of her cheap perfume on his hand: 'happy that I'd seen her again, sad at the memory of the hours spent in her company, of things unsaid, of opportunities unseized'.

That night they crossed into Romania: and when they opened the doors in the morning, they seemed already home. Green hills covered in vines, peasants dressed in black, with brown eyes and faces; signs in Roman script instead of Cyrillic, the words almost like Italian: *Paine, Lapte, Vin* . . . But then the illusion shattered, as though a pebble had been thrown in a pond: at a railway crossing, laden with sacks, stood not a horse, nor a mule, but a camel.

For a full week they rolled across the late summer landscape of Romania, Leonardo astounded by its beauty, Primo taking 'a delicate philological pleasure' in its lovely place-names – Galati, Alba Julia, Turnu Severin. But for the last three days the rain never stopped, the roof of their wagon leaked as usual, and their mood turned black. Then came Curtici: more rain, and the interminable week-long wait, as though the curse of the Ancient Mariner's ship had fallen on their train. That was too much for Lello. On the sixth day (Primo said) he left them. Whoever wanted to come with him was welcome, he said: *he* was going home by air. This time Primo did not accept the offer. Lello got on a train to Bucharest, he wrote, had many adventures, and eventually did arrive in Italy by plane, as he had planned: 'but that is another story, a story *de haulte graisse*, which I shall not recount, or shall recount elsewhere, only if and when Cesare gives me permission'.

Thirty-five years later Lello gave Primo permission: and this story *de haulte graisse* became 'Cesare's Return', published in *Lilit* in 1981. As we might guess from the Rabelaisian description, and from the long delay, it is the wickedest Cesare story of all; and as we might also guess, therefore, it is the one which – according to Lello – strays furthest from the truth, and into Primo's own imagination. Once again the adventures multiply: first Lello's in living it, then Primo's in telling it; and finally ours, glimpsing the receding truths, distortions, mysteries.

This is Lello's story, told reluctantly, and only after Primo's death. When they arrived at the Hungarian border, he heard that they would face forty days' quarantine in Austria before being allowed into Italy. Then he heard of a way out: the Italian government was offering to fly its citizens home from Bucharest. So this was not a mad wager, as Primo suggests, but a perfectly rational, indeed officially sponsored, move.

He told his group the news, and proposed that they all try it. Leonardo wouldn't abandon his medical responsibilities; and Primo declined too, for the same reason. (This is gallant of Lello: 'I refused because the adventure frightened me,' Primo said.) In the end four survivors decided to go with him, including 'Mr Unverdorben' and his friend, and Rovati, one of the ex-convicts from Milan.

They got to Bucharest without incident; but there their troubles began. The planes were no longer being provided by the Italian government (if they ever had been): instead the RAF would fly them home – but not free. Each seat would cost £16 sterling – a fortune, £380 in today's money, and none of them had any at all. So for the last time Lello 'organized' for a group of Auschwitz survivors. He went to the Italian consul, Luigi Dominici, who gave him the names and addresses of people who might help, Jews and non-Jews. It took him weeks, but at last he raised the sum they needed – and not just for six but for twelve, eleven Italians and one Russian, who had somehow managed to join them. Lello remembers some of those who helped – an Italian called Arditi, a Romanian Jew called Geller; and even more those who did not, who included an immensely rich Italian family called Crespi, owners of the *Corriere della Sera*, and of oil wells and a beautiful villa at Ploesti, near Bucharest. Finally, perhaps two weeks after Primo and the others had crossed the Brenner in their train, the RAF flew Lello's dozen home.

Now for Primo's version. Cesare, he wrote, wanted his return to be 'a glorious reappearance, an apotheosis': he wanted to arrive in Italy as free as a bird, not like a prisoner under guard, on a miserable, crawling train. When Primo declined to join him he made a quick arrangement with 'Signor Tornaghi' instead, a Milanese *mafioso* (i.e. Rovati); and on 2 October, the two disappeared.

Cesare, of course, had a plan, for which he needed some decent clothes. In Bucharest he and Tornaghi begged ('impartially', Primo said) from Catholics and Jews, until Cesare had the amount he needed; after that they parted. Now Cesare put his plan into motion: and we begin to see why Lello might prefer to disown it. It was to become (as Primo put it) 'a Latin lover': to find a rich girl, and to coax the money for his flight out of her family.

After a few unsuccessful attempts, Primo says, he found her: the daughter of the owner of the Ploesti oil wells, and of the beautiful villa 'whose gate was flanked by two marble lions'. Soon Cesare was engaged; and soon after that his future father-in-law agreed to make the happy couple a loan, while they waited for their marriage papers, and Cesare looked for a job. In all this, Primo wrote, the girl was a willing accomplice: she had understood everything immediately, and found it much to her taste; 'as for her father's money, she didn't give a damn'.

Shortly after the money was safely in his hands, Cesare vanished; and a few days after that he was on the plane. True, Primo wrote, he arrived after them; and 'the swindle had cost him a good deal, in compromises with his conscience, and in a love affair cut off half-way'. But he had returned like a bird, like a god, as he had promised himself and them, 'when we were stuck in the Romanian mud'; he had won his wager.

Well: no other survivors, in Primo's story, no selfless effort to raise money for them as well; no swindle in Lello's story, and no girl . . . Actually, Lello admits that there *was* a girl in Bucharest: she was called Gabi, and he did get engaged to her – but, he says firmly, she was poor. In other words, there was no scam, no 'Latin lover' plan; and as for 'the villa of the lions' and the oil wells, Primo borrowed them from his accounts of calling, begging-bowl in hand, on the Crespis.

I believe him – at least partly. I'm sure there were at least four or five other survivors with him – the ones he names, from the train. (I'm less sure their number really grew to twelve – numbers have a tendency to grow with Lello, like the size of fish with fishermen.) I believe him that Gabi was poor; and that he had no more to do with the Crespis' villa than to knock on its door.

But I can't help wondering if there wasn't *some* girl, and some scam, to help along the begging-bowl. In the letter Primo wrote to Lello when he sent him 'Cesare's Return', he admits that he has invented several things, 'to round out the story': for instance, 'that the girl was a willing partner in everything, including the scam' . . . Not that he invented the girl, or the scam, note; only the fact that she went along with it – which actually suggests that he had made the story of Lello's return less wicked than it was, instead of more.

Neither Primo's letter nor the story ends here, but the mystery only deepens. 'That Cesare descended on Bari from the sky there is no doubt,' the story says; but his triumph was as short-lived as the mayfly. As soon as his feet touched the ground he was arrested: because the dollars with which he had paid his fare were false. Now this too Primo lists in his letter as one of his alterations – but only in a curiously partial way. 'I have taken the liberty of not saying that the fake dollars came from a bank,' he said – so there *were* some fake dollars? – 'because it seemed to me indispensable to introduce the possibility that this was a reprisal by the swindled father-in-law' – so there *was* a swindled father-in-law? Since Lello has denied everything, I find I cannot ask if he was arrested on arrival, for paying his fare in fake currency. But Primo's letter suggests that there *was* some fake money, and a swindle; and that the only thing he made up was the one's being revenge for the other.

Can we see anything through these swirling mists of distortion and denial? I see the four who left Curtici with Lello – they are solid, named beings, and they are on the lists of Italian survivors. I see Lello working his magic on the rich of Bucharest. I see the villa of the lions, where they give him nothing; and a bank, where they give him false pound notes (not dollars) for the *zlotys*, *marks* and *pengo* he has collected. And behind a few of the *pengo* I see a girl and a father, and some small kernel of Cesare's scam. Finally I see Primo, removing the others, and keeping only the girl; borrowing the villa for her, and the bank's 'dollars'; and stirring the mix into the last escapade not of Lello Perugia, but of Cesare: hero of the interregnum, when fair was still foul and foul fair, but in comic, life-renewing mode.

Curiously, it is Lello who makes me believe Primo, and Primo who makes me believe Lello. The letter Lello presents as proof that there was no swindle is what makes me think there was. And what Primo writes about the truth of his story is what makes me think it isn't true. 'It may be inaccurate in a few details,' he says – which means that the great majority are true. But immediately he suggests the exact opposite, by fixing on the detail of the counterfeit 'dollars'. Counterfeit dollars and pounds were everywhere at the end of the war, he says. And then he tells the story of the Kommando Bernhard.

Around 1942 the Germans conceived a plan to destroy the Allied economies by flooding them with counterfeit banknotes; and founded the Kommando Bernhard to make them. It was a secret Kommando of about 140 prisoners, all experts in their fields, and almost all Jews: designers, engravers, photographers, counterfeiters. As long as they produced their perfect fakes, they would live. And so they did. As the Russians advanced, they were moved west from the camp of Sachsenhausen to Ebensee in Upper Austria, a subcamp of Mauthausen: to continue their work, Primo says, or more likely to be liquidated. They arrived too late for both, and were liberated by the Americans. All their plates, and hundreds of thousands of pounds' worth of counterfeit banknotes, locked into chests, were thrown into a deep glacier lake in the heart of the Nazi redoubt.

Thus Primo ends his story of Cesare's return: with an image of counterfeit, of deception. Did he mean Cesare's, or his own? In the end we can only guess, like everyone who has tried to retrieve the Kommando Bernhard's chests from the lake since 1945, and largely failed.

From now on all that was left was impatience. Everyone missed Lello – his vigour, his antics, his conjuror's skills. For three days they pushed across the plains of Hungary, through grey curtains of rain and mist. On 7 October, the twenty-second day of their journey, they reached Bratislava in Slovakia; on the 8th, Vienna. Here the train stuck for three days, pointlessly circling the city, from suburb to suburb, in a mocking echo of the larger pointless circle of the last three months of their lives.

They got out; they tried to change whatever money they had left, to find a shop, a market. But it was useless. The shops were half empty, or entirely shut; the markets were illegal and utterly wretched – shabby nervous people exchanging slices of bread, single cigarettes, 'small items of worn-out rubbish from their homes'. These were worse than the earliest markets Primo had seen with the Greek and Cesare. There was only one market they were like: the most miserable one of all, in the Lager. These Germans of the East Reich, Hitler's compatriots, had almost changed places with them: it was their turn to be on the bottom.

'We climbed on to our train with heavy hearts,' Primo wrote. They felt no joy in this reversal; though no compassion either. What they felt was 'a larger anguish': 'the heavy, threatening sensation of an irreparable and definitive evil present everywhere, nestling like gangrene in the entrails of Europe and the world, the seed of future harm'.

On 11 October they finally left Vienna. That evening they crossed the demarcation line into the West, at St Valentin near Linz. Primo said goodbye to the seven boy-soldiers of the Russian escort; and through them to all the barbaric and innocent young Russians of his return to life, from the parachutist of Katowice to the four young liberators of Buna-Monowitz. Now the Americans took over: warm showers and big, soft bath towels; and ten gigantic GIs in white suits, helmets and gas masks like spacemen, who sprayed them with DDT. The future had begun.

There was one more encounter with the past for Primo, before the future claimed him. On 15 October they entered Munich, and for the first time since Auschwitz, he stood on German soil.

'We felt we had something to say,' he wrote, 'enormous things to say, to every single German, and we felt that every German should have something to say to us.' *Did they know?* If they did, how could they 'look at their children, cross the threshold of a church?' If they did not, they had a duty 'to learn everything, immediately, from us, from me: I felt the tattooed number on my arm burning like a sore'.

But no one looked at him, no one asked for his tale. No German ever would, for a very long time. And when they did, they were different Germans, or the wrong Germans: the few just ones, or the grandchildren of the guilty.

That night they slept in the transit camp of Mittenwald, on the Austrian border. The next day they passed through Austria for the last time; and late in the night of 16–17 October, they crossed the Brenner into Italy.

Some – the less tired, Primo said; the younger, though not in years –

hugged each other in joy and triumph, cried and cheered. But he and Leonardo 'remained lost in a silence thronged with memories'. What, and whom, would they find at home? How many of their companions, and how much of themselves, had they left behind?

They did not sleep.

On 17 October they reached Verona, and here at last they separated, each to his own home. The next evening Primo and Leonardo boarded a train heading westwards.

19 October 1945

Their first sight of Turin, so deeply desired, was their worst moment. Through the train window they saw black gaps between the buildings and mounds of rubble. Could their own homes have escaped, their own families? Then the train emerged from the underpass: and there, on the corner of Corso Sommeiller and Corso Turati, was the great gothic pile of Arturo and Luisa Debenedetti's house, still standing; and the windows of their flat were open. If the worst came to the worst, Leonardo said gruffly, they could both spend the night there.

From Porta Nuova he telephoned; Luisa answered. Leonardo had a home, and a loving family. And now for the last question: Primo's.

In the Corso Re Umberto, Number 75 had lost bits of its walls and roof to the bombs; but it was still there, calm, intact and solid. And his mother, and his sister? – he could hardly believe it, but there they were, alive and well, and speechless with relief to see him. They had almost lost hope, as the last three months had passed without a word – but no, his mother had never lost hope; she had always known he was still alive. They could barely recognize him, he was so fat, with a round red face and a thick red beard; at first the concierge hadn't recognized him at all. But his eyes and his voice had not changed. Primo was home.

That afternoon Anna Maria rang his friends, and twenty minutes later everyone who was in Turin was there. Bianca ran all the way to the Corso Re Umberto. Primo opened the door to her. They did not kiss, or hug each other: this was Turin, in 1945. They just shook hands. Primo thanked her for helping his mother, and for taking Lorenzo's letters to her; no kiss could have touched Bianca more. Then they went in, and Primo began to tell his story to his family and friends. He did not stop for many days. In fact, he would never stop. He had found his task for the rest of his life.

PART THREE

Primo Levi, by Stefano Levi Della Torre, 1995

11. Levi Uomo:
1945–7

VETRINA DI OTTOBRE

PRIMO LEVI

ha scritto questo resoconto freddo e allucinante della più
tragica esperienza che un uomo possa aver vissuto.
È ancora un uomo chi di ora in ora, di prova in pro-
va, viene spogliato dell'aspetto fisico e distrutto nella sua
esistenza morale?
Questa è la domanda che PRIMO LEVI rivolge attonito
e amaro a se stesso e a tutti i fratelli del mondo:

se questo è
un uomo

FRANCESCO DE SILVA EDITORE - TORINO

If This is a Man flyer, 1947

Many years later there would be two writers called Levi: Primo, author of *If This is a Man*, and Carlo, author of *Christ Stopped at Eboli*. Both would be published (eventually) by Einaudi. In order to distinguish between their Levis, that great and grave publishing house devised nicknames for them. Since one was *Levi Primo*, the other was *Levi secondo*: and this, though he joked about it, must have pleased the competitor in Primo. But I think the other pair of nicknames must have pleased him even more: *Levi Cristo* for Carlo, and *Levi Uomo* for him.

All his life he had asked himself if he was a man, and feared the answer. But in Auschwitz, of all places, his fear had gone. He came back blasted, sick, suffocated by mounds of corpses; but he came back knowing that he was a man. He had not ceased to pursue virtue and knowledge, even there. And since he had, inexplicably, been given the chance, he would take it: not only to tell what he had learned of death, but to return to life – or rather, to seize life for the first time, to live it. It was a paradox, but at the same time natural: the first years after his return were his best ones. The shadow of death was still on him; he dreamt of the Lager every night, he spoke and wrote of it every day, 'with fury and method'. But he was young, Italy was young, and there was immense hope, both inside and outside him. Towards the end of his life he would say, with his fleeting, self-mocking, Della Torre smile: 'Yes, I suppose I've wanted that too, without achieving it – to be, myself, *un uomo completo*, a whole man.' Perhaps he was right: perhaps he was never, quite, a whole man. But the closest he came was now.

Of course it did not seem so at the start: it was not so at the start. When his soft bed yielded beneath him he was terrified, as though he were falling; his cousin Giulia remembers that he spent his first night at home on the floor. It was many months before he learned to stop searching the ground as he walked, so that his eyes seemed permanently fixed on his feet; nearly a year before he could go anywhere without food in his pocket, or leave anything he saw uneaten: if someone put three kilos of bread in front of him, he ate three kilos of bread.

He was, he would say later, deeply depressed: crushed by the weight of his memories, 'closer to the dead than the living'. The suffering he had known was waiting would wait no longer, and he grieved obsessively for Vanda. He grieved for all his friends: for Sandro and Emanuele, for Franco and perhaps – he feared – Alberto; for Diena, his first bed-companion, and Chaim; for Aldo Levi, father of Emilia and Italo, for Flesch the interpreter, Baruch the docker, Robert the professor, Glücksmann the soldier; and for dozens of others whose names we do not know.

And for all this weight of grief and memory he could think of only one remedy. He did not think even of it – he was driven to it, by instinct: the one instinct he always obeyed, and it saved him. *He had to talk.* He had to tell what the Lager was, and that it had existed; he had to make it known, to understand it, to make others understand it. He had decided that while he was there. But it had been an abstract decision, as everything is abstract until we do it. As always, I think, the one person he had not considered was himself. He had not realized that his mission to tell was not just for the drowned, but for himself; and more for himself than for them. As soon as he found himself at home, it was his own need that overwhelmed him – the need to be listened to, to be cleansed of his atrocious memories, even perhaps – he thought, many years later – to inspire awe and admiration, like Ulysses telling his adventures beyond the known world.

His need was so powerful it changed him. Primo Levi the silent one, the listener, who never started a conversation in his life, before or after, was transformed – it is his own image – into the Ancient Mariner: stopping every third person he met, holding them with his glittering eye, and telling his awful tale. It began even before he was home, on the train to Turin from Verona. He knew no one in his carriage except Leonardo; but suddenly it came over him – the need to speak, *now*, to everyone – and he talked and talked, and the whole carriage listened in horrified silence, like the Wedding Guest transfixed on his stone. Just as he had feared, no one had known: and from then on he couldn't stop. For months he went on talking to strangers on trains. Some were upset, some were interested, most thought him deranged, or at least eccentric. But he didn't care. No one could have been more surprised than himself; thirty and forty years later he was still surprised. But he had been driven.

And he noticed something: like the Wedding Guest, almost everyone listened. He had not expected that: he had feared the opposite, as they all had, in their most desolating dream. And indeed many of those who returned had to live that dream, even in their own families: they had suffered too much themselves, they were still suffering, and they didn't want to hear any more. But this didn't happen to Primo. His sister did not turn away, but listened to him first and for ever. His friends endlessly listened; even these poor strangers on their dreadful post-war trains listened. Perhaps, like the Ancient Mariner, his experience had given him 'strange power of speech'. Sometimes he wanted to think so; sometimes he even thought so. He had changed.

He must have wanted to do everything at once. But two things came first: to see Lorenzo, and to find out about Alberto.

Lorenzo

After that last, silent offering of soup, Lorenzo had disappeared. He had packed his dented mess tin, and his remaining rags of clothes; and set off to walk home.

He took with him the workmate with whom Primo had first met him: a bricklayer, probably from Friuli. Primo calls him Peruch, and that may have been his name. Lorenzo was tall, stooped and grey; Peruch was short and nervy, like a little horse. Primo compares them to Don Quixote and Sancho Panza, setting off to cross a continent on foot, with only a railway map (stolen from the Auschwitz station) to guide them. Lorenzo's family do not remember the map, and never met Peruch; perhaps he wasn't really like Sancho Panza at all. But Lorenzo *was* like Don Quixote, and not just physically. That, I think, is what Primo wants us to remember.

Because of their map, because of the war, and because they had to stop and work whenever they were hungry, it took Lorenzo and Peruch four months to cross Poland and Czechoslovakia. At the end of April they were in Bruck-an-der-Mur in Austria, where they were given exit visas to leave the Reich via Arnoldstein, near Villach. In these same days the German Army was fleeing in the opposite direction: a tank fired at them, but missed them. When they reached Italy they divided, and Lorenzo went on alone. He left only one trace on this part of his route, entering a refugee camp on 19 May, where he probably stayed for about two weeks. After that he walked on until he reached Turin.

In Turin he quickly found Primo's mother. 'He was a man who did not know how to lie,' Primo wrote; 'or perhaps he thought that lying was futile, ridiculous, after having seen the abomination of Auschwitz and the dissolution of Europe'. He told Rina that all the Jews of Auschwitz were dead, and Primo was surely dead too: it would be best for her to resign herself. That must have shaken even Rina: this ragged, cadaverous man, so patently honest and hurt, delivering his dreadful message in a voice he rarely used. But she did not show it. She sat him down at her table and prepared a meal for him, with many glasses of wine; then she tried to press money on him for the train home. But Lorenzo said that he had walked many thousands of miles from Auschwitz; he could easily walk the last few. And so he did. When he reached Genola, a few miles from Fossano, an old friend called Cino Sordo, passing on a cart, recognized him, and begged him to get on; but Lorenzo refused. Then a mile or two past Genola he stopped at another friend's house, and did not go on; perhaps he was afraid. In the meantime Cino had run to tell Giuseppe, who took his mule and cart to Genola to bring his son home. But still Lorenzo refused. He would walk, and in his own time.

Perhaps Giuseppe did not want to tell his wife that their son would not come home; or perhaps he didn't speak because he never spoke, and it was too late to change. Or perhaps the story is a family myth: dramatized, half-imagined, but such a powerful image that it is immediately believed. This is what it says: Lorenzo finally re-entered Via Michelini 4, emaciated, grey, his shoes in tatters and his feet covered in sores. He put his sack down on the floor, and it was crawling with lice. His young niece Emma stared at him, terrified. Giovanna, his mother, said sharply, '*Chi è Lei? Cosa vuole?*': 'Who are you? What do you want?' 'Mamma,' he said. 'I'm Lorenzo.'

Since this is a Perone story, it does not tell if Giovanna cried. It says only that she handed him a few things from his sack, among them the dented mess tin; and took the rest and burned it.

Three or four months later Primo came to Fossano. Now this is a Levi story as well as a Perone one; but neither, of course, describes the moment of meeting. The Perones say only that *il Dottor Levi* brought a knitted vest for Lorenzo, to thank him for the one Lorenzo had given him in the Lager. It was white, with a red border at the neck, and made of goat's wool; Lorenzo kept it until he died, but (they exchange a smile) it was so rough and scratchy he may never have worn it.

Primo says that he found 'a tired man'. Not tired from his long walk, but mortally tired; broken by all he had seen, in nearly three years of Auschwitz, and five months of walking through the rubble of Europe. And the Perones agree: Lorenzo had changed. Yes, he had been silent before, like all the family, especially the men; but now he hardly spoke at all. He began to withdraw from everyone, even from his mother, his sister Catarina, his niece Emma, to whom he had been specially kind; he grew half-savage. He no longer worked at his trade, but collected scrap iron and sold it at the market; Primo found him a mason's job in Turin, but he refused to come. And he began to drink in deadly earnest: not to relax, or even to forget, as he had probably done in Auschwitz; but to blot out the world completely, to blot out himself. He never spoke of Auschwitz, but he was perfectly clear. He had had enough, he said. He had seen the world, and he didn't like it.

Primo came to Fossano regularly over the next few years. He sent Lorenzo clothes, magazines, books (including his own); he wrote to him often, begging him to stop drinking, to take care of his health, to want to live. But Lorenzo did not want to live. He was permanently drunk, he had accidents at work; he would fall over, and then fall asleep in the snow. Finally, in 1952 he contracted tuberculosis. He was taken to the hospital in Savigliano, probably with Primo's help. Primo visited him every week. His brothers came often, his younger sister came from Turin, Catarina came almost every day. But he was not allowed drink in the hospital; and as soon as he could he ran away. He went home, where he must have been received with dismay – he was highly infectious, he had left the hospital illegally, and he was desperate for wine. The Perones contacted Primo, who wanted to have him brought to Turin. For the last time, Lorenzo refused. In the end the family notified the Savigliano hospital, and Lorenzo was returned. He died there, aged forty-seven, at the end of April, of TB, alcoholism, and despair.

'He, who was not a survivor,' Primo wrote, 'had died of the survivor's disease.' But it was not just that. Lorenzo's experience of Auschwitz was complicated, like Primo's own. There, he had been rich – 'at least compared to us', as Primo said; he had been able to help, to do some good in the world. And then it was over. He was poor again, he could help no one; it was he who needed help now. And as though to make the point doubly clear, it was Primo who helped him. Primo gave as naturally and silently as Lorenzo had done; he would have repeated that he was not giving but giving back, and even if he gave back all his life he would still be in debt to Lorenzo. And Lorenzo would have been as grateful, and as moved, as Primo had been. Nonetheless, their positions were reversed: it was as though Lorenzo was the Jew now, and would always be. The only thing he could do about help was refuse it. So that is what he did.

Lorenzo would never have told his family what he had done in Auschwitz. And even after Primo came and told them, they could not have understood. We all know what 'Auschwitz' means now: it is more than an instance, it is our model of human suffering and evil. But in Fossano in 1952 no one would have heard the name. The word 'Holocaust', which sums up years of historical discovery, did not yet exist. There was no language in which to understand.

In 1981, when all this had changed, Primo published 'Lorenzo's Return', in which he described Lorenzo's end as the death of a hero; and that is what it is now, clearly and simply. But in 1952 no one had heard of Primo Levi either. To the Perones he was the rich and kind Dottor Levi, *l'ebreu* who said that Lorenzo had saved his life, but all the life-saving they could see came the other way. To the Perones Lorenzo's death was not a martyrdom; it was a family tragedy, and a family shame.

His father had died in 1945, soon after his return; his mother was over eighty, and broken by her husband's death; his elder brother, Giovanni, was almost entirely withdrawn. Catarina was now the effective head of the family. And Catarina was the proudest of all the Perones. She kept Lorenzo's photographs, because she had loved him; and she kept his work papers, because to her his work *was* Lorenzo, or the unspoiled part of him. But everything else she gave or threw away: the mess tin in which he had taken his soup to Primo and Alberto; his clothes, including the white goat's-wool vest; his books, including his copy of *If This is a Man*, with Primo's dedication. She did not throw away Primo's letters, for the moment: perhaps because they proved that someone else had loved Lorenzo as well, and fought to keep him alive. But they also, therefore, proved something else: that he had been bent on self-destruction, that he was drinking himself to death. In the end the shame of Primo's letters grew greater than their consolation to Catarina, and to other upright, God-fearing Perones as well. Catarina herself, or one of the others, destroyed them some time later; just as, in 1945, Giovanna had burned Lorenzo's Auschwitz sack and everything in it.

This is sad, of course, for biography. But it is sadder still for Lorenzo, and for his family. By 1999, when his name was finally entered in the honour roll of the Yad Vashem memorial in Jerusalem, all his brothers and sisters had died except the youngest. He, and the next generation and their children, are all now deeply proud of Lorenzo. But they only began to be proud perhaps a dozen years ago. They loved him, they knew he was a good man underneath; but for forty years after his death they were ashamed of him. He had given up his work, he was a drunk, he had turned into the tramp his mother hadn't recognized. Even his tuberculosis was still a stigma in 1950s Piedmont; to this day the family say that he brought it back from Auschwitz, though it didn't appear until seven years later.

If we could blame them, this story would be only about them, and I wouldn't tell it. But it is about everyone: about how hard it is to understand what is happening to us until later; often until too late. We know about the Holocaust now, and depression, and 'post-traumatic stress disorder'; today there are other things, and other people, we are failing to understand.

But though this story is not only about the Perones, it is about them, as Primo's story was about their uncle, great-uncle, brother. So I am sorry if it hurts them, as his did too. But he wanted people to know that a great moral hero could be a rough, inarticulate man who died a drunk and a pauper. And now I think we should know that his own family could be ashamed of him for forty years. Because that is how heroism can be – especially the best, unrewarded kind: a historical glory, but a personal burden, not only for the hero, and not only at the time.

Alberto

By the early summer of 1945, a few months after the healthy prisoners had been marched away, the camp of Katowice had already been full of ominous rumours about their fate. But Primo held on to his conviction that he and Alberto 'would not be separated for very long'. It was his half of the pledge that had been doubtful; and though he'd made it in the end, it had taken him nearly a year. Alberto had always been quicker, cleverer, almost Einhorn-like in his capacity to solve, and dissolve, problems. He had probably slipped home like a fish, or flown like a bird, even faster than Lello. When he heard Primo's voice on the phone he'd probably say, quite calmly: 'Well, finally. Where have you been?'

But it was not like that. When Primo phoned the family, it was Alberto's mother who answered, and Alberto was not there. He was alive, she would have reassured him straight away, and so was his father: thank God, they had definite proof of that. But so far neither had returned.

Primo's heart must have sunk: half of this information, he knew, was false, so why should the other half be true? Perhaps Emma Dalla Volta explained her reasons now, or perhaps she promised to explain in detail when he came to see her. They made the arrangement for as soon as possible; probably within a week or two of Primo's return.

This first meeting must have been long, warm, and harrowing for them all. Primo told Emma and Paolo everything he could remember about Alberto and Guido in Buna-Monowitz: how the three of them had always been together, especially after the first few months; how Alberto had helped Guido, and Primo himself, and everyone; how 'no one, in that place, was loved as much as he'. He told them about Lorenzo, and Flora, about the cerium rods, and all Alberto's brilliant ideas. He told them that he owed his life to Alberto, and would never forget him.

He tried then, too, to tell them his fears. If anyone could have survived that march, it would be Alberto; but it seemed that almost no one had, and if he had not yet returned . . . But immediately Emma stopped him, and explained how they knew that Alberto, and Guido too, were both alive. As soon as they had returned to Brescia, at the end of April, Paolo had begun their search – everywhere, through the Red Cross and the Jewish community, through church, army and partisan organizations. Dozens of people came forward, with every kind of information: they'd seen Alberto, or Guido, or both, in a hospital, in a camp, on the way home. The Dalla Voltas didn't know whom to believe; they believed no one. Until someone had come whom they had to believe.

He was from a village near Brescia, and had been working for the Todt Organization in Silesia. When the Russians arrived they put him in a camp called (he said) Odenburg, or Odemburg: where he met another young man from Brescia, who had been in Auschwitz. This young man said that he had left Auschwitz on a forced march with other prisoners; that they had arrived at a railway station, from which they were to be transported to Germany; but that suddenly Russian soldiers had surrounded their column, their SS guards had run away, and their liberators had brought them to Odenburg. After a time the Russians said that anyone who wanted to leave could do so. The young *bresciano* decided to head for home; but the ex-Auschwitz prisoner had other plans. He asked his fellow-countryman to tell his family that he was safe: his name was Alberto Dalla Volta, and this was how to find them. And the boy showed Emma and Paolo a card with the address and telephone number of Guido's secretary on it, in Alberto's unmistakable hand.

That, said Emma and Paolo, was why they believed him. And they believed something else too, either because he told them, or because it came from someone in the same camp. Guido, they told Primo, was on the march too – many people had seen him. But he must have been separated from Alberto, and among those deported to Germany. Because in early March Alberto too left Odenburg, and went to Germany to look for his father.

Primo did not believe that Guido was on the march; but he knew that Alberto had been convinced his father was still alive. If he'd heard a report of him which – like his family – he believed, he would have been quite capable of going to the ends of the earth to find him. Perhaps, then, Primo was persuaded. Perhaps he now allowed himself to believe, with the Dalla Voltas, that Alberto might still return, because, like them, he wanted to. In the 'Story of Ten Days', written in December, he said of the nearly 20,000 healthy prisoners: *Almost in their entirety, they vanished during the evacuation march.* That was all. Only later did he add: *Alberto was among them.*

But if he was persuaded, it was not for long. In the spring of 1946, when he had refound Pikolo, he told him the Dalla Voltas' story in a letter. '*C'est bien mystérieux,*' he wrote; and added: 'I think it would be mad to hope for his return any longer.' Perhaps it was now that he added his sad, simple line of acceptance to the 'Story of Ten Days'.

Nonetheless, for the next several years he kept in close touch with Alberto's family, exchanging every scrap of news they heard about survivors of the march. To Primo each one seemed only to confirm his bleak conclusion; but not to the Dalla Voltas. A year or so after his first visit he went to see them again, and they told him what they had now learned, from many sources: both Alberto and Guido were still in Russian hands. Of this they remained certain, though their information changed over the years. Usually both Alberto and his father were reported to be working as chemists: first in an arms factory in Magnitogorsk; later in a scientific research centre called Oslov, or Coslov, which was secret, isolated and closed. There was never any official proof or record; the Russians denied that Oslov even existed. But then, of course, they would.

To watch the growth of this story was almost as painful to Primo as to watch Lorenzo's decline. And to know that he did not believe it was just as painful to the Dalla Voltas. At last their pain flared into the open. A year or two later, Primo visited once more. And this time he tried to tell Emma that she must stop deluding herself, it was only prolonging her agony: Guido, and Alberto too, were both dead. Paolo was furious, and cut him off in mid-sentence. Primo immediately withdrew, and returned to his usual gentle reserve. But the damage was done. He came again, they kept in touch, but increasingly rarely; and after the mid-1950s, not at all.

Over the years, the Dalla Voltas came to accept that Guido would not return. But when Emma died in 1973 she still believed that Alberto was alive. After the fall of Communism in 1989, Paolo renewed his investigations. When there was still no trace of Alberto, he began to admit to himself that his brother might have died – but later, long after the war, in Russia. Even so, he says, whenever there is a knock at the door today, he still thinks it might be Alberto.

Thirty years later, in his last book, Primo wrote that 'I did not have the courage to oppose my painful truth to the consolatory [one] that . . . Alberto's relatives had constructed for themselves'. But Paolo says he did, and I believe him. Primo Levi was one of the most rational men who have ever lived; that was his gift, but also his curse. I think he simply could not understand how someone could find consolation in an obvious delusion. I think he thought that if Emma Dalla Volta could stop hoping, she could stop suffering; she could put it all behind her. He did not understand that a mother cannot put her child behind her; she prefers to suffer.

But why, then, did he deny what he had done? Perhaps because he regretted doing it. And perhaps, then, as weak as the rest of us, he allowed himself to hide, or even forget, that he had done it. And to go on thinking that it would have been a courageous thing to do.

From the start there was something ambiguous in his treatment of Alberto. His love and admiration for him are immense, and expressed without reserve. Alberto Dalla Volta is the twin hero of *If This is a Man*, together with Lorenzo; but Lorenzo was not a prisoner. Alberto is Primo's model and inspiration in courage, dignity and freedom from corruption by the Lager; he is also his model in astuteness and practical wisdom. But he is not his intellectual equal. He is intelligent, but above all intuitive: he understands things in ways Primo cannot, without reason. In other words, he is half-way to becoming one of Primo's classic opposites. In *If This is a Man*, Primo is a chemist who enters the lab; Alberto is a third-year student whom we do not even see taking the examination. Primo speaks French, and enough German to pass the exam; Alberto knows only a little French, and no German at all. Now, Alberto *was* a third-year student; but he certainly took, and passed, the chemistry examination, though not well enough to enter the lab. And his languages were at least as good as Primo's – his French equally good, his German actually better. Why on earth did Primo suppress this – or perhaps forget it?

I think he probably forgot it. I think the transformation of Alberto Dalla Volta into one of Primo's opposites was not a literary device – nothing in *If*

This is a Man was a conscious literary device – but natural and unconscious; and much the same is true of all the others. Perhaps this was Primo Levi's flaw (and his secret guilt, against which he struggled): since his brain was the only part of him he – or others – had ever valued, it had to be better than anyone else's. Which it almost always was: except, perhaps, with Paul Steinberg, and we have seen how he felt about that. All those whom he loved and admired for being what he could never be could never be what he was either. Sandro, the first Alberto, Gabriella, Leonardo – they were all intelligent, but they were far from his intellectual equals. Alberto Dalla Volta came closer; but Primo could not let him be his equal either.

And then Alberto, who did come close, gave in to complete unreason. When his father was selected, he forgot all their hard-won understanding, and believed what he knew to be false. I think that deeply shocked and frightened Primo. If it could happen to Alberto, could it not happen to him? And then he met Alberto's warm, loving family; and it did, perhaps, happen to him. For a time he too may have given in to the temptations of unreason; to the distorting temptations of love.

Perhaps that is why he judged Alberto's delusion so harshly, and even more his family's about Alberto – because he had himself shared it. He judged them only in private for thirty years. But then in 1975 he published the story of Alberto and the cerium rods in *The Periodic Table*. At the end he wrote: 'Alberto did not return, and not a trace remains of him; after the war a man from his town, half visionary and half crook, lived for a number of years on the money he made telling his mother false consolatory tales about him.'

That sounds hard to me; and harder still in *The Drowned and the Saved*, when he tells how the story became more and more fantastic over the years ('Alberto was in a Soviet clinic, he was fine, but he had lost his memory . . .'). Paolo is as angry now as he was fifty years ago, when Primo tried to tell his mother that Alberto was dead. They never paid anyone, he says; and what they believed was their own affair. Well, it is long ago, and the details of the truth are no longer possible to establish. But that Primo was using living people, the family of his friend, to make a painful point about self-deception is undeniable. Nor did he warn them before, or apologize to them after. They never heard from him again; he never sent them any of his books, even – especially – the ones in which he mentioned Alberto. As any real writer will tell you, that is sensible. Never show anyone anything, they say. A book must be read *sub specie aeternitatis*, not from the point of view of someone's personal reputation. If it's worth doing, do it: and this was. But then all real writers are ruthless, like Primo Levi.

★　　★

And what about the others? For months – in some cases years – Primo set himself to find out what had happened to his friends and enemies from Auschwitz.

What was happening to Leonardo he knew. After the first joy of hearing Luisa Debenedetti's voice, his return was the opposite of Primo's. On that very first day all the hopes that had kept him alive were stripped away. The Debenedettis had to tell him that his mother had died of her stroke in Switzerland, even before he had entered Auschwitz. And they had to tell him that, nearly six months after the end of the war, there was still no trace of Jolanda. *Dottoressa* Nissim, who had recently returned, had no knowledge of her either: she could say only that Jolanda had never entered Birkenau. Poor Leonardo knew what that meant: Jolanda had been murdered the very night of their arrival. But her family did not know it, and he could not tell them. He was in despair; and until the Debenedettis had accepted the truth, he could not show it.

At first he returned to Rivoli. But that was even worse: he was alone in the life he had lived with Jolanda, and he could not bear it. Fortunately, the City of Turin soon opened a *concorso** for a doctor; Leonardo won it, and returned to Turin for good. For the next two or three years he lived with Jolanda's family, which had become his own. And slowly, surrounded by their love and affection, working once more night and day as a doctor, he recovered. But twice (at least) in those early years he nearly lost the will to live. At one stage, possibly as a direct result of the Lager, he developed a cancerous growth on his leg: 'Is this what I survived Auschwitz for?' he demanded, with rare bitterness. But he had X-ray treatment, and was cured. The other time was more mysterious. He was brought into the new Pinna Pintor Clinic confused, distressed, clearly ill. Perhaps he had had a breakdown, perhaps he had even tried to die; no one will say. But in 1947 he made a will, in which he thanked his new family for having helped him to survive 'the saddest and most tragic period' of his life. Without their loving kindness, he wrote, his solitude might have defeated him for good.

Lello, as we know, had reached home in early December, some time after his brother Angelo. There followed a difficult year in which, he still says bitterly, no one helped him. (If there was any truth at all in the story of Cesare's arrest on arrival, that might have had something to do with it.) Finally, however, in the autumn of 1946 he found the job which he would keep to the end of his working life, in the Poligrafo dello Stato, the government Stationery Office. From then on he began to build up his respectable middle-class life. He married and had two sons, one of whom

---

* A competitive examination, the standard entry to all public service posts in Italy.

would die at the age of eleven, run over outside their home. Lello has been, as Primo would write, 'sorely tried by fate'; and though he has been increasingly decorated, as a partisan and as a survivor, it was all, he feels, too little and too late. None of this surprises him. Primo was an optimist, he says, and so died of mortal disappointment; he is a pessimist, so nothing will ever get him down. He is right — nothing ever will. But only because, beneath his cynicism, there still runs Cesare's invincible gaiety, his delight in battle, and in his smallest victory.

Of the Chemical Kommando, Primo knew very soon that Silvio Barabas and Mendi the rabbi – whose real name was Menachem Chaim Davidowicz – had survived. For Bandi, Elias, Iss Clausner and many others he searched in vain. But Elias may also have survived. Around 1960, Paul Steinberg thought he saw him on the Reeperbahn, the notorious red-light district of Hamburg: having probably returned to pimping, one of his pre-war trades.

Primo also tried to find at least two 'from the other side': Dr Pannwitz, the perfect German, and Dr Meyer the imperfect German, who had armed himself in ignorance, like so many others, but had not quite succeeded. He would eventually find Meyer, as we know; but that event belongs to a particular season, and will be told there. In any case it was Pannwitz who was Primo's special prey. That look between them still haunted him. In the years after the war he searched the whole of Europe for Pannwitz, 'carefully, tenaciously, indefatigably'; but without success. Finally, it was Meyer who told him. Pannwitz had died in 1946: of a brain tumour, not of war. In the end he had behaved with the cowardice of someone whose power has been based on a myth, and on nothing interior at all: ordering his staff to stay and resist, he himself had slipped on to a train to safety at the last moment.

Finally, the French. Paul Steinberg managed to survive the death march, the transport to Buchenwald, and Buchenwald itself, still with the help of protectors. For fifty years he cut himself off from all but one or two of his fellow survivors, and thought and read as little as possible about Auschwitz. In the 1960s he tried to write a novel about his experiences, but put it away unfinished: the only end he could see for his hero was suicide, and that defeat he would not admit, even in fiction. Finally, when he had retired, he wrote a non-fiction memoir instead: *Chronique d'ailleurs*, which he published in 1995.* Here he admitted that Primo's portrait of him as an icy manipulator was true, but asked his question: 'Is it so wrong to survive?' He found no answer. He never regained the dignity he felt he had lost, and lived all the

---

* Translated into English as *Speak You Also*, Penguin Press, 2001.

more in his pride. 'I have paid for that,' he wrote. He died in December 1999, at the age of seventy-three.

Charles, we know, was back in Lusse by the end of July 1945. He had had only a month or so in the Lager, but his gentle nature was deeply shaken by what he had seen. He returned to his quiet, busy life as a country schoolmaster, and has rarely left his village since. He lived with his mother until she died. Later he married a fellow teacher, Andrée; with whom, in his late eighties, he still lives, in their small, neat house filled with kindness, which no visitor ever wants to leave. Charles is deeply religious, but – Jean says – free-thinking, always ready to criticize his Church if it fails to stand up for the poor and persecuted. He and Primo kept in touch faithfully over the years, and Primo came at least twice to Lusse, once in 1951 and once in 1974. Charles remembers visiting Arthur with Primo several times; Primo remembered only the last occasion, when Arthur was old and ill, and did not want to meet again, and stir up old memories. He died a few years later, in the 1980s.

In early March 1946 Primo and Jean finally refound each other, through Charles. They exchanged accounts of all they had gone through since they'd last seen each other, in the fateful January of 1945. For Jean, what happened after that was so atrocious that it almost completely wiped out his memories of the previous year. The march to Gleiwitz; the apocalyptic transport to Buchenwald, the corpses piling up on every side. Then the worst moment of all, for Jean: the death, from exhaustion, of his uncle René in Buchenwald. The next day he met a fellow Frenchman – Henri Kirszenstein, called Kiki, with whom he shared every moment and every crust for the last months of his ordeal. If it had not been for Kiki, Jean says, he would not have lived.

Together with Kiki he survived a month of hard labour, and another terrible march back to Buchenwald; where they managed to avoid the final evacuation, from which not a single person survived. At last, at four o'clock in the afternoon of 11 April, they were liberated by the Americans. Three weeks later Jean was home; and a month later his mother returned, having survived Birkenau, Auschwitz, Ravensbruck, Malchow, and evacuation marches of over 150 miles.

Jean had lost his father, his brother, his three maternal uncles and two paternal ones; he was the only man left in his family. He finished his studies in a few months, and took over the family pharmacy. He has run it ever since. Unlike Primo, but like Paul Steinberg and countless others, Jean did not speak of his experiences for nearly forty years: hardly at all to his children, a little more to his grandchildren, and never in public. Then, in 1980, he was asked to appear on German television, together with Primo; and the shock of speaking at last to Germans, in German, broke his silence. Slowly he began to accept the burden of witnessing. From the time of Primo's death he has accepted it more and more, since, as he says, the best witness of all has gone.

Of all Primo's fellow survivors – apart from Leonardo, who lived more or less next door – it was Jean whom he saw most often. But in all their re-meetings they would talk of the present and the future much more than the past; and when they did talk of the past, it was like old soldiers: avoiding bad memories, recalling only 'rare moments of reprieve, or eccentric episodes'. Jean did not want to go deeper, and Primo did not force him. This went back to the beginning. In May 1946 he sent him the 'Canto of Ulysses', which he had written before he knew that Jean had survived. But he did not translate it into French for him, because, he said, he could not do it well enough. Jean did not insist, and they never talked about the story. Then, when the first French translation of *If This is a Man* appeared in 1961, the 'Canto' chapter had been shortened; so that it was not until the second French edition in 1987 that Jean finally read *If This is a Man*, and the 'Canto' itself, whole. By then Primo was dead.

Charles and Jean, 1993

It may seem extraordinary that Jean was so uninterested in his own story, but in fact it was perfectly normal. It was Primo's need to ponder it that was extraordinary. In the same way, it was only Primo who remembered everyone's name, and tried to find them: because, as Jean says, 'He wanted to write.' Jean wanted to live. He kept in close touch with Kiki; but that was all. Not even he and Charles sought each other out. '*C'est bizarre*,' Charles says now, but Jean shakes his head. 'We wanted to forget,' he says. That only changed when Primo, who remembered for all of them, died. Jean telephoned Charles for the first time in 1988; since then they have had, in his own words, 'a warm and wonderful friendship'. They are the rememberers now.

Of the women, we know, Vanda did not return.

But Luciana did. From Auschwitz she had been sent to Hessisch Lichtenau near Kassel, as doctor to a labour camp attached to an arms factory. In mid-April the camp was evacuated, and Luciana became one of the hundreds of thousands of death-marchers driven towards the shattered heart of Germany. After a few days, she and her friend Henna slipped out of the column and dropped into a ditch. For four or five days they hid in a wood, drinking water from a pond; then, driven by hunger, they approached a farmer's wife, and ended by working as her scullery-maids. At last, on 24 April, a white flag was raised on the church tower, and the Americans entered the village. Luciana and Henna tore off their aprons and ran to the main square. There they picked out an American officer. 'We are Jews,' they told him. 'So am I,' he said. 'I am a Slovak,' said Henna, and 'So am I,' he said. 'I am a doctor,' Luciana said; 'So am I,' he said.

Thanks to him, a few days later they were in an American camp at Grimm. Luciana searched the camp for Vanda in vain. She stayed there for a month, working once more as a doctor. Finally, in early July, she took a train to Lake Constance. On 20 July she was back with her family in Biella; and three days later she saw Franco Momigliano again.

He too had had a dangerous and difficult war, including four months of prison, interrogations and beatings. Franco Sacerdoti was dead; like Primo, Luciana understood that very soon. And she had always known that Franco Momigliano was her man. In 1946 they were married.

Luciana threw herself back into life without a pause. In 1947 Vanda was stillborn; Luciana was ill for many months afterwards. But as soon as she could she began again. She trained as a psychoanalyst; Franco became an industrial economist. Before long they would both be famous in their fields.

Luciana is an immensely strong and generous woman, who all her life has looked forward and not back. In 1960, when she was forty, her son Alberto was born, but that did not slow her down either. Like Paul Steinberg, she cut herself off from other survivors; like Jean Samuel, she did not speak about her experiences until Primo, 'who spoke for all of us', had gone. It was not to spare herself pain, she says firmly, but because the past is the past, and there is too much else to do. She and Primo remained unbreakable friends all their lives, bound especially by the memory of Vanda. But perhaps she was too definite for him, too honest and abrupt. He never put her into any of his books, she noticed. Of course, she slightly minded.

Bianca Morpurgo, who had helped Vanda at the end, also survived, after many sufferings. At one point an SS officer forced her to beat an Italian prisoner, saying that if she refused he would beat them both himself; after that Bianca had a breakdown that lasted many days. She was in at least two other camps after Birkenau. In Malchow she worked once more as a doctor; but in Ravensbruck she was sent to dig trenches in the rain and snow, and sank almost to the level of a *Musulmann*. Finally, like Luciana, she was liberated by the Americans, in Leipzig.

At first she returned to Genoa, where she had been living before the war. She was emaciated, ill, and consumed with hatred for the Germans; a fellow survivor who saw her then thought she could not live. But she went home to Trieste, where she found that her other two sisters had survived. She had a family after all; and she recovered, though perhaps only on the surface. She returned to work as a doctor, and helped to bring up her nephew Edoardo. She remained a very strong character, Edoardo says, but a very silent one. Primo would certainly have looked for her at the start; and he did again later, at least once. But if she knew of his inquiries, she did not respond. She never spoke of Auschwitz. By her mid-seventies she hardly spoke at all. She died in 1996, still silent.

★   ★

Primo also sought eagerly for news of his earlier friends, before the great divide of Auschwitz. The first he asked about were his companions of Amay: especially Guido Bachi and Aldo Piacenza, whom he had last seen in the barrack cells in Aosta, in late January of 1944.

In March – Primo's first month in Buna-Monowitz – their cases were sent to the Tribunale Speciale. They were moved from the barracks to the Torre dei Balivi, the Bailiffs' Tower, a medieval castle keep which was the town prison of Aosta. Here conditions were brutish, and their new companions at first sight worse: drunks, down-and-outs, common thieves. But the newcomers to this underworld soon found that a secret solidarity reigned, which was extended to them. When Guido's comb was stolen, he mentioned it to a cellmate; and the next day the comb reappeared.

Here they stayed for interminable months, fearing a summons to the

Tribunale every day. When an offer of amnesty came Aldo reluctantly signed it (on Guido's orders, he says). As a result, after eight months of prison he was released, and brought before the local army commander, to be assigned to new military duties. Aldo decided to try his luck. His papers said *carcerato*, prisoner, he said, but the Maresciallo could see for himself that this was a mistake for *scarcerato*, released prisoner; would he not change it? The Maresciallo either believed him or pretended to; he added the 's', and assigned Aldo only one escort for the journey to his regional headquarters in Cuneo. At Cuneo Aldo refused to take the oath of allegiance to the Republic of Salò. Passing the buck, the Cuneo command ordered him to report to his home district of Racconigi. Aldo saluted, exited, and found that his escort had disappeared. Naturally he never reported to Racconigi. He lay low for a while; then ended the war as he had begun it, in a G. & L. brigade.

Bachi, meanwhile, was left behind. This was better than it sounds, and Guido managed it in style. After a month or so the Governor and Assistant Governor had summoned him before them. He was a graduate in commerce, they'd heard. Could he keep accounts? Certainly, Guido said, though in fact accountancy was his weak point. The Governor regularly recruited a *scrivanello*, a book-keeper, from among the inmates, and the current one was reaching the end of his term. Guido was apprenticed to him for a fortnight; and then took over.

Almost immediately, his life was transformed. He was taken from his cell of six or eight and given his own small room; he could even *turn out the light at night* (and fifty years later Guido still shakes his head in wonder). It took him a while to understand. There was a small detail of prison accounting which the *scrivanello* had not mentioned: how to cook the books to his own advantage. He was the first *scrivanello* in history to account honestly; and by doing so he had almost doubled the Governor's income, and the Assistant Governor's as well. The transformation of his life mirrored the one he had wrought in theirs.

This was only the beginning. Soon Guido was giving French lessons to the Governor's children. With the Governor's connivance he smuggled out a letter to his father, assuring him that he was alive and well. And as time went on he even managed, through the Governor's son, to contact a partisan band outside, and to help plan their operations from the improbable safety of prison. When Giustizia e Libertà offered to obtain his release, Guido declined. He was more use where he was.

His luck held: working together, his wife and his future wife – both Catholics – managed to have his case regularly postponed, and he was never tried. But, as the war approached its end, the position of political prisoners became more dangerous: they were the only cards left in Fascist hands. As soon as he heard of the Allied landings in June Guido began to plan his escape with the partisans of Torgnon. One guard helped them; others were made drunk on wine, or paid; and on 12 April 1945 the political prisoners of the Torre dei Balivi walked out into the night, while the common criminals watched, and kept silent.

The partisans led them over Monte Rosa, and for the first time in eighteen months Guido felt fear. But they arrived safely in Switzerland – whereupon he was promptly sent back again. He managed to rejoin his partisan friends; and ended the war, like Aldo, with them.

Afterwards both went home to Turin. Aldo returned to his legal studies, and has practised as a lawyer in Turin ever since. Guido stayed for several years; then in 1950 went as a representative of Olivetti to Paris, where he has remained: as charming, clever and rich as his fellow Parisian Paul Steinberg, but much happier. Like Primo, he loves a good story, especially against himself. Soon after their return, he recounts, they went together to testify against the spies who had betrayed them, and Guido re-met many of his underworld pals from the Torre dei Balivi. Once again, in their company, one of his possessions disappeared; and once again he told his old cellmate. But this time it was not returned. When he tried again, the ex-con shook his head: 'You are no longer one of us,' he said. And a smile of pleasure breaks over Guido's face.

And the spies, and those who had helped the little band of Amay?

Marie Varisellaz, the wife of Eleuterio Page, the owner of the Albergo Ristoro, was also arrested on 13 December, accused of 'being a danger to the nation, and housing persons of the Jewish race'. She too was held in the Cesare Battisti barracks, and regularly interrogated by Cagni. But she admitted nothing, and after fifty-two days she was released.

Cagni, De Ceglie and Bianchi were tried in May 1946. Cagni was condemned to death, De Ceglie and Bianchi, *in absentia*, to thirty years. Bianchi seems never to have been found, and may have been dead. Cagni and De Ceglie appealed. In June Togliatti, the Communist Minister of Justice, drew up an amnesty intended to heal the wounds of war, under which, one historian says roundly, 'even Fascist torturers escaped justice'. Cagni was one of them. In the end he probably served six years, De Ceglie none.

And last but not least, what had happened to Primo's fellow Jews and fellow partisans, who, like him, had decided to fight two long years ago?

Ada Della Torre, we know, had made her decision on the day she heard of his arrest. Since then she had been a G. & L. *staffetta*, moving first between

Turin and Ivrea; then in Turin alone from the end of 1944, living and working with Anna Maria. Silvio remained throughout with the *garibaldini* in the Biellese. In the forcing-house of war he came to the political decision he had been mulling over since the days of Milan: he became a Communist. This decision would dominate much of the rest of Silvio's life; Bianca's too, but Silvio's, perhaps, most of all.

Silvio was not among the friends who ran to Corso Re Umberto 75 on 19 October 1945, because he was not in Turin. He had gone to Vercelli, a small town forty miles away, as First Secretary of the Communist Federation there. But Primo came to see him in Vercelli, several times: especially after 1946, the year that Silvio and Ada married. On some of his early visits, Primo brought with him the chapters of the Lager story he was writing to show his friends. At the time Silvio was editing *L'Amico del popolo*, the Communist weekly newspaper of Vercelli (and writing most of it himself). He asked Primo if he could publish some of the chapters in his paper, and Primo agreed. The first, 'The Journey', appeared in March 1947, more than half a year before the book came out: so that, among his other achievements, Silvio Ortona can claim to be the first publisher of *If This is a Man*.

Silvio and Ada would stay in Vercelli for nearly twenty years, and all three of their children were born there. Silvio became Secretary of the Workers' Association, Ada a teacher and writer. In the late 50s Silvio had to flee briefly to Czechoslovakia, when he was about to be tried for the killing of some Fascists by the Bandiera, just after the liberation – in which he had not, in fact, been involved, but for which he had taken responsibility as leader. The anti-partisan trials, like the anti-Fascist ones, were eventually settled by an amnesty, and Silvio came home. Restored for the second time in his life to full citizenship, he was elected as a Communist Member of Parliament, and served for two legislatures.

These years must have been hard ones for Ada, who missed the city, her family and friends, especially Primo. But finally, in 1963, the Ortonas would return to Turin. From then on they would belong once more to Primo's closest circle.

The last Primo had heard of Euge was his refusal to join their little band, less than a fortnight before they were captured.

That was in December 1943. For six months Euge stayed on with his parents in La Salle. He contacted other groups, but none satisfied him. Then someone denounced him, and in June 1944 he too ended up in the Torre dei Balivi in Aosta.

There, of course, he found Aldo Piacenza and Guido Bachi. The moment he arrived Guido came to reassure him: Don't worry, I'll take care of you.

Guido ran the office, and had contacts with the outside; in effect, Euge says, it was Guido who was the Governor of the prison. And he laughs out loud in amazement and admiration.

Nonetheless, he wasn't keen to stay. He found a guard who was willing to talk, and opened negotiations. It would take a lot of money, the guard said. Euge's father and Carla Consonni went to Turin together to raise 30,000 lire. Then Carla went to the police superintendent who had arrested Euge. He pretended to be outraged; she fluttered her eyelids at him; and in the end the deal was done. She was to leave the money, in a yellow envelope, in the lavatory of a particular bar; the next day, at noon, Euge would be free. And so he was.

It was now July. He spent a week in hiding, with a member of the CLN. And now he found the right band: the Arturo Verraz, led by *alpini*, veterans of the Greek and Montenegran campaigns. On the bus up to Cogne Carla met him with clothes and equipment. At Cogne she surrendered him to the leaders of the band: 'And that,' she says, 'was my contribution to the cause.' As usual, it was not quite true. Back in Milan, she worked for the CLN, helping the families of captured and fallen partisans.

Euge spent the next four months with the Arturo Verraz. He was (says Luciana) a *bravissimo* partisan; and the Arturo Verraz did not disappoint him either. For that whole summer they controlled the valley of Cogne.

Nonetheless, by November their supplies were exhausted, and they had to retreat and re-arm. Euge crossed the Alps to France, with the hardiest of his band. After five days, he saw the village of Val d'Isère below him, and knew that he had survived.

Back home in Rome in December, he got his first architectural job still wearing his partisan rags; and he continues to practise today, at the age of eighty-six. Carla married Aldo Maestro. They too had a daughter whom they called Vanda. This Vanda would live.

Bianca and Alberto, like Ada and Silvio, saw each other only rarely during the twenty months of war. Once, determined to meet him in the Val Chisone, Bianca got caught in a round-up, and spent three days pretending to be a waitress in an inn, serving the same Fascists Alberto's band was trying to kill. Alberto himself, of course, lived close to the edge most of the time. He was a completely fearless fighter, his companion Giorgio Diena remembers: '*di una freddezza spaventosa*' – terrifyingly cool. Once, for instance, after a heated battle with a German patrol, they realized as they retreated that Alberto was not with them. An hour or so later, back at base, he sauntered in. Where the devil had he been? Oh, he'd chased after the Germans, to get in a few more shots at them, he said. *Alone*, with no one to cover him, to report his position if he were wounded? . . . But Alberto just grinned. The only time he saw him pale, Giorgio says, was when he put his hand in his pocket, and pulled out a grenade with the safety-pin removed.

Alberto would not have lasted long as an ordinary soldier, but in the guerrilla warfare of the mountains he came into his own. In the last terrible winter of 1944–5, for example, he went on two missions to France, to make contact with the Allied command.

The second mission left at the end of December. They were a large group, including Ada Gobetti, one of the founders and leaders of the Partito d'Azione, and her son Paolo; Alberto, his brother Bruno and Bruno's wife Juanita. On this leg all went well; they reached the Allied HQ in Grenoble safely, and Paolo, Alberto, and Paolo Spriano organized a liaison service which functioned to the end, bringing intelligence, arms and supplies back to Italy.

It was on the return journey, two months later, that the trouble began. They had chosen to cross the Colle del Gran Cordonnier, which in the summer would have taken half an hour. But it was February; the snow was frozen, their skis could find no hold, and for every step forward they slipped back two. After three hours Ada and Paolo could no longer move, someone was vomiting. 'It was Alberto,' Ada wrote, 'who saved the situation':

. . . Without saying a word, he went ahead; and slowly, laboriously, leaning on his ski-poles, he zig-zagged upwards, with infinite patience carving a staircase in the snow; up which, one after the other, we all followed.

When I read that description time kaleidoscoped, as it so often does with Alberto; and I almost seemed to have been there.

They made it home to Italy. But after that all but the two eldest, Ada and her husband Ettore Marchesini, were ill. Paolo had rheumatism, Alberto severe bronchitis. For weeks he lay in bed, tended by Bianca, furious that the war was ending without him. At last, on 30 April, Turin was free. By then Alberto was well again, he and Bianca were more in love than ever, and Ada Gobetti had become Deputy Mayor. Two weeks later, she married them.

If This is a Man

From the start Primo said many modest things about the writing of *Se questo è un uomo*. First, and earliest – from the 1947 Preface on – that when it came to it his conscious mission to testify dropped away, and he wrote as he talked, out of urgent personal need. That consequently he wrote 'at break-neck speed', without order or plan; starting with the most recent memories and writing backwards, not logically or chronologically, but 'in order of urgency' alone. That when he met Lucia, who would become his wife, his writing was transformed: but not into the work of a writer, who is concerned with style and form, who hones and polishes; rather into the work of a chemist, who is concerned only with content, who writes his report at the end of the week, and who does not reread, rewrite or alter. That, finally, he had not planned a book: that *Se questo* became one 'almost spontaneously', 'without my noticing', because when he told his friends the stories they said he should write them, and when he had written several they said he was writing a book, and he should finish it.

Almost from the start, people who knew *If This is a Man*, or the Lager, or Primo, found much of this hard to believe. In 1963, for instance, a journalist called Silori, who was also a survivor, challenged him. Did he see no contradiction between these modest amateur's claims and his being, by now, the author of two famous books? Primo repeated that writing *Se questo* had not been a literary ambition for him, but an immediate need, to liberate himself from his experience, and to understand it. But that, said Silori acutely, is precisely a writer's idea. 'I, for instance, never wanted to write about it,' he said. So why did you? And Primo had to fall back on a different explanation: that *Se questo è un uomo* was, after all, 'a kind of message'; that he wanted to explain certain things not just to himself, but to the world.

As *Se questo* became a much-studied classic, more and more people began to agree with Silori. The Turinese scholar Alberto Cavaglion, who discovered that *If This is a Man* was not, in fact, the first thing Primo published on the Lager, concluded that his claim to have written it haphazardly and without a plan was 'hardly credible'. Giovanni Tesio, who saw the original manuscript, and the typescript of the first edition, argued as long ago as 1977 that Primo had worked with extraordinary care on every word from the start; and that between the two published versions he had cut and added, polished and honed with (literally) the best of them. As for moving only slowly towards a book on the advice of his friends, at least two of them remember it rather differently. 'Primo told me that he meant to write this thing,' Euge says, 'and naturally, like all his friends, I said – Definitely, do.'

And by March 1946, just over a third of the way through the year of writing, he was telling Pikolo that he planned to collect his Lager stories into a book.

What was happening? Partly, it was his old diffidence and self-doubt returning. After Auschwitz they were less, or different, but they had not gone; they would never go. But I think there was something else as well: something to do with his true aim in writing the book, which was not only to cleanse himself, and to testify.

I think – though I do not know – that he had arrived at Auschwitz already defeated: convinced his life was about to end, not only without love, but without achievement. He, who had hoped to become a great scientist, had injected rabbits, and now he would die. But then he looked around and thought: *perhaps not*. If the Lager was, as it seemed to him, a monstrous experiment on human nature, it needed its scientist. He would be that scientist. He would observe and analyse it, and tell the world; thus, he would not only do his duty to the dead, but would make his contribution after all.

Perhaps writing *If This is a Man* was not a literary ambition for him. But it was a scientific and philosophical one: an ambition to contribute something fundamental to human self-knowledge. In the extreme circumstances of a death camp, this ambition gave him the sense of mission and self-worth he needed to survive. But back home, in normal life, it turned against him. It was hubris, it was putting himself forward, and above others: everything that was most impossible to him, and most repugnant. It was something he had to deny, immediately and for ever, or he could not have written the book then, or lived with himself after.

But we know, after all, that he had determined while he was there to report everything he could of the evil experiment of Auschwitz. That cannot have meant merely telling it to family and friends – or even writing it for family and friends, as he once claimed. He told Pikolo over and over in the camp that if he survived he would testify to what had happened there; and there would be no testimony without writing and publishing – if not a book, at least essays, reports, articles. *Of course* he intended to write, and to publish, if he could; much more than he had ever intended to talk. It was talking that he had meant to restrict to family and friends, the need to talk to strangers that took him by surprise. Writing to strangers must always have been part of the plan.

And in fact he had begun to write before *Se questo*, as Alberto Cavaglion discovered. Back in Katowice, the *Kommandantur* had conveyed to Leonardo a Soviet government request to survivor-doctors for reports on the medical conditions in their camps. Primo and Leonardo had written the report on the Monowitz KB together, in the summer of 1945. On their return, they worked on an expanded version, including accounts of the transports and arrivals, living and working conditions, the selections, gas chambers and crematoria, and the final dramatic ten days. It was published in 1946, a year before *If This is a Man*, in *Minerva Medica*, the most important medical journal of the day.

The *Report on the Health and Hygiene Arrangements of the Monowitz Concentration Camp for Jews* clearly shows that Primo's denial of any literary intention in *If This is a Man* was also untrue. It was at least half Leonardo's work, probably more. But the point remains the same: it would be hard to imagine anything more different from *Se questo è un uomo*. This is a truly impersonal, factual report; which shows that all the talk of the quasi-scientific detachment of *Se questo*, of its being modelled – as Primo half-seriously said – on the laboratory report, is more or less nonsense.

After his first foray into Lager writing, in Katowice, he had headed (slowly) home. Then, on 18 or 19 October, on the train from Verona to Turin, he had started to talk about that other world. And whatever his intention, this was the fact: he was a natural story-teller, and he had an audience of ordinary people. What he told were *stories*; dramatic, human tales of what had happened down there, of the brave and broken people he had known.

This is the part that surprised him: his own need to tell people face to face, to see them shocked, convinced, changed. He did it for weeks, for months, with friends, with strangers. So that when he came to write each episode, he had already told it many times. He knew it worked – and not just for him. It worked on *them*. On 27 January he had known that the first part of his plan had succeeded: every detail of the last year was fixed in his head, and he had survived. Now he knew that the second part could succeed too: *he could tell it*. He could make people believe what the Nazis had been sure no one ever would.

He began to write in November, as fast and furiously as he talked, and often in similar places – on trains, on trams, in his room at home. He wrote on pieces of paper, and in a school exercise book, perhaps in that order. By December 'the last chapters' were done, at least in this first handwritten version: certainly the 'Story of Ten Days', and probably 'The Last One'; perhaps also the chapter on entering the laboratory, or on the October selection. But now something else he had not foreseen happened. He had hoped that writing would purge the Auschwitz poison from his veins; and in the end it did. But not yet. He was falling deeper and deeper into depression.

It must have been now, I think, that Nico Dallaporta came to see him. We know what happened. Moved by the miracle of his return, and by the power of his stories, Dallaporta told him that he had surely been saved by God himself to bear witness. And Primo reacted with violence to this idea.

He thought it was monstrous, and said it was unjust – he who had just been describing truly monstrous and unjust acts with incredible calm. Now, his dedication to justice was lifelong, normal; but the violence of this reaction was not. The suggestion had touched 'an exposed nerve', he wrote later; and I think that was truer than he knew. Of course he had never imagined that God had chosen him to testify; but *he had chosen himself*, which made the injustice his own. I think that was why he responded as he did: because Dallaporta had almost stumbled on his secret ambition; and because he was too depressed to keep up his usual control.

The depression reached its peak, or pit, in January. There is no proof of this, but there is evidence: in Primo's poetry.

Poetry played a particular role for him: it was the one narrow bridge between his two halves, between his conscious mind, like a sunlit plain, and the dark abyss beneath, the thought of which had split the mind of his first creation, *L'Uomo*. The bridge opened rarely; and almost always under the pressure of emotions which could not escape him in any other way. Later he would note that there had been two main periods of poetry in his life, the first of them now, after his return from the Lager. When people asked why, he would answer that he did not know. But he did know. It was because they coincided with two of the worst depressions of his life – until the last one, in which he would not be able to write at all.

The dates tell the story. On 28 December he wrote his first Lager poem: 'Buna'. On 3 January he wrote 'Cantare', 'Singing', which is about a brief return to normality from a very different state:

> . . . But when we started singing
> Those good foolish songs of ours,
> Then everything was again
> As it had always been.
>
> . . .
>
> Once more we were just young men:
> Not martyrs, not infamous, not saints.★

★ Primo's friend Giorgio Vaccarino remembers an occasion soon after his return which may have been the one that gave rise to this poem. It was in a mountain refuge called Pavillon, above Courmayeur; Giorgio remembers that Anna Maria was there, and Alberto Salmoni, Alberto Levi, Franco Momigliano, Euge, and perhaps others – all friends who had seen 'killing and dying' like him (ll. 7–8), though not in the Lager. They sang mountain songs, and comic dialect songs ('Those good foolish songs of ours'); and Primo took part with gusto, Giorgio recalls. In fact, if it was this occasion (there were probably many more), he was making a last effort to stave off depression.

But this was only a truce. On 9 January came not one but two poems. 'The Crow's Song' is about the arrival of depression:

> 'I come from far away
> To bring bad news.
>
> . . .
>
> To find your window,
> To find your ear,
> To bring you the sad tidings
> That rob you of sleep's joy,
> That taint your bread and wine,
> Lodge every evening in your heart.'

The twenty-fifth of February 1944 was the date of Primo's last whole day on earth with Vanda. '25 February 1944' is only seven short lines, very close to silence. This, and its opening, show that Vanda was at the heart of his grief:

> I would like to believe in something,
> Something beyond the death that undid you.

Only twice more, in the very lowest depths of depression, would Primo's rational will crack like this, as even in the selection of 1944 it had not cracked.

On 10 and 11 January came the two great Auschwitz poems, 'Shemà' and 'Reveille', full of rage and despair. During the rest of January, three more poems of depression, in which the burden of loneliness grows.

> . . . And a man? Isn't a man sad?
> If he lives in solitude a long time,
> If he believes time has run its course,
> A man is a sad thing too.
>   ('Monday', 17 January 1946)

And:

> The time has come to have a home,
> Or to remain for a long time without one.
> The time has come not to be alone,
> Or we will stay alone for a long time.
>   ('After R. M. Rilke', 29 January 1946)

In early February, once more there are two poems in one day: 'Ostjuden' and 'Sunset at Fossoli', both written on the 7th. If the 'I' in 'Sunset at Fossoli' is speaking metaphorically, it may be Primo himself; if literally, Vanda. Or perhaps they have merged, or are merging, into one:

I know what it means not to return.

For the first time since before Auschwitz, he contemplated suicide.

If his solitude had continued, perhaps he could not have gone on. But as Alberto Dalla Volta had told him, he was lucky. '[D]estiny reserved for me a different and unique gift,' he would write later. Four days after 'Sunset at Fossoli' he met Lucia Morpurgo: and 'In a few hours we knew that we belonged to each other, not for one meeting but for life.'

It was a sudden, total reversal of the grey world of his depression, like the complete reversal of the normal world by Auschwitz, but with the opposite sign. 'In a few hours,' he wrote,

. . . I felt reborn and replete with new powers, washed clean and cured of a long sickness . . . [E]qually cured suddenly was the world around me, and exorcized the name and face of the woman who had gone down into the lower depths with me and had not returned.

He had been cured, not only of one long sickness, but of two: of his depression, and of his double bind. That is what these lines secretly mean. And what the poem he wrote for Lucia that day meant too.

> . . .
>
> Because you weren't there, in the long evenings,
> I considered the rash blasphemy
> That the world was God's error,
> Myself an error in the world.
>
> And when I was face to face with death –
> No, I shouted with every fibre.
> I haven't finished yet;
> There was still too much to do.
>
> . . .
>
> I came back because you were there.

★   ★

Not only was he suddenly cured, so was his writing. No longer was it frantic, solitary; but 'a lucid building', which gave him pleasure, even exaltation. The miracle of Lucia's love had healed his long self-doubt; and especially (I think) the crippling complex about his self-election. It is possible that, in February 1946, Lucia Morpurgo saved Primo's life. It is probable, on his own evidence, that she saved his book.

We can be almost completely certain which chapter Primo wrote, in that first moment of rebirth and release by love: 'The Canto of Ulysses', the humane heart of *If This is a Man*, its highest point of faith in man, and in himself – but echoing, too, Dante's fear of presumption, in the thirst for knowledge which would rival God's. That fear, the 'Canto' suggests, grazed Primo's mind at the time; when he came to write, I have guessed, it returned, and grew huge. But now the meeting with Lucia had banished it (almost) entirely, and renewed his faith in himself a hundredfold: and three days later, on 14 February, he typed out the final version. He had written almost the entire chapter, he would say, in half an hour of his lunch-break, 'in a kind of trance'.

The trance held. He continued to write wherever and whenever he could; then at night, in his room at the factory where he found work, he would type out the final versions. In February, for example, he also typed 'Kraus', in March 'Chemical Examination', in April 'October 1944', in June 'KB'. By December he had finished. The book was done.

'Of course I wanted it to be published,' Primo told a journalist who was also a friend. 'But I don't know if I would have offered it to a publisher if the few friends who had read [it] hadn't urged me on.' With his insecure, volatile confidence, his deep conflict over self-promotion, this may even have been true. But Anna Maria encouraged him, and Leonardo; probably Lucia (though she was even more private than he); perhaps his mother, though he never said so, and she may have found praise as hard to give him as affection. And more than a few friends: Silvio, Ada and Euge, Giorgio Lattes and Livio Norzi; his cousin Giulia, his old university friend Vanna Rava, his new Resistance friend Giorgio Vaccarino; and others as well. Anna Maria showed the typescript to a brilliant young scientist, Rita Levi Montalcini, Giorgio Lattes showed it to the head of the Olivetti school in Ivrea; both gave it their keen approval. And so Primo took that step too. He sent his book to 'a number of important publishers', he wrote later: 'three or four'. His first choice, and certainly his true hope and desire, was the great Turinese house of Einaudi. To Einaudi he delivered the book in person, walking the dozen or so blocks up the Corso Re Umberto with the typescript in his hand.

He was lucky: but not always. Having finally dared to put himself forward, he was – it must have seemed to him – instantly punished. He got rejections from all three or four, starting with Einaudi.

The others didn't matter to him. But the rejection by Einaudi was a blow which he never forgot. Particularly since it came from a fellow Turinese, a fellow writer, and a fellow Jew: the novelist Natalia Ginzburg.

At first it seemed, from Primo's account, that Natalia had merely been the one to tell him, because when he had returned to the Via Biancamano a few days later she had happened to be there. But over the years it became clear that it was Natalia who had made the decision, though perhaps not alone: two others had made it with her, she would say, of whom one was Cesare Pavese. Primo does not seem to have known about Pavese. But he knew about Natalia from the start.

Being Primo, he would not be angry, or blame her, especially in public. She was a good writer and an important editor; she was his friend Alberto Levi's sister, and the widow of the great Leone Ginzburg, one of the founders of Einaudi, and one of the first and fiercest antifascists, who had died of Nazi tortures only three years before. It was, he said, the wrong time – a time of hope, not harsh reflection: a book like his was an indelicacy, a rude reminder, like talking of the chimney in Auschwitz. Yet there were many such rude reminders pouring into the publishing houses in those days; and no house was busier than Einaudi, no editor busier than Natalia. Her only fault, if she had one, was haste: haste, and inattention.

Natalia herself said much the same, years later – or said that Pavese had said it: there were too many Lager books coming out, it would be better to wait. Now, this was true, but not of Einaudi. Lager diaries and memoirs were beginning to flow into all publishers; but they were flowing *out* only from small and dedicated ones, often with Resistance or other political affiliations. The mainstream houses would only join in later, when the tide of public interest had started to turn. Einaudi would not publish its first Lager, or Lager-related, books until 1954, and then only imported ones, whose great success had already been proved: Anne Frank's *Diaries* from Holland, and Robert Antelme's *L'espèce humaine* from France.

How did a reader like Natalia Ginzburg miss a book that seems today to tower above most others, and not only of its own kind? Of course we know it happens all the time, and usually to the greatest: to Proust, for example, and to Kafka; in Italy, to Svevo as well as to Lampedusa. But there were no doubt particular reasons here. Despite Einaudi's fabled seriousness, or because of it, they had to think very carefully of sales. They had to pick their lost causes carefully; and the Lager, especially in its racial aspect, was not one. That is not surprising about Pavese, or Giulio Einaudi himself. It is more surprising about Natalia Ginzburg, and at the heart of the question about her. But it is also, I think, at the heart of the answer. The closer a trauma comes to you, the more likely, not less, you are to repress it: the country that took the longest of all to read and write about the Holocaust was Israel. Perhaps Natalia Ginzburg read *Se questo è un uomo* hurriedly just because she was Jewish, just because she had lost her Jewish husband to the Nazis. In other words, the answer is personal; and even more personal than this. In 1947 Natalia had three small children, and had left her new (non-Jewish) husband behind in Rome. Turin oppressed her with 'a crowd of memories and shadows'; she thought constantly of returning to Rome, and eventually did. She had, we might say, her own problems.

But the answer is not only personal: it is also literary. Natalia Ginzburg was a novelist; she looked for narrative drive, for character and drama to catch the reader's eye. Eighteen months later she turned down another Lager memoir on just those criteria – and recommended that the author try De Silva's 'documentary' series. I think that she saw *Se questo* in the same way. She was wrong; but perhaps we can understand why.

The 1947 typescript of *If This is a Man* was even more chaste, even more reserved, than the book we know now: especially at the beginning. After the first five chapters it was much (though not entirely) as it would remain, with its astonishing events – the chemical exam, 'The Canto of Ulysses', the selection, 'The Story of Ten Days' – and its unforgettable characters – Lorenzo and Pikolo, Elias and Henri, the Last One, Charles. But in the first five chapters Primo would make many changes, before the final version: and with each change he would add more drama, more colour, more feeling. Above all, he would add more characters: especially humane and moving ones. In the first chapter Natalia saw there was no Emilia, in the second no Schlome, who welcomed Primo 'to the house of the dead'; there was no 'Initiation' chapter, and therefore no Steinlauf; in what is now the fourth chapter there was no Chaim, in the fourth and fifth (and later too) much less Alberto. Perhaps Natalia Ginzburg only read the first few chapters, and decided they were too dark, too austere. Primo would make the same decision himself ten years or so later.

Alessandro Galante Garrone was an activist-idealist: an antifascist magistrate under Fascism, and during the war a member of the Piedmont CLN for the Partito d'Azione. There he had met Anna Maria Levi. One day around the end of 1946 Anna Maria told him that her brother had written a book about his experiences in a Nazi concentration camp, which had just been turned down by Einaudi. He was bitterly disappointed and discouraged. He felt he had written something of value, and he had. Would Sandro look at it?

Sandro looked at it. He too was a writer – but a journalist, essayist and historian. He was instantly struck, and he knew exactly what to do. On the CLN he had also met Franco Antonicelli, its last President: and only a few months before Antonicelli had reopened his publishing house. Antonicelli agreed to see him; and together Sandro and Anna Maria took Primo's typescript to the offices of De Silva, four rooms above a bookshop on the Via Viotti. Here Antonicelli worked with four young editors, like a microcosm of heady, victorious, left-liberal Turin: Marisa Zini, daughter of

Zino, who had taught Primo herself all those years ago; Anita Rho, niece
of Barbara Allason, one of the earliest Turinese antifascists; Maria Vittoria
Malvano, private pupil of Augusto Monti; and a young ex-G. & L. partisan,
Lorenzo Zorzi.

Anna Maria's choice of route had been exactly right, and set the pattern
for the future. Primo's relations with the literary world would always be
awkward, on both sides. He would enter it sideways, like a crab, keeping
one eye fixed outside; and most literary critics and scholars would watch his
strange progress with suspicion, when they noticed it at all. His best readers
would always be, as he hoped, ordinary thinking people; and hybrids like
himself, who did not live by words alone. Franco Antonicelli was one of
these. He was a literary intellectual – critic, essayist and poet; but outward-
looking, avant-garde, and deeply political. In his early editorial work, with
the publishers Frassinelli, he had introduced moderns like Kafka and Joyce
to Italy; in his first De Silva period he had published unknown dialect poets,
and Goethe in translation, to remind readers of 'the Germany we loved'.
He was the perfect publisher for Primo; and he recognized the value of *Se
questo* straight away. The bitterness of the Einaudi failure lasted a few months
at most. When the first chapters began to appear in *L'Amico del popolo* at the
end of March, Silvio was able to announce: *From a book about to be published.*

That was how it began. But – despite what Primo would say – it was only
the beginning. This book – which 'grew like an antheap', which 'wrote
him' – had gone through two stages of writing, pre-Lucia and post-Lucia;
now it went through its first stage of rewriting.

To start with, the title was changed. Primo had already tried out several,
testing them on friends and acquaintances as usual. *Storia degli uomini senza
nome, Story of men without names*, had been an early one. For a time he settled
on *Sul fondo, On the Bottom*, the name of the second chapter: that was the
book's working title in *L'Amico del popolo*, and probably the one with which
it arrived at De Silva. Finally, some time before publication, he made his
final choice: *I sommersi e i salvati, The Drowned and the Saved*, the name of the
central chapter, and an echo of Dante. But this too was not to remain. At
the end of the fifth and last extract in *L'Amico del popolo*, Silvio included one
of Primo's 1946 poems, which still bore *its* original title: 'Salmo', 'Psalm'.
By the time the book was at the printers, the poem had become 'Shemà',
and the book's frontispiece. Its exhortation, 'Consider if this is a man', went
to the heart of its meaning: and Franco Antonicelli – perhaps at the suggestion
of his young editor Renzo Zorzi – chose the haunting question contained
in it instead. Primo was sorry to lose the link to Dante; but he recognized
the accuracy of this new title, and perhaps its power. He accepted.

He too had been making changes. Now, we do not have his original typescript (or the manuscript, of course; Giovanni Tesio only saw, and returned, both). But we do have copies of some very early typescripts of *If This is a Man*, which Primo sent to his cousin Anna Yona in the United States in 1946 or '47. There is no reason to doubt that these are copies of the typescript that both Natalia Ginzburg and Franco Antonicelli saw. And starting with them, we can watch Primo Levi becoming a writer.

First and foremost, he made the changes that a scientist would also make, or a historian: anyone seeking the maximum accuracy and clarity of communication with his reader. Thus, he corrected errors (only two typhoid sufferers in KB, not three), added explanations where they were needed (of the role of Pikolo in 'The Canto of Ulysses', for instance) and cut them where they weren't (e.g. on the meaning of *Blockältester* in 'October 1944', since by then we know). Above all, he added detail and precision: for example, in 'The Story of Ten Days' the stove was not just of 'metal' but of 'cast iron', and they found it in the ruins not just 'of the bombardment' but 'of the Prominents' Block'. Charles cried at his story not simply 'of the moment of my arrest', but 'of the armistice in Italy, of the dark and desperate beginning of the partisan Resistance, of the man who betrayed us, and of our capture in the mountains'. Many of these additions – like the last one – were already moving from the scientist's focus on precision to the writer's focus on the memorable and telling: the inspection he added to the list in 'On the Bottom', for instance, 'of the buttons of our jackets, which must be five'; or the description of the Buna's streets and buildings in 'A Good Day', which 'have numbers or letters instead of names', 'like us', '*come noi*'.

We have, then, already moved to another kind of change: a literary kind. First – as he said himself – the search for the right word, the right phrase: so that 'to have returned from Auschwitz', for example, from 'no small thing' becomes 'no small fortune'; and *Considerate la vostra semenza* – Ulysses' clarion call – is no longer like 'a draught of hot wine', but like '*la voce di Dio*', 'the voice of God'. But more important is what he didn't say. Already now, in 1947, the most important of his changes do not simply add more accuracy and rigour to his reporting: he can do that only a bit better than he already has. Instead they add things of which the 1946 typescripts *can* use more, and which, perhaps, Natalia Ginzburg had missed – colour, drama, emotion, even humour. And something else too. If we did not know Primo, we might guess that he clamped himself down to this chaste, objective text, that he ruthlessly cut all references to himself, all expressions of his own suffering and despair. *He did the opposite.* It was his nature to be clamped down, to leave himself out, to withhold expressions of feeling; and in this his chemist's training and his aim of witness both agreed. But something pulled him in the other direction. Perhaps it was people's reactions in trams and trains; perhaps it was something Natalia said, or Franco Antonicelli. But mostly, I think, it was his own writer's instinct. What he did was to *add* these things: to put himself and his feelings – just a little, just enough – back in.

Thus, for example, to the bizarre and frightening conversation with the Hungarian doctor on their first night, he added a touch of pathos and humour: 'Why is he in the Lager? Is he a Jew like us? "No," he says simply, "I am a criminal."' To 'The Canto of Ulysses' he added many little touches of immediacy and drama: *We have no time to choose, already this hour is less than an hour – Today I feel capable of so much – The sun is already high, midday is near – It is late, it is late . . .* In 'Kraus' he added Kraus's terrible epitaph – 'he will not last long here, you can see that at a glance'; and in 'The Story of Ten Days', very simply, Alberto's.

The chapters in which he made the most personal additions in 1947 were two of the greatest: 'The Canto of Ulysses' and 'Chemical Examination'.★ In the original 'Canto' he had barely hinted at his own unendurable longing: 'And the mountains when one sees them from the distance . . . the mountains . . .' Now, for one instant, if he does not let it out, he lets us in:

. . . oh Pikolo, Pikolo, say something, speak, do not let me think of my mountains, which used to show up in the dusk of evening as I returned by train from Milan to Turin! . . .

In 'Chemical Examination' he made two immediate, felt additions, moving from observation to expression, taking us inside him, and inside the moment, with a novelist's skill. One of these is in the middle of the exam, when he realizes it is going well – and suddenly the writer reconnects himself, and us, to the boy he had been, and under his convict's clothes still is:

. . . this sense of lucid elation, this excitement which I feel warm in my veins, I recognize it, it is the fever of examinations, *my* fever of *my* examinations, that spontaneous mobilization of all my logical faculties and all my knowledge, which my friends at university so envied me.

The other moment in this chapter is perhaps the boldest of all, in which he connects us not just to himself in the Lager, but to himself writing three

---

★ As far as we know, at least, since Anna Yona's copies consist of only ten of the original sixteen chapters. Altogether, with this proviso, 'The Canto of Ulysses' is the chapter which Primo reworked most in 1947: which rather belies his claim to have worked the least on his best pages, as his editor points out. (See Marco Belpoliti, *Opere*, Vol. I, p. 1404 (1997).)

years later, in a 'double leap, up and down', like the one at the end of 'Carbon':

. . . I know that I am not made of the stuff of those who resist, I am too civilized, I still think too much, I use myself up at work. And now I also know that I can save myself if I become a Specialist, and that I will become a Specialist if I pass a chemistry examination.

Today, at this very moment as I sit writing at a table, I myself am not convinced that these things really happened.

It may seem perverse to say that 1946 and 1947 were Primo Levi's best years. An acute depression, the second great failure of his life – how can these be good? But the depression was brief, and over by February 1946. After that these were his most fulfilled years. For several reasons, but one above all: during them he was writing a good, necessary book. And he knew it. In July 1947 he wrote to Pikolo with – for him – brazen confidence.

My book is at the printers . . . I've worked on it for a long time, with love and rage. I don't know if it is mediocre, good or very good; but I believe I have managed to do something more than free myself of an obsession, and save my memories from oblivion.

Lucia

Lucia Morpurgo was the other main reason for the happiness of these years. She was a year younger than Primo, slender, blonde, and attractive. She was not, like him, a true Turinese: her father was from Ancona, her mother from Casale, and she had been born in Perugia. But she had come to Turin as a child; and no one, in the end, was more Turinese than Lucia.

Her father, Giuseppe, was an immensely clever and erudite man: teacher of Latin and Italian, prolific author of school textbooks, scholarly editions of the Italian classics, and his own novels, of which the most successful was a peasant epic called *Beati Misericordes*. The family was Jewish, but not at all religious; and less culturally Jewish even than Primo's, as this very traditional, Catholic novel of Giuseppe's suggests. There were three daughters: Maria Grazia, the eldest; and then Lucia and Nella, who were twins.

Giuseppe was a bit of a Casaubon: scholarly, reserved, and, I suspect, rather pedantic ('a schoolmaster in life as well as work', says Giulia Colombo). His wife was livelier; but Giuseppe seems to have had more influence, at least on the twins. Lucia, especially, was highly intelligent, like her father; but like him reserved, serious, almost always alone.

Until 1938, she and Nella were at the Liceo Gioberti, like their father.
With the coming of the racial laws, they did their final examinations from
the Jewish School; after that, since university was barred to her, Lucia took
private lessons from the sculptor Roberto Terracini, together with Anna
Maria. Of course Giuseppe had also had to leave the Liceo Gioberti; he
became Headmaster of the *scuola ebraica*, from 1941 until it closed in the
summer of 1943.

Giuseppe, say Turin's antifascists, was not an antifascist. He had little
Jewish consciousness, he was a classicist, a member of the establishment, and
a traditional Jew of the Italian religion. He was one of those who hoped to
the end that if Jews only maintained their loyalty to Italy, Italy would not
fail in its loyalty to them. He was, of course, disappointed; and in 1943 the
Morpurgos fled Turin and went into hiding near Asti.

When they returned in 1945 the twins both resumed their interrupted
studies: Nella in pharmacology, Lucia in the history of art. In February 1946,
therefore, she was a student, half-way to her degree; and once again in the
same group as Anna Maria.

It was not through Anna Maria that she and Primo met, however; or
rather, that was not how they re-met now. For they had known each other
before: from at least 1938, when Anna Maria and the Morpurgo twins had
been at the Jewish School together; and very likely, in that small community,
from before that as well, from the time the Morpurgos had arrived in Turin.
They had seen each other, spoken to each other, been to the same events,
lectures, gatherings. But now something different happened.

When Primo was trying to evoke 1947 forty years later, and to explain
why people then did not want to read a book about dehumanization and
destruction, he said that they had more important things to do: to find work,
to rebuild their homes. They had other desires, he said: 'to dance, for
instance, to enjoy themselves, to have children'. On, or near, 11 February
1946, he went to a party in which young Jewish people were celebrating
their survival, and the end – they were certain – of war. Anna Maria was
not there, so he went with his cousin Giulia. Soon everyone was dancing.
Primo, who had never been to the Sala Castellino, the Sala Gay, the Sala
Debenedetti as a boy, turned to Giulia. He couldn't dance, he said, would
she teach him how? Oh no, Giulia said shyly, she couldn't, she didn't know
how herself. And there beside them was Lucia, usually so separate, so silent.
'*Ti insegno io*,' she said: 'I will teach you.' She took his hand, she drew his
arms around her, and they danced.

Avigliana

There was only one other thing Primo needed: work. At first, life being what it is, he needed it even more than love. He went back to Wander to settle his affairs, so abruptly abandoned two years before; he asked if he might still be needed there, but the answer was no. He went back to the Chemical Institute and applied to Ponzio's successor for a position as Assistant, but there was none available. If he went back to Ennio Mariotti, nothing came of it. He even went briefly to Paris, encouraged by Jean, but caught a cold and hurried home. Then he re-met Ester Valabrega, who was working for Chatillon in Vercelli. Might there be any jobs there? he asked. Ester inquired, and got him an interview. He may even have been offered something; but if so it was not enough. By the end of 1945 he was still unemployed, and without money; which was no small part of his mounting depression.

At last, however, he did find a job, in what he called 'the lakeside factory' in Avigliana, a few miles outside Turin. On 21 January 1946 he became Assistant Head of the Research Laboratory of Duco Avigliana, manufacturer of paints and varnishes, subsidiary of the worldwide chemical giant Dupont. It was the first chink of light in his depression; and a first step towards his recovery.

On a Monday morning, then, almost exactly three months after his return, he took the early morning tram up the Corso Re Umberto to Porta Nuova, and climbed on to a local train. This was yet another goods wagon, with wooden benches nailed to its walls; since there were no windows, the doors on both sides were left open, letting in not only light and air, but billows of smoke and soot from the engine. When he got off at Avigliana the factory site began at once, and stretched in a great horseshoe shape all the way to the lake. It had started life as an explosives factory, Dinamita Nobel – which was why, for safety's sake, the grounds were so large. Nobel still kept one explosives department, on the shores of the lake. The Duco factory itself was at the centre of the horseshoe, nearly two miles from the lake: so that Primo's 'lakeside factory' was the first of many romantic touches.

The reality, however, was romantic enough. The factory was neglected and battered by war, the vast site, when Primo arrived in January, covered in snow and ice. With bureaucratic perversity, only the smaller roads were tarred; the main one, along which the heavy lorries came and went all day, was a sea of mud – especially when the thaw came, a month or two after his arrival. But despite the freezing cold, the mud and ice, the location was superb. On either side towered the mountains of the Val di Susa, many of which he had climbed – Roccasella, Civrari, Ciambergia; on one rocky spur clung the Sacra di San Michele, one of the great medieval monuments of Piedmont, which you saw each time you walked out the door.

Here Primo not only worked but lived during the week, in the Casa Scapoli, the bachelors' quarters: also called the Casa Rossa, the Red House, because it was painted red.* His room, like all the rooms, was monkishly bare: a bed, a table and a pair of chairs; a cupboard, a basin, and a lamp in the middle. Here he sat in the evenings, typing his chapters; from the window he could see his mountains in the dusk once more.

Of his closest colleagues at Duco – the other laboratory heads, his assistant, the company doctor, whom he put into a story – I found only one still alive: Dr Luciano Colombo, head of the physics laboratory, and of one of the quality control laboratories.

Relying on a single witness is bad practice, even when he is as meticulous as Dr Colombo: just as there is no science of the single event (as Primo said), so there is no history with a single observer. But though Dr Colombo's reports cannot be compared to others at Duco, they can be compared to others *tout court*; and the results show great consistency, except on one point.

By the summer of 1946, when Colombo arrived, the marks of the past on Primo had healed. He no longer kept his eyes glued to the ground, or ate embarrassing amounts of bread. The strange, swollen roundness of his months of truce was long gone, and he had returned to normal: thin to the point of frailty, with a small, pointed face, and bright, expressive eyes. He was as quiet as ever, and at the same time as kind and helpful: 'as reserved, even withdrawn about himself as he was open and available to other people's problems', says Luciano Colombo. He was a brilliant analyst, and a font of creative ideas which put him 'a good head above everyone else'. 'If you wanted to know anything at all,' Colombo says – in almost exactly Giulia Colombo's words, or Primo's university friends' – 'you went to him'; and without fail or fuss he would have the answer. He showed no trace of his terrible experiences, but was invariably serene, always ready to smile, or even to laugh, in his contained way; especially to enjoy, and to tell, little jokes and stories. 'I remember him,' Luciano Colombo says, 'full of the will to live.'

Colombo remembers another happy thing from this time too: Primo's friendship with Felice Fantino. Fantino was a *collaudatore*, a tester, and also an *applicatore*: an expert on applying the more specialist products, whose job was to demonstrate the correct techniques to clients. In other words, he was

---

* Did Primo borrow this detail for Starye Dorogi? If not, he must have been powerfully reminded of that other strange place of only a few months before.

a skilled worker, rather than an educated *bourgeois*. He came from the village of Sant'Ambrogio near Avigliana, and was a famous speaker of Piedmontese, communicating with clients around the world in dialect with the greatest of ease. He was full of human warmth, and above all of happiness: 'a child of the sun', as Primo would write about Lello Perugia, 'very innocent and very civilized'. He was, in other words, a cross between two of Primo's ideal opposites, two of his more-than-half-fictional characters of the future: Cesare and Faussone. Perhaps something of Fantino even went into Faussone thirty years later. Now, certainly, the two men had long and happy conversations in Piedmontese; and Fantino already moved Primo to write. One of his earliest stories, 'Maria and the Circle', was based on something Fantino told him in one of their conversations; and Primo dedicated the story to him, as readers can see in *The Periodic Table*, where it became the strange fable called 'Titanium'.*

So far, Dr Colombo's memories fit with all we know of Primo. But now comes the one that conflicts: not with other people's, but with Primo's own. At Duco, he would say later, he was not only typing his chapters, but still madly telling them, 'to anyone and everyone, at the drop of a hat' – in the canteen, to 'the plant manager [and] the yardman' as they went about their work. And then he would type into the night, 'which was considered even crazier'. Now, according to Luciano Colombo, none of this is true. Yes, they all knew Dr Levi was writing something, and he did occasionally try out titles on them – but only for their sound. No one had any idea *what* he was writing, or any idea at all of the horrors he had undergone. He never breathed a word of that to anyone; not even, Dr Colombo is sure, to Fantino, who was far too open to keep secrets. And yes, Primo did type in his room in the evenings. But as to the idea that he typed like a madman, disturbing his neighbours deep into the night – Dr Colombo never heard anything like that at all. And though he did not live in the Red House himself, Dr Compagnucci, the head of the other lab, did. He asked him once, and Compagnucci assured him: Primo's typing was discreet and decent, and never disturbed a soul.

I must say this sounds very like Primo – more like him than his own description. Yet there is no doubt that he did have a time of talking obsessively to all kinds of people. Could it be that he did so only early on at Duco, and that by the time Colombo arrived this legacy of the past, like the others, was over? But Compagnucci and the others were already there; Colombo would surely have heard of it from them. No: I think the solution may be rather different. It was, in Primo's own words, 'the plant manager

---

* See below, page 527. Sadly, Fantino died a few years ago.

and the yardman' whom he stopped, 'the workers' who considered him 'a harmless kook' for his driven talk. I suspect that Dr Colombo is right, and that he never did speak of his degrading, dehumanizing, and still very recent experience to his fellow chemists: to those for whom he was an equal. I suspect he spoke only to labourers, and lowlier employees: with whom he did not work, and from whom he could get the human response he needed, without losing his difference from them. As for Felice Fantino, it is hard to say. He straddled both worlds; perhaps he lived too much in the upper one for Primo to let go. He liked to keep things, and people, separate; and still more so the parts of himself. So, his closest friends apart, those who heard his stories from him did not read them, and we who read them did not hear them from him; thus he kept apart his rational need to understand others from his secret need to be understood.

On 21 January 1946 Primo had entered the working world that would be his for the next thirty years: the world of organic chemists, 'bunglers', as he would write, expelled from the 'lost paradise' of inorganic chemistry, so simple and clean. From that day on, his particular continent would be that of paints and varnishes: that is, substances which, when spread thin, change from liquids into solids. And his particular country, in Duco Avigliana in 1946–7, was glycerophthalic resins, which I shall not attempt to explain.

His job was ill-paid; but, he might hope, secure, and even interesting. Ideally, he would write, chemists would like to do everything themselves – to set their own problems, 'beautiful and elegant', and find their own solutions; but this does not happen in the real world. Instead the Duco research laboratory, like that in any company, had to respond to clients' demands: for a shiny black paint, for instance, rapid-drying and extremely cheap, which needn't be long-lasting (this client, Primo explains, was a coffin-maker). Alternatively, they had to analyse their competitors' advertising samples, and, 'euphemism aside', copy them, if possible adding some marginal improvement: just as those same competitors were analysing, copying and attempting to improve on theirs. That, Primo wrote, is Technological Progress. It might occasionally prick one's conscience; but at least it wasn't boring.

In 1946, however, there weren't yet many competitors in Italy, and perhaps there weren't many customers either. In any case, Primo was not kept very busy with the normal research and development needs of his laboratory. He was, therefore, assigned several other tasks as well, which suited him even better. The director, Dr Debove, set him some detective problems to solve: and he could not have found a better detective. When Primo came to write of his adventures in chemistry many years later, two of the gayest and most successful came from Duco, and his very first year as a paint and varnish chemist.

A few months before he arrived, one of Duco's varnishes had developed an alarming disease. When first applied, it seemed fine. But after a few minutes it would recoil, picking up its feet like a swimmer who feels something nasty on the bottom; and little craters would form, through which the naked surface reappeared. This pitting of what should be smooth, like scars on skin, made everyone shiver; and the problem was dubbed *schivatura*, shunning or aversion, which referred almost as much to people's reaction as to the action of the varnish itself.

Primo set to and performed a long series of tests, watched with a certain irony by his co-workers, who had gone down the same path themselves. No use: nothing about the cans, the storerooms, the varnish itself had any ascertainable defect. He had found only one clue: some of the cans were made of shiny metal, some of a dull one; and only the varnish in the dull-metal cans 'shunned'. He had already tested both kinds of metal thoroughly, and both were entirely innocent. Nonetheless, he asked for a meeting with the supplier of the dull-metal cans: perhaps he had changed something in his production process recently?

The supplier came: no, nothing had been changed; his cans contained a bit of lead, as Dr Levi knew, but this had never given any trouble. Primo did know; that was a dead end. But now, as he looked into an empty can, he noticed something: around its base there was a minute gap, and yet neither it nor any of the others had ever leaked. Did the supplier, perhaps, use a sealant? Yes, of course he did, the man replied: welding was far too expensive. *What did he use?* Primo asked, his quiet voice rising just a fraction as he sighted his prey. Anything malleable, said the man: any kind of rubber gum, or soft plastic; or sometimes, in these difficult post-war days, *carniccio*. '*Carniccio?*' asked Primo. What was that? It was the remnants of flesh that tanners scraped off hides, the man answered. It made an excellent sealant; better than rubber, which sometimes swelled.

'Like a pirate who had spied a galleon', Primo prised off the bottom of a can with a pair of pliers, and unwound the thin worm of *carniccio* that ringed it. A tester painted some healthy varnish on a sheet of metal: perfect. Then he dropped a few small pieces of the *carniccio* on it. They waited, one minute, two. And then — yes! from each piece the horrified varnish recoiled, and a little crown of craters formed, exactly like pock-marked skin. This time, Primo wrote, the poxy mess looked beautiful to him. He had solved the problem of the *schivatura*.

For *The Periodic Table*, however, he did not choose this adventure to represent his time in Avigliana. Instead he chose the other: the adventure of

'Chromium', in which the deformation is subtly different. All paints and varnishes change from liquid to solid: it is small variations in how and when they change that make all the difference between success and failure. The 'shunning' varnish solidified wrongly; the anti-rust paint of 'Chromium' solidified too soon.

This is how Primo tells the story (and here too the 'how' matters). One day the Director said he had 'a little job' for him; and led him to the factory rubbish dump. Piled in a corner were thousands of strange, squashy orange shapes, the consistency of livers or lungs. They were, or had been, cans of paint that had gone wrong: in English, indeed, we would say that they had 'livered', in Italian that they had 'lung'ed'. The cans had been cut away, and the contents abandoned: still bizarrely retaining their shapes because of that unnatural solidification, rather like the cake of frozen soup from which, just a year before, Primo had caught his providential disease.

The paint contained a basic lead chromate and an alkyd resin (one of Primo's glycerophthalic resins). These were 'the two fornicators', Primo wrote, 'from whose embrace the orange monsters had sprung': the taint must come from one of them. Either the chromate was too basic or the resin too acidic. He went to the archives to check. First the resin, which the company produced itself: he read the 'birth certificates' of every batch just before and after the livering began. No, the resin was blameless: its acidity was variable, but always well below the danger mark. The chromate, then. That was bought in, and every batch tested. He got out the test list since January 1944: each one had satisfied the specifications, and had been duly approved by the analyst of the day. That was unexceptionable, except for one thing: every test had produced exactly the same value, 29.5 per cent of chromium oxide. 'I felt my inner being as a chemist writhe,' Primo wrote: such uniformity was not in nature. The analyst – 'poor wretch', bored and exhausted – had not been alerted; but the detective was. He found the Checking Specifications card: and here too all was unexceptionable except for one thing. For the checking of the pigment, it called for twenty-three drops of reagent. Now, that was absurdly high: it would flood the analysis entirely. The date on the card was January 1944; the livering had begun that February.

Once again the pirate had spied his galleon. Primo dug out the old CS cards: and there it was. All the previous editions had read '2 or 3' drops of reagent, not '23'. The last transcription had introduced the error; from then on any pigment that was too basic had passed unnoticed in the flood of reagent; and the damage was done. Primo said nothing yet; but after three long dull days of testing he knew he was right.

Still he said nothing: he was determined not only to understand the problem but to provide the solution. He experimented with various acids, but they had other noxious effects. So, he wrote, 'I thought of ammonium chloride,' which would bond with the free lead oxide that was causing the problem. His preliminary tests were promising. Now, put a few of the disgusting, slippery livers into a ball mill, add a calculated amount of ammonium chloride, and wait. Primo went home to Turin and Lucia, who listened to another impassioned tale of deformity and the hope of a cure.

On Monday morning the mill sounded right. Primo stopped it, opened the cover, and − 'Angels and Ministers of Grace!' he wrote, 'the paint was fluid and smooth, completely normal, born again from its ashes like the Phoenix.' His salary was increased; and as a special mark of recognition, 'I received an assignment of two tyres for my bike.'

How Primo told this story matters, I've said. He told it in his *Truce* tone, full of freedom and enjoyment; you can see his eyes lighting, his shoulders shaking in one of his contained bursts of laughter, like a held-in sneeze. He told it with his usual modesty, as though the problem were a minor, long-forgotten one, dug up for him because he had nothing else to do: a *jeu d'esprit*, like the story itself. In fact, the chromate-based anti-rust paint, Cromomarina, was one of Duco's premier products; the problem was a live and urgent one; and he was not working on it alone, but had many technicians under him. The '2 or 3' drops of reagent that became 23 *may* have been part of the problem, and its solution; but it is unlikely. The true cause was more complicated, and less amusing. The test solution used in the measurement of basicity was not the invariable standard it was meant to be, in those days of shortage; it was as hit-or-miss as everything else, and so, as a result, was the lead chromate. Primo led the research brilliantly, and the solution he just 'thought of' was his alone, and entirely original. Ammonium chloride had never before (or probably since) been used in the paint and varnish industry. But his challenge, and his victory, were very different from the ones in the story: not about a past problem but a present one; and not a solitary spiritual adventure, but a mainstream worldly achievement.

Why did he tell it that way? Partly because that was his natural myth, and his romanticizing impulse − chemistry as a lone adventure, when nowhere − least of all in a commercial factory lab − had it been anything close to that for two centuries. But also, I think, he told it that way quite deliberately. This was his high point: the moment when, he wrote in the story, 'I was ready to challenge everything and everyone, in the same way I had challenged and defeated Auschwitz and loneliness.' That is why he put the deformity back into the past; and why he made its resolution privately, almost secretly, his own: because the story is a parallel, a twin, to his other two victories of 1946 and 1947, especially to the one over Auschwitz.

That is also, I think, why he chose this chemical adventure for *The Periodic*

Table over the other: because the *schivatura* does not sow the 'forest of symbolic meanings' of the livering. The solidification of liquids carries a charge for us, because we are made of them. Our blood coagulates, Primo would write, beneficently outside our bodies, but fatally within them; '[and] everyone has heard of rigor mortis'. The 'livering' of the paint, like all forms of its premature solidification, is ugly, unnatural, obscene: a symbol, Primo would write, 'of the victory of chaos over order, and of indecent death over life'. It is, precisely, like death itself, and rigor mortis: the ghastly stillness and stiffness of what should be moving and warm. And he had, precisely, restored it to movement and life, like the Phoenix from its ashes. The resurrection of the paint is an image of his own resurrection, his own restoration to movement and to life, after the long imprisonment and dying of Auschwitz: an image, we might say, of his own deliverance.

By the time he came to write the story in 1973, however, it was a double image: not only of his life at the time, but of what it had become. And that, as always in Primo Levi, added a sombre note: happiness, freedom, victory never lasted long. In the story he is reminded of that long-ago triumph by a fellow chemist, who had worked at Duco Avigliana ten years or so after him; and who tells with rueful amusement how, to this day, ammonium chloride is still being added to its chromate paint, though no one remembers why.★ Primo then tells us why; and that once the post-war problems were over, the too-basic chromates disappeared, and his ammonium chloride was no longer needed. But formulas are sacred in chemical factories; the chloride had been in this one for years, it was not worth taking any risks. 'And so,' Primo wrote, 'my ammonium chloride, the twin of a happy love and a liberating book', was still being ground into Duco's paint twenty and thirty years later, though by then it was 'completely useless, and probably a bit harmful'. Following the parallel, its twins, his love and his book, would be the same: if not 'completely useless' by then, certainly less useful, and 'probably a bit harmful', to him.

Primo had done extremely well at Duco; he had even received (at least according to the story) a rise in salary. And yet, at the end of June 1947, three months before his marriage, he left, and went into partnership with Alberto Salmoni.

★ This forgetting Primo invented for his story: the miracle cure of the Cromomarina was far too important to be forgotten in ten or even twenty years. (After twenty years, in fact, Duco Avigliana closed down; so that by 1973 the company was no longer making paint 'on the shores of that lake', though it continued elsewhere.)

This was not like him, as he very well knew. Left to himself, he said, 'I would never have left the lakeside factory, and would have stayed there for all eternity, correcting varnishes' deformities.' But he was not left to himself. Alberto had insisted, he said, 'praising adventure, and the glories of a free profession'. Now, that is certainly like Alberto, who indeed admits it; and it is hard to resist Alberto in full flight of fancy. Perhaps it was specially hard to resist in 1947, when everyone was bursting with hope, including Primo; and when he was feeling so strong and capable of anything, as on that day in another June, when Pikolo had asked to be taught Italian.

All this may be true, but it still seems strangely improbable to me. Dr Colombo, however, has a possible explanation.

In *The Periodic Table* Primo mentions that he gave his colleagues a poem when he left: and Colombo has kept his copy. It is called 'The Last Will and Testament of the Assistant Laboratory Head', and it is a list of joke legacies: his broken desk and battered chair to Dr Binotto (Colombo's predecessor), 'the vexed question of the lead oxide' to 'the expert and benevolent care' of Colombo himself; plus half a dozen other provisions – except for poor Compagnucci, whose name is so long 'it would spoil my metre'. The last verse, freely translated, says:

> I choose new paths over old,
> Tardy, but not yet too tardy.
> I dwelt in Duco under the good Debove,
> In the time of false gods and Zanardi.

Zanardi, Colombo explains, was the Director General of Duco (or more precisely of the umbrella organization of which Duco was a part). And these gnomic lines, he points out, are a parody of part of the First Canto of *Inferno*, where Virgil says:

> *Nacqui sub Julio, ancor che fosse tardi,*
> *e vissi a Roma sotto 'l buono Augosto*
> *al tempo degli dei falsi e bugiardi.*

> I was born under Caesar, though late in the day,
> and lived in Rome under the good Augustus,
> in the time of the false and lying gods.

Bugiardi, for which Primo has substituted the rhyming *Zanardi*, is the part which means *lying*. And Dr Colombo's suggestion is that Primo left Duco because Zanardi had 'lied': that is, had made him false promises, perhaps of promotion, which, in the summer of 1947, were broken.

This seems to me much more likely. No doubt Alberto had been singing the praises of freedom for some time; perhaps Primo, in his bullish mood, was even tempted. But in normal circumstances he would never have done it. Then, suddenly, the circumstances were no longer normal: he no longer had the prospects he wanted at Duco, or the job he wanted, or perhaps any job at all. *Then* his bullish mood took over: and he left Duco not bitterly, or anxiously, but 'with absurd self-assurance'. He knew that this might be his last chance ('Tardy, but not yet too tardy') to experiment, to make mistakes, to change. And so he seized it. He had challenged and defeated Auschwitz, loneliness, and Matter. Now, surely, he could challenge and defeat himself. He wrote his poem, 'full of gay impudence', and set out to become an adventurer and a free spirit, like both his Albertos, at last.

The Truce

Except for rare lapses, Alberto Salmoni had never worked for anyone, and never would. Even now, when work was as scarce as everything else, he turned down a regular factory job when it was offered him. Something would turn up, he said; and since he was Alberto, it did. Bianca had two working-class friends who had started a small business mending and selling used tyres. She introduced them to Alberto, and for some months he worked with them. But this was only a stop-gap. He had no capital and no clients, but what he really wanted was to open his own laboratory: his own chemical consultancy, like Ennio Mariotti's. His parents were eager to help. He could use the family flat on the Via Massena, they said – just around the corner from Primo. The best room would be the one which opened on to the balcony; it happened to be their own bedroom, but *pazienza*.

This was the adventure which Alberto proposed to Primo in the summer of 1947. It was a classic Alberto enterprise – bold, full of vision, and underprepared. They never had enough money, or enough clients, lasted only six months, and ended in debt. Primo should have been consumed with anxiety the whole time, and on one level he probably was. But on another he enjoyed every minute of the Laboratorio Levi-Salmoni. When they were in the lab together, says Anna Cases, Primo was always smiling. And of the twenty-one chapters of *The Periodic Table*, three of the gayest came out of this adventure. Only his university years got as many; but they had occupied four years, not a mere six months.

It was not only Alberto who made Primo feel so relaxed – despite all the evidence, so paradoxically secure. It was Alberto's parents. Signor Salmoni was the ur-Alberto, as piratical as his son, but (I suspect) less of a dreamer. Primo had an unbounded admiration for him; and for 'the sweet and imperturbable Signora Ester' too, quieter and more orderly than her husband, but willing to do anything for her sons. They were warm, loving, 'ill-advised, long-suffering people'; and Primo loved being in their house, as he loved being in the Cases', or the Mariottis'.

And so his six-month adventure with Alberto became a second truce, between the two serious chapters of his life in chemistry; and he wrote about them as he wrote *The Truce*, with transforming gusto. Whatever real anxieties he felt at the time were dissolved away, or converted into humour, and in one case this chemical conversion itself became the subject of the story.

More than just the Salmonis' bedroom filled up with the reeking and dangerous tools of their trade. The hallway was crammed with demijohns of hydrochloric acid, Signora Ester's oven with flasks of stannous chloride, the balcony with vats of sulphuric acid. In the other direction, the flat was rapidly emptied of every usable container: soup tureens, enamelled saucepans, chamber pots. In the 'lab' itself, apart from pots and bowls and basins, they had two essential pieces of equipment specially made. One was a cylindrical reactor in which to distil pyruvic acid, set in a bed of bricks, and 'connected illegally upstream' to the electricity meter; the other was a large wood and glass ventilation hood, 'our pride, and our only protection against death by gassing'. Despite the hood, however, acid fumes filled the lab, and spread to all the rooms. The wallpaper yellowed, the doorknobs turned rough and grey; now and again a nail corroded through, and 'a picture, in some corner of the flat . . . crashed to the floor'. Not only Primo and Alberto but the elderly Salmonis, and even Bianca and Lucia, Rina and Anna Maria – all stank of acid, so that people in public places left little spaces around them, like the 'shunning' varnish.

Most of their jobs were of an agonizing dullness, like the production of the stannous chloride for the backing of mirrors. Primo, of course, picked out the few strange and comic ones to tell. One rather dubious client, for example, had the brilliant idea of a coloured varnish for teeth, on the model of nail varnish, removable by a (non-toxic) remover, but not by saliva; Primo tried out a green varnish on himself, and was so disgusted he declined to proceed. Another was very different: a strong and dignified old man, whose story Primo tells in *The Periodic Table*. He wanted some sugar 'chemistried'; duly chemistried, it revealed traces of arsenic. When Primo told him he nodded, satisfied. He was, he said, the cobbler of San Secondo,* where he had been making shoes by hand for thirty years. Now a young man had come and set up in competition, with all the latest machines. Well, *pazienza*:

---

* Primo had originally written 'the cobbler of Crocetta', his own district, and the Salmonis'.

there is room in the world for everyone. But the young man had not thought so, and had done all he could to steal the old man's clients. When that hadn't worked, this parcel of sugar had arrived; and he had suspected a plot straight away. Did he want a signed report, Primo asked, to press charges? No, no, the old man said, he didn't want to ruin the boy. He'd just take the sugar back to him, and 'explain a thing or two'. 'Yours is a fine trade too,' he added, looking around the primitive lab – 'like a junk shop', Primo said, 'or the hold of a whaler'. And then he left, 'with the tranquil dignity that was his by nature'.

I imagine Primo writing this story in 1973, with the modern world of chemistry (and not only of chemistry) all around him; thinking back with nostalgia to those days of poverty and simplicity.

But the key stories of this time of truce are the other two, 'Nitrogen' and 'Tin'. 'Tin' describes the lab, and Alberto, and his parents; we have already visited it, and will return. 'Nitrogen' recounts another chemical adventure: which, in the classic *Periodic Table* way, images another deep truth about Primo's life at the time.

The adventure was real. A client in the cosmetics business – he, indeed, of the tooth-varnish inspiration – was having trouble with one of his lipsticks. After a few hours it ran, spreading out along the lines around the lips; which made it, of course, entirely unsellable. He demonstrated the problem on a live model: one of a dozen over-made-up girls who lolled about the factory. A lipstick can only be evaluated practically, he said; the girls had to make up every morning, and he kissed them all eight times a day.

Primo and Alberto did their tests. The solution was simple: the client had used a soluble dye. They wrote their report, Primo cycled back to the factory and took their (very small) fee. But the client hadn't finished with them. He had just heard of a perfect dye: alloxan. Could they become his alloxan suppliers?

The client was unsavoury, and alloxan obscure, but Primo was twenty-eight, newly married, and still riding a bicycle to work. He would see what they could do. He went back to his old stamping ground, the Chemical Institute, and looked up alloxan in the library. As he had feared, it would be impossible to produce: the raw materials it required were far too expensive. Except for one, he noticed: uric acid. 'Just that,' he wrote, 'the stuff connected to gout, gluttony and bladder stones.'

He pursued alloxan along the library shelves. In man and mammals, he learned, who bind nitrogen into urea and eliminate it as liquid, uric acid is very scarce. But there are animals who bind nitrogen into the acid itself, and eliminate it in solid form; so that, for instance, 50 per cent of the excrement of birds and 90 per cent of the excrement of reptiles is the (now) precious stuff.★ Surely neither of these was expensive, and the former at least was hardly rare. Primo telephoned the client and promised the first delivery in a few weeks' time.

As Lucia had listened to the drama of the livered paint, so now she heard all about the pursuit of uric acid. She had even been a little jealous of the first adventure, Primo wrote; but this one she could share. The next day he planned a 'business trip': i.e. to cycle out to the nearest farms, in search of chicken shit. Lucia got out her own bike and went along.

There followed a classic Primo Levi lesson in harsh reality. Chicken shit was far from free, as he had imagined; gardeners had known about its nitrogen content long before him. And then you had to collect it yourself – together with earth and stones, chicken lice and feathers, grubbing about on your hands and knees on chicken coop floors. The young couple cycled back that evening filthy and exhausted, with a kilo of expensive rubbish in Primo's basket.

He tried to avoid the tussle with this muck by calling on a reptile exhibition. Pythons are bigger and cleaner than chickens, and their shit – as we now know – is almost entirely uric acid; this would be a quicker and easier operation. But he was thrown out on his ear. Pythons only eat twice a month 'and vice versa', he was told; their shit is worth its weight in gold, and contracted in advance to pharmaceutical companies.

So back he went to the Salmonis' ex-bedroom. He spent several days trying to sift out the chicken shit, and to oxidize its uric acid into alloxan. Without success. All he got were 'foul vapours, boredom, humiliation'; the shit remained shit, and he remained on his bicycle.

'Nitrogen', then, is a story of failure. But like *The Truce* – which was also about a long and painful failure – it is told with gusto. It is as hard to separate the celebratory elements of both from their monitory, minatory ones as it was for Primo to separate the precious shit from the rubbish. That is what makes 'Nitrogen' so profoundly characteristic of him; and so revealing. For it is about the attempt to extract human beauty from excrement: '*aurum de stercore*', as Primo said, gold from dung. *And that is exactly what he was doing in 1947*: extracting the gold of *If This is a Man* from the dung of Auschwitz, the gold of marriage from the dung of his loneliness, and the gold of adventure with Alberto from the dung of his fears.

But in the end that adventure failed. The last straw (or it may have been the first) was an accident with the vats of sulphuric acid on the balcony: one cracked, and the acid burned holes in the other balconies, all the way down.

★ Primo's old master, Ponzio, in his *Chimica Organica*, gives the figures as 25 per cent in birds and 90 per cent in reptiles. If that is right (and coming from Ponzio it must be), it makes the adventure of 'Nitrogen' even more of a wild goose chase than Primo paints it.

'I hoisted the white flag,' Primo wrote. He could not live on dreams and debts any more. He had defeated Auschwitz and loneliness, but not fear.

Except in writing. For from the dung of even that failure he extracted gold again, twenty-six years later: the gold of art and laughter, in 'Nitrogen'.

Alberto accepted his decision with sorrow, Primo wrote in 'Tin', 'but like a man'. He was not afraid of change, or risk, or of being poor; on the contrary, he had 'a restless frenzy for the new'. Immediately other plans possessed him, and he was not even very sad; whereas Primo was, and felt like howling at the moon, 'as dogs do when they see the suitcases being closed'. Together they dismantled the laboratory, to patient Signora Ester's relief. Slowly her pots and pans returned to her kitchen, her chamber pots under their beds. Primo does not say what happened to the pyruvic acid reactor in its well of bricks. But the fate of the ventilation hood becomes the final image of the story, and of Primo's brief truce. They had had it removed whole, and attached to a block and tackle, to be lowered safely to the ground. As they watched from the courtyard, the hood 'issued solemnly from the window' and paused, 'outlined against the grey sky'; then the chain broke, and it plunged down four storeys and shattered into tiny shards. Their will and daring were shattered with it, Primo wrote. But he spoke for himself. All Alberto said was: 'I thought it would make more noise.'

That was in December. In the meantime the two most important things in Primo's life after Auschwitz had happened. First, on 8 September he and Lucia had been married: first in a Registry Office, and then in a Jewish ceremony, conducted by Lucia's father. They went on a brief and frugal honeymoon – Primo was still a free spirit, and very poor. When they returned it was not to the Corso Re Umberto, but to a flat belonging to Lucia's elder sister.

And then a month later, on 11 October, he saw his book published. It was austerely beautiful: a plain white cover, with the title in red, and his name in small black letters beneath. The publicity flyer was equally striking, with his photograph on one side, and the title poem, in his hand, on the other; and words, almost certainly by Franco Antonicelli, which must have deeply pleased him, and deeply disturbed him. *No other book* on these tragic events, they said, has the artistic value of this one. *Primo Levi's* testimony is both that of a man, and that of a man of letters.

He was, he admitted many years later, excited and happy. I think he could hardly believe it. He had written, and published, his book. He had a beautiful young wife, his own home, and a free life in chemistry. September and October 1947 were the freest and most hopeful months of his freest and most hopeful years: the high point of his second truce.

If This is a Writer

If it had not been for Auschwitz, he probably would never have written. So Primo Levi often said; and it was both true and not true. He would have written essays, stories, poems anyway, because he had done so before, and because (as Silori said) writing was his natural response to experience. But he would not have written, and published, a whole ambitious book, at twenty-eight, or thirty-eight, or perhaps ever, if he had not felt he had to. The moral duty to testify overcame his Piedmontese reserve, his Jewish fear, his secret shame at having made human suffering his scientific study. It overcame all these, and released him to plan, to write and to publish a book – however much he still half pretended not to be doing any of these things.

And now the way that Antonicelli published the book helped him too. It appeared, not in one of De Silva's literary series, but in a special new political and documentary one, the 'Biblioteca Leone Ginzburg'. It was Number 3: Numbers 1 and 2 were war memoirs from the French and Russian fronts; Number 4 was an anthology of articles from the celebrated left-wing journal *La Rivoluzione liberale*. The presentation of *Se questo è un uomo* to the world could not have been more sober, more suited to its grave task; nor kinder to its shy and private author's needs.

The reviews started in November, and went on until the spring. There were ten or eleven of them, mostly in small left-wing journals; none in the major papers, apart from *La Stampa*, or by the famous critics of the day; and hardly any either in Jewish newspapers or magazines. All were positive, even warm; but most, says Alberto Cavaglion, remained 'conventional'. Above all, most praised it for its value as testimony only; thus starting a tradition which has lasted almost to the present day. But this was what Primo at least half wanted; and I imagine he was at least half satisfied.

Especially since there were several exceptions. The very first review was in *La Stampa*, Turin's own paper, on 26 November. It was by Arrigo Cajumi: scholar of French literature, London and Geneva correspondent of *La Stampa* in the 20s, and left-liberal, antifascist and independent *par excellence*. Cajumi's review was headed *Immagini indimenticabili*, 'Unforgettable Images', and he picked out those of three chapters in particular: the departure from Fossoli, the selection, and 'The Story of Ten Days'. When he compared *Se questo è un uomo* to Rousset's famous *L'univers concentrationnaire*, Cajumi wrote, the French book smelled to him of literature and party politics: whilst 'our chemist . . . writes cleanly and concisely . . . and arrives naturally at art'.

At least four others agreed. Aldo Garosci, writing in *L'Italia socialista* in December, called *Se questo* 'unequalled, and I think unequallable' in Lager literature, for its poetic and meditative qualities; Umberto Olobardi, in *Il Ponte*, said that it showed such a narrative gift, and such humanity in its author, that we were surely in the presence of 'a new writer'. The third was Cesare Cases – Anna's brother, a famous Germanist and a doughty fighter for Primo from the start. Cases broke the general Jewish silence. *If This is a Man* was a true work of art, he said, which proved that in the author himself at least 'the man placed in question in the title [had] survived'. The fourth, and perhaps the most acute of all, was Italo Calvino. *If This is a Man*, he noted, presented not just a record of facts, but a profound commentary, and a world of completely achieved characters. It was not only an essential work of testimony: it contained pages of 'authentic narrative power, which will remain . . . amongst the most beautiful of the literature of the Second World War'.

The other half of Primo – the confident, ambitious half – was thrilled.

But what all of him wanted, without conflict or complication, was readers. And he did not get enough of them. Antonicelli, he always said, printed about 2,500 copies of *Se questo è un uomo*, of which at most 1,500 were ever sold. De Silva was a small publisher, and its distribution system was poor; *Se questo* sold better than most of their books, but that still meant very small numbers. Perhaps no more than a few thousand people, most of them in Turin, read the first edition of the book, in its first ten years.

Primo was philosophical about this, as he had been about Natalia Ginzburg, as he was about most things: *signorile* – gentlemanly – as Alberto Cavaglion says, in the Turinese style. It was entirely understandable that people were reluctant to be reminded of a past from which they were still struggling to recover; if they looked back too soon they might never escape, like Lot's wife looking back on Sodom. When Anna Yona reported furiously that none of the American publishers she had approached was interested in his book, he only smiled and said, '*Pazienza*.' It had been very well reviewed, and occasionally he would receive a letter from a reader, or meet one. But by the spring of 1948 the reviews were over, and no one spoke of *If This is a Man* any more. A year or two after it was published 'it was a forgotten book', Primo said: 'it fell into oblivion', and remained there for many years. But he did not mind, he said. He had done his duty to the dead, and he had healed himself by writing: both his goals had been achieved. He was not a writer but a chemist; he went back to his real work, and his real life, and he did not think about his 'solitary book' any more. Nor did he think about writing anything else, or feel the need to do so: he had delivered his message, and there was nothing left to say. He did not write another word, he claimed once, for the next twelve or fifteen years.

That was his story, and he stuck to it. He had to. It was the heart of his protection against the two things he feared the most: failure, and the recognition of his ambition – especially for *this* book, built on the torment and death of millions.

The truth slipped out just once or twice. At the end of 'Nitrogen', for instance, where he wonders how he might escape from the mire of poverty and unsuccessful chemistry – 'I, the discouraged author of a book which seemed good to me, but which no one read'. And again in his last published book, *The Drowned and the Saved*, when he asks himself what might have happened if *If This is a Man* had been an immediate success. Perhaps nothing, he answers: probably he would have continued his daily grind as a chemist. But perhaps not. 'Perhaps . . . I might have let myself be dazzled and, with who knows what success, hoisted the banner of a life-sized writer.'

He was right the first time, I think: he would not have done it, no matter how many copies of *Se questo è un uomo* De Silva had sold. 'The Turinese do not leave the certain for the uncertain, or old roads for new,' he said. But he *had* hoped, he *had* dreamed. Seeing his sales, he said, he had abandoned the idea of becoming a writer. But in what spirit his next words show: 'It seemed to me an absolutely unattainable Utopia.'

And even this was not quite true. He did not abandon the idea of becoming a writer: only of becoming one full-time. When *If This is a Man* was finished, he told Pikolo that if it was successful he would go on and write the story of his return. And it *was* successful, with its few readers and reviewers. Cajumi's review in particular, he said later, was of fundamental importance to him, '*because it promoted me as a writer*'. With that encouragement – which he always needed – he did go on. He wrote the whole first chapter or more of *The Truce* during 1947 and 48; only giving it up slowly, discouraged by the failure of his hopes for *If This is a Man*.

There was one last lie, and it was the biggest one of all: that he didn't even want to write any more, and didn't, until he began *The Truce* in earnest in 1961. Not only did he begin *The Truce* straight away: he picked it up several times throughout the 50s, working on the chapter about the Greek on and off from 1954, publishing part of the chapter on Katowice in 1959. Between 1955 and 1957 he wrote all the additions to the Einaudi edition of *If This is a Man* – which were many and important. And from the beginning he wrote stories. 'I mnemagoghi', which he had told at university, and 'Argon', his work of family piety, he first drafted in 1946 – at the same time as *If This is a Man*, and in the same exercise book, as though he wanted to remember all his dead, and write everything he had ever imagined writing, as soon as possible, together.

And that is not all. He first thought of his playlet 'The Sixth Day' in 1946 as well, and wrote it (or typed it) in 1957. He wrote 'Titanium' in 1947 and published it in 1948. Between 1949 and 1961 he wrote and published at least another nine stories, including four which went into his first collection in 1966, two Lager stories which were finally collected in *Lilit*, and the first versions of two more chapters of *The Periodic Table*. And he still had not (officially) begun *The Truce*.

That is the truth about this reluctant writer, this non-writer between his first two books: from the moment he returned from Auschwitz, he never stopped writing.

Dancing

Vanda

'The clearer we are, and the more brightly lit,' said Calvino, 'the more we
are awash with ghosts and dark visions.' Primo Levi always tried to remain
on the cool, bright plain of his rational mind, and to avoid the abyss beneath.
But the longer he tried, the more the ghosts and dark visions grew.

The main ghost and untold story of his life is that of his depressions. He
had them before and after Auschwitz, but – except perhaps at the start – not
there. In the abyss of Auschwitz his own private abyss disappeared. That
happened to many, not only in Auschwitz – most ordinary ills, mental
and physical, are submerged or transformed in extreme experiences. But
afterwards they return, their fury redoubled. And so it was now for Primo
Levi. When he returned he had his Auschwitz depression; and though it
was caused by Auschwitz, and concerned Auschwitz, the heart of it was
private and personal once more.

We may guess from the poems of 1946 that Vanda was part of that heart. But we do not have to guess, because Primo said so, years later, to the woman he would call Gisella. In Fossoli, he told her, he and Vanda had fallen 'half in love', and 'loved each other as best they could'. And then he told her the truth: fearful, needy Vanda had fallen more than half in love with him. It was he who could still only half love a woman, who was still trapped in the 'bloodless female friendships' (as he wrote in *If This is a Man*) of his double bind. That is why he could not stop Vanda from falling into despair – because his love was still tormented, and not warm; because he could talk to her, but not touch her. As the weeks went on, things grew worse – Vanda's need for physical comfort, Primo's inability to give it. If he knew that she was flirting with the Commandant – and surely he did – he must also have known why. And yet he could not change, even for Vanda. Not even on the last terrible night.

That was the private anguish behind some of the most elegiac lines of the first chapter of *If This is a Man: Many things were then said and done among us; but of these it is better that there remain no memory.* That evening, he and Vanda, Luciana and Franco were together, as usual. When night came Luciana and Franco went to their room to make love; and firmly, gently pushed Primo and Vanda away together, so that they might do the same. But Primo could not. Perhaps that was why, in a madness of hope and despair, Vanda went to the Commandant instead. Then in the morning she tried to slit her wrists; and arrived in Auschwitz already wounded in body and mind.

For all this Primo felt unbearable guilt. If he had given Vanda the love she had needed that night, he thought, she might not have gone to the Commandant; if she had not gone to the Commandant, she might not have tried to kill herself . . . So he would say later, to Gisella; and so he began to think that dreadful night, and the next morning, and for five days pressed against Vanda in the cattle-car. That is why he told her those '*things which are never said among the living*' – which surely means his deepest secret, his double bind. Perhaps then Vanda said that nothing could have helped her abject fear: that was *her* worst secret. But then he came back alone; and blamed himself again, and more.

★   ★

He still had not changed a year later, when he fell in love with Galina in the Katowice infirmary. He was convinced she felt repulsion for him; and if she did it was not because of his Auschwitz rags and swollen face, but because of that conviction. A few months after that he was home, and something else happened, which made him more afraid than ever that he would never be able to love a woman. Finally – not in Turin, of course, but in Milan – in desperation he went to a brothel. But even that – especially that – he could not do. Perhaps that was when he thought of suicide. Two people saved him: Leonardo, to whom he spoke, and Lucia, who fell in love with him. Leonardo helped him to bear his isolation; Lucia at last freed him from it. That is how much he owed her.

★   ★

The other thing that happened, despite its outcome, was of the opposite sign. Beneath the lingering coils of his double bind, he *had* changed. He had changed so much that he had dared to invite someone to dance himself.

He'd done it immediately, within a week or two of reaching home. He'd gone to Gabriella Garda and told her he had always loved her, always regretted that he had not fought for her. And he asked her to leave her husband and marry him.

Gabriella was so moved, and so astounded, that for one wild moment she almost wanted to say yes. But it was only for a moment. She could never leave Ercole, and their small son Gabriele. Poor Primo, it was never possible. But she could not bring herself to tell him so. 'I'll write to you,' she said. She wrote him a long letter. It was the hardest letter he had ever received, Primo said. It closed a door of hope he had dreamed might still be open. He did not say where he had dreamed this, but she knew.

If he had come back for anyone, it was for Gabriella. He had not known that in the meantime she had had a child. The moment he realized that, he must have guessed it was too late. In fact, it had always been too late. *But he had tried.* It was one of the most selfish, and at the same time one of the bravest and most self-exposing things he would ever do. Its failure added to his deep grief, and soon to his depression. But I think it must have consoled him too: that he had dared to declare himself; that he did not, in the end, destroy a marriage; and that for the rest of their lives Gabriella knew that he loved her. It should console us for him too, because it shows that he did try to escape the closed world of his birth, and to join himself to his opposite for life. You may say that he did not try very hard, that he must have known he was doomed to fail. Perhaps: his other self may have known, on the other side of that narrow bridge inside him, and may have made, or welcomed, a different choice. But in October 1945 he made his first choice, and failed: that is what lies behind the last words of 'Phosphorus', that a throw of the dice had deflected him and 'Giulia Vineis' 'on to two different paths, which were not ours'. And behind the last words of 'Tin', perhaps, as well: in which he tells how, during the dismantling of the laboratory, he found, 'and greedily appropriated', an ancient yellowing paper: a decree of 1785, which *'orders, prohibits and severely commands that no Jew shall dare to take Lessons from Christians for any kind of Instrument, much less those of Dancing'.*

12. Levi Uomo II:
1948–63

Primo and his family, 1963

It is not possible to exaggerate what his marriage meant to Primo Levi. It meant, said his first biographer, all he had longed for since the Lager: 'an affirmation of the right, so fiercely denied him, to be a man'. That is right; except that he had longed for it not only since the Lager, but all his life.

For their first few months together Primo and Lucia lived in her sister's flat. That could not be permanent; and very soon they came to the first key decision of their marriage. They were extremely poor. Even after Primo found regular employment, he began on a pittance; and Lucia's first wage, as a teacher at the Jewish School, was probably still lower. At the same time she was young, active and intelligent, she disliked housework, and she wanted to work. When Primo proposed that they move in with his mother she accepted with alacrity. The flat was large and comfortable, far better than anything they would be able to afford for years. Rina was eager to do all the housekeeping, to help them in any way she could. It seemed an ideal solution to everyone. Their brief time alone together ended, as though it had been the honeymoon they had hardly taken. Primo returned to the Corso Re Umberto; and the life he would have for the next forty years began.

From the start it contained three people: himself, his wife and his mother. Very soon that grew to four, when his daughter Lisa was born on 31 October

1948; finally, after a gap of nine years, it settled at five, with the birth of Renzo on 2 July 1957.

Now Primo was not only a husband but a father, and his dream of normality was complete. His children gave him deep joy, especially when they were young; and especially, perhaps, Lisa. Parents often divide their children between them, or perhaps children divide their parents; and the Levis divided as many Italian families do (and Jewish ones, and many others): the father closest to his daughter, the mother to her son. Primo was a tender, gentle father, incapable of anger; perhaps too incapable of anger. Once, when Lisa was small, she tested both her patient parents with endless demands. But Primo refused to snap, and so (perhaps therefore) did Lucia; instead they discussed which of them should punish her. Ten or twenty minutes later Primo went into her room and smacked her – deliberately, and it must have seemed to her coldly, so much worse than in the heat of the moment. But Primo could never do anything in the heat of the moment; which is not always as selfless as it seems.

Lisa was very like her father – small, fragile, and extremely sensitive, with a strong self-governing will. When she was little, says Primo's cousin Giulia, she was wildly afraid of birds: 'Now she is a naturalist, and spends her time counting them.' Primo loved making toys for her, and watching her play with her friends; but most of the time his thoughts were elsewhere: 'his eyes on other horizons', as one of those friends recalls. Once, when Lisa was about six, she waited impatiently to show him a medal she had won at school. But he seemed not to understand what she wanted, until Giulia whispered in his ear; then he just said, 'Well done,' quickly, and changed the subject. Perhaps he was trying to train his daughter in his own self-effacing ways; or perhaps he could not bring himself to praise her, any more than he could praise himself. In either case he was silent because he felt so close to this child, not the opposite. But she could not be expected to understand that: not then, and perhaps not later either.

His thoughts, in those years, were very often still with the Lager; that was a large part of the problem. When Renzo was three years old he saw his father and Leonardo in their shirtsleeves, and asked, 'Why are you and Nardo written on?' Primo explained that once, long ago, they had been prisoners together. That was all. Renzo never asked again. He did not have to: the house was full of books on the Lager, almost every conversation he heard was full of the Lager. But he did not want to either; and nor did Lisa. Primo often told how he had decided to speak to each of his children, when they reached the age of fifteen, about his experiences in Auschwitz. But each in turn, nine years apart, had reacted in the same way: they had turned pale, started to cry, and ran away. Poor Primo: he wanted to talk to his children about what mattered most to him; it hurt him that he couldn't. But poor Lisa and Renzo: it had hurt them that he'd tried. Later, he understood that they had had to defend themselves against knowing such terrifying and vulnerable things about their own father. But he had not known it by himself; they had had to show him.

And this is a story of happiness, I hear you say, of the fulfilment of a lifelong dream? Yes. It is the story of a family: the family of a man who was a Colossus of thought, but like a child himself in matters of the heart. In everything intellectual he and his wife, he and his children, were much in accord: secular in faith, left-wing in politics (though Lucia was a good deal to the left of Primo). Both Lisa and Renzo were sent to the Jewish primary school, for its excellent liberal education, then on to ordinary Italian *licei*; both would become scientists, like their father. Like him, they would have their bat and bar mitzvahs at thirteen, then return to their secular and scientific lives. By the end of Primo's life neither had yet married; but he predicted that if they did, they would marry 'out'. He was right. Lisa is still unmarried; but Renzo's wife Silvia is not Jewish. Like his father, though, he must still feel some attachment to the tradition: Primo's grandchildren, whom he never knew, are called Emanuele and Miriam.

In 1948 not only Primo's life took the shape it would essentially keep for the rest of his days: so did Italy's. It was not the shape he would have chosen. When he had reached home in October 1945 his own party, the Partito d'Azione, still headed the first post-war government; but that lasted barely a month after his return. The Partito d'Azione was too moderate, and too small; from the start it was squeezed out by the two great blocs which were beginning to form, not just in Italy but in the world: right and left, capitalist and communist, the US and the USSR. In early 1946, under the pressure of defeat, it split ('It is not divisions which cause defeat,' says Vittorio Foa, 'but defeat which causes divisions'); and in the key elections of that year, which established the First Republic, the Partito d'Azione died. Over the next two years the right fought to control the disastrous post-war economy, and eventually succeeded; on the left the Communists fought for dominance, and also succeeded. In the spring of 1948, when Lucia was in the first months of her pregnancy with Lisa, and Primo was starting in the job he would have for the rest of his working life, new elections were held. The Christian Democrats won a huge majority; and for the next forty-five years, either alone or in a complex, Italian series of coalitions, they would govern the country.

Not the least factor in this victory of the right was American influence, and American aid. The Marshall Plan began in 1947; in 1948 George

Marshall himself warned that all aid to Italy would cease in the event of a Communist victory. When Marshall Aid reached the chemical industry in the 1950s, it rapidly became one of the stars of the Italian post-war boom. So Primo would benefit himself from the rabid anti-Communism of 1950s America, and its interference in Italian affairs. He would not have approved; but he would have disapproved with irony. He was sceptical of the Communist faith himself, as he was of all faiths; especially after his experience of Russia. 'No doubt you're right,' he would say, if someone tried to persuade him. 'But when I think of my own house, my own car . . .' And a small stubborn smile would lift the corners of his mouth.

But when he began his new job, in February 1948, American aid was in the future, and Italian chemistry was still very much in the past. He would do everything on his own, and on no money, especially at the start: on sheer hard work and chemical insight, and with the help of a few good people. It was exhausting, difficult, even dangerous; but this was the chemistry he loved. His last truce was over, and his serious life in chemistry had resumed. But for the first fourteen years of it he was often happy.

The new job had first appeared in December 1947. Livio Norzi's father, the famous *Ingegnere* Eugenio, had an enterprising young friend who was looking for a good chemist. And the *Ingegnere* knew one, who just happened to be in urgent need of a steady job. He introduced them; they took to each other straight away, and the deal was done.

Federico Accati came from Biella, the home of famously hard-headed businessmen. Before the war he had worked in his father's construction company in Turin, together with his two older brothers. After it, he decided to strike out on his own. It was hardly a propitious moment, he was not a chemist, and the chemical industry hardly existed. But that is what he chose. Perhaps he looked at the ruins of the cities, and thought that the world was about to change. But more likely he didn't think at all; he rarely did. He simply followed his instinct and his nose. On 10 February 1945, together with an older partner, he founded SIVA: the Società Industriale Vernici Affini, 'for the production and sale of chemical products: paints, pigments, colours, varnishes and allied wares'.

He began with ordinary paints, and started to do well very soon: he always had excellent contacts, and SIVA supplied paint to Montedison, to the city council of Rome, to the ship-building industry in Genoa. But Accati was not satisfied. Anyone could make paint, and far too many people did. Once again he used that nose of his, to sniff out an area in which there was hardly any competition at all, at least in Italy: insulating coatings for copper wire. (And considering that the great post-war industrial boom was about to start, especially in cars, in motors of every sort, in radio, television, communications – in everything that uses electrical conducting wire – he had used his infallible instinct too.) That is why he needed a good chemist; in particular, one who knew something about varnishes and resins. That is why, in other words, he needed Primo.

In 1948 SIVA was in Turin: at 264 Corso Regina Margherita, on the edge of the city, near the vast park called the Pellerina. Today the city goes on for miles, and the Pellerina is full of drug dealers and prostitutes; in 1948 there was nothing beyond them but open fields. But Number 264 itself was far from beautiful. It was a tiny, freezing shed; when the drier was installed the cellar, at least, became boiling hot; but so damp that no resin, and no human, was ever really dry.

When Primo arrived SIVA had only one other chemist, and ten employees. The chemist, Dr Gianotti, immediately approved of Primo; and so, I think, did the employees. They consisted of three girls who worked in the office, Maria, Renata and Rita; and seven labourers: Lorenzo Bergia, the janitor, a Turinese; Oreste Traversa, a *valdostano*; three brothers from Udine called Fracas; and Piero Selvestrel and Narciso Feltrin, both from near Treviso. Of these, Sante Fracas would stay at SIVA almost as long as Primo; Piero Selvestrel, and his brothers Redento and Egisto, who soon arrived, would all outlast him there by many years.

Apart from space and equipment, Primo had another serious problem: he really needed a qualified assistant. But Accati said firmly that there was no more money to be had: *after* Primo had developed their wire coating, perhaps, but not before. For a week or two he struggled on alone. Luckily, however, this was Turin, where he knew everyone, and where everyone tended to return. One day, on a tram, he met Gianna Balzaretti: a girl from his chemistry class all those years ago.

During the war Gianna had worked in Milan, and in Genoa, but after that jobs had become hard to find. She'd even taken a second degree in pharmacology, to improve her chances; still she'd only managed to find one horrible, lowly job since the war, which she'd soon chucked in . . . All this she told Primo – in a rush, I imagine, alternating self-pity with gusts of energy and humour, as she told it to me. He listened sympathetically; then he spoke, in the careful, reliable tone she suddenly remembered. He couldn't offer her a salary, he said, he had only just begun himself, and the work was hard. But if she could prove herself, let's say for a year, he thought he could promise that all would be well. She accepted without hesitation.

For the whole of that year, Gianna says, she worked like a *slave* – they all worked like slaves, especially Primo (she always starts with herself, then her natural generosity bursts in). The conditions were unbelievable, that first winter. At first there was hardly any equipment, and no help in the lab at all: she dried the resin with a hair drier, and lugged the great jars of acid around herself. After a while she did get a good young assistant, and the Selvestrels as well: now Egisto did the drying too, with a bicycle pump. They worked twelve, fifteen, seventeen hours a day; sometimes Egisto slept in the cellar all night, and she came back at two or three in the morning, just to check that all was well. The stink was apocalyptic – and the damp, and the cold, and the heat! First you'd stand for hours in the icy lab, then rush down to the cellar and boil, then back upstairs and freeze again. She borrowed her brother's fur-lined Russian jacket, but still she shivered and froze. Whereas Primo felt *nothing*: he'd just come back from Auschwitz, *poveretto*, it was nothing to him, he hardly noticed; whereas she, who had always had delicate health . . . He was so spartan, so dedicated, so far above anything physical; he couldn't understand when she complained. She did get angry about that; and he, in turn (though of course he hid it, and it was not Gianna who told me), was often goaded beyond endurance by her endless complaints.

Nonetheless, she stuck it: by the end of that awful winter they had their wire coating, and by the end of the year Gianna had her job. In fact, she says proudly, if Primo was the father of their resin, she was its mother: and Egisto Selvestrel agrees. He doesn't remember a single cloud between them; or if he does, he dismissed it as unimportant years ago. They were a perfect partnership, he says. Primo did all the theoretical work, all the invention – that is what he loved, says Gianna, and what he was good at. But he disliked the routine analyses, the endless checking, the patient boring follow-up work of the lab. All that he left to Gianna: and with her neat hands, her precision and practicality, she was exactly what he needed. He also disliked managing, much less disciplining, the workers, and was (says Gianna, but she is only the first in a long line) hopeless at it. Whereas she (says Egisto) was an elegant, attractive woman, and at the same time firm and clear: an excellent manager of men. That too, therefore, Primo left to her. 'He was the brain, I was the hand,' says Gianna: and a hand is what he always needed. If he had had a Gianna Balzaretti longer – she would leave in 1956, 'for health reasons' – he would have been happier for longer at SIVA.

The resin they developed together in 1948 was called Polivinilformale, or PVF, and it became the basis of SIVA's fortunes. No longer did it have to be expensively imported from the United States: they made it themselves, and combined it with other resins of their own; and improved the result year by year, until very soon SIVA became one of Europe's top suppliers of insulation coatings, and remained so for nearly fifty years. Of course Primo did not invent PVF entirely, out of nothing: no one ever invents something out of nothing, he would say, least of all in chemistry. He invented it as he describes chemists inventing in 'Tantalio': by analysing and improving – 'euphemism aside', by copying – an American formula. The competition at the time was American and German: and not the least part of his pleasure was in out-performing the Germans.

PVF was not the only new and better product he developed over the next twelve or fifteen years. In 1994 Renato Portesi of SIVA made a list of them for me (with one explanatory comment):

– Polymide resins and varnishes
– Many resins and varnishes no longer made (glycerophthalic, phenolic, ureic, etc.)
– Trimellitic anhydride (Bang!)

In 1995 SIVA stopped making PVF as well. Primo would not have been surprised; and I don't think he would have minded. He wanted to preserve memories, not things; he wasn't sentimental, and always eagerly moved on to the new in his own work, both in writing and in science. That is how Gianna Balzaretti remembers him, in those first years – always scouring the chemical abstracts, always seeking, and testing, new ideas. That is how Beppe Salvador, one of SIVA's long-serving workers, remembers him too: 'always in the lab'. Alas, it gradually became less true. In later years he would return as often as possible to the lab, but it could not be very often. If it had been, that too would have made him happier.

Through all these early months Federico Accati followed Primo's researches eagerly, and supported him without question, and without return, for as long as it would take. They too were a perfect partnership. Primo had found the last important opposite, and the last close friend, of his life.

Federico Accati was Cesare all over again: or rather, he was the Greek, with a dash of the Lieutenant thrown in. He was not as simple or as sunny as Lello Perugia. He was more driving, more striving, like the Greek: the opposite of cold, but darker somewhere, full of ambition, and also of rage. He was not a chemist, but like the Lieutenant he knew his job very well; he chose his staff with flair, and treated them with generosity – as long as they worked as hard as he did, and never complained, and never *ever* joined a union. In other words, he was a classic *padre padrone*. If people were loyal and obedient, and worked at least a twelve-hour day, he promoted and protected them, he hired their brothers and sisters, he lent them money and helped them buy their houses. But *guai*, woe, to anyone who stepped even an inch out of line. Then he bellowed like a bull, and banged his fist on his desk until it shook, and generally behaved with extreme and barely contained violence. Fortunately, perhaps, he had no sons, or his home would have been a battlefield. Instead he had four daughters, and was glad, because he thought they would obey him; a girl with a degree is the same as a man, he would say, with characteristic faith in the power of will, especially his own. He called his eldest daughter Luisa 'Luigi', and secretly admired her when she defied all his plans for her, became a university professor, and moved to the other side of Italy. It was his second daughter, Paola, who became the chemist, and the substitute son who took over his empire; he loved her, bullied her, and passed on to her his secret insecurity. He was narrow, crude and ignorant – and made himself seem even more so, perhaps out of pride. He claimed to believe all his life that 'Jew' meant 'free thinker' (which he approved of), rather than another kind of believer (which he didn't); and neither Luisa, who married one, nor Primo thought it wise to enlighten him.* Like the Greek, he measured everything by money; and like the Greek he admired tricksters most of all, who made something out of nothing – like the inventor of Levis, he would always say, which were cheap and ugly, hot in summer and cold in winter, and worn all over the world. When Primo began to make money with his books, he shook his head in admiration. As he himself grew richer, he collected paintings, and talked of them with tender pride; but only about how much they had cost him.

Of course he and Primo were the greatest of friends. Primo could not get over how clever Accati was, how daring, how much of a trickster himself: everything, again, that he could never be. Once, when they were having trouble with a resin, Accati dropped in oh-so-casually on a competitor. When the rival chemist hinted that he had just solved the problem, Accati coolly hinted that SIVA had as well. Whereupon the other chemist proudly recounted his solution, and Accati rushed back and told it, word for word, to Primo. That made Primo shake *his* head in admiration. Accati's violence must have shocked him at first; and he never defended himself against it, just bowed his head and waited until it was over. With Accati, though, this was an excellent ploy. He loved and respected Primo far too much to be really angry; and 'How can I be angry,' he would say, 'at someone who never lies, but admits his mistakes like a child?'

Accati relied more and more on Primo for the running of SIVA; and Primo relied more and more on Accati in the running of his practical life. He turned to Accati for advice on his literary contracts, and on dealing with his teenage children; when he began to earn larger sums, he handed them over to Accati for investment without even opening the envelopes. They

* Luisa married Primo's first cousin once removed, the historian Giovanni Levi, nephew of Ada Della Torre, and brother of Stefano Levi Della Torre.

told each other their troubles, in their reticent, masculine, Piedmontese way. If their wives were being difficult, a day in the country would solve the problem. If they couldn't sleep, it was overwork: real insomniacs took ten drops of sleeping draught, so they would just take two. Primo relied on Accati to restore his balance when things went wrong. 'That's it,' he would say in despair, 'I resign.' 'Have you called the plumber?' Accati would reply.

Theirs was a partnership of brain and heart, of brain and guts; and thirty years of hard labour on both sides.

Federico Accati

Very soon Accati was contacted by one of the leaders in their field, Bayer of Leverkusen, hoping to supply them with Bayer products, and generally to work together to their mutual advantage. Accati saw that this could be SIVA's big break: but how could he ask Primo to work with Germans? Luisa thinks he didn't ask; but Primo heard of the offer, and came to Accati himself, saying, 'Why didn't you tell me?' He was perfectly willing to work with Germans, he said. They started immediately; and to Accati's amazement it seemed to be true. Primo certainly worked very happily with his opposite number at Bayer, Dr Mielke. Primo in Germany was exactly the same as Primo at home: calm, polite, interested. If anything he seemed more relaxed here than he was at home – more ready to enjoy himself, to sample the local food and wine, to slip out to a museum in the afternoons. He neither attempted to raise the question of the past, nor avoided it. When people noticed his excellent German, or (once or twice, in the summer) the number tattooed on his arm, they would ask how he came by them; and he would answer. 'My name is Levi,' he would say. 'I am a Jew, I was at Auschwitz.' And he would wait for their response, with that intense alertness of his, carefully disguised. Alas, it was almost always disappointing: a shocked silence, followed by evasion; or hurried expressions of identification – almost everyone had a relative who had resisted, and who had suffered as well. Most of those he met were of his own generation, and of his own generation perhaps 98 per cent had been Nazis; but never (he would report) did anyone say: 'Yes, I was a Nazi myself, but I no longer am' – or even, 'and I still am today'. It was as though the past, of which he was the embarrassing reminder, had simply been wiped away.

Of course he was not surprised; and of course he understood the power of social unease. Sometimes he felt it himself: with a father and son in Bavaria, for instance. When the subject of Auschwitz had come up, in the usual way, the father had been particularly stricken, and so, therefore, had Primo. Afterwards the son told him that his father had been a local *Gauleiter*, but had harmed no one; nonetheless the Americans had made an example of him, parading him in front of the village, tied to a tank. Again, Primo would not have been surprised. It is easier to catch the innocent than the guilty; and those with the tenderer consciences, who are the least guilty, suffer the most.

But there was Primo Levi, in the 1950s and 60s, only five and ten and twenty years out of the Lager, and back in Germany – and not only in Germany, but in German chemical factories, some of which had used slave labour themselves; and all of which looked and smelled exactly like *his* factory, 'the same plan, the same trucks, the same corridors . . .' Can he really have felt as calm, as 'perfectly willing', as he seemed? He always disguised his feelings; was he not disguising them now? Well: probably. What he said, and allowed himself to show, was as much the result of a moral decision as what he wrote: that later generations were innocent, and Germany had changed; that even at the time the greatest blame lay with the leaders; that the important thing was to understand the power of totalitarianism, of propaganda, of charismatic leaders, and not to imagine that evil was safely isolated in one particular nation. Just once to a friend, and once to an interviewer (at least among the friends and interviewers I have found), did he admit that he did not, in fact, go at all happily to Germany, especially at the beginning. We will have to return often to this question of Primo Levi and Germany, just as he did: he spent the rest of his life, he would say, trying to understand the Germans. Now I think we must imagine this: that he went reluctantly, but hoping that what he found would yield what he always wanted – understanding; and not what he always avoided – feelings of anger, hatred, blame. And for a long time it did. And it yielded something else as well, which may be the key to what the Accatis saw. In around 1960 his cousin Giulia went to Germany for the first time after the war, and felt horribly uneasy, 'almost suffocated'. How on earth did *he* manage, she asked, for whom it must be so much worse? Unexpectedly, he smiled. '*Non hai idea com'è bello andare in Germania da uomo libero,*' he said: 'You've no idea how good it is to go to Germany as a free man.'

Until the mid-60s, he went at least once and sometimes twice a year, to Bayer, to Hoechst, to BASF; at least fifteen times altogether, he reckoned when it was over. In 1954 he went again; this time not to a chemical company, but to a concentration camp.

This visit shows that, for at least nine years after the war, he found more food for understanding than for anger in Germany. It does so because, by great good fortune, it included a special witness: someone who was already one of his readers, and who many years later would become a friend, and his second biographer.

In 1954 Gabriella Poli was a young journalist with the left-wing paper *Avanti*. She had already worked in the underground press during the war; and ever since she had heard the BBC report on the liberation of Belsen, she had been preoccupied, even obsessed, by the Lager. The report had told of piles of corpses, and of the living who were themselves corpses, barely able to lift themselves off the ground; it was searing, unforgettable, but it had not told her who the corpses were. With the Nuremberg trials, which she followed in detail, she had begun to understand. Then, towards the end of 1948, she had found a little book on a second-hand bookstall in Turin. It was *Se questo è un uomo*, by someone called Primo Levi; and when she read it she had understood the Lager. It was not simply mass murder: it was first the destruction of the soul, and finally the destruction of a people.

Now she had prevailed on her paper to send her to Buchenwald for the ninth anniversary of its liberation, so that she might meet some of the survivors, and hear their stories. As she climbed on to the train at Turin a thin young man climbed on beside her. Later, as she was taking down the story of a chemist from Ferrara, she noticed the thin young man again, sitting nearby. The chemist ended by saying, with pride, that the secret resistance committee of Buchenwald prisoners had played an important part in the liberation of their camp. 'In my camp, Buna-Monowitz, that wasn't possible,' the young man said quietly. 'We were not men, but *stracci*, mere rags; and rags do not rebel.' Gabriella recognized the gentle, shocking honesty of that voice; and found that she had met the author of *If This is a Man*.

Primo had been asked to accompany the journalists in the group as their interpreter and guide. And he was, of course, a superb guide: he knew everything, while they still knew almost nothing; patiently, calmly, he made the dark clear. Now, Gabriella already knew something about life, and death, in a concentration camp; most of it already from him. What she would especially remember was something else. Their group stayed in a school in Weimar, eight miles from the site of the camp. And every moment they were not in Buchenwald Primo would lead them around Weimar, asking people what they had known of the concentration camp on their doorstep, less than a decade before. He asked many dozens, perhaps hundreds of people; and no one had known anything. So they replied, and so Primo translated their replies: without challenging them, Gabriella remembers, without anger or surprise; just patiently asking, and noting the answers. 'You see,' he said to the journalists, 'these people didn't know. They didn't know then, and they don't know now.'

It seemed to Gabriella Poli, and it seems to me, that he believed them, and indeed that it was in a sense true. They did not *want* to know, because knowing was dangerous, and because if they knew they would have to do something. He understood this, of course: but so far it was, precisely, a matter of understanding. That is how people are, and have to be, if they want to survive; especially (but not only) in a totalitarian state. A totalitarian state is like a concentration camp itself, in which law and trust have broken down, and anyone can be a spy. The free man in a warm house can never be compared to the prisoner, condemned to death with no means of escape: even in a totalitarian state he is still responsible. Nonetheless, in 1954 Primo was still learning, and teaching, how free men had made themselves deaf and blind in Germany. The anger would come later.

In 1950 Dr Gianotti retired, or died, and Primo became Technical Director of SIVA. During the early 1950s the workforce more than doubled. Four new chemists arrived; and six or seven new workers were taken on, including Gianna Balzaretti's lab assistant, Giovanni Torrione, and a young man called Massimo Albertan, whom Primo employed because he was a fellow survivor of Nazi hospitality, and they had met somewhere on their infernal journey. By around 1953 the shed on the Corso Regina Margherita could no longer hold them all. Accati found a house in the suburb of Settimo; and SIVA moved to its lifelong home.

A house was still enough in 1953. Number 84 Via Leinì had (and still has) a tall wooden door, an old stone staircase, and wooden shutters over the windows. Primo's office was at the top of the stairs: a big, high-ceilinged room, with two tall windows like French doors, one facing him as he sat at his desk, the other on his left hand. Today they look out on suburban roads, lines of traffic, blocks of flats; but for years, once again, he saw only fields. Accati's office was next – even bigger, of course, with smart panelled walls; and then, all down one side, the lab, Primo's real domain. Downstairs was the kitchen, the dining-room, and a sitting-room, lined with sofas and chairs, where people could go for half an hour or so after lunch, to read, or doze, or play cards. It was like a home; and for many years SIVA was more like a large family than a company, especially around the three long tables in the dining-room.

Accati was expanding fast. In 1950 he had founded SCET, which produced the copper conducting wire, and coated it with SIVA's varnishes. In 1955 he would add SICME, to manufacture the enamelling machinery himself. SICME-SIVA-SCET would become a self-contained system for the production of insulated conducting wire; with SIVA and SICME also supplying the enamels and the enamelling machinery to other companies in the field. Over the next decades of industrial boom in Italy the group would become hugely successful, and make Accati a tidy fortune. SIVA, the source and seedbed, would eventually decline; but SICME and SCET are still going strong today, under Paola Accati.

Despite his office at the Via Leinì, by 1953 Accati was moving more and more towards the management of the whole group; and soon of SICME in particular, which quickly became a world leader. Primo was in charge of the move to Settimo, and from then on increasingly in charge of SIVA. He designed the laboratory, and all its work practices: the inventiveness and rigour of SIVA's science, which would last to the end, were his legacy. He organized, and often designed, the expansion of SIVA's production facilities into the fields behind the Via Leinì, which gradually grew to cover over 35,000 square yards. As Technical Director first, then as Director General, he would organize and oversee all its activities, from the ordering of equipment to the management of the staff; even, eventually, to the running of the commercial department.

This was Primo Levi's real life, as he would always say, for the next twenty-two years. Other writers often envied him for it – Calvino, for example, and later Philip Roth: it kept him in touch with the normal, everyday world. And Primo himself was glad and proud of it, as he would also always say. Chemistry was his first love; and though (he would insist) his was a 'low' chemistry, he continued to love it, and to draw from it a wealth of knowledge and experience 'which gives me an unfair advantage over other writers'. He was glad and proud that he had managed a chemical factory for a quarter of a century without any serious accidents; and he was glad and proud of his relations with his workers and employees, which were full of mutual respect, and mutual sympathy. He was recognized and respected as a brilliant chemist by everyone there; and by everyone in the wider world of industrial chemistry as well, one of thirty or forty world experts in his field. He always wanted to be top, and at SIVA he was: in it, says someone who knew him outside as well, 'He grew several inches taller.' SIVA took him out of his study, out of his house, and out of Turin; when he finally left it, he lost a great source of experience, of contact, of self-esteem.

On the other hand, he could not bear too much of any of these. Above all, he could not bear too much responsibility; and he got more and more of that every year. He loved chemistry, because he knew he was supremely good at it, and would not fail; he hated hiring and firing, fighting with Accati,* dealing with clients, because at these things, he knew, he was hopelessly bad. He hid his fear and reluctance very well, as always. But the few who were close to him at SIVA knew that he was more often unhappy than happy there, from quite early on. If he could have, he would have left – or so he often felt: certainly from the late 50s, probably even before. Gianna Balzaretti knew it; so did Francesco Cordero, a bright and eager young man whom Primo hired in 1957, and whom he taught and befriended.

Primo in the lab

By the end of the 50s he already began to have less time for the lab. At the
end of 1959 he wrote to his German translator: 'I cherish the secret dream
of retiring very soon . . .' His last entry in the SIVA Lab Book was on 23
November 1961. In 1962 he became Director General; and from then on
his research life had largely ended. Though the boom was about to begin,
his best years at SIVA had ended as well.

★   ★

When Primo told his German translator his secret dream in 1959, it must
have rested, once again, on *Se questo è un uomo*. His book had been forgotten
for ten years; he had resigned himself to that, though less happily than he
pretended. But perhaps now, with Einaudi as his publisher, with attention
and translations coming . . .

And all along, he had been writing anyway. We know that from the dates
of the early stories; and we know it too from a chance encounter.

In 1949 a young Tuscan called Marcello Franceschi had arrived in Turin
with a brand new degree in chemistry. Despite it, he had failed to find work;
and so – like Gianna Balzaretti – he had decided to take a second degree in
pharmacology. He found a modest room in a *pensione*, and became a student
again.

Franceschi, however, was no ordinary student. He was twenty-seven
years old, and had begun that chemistry degree eight or nine years before.
In between, he had been called up into the Navy. On 8 September 1943 he
had still been in training when the Germans arrived at his school in Istria.
Like many other unsung Italians, he refused to serve the Republic of Salò;
and embarked on a long Calvary of POW camps in Germany. For Italian
ex-servicemen there were no gas chambers, of course; but there were
starvation rations, forced labour, and German hatred and humiliation
only a step above those enjoyed by the Jews. Franceschi had survived; he
had restarted life, and found the girl he wanted to marry. But now, four or
five years later, he couldn't keep it up any longer. He was tormented by
nightmares, by memories of contempt; above all, by the horrible conviction that the Germans had been right, and he and his whole nation were
cowards, traitors, crawling worms. He was, in other words, in a deep
depression.

Recently, he had made a friend: a young law student in his *pensione*,
Guido Fubini. Guido was a friend of Anna Maria Levi's; and when he saw
what was happening, he thought of Primo. He was afraid for Marcello, and
certain Primo could help him. Would he talk to him? he asked. Primo
immediately agreed.

They met first in the very early 50s, 1950 or 51. And it went as Guido had hoped. Marcello told Primo his fear – that he had deserved the Germans' contempt, that he had done everything wrong, that he was a worthless coward. On the contrary, Primo said, he had done absolutely right, 'he was on the side of reason'; and he explained why. But it was not only what he said that mattered. More important was the feeling he gave Franceschi: a huge sense of goodness; a feeling of friendship for him, of respect and liking. There were deeper, more visceral feelings Primo could not express, to his family, to anyone. But this great human kindness he *could* express, to a stranger, to us, in every word he wrote. It was enough to cure Marcello Franceschi, and us, of despair; but not himself.

Franceschi called on Primo regularly for a year or more. They talked of their camps, and reminded each other how precious even the hardest times were now, and would always be, after that. They talked of chemistry, and why Italy was still inferior to the Germans in this too. ('*Abbi pazienza*,' Primo would say, 'be patient, our time will come.') And they talked about writing. Every time Franceschi arrived, Primo was in his study, writing. It was as necessary to him as breathing, Franceschi could see: 'He was a creator,' he says, kneading a shape in the air with his hands. 'I want to write,' Primo told him. 'How many books?' Franceschi asked. 'As many as possible,' Primo replied. So in 1951 or '52 Franceschi stopped calling on him, in order not to deprive him of the maximum number of books.

What was Primo writing when Marcello Franceschi arrived?

'Argon', 'I mnemagoghi', 'Titanio', 'La fine del Marinese' were already written. 'La fine del Marinese' was a Resistance story, 'Titanio' the mysterious tale he had heard from Felice Fantino. 'Argon' was his tender, comic tribute to his ancestors, his preservation of their curious essences in words. 'I mnemagoghi' was almost a picture of that activity: the story of an old doctor who has preserved his memories in bottles. Each bottle contains a solution which gives off an odour, and each odour evokes a particular place or person in the doctor's past: the death of his father, the peace of the mountains, a girl. He has never shown his 'mnemagogues' to anyone. When he finally shows them to the young doctor who is about to replace him, the younger man is painfully moved – by the horror of ageing, by the shame of having looked so deep into another's privacy. But he has only done so with old Montesanto's help; the bottled odours are intensely private, and evoke *that* father, *that* girl, only to Montesanto himself. All of which distils Primo Levi's ideas about memory and its communication with painful accuracy – and with extraordinary completeness, considering that it was one of the first things he wrote after Auschwitz, and that he had conceived it even before. Our memories are ourselves, it says, and it is unbearable that a single one should be lost; yet they are essentially incommunicable, and *will* inevitably be lost, or at best misunderstood – not only the old man's, but the young one's too, everyone's and everything's, even (though this is not part of the story) the memory of Auschwitz.

In 1950 to '52 Primo could have been working on parts of *La tregua*. Or on the story called 'Night Shift', which he published in *L'Unità* in 1950, and which would go into *The Periodic Table* as 'Sulphur': the account of a boiler almost exploding in a chemical factory, told by a workman called Lanza.* Or perhaps he was beginning one of the Lager stories which would end up in *Lilit*, 'Capaneo' ('Rappoport's Testament') or 'A Disciple'; or 'La carne dell'orso', the mountain adventure that would go into 'Iron': all these would be published first in the late 50s and early 60s. That is, he might have been working on one or another of his lifelong non-fiction subjects: the Lager, his life in chemistry, his mountains, his friends. But he might already have been writing something he wouldn't feel he could write for another thirty years: fiction; and fiction of a particularly original kind.

For there is one piece we *know* he was writing in 1952: a story in the form of a short play, called 'La bella addormentata nel frigo', 'The Sleeping Beauty in the Fridge'. And this story was the first of a new genre which he was, in effect, inventing: the moral fable about science.

'The Sleeping Beauty in the Fridge' is set in the year 2115, in Berlin. One hundred and forty years before, in 1975, the technique of cryogenics had been perfected, and a few of the most perfect human specimens had been chosen to time-travel into the future. The most perfect of all was a young woman called Patricia, who in 1975 was twenty-three years old (that is – with typical Primo Levi humour – she was born in the year he created her, 1952). In 140 years Patricia has 'woken' for a total of only 300-odd days; in 140 years, therefore, she has aged less than a year. Since around 2000 her fridge has been in the home of the Thörls, descendants of one of the original cryogenic scientists. During the course of the play Peter and Lotte Thörl entertain their guests, as usual, with Patricia's brief annual awakening on her birthday. Primo extracts much entertainment – and much pain – from the men's fascination with the ever-young Patricia, and the women's jealousy. One of the guests, Baldur, falls madly in love with her; and Patricia seizes the opportunity to run away with him. As they drive away, she coolly tells him the truth: she has no intention of staying with him; she simply had to

---

* Lanza was based on Sante Fracas, who tended SIVA's boiler just as Primo describes. Primo admired Sante's reliability and calm in a crisis, of which there were very likely several like 'Sulphur''s over the years.

escape. And not only because she is tired of endless freezings and defreezings: because of Peter Thörl's visits, at night, when he defreezes her just enough to enjoy her, but not enough for her to resist.

This is the first of the moral fables which would form the heart of Primo's first collection of stories, and part of his second. They have been compared to science fiction, and indeed called science fiction; but that is misleading. They are hybrids of science and literature, like the stories of *The Periodic Table*: about science, but much more about the meaning of science in human life. And fascinatingly for Primo Levi – the ultimate rationalist, and the ultimate scientific optimist too – fascinatingly for that Primo Levi, all these stories are as deeply pessimistic as the first. But what they are pessimistic about is not science. They are pessimistic about people, and the use they may make of this newest and greatest form of power: like Peter Thörl, who uses cryogenics to imprison someone, and to rape her with impunity whenever he pleases.

But Patricia is far from helpless: indeed she has her own ruthlessness, not only with Baldur, but with Peter himself. If there is a victim, it is Lotte Thörl; but she too has Peter in her power at the end, and intends to use it. The play is therefore not a tragedy, but a comedy: a satire, in which everyone is so shallow-hearted that we remain so as well. It is entirely characteristic of Primo that he should have taken this first new step in comic mode: in order to move as far as possible from the responsibilities of testimony; and in order, perhaps, to convince himself that this new direction was not serious, that it was mere entertainment.

He could not keep up that pretence for long. If there was anything more deeply rooted in him than humour, it was seriousness; and what could be more serious than the abuse of science, especially to him? Over half the pieces in *Storie naturali* would be science fables (rather than science fiction) like 'The Sleeping Beauty'; with shadows gathering.

He published the first of them ten years later, in 1962, though he may well have written it earlier. 'Angelic Butterfly' is also set in Berlin, this time in 1946. The Occupying Powers have found the traces of an obscene Nazi experiment, carried out by a Professor Leeb. After an examination of the evidence, they meet to hear their Colonel's explanation. 'In certain Mexican lakes,' he begins, there lives a creature called the axolotl. The axolotl breaks one of the fundamental laws of nature: it is neotenic, which is to say that it reproduces at the larval stage. Only a very few axolotls live long enough to metamorphose into their final forms: as though caterpillars reproduced as caterpillars, and only a very few became butterflies. Experiments had shown that giving axolotls thyroid extract hastened their moulting: so that all of them, and not just a few, could become what they were meant to be. Leeb had been convinced that other animals – perhaps many other animals – were neotenic; including man. He had been convinced that if we lived long enough, or if we could be specially treated, like the axolotls, we too could grow into what we were meant to be: that is, into angels. He had experimented on four prisoners, two men and two women; and something *had* happened, they had indeed changed. But not into angels: into hideous, terrifying vultures, unable to fly. The war had ended, local people had slaughtered the vultures, and Leeb had disappeared; but not, the Colonel fears, for ever.

This story is clearly a metaphor for the Nazi dream, which became a nightmare: the dream of becoming superhuman lords of the universe, which ended in their becoming subhuman monsters instead. And the connection to the abuse of science is precise: what else were the racial theorists, the doctors in the camps, the inventors of the gas chambers – even the generals with their tanks, the train drivers, the bureaucrats sending telegrams – but millions of abusers of reason and science? When Primo asked himself, as readers would often ask him later, if there was a link between his Lager writing and his fables, he answered that it was this: his fables were about deformities of morality and reason; and the Lager was the greatest of such deformities.

It was therefore no accident that, of the three darkest fables, two should be set in Germany. The second is called 'Versamina'; it is as powerful as 'Angelic Butterfly', if not more; and it introduces some of Primo Levi's deepest and most permanent themes about both life and science.

'Versamina' begins with Jakob Dessauer limping home after twelve years of exile and war. Home is once again, it seems, Berlin; and Dessauer is once again a scientist. He finds all his pre-war colleagues at the Institute dead or gone, including his friend Kleber, the most gifted of all. The only one to have survived is the old caretaker, Dybowski; and Dybowski tells him what happened to his friend.

Kleber had worked for many years on benzoyl derivatives. When he came to the forty-first he noticed a strange effect on his rabbits: they refused food, and tore at their own flesh until they died. He refined the compound until he reached Number 160, which he tested on dogs: all responded in the same way. He called his discovery 'versamina': the substance that converts pain into pleasure, and so turns all behaviour upside down.

The results are extraordinary, but horrible, like Leeb's. A student club stages orgies 'of a kind never seen before'; a versaminized battalion welcomes battle as eagerly as their leaders had hoped – too eagerly, and all die. Finally

Kleber himself becomes addicted to the delicious sensations which had once been pain. He can no longer eat or sleep, he scratches deep holes in his face and hands; in the end he dies in an 'accident' in his car.

Old Dybowski draws out the moral, comparing versamina to atomic energy, which ended, even before it began, in the atom bomb: 'Some believe that they can free humanity from pain, others that they can give it energy free; they do not know that nothing is ever free: everything must be paid for.' Dessauer understands, despite his own suffering: 'Pain cannot be taken away, must not be taken away, because it is our guardian.' But Primo understands still more, and does not let him stop there:

> . . . He also thought, contradictorily, that if he had had the drug in his hands he would have tried it, because if pain is life's guardian, pleasure is its purpose and reward. . . . [He] thought that if versamines could convert into joy even the heaviest and longest of pains, the pain of an absence, of a void around you, the pain of an irreparable failure, the pain of feeling you are finished -- well then, why not?

The Leeb in this case cannot return. But Dessauer is a scientist himself; and the foul work of delusion and destruction, we see, will carry on.

This is so startling that it is hard to understand how it can have received so little notice; but again it was Primo himself who covered his tracks, who distracted our attention from this side of his work, as from this side of himself, and convinced us that it was not important. On the contrary, it is very important. Here is the supreme humanist, who despite Auschwitz itself has just produced one of the strongest expressions of faith in humanity ever written; and his very next book is the exact opposite. More than half of it consists of satires on that same humanity: most of them apparently light – but only apparently, like all satire; and at least three openly despairing. No one who has read 'Angelic Butterfly', or 'Versamina', or 'Retirement Fund' (or several later stories either) can ever believe again that Primo Levi's faith in that Man whom he so endlessly interrogated was strong or steady. His doubts and his darkness are there on the page, in 1966, in 1962, in 1952; you do not have to wait for his last book, or indeed for this one, to know them, and to feel their power.

Pain cannot be taken away; everything must be paid for. Those are the laws of science, of life, and perhaps of these stories. Many years later Primo would hear the case of a good man, a pillar of his community, who suffered all his life from an irrational fear of animals. The psychiatrist who told his story suggested this explanation: he had unconsciously displaced his fear of man on to animals; thus he had preserved his positive image of human beings, and been able to go on loving them. His illness, that is, is what allowed him to be generous and trusting; it was the price he paid for not hating and fearing his own kind. Primo was very interested in this analysis, and wondered if it could be true. Now, he had his own similar fears, though not so severe; and he had his own severe psychological illness. I think he was wondering if this explanation could be true of him too; and I think it was. His depressions were the price he paid for his conscious, willed faith in humanity; and the dark fables of *Natural Histories* were the price he paid for *If This is a Man*.

'Retirement Fund' is the last of the five remaining science fables of *Natural Histories*. They were the latest to be published, and very likely the latest to be written. And they really are close in form to science fiction: which is no doubt how that idea of the stories arose, and spread to the entire collection.

All five use the same device: the unnamed narrator, a Milanese chemist, buys the newest fascinating gadget from his friend Simpson, the agent of an American company called NATCA. One or two of the NATCA stories are genuinely light-hearted. 'The Measure of Beauty', for instance, features the Calometer, which measures both male and female beauty – or rather, conventional ideas of them, or the buyer's own idea, depending on the model to which the machine is tuned; all of which allows Primo to make fun of social conformity and private vanity. In 'Full Employment' Simpson lets the narrator in on a little enterprise of his own: he has learned the language of bees, and through them he has begun to contract with other insects for their services – with dragonflies to harvest berries, with flies to carry messages, with ants to assemble resistors, to retouch photographic negatives . . . The opportunities are infinite; but for both good and ill. And ill has already happened: Simpson's partner has been arrested for bribing eels to carry heroin to the Sargasso Sea.

With the two stories about the Mimer the unease grows. The Mimer reproduces, atom by atom, any object placed in its cell, animate or inanimate; thus creating something from nothing (or at least from NATCA's *pabulum*), life from a primeval soup, as in the first days of the universe: 'the dream of four generations of chemists'. In 'Order on the Cheap' the chemist-narrator, like the discoverers of atomic energy, does not merely arrive at evil, but begins with it: his first thought is of the reproduction of banknotes, rare stamps, diamonds. He experiments with cigarettes and matches, beans and eggs, a spider, a lizard; the Mimer reproduces them all. He buys a small diamond and reproduces it exponentially, until the Mimer's cell is full; and 'On the seventh day he rested'. He summons Simpson: is a larger Mimer available, able to reproduce a cat? Or even . . . ? Simpson pales and walks away.

In 'Some Applications of the Mimer' the chemist-narrator has spent a month in jail for breaking the hastily drafted law on the use of Mimers.

During that month the next fatal step has been taken: his friend Gilberto has got hold of a Mimer.

Gilberto, Primo wrote, is a dangerous man: 'a child of our century', indeed its symbol; a tireless and gifted technician, but childishly curious and irresponsible, 'capable', the narrator has always thought, 'of building an atom bomb and dropping it on Milan, "to see what will happen"'. Two days after his return from prison Gilberto telephones, his voice trembling with excitement and pride. What has happened? the narrator asks. 'I've duplicated my wife,' Gilberto replies.

Gilberto has managed it all in his characteristically blithe manner, hiding his intention from himself and his method from his friend – he'd drugged his wife into unconsciousness – until the deed is done. And though he has violated 'a considerable number of human and divine laws', he is entirely untroubled: since he loves Emma (as he does, comments the narrator, 'in his own fashion, and so to speak from the bottom up'), 'it had seemed to him a good thing to have two of her'. But the chemist foresees trouble, which duly arrives. The two Emmas begin as identical as twins, but like twins they soon diverge; and Gilberto is faced with a difficult choice. But nothing is difficult for him. A month later he arrives at the chemist's office more radiant than ever. Gilberto has solved everything, he announces. But when the chemist congratulates him he explains. The credit belongs to Gilberto 1, not to him; he has only existed since last Sunday.

This is, in fact, a horror story, disguised as comedy by the hilarious, dangerous, childish Gilberto, the most fully developed character in the *Natural Histories*. Gilberto was, of course, based on Alberto Salmoni: which suggests two equal and opposite things. First, that Primo was beginning to see a darker side to Alberto's capacity for irresponsible and egocentric happiness; and second, that he still couldn't help smiling the moment Alberto appeared. That is what happened in life, whenever Alberto arrived at SIVA, for instance; now it happened in his work as well, making him laugh aloud at his fears. Alberto would have that effect on him to the end; or almost.

There is no Gilberto to lighten 'Retirement Fund', the last NATCA story. It brings together the two great brooding themes of the collection, and especially of 'Versamina' and 'Angelic Butterfly': the temptations of science, and the necessity of pain. Simpson retires, in order to develop his ant projects, and in order to enjoy his retirement present from NATCA: their latest invention, the Total Recorder, or Torec. This is what we might call today a Virtual Reality machine – which Primo Levi, therefore, was the first to imagine, like his hero Jules Verne with space travel and submarines. You put on the Torec helmet, and enter a tape in the player; and your brain is directly stimulated to undergo the experiences recorded on it – by a mountaineer, a deep sea diver, an astronaut, a seducer; by whomever, or whatever, you please. Every possible experience can be yours, without moving from your chair; while you have it, it is indistinguishable from reality; and though you remember it when you take off the helmet, as soon as you put the helmet back on you no longer do, so that each experience can be enjoyed over and over again, as though it were new.

The chemist tries several of Simpson's tapes – a soccer game, a fist-fight,★ an amorous encounter (which goes badly wrong; but that is not our subject here). He sees that the NATCA catalogue contains nearly 1,000 titles, arranged according to subject – 'Art and Nature', 'Power' (including 'Violence', 'War', 'Wealth'), 'Encounters' (these are mostly 'porn tapes', Simpson explains, like the unfortunate one the chemist has tried); and tapes too of mystical and religious experiences, of artistic creation, of heroic sacrifice; even tapes of the experiences of the newborn, the mad, the higher animals. The narrator is silent for a long moment. No other machine ever invented, he says, seems to him so dangerous: more dangerous than any drug. It will be 'the last great step, after mass entertainment and mass communications'; it will destroy all enterprise, indeed all activity whatsoever. With every pleasure – and pain, and adventure – available at the touch of a button, 'Who would ever work again? Who would take care of his family?'

Simpson agrees that controls will be needed (but admits that they have already been broken); and that users will need 'will and common sense' to use the Torec well, and not become addicted. But he is very happy to be a test case for his old employers, who hope eventually to sell the machine to every pensioner in the Western world.

'Poor Simpson!' the story ends. 'He struggled with the Torec like Jacob with the angel, but the battle was lost before it began.' He has gone from two hours a day in the helmet to five, to ten, to twenty. Between tapes he feels boredom 'as vast as the sea, as heavy as the world'; then he reads Ecclesiastes: *In much wisdom there is much grief, and he that increaseth knowledge increaseth sorrow.* But Solomon's wisdom, says the chemist-narrator, 'had been acquired in pain over a long life'; while Simpson's is fake, cheap, not his own. He knows it; and the only cure for his shame is to submerge himself once more in the Torec.

With Simpson heading for death (of which he is not afraid, having 'already experienced it six times'), Primo abandons the NATCA series. The rest of the *Natural Histories* explore other favourite subjects, to which he will regularly return: Primo Levi was as faithful a writer as he was a man. 'Censura

---

★ This is the experience of Primo's opposite, the Italian taunted by the WASP American, which was discussed in Chapter 3.

in Bitinia' is a satire on censorship, and thus on his old enemy, the totalitarian state. 'The Sixth Day' is a quintessentially Leviesque fable on his oldest subject of all, Man. Celestial experts – chemical, mechanical, psychological – debate at length what form this new being should best take, finally deciding that he should be a bird. Whereupon a messenger arrives: they are, as usual, too late. Man has been made without them, flightless, hairless, helpless. They can only wish him luck, and go home.

The remaining four stories explore the frontiers of man in Primo's usual way: by crossing them. Here he crosses the frontier between man and machines (in 'Il versificatore', 'The Versifier', about a poetry machine, and 'Cladonia rapida', about a disease of cars), and between man and animals. 'The Versifier' and 'Cladonia' are amusing *jeux d'esprit*, but did not take him very far. With his first two forays into the borderland between man and animals, however, he had entered a 'universe of metaphors' which would be even richer and more fruitful for him than chemistry. He would produce, by the end, literally dozens of stories, essays and poems about animals, plants, insects, bacteria – and *as* animals, plants, insects, bacteria: an extraordinary and nearly unique imaginative journey into the ultimate of opposite worlds. Once again the relative obscurity of the stories has hidden important things from us: and once again they were things which – like his secret doubts about science – he was happy to keep hidden, not only from us. One was how early his creative imagination flowered; another was how strange, and afflicted with their own deformations, were certain parts of his psychological constitution.

The first of these new Aesop's fables – and most likely the first he ever wrote – moves as far from humankind as possible: to the tapeworm, which can be its parasite. 'L'amico dell'uomo', 'Man's Friend', uses the form of a scientific report, as early novels used the traveller's journal. The first observations of the cells of *Tenium solium*, it begins, go back to 1905. In 1927 Flory presented the photographs which first displayed the 'Flory mosaic': long parallel lines of cells, with regular repetitions. But the breakthrough came only recently (and, we might note, from just that crossing of borders of which the story itself is the prime example). The Flory photographs were seen by an Assyriologist – because he himself was being treated for tapeworm. He noticed that the repetition of cells followed a strict poetic form, *terza rima*; and he had the wild unscientific courage to wonder if they weren't exactly that: acts of communication, poems.

After long and patient search, he showed that they were. Only about 15 per cent of adult tapeworms display a Flory mosaic; and of these many are primitive or fragmentary. But some are genuine poems, which the Assyriologist managed to decipher. There are poems to the worms' 'mysterious hermaphroditic loves'; even more interesting, there are poems to the host. These reach startling and disturbing levels, expressing love, guilt, hope, despair. The report quotes several examples, one of which has recently 'crossed the limits of specialized scientific writing', and entered an anthology of literature. *I have transgressed*, the poem laments. *I have defied the limits imposed on my kind by Nature, and manifested myself to you. So now I must go; and I ask for only one favour, that you receive my message.* But this last wish, the report concludes, was not fulfilled. The host, 'an obscure bank clerk from Dampier, Illinois', refused point-blank to look at the message from his own entrails.

In this little story lie coiled, like tapeworms themselves, many of Primo Levi's deepest and most tormenting themes. 'L'amico dell'uomo' is an allegory of despised love, of a despised lover: a lover so despised that not only his love but his language, his existence itself, are unrecognized; and when he can no longer be ignored, the beloved turns away in indifference, or worse. This may be the love of man for an indifferent God, or the murdered love of Europe's Jews for their countries; or it may be the love of one human being for another, who does not even notice his existence. Whichever it is, it is an allegory of depression: of being trapped in the vilest depths; of feeling a disgusting, worthless worm.

And it is an allegory of something else too: of the 'essential ambiguity' of our messages to each other, as Primo would write, many years later: of the difficulty, in the modern cliché, of communication. For 'whoever writes . . . writes in his own code, which others do not know; and whoever speaks as well': like the worm. No one was more aware than Primo Levi – who insisted on the possibility, and necessity, of communication to be clear, and who always strove himself for the utmost clarity – no one was more aware than he of the difficulty of what he was trying to do. No one was, in fact, clearer than he; but that was just because he knew how hard it was. Even when he was speaking to friends, one of them remembers, you could feel his effort, his moving dedication to the difficult business of being understood. 'To transmit a clear message is given to very few,' he wrote: 'Some are capable but not willing, some are willing but not capable, most are neither willing nor capable'; and some, he might have added, are both willing and capable, but others do not want to hear.

Last but not least, perhaps 'Man's Friend' is also an allegory of the unconscious: of hidden meanings deep inside us, which we reject and fear; but which are messages not only of guilt and sin, but also of love. Perhaps this little story was Primo's imaginative recognition that his rational half should make friends with the other, lurking in his entrails: that that half was human too. If so, its four short, light pages were among his most profound.

★   ★

All Primo Levi's stories are little known, compared to his books – almost a well-kept secret, even in Italy. But to us, his English-speaking readers, some are entirely secret, because they have never been translated. Of the *Natural Histories*, 'Censura in Bitinia', 'Il versificatore', 'Cladonia rapida' and one other are not available in English. The first three are minor entertainments, as Primo pretended all his stories were; very likely that is why his English publishers decided to leave them out. But the fourth was not minor at all; nor was it a one-off, like 'Censura' or 'Cladonia', but the first of several stories on the same themes. But it is undoubtedly strange, and so are they; and some of them have not been translated either.

The story is 'Quaestio de Centauris'; the themes are wild primeval dances of cross-fertilization, and their hybrid offspring. In 'Quaestio de Centauris', the hybrid is a centaur. The centaur is Primo's image both for himself – the Italian Jew, the 'grain of mustard' – and for mankind as a whole, that 'tangle of flesh and mind, of divine inspiration and dust'. His own deepest tangle was that second one too; and it is his own deepest tangle, I think, to which 'Quaestio de Centauris' returns.

The primeval dance in 'Quaestio', the 'second creation', Primo calls the *panspermia*. It took place in the time just after the Flood, when the earth was covered with a rich, warm layer of mud. In that hot mud every surviving seed and species was mad with desire, as never before or since; and every touch, no matter how fleeting, even across species and genera, was immediately fertile. So plants coupled with animals, and animals with birds and fish and stones; the earth coupled with the sky, and men with mares, and 'the whole universe felt love, until chaos nearly returned'.

From the great *panspermia* there resulted innumerable hybrids – the dolphin, for example, son of a tunnyfish and a cow, the butterfly, daughter of a flower and a fly; and also the noble race of centaurs, in whom the best of human and equine nature is combined. Trachi, the centaur of the story, was born in the Greek islands; when the story opens he is living with a family in the north of Italy. Like all centaurs, he is gentle and brave, wise and strong. But like all centaurs too, he is rare and different, and so he arouses suspicion in his human neighbours. Because of this, and because he is by nature very shy, as far as possible the family keep him hidden away.

The narrator, the young son of the family, becomes Trachi's particular friend. He tells us certain other strange and interesting things about Trachi. From his panspermic origins he has retained a deep link to everything wild and creative in nature: he senses the approach of storms, and the growth of seeds in the ground; subconsciously he also senses every desire, and every coupling, that takes place around him. Yet, like all centaurs, he is himself solitary and chaste; so that this unconscious awareness troubles him, and makes him anxious and restless every spring.

The years pass, and inevitably the crisis comes. When the narrator's childhood friend, Teresa, returns home after a long absence, he falls timidly in love with her. And so does Trachi — wildly, and impossibly. That is the tragic fate of centaurs: to love human women, half of whose nature they share, but to be banned from them for ever by the other half of themselves.

One evening, as they walk in the woods, Teresa and the young narrator make love. That night Trachi does not come home; he never comes home again. Over the next days the narrator pieces together what has happened. On that first night, in the same part of the same wood where he had possessed Teresa, Trachi exploded in his own 'gigantic wedding night', with a mare stolen from a neighbour's stable. In the next five nights he perpetrates five more violent rapes down the length of Italy. He is last seen by a fishing boat near Corfu, which reports 'a man riding a dolphin' across the Ionian Sea.

Primo would write two more stories about *panspermiae* and their products. They are ambivalent, but threaded with hope. In 'Quaestio de Centauris' there is no hope. Trachi is irretrievably different, and irretrievably divided; and his difference and division bar him from human women for ever. When he falls passionately in love, there is no way out for him: only, in the end, an explosion of violence. When Primo was himself in this double bind, before 1946, he never thought of turning his frustration outwards, like Trachi, but only in. And we must fear now, reading 'Quaestio de Centauris', that that dilemma had not quite ended after all.

★   ★

Meanwhile, Primo never forgot *Se questo è un uomo*. In 1949 De Silva was sold to Nuova Italia of Florence; whereupon he instantly pressed his new publishers to reissue his book. They refused, saying they had 600 De Silva copies left. Then, in 1952, he was offered an entrée to Einaudi, characteristically through a back door: Paolo Boringhieri, then head of Einaudi's scientific publishing, asked him to be a reader, translator and adviser on the scientific side. Primo agreed, and for the next year or two worked hard on the translation of the first two volumes of a huge work in English, Henry Gilman's *Advanced Organic Chemistry*. And immediately he took advantage of this new contact. In the editorial meeting of 16 July 1952 Boringhieri reported that one of their best scientific translators, Primo Levi, 'wished to know if Einaudi would be willing to issue a new edition of *Se questo è un uomo*, which was now almost sold out'. The Council was favourable; but Giulio Einaudi himself, ever mindful of money, doubted there would be any in *Se questo*, which had already had two publishers, and clearly hadn't made much for them. 'No decision was taken', the minutes of the meeting conclude.

Primo seems to have given up for the next few years. But in just these years things began to change. Rousset, Antelme and Vercors, Leon Poliakoff, Anne Frank and Piero Caleffi were all published – Anne Frank and Antelme, as we know, by Einaudi itself. There *was* interest in the Lager; and there was interest in *If This is a Man*. As Primo discovered himself, in 1955.

It was the tenth anniversary of the liberation, both of Italy itself, and of the camps of the Nazi Reich. He had written a sombre piece for the occasion, in which he had warned that the Lager was being forgotten, or had never been recognized – like his book, though he did not say so. Then he was asked to speak at an exhibition on the deportation of Italy's Jews: to explain to people the photographs of cattle-cars, of barbed wire, of shaven heads. And to his amazement, he was besieged by hundreds of young people, who had all either read his book or wanted to read it, and who plied him with sympathetic questions. Instantly he returned to Einaudi, and put his case to the Director, Luciano Foà. Foà passed it on to the Council, like Boringhieri before him; and this time no one had any reservations. At last, on 11 July 1955, Primo signed a contract for *Se questo è un uomo* with Einaudi.

But in 1955 Einaudi was in one of its regular financial crises. It had turned itself into a joint stock company to find new investors; Primo contributed his advance royalties. Still months passed and nothing happened. Primo wrote to Foa, and went to see him. In 1956 a new contract was signed; nothing. A new promise to publish in May 1957: still nothing. In January 1958 Primo sent a stern rebuke to the publishing house. One more date was set, in early 1958, and promptly passed. *Se questo è un uomo* finally appeared in June, three years after the original contract was signed, and (in Giulio Einaudi's words) 'after repeated insistence by the author'.

Einaudi was cautious, printing only 2,000 copies, 500 fewer than De Silva eleven years before. By the end of the year they were gone, and Einaudi promised to reprint. When they still had not done so by the end of 1959, Primo insisted once more. But that was the last time he had to insist. In February 1960 another 2,000 copies were printed, in 1963 another 2,000. By 1970 *Se questo è un uomo* had been reprinted twelve times. By the mid-1990s it had gone through thirty editions and sold over 300,000 copies in its original form alone; not counting the schools editions, the combined edition with *La tregua*, and finally paperback editions. By the last years of Primo's life Einaudi was selling 20–30,000 copies of *Se questo* every year; by ten years after his death, nearly a million and a half copies had been sold in Italy alone. By his own calculations, this means that by now well over 3 million of his countrymen have read Primo Levi's testimony to the Lager; plus several million more worldwide. They may not always be the ones who should read it, who are most at risk of repeating the calamities it describes. But I think we may say that his aim has been achieved.

Primo used the three years he was kept waiting by Einaudi well. Already in the first revisions of his book, in 1947, he had brought his writer's skills to bear on the scientific austerities of his original plan. Now he had been practising those skills for a decade in his stories. As soon as he knew that Einaudi would republish *Se questo è un uomo*, he began making more revisions, with all his new and greater art.

He began with himself. *Se questo* had originally opened in Fossoli ('In mid-February 1944 there were 600 Italian Jews in Fossoli camp'). Now it opens instead with the line: 'I was captured by the Fascist Militia on 13 December 1943'; and continues for five new paragraphs, telling us how he came to be there.

This is the key to almost all his additions. He had eliminated himself so ruthlessly: too ruthlessly. He seems to have realized that now. We want to know, we *need* to know, the narrator's story, as well as other people's; and there is nothing wrong or selfish in telling it, since it is as representative as theirs, as much a story in this 'new Bible'. Thus, for example, in a long addition to Chapter 2 which begins with the tattooing of numbers, there is one of the most emblematic exchanges in the book: when the guard tears the icicle from Primo's hand, and to his 'Why?' replies, 'There is no why here': '*Hier ist kein Warum.*' He had not told this before, despite its awful summary of the truth about this place. Now he realizes that its power is more important than his instinct to keep himself out of the story; and he lets it in.

Even more important, letting in more of himself meant letting in more of his encounters: more of his own friendships, and his own feelings. Thus, in the same long addition to Chapter 2 there is his encounter with Schlome, the Polish Jewish boy, little more than a child, who welcomed him 'on the threshold of the house of death'. Schlome is amazed that there are Jews in Italy; he gives Primo his invaluable advice not to drink the water, and timidly embraces him. Schlome transforms the entry into Auschwitz for us, as he did for Primo: not by cancelling the horror – nothing could do that – but by showing us that humanity can nonetheless survive in it, which is what the book itself will do.

Again in Chapter 2, Primo added Flesch the reluctant translator, for whom, he wrote, 'I feel an instinctive respect, as I sense that he has begun to suffer before us'; and in Chapter 4 Chaim, his early bed-companion, who explains as much as he can to him, and whom Primo trusts blindly. Then there is Steinlauf, the hero of the whole new chapter Primo added, 'Initiation':* Steinlauf — that is, Glücksmann — who gave Primo his first sense that resistance and the retaining of one's dignity were not only possible but necessary, even here. Perhaps, indeed, it was now — Primo puts it after only one week — that he first conceived his own plan of resistance: his determination to observe and report on this abomination. He does not say that it was 'Steinlauf''s example that gave him the idea; he will not let himself that far into the story. But the chapter is full of gratitude for a lesson learnt and 'not forgotten, then or later'. I would like to think that this *was* the moment of conception of *If This is a Man*; and this new chapter Primo's *ex voto* to the good soldier, Eugenio Glücksmann.

All these additions are similar, and not only because they are personal encounters of Primo's. *They are moments of reprieve*: warm, human meetings, like the ones with Reznik and Pikolo, Lorenzo and Charles, which join their side of the book's balance, and make it still stronger than it was before. And there is one more, which comes later, but which is by far the most important: almost the whole of Primo's friendship with Alberto. Alberto appears only three or four times in the De Silva edition; all we know is that he is a chemistry student, who vanishes in the evacuation march; and we hear only at the end, when he comes to say goodbye, that for six months he and Primo 'had shared a bunk, and every scrap of food "organized"'. All the great passages about Alberto Primo added now — his quick understanding of the necessity of war, yet his utter uncorruption; his free spirit, his generosity, his cunning ideas. In the first telling this friendship had remained private, its importance only hinted at in passing. But after ten years poor Alberto *had* to be dead; and Primo was released to add their story to his witness. That meant adding, as his editor says, *joie de vivre* and even humour to the first version; and adding immeasurably to the victory of human solidarity, love and hope over the forces of darkness.

Primo made many other kinds of addition now as well. He added new descriptions and reflections, on the transport, on KB (the whole first page of Chapter 5), the famous paragraph on shoes. He expanded the descriptions of Null Achtzehn and of Alex the Kapo; he added a comic version of Dante's Charon at the gates of hell, who instead of crying *Guai a voi, anime prave*† asks them, courteously, for their money and watches, 'since they will be no use to us any more'. He added two more inward moments — his impulse to run away from the chemical examination; and, in 'October 1944', the terrible thought

---

* Chapter 3. This new chapter also includes Diena, Primo's even earlier bed-companion, who receives him kindly as well.
† 'Woe to you, wicked souls': Canto III, line 84.

that René might be going to the gas chambers in his place: 'I do not know what I will think tomorrow, and after; today I feel no distinct emotion.'

These too add depth, realism, power. But the most important changes are the first ones we mentioned: the addition, or expansion, of strong and sympathetic characters, from Schlome and Steinlauf to Alberto. It is striking how much of the positive, humane life of the book was grafted on to it only now, a decade after it was first written. Primo's growing skill as a writer was not the only reason. Those ten years had given him other things as well: distance, on the one hand; and on the other a much-loved family, especially a much-loved daughter. Perhaps she was the reason why one more character came back to him now. Little Emilia, daughter of Aldo and Elena Levi, sister of Italo, had not been in the first version of his new Bible either. Now he added her, that 'curious, ambitious, cheerful, intelligent child'; and no one who has read *If This is a Man* will ever forget her.

Emilia and Italo Levi

★

From the moment of its republication the book was a success. Antonicelli hailed it as a masterpiece in *La Stampa*; followed by Piero Caleffi himself in *Avanti*, by *L'Unità*, *Il Mondo*, and many others – still mostly the left-wing press, at first, but all unanimous in their praise. Six months later the first 2,000 copies had sold out. The long adventure of Primo's first book had begun; and not only in Italy.

Two years before, in 1956, a young English historian had arrived in Turin. Since he was introduced by Franco Venturi, he was accepted into the small tight world of Turin intellectuals with record speed; and since he was Jewish, he soon met the Arturo Debenedettis, whose daughter Anna he would marry. Inevitably, as he says, he was given a copy of *Se questo è un uomo*, still in the De Silva edition. And with the arrogance of youth (as he also says), he decided that he would be its English translator.

Detto fatto – no sooner said than done. The Debenedettis introduced him to its author. No, he had no publisher, he admitted to Primo. But Einaudi, who were about to publish, might not think about translators for years; and this young man was intelligent, articulate and eager. Primo agreed.

For nearly a year Stuart Woolf went to Corso Re Umberto 75 two evenings a week at about nine. He would see Lucia briefly when he entered; then they would go into Primo's study and work for two or three hours, sometimes more. Stuart would have left Primo the latest pages; Primo would have made his marks and comments; they would discuss them, and settle on a final version. Primo was as minute and thorough as Stuart expected, and a great deal more firm. He was so modest and gentle in other things, but in this he was completely certain. 'He never had any doubt about his own writing,' Stuart says, or about other people's either; about language and its use he was passionate, definite, even dogmatic. He was also tireless, despite long days at the factory, and having to get up again at six o'clock the next morning. Auschwitz had left him tough and resilient, Stuart thought, as Gianna Balzaretti had thought before him: he didn't need much sleep, and spent every spare moment reading. He had read everything, it seemed to his young translator, in English as well as Italian: and he appeared to remember all of it, quoting whole chunks of the Authorized Version, and passages from his favourite English-language authors – Melville, Swift, Conrad. As time went on they worked less and talked more; with his usual mixture of courtesy, reserve and interest, Primo wanted to talk more about Stuart than about himself, and quizzed him about the life of an Ashkenazi Jew in England. Like Luciana, and perhaps Bianca, Stuart has always been surprised (and I think a little disappointed) not to find himself in any of Primo's books or stories.

When the work was finally done, Primo gave his first translator two very characteristic presents: a book by the ex-Fascist Guido Piovene, and a meal at his table, cooked by his mother – *gnocchi romani*, Stuart remembers, and very good. For a long time afterwards Stuart felt lost on Tuesday and Friday evenings. It had been a hugely lucky, transforming experience; and his is the translation of *Se questo è un uomo* (and of *La tregua* too, done six years later) we still read today, both in Britain and America.

After a complicated journey, *If This is a Man*★ was published by a small house, Orion Press, in late 1959 in the United States, and in early 1960 in the United Kingdom. And now it repeated the *rite de passage* which seems to have been its fate: having been greeted as a great work of art and testimony by a few discerning critics, it fell straight into oblivion. This time it would remain there for even longer. Britons and Americans, the fortunate victors, whose lands had not been invaded, and whose Jews had not been destroyed, would take two more decades to be ready to face the Holocaust, and Primo Levi.

Primo resigned himself, as he had done before. He wanted readers in Britain and America, he wanted readers everywhere. But when, in 1959, he heard that a German publisher had bought *Se questo è un uomo*, he forgot everything else. He had written this book for Italians, for all those who did not know, for future generations. But underneath he had written it for Germans. It was the Germans at whom it was aimed 'like a gun', he would write; and now 'the gun was loaded'.

He did not know that Fischer Verlag was a Jewish house, and he did not trust them. He wrote a fierce letter – he was capable of very fierce letters, especially to publishers – requiring to see the translation in advance, chapter by chapter, so that he could check that not a single word had been removed or changed. In mid-August the first chapter arrived, together with a letter from the translator. The chapter was excellent, the letter in faultless Italian. The translator introduced himself: his name was Heinz Riedt, he was exactly Primo's age, and an Italianist, translator of Manzoni, Pirandello, Gadda and many others, but especially Goldoni. Fischer had shown him Primo's letter, he said, and he was eager to reassure him. He was (this was Primo's summary) an 'anomalous German'. His father had been a diplomat, Riedt told him, and he had grown up in Naples and Palermo. When he was called up into the Wehrmacht he had faked an illness, and been allowed to take up his pre-war place at the University of Padua. There, after September 1943, he had secretly joined a group of G. & L. partisans, and fought an underground war against his own people. In 1950 he had returned to Germany, where he now lived, in the Eastern sector of Berlin. He was married; his wife's father was Jewish, and an Auschwitz survivor. He had been offered *Se questo* by a

---

★ Later on its American title was changed to *Survival in Auschwitz*, as it has remained.

lucky chance, he concluded: nothing could be closer to his heart than to bring the terrible truth to his misguided country.

Primo's response shows how far he really was from the cool and measured being he liked to appear — how close still to the boy who veered between heaven and hell, to the young man who hoped every day for 'the heavenly message that changes your life'. 'Dear Herr Riedt,' he wrote. 'Your letter fills me with joy and gratitude . . . Perhaps you are the person I have been hoping for years to meet.' On the outside this unknown messenger was his furthest possible opposite, his enemy, a German; but on the inside he was very close to himself — a G. & L. partisan, a lover of language, a translator between peoples. He summed up Primo's highest hopes — the abolition of difference and distance; the possibility of crossing the abyss between himself and Pannwitz, of understanding the Germans.

Eagerly they set out on the work together. Riedt sent his chapters and lists of questions; Primo returned his answers, his own queries, and his closely argued suggestions, never fewer than two pages of them, often three or four. They laboured to find hundreds of right words for the life of the camp, Riedt always pushing for correct and comprehensible German, Primo fighting for the harsh, subhuman sounds fixed in his memory like fossils. Loading and aiming the seventeen chapters of *If This is a Man* took twenty letters and ten months. It also took more than trouble on both sides. In 1960 the Italian *Wirtschaftswunder* really took off, and Primo came home later every night, too exhausted to pick up a pen. Riedt's trouble was more sinister. He was already marked out as a traitor. Now he was working for a West German company, which was strictly forbidden in the East; worse still, it was a Jewish company, and he was translating a Jewish book, a Jewish accusation. For the second time in his life, he was forced underground: all his correspondence with Primo, as well as his payment from Fischer ('which was not very much'), went through his father-in-law in West Berlin. Primo did not know it, because Riedt did not want to complain: but his gun was loaded against the Germans in secret, as though the war was not over. Which, of course, it wasn't.

'And so we are finished,' Primo wrote to Riedt on 13 May 1960. He was pleased with the result, and grateful; and sad that this work, which was the culmination of all his work, indeed of his life, was over. Of all the aims he had set himself so far, he wrote, this was the clearest: 'to make my voice heard by the German people, to reply to the SS man who laughed at the truss, to the Kapo who cleaned his hand on my shoulder, to Dr Pannwitz, to those who hanged The Last One, and to their heirs'. He had survived, not only his year of Auschwitz, but long enough to achieve this aim; and he was content. Now all he could do was await the response.

Once again the wait was not short: eighteen months passed before *Ist Das ein Mensch* finally appeared in November 1961. But then — at least at the start — he was pleased. Fischer printed 50,000 cheap and affordable copies — compare that to Einaudi's 2,000! — and all 50,000 sold out in a few months. There were very few reviews; but those there were were intelligent, anguished and full of praise. 'No other eye-witness,' said one, 'has managed as well as he . . . to put the inexpressible into words.' 'Is This a Man?' asked another. 'Yes! Primo Levi is a man . . . [His] book deserves a place of honour on German shelves.' Best of all, perhaps, was the review by a critic called Heinz Beckmann, in *Der Rheinische Merkur*. 'Helplessly we ask ourselves how these people, with such hell in their souls, could go on living,' he wrote. 'But then we feel ashamed of our question, which should be the other way around: How can we go on living, in whose name all this was done?'

And then there were the letters. Primo had done an inspired and very Primo-like thing. When Fischer had asked for an Introduction, he had hesitated; and then suggested they use part of his May 1960 letter to Riedt. Thus this very personal letter had become part of the German edition of *If This is a Man*: so that in this edition more than any other he reaches out to touch his reader directly, immediately, as he would touch us all in 'Carbon'. In his letter he spoke, as we know, of his desire to answer his tormentors. But he also said:

. . . I am sure you have not misunderstood me. I have never harboured hatred for the German people; and if I had, I would be cured of it now, after knowing you . . .

But I cannot say I understand the Germans. Now, something one cannot understand constitutes a painful void, a sting, a permanent stimulus that insists on being satisfied. I hope that this book will find some echo in Germany: not only out of ambition, but also because the nature of this echo will perhaps make it possible for me to understand the Germans better, to placate this stimulus.

In the first few years after the book appeared he had around 35 or 40 letters from German readers. They kept coming after that too; but fewer and 'paler', as Primo said, over the years, until the German letters were hardly distinguishable from the others. The first thirty-odd were different: written by men and women who had been alive at the time, or by their children. He answered them, and answered their answers; he pondered them for many years, and finally wrote about them, in the last chapter of *The Drowned and the Saved*. By then his early satisfaction with the German response to his book had drained away. Fifty thousand copies was a large number — but it was only one in 1,000 Germans, and that was only counting the West. And for the next twenty years Fischer refused to republish, pleading lack of interest.

And about the letters too he had changed. What struck him at first was that none was hostile; a few attempted to find excuses, but most were riven with guilt and shame. Later he would notice the first kind more than the second. But what, perhaps, he came to notice most of all was the size of the task he had set himself, the huge difficulty – perhaps the impossibility – of 'understanding the Germans'. Almost all his correspondents were moved to write to him by the part of his preface in which he told Riedt of that hope. They all tried to help him; but they all failed. They did not understand the Germans either, they said; they did not understand 'the German', either perpetrator or bystander, in themselves (and at least one brave bystander admitted to having been one).

I don't know when Primo began to despair of his great project of understanding, or even if he did. But I fear so. Riedt had told him in his last letter that he did not understand 'the German character' either; and Primo's longest, closest and most trusted German correspondent, who would soon appear, would tell him: 'You will certainly never be able to understand "the Germans": even we are unable to do so . . .' For by understanding 'the Germans' he meant understanding evil: understanding how ordinary people could do the evil ordinary Germans did. And understanding this, wholly and truly, may be beyond human reach, without either entering it oneself, or going mad. But the only alternative to understanding evil is hating and fighting it, which Primo could not do. Or – even worse – simply accepting it, which he could not do either. In Bernhard Schlink's *The Reader* an older man who has lived through the war says mockingly to a younger one, who hasn't: 'You want to understand how people can do such terrible things?' But executioners do terrible things too, he says: and not out of hatred, or in war, or even because they are under orders, but just because it is their job. And the young man feels a great emptiness, as if he had been searching for something 'not outside but within himself, and had discovered there was nothing to be found'. He survives (or half survives) that moment. I'm not sure Primo Levi could.

Three more translations of *Se questo è un uomo* came out in these early years: the French in 1961, the Finnish in 1962 and the Dutch in 1963. The most important, the French, was – he felt – a shambles. The text was cut, the title wrong (*C'était un homme*), the translation terrible. And all this was done without consulting him, so quickly that he had no time to act. He was furious, and watched all translations from then on like a hawk – especially, of course, the second French one of *Se questo*, a quarter of a century later.

His letter to Einaudi about that first French mistranslation was one of the harshest he ever wrote (it was 'literally unreadable', he said, 'beyond belief').

But even here he could not remain angry for long. It seemed only reasonable to him, he said, to want one's books to travel the world 'in good health'. It was an epistolary version of the Della Torre smile.

★   ★

From the moment of his return Primo Levi had two careers, not just one; and despite his denials he preferred writing to chemistry from the start. A decade or so later he added a third. This time he didn't say: only Auschwitz made me a speaker. But this time it was true.

When he was nineteen years old, and attending the meetings at the *scuola ebraica*, he had agreed to give a paper like all the others. But when it came to his turn, he had had a new and shocking experience: he was overcome by panic. He read terribly badly; it was all he could do to read at all. He promised himself fervently that he would never speak in public again.

In the normal course of events that would have been an easy promise to keep. But events, of course, were not normal. One evening, some time after the first publication of *Se questo è un uomo*, he went to a survivors' conference with his cousin Giulia. It was in the Teatro Gobetti, a tiny theatre with just two rows of seats; there cannot have been more than a few dozen people there. All went well until one of the speakers said: 'If the author of *If This is a Man* is here, we would very much like to hear from him.' Giulia turned in delight to Primo – but the chair beside her was empty. He had fled.

He continued to flee, even from meetings with only one or two people – unless, like Marcello Franceschi, they were fellow-survivors in need. And then, one day, he couldn't. It was at the 1955 exhibition, where he had agreed to explain the photographs of deportees. Even at this prospect he must have quailed. But people were listening at last; and it was only explaining the pictures, like a guide in a museum. He went – and found himself besieged, almost suffocated, by those crowds of eager young people. He was terrified; but at the same time moved and encouraged. That was the moment when he took his book back to Einaudi. It was probably also the moment when he decided that, if it was required of him, this too would have to be done.

After the Einaudi *Se questo* came out in 1958, and perhaps occasionally before, it *was* required of him. In those days the schools were not yet interested in deportation, either racial or political, or in anything to do with the war, which was still too close for comfort. The earliest requests came from exhibition organizers, from Resistance groups, from cultural organizations; and slowly Primo began to accept them. It was extraordinarily brave of him. To stand up, to stand out, to be looked at – these were things he literally could not bear. But he called on his iron will, and made himself do them. He had never asked more of himself, even in Auschwitz; and he almost didn't succeed. In the beginning his terror was intense, palpable, almost unbearable to see; those were desperate sessions, in which the audience was almost as frightened as Primo, and almost as brave. But they kept coming; and so did he. Gradually, by sheer effort of will, he turned himself into a speaker. Not an orator, of course, not an expansive, dramatic performer. He spoke as he wrote, quietly and unemotionally, never raising his voice, even when others did, refusing to make grand gestures, or any gestures at all; but managing, with that gift of his for making the dark clear, to make even children – especially children – understand that the Lager could be anywhere, even amongst themselves: since its essence was death, not by starvation, or the gas chambers, but by contempt: by the destruction of another's human dignity, after which his physical destruction is easy, and almost unimportant.

From 1960 on, and especially after *La tregua* in 1963, he began to receive endless invitations to speak in schools – so many, he said, that if he had accepted them all his third career would have left no room for the other two. But he accepted as many as he could: and not only out of a duty to testify, but because he almost came to enjoy it. Not that children and young people were easy audiences – on the contrary. They were as searching as adults, and less inhibited; it was also harder to convey the reality of the past to them. But Primo liked and respected the young, and he was determined from the start that they were the most important recipients of his message. Within a few years of those agonizing early meetings he had become the best-known speaker on the Lager in the schools of Piedmont: *la voce della deportazione*, as one of his fellow-speakers said, the living voice, as well as the writer, of deportation.

⋆   ⋆

It is one of Primo Levi's chief characteristics as a writer that – except for the first – he gestated each of his books for years; so that not only his whole writing career but each book in it has its roots much further back than we imagined.⋆

The first example of this, as we know, was *La tregua*, which goes back to the beginning. Since 1947 – or even 1945 – Primo had been telling its episodes to friends; from 1958 he began to tell them to young people inside and outside schools. By now he had paced each adventure to perfection, and knew how well they worked with every kind of audience. In late 1959 he wrote to Heinz Riedt that he thought 'every Sunday' of sitting down

---

⋆ This is one of the key observations made by the editor of the *Opere Omnia*, Marco Belpoliti. I thank him for our detailed discussions of it, even before the *Opere* were published.

and writing the story of his return; but he never found enough time, or enough desire.

Two years later he finally did. He was encouraged by the easing of the Cold War, he always said, and by the growing optimism and ease in Italy. He was encouraged even more by the success of *Se questo*, now on its second printing, making its way abroad, and amongst the young. But most of all, being Primo, he was encouraged by the approval of friends. Some time before, he had sent Italo Calvino the first set of stories which would become *Storie naturali*: and in November 1961 Calvino sent him a positive, even enthusiastic letter, urging him to carry on.★ Then, probably also in November, he found himself in a group of friends at the house of Alessandro Galante Garrone, who, together with Anna Maria, had taken *Se questo è un uomo* to Franco Antonicelli. As usual, Primo was listening rather than talking; until Galante Garrone remarked that *Se questo* had ended too soon, leaving one anxious to know what had happened next, and whether Primo and his companions had ever reached their homes. Reluctantly at first, Primo answered; but soon his joy in story-telling took over, the room fell silent in pleasure and horror, and he talked for an hour. At the end Galante Garrone asked why he didn't put his extraordinary adventures into a second book. Because, Primo said with his hint of a smile, it was a law of literature that a successful first book had to be followed by a failure. But when *La tregua* came out fifteen months later, Galante Garrone saw that Primo had dated it *December 1961 – November 1962*; and at its presentation Primo took his arm and said, 'This book was born in your house.' It wasn't, of course; Galante Garrone guessed immediately that Primo had thought of writing it many times before. But he was happy to have helped deliver both of Primo's first two books to the world; and touched when, years later, Primo wrote in his copy of the sixth: 'To Sandro, who always believed in my stories even before I wrote them.'

In fact, he had picked up his chapter on the Greek and finished it many months before, in March. But now he began again in earnest. In November he wrote the chapter about the Little Hen – it had probably been the high point of his performance at Galante Garrone's, and he wanted to fix it on the page with his friends' laughter still in his ears. After that he went back to the beginning, and worked his way steadily through the story: Chapters 1 and 2 in December; Chapter 4 (since the Greek was Number 3) in January 1962, Chapter 5 in February, 6 and 7 in March, 8 and 9 in May, 11 (since

---

★ Calvino was especially enthusiastic about 'L'amico dell'uomo' and 'Quaestio de Centauris'; but less enthusiastic about some Lager stories Primo had also sent him (probably 'The Disciple' and 'Rappoport'). Even the greatest readers and writers can be wrong.

10 was the Little Hen) in June, 12 in July, 13 and 14 in August and September, 15 in October, and 16 and 17 in November. He wrote in the evenings after supper, on weekends, in the summer holidays; of the chapters dated to a particular day, almost all were written on Saturdays and Sundays. All except the last three were written in the olive-green school exercise book with '*Primo Levi: Italian*' on the cover; in Primo's small, neat hand, in blue fountain pen, with corrections in red and blue biro. He made many small corrections even now, after so many tellings – and some bigger ones as well, removing the whole of 'A Disciple', for instance, and the anticipation of grief for Vanda. Throughout, he pursued his goals of clarity and power: substituting ordinary Italian for Cesare's Roman dialect, for example; and in the last chapter adding the stark summary his friends did not need: 'Of 650, our number when we had left, three of us were returning.'

He took the typescript to Einaudi as soon as it was done. This time there was no delay: the contract was signed on 4 December, a few weeks at most since he had written the last words. His problems with his publishers were not over; no writer's ever are. But this was the first sign of change, like a door silently opening.

Something else also emerges from the contract for *La tregua*: it had originally had a different name. That had happened before, and would happen again; Primo mulled over his titles as long and hard as over everything else. But this debate was not only a literary one. He had first called his book *Vento alto*, *High Wind*: an image which connects to two of its key passages. The first comes at the beginning of his long odyssey, early in Chapter 3. 'In those days and in those parts,' he wrote,

a high wind was blowing over the face of the earth; the world around us seemed to have returned to primeval Chaos, and was swarming with scalene, defective, abnormal human specimens; each of them bestirred himself, with blind or deliberate movements, in anxious search of his own place, his own sphere, as the particles of the four elements are poetically described as doing in the cosmogonies of the Ancients.

It was like the 'second creation' of 'Quaestio de Centauris' and the other stories of fertile chaos – the vast possibility of beginnings, in which there is more hope than there will ever be again, but also more danger. But if in the stories, apart from 'Quaestio', hope and fear are mixed, in this image there is only ill omen: for the creatures who are about to repopulate the earth are all (even Noah) deformed, as Trachi will be. This chaos is the chaos of war and of the Lager, which we will meet again at the end, in Primo's dream: '*I am alone in the centre of a grey and turbid nothingness, and now I know what this means, and know also that I have always known it: I am back in the Lager, and nothing is true outside the Lager.'* *This* high wind can spawn only the war and the Lager from which it blew.

It is the same vision evoked by the word 'truce': a brief, illusory moment between war and war. 'Truce' is clearer, and Primo chose it for his title. It was the right choice: *High Wind* was too fanciful for this picaresque adventure. But the fact that Primo intended it for his all-important second book, right to the brink of publication, shows what a hold the idea of that fertile, fearful wind had on his imagination in those years. Quite soon we shall have to ask why.

The Truce was a key step in Primo Levi's career as a writer. It was, as he would say, his first consciously literary book, in which, though the events were once again true, he allowed himself much more freedom in the telling. And it was the first of his books to be immediately, almost automatically, accepted by his publisher.

That was even before it appeared. Afterwards it brought the biggest change of all: fame. Primo's fame started slowly and locally; he resisted it, and so did the Italian literary establishment. But after *La tregua* neither he nor they could stop it. We know him well enough by now to guess that it would be a complicated gift for him. And not only for him. His family hated exposure as much as he did; and those things he did desire – intellectual honour, human communication, the spread of his message around the world – were not the rewards to them that they were to him. His books already took him away from them in the writing; they would take him immeasurably further away as his readership grew. That is the common fate of all families of successful workaholics. But if Primo bore his success particularly badly, so did his family. With every step of his fame he went into crisis; and so, I think, did they.

That began with *La tregua*. When it came out, Lisa was fourteen. She went to the presentation with the rest of the family. The tables were piled high with copies of the book, each with its photograph of the author on the cover: just his face, as usual. As Giulia Colombo went up to one table, she met Lisa turning away; and instead of pleasure, or teenage boredom, what she saw on her face was pain. 'What's the matter?' Giulia asked, frightened. Nothing, Lisa replied. She just couldn't bear the photographs. 'It's like seeing my father cut to pieces,' she said. That is how Primo's fame would feel to his family: something that killed him for them, then cut him up and kept the pieces.

Corso Re Umberto 75

The one person Primo Levi kept out of his stories was himself: even out of his first book, until slowly he put himself back in. At the centre of his world there is a silence, and not only about himself. He never wrote or spoke about his mother; and with tiny exceptions he never wrote or spoke about his wife either.

Once he told an interviewer that it was she and their children who had helped him back to normality; once he said that she 'has helped me all my life'. That was all. To colleagues, acquaintances, even friends (except the most intimate), he did not speak of her at all, or of his children either. Everyone noticed; Turin is a monument to privacy, but Primo Levi was like a tomb. It was almost as though he had no wife and family – some people even thought he hadn't, and were surprised when they learned the truth.

In his writing his wife appears very rarely. There is the poem of their meeting, '11 February 1946', and the few festive pages of 'Chromium' and 'Nitrogen', about their meeting and earliest days. Finally, after thirty-four years of marriage, there is a poem for her sixtieth birthday, tender but terrible. 'Have patience, my weary lady,' it begins:

> Patience with worldly things,
> With your journey's companions, myself included,
> From the moment I fell to your lot
>
> . . .

Have patience, my impatient lady,
So ground down, mortified, flayed,
You who flay yourself a little every day
So that the naked flesh hurts still more . . .

It is a cry of pain for both of them. But it was never repeated. He wrote out the public suffering of his life; but the private one remained sealed up, like the flayed body of his poem, in his family tomb.

★   ★

There is a famous hellish marriage in Italian literature: Pirandello's. Everyone knows about this one, because Pirandello spoke and wrote about it obsessively; it was the cauldron of his art.

Despite their immense differences, as men and as writers, Luigi Pirandello and Primo Levi had had several similarities as boys. The delicate son of a powerful, philandering father, Pirandello had tortured his adolescent desires with impossible ideals, and thought he would never fall in love. At twenty-seven he married a girl chosen for him by his father, and immediately fixed both his ideals and his desires on her. She would be his salvation, he told her: this girl whom he hardly knew, whom he could only see in an army of aunts and uncles, and who was not allowed to raise her eyes to his face until they were married.

For the first nine years or so their marriage seemed almost normal. Pirandello wrote and taught; Antonietta bore him three children. But Antonietta was not normal. She had inherited her family's obsession, and especially her father's: a pathological jealousy. Her father had kept her locked up in his house as much as he could; when she went to school, he had followed her as she walked with the other girls, and if she raised her eyes from the ground he had made the most violent scenes.

In 1903 Antonietta had her first breakdown. She seemed to recover; but from then on she fell ever deeper into jealousy, and finally into full-blown paranoia. She suspected Pirandello of having love affairs with all his students, and accused him without cease; she spied on him in the street, and made appalling scenes, just like her father. Once she tried to attack him with a pair of scissors. Eventually she even accused him of incest with their daughter, Lietta; and in despair Lietta tried to kill herself. That was the end for Pirandello, who until then had been unable to let Antonietta go. When his elder son returned from the war in 1919, he had his wife committed. Even then he went on trying to bring her home for years, and only gave up, at last, in 1924. Antonietta lived on in her clinic for over twenty years more, finally dying after the Second World War.

All this terrible suffering Pirandello transmuted into art. It was, his biographer says, both 'the obsessive stimulus of his creativity' and his best subject. His greatest plays, *Six Characters in Search of an Author* and *Henry IV*, are both, in their ways, about madness; and about the power of the mind to create its own truth, so that we are not only who we think we are, but also who others think we are. In the stories, for instance, there is poor Piovanelli, whose wife 'hated the whole human race' because of her terrible jealousy – but especially, and insanely, him:

. . . Jealous of him! Of him, as faithful as a dog by nature . . . shy with women, so shy he even pitied himself . . .

And now he, who had always behaved with the greatest respect and reserve to women, who had never dared to do or say anything that might seem at all risqué, who had always believed every sentimental conquest to be terribly difficult – he felt ambushed on all sides, and walked down the street with his eyes on the ground. And if a woman looked at him, immediately he looked away; if a woman barely squeezed his hand, he turned all the colours of the rainbow.

All the women on earth had become his nightmare, the enemies of his peace.

★ ★

The main person who kept herself out of this story is Lucia. She is its most Pirandellian character: a shadow creature made up of others' visions, not even in part her own author.

Even in these visions, she is not Antonietta. Antonietta was mad; Lucia is not. But her tragedy, and Primo's, was similar.

When Lucia fell in love with Primo it seemed like a miracle to him, and it was. He was deep in the pit of his sexual fear, which had made Gabriella Garda (and Galina, and all the earlier girls) turn from him, despite their love or liking. And now he was in the pit of depression as well. When he came so often to see Anna Cases, in the winter of 1945–6, she suddenly wondered if he was hoping they might try again: and was terrified, because she sensed the depth of his need. When she heard that Lucia was going to marry him, she remembers, she felt enormous admiration for her courage.

But was it really courage? It is part of all passionate love to want to be all in all to one's lover: to make him completely happy, to be all he needs to be happy for ever. But a woman who falls in love with a wounded, suffering man wants that more than others. Lucia wanted that more than others; and it must have seemed that with Primo she could have it. Neither of them knew yet how strong he really was, and how much he would need his freedom; nor how weak he was, and how little he would dare to seize it.

Primo never wrote a word of this: except perhaps once or twice, briefly and obliquely. In his novel *If Not Now, When?*, for instance, his hero Mendel falls painfully in love with Line, a strange, contained, imperious young woman. Before him, Line had taken the desperate young Leonid as her lover. What did Line see in Leonid? Mendel asks himself; and answers:

. . . Perhaps only a drowning man; there are women born to rescue, and perhaps Line was one of those . . . Or perhaps it's something else: Line isn't looking for a drowning man to save, but on the contrary for a humiliated one, to humiliate him more . . . There are people like that: they harm others without knowing.

But if Primo never transformed his marriage into art, like Pirandello, someone else did. In *The Marriage of Raffaele Albanese*, Piero Rinaldi remains based on Primo, Luisa Accati says – once again fused together with her other sources in her novelist's imagination.*

When Piero returns from the war, he marries Alda and brings her home to live in his mother's house. Everyone expects trouble between mother-in-law and daughter-in-law: but there is none, especially at the beginning. Alda wants to work; she hates food and cooking and housework, and is happy to leave it all to Maria. Maria, in turn, is happy to keep everything in the house to herself. 'If I need any help I'll ask,' she says; and naturally she never does.

From the start Alda tries to keep only one thing to herself: Piero. Whenever he suggests that they might see one of his friends she says, 'Oh no, not today.' When Maria invites someone to dinner, Alda is silent; after a while she says, 'Please excuse me, I've work to do,' and disappears. This happens not once or twice but always; and it soon becomes clear that her hostility to anyone who enters the house is much more than the shyness of a new bride. Rather – says Anna Rinaldi, daughter of Piero's brother Emilio – it is the sign of a deep misanthropy, which makes her unable to bear anyone but Piero and Maria; in truth, anyone but Piero. For though there seems to be no shadow between mother-in-law and daughter-in-law, there are, before long, many other shadows; and according to Anna's parents they come from this: that Alda has to live like an unwelcome guest, like an intruder, in another woman's house. Emilio tells Piero so: he is wrong to force his wife to live with his mother. But Piero denies that he has forced her: Alda has freely agreed, and in fact the arrangement suits her. If she is difficult, it is not because she has to live with her mother-in-law; it is because that is how she is.

There is no doubt that that is how she is; the only question is how it

---

* See *The Hare and the Tortoise*, p. 62 above.

began. Anna takes Piero's side and blames Alda; but Anna's mother Emma defends her. Alda is in an impossible situation, she says. It is true that she has rejected Piero's friends – but only because Piero's friends rejected her. It is true that she wanted to own him – but then she discovered that he was already owned by his mother, and there was very little left for her. The less she could have of him, the more she tried to keep the little she had; but the more she tried to keep of him, the more he had to save something for himself. Even to the point of betraying her, Emma says. Not sexually – his hatred of his father's philandering made that impossible. But with intense female friendships, including one with someone he had loved before his marriage. Yes, Alda was jealous, even pathologically jealous and possessive: but which came first, her jealousy or Piero's betrayals, starting with his mother?

And yes, Piero was in an impossible situation too. And yet, says Emma, it also suited him for Alda to be as she was: the dark destroyer of his life, in his friends' eyes. 'To some extent, Piero always thought of his wife as the dark side of himself as well,' she says. This last defence of Alda she does not explain.

★   ★

It seems fantastic that the inner story of Primo Levi should be anything like this, and a moment later it seems natural. In almost every friend and every woman he sought freedom from himself – from his depression, his self-suppression, his bondage to his mother. And in almost all of them he found it, at least a little. But in his two closest friends, Giorgio Lattes and Livio Norzi, he found – and perhaps sought – not difference, but similarity, even an exaggeration of himself: stasis, enclosure. And in the one key choice of a woman in his life he did the same. It was as though, at the last minute, his courage failed him; and he slammed the window shut, as he had done once before, and turned back into his room. And perhaps that was inevitable. It was the only kind of relationship for which his mother had prepared him.

Piero was always shy and withdrawn, says Maria in *The Marriage of Raffaele Albanese*: it's natural that he should choose a wife who is even shyer and more withdrawn, and he is happy that way. But it is only *she* who is happy that way, or as happy as she could hope to be, having to share him at all. Now, Rina did not choose Lucia, as Maria has in truth chosen Alda; but in the same way it was only she who was happy in Primo's marriage, or as happy as she could be, having to share him at all. For Piero in the novel it is the end of any hope of happiness, or at least of freedom; it is like closing the door and locking himself in. He marries Alda, we understand, because she is willing to share him with his mother. And perhaps that was one reason, at least, why Primo chose Lucia: to save him from his desire for escape; to close the door as well, and lock him in.

As Alda is to Piero, so Lucia was to Primo: not an opposite, but an extreme version of himself. If he had often been depressed from childhood, Lucia had been more so: isolated, withdrawn, 'unhappy from birth', Primo would say. If he was self-denying, self-effacing, more Turinese than the Turinese, she was even more so: 'Calvinist', Primo would say, opposed to any indulgence, and most of all to any show. And if Primo was shy, ill at ease outside his closest circle, Lucia was even more so. She knew that people blamed her for it, but it was beyond her control. And so a vicious circle of rejection grew up between Lucia and Primo's friends, like the one between Alda and Piero's friends in the novel. She sensed that they did not think her good for Primo, they sensed that she thought the same of them, and it was impossible to say who began. But the result was stark, and came soon, as soon as they were married. Like Alda with Piero, Lucia would almost never go to Primo's friends with him: not even to the Accatis, whom she liked, and who liked her. 'Outside the house,' one friend says, 'you only ever saw Primo alone.' And in it he had to be alone with her, or alone with her and Rina and the children. Hardly anyone was allowed to enter the family circle: only Leonardo, who was almost family himself; and occasionally one or two others – Jean and Claude Samuel, for instance, on their brief visits to Turin. Livio Norzi was not welcome, nor Giorgio Lattes, nor even, always, Bianca; Primo would go to them, alone. If he invited a guest against her will, Lucia would not appear, or would soon disappear, like Alda.

And at the heart of it all was a huge protectiveness. 'Lucia could not conceive that Primo could be well and happy with anyone but her,' says one of the friends. She was fearful of all his friends, men and women, but especially of women. In order to avoid Antonietta's scenes, Pirandello would pre-announce his departures and arrivals, and keep to them exactly. Primo did the same. He was always looking at his watch, making sure he would be home in time for lunch or supper; if it got late, he would grow restless, and bolt. But all Pirandello's anxious care did not reassure Antonietta; nor Primo's Lucia. Perhaps at the beginning, like Alda in *The Marriage of Raffaele Albanese*, she took his telephone messages from his women friends, and felt complicit in her own betrayal. But if she ever did she soon stopped; and Primo told his female friends not to call him at home.

But his closest female friends of all were inside the house, and always had been, long before her. After the war and the death of their father, Primo and Anna Maria were closer than ever. It would not have been easy for any pair of sisters-in-law to live together in these circumstances; but for this pair it was impossible. Anna Maria left the Corso Re Umberto soon after Primo's marriage. She went to work for Adriano Olivetti's *Comunità*, first in Ivrea, then in Rome. She married in Rome and settled there. She has rarely returned to Turin since. Like Emilio in *The Marriage of Raffaele Albanese*, Anna Maria is the one who got away.

That left Rina. But Rina could not be expelled, or even visibly resisted. She could only be accepted, if Lucia wanted to keep Primo: just as Rina had to accept her, for the same reason. That was the Faustian pact that their natures imposed on all three of them. But at least Rina could help the family; or so Lucia imagined. But it did not turn out as she imagined. As Rina had always ruled Primo, so now she ruled his family, and especially Lucia. Lucia had hoped that Rina would be a helper in her house, but it turned out the other way around. *She* was a helper in Rina's house: and the only escape would have been to leave it, to ask Primo to take her and the children away. But escape was not Lucia's way. Her way was, as usual, an extreme version of Primo's: to submit, to endure; and beyond that 'to flay herself a little every day', and thereby, in the end, to win after all. So when, like Emilio in the novel, Federico Accati told Primo that he was wrong to force his wife to live with his mother, Primo gave Piero's reply: he had not forced her, it suited her too. Later he would realize that Accati was right, and that this had been the greatest mistake of his life. But later would be too late; and his guilt would become part of their battle.

It was as Luisa Accati wrote in her novel: *Total dedication is a bottomless pit which swallows up all who approach it.* Inevitably the desirer will be disappointed, because no real dedication will be enough; and inevitably the desired will be repelled, and even frightened, because he soon learns that this is true. Lucia wanted to be Primo's only rescuer, listener and friend, but she must have realized very soon that she was not, and never would be. His mother, his sister, his friends were there before her, and she never managed to remove any of them. And then there was something else as well. It must have seemed an exceptionally cruel trick of fate when her husband, of all people – her timid, submissive, self-effacing husband – turned out to be a genius, a creator of steely dedication, and a famous man. All she wanted was for him to be with her, and with their family: *but he never was*. It was all right for him to be at the factory all day – that was normal. But as soon as he was at home, what did he do – every evening, every weekend, every holiday? He wrote, alone in his study; or he went off to talk to conferences, exhibitions, schools. She wanted to be his only listener; but he wanted more and more and more. He wanted a whole world of listeners – and he would have them. To her old rivals, his mother, his sister, his friends, there would soon be added a new and innumerable kind: his readers. She feared everyone he needed; but perhaps she fears his readers most of all. We are invisible and immortal; against us she cannot win. But she could never really win, any more than he could. Their marriage (says another friend) was a trap into which they both fell, equally blamelessly, or equally to blame.

Antonietta's jealousy of Pirandello was insane, because he was innocent of all her suspicions, and, despite everything, in love with her to the end. Lucia's jealousy of Primo was obsessive, like Alda Rinaldi's, but it was not insane. Like Piero, Primo had an earlier love, whom he continued to see, and who – he would tell the world – but for 'a throw of the dice' would have been his life's companion instead of her. And there would be other intense female friendships: here too Lucia was more like Alda Rinaldi than like poor deluded Antonietta. But here too the vicious circle blurs and spins. Did Primo's female friendships push Lucia's possessiveness into obsession? Or did Lucia's possessiveness push Primo towards other female friends?

Despite their sympathy for her, the Accatis thought Lucia's jealousy irrational from the start. Once, they remember, among the photographs Primo and Accati brought back from a trip was one which had happened to catch two unknown girls standing near them: and Lucia was tormented by suspicion for weeks. As for any woman who worked closely with Primo – that was quite impossible. Lucia was jealous of all of them, starting with Gianna Balzaretti. And she was not completely wrong. Primo hid his interest in women, because of his own ancient shyness, and because of Lucia. But he *was* interested in women; and women, especially, knew it. If there were men and women in a room, Primo talked to the women; if there were pretty women and ugly ones, he talked to the pretty ones. Gianna Balzaretti *was* pretty, very lively and feminine; and (as long as she wasn't complaining) Primo visibly enjoyed her company. It was almost certainly no more than that; but there was no convincing Lucia.

Like Antonietta spying on Pirandello, we can catch two glimpses of Primo with women in these early years. One was very early: September 1948, exactly a year after his marriage. He had attended an International Congress of antifascists in Venice, which went on for an exalting three days. On the train home he sat beside a young woman. They began to talk, and never stopped. Primo was reserved, says the young woman – who is of course no longer young, but still seems so – but he was not cold. On the contrary, he was intensely open. 'He wanted contacts,' she says, 'not just intellectual contacts but all kinds, real exchanges.' She pauses; and then she repeats, with a small change: 'He wanted contact.'

She had read *Se questo è un uomo*, so they talked of that, and he told her things he had not written, for instance about Vanda. They talked about books, and politics, and Israel; they talked all night, about everything under the sun. Primo was so intelligent, so interested in everything, talking to him was a rare adventure. After that one night, the young woman felt as though she had known him all her life, and would go on knowing him all her life from then on. He must have felt the same, because when they arrived in Turin he turned to her sadly. He had not said a word about a family so far. But now he said that he was very sorry: they would not be able to speak again, because his wife would be too unhappy. When the young woman reached home and told her mother, her mother said, 'We'll invite them both, then.' But Lucia would never come.

The second glimpse comes thirteen years later, in 1961. Two young Polish Jewish women, both survivors, were on holiday in Riccione, in a beautiful small hotel. Their husbands joined them rarely, or not at all, remaining in their offices in distant cities. For three weeks of high summer the two friends had a marvellous holiday, lying in the sun all day, and dancing every night with lines of eager, handsome men. On the second or third evening, on the hotel terrace, a small, thin, young-looking man came up to them. Was it Polish they were speaking? he asked. Yes, they replied. In their common language, French, he told them that his name was Primo Levi, he was Jewish, and he had been in Poland, in a Lager. Instantly, they were friends. On many evenings after that the three had long conversations. Primo wanted to know everything they could tell him about the world of Polish Jewry before the war; he told them about the Resistance in Italy, and about his journey home; they talked long and hard about Israel, because the two young women were Zionists, while Primo had serious reservations. He told them that he had written a book about the Lager, and was writing another, about that journey home.* They did not rush off and buy his book, reluctant to break the happy spell of their holiday. But when they looked for it years later, they found – like so many survivors – that it was the one Lager memoir they could read. They regretted then that they had not exchanged addresses with the quiet chemist from Turin, as he had suggested; but at the time that too would have threatened the peace of their brief truce. For he was extremely interesting, with 'penetrating eyes', and they very much enjoyed their evening meetings. But he was melancholy, lonely, very shy. His conversation was witty and ironic, but he never laughed. They never saw him on the beach, or in the nightclub; he never mentioned a family or friend. He simply appeared, by himself, in the early evening, and an hour or two later disappeared again. Everyone at the hotel dressed to kill in the evenings, but he was always the same, in modest, inexpensive shirt

---

* In the summer of 1961 Primo was writing Chapters 12 to 14 of *La tregua* ('The Wood and the Path', 'Holidays' and 'The Theatre').

and trousers. His voice was particularly calm and quiet; he never raised it, even at a dramatic point in a story, or when they argued about Israel. And though he repressed it, they sensed something else as well: he was deeply attracted, especially to one of them. If she had given him the smallest encouragement, they thought . . . But she didn't. She was happily married; she only wanted a little holiday excitement. That was clearly not this lonely man's line; and besides he was not at all attractive. She preferred her handsome dancing partners. Her friend (who is the one who told me this story) has an abiding image of Primo, on that brief summer holiday: as the evening darkens, he walks away.

These two encounters are themselves images, prefiguring later ones: one at the deepest level spiritual ('We were like two schoolfriends,' says the young woman from the train), the other disturbingly physical; and both happening away from home. Primo's relationships with women were always *tregue*, brief truces in the war at home. Rina and Lucia fought each other for him, he fought each of them for the other and for himself, and last but far from least he fought himself, as he had always done. In this war no one yielded, no one rebelled, and no one won, except perhaps Rina. Primo's friends told him incessantly that he should rebel against Lucia's control; but he never did. He had never been able to rebel against anyone, to impose his will on anyone – so how could he do so with her, to whom he owed everything – his family, his first book, even his life?

I say that no one won, except perhaps Rina: she kept her home, her son, her grandchildren, and tolerated her daughter-in-law no more than she had to. Certainly neither Primo nor Lucia won. Lucia lost to Primo's mother, to his women friends, to his writing, to his readers: fighting not to share him with any of them, and having to share him with all. And Primo lost his freedom, or what little freedom he had. If a message could have been sent from the Lager, he had written in 1946, it would be this: 'take care not to suffer in your own homes what is inflicted on us here'. He had already known then that such suffering was possible outside the Lager. His marriage was an attempt to escape an old bondage; but instead it added a new one. All his close friends knew this, though they could not say so openly, especially to him. They said it privately, to each other. Euge said and says: 'Primo was always a prisoner.' And Ada Della Torre said: 'Primo built himself a Lager.'

That was, perhaps, the underlying truth of it. It is a classic ploy of artists (and not only artists) to have fierce wives: to have someone else to guard their gate, and to take the blame for turning their friends away. Primo turned Lucia away to write, but she turned them away; and only she knew where the blame really lay.

And perhaps, on a still deeper level, he needed the worst aspect of her jealousy as well: his imprisonment from other women. His double bind had not entirely released him, and it never would. He still both longed for women and feared them: but now he could blame someone else for his fear. He could say, 'I am very sorry, but we cannot meet again, my wife is too jealous': and it was true, but perhaps not all the truth. And when one day he didn't say it — when he nearly leapt, when he nearly escaped after all — it was impossible; and all he wanted was for Lucia to lock him in once more.

This leaves the deepest level of all: the level of Primo's first bondage, to his mother. I wonder whether that is what Emma Rinaldi meant, in her last mysterious remark: that Piero 'thought of his wife as the dark side of himself'. I wonder if she meant that *he* could not be bad, and defy his mother, but hoped that *she* could and would. And she did. The only trouble was that Piero's mother was worse; and that when Alda lost, she turned on him.

On all these levels, perhaps, Primo needed Lucia to be as she was. Several of his friends knew it, including Ada ('Primo built himself a Lager'). And unconsciously, at least, I think he knew it too, from the very beginning. I think that was why he was so struck by Felice Fantino's story of the magic circle in 1946 or '47, and why he put it into *The Periodic Table*, 'for chronological reasons', at that point in his life.

Alberto Cavaglion has suggested that 'Titanium' may be an allegory of authoritarianism, or of Fascism. But that does not seem plausible to me. The painter who is turning little Maria's room a magical white seems strange and powerful to her, but also 'quite nice and friendly'. When he says the word '*titanio*', and she hears '*ti taglio*' — 'I cut you' — she is not really afraid: rather, she feels 'a delicious shiver of fear, as when the ogre appears in a fairy-tale'. That is what the man is to her: a fairy-tale ogre, more thrilling than genuinely frightening. Then he encloses her in his chalk circle; and that *is* 'unexpected and terrible', but still only in a fairy-tale way. When at last he has finished painting, she asks him to release her; and laughing, he rubs away the circle 'very carefully, to undo the magic spell'.

This is not a baleful experience of tyranny, but a magical one of containment. It is as much protection as imprisonment; and when it is over, the child is the opposite of traumatized. 'When the circle had disappeared,' Primo wrote, 'Maria got up and left, skipping, and she felt very happy and satisfied.'

'Maria and the Circle'* was written in 1947, the year of his marriage. *That*, I think, is its secret subject: the magic circle he hoped Lucia would draw around him. By 1975 he knew she had drawn one, but that it was

---

* The story's original title.

different from Maria's. In order to make the story fit into *The Periodic Table*, he added the exchange about titanium, and changed the title. Titanium dioxide is a white pigment; '*titanio*', therefore, is required by the story. But Maria's mistake is not required. It is a favourite device of these stories: 'Vanadium', for example, will also contain a mistake for a chemical term. But 'Vanadium' will turn on that mistake; whereas nothing, in fact, turns on Maria's. '*Ti taglio*', 'I cut you', she thinks the friendly ogre says, before he draws his magic circle. It is as though, looking back on his young self, Primo marked his hopes of containment with an ironic, useless warning.

13. Centaur:
1963-75

Primo in 1967

La tregua came out in April 1963. On its cover was an acute summary – unsigned, but by Italo Calvino. About the atrocities of Auschwitz, Calvino said, Primo Levi had written a book of classical equanimity; now, about freedom and a new beginning, he had written one tormented by 'a sadness which could never be cured'. Calvino saluted the book's extraordinary portraits – the Greek, Cesare, Hurbinek, 'who had never seen a tree'; and summed up its tensions – on the one hand, the plague that had blasted Europe; on the other, the Russia of Pushkin and Gogol, comic and tragic, epic and absurd.

The reviews would all echo Calvino (or simply repeat him, as reviewers often do). First off the mark was Franco Antonicelli, writing in *La Stampa* even before the book came out, in a clear bid to set the tone. Like Calvino, Antonicelli saluted Primo's most 'splendid' pages, including the ones on Hurbinek, and noted that despite its 'tumultuous vitality' *La tregua* was, in the end, a 'desperate' book. Primo had to wait a month to see if Antonicelli's example would be followed; but finally it was. One of the most important critics of the day, Paolo Milano, wrote a long and powerful piece in

L'Espresso on 21 April, calling *La tregua* 'incontrovertibly convincing', far more so than other memoirs, 'not to speak of fiction'. This time the left-wing press followed, rather than led: the *Gazzetta del Popolo*, *L'Unità*, *Rinascita* all echoed Calvino's, Antonicelli's and Milano's praise, and also their reflections on the strange recurring anguish in this vivid, picaresque tale. The most enthusiastic (and far-sighted) of all was Giancarlo Vigorelli in *Tempo*, who said that every page of *La tregua* had the weight of truth, and that such was Primo Levi's narrative gift that he might soon give us a book on quite a different subject.

Apart from Vigorelli, however, most of the major critics also followed Antonicelli and Milano in preferring the first to the second half of the book, and in regretting the darkness of its end. Not so the provincial reviews, almost all of whom began with undiluted praise for *La tregua*, and never changed. This reflects a central truth about *La tregua*'s success, and about the success of all Primo Levi's work: it started from the bottom up. Milano, and later the other premier newspaper critics, such as Walter Pedullà and Carlo Bo, recognized the value of this literary outsider before the academic ones did; but before them came the 'outsider' critics, and before *them*, the readers. Primo's fame would always have this pyramid shape, based on a sturdy foundation of ordinary readers. It was the only thing about it that pleased him without reservation.

The pattern began now with *La tregua*: and not only with its reviews. The premier literary prize in Italy, the Strega, also comes first in the year, in early July. *La tregua* had only appeared in April. Einaudi had already put forward the year's front runner, Natalia Ginzburg's *Lessico famigliare*, and had no intention of introducing a competitor. No literary school or circle proposed Primo Levi, since he was equally outside all of them; since he was neither Catholic nor Communist – the two broad bases of power in Italy until not very long ago – no one else proposed him either. But *La tregua* had what every writer longs for – word of mouth power, reader power; which at the last moment propelled him into the list of six finalists, published in late June.

So began Primo's first skirmish with fame; and a painful one it must have been. Part of him – the competitive part, the first reaction he always suppressed – must have thrilled at the dream of beating Natalia: what sweet revenge for *Se questo* that would have been! But Primo would have banished that thought before he had it. Instead he would have fretted – was he not putting Einaudi in a difficult position? And his family? Only a few weeks earlier Lisa had turned away in horror from the picture of his fame: and here it was already approaching. So he pretended it wasn't. He had no intention of attending the prize ceremony in Rome, he told a journalist – but Cesare

Lupo, his proposer, rang to say he might even win, and in order not to offend anyone he changed his mind. At work most people didn't even know he was a writer; he told them he was going to Rome to see his sister. 'I feel like a Martian here,' he said, when he arrived in the glittering surroundings of the Villa Giulia. And that, at least, was true.

On the evening of 4 July, Natalia Ginzburg won, with Primo in third place, eight votes behind (and the novelist Tommaso Landolfi in between). He breathed a sigh of relief, and went home.

But his first dance with fame was not yet over. Several articles appeared, saying that the real discovery of the seventeenth Strega had been Primo Levi. And then, suddenly, he was in the running for another prize; and this time he would win.

The Campiello was the right prize for Primo Levi. It was brand new, begun that year by a group of Venetian industrialists; and it aimed specifically to avoid the literary intrigue and infighting of the other major Italian prizes, which had reached an all-time high, or rather low. To achieve this aim, the founders had invented a jury system that had the simplicity of genius, and a complexity only Italians could imagine surviving. There were two juries: a small one, of nine writers and critics, who chose the short-list of five titles; and a vast one, of 300 ordinary readers, who would decide the winner. Apart from some housewives, workers and students, most of the 300 were really far from ordinary, since they included MPs, ministers, journalists, academics, and famous figures in the arts world (for example, Federico Fellini). But they were not literary professionals; and they were still, therefore, the perfect jury for Primo.

This time, Einaudi did not wait for word of mouth, but entered *La tregua* themselves. Their decision to submit his book for the prize had fallen on him 'like a meteorite', Primo said; he had had nothing to do with it, it had all happened without his will and without his knowledge. He hoped the Belloncis – the founders of the Strega – wouldn't mind . . . Then in August he was awarded another prize,* and had to turn it down, in order not to withdraw from the Campiello. Another conflict, another situation in which, whatever he did, he would offend *someone*. That is what praise and prizes already seemed to him: demands, half of which he would be bound to fail.

This time there was no question about his attending the prize-giving on 3 September, since for at least the last month he had been predicted to win. Once more, however, he went alone. A journalist called Giancarlo Meloni spotted him on the train from Turin: sitting very upright in a seat too big

* The Alpi Apuane, which had been won by Fenoglio, among others, but which was certainly minor compared to the Campiello.

for him, never raising his eyes from a book of Isaac Asimov's science fiction stories in English. He looked – Meloni noted – extraordinarily young, with thin lips, protruding ears 'like a student priest's', and extremely sharp blue eyes. When Meloni suggested that the prize 'was in his pocket', he replied that perhaps they might want to avoid saying that a *Primo* was *secondo*, and gave his suppressed laugh; and 'You can't tell,' Meloni wrote, 'if he's laughing at himself, or his joke, or you.'

Despite its democratic ideals, the Campiello ceremony was held in surroundings as splendid as the Strega's: the *salone d'onore* of the Fondazione Cini, on the island of San Giorgio Maggiore in Venice, amid the flower of the literary world 'and the descendants of the Doges', as Primo would say. It was a very Italian evening. First there was music (a great deal of music), messages from every important person who was not already there, and endless erudite speeches, for which Italian audiences have an astonishing patience, perhaps as a result of long childhood training in their churches. Finally, at half past eleven, or even midnight, a notary read out the results of the 245 valid and completed votes of the 'ordinary' jury. And Primo Levi was *primo*, with 104 votes, forty ahead of his nearest rival.

Not even he could hide his emotion. He looked – said the various reporters – 'shy and confused', 'visibly moved', 'terrified'. 'I'm very happy,' he told the official interviewer. To the *Avvocato* Valeri Manera, head of the prize's founders, he said, 'with a certain solemnity', that he 'would make certain decisions in his life' now. When he ran into Giancarlo Meloni, the journalist from the train, he said, 'You know, I feel ready for anything,' and blushed.

Then he went home, and didn't make those decisions after all. Or rather: he didn't make them on the surface. He went on being a chemist, and calling himself a chemist (not only publicly) for another dozen years. But inside him something had changed. *La tregua* was his first literary book – he'd 'buffed it up', 'rounded it out', as Faussone would say: taken literary liberties with his material. It was also, therefore, the first book to cause him guilt and struggle. It had been necessary, it had been *right* to write *Se questo*, and the grain of ambition in it was easily hidden, even from himself. But *La tregua* was more like a normal book: that is to say, gratuitous. So he had worried about it, as he would worry about *Storie naturali*: should the author of *Se questo* have written it? Should the author of *Se questo* write any other books at all? But he *had* written it, and there was no going back now. Half of him disapproved of being a writer; his wife disapproved of his being a writer. But he wanted to write; and now he knew that his readers wanted him to write as well. This, then, was the turning point for him: when *La tregua* received the Campiello, inwardly Primo Levi became a writer. Briefly, he even let it show. 'Perhaps I enjoy writing more than being a chemist now,' he said to Enzo Fabiani of *Gente*, a fortnight after the Campiello. For this interview Lucia and the children posed with him for a photograph: Primo at his typewriter, his wife and daughter smiling down at him.★ It is the only such photograph I have ever seen – Primo Levi as a writer, with his family around him. Perhaps that's why he let the truth slip out now: because at that moment they didn't seem to mind.

But the reality was that they did mind, deeply and painfully – and so did he. His division over being a writer was not a small thing: not just ordinary Turinese shyness, and an ordinary Turinese reluctance to leave a good paying job. It *was* shyness, and reluctance to leave his job; but in Primo these were neither ordinary nor small. They were deep cracks in his constructed self, which plunged straight into the abyss of his real self below, like the abyss of the Man's mind in his first story. It was not just that he found praise, success, attention difficult to receive: he found them impossible. And yet at the same time he wanted them, he even needed them – because although he knew he was good, he could never feel he was; and whereas excellence in chemistry is easily proved, in writing there is no proof apart from readers' and critics' reactions. So he both wanted and didn't want success and recognition for themselves. And even more for their consequences. A successful writer was asked to speak to people, to travel around the country, around the world: and what did he both want and fear more than to speak to people, and to travel around the world? Only one thing, perhaps: to be desirable to women, at last, and to lose his fear of them. And didn't success hold out that prospect too? Famous men were attractive to women; even Primo Levi, if he were famous, might be attractive to women . . . Perhaps he never had this thought consciously, and perhaps Lucia didn't either. But it would become part of their battle, because it would happen. In fact it may already have happened. All Primo's conflicts with fame began at its beginning: that is, with *La tregua*.

The image of the hybrid, the centaur, had been with him from the start: from at least 1946, when he'd first sketched 'The Sixth Day'. What will this creature 'Man' be? asks Ormuz, the ultra-rational planner. 'He will be double,' he answers: 'Human to his heartstrings, and beast below.' From then on the image would resurface regularly in Primo's writing, from Trachi in *Storie naturali* to the multiple hybrids of 'Disfilassi' in *Lilit*, after 'the iron barrier between the species had broken down, no one knew yet whether for good or ill'. But it would resurface still more in his conversation, as his image of himself. 'I am an amphibian, a centaur,' he said in 1966, 'divided

★ See p. 476.

into two halves.' He would identify his halves in several ways – Italian and Jewish; chemist and writer; rationalist, 'but even I have a scrap of subconscious'. Of these it was mostly the middle pair he meant. Looking back, he would note how much they had, in fact, crossed and combined – how chemistry had enriched his writing, and vice versa, making him see writing with a chemist's eye, and his chemist's labours with a literary one. But at the time, what he felt most keenly was a 'paranoid division'. He kept his two halves strictly separate, and moved between them like Jekyll and Hyde. Every morning entering his factory, every evening entering his study, he remade himself from writer to chemist and back again; and this second transformation especially 'took a good hour'. 'Being a chemist in the eyes of the world,' he wrote in *The Wrench*, 'yet feeling the blood of a writer in my veins, I felt as if I had two souls in my body, which is one too many.'

In *Storie naturali* Trachi explodes in violence when one half of him makes impossible what the other half desires; in *Vizio di forma* the Golem will similarly explode when his two masters, who are his two souls, disagree. Primo clearly knew something about division – and one so deep that it cannot have been only between the chemist and the writer. He would talk about that one precisely because it wasn't the most important. Most important was the third division he mentioned, between the rationalist and his 'scrap' of subconscious. And almost as important as that was one he didn't mention at all: between the part of him that wanted success and the part of him that feared it; between the family man, to whom his family meant being human, and the newly famous, possibly desirable writer.

After his return from Auschwitz, Primo no longer did the most difficult kind of rock-climbing: except once, in the early 1960s. Although he was already over forty, he climbed Testa Grigia near Gressoney, alone: 'I wanted to prove to myself that I still could,' he said. Once he had passed that test he was content with less dangerous expeditions, often with Silvio – though even these would remain quite spectacular to the end. And for the rest of his life one of his most constant pleasures was walking in the mountains with his friends. Almost every weekend he would walk with Bianca and the Bobbios, or with Nicoletta Neri and Carla Gobetti, or with friends from Einaudi and *La Stampa*. They would go to the Val Susa nearby, or to the Val Pellice; to Monte Freidour, to Rocca Patanüa, to Musinè. Primo would explain every rock and bud and bird; he would tell the latest funny story he was writing, and be happy.

Once he had settled at SIVA he found another hobby. He was a creator, as Marcello Franceschi said; and he loved to use his hands as well as his head. From the factory floors he collected the discarded ends of copper wire, and all sorts of scrap no one had any use for: like Ponzio in his university laboratory long ago. Primo made no funeral pyre, however, but went straight to the stage of salvage. Out of the scraps of industrial rubbish he made collages; and out of the copper wire he made sculptures – birds, animals, insects; creatures of every kind. Perhaps he made fewer collages, or did not keep them in his study: none of his interviewers has ever described them. But he made dozens of wire sculptures over the years, and hung them in his study, and gave them to friends. Silvio has a crocodile and a kangaroo, Gisella has an ant – perhaps the Ant Queen of Primo's story;* in his study there were, at different times, a green owl and a red butterfly, a gull, a penguin, a bug, and assorted mysterious creatures, including (according to Philip Roth) 'a Jew playing his nose'. It is as though Primo had made visible his world of animal metaphors, and stood them around to keep him company.

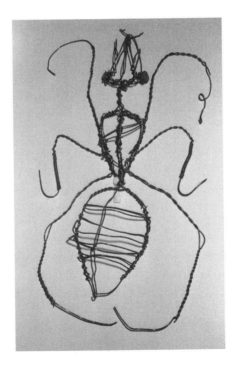

The Ant Queen

*

---

* 'The Ant's Wedding', in *Stories and Essays* (translated in *The Mirror Maker*). See Chapter 15.

Apart from learning to lose his Piedmontese accent when he spoke in public, Primo Levi never changed. He spoke quietly, dressed badly, and sat in the last row of every gathering till the end of his days. He was 'faithful in everything', as he said; but especially to his friends. Throughout the steady growth of his fame he never abandoned an old one, and hardly made a new one (with one or two exceptions, as we shall see). He stuck, above all, to friends of his own age; though he might be interested, welcoming, even warm to young people, he never made a close friendship outside his own generation.

The only exception to this rule lay in the other direction: Leonardo. For the rest of their lives after Auschwitz Leonardo and Primo remained like father and son – or, since both had their childlike sides, like brothers. Leonardo became Renzo's godfather. Lucia accepted Leonardo, as we know, and probably loved him. Alone among his friends, Leonardo became part of Primo's family; and Primo became part of his.

By now Leonardo had not just one family but two. For the first year or two after his return from Rivoli he lived with the Arturo Debenedettis – and Arturo and Luisa became good friends of Primo's too. Then, in 1947 or '48, Leonardo moved: to Corso Re Umberto 61, only a block away from Number 75. He moved in with his oldest and closest friend from medical school, Arrigo Vita, and Arrigo's two unmarried sisters, Laura and Giulia. The flat was enormous – it had been home to seven brothers and sisters, before the other four had married and left. There was plenty of room for Leonardo, and not only physically. He lived with the Vitas for the rest of their lives.

When people talk about Leonardo and the Vitas, they smile – much as they do about Alberto Salmoni, but with nostalgia for something that has gone. All three unmarried Vitas were short, plain, clever and good, and of an immense old-fashioned culture. People called them *le signorine Vita*, the Misses Vita; or sometimes, recalling the whole family, *i sette nani*, the seven dwarves. Arrigo was an oculist, Giulia taught literature in *scuola media*, and Laura, the eldest, kept house for all four. Giulia was the most severe; after living with Leonardo for twenty years, she still addressed him with the formal *Lei*. Arrigo presented a rebarbative Turinese front to the world, but behind it he was a doctor like Leonardo, who gave every ounce of himself to his patients. He was also eccentric, with a passion for going on long cycling holidays with only one change of clothes; when he treated himself to a hotel room on one of these, the manager rang his sisters to say that someone had stolen Dr Vita's identity card. And Laura – Laura was the ur-Vita, the kindest, homeliest, and most surprising of all. It was Laura who had smuggled messages to the antifascist exiles in France in her shopping basket, because she looked so harmless. She was a good deal to the left of her siblings, and after the war was the first female president of the Turin Jewish Community. But her independence was as quiet as her courage. She had never worked, except as a volunteer for many years with handicapped children; she was the sweet, soft one, and she became Leonardo's companion. They never married: perhaps because Leonardo did not want anyone to take Jolanda's place; perhaps because he too had his surprises, which included another woman, whom he did not marry either. But he and Laura Vita lived together in mutual happiness until she died. Two people with a gift for affection had found each other; which is a rare good fortune, and must have amazed and delighted Primo for his friend.

In all, Leonardo would live at Corso Re Umberto 61 for over thirty years. His consulting-rooms faced Arrigo's; streams of patients flowed through them, both private and public, and as often as not neither paid. Leonardo also worked as doctor to the Jewish orphanage, and later to the Jewish old people's home; he worked every hour of the day and night, as he had always done. When he wasn't working he read, or went to the cinema, or pored over the photographs he had taken on his holidays with the Vitas, which he loved even more than the holidays themselves. But, apart from his work, the main centres of his life were Auschwitz, and his family and friends. He joined the Italian section of the International Committee for Auschwitz; he kept in close touch with every ex-prisoner he'd ever known; he dedicated endless evenings to showing young people his photographs and slides of Auschwitz, repeating, quietly, that this had really happened. And every day of his life he went to lunch or to supper with a relative or friend: twice a week with the Arturo Debenedettis, once a week with Nella Fubini, and later with her daughter, Sandra; once a week at least with one or another of his married friends. The children and grandchildren of both Debenedettis and Vitas became his own; he never missed a birthday, an illness, a sorrow or joy. 'Officially alone', as Primo would write, Leonardo was the least lonely person who ever lived.

Primo was the opposite: the head of a family, loving and (even too much) loved; but in his deepest nature alone. Leonardo's mere presence 'eased the heart', he would write; not least his own. And for thirty years he was practically next door, in the perfect setting of No. 61. '*Il sessantuno*', as it was known in the Vitas' family, was an island of openness in the exclusivity of Crocetta and Turin. Students, patients, friends and family poured in. 'If Fascism ever returns,' the family would say, 'the first thing they'll have to do is close *il sessantuno*.'

To this island of openness Primo came whenever he could: in the evenings as long as he worked; often for lunch when he had retired, and Lucia was still teaching. Being at No. 61 was like leaving Turin without leaving it. Being with Leonardo was both remaining faithful to his Auschwitz past and yet escaping it, because Leonardo was entirely untainted by it, and despite everything a happy man. Primo always needed someone else's happiness to draw on, because he didn't have his own: and in *il sessantuno* he regularly found it.

He had another happy friend, of course: Alberto. After their joint hopes had crashed to the ground, Alberto had also entered a small chemical company – as a partner, unlike Primo. That had not lasted long, because he and his partner did not agree; and Alberto had moved to a third company, first as a chemist, but soon as a partner once again. Here he stayed for the next twelve or fifteen years. But by the time he reached his mid-forties, Alberto decided that chemistry had become too restrictive for him, and too responsible. So – with a freedom which deeply shocked his Turinese friends – he abandoned his trade, and launched himself as a businessman-entrepreneur. First he ran a beautiful gift-cum-toyshop, which must have given pleasure to both the aesthete in him and the child. But this would not last forever either. Primo would know of one more change in his friend's career, a stationery store on the Via Mazzini; after his death there would be another, a small agri-business in Umbria. These too, I think, would please Alberto, but not satisfy him. Probably nothing real could ever satisfy him: realizing each dream just made him start up another, like a boy who is always chasing the next butterfly. These were the years – the 60s and after – in which Primo wrote several times about Alberto:* but never about this quality of his, of the insatiable and drifting dreamer. It seems strange that Primo Levi should ignore such a fascinating human trait, so clearly displayed, and so close at hand. I think it shocked his Turinese soul, and in the end saddened him. But he could not bear to associate sadness with Alberto: and indeed it is impossible, Alberto will no more mix with sadness than water with oil. To the end his presence would ease Primo's heart: almost, if not quite, like Leonardo's.

His two other old and unchanging friends were of the opposite stamp, as we know. Between them they had every sterling quality but happiness. Livio Norzi was a man of huge scientific erudition and mathematical brilliance, to whom Primo himself came to learn; a good sportsman and mountaineer as well, gifted at whatever he touched. But he touched almost

---

* In 'Carne dell'orso', in the early 60s; 'Alcune applicazioni del Mimete', in the mid-60s; 'Tin' (and indirectly the other two stories of their joint adventure, 'Arsenic' and 'Nitrogen') in the mid-70s.

nothing. He was interested only in science, and in a few other brilliant, narrow people; everyone else, and any opinion other than his own, he dismissed with fierce disdain. For a time in his thirties he was engaged; but his fiancée died in a mountain accident, and he never had another. For the rest of his life he lived with his clever, overwhelming mother, and almost certainly died a virgin. He was even more oedipal and untouchable than Primo; and even more subversive of his own success, which he nonetheless desired. He could have made a (still) more brilliant career, he could have published his ideas on engineering and science, but he never did. His morbid shyness, like Primo's too, was close to pride; but in Livio's case it crossed over.

Giorgio Lattes was a great bear of a man, the warmest and least isolated of the three. His troubles were different, and came later. The girl he had fallen in love with in youth, Giuliana Orefice, had married someone else; he had waited until her marriage was over, then married her himself, and became a loving father to her two sons. After the war he had worked for a while for Olivetti in Ivrea, like most of Jewish Turin; later he opened his own small engineering firm. He lacked the powerful, focused intellects of the other two, but beneath his slow speech he hid a deep culture and a fine mind. Like Livio, part of him would have liked to have done more. But like Livio too, he did not begrudge Primo's success, but on the contrary celebrated it, and thought it was not enough. He was a gentle, generous, passive man, even less of a fighter than Primo, but someone whom everyone loved. Primo loved him, and deeply trusted him.

Primo saw these two oldest friends, alone and together, almost every week of his life. He and Livio fought long chess battles, as they had done since university. The three talked endlessly, about science and maths, about history, philosophy and politics; they had long political arguments, because Livio, alone of the three, was on the right. They had – says Alberto Piazza, one of Giorgio's sons – a world of their own; and almost a language of their own as well, a sort of family language, full of their own private references. In this language they would play impenetrable intellectual games, and hold long conversations 'on quite fantastic and useless subjects', says Alberto, 'for the sheer joy of mental exercise': like the distant rabbinical generations they had left behind. This secret language strikes me as extraordinary: the symbol of another mystery in Primo's life, this strange hermetic friendship, based on a passion for pure knowledge which hardly exists any more. What were some of their 'useless' subjects? I ask. Alberto remembers one, which would have been introduced by Livio: mathematical abstractions, and the beauty of mathematical forms. And suddenly I remember another, though I wasn't there: centaurs. The *envoi* to 'Quaestio de Centauris' is the clue:

Quaestio de Centauris et quae sit iis potandi, comedendi et nubendi ratio.
Et fuit debatuta per X hebdomadas inter vesanum auctorem
et ejusdem sodales perpetuos G.L. et L.N.

The Question of Centaurs: an account of what they eat, drink and desire,
being a subject debated for ten weeks by the present author and his lifelong companions,
G.L. and L.N.

This subject, of course, would have been introduced by Primo. I try to imagine these three *geni* (though not all *piccoli*) discussing the end of the story — Trachi's explosive rapes — even in their secret language; and fail. Surely that was Primo's private imagining.

In 1963 another pair of old friends reappeared: Ada and Silvio came home from Vercelli. Both were as *engagé* as ever, and very busy: Silvio with the *Camera di Lavoro*, Ada with her teaching, her writing, her three children. Primo and Silvio climbed together whenever they could, on weekends and holidays, and saw each other at the Saturday evening gatherings I shall describe. But until the mid-70s, when they both retired, there was no time for close friendship. That would come later. For the first dozen years or so after the Ortonas' return, Primo's real closeness was with Ada.

Ada did not see Primo as much as she would have liked either, because of their over-stretched lives, and because of Lucia's jealousy. Still, they could see each other more often than before; and the renewed link was precious to Primo. Ada was his cousin as well as one of his oldest friends; theirs was a family closeness, like sister and brother — a substitute for Anna Maria, whose special understanding Primo had lost all those years ago. He had a father-substitute in Leonardo, a mother-substitute in his Aunt Jole, whom he often went to see, and now a sister-substitute in Ada. He needed all of this, and more, because he lacked a natural sense of family support as much as he lacked happiness. But he had it all, and more, from his friends. I think he would have said, without irony, that Alberto Dalla Volta was still right, and he was a lucky man.

And what about those Saturday evening gatherings? They happened, not on every Saturday but on many, for a decade or more after the Ortonas' return. Ada kept open house: open to her children's friends during the day, and on these evenings to hers. But 'open' at the Ortonas' was still super-Turinese. Primo described something very like this group of friends in a story called 'Psicofante'.★ They are passionately open and universalist, they fiercely disapprove of any division by class or race; yet somehow 'it

---

★ Written in the late 60s and published in *Vizio di forma*.

would seem to us unnatural to receive anyone who lives north of Corso Regina Margherita or west of Corso Racconigi' – that is, outside middle-class, mainly Jewish Crocetta. Very few 'external' friends of the friends are ever accepted, nor even (Primo wrote) all their spouses; 'in the course of thirty years', therefore, the group has hardly changed.

He could hardly explain this to himself, he wrote, and it did not make him proud. But Bianca has an explanation. It went back, she says, to 1938 and the racial laws: the shock that had driven her open, trusting Jewish friends into a tight protective circle. Immediately after the war, those who had survived returned to that circle: Primo, Livio and Ada (until she married Silvio and moved to Vercelli), Alberto and Bianca, Euge and his wife Olda, Giorgio and Giuliana, Luciana and Franco Momigliano and Franco's sister Mila; plus Alberto and Miranda Levi, Giorgio Segre and his first wife, Guido Bonfiglioli and his, Edith Weisz's brother Rudi and his wife Sandra, and – apart from Bianca – just one 'representative of the *goyim*', as he says himself, Giorgio Vaccarino. Soon Luciana and Franco, Euge and Olda, the Segres and (later) the Bonfigliolis would move away from Turin; but the others would remain at the heart of that closed Jewish group which would 'hardly change for thirty years'. That is why Primo found it so hard to explain: because it was the result, and the preserved image, of the worst shared trauma of their lives; and he never liked to think that trauma, rather than reason, ruled human behaviour, least of all his own.

Despite this, or because of it, these were the people amongst whom he felt most at home. Whenever they met, he wrote in 'Psicofante', they noted with joy that they 'still spoke the same language' – not only metaphorically but actually, a family language like the one Primo spoke alone with Giorgio and Livio, and no doubt an extension of it. With them he relaxed, he expanded, he told his absurd, ironical, sharply observed stories, and was – in a quiet, homely way that did not upset him – their acknowledged star. When they exchanged news, Primo was interested in everyone's, but everyone was interested in his; 'We talked a lot about what Primo was doing and writing,' Silvio says. And then they played intellectual games – again like an extension of Primo's friendship with Giorgio and Livio. They exchanged sets of rhyming words, on which the other person had to construct a sonnet; they played complicated kinds of charades. And these games, too, suited Primo – his childlike side, his great need for fun and relaxation, so rarely satisfied; and his secret need to shine, because he and Ada were by far the best at them. Silvio remembers one particular triumph. In one of their charades, you had to act out a scene which ended on a given line. The setting, an upturned bucket in the middle of the room. Enter a guide with two tourists. Guide: 'And now for the famous statue of *Discobolus*!'

The eager tourists turn to the bucket – and shock! horror! it is bare. In runs Primo, with a plate in his hand. He leaps on to the bucket, bends and stretches into position, and speaks his line: 'I had to go out for a moment.'

This group of friends was his home. But he had one other, which intersected and overlapped with it, for example in the person of Bianca. This was a group of ex-Partito d'Azione and Giustizia e Libertà antifascists, most of them non-Jewish, and many of them slightly older, who gathered around the charismatic figure of Tina Rieser – Pavese's *donna della voce rauca* – and her kind and clever husband Henek.★ They too were middle-class and intellectual. Bianca herself was rapidly becoming a famous and extremely busy left-wing lawyer. The others included figures such as Norberto Bobbio – now one of the elder statesmen of Italy, already then a distinguished political philosopher – and his wife Valeria; Carlo Mussa, who was a chemist like Primo, and his wife Franca, who would become a psychoanalyst; an engineer called Gino Sacerdote and his wife Cesarina, who *were* Jewish; Giorgio Vaccarino and his wife Lela; and Nicoletta Neri, who was a professor of English literature, and the sister of the tragic boy who had killed himself in Primo's Qualitative Analysis laboratory, in the long-ago world before the war.† They met first at Tina Rieser's; then after Tina's death, at the Sacerdotes', and occasionally *chez* other members, including Primo and Lucia. For in this group Lucia did occasionally take part: perhaps because its solidarity was political, rather than ethnic; but mostly because these were not Primo's most intimate friends, the ones who predated her in his life, and with whom, therefore, she was locked in battle. To the meetings of *those* friends – the Jewish friends – she almost never came.

In the antifascist group I think we must imagine Primo happy, but less entirely at his ease. He admired Bobbio very much; and Bobbio, Bianca and Tina Rieser were the great leaders and talkers here. In this group, as in all groups except his own, what Primo did was listen. One evening Nicoletta Neri, just back from India, told them a harrowing traveller's tale: she had seen whole families making their homes in the water pipes waiting to be

★ Primo combined these two groups of friends in 'Psicofante', I think: making Tina and Henek the hosts, as they were in one, but the Alberto Levis and Giorgio Latteses guests, as they were in the other. (He gave all the other friends fictional names – or perhaps invented them; none of the survivors recognizes him- or herself, or admits to doing so.)

† See Chapter 4, p. 127 above. Nicoletta was one of Primo's walking friends. Others in this group were, for example, a fiery left-wing teacher, Elda Mancini, the Bovero sisters, Anna and Clara, Ester Valabrega's older sister Elda, and Joan Franzinetti, a Welsh woman who taught at the University.

laid in the streets of Calcutta. Years later Primo rang her, and asked if he could use her story of the pipes in the book he was writing.★ That was typical of Primo's extraordinary memory, Nicoletta says; and of his writer's instinct as well, because we can be sure he went home that night and wrote it down, certain it would fit into one of those many books he hoped to write, though he did not yet know which one.

These, then − plus a few families, the Accatis, the Mariottis, the Galante Garrones − were Primo's friends for the rest of his life; and the older the better. Though the most important inner movement of his life was into literature, he would have hardly any literary friends. He liked and admired Calvino, Natalia Ginzburg, and several other writers he would meet on the way − Fulvio Tomizza, Carlo Sgorlon and Rocco Scottellaro, for instance; but they remained on the edge. Or rather: Primo remained on the edge, which was his natural position. He made only two real friends among writers: both of them outsiders like himself.

The first was Mario Rigoni Stern, like Primo the author of a single famous book, and expected to remain so. Rigoni Stern's was *Il sergente nella neve*, *The Sergeant in the Snow*: a work of witness as simple and as infinitely pitiful as *Se questo è un uomo*, this time to the Italian retreat from Russia in 1943. Like Primo, Rigoni Stern went on writing, but almost secretly: stories of the high tablelands which were his home, published occasionally by Calvino (again!), or by Elio Vittorini, in left-wing magazines. After nine years Calvino suggested that there were enough stories to collect in a book, and proposed the title *Il sergente degli urogalli*, *The Sergeant of the Capercaillies*. But '*Basta con il sergente*' − 'That's enough of the sergeant' − said Rigoni Stern, who is a profoundly emotional man, but not a sentimental one. The book was published as *Il bosco degli urogalli*, *The Capercaillie Wood*, and praised for its beauty by discerning critics, led again by Franco Antonicelli. Like Primo, Rigoni Stern felt confirmed; from then on he would go on writing.

Primo had read *Il sergente* − and immediately reread it − when it came out in 1953. In 1962 he was working on his own second book when Rigoni Stern's appeared. It must have been like finding a twin he didn't know he had. He wrote at once to Rigoni Stern, telling him that *Il bosco* had given him special pleasure. It 'filled a gap in our literature', which had so little of ordinary life and of the natural world in it; and it was written as books should be written, honestly, exactly, and in the fewest possible words. He could have been describing his own hopes and aims in writing; except that there

---

★ You can find it in the ninth chapter of *The Wrench*, with Faussone's tough conclusion: 'and they were lucky, because most people slept on the sidewalks'.

was at the same time something very different in Rigoni Stern's. And that difference, I think, drew him even more. 'I hope you will go on writing,' he told Rigoni Stern; and 'I hope, too, we may find an opportunity to meet.'

Mario rarely left his high fortress near Asiago, and time passed. At Christmas Primo said in an interview that he would like to spend it in a mountain refuge with Rigoni Stern. Mario wrote to him and said 'Come'; but Primo couldn't come. Finally, however, even Mario had to see his publisher, who was also Primo's. The two met at Einaudi. Mario Rigoni Stern was not only a writer after Primo's heart: after the retreat from Russia he had had twenty months in Nazi Lagers. They became friends instantly, with a few words.

Given their situations, however, they saw each other rarely. They spoke on the phone, they exchanged letters; they met at schools and talked about their Lagers. And once or twice Primo and Lucia came together to Asiago. Mario and his wife Anna have a warm Alpine house, with rugs on the walls as well as the floors, in the Austrian style; it feels welcoming, secure. But the springs of Rigoni Stern's imagination are outside, in the woods and wide spaces he writes about in his spare, sensual prose. Primo envied his friend this vast, high, open world, which seemed to him empty and silent, but in which birds and animals lived their separate animal lives, and Mario could sense and almost share them. Primo loved Mario's country dweller's lore: how he could spot the small, sticky balls of skin and bone which are the 'vomit of owls' — all the bits of their prey they cannot digest, and redeposit on the ground; or the tiny snaking hillocks of snow, where a mouse runs past you underneath it. Such observations Primo would pass on eagerly to his friends on their mountain walks as soon as he got home.

But Mario's relation to his land was more than this, even more than a deep knowledge and celebration. It was an acceptance, an identification, a belonging; and this Primo deeply envied, but could not share. Mixed into his own fascination with nature was more than a grain of the scientist's detachment, and the city dweller's fear. Rigoni Stern remembers one spring morning on the Levis' first visit, when Primo asked to see his bees. Lucia came and stood beside him as he opened the hives; but — even though it had been his idea — Primo hung back, afraid. They won't hurt you, Mario said; but Primo recalled a story of bees who had drunk *grappa*, and had sacked other hives, like drunken, rampaging humans. They don't have to get drunk to do that, Mario said, they just do it sometimes. But that only confirmed Primo's feeling: at its heart nature was cold and cruel; animals had instincts, but no feelings, and if a doe resisted a buck he would rip her apart with his horns. That is true, Mario would say, but life must go on; it is neither idyllic nor cruel, but simply as it is. Primo would tease him when he smiled to see a rabbit nibbling the grass beneath his window, or a squirrel scratching for bread at his door: 'They come because they're hungry,' Primo would say, 'not to please you.' Of course Mario knew that; but he could not help being moved, any more than Primo could help his scepticism, or his fear.

Primo admitted his deep envy of Rigoni Stern's love of the land to his urban friends; but with Mario himself he argued and sparred, and defended *his* land of technology and science. When Mario railed against the pollution of the cities by science and industry, Primo said that only science and industry could cure it: if necessary, we would walk the streets with masks on our faces, and oxygen tanks on our backs, and life would carry on. That would not be life, Mario would say; but Primo would only smile. Of course we will always try to improve things, Mario would say, we needn't be nature's slaves; but neither will nature be ours, it will rebel and go its own way. Maybe you are right, and science can solve the problems of pollution; but it cannot make a leaf. Then Primo would smile again and say, one day science will do that too. And it seems now he was right, though he has not lived to see it.

In the same year that Primo first wrote to Mario – 1962 – Einaudi published another great book of witness to the war: *La guerra dei poveri, Poor People's War*, by Nuto Revelli. Nuto was a Piedmontese like Primo, born and bred in Cuneo. In 1942 he had been a patriotic Fascist, and an eager young officer whose father had dreamt of seeing him a General one day. Then came the Russian front, with his poor *alpini* who had only mules against the Russian tanks, who were underarmed and underfed, trained for the mountains and sent to fight on the plain; and after that the retreat, in which they died like flies, abandoned and despised by their German allies. By the time he reached home Nuto was almost mad with anger and despair. He fought passionately against the Fascism that had misled and betrayed them, first for the eighteen months of the partisan war, then, like Primo and Mario, in years of writing.* He had kept a war diary in Russia (in microscopic

---

* After *La guerra dei poveri* he would publish a collection of interviews with forty survivors of the Russian retreat, *La strada del davai*, in 1966, and in 1971 *L'ultimo fronte*, letters from soldiers who were declared missing, but whose bodies were never found. In the 70s and 80s he published two extraordinary books of interviews with the rural poor of the Cuneese (*Il mondo dei vinti*, 1977, and *L'anello forte*, 1985); in the 90s he returned to the theme of the war with *Il disperso di Marburg* (1994).

Mario Rigoni Stern's later books are: *La guerra della naja alpina* (1967), *Quota Albania* (1971), and *Il ritorno sul Don* (1973), all on the subject of the war; and *Storie di Tönle* (1978), *Uomini, bosche e api* (1980), *L'anno della vittoria* (1985), *Amore di confine* (1986), *Arboreto selvatico* and *Il libro degli animali* (1991), like *Il bosco degli urogalli* evocations of his land.

writing, because he had been afraid to run out of paper); on that he based his first book, *Mai tardi*, written immediately, like *Se questo è un uomo*, and published in Cuneo in 1946. Now, for *La guerra dei poveri*, he added his diary of the partisan war; and his pity and fury leap off the page.

Primo read *La guerra dei poveri*, Nuto read *La tregua*, and when they met some time after that, Nuto says, 'we were already friends.' They did not meet often either: twice or three times a year, when Primo went to speak to a school in Cuneo, or Nuto to one in Turin, or when they spoke at one together. But each time they met it was as though their conversation had ended only the day before. They rarely spoke of the past – they had read each other, and heard each other's stories often in schools (and even after many times, Primo was moved). Instead they laughed and joked, and talked about work; Primo was fascinated by Nuto's researches for *La strada del davai*. Later, in the mid-70s and 80s, when they had a bit more time and money, they went to the wonderful local restaurants of the Langhe together, like good Piedmontese; Nuto introduced Primo to Bartolo Mascarello, one of the great producers of Barolo wine, and Primo would relax and enjoy himself so much he would buy several of Mascarello's delicious and expensive bottles.

Everyone knew these three witness writers – Levi, Rigoni Stern, Revelli – were friends. At Einaudi they were called 'the Ponchiroleans', because (until his sadly early death) Daniele Ponchiroli was their editor, champion and friend. In Turin they were called *il trifoglio*, the three-leaf-clover – not only, I think, because they grew from the same stem, but because together they seemed a lucky charm, a triple proof that it was possible to emerge whole from war, and tell the tale. All three were mavericks, outsiders, thorns in the side of the literary world: Primo a humble chemist, Mario an official in the Land Registry, Nuto a salesman of metal products. All three were *scrittori civili*, 'civic writers' awarded moral but not literary stature – whereas, in fact, all three were artists in prose, and creators of rich worlds. And yet at the same time they were utterly different, as writers and as men. Mario is a poet-storyteller, Primo a philosopher-storyteller, Nuto an historian-storyteller. Primo was, of course, the rationalist of the three: both Mario and Nuto are instinctive writers, and deeply emotional men. Both are Primo's opposites: soldiers and fighters, strong but at the same time gentle. Nuto would laugh at that. He is bad, he says, *cattivo*: the primitive, aggressive one of the three, who hated and killed Germans for all of them. But that was more than half a century ago. If Primo's goal since then was to understand Germans, Nuto's was simply not to hate them; which was almost as difficult, but not impossible. And in his latest book, about a missing German soldier, he achieved it. For him, he says, the war was finally over in 1994. I think it is over for Mario too, healed by the constant renewal of seasons. That was the last difference between Primo and his only literary friends.

Already in the writing, his short stories made him feel guilty, afraid of offending both his survivor friends and his readers. Would they not think (like Franco Antonicelli) that Primo Levi should remain the author of his first book only, or at most of his first two? Was offering them these 'entertainments' not a kind of fraud, 'like someone who sells wine in bottles made for oil'? He felt, he would say later, a deserter from his cause.

He was not wrong. When the stories first appeared in newspapers, he had several dismayed and even angry letters from readers: as he had feared, they felt betrayed. There was nothing he dreaded more than hurting people, especially these people. And yet, and yet . . . He knew perfectly well that his stories were not really entertainments, but satires on human hubris very like that which had led to the Lager – sometimes, indeed, the same. He was fond of them, even proud of some of them; and he did not at all agree that he should remain the author of one or even two books. He *wanted* to publish them – and not only in newspapers, but in a book, 'so that they would not be lost'.

Between them, Primo and his publisher worked out a solution to his dilemma, which promptly made it worse. Perhaps because of this, it is hard to be absolutely certain whose idea it was. Sometimes Primo said it was his, sometimes that it came from Einaudi, specifically from their commercial director, Roberto Cerati. Cerati says it was his idea; and a letter he wrote to Primo at the time appears to confirm it. Certainly Einaudi were as worried as Primo that this book would shock his readers. So Cerati, it seems, proposed that *Storie naturali* be published under a pseudonym; and Primo readily agreed.

That was not the end of it, however. 'Primo Levi' on *this* book might shock, but it was a well-known name; while for obvious reasons no one had ever heard of 'Damiano Malabaila', the pseudonym Primo had chosen. Besides, Einaudi hoped that once his readers knew that Primo shared their worries, they would forgive him; and no doubt so did he. So Cerati conceived the whole thing as immediately transparent, a cover meant to be blown; and once more Primo agreed. The book was printed with the name Damiano Malabaila on the cover; but with a blurb – once again by Calvino – which included a long quotation from the author, expressing his doubts and hesitations, and with every word (especially 'I entered the world of writing with two books on the concentration camps') clearly identifying him as Primo Levi.

It didn't work. Reviewers might indeed have been shocked to find Primo

Levi's name on this book; but when they found Damiano Malabaila's covering it – and only just, like a teasingly short skirt – they were insulted.★ Paolo Milano cast his early and important review in the form of an open letter to Primo, refusing to believe that he would partake in a publicity stunt, and thus instantly convincing everyone that he had; and pointing out that if it was wrong for Primo Levi to write 'entertainments', simply signing them with another name would make no difference. That took up almost half his review; and other critics followed. Many said rather crossly that the link between these stories and the two great books was perfectly plain – man and his deformations – and implied that Primo needn't have bothered to explain. One – Vittorio Spinazzela – was so annoyed he said so openly, and went on to demolish the stories, especially the best ones ('generic and outdated moralizing').

In fact, however, even he had some kinder words for their style; and in general, underneath the criticism for 'Damiano Malabaila' there was a good deal of praise for Primo Levi. Several reviews – including the first, in *La Stampa* – were unreservedly positive. The most intelligent – such as one by Giorgio Calcagno, a *Stampa* journalist who would later become a friend – said that the stories were uneven in quality and tone; but that the best were glorious, 'amongst the most successful [pages] of our recent fiction'. Milano himself – when he got to the stories – said much the same. The greatest praise, from him and others, came for 'Angelica Farfalla', 'Versamina', 'Trattamento di quiescenza' and – from Calcagno, for instance – for 'L'amico dell'uomo'. 'The reader need not fear,' Calcagno wrote. 'Primo Levi's wine is good, and has been poured into the right bottle.'

On the whole, then, the *Natural Histories* themselves were more approved than disapproved of by the critics; and in January 1967 a jury which included Dino Buzzato and Eugenio Montale awarded the book the Premio Bagutta – the poorest and purest prize in Italy, worth only 100,000 *lire*. That perhaps consoled Primo for the conflict over Damiano Malabaila, and for the first harsh criticism his work had ever received. For there was some, apart from Spinazzela's. The editors of the *Quaderni piacentini* were so intemperate ('a hybrid failure: bad literature, worse science fiction') that Cesare Cases was

---

★ And why did he pick *that* name? they wondered. Surely 'Malabaila' was a play on '*cattiva balia*', a bad wet-nurse – that is, a symbol of the book's theme, poison in place of nourishment, 'fair is foul and foul is fair'? Primo naturally avoided all analytic explanations of his actions, and he did so again here: it was a name he saw over a shop he passed twice a day, he said; he simply liked it, and used it, and its meaning did not occur to him until later. I suspect this seemed like another evasion; adding to people's impression that he was hiding from them, that he was afraid of their response to this book. Which, of course, he was.

moved to write a long and brilliant letter in Primo's defence. Lorenzo Mondo – another *Stampa* journalist who would become a friend – rated only the most serious stories, and dismissed the satires as too comic for their intended effect; and one or two others agreed. Walter Pedullà, on the other hand, thought that the *Storie naturali* weren't comic enough; which only goes to show that no matter what you do, someone will disapprove. The problem was that this was Pedullà: which meant that the only top critics to review the book, Milano and Pedullà, were largely negative. Even worse, others – Carlo Bo, for example, and Primo's first champion Franco Antonicelli – didn't review it at all. Antonicelli's abstention in particular must have hurt. Primo would always long to write fiction, and yet fear it. His fear had added to the difficult birth of *Storie naturali*; and now the difficult birth of *Storie naturali* added to his fear. He already had the idea for his only novel, *Se non ora, quando?*; but he wouldn't write it for another fifteen years.

★   ★

In fact, something unusual happened after *Storie naturali* – something unique in Primo Levi's life after Auschwitz. He stopped writing. It is not clear exactly when: when the last of the *Natural Histories* was written, either in 1966, or already in 1964.★ This pause lasted until 1968. In that year a great wave of new writing began – the twenty stories of *Vizio di forma*, all written over the next two years; and several of the stories about chemistry he had first talked about in 1963, and had started then or soon after, but which he'd felt were failures, and had abandoned. It was as though in 1968 a dam burst, which had been firmly fixed for the previous two (or even four) years. Now, we must not exaggerate – if on one level Primo was infinitely discourageable, on another he was not at all. And there were many reasons for the dam, as we shall see. But his fears for *Storie naturali*, and their painful confirmation, were surely among them.

And the others? Both Fiora Vincenti and Gabriella Poli say that the mid-60s were years of intense reading and re-reading for Primo, both in science and in his favourite authors, Conrad, Rabelais, the poets Belli and Porta. They were years in which he began to write occasionally for *La*

★ Five of the stories appeared in *Il Giorno* at approximately six-month intervals between 1964 and 1966. This may have been Primo's rate of production, or else *Il Giorno*'s rate of acceptance; it is hard to say which. Fiora Vincenti says firmly that the writing of the *Natural Histories* was over by 1964, which must be what Primo himself told her. On the other hand, in *Echi di una voce perduta* Gabriella Poli implies that he wrote several of the stories of *Storie naturali* (and several 'essays' as well) after the radio production of *Se questo*, i.e. after April 1964.

Stampa and other papers – on science, on the Lager – and for an increasing number of conferences and publications on deportation. They were peak years for his 'third career', with *La tregua* appearing in a schools edition in 1965. And they were years of travel: for SIVA, to Germany, England, Scandinavia, and to Russia for the first time; his one and only visit to Israel, in 1968; and in 1965 to Auschwitz, together with Leonardo and Laura Vita, and another survivor and friend, Giuliana Tedeschi. It was twenty years since the liberation; there were ceremonies, speeches, 'everything cleaned up', Primo said, both the place and the people. This first return had little effect on him; the second would have more.

Above all, however, there would be two clear reasons for the gap in his writing after *Storie naturali*. And there was also one more.

The first reason was SIVA. In 1965 or '66 the company got its first big Russian contract, and its heyday began. For the next seven or eight years, until the oil crisis of 1973–4 stopped Western industry in its tracks, SIVA boomed and grew, and Primo's day-job with it. He was in the office every day 'from 8 to 8' – or at any rate from 8.15 to 7; at nights, on weekends, on holidays he was on call – and 'every blessed day', he said with pardonable exaggeration, the call came. He had never had enough time to write; now he had no time at all.

Still there were, in these boom years, many compensations. Success was quite pleasant in itself, and no doubt his salary benefited as well. SIVA was a wonderful source of stories, both chemical and human: he loved telling factory anecdotes, especially in these years; and most of the ideas for *Vizio di forma*, he would say, had come to him in the laboratory. Several of the stories show an intimate knowledge of the problems of working with hostile, competitive or incompetent colleagues; and Primo naturally had his share of those. But most of his fellow-workers were congenial, and several were almost friends.

First, for instance – from the late 50s to 1970, when he left – there was his 'pupil', Francesco Cordero; and from 1965 Renato Portesi, who was a trained chemist, but also a kind of autodidact – a voracious reader, and a collector of degrees, of which (at last count) he holds three. For men like these – serious, modest, eager for knowledge – Primo had great respect, and also sympathy; perhaps they reminded him of the few things he liked about his father, and about himself. To both he talked openly of the Lager; to Portesi he told some episodes so terrible that, as he spoke, his hands trembled. He showed the chapters of *The Periodic Table* to them, and asked for their opinions; he even 'put me into the book', Cordero says with pride – turning his younger pupil into his teacher, 'Signor Giacomasso Olindo', who was 'over seventy, and had been making varnishes for fifty years'. Primo was fascinated by the expressions and sayings Cordero had brought from his corner of Piedmont – and Cordero does him to the life, leaning forward like a dog on a leash, barking 'What did you say?', and writing them down. When Cordero heard Piero Selvestrel turn '*gomma Manilla*' (Manila rubber) into '*gomma maniglia*' (handle rubber), he rushed this gem to Primo straight away, for his inventory of domesticated alien words.★

With Portesi he talked of books – of Mann, of Joyce, of Kafka, of Manzoni; and of many many more. His private opinions were the same as his public ones, here as elsewhere. Mann was his favourite, *Joseph and his Brothers* 'the greatest novel of the nineteenth century'; he lent it to Portesi, and insisted he read it. About Joyce's *Ulysses* he said, 'Ah, the great insanity of *Ulysses*' – but wonderingly, admiringly, Portesi says; just as, though his gospel was clarity, when he read a wild obscure book like Stefano D'Arrigo's *Horcynus Orca* 'everything [flew] out the window', and *Horcynus Orca* flew into *The Search for Roots*, his anthology of personal favourites – together with difficult, brilliant Paul Celan. Altogether, Portesi says, Primo spoke as he wrote, *was* as he wrote. When he, Portesi, reads him, it is as though Primo is standing once again before him. His quiet, clear way of speaking, so that you understood immediately; and underneath always the hint of an ironic smile . . . And now Portesi imitates him too – just like Cordero, and just as well. Primo seems to have impressed both these men as he imagined could only happen in youth, 'before the wax hardens': so that, for a moment, they almost become him. Portesi hunches his shoulders a little, like Cordero, and leans forward a little too. '*Vede, Portesi,*' he says, in Primo's voice – 'You see, Portesi'; and he gives me Primo's lesson on thrift in boiling water: 'Water boils at 100°. If you heat it higher, it boils desperately; but still at 100°.' And the solemn way he says 'desperately' is irresistibly comic.

Both Cordero and Portesi loved Primo, but only Portesi understood him. Cordero is like a one-man symbol of post-war Italy: the son of a poor farmer, who with volcanic energy and ambition transformed himself into a modern industrialist, and a major employer in the place where he was born. *Il Dottor Levi* was his university, he says; everything he knows, and so everything he has, he owes to him. If he had had any ambition at all, he could have won the Nobel Prize, or built an empire bigger than Accati's, or Cordero's own. But he hadn't, not an ounce. All he wanted to do was write, Cordero says, shaking his head; and he opens his hands in front of him, like someone giving away everything he owns. That, I see, is his vision of Primo;

★ It's not in the final version of the *jeu d'esprit* Primo wrote on the subject, 'L'aria conges- tionata' ('Air Congestioning'), but it probably was once. He revised his list, Cordero remembers, every year.

and suddenly it gives him a new vision of himself. He went away, he had
his great success, and he never thanked Primo, he says; and his eyes fill with
tears.

With Portesi it was different, because Primo and Portesi were rather the
same. Portesi too is shy and unworldly; and a quietly humorous, quietly
observant man. His pictures of Primo are sharp and tender. Primo's extraordinary precision and pleasure in the laboratory, 'like an eighteenth-century
chemist', wanting to do everything himself, and with his own nose, mouth
and hands. His childlike pleasure in telling stories, in playing games ('You
are on a desert island, how do you invent steel?'), in getting Portesi to guess
the model for a character in a story: 'Think hard, think hard! Can't you
tell?' His gentleness, even meekness – but to a bully, or a show-off, his
condemnation would radiate as he turned away. To Renato Portesi, Primo
was a hero; but at the same time he felt his sadness. It was Portesi who
noticed the intensity of Primo's effort to communicate, as though he had to
do it perfectly, to have any hope of success at all. And it is Portesi who says
one of the saddest things: 'Perhaps Primo Levi was continually disappointed
by the world.'

There were, finally, two other, very characteristic friends. One was Marco
Magnanti, a chemist who came to SIVA in the early 60s, and lasted only
about five years. He was a lazy, fun-loving Roman; in Primo's own words,
he was 'the Cesare of the situation'. Primo loved laughing at his jokes, and
teased him if he didn't produce them. When Magnanti left to go back to
Rome, Cordero says, 'Primo suffered'.

The last friend, happily, lasted much longer: from 1956 to 1973. This was
Signora Orsola Azzario Ferrero: Orsolina, the redoubtable SIVA cleaner.
Orsolina, like Cordero, came from Piedmontese peasant stock; like Cordero,
she was a prodigious worker, and very intelligent – 'The most intelligent
person in this company is Orsolina,' Accati used to say, and not only when
he was angry with all the others. But she was one of sixteen children, and
like the rest she started work at fourteen. By twenty-eight she was a widow
with two young sons. At forty-two she arrived at SIVA, and promptly took
it over.

Well, she says, they needed her. It was so grey, so dull. The women all
looked like nuns, in long dark aprons, and not a touch of colour on their
faces; she is a deeply pious Catholic, but a woman should look like a woman,
even at work. She told them so (most of Orsolina's stories begin, 'I told
them so'); and soon bits of colour began to appear, 'shyly at first, like flowers
in a meadow'. Then she set about the old house in the Via Leinì, and cleaned
it to within an inch of its life; and kept it that way for the next seventeen

years – all by hand, she says proudly; to this day she won't have a machine in her house. After that she would go on little errands for everyone; and finally – by now it might be eight at night – out to pick daisies in the field behind the factory, and put them on the desks of her favourite people, especially Primo.

For Orsolina, too, deeply loved him. '*Ah, mio bambino,*' she says, '*il bambino del laboratorio*' – the baby of the laboratory. He was a saint, she says, and now her eyes too fill with tears. He was so kind, so fair, so good to everyone, in particular to her. Once, when there was a special display of Christmas lights in the Via Roma he took her to see them – 'And he a Jew, Signora!', and an atheist himself, as he told her. But he had such respect for everyone, and especially for religion. (But everyone likes to think that he secretly preferred whatever they did – chemists chemistry, writers writing, the religious religion.) When her son Mario was ordained, he was so interested, and wanted to meet him; they went to the Corso Re Umberto and met his family – and you should have seen the concierge, Orsolina laughs, when a priest came to call on the Levis!

And of course she taught him things too: how to smile, she says, and how to talk. When she came to SIVA he was so serious, all he did was work. But with her he would relax, he would chat, 'he would even laugh'. That is what he needed, she says – someone to make him laugh, to distract him from his obsessions: work and the Lager. When she left, he missed her. She

Orsolina's farewell, 1973
Primo and Orsolina are on the right, with Renato Portesi (in glasses)
in front of them

came back on a visit once, and when he saw her he leapt up from his chair and *hugged* her. His friends, his family – they were all too complicated, like him; they couldn't help him, especially at the end. Now Orsolina holds out her hands too, but in a different gesture from Cordero's. 'I would have caught him,' she says.

In truth, Primo had another SIVA friend: but this was a more complicated story.

It started in 1966, when the Russian connection began. SIVA needed a Russian speaker – and possibly also an English and French speaker, if such a multiple linguist could be found. One was: a young woman called Tullia Ami. She was hired, and given the office next to Primo's.

Tullia was a very different kind of woman from Orsolina, especially for Primo. Orsolina came from another world entirely; she was older, simpler, and of a transparent religious chastity. Tullia was nearly twenty years younger than Primo, married but without children; and she came from his own world. Her Russian was excellent, her English and French as good as, if not better than, his; she had a degree in English literature, and had spent a year in America, which he had never seen. She was direct and combative, certain of her own opinions, and determined to push them through without charm or manipulation. This was unusual for a young woman in Italy; and so was her appearance. Italian women seem to be born beautifully dressed, with extreme feminine grace and expensively cut hair. Not Tullia Ami. She chopped her hair short, walked like a man, and wore unflattering clothes. In fact, if you looked carefully, she had a good face and a tiny, slender body. Most men didn't look, which was no doubt her intention. But Primo the observer, the outsider, ill at ease in his own body, did look. And she looked back at him.

That there was something between them everyone could see; but what it was no one could tell. Primo had an English friend, a fellow chemist called Keith Barnes; not even Keith, who is not Italian, could see through Tullia's disguise, or for that matter Primo's. There *couldn't* be sex between them, he thought; and yet there was a very powerful feeling. It baffled Keith, but he was sure: Primo was in love with someone, and it was Tullia Ami.

He was wrong, I think, for a reason we shall soon see. What was between Primo and Tullia was not love, but something else: a fascination with each other's difference, perhaps, and a strong intellectual sympathy. But that too ends in sex, if at all possible; and for Primo the possibility could best exist away from home. In 1968 Tullia moved away from SIVA to SICME; but he made at least two trips to Russia with her in the early 70s. Lucia was desperately jealous, and this time she was probably right. But by then Primo had given up any real hope of sexual love. His affair with Tullia Ami, if it was one, began and ended in Russia. Alas, we cannot ask her (though she would not have told us anyway): she survived him by only four years, dying of cancer at fifty-four.

Around 1965 or '66, then, SIVA began to interfere with Primo's writing even more than before. It took more time, and it took more toll on his nervous energy.

He liked to keep things in separate compartments; but then the compartmentalization itself became a strain. At SIVA everyone really knew he was a writer, but he tried to keep it hidden. Apart from closer friends like Cordero, no one ever saw him take a note. He never talked of his other life; sometimes he even denied it. Once, for example, a visiting Yugoslav chemist asked if he was the Levi who had written 'the famous book'. Primo's expression darkened for an instant; then 'calmly, and with a strange glint in his eye, he said: "There is a Carlo Levi who has written a famous book, and who is also a great painter; perhaps you are thinking of him."'* But when SIVA workers asked him to sign his books for them, he did so willingly. And as his fame grew, Accati started to present his books to clients, even asking him to sign copies for the best and favourite ones. At first he was very reluctant, Paola remembers; but soon she felt that he was also secretly pleased. That was his struggle, which did not end.

And then there were the accidents, and the fear of accidents. When interviewers asked him in 1980, long after he had retired, if he had made any terrible mistakes in his life, he said no. Many many ordinary ones, of course, but nothing truly terrible: he was at peace with himself, he said, because he had got through nearly thirty years of chemical responsibility without a fatal accident. Now, that was true, but also not true. There had been no fatal accidents, but there had been many others; and if he could face them peacefully now they were safely over, that hadn't been true at the time.

We already know of two fires and one near explosion; and there were at least half a dozen more. One involved Orsolina – a faulty mixing machine flung hot acid in her face, and Primo came running with a mirror, to reassure her that the damage was not serious. Another happened while he and Portesi were working on a new product together. Again there was a violent explosion, one wall collapsed, and the product was abandoned. Among Primo's retirement presents were test-tubes of all SIVA's resins; and one broken, blackened tube, with the name of this disaster on it.†

---

* From an account by Felice Malgaroli, another friend and sensitive observer of Primo at SIVA.

† It was the 'trimellitic anhydride (Bang!)' of Portesi's list (see page 482 above).

All these, however, had one saving grace: as Director he might be ultimately responsible for them, but they were not *his fault*. It was that he could not bear. He narrowly escaped it once, on that freezing, foggy New Year's Eve when the petrol tanker overturned outside SIVA's door. But from this point in the mid-60s on, three times altogether he did not escape, but was personally responsible for serious accidents.

One happened a little later, in the early 70s. It involved a storage tank for phenol, which he had designed himself, with a special valve for releasing controlled amounts under pressure. His design was faulty, the valve broke, and hundreds of gallons of the stinking and highly toxic chemical escaped before the situation was brought under control. This time he was away, and didn't hear of the disaster until it was over. That was slightly easier; he accepted responsibility immediately, and (perhaps) without too much pain.

In 1967, however, there was an event which affected him more closely. In that year SIVA's famous tower was built, which until a few years ago

The SIVA tower

could be seen from the Turin–Milan motorway. Ironically, this tower was an early monument to Primo's concern for safety: for its function was to separate the acetic acid from the water which had been used in the PVF process, and thus to discharge clean instead of toxic water into the Settimo waste system for the first time in fifteen years. But this huge ecological improvement was at first a near disaster; and it was Primo's fault. He had designed the tower, directed its construction, and instructed the workers in its use. For the first few nights he had stayed at SIVA, to make sure all was well. Finally he went home – to be called back almost immediately. What greeted him was so terrifying that he put it in detail into *The Wrench*, ten years later. In Faussone's words, the tower had developed 'like an attack, every five minutes'. It started with a hum, then a vibration, then a dreadful, mounting shake, like an earthquake; until finally there was a muffled *swoosh*, and once again the hum. No one had any idea what to do, or what the problem could be; but if the central tube cracked, or exploded, half of Settimo would be flooded with acid water. Now, despite his fear before and his guilt after, Primo was good in emergencies: his habit of self-control took over, and he was focused and cool. In *The Wrench* the tower's designer (the only one who knows how) comes and shuts the whole process down; and I think that was what happened. The designer – that is, Primo – shut the tower down safely; at last there was silence, and he had not drowned Settimo in acid.

Slowly he worked out what had gone wrong: the ceramic rings they'd used to line the tube had crumbled under the pressure. The debris had to be flushed out, and stainless steel disks put in instead: by someone crawling, inch by inch, up 100 feet of dark tube, 'like a rat in a snake's belly'. Primo writes with great feeling of this experience, though he wouldn't have had it himself: putting into it all his horror of entrapment, and of that narrowly escaped disaster.

Later, in *The Double Bond*, he would write about his third and last calamity, once again, I think, from the early 70s. This one was not a brief emergency, but a long-drawn-out crisis; and it was nearly fatal not to individual people, but to SIVA as a whole. Once again he would put it into *The Wrench*: but in disguised form, so as not to give away (he said) company secrets.★

In fact, what the disguise of *The Wrench* covered was not so much SIVA's secrets as his own failure: for there the problem is someone else's fault, and his company is absolved; whereas in reality the opposite of both was true. A complaint had arrived from a client: SIVA's copper wire had developed a fault. For welding purposes, the client company needed to coat the ends of

★ See 'Anchovies' I and II, the third-to-last and last chapters of *The Wrench*.

the wire in tin, which they did by dipping them into the tin in molten form. With SIVA's competitor's wire – and with SIVA's own wire, up to a few months before – this was a quick and easy procedure. But no longer: now, when they immersed SIVA's wire in the molten tin, it carbonized, and the tin would not adhere.

At first this did not seem a major disaster, but it quickly became one. The competitor spread the word, and more and more clients defected. Primo spent whole days and nights in the laboratory, as though he were back in Avigliana with his blocks of livered paint. After a while he started to close in on his prey: but only slowly, because he was afraid it was himself. For years now their formula had been perfected, their sales excellent and their clients satisfied; there had been nothing to do but sit back and sell. There had been only one tiny defect in their enamel: one of the solvents it contained reacted with the iron of the tanks in which it was stored, and if it was kept for long, it turned brown. This didn't affect its function, and was a purely aesthetic failing; but out of pure perfectionism, Primo decided to solve it. He checked that the solvent did not react with zinc; and then he had all the tanks containing both it and the enamel zinc-lined. Now SIVA's enamel not only *was* perfect, but looked perfect as well.

The trouble was that suddenly it wasn't perfect any longer. After several weeks of evasive tests, Primo forced himself to carry out the one that really mattered. He divided some of the enamel solution among three containers, and put a glass ball into the first, a zinc-covered tin into the second, and an iron drum into the third. After a week, though the enamel in the third container had turned brown, it accepted tin as well as the first. But copper wire covered with the second sample carbonized, and savagely rejected the tin. The culprit had been found – or rather, two culprits: the zinc, and the Director.

This crisis, Primo wrote, was the worst in SIVA's history; it cost him many sleepless nights, and 'a virtual nervous breakdown'. He did not say the same of the tower crisis, which was indeed less severe. But it was the first serious accident for which he was personally responsible; and we can be certain that it profoundly disturbed him. One reason for the gap in his writing after *Storie naturali* was probably 'a virtual nervous breakdown' around 1967.

The second reason was a happier one, especially at the start. He was experimenting with a new medium for things he had already written: drama.

In fact, he had always been interested in dramatic form, as he had always been interested in poetry; only his identification as a *scrittore non scrittore* meant that it was a long time before anyone noticed. Already in *La tregua* the theatre scenes carry many of his key meanings. And three of the fifteen stories of *Storie naturali* are in the form of plays – including two of the earliest, 'The Sixth Day', which goes right back to 1946, and 'The Sleeping Beauty in the Fridge', which goes back to 1952. In the early 1960s the RAI began to commission radio plays from writers; and – again, perhaps, through Franco Antonicelli, with his wide cultural contacts – Primo Levi was among them. 'The Sleeping Beauty in the Fridge' was recorded in Florence in June 1961, and broadcast in November. Primo did not say whether he enjoyed this experience; but we can guess. That same month he sat down to write *La tregua*, and finished it a year later. Soon after it was published he received a letter from Canada: the CBC had produced a radio version of *Se questo è un uomo*. The script and tape-recording soon followed. These were among the best presents he had ever received, Primo said. The authors had seen deep into one of his main themes: the dehumanization of the prisoners by the inability to communicate, by the babel of mutually incomprehensible languages. This babel of voices they had made the heart of their play. Primo was so thrilled – both by the play itself, and by the possibilities of radio that it revealed to him – that he immediately wrote his own version, and proposed it to the RAI. It was accepted in early 1964; and he had embarked on the work which would occupy the next four years.

The mid-60s was a time of great French influence on Italy, especially in student politics – up to and after *les événements* – and in the arts. The *nouvelle vague* was shaking up cinema all across Europe, spilling film-makers out of the studios and on to the streets, and making them look for their actors among ordinary people. The gifted young director chosen by the RAI, Giorgio Bandini, was at the heart of this movement; it was perfect for *Se questo è un uomo*, and for Primo; and this radio production was one of his happiest experiences.

They recorded its scenes outdoors, in the village of Brozolo in the Monferrato, about twenty-five miles from Turin: the people there still wore clogs, and the village streets sounded exactly like the roads of Auschwitz. Not during the day, of course, with cars and crowds and Piedmontese voices: so they worked at night, from nine to midnight, under the lights of reflectors. It was late winter, the nights were cold and dark and veiled in fog; the reflector lights were not enough, and the actors had to wear torches around their necks to see their scripts. Among them were only three or four professionals, including Nanni Bertorelli, who played Aldo (the name Primo had given himself), and a French actor who played Pikolo. The rest were ordinary people: many of them foreigners living in Turin, because Primo was eager to keep to the Canadian theme of Babel. There was a Russian, for instance, and an Italian Russian expert; a Polish industrialist, and the

German-Jewish wife of the RAI's doctor, who both spoke Yiddish; and four poor Germans who played SS officers, and whom everyone couldn't help hating.

Primo was fascinated by the whole process of re-creation, especially its new and technical aspects – the sound effects, the microphones, the recording. He chatted happily with the actors, he followed every aspect of the production with eager attention. But these dark nights – with their tall lights piercing the fog, with the sound of the clogs and the babel of voices – these nights were indeed evocative of Auschwitz, not only for the audience. Once or twice the young actor playing Alberto saw Primo glance up uneasily at the lights; and once, when they set a door on fire to reproduce the crackling of flames, Giorgio Bandini saw him pale and walk away.

The work took two months (two months, and forty-seven actors! – those were the days, says Bandini), and the original result was two and a half hours long. Primo left the cutting to Bandini. *Se questo è un uomo* was broadcast on 24 April, the eve of the nineteenth anniversary of the Liberation. It was much praised; and started a new cycle of attention to the book and its subject, which must have pleased Primo most of all.

Success encouraged both him and everyone else, and other work followed. For years Massimo Scaglione, director of Turin's experimental Teatro delle Dieci, had been asking Primo for a play. In 1965 Primo offered him the three playlets of *Storie naturali*; and in February 1966 they appeared, in the tiny Teatro Romano (which was really the foyer of a cinema, lent for many seasons to the young company). At the same time the RAI commissioned the same three playlets for the radio, as well as radio versions of 'Angelica Farfalla', 'Versamina' and 'Some Applications of the Mimer': all directed by Scaglione, and all broadcast during 1965 and 1966. 'The Versifier' was done again in 1967, and 'Retirement Fund' in 1968; after which Primo went back to the page.

Apart from a major (seven-part) production of *La tregua* in 1978, that was the end of his radio career. It had been a fascinating excursion; but once he had worked out the linguistic inspiration of the Canadian script for both his Lager books, he had got what he wanted out of radio. The rest was entertainment. In the late 70s he would have a brief affair with television, with 'The Versifier' appearing in 1977, and 'The Sleeping Beauty', 'The Sixth Day', and a *Vizio di forma* playlet, 'Procacciatori d'affari', in early 1978.* This too he very much enjoyed: seeing his characters come to life;

---

* All again directed by Scaglione, Primo's main theatrical collaborator from 1966 to 1980. Scaglione had already directed 'The Versifier' for television once before, in 1970. For both the TV version of 'Procacciatori' and a later stage one the title was changed to 'Nascere sulla

watching experts – actors, technicians – practising their trades. But *his* trade was on the page. Outside these years, only one thing could tempt him away: the chance of finding a wider audience for his books of witness. So he always welcomed film-makers' interest in *The Truce* (though the film was only made ten years after his death, in 1997); and so too, in the summer of 1964, he agreed to a stage version of *If This is a Man*.

In fact, he had hesitated a long time before he agreed. The idea came from the young actor who had played Alberto in the radio play of *Se questo è un uomo*, Pieralberto Marché. Primo worried that *Se questo* was being over-exposed, and so was he. The live theatre was a new experience, and though he was always drawn to new forms, this one frightened him. 'Readers,' he said, 'and radio listeners too are far away, hidden, anonymous; your theatre audience is right there, it looks at you, it lies in wait for you, it judges you.' But Marché reported that several theatres were interested; and Primo thought that this was a chance to reach a new audience in a new way, more directly than ever before. All right, he said to Marché, but you do it. Impossible, said Marché, without Primo's help the adaptation would be inauthentic, full of mistakes, plain wrong. Very well, Primo said: you start, then we'll see. Marché took the book with him on holiday. On his return, he brought what he'd done to Primo. Your dialogue is good, Primo said, but you were right – *this*, for example, is plain wrong. He was hooked; Marché had won.

From then on they worked together. Each would write a scene, and show it to the other. Marché would shorten Primo's speeches, and read them out loud to see if they worked; Primo would correct Marché's mistakes and misunderstandings. On the important points they were agreed. This was not one person's story, but millions': Aldo, therefore, must not narrate, but must be one character among many. The play must not declaim, but must lead the audience to its own conclusions, like the book. It must not fall into 'excessive realism', as Primo said, by trying to portray horrors: the last thing he wanted was to inspire pity, which is for things that can only happen to other people. As always, he wanted to inspire understanding: above all, of the process of dehumanization, especially through the deprivation of a common language. About the means, too, they were mostly agreed. Once again, the babel of voices must dominate. The SS should not appear: only their voices should be heard, through the loudspeakers. And

---

terra', 'To Be Born on Earth', and an alternative ending was devised by Scaglione (with Primo's consent): instead of refusing all advantages of birth, in order to share in ordinary human fate, the hero accepts them, in order to change it. When he was asked which ending he preferred, Primo said, 'Mine.'

the prisoners should not be shown as skeletons, as walking dead; but in their ordinary humanity, as it is slowly but surely taken away. Only on one point did they disagree. Marché wanted to have a chorus, who could express some of the book's most important reflections, in some of its most beautiful, almost biblical language. Primo objected to the idea, perhaps because he feared that it might seem pretentious. But the reflections are the heart of the book; and he soon saw that it was impossible to fit them all into realistic dialogue. Marché got his chorus.

The script took them two years. When it was finished, it had several false starts, including one with the Venice Biennale. Finally it was accepted, at the highest level: Turin's Teatro Stabile (Civic Theatre) would present it as the Italian entry in the Second International Festival of European Civic Theatres in Florence. At first this must have pleased and reassured Primo: his play would be produced with the utmost seriousness and integrity, for a serious and cultured audience. As indeed it was. Nonetheless, this was a very different world from any he had dared to enter so far. Bandini at the RAI, and Scaglione with his Teatro delle Dieci, were counter-culture outsiders like himself. Gianfranco De Bosio and the Teatro Stabile of Turin were distinguished and even innovative professionals, but part of the theatrical establishment. From the start Primo found the world of theatrical careerists as bad as that of literary ones. There were the usual endless quarrels, political manoeuvres, clashes of egos; he worried that the rehearsal period was too short, and that a week after it began, most of the actors were still without contracts . . . He was still fascinated – especially by the technical side, the sets, the costumes, the props. Here he became deeply involved, and eager to take responsibility, as he had with Marché: giving meticulous advice on the construction of the bunks, on the size of the soup tins, on the right material for the prisoners' uniforms; and on that item that could kill them first, their shoes. With these things – and these people – he was happy. The rest was all he could not bear.

The rehearsals were taking place in Prato, near Florence, which meant that he could only rarely attend them in any case. In the event he attended hardly any; but delegated Marché as his representative, to ensure, he wrote to De Bosio, that the production would remain true to his conception. This cannot have made the atmosphere easy, to put it mildly. But then something infinitely worse happened. On 4 November, only days before the play's scheduled first performance, Florence was devastated by a flood. At least seventeen people died. Shops and homes were ruined, many hundreds of art treasures, and around a million precious books and documents, were damaged or destroyed. Many of the actors lost their cars and most of their possessions. The 600 remaining copies of *Se questo è un uomo*, in their

Florence warehouse, were lost as well; and the Festival was cancelled. All through October the grudging reviews of *Storie naturali* had been appearing; and now this. Primo had strayed twice from the strict path of witness this year. Within a few weeks of each other, both were being punished.

In the end, the play opened in the Carignano Theatre in Turin instead, on 19 November – after ten more days of rehearsal, which both Primo and Marché thought it needed. That, at least, was to the good. And so, in the end, was the opening night itself. Lucia came, and looked happy; when Turin recognized Primo's achievement, she was proud. Primo, of course, was nervous, and tried not to be seen. But the audience gave both the play and its author a standing ovation at the end. He was overwhelmed, moved, and on the whole pleased. The production *had* remained true to his main theme, the loss of humanity in that Tower of Babel. The fifty-three actors – from Germany, Austria, France, Israel, Poland and Hungary as well as Italy – had all spoken in their own languages; yet everything it was important to understand had been understood. The abstract design, by Gianni Polidori – a half-circle opened to the audience, like one of Dante's circles of Hell – had worked well; so too had the more abstract scenes, such as the terrible marches – almost dances – to 'Rosamunda'; and the small, personal ones as well, such as Aldo's meeting with Lorenzo, and the 'Canto of Ulysses'. It is impossible to imagine what Primo felt as the past – *that* past – came to life again before his eyes. Perhaps for a few nights his nightmares returned. But that night, as he waited, and for a moment the audience was stricken into silence, then broke into passionate applause – that night, I think he thought it was worth it.

Audiences continued to fill the Carignano, and to be enthusiastic and moved. In early 1967 – like *Storie naturali* – *Se questo è un uomo* was given a prize: the Italian Institute of Drama's award for the best new play of the year. But with very few exceptions, the reviews were not good. In fact they said what Primo himself thought: that the lyricism of the chorus worked; so did the mass scenes – the marches, the selections – and the personal encounters. But in between the production had not managed to avoid the 'excessive realism' he had feared. Sobs, groans, hangings, poor Sómogyi's chorus of *Jawohls* – these were bathos, or worse. The reality of Auschwitz could not be rendered on a stage. It was a noble and worthwhile effort; but it had failed.

Primo's and Marché's contract said that there was to be a full season of performances at the Carignano, followed by a tour of Italy. But the reviews were poor, and the production expensive. In the end the play was given only fifty performances in Turin, and a tiny tour of Piedmont. Then, despite its prize and public success, the contracts were terminated and the company dissolved. Marché was furious; and after some characteristic hesitation, so was Primo. Together they sued the Teatro Stabile for breach of contract. Eventually – it took several years – they won, and were awarded damages. Justice had been done; but the play was never shown again. This was a bitter ending for Primo. He had never wanted to make money out of *Se questo* – on the contrary, profiting from the deaths of his companions was one of his obsessive fears. All he had wanted was to find the largest possible audience for it. And what had he got? Too much money, and no more audience at all.

That was effectively the end of his theatrical career. Scaglione would direct one more production of *Nascere sulla terra*, in 1980; and in 1986 Primo would permit an amateur company of students and workers to produce a stage version of *The Wrench*. Both were enthusiastically received; but he was not tempted to return. The theatre was a huge adventure, attractive and impossible at the same time, as all adventures were to him. And he *had* tried it. He had enjoyed watching actors at work, as he enjoyed all his excursions into other people's trades. But in rehearsal he was at his most humble, his most careful, and would never breathe a word of dissent or advice about what was being done to his words (like Giovanni Arpino, Scaglione says, who would say 'Pretend I'm a dead writer'). The theatre was not his world. It was not one of his unrequited loves, like zoology or philology, but only 'platonic', he would say – 'a love from a distance'. It took only one shock to convince him of this. After the failure of *Se questo*, he withdrew.

There was one more reason, I have said, for the gap in Primo's writing in these years. By the mid-60s his home had been turning into a prison for almost twenty years. In Aosta, in Auschwitz, he had thought *No* – he was not yet ready to die, he had not yet lived. I think he thought it again now. He wanted, at last, to live. He wanted to escape the prison of the Corso Re Umberto, and of his double bind. And he had found someone he wanted to escape with. That is why he was not in love with Tullia Ami: because he was in love with *her*.

He had known her for many years; everything important in his life had deep roots, and grew slowly. Perhaps – probably – she was already in his mind when he wrote of the Centaur's impossible love in 1959. A few years later, when he wrote *La tregua*, they knew each other well enough for him to tell her every word.

And then, in September 1963, she and her husband were guests at a dinner to celebrate his winning the Campiello. That evening she told him something she had not told him before: that when she read *Se questo è un uomo*, which she had done more than once, she had to keep a piece of bread beside her, or an apple. She always remembered that afterwards, and told it to me more than twenty years later, though she did not say why. Perhaps she realized at that moment – or he did, or they both did – how close she was to him, so that when she read his words, she felt his hunger. That is the communication he longed for – the communication, which is communion, of 'Carbon'.

The adventure of falling in love, of course, was the one he longed for most of all, but also feared most of all. Perhaps what she said now re-minded him straight away of Lilith, the girl he saw in Auschwitz just as he was biting into a piece of apple – and now *she* was reading him, and biting into an apple too. Two years or so later, in the middle of this time, he wrote a poem about the original Lilith, the she-devil with whom men – and even God – sin:

> It is written in the great book
> That she is a beautiful woman down to the waist.
> The rest is will-o'-the-wisp and pale light.

And years later, when he spoke of *her* (as he almost never did), he called her Lilith, a temptress for whom he had nearly ended his marriage.

Lilith herself – I shall call her Lilith too – would tell me very little. That he loved her. Not that she loved him: but she let me see it in her face and eyes. Not how long it lasted, or who ended it, or why. But she did not have to say these things either, because I knew. Primo told the woman he would call Gisella that there had been only one real love in his life, apart from Lucia. But it had been brief; it had to be, or 'he would have gone mad'. He had ended it, he said, because he could not end his marriage. When Lilith heard that, for once she allowed herself to speak. 'I was not free either,' she said.

It had begun, I have guessed, in late 1963; by 1968 it was over. In that year Primo and Lilith found themselves away from Turin together: only briefly, and by accident. But as always, Primo was different away from home. Perhaps he made himself end it then – or perhaps, on the contrary, that was its highest moment, and he knew he would have to decide. He could not bear the burden of deceit any longer, or the burden of possible freedom. Already in late 1964 he was longing to stop, to give in. In September – exactly a year after the Campiello dinner – he wrote his only other poem of these years, 'Landing' ('Approdo'). From it he took the title of his first collection, *L'Osteria di Brema*, *The Bremen Beer-hall*: and in it he put all his inability to bear hope and fear and pain: the life he longed for.

Happy the man who has made harbour,
Who leaves behind him seas and storms,
Whose dreams are dead or never born,
And who sits and drinks in a Bremen beer-hall . . .

. . .

He fears nothing, hopes for nothing, expects nothing,
But stares fixedly at the setting sun.

'Happy' *means* happy – relieved, at peace, no longer in torment. But of course it also means: in utter despair. In 1945 Primo had found a remedy for despair: to write, to work out the agony in words. That is what he did again now. But even the first time it had not worked on its own, but had driven him deeper, until he was rescued by love. This time he must have written feverishly: where the fifteen stories of *Storie naturali* had been spread out over twenty years, the twenty of *Vizio di forma* were written in little more than two. But once again it did not work. In 1968 or 1969 he had a major depression, one of the worst so far. This time he could not be rescued by a new love: that was itself the depression's cause. But perhaps he was rescued by his old one. Whether or not Lucia knew about Lilith, whether or not she was also punishing Primo, when he was down she helped him. He recovered, and finished his book, just as he had done the first time. He was hers again, as he had chosen.

★   ★

Vizio di forma was, Primo said, 'the most neglected of my books', the only one never translated, never given a prize, and universally reviled by the critics. Not all of this was quite true. The book made it to the long list for the Campiello – though no further – and received a good deal of praise among the brickbats.★ Old admirers like Giorgio Calcagno and Giulio Nascimbeni remained loyal, and so did *Il Giorno* (though it didn't publish any of the stories this time). But Carlo Bo in the *Corriere della Sera* complained that the restraint of *Se questo* seemed to have become abstract, almost inhuman. *Paese Sera, Rinascita, Avanti* and several others were damning, saying (truly) that the stories were uneven, and (untruly) that they were grey, schematic, cold. But worst of all was Milano. He did remark that the stories were 'all considerable', and 'three or four profound'; but Primo didn't notice that. What he noticed was that Milano accused him of being (to

---

★ Many of its stories have also been translated, at least into English (in *The Sixth Day*, combined with most of the stories of *Storie naturali*). But this only happened after Primo's death, in 1990.

borrow the word from his other subject) a forgiver. He was, Milano said, too indulgent of the evils he exposed, too hopeful that they could be conquered. *Vizio di forma* was the peak of Primo's effort to balance his private despair with a public dedication to faith in man, in mind, in science. And now Milano told him it wasn't worth it – indeed, it was harmful, and he should have scared his readers more. And the critic in *La Stampa*, his own paper, promptly echoed Milano. Primo laughed at this, but never forgot it.

He was right to laugh. *Vizio di forma* was an unpopular book for exactly the opposite reason: despite all his efforts, it was pervaded by hopelessness. Primo tried to deny this, both as a social duty (despite Milano) and for self-protection, but many readers who wrote to him, and several critics, remained unfooled. One of these was the critic of *Catholic Studies* (Catholics, for whom the world is the realm of sin, would always be sensitive to Primo's pessimism). Another was Fiora Vincenti, his first biographer, who came to interview him some time after the publication of *Vizio di forma*. Perhaps this alerted her to the darkness in his book: since in person, she says, he was 'terrifyingly pessimistic', saying that he had had no real hope for mankind since long before Auschwitz. (She had probably found him in a new depression; there were many in the 70s, as we shall see.) In any case, she saw it. The *Natural Histories* still had a 'youthful exuberance' behind their irony, she wrote (with some exaggeration). In *Vizio di forma* this had completely disappeared. In its place were bitterness, anguish, unease; above all a sense of withering, of hardening, as both nature and love recede from the characters, leaving only regret and nostalgia behind. As Primo would say a few years later to *Uomini e libri*, the literary magazine edited by Vincenti and her husband: 'A book runs away from its author: it says more than he intends.' She had read in *Vizio di forma* the depression out of which it was written.

Of its twenty stories, about half are still satires, like the *Natural Histories*: often sharp, even black, but contained. Among these are 'Procacciatori d'affari',★ which would become *Nascere sulla terra*: in which three celestial salesmen attempt to persuade a soul in waiting to choose Earth as his home;

★ Translated as 'The Hard-Sellers' in *The Sixth Day* (though perhaps 'Touting for Trade' would have been better). The other eleven stories translated are 'Verso occidente' ('Westward'), 'Visto da lontano' ('Seen from Afar'), 'Lumini rossi' ('Small Red Lights'), 'A fin di bene' ('For a Good Purpose' – though again 'Best Intentions' must have been better), 'Psicofante' ('Psychophant')', 'Recuenco: la nutrice' and 'Recuenco: il rafter' ('Recuenco: The Nurse' and 'Recuenco: The Rafter'), 'Il fabbro di se stesso' ('His Own Blacksmith' – or better, 'His Own Maker'), 'Il servo' ('The Servant'), 'Ammutinamento' ('Mutiny'), and 'Ottima è l'acqua' ('Excellent is the Water').

trying, and failing, to hide from him its *vizi di forma*, its deformations – wars, death, disease. Among them, too, are several stories on Primo's perennial subject, Man; three or four science-fiction-style thought experiments, and a satire on advertising; 'Psicofante', which is hard to categorize; and two Pirandellian tales about writing, in one of which a character turns the tables on his author and writes about *him*.

Several of these are profound, funny and disturbing – 'Procacciatori', for example; and 'A fin di bene', 'For a Good Purpose', in which a telephone network, on reaching a certain size, becomes a primitive brain, and begins to make disastrous decisions on its own. But they are uneven, as the critics said, and the weakest ones are much weaker than the *Storie naturali*. It is the others – the ones which came straight out of Primo's despair, and which betray it – which are the best. The feelings in them may be negative, but they are very powerful. And because Primo cannot quite contain them in rational packages, they emerge richer and more mysterious: less like morality tales, and more like poetry.

The story that struck everyone most, and has gone on doing so, is 'Verso occidente', 'Westward'. In it a group of scientists is studying lemmings: that is to say, the impulse towards suicide. Is it hunger, or over-crowding, perhaps, that drives whole populations to throw themselves into the sea? No, one of the scientists dares to suggest: it is because they want to die. Most living creatures want to live: but not all. 'Individuals without love for life can be born,' he says; 'others may lose it for a short or long time, perhaps for all the life they have left.' And indeed, he adds, they are not wrong. 'Life does *not* have a purpose; pain always prevails over joy; we are all sentenced to death, and . . . condemned to watch the end of those dearest to us; there are compensations, but they are few.' The will to live is incised in us; but it covers up the truth, which is the void.

Having reached this point in theory, they embark on practice: to find 'the hormone that inhibits the existential void'. They find it, and call it Factor L. It works on people who have lost the will to live: who feel, Primo wrote, 'useless . . . drowned in a sea of uselessness. And alone even in a crowd: buried alive, among everyone else buried alive.' It does not work (as it turns out, in a gruesome ending) for the lemmings; nor for the Arunde, a tribe for whom suicide is equally normal, because they do not believe that anything in heaven or earth cares for them, and attribute no value to their own survival. The scientists send a package of Factor L to them; but they return it. 'The Arunde people, soon to be no longer a people, greets you and thanks you,' they write. But they decline the gift, because 'we prefer freedom to drugs and death to illusion'.

'I wrote that story in a moment of depression,' Primo said in 1986, just as he was entering the last one. We know how that one ended. In all the other major depressions we know of, he thought of suicide; 'Westward' suggests that he thought of it in 1968 or '69 too.

Of the other stories which image and express depression, two are dealt with elsewhere.★ Two are thought experiments, like 'A fin di bene'. 'Knall' is about an object, almost a toy, whose name in German (of course in German) means 'crack' or 'bang'. Pointed at a person, the knall kills immediately. It also cracks stone, melts metals and starts fires; young men light their cigarettes with it, to show off to girls. The only reason why the knall has not become a serious social danger, the story concludes, is because it does not spill blood, which is what really stirs us, 'like sharks or bulls'. But this new, silent ability to kill, which anyone can buy for a few *lire*, has changed social behaviour. Since the knall only works at a range of under a yard, people keep at least a yard away from each other in public places; and increasingly they stay at home. '*Alone even in a crowd*', '*buried alive*', just as in 'Westward': because if anyone comes close, it may be to kill you.

In 'Excellent is the Water', a young physicist is given a useless job: to measure the viscosity of water. As though this weren't bad enough, one day the figures do not tally: they show a minute, but impossible, increase in viscosity. When he tells his superior, he receives only abuse. Then, sitting on the banks of the Sangone, nursing his grievance, he notices something wrong with the water. It seems to be flowing more slowly, its murmur is muted. He runs back to the laboratory with a sample, and it is monstrous: 30 per cent more viscous than normal.

Within days the other small rivers of Piedmont thicken, and within a month the Po; then viscous rain falls over the whole of Europe, and soon the world. Trees die; all the machines that use water become slower and slower to fill and to empty. And in less than a year mankind itself is affected. The sick die and the healthy sicken. We move slowly, we can hardly digest, we cannot weep. The Amazon – the story ends – has become a swamp, and the 'Caribbean Sea no longer has waves'.

Of course this is 'science fiction': a thought experiment to show how beautifully balanced our world is, so that if it changed even a little, life would become impossible. But it is also an exact account of depression, fixed, like a tombstone, at the end of the book. Everything slows, everything stops, there is no way out. Unlike 'Westward', 'Excellent is the Water' never mentions depression: but it makes you feel it.

★ 'I sintetici', 'Synthetics', discussed in Chapter 3, in which Primo explores the sense of being abnormal, non-human, 'better possibly, but different'; and 'Il servo', 'The Servant', the story of another non-human, the Golem, discussed in Chapter 15.

There are two great losses in *Vizio di forma*, which are really the same loss, as Fiora Vincenti saw: the loss of nature, and the loss of love. 'Ammutinamento', 'Mutiny', is about the first – and dedicated, therefore, to Mario Rigoni Stern, the friend who represented to Primo that deep bond with the natural world which he had never had, and the last chance of which he had now lost.

The heroine of 'Mutiny' is a young girl, Clotilde, who is eleven years old, and reminiscent of that long-ago Lidia with whom Primo had fallen in love when *he* was eleven. Lidia had had a magical relation to animals; Clotilde has a magical relation to plants, and understands their language. She knows, therefore, that not all plants agree. Some are domesticated, like cows, and could no longer live without us. But others resent their enslavement, and want to escape it. One day, Clotilde takes the narrator to a clearing deep in a wood. This, she says, is a tree school: 'a secret place where trees taught each other to walk, in hatred of men'. The juniper has moved at least three feet in four days; and the cherry tree is telling the others that they must no longer bear fruit for man, nor purify the air for him, but should pull up their roots and leave.

So nature hates us, and wants to leave us; and it does. Luigi in 'Lumini rossi' ('Small red Lights') works alone in a dark room, obeying the orders of red lights, to what effect he does not know. To and from work he must obey more red lights – traffic lights, lift lights, the security lock light – to reach the saddest order of all: the red light at the base of his wife's throat, which shines on the fertile days of all married women who already have the permitted number of children. He calculates that the red lights of each of his days come to 200: '70,000 in a year, 32 million in fifty years of active life,' Primo wrote. And it seems to Luigi that 'the top of his skull was hardening': as though he was growing a rhinoceros horn, 'but flatter and blunter', 'excellent for battering against walls'. In 'Protezione', 'Protection', everyone lives, not with an oxygen tank on their backs, as in Primo's debate with Rigoni Stern, but in full metal armour, to protect them from the meteor shower through which (according to the Authorities) the Earth has been passing for twenty years. Elena feels protected by her armour, not just from meteors but from everything: from other people, from the future, from herself. Marta is less happy, but resigned. Her affair with Elena's husband Roberto has been over for ten years, and she knows she will never have another: not least because of the armour itself, which means that she will never see a stranger's face and body again. All she can touch is Roberto's hand, when they say goodbye: this fills her with a glow of sadness that 'kept her company inside her armour, and helped her to live for several days'.

With these two stories we have moved openly to the loss of love. There is one more: the most anguished of all. It is called 'Vilmy'.* A Vilmy is a graceful, evil, catlike creature, whose milk has introduced a new *vizio di forma* into the world. It contains a chemical as vital as Factor L: N–phenyltocine, which creates the attachment between infants and their mothers. In animals the concentration is low, and the effect soon disappears. In humans it is higher, and the attachment to the mother lasts many years. But in the milk of the Vilmy it is twenty times as high as in humans'; so that not only the Vilmy's own children, but anyone who drinks its milk is tied to it by 'an almost pathological bond', instantly and forever.

This has happened to the narrator's friend, an Englishman called Paul Morris. Paul tells the narrator of his torments, ever since he laid eyes on the first of his three Vilmies, each more skilled in the arts of seduction and humiliation than the last. *Never* taste the milk, he tells his friend. The desire it inspires is unlike any other, because it is hopeless. Even the most doomed love for a woman is not completely hopeless; it could at least in principle be satisfied. But the desire for the Vilmy, or for her milk, cannot be satisfied. You drink, and immediately you must drink again: the desire remains desire, without end.

This is not only the most anguished story, but the most mysterious. It cannot pretend to be about some possible external catastrophe, like 'Excellent is the Water', or even 'Protezione'. Was the Vilmy a symbol of women, who had always inspired in Primo both intense desire and intense fear, and still did, so that he knew now that his desire would never be satisfied? Or was the conceit of the mother's milk deliberate, and the Vilmy a symbol of the '*malabaila*', the bad mother, who leaves her child with 'an almost pathological bond' to her, because she has never given him what he needs? That need *is* hopeless, because it is the infant's need, and could only have been satisfied in the past, which is irretrievably gone. The grown man who continues to have the infant's need inside him is exactly like the hopeless addict Primo describes, whose desire cannot even in principle be satisfied. And Primo *was* exactly like that man. But then he was exactly like the other one as well, and like Marta in 'Protezione', who have lost their last chance of love, and know, or think, that they will never have another. Luckily, we do not have to decide. 'Vilmy' is an extraordinary work of imagination, which can bear both meanings, and probably more. I think the Vilmy is at least both: both Primo's impossible desire for women, and his impossible

---

* Unfortunately, neither 'Vilmy' nor 'Protezione' is translated into English. Nor are 'I sintetici' or 'Knall'. (Nor the two stories on writing, 'Lavoro creativo' and 'Nel parco'; the new version of 'The Sixth Day', 'Le nostre belle specificazioni'; or the satire on advertising, 'In fronte scritto'.)

need for his mother's love; a symbol of both his double binds, and one of the deepest glances into the abyss of his soul in all his writing.

★   ★

On the cover of *Vizio di forma*, Primo had expressed his fears for the next decade. All the signs had turned baleful, he wrote – 'DDT in the fat of penguins, carbon monoxide in the atmosphere, lead in our own veins'. And they had done so quite suddenly.

> . . . In the course of a few years, almost from one day to the next, we have realized that something final has happened, or is about to happen: like someone travelling down a peaceful river, who suddenly notices the banks slipping away behind him, the water filling with whirlpools, and the sound of the waterfall already near.

'An old man should not confuse his weakness with the weakness of the world,' Vittorio Foa says at the end of his autobiography: 'if he can no longer hope, others can'. Surely this is what Primo was doing, I thought – confusing his despair with the earth's. It was only to him that 'something final' had happened, not to the entire globe. That was getting worse, but it always had; and like a young person, which he no longer was, it was extremely resilient. He had projected his fears, as a psychologist would say: it was really he, not the earth, who was suddenly in danger.

But this is only partly true. In fact he was right in his forebodings: he had only slightly misplaced them. It was not (yet) global ecology that was about to collapse, but Italian society. The 1970s were the *anni di piombo*, the 'years of the bullet', in Italy: a decade of social unrest, terrorism, and a resurgence of fascism. In the 70s Primo's working life was almost all frustration, his home was what it was, and he had lost his last battle against his double bind. That was bad enough. But there was one thing he especially couldn't bear: violence. And violence, in the *anni di piombo*, was everywhere.

The 1970s were paying for the 60s – for their colossal social changes and economic growth, and for the collapse of their hopes. Turin was both a centre and a symbol of all these, changed beyond recognition by the end of the 60s, swollen into a modern industrial city by twenty years of immigration from the south. Throughout the 60s, centre-left governments in Rome had talked of reform – social, economic, educational – to keep up with the pace of change. But as so often, especially in Italy, nothing was done. Finally, with the example of France before them, students and workers began to take things into their own hands. There were some heady moments in the late 60s and early 70s, when it seemed that the grip of Church and State might be loosened, and 'power to the people' might make some real gains; but factionalism and anarchy soon took over, and only a few lasting victories remained.* And in the meantime, a right-wing backlash had begun. By 1971 the boom of the 60s faltered, by 1973 it was over, and economic tensions were added to political ones. It would take the rest of the decade to work them out.

Violence had already started in the late 60s. In December 1969 a bomb killed sixteen people in the Piazza Fontana in Milan. Police blamed anarchists, and arrested several people, one of whom died in custody; they all turned out to be innocent, although it took until 1985 for the last one to be cleared. From the start the left suspected a neo-fascist plot, with connections to the government: a 'strategy of tension' to justify a crackdown on workers and students, and to reawaken Italians' desire for strong government, which is the other side of their natural anarchy. Primo shared these suspicions, and they deeply disturbed him. Later in the decade, with the extreme-left terrorism of the Red Brigades – like that of the Baader-Meinhof gang and Rote Armee Fraktion in Germany – the worst violence and excess spread to the other side. Indeed (as the right would no doubt say) it had started there, with violence deliberately adopted as a revolutionary tool by students and workers, and regularly breaking out in their strikes and occupations. But in the early 70s the main danger seemed clear, especially to Primo and his generation: fascism, with its bullying, intolerance and worship of might for its own sake, was returning.

And it was happening not only in Milan and other places, but right there, in Turin. Starting in 1969, local fascists had resurfaced: defacing Resistance monuments and graves; disrupting meetings of trade unionists, workers, and left-wing parties, and raiding and fire-bombing their offices. And they focused much of their effort on the young. Groups of young fascists waited outside schools, and handed out propaganda leaflets to the students; anyone who refused them was immediately attacked. As time went on the attacks grew in number and in violence. Students were punched and pushed, beaten with whips, chains, knuckledusters, iron bars. By the end, in late 1974 – after that the Red Brigades took over, and real terrorism began – a gang of fifty fascists surrounded the Liceo D'Azeglio and pelted it with stones; one of them was carrying a gun.

Nothing could have disturbed Primo more than this targeting of the young – especially since these years, 1969 to 1974, almost exactly covered his own son's time in *liceo*. Fortunately, Renzo seems to have escaped injury. But several boys were badly hurt; the son of one of Primo's antifascist friends

---

* For example, in workers' rights, regional government, and the first divorce law in Italy, passed in December 1970. See Paul Ginsborg, *A History of Contemporary Italy*, Chapter 9, 'The Era of Collective Action, 1968–73', from which this account is largely taken.

had his nose bloodied, and Alberto and Bianca's son Fabrizio was arrested for fighting back. The police did little – or worse than little, as Fabrizio's case shows. Clearly something had to be done.

Something had already been done in other cities with the same problem – in Milan, for instance, and in Rome. Antifascist parents and teachers had come together to help their children defend themselves, in an organization called Cogidas.* In March 1973 a Turin branch was formed. Its first President was Alessandro Galante Garrone; among its first officers were Valeria Bobbio, Tina Rieser and Primo Levi.

For the next year or so Primo fought against fascists for the second time in his life, as though the clock had turned back nearly thirty years. He and Lucia – for Lucia joined in his Cogidas activities – took regular turns with other parents to watch outside schools, to note serious incidents, and to report them to the authorities. On Saturday 29 May, for example, the two Levis, together with Alberto, Bianca, and Ada Ortona (that is, Ada Della Torre), were posted outside the Albert Einstein Institute on the Via San Secondo. A group of about ten young *squadristi*,† giving Roman salutes and singing fascist songs, handed them leaflets, which they immediately destroyed. The boys then threatened them. A passer-by called the police; who, when they arrived, seemed to know the young fascists by name, and allowed them to distribute their leaflets to the students.

On Thursday 15 November Primo wrote Cogidas' report of the worst incident so far. Three boys, apparently alone, handed out the leaflets; but when students began to refuse, a larger group of well-known thugs suddenly appeared, and attacked them with clubs and chains, wounding several. This report was signed by fifty-five teachers and forty-seven parents, and submitted to the Turin Tribunal for prosecution. As far as I have been able to establish, nothing happened.

We know how Primo felt about his first antifascist war: incapable and out of place; on the right side, but in the wrong role. Since he never spoke of it, we cannot be sure how he felt about this one. It was very different: he had his best friends with him, including Alberto, and his wife by his side; he did not have to bear arms, or join in violence himself, but only report it, which was much more his strength and style. Still I cannot think he felt at ease. To watch schoolchildren being terrorized and brutally attacked, to be in danger himself, and even threatened – all this must have brought back fears he could hardly bear. Just to know that fascism was not dead – that it

---

* Centro Operativo fra Genitori per l'Iniziativo Democratica Antifascista nella Scuola: Parents' Operational Centre for a Democratic and Antifascist Initiative in Schools.

† Members of fascist action squads.

was unkillable, like a weed – that alone must have made him despair. He must have remembered the Greek: '*There is always war.*' And it was always the same war. Thirty years later, his son was having to fight the same enemies he had fought; and amongst them was the son of the Sportsman.

★   ★

By the 1970s, Primo's working life was all frustration. For over twenty years now he had been bound hand and foot to his trade; it interested him less and less, and he felt more and more like a slave. Then in 1972 Giovanni Torrione, who had entered SIVA as Gianna Balzaretti's first assistant, died suddenly in an accident. He had overseen the day-to-day working of the factory – the management of the workers and the plant; suddenly all that became Primo's direct responsibility too. And at the same moment, this whole area became much more complicated. Despite his best efforts, SIVA's safety practices were not much better than those of most chemical factories of the time. But the regulations governing the industry were growing tighter; and now a new young trade-union leader in the company took up the cause, and led a tough campaign for radical (and very expensive) improvements. Primo was certainly sympathetic, at least in principle; but Accati was furiously opposed, and indeed if it had all been done at once the company would have been ruined. Primo was caught between Accati and the workers; between the knowledge that he was powerless, and the fear that he would be blamed. And there he remained, like a man in crossfire, for the next few years.

Finally, in the autumn of 1973, the oil crisis erupted. Overnight, OPEC raised prices by 70 per cent and cut production by 10. The whole of the West reeled under the blow; but especially oil-dependent Italy. Over the winter of 1973–4 oil prices soared, inflation became (and remained) the highest in the western world; Italy went into deep recession, and, with minor ups and downs, stayed there for the rest of the decade. It was not a good time to be running a factory.

And then it got worse. After nearly thirty years of effort and success, Federico Accati suddenly saw his whole empire under threat. He also saw what had to be done – what always has to be done in hard times: slash costs, 'downsize', fire people. And he couldn't do it. He may have been a stubborn, selfish father; but the companies were his family, the employees his children. Now he too was in a double bind; and it had the effect on him it regularly had on Primo. He fell into a depression. He, whose life had been his work, could not face going to work in the mornings. His wife had to drive him to the factory gates; and even then, more often than not he could not go in. He may have thought of selling out altogether. But then an alternative appeared. There was a clever and ambitious young man who had made his way up through the companies, and who several years before had pulled SCET out of a similar period of losses. He was not handicapped by feudal loyalties, and he offered to do what was necessary. With a sigh of relief, Accati accepted.

It was not a good solution, and Accati knew it. He remained depressed for a long time; which was to his credit, but to everyone else's cost. I think he could not bear to know what was happening; but at the same time he could not stop it, if he wanted to save his life's achievement. He withdrew, and left the Downsizer in charge.

This was the last straw for Primo. His indomitable friend, his life-long partner, was gone: defeated by a conflict he could not resolve, in a way Primo knew so well, but had never dreamed to see in *him*. And the company he had worked in for a lifetime was going. The Downsizer had begun with SICME; but he soon turned his attention to SIVA, which he thought small beer, badly managed, and very likely not worth keeping open at all. He plainly disliked Primo; and for once Primo disliked him in return. And to *this* man he had to turn for his directions; *this* man was now his superior. He bore it as long as he could, but even he could not bear it for long. At the end of 1974, after twenty-seven years with SIVA, he handed in his resignation.

Of course, being Primo he did not simply walk away. He resigned as Director; but agreed to carry on as 'Senior Consultant' until a successor could take over. For the next three years he continued a half-life at SIVA, still spending every morning in the office.* He was – thank heaven! – no longer responsible for the lives and livelihoods of eighty people; and immediately he grew his beard, like a sign of liberation, of celebration, of being a writer in a chemical company, not the Director of a chemical company who occasionally wrote. But the writer was still in the chemical company; the economic situation was still dire, the Downsizer still downsized, and altogether his burden had been reduced, but not changed. And in one way those last years were even sadder than the others, because his relationship with Accati was becoming strained. First the Downsizer had come between them; and now – perhaps out of fear of his influence – Primo was not his usual trusting self with Accati, but presented him with a carefully calculated demand for his severance pay. Accati was shocked and hurt – and immediately thought the claim was far too high, though in fact it was exactly the amount to which Primo was entitled (that was the point of the calculations).

---

* Primo always says two years, 1975 to 1977; but since he resigned at the end of November 1974, and only left in September 1977, it was in effect three.

Then, around 1975, they were both served with indictments alleging serious neglect of safety standards. Accati went to a famous right-wing lawyer for his defence; Primo went to Bianca. That made another breach between them. In the end, the law's delays, and then an amnesty, took them beyond the mandatory five-year period, and the case would never be brought. The two old friends settled their differences, and refused to become estranged. But forgiving is not forgetting; and somewhere a trace must have remained.

The truth is that Primo's last three or four years at SIVA, from 1974 to 1977, were very miserable. This main story in his life, like so many others, both lived and told, ended badly. By the time he could leave for good in 1977, he almost leapt for joy. And not only because *now he could write*, as he said: because he had been in the bad ending of that story for too long. After he left he would ring Portesi occasionally and ask '*Come sta la Orsolina?*' – 'How's Orsolina?', whom he knew Portesi saw. But that was all. He left, and he rarely returned. People at SIVA imagined he missed it, and that a visit would make him too sad. But that was out of company loyalty, and because they forgot, or never knew, about his bitter last years. Primo wanted to forget them; that is why he stayed away.★

★   ★

When he had made his fearful predictions on the cover of *Vizio di forma*, it was as though he had foreseen not only Italy's future, but his own. The river that began its rush to the fall in the 70s was his own life. It had hardly been peaceful before; but now the whirlpools of depression were everywhere. In the first half of this difficult decade he had at least one bad one every year. In 1971 *Vizio di forma* came out in the spring, to its lack of praise; by the summer he was very depressed, and went on being so at least to October. In retrospect, he did not count this among his really serious depressions. Indeed, it was not a major episode; nor were any of his 1970s depressions, as we shall see – he could still work, he could still write, he was not driven to the brink of suicide. Yet even these despairs were so terrifying that it is hard to imagine anything worse.

In August 1971, for example, he wrote from holiday in Pietra Ligure to Leonardo. In previous years, he wrote, he hadn't minded this seaside life, he had even enjoyed it. But this year it seemed to him little less than a Lager. He could not bear the crowds, the heat, the loneliness; he could not escape

★ SIVA survived the Downsizer, and lived on until 1998, but in reduced form. The paint department, for example, was closed altogether – to the despair of the Selvestrel brothers, whose final departure was still more bitter than Primo's.

the thoughts that pursued him. After sundown he had a few hours of peace, and at night he slept, with the help of sleeping-pills. But each day was a nightmare he thought would never end. He had had enough, he did not recognize himself any more. He desperately needed to talk to Leonardo, to whom he could tell things he would not tell Lucia, or perhaps anyone.

Though this was not a major depression, it was very similar. The image of the Lager, and the tormenting circle of thoughts; the effort to protect Lucia from knowing the worst – and to protect himself from dependence on her: these would be the marks of all his depressions in the coming years.

In late 1972 he had another, which lasted about two months, and ended very suddenly, like all the others. Then in the autumn of 1973 came the oil crisis, and as a consequence SIVA's, and Accati's; and even more distant friends began to notice that Primo was worrying obsessively, and feeling responsible for things which were not his fault. In early 1974 he replied to Hermann Langbein, who had written to remind him that it was up to politicians, not chemists, to find a solution to the petrol crisis. He agreed; but Langbein would understand, he wrote: he had not felt in such a critical situation 'since 1945'. That is, since the Lager. He was in another depression.

He must have realized he could not go on like this. He had already yielded to sleeping-pills; but they were no longer enough. If he wanted to save himself, he had to do more. So, in around 1975, he did. For the first time, he went to a psychiatrist.

He was still reluctant, and very cautious. He chose someone far away from Turin; he went only once; and perhaps he obeyed the habit of a lifetime, and did not speak of his present and most private troubles. But in any case the psychiatrist, who was excellent and experienced, would not have been fooled. He found that Primo was not, at this stage, clinically depressed. When he saw him again a few years later he would change his mind.

★   ★

And yet – perhaps those two words should be on Primo's gravestone, after the stark number *174517*. *174517*: and yet *If This is A Man*, and *The Truce*. Now all the troubles of the early 70s: and yet his third masterpiece, *The Periodic Table*.

It had been in his mind since *La tregua*, or even before. At the same moment as he had begun to talk of his split between chemist and writer, he had begun to talk of healing it. It would be, he said, a hope 'to cultivate in secret': 'to find a meeting point' between his two halves, by telling the story of his day half, the chemist, with his night half, the writer. 'Perhaps', he said in that happy interview after the Campiello – the one in which his family had joined him – perhaps he had even begun.

He had certainly begun. In fact, he'd begun more or less at the beginning – with 'Sulphur', which we know was written by 1950. Now, or recently, he may have begun again – with 'Carbon', which appears and reappears several times in his story of his life; or perhaps with another line of chemical stories, which he would take up again after *The Periodic Table*. But one of these lines, or both, were not working. By the beginning of 1966 he had abandoned his attempt to write about his day-job. 'They are my worst [stories],' he said. 'I'll never succeed, I'm sure.'

But that was in the middle of the gap in his writing. And in 1968, along with the stories of *Vizio di forma*, he took up his chemical tales once more. By October of that year he had written two chapters of what had now clearly become his whole chemical autobiography: 'Hydrogen', which was then the first, and 'Carbon', which would be the last. But these were early drafts, and perhaps very different from their final versions; once again, he was not satisfied. 'I've read ["Carbon"] to a few people,' he wrote to his Croatian translator, Mladen Machiedo. 'In general, they found it boring; but the scientists liked it, which is a bad sign.' Two years later, in October 1970, he took out 'Carbon' and rewrote it in the form we have now. Even so, in October 1971 it was still in his drawer. But that was the tail end of his *Vizio di forma* depression. A few months after that he started 'Tin'; and from that point on he did not stop. He wrote 'Tin' and 'Zinc' in 1972; and all the other new stories – ten of them, plus rewrites of 'Argon', 'Iron', 'Lead' and 'Mercury' – in the miserable years of 1973 and 74. The last story to be written, 'Vanadium', was finished in September 1974; he resigned as Director of SIVA in November. The great project of joining his two professional halves was at last achieved: but in imagination only, like all Primo's greatest achievements, and while his chemist half was in its terminal decline.

We have explored most of the stories of *The Periodic Table* in their places in Primo's life. The last four remain: 'Uranium', 'Silver', 'Vanadium' and 'Carbon'.

'Silver' picks up a theme that recurs in Primo's chemical stories like a chorus: the large effects of small causes. It started in 'Potassium', with the difference between sodium and potassium (and between the narrator and his much admired mentor). From then on it would reappear in many of Primo's chemical adventures – which are mostly misadventures, for which the small elusive cause must be found: in 'Chromium', in 'Anchovies' in *The Wrench*, and in Chapter 5 of *The Double Bond*, in which after long pursuit the hunter corners his prey; but also in 'Sfida della molecula', 'Stabile/Instabile' and 'Riprodurre i miracoli', in which he fails. And then this idea of small causes, which is itself only apparently small, ends up in other stories as well. It is a tiny cause which leads Primo in his hunt for another kind of prey, in 'Vanadium'; and finally, in 'Pipetta di guerra', written in 1985, it is the smallest difference between Primo and his twin Alberto Dalla Volta – having had scarlet fever in childhood and not having had it – which makes the difference between life for one and death for the other.

Primo put many of his SIVA problems into 'Silver': especially the burdens of responsibility, which make you 'lose sleep, lose your appetite, get ulcers or shingles' – of which he would have several attacks himself – and which in general induce 'terminal managerial neurosis'. In 'Uranium' he put another set: the horrors of Customer Service. About these he is both funny ('my Bologna colleague has a collection of dirty jokes continually brought up to date, and reviews them diligently together with the technical bulletins'), and, in relation to himself, acute: 'I tend to be brusque and impatient with customers who are impatient and brusque, and to be mild and yielding with suppliers who, being themselves CSs, are just that, yielding and mild. In short, I am not a good CS, and I fear that by now it is too late for me to become one.' But just as 'Silver' is really about the unending war against small causes, so 'Uranium' is really about another, more private theme.

On a CS mission to a small, grimy factory, Primo is sold something instead: a tall story. Bonino, the head of department, recognizes him as 'the fellow who wrote a book', and tells him his own war story. Right at the end of the war two Nazi airmen gave him a lump of metal, which 'they didn't need any more': it was uranium, he says, and he has kept it, secretly, ever since. He'll send a piece to Primo, as proof. Now follows a page of chemical testing, which should be boring, but – as always in Primo's hands – is funny and dramatic instead; and this time also moving, because he is an ex-chemist back in the laboratory, which brings back a sense of youth and joy, 'of an indeterminate future pregnant with possibilities, that is, of freedom'.

Of course the metal is not uranium, but cadmium. Its origin, Primo concludes, is not interesting – probably the cadmium–plating department of Bonino's factory. What *is* interesting is the origin of the story: which is Bonino himself, alone. He, Primo, may have a desk twice the size, but he is still caught 'in the CS net of duties', not only in life, but 'to verisimilitude' in his writing. Bonino may be shabby and powerless, but he has 'broken the barrier'. And what lies on the other side of this narrow strait, beyond which *l'uom più oltre non si metta*? The 'boundless freedom of invention': the freedom 'to build for himself the part that suits him best, to stitch around him the garments of a hero, and fly like Superman across centuries, meridians and parallels'. That is, the forbidden freedom of fiction: of imagining a different past for himself, as Primo himself would do in *Se non ora, quando?*; of imagining himself not a self at all, but 'flying across centuries, meridians and parallels', as he had already done in 'Carbon'. Underneath its CS satire, 'Uranium' expresses Primo Levi's longing to escape: from reality, from his first book, from himself.

Secretly, he had already broken the barrier of fiction, and not only in 'Carbon'. But he did not like to admit it. After *The Periodic Table* was published he challenged the physicist Tullio Regge to guess which one of its stories he had 'faked'. In fact he'd faked many, even most, if by 'faking' he meant 'rounding out', adding a few dramatizing, symbolizing details;★ if he meant more than that, he hadn't faked any. But when Regge guessed 'Nickel', Primo smiled and said no. Perhaps he named the one he did for effect, because the core of the prohibition centred on the Lager. But the story he admitted 'faking' to Regge was 'Vanadium'.

What he had faked most of all, I think, was its beginning: the extraordinary way he finds 'Dr Müller' of the Buna laboratory. He receives a letter (he recounts) from a German supplier – a descendant of I. G. Farben – signed by someone of that very common name: so common that he refuses to wonder if it could be the same. But suddenly he realizes that this Müller makes the same mistake as *his* Müller did, so long ago: saying 'naptenate' for 'naphthenate'. That is the small cause that sets him on Müller's trail.

In fact, the person who found the real Dr Müller, Ferdinand Meyer, was not Primo, but his friend Hety Schmitt Maass, whose ex-husband had been a colleague of Meyer's at I. G. Farben. Until their correspondence is released we cannot be absolutely certain; but I am quite sure there was no 'naptenate' in the real story. Rather, it was Hety's connection to I. G. Farben that made her specially sensitive to Primo's story in the first place, and she must have mentioned it to him straight away. He saw his chance, at last, to find out about – perhaps even to find – some of those 'on the other side'; and he gave Hety the names he remembered: Pannwitz, Meyer, probably others. The others meant nothing to her, or had disappeared; but she immediately recognized Meyer. She told him about her new friend, and his book; and it was Meyer who wrote first to Primo, not the other way round. That is how the connection was made. The 'naptenate' mistake was a dramatic device Primo invented to draw us into the story.

There are other interesting differences too between the story and what

---

★ See, in 'Lavoro creativo', the conversation between Antonio and his character James about the stories James has written about him.

'"True stories?" gulped Antonio.

"Well, basically yes. A little rounded out: you're in the business, you know what I mean."'

really happened. In 'Vanadium' Primo's approach to Müller is distant, wary; his response to his second long letter is critical, and his reply to his plea for forgiveness deliberately hard. Müller had been better than most in Buna, he tells us, and he was better than most now: he had a conscience, and was struggling to deal with it. But he exaggerated his goodness at the time, and made mad excuses for I. G. Farben. According to the story, Primo drafted a reply, which, he says, he never sent. In it he 'tactfully' described two cases of Germans who had behaved much more bravely towards them than Müller had; he said that Müller had been 'honest and unarmed', but that in the face of Auschwitz this was not enough; and he 'did not say a word' about a meeting Müller had proposed on the Riviera.

Now, we do not have this correspondence either; but I am inclined to trust Primo's account of 'Müller''s second struggling letter – 'clumsy', 'moving', 'only half-sincere'; 'he was trying to settle his accounts with the past, and they did not tally; he tried to make them tally, perhaps by cheating a little'. It is possible that his own response hardened in return. But the one letter we do have – Primo's first to Meyer – is rather different. It is warmer, kinder, more open. As Frau Schmitt Maass will have told you, Primo wrote, my memories of you are good ones. He recalled Meyer's note entitling him to be shaved twice a week, to receive a pair of leather shoes and a clean shirt; he recalled his question, 'Why do you look so afraid?' He had sensed then that Meyer felt sorry for them, and even ashamed; he was amazed and grateful now to learn that Meyer had known their names; and he believed him that he was 'on the other side' against his will.★ In this first letter, at least, he also emphatically agrees that they must meet.

Did he harden in his second letter, which in fact he sent? Or did he harden only later, in the telling? – because face to face, as he says, 'my opponent distracts me, he interests me more as a man than as an opponent . . . It [is] best for me to stick to writing.' Until their correspondence is released, once again we cannot know. We have only what Primo wrote in 'Vanadium'. He asked Meyer to tell him all he had done; then wrote to him that he did not need absolution: he had not been a hero, but nor had he committed any crime; he might live in peace.

But Meyer was not satisfied with this. It is true that he telephoned Primo and asked to meet him, and that Primo agreed. And it is true that before the meeting could take place, he suddenly died. Primo leaves the end of the

★ Hermann Langbein also judged Meyer positively in his book *Menschen in Auschwitz*, partly on Primo's testimony. Langbein further accepted Meyer's claim that he had attempted to help other Jews as well, despite orders to the contrary from his superior – that is, from Pannwitz.

story open. We may imagine that Meyer committed suicide; or that – like Franz Stangl, the commandant of Treblinka, when he had finally confessed to Gitta Sereny – his heart simply stopped of its own accord. But we should probably imagine neither. Outside 'Vanadium' Primo said – sometimes thankfully, sometimes bitterly – that Dr Meyer died a natural death.

So we come to 'Carbon', which is both the end and the beginning of this rare book, and both the beginning and the end of all Primo Levi's work, the achievement of everything he aimed at in his writing.

Its own age and origins are as mysterious as those of its hero, the atom of carbon. Did he first think of it in Auschwitz, in prison at Aosta, in Milan, or as early as *liceo*? Did he first write it in 1968, or as early as 1960, or 1961? He suggested all of these. But two things he clearly said: that 'Carbon' was his first literary dream, and that it was the first story of an element he ever wrote. From it grew the idea for a whole book of elements: so that the whole of *The Periodic Table* was born from its end; and in particular from the end of its end, from the atom of carbon that enters the writer's brain, and there meets the idea of itself that has been waiting for it for the human equivalent of the story's geological years.

'Carbon' begins – after an introduction to which we will return – with our atom bound into limestone, as it has been for hundreds of millions of years. This imprisonment 'cannot be thought of without horror'; but it is about to end. Suddenly, with a blow of a pickaxe, it is freed; and as the impurity of carbon dioxide it begins a wild dance of movement and change. For eight years it is flung around the world on the wind, until it is captured again, and its adventure becomes organic: it is photosynthesized into the leaf of a vine. From the leaf it migrates to the sap, from the sap to a grape, from the grape into wine; the wine is drunk, the drinker expels our atom in his breath, and once again it is carbon dioxide in the air. The dance is repeated: it is caught in the trunk of a cedar, eaten by a woodworm, and left in the slough of its carapace for 100 years; until the carapace at last dissolves, and 'the ex-drinker, ex-cedar, ex-woodworm' is freed once more. Three more times it flies around the world, until this time it is caught in a glass of milk. It is swallowed; it enters the bloodstream, and from the bloodstream, a cell. 'The cell belongs to a brain, and it is my brain,' Primo wrote. That cell, and so our atom, 'is in charge of my writing, in a gigantic minuscule game which nobody has yet described'. Thus, in a last dance – the 'double leap, up and down' – it guides his hand in that moment of supreme communication, as he marks on the paper *this dot, here, this one*.

So many ideas that were deeply important to Primo Levi are here. First, that pitiless geological imprisonment, which is 'worthy of a Catholic Hell':

584   <i>The Double Bond</i>

and yet it is entry into life which is an imprisonment, a binding into a long chain; release is not into life, but back into its raw material, which only with a new, miraculous capture is seized into the chain of life again. And then, that life-giving impurity of carbon dioxide, from which we come, and to which we return; and its rarity, only 0.03 per cent of air, like the vivifying impurity of Jews, only 0.07 per cent of Italy. And last but not least, the image of the dance, the 'perpetual, frightening round-dance of life and death' — perpetual and frightening, but a transcendent miracle as well.

'Carbon' itself is a kind of miracle. In <i>The Periodic Table</i> as a whole Primo achieved his dream of uniting his two halves, the chemist and the writer: but in no chapter more than 'Carbon', which is almost pure science, and almost pure poetry. And in 'Carbon' he also achieved another dream, which he would explore again and again, but never better than here: the dream of breaking barriers, of escape from himself, of 'boundless freedom'. In 'Carbon' he became even more than the other — he became Other, 'flying across centuries, meridians and parallels'.

That that is what he desired is clear from the introduction to the story, to return to that now. <i>The Periodic Table</i>, he claims there, is not autobiography: but it plainly is. The claim is true only of 'Carbon'. With 'Carbon' he escaped autobiography even in his autobiography. And yet, at the same time, he took us with him. For 'Carbon' is as much our history as his. It is a circle which binds us to him in its own 'double leap', uniting his writing and our reading in a single act. That is his deepest dream: to communicate; to be listened to; to touch another human being. When we read the dot he made, like Lilith with her apple we fulfil that dream.

Lilith

Lilith rationed our meetings, charmingly but firmly, and often many weeks would pass before she would agree to see me again. In the meantime I looked for her everywhere in Primo's writings. Surely she was in Gisella of *The Double Bond*, at least a little – hadn't she admitted that, smiling in her special way as she quoted the line *You always put up a barrier of smoke around you*? And was she not also, a little, in Line, in *If Not Now, When?* – in Line's containment and elusiveness; and in her low, veiled voice, the 'slightly husky' voice, once again, of a smoker? Perhaps it was because I was looking that, in a week in which I was forbidden to see her, I thought I found her in two of the stories of *Lilit*; and that in one I even thought I saw a shadow of myself.

This story is called 'La ragazza del libro', 'The Girl in the Book'. In it, Umberto meets a slim, vivid old lady with an extraordinary name: Harmonika Grinkiavicius. Not long afterwards he comes across the name again, reading the adventures of an English soldier in Italy during the war. In the book Harmonika is a partisan (like Line, I thought), with whom the Englishman falls torrentially in love. She is fearless in both love and war; and for thirty pages their 'heroic nights' are celebrated in glorious detail.

From then on Umberto can think of nothing but the vivid old lady and the girl in the book. As soon as he can, he returns to the town where he met Harmonika and knocks on her door. Beneath her white hair her face is still young, her eyes still full of laughter. Is she Lithuanian, he asks, does she speak many languages? Yes, she says, how does he know? From this book, he replies. She takes it from him and begins to read. And as she does so Umberto realizes that that is what he has come for: 'to see Harmonika in the act of reading the adventures of Harmonika'.

Half an hour later she gives the book back to him. *Is it true?* he asks. The old lady is silent; but then she smiles. She would like to be the girl in the book, she says, but she is not. Her memories are different from the Englishman's. And now hers have faded, while his have become brighter and more highly-coloured. 'I do not know which are more beautiful,' she says. 'You choose.' And charmingly but firmly she sends him away.

*　　*

A week later, Lilith is waiting for me at her door. She looks as young as Harmonika – younger, because her hair is not white. She *is* beautiful, I think (I don't want to be like the Englishman, making things more glamorous than they were): especially her eyes, which seem to be a different colour every time we meet – green, grey, blue, amber.

We sit for a while in silence. Lilith is very good at silence: she is happy to sit still for a long time, just tapping the ash off her cigarette now and again. As usual, I speak first. I have brought a chapter of *The Double Bond* which Primo didn't show her; and she has a chapter I have never seen. Shall we exchange them, as we decided the last time? No, she says – quite calmly, though she sees the disappointment on my face; you cannot change Lilith's mind by looking hurt. 'I'd forgotten what was in it,' she says. 'He might have wanted to change it, or I might.'

'So this chapter, at least, is about you?' I say quickly.

'No, no,' she replies, her eyes laughing, like Harmonika's. 'Only in small ways – and as he saw me, which perhaps was right, and perhaps was wrong.'

'What was wrong, for instance?' I ask.

She smiles. 'You should not look for the real women behind Primo's fictional loves,' she says, 'because there weren't any. The women he loved were the fictional ones.' She reaches out to the table beside her. 'In fact, that is one of the main points of this chapter. That part, I think, you may hear.' And she picks up a little pile of pages. She has prepared this all along.

For the next half hour I listened to Lilith reading in her husky voice. She read the first two pages, which were about depression – what Bertrand Russell called the Byronic desire for desire: having no desires, or only impossible ones. This desire for desire – Lilith read out, in Primo's words – he suffered as well; and since he had set himself the task of understanding, he was trying to understand this too. Here she stopped, and read a page or two in silence. Then, with many other silences, she read out his warning to the Lady: he turned people into characters; perhaps he had already done so with her. Do you remember Pygmalion, she read, who suffered so atrociously for love of his statue that the gods took pity on him, and turned her into a living woman? And many silences later, she read: I recommend to you the loveliest pages of *Don Quixote*, in which the Knight admits to Sancho Panza that Dulcinea is the pure creation of his imagination; and so are all the Amaryllises, the Sylvies, the Galateas of all the writers in the world.

She turned another page or two in silence, then put the chapter back on the table. That was my answer: Lilith was not the girl in the book either. And she herself had chosen which was more beautiful, to preserve certain memories in words, or to let them die. I had seen Harmonika reading the adventures of Harmonika; but neither I nor anyone else would ever read them in a book. She lit another cigarette, and smiled at me through the smoke.

Now it was my turn. In fact, I had also hesitated over giving her my whole chapter. It was the one about Primo's double bind, which had driven him to the brink of suicide several times, once (I'd guessed) with her. If he had not shown it to her himself, it was because he had not wanted her to know the depths of his disturbance. But then she must have known it already; perhaps no one knew it better than her. I took the copy I had made out of its folder and handed it to her.

She said, 'Thank you,' with that special look of hers, which is like a touch. Then she took it and put it away in the drawer of her table.

I hadn't imagined that, though as soon as she had done it I saw it was right. Of course when she first heard Primo's voice again they must be alone. But then she surprised me again. 'Am I in this chapter too?' she asked, as though she had not just read me the lesson of Dulcinea, peering through her smoke to make sure I had understood.

Yes, I said, I thought she was. The chapter was about his trouble with girls. 'Ah,' she said. He tells how it went back to adolescence, even to childhood, I said, and how it regularly drove him to despair. Then he tells how, finally, someone saved him. 'Yes,' she said. 'Lucia.' But at the end, I went on, he says that it is coming back again, with the Lady to whom the letters are addressed. She said nothing, but she looked very sad. He says, I concluded, that he saw her yesterday, in the Via Pietro Micca. He started to go up to her. But though he is famous now, that doesn't mean that he has anything left to say. And so, in the last moment, he turned the corner and slipped away.

'He turned the corner . . . ,' she repeated. She groped unseeingly for her cigarettes. 'That was Primo. He didn't dare.'

'But he wanted to,' I said.

'Did he?'

'He just stopped himself. Do you remember what he said? "I have no instincts; or if I do, I repress them." '

She laughed aloud, but only for a moment. 'I don't think he stopped himself,' she said. 'He simply wasn't capable of strong emotions. They just weren't there.'

I gaze at her in shock and sadness. This is the woman for whom Primo went through torment, for whom he nearly broke every rule of his society and his nature; and she does not think he was capable of love. For that must be what she means.

She widens her eyes at me, and gives her searching, quizzical smile.

'Have you ever heard of an interview,' I ask, 'towards the end, when he was asked if there was anything else he would have liked to be, if he hadn't been a writer?'

'No,' she says, 'what did he say?'

'A dancer,' I say. 'He said he would have liked to be a dancer.'

Now she is so sad I wish I hadn't told her. And I think: if Primo could make Lilith so sad, can anyone imagine the sadness of Lucia?

★   ★

The second story is called 'La valle di Guerrino', 'Guerrino's Valley'. Guerrino, the narrator tells us, was an artist: a lone itinerant painter of Madonnas and Nativities in the rustic churches of his valley. He was entirely untrained, but a born painter. At least one of his works deserves to survive, the narrator claims: a Last Judgement, full of irony and pity, presided over by a Saviour with staring eyes, whose features are a self-portrait of Guerrino.

Indeed, it was Guerrino's trademark to include at least one portrait of a living person in each of his paintings. Sometimes they were acts of homage to a patron, or of revenge on an enemy; often, as in the Last Judgement, they were visions of himself. But most often – always, in his paintings of Madonnas – they were portraits of his innumerable girls. These portraits are his most beautiful creations, but the stories behind them are barbaric. Guerrino was like a human Trachi: he rampaged through the valley, raping every young girl he found; leaving behind him a trail of children, and his 'ethereal images'.

There is, however, one other legend of Guerrino. When he was already over forty he fell in love with a young girl, whom he saw only from a distance, standing at her window. For the rest of his life he returned regularly to pay court to her; but every time she sent him away. Many people believe, says the narrator, that it was because of this love alone that Guerrino became Guerrino; but this love alone he never portrayed.

Not even I think that Guerrino's woman in the window was any one woman in Primo's life. She is all of them, starting from *his* girl in the window, when he was fifteen. And Lilith is right. Guerrino has never touched his love, or seen her from closer than the street below: even though she is real, what he loves is a creature of his imagination. What the story seems to say is that the artist – at least this artist – cannot love a real woman, and it is this that has made him an artist. But it has also made him a rapist, out of despair for his impossible, imagined love; and perhaps out of disappointment with the real ones. And I remember the girls who'd been 'in danger' with Primo when he was young; and what the young poet said to the doctor, in another of the stories of *Lilit*: that he wanted to punish his ideal woman, to accuse her of deceiving him, of trying to seem better to him than she was.

★　　★

This is my last visit – Lilith is going away, and then I am, and I don't know when I shall see her again. So this time I must follow *my* plan, not hers, as we have done so far.

The same thought always strikes at my heart when I enter her building: *Primo could have killed himself here.* It is so like the Corso Re Umberto, with its high hall, its curving stairs, its old, ornate lift cage. Does Lilith ever have this thought herself? I wonder. Probably not. There are many buildings like this, all over Turin; there is no reason to connect these two in particular. Still, I wonder if she does.

I didn't ask her, of course; but in a way she told me. I had left 'La ragazza del libro' with her on my last visit, saying that perhaps Primo had foreseen her dilemma, and her solution. As soon as I came in this time she gave it back to me, without comment. What had she thought of it? I asked, surprised. Nothing, she said: she hadn't read it. She hadn't been able to read Primo since he died. She had tried again, for me; she had even wanted to read this story. But there it was: she couldn't. 'But you can read *The Double Bond*,' I said. 'That's different,' she said. 'I don't know why.' I waited; but she said no more.

'You don't know why?' I asked.

She shook her head and smiled. Lilith is very good at this sort of silence too: if she doesn't want to answer, she keeps silent. Not many people can do that, I discovered. But this time she changed her mind.

'Perhaps I still blame him for his death,' she said. 'It was very aggressive, you know. Suicide is always aggressive; but to do it *inside* the house . . . Poor Lucia.'

'You mean he was punishing Lucia?'

'Not only Lucia – all of us. We shouldn't have left him alone at the end.'

'So really,' I said, 'it's not him you blame, it's yourself.'

'You mean,' she said slowly, 'that's why I can't read him? *Può darsi*; maybe. I must look inside myself one day, and see if I can tell. But I warn you I am not good at that. And besides, I am very lazy.' And she gave one of her catlike smiles, as though to prove it.

It was time for my plan, I thought. It was not quite true that she had told me nothing at all. If you really want to tell someone nothing at all, you must refuse to see them; once they're across your threshold, even your silence will give something away. But Lilith was an admirable opponent. She had made up her mind to tell me very little, and she had told me very little. If she didn't want to answer a question, but thought it admissible, she widened her eyes; if she thought it inadmissible, she closed them. She had a dazzling repertoire of smiles, which she played like music – encouraging, questioning, mysterious, stubborn, sly. She would never tell me her story; so I had decided to tell it to her.

I think you are Primo Levi's *donna della voce rauca*, I said, and I want to tell you her story. She smiled and widened her eyes. You can say yes, or no, or nothing, I said. She lit a cigarette, and watched me through the curls of smoke. I told her the story I have already told here: the Campiello dinner, and the apple; the four years of growing torment; the moment away from home, which was perhaps its height; his ending it, because he could not end his marriage. That was when she said, 'I was not free either.' When, at one point, I said *He fell in love with you*, she looked sad again, sadder than I had ever seen her. To the rest, of course, she said nothing at all.

At the end we sat for a long time in silence. Then she said quietly, 'He did try to leave his life with me. But . . .' She stood up. 'And he told me he loved me to the very end. Now we must have some coffee, I think.'

We had coffee, and talked of other things for a while. Then she took me to her door. 'Be careful,' she said. When I looked back from the lift she was still standing there, like Guerrino's woman in the window.

Since then we have exchanged several letters. Hers are short and often humorous. In one she told me that she could read Primo again: she'd just finished *La tregua*, which was very beautiful. She never asks about this book. I haven't asked if she ever looked inside herself again; if she did, she hasn't told me what she saw.

14. Writer:
1975–85

Primo in 1982

They were his worst stories, he'd said – he would never succeed with them, he was sure. And nine years later *The Periodic Table* was the biggest and happiest success of his career.

There wasn't a paper in Italy that didn't review it. Lorenzo Mondo led the chorus of praise, closely followed by Natalia Ginzburg, which pleased Primo a good deal. His friend Roberto Vacca, who never reviewed, wrote a rave; Paolo Milano was also keen; and if Carlo Bo didn't review the book, it was because he was backing it for the Viareggio. Almost every story was somebody's favourite, with 'Iron' and 'Argon' leading; even 'Mercury' got one critic's vote. Everyone noted that with this book Primo Levi had returned to autobiography; but *Il Ragguaglio Librario* said that in Levi non-fiction was so close to 'creativity' that no distinction was possible; and *Rinascita* declared roundly that *The Periodic Table* was a novel, 'in the classic and traditional sense of giving a form to experience'. The Milanese Jewish writer Guido Lopez summed up the general response in midsummer: of all the books in the world, there were now three by Primo Levi we would have to save.

In July *The Periodic Table* missed the Viareggio by one vote (or possibly three, depending on which leak you heard). In September came the Prato, with two prizes, one for fiction and one for non-fiction: and Primo won the fiction category. Within a year *The Periodic Table* had gone through five editions and 32,000 copies sold. Immediately there was a huge leap in its author's fame. In June he was interviewed by his friend Carlo Mussa in front of a large audience in the Teatro Carignano. In September he made his first reluctant appearance on television, interviewed by Mondo, and questioned by a posse of professors. After that the requests to speak to schools, to universities, to literary circles came thick and fast. Primo went to a youth club in Cuneo, and to one of Turin's 'Literary Fridays', in November; in 1976 he agreed to a tour of five Swiss cities, starting at the University of Zurich. But apart from these, and the ones from schools, he turned down most of the invitations. He was a hardened speaker now; but it was all too much. And it was not only the invitations. His post was beginning to swell, and to include more and more manuscripts from young hopefuls. He was beginning to be stopped on the street, and asked for his autograph on the backs of tram tickets, or whatever else came to hand. He felt flattered, but also invaded. 'If this goes on,' he said, 'I'll have to shave off my beard.'

The Periodic Table was the turning point – indeed, it was a double turning point. First in Italy in 1975, and then in the United States in 1984, it was the book which promoted Primo Levi from a respected figure to a famous one, and from a witness-writer to a full, non-hybrid one. It was his most literary book so far, and perhaps his most literary book altogether: as original as *The Wrench*, as full of invention as *Se non ora, quando?* (as he admitted to the professors), and far richer in both imagery and feeling than either. It was a return to autobiography and memory, but that was *terra firma* to Primo, and he felt happier there. At the same time, the literary quality of this fifth book was recognized and praised more than it would be in either of his later novels. And though it began the second stage of his difficulties with fame, they were still only beginning. *The Periodic Table* healed the breaches in Primo Levi between chemist and writer, between hybrid writer and complete one; and perhaps even, for a while, between the man who needed recognition, and the one who could not endure it.

A few years into his retirement, Primo would wryly announce that things had not gone as expected: with his new 'avalanches' of time, he had imagined writing another twenty or thirty books; instead he'd written hardly any. But this was also a few years into his narrowing depressive cycle, and it wasn't true. In fact, he wrote a prodigious amount in the last dozen years of his life

– 'as though he wanted to make up for lost time', Lorenzo Mondo says; and towards the end published almost 'frenetically', as his editor, Marco Belpoliti, puts it. True, he had written three books before 1975, and he wrote three books after. The difference came in the stories. If we do a Levi-like calculation, and assume that instead of three hours in the evening he could now – in theory – work eight hours a day, that is an increase of just under three times; whereas his production of stories increased half-way to four.

The reception of *The Periodic Table* convinced even Primo that he had been wrong to despair of his chemical stories. In late 1976 he made his famous remark to Gabriella Poli: 'My books come to me as twins.' First two books on the Lager, then two books of stories; and now he wanted to give *The Periodic Table* a twin too. In *The Periodic Table* the chemistry had been inorganic; this time he would move to organic, as he had done in life. A few months earlier he had been at the thirty-fifth anniversary dinner of his year in chemistry, and told his fellow-chemists of his plan. They had come up with a title: *Il doppio legame*, the difficult double bond of living substances. Yes – that was good, he had accepted gratefully. So he had his title; now all he needed was the book.

He had begun it: perhaps already in 1963, when he'd first talked of 'a book about chemistry and chemists'. If so, he re-began it now. But it was not easy. Inorganic chemistry had been a 'lost paradise' of solidity and clarity in writing, as it had been in the hopeful studies of his youth; organic chemistry was the opposite in both. It was, he wrote, 'bungling': feeling your way in the dark, full of false starts, failure, and sin. He wanted to write about that now, he even needed to. His own chemical sins weighed on him – all those accidents, over thirty years; dumping acetic acid into Settimo's sewage system for fifteen. And his friends' weighed on him as well: the sins of Giorgio Lattes, for example, who was having to change many of his factory's practices now, under the new laws, and fighting to survive, like Federico Accati; perhaps also the sins of Alberto, which he had probably forgotten, but which had surely been among his reasons for leaving chemistry, all those years ago.

So Primo began. He showed the opening lines, in another school exercise-book, to Gabriella Poli this time: 'For fifteen years Z. had been living in sin, and he knew it.' Z. was a chemist, the owner of a factory which made combs, spectacle frames, and other things out of fake tortoiseshell. Z.'s sin, which profoundly tormented him, was the same as Primo's: his factory polluted the land and water around it with toxic waste. The story was excellent, Gabriella remembers. Nonetheless, Primo did not go on with it: the first *Double Bond* stopped there. Instead, he wrote the first story about his freest and most fulfilled hero, Libertino Faussone, and published it in *La*

Stampa in March 1977. It was as though he had 'turned the corner and slipped away', as his narrator would do in the second *Double Bond*, with the Signora; it was as though he had even bolted. In that year, 1977, a young student who came to hear him speak saw the same movement in the central mission of his life, his testimony. He spoke on two levels, Claudio Cavallini remembers: one willingly and openly, the other unwillingly, and with difficulty. The first level was the brave and positive one, on which he told about Alberto Dalla Volta, about Lorenzo, about all those who miraculously resisted 'the weapons of the night'. The other was the night side, 'the monstrous in man', says Claudio, which he would recognize, but immediately abandon. He was talking to the young; it was more important than ever to show the possibility of resistance, and not to sow despair. But it was not only this – the conscious and moral decision he always made. It was a deep inner need to avoid the dark, because in it he himself might drown. He obeyed it in his testimony, and not only to students: recognizing the worst in man – the grey zone – in his first book, then abandoning it until his last one. And he obeyed it now with his own dark side, in *The Double Bond*. That would be the very last thing to which he would return.

For the next year or more, therefore, he would do the opposite of what he had first set out to do: to give *The Periodic Table* its difficult, organic twin. Instead, he stripped *The Double Bond* of all its darkness – Z.'s sin, and his remorse; Dr Levi's errors – and used the rest for his most optimistic, most entertaining book, *The Wrench, La chiave a stella*. He wrote it, he said, with extreme ease, and (it's clear from every word) extreme pleasure: we may guess, in a kind of relief.

At the same time, he began his great production of essays and stories. At the beginning of 1975, thirty years after the liberation of Auschwitz, Arrigo Levi, editor of *La Stampa*, asked him for an article to mark the occasion, and published it in early February, on the first page. Later that month, *La Stampa* also published a chapter of *The Periodic Table*, which was still to appear; and in June, one of the Lager stories that would open *Lilit*. In 1976 it started to grow – two of the stories of *Lilit*, two essays, two poems, two book reviews and two other pieces (one of which was the 'Afterword' to *Se questo*, added in that year). In 1977, a huge jump – two chapters of *La chiave a stella*, six *Lilit* stories, six essays, three other pieces and a poem: a total of eighteen contributions by Primo Levi. In 1978, twenty-four, in 1979, seventeen, in 1980 nineteen; and through the 80s, never less than thirteen (that was 1982), and over twenty in each of the last three full years of his life. That's two a month, from a man in his mid-60s, who was not a journalist, and who was completing his last, dolorous book on the Lager. 'Frenetic' does not seem far off the mark to me.

Would he have written as much without the platform of *La Stampa*, which he could rely on to publish whatever he offered? It is hard to say: the counterfactual proof does not exist, as he would say. But his use of the platform was very determined. Mondo and Arrigo Levi often asked him for comment on events in the news, Piero Bianucci at *Tuttoscienze** asked him for articles on science; but he firmly refused. He wrote what he wanted, when he wanted: the occasional book review, or topical piece on his special subjects – technological advances or disasters, Israel, the Lager; but mostly his own stories, essays and poems. Every now and again he would arrive at the newspaper's offices, often unannounced. He would call on his friends – old ones, like Carlo Casalegno, about whom we shall soon hear more; and new ones, like Calcagno and Bianucci, and two more Albertos, Papuzzi and Sinigaglia; and above all Gabriella Poli, whom he re-met now, after twenty years, and who would soon join the circle of his trusted readers. Then he would walk over to *Tuttolibri*, his little black plastic briefcase under his arm, take out the latest story or poem, and offer it to Mondo. *La Stampa* almost never publishes poems; but of course, says Mondo, we always took it. This was Primo Levi.

Nineteen-seventy-five may serve as a snapshot of the busy, difficult years 1975–7, when Primo was still in his larval stage, like one of the tadpoles he'd watched as a boy, waiting to emerge definitively as a writer.

He was still speaking in schools, though it was becoming harder. In the 60s the Second World War had been real to young people, something that had happened to their own parents; by the 80s it was history. The 1970s were a transition time in this too. He was beginning to feel old and irrelevant, 'a *garibaldino* with a white beard'; the students' questions were beginning to be stereotyped, and all the same; they were beginning to ask if it was all true. In late 1975 he wrote out his answers to the eight most frequently asked questions, to be added to the schools editions of *Se questo è un uomo* and *La tregua*. Eventually – but not yet – they would replace him.

By now he was no longer active in Cogidas, but something else had grown out of it. As part of the 'people power' measures that followed 1968, the *Decreti delegati* – Delegates' Laws – had been passed in 1974, allowing (among other things) for parents to be involved in the running of schools. The D'Azeglio parents founded their own *Consiglio*, or parents' council; and in early 1975, by a large majority, they elected Primo Levi their President. He was President for a year – and then a bit more, until the next President could take over (after which the popularity of parent power declined in any case, defeated by bureaucracy and boredom).

---

* The science section of *La Stampa*, as *Tuttolibri* is the books section.

In the first few sessions he saw a few of his own motions carried – for a celebration of the Liberation on 25 April, for instance, and for a declaration of solidarity with antifascist demonstrations; and there were always important issues to deal with – new, experimental teaching arrangements, for example, and students' demands for '*autogestione*', or self-management; questions of how to deal with fascist interventions in student meetings, with disputes between teachers and students, with new courses (including one on sex education). But the bureaucracy and boredom overwhelmed Primo very soon. It soon became clear to him that they would achieve little or nothing; they focused more and more on self-interested and explosive questions, such as the rules for new admissions, or on essential but deadly dull ones, such as money – for student trips, for the gymnasium, for a new photocopier. He was extremely scrupulous, and missed only one of the thirty-two meetings in his term of office; but everyone could see he was not happy, and privately he was desperate. His spell as President of this small and well-meaning group, he told Giorgio Calcagno, was 'the worst time of my life' – forgetting to mention his partisan period, or even Auschwitz. Of course this was a passing mood; but it explains, Calcagno notes, why Primo Levi could never join a political party, or any party at all.

And then there was SIVA; and then writing. In the autumn of 1975 he was translating the great German-Jewish poet Heinrich Heine: for the next two years all the poems he would bring Lorenzo Mondo in his little black briefcase would be translations, mostly of Heine. He had just finished another translation in August: this time of a book of science, *Natural Symbols*, by the English anthropologist Mary Douglas. And as soon as that was done he wrote to Luciano Foà, former Director of Einaudi, now owner of Adelphi, proposing a new and very different translation.

Some time ago, he told Foà, he'd come across a book published in Holland in 1957. It was by a Dutch-Jewish historian, Jacques Presser; it was called *De Nacht der Girondijnen*, *The Night of the Girondists*; and it was the story of a young Dutch Jew who manages to stay alive in Westerbork⋆ by helping to load his fellow Jews on to the trains. He had read it and reread it; it was ruthlessly truthful, and he could not get it out of his mind. At the end of September Foà accepted his proposal; and Primo sat down to his translation.

La notte dei Girondini was his first re-encounter with the dreadful subject of the 'grey zone' – the twilight world of Schepschel, Alfred L. and Henri, of the Block elders, Kapos and spies; all those who saved themselves by collaborating, more or less willingly, with their persecutors. He had never

---

⋆ The Dutch equivalent of Drancy, or Fossoli: the holding camp from which the transports left for Auschwitz and the other end-stations of the Reich.

smoothed over its existence: he had examined it in his first book, and returned to it in his portrait of Rappoport, for instance, written in 1959; it had never disappeared from his conversation. Nonetheless, since 1946 he had not given it his characteristic, un–selfsparing attention in writing; on the contrary, with the portraits which would go into *Lilit*, and with 'Cerium' in *The Periodic Table*, he had allowed himself to dwell instead on 'moments of reprieve'. Now, he wrote, the time had come to explore this space between the victims and their executioners, which only a Manichean could think was empty. In fact it was full; and 'if we hope to understand the human race' we must recognize this, though the knowledge 'stings like a burn'.

He made himself recognize it now, passing each of Presser's burning words through his own mind, and into his own language; and it was almost unendurable. Translating Presser, he told Gabriella Poli, he relived Auschwitz; for the whole time it took him, from October to nearly the end of December, he was afflicted by 'violent emotion'. He was forcing himself to do what he could not bear to do: to face 'the monstrous in man', as Claudio Cavallini said, without bolting. He did it, and he would do it again; but we cannot guess how much it cost him. Or perhaps we can.

In 1975 Primo Levi began to come out as a writer. Not only did he publish *The Periodic Table*, which showed the world that chemistry could also be literature; barely a month later he published *L'Osteria di Brema*, which showed the world that *this* chemist was also a poet.

So far only his close friends knew that he wrote poetry; in writing terms, it was his best-kept secret. Five years before he had had twenty-three of the poems he'd written so far – minus the one to Lucia – privately printed; or rather, not even printed, but typed and bound in thin cardboard covers, not unlike his favourite school exercise-books. He had made (he would say later) 300 copies of this slender, anonymous, untitled booklet; but though he was probably dramatizing when he said that 'no more than fifteen people [had] read it' in its first year, we can be certain that only a small fraction of the 300 was actually distributed.

Over the next five years he had added another four poems, so that there were nearly thirty; and at some point he had mentioned the fact to his publisher. But thirty-odd poems were still too few; his poetry was even more maverick than his prose, and like the stories, it was uneven. The Einaudi editors said no. Primo took the rejection with his usual self-control. But now – 'by chance', he told Einaudi – he had come across the small Milan house of Scheiwiller, which had offered to publish the twenty-eight poems. I don't suppose it was by chance at all. He had decided it was time to come out as a poet as well.

There can be no stronger proof of his determination to be taken seriously as a writer than this. For it was as clear to him as it was to his critics, biographers and translators – to Giovanni Tesio, for instance, to Gabriella Poli, to Ruth Feldman – that his poetry was where his darkness found expression: his sadness and isolation, his anger and fear – everything his moral and rational self suppressed, and his instinct of self-preservation as well. Of the fifteen poems of his first 'attack', in late 1945 and 1946, just under half were about Auschwitz. Two others were about, and to, Lucia, one was a (mostly) humorous piece about Monday mornings, and one a sinister little poem called 'The Witch', in which a woman burns an effigy of the man she loves. The remaining four poems are all expressions of anguish: different kinds of anguish, but none of them directly linked to the Lager. Between 1949 and 1974 came a dozen others: of which only two, now, are directly linked to Auschwitz, and indirectly two more. Then there is 'Epitaph', about a murdered partisan,★ 'Lilith' from 1965, and a 1970 poem connected to 'Carbon'. All the rest – at least five – are once again poems of depression and despair, for which any link to the Lager must be supplied by the reader's knowledge and imagination. The crow, for example, had been Primo's image of death and desolation since 'The Story of Ten Days': in 1953 it returns for the second time in these poems, a 'small black shadow' waiting for the poet everywhere – 'useless, useless to flee!' In 1964 came 'Approdo', 'Landing', the longing for easeful death which we already know. 'Via Cigna', in 1973, is like a prose version of *Vizio di forma*'s 'Small red Lights'. 'Black Stars', of November 1974, is a cry of horror at the universe ('And all of us human seed, we live and die for nothing, the skies perpetually revolve in vain'); 'Leavetaking', of December 1974, a quieter but equally defeated poem about ageing ('It has grown late, my friends . . .'). If Primo was not in his second (or later) depression of that hard year, I'll eat my hat.

Many of these are wonderful poems – 'Shemà' and 'Reveille',† 'There Were a Hundred', which Primo would use for the *envoi* to *Vizio di forma*, 'Waiting', both 'Crow' poems, and several others. What we should note, however, is this: that if Primo Levi had wanted above all else to preserve his image as the serene sage, he would not have published his poems. He did want to preserve that image; but he wanted something else more. To write, he said, was to bare oneself to the world, even in one's most carefully polished work. How much more must that be so, for him, in poetry – which came from his heart and not his mind, which 'caught him in flagrante', which struck him like 'a rash', like 'an infection'?

★ This is a memory of the sentence carried out at Amay.
† Respectively the *envois* for *If This is a Man* and *The Truce*.

In fact he said so, to an aspiring writer whose work he would admire and champion. When Mario Macagno first asked for his advice on poetry, he tried to discourage him. 'You know,' he said, 'that writing poetry means stripping yourself bare?' He knew the risk he was taking. But he wanted to prove himself a writer, even at the risk of being understood.

★   ★

In September 1977, at the age of fifty-eight, Primo Levi's half-life as a chemist was finally over. His trim rabbinical beard had become part of him, giving his face a puckish, humorous point that balanced the intensity of his eyes. And now his clothes changed too. His shirt-collars opened, his jackets loosened, his trousers grew less narrow – sometimes they even flared, in the 70s style; and slowly – very slowly – the smell of the factory faded from them, and from his shoes. He had metamorphosed; he was free.

Nineteen-seventy-eight began well, under this new sign of freedom. The three short plays which he and Scaglione had adapted for television, and which had been filmed in early 1977, were finally shown in January of this year; Primo went to the preview of 'The Sleeping Beauty' at the Turin studios of the RAI, and told everyone, 'This is a holiday for me.' Meanwhile, the radio version of *La tregua* was also being made, in the first few months of 1978; and now he was free he could go to as many of the recording sessions as he pleased. He went to them all. The return to radio, and to his first great story of liberation, was thrilling: 'a wonderful experience', he said.

But it was not as wonderful as it should have been. It was spoiled for him – as the television plays were too – by a long attack of shingles, which lasted for the whole first quarter of this year. It was probably not his first; but it was the longest and most severe. This was a cruel blow. Here he was, completely free for the first time since he came home from Auschwitz; and immediately he had his first serious illness since Auschwitz too. He was furious; and worse than that, afraid. He was in pain, and his body was failing him. He could not bear either. During all this happy holiday, he was in a depression. Finally, at the end of March, the fourth treatment worked, and the depression disappeared together with the shingles. But it had been a warning. 'I realize I am vulnerable,' he said.

It was also a sign, because shingles is a stress-related illness. In fact, it was the sign of something so ironic, and so painful, that it might have been a story by Primo Levi rather than about him. It was this: that the beginning of his real release was also the beginning of his real decline.

Why? Was he so afraid of freedom as a writer – as afraid as he was of freedom from his marriage? No. He *was* afraid; but in the case of writing, unlike the other, his desire was greater than his fear. There were other reasons, of which two were the most important; and those two, especially, were the story of his last years.

The first reason was a general and public one: the worsening of the violence around him. In the autumn of 1974 Piedmont had been the first Region in Italy to begin an investigation into neo-fascist activity; and by 1975 that was dying down. But almost immediately the Red Brigades took over. They had been attacking factory bosses and right-wing trade unionists since 1972, setting their cars on fire, beating them, and issuing long communiqués. But in 1975 the attacks radically increased, and became more professional, until bombings, kidnappings and shootings became (as the Region's report put it) 'an everyday part of Piedmontese life' for the next three years, especially in Turin. In 1976 came yet another intensification of violence, both in Piedmont and in the rest of Italy. In that year eight people were murdered by the Red Brigades, including one in Piedmont, a police official in Biella. In 1977 seven people were assassinated, two of them in Turin: another policeman, and a lawyer who had acted against the Brigades. From policemen and the legal profession they then turned their attention to journalists. In June the editor of *Il Giornale Nuovo*, Indro Montanelli, was shot and wounded; in September Nino Ferrero of *L'Unità*. Also in September, a bomb exploded outside the offices of *La Stampa*. Finally, on 16 November, Primo's friend Carlo Casalegno, the Deputy Editor of the paper, was shot outside his house on the Corso Re Umberto, only a few streets away from Number 75. The assassins had not aimed for his legs, as they usually did: this time they had shot to kill. Casalegno had two bullets to the head, and one in the neck. He clung to life with remarkable strength, but died thirteen days later.

Casalegno was a *dazegliano* and an ex-G. & L. partisan; Primo met him often at *La Stampa*, and at Azelia Arici's literary evenings on the Corso Galileo Ferraris. The violence had almost literally come home. Primo had never made a public political statement before. But *La Stampa* published an 'Appeal against Violence' by a group of Turinese intellectuals: and to that – together with Norberto Bobbio, Italo Calvino, Alessandro Galante Garrone, Massimo Mila and others – he put his name.

The death of Casalegno was a turning point for Turin. Thousands of people demonstrated against his shooting in the Piazza San Carlo; nearly a quarter of a million signed a petition to hold the trial of the Red Brigades, scheduled for March 1978, in the city. It began there on 9 March. On 16 March Aldo Moro was kidnapped; in early May his body was found in the heart of Rome. The government had wavered, but held firm; there had been no compromise with terrorism. The trial ended in June with convictions for all the Brigade leaders. The violence continued for months, even for years; but the Red Brigades' back was broken, and the whole country condemned them. By 1980 the *anni di piombo* were finally over. Italian democracy had survived, and so had Primo Levi. But it was as well for both, I suspect, that it had taken no longer.

The peak of external violence, for him, had coincided with the first moments of his freedom, in late 1977. That was cruel; but at least it eventually stopped. The other painful ironies of timing did not. They began now, and went on to the end.

First of all, his freedom was not only an escape, but also a loss. SIVA had brought him company, variety, and material; it had given him friends as well as enemies, and satisfaction as well as shingles. Above all, SIVA had given him a life outside the Corso Re Umberto. Not an easy one; and in the end having two lives had begun in itself to split him apart. But when that other life ended, his world closed in for good. He had *La Stampa* to go to, and later also Einaudi. But it wasn't the same. He was welcomed, especially by his friends (not by all at Einaudi, with his doggedness over detail, and over payment too); at *La Stampa* he was even treated like a celebrity, like an elder statesman. But these were busy places, and they were not his own. He dropped in discreetly, and hurried away again. There was no excuse to stay.

With the end of SIVA the door of his home closed behind him for the last time: not just psychologically, but really. He had no reason to go anywhere else, to see anyone else, to telephone or be telephoned by anyone else any longer, except for the inadmissible one of his own pleasure. And so he did not; or he did so much less, and with infinitely greater difficulty. So, for example, he almost lost touch with his oldest love, Gabriella Garda. Until he retired, he went to Milan several times a year; when she came to Turin she could see him at the factory. She will never forget, she says, one day in particular, when he showed her his tower, and all SIVA's latest technical marvels, so unimaginable in the poor, pre-war chemistry they had shared. It was like a homecoming, Gabriella says – like being back at Wander together, with the smells of their laboratory around them. After 1977 such meetings were no longer possible. In the last ten years of Primo's life she saw him only rarely; in the last year, not at all.

It was not only Gabriella Garda on whom the door closed, after 1977, but any woman, real or imaginary, outside Turin. The days of meeting girls on trains were over. In 1976 Primo wrote a story about an encounter on a train, like a parting present to that old adventure. Riccardo longs to pour his heart out to the girl, to tell her of his unhappiness, and of his certainty that one day he will be a famous poet. But he is slow and shy, and when he finally asks her to come to Naples with him, she refuses. The story is called 'Breve sogno': 'A Brief Dream'.

Other things weighed heavily on Primo too, at the end of the 70s. The charges against him from his years at SIVA, for example, were still pending: and if Primo Levi, champion of the oppressed, had been publicly accused of endangering the lives of the workers in his care, I cannot imagine he would have survived. Still, that was only a fear, however awful; it didn't happen. But two things did happen: the two which were the most important reasons for his decline.

The first was to do with his mother. In 1975 Rina had turned eighty. She was still in good health for her age – she had problems with her eyes, and the usual frailties, but nothing serious. They were enough, however, to threaten her hegemony. She could no longer keep house adequately, or even at all. Lisa had left home, Renzo was starting university; the family was changing, and she was losing her absolute rule. Though she was not ill, therefore, she began to become so. By 1976 Primo was already beginning to refuse engagements on the grounds of his mother's health, especially if they meant leaving Turin.

For a while this was still manageable, sporadic. In 1978 – Primo's first full free year – it became much less so. In that year Rina became old. Her eyes were worse, she had palpitations, she no longer left the flat. At the same time, Lucia's mother, who was four years older, seemed to worsen as well. Lucia began to dedicate herself entirely to the care of the two old ladies. Primo did not have to help a great deal with her mother, except no doubt with sympathy and moral support. But he could not let his wife do everything for *his*, and do nothing himself. At the very least he had to be there, to help her, to do his share of the household tasks. It was no longer just at mealtimes now that he hurried home from friends' houses, even from meetings: it was when the shopping had to be done, or medicines fetched, or his mother's lenses changed. By 1979 he felt in a state of siege. By 1981 he and Lucia no longer left Turin, even in August.

About this last imprisonment of Primo Levi everyone knew, even to the outermost circle of his friends and acquaintances. He could not hide it, and he did not try. It was, after all, like Auschwitz: a natural and external explanation of his difficulties; even of depression, when that too became impossible to disguise. And it was true: from 1978 onwards his depressions were triggered very largely by his mother's decline, and by its consequences. But it was also not true, because neither was natural or external. The truth was that his own relationship to his mother was pathological; and so was the level of care Lucia required them both to give. These together were quite enough to depress him on their own.

But they were not left on their own. The second main nightmare of his last years also began its squalid existence now, in the last months of 1978.

In November Louis Darquier de Pellepoix, Vichy's commissioner of Jewish affairs, was interviewed in the French magazine *L'Express*. Auschwitz, he said, indeed the whole so-called Holocaust, was a myth invented by the Jews. All the statistics were false, the photographs fakes; there had been deportations, but to unknown destinations; there had been gas chambers, but they murdered only lice. (The interview was headed 'Only Lice Were Gassed in Auschwitz'.)

In December Robert Faurisson, professor of literature in Lyons, also finally managed to publish his claims in France. For nearly twenty years he had been arguing that the gas chambers had never existed. His university had suspended him for teaching this non-history to his students; for four years *Le Monde* had been refusing to debate his views. Now it changed its mind. On 29 December it published his article, 'The Rumour of Auschwitz': the descriptions of the gas chambers were not credible, were indeed impossible; there had been none at Buchenwald, at Bergen-Belsen, at Dachau; therefore there had been none at all.

This was negationism: the first and most extreme form of Holocaust denial. It had been growing in France since the late 40s, and in Britain and America since the 50s and 60s (not in Germany, which however would provide the world leaders in later and more subtle forms). Up to now it had been a lunatic fringe. But with these two publications in highly respectable papers it broke a barrier, and entered the larger world. From now on it would be as hard to eradicate as that other noxious weed, fascism. In Britain, for example, David Irving had also published his *Hitler's War* in the late 70s, claiming that Hitler neither ordered nor even knew about the genocide of the Jews; Irving is still a leading Holocaust denier today.

Primo replied to the negationists immediately, in a barrage of articles in *Corriere delle Sera*, *La Stampa* and elsewhere. Darquier was eighty-five years old and clearly senile, he said; since he himself had sent 70,000 French Jews to their deaths, he was hardly a disinterested party. As for Faurisson, he was probably deranged: the only motives for such gross denials of fact were guilt or madness, and since Faurisson was too young for guilt (he was only fifty), he must be mad. How can you begin to answer a madman? In all the trials so far – the Nuremberg trial, the Eichmann trial, the Auschwitz trial in 1965 – the accused had defended themselves in all sorts of ways: they had done nothing themselves, they were under orders, they did not know. But none had ever said it hadn't happened. There had been 17 million Jews in Europe in 1939, and 11 million in 1945: where were the missing 6 million? Come and talk to us survivors, Primo told Faurisson: you can do so without leaving France, there are plenty of us there.

He did not mean the first part of this invitation. In the face of such irrationality and naked bad faith his belief in rational argument failed: he could not debate, or even read, those who denied the crimes he had devoted his life to recording. They, and they alone, brought out in him absolute intolerance; and a violence of language ('senile', 'stupid', 'mad') which was to him the essence of the Lager, and normally beyond the pale. The appearance of Faurisson and his ilk was the deepest shock to him: perhaps as deep as the shock of Auschwitz itself. These new Nazis lived in peace and safety, unlike the original ones. They had all the evidence before them. His outrage against them remained raw, personal and powerful to the end. In 1986 he wrote of their 'ugly enterprise': they claimed innocent neutrality, while devoting pages and pages of intellectual gymnastics to showing that 'we did not see what we saw, did not live what we lived'.

It was not only Holocaust denial that appeared at the end of the 70s: the Holocaust itself was at last emerging into public consciousness in these years, a generation after the end of the war. In April 1978 American television broadcast the series *Holocaust*, and immediately sold it to fifty countries. In January 1979 it was shown in Germany, and in May in Italy. It was, Elie Wiesel complained, cheap and even offensive: a melodrama made for money, a soap opera instead of a tragedy. Everyone agreed, including Primo. But with his usual detachment, he was one of the first to put what has become, with time, the general view. Yes, *Holocaust* was crude, commercial and simplistic, but on the whole its intentions were respectful. And most importantly, it worked. Just those aspects of it which were most ambiguous – its soap-opera form, the mass-medium nature of television – meant that it was infinitely more effective than any book or sober documentary in making the genocide of the Jews known to the world. Many millions of people saw it, especially in Germany.★ There it broke three decades of silence, and caused the first (and perhaps the last) convulsion of public self-examination of the recent past. In sum, it was worth it; like the book on which it was based, which was equally dubious, it was 'nonetheless an ally'.

For several years Primo had been trying to cut down on his 'third career'. By the late 70s he spoke in schools only rarely, when asked by friends, and wanted to stop altogether. But now suddenly there was all this new interest; and this new attack, which would last a good deal longer. In March 1979 a group of young hooligans had screamed abuse at an Israeli basketball team

★ Over 20 million Germans watched the series, which meant, one critic pointed out, every second adult in the country.

in Varese – '*Ten, a hundred, a thousand Mauthausens!*' Soon after, the Jewish Youth Federation called a national conference in Rome, to which Primo was invited. He went. He could not give up the battle, as he longed to. Together with Lidia Rolfi, with whom he had often toured the schools of Piedmont, he rededicated himself to it now. Over the next few months he travelled the length and breadth of Northern Italy, talking to students about his new book, *La chiave a stella*; but also, once again, about *Se questo è un uomo*, and the terrible, unanswerable question of racial hatred.

By the end of that time he was exhausted, and his sense of distance from this new generation had grown. His 'strange power of speech' had left him, he felt; his message had to cross a gap of too many years now to reach the young. They felt it too. Like Renato Portesi, they sensed the immense effort he was making to reach them, and the underlying fear that it was impossible: that experience, and especially *this* experience, was not communicable after all. After sixteen years, and around 150 schools, he quietly stopped going, and left talking to the young to Lidia Rolfi, Giuliana Tedeschi, Ferruccio Maruffi and the others.

At the time it seemed as though he had bolted from the subject for good. In the first six months of 1979, with the shock of negationism, no fewer than eleven Holocaust-related articles had appeared under his name. After that, two of the Lager stories of *Lilit*, also in 1979, and one in 1980; in 1981 *Lilit* itself, with twelve Lager (or Lager-related) stories in it. But then nothing. In 1982 came the counter-Lager novel *Se non ora, quando?*; in this, and in other pieces over the next few years, there was a new interest in Judaism and Jewry, but very little about the Holocaust. When *The Drowned and the Saved* appeared in 1986 it took everyone by surprise. Primo's campaign to escape the label of 'witness-writer', and to be accepted as a literary writer *tout court*, had begun to work. Then suddenly after five years it was all reversed, and Primo Levi the witness and analyst of the Holocaust was back again.

But the truth was that he had never gone away. Primo Levi gestated most of his ideas for years, like an elephant; but after 'Carbon' and *Se non ora, quando?*, the longest gestation was for *The Drowned and the Saved*. It went back to 1975, and his first re-encounter with the grey zone, in his translation of Jacques Presser. He had begun it then, perhaps with the story of Chaim Rumkowski. Then he'd put it away, and gone back to it, and put it away again, several times over the years. But he did not give up. In 1979 Faurisson and negationism renewed his resolve. In mid-1980 he picked it up again, and started (or re-started) what would become Chapter 1, 'The Memory of the Offence', in earnest. The book caused him 'great and profound anguish', says his second biographer, Gabriella Poli. He could not write more than a

page a day, and he did not finish 'The Memory of the Offence' until early
1981. After that he continued, slowly and painfully. By 1985, six chapters
were finished. He wrote the last three, and the Conclusion; and extracted a
bit of a 1982 text for the Preface. By January 1986 it would be done.*

It would cost him everything. Together with his suffering over his
mother, it would push him down into the next circle of depression. And
because it was a great book, and his last to be published, it would close the
circle: returning him to his condition of hybrid writer, and costing him
some of the purely literary recognition he had worked so hard to secure.
But that, at least, he would not know.

At the end of 1976 he was still struggling to write the first *Double Bond*.
Three months later *La Stampa* published a new Primo Levi story: and there,
fully fledged, was Libertino Faussone – Piedmontese, rigger of cranes,
derricks and bridges: tall, thin and lugubrious-looking; passionately devoted
to his demanding trade, which takes him all around the globe, to the
exclusion (or almost) of any lasting human bond.

What had happened? How had this brand new character suddenly
appeared in Primo Levi's life? Well, of course his appearance wasn't really
sudden at all. He is such a typical Piedmontese craftsman that everyone in
Turin, even today, knows a Faussone. Primo had been surrounded by
Faussones all his life, especially at work; and for a long time he had wanted
to write something about them. Then – he said – several things happened.
First, he returned to Russia, scene of his own first (and only) foreign
adventures; and there he met 'not Tino Faussone, who doesn't exist', but
dozens of his twins: Turinese technicians building a Fiat factory. That was
when Faussone was conceived – somewhere in the early 70s, in Togliattigrad.
But so far he had no story to tell. Then – in the spring of 1977, or a little
earlier – Primo went to Barolo with Nuto Revelli, Bianca and others, to
meet Bartolo Mascarello (and to buy several bottles of his wine, as we
know). One of the others on this happy outing was Giovanna, daughter of
Alessandro Galante Garrone. On the way home Giovanna told a story she
had heard from her singing teacher, the folk-musicologist Roberto Leydi.
In a certain factory in Milan, whose workers were mostly from the south,
the shop stewards were in conflict with the boss, as usual. But their solution
was far from usual: they put a curse on him. It wasn't a serious curse; they
only meant to produce a rash, or boils – just enough to demonstrate their

---

* This adds up to nine chapters, whereas – readers may note – in the published book there
are only eight. Intriguingly, there are indications that Primo may have cut one. Alternatively,
one of the first six may have been an early version of one of the last three.

bargaining power. But it worked too well, and a few weeks later the boss was dead.

Primo was still locked in his own battles with the shop stewards at SIVA, though I don't suppose that was the only reason he was riveted by this tale. He turned his special, intense writer's gaze on Giovanna, and quizzed her on every detail. He had found the first story for Faussone to tell. Then he gave him another; and soon he remembered more stories, or found new ones, and realized that there might be enough material for a book. There was. He wrote six more chapters from the summer to the end of 1977, and three more from April to June of 1978, after the shingles had left him in March. By now he had realized that the Marlow-like narrator should also speak, for variety and balance; besides, he said, he wanted to tell some of his own chemical adventures as well. He had found a way of using the material of *The Double Bond*. In the summer of 1978 he recast three of its chapters, and the book was done.

That was (with a few additions from Giovanna Galante Garrone) Primo's story of writing *The Wrench*, and it was substantially true. One chapter, he always said, he had entirely invented ('The Helper', about Faussone's best friend on his travels, who turns out to be a monkey). One, 'The Bridge', he took largely from a 'wonderful book on bridges', with help from Livio Norzi; here he also inserted Nicoletta Neri's traveller's tale. One – 'Beating Copper' – he got from his technician friend at SIVA, Felice Malgaroli, whose father had been an old-style coppersmith: though Faussone was not a real person, Primo said, his father was. Felice had also worked on derricks, and had lived and worked in many countries of the world – Venezuela, Pakistan, China and Japan. Primo quizzed him about derricks as he had quizzed Giovanna about her story of the curse; with another SIVA technician, Walter Strozza, and the brother of a third – Mosca, who was a rigger – he had long and passionate conversations about cranes. He checked every fact with experts, and in technical articles and manuals; then he checked them all again with Giorgio and Livio, and with his engineer-writer friend Roberto Vacca. He had a splendid, pedantic, technical time; and then he performed his alchemical magic, stirred it all together and invented Faussone.

That is what he always said in public: that Faussone was imaginary, a mixture of every Turinese craftsman he had ever known. In private he occasionally said that there was one model in particular; but he never named him, and the only real Faussone he ever described was the son of the coppersmith, Felice Malgaroli. This is where he moved very slightly away from the truth, if only by omission. For there was one main model for Faussone; but it wasn't Felice, who is a complicated man, a painter, writer, and survivor of Mauthausen.

Why did Primo never say so? Writerly pride, perhaps, in his first invented hero (though Cesare, for example, was equally invented, on the base of Lello Perugia). But for other reasons too. The clue to one is on the typescript of *La chiave a stella*. There Primo made a list of people he wanted to thank, which was never published. It included 'L.N.', 'G.L.', 'Rob. V.' and 'G. G. Garrone'; and also (added in Primo's hand) 'T.A.' That is to say: Tullia Ami. If Tullia Ami had anything to do with it, he couldn't say so; and not only because of Lucia.

Tullia herself was not Faussone, of course. The main model for Primo's hero was Renzo Groff, SICME's best-known technician, who went all around the world installing and repairing its machines.

Groff joined SICME in 1966, and Primo first met him in the early 70s. Like everyone else in the group of companies, Primo thought Groff the best and most dedicated craftsman they had, or could hope to have. That is the heart of what Groff gave Faussone: a fanaticism of work, and of work well done – the Piedmontese religion of *lavoro ben fatto, travaij bin fàit*. And this too may be one reason why Primo never named him: for Groff, the high priest of *travaij bin fàit*, was not even Piedmontese. His name evokes distant Germanic rather than Gallic ancestors; and he came, in fact, from Trento.

Now Groff is not a rigger, so the details of Faussone's technical adventures did not come from him. But he is exactly Faussone's age, and – it strikes me when we meet – not unlike him physically. True, he is neither thin nor bald, though he's fifteen years older than Faussone now; but he is tall and very clean-shaven, with a big, heavy, deliberately inexpressive face, like Faussone's. Of course he is a modern, middle-class man, unlike Faussone: one of his sons has been to university, and he is wearing a smart, expensive suit. Primo returned him to his working-class roots for Faussone, as he had done with Sandro Delmastro; or rather, for this side of Faussone he kept to the general type of the Turinese artisan.

Since Groff is a married man, he does not admit it: but I guess from the look in his eye when I ask him that the two adventures with girls may have had something to do with him. It is his character, he says, that he himself recognizes in Faussone: and even after one short conversation, I agree. Faussone is very intelligent, but very silent; he has put all his intelligence into his hands, which are much more expressive than his face, and until he meets Primo he has never told, or even thought about, his stories. Groff is even more intelligent than Faussone; he understands himself very well, and describes his character to me in a few brief and pithy phrases. But he does not think it is important. He cannot understand why I am interested in Primo Levi, or in Faussone, or in him. You need to know how machines work in order to control them, he says, but controlling people is not a matter of knowledge. I don't want to control people, I say. 'Oh really?' he says politely, and gives me a sceptical grin.

Faussone is proud, perfectionist, honest, loyal, restless, and secretly very lonely. Groff is more Faussone than Faussone. 'My work has to be perfect,' he says, 'and it always is. I'm as stubborn as a mule, I'll take a machine apart from top to bottom rather than let it beat me, and as for another human being . . . I have to win, and I always do. I don't do anything twice, either: not out of laziness, you understand, but on principle, because my work represents *me*: it has to be right the first time. All the work I do is for myself, in that way. I don't work for money. If you work for money, you're off at the first offer. I've had hundreds of offers, for more and more money, but I'm not interested. SICME is good to me, and I'm good to it in return; your company isn't a car, that you trade in as soon as a better one comes along. So I work for SICME, and everybody knows where to find me. But more than that, I work for myself. So everybody knows my name. I go round the world as Groff, and it's Groff they ask for. I make sure of that.'

Like Faussone, Groff speaks a little of the language of most of the countries he visits. He has more friends abroad, he says, than at home, where he has spent only half of every year for the last thirty years. He's fifty now; and Paola Accati has told me that he complains about the travelling, but after a week in the factory he gets sad and bad-tempered, and only cheers up when his next trip is planned. He has always been like that, he says – restless and striving, he doesn't know why. It has hurt his family; perhaps he should never have married. Really he is best alone with his work . . . Then he stops, and shakes a finger at me. 'You see?' he says. 'That's what happens when you think about things too much, you get gloomy. So, what else do you want to know?'

I want to know how Primo got to know so much about him, I say, ignoring the irony in his voice. And now Groff's reply is quite surprising. Not from him, he says: they spoke only about technical matters, and not very often. It was Tullia Ami to whom he told his SICME adventures, when they went on long and boring Russian trips together. Then, when Primo had to go with her as well (Groff is one of those men who could not see the point of Tullia), she passed them on to him. So *that* is where Tullia Ami came in. Primo had known many Faussones, especially in SIVA; and seeing them in Togliattigrad gave him the idea of writing about them. But it was Tullia, telling him about Groff, who gave him the deeper character – Faussone's immense pride, which is also loneliness and insecurity, like Primo's own.

My admiration for Tullia grows: she must have told those stories very well. And then what? I ask Groff. Did Primo ask if he could use you for

Faussone? Did he give you a copy of the book, with one of his witty apologies, or thanks? (On Giovanna's, for example, he wrote 'To Giovanna, who gave me *la chiave*.') No, Groff replies. Primo never said a word to him. It was Tullia Ami, once again, who brought him the book. '*Il dottor* Levi would like you to have this,' Tullia had said, 'because the hero is a bit like you.' Primo had written a brief dedication to him on it: friendly and courteous, but saying nothing about having based much of Faussone on him. As a result, he didn't read it until long after; and only then realized how like him Faussone was, and how it must all have happened through Tullia Ami.

He has told all this in his factual, Faussone-like way, with no emotion in his voice. Was he surprised when he finally read it? I ask. Was he pleased? – Faussone is a splendid character, after all, 'Primo Levi's ideal man', as many of the critics said. Or was he, perhaps, annoyed? Did he feel that Primo had stolen his soul for a book, and never even thanked him? No, no, Groff says, and his face does not look guarded, but bemused. Primo was welcome to his soul; it isn't worth much, as he has already told me. Besides, Faussones are ten a penny; these *piemontesi* know how to work, he has to give them that – only (with a grin) not *quite* as well as him.

Well, that's true. Even so, I'm amazed he doesn't mind. And then he amazes me again. Can I see his copy of the book? I ask. I'd like to read Primo's dedication to him. Sorry, he says, he doesn't have it any more; it got lost somewhere along the way. I look at him carefully for any signs of triumph, but there are none. He has lost the book which recognized his greatness, and gave him the distinction he craves. Simply that: lost it. I'm baffled. But then I remember Primo's encounter with another real Faussone – an even realer one. Soon after the book came out, a young man came up to Primo at a presentation in San Mauro: his name was Faussone, and he was a rigger. Astonished and amused, Primo proposed that Faussone come with him to a television interview he was about to do: the Author and his Hero together, like Antonio and James in *Vizio di forma*. But Faussone refused. He said (Primo reported, with pleasure) that an interview 'was not a serious thing, while his was a serious trade'.

So that was how *La chiave a stella* was born, in place of *Il doppio legame*. Instead of writing about himself, Primo was writing about his opposite: a rough, free wanderer, like Rodmund in 'Lead'. Instead of writing about his day-job, he wrote about someone else's; and instead of writing about sin and guilt and pollution, he wrote about the happiness and fulfilment of a solitary, perfectionist craft. It was as though he had performed an Inversion of Walden – a total reversal, transforming the hardest book he'd ever tried to write into the easiest, the darkest into the lightest, the most graven with responsibility into the freest. And when in the end he put *The Double Bond* itself into the new book, he doubly reversed it: his tower disaster was transferred to Faussone; his other disaster kept as his own, but disguised and redeemed.

And who can blame him? All around him Italy was deep in crisis: but for the first time in his life he was free. He needed to compensate, and also to celebrate; and where better to do both than (as always) in a book? In fact he gave Faussone his own dark side too, the costs of his solitude and striving – his own hidden fears of water and entrapment; even his shingles. But that only makes Faussone more real. *La chiave a stella* is Primo Levi's happiest, most celebratory book: it was to write, and it is to read. He put into it everything he loved. Work, first and foremost – good, clean craftsman's work, done with head and hands, like Faussone's, and (on good days) like both his own, chemistry and writing. Turin, home *par excellence* of such craftsmen, and his own home, which he deeply loved. ('To Primo Turin was heaven,' says Keith Barnes, 'the most beautiful city in the world.') Travel, which he had always longed for, and so rarely achieved; Faussone's 'perpetual flight' was perhaps the greatest compensation of the book for Primo. Russia, the scene of his own few adventures, which he had loved since his first liberation, but which had always maddened him as well. The Russians hadn't changed, he discovered in the 70s: they were still the opposite of the Piedmontese, hospitable, mercurial, and disorderly beyond belief. Now they had modern factories and assembly lines, like everyone else – but in their high-tech ovens they cooked sausages, and half their assembly lines didn't work; when Primo asked why they said, 'That's not what we had a revolution for.' As for Russian travel, that had not changed either. Some of this he put in the end of *The Wrench*, as he and Faussone head home. 'Are there three of you?' the driver asks. 'No, two,' says Faussone. 'French?' 'No, Italian.' 'Are you going to the station?' 'No, the airport.' 'Well then, get in.' And some of it he didn't put in: the days on trains that supplied no food, so that he always brought a huge box of biscuits from home; the time the pilot of a very old, very late plane said '*Tovarisch*, there will be a delay to the schedule of delays.'

On a deeper level, too, *The Wrench* is about the things he loved best. Equality between men, for instance, and the debunking of snobbish élites: for if all Primo Levi's books are deliberately 'non-literary', this one is something more. He had set out, he said, to write an *anti*-literary book, with an anti-literary hero, of a kind that had hardly appeared in literature before. He had set out to build a bridge not between art and science this time, as in *The Periodic Table*, but between art and technology, as he always called his own industrial chemistry. And not only between art and 'ordinary' readers this time, as he tried to do in all his books: but between art and 'non-readers' – often working-class men like Faussone, who were not interested in literature, because literature was not interested in them. And *The Wrench* did reach such non-readers – dozens of them wrote to him to say so; and these letters, unlike many he received, he cherished without reserve. One of his best moments was when he heard that the forty-six riggers of the Società Fratelli Peyrani of Turin had all read the book, grinning with pleasure – had indeed all read the *same* book, passing it from hand to hand. Not all writers would have been thrilled by that; but Primo was delighted.

And *La chiave a stella* is about writing. It is about the art of story-telling, which is as delicate as crane-rigging, though not as dangerous. Primo comments often on Faussone's failures as a story-teller – not out of competition (or not only out of competition), but because in writing, as in crane-rigging and chemistry, it is through your mistakes that your art makes its requirements clear. It is about Primo's own move from chemistry to writing, which he is on the brink of making. It is openly about writing in the chapter called 'Tiresias'; and secretly about it in everything Faussone says about his lonely, perfectionist trade.

Finally, *La chiave a stella* is about Primo's greatest unrequited love: language. Primo Levi was, in fact, a very ambitious writer, and *La chiave a stella* was his most ambitious book. He wanted to write a book, he said, 'that had never been written before'. It would have a new subject, work (which, as he said, occupies 80 per cent of our lives, but hardly any of our literature); and a new hero – a machine-man, a modern industrial technician. But above all, it would have a new language: not the classical Italian of most of his country's literature, and of his own books so far; nor yet the dialects of his favourite poets Belli and Porta, or of Pasolini and De Filippo. It would be a language which he partly heard, and partly invented, and which he called '*la parlata italo-tecno-piemontese*': Piedmontese-techno-Italian.

This new language – says the philologist Gianluigi Beccaria – wasn't simply Piedmontese translated into Italian: rather, it was Italian ' "thought" in Piedmontese', and in the terms of Faussone's trade. It is full of slang ('like an attack every five minutes'); of repetitions ('either I tell you the country or I tell you the event; if I were you I'd choose the event, because it's a good event'); of grammatical errors and elisions (Faussone uses '*che*', 'that', to do every connective job, like his wrench: for 'where', 'while', 'because' and many others). Best of all, it is full of Piedmontese words and expressions, Italianized to comic effect: so Faussone pictures his frozen companion, for example, as '*duro come un merluzzo*', 'as stiff as a cod', from the Piedmontese '*duro come un baccalà*' – but *baccalà* is salt cod, as stiff as a board, not soft and sinuous like a *merluzzo*. And then there are Faussone's trade words, made part of his ordinary speech – so that he says about the dearth of girls in Togliattigrad '*articolo ragazza, si tirano un po' verdi*': 'in the girls department we're a bit short-stocked'; about a brilliantly starry sky that it looked '*fuori tolleranza*' – that is, outside the range of error allowed for in a project or plan.

The Turinese, of course, pick up every word of this alchemical transformation, and laugh like drains; for many *La chiave a stella* is their absolutely favourite Primo Levi. Other Italians (Primo said) get around 70 per cent of the jokes; in translation, alas, we probably get no more than half. But that half is sharp, real, and still very funny. Primo's challenge to himself had succeeded – he *had* written a book no one had written before, in a language no one had written before. *The Wrench* is not over-stocked in the usual novel departments – love, sex, society; in a word, in human relations. But it is funny and profound, and a considerable literary achievement.

Primo had thought of no fewer than nine titles for his book, including *Faussone the Rigger* and – his own favourite – *Vile Meccanico, Base Mechanical*, which was a quotation from Manzoni. Fortunately Einaudi voted against *Vile Meccanico*; and Primo chose *La chiave a stella* for (he said) the sound.

It was published in early December 1978, very close to 'La rumeur d'Auschwitz' in *Le Monde*. The reviews and interviews began at once and went on for months; *La chiave a stella* brought Primo more attention than any of his books so far, and marked another step in his fame. The majority of the avalanche of reviews was enthusiastic, though there were the mandatory one or two stinkers. More or less everyone noted the novelty of the subject, and especially of the style. Giovanni Raboni in *Tuttolibri* hailed the discovery that the rigging of a crane could make a thrilling story; and Lorenzo Mondo and Giorgio De Rienzo in *La Stampa*, Enrico Deaglio in *Lotta Continua*, Geno Pampaloni in *Il Giornale Nuovo*, Mario Lunetta in *Il Messaggero* and Paolo Milano in *L'Espresso* all celebrated the capture of a whole new language on the page. Apart from praise for Faussone's language, Milano was rather lukewarm, pleading 'shameful ignorance of everything to do with machines' (with a touch of that secret scorn Primo so deplored in literary intellectuals). To make up for this, Primo got his first review from the academic Alberto Asor Rosa, who would later put him into his encyclopedia of Italian literature; Asor Rosa's own prose is professionally neutral, but it is clear he meant to praise.

Primo collected all his reviews assiduously, and reviewed them in turn: five marks each for their assessment of *La chiave*, five for *his* assessment of *them*. (Raboni, Gabriella Poli tells us, got ten out of ten.) From a literary point of view things were going very well. The problem – because of course there was one – was political. These were years of economic crisis, high unemployment, and intensive left-wing campaigning against the exploitation of workers. And now along came this hymn of praise to work, this counter-revolutionary claim that, except for 'miraculous and isolated moments', loving your work 'represents the best, most concrete approximation of happiness on earth'. Trade unionists removed Primo's name from their guest-lists, wrote one satirical journalist; 'industrialists decided not to send him their Christmas greetings, with the usual bottle of Asti Spumante'. Who was this Primo Levi anyway, and this character of his, Faussone? Just another middle-class intellectual sticking his nose into things he didn't understand, said a metal-worker from Modugno, in a letter to the far-left paper *Lotta Continua*; as for Faussone, he was an aristocrat, one of the privileged: what could *he* say for the ordinary worker, any more than his creator? This second question was thrown at Primo from the start, by students, trade unionists and journalists. The heat of the reaction shook him; but he had expected it. He had written *The Wrench* precisely to take up arms against the ideological attack on work, and he was willing to go on. He pointed out that he had noted all the objections in the book itself: that 'It is sadly true that many jobs are not loveable'; that praise of work from certain quarters was quite rightly suspected; that 'We can and must fight to see that the fruit of labour remains in the hands of those that work'. But it was senseless and absurd to condemn all labour absolutely, biblically, as though it were 'something we could do without, not only in Utopia, but here, today'; as though merely to refuse to work, or not to know how, meant that you were free. On the contrary, it meant the opposite. It was having a trade, and practising it well, that freed you. That was the message of his book, if it had one; and he never changed his mind that it was right.

Slowly the controversy faded; several critics – including the distinguished Communist Corrado Stajano – defended him; and by May, when the long list for the Strega was announced, *The Wrench* was already being tipped to win. There were the usual intrigues, the usual dramas: the day before the final vote an advertisement appeared for the book with *Winner of the Strega* already on it, and a furious campaign was mounted against it at the last minute. But the judges were not moved. Up to the fiftieth vote, Ferruccio Ulivi was ahead; at the 100 mark, Primo overtook him. At 150 the result was already clear, though there were nearly 300 votes to go. At midnight on 5 July, Maria Bellonci declared the winner of the thirty-third Strega: *La chiave a stella*, by Primo Levi. After the applause and the flashing of camera bulbs had died down, she came and embraced him. 'Imagine it's sixteen years ago,' she said, 'when you were in the running for *La tregua*. You should have won then.'

After the controversy which attended its birth, *Chiave* was a runaway success. In September it won the Bergamo Prize as well; by the end of October it had sold 140,000 copies – twice as many as *The Periodic Table*. Primo was thrilled and happy – and also, briefly, depressed. Perhaps it was the strain of battle; or disappointment that more attention had been paid to the battle than to the literary achievement of his book. But probably not: that was only a failure, after all. More likely it was *La chiave a stella*'s success. He thought that quite possible himself, looking back: '*La mia nevrosi di successo*', 'my success neurosis', he called it (or rather his doctor did). *Chiave* was his biggest success so far: and he was depressed. A still bigger success lay ahead, with *Se non ora, quando?* We can guess the consequences; fortunately Primo couldn't.

But 1979 wasn't only the year of *La chiave a stella*. It was also the year of negationism, and of his rededication to witnessing, in schools, in *La Stampa*, in the *The Drowned and the Saved*. It was also the second year of the siege, as he had begun to call it, of the two old mothers. When he gave up speaking to schools after all, at the end of 1979, it was because he had to: he was in a new depression. He still saw friends, he even travelled; in Vienna for a conference he met, with joy, an Italian who remembered him arriving at the Kraków barracks with his Greek. In other words, it was still not a depression of the worst kind. But it was bad enough.

In September he wrote a valedictory poem, 'Toward the Valley':

> It's late for living, late for loving,
> For fathoming the sky, understanding the world . . .

In June he had written another, full of horror, called 'Annunciation': an angel – who, like one of Professor Leeb's monsters, looks more like a bird of prey – brings a new Annunciation to a new Mary: she is about to bring forth the opposite of that earlier Lord, one who will be a sower of death and hate. In July he had published in *La Stampa* the story of Pasquale, who has also written a poem called 'Annunciation'. It is the best poem he has ever written, but it quite literally runs away from him; he cannot rewrite it, and he can never write another . . . That was always Primo's deepest fear, in depression: that he cannot write, that he will never be able to write again. In this one it came to him.

In late December he published 'In una notte', 'In a Night' (or 'In One Night'), in *La Stampa*. A train enters a frozen, empty landscape, like the one outside space and time through which the Man had approached the world in his first story. It is forced to stop, in a cloud of burning leaves; and out of a wood emerges a group of small people, wrapped in dark, padded clothes. They bring out saws, hammers and shears, and with one accord they begin to dismantle the train. Silently, relentlessly they work through the night; by dawn the train is demolished, down to the last bolt. Then they begin on the track, and then on the birch trees of the wood; as the sun rises, in twos and threes they attack each other, and finally, blindly, themselves.

This is, once again, like the story of *l'Uomo*: in one freezing night, the mind cracks. But now, nearly forty years on, it does not merely crack: it is entirely dismembered and destroyed. After that fearful vision, or around it, darkness descended. He could not write, he had nothing to say. 'I feel on the brink of a shipwreck,' he said. But he didn't drown; not this time.

★   ★

In his last decade, Primo's life went up and down like the waves of that sea he imagined: and each time it was a book that saved him. During the *anni di piombo* of 1977 and '78 it was *La chiave a stella*; and now a new book would take hold of his mind. After the trough of late 1979 and early 80, it would raise him up again; and this time the high would last for most of the next two years. Despite the siege of the mothers, 1980 and 1981 would be essentially good years, because he was researching, and then writing, *Se non ora, quando?*

I have already called it his anti-Lager book, and that was the heart of its power. *Se non ora* was more than compensation: but as depression closed in on him, his need for compensation grew. With Faussone he had been able to inhabit a man simpler, stronger, and freer than himself. With Mendel of *Se non ora, quando?* he would inhabit one who, while Primo Levi was trapped like an animal in Auschwitz, fought back like a free man. This compensation bore the sign of revenge: of returning the blow. That is new in Primo Levi, even in imagination; and perhaps it signals the first weakening in his systems of control, the first piece stripped from the train by the small night people. But there was another compensation of these years as well, which still bore the old sign of understanding and reconciliation. That had started as soon as *Chiave* was finished, in the autumn of 1978. He had joined the Goethe Institute of Turin to study German.

Many survivors (and not only survivors) still feel a shiver of unease and distaste when they hear German. Not Primo. It had happened to him too, he admitted, immediately after the camp: but 'I tried hard to banish these feelings in myself, and I succeeded.' German was not only the language of the Nazis; it was also the language of Goethe and Heine, of Freud, Marx, Kafka, Einstein. He had learned it the hard way; why deprive himself of the rewards that it could offer?

This was a very Primo Levi way to put it. So was the reason he gave in 'Tornare a scuola', 'Going Back to School': 'pure intellectual curiosity'. But that little essay is all about overcoming: overcoming 'shyness and laziness' to go at all; overcoming the trauma of a new and awkward situation – he is 'a Martian', a sixty-year-old man among university students, most of them girls; overcoming the handicap of elderly eyes, ears, memory. At the same time the story is full of pleasure and humour. This return to school brings back the flavour of childhood, 'delicate and long-forgotten'; 'giving oneself the gift of a pleasant and pointless activity' is a rare luxury. I think this was still an overcoming exercise – as indeed the Germans call it: *Die Bewältigung der Vergangenheit*, the overcoming of the past. And just for that reason, he enjoyed it.

In fact, his German was very good: he would not have gone back to school if it had meant making mistakes in front of a roomful of students. But he did ask questions – often very difficult ones, about modern expressions he hadn't heard before, or etymologies he didn't understand. Sometimes the teacher didn't understand them either; and then he and Primo would go off to the library together, deep in conversation. Once Cesare Cases, who is a very distinguished Germanist, arrived at the Goethe Institute to find the teacher 'desperate' – Cases is also a wicked story-teller – because Primo had asked him a question he couldn't answer. Fortunately Cases could, and told him; and off he went, delighted to be able to pass on to his star pupil a point of German grammar so abstruse not even he himself had known it.

This teacher was also part of Primo's *Bewältigung der Vergangenheit*, and for a long time a happy one. For Hans Engert was a good German, indeed a delightful German: the kind of German, as Primo had said to Heinz Riedt, that he had always hoped to meet. Engert had been only twelve years old at the end of the war: too young to have faced the test, like Riedt, but also too young for any responsibility. Like all the staff at the Goethe, he was a typical member of the self-critical, passionately liberal 'second generation' of Germans. Like Riedt, he had left Germany young and come to live in Italy; like Riedt, therefore – and like Primo too – he was an essential outsider, an eternal non-belonger; for reasons of his own as well. He was an excellent linguist, teacher and translator, and an extremely nice man; and he and Primo became friends. Primo called him '*Professore*'; they never used *tu* to each other, but only *Lei*; and perhaps there was that touch of competition between them that Cases noticed, and which always spiced Primo's relationships with other intellectuals. But it was a good friendship, small but strong, which even extended beyond the Institute: Primo would telephone Engert about their favourite philological questions, and once or twice he went to gatherings at Engert's house in Moncalieri.

Its ending, then, was all the sadder. Primo attended Engert's class for two

years. In it he also made another friend: Anna Savoini, one of the only two
'*signorine* over thirty' – who were, in fact, both married women close to his
own age. At the registration evening for their third year, in the autumn of
1980, Primo suggested to Anna that they try another class, for a different
experience of German; so together they switched to a new teacher who had
just arrived from Berlin. Primo told Engert their reasons, and the friendship
seemed undisturbed. But a year later something shocking happened. In
November 1981 Engert suddenly died, almost certainly by his own hand.

Primo hadn't re-registered in September; Anna had tried to persuade
him, but he was working on a book, he said, and had no time. So very likely
he hadn't seen Engert for many months when it happened. The story was
in *La Stampa*, and Bianca had been professionally involved; he must have
known all the details. Hans Engert was a homosexual. For some time – who
knows how long – he had been blackmailed by a young Arab. Finally he
had reported the boy to the police; and now the case had come to trial. But
in the last minute he had lost heart. On the opening day of the trial, according
to *La Stampa* – or when it was over, as Bianca remembers, and the boy had
been convicted – he hanged himself in his Turin flat.

Primo was deeply distressed by this terrible death. He even worried that
Engert might have felt abandoned by him the year before. He had so liked
and admired his gentle, intelligent, civilized friend; and now he knew that
he had had this secret suffering all along, and that in the end it broke him.
Like Agostino Neri's death when he was not yet twenty, it came, I think,
too close to home. He did not return to the Goethe Institute; and when a
memorial service was arranged a year later, he did not go. Probably he could
not face it; and by then his own despair was close to Engert's.

That was the end of his friendship with the good German.

'After thirty-five years of apprenticeship,' he wrote, 'one day I decided to
leap over the barrier, and try to write a novel.' That had been his phrase for
it, ever since Ulysses had come to him in the mud of Auschwitz – to hurl
himself over a barrier, and set out on the open sea, to break down the barrier
and fly. The day came, some time in the early spring of 1980: perhaps
because his depression had gone, and he felt ready for anything; or perhaps
because he realized that night was falling upon him more often, and if he
was ever going to do it, it had better be now.

It was an aspect of the new and anguishing Holocaust discussions that set
him on the path: the idea of the new generations, in Israel and elsewhere,
that the Jews of Europe had gone to their deaths 'like sheep', without
resistance. It reminded him of the boy who had advised him to escape next
time: it was absurd, profoundly ahistorical, and betrayed a prejudice which

had still not disappeared. There were circumstances in which resistance was possible, and others in which it was not: in Auschwitz it was not, and not only for Jews.

But this made him remember two stories of Jewish resistance: one his own, and one someone else's. He had told his in *La tregua*: the young Zionists who had hitched their coach to the Italians' train in October 1945, because a ship was waiting at Bari to take them to Palestine. The other was told him by a friend, Emilio Vita Finzi, who had worked at the centre for Jewish refugees on the Via Unione in Milan just after the war. One day a doctor had called him to come and deal with an extraordinary group of young people: he was trying to operate on one, a young girl, her friends didn't trust him, they were besieging the operating theatre and threatening him . . . Emilio and his friend Marcello Cantoni rushed over, and found the situation just as the doctor described. Amid the throngs of bewildered refugees was a band of young Jewish partisans, armed to the teeth, fiercely resisting any orders that were not their own. Emilio and Marcello calmed them down; the girl was saved; and the two young Italians spent the next few hours listening to hair-raising tales of guerrilla warfare behind German lines.

Emilio had told Primo this story years and years ago, around 1965 or '66. Primo had jotted it down, and filed it away in his 'ideas in waiting' drawer – the same one, no doubt, in which he would put Nicoletta Neri's Calcutta story. He went to the drawer now: yes, there it was. And he decided to write a novel.

He rang Emilio and asked if he remembered the partisans' tales, but of course it was too long ago. So Primo set out to research his subject, as he had researched into bridges and cranes for *La chiave a stella*. He studied Yiddish, he read histories and novels of the *shtetls*. His friend Giorgio Vaccarino, historian of the Resistance in Europe, lent him everything he had: his own article, 'Soviet Partisans in the Second World War'; a massive American work, *Soviet Partisans in World War II*; and two very rare memoirs by Soviet partisan leaders in the Ukraine, published in France soon after the war: *L'obkom clandestin au travail*, by Aleksei Fyodorov; and *Les partisans Soviétiques* by S. A. Kovpak, which has a linear, chronological form much like *Se non ora, quando?*'s. Primo also heard about another memoir, again about a band of partisans in the Pripet Marshes, which he remembered well: this group too had passed through Italy, and eventually published the memoir in Buenos Aires. He tracked it down in the Bibliothèque Nationale in Paris: *Di milkhomeh fun di Jiddische Partisaner in Mizrach-Europe*, by Moishe Kaganovich – two volumes, in Yiddish; and he translated every word, to impress on his memory not only the remarkable events, but 'how you think and write in Yiddish'. Many of the episodes and expressions in *Se non ora*, he would say later, came from this extraordinary diary.

He didn't stop there. He found the story of Polina Gelman, daughter of a Russian rabbi, who flew between partisan bands in a wooden plane, and put her too into his story. He read the *Pirke Avoth, The Sayings of the Jewish Fathers*, he read books of Yiddish proverbs, Yiddish grammar and Jewish jokes. For eight months, apart from studying the other side's grammar, he did nothing but immerse himself in the lost world of East European Jewry and its last defenders. It was another *ex voto*, like 'Argon' – a memorial to forgotten ancestors, on a much larger scale; and another, longer 'moment of reprieve' – a tribute to characters like Rappoport, Ezra, Wolf, Tischler; but ones who had managed, by luck or courage, not to be caught. It was also a positive orgy of research, for his first complete fiction: a way of preparing solid ground for his leap. And, as in his research for the adventures of Faussone, I think he enjoyed every minute.

About the writing we do not have to guess. Primo Levi began his leap into fiction in January 1981, and did not land until December. He marked the exact dates, not only at the beginning and end of his typescript, but at the end of the published book: *Torino, 11 gennaio – 20 dicembre 1981*. When Guilio Nascimbeni asked him why, he replied: To mark a happy year. He had written all his books with joy, he said; but the joy of writing *Se non ora, quando?* was new, different, extreme. To write was always to be free: but to write fiction was a super-writing, and a super-freedom. It was not just to leap – it was to fly.

His newest and most different freedom was the creation of characters – not one this time, but thirty, and out of nothing, out of his own imagination. At first this seemed daunting. Writing Faussone's stories had been as easy as recording – indeed it had seemed to him as though he *was* recording; as though the Faussones he'd known all his life came into his room and spoke. But these people, whom he did not know, spoke a language he did not know either . . . The first thing he wrote, on 11 January, was to them, or about them – these strange unborn creatures, who 'wait, hope and fear' to make their entrance. But then he began – and it worked, they poured out, a whole herd of them, and that was the moment of his greatest freedom. After a while, then, they took over, and did what they wanted, not what he had planned; but of course that was even better. Only later, looking back, did he notice other limits on his freedom: that all his creatures contained a little of himself, and his hero, Mendel, more than a little; that the others all contained fragments of people he had known, in life or literature. Thus Gedale and Leonid, for instance, were both based on real people, White Rokhele on women in the *shtetl* tales he'd read. (And in Line, I have guessed, were fragments of all the women in his life – Lucia, Lilith, Gisella.) The absolute freedom he had imagined was an illusion; but not the rest. Whatever the fate of his novel, writing it had been glorious – a whole year, it had felt to him, of flying.

So he always said, and I am sure he meant it. But there were also signs of a different feeling. This was a challenge he had avoided (or pretended to avoid) for thirty-five years – this was the barrier, as he said, the narrow strait beyond which, perhaps, he was not meant to go. When he felt he was succeeding, he flew; but when he was uncertain he was deeply anxious. Was it worth it? he once asked Oreste Molina at Einaudi. There were dissensions amongst his *Tribunale* of readers – Lucia said he should not have killed Leonid, for example, and Gabriella Poli said the same about Dov. After a struggle, he decided that Leonid must die; but that Gabriella was right about Dov, who was accordingly resurrected. Later, when the book was finished, Bianca said – for the first time – that she thought it needed more work; the characters needed more development. And for the first time he took criticism badly, and did not listen. Perhaps, Bianca says, he felt time passing: he must write as much as possible while he still could. That is the feeling the typescript of *Se non ora* gives me. Primo marked the dates of composition of every small section of it, every few days, often every day – as though to warn himself how quickly time was passing, or to prove to himself how much he had achieved. Looking back on his flight a year later, his descriptions carried both signs. Writing a novel, he said, you fly with all the emotions of the early pioneers: both the excitement and the fear.

In the summer of 1980 Giulio Bollati had an idea for a new series of books for schools: selections from their favourite authors by famous Einaudi writers, with short introductions explaining their influence on their work, or their importance in their lives. He invited several writers to partake – Italo Calvino, Leonardo Sciascia and Paolo Volponi, for example, as well as Primo Levi. Primo was in the middle of the research for his novel, as well as a busy year of writing for *La Stampa*. But he liked the idea immediately: 'It appealed to my natural narcissism,' he said. He accepted, and the others did as well. In September – three months ahead of schedule – he handed in his 'personal anthology'. Typically, he was the only one; the others never finished theirs. There was no series; and Primo's choices and introductions were too sophisticated (and perhaps too tragic) for the young readers Bollati had in mind. In December it was decided to issue *La ricerca delle radici*, *The Search for Roots*, as a normal Einaudi book. Primo was pleased. All it needed now was a longer and fuller introduction than he had originally provided. He gave that to Einaudi in March 1981, and the book was published at the end of April.

Without the company of Calvino and the others, there was a risk that it might seem an exercise in that narcissism to which Primo had pretended. But that didn't happen. *La ricerca delle radici* was received with almost universal admiration and respect. Calvino gave Primo's 'personal anthology' a long and generous review, even though he hadn't written his own, and probably knew he never would. All Primo's regular admirers – Lorenzo Mondo, Giulio Nascimbeni, Claudio Marabini, Geno Pampaloni – added their approval. By now, it is clear, Italian newspapers and their readers accepted Primo Levi as a master: a decade or more before the academy.

Radici, then, was a gamble which paid off. Like *Se non ora*, it was a book he had seemed to enjoy writing, and of which he remained fond. But like *Se non ora*, it was also deeply ambivalent. When he was young, Primo had insisted that you could create yourself, ignoring your roots as a Jew; since then he had written so often about self-creation that it had become a major theme. For him the whole project of exploring his roots was a reversal – especially, perhaps, his roots as a writer, the self he had most publicly made. It is quite strange that he accepted it; and 'in a few seconds', as he said.

The reason he gave was equally strange. About a year after the book was published, he said in an interview: 'To open your belly and expose your guts is an exhibitionist idea which tickled my fancy.' Primo Levi an exhibitionist? – Primo Levi talking about his guts, his belly? But it was not a mistake: the same strange exhibitionism was already in the Introduction. But there it is much more complicated. In putting together this book of roots, he wrote, he had felt more exposed, more vulnerable, than in writing his own books. 'I felt naked,' he said; but 'not in the manner of the exhibitionist', who simply enjoys it. Rather: 'in the act of opening myself, I felt like Mohammed in the ninth *Bolgia* and in the illustration by Doré, in which moreover the masochistic satisfaction of the damned is enormous'. There *was* pleasure; but it was perverse, and inseparable from pain.

'I have never had either psycho-analysis or a surgical operation,' he had written in the first version of the Introduction, but this work of literary self-exploration seemed to him the same. I think he had identified the deep, dark coils of the gut with the deep, dark coils of the unconscious for a long time: certainly since 'L'amico dell'uomo', written at least fifteen years before. And I think he still did. This would be an extra source of anguish in the future, when he *would* finally have to have an operation, and his belly would be literally opened. And it was a source of anguish – or an ambiguous pleasure – now. He made the connection himself between *La ricerca delle radici* and his subconscious. 'However much I want to deny it,' he wrote in his Introduction, 'there is a trace of *id* in me too'; and it was his *id*, not his ego, he said, that had been at work here. That phrase – 'There is a trace of *id* in me too' – was beginning to appear in the things he said about himself now. His 'trace of *id*' had always broken out in his poetry; but now it was breaking into his prose as well. His night work was invading the day more than he had intended; and 1980 – with the conception of *Se non ora, quando?* at the start, and the writing of *La ricerca delle radici* at the end – was the year it began.

Despite the critics' recommendations, *La ricerca delle radici* was hardly a popular kind of book, and it has never had many readers.* I do not suppose Primo minded. The books for which he desired an audience were his 'daylight' ones, which expressed his responsible optimism, and moved 'from the darkness to the light'. Perhaps instinctively, certainly successfully, he hid his night side where it was less likely to be found: in his poetry, his stories, and now in his literary self-analysis. No one who reads *The Search for Roots* can continue to imagine that Primo Levi was a serene or hopeful man. His literary roots begin with the Book of Job and end with an article from *Scientific American* on black holes; they move from one to another along four paths, which he names: 'Man suffers unjustly' (which includes Thomas Mann, T. S. Eliot, Isaac Babel); 'The stature of Man' (including Homer, Conrad, and his chemical father Ludwig Gatterman); 'Salvation through laughter' (e.g. Rabelais, Porta, Sholem Aleichem); and 'Salvation through knowledge' (e.g. Darwin, Russell, Bragg).

As Calvino pointed out, these are 'four lines of resistance to . . . despair'; four stoic responses to a universe which is at best indifferent to us, at worst (in Primo's own words, in his last short Introduction) 'hostile, violent, alien'. They are Primo Levi's private bible of overcoming injustice and anguish with laughter and understanding. He was right: he is naked here.

Nineteen-eighty-one, as Primo's last editor notes, was the peak of the frenetic literary activity of his last dozen years. Apart from writing *Se non ora* throughout, he also wrote the new long Introduction to *Ricerca*, and published the book; published sixteen pieces in *La Stampa*; pressed on with the slow, dolorous work of *The Drowned and the Saved*; and finished, arranged and published his third collection of stories, *Lilit*, at the end of the year.

Lilit was divided into three sections, past, future and present. The first – as Primo explained on the inside cover – took up the themes of *Se questo è un uomo* and *La tregua*, the second those of *Storie naturali* and *Vizio di forma*; the third was set more or less in the present, and connected, perhaps, to *Il sistema periodico* and *La chiave a stella* (though this was more the critics' idea than Primo's).

---

* It was also the last of his books to be translated into English, as already noted.

Lilit was by far the best received of Primo's books of stories so far, and the main reason was the first section, 'Passato prossimo'. Claudio Marabini, Carlo Bo, the University of Turin professor Giorgio Bàrberi Squarotti, who had become an admirer with *The Periodic Table*, led the chorus of high praise for Primo's new Lager stories, about those who had remained men, for better or for worse. Bandi, Wolf, Tischler, Ezra and the others, the returns of Cesare and Lorenzo, the adventures of 'Avrom' and Joel,* the desperate tale of Chaim Rumkowski, president of the Łódź ghetto – these touched people's imaginations then as they still do now, not more than some of Primo's other stories, but without exception.† It is not only their extreme subject-matter which makes them more stirring to us, and – more importantly – to Primo, so that they have an emotional directness and colour he rarely released elsewhere. It is that, more mysteriously, this subject always called out his best writing: not just the warmest and most profound, but the richest in imagery, structure and expression. Primo Levi also wrote other very fine books and stories: but it remains true that the Lager and its aftermath inspired his greatest work, and that on that subject every word he wrote was extraordinarily adequate to its terrible task.

Nonetheless, the other stories of *Lilit* were also far better appreciated than those of *Storie naturali* or *Vizio di forma*. Many were singled out regularly for praise – 'La valle di Guerrino', 'Breve sogno' and 'La sfida della molecula', for instance, which we already know; and several which we will explore later – 'Tantalio', for example, 'La bestia nel tempio' and 'Disfilassi'. These *are* all wonderful stories; but so were many in poor, neglected *Vizio di forma*. In ten years the tide had turned: in 1971 you had to go against it to notice a good Primo Levi story; in 1981 you had to go against it to see a bad one. With Leviesque irony, the year his night people began to threaten his prose from the inside was the same year it became, on the outside, firmly established.

★   ★

---

* Joel König and Marco Herman – 'Avrom' – both wrote extraordinary memoirs of their escape as teenagers from the Nazi genocide, for which Primo wrote the Prefaces for the Italian editions (*Sfuggiti alle reti del nazismo*, *Escape from the Nazi Dragnets*, Mursia, 1973, and *Diario di un ragazzo ebreo*, *Diary of a Jewish Boy*, L'Arciere, 1984). Primo met and admired both of them; for Marco – who had ended the war with the partisans of Cuorgné – he had a special, Cesare-like feeling.

† The American publishers Summit Books shared this response, and published the first part of *Lilit* separately, as *Moments of Reprieve* (New York, 1986). (Adding three other Lager pieces: 'Last Christmas of the War', 'The Quiet City' and 'Small Causes', which Primo wrote later.)

In late December and early January Primo made a few adjustments and additions to his book (to action and dialogue, not to the larger question of the characters raised by Bianca). On 7 February he finished the Note to be added at the end; and ten days later the contract was signed. Einaudi took his ninth book 'sight unseen', he told Guido Lopez: he had brought it in on the same day.

Se non ora, quando? was published at the end of April. A few days later Einaudi had to rush to reprint another 50,000 copies: Primo Levi's 'first real novel', as the publicity proclaimed it, was an instant best-seller. He was as excited as a child. Could it be that it had worked? Had he leapt the barrier and *not* been punished, 'as pleased Another'? Had he dared at last, and won?

Yes, emphatically and extraordinarily – and also no. For six months the reviews poured in, from popular magazines as well as the papers – *Panorama*, *Epoca*, *Gente*; Primo kept them all in a folder, as usual, and it must have been the biggest folder on his shelves. There was a torrent of praise, and for once no real stinkers at all. *Se non ora, quando?*, said *Il Sole 24 Ore*, was the complete confirmation of Primo Levi as a writer; no one, said *Avanti*, remembers Levi the chemist any more. Pampaloni, Marabini and Mondo, Nogara and Romano, Sgorlon and Vacca all praised its clarity, humanity and irony; its stunning landscapes and epic sweep; the biblical resonance of its language, and the picaresque excitement of its story. Primo's letters told him that people couldn't put it down; wives complained that husbands snatched it from them before they'd finished, husbands said the same about wives. In June it won the Viareggio (among the judges, Umberto Eco, Carlo Bo, Giovanni Raboni, Paolo Volponi), and was already a strong favourite for the Campiello. With his usual scrupulousness (and some old-fashioned Jewish fear of native resentment), Primo wrote to withdraw from the Campiello; but after a scolding from friends, he withdrew his withdrawal. And in Venice in September he won hands down, 100 votes ahead of his nearest rivals, Goffredo Parise and Ferruccio Parazzoli. He was the only person to have won the Campiello twice, in its first year and now in its twentieth; in the same evening he had been up for the 'Campiello of Campiellos' too, though that went to Ignazio Silone. The Viareggio and the Campiello each meant an extra 30–40,000 books sold, and Einaudi had to reprint twice more. By the end of the year *Se non ora, quando?* had sold 110,000 copies, and was still at the top of the best-seller list. It was by a wide margin the most popular and successful novel of 1982.

And yet . . . This time, alas, the 'and yet' moves in the other direction. Though all Primo's best critics praised the book, none praised it without qualification. Carlo Sgorlon spoke for them all when he said that *Se non ora, quando?* was very fine, the best novel of the season, but it was not quite a masterpiece. So did Claudio Magris, when he said that not even Primo Levi could write a novel about the Holocaust: his own books of testimony were incomparably superior. *Se non ora* was too long and detailed, Marabini and others said; its characters were a little too *à thèse*, and even a little 'socialist realist' – Gedale, for instance: too noble, good and strong. And the end (even *Panorama* agreed) was a little contrived. Primo had changed the operation on the girl partisan in Milan to the birth of Isidor and White Rokhele's child: and placed it on 7 August 1945, the day the atom bomb fell on Hiroshima. When *La tregua* had ended with his own *Wstawàch* dream, the warning had been desperately convincing. This one, with its obvious symbolism, seemed much less real.

None of this, wrote Marabini, reduced Primo Levi's victory in the battle 'between history and poetry, between reality and imagination', which he had finally won. But of course it did. Primo responded to his critics with irony: they accused his characters of talking 'like the heroes of a romantic novel', he said – but that was exactly what they were. He accepted their criticisms, he even agreed with them. But when he talked of them, he smiled: an inward smile, said a famous reporter, full of obscure meaning.

If he had ever wanted success for a book, it was now. His family was no happier with his fame than they had ever been; but his children were grown up now. His real life had been his writing for many years, in truth for ever; and this was his great test of himself as a writer. It was dangerous to make so much hang on one book. It was also foolish, since he was reaching for an ideal of pure invention which he himself knew was unreal (fiction, he wrote, 'seethes with memories'). But unreachable ideals were his vice, his habit. He didn't dare to take ambitious risks in love or money; but he did in ethics, and in writing. That was sensible, since he was better at them. But they were not safe either, and there was just as far to fall.

Se non ora was a huge success – but only really with his faithful public of ordinary readers, who unlike the literary professionals had no reservations. That should have been enough for Primo. But he was human after all, and he wanted the critics as well.

In fact, his risk-taking with *Se non ora* had been more than ambitious, it had been positively wild. Not only had he written a book about people he did not know, except on the page; at least the (Italian) critics didn't know them either. He had also written a big, baggy old-fashioned monster of a novel, in every genre they despised – historical novel, adventure story, popular saga – and still hoped to win them over. *And he had.* He should simply have been pleased at the praise he had managed to wrest from the literary establishment with such an unfashionable book. But that was another of his vices. He wanted to go his own way, against the tide, and still be completely accepted; which is a good deal to ask of the world, even for a genius.

His pure happiness lasted no more than a month. The earliest reviews had been excellent; but in June the reservations began – Marabini, Sgorlon, Magris, Pampaloni . . . In early July he gave his subtle smile to Oreste del Buono. And by then his friends would all have read his first novel. Alberto loved it, and said so; so did Gabriella Garda, and very likely many others. But many didn't. Bianca had told him so; so, now, did his cousin Anna Yona. The others didn't tell him, but they agreed with Claudio Magris: *Se non ora, quando?* was inferior to *Se questo è un uomo* and *La tregua*. Primo's leap into fiction had not succeeded, or not as he had wished: his non-fiction was infinitely greater. His earliest champion Cesare Cases thought so; so did Norberto Bobbio and Vittorio Foa, both of whom Primo admired as others admired him. So did Oreste Molina, to whom he had admitted his own doubts early on, and Agnese Incisa, another great friend and supporter at Einaudi. They didn't tell him, but I'm sure he knew.

And then, still in June, there was more. First of all, he returned for a second time to Auschwitz. This time he went with a group of students and survivors from Florence; and with a team from *Sorgente di vita* ('Spring of Life'), a television programme on Jewish culture. When he wasn't being interviewed by the programme's director, Daniele Toaff, he was surrounded by the students and their parents: all deeply shaken, and all turning to him for help. They asked the questions people always did, and which he had escaped for the last three years; then, with the shock of the reality around them, they asked many more. He answered in detail, for several days, with the reality around him too: especially in Birkenau, which he had not seen the first time, and which has been left much as it was, with the railway ending in nothingness. Forty years on, he went to restaurants in Auschwitz, he stayed in a Holiday Inn in Kraków: and at the same time he saw the sealed freight cars again, smelled the Lager smell of burning coal, heard the Lager sound of barracks Polish from two drunks cursing each other in a lift. He was both in the absurdly changed present, and back in the past again. This visit was far more harrowing than the first; and he would not go back again.

The other thing happened almost simultaneously: Israel, under her Minister of Defence, Ariel Sharon, invaded Southern Lebanon. It was the beginning of a disastrous occupation, which would include the infamous massacres of Sabra and Chatila (committed by Arab Christian Falangists, while the Israeli Army turned a blind eye) and which would not end until 2000. A group of Jewish leaders and intellectuals, including Primo's friends and

fellow-writers Edith Bruck and Natalia Ginzburg, wrote an open letter to
La Repubblica, calling for the withdrawal of Israeli troops, and the recognition
of the rights of 'all the peoples of the region'. They asked Primo to sign it;
and on the eve of his departure for Auschwitz, he did.

He returned to a battle on two fronts, which lasted for many months.
The first front was *Se non ora, quando?* Suddenly his reminder that Jews, too,
could take up arms and fight was tragically – even comically – out of place.
The Jewish fighters of 1982 were no longer a persecuted and oppressed
minority, fighting for their freedom, but – it seemed to many, including
many Jews – the new oppressors, fighting to deprive another minority of
theirs. Suddenly Primo's reviews and letters were full of Lebanon. 'Everybody is somebody's Jew', *Manifesto*'s reviewer quoted him: 'And today the
Palestinians are the Jews of the Israelis.' Half his letters, Primo said, accused
Se non ora of being Zionist, the other half of not being Zionist enough. For
a long time no one could read his novel as a novel, as though the moment
he had crossed the border into fiction, history had moved it. It did not hurt
his sales or his success; but it hurt him.

The second front was himself. He quoted Sholem Aleichem: 'It is difficult
to be a Jew.' In 1982 it was more than difficult, it was impossible. A civil
war raged in his mind, in his body: in his entrails, he said, where he hid all
his worst conflicts.

He had been divided about Israel from the start. During his university
years he had admired the ideals of left-wing Zionism, though he had not
been a Zionist. In Auschwitz and after he had become one, for others if not
for himself: Israel must exist, the most persecuted people in history must
have a home. But immediately he had had doubts and reservations: about
the Palestinian expulsions, about the nascent militarism of this homeland
born of war. When Israel was attacked, she must defend herself: and in 1967,
Renato Portesi remembers, he even collected money at SIVA for her
support in the Six Day War. But when Israel was the aggressor, he would
not give a penny, and he would not defend her. He had a deep emotional
attachment to Israel: deeper than that of many Jews who did defend her, for
the obvious reason of his past. But this is the point at which he said: 'I do
not have instinctive reactions. If I do, I repress them.' He was a Jew, but
before that he was a democrat. We must repress our emotional reactions,
and criticize Israel like any other country when she does wrong, he said.
And he did.

In fact he had already done so, as long ago as 1969: signing a protest against
Israeli policies of the day by a group of left-wing Jewish intellectuals in Turin.
That too had created a furore. The Segres – Sion and Ilde – had begged him
to think again: he was an important representative of Jews in Italy, indeed in

the world; and though a Jew *in* Israel might – perhaps should – criticize his government, to do so from the outside only gave comfort to her enemies. Primo listened, and even agreed ('I take pains to listen [to my opponent], and run the risk of believing him'); but he did not change his mind.

He was more famous now, the situation more extreme, and the furore accordingly worse. But he was not (or tried not to be) deterred. On his return from Auschwitz, he wrote an anguished piece in *La Stampa*. He was not ashamed to admit his anguish, he said: Israel felt like a second homeland to him; he wanted her to be different from other countries, and suffered when she wasn't. She *had* been sorely provoked and besieged; nonetheless, this attack was out of all proportion, and had outraged the world. For several weeks reporters flocked to his door, and he continued to say the same things: *No*, Begin and Sharon were not Nazis, and the Palestinians were not the new Jews: there was no state policy of extermination in Israel; Palestinians were killed because they were fighters, not because they were Palestinians. Nonetheless, Israel had over-reacted; she was becoming as bad as her enemies – aggressive, militarist, unwilling to compromise; she was becoming her own worst enemy in the eyes of the world.

He had family in Israel, and friends, some of them fellow survivors. They began to write to him, saying the things the Segres had said in 1969: one had to close ranks in time of war. Leonardo agreed; and Primo's oldest and most important Auschwitz friendship came under strain. In early July he faltered, and sent away a reporter from *Corriere della Sera*: 'I do not want my name connected to this war any longer,' he said. He gave several more interviews nonetheless, but refused all invitations to join live debates on Israel. Those he couldn't face.

And then, in September, came Sabra and Chatila, and he had to speak out again. He signed an open letter urging Italians to demonstrate against the atrocities, and a telegram signalling this support to the protest movement in Israel. And, reluctantly, he gave a last long interview to *La Repubblica*. Begin and Sharon should resign, he said; they were making Israel a pariah, and blackening the name of Jews throughout the world. For Israel's own sake, for their own sakes, Jews should strangle their impulse to support her, and help Israelis to get rid of this terrible government.

That was his last word on the subject for many months, and one of the last in his life.* The reason is clear from the interview. His post from Israel

---

* In February 1983 he called once more for Begin to resign; and in September 1984, in a period of relative calm, he gave a long interview to Gad Lerner for *L'Espresso*, in which he repeated his plea that Israel withdraw from Lebanon, and halt the building of settlements in occupied territory.

had become unbearable. His friends – who had fought in earlier wars, and lost soldier-children in later ones – wrote in pain and anger. Was he blind, they asked, to their blood, to all the Jewish blood spilled over the years? He was not; if only he could have been. But he refused to privilege Jewish blood over any other, he said, or to allow the sufferings of the Holocaust to justify everything. 'You can reason very coldly,' the interviewer said.

He had to; his reason was himself. He had not given it up in Auschwitz, and he would not give it up now. But this standing apart from friends, from fellow survivors, was his ultimate going against the tide of these years – far harder than the others, which were only a matter of literature. He did it, but it tore him apart.

And what was he doing all this time? He was back in the Lager. All through the summer he was translating a book, which was not about the historical Lager, but something worse. 'Take care not to suffer in your own homes what is inflicted on us here,' he had written. That is what it was about: the Lager in life, in the mind.

The book was Kafka's *Trial*. The translation was proposed to him by Einaudi, indeed by Giulio Einaudi himself, whose idea it was. It was a hard proposal to resist. There was to be a prestigious new series, *Scrittori tradotti da scrittori*, *Writers Translated by Writers*: it would include, for example, Natalia Ginzburg with *Madame Bovary*, Fruttero and Lucentini with *Dr Jekyll and Mr Hyde*, and Italo Calvino with *Lord Jim*; and once again Primo Levi would be the first, the flagship of the series. It could be very lucrative, too: the authors to be translated were classics of world literature – and out of copyright, leaving all the royalties to their translators; Einaudi produced the books beautifully, and cheaply (at 7,500 *lire*, about £7.80 a copy). Primo had just had one best-seller; he might instantly have another. That was no doubt why Giulio Einaudi thought of him, in his canny publisher's way. And Primo was not immune, either to flattery by the house that had once turned him down, or to the prospect of earning a nice amount of money with less effort than usual: for as Carlo Fruttero said, 'It is always easier to translate a good book than to write one.'

On the other hand, Kafka . . . Primo admitted to everyone that Kafka was not a favourite of his: a great writer, but not his kind. He, Primo, always sought to move from the dark to the light, from anguish to understanding. Kafka remained in the dark, like a mole. He moved in the endless, aimless, winding passages of the unconscious, and never sought to emerge; he was a writer of fear and shame, in a hostile, incomprehensible world. In fact, he was Primo's negation, he cancelled out all his efforts; and Primo was afraid of him, 'like a huge machine advancing on you, like a prophet who tells you the day of your death'. Kafka 'set off unconscious defences' in him, he said. A year before, when he had had no idea he would soon be asked to translate him, he had remarked that Kafka inspired in him 'repulsion of a psychoanalytic kind'.

With hindsight, it seems extraordinary that he accepted this commission. He knew what translation was – he had suffered badly enough with Jacques Presser, seven years before. Since then he had had another bad depression; he knew that he was vulnerable. But he had always lived on his will, and I suppose he could not know it was failing until it had failed. He accepted 'lightly', he said, 'to see what would happen' (like Gilberto in *Storie naturali*). Besides, each time he finished a book he felt he had nothing left to tell; now, at last, he had written his novel, and the feeling was stronger than ever. 'I didn't know what to do with myself,' he said. *How about nothing?* I want to shout at him, across the years; and perhaps Lucia did. But he was clearly not capable of that. Giulio Einaudi offered him Kafka, like a lifeline; and he took it.

By May he was hard at work. In June and early July came the terrible interruptions of Auschwitz and Israel. After that he was alone with Kafka – with a shock, he said, an attack, a maelstrom, a jungle, an infection. At the heart of Kafka was an illness, a motiveless shame: 'He fears punishment,' Primo wrote, 'and at the same time desires it.' Immersed in that illness, he said, it became his own. But I think it was his own already, and always had been, long before Auschwitz. 'He fears punishment, and at the same time desires it': that may be the closest he ever came – and the closest we will ever come – to a key. But it did not release him; on the contrary. Kafka's illness was so close to his own that it called it up, like a spell. In September, when the translation was finished, the 'huge machine' he had really feared closed in on him: not Kafka, but depression.

In his last year or two, he did not hide this depression from interviewers – especially foreign ones, far away from home. To Germaine Greer, for instance, he attributed it entirely to Kafka: the translation, he told her, sent him into 'a deep depression', which lasted six months. In fact Kafka was only the last of many causes. There was the great success of *Se non ora* – and then it was over, and he was left alone with his doubts and fears. There was Lebanon, having to take a public position, the agonizing letters from friends. And underneath all the time the private causes grew, as we shall see.

Any one of these would have been enough to bring him down. Together they produced his worst depression since the late 1960s and the end of love. It lasted nine months, not six. This time the Rome psychiatrist diagnosed his condition as extremely serious. A Turin neurologist was called in, Dr Renzo Gozzi, who prescribed a powerful anti-depressant, Parmodalin. Even so Leonardo was afraid that he might not come out of it, that this time he might not survive. As in all his worst depressions, he thought obsessively of suicide. As in all the worst ones too, he could not write, and feared he might never write again. These two were the same, for him: if he was dead as a writer, he might as well be altogether dead. Just before the dark completely descended, he wrote a poem so rough with fear that it was never collected. It was called 'Alla Musa', 'To the Muse'; and it was like a warning. Why, he asked her, did she visit him so rarely? If she did not hurry, he wrote,

> *The next time you will find your poet*
> *Insane, or dead, or enraged.*

The pit of this grave depression came in the last months of 1982. Even so he continued to publish in *La Stampa*, though some things were surely written before: the beautiful 'Stable/Unstable', for example, published in November; and perhaps also the half-defiant 'Vecchio io?' ('Me, Old?') of the same month:

As a rule, I do not feel old . . . I love nature still . . . Organs, limbs, memory, imagination still serve me well. Yet I am acutely aware of the ominous sound of that word, which I have just written twice: *still*.

After that, with the help of the Parmodalin he climbed back to a grey half-life. As soon as he had any will at all, he put it to the test, and attempted a return to schools; but gave up immediately, and never returned. In February, when the report of the Israeli Supreme Court on Sabra and Chatila held Begin and Sharon partly responsible, he gave his interview to *La Repubblica*, calling once more for them to resign. Still the Muse stayed away; so he returned to translation, and in January signed the contract for another, much more congenial book: *La voie des masques*, by the French anthropologist Claude Lévi-Strauss. During the last five months of depression he worked on it whenever he could: which meant sporadically, with long pauses. Towards the end *The Trial* came out, and he had to talk about it to journalists; whether that relieved him or dragged him back again is hard to say. Mostly he read and reread, especially Pliny.

At last, in May, it was over. He was euphoric with relief. He threw open his doors to interviewers, to students, above all to friends. Everything had lost its savour during his long torment – even his oldest joy, climbing and walking with his friends. Now he began again: climbing with Silvio, walking with Bianca, with the Bobbios, with all his friends. On 31 July, his sixty-fourth birthday, he and Silvio climbed the Pian della Turnetta together, in Cogne: 2,479 metres high, on the top of the world. His limbs still worked; he was himself again.

Primo on Pian della Turnetta, 31 July 1983

That summer he had an experience which in a weaker season might easily have derailed him. A left-wing Resistance friend of Giorgio Vaccarino's had a son who had gone violently in the other direction, becoming a neo-fascist, and a convinced Holocaust denier. The distressed parents asked their friends to speak to him; and Giorgio asked Primo if he would do so as well. Primo resisted: he knew from experience that Holocaust denial was a fanatic faith, not subject to rational discussion. Finally, however, he agreed. But to his horror, on the appointed day two boys turned up instead of one, bristling with books and arguments: clearly a self-appointed committee to convert their most important opponent to their cause. The gas chambers had never existed, they assured him; in any case, Zyklon B could not kill people. Primo showed them the number on his arm, and gave them Schmulek's lesson: if his number was 174517, and there were 10,000 men in Monowitz, where were all the others? Out of 8,000 Italian Jews deported, 7,400 had not returned: where were they? In the Turin cemetery alone there was a memorial with 800 names on it. Either they were not really dead, in which case the boys could find their names in the telephone directories of Turin, Alessandria, Casale. Or else they *were* dead, in which case why so many, and all in the same years? Coincidence, the boys replied; starvation and disease. Besides, it wasn't six million altogether who had died, but only two. *Only two.* When Primo told that to his friends, he flushed with indignation.

He was not yet strong enough, however, to return to his book on this subject. Instead, in September he agreed to translate a second book by Claude Lévi-Strauss, *Le regard éloigné*, and worked on that for the next six months, with pleasure and profit.* In September, too, he had an important meeting, or rather re-meeting: with Elie Wiesel, the other great survivor-writer who had been in Buna-Monowitz.† Wiesel had written to Primo in the 1960s, asking him to join a panel of literary judges for memoirs of Bergen-Belsen; since then they had met once or twice at conferences in Italy. But Primo dated their friendship from this moment. Wiesel was an extreme opposite – a mystic and a believer, deeply identified with his religion and his tribe. They disagreed on everything, especially God and Israel; but theirs was immediately 'a meeting of brothers', Primo said, and from then on he wrote or spoke to Wiesel several times a year. 'Put the two of us together,' Wiesel says, 'and you get one *être concentrationnaire*.' Even in his way of being a survivor, Primo sought not confirmation, but completion.

The second half of 1983, then, brought recovery. But it also brought loss. First, Hety Schmitt Maass died suddenly, at only sixty-five; and Primo had lost his best German friend. That was in early August. Then, in October, came worse: he lost perhaps his best friend of all.

Leonardo was only three years younger than Primo's mother, and was ageing along with her. One by one the Vitas had died and left him. First Laura, the second companion of his life, in 1967; then Giulia, a year later. Leonardo and Arrigo drew closer and carried on. But then, in the mid-70s, Arrigo too became ill. Leonardo fought hard to save him, but in vain. In 1976 Arrigo died; and Leonardo was left alone in the huge flat at No. 61. Still he had his patients, his surrogate families, his friends, and for four more years he managed to continue on his own. But he was in his late seventies now, then his early eighties, and even he had to admit that he had developed a handicap, for a doctor: he was as deaf as a post. When he couldn't hear a word any more, he finally retired. In 1980 (just as Rina, too, became old), he gave up his job as doctor to the Jewish old people's home, and entered it as a resident.

At first he struggled, of course, to adapt from doctor to patient, from a lifetime of usefulness to one of dependence. But Leonardo was a great accepter of reality. He had his own bedroom and small sitting-room, his own books and furniture; above all he had a constant stream of visitors, including Primo. He enjoyed another two good years of life. Then, in the spring of 1983, his heart warned him that it was about to give out; and by

---

* Marco Belpoliti points out that there are traces of *Le regard éloigné* in *The Drowned and the Saved*: especially of the chapters 'Race and Culture' and 'The Anthropologist and the Human Condition'.

† They had even been in the same Block at one point, they worked out; but they had not known each other there.

now he had Parkinson's disease as well. Still, says Ferruccio Maruffi, he was a happy man. He treated himself, Primo wrote, according to his long experience, and went on peacefully and without fear. He was determined to die on his feet, when the time came, and he more or less did. On 16 October he had a heart attack sitting in his chair, and died instantly.

Primo rang Ferruccio and asked him to come with him to the *casa di reposo*. He was calm and contained, as always, Ferruccio says, but the request itself showed how shaken he was. At that moment he needed to be with another survivor, because only another survivor could understand what he had lost: a witness to their shared past. With Leonardo's death Primo lost a vital support: friend, doctor, brother, fellow survivor. If Leonardo hadn't died, perhaps Primo wouldn't have died either. I think Ferruccio thinks this, sometimes, and so do I. But it is more a wish than a belief. No one – not even a Leonardo – can save another person from himself.

Leonardo

★   ★

Nineteen-eighty-four was the year of poetry for Primo Levi. Since *L'Osteria di Brema* he had been adding three or four or five poems every year, 'at an uncertain hour': often the same hour as the crow of depression returned. There were other occasions too – his wife's birthday, Passover – and other fears: the nuclear threat, the return of war; and most often, time running out, especially for his difficult book of essays on the Lager. The first poem he wrote after *L'Osteria* was secretly about this book, I suspect: or about his plan for it, since it was only just begun. In the poem Pliny pleads with his friends not to stop him sailing across the strait to observe the eruption of Vesuvius. 'Don't worry, sister,' he says: he's careful and experienced, he'll be back soon. Now, Primo's own sister was worried about his new Lager book; she could see what it was costing him, I suppose, and was afraid it would cost him more. And Primo knew she was right to be afraid: famously, Pliny went too close to the volcano, was poisoned by its fumes, and died; and that was the point of the poem. But Primo's Pliny hopes that the chapter he will write on Vesuvius will outlive him; and he is not afraid, or at least he is not deterred. 'Sailors, obey me,' he says – just like Ulysses: 'Launch the boat into the sea.'

Then, in April 1981, Primo wrote 'Le pratiche inevase', 'Unfinished Business': 'Sir, starting next month / Please accept my resignation . . .' The speaker has left a lot of work undone – clients neglected, cities unvisited, a house unbuilt. And 'Above all, dear Sir,' he says, 'I had in mind a marvellous book':

> You'll find the outline in my drawer,
> In the back, with the unfinished business.
> I haven't had time to see it through.
> Too bad.
> It would have been a fundamental work.

For '*In fondo*', 'In the back', he had originally written '*Nel fascicolo verde*', 'In the green file': and in that particular green file (he would tell Giovanni Tesio) he kept what he had written of *The Drowned and the Saved*.

In January 1983, half-way through his terrible depression, he wrote 'Un topo', 'A Mouse'. 'Talky, sententious, equestrian', it preaches to him about wasting time: 'Because life is short and art long',

> And at my back it seems to hear
> Some winged curved chariot drawing near.

In the twinning of Primo's books, Tesio says, *Ad ora incerta*, his collected poems, should be paired with *I sommersi e i salvati*, as the dark side of Primo Levi. I think he is right; and that Primo twinned them himself, turning to poetry when he still could not return to *The Drowned and the Saved*.

That must be what happened now. For suddenly, in 1984, Primo had his second 'rash' of poetry: writing – instead of one, or none, as usual, or even five or six, as in the last few years – fifteen poems in the course of the year. When people asked why, he said he didn't know: poetry just came naturally after Auschwitz, and after *Se non ora, quando?*; and it simply didn't come in his chemical years, when he could only write at certain hours, and not at uncertain ones. This was not untrue: but it was far from the whole truth, as he knew. He wrote poetry in his Ancient Mariner moments, whenever 'that agony returned' – when he *had* to talk, when he had to tell everyone of the ghastly journey he had just survived. His two 'attacks' of poetry came in 1945–6 and 1983–4 because these were the times of (or just after, in 1983–4) the two worst depressions in his life until the last one. That was the reason; but that reason he did not tell.

He had just survived another ghastly journey; he was not yet strong enough to push his boat back out into the dangerous waters of his abandoned book; and perhaps he never would be. In the meantime he had to write – he always had to write; and he had, at least secretly, to tell. For that, poetry was perfect – and stories and essays too, of which *La Stampa* published thirteen in 1984, the highest number in any year so far.★

Not all the poems of 1983–4 secretly tell. The first poem of 1984, for instance, does the opposite, celebrating the moment when the Muse arrives, and the poet feels 'Not lazy, not lost, not forever useless' ('Just take nothing for granted', it ends). But all the others, in one way or the other, do. The next two, 'Fuga' ('Flight') and 'Il superstite' ('The Survivor'), are nightmare poems: the first an echo of *The Waste Land* ('Rock and sand and no water'), with a horrifying end; the other a (marvellous) Auschwitz poem – a very rare return now, the first since 'Annunciation' in 1979. After that came a much more common kind of poem for Primo's later years: one in which he speaks as an animal or plant (as he'd done in 'Old Mole', for example, of late 1982), or occasionally to one (as in 'The Mouse', of early 1983). These *persona* poems are almost all secret tellings of psychic suffering, loneliness and fear. In this one, 'The Elephant', an elephant who died carrying Hanni-bal's army across the Alps speaks from his snowy grave, thousands of miles from home: 'I've hurled my useless dying trumpeting / At these peaks, / Livid in the sunset: "Absurd, absurd."' So, for instance, Primo had also

---

★ Though as always some may have been written before. (One certainly was: 'Polvere olimpica', part of 'Un lungo duello', written in 1982. See p. 654 below.) Altogether – including the thirteen stories/essays, eight poems, one article, and an extract from his *Dialogue* with Tullio Regge, also published this year – twenty-three pieces by Primo Levi appeared in *La Stampa* in 1984: also the highest number ever, exceeded only by twenty-five in 1985.

spoken as the Agave, which flowers only once in its life ('It's our way of shouting: / I'll die tomorrow. Now do you understand?'); as the Pearl Oyster, as the Snail: 'Why run and risk adventures when all you need / Is to close tightly to have peace?' So too, though, he had spoken of the horse-chestnut tree on the Corso Re Umberto, exactly his own age, dusty and deafened by the city's noise: yet 'Still, in its sluggish wooden heart / It feels and savours the seasons' return.'

At the end of *Ad ora incerta* (though not of the year), he wrote two fierce, mysterious poems of war, using the metaphor of chess. In the first, the White Queen speaks, who has just defeated her 'enemy for all time, / The abominable black queen', and asks: 'When will we play again?' In the second, one opponent speaks to the other:

> You mean that, half-way through,
> With the game all but over, you'd like
> To change the rules of play?

No, no, he (or she) says, you know that's not allowed. So why not give up now?

> To foresee my moves,
> Greater knowledge than yours is needed.
> You knew from the start
> I was the stronger of the two.

The opponents could be anyone: God and man, two human enemies, Primo and Lucia. But on one level at least they are Primo and his most implacable enemy of all, his own black depression: which he had always defeated so far, but which he knew would return; and which he knew was stronger than he.

The last five poems of 1984, written between September and December, came too late for *Ad ora incerta*. The first, 'Il Decatleta', was another dark poem: a veteran decathlete, worn out by victory, hears whistling from the stands. The next three were more balanced poems; 'Una valle', 'A Valley' especially is mysterious and beautiful. But the last one darkens again. It is called 'Carichi pendenti', 'Tasks Pending', and it is like a reluctantly abandoned suicide note.

> I've no wish to disturb the universe.
> I would like, if possible,
> To cross over in silence,
> With the light step of a smuggler,
> Or like someone slipping away from a feast . . .
>   . . .

> If it were not for the tasks still pending,
> The debts outstanding,
> The unbreakable commitments made.

His family – Primo told Giovanni Tesio – were worried by 'Unfinished Business', in 1981. This poem must have worried them still more.

L'Osteria di Brema had contained twenty-eight poems, written over thirty years. By March 1984 Primo already had thirty more. He had written them to tell, however secretly; and again, despite the risks, he wanted readers. Scrupulous as ever, he took his new collected poems to his publisher. But he must have been certain they would turn them down a second time; and in effect they did. It was no longer possible for Einaudi to refuse to publish Primo Levi. Instead, they simply didn't respond.

The reason was that Einaudi was once more in crisis, and this time it was almost terminal. The trouble – like all Italian economic troubles – went back to 1973. For nearly a decade it grew silently. Then in 1982 it began to show – with Primo's impeccable timing, the year of his first best-seller. By 1983 Einaudi owed him 100,000,000 *lire* in royalties for *Se non ora* alone. By early 1984 the house was in collapse, a new administrator was brought in, and all royalties were frozen. Calvino left, Sciascia left; of the great old names only Primo, Lalla Romano and Natalia Ginzburg stayed. Staff were leaving too, including Primo's friend Oreste Molina, who would go in 1985. All this was deeply disturbing to him: 'like losing a piece of your country', he said. And then, of course, there was the money. He had his SIVA pension; but his mother needed more medical care every year, and his costs were spiralling. He watched his literary earnings carefully, and collected them regularly, in person, as long as he could. When they stopped it was a bad blow.

In the circumstances, it was quite extraordinary that he offered Einaudi his poems at all, and he was probably relieved when they didn't reply. In March he signed a contract with Garzanti instead. By June, he had another five poems which they let him add; and *Ad ora incerta* was published at the end of October.

Apart from a few of Primo's most devoted admirers, no one noticed. There was one (excellent) review by Giovanni Raboni in *La Stampa*, one long interview by Giulio Nascimbeni, and a short one by Giovanni Tesio; and for a long time that was all. Finally, in the summer of 1985, there was a gently negative review by Claudio Marabini. Primo's poetry was too plain, and too old-fashioned, for almost all professional readers. Still, I think he was not wholly disappointed. He wanted ordinary readers even more in poetry than in prose, and he got them. And his 'success complex', which had taken a short holiday with *Se non ora*, would surely have returned with a vengeance if he had received too much attention for this narcissistic (and revealing) art. In fact he did receive some, winning the Carducci Prize for *Ad ora incerta* in July: but no one noticed, so he could enjoy the tribute undisturbed.

Despite Einaudi, then (and money, and his mother), 1984 was a year of renewal. First and most important, he had renewed himself, through poetry. Then he found a perfect new instrument: his Apple Macintosh computer, which he fell in love with in the summer of that year. Once his son had taught him how to use it, it would become his inseparable companion. On it he would not only write, but play chess, invent puzzles, and return for the first time since his youth to the pleasures of drawing. The first thing he wrote on it, Gabriella Poli tells us, was a poem.

And then at the end of the year, suddenly and astoundingly others renewed him, in the best possible way: made him new as a writer.

It happened in November, a month after *Ad ora incerta* appeared. *Survival in Auschwitz* – that is, *If This is a Man* – had sunk without trace in the United States of the 1960s. But now *The Periodic Table* was finally published there: and America discovered Primo Levi. John Gross in the *New York Times*, Neal Ascherson in the *New York Review of Books*, Paul West in the *Washington Post*, all hailed this 'enchanting', 'original', 'beautiful' book. Alvin Rosenfeld in the *New York Times Book Review* – which was, and still is, the maker and breaker of literary reputations in the US – wrote an especially thrilling review, conveying his own excitement at 'this beautifully crafted book', a 'synthesis of scientific learning and poetic sensibility'. But most important of all was not a critic – even these critics – but a fellow writer. Saul Bellow chose *The Periodic Table* as his book of the year, saying: 'We are always looking for the book it is necessary to read next . . . There is nothing superfluous here, everything this book contains is essential.'

The Periodic Table leapt to the top of the American best-seller lists. Suddenly everyone wanted to translate it, and everything else Primo had written too. His phone never stopped ringing with offers from publishers, invitations to speak, requests for interviews from all over the United States; culminating in a long list of eight questions from the *New York Times*, for which, 'amazed and exhausted', he went to the RAI's studios in Turin and recorded his answers.

This was the moment at which Primo Levi became not just an Italian writer, or a European writer, but an international one. Within weeks – as is the way of the world – he was loved and prized at home as he had never been before; within months he was being mentioned for the Nobel Prize. His finances would be transformed. If he had lived long enough, perhaps his life would have been transformed as well. It was mysterious: for decades he had been almost unknown in America. And now this. How did he explain it? asked Giorgio Bocca. For once, he was happy to have no answer. 'It's a kind of miracle,' he said.*

As soon as he was restored, of course, he returned to the fray. In early 1985 he wrote a long and careful introduction to the autobiography of Rudolf Höss. This oppressive book, he argued, showed that even the Commandant of Auschwitz, one of the greatest criminals in history, was not a monster, but something worse: a more or less ordinary man. No one who read this Preface had to wait for *The Drowned and the Saved* to know that the emphasis was shifting in Primo Levi's vision of man.

At the same time, and despite Einaudi's troubles, he also published a book of his own. It wasn't a commercial book, and indeed it sold badly – even worse than poor *Vizio di forma*. Yet it was one of his most delightful and original, and one of the most *primoleviano*, to borrow a term from Calvino. This was *Altrui mestiere*, *Other People's Trades*: a collection of fifty-one of his essays, almost all from *La Stampa* of the last ten years.†

Despite Primo's new status as national treasure, *Altrui mestiere* was scantily reviewed. Nonetheless, everyone who did review this odd book loved it, and with the usual Primo-Levian effect, loved him. Seeing all fifty-one pieces together was astonishing. It was like being one of his friends, and listening to his fascinated, encyclopedic talk every day. '*Primo sa tutto*' – 'Primo knows everything': with *Altrui mestiere* we feel that too. And he tells it all with such excitement, such pleasure – as he had always done, since Anna Maria was old enough to listen – that we are excited too, amazed at the variety of the world. *Other People's Trades* is Primo's great book of curiosity. It is the

---

* Miracles have their means, if not their explanations. Several people were responsible for Primo's. First – as he went on to say – the American Italianist Raymond Rosenthal, who would become his main English-language translator: Rosenthal came across *The Periodic Table*, and took it instantly to Emile Capouya, editorial director of Schocken. Next, Capouya, who accepted it; when Einaudi had offered it around the US in 1975, twenty publishers had turned it down. Then Rosenthal again, who sent the proofs to Bellow, and when Bellow didn't react immediately, wrote him a furious letter – 'I send you this marvellous book, and you don't even reply!' And last but not least, Schocken's director of publicity, Irene Williams, who worked passionately for *The Periodic Table*, getting Bellow's puff through Rosenthal, and ones from Italo Calvino and Umberto Eco, the most famous Italian writers in America, through Ugo Stille, the editor of *Corriere della Sera*. Irene also took devoted care of Primo and Lucia in New York, and remained a friend until his death.

† Most of these (forty, plus four from *Stories and Essays*) are translated into English in *Other People's Trades*, Michael Joseph, 1989.

book of his real adventures, not his compensatory ones: intellectual and imaginative adventures, adventures of the mind. It is, therefore, the book of his real passion, and we feel that too. It is not true that great intelligence is cold, said Giulia Massari, the critic of *Il Giornale*. On the contrary, it is an instrument of great human warmth: especially in Primo Levi.

Altrui mestiere consisted of 'invasions of territory', Primo wrote in his preface – 'poachings in [the] private hunting grounds' of his favourite unrequited loves: zoology and philology, above all; and astronomy, space science, literary criticism. It also contained travels in his own lands – in chemistry, in writing, in his own life, past and present – which amounted, he admitted in his cover note, to a 'brief but truthful autobiography'. In fact, if we add up all the essays about chemistry (six), writing (six) and his life (nine, including the wonderful pieces on his house, his uncle's shop, his long duel), the 'brief autobiography' almost exactly balances his voyeur's invasions – six essays on zoology, five each on philology (including 'L'aria congestionata') and literary criticism, and one each on astronomy, space science, Jewish ritual and Yiddish. Still, that leaves ten essays on subjects that belong to everyone and no one, but most of all to him – including the most fascinating ones of all, 'Stabile/Instabile', which we already know, essays on pain and fear, on the archaeology of chewing-gum, on the making of sealing-wax from the resin of insects, in which the last stage was once the use of 'girl-machines': they bent, seized the blocks of wax in hands, toes and teeth, and quickly rose, opening their arms wide, to create thin star-shaped sheets, over and over again. Only Primo Levi could describe this 'comic, kind and cruel ballet', in which humans became like plants bursting endlessly into flower; or like machines, in which 'the mouth, workshop of the word, once again became an instrument for biting'.

Everything strong in him is in this book: his scepticism, tolerance and humour; his willingness to explore difference – and what can be more different than the spider he fears, the beetle whose instincts have not changed in a hundred million years? Yet even beetles – 'the aliens, the monsters' – he converts into objects of fascination: making gold out of excrement once more, like the scarab beetle itself, which feeds its larva on dung, 'now no longer ignoble'.

Yet even in *Altrui mestiere* fear and melancholy are not absent, since they are a part of life, especially Primo's. The cover, which he drew himself, on his new computer, betrayed this, in one of his acts of saying more, perhaps, than he meant to. It was in shades of blue and grey, and showed three owls, all the same. The owl, Primo told his friend and fellow-writer Gina Lagorio – night owl, wise owl, owl of Minerva? – was himself.

★   ★

Altrui mestiere came out at the end of February – his twelfth book, not counting the translations. By then, however, his mind was elsewhere. He had agreed to go to the United States.

The invitation came from not just one but two American publishers: Schocken Books, who had published *The Periodic Table*, and Summit, who were about to publish *If Not Now, When?* Primo was in one of his schizoid situations. Travel was his greatest unrequited love, and the United States his greatest gap; when Bianca had gone there a few years before, he had insisted on a minute account, and hung on to every word. On the other hand, there were the usual impediments. Or impediment.

His mother was in a desperate state by now. Not physically: at ninety she was never quite well, but she wasn't ill. The trouble was mental. She had become senile: anxious, forgetful and demanding. 'She is very agitated, and agitates us too, day and night,' Primo had already written to Ruth Feldman, the American translator of his poetry, two years before. They had to have help. A young Israeli medical student at the University, Amir Eshel, had already taken care of Corrado and Gustavo, who were ageing faster than Rina, and who would both die in 1984. Around 1983, therefore, Amir came to Rina as well. He would arrive in the morning, or sometimes in the early afternoon, and take her out for walks to the little park on the corner, or along the Via Sacchi. She would set out and return in her chair; but in the middle, with starts and stops, and with encouragement from Amir, she could still walk. She was strong, Amir says, much stronger than her brothers; and with him, at least, she was mentally strong as well. She didn't talk a great deal, he says: like her son, she was reserved, and you had to coax her into conversation. But when she did speak she didn't repeat herself, and her memory was good; she would tell him stories about her childhood, or about the other old people they met in the park. It is common for very old people, like small children, to behave worst with their own families; and no doubt there is an element of control in their behaviour – control through weakness now, since they have lost all other kinds. But this was especially true, I think, of Rina, whose rule had been absolute for so long. She still dominated the household, Amir says, 'like an old monarch'. Her schedule and her needs were everyone's: her food had to be cut up just *so*, her tea served just *then*. Lucia was as dutiful as ever – more dutiful than ever; and so, of course, was Primo. They hadn't left her alone for years: only very occasionally for an evening, while Amir baby-sat. They had very rarely visited friends together anyway; now it was impossible. They could not leave Primo's mother, they would say – and so would she. Once Valeria Bobbio rang to ask Primo to come round after supper, and Rina picked up the phone. When Valeria explained, she said: 'They can't. They have to take care of me.'

If he couldn't go to the Bobbios, a few streets away, how on earth could he go half-way around the world? Besides, he had hesitations of his own. It was so long since he had left Turin he had almost forgotten how. And would he understand what people were saying, with his reader's English, and their American accents? Half of him longed to escape, and to make Lucia escape, their servitude. The other half was terrified. For once the desire to escape won. He took English lessons with an American teacher, he asked Anna Maria to come and stay with their mother; and he went.

America was Primo Levi's last big adventure. He and Lucia were there for two weeks in mid-April 1985. In those two weeks they visited six cities – New York, Los Angeles, San Diego, Indianapolis, Bloomington and Boston; Primo gave six lectures and (he always said) twenty-five interviews. Every lecture was packed; the first, at the City University of New York, was so crowded that people sat on one another's laps. Primo was too uncertain of his English to do what he did at home, and open the whole evening to questions. Instead he read out a talk called 'Beyond Survival', which he had originally delivered at a conference of Jewish writers in 1982. His Italian accent was strong, and his English indeed not good enough to deal very well with questions; he also refused most radio interviews, and all television ones, pleading his poor English ('I am Italian, and can only talk with my hands'). Despite all this, the tour was a great success – so great that Professor Dante Della Terza invited him to come and teach at Harvard, and Arthur Samuelson of Summit begged him to return the next year, for the publication of *The Wrench*. This small, upright figure, radiating both an intense energy and a contained weariness, impressed audiences just as his great book does, in every language: with a sense of deep, embattled humanity.

As for Primo himself, this last adventure came too late, like his fame. Of course some of it was marvellous. He was profoundly pleased to be treated as a literary writer, with *The Periodic Table* and *Se non ora* in the foreground, and *If This is a Man* in the background – the book which had freed him as a writer, but which for many years now had oppressed him instead; and did so still at home. He was thrilled and astonished by America – by its openness and daring, its superb technology, its thirst and respect for culture and art. On the other hand, he was disappointed in it ('Perhaps he was continually disappointed by the world'). His hosts – publishers, professors, scientists – were civilized and often left-wing intellectuals, with whom he felt at home. But the average level of American communication shocked him. After a few unhappy experiences, he decided to refuse all interviewers who had not read at least one of his books; but had to retreat very soon. And he was shocked, too, by the large number of beggars and street sleepers – 'black and white (but mostly black)' – in the richest country on earth: a benefit of unbridled capitalism which did not flourish in Europe until after his death. Once, emerging from a lavish cocktail party, they saw a very ragged beggar outside the door; Irene Williams has never forgotten the look on Primo's face.

Above all, however, he was amazed, and also dismayed, at the very different business of being a Jew in America. Jews were so secure here, so far from a minority – almost a majority, it seemed, especially in New York: and paradoxically, that didn't seem to him an entirely good thing. Being a minority was a school for tolerance, he had recently said: but Israel, and the Jews of America – at least, many of those he met – were not tolerant any more. They had become like everyone else, when he wanted them to be different. They were sufficient unto themselves, and did not mix, as he had written (but only half seriously) of his ancestors. In his entire time in the US, he said, he met only Jews: where were the others? he and Lucia wondered. They asked him only Jewish questions, and saw him only as a Jewish writer: 'They put a label on me,' he said. When someone at one of his lectures asked if he was a Jewish writer he answered, 'I don't like labels. Germans do.' He made jokes which were not appreciated by his Jewish audiences, saying about Fossoli, for instance, that it was his 'first exclusively Jewish environment'. Once, when he was asked a serious question about Israel, he began a serious answer, to the effect that in historical terms its establishment had been an error; you can imagine the reaction. Altogether, some of his listeners, especially in New York, found him 'not "Jewish enough" for their liking', as Ruth Feldman puts it; this upset him very much at the time, and even more later.

And then there were the parties. Primo hated literary parties in Italian; in English they were a torment. He was reduced to pretending to understand, and responding with vague noises: given the general cacophony, he said, it made little difference. At publishers' parties people concentrated on impressing each other and ignored him, at the others he was mobbed by frantic admirers; of the two he preferred the first. The worst party of all came after he and Saul Bellow had received the Kenneth B. Smilen awards together, Bellow for a collection of stories, Primo for *The Periodic Table*. He had looked forward very much to thanking the man who had made him famous; but for mysterious reasons of his own Bellow was curt, and Primo was deeply wounded. The only good party, for him, wasn't a party at all, but a meeting with representatives of the New York Jewish community. Among them was a group of Jews from Salonika, Leon Levi's home: they talked to him about *If This is a Man*, and Salonika, and the Ladino they still spoke, and Primo had a wonderful time.

His US adventure was a very Primo-Levian story: outwardly a success, but inwardly a disaster. He had hoped, naïvely, to have more time to see things, and less time being seen. His 'success complex', his attention complex, his fame complex all rose up to haunt him. He hated selling himself in the American way, and he was horrified at the American desire to make writers into oracles, with simple, uplifting answers. And he was, he had to admit, 'no longer a young man'. By the end he was exhausted, and in his own words 'half crazy'.

The truth was that his strength was going. He had made impossible demands on himself all his life; they often broke him, but for most of his sixty-five years he had managed to live up to them. That was ending now. He wanted his communication to be perfect, even in English, and it couldn't be. He wanted Jews to be better than they were, he wanted Man to be better than he was, he wanted himself to be better than he was: to fellow prisoners, to audiences, to his wife, to his mother. Above all to his mother. She had always been his central torment; but since she had begun to age it had become infinitely worse. He had been so unhappy watching her decline that he had only longed to get away; but now he was even unhappier *not* watching it, not knowing whether it had worsened. Away from her his slavery was not less, but almost more. And his control was slipping. He had always been able to hide his feelings, to look serene and detached, even when he wasn't. Not now. He hadn't been able to hide his anguish at Bellow's coldness; and he couldn't hide his loneliness and vulnerability in America. He had written to tell his old university friend Edith Weisz, who lived in America, that he was coming there on tour, and she came to one of his New York lectures. When he saw her, she says, he came and hugged her – 'a real, warm hug'. She was astounded: the old Primo Levi – that is, the young Primo Levi – would never have done such a thing. She was delighted, and hugged him back. But it was not, as she thought, the result of greater ease. It was the result of greater need: so great that he had even shown it in front of Lucia, who was cold and cutting to Edith from then on. It would happen again soon, this sudden betrayal of need to a friend. It was not a good sign.

Back home again, he slowly recovered; or recovered as much as he could. At the end of May he wrote a poem about flying home – being lifted body and soul into the sky, like the Virgin into heaven. 'Are we worthy of this Assumption?' he mocked. But he managed to end on a (just) positive note: 'I do not think it was a wasted journey.'[*]

---

[*] The poem also ends with the sight of 'Lisa, with her keen, clear face', waiting for them at Malpensa: a new private note, which seems to me like another hug of need – the only time he ever named one of his children in his writing.

International fame and its ambiguous pleasures had flown home with him, and took up residence for good in the Corso Re Umberto. In the summer of 1985 he did long interviews for Italian television, for Swiss Radio, for the BBC. In early June *Altrui mestiere* won the Aquilea prize, beating both Leonardo Sciascia and Primo's hero Norberto Bobbio. The letters were flowing in from America now, to add to the rest; so many of his books were being translated, in so many countries, that he made a chart and hung it on his wall to follow their progress. Throughout the summer the reviews of *If Not Now, When?* flowed in from America too, many of them critical: still he filed them all as neatly as ever – more neatly than ever, with the aid of his computer. And despite all this, he returned to *The Drowned and the Saved*, and completed it now – more quickly, but not more easily, than before. The end of the year would be under the sign of this last, most difficult book, which would leave him drained. And it would be under another sign as well, which would close the circle: that of Italo Calvino, whose first book had appeared alongside his, in long-ago 1947.

Calvino wrote to him in early August. He had a favour to ask, he said, 'and once again it's to do with Queneau'. Calvino was a great admirer of Raymond Queneau – poet, novelist, editor of the *Pléiade*, and polymath and invader of territories equal to Primo. Despite Queneau's often ferocious obscurity, therefore, Primo was an admirer too. A few years ago, in the early 80s, he had attended one or two of Einaudi's summer meetings, at Rhêmes Notre Dame in the Val D'Aosta; and at one of these Calvino had already consulted him about Queneau's *Petite Cosmogonie Portative*, which he was translating. Queneau was a champion of science-in-literature after Primo's own heart ('*On parle des bleuets et de la marguerite / alors pourquoi pas de la pechblende pourquoi?*' he wrote★); and it was with the forest of obscure scientific terms that Calvino had asked for Primo's help. For several mountain evenings they'd worked together very happily, Primo said; attended with fitting surrealism by a cat, 'who every now and then tried to turn the pages with its paw'.

This time Calvino wanted his help with an even more scientific *jeu d'esprit* of Queneau's, *Le chant du styrène*, *The Song of Styrene*. 'I expect you're away on holiday,' Calvino wrote; he would wait for Primo's return. Poor Primo, however, hadn't had a hot, oppressive August away from Turin for several years. He rang Calvino straight away. He was delighted at the prospect of another 'spiritual feast', and had already had a look at the first draft Calvino had sent him. The chemistry seemed fine, but he had a few ideas for the

---

★ 'We speak of the cornflower and the daisy / so why not of pitchblende why?' It goes on: 'We speak of the forehead the eyes the nose the mouth / so why not of chromosomes why?'

mechanical part. Mechanics wasn't his subject, he said modestly; and Calvino seems to have assumed that he would do no more. But Primo always did more, and this time it was a pleasure. He was still working on the draft of *La canzone del polistirene* when he heard the news: at only sixty-two, at the height of his powers, Calvino had suddenly died.

That was in September. In his obituary Primo spoke of the books Calvino would never write now: perhaps he was thinking of his own unfinished book too, and perhaps Calvino's death was one reason why he made himself go on with it, despite everything. And then another blow fell. In October he was savagely attacked in *Commentary*, the magazine of right-wing American Jewry.

'Reading Primo Levi' was written by the journalist and novelist Fernanda Eberstadt. But Primo knew that it represented the views of a whole group of people: those Jews who did not think he was 'Jewish enough', or his first book Jewish enough either. Eberstadt's main point is this second one. *If This is a Man* is 'a social and psychological study elevated into a work of art', she says, truly and rather well – but that is exactly what is wrong with it. Its intention is to explore '[what] makes human nature human' – once again true, and well put; but unacceptable to her. The catastrophe of Auschwitz was a catastrophe of the Jewish people; that is the vital point for her, and that, she argues, Primo Levi ignores. It is not true, but it is nearly true; and in the view of Eberstadt and those like her, it makes *If This is a Man* an illegitimate response to the Holocaust. She proceeds, therefore, to demolish the book, accusing Primo of pseudo-science, hackneyed psychology, and 'a tin ear for religion'; and (in the story of Rumkowski, in *Moments of Reprieve*) of 'muddled sentimentality' and 'educated cliché'. She surely has a tin ear for writing; but entirely as a result of her political position. When it comes to *If Not Now, When?* her criticism is cruelly exaggerated, but not false: she calls the plot schematic, the conversation 'leaden' and the novel a failure. Not content with destroying *If This is a Man*, *Moments of Reprieve* and *If Not Now, When?*, she also mounts a personal attack on Primo, saying that he only 'found the will to resist' after Fascism had fallen, and that he only declared himself a Jew on arrest because he 'thought it safer': that is, she calls him a coward.

Primo put on a brave face, but really he was devastated. He was used to being ignored, and politely underrated: but this was excessive violence, not unlike the kind he had just been writing about in *The Drowned and the Saved*. He was particularly hurt by the personal insinuations, and outraged by their ignorance. Still, left to himself he would probably have suffered in silence. But Ray Rosenthal wrote a furious letter to *Commentary*, and so did one of Primo's (or rather Lucia's) American relatives, Alan Viterbi; and very likely urged on by them, Primo wrote his own reply. He defended himself against the imputation of cowardice with quiet irony: if armed resistance only began in Italy after the German invasion (as in every other country in Europe, incidentally), there might be a good reason: you cannot fight an enemy who is not there. As to his reasons for declaring his Jewishness, they were all in *The Periodic Table*, including 'an irrational surge of pride'; Eberstadt had ignored everything that did not suit her purpose. Then he turned to the central point. His analysis of the Holocaust as an extreme case of xenophobia was inadequate, Eberstadt had argued, since 'the destruction of the Jews was conceived precisely at a time and in a place in which [they] had become thoroughly assimilated'. That is the hidden agenda of the piece – to persuade Jews that assimilation, far from protecting them, itself led to the Holocaust. Primo dismisses this specious argument with ease. The Jews were not assimilated in Spain in 1492; they were assimilated in Italy, where they would have continued to live in peace with their neighbours if it hadn't been for the war. They were assimilated in Bulgaria, whose (pro-fascist) government protected them; they were not assimilated in Poland and Russia, where there were pogroms for generations. By implication, Eberstadt had criticized him for being an assimilated Jew: well, he was. All Jews in the Diaspora were, at least to the extent of speaking the language of their country. Had Eberstadt herself not attacked assimilation in English?

That was his only underhand blow, and I hope he enjoyed it. But in fact he hated the whole thing. He hated controversy with anyone; and Eberstadt was speaking for his fellow Jews, the Polish and Russian Jews for whom he had written *If Not Now, When?* (but they didn't like that either); some of them – even many of them – were probably survivors. It was like the dark days of Lebanon all over again. He hadn't backed down then, and he didn't now; but it was almost as hard.

In October Jean and Claude Samuel came to visit the Levis. This would turn out to be the last time Jean would see Primo. He found him changed: 'sadder', he says, 'more worried' – Jean refuses to use the word 'depressed' about his oldest and best Monowitz friend. He had just heard Ernst Nolte on German television: a new and subtler stage of negationism was beginning. It would be another year before it reached Italy, just in time to play its part in Primo's final despair. But he heard about it from Jean now, perhaps for the first time; and it added to his black mood. But that was already there. He did not mention America, or Fernanda Eberstadt; or if he did, Jean does not remember them. But he did say that he was finishing his book of essays on the Lager. And for the last time Jean understood him, without the need for explanation. 'Writing *The Drowned and the Saved* had left a deep mark on him,' he says.

Primo finished the last chapter on 28 December, and on 3 January the Conclusion. A few weeks later he also completed his tribute to Calvino. *La canzone del polistirene* was being presented in Milan, and he was asked to take part, together with the publisher, Vanni Scheiwiller, and several others. Primo read out his *Calvino, Queneau and Science* in a voice veiled with sadness. At the end, as they were all filing out, he found himself near a tall man with a great beak of a nose. His memory was infallible, not only for the Lager: and though he had not seen that nose for nearly fifty years, he recognized it instantly. It belonged to Pierluigi Olivetti, whom he had known in *liceo* – a charming, sunny, open boy, son of the founder of Confindustria, the huge industrialists' association, who had been born a Jew. 'Olivetti!' Primo called out – he who almost never spoke the first word, even quietly. Olivetti turned to him, delighted to be recognized. And then it happened again. Primo embraced him, Olivetti remembers, with touching affection. Then he asked him to come and see him in Turin. 'It's a wonderful memory,' Olivetti says now – or rather, writes down for me, because a few months after Primo's death he had a stroke, and has never properly recovered his speech. Yet he is not at all sad. He is a lion, like Gabriella Garda, like Alberto Salmoni; and like Edith Weisz too, and another, as we shall see. Primo's instinct for helpers was still as infallible as his memory; except that they could not help either.

The Double Bond

The last lion in Primo's life was the woman he called Gisella. She is not the whole Gisella of *The Double Bond* either – no one is that Gisella, as Lilith had warned me. The secret love in his letters is for the woman in the letters. But of all the real women in the last years of his life, it was most of all for her.

She is the opposite kind of lion from Gabriella Garda – a brisk, dismissive one, when I turn up at her door. I am wasting my time and hers, she says, if I think she has anything to add to the usual pieties about Primo Levi; ask anyone in Turin. I already have, and they agree. It has baffled me how she and Primo managed to keep their relationship secret in this small city. But just looking at Gisella, it is clear. He needed secrecy, and she gave it to him, without reserve and without exception. She is small and upright, like him, and I can see in her lioness's eye that she is not about to change.

Nor did she, ever. Shortly after that first meeting she had to admit a small defeat. Neither Gabriella nor Lilith knew her name, because Primo did not tell them. But he told them other things, which they told me; and since I have a pathologically detailed knowledge of everyone he ever met, I identified her without difficulty. At first she denied it, very convincingly; but when I told her some of the things Primo had said, she had to turn her head away to hide her tears. Very well, she said. She had known him well, and tried to help him, towards the end. But that was all she could say. When I saw what even these few words cost her, after so many years, for a moment I wanted to stop. But then I watched her regain control of herself, and thought how different Primo's women were – Gabriella, who didn't care about control, and cried as easily as she laughed; Lilith, who didn't need it, since she accepted everything from the start; and now Gisella, who lived by it, like Primo, and like him tore herself apart. And I thought that perhaps I'd been wrong about everything, and *this* is what he really needed, not an opposite at all; and I was hooked again on the wild goose chase for human truth, and went on.

So Gisella and I began a long battle. She refused to tell me anything personal about her relationship with Primo; she never used the word love. She told me only that it began in 1974 and ended on 8 April 1987, when he made his last telephone call to her. At the beginning especially it was full of fun: he loved to laugh and joke and be lifted up, and she went on doing that for him, as much as she could, as his moods darkened. Of course *he* was very witty and funny when he was happy, and loved to tell her Jewish jokes and stories; like the one about Goldberg and Cohen, who have delicatessen shops next door to each other. Goldberg's shop (he recounted) is always packed, while Cohen's is empty; so finally Cohen asks his friend what on earth he is selling. 'Lark paté,' Goldberg tells him. '*Lark paté?*' gasps Cohen. 'But how can you afford it?' 'I add a bit of horse,' Goldberg replies. 'How much?' 'One lark, one horse,' says Goldberg.

This is the kind of story Gisella is glad to tell me. About the rest she has remained silent, and all I know is what Primo told Gabriella and Lilith. That this was his last, best love. That she was endlessly generous and loving, that she asked nothing of him, and never frightened him (this is from Lilith, who did). That there was an open happiness between them, and a profound spiritual communion (this is Gabriella). That she was essential to him, and made his last years possible. That she gave him life, and helped him to stave off death (but this is me now, not Primo). That she was his Factor L, his Double Bond.

The battle we have fought has not been over this, since even I was willing to stop there. Whether he finally shed his double bind, or finally accepted it, because she did, we will never know; and that is right. The central suffering of his life, therefore, remains a mystery, both in its beginning and in its end; and that is right too.

Our battle has been over books. Primo gave Gisella everything he ever wrote, published and unpublished, including of course his letters to her (or rather to the Gisella of *The Double Bond*). That was not a battle: he wanted the world to see them eventually, and most of what I have been able to say about them here comes from her. When she dies, however, they may be burned. We know about them now, she says, which is all that matters; the letters themselves are hers, and she may take them with her. We are still fighting over that. But our main battle has been about something else.

Gisella lived through Primo's last two major depressions with him, and many smaller ones; she watched the noose tighten, and feared that she would lose him. And like him, she found order and relief in writing. She kept diaries; and increasingly over the years they filled with the details of Primo's depressions, scribbled down when he had left her, almost illegible with anguish.

These are the books at the heart of our battle: not his, but hers. She has made her decision; our battle is over, she says. This decision is the same as the other, over the letters to Gisella. The diaries will be burned: she is immovable about that. They contain much else about her own life, which is of no interest to anyone. Can you not remove the pages about Primo? I plead. But she cannot bear to go through them again. I remember her suffering when she did, and I cannot ask her. She has done enough.

But there is another part to this decision, just as there was over the letters. We should know what lay behind the order and light of Primo Levi's books, she agrees: the great price he paid for that light, and why he needed it. And we should know what was behind his death. So she did go through the diaries, for the first time since that terrible day. She made notes from them and sent them to me, with instructions to burn them; once she read her notes to me, then tore them to shreds before my eyes. She wants us to know, and doesn't want us to know. I put her too in a double bind. I'm sorry.

I am not allowed to describe her. I will only say – and she will think it far too much – that of all Primo's loves, she is the most Turinese: honest, faithful, self-denying. Once she made up her mind, she has been as loyal and generous to me as she was to Primo. Our battle *is* over, thank heaven; but hers is not, I know.

★   ★

Once they sat down and made a list of Primo's serious depressions (he never called them depressions, Gisella remembers, only 'being tired', 'being down'): it came to five or six altogether, some time before the end. There had been three before they met, he said: one around the time of SIVA's move to Settimo (that is, in the early 50s); another SIVA one, in the 50s or 60s; and one after *Vizio di forma* in 1971, which he ran together with the one after the loss of Lilith, about which he only hinted to her. (In these he did not include the first big depression, after his return from Auschwitz; Gisella does.) But around and among all these there were always small ones: 'at least once a year, like flu', Gisella says. Anything could set them off, even, or especially, little things: 'Every little thing was a tragedy to him,' she says. As long as he was working, it was usually work. In the first years of their friendship it was almost always illness: he had 'a terror of physical ailment', she says (he would say so too, towards the end); and not only his own. When she had a finger in plaster once, he recoiled in shock; when she had a lung infection, he rang her twenty times a day, certain she was dying. He was always certain *he* was dying, even from shingles. In 1976 he had a depression after surgery on a gum; in 1978, during the shingles. After both of these he said, '*Capisco che sono molto fragile*': 'I realize I am very fragile.' From 1978 on the causes were almost always the mothers, especially his; until the last one, when everything came together, his mother's illness and his own.

He had depression inside him from the start, Gisella says. Only it had begun to rise like a river more and more often, with ever shorter periods of grace.

Notes from Gisella's diary, 1982–3

Depression growing slowly, with success of Se non ora, quando?

4 September 1982   In Venice for the Campiello. Takes part in all festivities, but with effort: the verruca on his left foot is painful. ★

4 October   Interview with Dina Luce
  [Q: What are you afraid of?
  A: Of physical pain, my own and others'.]

20 October   Operation on the verruca, not wholly successful

22 October   Sabra and Chatila
  A wave of antisemitism in Italy
  Attack on the Rome synagogue: 1 child dead, 40 wounded
  Harsh letters from Israeli friends
  His friends ill – Ada, Giorgio
  His mother confused, in bed: 'She has become a memento mori *to me.'*
  He spends his time inventing and solving cryptograms in English and German.
  He says: This depression started after Se non ora, quando?, *and after writing 'Un lungo duello'.*

★ He caught this verruca at the swimming-pool, where he went once a week for exercise. Of course he feared it was cancerous, and would kill him too.

5 November   He writes 'Old Mole'
> *He says: 'I'm afraid I have said all I have to say, and that I won't be able to write any more.'*

18 November   He doesn't seem changed, but: 'The trouble is the way you feel inside.'
> *'Nothing interests me any more. What if I stay like this, like a worm?'*

19 November   Last night, supper with Camon; told him 'I am in a depression.'★
> *Another terrible letter from Israel*
> *'I have nothing more to say.'*
> *'I don't know what to do with myself.'*
> *'This is the fourth depression of my life. I want to end it. But the third floor is not high enough.'*

26 November   He does not want help. 'Let me manage by myself,' he says.
> *'My novel has won three prizes, but the very thought of it makes me sick.'*
> *'I need to talk, talk, talk.'*
> *'How can I help?' 'By listening.'*

He says: 'Maybe it's really because of the success of Se non ora. *But Kafka contributed too.'*
He says: 'I was stronger in the Lager.'
He says: 'When I think of myself, I want to be sick. I wish I could kill myself.'
He says: 'Don't be frightened. I'm not in danger. Not yet.'
At the end of the year he says: 'I'm looking for God, but I can't find him.'

Then came the psychiatrist, the neurologist, the Parmodalin.
Finally, on 24 May 1983 it ended, like a plug being pulled.

He says: 'A man sits on a sofa with a newspaper in his hand, which he cannot read. He is in darkness, all he can think of is death. And all of a sudden – it's gone. He stands up and says: "Let's go out."'

Gisella says: Afterwards he was so relieved, he laughed and joked, he was totally happy. And that frightened me more than anything.

★   ★

★ What he had actually said appears in Camon's *Conversations*: 'It may seem strange to you, but I've had . . . a stupid depression [recently], over very little: I had a small operation on a foot, and that made me think I'd suddenly grown old.' Primo had wanted to talk to Camon about his troubles – his mother, his wife, his depressions; but his control was still too good, Camon had no idea how desperate he was, and he wasn't interested.

'I am a talker,' Primo told Camon. 'If you stop up my mouth, I die.'

That is the essence of Primo Levi. It was the essence of his experience of
Auschwitz: if you deprive a man of communication, you deprive him of
humanity, and soon of life. It was the essence of his writing, in which his
whole aim, as Gabriella Poli says, was 'to communicate experiences': whoever did not communicate, or communicated badly, he wrote, was unhappy;
and whoever did not want to communicate did not want to live. The motto
of his autobiography was *'Troubles overcome are good to tell'*. Telling, he said,
was one of the pleasures of life, and more: a basic human need. His image
of that need is himself, stopping strangers like the Ancient Mariner to tell
his tale; and Hurbinek, the child of Auschwitz, whose need to speak
charged his stare with judgement, and who died having uttered only one
incomprehensible word.

   But 'If you stop up my mouth, I die' is not only Primo Levi's report of
Auschwitz and of writing. It is also, quite simply, his report of himself. *'How
can I help you?' 'By listening'* . . . All Primo Levi's loves were his listeners.
First Lucia, who had listened to him more than anyone else after Auschwitz:
and 'That is why, for good or ill, I am bound to her for life,' he said.
Gabriella listened, and Lilith listened; but Gisella listened most of all. And
she listened in the worst times of all – even worse, he would say, than the
Lager. She listened as only one woman had ever listened before, even more
than Lucia: like Vanda, who had travelled with him towards death, and to
whom he had told things that are never said among the living.

15. The Drowned and the Saved: 1986

Primo in 1986

At last, in early January 1986, *The Drowned and the Saved* left its green file, and was safely delivered to Einaudi.

Primo's relief must have been enormous. But this liberation, like his first, could not be a simple moment of joy and celebration. He had forced himself to face the offence to the end – and to make us face it too, as we shall see. *The Drowned and the Saved* was a fundamental work, and he had seen it through. But this telling, and this understanding, did not relieve him. On the contrary. It left the same mark as the offence itself had done, the same weariness and contagion.

By now he knew only one sure solution – to go on writing. But what could he write? Then suddenly he had an idea. It was completely different, it might even be shocking, after *The Drowned and the Saved*. But when had that ever stopped him? On the contrary, it was another of his vices, of his favourite dangerous things.

People often asked him everyday chemical questions, and he loved to answer them. What made jam gel? (That was Anna, Leonardo's niece and Stuart Woolf's wife.) What made mayonnaise go wrong – or right? Why did an egg go hard when you boiled it, instead of soft, like most things? (Both of those were Lucia.) Then there were the wider questions of science, which he loved to talk about to Gisella: what were molecules and atoms, what was electricity? Perhaps he could take refuge in his two most requited loves: science and a listening woman.

For a few weeks nothing happened. Then at the end of January he gave his talk on Calvino in Milan. *La canzone del polistirene* was sponsored by Montedison; and at that meeting the Montedison magazine editors almost certainly asked him to write something for them. It would have to be something chemical, of course. Why not that scientific story he had been mulling over? And two days later he began.

This was *The Double Bond*, which he would never finish, and never publish in the Montedison magazine or anywhere else. Nothing was left of the original *Double Bond* except the title, and the idea of an organic twin for *The Periodic Table*. Both these he took over for the new one. It would be – he had decided – a collection of letters from a chemist to a lady, on the model of eighteenth-century books of instruction for young women. But the bond between the chemist and the lady would be double from the start – difficult, organic, unpredictable. On the surface his letters would be merely pedagogical, answering the scientific questions she had asked; while underneath they would be shyly personal, hinting at the growing feeling of the elderly, valetudinarian chemist for the Lady. And the title, too, was deliberately double now. Primo had learned the psychological meaning of *il doppio legame*: the double bind, the 'contradictory message' (that is how he put it to the real Gisella) which both must and cannot be obeyed. His double bond with the Lady is also a double bind for him – indeed, his oldest double bind; and that too he would explore in these letters.

He began the first letter on 1 February and finished it on the 17th. It begins 'Gentile Signora', which is friendly but formal. Indeed, the first letter is altogether friendly but formal. Only the gallant, teasing humour, and a certain note of suppressed pleasure, suggest that this is already more than a simple pedagogical exercise. And perhaps the fact that he does not come to the scientific point immediately, but entertains her with 'digressions' – which are one of the great joys of life, he says, just as he had said about telling. He begins with a digression about himself (he prefers writing to the telephone, he tells her, which reveals his shyness straight away); and with one about machines as metaphors – they are as good as animals, he claims, and he undertakes to use 'as annoying as a busy telephone line' instead of 'as a fly' from now on.

After a few similar 'digressions' he turns to her question: the definition of 'volt' and 'ampere'. And now we see that his digression into metaphor was no digression at all, since his explanations are metaphors themselves – not machines for man, this time, but the other way around. Electrical charge is like anger, he says, a feeling with which even she is certainly acquainted: a volt is a touch of anger, rather than a great rage. Like anger, electricity can stagnate, can evaporate, can explode; and most usefully, like anger too it can be channelled and used.

What matters more than volt and ampere is *voltage* and *amperage*, which are intensities of current, he explains; and even more important still is the work which can be extracted from them – on which there is always a small loss, a small payment to be made. If the Signora eats, say, 2,500 calories a day (and even she must eat, he apologizes), will she have 2,500 calories of energy to work with? Alas, no, he replies; but this too is a digression. Perhaps he will return to it one day.

After this he goes on to explain watts, kilowatts and kilowatt-hours, where once again what matters, and what has value, is work. You cannot ask how much 100 watts cost, he says, any more than how much the distance from Genoa to Palermo costs; but you can ask how much it costs to move something from Genoa to Palermo, or to buy something which produces 100 watts, like a light bulb. This question of cost has human implications, he adds. You can't ask how much a human being costs today, but in the age of slavery you could; and even today you can buy footballers everywhere, and in some places wives.

There is a good deal more along these lines, including a comic SIVA story about an electrocuted horse, to illustrate alternating current. Naturally, he says, the Signora will have to make some effort to absorb all this information (which, however, will use less than a millionth of a kilowatt per hour, no offence intended to her brain); she is also warned that if she asks long questions, she will get long answers. And he is very cordially hers.

This was a delightful start, rich with the pleasure and irony of *The Periodic Table* and *Other People's Trades*. Primo gave a copy to both his secret models, Lilith and Gisella. He showed it to Lucia, who always saw everything first; and to Silvio, who liked it very much. He would also show it to Gabriella Poli, and (later) to Ernesto Ferrero. But that was all. Neither Bianca nor Alberto ever saw it, nor any other chapter of *The Double Bond*. Perhaps he was already unhappy about it, not knowing – or knowing – where it would go. Or perhaps he just didn't have time, until he was too unhappy about everything again.

For this first letter to Gisella, written in the first half of February, was not false about his mood, but it was misleading. He had recovered from his worst exhaustion after *The Drowned and the Saved*. He had not lost his curiosity for the world around him, or for people. A new book still filled him with eagerness and energy. And he was still in control: to most people, in public and even in private, he seemed his usual alert, ironic, optimistic self. But underneath the sadness was growing. It was as though, after *The Drowned and the Saved*, he had dropped down a stage. There were still high moments in the last year of his life – even very high moments, because he was so glad to have found them. But inside the darkness was quietly lapping, like small insidious waves.

And the trouble was that 1986 was a cruel year. I had wondered why Primo gave the first chapter of *The Double Bond* to Silvio, and not to his other closest friends. One reason was that he saw Silvio most regularly now; and the reason for that was the first great cruelty of the year.

Ada – his sister-substitute, the third or fourth great listener of his life – had been ill for years. Any long illness is terrible, but hers was insupportable. Brilliant, strong, vital Ada had Alzheimer's disease. She was only in her late fifties when she had begun, slowly and insidiously, to change. When the disease first gripped her she talked obsessively of Milan in the war – the Via San Martino, all the friends together, when they were so happy, despite everything. By 1981 her mind was destroyed. Primo no longer came to see her; he was too vulnerable, he literally could not have borne it. I am sure Silvio understood that, though it is not the sort of thing he will say. In any case, he did not blame Primo; on the contrary, they took refuge with each other, as each struggled with the illness that filled his home. Now, five years later, the end was approaching. Ada had to have full-time nursing; Silvio feared she would have to go into an institution. But before that final decision had to be made, she died. Amid their grief, I am sure Primo envied Silvio his release.

We have a few glimpses beneath the surface in the early part of the year. It is not a coincidence that they reveal the same preoccupations that submerged him in late 1979, in 1982, in the end. All Primo's depressions were one depression, with long (or once long) periods of truce between.

In mid-January he wrote to another friend of his youth, Emma Vita Levi, who had invited him to Como. 'It is true that Como is near to Turin,' he replied, 'but Turin is far from Como.' And he gave the reason for that precise little joke: the state of the two mothers, now ninety-one and ninety-four, had got very much worse.

Twice – probably in late February, and again in March – Pierluigi Olivetti came to see Primo, as he had promised. They talked about their schooldays, and what had happened to everyone – or rather, Primo *el memorioso* did, with pleasure and longing, almost as Ada had talked of Milan. Pierluigi, like most of us, remembered very little of fifty years before. But in return he told Primo about his twenty years in Argentina, where his family had had the good sense to withdraw in 1938, and where he still regularly returned on legal business. Primo was as hungry as ever for travellers' tales; and for a while he was his old self again, curious, lively, eager to laugh. But it would not last long. Soon his eyes would cloud; and he would return to where he had begun, talking of his troubles. There were two of these which he repeated over and over to Pierluigi: he could not write; and his mother's illness was dragging him down. Whenever Olivetti arrived (and he would come once again, later in the year), he found him alone with his mother. And that is what he felt, though Primo must have told him that he had married and had a family: *Primo is alone with his mother.*

The last glimpse comes in an interview he gave to a Piedmontese magazine in March. For years now he had received an 'avalanche' of letters from readers, at least one or two a day (sometimes he said four or five), often with manuscripts attached, asking for his judgement, his help, and above all for his answers. In the last few years the questions had become more and more religious; especially those from young readers. How could God have permitted such things? they asked him. *Please explain the evil of the world.* He did not know how to answer; but he did not know how not to answer either, and he struggled to respond to every one.

'How do you experience fame?' the interviewer asked. 'In fits and starts,' he replied. 'In particular at ten o'clock in the morning, when the post arrives.'

In April he had his very last adventure: together with Lucia, he went to England, and then to Sweden, for the publication in those countries of *If Not Now, When?*

It was much the same as the previous year: twelve or thirteen days away, arrangements like a military campaign to be made, Anna Maria asked to come up from Rome once more. It must have been arranged at least a year before; he wouldn't have agreed to it now. But London and Stockholm were only a few hours away by plane; it was much the same as if they had gone to Cogne or Pietra Ligure by car. And Primo had learned, I think, from his American experience: they would visit only the two capital cities, and keep most of the time for themselves. This turned out, therefore, to be a happy break. He should have had many more – many small holidays, short enough to cheat his guilt, long enough to break the cycle of despair. But then he should have had them all his life; it was a little late now.

He gave only two talks in London, one at the Italian Institute, and one at a Festival of Italian Jewry; and two interviews, one to the *Guardian*, and one to the writer and publisher Anthony Rudolf, who had been the first publisher of his poetry in English, ten years before. That was a happy meeting, almost one between friends; and so were most of Primo's meetings in England. The British reception of *If Not Now, When?* was enthusiastic – partly out of ignorance, as he was perfectly aware;★ nonetheless, it was balm to his soul. British Jews were almost as assimilated as Italian ones; no one put a label on him here. And it was not only the Jews he found congenial. When he got home he wrote an essay about the 'twinship', between the British and the Piedmontese, which despite the decline of both since he wrote – or even before – still seems to me largely true. (Though the piece is itself very Piedmontese/British, and not to be taken seriously.) They shared, he said, military efficiency, entrepreneurial spirit, and 'a general lack of talent for music'. Plus: 'The love of work well done, of law and order. The rejection of exhibitionism, of abstraction, of grand gestures, of rhetoric . . . Respect for human rights. Harshness of class warfare.' And, he might have added, politeness to the point of cowardice, irony, endurance, sheer bloody-mindedness. All of these things he laughed at, and loved, in the British.

But this visit was so brief, it included two other important meetings. One was with the great American novelist Philip Roth, who was then married to Claire Bloom, and living in London. As writers, these two could not be more different – brilliant, subversive, sex- and self-obsessed Roth, and patient, observant, tragic, ironic Primo Levi; they took to each other instantly. Primo struck Roth as happy, 'a free and lively spirit': 'Well, I got him completely wrong,' he says, with a grin. But of course he wasn't wrong: he was exactly half right. Claire, his wife, would sense the other half: Primo's despair. 'But then Claire is an actress,' Roth says. He picked up Primo's mind – his lively, free, happy mind; she picked up his miserable, broken, blocked feelings. Neither was the 'real' Primo Levi; they both were.

But this is moving ahead to the consequence of this first meeting: their next one, five months later, out of which would come the best interview with Primo Levi ever written. Now, however, another group of people were clamouring to take him over.

He told the story when he got home. It began, like so many of his stories, in Auschwitz. At the end of 1944 the Kapo of the Chemical Kommando was Jup Lessing, the Dutch Jew who also played in the camp orchestra. Like

---

★ There is nothing like the strength of Yiddish culture in Britain that there is in America, because of the high degree of assimilation I go on to mention. Also – and again very like Italy – many British Jews are of Sephardic rather than of Ashkenazi origin, especially amongst the oldest and most influential families.

everyone in that place, he favoured his own countrymen; and the four or five Dutchmen in the Kommando wanted to keep it that way. One of them, who had been a printer in his previous life, made a New Year's card out of a scrap of cardboard, which all the Dutch prisoners duly signed. Curiously, Primo noticed, another prisoner signed as well: Goldbaum, who was not Dutch, but Austrian. Ten days later he entered KB, the endgame began, and he forgot all about the New Year's card. But of course he did not really forget; he remembered that detail, like every other detail, and he did not forget Goldbaum. Later he learned that Goldbaum had died on the evacuation march; and he did not forget that either.

Thirty years later he recalled Goldbaum in 'Vanadium', as the prisoner whose name 'Dr Müller' had known, even though he had not mentioned it in *If This is a Man*. Ten years after that, *The Periodic Table* was finally published in Britain. A few months before he was due to go there, a letter arrived for him from England. It came from a Jewish family from Bristol called Zinober, and was signed by one of them, Dr Vivienne Zinober Joffe. Dr Joffe explained that her uncle, Gerhard Goldbaum, had been deported to an unknown destination; the family had found no trace of him ever since. She knew that Goldbaum was a very common name; nonetheless, did Primo remember any more? Would he tell her, on the off-chance that his Goldbaum was the Zinobers' uncle? She would be more than willing to come to Turin.

If she could wait until April, Primo replied, she would only have to come to London. And so it was arranged. The whole family turned up to the appointment: seven people, spanning three generations. They showed him two photographs of their uncle, taken in 1939. And – Primo wrote – like a flash another of his pathological memories leapt to life. He could hardly believe it, and nor could the Zinobers: but it *was* the same Goldbaum, he remembered the face perfectly. They could not speak for emotion, and then they could not stop. They 'enclosed me like leucocytes around a germ', he wrote, and bombarded him with questions. He could only repeat to them Goldbaum's fate, which they had already read in 'Vanadium'; and reassure them that he had not suffered extremely before it. Goldbaum had been taken into a laboratory, like him; that is how Dr Meyer had known him. In return, forty years later the Zinobers were able to clear up the puzzle of the New Year's card: Goldbaum had fled from Austria to Holland, and lived there until the German invasion. He had joined the Dutch resistance, they told Primo; he had been arrested as a partisan, then recognized as a Jew. Just like Primo himself, in fact. Goldbaum, of whom he had only known that puzzling signature, his face and his death, had been another twin.

★   ★

He returned to find many demands waiting: the post piled up on his desk; requests for interviews and meetings, both Italian and foreign, including the first one for a long time with students. All the schools of Pesaro, near Ancona, were brought together; and this time the problem was the opposite of the usual one – the young people were very well-prepared, and bombarded him with intelligent and searching questions for ages, until he almost had to beg them to stop. Back home again he found good news – and more demands. Hanser Verlag had decided to reissue all his books in Germany, starting with a new translation of *If This is a Man*. They invited him to Germany; and Summit invited him back to America for the publication of *The Monkey's Wrench* in November, proposing a huge tour of major East and West Coast cities, and several in between. He didn't know whether to laugh or cry. He turned both invitations down.

Then, at the end of May, *I sommersi e i salvati* was published, and a new round of applause and demands began.

This gravest of all Primo Levi's books was firmly in his dangerous tradition of standing outside and against every accepted idea: and this time it was more dangerous than ever. He had had three motivations for writing the book, he said. First, to bring home, especially to the young, that these events were only just past, and possibly also future; not ancient, half-mythical history, like the agonies of the Christian martyrs. Second, to dislodge the comforting, dangerous stereotypes of black and white: satanic oppressors and saintly victims, of which the reader could only be the latter. And finally, to answer the deniers once again, with a clear and conclusive analysis.

All of these were reasons behind the book, and also results of it (though naturally never complete). But only the second was in it. *The Drowned and the Saved* does destroy the black and white stereotypes of torturer and victim, *by making them both grey*. In 'Useless Violence', and in the last pages of his Conclusion, Primo repeats the point he had often made before: that (with a few exceptions) the SS were not monsters, but only 'averagely wicked': averagely stupid human beings who had been 'badly reared' – miseducated and deformed by the vast power of a totalitarian regime. And then, in the most important chapter of the book, 'The Grey Zone', he does the same thing to the other side. As the torturers were not monsters, so the victims were not martyrs and saints: they too were average human beings, corrupted in the same proportion – that is, with very few exceptions, who *were* martyrs and saints, or very near them – by the infernal system to which they were subjected. That had been the greatest shock for the new prisoner; it was the one for which he himself had felt the greatest need to account from the start, so that already in *If This is a Man* the portraits of Kuhn, of Henri, of Alfred

L. sear and wound as much as if not more than those of Pannwitz, of Fräulein Liczba, of Alex. That account is concluded here.

It was dangerous in both directions: it might bring comfort to his enemies, and pain to his friends. He knew it, as he'd known it about Israel; but he did it anyway, as he'd done it then. Because, he said, it was necessary, 'if we want to know the human species'; and 'if we want to know how to defend our souls', should it ever happen again.

Thankfully, neither danger materialized. Some fellow survivors *were* shaken: perhaps even more by his warnings about memory than by 'The Grey Zone', which was a truth they had known for forty years. Primo had told everyone that truth now: but he had also required them to suspend judgement. No one could judge those who had been subjected to such unimaginable sufferings, he wrote: certainly not those who had not shared them; not even those who had. They had truly had no choice: unlike their oppressors, for whom the choice was hard, but not impossible. He knew of no human tribunal that could judge them, he said: even, or especially, those in the most extreme situation of all, the members of the *Sonderkommandos*. Even they – above all they – were not monsters, as one of them said; and Primo quotes him: 'You mustn't think that we are monsters; we are the same as you, only much more unhappy.' And despite everything, it was precisely the last *Sonderkommandos* who had found the desperate courage to rebel. 'I ask that we meditate on the story of "the crows of the crematorium" with pity and rigour,' he said, 'but that judgement of them be suspended.' Here more than anywhere he puts the blame where it belongs – on those who, far away, all-powerful, inviolably safe, devised this plan, and required others to carry it out. 'Conceiving and organizing the Special Squads,' he wrote in 'The Grey Zone', 'was National Socialism's most demonic crime.'

The other danger would have been even worse, but he had guarded against it too well. Over and over again he made his message clear. Victim and oppressor are 'both in the same trap': but 'it is the oppressor, and he alone, who has prepared it and activated it, and if he suffers from this, it is right that he should suffer; and it is iniquitous that the victim should suffer from it, as indeed he does suffer from it, even at a distance of decades'. And: 'The oppressor remains what he is, and so does the victim. They are not interchangeable, the former is to be punished and execrated (but, if possible, understood), the latter is to be pitied and helped.' He excoriated (not for the first time) sensationalist psychology like that of Liliana Cavani, the director of *Night Porter*, who said, 'We are all victims or murderers, and we accept these roles voluntarily.' 'I do not know,' Primo wrote, whether in my depths there lurks a murderer, but I do know that I was a guiltless victim and I was not a murderer. I know that the murderers existed, not only in Germany, and still exist, retired or on active duty, and that to confuse them with their victims is a moral disease or an aesthetic affectation or a sinister sign of complicity; above all, it is a precious service rendered (intentionally or not) to the negators of truth.

After that, not even the negators themselves could use his book against him.

The reviews were quiet, overwhelmed. *I sommersi e i salvati* was one of Primo Levi's finest books, said his oldest admirer, Cesare Cases; a masterpiece of the essay genre, said an important new one, Pier Vincenzo Mengaldo. Lorenzo Mondo saluted him as a great moral thinker, which is surely exactly right. Each of the eight chapters was picked out for its special value: most often 'The Grey Zone', but also for example 'The Memory of the Offence' (Cases, in *L'Indice*), 'Shame' (Sergio Quinzio in *L'Espresso*), 'Letters from Germans' (the *Quaderni del Centro Studi della Deportazione e dell'Internamento*). In 'Shame' Primo retold his own obsessive story of 'Daniele' – that is, Luciano Mariani – and the drops of water he had not shared with him; the shame of that remained, 'concrete, heavy, perennial', though Luciano had been dead for many years. In 'Stereotypes' he told his other obsessive story, of the schoolboy who had advised him how to escape 'next time': that too, in front of the ignorant, innocent young, is obscurely and unjustly a story of shame. In 'The Intellectual in Auschwitz', his reply to Améry – and indeed throughout the book – he deals with forgiveness: the question, he said, he was most often asked. He repeated once and for all that he was not, as Améry had said, a 'forgiver'. He had not forgiven his enemies, unless they had repented, and not only in words; but he required justice, not personal revenge. He had been glad to see the most responsible punished at Nuremberg, at Frankfurt, in Jerusalem. If he were a judge himself (he had written to a German reader years before, but published now), he would not hesitate to punish those still alive and outrageously free today.

As for the Germans as a whole, he had always refused to pronounce a collective verdict on a people: that was what *they* had done, and it was always false, iniquitous, absurd. Nonetheless, since the 1950s and 60s he has changed his mind. He is careful; he speaks of 'almost all'. But he says now that the great majority knew; and that the collective crime 'of almost all Germans of that time was . . . lacking the courage to speak'.

The gravest of Primo Levi's books: that seems quite clear now. Its most urgent question, he wrote, was: Is Auschwitz dead, 'like slavery and the duelling code?' Or might it return? For years he had been repeating that, though similar horrors were spreading like weeds elsewhere – in Vietnam, in Cambodia, in the Soviet Gulags – in Western Europe at least it was unlikely: the six years of the Thousand Year Reich had surely 'vaccinated' us against a repetition. But the conclusion of *I sommersi e i salvati* was different: 'It happened, therefore it can happen again: that is the core of what we have to say.'

He had not really changed his mind about this as well: he still thought a return of Auschwitz was unlikely. But *The Drowned and the Saved* is a warning; and the time of warning is not the time for reassurance. It was the same in 'The Grey Zone'. He had described this zone before, in his first book. But there he had described its opposite as well, smaller but redemptory, which contained figures like Lorenzo and Alberto, Schlome and Chaim, Jean and Charles. His aim was narrower now: to analyse the grey zone, and to warn us of its size. So that is what he did. When he says that 'Preferably the worst survived', he does not mean that *only* the worst did. He was innocent, and he survived; so (though he doesn't say so here) did Lorenzo and Jean and Charles. He means that usually, typically, the selfish and unscrupulous survived: 'It was not a certain rule . . . but it was, nevertheless, a rule', and he and the others were the exceptions that proved it. That is his point now, and alas it is simply true. You are more likely to survive any disaster if you take care of yourself, and do not go back into the burning house to help the others.

The darkness of *The Drowned and the Saved*, then, is mostly technical: the result of its limited aim, rather than of any fundamental change in Primo's views. But there have been changes. There is the new conviction that most Germans knew, based on facts which took many years to emerge. And there *is* also a fundamental change, which is not about facts, but something deeper. He has not forgotten Lorenzo and the others, the few who once redeemed man, and still do. But in his first book they *were* man: they were the essence of man. That essence was vulnerable, and could be destroyed; it was even inevitably (although not easily) destroyed, in the extreme circumstances of the Lager. But man was made for virtue and knowledge, not for bestiality: that had been Primo Levi's message from the Lager. Now 'The Grey Zone' does not say that he was made for bestiality either. What it says is that he was made for neither: he was made for nothing. With a few exceptions on either side, man is grey: equally open to good and to evil. That is the message of *The Drowned and the Saved*.

I think it is the truth, and not just in the Lager: as Stefano Levi Della Torre says, '*La zona grigia è la normalità.*' Most of us do not torment ourselves over this; we are realists, like Cesare. But for Primo Levi it was a surrender. In the Lager he had found an answer to his question about man which had sustained him for many years: right up to its happiest expression, in *La chiave a stella*. Now it had gone, and it was like losing a faith. And if Lorenzo was a man, then he was a man; if the grey zone was normality, then he was abnormal, as he had always feared. The darkness of *The Drowned and the Saved* is real. Life – not the Lager – had pushed Primo Levi back to his first, despairing answer to his question.

That darkness is very plain to us now. English and American readers, who received *The Drowned and the Saved* a year after Primo's death, saw in it a new pessimism, anger, despair: in its grave warning, in its harsh judgement of Germans (but they had not read his remarks in the Italian press over the years); in that rare exaggeration that 'the worst survived, the best all died'. We read it from the start as 'Primo Levi's suicide note', in Cynthia Ozick's phrase. Some of his friends reproach themselves that they did not: we should have read it more carefully, Bianca says. But in the summer of 1986 none of the Italian critics saw any change in Primo Levi. Cesare Cases, Lorenzo Mondo – all Primo's best readers still emphasized his enduring faith in man and in mind. Only an anonymous fellow survivor, writing in the journal on deportation and internment, recognized the darkness of *The Drowned and the Saved*. Bianca and the others should not blame themselves: without the benefit of hindsight, Primo was still as controlled on the page as in their conversations, or even more.

★   ★

This was testimony once more, and urgently needed: not self-advertisement, but duty. Even so, for the first time Primo was not just half reluctant to present his book around Italy, but wholly reluctant. He could not leave his mother again; still less could he leave Lucia to look after her alone.

The furthest we know he got was Milan, in mid-June. Oreste Del Buono introduced him, on the little square outside the Einaudi bookshop on the Via Manzoni. It was a wet evening and there were no chairs. Nonetheless 200 people came, many of them elderly survivors and ex-partisans, many young students; they stood for over an hour, listening to him answer Del Buono's questions, and then their own. There are not many writers in Italy (or anywhere else) for whom readers would do as much. But Primo Levi was 'loved as a writer, loved as a man', wrote *L'Unità*. I hope he felt it.

Very likely it was clear that his mother's health was worsening: perhaps that was one reason why he was particularly loath to leave. And then what he must have been dreading for years finally happened. On 28 July, three days before his sixty-seventh birthday, Rina had a stroke, and was removed to hospital. Primo watched, pale as a ghost, as she was taken away.

She did not die. She remained in hospital for several weeks. Then she came back to the Corso Re Umberto: paralysed on her left side, unable to do anything for herself, only intermittently lucid. His last Calvary had begun.

★   ★

Amir finished his medical training this summer and left for the United States. There was still the maid, Concetta, who had helped to cook and care for Rina for years; but that was no longer enough. Rina needed full-time nursing now, like an echo of Ada. Primo hired a day nurse and a night one. They were kind, efficient women; especially the night nurse, who was a nun. The burden should have been lifted from him and Lucia now: the physical burden at least, if not the psychological one. But even that did not happen. They had to be there when the shifts changed, and most of the time in between. Despite the nurses, Lucia still did many of the more intimate things for her mother-in-law; and so, it seems, did Primo. And more than ever he was at her beck and call. He spent long hours at her bedside; when he left she called out to him constantly. He got no rest day or night, he said. Sometimes he would not leave the flat all day, until in the evening he would have to escape, if only for half an hour. He would put on his coat and open the front door; and then she would call him. He would take off his coat, and close the door again.

This was not new: it had been going on for at least three or four years. But it was much, much worse, and soon he was very low. Then for a change there was some good news. Philip Roth had proposed an interview with him to the *New York Times Book Review*, and it had been accepted. Roth wrote to suggest a meeting in September. So he would see his amazing new friend again: and even better, Roth was bringing his wife.

Primo was hugely lifted up by such moments of reprieve, almost as much as by the ends of his depressions. He rang Renato Portesi in great excitement and told him. Did he realize who Philip Roth's wife was? Claire Bloom, the heroine of *Limelight*! Portesi was delightfully envious. *Limelight* had been an important film for him, he said. 'Even more for me!' Primo replied. Then he rang Paola Accati, who had lived in London for several years, and spoke excellent English. 'I can't do two things at once,' he said, 'speak English *and* drive.' Would she come and speak English to them, while he drove?

The couple came for a long weekend in early September; and it was, as Roth says, a very happy time. Primo had been 'a good boy', of course, and had written out all his answers to Roth's questions; for an hour or so in the mornings the two discussed them, Primo expanded them, and with the help of a dictionary they translated them into English. Then Claire joined them, and occasionally Paola, as arranged; and they walked or drove around Turin. They went to a famous café (Roth doesn't remember which, perhaps

Fiorio's, or the Bicerin); they went to the Luxembourg, Primo's favourite bookshop, and Roth signed some of his books in English. One evening they all went – both Levis and both Roths, accompanied this time by Ernesto Ferrero of Einaudi – to the Cambio, famous for having been Cavour's retreat during Italy's first Parliament: one of the most exquisite, and also one of the most expensive, restaurants in Italy. Primo looked around with comically exaggerated innocence; Roth entertained everyone with stories about the reactions to *Portnoy's Complaint*, which Primo much enjoyed, without a hint of embarrassment. 'Perhaps I dis-inhibited him,' Roth says. He did. So did thrilling, sympathetic Claire Bloom; so, above all, did his brief escape itself, and Lucia's even briefer one. It was not only because of his curious, lively mind that Primo seemed happy to Philip Roth. It was also because, on both of the brief occasions they met, he was.

The most important part of their encounter, for Roth, was not the Cambio, however, or even the hours spent in Primo's study, coaxing more memories out of this quiet man. It was the day they went to SIVA.

Roth had specially asked to see Primo's factory. Paola was telephoned, Claire Bloom joined them, and they all drove out to Settimo. Primo showed them around proudly. Everyone who saw him came running up with startled pleasure, as if, Roth says, 'a favourite elf had returned'. One man who stepped out of a room to find Primo in front of him was so pleased and surprised he embraced him. Claire Bloom thought: 'Everybody loves him.' Roth thought: 'This is what Primo loves.' A few months later he would think: If he hadn't left the factory, he wouldn't have died.

It wasn't true, we know: the factory had been as full of suffering as the rest of life for Primo. After the tenth or twentieth person had greeted him in delight, he said 'Ghosts! They're all ghosts.' Rather: it was half true, like most things about Primo Levi. To Philip Roth he was the most rooted writer in the world, rooted in his job, his city, his family – in reality, not words. And 'I envied him,' Roth says. But in truth Primo was only half rooted in these things, and half was almost too much for him.

Still he was proud and pleased to be back, and they had another happy day. After it Primo and Paola took the Roths back to their hotel, then went for a drink together in a bar. That was an extraordinary experience, Paola says. She had always been a little in awe of Primo, even afraid of him. She is her father's daughter, direct and emotional, and she didn't know what to do with someone who never expressed any emotion at all. For a time she had lived near him, and he had driven her to SIVA every day; she had painful memories of long silences in that car. She had never seen him really relaxed: or only once, ages ago, when he had stayed with her in London for a day or two, and they had got lost on the Tube together. But now he was like that again. They talked about people in SIVA, they *gossiped* about Roth and Bloom; Primo said that she was just as fascinating as he was, and much more beautiful. They laughed so much, Paola says, that if the bar had been a train they would have got lost again.

Out of this happy visit came the excellent *New York Times Book Review* interview, which Primo himself liked very much. Everyone ought to be interviewed by our best novelists. Philip Roth described Primo as 'inwardly animated . . . in the manner of some little quicksilver woodland creature'; 'keenness trembl[ed] within him like his pilot light', he said. Roth is a tremendous listener, as good as Primo himself, and he inspired some of Primo's most open confidences: about his youthful inhibitions, for example, and his relief on retirement; above all, about his anthropologist's attitude to Auschwitz.* In return, Primo was intrigued by Roth's difference: in particular, by the open sexuality in his writing. 'He wondered what kind of creature I was,' Roth says, 'whether I walked around with my flies open . . . Writers always do that when they meet. Each of us thinks, "Is he as crazy as I am?"' It's a shame that Primo never wrote the mirroring portrait: Philip Roth by Primo Levi. That would have been something, as Roth himself might have said.

Primo and Philip Roth, 1986

* It was to Roth that Primo said that he had lived his whole Auschwitz year 'in a condition of exceptional spiritedness', constantly pervaded by curiosity: 'the curiosity of a naturalist who finds himself transplanted into an environment that is monstrous but new, monstrously new'.

By the end of the weekend they had become 'mysteriously close friends', Roth would write elsewhere. Claire Bloom felt the same. She hardly knew Primo, she says, but she knew that he felt despair. What kind of despair? And she knows that too: he was finally free, she says, from the factory, from financial worries, from everything; *but he could not move.* They said goodbye outside the Roths' hotel on the *collina.* 'I don't know which of us is the younger brother and which is the older brother,' Primo said to Philip. Both visitors were on the verge of tears; and Roth was startled to see that Primo was as well. Then Primo hugged him too, 'as though we might never meet again'. As it turned out, of course, they never did.

The reprieve did not last. It probably ended as soon as the Roths had gone; or even before, with that embrace.

There was only one thing, I've said, which could disturb Primo more than his mother's illness: his own. As soon as that began his defences crumbled, as they had with his last physical crisis, in September of 1982: September again, the swan-song of the year.

Only his doctors know the exact order of the last events of his life. But I think they went like this. He had the classic symptoms of an enlarged prostate: retention of urine, and the need to urinate often. (Another reason, perhaps, why he had been so loath to leave home earlier in the summer.) He finally brought himself to go to the doctor. The first line of defence was to stop taking his sleeping-pills immediately: they aggravated the problem, and had no doubt helped to cause it. The only trouble, of course, was that he needed them: they were a defence too, and now they were gone. He was ill, his illness was embarrassing, and he no longer had the help he needed to get through the night. By August he was sinking into depression. By the middle of September even Silvio – his most rational, most Turinese friend – had to admit that something was seriously wrong. On the 14th he, Primo and Bianca went for one of their long mountain walks, along the Via Sacra, on the Monte Ciambergia. It was a beautiful late summer's day. They remarked to each other with sadness (and the inevitable touch of pride) that their little band of stout walkers grew smaller every year. But Primo became more and more silent. Finally he admitted he wasn't well. They cut their walk short and went home.

He was still himself, however. Ten days later he sat down and wrote the second letter to the Signora; and it was as good as the first, if not better. This time the subject was Lucia's: the mysterious hardening of a boiled egg. Immediately – or almost immediately, digression being his favourite sport, as he says – he launches into a gorgeous *primoleviano* paean to the egg. An egg is a marvel, a Botticelli, a jewel, he says; as long as he lives he will never cease to wonder at it. A fertilized egg contains both a traveller and all he needs for his journey; that is why it can also nourish us. Even an unfertilized egg contains the recipe for an individual, like all seeds; and yet we eat seeds, even the vegetarians among us – who do not, he knows, include the Lady. We animals, he tells her, are not like the good plants of this world, who create life out of non-life, and order out of chaos; we cannot live on minerals and air, but must destroy other life to create our own.

Now, the yolk and the white of an egg consist mostly of proteins, he says, and to describe proteins he will need Dante's inspiration. But he will try. He begins with the molecule, which is, he explains, the smallest autonomous object. The molecules of albumen are long chains, like the coaches of a train. (Both nature and man, he instantly digresses, have a fanatical preference for arranging things in chains, in a single dimension: as, for example, the words in sentences, such as his to her now.) The links in albumen chains are like the letters of the alphabet, which combine in different ways to make words. But not in unlimited ways: like human languages, they have their favourite combinations, and ones they cannot abide. (So English has an inexplicable love for *th* and *wh*, he notes, and hates vowels at the ends of words.)

Now, he says, boil your egg: and what happens? His answer is a battle scene – the molecules of boiling water hurl themselves against the shell, whose own molecules shake violently, like the walls of a house hit by an earthquake; the molecules of water in the egg seize this wild energy, and in turn hurl themselves against the molecules of the yolk and the white. In this violent attack the latter's favourite quiet combinations are destroyed, and pushed into new, disorderly order, like the letters of a word which is no longer a word. And that is her boiled egg.

This process only seems different from the opposite one, he concludes, in which materials like glass and metal melt instead when heat is applied. In reality the two are the same: a movement from order to disorder, like soldiers falling out of line. And there you are, he says: that is the only protein story he knows. All the stories of life are protein stories – health and sickness, growth and age, above all the story of thought. He gets dizzy just thinking of them: how few we know; how many we might know one day, but then it will be too much for any one person, or even any group of people, to put together.

This is his answer to her question of the egg, and like all Primo's scientific answers, it goes far beyond the limits of science. But in this letter he begins to push against other limits as well, as he had planned. The relationship between the writer and the Lady is starting to emerge. They have known each other for many years; they have eaten pizza together a few nights ago. Unlike him, she is a proper 'Indo-European' – that is to say, she is not Jewish. That she is younger than him is the assumption of the whole enterprise; but not hugely younger. There is that acquaintance of 'many years'; and she has a daughter who is old enough to come with her to a concert, where he has seen them together.

Even more than the past, however, this letter begins to reveal their present. The chemist is still shy, still armoured in irony; but this is almost openly a love-letter to his Lady. He writes to her for many reasons, he says, and lists three, starting with his dislike of the telephone: the fourth reason, he adds, he leaves to her imagination. He wants to court her, he says, he wants to amaze her – it's one of his aims in life. At the end of the letter he recalls seeing her at that concert with her daughter. She smiled and waved at him; and this too is a protein story, which he proceeds to tell her. She felt (he hopes) pleasure at seeing him; that pleasure, translated into proteins, contracted the muscles of her mouth, and made her smile. The other story that he read in her smile, he says, is too obvious to tell her; and too sad, since he is a gentleman of more than middle age.

Primo showed this letter to the same few people: Lucia, Lilith and Gisella; Silvio Ortona and Gabriella Poli. Gabriella gave it unqualified approval: the shy growth of the chemist's *tendresse* for the Lady was particularly good, she said; and I agree. But Silvio reacted differently this time. He was alarmed by this letter, he says: he saw in it not the Primo he knew but 'a mental illness', perhaps the one he had glimpsed on their walk, ten days before. Perhaps he is confusing the second letter with the next one; but he is certain it was the second. He told Primo that something was going wrong, and he should stop writing the letters. Primo did not stop; but he did not show Silvio any more.

There is only one part of the second letter, I think, which could have frightened Silvio. It comes in the protein story of the Signora's smile. He is – says the elderly chemist – very interested in what goes on under her skin: in that play of the muscles around her mouth, for instance, which he will go on to describe. In fact, he has a positively fetishistic interest in her viscera. He does not care for women who do not eat or drink or sweat (at this point I think of Claudio in 'Psicofante', to whom women are unreal until he sees them eat). Perhaps he is a sexual deviant, he says lightly; but it is not very important, and he tells her now only as background to his story of her smile.

Maybe this did seem deviant to Silvio, and maybe it is. For once, though, I am not inclined to see Primo himself in it: at least not his conscious, daylight self. That self precisely preferred his women disembodied, especially disembowelled: he could hardly think about his own viscera, never mind theirs. But here too, perhaps, there was a night-self underneath.

He resisted; he would always resist. But it was like resisting the sea, the night, the huge machine he had seen behind Kafka. The two worst things had happened. His mother was not herself any more, but only an old sick body, of which she was no longer in control: viscera, precisely. And now he himself had embarked on the same fearful road, like Ada before him, and the *Musulmänner* of the Lager.

And there was also a third thing. *If Not Now, When?* was a flop in America: that was incontrovertible by now, and he told Philip Roth so in September. It had only convinced those who could not judge; those who could, like the Americans, knew that its *Yiddishkeit* was unreal and secondhand. And they were right, he said. Perhaps Bianca had been right too, and Magris and Marabini, Bobbio and Foa . . . Perhaps – though he didn't say this to Roth – he had failed as a 'real' writer.

It was the same as in 1982: any one of these would have been enough to push him over the border. Instead they all came together. By the end of September, a fortnight after his walk with Silvio and Bianca, his last depression was already profound.

Primo and Bianca on their last mountain walk, 14 September 1986

★

It was the same, but worse. Roth asked him to come to England, to America: he couldn't go. He had invitations to lecture in England, in Germany: he turned them down. He didn't want to see anyone, to speak to anyone. He had nothing to write, nothing to say.

Then in mid-October there was a brief reprieve. I don't know whether it started because he had returned to *The Double Bond*, or whether he could return to *The Double Bond* because it had started. In any case, around 15 October he began the third letter; and this time it was a very different thing.

I have already suggested, at the beginning of this book, what I think happened. His disease had caught him again, harder and faster. I think he decided that he must try to face his demons at last, instead of forcing them back into their mist, like his drowned companions in 'The Survivor'. Perhaps if he told *everything*, it would all go away. He did tell everything, to the real Gisella; and it did go away then, but only for a while. Telling her was like telling himself: it remained secret. If he wrote it to his readers, the secret would be out. He had feared that all his life, and the more famous he became the more he feared it. But perhaps that was exactly what had to be done. You had to face your greatest fear, and survive it. Then there would be nothing to fear any more.

I don't know, of course, if he said this consciously to himself. But ever since his first book he had written to cure himself, among other things. The letters to the Signora had not begun as one of his telling cures, like *If This is a Man*, and most of the poems, and many of the stories. But that is what they now became.

We have already looked at this third letter, in the account of Primo's schooldays. In it he tells the Lady about his long, lonely sexual suffering. His shock, at eleven or twelve, when he understood from half-heard jokes and stories that – as Yeats said – love had pitched her mansion in the place of excrement. His long wait, in vain, for the strange and unnatural instinct to appear. His constant falling in love, but 'bloodlessly', as he had said in *If This is a Man*: terrified of being touched, frightening the girls off with his torment. The confirmation of antisemitism and the racial laws; the boy at school who said that circumcision was castration – not for all Jews, perhaps, but certainly for him. Seeing the young laundress naked at her window when he was fifteen; and closing his own window then, in effect for ever. Remaining trapped in his untouched solitude for years, overcome every so often with such despair that he thought of suicide. Escaping it, at last, only after Auschwitz, in the miraculous meeting with Lucia. Finally, his determination before that, at twenty-one, to prove his own solution to Walden's Inversion; his tragi-comic, Primo-Levian failure, and the moral he drew from it, then and now: *Woe to him who presumes upon his powers*. Which, perhaps, he was still doing in love and sex, despite his fame, and despite Lucia. For the letter ends with the return of his shyness with the Lady, and his conclusion:

perhaps, after all, avoiding her on the Via Pietro Micca was the right solution.

He had stripped himself more than bare in this letter, not unconsciously but openly, and he was very anxious to know his first readers' reactions. If Silvio's negative one did come now, it must have shaken him badly. On the other hand, on 17 October he showed Ernesto Ferrero what he had written so far, which may have included a first version of this chapter; and Ernesto strongly approved. The letters were beautiful, he said, he wanted to read more. Primo must carry on. Gabriella Poli approved of this chapter too, though it is not clear which version she saw either. Gisella saw everything, always, and always encouraged him. Only Lilith did not see it. Primo had fought his last battle against his double bind with her; he did not want her to know how hopeless it was.

Writing this confession did help, at least briefly. Exactly half-way through it, on Saturday 18 October – the day after Ferrero had given his *placet* – Primo was invited to Acqui to collect a prize for *The Drowned and the Saved*. Not only did he go; he was in a moment of high happiness, like a man in remission from a fatal disease.

The prize was the distinguished 'Testimoni del tempo', 'Witnesses of our time'. Bobbio had been among the winners in 1984, and Alessandro Galante Garrone in 1985; this year Primo shared it with Vittorio Foa, Carlo Bo and Susanna Agnelli. The scene was a theatre, packed with people; there were speeches – including his own – interviews with TG2, the usual worldly fuss and fanfare. And still he enjoyed every moment. Vittorio Foa, his cousin and friend, knew how depressed he'd been: when he'd wanted to call on him, not long before, Primo had said he was too depressed to see anyone. But now he was completely changed, Foa remembers. And he tells a story which shows the power of relief – and of his company, since Vittorio Foa is another great opposite, with a lust for life that precedes him into a room like laughter. The *testimoni del tempo* were to receive their prizes first (there were half a dozen other awards as well). But they had to wait: Susanna Agnelli had not yet arrived. Primo and Vittorio stood in a corner, forgotten, while the glamorous Agnelli swept in, and all along her route men seized her hand and kissed it, like corn bending in a wind. The two cynical Della Torres thought this was very funny, and Vittorio began – surely it was Vittorio who began – to mock it. He and Primo had a marvellous time, he says, grabbing the hands of all the women in reach, and kissing them with the utmost ostentation. Primo could be like this with his friends: like a schoolboy let out of school. But now, and in this extraordinary way – kissing the hands of strange women . . . It was like a last glimpse of *la leggerezza della vita*, all the fun and lightness of life which he had never had: like that moment forty-three years before, when he had heard the Dora flowing by outside his Aosta prison cell, bearing away its gold.

★   ★

By the end of October the reprieve was over. He went back to *The Double Bond*.

Yes, he wrote to the Signora on the 27th, he knew it well. In fact he was going through it at this very moment. And he must try to understand it. That was the career he had chosen: 'to understand the why of things'. Now he must try to understand the why of this too.

'This' was depression. First his double bind, then depression: these were the cracks in the Man's mind, and he looked deep into both of them in these letters. The obvious answer to *why*, he says, would be failure and frustration. But in fact it is just the opposite, at least for him. He is successful, he is even famous, and that should make him happy. For a short time it did, he says. But not any more. And he tries to tell her why.

This fourth letter is the one which Lilith read to me, skipping more than half the pages; it is also the only one which Gisella did not keep, for reasons which will appear in a moment. The result is that – unless Lilith changes her mind, or Lucia does, and one or both release this letter – what Primo finally understood of his depression will remain, in part, a mystery, like the final state of his double bind.

Still, Lilith did send me most of the first two pages, and a tiny strip of the third. In them Primo says little that is new; but the repetition itself confirms the heart (or part of it) of his trouble.

He begins with Bertrand Russell, whose name for the melancholy of depression was 'Byronic infelicity'. Its sufferers, like Lord Byron, and like Russell himself, may lack nothing; they may be rich and famous, like both of these – a great deal richer and more famous than Primo Levi. What they lack, says Russell, is desire: a possible desire, for a possible, achievable goal. Depression – Primo agrees – is the absence of desire, or its impossibility. Depression is the desire for desire: though that is an illusion too, since even if they find something reasonable to desire, and achieve it, the next moment they will be as unhappy as before.

This is exactly like the story of the Vilmy, which Primo had told more than fifteen years before. And it is like the psychoanalytical double bind: stasis, blockage, for what may really be desired is impossible.

From this general analysis Primo moves on to his own case: which similarly has nothing to do with failure or frustration, but with success, which no longer satisfies him. He tries to understand why; and finds (on the pages Lilith allowed us) three reasons. First, success is 'a past participle':* by definition it is something which has already happened, which is finished and

---

* Literally, in Italian (but unfortunately only in Italian, Primo noted): *successo*, the past participle of *succedere*, to occur or to follow in time.

gone. It is as though *you* haven't done it, Primo wrote: you have gone back to being your ordinary, useless self, and all the praise is for your brother, who is better, and always younger, than you. Success is like a drug (like the Vilmy's milk, we may add): it is never enough, you always need more.

The second and third reasons are more reasonable, he says. One is that fame means conferences, congresses, literary festivals, which he can't abide. Of course he needn't go; but that means saying no, and he doesn't like that either. The other is more important. Fame means letters from readers, with their impossible requests for peace of mind, for love of life, for an end to loneliness; and for a 'judgement', which means praise, for their work. He gets two or three a day now; and he was brought up to answer letters. Then he says it again: every morning when the post arrives is a moment of dread for him.

Here his investigation ends; or rather, Lilith ended it. In the pages she cut out there was, she said, a 'private episode'. There was also a growing portrait of the Lady, Gisella recalls: a beautiful woman, an ex-teacher (like Gabriella Garda this time!), in conflict with her husband . . . Then, in the bits and pieces Lilith so carefully stuck together is his warning, and hers: Gisella is no real woman, but Primo's own creation – his Dulcinea, his Galatea.

Primo finished the fourth letter on 11 November. He was very anxious about it, even more anxious than he'd been about the third. No one saw it but Lucia, Lilith and Gisella. He did not show it to Gabriella Poli, or to Ernesto Ferrero; nor any of the later ones either. No one knew that he had written more than three letters; not even Lilith would know that he had written the last two.

On 14 November he gave Chapter 4 to Gisella and begged her for her reaction straight away – he would ring her the next day. Then the next day he rang, early in the morning, and said he must have it back immediately. Lucia had said it must be changed. Gisella gave it back to him, probably the same day; and that was the last she saw of it.

The only change Primo told her Lucia had required was of the Lady's name. (Perhaps because they knew a real Gisella, Gisella says: it is not, of course, her own real name.) But it is clear that that was not the only problem. There was that 'private' – that is, erotic – episode. Much of the letter was about the female body, in particular the Signora's: and once again the chemist's interest was less in her surface than in her interior – in the movement of blood in her veins, of molecules in her eyes; even, Gisella remembers, in her viscera. Surely, Primo said to Lucia, she couldn't be jealous of a fictional character, of a woman who did not exist? But for once, perhaps, it wasn't only jealousy, but also a reaction of alarm, like Silvio's.

Mostly, I imagine, Primo was trying to transform science into literature again, as he'd done in *The Periodic Table*, and as he agreed with Queneau was almost never attempted, but ought to be: *On parle du front des yeux du nez de la bouche / alors pourquoi pas de chromosomes pourquoi?* Or perhaps the viscera of women he loved did secretly attract him, for the same reason his own repelled him – because they were identified with the unconscious in his mind, and he was as eager to know what went on in theirs as not to know what went on in his own. I don't know if he ever made any changes to this chapter: whether the bits Lilith cut out of my copy, for example, were still the same. But I suspect they were. I suspect he gave Lilith 'her' chapter privately, but decided to leave it, at least temporarily, out of the book he was planning to publish. When he started Chapter 5 at the end of November, he began on the same page number again, and called it Chapter 4.

Primo had probably returned to Dr Gozzi as soon as his depression began. Despite his prostate problem, something clearly had to be done, and Gozzi put him back on Parmodalin. But throughout November the depression deepened, and Primo went back again. By December Gozzi had changed his medication, probably to Trittico. That would not work either.

Still he managed to carry on. On 22 November he spoke for the last time in public: at an international conference on the central subject of his life, the testimony to the Nazi Lagers. Hermann Langbein came, and Maurice Goldstein, president of the International Committee for Auschwitz; plus forty scholars and writers on deportation from all over Europe. Primo spoke on the second day, to present the book at the heart of the conference: a collection of interviews with 200 Piedmontese survivors, *La vita offesa* (*Offence Against Life*). This was the culmination of an undertaking which had begun in the early 80s, inspired by ANED, the association of ex-deportees, and coordinated by Primo's friend Bruno Vasari, survivor of Mauthausen, and addressee of *The Survivor*. Primo had been involved in this extraordinary project from the start – helping to prepare the interviewers, giving an interview of his own, advising the book's editors. Now he had provided its Preface, in which he spoke once more of survivors' own burning need to tell; and of the need that they continue to do so now, against the 'ugly enterprise' of the revisionists – to whom, he said, although their names did not appear on the title page, this book of witness was dedicated.

In his speech Primo talked once again of the undiminished necessity of witnessing, especially to the young. Then he touched on two of the recurring themes of his last months. He received hundreds of letters, he said, especially from young readers, and many asked the same things: *How could Auschwitz happen? Could it happen again?* He didn't believe in prophets, he said, and least of all in himself as a prophet; but he felt obliged to reply. And he handed out to the audience two sets of his replies: the last chapter, 'Letters from Germans' from *The Drowned and the Saved*; and the answers to his Italian, English and American readers, which make up the Afterword we have to *If This is a Man* today.

For the last time he was applauded and besieged. Young people gave him their programmes to sign; those who had no programmes gave him tram tickets, those who had no tram tickets held out the backs of their hands. We are their grandfathers now, he said to a fellow survivor, back on the podium. It is not easy to understand each other. But we must go on.

He went on writing and publishing too. In July and August he'd written the two pieces inspired by his English visit, 'A Mystery in the Lager' and 'Bella come una fiore', even though the high summer months were always hellish, and his physical symptoms were probably growing. In late July he also published 'Forza maggiore', that terrible story of humiliation and defeat: an image of the Lager, he agreed when Jean Samuel asked him; but perhaps even more of the illness he saw approaching. At the end of August he wrote an insect poem, 'The Fly'. '*I am the messenger*,' the fly says: and this messenger is not the eagerly awaited one of his youth, like his friend the Lieutenant, dead now several years. Rather, it is like 'the prophet who tells you the day of your death': repeating to those about to leave it the only message of this world – a monotonous, meaningless buzz.

Like 'Force majeure', this was already an expression of depression, of its shadow creeping towards him. Yet as it descended he wrote two lighter pieces: a *jeu d'esprit* about time; and an essay on one of the favourite ideas of his last year – which was quintessential, deliberately hopeful Primo Levi. All scientists should take a kind of Hippocratic Oath, he suggested, to pursue beneficial research, and not the other kind. Of course it will not always be clear, and of course some will always be corrupted; but even the small difference it might make would be worthwhile.

Even afterwards he went on writing. On 24 October he published 'Il mitra sotto il letto', his story of his brave partisan sister and the Beretta that ended up in Brazil: his last light-hearted piece, probably written in the brief truce of a week or two before. That went straight into *Racconti e saggi*, *Stories and Essays*, a collection of further pieces from *La Stampa*, which the paper's publishing side issued in late November. In October too, therefore, Primo wrote the brief introduction for it: returning again to his distrust of prophets, and his rejection of the role for himself. Please do not look for messages in this book, he asked the reader. To be treated as a prophet sent him into crisis, he wrote. He was not a prophet: he was 'an ordinary man of good memory' who had stumbled into an abyss, and who had retained an interest in abysses ever since. People took this as the usual display of Primo-Levian modesty, to be admired but not believed, and looked for messages anyway. In fact, it was a great deal more: a plea not to be given responsibilities he couldn't bear. That is a classic depressive fear; and it casts its dark light backwards. Behind his passion for normality, his determination not to seem the genius he was, there was not only modesty from the start, but this same depressive fear.

By late November he was very bad. On the 24th he wrote his last *persona* poem, 'Il dromedario', 'The Dromedary'. Is there no water? He will do without. No food? He has his hump. Is his voice ugly? He stays silent. Is *he* ugly? It doesn't matter to his female. He is a slave, but he has his realm: the desert.

> *My realm is desolation;*
> *It has no limits.*

Then, at the very end of November, he returned to *The Double Bond* – but to a very different *Double Bond*. From an idea which combined science and love, in the first two chapters, it had mutated into an effort to understand the one thing he had never explored: himself. That had lasted for the next two chapters, with the result we know. He must always have feared that if people really knew him, they wouldn't like him; and now it seemed that Lucia agreed. It had been hard enough to expose himself in writing before; *he did not want to write this book*, he told Gisella. But now it was impossible, and not only because of Lucia. Like his other treatment, this one wasn't working: after two sessions on his writing couch, he was more depressed than ever. And so *The Double Bond* mutated again. He turned away from pursuing himself, as his *alter ego* had done with the Lady. Chapters 5 and 6 would not be about himself, nor about love, but only about science. He had bolted.

This was a defeat, and he gave up too soon: if he'd continued, perhaps just for himself, maybe the treatment would have worked after all. Nonetheless, in itself Chapter 5 is quite delightful. Without the delicate gallantry of Chapter 2, it is like an essay from *Altrui mestiere*, or a chapter of *The Periodic Table*. In fact it is very like 'Stabile/Instabile', including the tale of several more factory disasters; and even more like one of the best essays he'd written in 1985, and just published in *Racconti e saggi*: 'Una bottiglia di sole', 'A Bottle of Sunshine'.

In 'A Bottle of Sunshine' he had proposed, only half jokingly, a new definition of man: not an animal who speaks, or uses fire, or buries its dead, but an animal who makes containers. Making things to hold other things, he says, displays two uniquely human characteristics: the ability to think of the future, and the ability to foresee how one material will react with another. He gives us a glorious list of containers, from boxes and bags and jars to cages, postboxes, 'gasometers as big as cathedrals', cradles, coffins and urns. Containers must not only contain something, he says: they must also let other things through. Wine bottles, for example, contain wine, but let through light; sieves contain solids, but let through liquids and other things – think of filters of every kind, of mosquito nets, of fishing nets, of the barbed wire of prison camps. Windows let in light but exclude air, shutters let in air but exclude light. Curtains let in a little light and air but not images, frosted glass lets in a little light but neither air nor images; gates let in light and air and images, 'even cats and outstretched hands', but not whole human bodies (except very, very thin ones, we remember from another story).

Our future, he had concluded, depends entirely on the question of containers. Scientists must find a container for some of those fearful energies to which he had alluded at the end of 'Stabile/Instabile': especially for the energy imprisoned in hydrogen, which can be released only by temperatures almost as fierce as the sun's. They must find 'a bottle for the sun' (whose walls, he notes, will almost certainly be magnetic fields): and we must wish them every success, since no one wants to imagine what will happen if *that* bottle breaks.

This is not the first time Primo had been drawn to the theme of containers. In 'Cerium', in *The Periodic Table*, he had described the problem of stealing in the Lager: and this too was largely a problem of containers. Gasoline and alcohol, for example, fetched high prices, and were plentiful in his laboratory; but how could he smuggle them into the camp? 'This is the great problem of packaging,' he'd written, 'which every chemist knows' – and which, he added, God Almighty solved brilliantly, with the membrane of cells, the peel of fruit, and not least with our own skins, since 'after all we too are liquids'.

As all these quotations show, 'the problem of packaging' releases some of his most extraordinary flights of writing, as rich and unique as his writing on the Lager. This suggests that it touches on themes – even obsessions – which profoundly move him; and I think that is true. Containing, packaging, imprisoning – these are ideas which push him into imagery, because they attract and repel him equally. The walls of containers are frontiers which both must and cannot be crossed, both from inside to out, and from outside to in. In the first direction, which does he want or fear more, to escape or remain contained? I think he could never say. And in the other, what he needs must enter, what is noxious must be barred; but these are not so easily distinguished either. We are back to the unconscious, and to viscera as well, and how much of the flora and fauna that inhabit them he should befriend. I have often said that he wrote about others, not himself: about himself only through others. But the opposite is also true. More and more he wrote about himself, in the guise of writing about others. When he defines man as the maker of containers he is surely wrong: birds build nests, bees build honeycombs, even moles and rabbits excavate their homes. The question of containers defines not Man, but this man: Primo Levi.

When he returns to containers now, therefore, he is bolting – but only consciously. He has explored his double bind and his depression openly; now he explores his neurosis of containment secretly. Have you ever thought, he asks the Lady, about the philosophy of containers? He repeats his idea that our containers distinguish us from animals (apart from certain ants, he adds now, with a shiver, who store their food in other ants' bodies). Containers divide outside from inside, he says, like our skins; or like the frontiers of countries, which can also be broken, or infiltrated, or legally crossed. Then he turns to her kitchen, and considers her pots and pans, and the changes wrought in them by the move from copper to aluminium – indeed, the changes wrought in the whole world, since wars were fought over copper, which is rare; whereas aluminium is common, so that happily there will be no aluminium wars.

This is all delightful, as I've said, but it is only the preface to the main business of this letter, which is to tell her some of his encounters with containers. He tells her four: the disaster of the *schivatura* at Duco, which he had traced to the tannery scrapings in the cans; the disaster of the zinc-lined vats at SIVA, which he had traced, alas, to himself; and two others, also at SIVA.

Introducing these, he remembers another container long ago, in another place and time. He was inside this container, cleaning it, with his companions: and because outside was all horror and danger, this cave of rust was like a refuge. No doubt experts would say it was a return to the womb, he remarks. And he moves straight to the first new SIVA story.

At SIVA, he recounts, they had a herd of tanks, some of them underground. From one of these the solvent was regularly pumped out for sale, under the supervision of (it's clear) Sante Fracas. One day Sante came running into his office, his eyes staring as though he'd seen a ghost. *The earth above the tank was moving*, he panted. Primo ran back with him and stopped the pump, but the damage was done. During the operation a valve was opened to allow air in, after which the solvent would be replaced. Sante had opened the valve as usual. But then he had put his notebook down over it; the air had been blocked from entering, a vacuum had formed inside the tank – and the steel walls, seven millimetres thick, had buckled.

They poured air into the tank with ventilators, and cleared it out entirely; and three days later they climbed down inside. They found a sinister scene. The walls leaned inwards in sickening folds, like a squeezed lemon; or like

– Primo wrote – an intestine. He got out as soon as he could, with his conviction confirmed that human beings are not made to be contained. That is why, he said, prison is the worst and oldest punishment; and why mining is the worst work, where the first workers' revolutions began.

This time his conclusion is true for all of us, not just for Primo Levi. And no doubt none of us would have enjoyed being inside that crippled tank, with its eerily bulging walls. But Primo's reaction confirms that the claustrophobia he gave to Faussone was his own; and that the very last place he wanted to be was back in the womb. It reminds me of 'Fear of Spiders': the spider as the symbol of the suffocating mother, who wants, precisely, to force us – him – back into her womb.

If this story is an ultimate image of imprisonment, the last SIVA story is the opposite. Years before, Primo tells the Lady, another underground tank had chosen liberty. After a month of rain, the water table had risen until it reached the level of the tanks. Swollen and still growing, it lifted this tank – the only empty one – up through the metre of soil above it, and right out into the air, where it stopped and basked in the sun, streaming earth and rust and water. In the story of the crushed tank, Primo had felt like Jonah in the belly of the whale. In this one, it is as though the whale itself has miraculously burst free of the sea.

It didn't help. Soon after, he took 'her' letter to Lilith: that was the last time he would see her. Then he sat down and wrote the sixth chapter. It would turn out to be a last time too.

Chapter 6 is the most scientific of all.* In it Primo turns to some of the most fundamental questions of science: the nature of matter and of time; whether time is as discontinuous, as atomic as matter. These questions are not Gisella's, but his own. So is the last question, to which he devotes his last three pages: the distinguishing features of the molecules which are the fundamental building blocks of life; and how and why they could have arisen in the world.

This too is a subject he has tackled before, in even greater depth: in the most purely scientific essay of his career, which he published in the science magazine *Prometeo* in 1984. The link between *The Double Bond* and 'L'Assimetria e la vita', 'Asymmetry and Life', goes back even further: to 1941, and Primo's sub-thesis on Walden's Inversion, which he has described to Gisella in Letter Three. For Walden too is about the asymmetry of carbon atoms, which is to say (poetically and Primo-Levianly) the asymmetry of life: that

---

* Almost certainly. In the copy Gisella gave me the first four pages are missing: but according to her they were as purely scientific as the rest, and I think we can believe her.

was the first subject on which Primo had hoped to make his scientific contribution, and in his *Prometeo* article it is also the last.

Very roughly, his thesis in 'L'Assimetria e la vita' is that all the elements of life – proteins, cellulose, sugars, DNA itself – are made up of asymmetrical molecules. Not all asymmetrical substances are living, but all living organisms are asymmetric, from viruses, to oaks, to fish, to man. And not only that: the asymmetry characteristic of life on earth is almost without exception left-to-right asymmetry, and not the other way around.* Primo wonders how this came about, and speculates (among other answers) that there may have been millions of years of silent struggle between left-hand life and right-hand life, until left-hand life finally won.

Now, in the sixth letter of *The Double Bond* he returns once more to the molecules that make up life, and this time points out another distinguishing characteristic: they are all long chains of atoms. Again, not all substances made of long molecules are living, but all living substances are made of long molecules; and this universal length of life is as mysterious as its asymmetry. Each living species, in particular, reproduces itself by means of a special long molecule, which is its DNA: again this links bacteria to oaks to man. And again Primo asks how this extraordinary and improbable long molecule of life could ever have begun.

This time he considers three answers: a divine plan; sheer chemical chance; a source in space. He dismisses the third in a few lines: it only moves the question of origin to another place. He also dismisses the first, with a harsh, despairing question, not about God but Man: why should *we* be the aim of creation, creatures covered in blood, creators of an immense weight of pain since the beginning of history? He casts his vote, with Democritus, for chance. But here too he asks: was there not most probably a war, in the immense abysses of time, amongst all the different DNAs, until one emerged victorious? And would that not mean that war and the abuse of power are written into our very origins?

That is what has become of his faith in Man.

Dear Gisella, he ends, have I conveyed to you the poetry of these enormous and minute events? Or have I annoyed and upset you instead? If so, tell me, and I promise I shall stop.

The date at the end was 19 December.

★   ★

---

* Asymmetric molecules are ones that can exist in two mirror-image forms, which possess the property of being able to rotate the plane of polarized light in different directions. Amino acids, the building blocks of life, are asymmetric and are found to be entirely of the form that rotates the plane of polarized light to the left.

And yet: there was one more *and yet*. In the last days of 1986 he gave three interviews – including one for television, a medium he'd always dreaded.

The easiest interview was for Mario Miccinesi of *Uomini e libri*, whom he'd known for years. Miccinesi had recently founded a 'Club for the Sciences of Peace'. In its name, he asked eight scientists and writers how they thought a 'culture of peace' might at last be substituted for our millennial history of war. The question was one of Primo's hobby-horses at the moment; Miccinesi put it to him by telephone, and asked for his reply by letter, thus hardly disturbing him at all. Primo replied immediately. Italians could do very little, he said, but that little must be done. And he repeated his proposal for a scientific Hippocratic Oath. It would appear in *Uomini e libri* for January–February 1987: the last interview published in his lifetime.

The television interview was for a new weekly programme called 'Focus', on the great cultural questions of the day. Primo was filmed coming home and sitting down at his desk. We have split the atom, the interviewer said, conquered space, begun to penetrate genetics: how will we manage in this brave new world? And for the last time Primo gathered up his strength and lied. It was true, he said, that we faced the unknown, with nothing to guide us. That was both positive and negative, it bore both signs: for unimaginable progress, and for unimaginable peril. But he saw hope, for example in the new environmental movements; and also in the old ideal of democracy, in which he continued to believe. He repeated, for the last time, his proposal for scientific self-restraint: it was naïve, but naïve ideas sometimes worked. And so it came to the last question. Did he still believe in man? Would he still be willing to bet on him? Yes, he would, he replied.

. . . If that faith in Man didn't exist – which in effect means faith in the young – it wouldn't be worth going on.

That was three days before Christmas. Three days after Christmas, on Sunday the 28th, he gave the last interview of his life; and it was quite different.

The interviewer was a young journalist, Roberto Di Caro. When Roberto heard the news on 11 April, three months later, he was not surprised. The man he had met on that winter Sunday, he felt, had always wanted the world to be more orderly than it was. He had always struggled to order it, both in life and in writing, and up to now he had succeeded. But he was beginning to fail: disorder was taking over. Still, it had not taken over yet, Roberto felt. Primo was still alert and interested; he still wanted to do new things – for instance, in this interview.

People always asked the same questions, he told Di Caro. About the relationship between chemistry and writing; about why he didn't hate the Germans, why he hadn't escaped, if the things he'd written were still valid, if they would ever return. Let's do something different, he said. So they talked, first of all, almost exclusively about writing. Primo said that writing was a technical problem for him, like building a piece of equipment that would work. He said that he couldn't understand now how he had found the time to do both things for thirty years. He talked about a letter from a reader which had pleased him, because she said that his book had helped her to solve her problems: but she had not told him what they were, nor had she signed her letter, so that she had asked no more of him than he had already given. He talked about *The Wrench*, and about poetry, and about his style, which he kept as plain as he could; and he said yes, he was writing another book, but reluctantly, and he would rather not talk about it.

And then came the second difference. He had already spoken openly about his usual difficulties – his fear that his stock of stories might be exhausted; his increasing immobility, partly because of his 'complicated family', and partly because he'd internalized the problem by now, and found it hard to travel himself. These things were not new; he'd been saying them to journalists for several years. But half-way through the interview Di Caro reminded him of its start. You wanted different questions, he said: is there one you would like to answer, which no one has ever asked? And Primo chose one. There is, he said, the question of the difference between the writer as he appears in his books, and the man as he really is. And he proceeded to destroy the image he had so carefully presented all his life – not only to his readers, but even to his friends; and not only since he had become a famous writer, but since he was a small boy.

People found a strength and wisdom in his books, he said, which he did not have. They saw him as a guru, a prophet: and he was not. Any reader of palms and tea-leaves was a better prophet than he. He had meant what he said in his introduction to *Racconti e saggi*: he deeply distrusted prophets, he more than distrusted them – they were a plague, and always had been. He was not a prophet, and he was not strong. Not at all. His readers thought that he was, because he had survived the Lager: but that was not strength, it was only endurance. It was not their fault, however, that they had this false idea of him; it was his own. He had put a false image of himself into his books. He had not pretended to be brave, or clairvoyant; but he *had* always presented himself as balanced and serene. And he was not. He went through long periods when he was not serene at all – perhaps because of the Lager, he added. He did not cope well with difficulties. But about that he had never written.

Would he ever write about it? Di Caro asked. Perhaps one day he would, Primo replied (not admitting that he already had).

After that they talked for a while of other things: Primo's need for order, for example, and his fear of slogans; the sad unpredictability of the world. That brought him back to himself: the unpredictability of his success, and its bad timing. And once again he spoke more openly than he had ever done before. If it had happened ten years ago, he said, he would have enjoyed it more. Now he thought: *what for?* Once, whenever a new translation arrived it was a cause for celebration. Now it caused nothing but work. He was tired, he said. He felt his age.

He was more depressed than Di Caro realized, and less in control. But I think that this was not only depression; it was also a decision. In his last depression Primo Levi decided that his pretence of strength was destroying him, and he had to give it up. He was beginning to give it up: first in *The Double Bond*, and now here; and once more, very soon. Perhaps he would have given it up entirely, though the last two chapters of *The Double Bond* suggest otherwise. But it was too late. We will never know.

At Christmas, Agnese Incisa went to see him. He was at his computer: his constant companion, 'his concubine', he said. He showed her all its functions – word-processing, graphics, chess. 'It was the last time I saw him happy,' she says.

Giovanni Tesio rang him at Christmas too, but found him in a very different mood. He wasn't writing, he told Tesio. He felt empty, like a rifle which has fired its last round; he had nothing left to say.

Like almost everyone, Tesio had always believed in Primo's serenity – because it made one feel serene oneself, as he acutely says. But this time he heard something new in Primo's voice: an unguarded note, 'an abandonment'. Suddenly he sensed a crack in the façade Primo presented to the world. And he heard himself proposing that they fill this empty time together. You can tell me your life, Tesio suggested, and I'll record it; then I can write it, under your supervision. An 'authorized biography', in other words – even an authorized autobiography, since he would submit every word for Primo's approval. Primo accepted immediately, even gratefully: he was being given another chance to tell. They arranged to meet in early January.

He wrote a poem for the New Year, 1987: and it was an echo of the harsh words he'd had for Man in Chapter 6 of *The Double Bond*. The earth and all its rivers and seas obey the laws of creation, he wrote, along with 'Suns, stars, planets, comets'. Only we rebel; only we corrupt and destroy.

Fast, fast
We are spreading a desert
In the forests of the Amazon,
In the living hearts of our cities,
In our own hearts.

★   ★

One of Primo Levi's favourite story forms is failure, especially his own –
'Hydrogen', 'Potassium', 'Nickel', 'Phosphorus', 'Nitrogen', 'Tin'. On the
brink of success, at the height of ambition, there is an explosion, a crash, a
fire; or simply a failure of nerve, or an error. That was his humour, and his
depression. But it was also his experience. He was allowed such lucky timing
when it really mattered – the 'good fortune to be deported to Auschwitz
only in 1944', and to fall ill in January 1945 – that it seemed to use up his
allowance. After that, bad timing really did seem to dog him at the most
important points. His first book came out too early. Both his novels, *The
Wrench* and *If Not Now, When?*, came out at the wrong times. The moment
he finally retired, and could dedicate his life to writing, Italy plunged into
violence, he got shingles, and his mother began her decline.

That ironic pattern culminated now. In 1986 he was still only sixty-seven
years old. He published two books, one of them his most fundamental work
since *If This is a Man*. It was not true that he was 'written out' – he felt that
with every depression, with every book, and it would have passed now as it
had done before, until the next time. He was finally reaping what he had
sown, as he wrote to Hermann Langbein. He was famous in Italy, and
beginning to be famous all around the world. He had not won the Nobel
Prize this year – Elie Wiesel had instead. But Wiesel had been given the
prize for peace, not for literature; that was still a possibility, therefore,
though not for several years. His Collected Works were being prepared for
publication; even his orphan child, *Vizio di forma*, was about to be reissued.
Every school child in Italy read his books and knew his name. But it had all
come too late. He had never found it easy to enjoy success, but now he
couldn't enjoy it at all. He was rich and famous, the whole world was
listening, and three months later he was dead.

★   ★

Please don't look for messages, he begged the readers of his *Stories and Essays*
that autumn, but they promptly did. I shall do worse, and look for secret
messages: ones he put in these small bottles, because he half hoped they
would never be found. Perhaps messages in bottles is the wrong image,
then. It is more like looking for the suicide note he didn't leave.

He often put his fears and obsessions quite openly into his stories – spiders, beetles and ants, for example, nuclear power, the monstrous in man (the latter in 'Angelica Farfalla', for instance, 'Knall', 'The Commandant of Auschwitz'); and more mysteriously too, as in 'L'amico dell'uomo', 'Vilmy', or 'Forza maggiore', written this year. In *Stories and Essays* he had added another Lager story, written in 1984: 'Auschwitz, Quiet City', the tale of another opposite and twin: an 'almost-me', a Primo Levi turned upside-down. This was another Buna chemist, like Meyer, whom Primo had heard of through Hety Schmitt Maass and Hermann Langbein as well, very likely at the same time. In the story Primo calls him Mertens; his real name was *Diplomingenieur* Reinhard Heidebroek.

In 1941 Heidebroek was a young chemist in Ludwigshafen. He was offered – almost ordered – a move to the Buna-Werke in Auschwitz. He went to see the factory; he returned, married his fiancée, and moved to Auschwitz. In August 1943 he came home on holiday (since even in the middle of losing a World War, Primo wrote, in August Germans go on holiday). His friends pressed him – there were rumours about Auschwitz, were they true? Heidebroek did not reply. Instead he played the piano all evening and drank without cease. Finally his friends insisted. Auschwitz was a Lager, Heidebroek said. He and the other German employees were not allowed to speak to the prisoners. Once, his wife began, a woman prisoner had asked her for bread, but – Be quiet, Heidebroek snapped, and would say no more.

Years later, after the war, Langbein interviewed Heidebroek, as he had Meyer. Heidebroek repeated that he did not speak to prisoners, for fear of SS spies; but he was appalled by their condition, he said, and tried to get them warmer clothes. Langbein accepted that Heidebroek, like Meyer, was an 'inward dissenter'. Primo did not think this was enough. He wrote to Heidebroek, saying that Hitler had only been able to destroy Europe, and Germany herself, because of 'good citizens' like him. He wanted to ask Heidebroek several questions, but Heidebroek never replied; and he too died a few years later.

This was a very different story from 'Vanadium'. Meyer was older, and had been Primo's own superior down there: he was not a perfect enemy, but he was an enemy nonetheless. Primo had not known Heidebroek in Buna; he was simply a young chemist of his own age. Primo did not want to meet him, for reasons of which, he said, aversion was only one. This, and the imagery of twinship, show what the story does not explicitly say: that if Hitler had been Italian, and Primo a Catholic, he might himself have been a Heidebroek; an 'inward dissenter' only, a coward, an enemy. Man, now, is much worse than fallible; and now Primo Levi is a man.

This is a bad enough fear: that though he did not enter the grey zone as a victim, he might have as a perpetrator. But it is only a might-have-been; a thing that didn't happen, like the prosecution for endangering the lives of his workers. He would not kill himself over a might-have-been. This is not the suicide note I am looking for.

I find it in two very different kinds of stories. One kind goes back to 'Quaestio de Centauris', and is Primo's exploration of deep inner division. The other goes back to another element in 'Quaestio de Centauris', and to stories like 'Angelica Farfalla', 'Un lungo duello' and 'Carbon': it has to do with what is at once Primo Levi's greatest hope and greatest fear.

In 1977, on the eve of his full release as a writer, he wrote a story called 'La bestia nel tempio', 'The Beast in the Temple'. A couple on holiday are taken to see an ancient temple on an island in the middle of a lake. From their first glimpse of it the temple is like a mirage. Its walls are thick and uneven, it has few windows and no doors. Inside it is as big as a city, crumbling and filled with weeds. Their guide leads them into its central chamber: a vast, dark, impossible arena. The blocks of seats are insanely irregular; a whole section leans inwards, like the walls of the crushed tank at SIVA. All around and between them are columns, which are the most impossible objects of all. Whenever you try to follow a column with your eyes it turns into a gap between columns, and vice versa; so that both, but especially the gaps, are clearly illusions. Then the guide points out a massive shape: the Beast. The Beast hears them, and begins to gallop around the arena, faster and faster, seeking an escape. Each time it hurls itself against a narrow opening, bits of the walls collapse, and the opening is narrower still. The narrator's wife says: It is making its own prison. It is closing every exit itself.

When they emerge a group of people are setting up their tents outside. They come to wait for the Beast, the guide says. They have always done so, since the temple was built. When it finally escapes they will kill and eat it, and the world will be cured; but the Beast will never escape.

No one ever seemed to ask what Primo's most nightmarish stories might mean: poetry and imagination are ends in themselves to Italian critics, and receive only praise. But 'La bestia nel tempio', like 'Quaestio de Centauris', seems to me a glimpse of horror, which should have frightened Silvio Ortona, for instance, far more than Chapter 2 (or even 3) of *The Double Bond*. What is the Beast, and what is the temple? Surely the temple could be a mind – a dark, dreamlike, misshapen mind: Primo's subconscious mind, or the depression hidden at its heart. And the Beast? – is the Beast not Primo himself, desperate to escape, and each convulsive effort to force his way out only closes him in more? Or is it his depression again, or its cause? – which has always been there, but if it could only be expelled (told?) and destroyed all would be well, but it never, ever will.

Then there are two stories quite clearly about a double bind. The first is the oldest story of this group: 'Il servo', published in *Vizio di forma* in 1971. This is Primo's reworking of the legend of the Golem, the fabulous servant of clay built by Rabbi Arié in the year 1579 to defend the Jews of Prague. Primo's Golem is like the Beast (or rather, the Beast is like the Golem): superhumanly strong, but unable to achieve an ounce of his own desire. The Golem does not have his own desire, since he does not have his own mind; at least, Rabbi Arié did not give him one. He gave him what was needed for his task: courage, obedience, pride and rage. For many years he is a perfect servant and invincible defender; and when Arié notices small acts of disobedience, he is happy as well as afraid.

The Golem's mind is the Name of God, which the rabbi has written on a scroll, and which he places between the Golem's teeth whenever he wants him to act. Arié is careful to withdraw the scroll every Sabbath, since the Law requires that not even a servant work on the Sabbath. And then, one day, he forgets. The sun sets, and the Golem is still working. Arié tries to reach the scroll, but the Golem brushes him off like a fly. Then he lifts his axe, and destroys the rabbi's house and everything in it, all through the night, like Trachi the centaur sowing violence and terror down the length of Italy.

By the morning, Arié understands. The Name of God is the whole of His Law: that night, therefore, the Golem was told 'Obey thy master' and 'Thou shalt not work upon the Sabbath' at the same time. And he was driven mad, because *Nothing maddens more than two conflicting orders.* That is what Arié tells us: or rather it is what Primo Levi tells us, since this explanation is unique to his version of the story.

And then there is Fassio, in 'Tantalio', one of the stories of *Lilit*. Fassio is a friend of the narrator's, who is a chemist in a varnish factory (and who has several colleagues, incidentally, with the same names as Primo's at SIVA: Palazzoni, for example, and Molino). One day they receive an unusual request from a client. Would they please analyse a varnish which protects whatever it covers from evil? They suspect a practical joke, but the proofs pour in: a fishing boat treated with the varnish suddenly brings in miraculous catches; a printing press no longer produces a single printing error (a writer's joke, that one). They do the analysis, and find that the chief ingredient is a rare metal, tantalum. They do tests, and find that it works; whereupon they varnish themselves, and find that their luck is transformed.

The narrator thinks of his friend. Michele Fassio has always been suspected of having an evil eye, since disasters have followed him around since childhood. As a result he has never married, and leads a lonely, withdrawn life. The narrator writes to him, and Fassio replies eagerly: he will come immediately for tests. The chemists test his gaze carefully, and establish that indeed his right eye has a noticeably damaging effect, even on steel; but if the steel is covered with their varnish, or if a piece of varnished glass is placed between it and Fassio, the effect disappears. Fassio is overjoyed at the thought of shedding his lifelong curse, and begs them to varnish his glasses immediately. They do so; he puts the glasses back on, and drops dead at their feet.

The doctor talks vaguely of an embolism, a heart attack. He could not know, says the narrator, that the gaze of Fassio's right eye, no longer able to direct its power outward, had been reflected back on himself, and killed him instantly.

Primo had never directed a baleful gaze on anyone but himself. Nonetheless this seems to me the clearest suicide note of all. When his rage grew as great as Trachi's, as the Beast's, as the Golem's, it still could not escape; and the result was what he had imagined for Michele Fassio. I think he knew he was writing about himself in all of them; especially in Fassio. There are no other Micheles in his stories; and Michele was his own, and also his suicidal grandfather's name.

The other suicide notes are also birth notes, and rebirth notes — a unique, Primo-Levian mixture of desire and fear.

What was his desire? It was always to do with crossing borders, leaping over barriers, passing through gates — with overcoming gaps and divisions, between people, between himself and the world, within himself. And what was his fear? All of these; the same.

It goes back to the centaur, his image for himself. The centaur is the result of crossing the gap between species — indeed, in Primo's imagining of the *panspermia*, the breakdown of all the barriers in the world. Despite this, the poor centaur turns out no better than man in the end. But in several later stories there is (perhaps) a more hopeful vision. In 'Disfilassi', for instance, the barriers between the species have broken down, and almost every creature is a hybrid, conceived from the seeds and pollen in the air: Amelia, who is one quarter larch, hopes that from this new, airy conception a better man may be born. And in 'The Great Mutation' another young girl, Isabella, grows wings and becomes half-bird, like more and more people around the world. This time — unlike in 'Angelica Farfalla' — there is no failure, no punishment, but only a new freedom. The weight of Isabella's body had become hateful to her, Primo wrote, and the moment her feet leave the ground she feels a great sense of peace. Why did people think flying was difficult? she asks herself. It was the most natural thing in the world.

This longing to be rid of the body is also, of course, a vision of death: death as release, 'easeful death', as Keats wrote, who also desired it. This vision too Primo had had for a long time. In *Vizio di forma*, for example, he wrote – humorously – of the 'death' of fictional characters in their National Park. As long as a book is read, its characters live; so that many, like Hamlet and Panurge and Don Quixote, live for ever. If a book is forgotten, however, so are its characters; and that is death in the Park. But it is not the agony it is on earth. Simply, people slowly lose substance, become thinner and more transparent, until they are as light as air, and you can't see them any more.

When the writer, Antonio, is old, he decides that the ambivalent immortality of a literary character may be his best hope for the future. He writes his autobiography (full of adventures he has never had), and two weeks later is duly carried off to the Park. There he spends three pleasant years. Then one day, when he holds his hand up to the light he notices that it is transparent. When he can see the grass through his feet, he knows that his end has come. He says good-bye to his friends, and waits peacefully to dissolve into light and wind.

Now, in the spring of 1986, Primo wrote a story which united all these themes – imprisonment and the body, escape and death; and something else as well. It is called 'Il passa-muri', 'The Man Who Went Through Walls'. Memnone (the Memorious, like Funès?) is an alchemist and a heretic. He believes that matter is not continuous, like water, but made of atoms, like sand; he has written this, and taught it, against the strict orthodoxy of his guild. For his defiance he is thrown into prison, from which only a retraction can release him. He will not retract; so there he remains for many years.

But he does not waste his time. From his cloak he tears a piece of cloth, and fills it with dust and stones from his cell floor; slowly and carefully he rubs and stretches it until he has made a filter of his own secret design. Through this he filters all his food, eating only the thinnest part. At first he only grows weaker; but at last he sees the effect he has hoped for. His own matter is thinning, the gaps between his atoms growing, until he is more space than flesh. He too begins to see light through his hand; until he can see the bones themselves, and they too are as thin as veils.

He knows that his prison walls are also made of atoms, and therefore of gaps; and now that his own atoms are so widely spaced, they should be able to slip through the wall's spaces like sesame seeds through a sieve. He waits for a moonless night; and then he tries.

It works. His hands enter the stone, his arms, his head. He is invaded by nausea as he feels the stone of the wall mix with his brain. Still he presses on until his feet leave the ground. The wall cannot be much thicker than he is long; but for a long time he is stuck, like a fly in honey, since every time he pushes against the wall he sinks deeper in. Still he slowly inches through; and at dawn he emerges, like a butterfly from its cocoon.

At first he is heavy with stone, unable to move. When he extracts his own mesh-like substance it sinks into the ground at every step, and despite his fatigue he has to run. When he reaches home at last the only place he can rest is in bed, with his diaphanous body spread across the feathers. Hecate his wife fetches him food; he must restore his substance, and become, once more, opaque.

Many years have passed, but Hecate's skin is still smooth and sweet-smelling. Memnone is overcome by desire. Forgetting his new condition, he embraces his wife. In the last second he remembers, and tries to withdraw; but Hecate's arms are too strong. He feels the same vertigo he felt in the wall, but this time 'delicious and mortal'. They disappear together into 'perpetual, impossible night'.

Sex means death, we might say, for Memnone, who is more than half air. But death also means sex: something forbidden, but intensely desired. Memnone's death seems to me an apotheosis of everything Primo desired: release from the body, and bodily release; his own death, and his wife's.

In these stories which I have called suicide notes, he imagined conception in the wind, life in the air, and death as becoming light and air. It returns him to the atom of carbon, which is the beginning and the end: flying across meridians and parallels in wind and light and air.

The Double Bind: 1987

Giorgio De Chirico, *Ulysses' Return*

In the summer of 1986 Primo had received a phone call from a stranger in England. He was a retired doctor, the stranger explained, a student of Italian, and an admirer of Primo Levi's books. He would like to do an interview with him. Which books had he read? Primo asked quickly. The doctor named them; he had read them in Italian, he spoke about them with intelligence and enthusiasm. To his amazement, Primo agreed.

The doctor had tactfully not explained that the interview was for Primo's obituary, which a newspaper had asked him to write for their reserves. Since Primo had equally not explained that his health was poor, that was just as well. A month or two later they met. To the doctor's delight, Primo was kind, welcoming, and as interested in his unpractised interviewer as his interviewer was in him. In return Primo found the doctor sympathetic. His name was David Mendel; he was a sceptical Jew like Primo, and close to him in age. He was also intelligent, humorous, and sensitive to Primo's insecurities, since in a less profound and damaging way he shared them. Above all, he genuinely loved Primo's books, and now Primo. The two became friends.

When, in the first weeks of 1987, Primo's depression entered its acute stage, he thought of David. He was a doctor, a friend, and far away from Turin. On 7 February he wrote to him and told him that he had fallen into 'a rather serious' depression. He could not write or even read, he did not want to do anything or see anyone. 'I ask you, as a "Proper Doctor",' he wrote – David had sent him his book, *Proper Doctoring* – 'What should I do?' David rang him immediately, and asked him to send him details of his treatment; and the next day Primo replied.

The depression had started around October, he said. He had had an attack before, which had been rapidly cured by Parmodalin, so he had started on it straight away. There'd been some improvement, so on 1 January the dose had been doubled; but that had caused urine retention, a urologist had diagnosed a 'slight' prostate enlargement, and he'd been taken off Parmodalin. He was now on Trittico – and a week later, he would report, on 'Cantor Midy'. He sent David descriptions of each of these.

This was, as he said himself, a 'confused account', because most of it wasn't quite true. His depression had started in August, not October. Parmodalin hadn't cured him 'rapidly' in 1982, and had not produced any improvement at all this time – on the contrary;* as a result he had first changed drugs before January, if Lilith has remembered rightly. The prostate problem was not 'slight', and had begun long before January as well. About the drugs themselves he was more accurate, because he wanted David's opinion of them; but even here it is possible that by the time he asked David about them he wasn't even taking them any more.

Parmodalin was one of the first generation of antidepressants, called MAO inhibitors; Cantormide (almost certainly what Primo meant) was one of the tricyclics, developed soon after. The change was a mildly helpful one for Primo, since tricyclic drugs have a less damaging effect on smooth muscle, and therefore on the prostate; nonetheless they still have some, so that the problem was not solved. Today's serotonins have none; but they came too late for Primo.†

In January, then, he was on Trittico – or perhaps on Nicolin, another drug he tried at some stage. Whichever it was, it wouldn't work either. Still he managed to keep going. On the 12th Tesio came for their first meeting.

---

* As he seems to have admitted to David later, probably on the phone. As things grew worse he began to cover up less, no doubt because he realized that David could hardly help to change the real facts unless he knew them.

† Most of this information comes from Dr Jeremy Mack, who has made a study of Primo's last illness ('Primo Levi: His Last Days', paper delivered at the University of Pennsylvania conference 'The Holocaust in Italy Ten Years after Primo Levi', 1997). Any mistakes are mine.

He arrived at three and stayed for two hours; that would be their routine. He did not ask questions; Primo should simply start at the beginning, he suggested, and carry on. In this first session Primo talked of his childhood: a lot of his father, the great reader, and 'a bit of a womanizer', but not at all of his mother; of his grandparents, aunts and uncles, and of his teachers, especially Glauda; of himself as a boy, precocious and shy. Tesio is careful in what he says about all three meetings, since Primo is no longer here to approve. But Primo himself was most careful in the first; still most in control. Tesio felt, for example, that there was more to his refusal to talk about his mother than he would say; and when he suggested that he might go and interview some of the family as well, Primo firmly discouraged him. '*Non è il caso*,' he said: 'There's no need.'

On the 16th he left Turin for the last time, to collect his last prize: the Premio Marotta, for *The Drowned and the Saved*, awarded at the Villa Pignatelli in Naples. The writer and critic Michele Prisco talked to him, and noticed no crack in Primo's public façade. I saw the same man I had always seen in his books, Prisco said: a superior man, and above all a serene one. These were, very likely, stronger days, and Primo always tested himself as soon as he could. On the 20th, four days later, he suddenly made his last public appearance, at an ANED round table on the forty-fifth anniversary of the Wannsee Conference. He had said he could not come, and had no talk prepared. When it was announced that Primo Levi had joined them after all, and he took a hastily prepared seat next to Maurice Goldstein, the audience broke into applause. Goldstein saw that his eyes clouded, and turned to the ground. He asked to say a few words of greeting soon, because he had to return to his mother's bedside. As soon as the next speaker, Vittorio Giuntella, began, Primo got up to slip away. As he passed behind Giuntella, he touched his shoulder in apology. Giuntella stopped and said to the audience: 'Excuse me, I cannot let Primo Levi leave without saying goodbye.' He turned and embraced him, saying, 'Remember we love you'; and again the audience applauded. Somehow he had found the will to come; but it had ebbed like a tide. This time everyone sensed his suffering, and Giuntella spoke instinctively for all of them.

The very next day he was called to his duty for the last time, like an old soldier ('On your feet, old men,' he'd written a few years before, in *Partisan*: 'for us there's no discharge'). In June 1986 Nolte had published the article which set off the *Historikerstreit* in Germany: 'Vergangenheit, der nicht vergehen will', 'A Past Which Will Not Pass Away'. News of it had begun to filter through to Italy then. Now, on 21 January, two articles were published in *La Stampa* which brought the new revisionists' 'ugly enterprise' to every breakfast table in Turin. The journalist Paolo Mieli summed up

Nolte's arguments: that what Hitler had done – mass deportations, massacres, concentration camps – had already been done by Stalin, in the Gulag Archipelago; the historian Ernesto Galli della Loggia added a few more of his own – that the 'uniqueness' of the Holocaust was invented by the Western allies, and especially by the Soviets, to diminish their own responsibilities.★ Primo's reply was called 'Buco nero di Auschwitz', 'The Black Hole of Auschwitz', and it was published in *La Stampa* the next day. It betrayed no signs of his depression, but was as solid and hard as a diamond, and cut like one. It was true that the Gulag came before Auschwitz, he wrote, and the Soviets cannot be absolved. But the aims and motives of the two infernal systems were not the same. The aim of the barbaric Gulag was slavery, not death; the mortality rate there was cynical and abominable, but it was not the whole point and intention of the system. Only the Nazi state devised a system with that aim; only the Nazi state invented Chelmno and Treblinka, where not only men but also women and children were brought, only to be murdered, and only because of their race. There were no selections in the Gulag, and no gas chambers; and that detail was not as marginal as Nolte implied. The gas chambers were entirely German – the gas produced in Germany, the clothes and hair and gold teeth of the victims sent back for use in Germany. '*No German should ever forget that,*' Primo wrote; nor that only Nazi Germany sent to their deaths the just born and the already dying, in the name of a ferocious racial ideology that has had no equal in modern times. 'If Germany wants to keep her place amongst European nations today,' he said, 'she must not and cannot whitewash her past.' That was his last message to the German people.

On the 26th Giovanni Tesio came for their second session. This time they talked about Primo's adolescence and young manhood. First, the *liceo* years: his schoolmates – he much admired Ennio Artom – and his teachers, especially Azelia Arici; his inhibitions ('but these are things not to be told'). Then the Milan years, and his first story, which he described very accurately: 'about a man who lived outside time, who entered time, was dragged into time . . .' Then the mountains, Amay, Fossoli. They stopped, Tesio says, at the Lager: about this Primo had written always and often, and the facts were known; they could return to it later.

Tesio, as I have said, is very careful in what he says about these meetings; especially now, with the distance of years. Primo told him nothing new, he says firmly. The only difference from all the other interviews he had given was in his tone. He had been open in some (almost all of them – though

---

★ Galli della Loggia's position was ambiguous, to say the least. Mieli, on the other hand, presented the arguments against Nolte as well, in an objective report.

Tesio doesn't say this – in the last five years); but now he was more open than he had ever been before, 'at least with me'. Sometimes he would ask Giovanni to turn off the tape recorder; sometimes Giovanni would turn it off himself, without waiting to be asked. In Primo's voice, in his expression, there was that new note Giovanni had first heard at Christmas: of abandonment, of letting go. And though Tesio will not say so, Primo did speak to him about some things he had never mentioned to interviewers before: those 'inhibitions' which were not to be told, for example. In fact, it was Tesio himself – or rather his daughter Silvia – to whom he had let out the first word of them, exactly a year before. Perhaps that made it easier now; and perhaps that was not the only new thing that Primo told him. We know how much he had opened up to Roberto Di Caro, a month earlier: perhaps deliberately, as I have guessed, as part of a final, radical telling cure. I cannot imagine that he did not continue it, at least in part, with Giovanni Tesio; and there is some evidence that he did, as we shall see.

With friends who lived further away, however, he could still keep up a façade. When Clara Moschino rang from the Lago di Garda he was very silent, but insisted there was nothing wrong. With his artist friend in Bardonecchia, Eugenio Bolley, he even managed to joke: '*Ho il sistema idraulico a pezzi,*' he said, 'My plumbing system's shot to bits.' And with his readers he used the same detached, ironic Della Torre tone. Some time in January he wrote the Introduction to the new *Vizio di forma*. Don't worry, he said. Our water will not become viscous; all our seas will preserve their waves. It was his last lie.

He could not write, he had told Tesio at Christmas. It was still not finally true, but almost. 'Almanac' was written at the turn of the year, and published in *La Stampa* on 18 January. 'Buco nero di Auschwitz' was written on the 21st and published on the 22nd. One piece did appear after that – 'Argilla di Adamo', his review of a book on a new theory of the origins of life, which was published on 15 February. But this had been written some time before; possibly in December, since it explores some of the same arguments as Chapter 6 of *The Double Bond*. 'Buco nero di Auschwitz' was the last piece he wrote for *La Stampa*.

A week before 'Almanacco', however, on 11 January, there'd been what was probably, therefore, his last book review: of a new translation of *The Call of the Wild*, one of the favourite books of his childhood. That was a kind of coming full circle; and so was the review. Buck, Primo wrote, the good bourgeois dog, is deported into slavery in a distant, freezing land; his dignity is not destroyed, but he must adapt, and learn new and terrible

things. He becomes the leader, the *capo*, of his team – 'the Kapo?' Primo
asked – by killing the reigning one. And Buck's creator, he said, was no
ordinary inventor of stories: rather, he was a man 'who fought to the bitter
end for life and for survival, and drew from that battle his reason to write'.
Once Primo Levi had written only of others, and almost strenuously avoided
himself. Now he sees only himself everywhere. It is an image of his illness,
and a symptom. But it is also an image of why he became ill in the first
place, and of his last-minute effort to cure himself.

In January one other piece appeared as well, though not in *La Stampa*: a
journalist's interview with a mole, under the title 'Zoo immaginario',
'Imaginary Zoo', in the magazine *Airone*. The subtitle said 'The Natural
Histories of Primo Levi', as though there were more to come; as indeed
there were. Four more 'interviews' followed, one in each of the next
months: with a germ in February, a gull in March, a giraffe in April; and a
last one, posthumously, in May.

This 'Imaginary Zoo' was Primo's last little book, or his last idea for one.
He had clearly planned the series, and he carried it out, despite everything.
In fact the mole and the *E. coli* had been written before, in November. But
the other three he wrote now, in January and February. After that '*I cannot
write*' was finally and completely true.

The imaginary zoo is once again classic Primo Levi: a Calvinian,
Queneauian attempt to leave the well-trodden paths of our own lives, and
imagine completely different ones – *pourquoi pas les giraffes pourquoi?*, as
Queneau might have said. It is funny, and full of extraordinary information
we never knew, and now will never forget: that the mole's fur can be turned
against the grain, or he could not back up in his narrow tunnels; that the
giraffe's long neck is fitted with not just one glottal pump, like ours, but a
whole series, all along its length, or he could not swallow. At the same time,
each of these creatures is not only our opposite but our mirror, and sometimes
our warning: as Primo has always used animals, like chemical elements, as
our reflection, and his own.

The idea went back not just to November, but before: to April 1986,
when he wrote 'The Ant's Wedding' – the first animal interview, and the
best. Here there is still flight, transcendence, nostalgia for love: that splendid,
single moment in the ant queen's life, and the instant death of her young
husband; then her return to the nest, 'no longer virgin aviatrix, but widowed
mother, gravid with millions'. The rest, which is satire, is equally fine. We
have never understood your system, the queen says to the journalist (who is
female like herself). The honeymoon is nice, but why all those repeat
performances? A waste of good working time. And why all those men?
Fifty–fifty is really absurd, one male for every fifty females would be more

than enough, even in your current state of evolution. But what about the other forty-nine? asks the journalist. 'It would be best for them not to be born,' the queen replies. 'Otherwise, you'll have to see: kill them, or castrate them, or make them work; or let them kill each other, since they seem that way inclined.'

Primo had always been afraid of women. That is what his double bind meant, or came from. But it was not only fear, it was genuinely double: desire/fear, love/hate, both together. In his early stories there had been the Vilmy, and Lilith, who combs her long hair, and laughs at the two starving men; in the poems there had been the mysterious witch, and Lilith again. But there were also all the young girls, from Lidia to Clotilde and Amelia, who are precious connections to nature for the narrator; and all the girls and women in *The Truce*, *The Periodic Table*, *If Not Now, When?*, who may be elusive, or unattainable, but who are also loved, and deeply desired. By 'The Ant's Wedding' that side of the bind was weakening; in the others it has gone. Whenever the last 'natural stories' stray from their Queneauian combination of science and wit, it is to fear of the female, disguised as humour.

In fact this began even before 'The Ant's Wedding', in a *jeu d'esprit* Primo wrote in late 1985 or early 1986. It is called 'Le fans dei spot di Delta cep', 'The Advert Fans of Delta Cep', and it is a letter to Primo's friend Piero Bianucci from an inhabitant of Delta Cep, the eighth planet in the galaxy of Delta Cephei. She and all her friends are great fans of earth television, she tells Piero, especially of the adverts for preserves, which are of much interest to them, given Delta Cep's inhospitable climate. She proceeds to tell him various absurd and entertaining things about her planet, chief among them the sexual arrangements. On Delta Cep, it appears, life is organized much as it is among the ants. The inhabitants are almost all female. Their males are ten or twelve centimetres long, thin and headless like asparagus; they cost 20–50,000 *lire* each, depending on age. Fertilization is accomplished, she explains, by placing one for two or three minutes under an armpit, 'as you do with thermometers'. Because of the extreme climate, much of the year is spent in caverns underground (hence the interest in preserves): during these times the Delta Cepians watch television, organize literary prizes, and allow themselves to be fecundated by three or four different males, for variety, 'and because it's the fashion'. After that, we gather *en passant*, the usual practice is to send them off to be pulped.

When his depression began, and the blank page stared up at him, Primo must have remembered the journalist interviewer of 'The Ant's Wedding'. He had no new ideas – that was always his feeling in depression, both effect and cause. *But he could use some old ones*. He had several animal poems; could

he not turn them into interviews as well? I think that must have been his
idea; it is certainly what he did.

'Old Mole', which he'd written when his last depression began, even
started like an answer to a question: *'What's strange about it? I didn't like the
sky . . .'* The interview he now wrote followed much the same lines as the
poem. The journalist's question is similar – does he never miss the beautiful
surface of the world? – and so is the mole's answer: he may live in darkness,
but also in peace. His strong hands are the same, and his lone entertainment,
which is frightening dogs. Above all, the theme of the female is the same.
In his youth, the Old Mole had said, he had followed females: no more.
Now the mole asks the journalist if he is male or female. Male, answers the
journalist (as he is from now on), but what difference does it make? A good
deal of difference, answers the mole: females are not to be trusted. They
only interest him for two weeks of the year; apart from that, he's better off
alone. Later he relents: his wife is young and beautiful, and digging towards
each other in the mating season is an exciting adventure. But the marriage
of moles in their dark and narrow tunnels is not the same as the ants' wedding
in the air; and nowhere in these last interviews does Primo's writing take
flight either. His wit remains, and his knowledge; but the thrill has gone.

For the second interview, with an *E. coli* bacterium, he had no previous
material, except his abiding interest in intestines. This interview is like one
of the original *Storie naturali*, complete with a satirical moral: watch your
test tubes carefully, the *E. coli* warns, in which you perform your genetic
experiments on my cousins 397 times removed. I am good-natured, but I
cannot speak for them, especially since you have changed their central
switchboard.

For the third interview, however, Primo turned once again to earlier
work: his poem 'The Gulls of Settimo', written in 1979. The theme is the
same: the unnatural fate of seagulls in our polluted world, which forces them
further and further inland, to survive on our garbage. The herring gull of
the interview is prickly and proud, but he admits it: yes, he has to steal fish
from the zoo, or his wife's eggs will crack when she sits on them; yes, he
has to hunt rats, and even rubbish. He draws the line at some things, but
his children will eat anything: dead kittens, watermelon rinds. 'The next
generation frightens me,' he says. Sir, the journalist replies, you are too
pessimistic. They have cleaned up the Thames, and one day we'll clean up
our rivers too. Take heart, and don't forget the sea.

That was written in January. On 1 February he wrote 'The Giraffe',
which was once again new. This one contains the most startling information,
at least to me. The giraffe has the same number of vertebrae as a man or a
mouse: seven. The length of his neck, however, does cause him special

problems, even with those extra pumps; in order to drink from a river, he has to spread his front legs wide, however awkward it may look. And what about your blood pressure? asks the journalist. With the length of his neck and legs its must be tremendous, probably three times human blood pressure, which is already problematic; and what happens when he runs, or suddenly stands up? We never suddenly stand up, says the giraffe, since we never lie down: we leave that to cattle, and to you. We have hypertension, but it doesn't bother us: nature has fitted our legs with inbuilt elastic bandages. And now the interviewer must excuse him, but he has to have some exercise: it may be only in the miserably confined space of the zoo, but he must run.

In this interview, like the mole's, Primo's own concerns are creeping back in (blood pressure, both high and low, was a serious problem for someone on antidepressant drugs). And then came the last one.

By now it was the end of February, and he was very deep in depression; it is a miracle that he wrote anything at all. That he did so is a measure both of his indomitable will, and of his fear. His fear gave him the impulse and the need; and with his will he searched out everything he had written before, and reworked it.

The last interview was with a spider. The journalist, who is human, is male again; the spider female. The first, shrill question is hers: 'Are you edible?' So is the next: Is he good at catching flies? He is so big, she cannot imagine the size of his web. To tell the truth, he says, human beings use rather different methods; may the interview begin? First he asks why she hangs upside down. Her answer develops Primo's poem 'Arachne', like variations on a musical theme. '*My patience is long, my mind short,*' she had said there; and repeats it now. She has no mind and no imagination, she has only perfectionism, a plan, and monstrous patience. All this is in 'Arachne'; and, in even closer detail, in an essay called 'Romanzi dettati dai grilli', 'Novels Dictated by Crickets', in *Other People's Trades*. The spider, the beetle, the ant horrify Primo, because they are mindless; they are not individuals, but only units, and they will never change, but will execute the same order for eternity. They are like *Musulmänner*, like Nazis, like depression.

And they are, of course, like women, or like the women he fears. And now the interview draws very precisely on the central paragraphs of his essay, and the central lines of his poem. The female spider is almost always bigger and stronger than the male (like the girls of Delta Cep, with their asparagus lovers), and after sex they almost always eat their husbands. The spider explains it to the journalist now in almost exactly the same words Primo had used in 'Arachne', five years before: she likes the male both as husband and as food; he fills her belly and her womb at the same time. But sometimes (and now Primo returns to 'Romanzi dettati dai grilli') the male defends himself; and now the universe of metaphors that opens up contains the strangest and most dangerous solutions. There are males who bring the female a gift of food, so that her stomach will be full before they begin. Others spin a web around her in a nuptial dance, and only impregnate her when she is helpless and immobile. And some steal an immature female, imprison her, and feed her very little, like Memnone, so that she never grows strong. When she is sexually mature they impregnate her, release her, and run away.

These uxoricidal solutions to the fear of the female were the last things Primo Levi wrote, or rewrote, in his life, as far as we know.

★   ★

On 8 February Giovanni Tesio came for their third meeting. They had ended at Fossoli two weeks before; now they began again after the war. Duco, the *Laboratorio* Levi-Salmoni, thirty years of SIVA; and in the evenings, writing. Primo looked back on himself in amazement. How had he found the will, the strength, to live not just one life, but two? 'It's a mystery,' he said.

It is not possible to be certain exactly what happened at any of these meetings, because of Tesio's discretion as the authorized biographer who can never now be authorized. But this one, which turned out to be the last, is the most obscure. What Giovanni said in 1987, in the first shock of what happened, and what he says now are slightly different. I would like to think that he was more open with me than with the crowds of journalists, fifteen years ago; but it is very likely the other way around.

By now Primo was clearly ill. He had a new foot problem, and possibly also a recurrence of the shingles.★ And the real pit of his depression had begun. It was so bad that only the day before he had written to David Mendel for help, saying that he had lost interest in everything, and did not want to see anyone. It was so bad that he could not hide it any more. With Tesio now he went over some memories over and over again; others he would begin on, then stop and withdraw. From a collection of the facts of his life, with the problems postponed, their meetings had become (Tesio was reported to have said) like a 'psychoanalytic operation'. And Primo's anguish was visible. He seemed to relive many of these memories with a new and intense suffering. Giovanni would give no examples, except one:

★ The foot trouble was almost certainly a legacy of the Lager, an ulcer which had reopened before (see page 723 below). The shingles is reported by Miryam Anissimov in her biography; to me Tesio implied an earlier date.

Primo dwelt obsessively on the memory of a fellow prisoner whom he had not helped. That was the memory of 'Daniele' again, and the drops of water he had not shared. By now it had come to stand for all his nameless crimes; or perhaps it was the only one he dared to name.

At the end of this session, or some time after, Primo told Giovanni they would have to stop. The reason he gave, as Giovanni remembers it now, is that he had to go into hospital for an operation. At the time – that is, on 11 April – the reason the journalists reported was different: that their interviews had so exhausted Primo that he couldn't carry on; that he'd said 'I don't feel up to it any more.' Probably he had said both things; and out of discretion, and perhaps also guilt, Tesio had only mentioned the second. At such a moment everyone asks himself anxiously whether *he* might not be responsible – as Primo himself had done with Hans Engert. But it was Primo's depression, not Giovanni's 'psychoanalytic' sessions, which had exhausted him.

Something else may have happened at the end of this meeting. Tesio remembers that it happened, but not when: he is a sensitive man, and I think this whole session was more than he could bear. They went to the door together and said goodbye; and Primo embraced him. Nothing like it had ever happened before, Giovanni says. Primo was the most controlled person he had ever known; he had never seen him make the smallest unguarded gesture. And now this. The others had been touched, because they did not really know Primo, even if they'd met him fifty years before. Tesio was touched too, though he is much too reserved to say so. But he knew Primo well, and he was also deeply alarmed.

In February Primo still tried desperately to save himself. On the 14th he wrote for the second time to David Mendel, describing his symptoms in detail. He couldn't read or write, he couldn't concentrate at all, and hardly drove any more (he soon gave up altogether). The post terrified him, with all its demands; the prospect of travel terrified him – having to take a plane, speak an unknown language, remember unknown faces . . . Even the smallest things were impossibly hard. The only thing he did well was sleep, with the aid of sleeping-pills. He spent all day in a state of anxiety, waiting for the oblivion of sleep. In the afternoon he took two glasses of wine so that he could sleep. Only in the evening did he feel a little better, knowing that sleep was near.

On the 19th he wrote to Ruth Feldman in America. Summit were pressing him to come to the States again, even though he had told them he couldn't. He was in the grip of a bad depression, he said. He hoped with all his heart it would pass soon. (He knew it would, he had told David Mendel

– but only rationally; he *felt* he would never escape.) 'I am going through the worst time of my life since Auschwitz,' he told Ruth: 'in some ways, even worse than Auschwitz, because I am older and less resilient. My wife is exhausted.' 'Forgive me for this outburst,' he wrote. And he signed his letter: 'Best wishes, but "de profundis".'

Ruth was deeply shocked. It had taken Primo's letter a month to reach her, but she replied immediately. If only, she suggested, his wife could get more help with the old mothers, 'to ease the burden on her, and on you'. David Mendel had sent good advice too – Primo should remove himself from the depressing conditions in his home, and come to the Mendels on holiday. That was completely logical, Primo replied, but it was just what he couldn't do. He may never have read Ruth's letter. But if he did, he could have answered: that is just what Lucia couldn't do.

In the autumn, and even up to February, he still went out whenever he could, to find the help he needed. He saw Alberto and Bianca regularly to the end – though separately now, as he'd had to do for several years; they had divorced, and Alberto had remarried. I suspect he saw less of Silvio now. Silvio had remarried too, and was rebuilding his life with his new wife, Primo's gentle, intelligent chemist cousin, Ada Luzzati. Besides, Primo only wanted to talk about one thing: his depression. Silvio would listen kindly, and have intelligent things to say; but he was too rational himself, too eager for reason to win, and for all the devils to be packed away. It was like the letter Primo had written to his friend Roberto Vacca, about a little book of Vacca's on learning new things: it was a wonderful book, he said, but 'it's harder to change oneself than you say'.

He saw Giorgio and Livio on alternate Sundays, but Giorgio was so low himself now that that only added to Primo's depression. Olivetti had gone to Argentina on business, and wouldn't return until the eve of his friend's death. Now Primo sought out another friend from *liceo*, whom he went to see every Saturday. Vittorio Daneo was a doctor, like David Mendel. He was principled, melancholy, extremely reserved. If Olivetti was Primo's last opposite, like Alberto, Daneo was a last friend like Livio, closer to himself. The circle was closing in every way.

Up to around the middle of February too, Primo continued to go occasionally to *La Stampa* and to Einaudi. His friends watched him getting steadily worse. They rang him regularly and asked for his news. *La Stampa* asked him for articles, Einaudi asked him for the chronology of his life for the Collected Works; Ernesto Ferrero begged him to carry on with *The Double Bond*. At the Via Biancamano they offered him a room where he could come and work. He accepted gratefully, and never came. Let's just kidnap him, they told each other, and take him around the world for a week or two. It's the sort of thing you say, Ernesto sighs. Then afterwards you think: we should have done it.

In the last months Agnese Incisa was especially solicitous. She teased Primo, she listened to him, she tried to lend him some of her own energy and optimism. Once she telephoned him and asked him to come for a walk – not just some time, but now, today; and he actually agreed. When shall I come and fetch you? she asked quickly. And immediately he retreated. It wasn't possible, he said. He talked to her about his mother – her endless demands, the constant terrible reminder of her presence. Agnese asked him direct questions, as no one ever does in Turin, and he answered. Was this his first depression? she asked. No, they came in cycles, he said; but this one was the worst.

Then he began to come less often, and to look more harrowed. No one at Einaudi had ever seen him like that before. No one anywhere had. Felice Malgaroli, his friend from SIVA days, saw him on the street one day, his back bent, his face tormented. The last horror had happened.

He had been on antidepressants for five months, and back on his sleeping-tablets as well. His prostate trouble had become severe, and one day he noticed blood. Dr Gozzi suspended all his drugs immediately, and an operation was urgently arranged. It would not be many weeks – six at most, I think, possibly as few as three. But for all that time, waiting for what he feared the most, he was without the support of any medication.* It had not cured him; he felt that it had not helped at all. But it must have done. He did not think he could get worse, but he did.

The last time he came to Einaudi, Agnese says, he shocked and frightened her. His eyes were fixed, as though he were looking into an abyss. He began on his troubles straight away – he couldn't write, his mother called him all the time . . . For God's sake, Agnese said, put her into a home. And Primo went quite white and began to tremble. Agnese ran and fetched him a cognac from a reliable Einaudi tippler. How can you say that? Primo said to her. My mother would die. I'm sorry, I'm sorry, Agnese said. But then she took him by the shoulders and almost shook him. Primo, she said, your mother is ninety-one years old. It's better she should die than you.

After that he did not appear any more. He refused all invitations – to

---

* Primo even told Agnese Incisa, in one of their meetings, that he had stopped taking the drugs himself, before the doctor told him to, because they weren't working. I don't know if we should believe this. He did not say it to Gisella; and it is out of character – he was obedient, and trusted scientists. On the other hand he was depressed; and in depression the only character that counts is the depression's – now and later.

Holland, to Berlin, to the US for *The Drowned and the Saved*, to Canada for a literary festival. He declined to join the Leopoli (Lvov) Commission: an investigation into the massacre of 2,000 Italian soldiers in the Ukraine in 1943, on which he would have served with several friends, including Mario Rigoni Stern. 'I am suffocated by all the things people ask of me,' he said, 'and by the piles of post. I say no to everyone, forgive me.' On the 19th he wrote that letter to Ruth Feldman: this was the worst time since Auschwitz, worse than Auschwitz. On the 27th he said it to Gisella: 'I am worse than I was at Auschwitz.'

I don't know who it was who thought that it was time for a psychoanalyst. There was no question of Primo's returning to Rome; one would have to be found in Turin. The friend (it must have been a friend) contacted Luciana Nissim; and Luciana came to see Primo.

She had known nothing of his previous depressions; he had never asked her for a word of advice. But he hid nothing now; he probably couldn't. She found him in desperate need of help. She rang Anna Maria and told her – though not quite how bad it was; afterwards, of course, she thought she should have, but she didn't want to frighten her. But perhaps Anna Maria knew. She made inquiries; and a good analyst was found in Turin.

Primo went for the first time on 26 February. The analyst was a woman, kind, direct, very intelligent. A listening woman: it should have worked. But it didn't. She was too young, she says – she understood that about him very soon. He was too far gone, I say, and too resistant: but of course she won't say anything about him. No, that is not quite true. She mentions two factors in his depression: perhaps the two most important, perhaps just the two she feels she can say. One was the operation he was facing. And the other was the post: *l'angoscia dell'ora della posta*, the anguish of the moment the post arrived. He talked about that, she says.

Primo told Gisella that he went only twice to the analyst: that first time, and once again a week later. The analyst says it was more, five or six times; but she says it from memory, without checking her records. In any case there was nothing she could do.

★   ★

There were two and a half weeks of March to live through before he would enter hospital. He rang friends who had had the same operation, like Bruno Vasari and Vittorio Foa, and asked them about it. Vittorio told him that it was a miracle, it would make him young again. *'Quell'estremista!'*, 'That old extremist!' Primo said fondly, and didn't believe a word.

Such moments apart, he only narrowly survived the waiting. He did not want to see anyone, he did not want anyone to see him. He asked friends not to call, not to come to the hospital, not even to ring and ask Lucia how he was. *Non era il caso*, it wasn't necessary, he would ring himself as soon as he could. They protested, but of course they obeyed. He was left alone.

He hardly ate any more: he took a bite, and all appetite left him. He was losing his memory, he told Gisella, even for things that had just happened, for the simplest things, for everything. He was tired of everything, he was utterly useless.

Just before the operation he rang both Lilith and Gisella. He asked to see Lilith; then fifteen minutes later he rang back, and said he couldn't come. He begged Gisella to tell him again that this depression would end, like all the others. Even she had never heard such anguish in his voice before.

He went into the San Giovanni Maggiore Hospital on Tuesday 17 March; the operation was the next day. The surgeon was Professor Giovanni Sesia, from the Pinna Pintor Clinic. The surgery went normally, but there was a problem with the anaesthesia. Primo had to be anaesthetized more than once during the operation; then when he was brought out he was clearly in pain, and had to be taken back into the operating theatre immediately. The problem was minor, the doctors assured the family; and afterwards Primo did not remember it.

In the recovery room after the operation one of the doctors, Roberto Pattono, asked him what illnesses he'd had. The only serious illness he'd had in his life was this, Primo replied, pointing to the number on his arm. After his death this remark seemed like a fatal and dramatic explanation. It *was* a little dramatic (as Primo could be, Philip Roth had noticed: 'After all, he was a writer'). But it was not an explanation. It was simply true: until his shingles, and now this, Primo had never had a physical illness to compare with the assault on his life and health of Auschwitz.

He stayed in the hospital for the usual post-operative period of just over a week, and seemed to his doctors to be recovering well. For three days he was fed intravenously, and fitted with a catheter; he didn't like either, but then (says Dr Pattono) no one does. Pattono saw no signs of depression: Primo seemed to him full of hope and plans. Plinio Pinna Pintor, on the other hand, the senior physician in charge of Primo's case, and an old G. & L. friend, found him deeply depressed: so depressed, he said, that he feared that that was his most dangerous disease.

Pinna Pintor was right; but Pattono was not altogether wrong. Primo did hope, at first, that the operation would cure his depression. But it didn't; and if you've glimpsed a hope of escape, and then lose it again, you are worse off than before.

Still, the operation was over, he was recovering, he was alive – he *must* have had moments of hope and relief, and so must his friends and family.

The doctors had suspected cancer: that was almost certainly why they had operated so urgently. But the biopsy showed that he didn't have cancer after all. That was another marvellous reprieve. He was healthy; he could have made a complete recovery. As Pinna Pintor said, the danger was not in his body, but in his mind.

Should they have operated at all, on such a deeply depressed man? Did the complications of the operation – the extra episodes of anaesthesia, the return to the operating theatre – add to the physiological causes, and symptoms, of his depression? It is hard not to ask these questions; but it is even harder to answer them. Today the treatment of both depression and prostatic hypertrophy has changed in ways that mean that Primo would probably not have needed an operation at all, or could have had a less invasive one. But that does not help him, or his doctors either.

★   ★

He came home on 26 or 27 March. On the 31st the stitches were taken out. He had returned to Dr Gozzi, and was presumably back on antidepressants, with the same results as before: his depression was 'horrendous', worse than ever. Anna Maria had come to Turin for his operation, but now she went home. For the next two weeks he remained completely isolated, except for the telephone.

The consequences of the operation obsessed him. He could not bear the sense of being out of control of his body, the humiliations of physical care. He was told he did not have cancer, but that did not stop his fears. He had pains in his legs; he thought it might already have spread to his bones. He rang Cesare Cases, who had a relative who'd died of prostate cancer which had metastatized to bone: How exactly had the disease proceeded? he wanted to know. He rang Federico Accati, who was living with the condition, and would live with it reasonably well until his death two years later. Federico reassured him, as everyone always did, with the usual result: as soon as he had hung up, it was the same as before.

Many friends telephoned him. Mario Rigoni Stern had already phoned in the hospital, ignoring the ban. Ernesto Ferrero rang every day, trying to distract him with news of translations, honorary doctorates, the progress of the Collected Works. Paolo Spriano rang and asked how he was. 'Bad, bad,' Primo said. Rita Levi Montalcini rang and heard the anguish in his voice. Euge rang from Milan. Primo said, 'I can't do anything any more. I can't go on.' Giorgio Vaccarino rang, and Primo repeated the same things: 'My mind doesn't work. I can't go on.' They all encouraged him, told him it would pass, and thought it would.

Bruno Vasari rang – or rather, Primo rang him, to thank him for a new book of his Vasari had sent. Primo said he was expecting a phone call from America, and was very worried, because he could no longer speak English at all. Francesco Rosi rang, and told him that he was still determined to film *La tregua*. Primo said, 'You've brought me the only good news in a dark time.'

When Edith Bruck rang, Primo said he was tired by many things and had no more hope. *No hope?* she cried, and felt afraid for him, because he had always said that without hope one couldn't live. He couldn't write, he said, he couldn't remember anything any more, not even his own life; if people asked him things he had to go and look them up in his books. And she was afraid again, because she knew that without writing he couldn't live either. Then he said it again, even to her, who knew what it meant: '*It was better at Auschwitz. At least then I was young, and believed.*' He did not say what he had believed in at Auschwitz, and no longer believed in now. Man, reason, himself, the possibility of understanding? All of them, perhaps; for him, they were the same.

Alessandro Galante Garrone rang, and told him he must not give in to despair. Primo Levi was needed, he said, no one could replace him. Primo thanked him for his kindness in a low, vague voice. Galante Garrone said he wasn't being kind – how could Primo say that, as though he were a stranger? He was an old friend, and he meant it most sincerely. But Primo only repeated it again, as though he hadn't heard: '*Grazie, sei molto gentile.*' Galante Garrone had spoken in love and concern. But these were exactly the words Primo could not bear to hear: *You are needed. You cannot give in.*

He hardly went out. He did nothing: just waited for sleep, as he had told David Mendel. He sat for hours in front of his computer, doing nothing. And he sat for hours by his mother's bedside, as he had done for months, even years. But there, perhaps, he did something. He didn't say so to Gisella, or to anyone else, as far as I know: only to Edith Bruck, fellow writer and fellow survivor. To Edith he said that he was writing down the things his mother said: 'annotating', Edith wrote in her own book, 'his mother's sensations'. 'Do you understand?' he asked her hurriedly. 'I don't know if they'll make a book.'

I am sure it was true. His suffering now, mental and physical, was worse than Auschwitz, and it was mirrored in his mother. He had overcome Auschwitz by writing about it: turning that grotesque and useless violence into science and understanding. In the last weeks of his life he was trying to do the same with his mother.

And yet: no one imagined that he would not get over this depression. Those who knew he had survived depressions before thought he would again;

those who didn't know thought this was an aberration, and would pass. He talked of it only to his friends, and not to all of them: Norberto Bobbio, for example, said that until the day of his death he had thought Primo Levi 'the most tranquil and serene person in the world'. He could 'put on a good face', as Amir Eshel says; he had practised all his life. And it was not only a face. He felt that he would never escape; but he thought that he could. And he wanted to. What people said afterwards was true: he would never have chosen to die. When he was well he was still interested, engaged, amused. And he disapproved of suicide. Suicide was like obscure writing: a flight from the world, and from people; a betrayal of the aims of life, which was his only religion, and of our responsibility not to spread despair. Even in the pit of his worst depressions he tried to see over to the other side, when he would be well again; and the instant he felt minutely better he hoped and pretended he was already there. Whenever he turned down invitations, he always did so not just politely but hopefully. 'May I ask you to return to this subject later on, say by the end of August?' he wrote to the director of the Canadian literary festival on 1 March. He would be glad to take part in her film, he wrote to a French film-maker, but not just now – when 'now' was 8 April, three days before he died. No one who received such a letter could believe that he was planning to kill himself when he wrote it; and in that they were certainly right.

There were several examples closer to home. In January, for example, a fellow writer-survivor, Liana Millu, wrote to him, enclosing something small and hard with her letter. It was a tiny, bitten stub of pencil: the pencil she had found in a house in Mecklenburg, on the day of her liberation, and with which she had begun her memoir, *The Smoke of Birkenau*, soon after. Liana had had a sudden impulse to save her Mecklenburg pencil from her own death, and sent it to Primo. On 7 January he replied. His days were shortening too, he said. But he deeply appreciated her 'strange and precious gift'; and he promised to keep it. '*Lo conserverò*', *I shall keep it*, Liana Millu repeats, in her fine, deep voice: words full of the future, and of his place in it.

That was before the operation. After it, in April, Agnese Incisa moved to Bollati Boringhieri, who were publishing Jean Améry's *Beyond Guilt and Expiation*. Primo had only recently come home from hospital, but Agnese rang and asked if he would write the Introduction for the book, which was due in October. Primo said, 'Yes, let's talk about it.' Agnese was extremely pleased, both for Primo and for the book. She had to go to Rome, she told him, she'd be in touch as soon as she was back. In Rome she called on Natalia Ginzburg on the 11th. When she arrived, Natalia told her the terrible news.

And there were other such events too, as we shall see.

The truth is, I imagine, that he had better days and worse ones. As always, he had a better day (or moment) with Alberto. Of his very oldest friends, Alberto had remained the closest, in this last and worst time. Giorgio Lattes was too low, Silvio too reserved, Livio too withdrawn. Only Alberto was as healthy and happy as ever, he loved Primo, and he took no notice of any ban. He came to the Corso Re Umberto, he'd even come to the hospital, as Bianca had as well. And now, about a week before the end, he managed to persuade Primo to come for a walk on the *collina*. They drove across the river and up the hill, probably right up to the Colle della Maddalena at the top. There they got out and walked a little together, in the pale spring sun. From the height of the *collina* you can see the whole of Turin, laid out along the curve of the Po. As the two friends looked down on their city, Primo said: 'How much we've seen and done together, you and I.'

A few days later it was Bianca's turn. In these last months Primo had said to her often: Help me, ask me out, and if I refuse, insist. She had, but it had rarely worked. Even when he'd come, he couldn't stay, but would excuse himself early and bolt, as he'd done at the round table on Wannsee: 'like a man with a fire behind him', Gabriella Poli says. But now, just a few days before his death, Lucia rang her and said: Please come and take Primo out, try and get him out of this mood. The very next day the case Bianca was working on finished early, by mid–morning. She rang Primo and said: Come for a walk. No, no, Primo said, I don't feel like going out. But now Lucia said: Go on, go for a walk with Bianca. So he did.

They went to the Valentino together, and walked along the path by the river. Bianca tried to distract him, to tell him about her cases, about anything that came into her mind. But Primo couldn't listen. He stopped her, saying, I'm sorry, you're right to try, but I'm not well. And then Bianca did something which, she says, she had never done before: she asked him what he thought had caused his depression. Was it Auschwitz? she asked. And Primo said, quite clearly and firmly, No. He did not think so. He had survived, he had testified. That was not the reason.

If he told Bianca the reason, or a reason, then, she will not say. She drove him home to the Corso Re Umberto, and he went back inside.

He did not come out again, except perhaps once or twice, to the shops across the road. Bruno Erber, who was a doctor and a friend, met him in the street only a day or two before he died. He tried to ask him how he was, but the same thing happened. Primo stopped him, rudely and abruptly, for Primo. I don't want to talk, he said. Bruno went home, shocked and worried.

April the 8th, a Wednesday, was a better day; certainly one with more energy. He wrote to the French film-maker to make his excuses for the moment. He phoned the offices of the Jewish Community to ask if the matzos for Passover had arrived; the next day Lucia would come to fetch some. He phoned Einaudi to ask if they had sent *The Drowned and the Saved* to Gallimard. And he wrote to Ferdinando Camon to report their answer.

Ever since the first flawed translation of *If This is a Man*, Primo had had little luck in France. *The Periodic Table* was only being published there now, and he was still far less read in French than in English or German. He minded very much about this, and had said so to Camon, who had many dealings in France. Camon offered to help. He was writing an article for *Libération*, to introduce Primo to French readers; and he'd sent *The Drowned and the Saved* to Gallimard many months ago. They now said they'd never received it; hence Primo's call to Einaudi. He thanked Ferdinando sincerely for everything he was doing, and hoped very much that Gallimard would take *The Drowned and the Saved*.★

This letter didn't quite get lost in the post, but nearly: it didn't reach Camon in Padua until the 14th, three days after Primo's death. When he saw it Ferdinando thought, with grief, *He wanted to say goodbye*. Then he opened it, and found the opposite: a letter full of the future, like Liana Millu's. And it only arrived on Tuesday. It cannot have taken six days to come from Turin, or even five or four, he says. It would usually take no more than three: and Camon is convinced, therefore, that the letter was posted on Saturday, and by Primo himself. On that conviction he has based his determination that Primo cannot have committed suicide. 'It is impossible to think,' he has written, 'that he posted this letter, and a quarter of an hour later killed himself.'

The trouble with this is that it is the purest speculation. In my experience letters can sometimes take any amount of time, especially (though not only) in Italy. The date stamp on the envelope is indecipherable, even by the Padua Police Department's forensic laboratory, where Camon took it; and not even a forensic laboratory could say who had posted it. Since then Camon, and therefore others, have talked as though both the posting of this letter on the 11th, and its having been Primo who posted it, were established facts. In reality they are imagination and wishful thinking only; which does credit to Ferdinando's heart, but not to his head.

Nonetheless, this remains true: Primo wrote it on the 8th; and on the 8th, therefore, he intended to live.

★ In fact Gallimard were not keen at first, though they did publish *The Drowned and the Saved* two years later.

On the same day, possibly in the afternoon, he received a visit: Giulio Einaudi, his publisher, came in person, to ask him to become President of the newly resecured publishing house. If only *that* had happened ten years before – though even then Administrative Councils and Presidencies were hardly his style. He was flattered to be asked, since it certainly marked a change in his standing in Einaudi since the rejection of his first book, forty years ago. He did not say no straight away, and later rang Norberto Bobbio for his advice. But really his mind was made up. He couldn't do this, even when he was well. Now that he was ill it was just another burden, another thing that was being asked of him, but was beyond his powers. He declined.

Giulio Einaudi knew that he was depressed, and found him so that day. Primo was afraid that he would never recover from his operation, he says, that he would never be able to write again, that what he had already written – especially *The Drowned and the Saved* – would be forgotten. Whenever he spoke of himself, Einaudi says, his gaze darkened, he looked like a man 'who saw no future'. But as soon as they talked of other things – of the rebirth of the publishing house, of his computer – he cheered up. He told Einaudi he must have a PC; if he wanted lessons, he, Primo, would be glad to give him some.

That evening (probably in the evening, when careful people make long-distance calls), he rang several more friends. One was Lello Perugia in Rome; to Lello too he said that he feared his books were not being read, and that Nazism still flourished in the world. He said the same to Mario Macagno, though on which of these last days Macagno is not sure: *The Drowned and the Saved* would be forgotten; Fascism had not disappeared. 'Nor has antifascism,' Mario replied, trying to cheer him: 'For every fascist there are millions of antifascists now.' What did Primo reply? *'Non sono convinto,'* 'I'm not convinced,' Mario says, in Primo's most ironic tone.

He phoned Elie Wiesel in America; probably he said the same things. Wiesel said 'Come to New York' – just as Roth had said, as David Mendel had said, as the Einaudians had felt: *Get him away.* That was what was necessary, and impossible. He rang Bolley in Bardonecchia, and probably said the same things once again. Bolley, who is a passionate Christian, tried to speak to him of Jesus; he told him that Lorenzo Mondo had said he would certainly be given the Nobel Prize one day. Primo said 'I just don't care.'

That night he also spoke for the last time to Gisella. He said it all once again: he was no better, he couldn't write, he couldn't remember. He thought only of death, he said. While we've been talking have you thought about it? she asked. No, he replied. But he did not telephone her again.

★

On Thursday afternoon Ernesto Ferrero rang him as usual. He gave him the latest news — the Dutch wanted to publish his last books now. Then he tried to cheer him up even more: you'll have to pack your bags soon and go to Stockholm, he said, one day the Nobel Prize will be yours. Primo only said, you're joking. He was tired, he complained. Yet that day (or possibly another of these last days) he also said: perhaps I am getting better.

He may have made another call on Thursday as well. Ten years later, during the commemorations for the tenth anniversary of his death, Elio Toaff, the Chief Rabbi of Italy, said publicly for the first time that Primo had called him too. According to the newspaper reports, Rabbi Toaff claimed that Primo had rung on Saturday morning, 'ten minutes' before he died. Primo said that he could not carry on, Toaff remembered; his mother was ill with cancer, and every time he looked at her he saw the *Musulmänner* of Auschwitz.

Much of this cannot be right. Rina did not have cancer, and Primo cannot have rung on Saturday, when orthodox Jews cannot answer the phone. Nonetheless, I'm sure it was true that Primo did telephone the Chief Rabbi, and talk to him of his despair. Toaff had already said so privately, some years earlier. And in these last days Primo phoned everyone. His own rabbi, Emanuele Artom, was too close to home; when he had to turn to anyone but a friend, he did it away from Turin. A rabbi might be able to say something new, something that would convince him at last, as even Gisella could not convince him. Still, he did not tell Toaff that he wanted to kill himself, and Toaff did not guess. The rabbi did not say the one transforming thing that could have saved him. I do not think it exists.

On Friday Primo called Livio. He may have repeated the same things again: he couldn't write, he couldn't remember English any more. But on Wednesday he had done so much, on Thursday (perhaps) he had thought he might be getting better. And in these very last days, despite everything, perhaps he was. To his cousin Giulia on Friday he did not talk about his mother. They chatted for a half an hour about ordinary things. He asked Giulia how she was: however banal, that was new. He wasn't better yet, he said, the effects of the operation were still the same. Don't worry, she said, it'll pass. '*Esperienza personale?*' he said. Perhaps it was bitter; but there was a flash of his old wit as well. Giulia promised she would bring him some of her Passover cakes the next day.

We know of two other phone calls on Friday. One was from, or to, Rita Levi Montalcini: and this time, she says, he sounded in much better spirits.

The other was with Giovanni Tesio. Again it is not quite clear whether Primo rang him, or he Primo. At the time the papers all said that Primo rang: that would be even better. Now Tesio says that he did. He had continued to respect Primo's ban; but he always phoned for Christmas and Easter, so he did again. And the result was surprising, wonderful. As soon as Primo heard his voice he said, 'Ah, Giovanni! If you like, we can go on now.' On Sunday a photographer was coming; but after that Giovanni should ring, and they could decide when to start their work again. He sounded much better, quite recovered, Tesio said in 1987. Back to normal, he says today: 'No, more than normal – very happy.'

At that moment he must have been thinking: *At last the plug has been pulled. It's over.*

★   ★

And then it happened. At around 10.15 on Saturday morning the local police station, ambulance station and forensic department were ordered to send officers and vehicles to Corso Re Umberto 75. There they found Primo's body at the foot of the stairs. He was examined and pronounced dead. An hour or so later his body was removed to the University's Institute of Forensic Medicine for an autopsy. The police took statements from the concierge, Jolanda Gasperi, and from Rina's day nurse, who testified that he had recently undergone an operation, and was severely depressed. No evidence was found of 'third-party involvement'. Both the police and the ambulance service filed their reports under suicide.

Reporters arrived almost immediately, and the news was on the radio by noon. Giuseppe Di Chio, the family's lawyer, went to the house immediately, perhaps notified by the police. A neighbour telephoned Bruno Salmoni, who phoned Alberto, then went to the house as well. Bianca arrived, the Mussas, two people from Einaudi. Other people started to arrive too – strangers, students, readers, with bouquets of flowers, which they left at the door. David Mendel, who had flown in the night before especially to see Primo, heard the news in his hotel room. Mario Rigoni Stern heard it from a reporter who rang for his reaction. Nuto Revelli and Alessandro Galante Garrone heard it in Angrogna, in the Val Pellice, where they had come to talk to students about the Resistance; instead they spent the afternoon talking about Primo Levi.

Euge, in Milan, was told that Primo's cousin had called him: 'I knew,' he says. Bruno and Eva Erber were listening to the radio. When the news-reader began: *A distinguished Italian has died in Turin*, Eva clutched Bruno's arm. 'It's Primo,' she said. Amir was in Israel for Passover. When his fiancée Emma called from Turin and said, 'There's bad news,' his reaction was the same: 'Primo!'

Almost everyone else refused to believe it.

The autopsy was done as quickly as possible; Jews are meant to be buried within twenty-four hours. Primo's skull had been smashed and most of the bones in his body broken. But his face was unmarked.

'Suicide is a grave sin,' he had noted from the *Shulkhàn Aruch*, the compendium of ritual laws, 'and the suicide must be given no funeral celebration. In doubtful cases, it is obligatory to accept other explanations.'* Rabbi Artom decided that Primo's case was doubtful, and he should have a proper Jewish funeral. It would have to be minimal anyway. So the family wanted, so Primo would certainly have wanted; and so the law required, since they were on the brink of Passover, during which no celebrations are allowed, neither weddings nor funerals.

The family had also wanted the funeral to be private: but that was not possible. By 2.30 on Monday 13 April, 1,000 people or more had gathered outside the Institute of Forensic Medicine on the Via Chiabrera, near the river. Inside, Rabbi Artom said the *Kaddish*. Six fellow survivors of the Lagers lifted the coffin on to their shoulders and emerged. For a few hundred yards the funeral procession moved slowly and in silence. People from all the parts of Primo's life were there. All his friends and family. At least fifty survivors, their neck-scarves marked with the names of their camps. All of SIVA, all of Einaudi, most of the Turin Jewish community. All the great and good of the city, the Mayor and Councillors. City flags, regional flags, the flags of ANED and ANPPI, the ex-prisoners' associations.

The bearers lowered the coffin into the hearse, and the funeral cortège drove to the City Cemetery. Five hundred people came to the burial. The rabbi said the final prayers, and dropped the first spadeful of earth into the grave. Then Lucia, Renzo, Lisa. When the grave was filled a small marble strip was placed on top, with Primo's name and the dates of his birth and death. Later, on the permanent stone, his number would be added: 174517.

★   ★

That evening there was a civic commemoration in the Palazzo Lascaris. The Mayor spoke, Bianca spoke. All weekend telegrams poured into Corso Re Umberto 75 from around the world. The windows and doors of Primo's

---

* Primo listed this, among other rules and prohibitions, in a letter to a friend in 1980. The *Shulkhàn Aruch* continues: 'There is no sin if the suicide is a child, or an adult in a state of depression, madness, or fear of torture.' He would have passed anyway.

apartment remained closed, but people lined up outside to leave their flowers. At the end of the week the family thanked everyone through the pages of *La Stampa*.

The papers bulged with reactions and tributes, from Elie Wiesel, Philip Roth and Giulio Einaudi, from Natalia Ginzburg and Claudio Magris, from Mario Rigoni Stern and Nuto Revelli, from all Primo's most loyal critics and friends. Giovanni Arpino said Primo had been loved and left alone in Turin, 'fatal city', where writers killed themselves: Salgari, Pavese, now Levi. Luigi Firpo, who had known Primo since *liceo*, said that he had been profoundly unhappy, and that his 'rationalism, taken to the extreme', had driven him to this point of desperation. Ferdinando Camon spoke for almost everyone, saying that he could not reconcile the Primo Levi he had known with this death. If it *was* suicide, Camon said, all he could think was: '*Then he was pretending.*' In his books, so cool and controlled, in his talks and interviews, 'so low-voiced, so imperturbable', he must have been pretending.

Over the next days and weeks people asked each other over and over what could have happened. One of the first ideas was that he must have been murdered – by Fascists, Nazis, skinheads. An Israeli friend of Emilio Vita Finzi's rang him from the embassy in Rome and asked if that was what had happened. Rumours flew in the neighbourhood that Primo had had death threats. It was not impossible: Elie Wiesel has had them; so have Nuto Revelli and Alessandro Galante Garrone. But Primo never said a word about any such thing. We can exclude murder, as the Italians say, *nel modo più assoluto*, absolutely.

The next idea was put forward by Primo's friend Rita Levi Montalcini. She knew how depressed he was: she too suffered from depression, and they'd discussed it together in detail. But she also knew that he had not given up, that he had plans and engagements. And like Ferdinando Camon, and Liana Millu, therefore, she was convinced he could not have committed suicide. Not like *that*, she says, and many have repeated after her: in a manner that was so dramatic, so violent, and so uncertain. Primo was a chemist; if he had decided to kill himself, he would do so in a decent, reliable, Primo-Levian way. No, she said (and continues to say): at the most he had a sudden '*raptus*', or brainstorm, caused by the depression; or more likely an attack of faintness, caused by the depression again, and by the operation from which he had not yet recovered.

This line was taken up by David Mendel, who had determined to carry Primo off like a knight on a white charger, and had arrived, he must have felt, just hours too late. Primo had told him he was no longer obsessed by Auschwitz; to David his life seemed better than it had ever been (as indeed it was); and he knew that Primo was hugely intelligent, rational, and 'the soul of kindness'. How could he have thought that the best solution to his problems was to kill himself, and to leave horror behind him? Not possible, David concluded. He was on antidepressants, which are well known to lower blood pressure. The banisters in Primo's building are low, reaching at most to his waist.★ What must have happened was this: he felt faint, reached for the banister, and fell.

Finally, there are one or two people who believe that Primo chose his death consciously and clearly. Not normally: he would not have chosen it if he had not been depressed. But not in a '*raptus*' either: not, as the courts say, when the balance of his mind was disturbed. He chose to die, they think, because of the pain of depression, not because the balance of his mind was disturbed. The two things are not the same.

The first person who believes this is Roberto Di Caro, the last journalist to interview Primo, at the end of 1986. He was certainly depressed, Roberto says. But even in depression he was lucid. He had always found life hard, now he found it even harder; if it became too hard, there might be only one

---

★ The height of the banisters has now been measured (and see page 725 below): they are 96 centimetres high. Primo was about 170 cm (about five foot five) tall.

solution. He did not say this to Di Caro, but Di Caro felt it in him. That is why he was not surprised, as he says, when he heard the news.

To the other person Primo *did* say it, or almost say it, and more than once. In 1985 he had an ulcer on one of his feet (that legacy of the Lager, which he seems to have had again in 1987). It made him walk badly, and this in turn gave him trouble in a knee. So he went to a physiotherapist for a month or so. The physiotherapist was a young woman called Raffaella Pagani; she was the other person.

During the course of Primo's treatment the two became friends; and after it Raffaella went to see him several times. She is an active, independent person, who nonetheless hides her insecurity less well than Primo. She began to tell him her troubles. Her childhood had been difficult, and now her marriage was breaking down; she told him about both. He did not give her any advice, she says, and he did not tell her his troubles in return. He simply listened. And she felt eased, supported, understood as she had never been before. It was the last flowering of Primo Levi's great ability to listen, the mirror image of his great need to tell.

One day Raffaella told him that in her late teens she had wanted to kill herself. She had suddenly thought: *there is no way out.* She had gone to throw herself under a car, and only changed her mind in the last minute. After that she and Primo often talked of suicide. He seemed to her very interested in it, even fascinated by it, but in a calm and normal way. He talked about suicide without fear, she says, as though it was a perfectly ordinary thing. He said that Pavese had chosen his quite consciously. He told her that it was in his family, that a close relative had killed himself. It seemed to her that he had thought about this for a long time, and had concluded that, in some circumstances, suicide could be a choice like any other.

She watched him becoming more and more depressed, towards the end; and in the last few months of his life she no longer saw him. But like Di Caro, when she heard the news she was not surprised. And when she read Rita Levi Montalcini and the others, she thought: No. He said it was a choice, and now he's made it.

★   ★

Apart from his family, the first person to see him that morning was a friend of Renzo's, who had called on Renzo in his flat next door. Either Primo's release had lasted through the night, or he was putting on his best face. He seemed to Renzo and his friend completely normal and serene; when the two young men left they all said, *'Ci vediamo'*, 'Be seeing you', as always.

At around half past nine (at least according to one reporter), Lucia left to go shopping. At around ten, as always, Jolanda Gasperi brought Primo his post. She took the lift up to the third floor and knocked on his door. Primo answered himself. Jolanda knew he had been depressed, but he smiled and thanked her as usual. Jolanda asked after his mother: she quite often went in to talk to her. 'She's asleep,' Primo said. They agreed that Jolanda would come for a chat another time. Primo closed the door, and Jolanda took the lift back down.

She fetched her broom, opened the door between the inner hall and the long outer one, and the main door to the street as well. She chatted for a minute or two to some people passing, then began to sweep. Perhaps fifteen or twenty minutes had passed since she had given Primo his post when she heard the sound: a thud, in the inner atrium. She went in and saw Primo's body. She recognized him right away. At first she thought he had been taken ill, or slipped on the stairs. She ran to her lodge, shaking, and rang the Red Cross, but there was no answer. Then a cleaner came out of one of the first-floor offices: he had heard the thud too. He rang the police and ambulance service.

Jolanda knew that Lucia was out: what should she do? She called Renzo on the *citofono*, the intercom system from the entrance. She said that his father had been taken ill, or had an accident – she still wasn't sure. Renzo came down, and was the first to see his father.

Renzo telephoned Lisa. The police and ambulance arrived. Francesco Quaglia, a resident who had known Primo since *liceo*, heard the hubbub and came down. And before the police could remove Primo's body, Lucia returned. She embraced Quaglia in tears, saying, 'He was tired, demoralized . . . You saw it too, didn't you?' According to several reporters, she said that Primo had been very depressed for some time. According to one reporter she said: I was afraid of it, we all were. We tried not to leave him alone. And according to another observer she said: '*Aveva il coraggio*', 'He had the courage.'

★   ★

It was said at the time, and has been repeated ever after, that Primo left no will. It is not true: he left a perfectly normal one, leaving his estate to his children, with the use of it during her lifetime to his wife. It was also said that he left no note, and that, by contrast, is almost certainly true. They looked everywhere – even on his computer, Giulia Colombo says; but there was nothing. Of course there was nothing. About that the suicide-doubters are right. Primo Levi would never have planned to kill himself in cold blood, and sat down to explain to his family why he was doing this to them. He did not want to do it to them at all.

It was reported at the time that the day's mail contained only magazines, a book, some circulars. Jolanda Gasperi says now that there were also letters: many letters, as there always were. But the police examined them, and found nothing that could have distressed him, she says. (What would the police think was something, though? Gisella wonders.) More reliably, Lucia has also said that there was nothing terrible in the post. But then Primo tried to keep his worst suffering from her; and perhaps she did not realize what would seem terrible to him either.

From the start people said that there were many means of death more certain than leaping off a third floor — as Primo had noted himself, as long ago as 1946; that leap might not have killed him, they say, but only left him paralysed. But first of all this is not true: it is a fifteen metre fall at least, with a stone floor waiting. There were chemicals, for instance, and Primo was a chemist, says Rita Levi Montalcini; he could have taken an overdose of his own antidepressants, David Mendel adds. That would have been clean, painless, private — much more in character than that cruel public death. That is true. But — as they say — Primo wasn't trying to die. On the contrary — *he was trying not to die.* He quite likely put all temptations out of reach, in Lucia's care, or perhaps the nurses'. That would leave him nothing when the time came. Nothing but the void — the void which had drawn his grandfather, which draws all deep depressives, like a call.

But Rita Levi Montalcini, who knew Corso Re Umberto 75, said something else as well: the void into which Primo was supposed to have leapt was hardly a void at all. And that is true. If you look down from the third floor, you don't see space, but a narrowing spiral crammed with obstacles — the circling banisters, the lift cage, the hard white edges of the stairs. Recently the space between the lift and the stairs, on the side where Primo fell, has actually been measured: at the widest point it is no more than 170 centimetres (about five and a half feet), at the narrowest barely a metre (just over a yard — about three and a third feet). It would be possible, even likely, for a falling body to hit the sides of that tiny tunnel before the floor. This is desperately far from Primo's fantasies of flight, and beyond imagination.

And there is one other point which may be on the doubters' side. In her deposition to the police, Rina's nurse said that 'around ten o'clock' Dr Levi called her, and asked her to answer the telephone, if necessary, because he had to go down to the concierge's lodge. She then returned to Rina's room, which was at the far end of the corridor from the front door; and heard and knew no more until Renzo appeared with several police officers, some time later.

Perhaps it does seem strange that a man in the last seconds before suicide would bother to make sure that his telephone was answered after his death. But only if he has consciously planned to die.

Despite all this – despite the *'Ci vediamo'*, the narrowness of the space, the request to the nurse – I think it is quite certain that it was suicide. Primo's analyst is certain it was suicide, though she will not say why. Lucia accepted that it was from the start, as the reports show. Anna Maria accepted it, telling friends that Primo had killed himself because he was depressed. Primo's cousin Giulia accepts it, though she is certain it was not premeditated. Bianca and Alberto accept it, Euge accepts it, Silvio and Ada Ortona accept it, or do not deny it. Both Lilith and Gisella accept it utterly.

That is: those who knew him best cannot deny it. Only those who knew him less well can: his fellow graduates of 1941, for example; and we, his readers. The further away we are from him, the easier it is to believe he did not kill himself. In his death as in his life, Primo Levi's kindness worked best for strangers.

No one wants to believe it: not just for his sake, but for our own. It is as though Primo Levi held up a light for us – almost the only human being who did, in that worst place and time. It is as though, as Jeremy Mack says, he helped us to regain our self-esteem. And if he laid down that light himself, was he not saying that he no longer believed in it – that he no longer believed in us? (And did we not already suspect that, from *The Drowned and the Saved*?) And if he no longer believed in us, how could we? That is what many people felt. Most painfully, perhaps, his fellow survivors. 'The most loved, the most listened to, the most read [of all of us],' Edith Bruck wrote. '*If he did it*, what a betrayal, I cried, what pain, what paralysis: *then I can do it too.*' But it was painful for everyone. 'If *he* couldn't live with such memories,' Clive James said, 'who can?' 'Our fear,' wrote the *New Yorker*, 'was that the efficacy of his words had somehow been cancelled by his death – that his hope, or faith, was no longer usable by the rest of us.'

These are inevitable but unfair feelings, like the feeling of children whose father has died that he has deliberately abandoned them. It is absurd to think that what a man says at sixty-seven, when he is exhausted and clinically depressed, could cancel out what he said when he was twenty-seven, in the flower of his moral and intellectual strength. If a man sees crawling monsters when he is mad, we don't believe him, or blame him, but treat him. Primo Levi's death is not part of his testimony, but only of his disease.

In any case, there is another step here, which we have taken almost without noticing. Primo Levi's depression caused his suicide. But only if Auschwitz caused his depression is there any reason to take that step: to say that even Primo Levi could not survive Auschwitz after all. People simply assumed the link from the start. The reports of his death bore headlines like *'Auschwitz killed him 40 years later'*. Renzo, his son, said it, or was said to have said it: 'Read the ending of *La tregua* and you'll understand.'* All the survivors said it: Elie Wiesel, Maurice Goldstein, Bruno Bettelheim. Famous friends like Natalia Ginzburg said it, and well-known critics like Claudio Marabini and Carlo Sgorlon; and all were quoted ever after.

But to the best of our knowledge it is not true. Primo himself denied it, to Bianca, to David Mendel. All his closest friends are convinced it is not true: Bianca and Alberto, Silvio and Euge, the Accatis; Gisella, Lilith and Gabriella Garda; and others who were close to him at the end, like Vittorio Daneo, Rita Levi Montalcini, and Luciana Nissim, who is also a survivor; his biographer Gabriella Poli, his best critic Cesare Cases. Of course an experience like that of Auschwitz remains the determining experience of a lifetime; it is part of everything ever after. But – as he said to Bianca – Primo had returned, and he had testified; he had resolved and transformed the experience; its poison no longer ran in his veins. Indeed, he said more, and more is true. He was careful, and we must be too. But recalling all the horror, for him and for all who suffered it, the central, painful and paradoxical truth of Primo Levi's life seems to me to be this: that for him Auschwitz was an essentially positive experience. It gave him a reason to live, to communicate, to write; it gave him the subject for the contribution he had always known he could make. It was, as he always said, his adventure, his time in Technicolor, his university, for which he could even feel nostalgia, as we do for the ordinary hard times we have survived. It was the moment when his highest conception of humanity, and his best belief in himself, came together, and lit that light which is *If This is a Man*.

The central, painful and paradoxical truth is that Primo Levi was depressed before and after Auschwitz, but not in it. He thought of suicide before and after Auschwitz, but not in it. Depression and suicide were in him from the start. It is even possible that without the experience of surviving Auschwitz, and without the mission to understand and testify to it, they might have claimed him sooner.

Primo Levi's death was personal. It was a tragedy, but it was not a victory for Auschwitz.

*   *

In the pit of depression he always thought obsessively of suicide. This worst of blind instincts he resisted most of all, and hid most of all. He may not even have told his doctor, Gozzi (though he must have told his analyst: in

---

* The ending of *La tregua* was the return of the Lager, and of the dreaded command: Get up, *Wstawàch*.

any case, she knew). He did not tell Bianca, unless she is hiding too. He surely did not tell his children; and he surely did not tell Lucia either, though like the analyst she knew. But he did tell at least two people.

He told Gisella, openly, as always. She cannot bear to remember very much about his last depression; but she remembers his last conversation, as we know. '*Penso solo a sopprimermi*,' he had said: 'I think only of killing myself.' And no, he had not thought of it while they were talking; but he had not talked to her again.

The other person he told was Alberto, and Alberto's wife Marcella, who was with them. With Alberto and Marcella he was more careful. After he had repeated his agony – being trapped in the house, caught in the siege of the two old ladies – he said, quite calmly: '*Devo confessare*, I must confess, I sometimes think of suicide.' But Alberto saw through his calm, and was very worried. So worried that he went to Lisa and told her: they must get Primo out of that prison. But Lisa had grown up in it herself. There was nothing she could do.

Indirectly, Primo also told Raffaella Pagani. She was a new, young friend; and he was not yet depressed when he talked to her so calmly of suicide. But he had been depressed before, and he must have known it would return. He was trying to think about it calmly while he still could. As Camon said, he was pretending.

So he had impulses to suicide – even constantly, towards the end. But he had resisted them before. Why not this time?

Because this time his depression was worse. He was terrified of operations, of illness, of pain, of losing physical and mental control: of becoming an invalid, a *Musulmann*, like Ada, like the two old mothers. And now it had begun, or seemed to him to have begun. Even the verruca on his foot had tipped him into an acute depression. Now he had a genuinely serious illness, and he literally could not wait to get well. He could not bear the physical humiliations, the dependence. He had hated injections since he was a boy, and now he had to have one every day. Everyone told him it would pass, and he knew it would. But he couldn't believe it.

His loss of memory and concentration was (or felt) worse, because his depression was deeper. His fear that his testimony had failed was worse, because of the new wave of revisionism in Germany itself. His fear that he was not a 'real' writer was worse, because he had tried and failed. His fear that his project of understanding had failed was, perhaps, no worse than it had been for the last few years; but that was bad enough.

But more than any of these, what was worse was his prison. This was the last double bind: bound once by his wife, and once by his mother.

The strongest bind was his mother's. She was the Vilmy, the *malabaila*, the mysterious root of everything in his life. This woman, 'so intelligent, so imperious', as Norberto Bobbio said, had ruled him from the start, and ruled him entirely at the end. Everyone, from his closest friends to casual contacts, could see that his relationship to her was abnormal. Analysts, and analyst friends, would say that he had never separated from her. The child everyone felt in him was her child, the need for affection her affection, which he had never had. When he *was* a child, and completely in her power, he had grown the carapace of equilibrium which made him seem old. When he was old, and her power was ebbing away, the carapace began to crack, and the lost child emerged. When he was a boy he also had a father, when he was a man he had a wife; but from start to finish visitors to Corso Re Umberto 75 felt, and even sometimes believed, that he was alone with his mother. Philip Roth says, 'You felt the presence of his mother through him. Wherever he was, you felt that in some room nearby there was his mother, waiting.' When Raffaella Pagani went to see him, Primo would put his mother's wheelchair in the light at the end of the corridor, and they would go into his dark study. They would sit in the dark, and his mother in the light, where he could see her.

At the end everyone knew that his mother's illness was consuming him, that it was a main factor in his depression, even the most important of all. He talked about it obsessively to everyone, to Giulio Einaudi, to everyone at Einaudi, to his last interviewers, to his neighbour Francesco Quaglia, to Rabbi Toaff, to Bianca in their last conversation. And he talked about it, of course, to Gisella. He said: I go to the door of my mother's room and I feel the weight of the whole world on me. He said: She is paralysed, and she paralyses me. He saw himself becoming her: losing control like her, dying like her. His mother was incontinent, like an infant, and so was he. He was so fastidious, so shy, that this was a torment to him anyway: he asked Gisella, he even asked Rina's nurse, what he should do, especially if someone was coming to see him. But when Gisella suggested that – just briefly – he wear incontinence pads, he couldn't. Then I should be exactly like my mother, he said.

The trouble was, he really wanted to be rid of his mother at last; he really wanted her to die. That is why, when Agnese Incisa first suggested that he put her away, he had nearly fainted. She would die, he had said. Better her than you, Agnese had replied. The same thought had been buried deep in his brain. Now Agnese's words had found it; he had been found out. He wanted someone to die in his place – and not just someone, but his mother. He wanted his mother to die, he told Ferruccio Maruffi in anguish. Everyone wants their old mothers to die, Ferruccio said, but he wasn't consoled. Still he began to tell more and more people. 'These old mothers who won't die,' he said to Franca Mussa, to Ernesto Ferrero, to Massimo Scaglione. 'It is her or me,' he said to Gisella, to his cousin Giulia, to people at Einaudi. 'One of us will have to go.'

It could not be his mother, of course. In the end she outlived him by four years, dying in 1991, at the age of ninety-six. Lucia took care of her to the end. She was told that Primo had had a heart attack, but did not believe it. I do not suppose she ever knew how her son died.

After the first shock of recognition that he wanted to save himself at the expense of his mother, Primo tried to. He told Lucia that he wanted to put his mother into a home. But Lucia would not hear of it; and not for her own mother either. Her slavery went on; and so, therefore, did Primo's.

Then he was ill too, and she took care of him as well. To his guilt he was adding a debt, neither of which he could ever repay. When Dr Gozzi suggested that he would have to break some of these bonds of guilt and obligation if he was ever to be well, Primo was angry. In the end he was willing to sacrifice his mother, but not Lucia. He could never leave her; for a short time (perhaps during his analysis) he left Gozzi instead.

It was clear to everyone who knew them that Lucia's dedication to the two mothers was extreme, even pathological, and that she used it to bind Primo to her. But some also understood the other side: that Primo needed to be bound. He wanted to sacrifice his mother, but he also wanted to be stopped from sacrificing her; and Lucia stopped him. Lucia always stopped him doing what he wanted. That is what he needed her to do.

We have only glimpses of that morning. The rest we can only guess.

I think he still felt better: perhaps completely well, certainly well enough to put on a good face for Renzo and his friend. Perhaps that was why Lucia decided she could leave him and go shopping.

It was a beautiful, sunny day, the first one that spring. His mountains looked near enough to touch. I think he had greeted that day, had hoped to enjoy it at last, like everyone else – much more than anyone else. And then he realized he couldn't. He wasn't better. It wasn't over after all.

Perhaps it happened before the post, but certainly by then. He had talked of it so often – *l'angoscia dell'ora della posta*. His terror of the post, as he said to David Mendel, because it might leave him 'no way out'.

There was nothing in the post, Lucia said. But if there were letters, and if he opened them, as Jolanda Gasperi thinks he did, just an invitation from abroad, a request from a reader, could have sent him back into his universe of dread. Even if he didn't open them, a foreign envelope could have been enough. And even if there were no letters at all, the moment before he opened the door could have been enough as well.

He went to the phone and called Dr Gozzi: we know that. '*Non ne posso più*,' he said, 'I can't go on.' Wait, Gozzi said, I'm coming. But he couldn't wait. He called the nurse, and told her to answer the phone; we know that too. In case someone might call and stop him in the last second? Because he just needed to get out, and really thought he might walk downstairs? He opened the door, and found himself outside.

It wasn't the light and air he had dreamed of, but it was a deep void. One last time the thought knocked at his brain, and found the place waiting there. I think he looked for Lucia to stop him. He leaned and looked, but she wasn't there; and he let go.

Notes

Quotations and some individual lines are separately identified and sourced. Otherwise sources are given for paragraphs as a whole, identified by ¶ plus the opening words.

The following abbreviations have been used in the Notes for sources that occur frequently:

ANED: interviews with Piedmontese deportees by ANED (Associazione Nazionale Ex Deportati)

AP: Aldo Piacenza

AS: Alberto Salmoni

Ateneo: *L'Ateneo, Notizario dell'Università degli Studi di Torino*, Anno XIII, No. 3, May/June 1997

BBC *Bookmark*: BBC2 TV *Bookmark* programme on Primo Levi, 1985

BGS: Bianca Guidetti Serra

Belpoliti 1998: Marco Belpoliti, *Primo Levi*, Bruno Mondadori, 1998

Blakeway: *The Memory of the Offence*, BBC2 TV, 1992, director Denys Blakeway

Bocca: Primo Levi interview with Giorgio Bocca, 'Prima pagina', Canale 5 TV, 13 January 1985

Carpi: Daniele Carpi, 'The Development of Fascist Antisemitism in Italy', in *The Catastrophe of European Jewry*, ed. Gutman and Rothkirscher, Yad Vashem, 1976

Cavaglion 1993: Alberto Cavaglion, *Primo Levi e Se questo è un uomo*, Loescher Editore, 1993

Conversations: Ferdinando Camon, *Conversations with Primo Levi*, trans. John Shepley, Marlboro Press, 1989

Conversazioni e interviste: *Primo Levi: Conversazioni e interviste*, ed. Marco Belpoliti, Einaudi, 1997.

CP: Primo Levi, *Collected Poems*, trans. Ruth Feldman and Brian Swann, Faber, 1988.

De Felice: Renzo De Felice, *Storia degli ebrei sotto il fascismo*, Einaudi, 1993 (originally 1961)

Dini & Jesurum: Massimo Dini and Stefano Jesurum, *Primo Levi: le opere e i giorni* (*Primo Levi: Life and Work*), Rizzoli, 1992

DL: *Il doppio legame* (Primo Levi's last unpublished work)

Donne: Luciana Nissim and Pelagia Lewinska, *Donne contro il mostro*, Vincenzo Ramelli Editore, Turin, 1946

D. & S.: Primo Levi, *The Drowned and the Saved*, Michael Joseph, 1988

Echi: Gabriella Poli and Giorgio Calcagno, *Echi di una voce perduta*, Mursia, 1992

EGT: Eugenio Gentili Tedeschi

Fadini: Primo Levi interview with Edoardo Fadini, *Unità*, 4 January 1966 (in *VM*, qv.)

Ferrero, *Antologia*: Ernesto Ferrero (ed.), *Primo Levi: un antologia della critica*, Einaudi, 1997

GB: Guido Bachi

GCD: Giulia Colombo Diena

Grassano: Giuseppe Grassano, *Conversation with Primo Levi* (included in an abridged version in Grassano's *Primo Levi*, La Nuova Italia, 1981, and in *VM*)

Greer interview: Primo Levi interview with Germaine Greer, *Literary Review*, November 1985 (in *VM*)

INNW: Primo Levi, *If Not Now, When?*, Abacus paperback, 1987

ITIAM: Primo Levi, *If This is a Man*, Abacus paperback, 1987

'Itinerario': Primo Levi, 'Itinerario di uno scrittore ebreo', *Opere II*, p. 1213 (published in English as *Beyond Survival*, trans. Gail Soffer, Prooftexts 4, Johns Hopkins University, 1984)

JS: Jean Samuel

LDB: Leonardo De Benedetti

Lucarini: Primo Levi interview with Paola Lucarini, *Firme Nostre*, Anno XXV, No. 100, September–December 1983, pp. 3–4

Mondoperaio: Primo Levi interview with Rita Caccamo De Luca and Manuela Olagnero, *Mondoperaio*, No. 3, 1984 (in *VM*)

MR: Primo Levi, *Moments of Reprieve*, Abacus paperback, 1987

Museo: *Fossoli, Il Museo Monumento al deportato a Carpi*, Guide Artistiche Electa, ed. Roberta Gibertoni and Annalisa Melodi

Nicco: Roberto Nicco, *La Resistenza in Valle D'Aosta*, Istituto Storico della Resistenza in Valle D'Aosta, Musumeci Editore, 1990

Opere I: Primo Levi, *Opere I*, ed. Marco Belpoliti, Nuova Universale Einaudi 225★, 1997

Opere II: Primo Levi, *Opere II*, ed. Marco Belpoliti, Nuova Universale Einaudi 225★★, 1997

OPT: Primo Levi, *Other People's Trades*, Michael Joseph, London, 1989

Papuzzi: Alberto Papuzzi, 'L'alpinismo? E' la libertà di sbagliare', *Rivista delle montagna*, March 1984 (translated as 'Mountaineering' in *VM*)

Piemonte letterario: Giovanni Tesio, *Piemonte letterario dell'otto-novecento*, Bulzoni, 1991)

PL: Primo Levi

PT: Primo Levi, *The Periodic Table*, Abacus paperback, 1986

Rapporto: Primo Levi and Leonardo De Benedetti, *Rapporto sulla organizzazione igienico sanitaria del campo di concentrazione per Ebrei di Monowitz (Auschwitz Alta Silesia)* in *Minerva Medica* XXXVII, July–December 1946, pp. 535–44 (part quoted in Alberto Cavaglion, *Primo Levi e Se questo è un uomo*, pp. 40–41, fully quoted in *Opere I*, pp. 1339–60)

Regge: Primo Levi and Tullio Regge, *Dialogo*, Princeton University Press, 1989 (in English)

Roots: Primo Levi, *The Search for Roots*, Allen Lane, The Penguin Press, 2001

Rosenfeld TV: *Primo Levi*, VPRO (Dutch Television) programme, directed by Netty Rosenfeld, 1988

Roth: Primo Levi interview with Philip Roth, *New York Times Book Review*, 12 October 1986 and *London Review of Books*, 23 October 1986 (in *VM*)

Rudolf: Primo Levi interview with Anthony Rudolf, *London Magazine*, October 1986 (in *VM*)

S. Salvatore: *Primo Levi: Memoria e invenzione*, ed. Giovanna Ioli, Edizioni della Biennale 'Piemonte e Letteratura', 1995, papers given at the Primo Levi conference at San Salvatore Monferrato, 26–8 September 1991

SO: Silvio Ortona

TMM: Primo Levi, *The Mirror Maker*, Methuen, 1990 (and Abacus paperback, 1998)

TSD: Primo Levi, *The Sixth Day*, Michael Joseph, 1990 (and Abacus paperback, 1991)

Vincenti: Fiora Vincenti, *Invito alla lettura di Primo Levi*, Mursia, 1973

VM: *The Voice of Memory*, ed. Marco Belpoliti and Robert Gordon, trans. Robert Gordon, Polity, 2001 (translation of *Conversazioni e interviste*)

Waitz: Robert Waitz, 'Auschwitz III (Monowitz)', pp. 467–99 of 'De L'Université aux Camps de Concentration, Témoignages Strasbourgeois', in *Les Belles Lettres*, 1947

Introduction

p. xxiii
'Primo Levi . . . identified it . . .'   Author interview with Giorgio Calcagno.
p. xxiv
¶ 'Except for one year . . .' PL, 'La mia casa', *Opere II*, p. 633, translated as 'My House' in *OPT*; Roth, in *VM*, p. 14; PL, interview with Giulio Nascimbeni, *Corriere della Sera*, 28 October 1984 (in *Conversazioni e interviste*).

¶ 'His mother's family . . .'   Author interviews with GCD and Giorgio Luzzati.

¶ 'A year and a half later . . .'   Birth certificate Anna Maria Fortunata Levi, No. 447, Ufficio No. 2, Parte 1, 1921 (27 January 1921); Blakeway; Vincenti, p. 32; author interviews with GCD, Giorgio Luzzati, and Vera Gay Marconi. See also *Numero Unico* for 1936–7, 'D'Azeglio sotto spirito', p. 19. The typewriter image is Signora Marconi's.

¶ 'Their parents both . . .'   'Itinerario'; Risa Sodi interview, *Present Tense*, May/June 1988; Daniella Amsallem, 'Primo Levi "juif de retour"', *Les Nouveaux Cahiers*, No. 114, Autumn 1993, especially p. 38; Stefano Jesurum, 'Primo Levi', in *Essere ebrei in Italia*, Longanesi, 1987; author interview with Paolo Avigdor.

¶ 'But not wholly . . .'   *PT*, p. 5; author interviews with Sergio Valvassori and Mario Rigoni Stern. For sources for PL's bar mitzvah period, see Notes to Ch. 3.

¶ 'That is, at least . . .'   Laura Archera, quoted in Alberto Papuzzi, 'Huxley, la violinista e il sibarita', *La Stampa*, 24 July 1994, p. 17; PL, 'Meccano d'amore', *Opere II*, p. 882, translated as 'Love's Erector Set' in *OPT*; author interviews with GCD and Giorgio Luzzati.

p. xxv

¶ 'Later he would do . . .'   *PT*, p. 26, and PL, 'Il mondo invisibile', *Opere II*, p. 800, translated as 'The Invisible World' in *OPT*.

¶ 'His father . . .'   *PT*, p. 19; Regge, pp. 12–13; *Roots*, p. 4.

¶ 'How many times . . .'   PL, 'Ranocchi sulla luna', *Opere II*, p. 890, translated as 'Frogs on the Moon' in *OPT*; author interviews with GCD and Ferruccio Introna.

p. xxvi

¶ 'They would follow . . .'   PL, 'La mia casa' and 'Wooden Heart', *CP*, p. 39; author interviews with GCD and Paolo Avigdor.

¶ 'But to him . . .'   PL, 'Ranocchi sulla luna' and 'Meccano d'amore'.

Chapter 1: Paradiso

pp. 5–9

Historical information from: *Ebrei a Torino, Ricerche per il Centenario della Sinagoga (1884–1984)*, Allemandi, Turin, 1984: especially PL's Preface (in *Opere II*, p. 1251), and material on demographic history by Luciano Allegra and on *ebraico piemontese* by Paola Diena. And from: Umberto Eco, in *Trovare Torino, La Stampa* supplement, 3 November 1987; Ernesto Ferrero, Introduction to *Primo Levi: I racconti*, Einaudi, 1996; Salvatore Foa, 'Ebrei a Torino', *Lunario Israelitico 5962*, F. Servi, Turin, 1932; EGT, 'Primo Levi: Parcours de la laïcité à la Résistance', talk delivered to PL conference, Paris, June 1999; Ivo Herzer (ed.), *The Italian Refuge*, Catholic University of America Press, Washington, DC, 1989, especially the Introduction by Herzer and essays by Paul Bookbinder, Andrew Canepa and Daniele Carpi; Stefano Jesurum, 'Comunità Italia', *Gli speciali di Sette*, 1995; Arnaldo Momigliano, *Pagine ebraiche*, Einaudi, 1987; SO, *Ortona, Della Torre, Casale Monferrato, ecc.*, private family monograph, May 1993; Alexander Stille, *Benevolence and Betrayal*, Jonathan Cape, London, 1992; Stuart Woolf, 'Primo Levi: Drowning and Surviving', *Jewish Quarterly*, Vol. 34, No. 127, 1987; Davide Yona and Anna Foa, *Noi due*, Il Mulino, 1997; interviews with PL by Barbara Kleiner, *Neue Musikzeitung*, August–September 1986 (in *Conversazioni e interviste*), and Rudolf; and author interviews with Giulio Bollati, Guido Davico Bonino, Alberto Cavaglion, Angelo D'Orsi, and Ernesto Ferrero.

p. 9

¶ 'He wrote . . .'   *Ebrei a Torino*; Angelo d'Orsi, *Torino*, ed. Valerio Castronovo, Laterza, 1987; author interviews, including Luciano Allegra, Alberto Cavaglion, Elena Deangeli, and Angelo d'Orsi.

pp. 10–12

The Famous Reserve of the Piedmontese   Information from: PL, Preface to *Ebrei a Torino*, and PL, 'Bella come una fiore', *Opere II*, p. 926; *Echi*; Regge; Stille, *Benevolence*. Also from: Norberto Bobbio, *30 anni di storia della cultura a Torino*, Società Piemontese CRT, 1977; *Conversations*; Carlo Casalegno in *Annuario D'Azeglio 1967–8*, pp. 62–7; d'Orsi, *Torino*; Luigi Firpo in *Dieci anni del Circolo della Stampa*, 1990; Giorgio Martellini, *Ritratto di città con persone*, GCC, Inner Wheel Club, Turin, 1986; *Torino come eravamo*, supplement to *La Stampa*, 20 January 1978; *Trovare Torino*, supplement to *La Stampa*, 3 November 1987; *Torino e dintorni, TuttoCittà*, city guide 1991; Greer; Gad Lerner, 'Torinesissimo Primo Levi', *La Stampa*, 7 February 1997, and 'Very Important Piemontesi', RAI Torino radio, 21 May 1981; author interviews with Alberto Cavaglion, Carla Gobetti, Fabio Levi, and Giovanni Tesio; author's cuttings 1993–5, including Giorgio Bocca, Oreste del Buono, Paolo Guzzanti, and Alberto Papuzzi.

p. 12
'In 1946, alongside *If This is a Man* . . .'   *Piemonte letterario*.
¶ 'When he returned . . .'   *Echi*, p. 84; and see 'Itinerario'.
'The chapter . . .'   Greer interview.
¶ '*The Periodic Table* . . .', and all subsequent material on *ebraico piemontese*: PL, 'Argon', *PT*; 'Itinerario', and 'Il fondaco del nonno', *Opere II*, p. 827, translated as 'Grandfather's Store' in *OPT*. Also Paola Diena, degree thesis, University of Turin, 1979–80, *Il Giudeo-Piemontese* and material in *Ebrei a Torino*; Luciano Allegra material in *Ebrei a Torino*; and further material on *ebraico piemontese* kindly given to me by Elena Vita Finzi and Professor Gino Sacerdote.

p. 14
¶ 'From childhood . . .'   'Argon' and 'Itinerario'.
'reflects another . . .'   'Argon', p. 9.

p. 15
'have in common . . .'   'Argon', p. 4.
¶ ' "Gratuitous discussion" . . .'   Author interviews with Alberto Piazza and Antonia Levi.
¶ 'He knew this . . .'   See 'A un giovane lettore', *Opere II*, p. 845, translated as 'To a Young Reader' in *OPT*.
'On it he had written . . .'   See Alberto Cavaglion, 'Argon e la cultura ebraica piemontese', in *Il presente del passato*, Franco Angeli, 1991, p. 170.
'. . . it is still on the final typescript . . .'   In the Einaudi Archive, Turin. All future references to PL typescripts will be to this archive, unless otherwise indicated.

p. 16
'there were also . . .'   *Echi*, p. 223.
¶ 'Once again . . .'   *Echi*, p. 223; SO, *Ortona . . . ecc.*, p. 77; author interviews with SO.
¶ 'Thus, Primo's *zia* . . .'   'Argon'; SO, *Ortona . . . ecc.*; Cavaglion, 'Argon e la cultura ebraica piemontese'; author interviews with Jole Segre. Note that there are several errors in the English translation of 'Argon': e.g. 'eighty-six' for 'sixty-eight', on p. 15; and 'your winds' for 'my winds' on p. 12.

p. 17
The first three ¶¶ are all taken from 'Argon'. The rest of the page (the story of Barbaricô) is taken from 'Argon' as well, plus background information from author interviews with Jole Segre, GCD, Andrea Levi, and Anna Foa Yona. All confirm that (as PL says in *Echi*, p. 84), the story of Barbaricô is true.

p. 18

The story of Barbabramìn: 'Argon'; author interviews with Jole Segre, GCD, Anna Maria Levi Bassan. Again all confirm that the story was essentially true, though *zia* Jole says, for instance, that Barbabramìn spent twelve years in bed rather than twenty-two.

p. 19

'The first draft ends here . . .' See Alberto Cavaglion in *Il presente del passato*, who includes the draft with his talk.

pp. 19–21

Most of the information about the Della Torres comes from Silvio Ortona, *Ortona . . . ecc.* I would like to thank him for allowing me to use his researches in this book. Also from: 'Grandfather's Store'; Vittorio Foa, *Il cavallo e la torre*, Einaudi, 1991; Stille, *Benevolence*; and author interviews with Jole Segre, SO, and Giovanni Levi.

pp. 21–3

Luzzati information from 'Grandfather's Store', and author interviews with Jole Segre, GCD, Lea Segre, Ada Ortona, and Giovanni Levi.

pp. 23–4

Levi and Sinigaglia information from author interviews with GCD, Elena Bachi Pollone, Enrica Finzi Levi, Silvia Levi Salaspini and Anna Maria Levi Bassan. Also from PL's Introduction to *Roots*, and Regge.

' "They were very fond of each other . . ." ' *Roots*, p. 4.

PARADISE LOST

Historical information on Bene Vagienna from: *Bene Vagienna: storia di una città* and *Notizie storiche sulla città di Bene*, both published by Gli Amici di Bene (The Friends of Bene), and both kindly given me by Dr Michelangelo Fessia. Historical information on the Jewish Community of Mondovì from: Dino Colombo, 'Il ghetto di Mondovì', *Rassegna mensile di Israele*, April 1968; Roberto Arnaldi, 'Immagini di un passato ebraico nel Monregalese', *I Quaderni de 'La Ghisleriana'*, 1982, both kindly given me by Dr Mario Levi of Mondovì. Birth, marriage and death certificates from the City Archive of Mondovì.

p. 26

¶ 'In Bene Ricchetta's husband . . .' 'Argon', p. 19; *Gazzetta del popolo*, 3 August 1888, p. 4; Salvador David Levi death certificate, Atto No. 222, Ufficio 2, Parte 1, Anno 1935, Città di Torino.

p. 31

Paradiso information from author interviews with Dr Fessia and Contessa Soardi of Bene Vagienna.

p. 33

Information on Dr Rebaudengo from Jole Segre and Contessa Soardi.

'. . . six months after Michele's death she won . . .' Case documents, Tribunale di Mondovì, 14 December 1888, kindly provided to me by the Archivio di Stato (State Archive), Cuneo.

¶ 'Michele Levi married Adele Sinigaglia . . .'   Marriage certificate Michele Levi
– Adele Sinigaglia, Atto No. 744, Ufficio 2, Anno 1877, Città di Torino (date
13 November 1877); case documents, Tribunale di Mondovì, 17 November
1888.

¶ 'After two years . . .'   Giacomo Levi death certificate Bene Vagienna, Atti di
Morte No. 70, 1887.

* e.g. the *Gazzetta del popolo*, 20 October 1888 and several case documents refer to
the *vivente*, i.e. living, Giuseppe Levi.

p. 34
¶ 'By then . . .'   *Gazzetta del popolo*, 3 August 1888, p. 4; *Gazzetta di Cuneo*, 25
September 1888, p. 2; *Sentinella delle Alpi*, 1–2 August 1888, p. 3 and 2–3 August
1888, p. 3.

Information on the rest of this page and the next from the *Gazzetta del popolo*, 3
August 1888, p. 4 and 27 July 1888, pp. 3–4; *Gazzetta piemontese*, 26 July 1888,
p. 3; *Sentinella delle Alpi*, 2–3 July 1888, p. 3; *Gazzetta di Mondovì*, 4 August 1888,
p. 2.

* Death certificate Salvador David Levi, as before.

p. 35
'His death was registered with the notation . . .'   Archive documents, Ospedale
(Hospital) San Giovanni Battista, Turin, *Rubrica Anno 1888, Uomini* (Men).

'without malice'   'Argon', p. 5.

¶ 'Although Cesare Levi . . .'   PL birth certificate, Atto No. 1610, Ufficio 2, Parte
1, Serie 1, Anno 1919, Città di Torino; author interviews with Jole Segre,
Giovanni Tesio, Raffaella Pagani.

¶ 'Long after my visit . . .'   *Il filo della memoria*, by Paolo Levi, Rizzoli, 1984.
Chiusa di Pesio is a real village near Cuneo.

Chapter 2: Botticelli Angels: 1919–30

p. 37
¶ 'Primo's cousin . . .'   Vittorio Foa, *Il cavallo e la torre*, Einaudi, 1991.

'I remember . . .'   Foa, *Il cavallo e la torre*, p. 9.

pp. 37–8
Information on PL as a child from PL, 'The Invisible World', *OPT*; Vincenti,
p. 37; Regge, p. 13; Giovanni Tesio, 'A proposito di una biografia mancata'
('About an Unwritten Biography'), in S. Salvatore, p. 267; David Mendel,
'Autobiography in the Writings of Primo Levi', talk delivered at the Italian
Cultural Institute, London, 4 April 1995; Rosenfeld TV; author interviews with
GCD, Lea Segre, Ferruccio Introna, Sergio Valvassori, Vera Gay Marconi; and
undated letter to the author from Giovanni Tesio.

p. 38
¶ 'His father was responsible . . .'   Vincenti, p. 36; Davide Yona and Anna Foa,
Noi due, Il Mulino, 1997; author interviews with Anna Yona; letter from PL to
Anna Yona, 7 September 1971.

p. 39

¶ 'As a child . . .'   PL, 'Lo scriba', *Opere II*, p. 841; interview with PL by Giuseppe Grieco, 'Io e Dio', *Gente*, December 1983 (translated as 'God and I' in *VM*); author interviews with GCD.

¶ 'There was one other thing . . .'   Interviews with PL by Roberto Di Caro (transcript of 'La fatica di scrivere', *L'Espresso*, 26 July 1987) and Paolo Terni, RAI Radio, 'Pomeriggio musicale', 13–17 February 1984; *Conversations*, p. 6; author interviews with GCD and Jole Segre.

¶¶ 'He had a good ear . . .' and 'At around the same time . . .'   *PT*, p. 111; author interviews with GCD; interviews with PL by Paolo Terni, as above, and Alberto Gozzi, RAI Radio Due, 7 January 1985.

p. 40

¶ 'He had many very clear . . .'   Interviews with PL by Giuseppe Bonura, *Avvenire*, 9 February 1984, and Paola Valabrega, private interview for degree thesis, 1981 (in *VM*).

¶ 'He does not write . . .'   *PT*, pp. 19–20; author interviews with Jole Segre.

p. 41

'and the monster was there . . .' and following ¶   PL, 'Paura dei ragni', *Opere II*, p. 755, translated as 'The Fear of Spiders' in *OPT*.

p. 42

School, all three ¶¶   Rignon School records; Vincenti, p. 32; Dini & Jesurum, p. 2; author interviews with GCD and Sergio Valvassori; undated letter to the author from Giovanni Tesio; letter to the author from SO, 7 February 1997.

¶ 'Its real source . . .'   PL, 'I mnemagoghi', *Opere I*, p. 401, translated as 'The Mnemagogues' in *TSD*, and 'Leggere la vita', *Opere II*, p. 682. The quotation 'extreme introversion' is from Vincenti, p. 32.

¶ 'He and Sergio . . .'   PL, 'Fra Diavolo sul Po', *La Stampa*, 14 December 1986, p. 3 and *Opere II*, p. 1310; GCD in Rosenfeld TV; author interviews with GCD, Ferruccio Introna, and Sergio Valvassori.

p. 43

¶ 'What this quizzical . . .' and next ¶   'Bella come una fiore'; Tesio, S. Salvatore, p. 267 and undated letter to author; Rignon School records; author interviews with GCD, Ferruccio Introna, and Sergio Valvassori. Emilia Glauda retired in 1940 after forty years' service, and died around 1980, at the age of 100 ('Bella come una fiore'; letter to the author from Rignon School).

p. 44

¶ 'In fact it wasn't unusual . . .'   Author interviews with GCD and Guido Bonfiglioli. Reasons are nonetheless given in e.g. Vincenti, p. 32, and Rita Levi Montalcini, *Senz'olio contro vento*, Baldini & Castoldi, 1996, p. 94.

'. . . several of the family say . . .'   Felice Malgaroli, letter to Norberto Bobbio, 10 August 1994, citing 'cousins'.

¶ 'If this *was* the plan . . .'   Information about Marisa Zini from Vincenti, p. 32, and Giovanni Tesio, undated letter to the author.

¶ 'And once he was . . .'   Ginnasio/Liceo Massimo D'Azeglio records, Classes 4A (*ginnasio*), 1932–3 and IIIB (*liceo*), 1936–7; PL, 'I sintetici', *Opere I*, p. 588.

p. 45

'Sono andato . . .'   D'Azeglio magazine *Numero Unico*, 1932, title 'Vecchio d'Azeglio', p. 2.

Anna Maria   'The Invisible World' and 'Frogs on the Moon'; Lucarini; author interviews with GCD, EGT, Sergio Valvassori, Vera Gay Marconi, Enrica Finzi Levi, and Anna Maria Levi Bassan.

'It would not be accurate . . .'   Vincenti, p. 31.

¶ 'Where did his timidity . . .'   PL, Preface to *La tregua* schools edn, 1965, p. 5 (in *Opere I*, p. 1141), and 'Argon'; Greer; author interviews with GCD. Information on the Levis in this ¶ and the next from: PL, Preface to *Roots*; Paolo Levi, *Il filo della memoria*; author interviews with GCD and Jole Segre. *Il filo della memoria* confirms almost all PL's portrait of Nona Malia and Dr Rebaudengo, except for the mouldy chocolates. Nona Malia died in April 1932, aged seventy-five, not at over eighty in 1928, as PL says in 'Argon' (*PT*, p. 18).

p. 47

¶ 'The contrast . . .'   Author interviews with GCD.

pp. 47–50

Information on *nonno* Luzzati and his sons Corrado and Gustavo from: 'Grandfather's Store' and 'Tempo debito', *Opere I*, p. 131; Tesio, S. Salvatore, p. 267; author interviews with GCD, Paolo Avigdor, Giorgio Luzzati, Silvio and Ada Ortona, Anna Yona, Jole Segre, and Lea Segre. For the Della Torre smile, see also Foa, *Il cavallo e la torre*, p. 9.

pp. 50–52

Rina   Esterina Luzzati and Cesare Levi marriage certificate, Atto 851, Ufficio 1, Parte 1, Serie 1, Anno 1918, date 17 October 1918; 'My House'; Vincenti, p. 31; Roth interview; Giovanni Tesio, undated letter to the author; author interviews with GCD, Jole Segre, Lea Segre, Paolo Avigdor, Ada Ortona, Anna Yona, Antonia Levi, Enrica Finzi Levi, Vera Gay Marconi, Sergio Valvassori, Salvatore Roggero, and Giovanni Tesio.

p. 52

'His mother too . . .'   *ITIAM*, p. 117.

¶ 'This is about . . .'   Author interviews with JS and Bruno Testa.

pp. 52–5

Cesare Levi information from: 'The Invisible World' and 'Argon', p. 19; Vincenti, p. 31; Dini & Jesurum, p. 16–18; *Conversations*, pp. 6–7; Regge, p. 13; Tesio, S. Salvatore, p. 266; Lucarini; Gozzi, RAI Radio Due, 7 January 1985; Giorgio De Rienzo, 'In un alambicco quanta poesia', *Famiglia cristiana*, 20 July 1975, p. 43; Ernesto Ferrero, 'Primo Levi scrittore' in *Notiziario dell'Istituto Storico della Resistenza in Cuneo e provincia*, No. 32, December 1985; and author interviews with GCD, Paolo Avigdor, Jole Segre, Lydia Levi, Anna Yona, and Giovanni Tesio.

p. 56–7
Background information on the ethos of the 20s and 30s in Turin from author
    interviews with GCD, Anna Yona, Fernanda Pivano, EGT, Luisa Accati and
    Giovanni Levi.

p. 57
¶ 'Apart from the memory . . .'   'My House' and 'Frogs on the Moon'.

p. 58
¶ 'By contrast . . .'   PL, 'Il mitra sotto il letto', *Opere II*, p. 917, translated into
    English as 'The Tommy Gun under the Bed' in *TMM*.
'The reason he gave for not . . . speaking about his mother . . .'   See Valabrega
    interview, 1981, *VM*, p. 140; and author interviews with Giovanni Tesio.

pp. 58 to end of chapter
Where sources are nameable, they are given in the text; otherwise protected sources.

p. 63
Quotations 'reverence' and 'natural authority' from author interviews with Sergio
    Valvassori and Salvatore Roggero.

Chapter 3: *Primo Levi Primo: 1930–37*

p. 69
¶ 'By the 1930s . . .'   *PT*, p. 51; Bobbio, *30 anni*, p. 42; Stille, *Benevolence*; *Piemonte
    letterario*, p. 142; Preface by Alessandro Galante Garrone to *Moralità armata*, ed.
    Alberto Cavaglion, p. vii; presentation of *PT* at the Unione Culturale, Turin, 4
    June 1975, p. 12 (typescript kindly given me by Gabriella Poli); Carlo Casalegno
    in *Annuario D'Azeglio 1967–68*, Vincenzo Bona, Turin, 1968, pp. 60–61. On
    Azelia Arici: PL, 'Ricordo di Azelia Arici', *La Stampa*, 7 July 1978; interview
    with PL by Gianni Milani, *Piemonte VIP*, Anno III, No. 3, March 1986, p. 18;
    author interviews with Sergio Valvassori.
¶ 'Still, the school's . . .'   *Piemonte letterario*, p. 142; author interviews with Angelo
    d'Orsi.
¶ 'Throughout . . .'   Ginnasio Liceo Massimo D'Azeglio records, *ginnasio superiore*.
¶ 'These marks . . .'   Author interviews with schoolfriends, e.g. Alfredo Fedele,
    Bruno Foa, Pierluigi Olivetti, Enzo Levi, Maria Augusta Borelli, Nerina Freschi,
    Fernanda Pivano.

p. 70
¶ 'Many of the teachers . . .'   Vincenti, p. 32; Tesio, S. Salvatore, p. 267 and letter
    to author; author interviews with Fernanda Pivano.
¶ 'But one teacher . . .'   *Piemonte letterario*, p. 143; Azelia Arici, 'L'insegnamento
    di Dante', in *Scritti e conferenze 1939–1976*, Edizioni EDA, Turin, 1979; author
    interviews with Signora Barberi, Carla Vernaschi Fischer, GCD, Enzo Levi,
    Fernanda Pivano.

Next three ¶¶   Lucarini; author interviews with Alberto Papuzzi, Alfredo Fedele, Salvatore Roggero, Carlo Martinola.

¶ 'Unsurprisingly . . .'   Vincenti, pp. 37–8; Tesio, S. Salvatore, p. 268; Regge, p. 12; PL, Preface to *Roots*; Paul Bailey in Blakeway; author interviews with GCD.

¶ 'And what of . . .'   PL, Preface to *La tregua* schools edn, 1965; *Piemonte letterario*, p. 149; Regge, p. 12; *Echi*, p. 153; Risa Sodi, 'An Interview with Primo Levi', *Partisan Review*, 1987, p. 366, in *Conversazioni e interviste*; Fadini, in *VM*; Paul Bailey in Blakeway; author interviews with Jole Segre, Giovanni Tesio, Guido Bonfiglioli.

p. 72

¶ 'The mystery . . .'   Quotation from Laura Mancinelli interview with PL, *Il Secolo XIX*, 23 April 1985.

¶ 'At first . . .'   Tesio, S. Salvatore, p. 267 and letter to author; author interviews with Fernanda Pivano.

¶ 'What is certainly true . . .'   Regge, p. 14.

¶ 'Arici was . . .'   Author interviews with Signora Barberi, Bernard Delmay, Fernanda Pivano, Enzo Levi, Carla Vernaschi Fisher.

p. 73

¶ 'For his part . . .'   Regge, pp. 14–15; *Echi*, p. 153; Ernesto Ferrero, 'Primo Levi scrittore', December 1987, p. 185; Tesio, S. Salvatore, p. 267.

¶ 'He was polite . . .'   'seeing inside' from Carla Vernaschi, *allievo normale* from Signora Barberi, 'certain aversion . . .' from Tesio, S. Savatore, p. 267.

¶ 'Nonetheless, she *was* . . .'   PL interviews with Lucarini, Mancinelli, Greer; author interviews with Signora Barberi and Carla Vernaschi Fischer; Giovanni Tesio letter to author.

¶ 'This is how . . .'   Massimo Mila, quoted in Davide Lajolo, *Pavese: il vizio assurdo*, Rizzoli, 1984, p. 53; other quotations from 'Hydrogen', *PT*, and Regge, p. 14.

p. 74

'I would watch . . .'   *PT*, p. 23.

¶ 'And his short-cut . . .'   *PT*, p. 22; *Conversations*, p. 66; Regge, p. 14; presentation of *PT* at Unione Culturale, p. 15 (quoted in *Echi*, p. 80).

¶ 'He chose chemistry because . . .'   BBC *Bookmark*; Rudolf, *VM*, p. 30; 1975 presentation of *PT* at Unione Culturale (quoted in *Echi*, p. 61); Leo Club, Cuneo talk, 1975, quoted in *Echi*, p. 80 (typescript kindly given me by Gabriella Poli).

¶ 'He chose chemistry, then . . .'   *Conversations*, p. 66; Regge, p. 13; Lucarini; *PT*, pp. 52–3.

p. 75

'For me . . .'   *PT*, p. 23.

¶ 'His desire . . .'   Vincenti, p. 34.

'are a bit shocked . . .'   Valabrega interview, 1981, *VM*, p. 144.

¶ 'When he looked back . . .'   'double leap' quotation from 'Carbon', *PT*, p. 233.

¶ 'But of course . . .'   'almost prohibited' from Ferrero, 'Primo Levi scrittore'.

p. 76

'I have often . . .'   PL, 'Il linguaggio degli odori', *Opere II*, p. 837.

Bar Mitzvah

¶ 'Religion made only . . .' and next ¶   PL in interviews with Stefano Jesurum, 'Primo Levi', in *Essere ebrei in Italia*, Longanesi, 1987; Daniela Amsallem, 'Primo Levi, juif de retour', in *Les Nouveaux Cahiers*, No. 114, Autumn 1993; Alberto Gozzi, 'Conversazione con Primo Levi', RAI, 13 January 1985; Giuseppe Grieco, 'God and I', in *VM*.

¶ 'Primo never went . . .'   PL in interview with Silvia Giacomoni, 'Il mago Merlino e l'uomo fabbro', in *Conversazioni e interviste*, in section omitted from '*The Wrench*' in *VM; PT*, pp. 35–6; PL in contribution to 'La festa più bella', *Shalom*, August 1981.

¶ 'But he didn't . . .'   'Le parole fossili', in *Opere II*, p. 819 (untranslated); author interviews in GCD.

¶ 'Then in his thirteenth . . .'   PL in interviews with Gozzi and Grieco, as above.

p. 77

¶ 'When the writer . . .' and next three ¶¶   PL in interviews with Gozzi, Grieco, and Jesurum as above.

p. 78

¶ 'At the end of his life . . .'   PL in Jesurum, summarized in *Echi*, p. 291.

¶ 'He seemed so calm . . .'   'I was extraordinarily shy . . .' from Tesio, S. Salvatore, p. 267 and letter to author.

p. 79

'between the heaven . . .'   *PT*, p. 22.

¶ 'Perhaps this was . . .'   From author interview with Mario Piacenza.

¶ 'Of course the most . . .'   Valabrega interview, 1981, in *VM*, p. 139; Dini & Jesurum, pp. 19–20; Tesio, S. Salvatore, p. 267 and letter to author. On the habit of blushing, see also PL, 'Trattamento di qiuescenza', *Opere I*, p. 559, translated as 'Retirement Fund' in *TSD*, see p. 117.

¶ 'As late as seventeen . . .'   *DL*, Ch. 3; Dini & Jesurum, pp. 18–19; *Conversations*, p. 66.

¶ 'For his lack . . .' and next three ¶¶   *DL*, Ch. 3.

p. 80

¶ 'What was this? . . .'   Taped interview with PL by Silvia and Giovanni Tesio, January 1986; *Conversations*, pp. 66–7; Tesio, S. Salvatore.

¶ 'A year later . . .'   Tesio, S. Salvatore, p. 268; author interviews with Ernesto Ferrero.

¶ 'Primo wrote Chapter 3 . . .' and next eight ¶¶   *DL*, Ch. 3. Typescript kindly given me by Ernesto Ferrero.

p. 82

¶ 'This is not how it looked . . .'   'I haven't left it . . .' from 'Very Important Piemontesi' radio interview, 21 May 1981; 'I am faithful . . .' from Valabrega interview, 1981, *VM*, p. 141; author interviews with GCD, Luciana Accati, AS.

¶ 'But they were not . . .'   'most of his friends at school . . .' from PL interview by Giuseppe Grieco, 'God and I', *VM*, p. 274.

'Agli amici', *Opere II*, p. 623, my translation.

pp. 84–9

Enrico   Most of the information in this section comes from author interviews with 'Enrico', Mario Piacenza (actually faxes, since Dr Piacenza lives in Peru). Also from Regge, p. 15. All quotations are from 'Hydrogen', unless attributed to Mario Piacenza.

p. 86

¶ 'This possibility of explosion . . .'   'Throughout his life he repeated': see e.g. *Echi*, pp. 18, 72, 97–8. Also e.g. in Grassano, 'Conversation with Primo Levi', *VM*, p. 127. The complete typescript was kindly given me by Gabriella Poli.

p. 87

'What were we able . . .'   *PT*, p. 24.

p. 89

'We left . . .'   *PT*, pp. 27–8.

¶ 'In later life . . .'   See e.g. PL, 'L'Intolleranza razziale', *Opere I*, p. 1293 (talk given in November 1979; see p. 1310); and PL interviews with Gabriella Monticelli, *Epoca*, 10 October 1981, Angelo d'Orsi, 1983/5 (tape kindly given me by Angelo d'Orsi), and Mario Miccinesi, *Uomini e libri*, No. 112, Anno XXIII, January–February 1987 (in *VM*).

¶ 'At school, however . . .'   'reasonably well . . .' from Angelo d'Orsi taped interview; 'We were talking . . .' from Giovanni Tesio, undated letter to the author.

¶ 'To the Catholic journalist . . .'   'As a Jew . . .' from *Conversations*, pp. 6–7, and Vincenti, p. 34; interview by Massimo Dini and Pier Mario Fasanotti, in Dini & Jesurum, pp. 18–19.

p. 90

'I was nineteen . . .'   'Retirement Fund', *TSD*, p. 116.

pp. 91–5

Guido   This section is based on the story 'Un lungo duello', *Opere II*, p. 831, translated as 'A Long Duel' in *OPT*.

p. 93

'On some pretext . . .'   'A Long Duel', p. 56.

p. 94

'Now I noticed . . .'   'A Long Duel', p. 57.

p. 95

Man-made

¶ 'Apart from "Hydrogen" . . .'   'waiting . . . for the surgeon . . .' from PL, Preface to *Roots*, p. 5.

¶ 'The story is called . . .', and the rest of this section   'I sintetici', *Opere I*, p. 588.

p. 98

¶ 'Primo himself certainly . . .'   'tried not to be different' from Fadini, *VM*, p. 85; 'neither Italian nor Jewish . . .' from Angelo d'Orsi taped interview.

p. 99

'. . . but never tried to impress . . .'   Author interviews with Fernanda Pivano.

p. 100

¶ 'Sixty years later . . .'   For obvious reasons of discretion, the Bad Boy will remain unidentified.

¶ 'By his last year of school . . .'   '. . . with Vittorio Daneo and Alfredo Fedele . . .' Author interviews with Alfredo Fedele.

p. 101

¶ 'It shows in something . . .' and next ¶   Information on the history of *Numero Unico* from Clelia Guglielminetti, 'Stampa "dazegliana" degli anni Trenta' in the D'Azeglio *Annuario 1967–68*, pp. 282–90.

¶ 'And the portrait . . .' and quotation 'Any student . . .'   *D'Azeglio sotto spirito*, p. 28 and p. 26 (my translation).

¶ 'However, he was not . . .'   Information on Panetti and Dolza from *D'Azeglio sotto spirito*, pp. 10 and 16; and author interviews with Alfredo Fedele.

p. 102

'You Don't Know How to Study!'   *D'Azeglio sotto spirito*, p. 12 (my translation).

p. 103

¶ 'The Primo Levi who approached . . .'   PL, 'Fra Diavolo sul Po' and author interviews with GCD.

¶ 'Primo certainly felt . . .'   'Fra Diavolo sul Po'; *ITIAM*, p. 112.

¶ 'And then it happened . . .'   e.g. Vincenti, p. 35; Dini & Jesurum, p. 29.

¶ 'The family . . .' and next ¶   Author interviews with GCD and Fernanda Pivano; Fernanda Pivano, 'Il mio compagno Levi ed io', *Corriere della Sera*, 18 April 1987, p. 4, and 'Quella misteriosa bocciatura in italiano', *Elle*, No. 7, July 1994, pp. 41–2. For PL's choosing the Spanish Civil War as well, see Vincenti, p. 35, and e.g. interview with PL by Gian Franco Colombo, *Il Sabato*, 8–14 December 1984, p. 25.

p. 104

¶ 'Over the years . . .'   Different accounts: Vincenti and Dini & Jesurum say that PL handed in a blank paper; to Colombo PL said his essay had been 'drearily obsequious', in 'Fra Diavolo sul Po' that it had been thin.

'the same account of why . . .': in all these; and GCD agreed.

¶ ' "At the time" . . .'   The quotation is from 'Fra Diavolo sul Po'.

¶ 'When I picture . . .'   'Fra Diavolo sul Po'.

p. 105

¶ 'This was not the only . . .'   Colombo interview, *Il Sabato*; Fernanda Pivano, 'Il mio compagno' and 'Quella misteriosa bocciatura'.

¶ 'In October . . .'   D'Azeglio records.

THE HARE AND THE TORTOISE II

p. 106

'Despite his weak . . .'   Vincenti, pp. 32–3 (my translation).

p. 107

¶ 'Then one day . . .' For reasons of discretion, neither the distinguished old gentleman nor the Sportsman will be identified.

p. 109

¶ 'He stares at me . . .' The *La Stampa* edition of the story is 'Polvere olimpica' ('Olympic Dust'), *La Stampa*, 14 August 1984.

p. 111

¶ 'As it turned out . . .' The confirmation of the slapping game and of the Sportsman's identity were given me by the woman I call Gisella.

Chapter 4: Chemistry: 1937–41

p. 112

¶ ' "Night lay . . ." ' Quotation from 'Iron', *PT*, p. 37.

¶ 'Freedom . . .' and next two ¶¶ PL, 'Il segno del chimico', *Opere II*, p. 810, translated as 'The Mark of the Chemist' in *OPT*; author interviews with Gabriella Garda Aliverti, Gianna Balzaretti, Vittorio Berardi, Guido Bonfiglioli, Sidney Calvi, Nico Dallaporta, Silvia Delleani, Leo Gallico, Franco Momigliano, Clara Moschino, Nereo Pezza, Vanna Rava, AS, Vittorio Satta, Ester Valabrega, Emma Vita Levi, and Edith Weisz; and letters from Liborio Casale, Gabriele Pelli, and Marino Revelli.

p. 113

¶ 'But during . . .' Regge, p. 21; Roberto Berardi, *Un Balilla negli Anni Trenta*, L'Arciere, Cuneo, 1994; Bobbio, *30 anni*; 'The Little Theatre of Memory', radio interview with PL, in *VM*, p. 49; Clemente Granata, 'Università, la grande scommessa', in *Trovare Torino*, p. 33.

¶ 'Not a single one . . .' *PT*, p. 40; Regge, pp. 19–21; 'The Little Theatre of Memory'; 'The Mark of the Chemist'; PL letter to Emma Vita Levi, 5 July 1984.

★ Granata, 'Università', p. 32; Yona and Foa, *Noi due*, p. 151.

p. 114

¶ 'In 1937 . . .' Granata, 'Università', p. 33; *PT*, p. 31; author interviews with Gianna Balzaretti; letter from Gabriele Pelli.

¶ 'After the first few . . .' *PT*, pp. 31, 38–9; 'The Mark of the Chemist'; author interviews with Ester Valabrega and Emma Vita Levi.

¶ 'The day started . . .' and next ¶ Granata, 'Università', p. 33; 'The Little Theatre of Memory'; 'The Mark of the Chemist'; author interviews with Gianna Balzaretti, Vittorio Berardi, Clara Moschino, and Vittorio Satta.

p. 115

¶ 'During their four . . .' On PL's *100/100 e lode*: PL made the remark about its reflecting his professors' antifascism more than his own merit to e.g. Regge (p. 21) and in the Angelo d'Orsi taped interview. Nico Dallaporta says on the contrary that a special mark had to be invented on one of PL's papers to reflect his achievement. And Gianlorenzo Marino, in 'Primo Levi chimico e scrittore',

CNS (La Chimica nella scuola), No. 4, September–October 1993, points out that *100/100 e lode* was very rare for Jewish students (p. 3). Certainly PL was the only one in his class to receive it; though both Leo Gallico and Emma Vita Levi got 98 (University of Turin records). Rest of ¶: *PT*, p. 38; 'The Mark of the Chemist'; Regge, p. 19; *Echi*, p. 62; University of Turin records.

pp. 116

Year One: The Racial Laws   For an excellent summary of the history and effects of the racial laws in Italy, see Carpi.

¶ 'His university years . . .'   *Echi*, p. 62.

¶ 'When he arrived . . .'   'Itinerario'; Stille, *Benevolence*, pp. 21, 50–52, 101–2; Angelo d'Orsi taped interview. In fact the early leaders of Giustizia e Libertà in Turin had not been Jewish; but when they were neutralized by a police crackdown in 1933, the new young leaders – Leone Ginzburg and Carlo Levi – were. Hitler had come to power in Germany in 1933, and the most politically sensitive young Jews were already turning against Fascism. PL's cousin Vittorio Foa, for example, joined G. & L. in 1933 (Stille, *Benevolence*, p. 102).

p. 117

¶ 'From 1934 to 1937 . . .'   See Carpi and e.g. Stille, *Benevolence*, pp. 44–9 and 140.

¶ 'In 1937 . . .'   Carpi; Stille, *Benevolence*, pp. 65, 140; Yona and Foa, *Noi due*, p. 190; and De Felice, pp. 214–15.

¶ 'This was the atmosphere . . .'   Regge, p. 21; author interviews with BGS.

¶ 'In March 1938 . . .'   Stille, *Benevolence*, pp. 70, 140; Yona and Foa, *Noi due*, p. 193; De Felice, pp. 555–6.

¶ 'The government . . .'   Carpi; De Felice, pp. 567–8, 576–82; Stille, *Benevolence*, p. 77.

p. 118

¶ 'The racial laws . . .'   De Felice, p. 218; Stille, *Benevolence*, p. 141; Berardi, *Un Balilla*, pp. 75, 110; EGT, 'Primo Levi: Parcours', p. 4; PL interview with Giorgio De Rienzo, *Famiglia cristiana*, 20 July 1975, and letter to Rosanna Benzi in *Gli Altri*, 3rd trimester, 1979, in *Opere I*, p. 1283. The story of Victor Emmanuel II comes from Mirella Serri, *La Stampa*, 9 February 1997, Special Supplement on *La tregua*, p. 2.

¶ 'Nonetheless . . .'   Rudolf, *VM*, p. 24. Mixed marriages among Primo's classmates: Sandro Delmastro tried to marry Ester Valabrega, but failed (see below, page 144); both Emma Vita Levi and Lilia Beer married Catholics.

¶ 'Of course it was . . .'   Author interviews with GCD.

p. 119

¶ 'As a result . . .'   On the university rules about Jewish students, see Cavaglion 1993 and Marino, 'Primo Levi chimico e scrittore'. Also author interviews with Ester Valabrega and Maria Vittoria Malvano.

¶ 'In the first moments . . .'   Vincenti, p. 39; PL letter to Rosanna Benzi in *Gli Altri*, and Preface to *La tregua* schools edn, 1965, p. 6. The quotation on PL's withdrawal comes from *PT*, p. 40; the information on the other students' not withdrawing comes from author interviews with Gianna Balzaretti, Vittorio

Berardi, Sidney Calvi, and Nereo Pezza, and from her letters from Gabriele Pelli and Marino Revelli. One of the other Jewish students, Leo Gallico, agreed.

¶ 'On this level . . .'   Quotation from Vincenti, p. 39.

'But on another . . .'   Quotations from PL, Preface to *La tregua* schools edn, 1965, and interview with Giorgio De Rienzo, *Famiglia cristiana*, 20 July 1975.

p. 120

¶ 'He did not admit . . .'   *PT*, p. 35; letter to Rosanna Benzi in *Gli Altri*; Angelo d'Orsi taped interview; Dini & Jesurum, p. 115.

¶ 'By the end . . .'   Author interviews with Vanna Rava and Guido Bonfiglioli.

¶ 'The racial laws . . .'   Author interviews with Ester Valabrega, Nereo Pezza, Vittorio Satta. The story of the Mineralogy exam in this and the next two ¶¶ is from author interviews with Guido Bonfiglioli.

'At the end . . .'   Also University of Turin records; PL letter to Emma Vita Levi, 5 July 1984.

pp. 121

Zinc   The main source for this section is 'Zinc', *PT*. Background information on Ponzio is from PL's taped interview with Angelo d'Orsi; Levi Montalcini, *Senz'olio*, p. 95; and author interviews with Gianna Balzaretti, Silvia Delleani, Bernard Delmay, Clara Moschino, Emma Vita Levi and Vittorio Berardi, and her letter from Marino Revelli.

p. 122

¶ 'Ponzio's instructions . . .'   Professor Ponzio's notations on the purity of zinc (*PT*, p. 33) are exactly as PL said: I thank Bernard Delmay for sending me page copies from Ponzio's book (*Preparazioni, reazioni ed esperienze di Chimica Organica per l'anno academico 1939–40*, Litografia Felice Gili, Turin, 1940), including p. 238 on zinc sulphate.

p. 123

'the praise of purity . . .'   *PT*, p. 34.

'add a drop . . .'   *PT*, p. 34.

p. 124

¶ 'In the original . . .'   Typescript in Einaudi Archive.

¶ 'As soon as I suggested . . .'   Author interviews with AS, Gabriella Garda Aliverti, Ester Valabrega, Vittorio Berardi, Silvia Delleani, Nereo Pezza, Vanna Rava, Emma Vita Levi, and Edith Weisz.

'When I met her . . .' and next three ¶¶   Author interviews with Clara Moschino.

p. 125

'I was desperate . . .'   *PT*, p. 35.

¶ 'The real Primo . . .'   The *La Stampa* version of 'Dialogo di un poeta e di un medico' was published on 2 October 1977. Again (as with 'Polvere olimpica' and 'Un lungo duello'), this version is shorter, and leaves out the more personal material. The Einaudi typescript includes this material, and is dated 25 September 1977: clearly, therefore, PL cut it out for *La Stampa*, rather than adding it later.

'The universe . . .' and 'He hesitated . . .'   'Dialogo di un poeta', *Opere II*, p. 114.

p. 126

¶ 'In the young poet's description . . .'   See e.g. PL's debate with students at

Pesaro, 5 May 1986 (typescript kindly given me by Gabriella Poli). The references to Leopardi are in *DL*, Ch. 3.

¶ 'Even without . . .' Information about Primo's going to a doctor for the first time comes from the doctor himself, who wishes to remain anonymous.

¶ 'In his second year . . .' University of Turin records; *PT*, pp. 38–9; 'The Mark of the Chemist'.

p. 127

¶ 'Luckily . . .' Information on De Paolini and Fenoglio from University of Turin records; PL letter to Emma Vita Levi, 5 July 1984; and author interviews with Gianna Balzaretti, Vittorio Berardi, Sidney Calvi, Leo Gallico, Clara Moschino, Vittorio Satta, Ester Valabrega and Edith Weisz, and her letter from Marino Revelli.

¶ 'There was another suicide . . .' Author interviews with Gabriella Garda Aliverti, Gianna Balzaretti, Clara Moschino, Nereo Pezza, AS, and Emma Vita Levi; *PT*, pp. 32–3. For Agostino Neri's marks and Caselli's service, University of Turin documents. Neri was the son of the Professor of French at the university, and brother of a future friend of PL's. Caselli was born in 1885, so was about fifty-three in 1938–9; he died only four years later, in 1942.

¶ 'When the racial laws . . .' Author interviews with SO, EGT, and BGS. AS's family was so assimilated that all three brothers married 'out'.

¶ 'When Vittore Veneziani . . .' Author interviews with Guido Bonfiglioli, GCD, BGS, Maria Vittoria Malvano, and Ugo Sacerdote.

p. 128

¶ 'Primo took part . . .' Author interviews with GCD.

¶¶ 'He would already . . .' and 'He too . . .' Author interviews with Gabriella Garda Aliverti, Luciana Nissim, GCD, Clara Moschino, EGT, Gianna Balzaretti, Leo Gallico, and Renato Portesi. See also Annamaria Guadagni, 'La memoria del bene, Ritratto di Luciana Nissim' in *Diario della settimana* (*Unità* weekly), 26 February–4 March 1997, pp. 14–21, on p. 15.

pp. 128–9

Information on AS and his family from: Cesare Cases, 'Ricordo di Primo Levi' in *Tre narratori*, ed. Gianfranco Folena, Liviana Editrice, p. 99; and author interviews with BGS, AS, Bruno Salmoni, EGT, and Nico Dallaporta. AS sees his friendship with PL in terms of opposites himself.

Information on BGS: author interviews with BGS; BGS in Blakeway and Rosenfeld TV.

pp. 129–31

Information on SO: author interviews with SO, and her letter from him, 17 December 1999.

Information on EGT: author interviews with EGT, and her letter from him, 3 February 2000.

Information on Franco Momigliano: author interviews with EGT, AS, and Luciana Nissim; also Guadagni, 'La memoria del bene'.

Information on Luciana Nissim: author interviews with Luciana Nissim and Guadagni, 'La memoria del bene'.

p. 131

¶ 'Of course this wasn't . . .' Information on others in the Jewish group from author interviews with GCD, SO, EGT, AS, Luciana Nissim, Guido Bonfiglioli, Maria Vittoria Malvano, and Renata Gaddini.

Drawing of Italo Diena from *Chronache di Milano*, text by Ada Della Torre, drawings by EGT, 1943; now reproduced in *I giochi della paura*, Le Chateau dizioni, Aosta, 1999.

¶ 'No: by the *piccoli* . . .' and next two ¶¶ Information on the Artoms from *Moralità armata*; PL, 'Un parco dedicato a Emanuele Artom', *La Stampa*, 1 April 1984 (in *Opere II*, p. 1211); and author interviews with Luciana Nissim, Maria Vittoria Malvano, GCD, Guido Bonfiglioli.

pp. 133–4

For the story of Emanuele Artom: as well as *Moralità armata* and 'Un parco dedicato a Emanuele Artom': PL in *PT*, p. 52, and *Mondoperaio*, in *VM*; Benvenuta Treves, 'Emanuele Artom (1915–1944)', *Eco dell'educazione ebraica*, No. 7, April 1955, p. 13; Donatella Gay Rochat, *La Resistenza nelle valle Valdesi*, Claudiana, Turin, 1969, pp. 13, 99–100; Antonio Prearo, *Terra ribelle*, Silvestrelli, 1948, pp. 119, 126; Michele Fiorio, *Resistenza e liberazione nella provincia di Torino (1943–45)*, Gribaudi Editore, 1993, pp. 126–7; Ada Gobetti, *Diario partigiano*, Einaudi, 1956, p. 114.

p. 134

¶ 'In Primo's second year . . .' Quotation from *PT*, pp. 50–51.

¶ 'What we know now . . .' *Mondoperaio* and Angelo d'Orsi taped interview; author interviews with BGS, SO, and Guido Bonfiglioli.

¶¶ 'Whenever people . . .' and 'Above all . . .' Author interviews with Anna Cases, GCD, BGS, and Guido Bonfiglioli.

p. 135

¶ 'Primo felt . . .' Annamaria Guadagni, 'Primo Levi', *Unità*, 21 February 1993, p. 18; author interviews with AS.

¶ 'Primo had started . . .' and next ¶ Papuzzi; author interviews with Luciana Nissim.

p. 136

¶ 'That he did so . . .' Alberto Cavaglion discusses mountaineering as a key to PL in *Primo Levi e Se questo è un uomo*, pp. 46–7. Also: Massimo Mila, 'Alpinismo come cultura', *Il Ponte*, Nos. 8–9, 1947, pp. 910–14; Bocca; and author interviews with Carla Gobetti.

¶ 'One reason why . . .' SO in Blakeway; *PT*, p. 45; Papuzzi, in *VM*; *Echi*, p. 240; author interviews with Carla Gobetti and Guido Bonfiglioli; letter to the author from Guido Bonfiglioli, 10 November 1995.

¶ 'But essentially . . .' 'L'Alpinismo? E' la libertà di sbagliare' is the title of Papuzzi's article on PL as a mountaineer.

'There is a way . . .' Mila, 'Alpinismo'.

p. 137

¶ 'All mountaineering . . .' PL, 'La carne dell'orso', *Opere I*, p. 1125; Papuzzi, *VM*, p. 60.

p. 138

¶ 'To Primo . . .'   Author interviews with Anna Cases and Clara Moschino.

¶ 'Sandro was born . . .' and next three ¶¶   'Iron', *PT*; author interviews with Ettore Delmastro, Ester Valabrega, Gabriella Garda Aliverti, and Clara Moschino.

p. 139

¶ 'Sandro was a loner . . .'   University of Turin records; BGS in Blakeway; and as well as those cited for the previous ¶¶, author interviews with AS, Edith Weisz, and Nereo Pezza.

'did not belong . . .'   *PT*, p. 44.

¶ 'He spent every Sunday . . .' and next seven ¶¶   'Iron' and 'La carne dell'orso'; and author interviews with AS and Ettore Delmastro.

p. 141

'And now . . .'   *PT*, p. 48.

¶ 'This rare adventure . . .' and next ¶   Author interviews with AS, Ester Valabrega, Ettore Delmastro, and Tullio Regge. On PL's problems with the Delmastro family over 'Iron', see also Greer, *VM*, pp. 6–7. In interviews with me, Ettore Delmastro put the family's objection as 'Sandro wasn't a Communist.' But since 'Iron' doesn't say that he was, this was clearly a distortion. Ester Valabrega is clear that their real objection was to the suggestion that they were 'poor, simple people', who needed the money Sandro could bring in (*PT*, p. 41): and 'Indeed it is true,' she says, 'that the Delmastros never cared about money.'

p. 142

¶ 'He knew himself . . .'   PL letter to Emma Vita Levi, 5 July 1984.

¶ 'There is a way . . .'   e.g. AS and EGT suggest this way of reading PL.

¶ 'Now this is certainly . . .'   Quotations are from the poem 'Agli amici' and *PT*, pp. 40 and 44.

¶ 'And yet it was . . .' and next ¶   'Iron'; author interviews with Ester Valabrega, Ettore Delmastro, Edith Weisz, and Gianna Balzaretti.

'Today I know . . .'   *PT*, p. 49.

p. 144

¶ 'Sandro was the first . . .' and next thirteen ¶¶   Author interviews with Ettore Delmastro and Ester Valabrega.

Also:

¶ 'Primo, who had hoped . . .' and next ¶   Author interviews with EGT and AS; Gay Rochat, *La Resistenza*, pp. 43–4, and Prearo, *Terra ribelle*, pp. 50–51; Gianni Aliberti interview for ANED, May 1982, p. 6. Sandro had hoped to fight alongside Primo as well (author interviews with EGT).

★ Prearo, *Terra ribelle*, p. 27; Gay Rochat, *La Resistenza*, p. 44; Gianni Aliberti, ANED interview.

p. 145

¶ 'Back in Turin . . .'   *Notizario Gielle*, April–May 1948, Anno II, No. 45, p. 6, 'Sandro Delmastro'; *25 aprile: la Resistenza in Piemonte*, ANPI, Comitato provinciale di Torino, Orma, 1946, p. 36 (republished 1984).

¶ 'Giorgio Agosti . . .'   *Un'amicizia partigiana*, ed. Giovanni De Luna, the wartime letters of Giorgio Agosti and Livio Bianco, leaders of Giustizia e Libertà: letters of 16 May 1944 (p. 107) and 11 December 1944 (p. 360).

¶ 'He was taken . . .' and next ¶   Author interviews with Nuto and Anna Revelli. The quotation is from 'Iron', p. 48.

p. 146

¶ 'After the war . . .'   *La guerra di liberazione 1943–45: I caduti in provincia di Cuneo*, Istituto Storico della Resistenza, Cuneo, 1989, p. 27.

¶ '"Every time . . .'   'La carne dell'orso'; Vincenti, p. 41.

¶ 'In the last two years . . .'   *PT*, pp. 51–2; author interviews with AS and EGT. AS began talking to more political friends like Franco Momigliano in the last years of university, but made no active move to join them until 8 September 1943.

¶ 'In his third year . . .'   University of Turin records; author interviews with Emma Vita Levi, Clara Moschino, Vittorio Berardi, Vittorio Satta, Ester Valabrega, and Tullio Regge; and Regge, p. 21. PL's minor thesis under Milone was *I raggi elettronici, Electronic Rays*. Milone was Co-Director and then Director of the Chemical Institute from 1948 to 1980, and was made Professor Emeritus in 1982. He died in 1985. (University of Turin records.)

p. 147

¶ 'In *The Periodic Table* . . .'   *PT*, pp. 52–3; *Echi*, p. 81; Lucarini; PL, 'L'Assimetria e la vita', *Prometeo*, Anno 2, No. 7, September 1984, p. 62, in *Opere II*, p. 1231.

¶ 'As usual . . .' and next ¶   University of Turin records; Mancinelli interview; Roth; author interviews with BGS, Vanna Rava, Ester Valabrega. For PL being capable of becoming a research scientist: author interviews with Nico Dallaporta and Tullio Regge; also Regge in *Ateneo*.

p. 148

¶ 'And what of that last . . .'   Author interviews with BGS, Guido Bonfiglioli, Sidney Calvi, and Leo Gallico, and letter from Liborio Casale.

¶ 'In those last two . . .'   University of Turin records; *Ateneo*, p. 6; Regge, p. 20; author interviews with Clara Moschino, Nereo Pezza, Emma Vita Levi, and Edith Weisz.

¶ 'The explosion of energy . . .'   'Potassium', *PT*, p. 53; Regge, p. 21. Ponzio also refused Emma Vita Levi. She and Leo Gallico were both finally taken on by Professor Corbellini at the Polytechnic Institute.

¶ 'He did finally . . .'   Regge, p. 21; *Ateneo*, p. 8.

p. 149

¶ 'With his *100/100* . . .'   University of Turin records; author interviews with Edith Weisz and Ester Valabrega.

¶ 'So – except . . .' and next ¶   For PL's fear that a degree would be useless to a Jew in 1941, see the original opening of 'Potassium' in the Einaudi Archive: 'I had probably got a good degree. But what could I do with it?' For the rest of the ¶, and the next, author interviews with AS, Ester Valabrega, Leo Gallico, Emma Vita Levi, and Edith Weisz.

p. 150

¶ 'In the late 70s . . .'   Regge in *Ateneo*, p. 22, and author interviews with him.

¶ 'In 1941 . . .'   *PT*, p. 53; Regge, p. 21.

¶ 'Dallaporta was . . .'   'Potassium'; author interviews with and letters from Nico Dallaporta; author interviews with Guido Bonfiglioli.

p. 151

¶ 'By January . . .'   *PT*, pp. 50, 54, and original typescript of 'Potassium' in Einaudi Archive.

p. 152

¶ 'At the time . . .'   *PT*, pp. 55–6; author interviews with Nico Dallaporta; University of Turin documents; Regge in *Ateneo*, p. 7.

¶ 'This time . . .' and next four ¶¶   'Potassium', pp. 55–7; author interviews with and letters from Nico Dallaporta.

p. 154

'During those months . . .'   *PT*, p. 57.

¶ 'The closer one looks . . .' to end of section on 'Potassium'   'Potassium'; author interviews with and letters from Nico Dallaporta; author interviews with AS and Guido Bonfiglioli.

p. 155

¶ 'Primo spares us . . .' and next five ¶¶   'Potassium', pp. 58–60. On PL having written several times about rejecting the consolations of religion: in *ITIAM*, and e.g. in 'Verso occidente' in *Vizio di forma* (*Opere I*, p. 578, translated as 'Westward' in *TSD*).

p. 157

'because it . . .'   *PT*, p. 58.

'a double leap . . .'   *PT*, p. 233.

¶ 'For the first months . . .' and next ¶   *DL*, Ch. 3.

p. 158

¶ 'In fact . . .'   Author interviews with Guido Bonfiglioli, and letter from him 1 November 1998.

¶ 'Walden's Inversion . . .' and next four ¶¶   *DL*, Ch. 3; Guido Bonfiglioli letter to author, 1 November 1998; Enzo Borello, 'Primo Levi studente di chimica', *Ateneo*, p. 7; PL, *L'inversione di Walden, Tesi di Laurea in Chimica Pura, Regia Università di Torino, Anno 1941* (*Walden's Inversion, Thesis for the Degree in Pure Chemistry, University of Turin, 1941*; supervisor Professor Giacomo Ponzio): conclusion on pages 37–8. This thesis was printed and bound in 1997, as part of the commemorations for the tenth anniversary of Primo's death.

p. 159

¶ 'On the text-book . . .' and next two ¶¶   *DL*, Ch. 3; author interviews with Guido Bonfiglioli.

ALBERTO

The translation of Dante used is the author's.

Chapter 5: Nickel: 1941–2

p. 167

¶ 'When Primo . . .' Author interviews with GCD, Antonia Levi; PL, 'Fra Diavolo sul Po'.

p. 168

¶ 'Clara Moschino . . .' Author interviews with Clara Moschino; Lucarini.

¶ 'Then, as though . . .' Author interviews with GCD and Jole Segre; Cesare Luzzati death certificate, Atto No. 1313, Ufficio 1, Parte 1, Serie 1, Anno 1941, date 26 June 1941.

¶ 'A few months . . .' Alberto Cavaglion, *La scuola ebraica a Torino (1938–1943)*, Pluriversa, 1993, p. 53; PL, 'Lettera a Euge', *Ha Keillah*, No. 4, April 1978.

p. 169

¶ 'Shortly afterwards . . .' and next two ¶¶ EGT, 'La Resistenza ha cominciato in Via Roma', *Ha Keillah*, No. 3, February 1978, and in Rosenfeld TV; PL, 'Lettera a Euge', *Ha Keillah*, No. 4, April 1978, and in Angelo d'Orsi taped interview.

¶ 'He explained why . . .' For PL starting his Balangero job in December 1941, see *Ordine dei Chimici* records, Turin; for its being 7 December, see Vincenti, p. 42, and *PT*, p. 64. For the poster nights being in mid-October, see Emanuele Artom's diary entry for 18 October, in Cavaglion, *La scuola ebraica*, p. 53; and *Hatikwa*, Rome, November 1960, p. 3, which gives the date as 15 October.

p. 170

¶ Primo Levi, then . . .', next two ¶¶, and 'Guido . . .' EGT and PL letters in *Ha Keillah*.

¶ 'This was Primo's position . . .' See *PT*, p. 61.

'The doorbell . . .' and next three ¶¶ 'Nickel', *PT*; *Ateneo*, p. 11; Bocca, p. 4 (typescript kindly given me by Gabriella Poli).

pp. 172–8

Nickel 'Nickel', *PT*; Vincenti, p. 42; Bocca, p. 4; PL interview with Enrico Boeri, *Techniche chimiche* 12/83, p. 30 (in *VM*, p. 65); Ennio Mariotti documents and letters, kindly given me by Signora Mariotti; author interviews with Signora Mariotti and Vanna Mariotti Grosso; articles on the asbestos mine at Balangero in *La Stampa*, 1 and 3 October 1995. The mine finally closed in 1990, and has since been sued several times by employees who contracted lung cancer there.

p. 177

¶ 'Primo Levi wrote . . .' On PL's telling the events of Balangero straight away: author interviews with EGT. EGT thinks that PL wrote the stories down straight away as well, just as BGS thinks about 'The Mnemagogues'. The quotation 'they felt ill at ease with me . . .' comes from *DL*, Ch. 3.

pp. 178–81

Lead and Mercury *PT*, pp. 79–108. *Re* Auschwitz stopping PL from becoming a conventional literary writer, see also Paul Bailey in Blakeway, and Giovanni Tesio in *Piemonte litterario*, pp. 149–50.

p. 181

¶ 'On the morning . . .'   Death certificate Cesare Levi, Atto No. 648, Ufficio 1, Parte 1, Anno 1942, date 24 March 1942; Vincenti, p. 42; author interviews with GCD.

¶ 'It was the end . . .'   For PL suffering over the death of his father: Lucia Levi letter to Anna Yona, 29 November 1988.

¶ 'He returned . . .' and next five ¶¶   'Phosphorus', *PT*, p. 109; author interviews with Gabriella Garda Aliverti, GCD, and SO.

BURNING

All information on Ennio Mariotti from Signora Mariotti and her daughter, Vanna Mariotti Grosso; and from all the patents, letters, *curricula vitae*, etc. of Ennio Mariotti's life which Signora Mariotti kindly gave me.

p. 186

¶ 'Acids, caustics, fires . . .'   For PL's worry about accidents, see e.g. Lucarini; and pp. 555–8 below. For responsibility driving him into depression, and making him want to resign: information from Gisella.

¶ 'But like all his failures . . .' and next five ¶¶   For the date of 'Sulphur': the typescript in the Einaudi Archive is dated 31 August 1950. For the rest of the ¶¶: PL, *La chiave a stella (The Wrench)*; Boeri interview, *VM*, pp. 56–7; PL, 'La forza dell'ambra', *Opere II*, p. 759, translated as 'The Force of Amber' in *OPT*, and 'Stabile/Instabile', *Opere I*, p. 778, translated as 'Stable/Unstable' in *OPT*.

p. 188

'to our social behaviour . . .'   'Stable/Unstable'.

¶ 'In late 1996 . . .'   Giuseppe Bottai was the Minister of Education (Vincenti, p. 39). On his being one of the fiercest antisemites, see De Felice, pp. 242, 282, 302–4.

p. 189

¶ 'My friend the Biographer . . .' and next two ¶¶   See Michael Holroyd, 'Smoke with Fire', in *Works on Paper*, Little, Brown, 2002, pp. 10–19; extra details from private conversation.

Chapter 6: Milan: July 1942 – 8 September 1943

p. 195

¶ 'In 1933 . . .'   Letter to the author from Ada Ortona, 22 December 1999, and author interviews with Silvio and Ada Ortona.

¶ 'Then as now . . .'   SO in Blakeway; author interviews with EGT and Anna Cases; letter to the author from EGT, 3 February 2000. Also PL interviews with Giorgio Bocca, as above, and with Enzo Biagi, in *1935 e dintorni*, Milan, 1982, p. 87. EGT arrived in Milan in January 1941 (EGT, 'Primo Levi: Parcours', p. 5).

p. 196

¶ 'The next to arrive . . .'   Author interviews with SO and EGT, and letter to
the author from SO, 17 December 1999; 'Gold', *PT*, pp. 127–8; Annamaria
Guadagni, 'Primo Levi', *Unità*, 21 February 1993; Ada Della Torre, *Messaggio
speciale*, Editori Riuniti, Biblioteca Giovani, 7, 1979, pp. 14–15.

Drawings throughout this chapter come from *Chronache di Milano* by Ada Della
Torre and EGT.

p. 197

¶ 'The next to appear . . .'   Author interviews with SO and Carla Consonni Maestro.

¶ 'When Primo arrived . . .'   He arrived at Wander in July 1942 (*Ordine dei Chimici*
records). 'Phosphorus', *PT*; author interviews with Gabriella Garda Aliverti and
SO.

p. 198

¶ 'And so the time . . .'   Author interviews with SO, EGT; 'Gold', *PT*, pp. 128–
9; PL, 'L'Europa all'inferno', *La Stampa*, 27 August 1979 (*Opere I*, p. 1286), 'Il
faraone con la svastica', *La Stampa*, 9 September 1983 (*Opere II*, p. 1190), and
ANED interview, 1983, *VM*, pp. 235–6; PL interviews with Enzo Biagi in *1935
e dintorni*, p. 87, and deposition in trial of Friedrich Bosshammer, 1971, *La
Stampa*, 25 April 2001.

¶ 'Politics excepted . . .' and next ¶   Vincenti, p. 43; Della Torre, *Messaggio*, p. 13;
Guadagni *Unità* article, 1993; 'Gold'; *Chronache di Milano*; author interviews with
SO, EGT, Gabriella Garda Aliverti, Carla Maestro, and Anna Cases, and author's
letter from SO, 17 December 1999.

p. 200

¶ 'In all this Primo . . .'   Author interviews with Gabriella Garda Aliverti, Carla
Maestro, and Anna Cases. See also Luciana Nissim in Silvia Giacomoni, *La
Repubblica*, 16 February 1997: '*tra gli amici, era il più fine, aveva qualcosa di speciale*':
'amongst the friends, he was the most refined, he had something special'.

¶ 'Euge, Silvio and Primo . . .'   'Gold', *PT*, p. 129; SO, *Disgrazia (Monte)*, 28 June
1983, kindly given me by SO; author interviews with him. EGT says that they
went climbing every week.

¶ 'They set off . . .' and next six ¶¶   PL, 'Fine settimana' ('Weekend'), *Opere I*,
p. 192; SO, *Disgrazia (Monte)* and interviews with the author.

p. 204

¶ 'Primo even says so . . .'   'Gold', *PT*, p. 129; author interviews with Gabriella
Garda Aliverti, Carla Maestro, and Anna Cases.

¶ 'Anna was small . . .' and next two ¶¶   Author interviews with Anna Cases and
Gabriella Garda Aliverti.

pp. 205–8

Phosphorus   'Phosphorus'; typescript of 'Phosphorus' in the Einaudi Archive;
author interviews with and letters from Gabriella Garda Aliverti. The poem on
page 208 is 'Lilith', dated 25 May 1965, in *CP*, p. 26.

p. 209

¶ 'Gabriella married . . .'   'Gold', *PT*, pp. 127–8; author interviews with Gabriella
Garda Aliverti.

¶ 'Did the group . . .'   'Sereno', 'equilibrato', 'sempre lo stesso' (serene, balanced, always the same) is the single most common description of PL throughout his life, by everyone from intimate friends like BGS and SO to distant acquaintances. Rest of ¶: author interviews with Anna Cases, Carla Maestro, and Gabriella Garda Aliverti.

¶ 'Carla Consonni was Euge's . . .' and next ¶   Author interviews with Carla Consonni Maestro.

p. 210

¶ 'When no one . . .'   Author interviews with Anna Cases and Carla Maestro.

¶ 'Vanda Maestro was . . .'   'Gold'; author interviews with Gabriella Garda Aliverti, Anna Cases, GCD, EGT, Carla Maestro, SO, and Ester Valabrega.

¶ 'She hadn't always . . .' and next five ¶¶   Background information on Vanda Maestro and her family from Renata Gaddini, Enzo Yacchia, Guido Bonfiglioli, Carla Maestro, Maria Vittoria Malvano, and Graziella Diena. See also the portrait of Vanda Maestro in *Donne piemontesi nella lotta di liberazione*, Commissione Femminile dell'ANPI provinciale di Torino, 1953, pp. 87–8, which I am certain on stylistic grounds was written by PL. (See below, Notes to Chapter 7, page 763.)

p. 212

¶ 'The new version . . .'   Guadagni in *Unità*, 1993; author interviews with SO, Ester Valabrega, and EGT. Ada was echoing *Inferno*, Canto IV, lines 104–5: 'Così andammo infino alla lumera / parlando cose che 'l tacere è bello' ('Thus we went on as far as the light, / talking of things which are best left in silence'). PL echoes them in *ITIAM*, p. 22.) I thank Giovanni Tesio for finding these lines for me.

¶ 'Everyone was writing . . .'   'Gold', *PT*, pp. 127–8; author interviews with EGT, Carla Maestro, and SO.

p. 213

¶ 'On top of all this . . .'   *Libri segreti*, 28 October 1942, now reproduced in *I giochi della paura*, Le Chateau Edizioni, Aosta, 1999.

¶ ' "I . . . fantasized . . ."'   'Gold', *PT*, p. 128. Tesio, *Piemonte letterario*, p. 149, and interviews with the author suggest that PL first thought of 'Carbon' in *liceo*; *Ateneo*, p. 10 and BBC *Bookmark* suggest that it was written *c.* 1961–2. For Ada and SO writing poetry: as well as 'Gold', author interviews with SO, EGT, and Carla Maestro. For PL's Milan story having been intended as a short novel, Vincenti, p. 43.

p. 214

¶ 'Only one . . .' and next ¶   'Crescenzago', *CP*, pp. 3–4.

¶ 'These hopeless . . .'   For 'Many years later he told Silvio . . .': author interviews with SO.

p. 215

¶ 'Primo recognized . . .'   'Gold', *PT*, p. 128; Vincenti, p. 43. On PL's poetry as a locus of expression for his unconscious, see *Echi*, Ch. 4, 'Poesia, curiosa infezione', especially pp. 88–91.

¶ 'He himself made no . . .'   PL, ANED interview 1983, *VM*, p. 224; Papuzzi, *VM*, p. 62; *Conversations*, p. 60; Vincenti, p. 43.

pp. 215–18

'Uomo' 'Uomo' is unpublished, and has never been seen by anyone else, as far as I know. I thank Gisella for showing it to me. All quotations in this section are from her typescript.

p. 218

¶ 'The journey from before . . .' For split and division as PL's most common image for himself, see e.g. Fadini, *VM*, p. 85, and Tesio's interview with him, 'Credo che il mio destino profondo sia la spaccatura' ('I think my profound fate is division'), *Nuovasocietà*, 208, 16 January 1981 (in *Conversazioni e interviste*). The 'Argon' quotation is in *PT*, p. 9.

¶ 'That future . . .' 'Gold', *PT*, p. 129.

¶ 'Some time before . . .' Author interviews with Camillo Treves.

¶ 'Around the end of 1942 . . .' and next ¶ 'Gold', *PT*, p. 129; Della Torre, *Messaggio*, pp. 9, 12–13; author interviews with SO and EGT; and EGT, *La Resistenza a Cogne*, June 1997, p. 2. I thank Eugenio Gentili Tedeschi for giving me this and other as yet unpublished writings.

p. 219

¶ 'But their preparation . . .' and next ¶ 'Gold', *PT*, p. 130; Della Torre, *Messaggio*, p. 13; Paul Ginsborg, *A History of Contemporary Italy*, Penguin, 1990, pp. 12–13; Sergio Favretto, *Casale partigiana, 1943–1945*, Libertas Club, Casale Monferrato, 1977, p. 9.

¶ 'The friends knew . . .' and next three ¶¶ Della Torre, *Messaggio*, p. 13 and Ginsborg, *A History*, p. 13; PL, 'Il faraone'; author interviews with SO and EGT.

★ Author interviews with BGS.

p. 220

'The news . . .' 'Il faraone'.

¶ 'But Silvio . . .' Author interviews with SO and EGT.

¶ 'But even for Primo . . .' 'Il faraone'; Ginsborg, *A History*. For the Italian Army attitude, see e.g. Revelli, 'Il sergente nella neve', and Berardi, *Un balilla*.

p. 221

¶ 'At that moment . . .' and next ¶ 'Gold', *PT*, p. 130; 'Il faraone'; and author interviews with SO, BGS, and Renata Gaddini.

¶ 'Ada was . . .' Author interviews with EGT, SO, and Carla Maestro.

¶ 'Primo watched . . .' Vincenti, p. 42; 'Gold' and 'Il faraone'; author interviews with Carla Maestro.

¶ 'Soon after . . .' and next ¶ Della Torre, *Messaggio*, p. 13; author interviews with SO. Annamaria Guadagni, in 'Prima del grande buio', *Diario della settimana*, 2–8 April 1997, p. 53, says that the house was bombed, but rebuilt.

p. 222

Caption to illustration: Ada's last line – 'The love which moves / Sun and stars wills our end' – echoes the last line of the *Divina commedia*: 'L'amor che muove il sole e l'altre stelle', 'The Love that moves the sun and the other stars'.

p. 223

¶ 'No one had any intuitions . . .' Author interviews with Gabriella Garda Aliverti and EGT.

All from meetings and interviews with, and letters from, Gabriella Garda Aliverti. The quotation on page 228 is from 'Phosphorus', *PT*, p. 126.

Chapter 7: Amay and Aosta: September 1943 – January 1944

p. 230

¶ 'When Primo arrived . . .'   'Il faraone'; Biagi, *1935 e dintorni*, p. 88; author interviews with Paolo Avigdor.

¶ 'Of the Turin . . .'   *Corriere del Piemonte*, 20 May 1945, p. 2.

¶ 'In fact, she'd . . .'   Author interviews with Paolo Avigdor and GCD.

p. 231

¶ 'In order to . . .'   Author interviews with SO. For the bombing of Turin, see *Torino in guerra 1940–45*, background material for the exhibition of that name in the Mole Antonelliana, Turin, 5 April – 28 May 1995, edited by Giovanna De Luna.

¶ 'Everyone was doing . . .'   *Torino in guerra*; author interviews with Renata Gaddini and Luciana Nissim.

¶ 'The next day . . .' and next ¶   Author interviews with Renata Gaddini.

★ Author interviews with Paolo Avigdor.

p. 232

¶ 'Giulia Colombo remembers . . .'   Author interviews with GCD, Giorgio Luzzati, and Lea Segre, and letter to the author from Ada Ortona, 22 December 1999; Stille, *Benevolence*, p. 164.

¶ 'In the Val D'Aosta . . .'   'Il faraone' and 'The Tommy Gun under the Bed'; Vincenti, p. 44; Nicco, p. 26; author interviews with GCD, Jole Segre, BGS, and BGS in Blakeway. On Franco Tedeschi: author interviews with GCD and Maria Vittoria Malvano; and *Torino in guerra* exhibition, letter from the Jewish Community of Turin to DELASEM, Salzburg, looking for Franco Tedeschi: saying that he was deported to Sosnowitz in April 1944, transferred to Mauthausen in January 1945, and seen in Mauthausen up to mid-March. The letter also adds the current rumour that he was seen in Ebensee after its liberation; but this was probably a false lead, like so many.

p. 233

¶ 'Primo's movements . . .'   Author interviews with GB and AP; 'Il faraone'; and the Preface to schools edn of *La tregua*, p. 6.

¶ 'All three Levi . . .'   Information on Enrico and Lisa Levi from Antonia Levi, Enrica Finzi Levi, and *Il filo della memoria*.

¶ 'Mario was the oculist . . .'   Author interviews with GCD and Elena Bachi Levi Pollone. Carpi says (p. 290) that nearly 4,000 people seceded from the Jewish communities of Italy in 1938–9.

p. 234

¶ 'A year or two before . . .', and next two ¶¶   Author interviews with Elena Bachi, and with Carla Pellegrino and Gianna Travaglini of Orta; Mario Campiglio, in *Bollettino Storico per la provincia di Novara*, Anno LXXXV, No. 1, 1994, pp. 20–21. Roberto Levi was born on 17 April 1920 (birth certificate Atto 1696, Ufficio 2, Parte 1, Anno 1920, Città di Torino).

pp. 234–7

The story of Mario and Roberto Levi at Orta: author interviews with Elena Bachi, and with Carla Pellegrino, Gianna Travaglini, Don Erminio and Maria Giulia Cardini, all of Orta. And: letter to CDEC, Milan, from Elena Bachi, 13 May 1968, kindly given me by Elena Bachi; Campiglio, *Bollettino*, pp. 21, 25; 'Eccidi di ebrei in Italia', section on Lago Maggiore, p. 31, from a book whose title I regret to say I did not record; Aldo Toscano, in *Bollettino Storico per la provincia di Novara*, Anno LXXXIV, No. 1, 1993, pp. 9–12; 'La soppressione dei Levi a Orta perché ebrei' by F. B., and 'Sulla morte dei Levi perché ebrei', letter from Peppuccio Galli (son of *Avvocato* Galli), *La Campana*, Orta, January 1987, pp. 3–4. Amongst the other Jews whom Don Giuseppe Annichini assisted were the politician Umberto Terracini and his family, whom he helped to escape to Switzerland (information from Don Erminio). I thank Cesare Bermani for directing me to the best historical sources on the early Nazi atrocities in the area.

p. 237

¶ 'Ada had worked . . .'   Della Torre, *Messaggio*, p. 14; Riccardo Levi, *Ricordi politici di un ingegnere*, Vangelista, Milan, 1981, p. 54; EGT, *I giochi della paura*, 'Il segreto dei Libri segreti', p. 18.

p. 238

¶ 'In October . . .'   Della Torre, *Messaggio*, pp. 11, 14, 32; R. Levi, *Ricordi*, pp. 54, 57–9; author interviews with GCD.

¶ 'Once her mother . . .'   R. Levi, *Ricordi*, pp. 30, 59, 61–2; Della Torre, *Messaggio*, pp. 12, 32–3.

† Nicco, p. 30; and Italo Tibaldi, lists of survivors and non-survivors from PL's transport. I thank Italo Tibaldi for giving me this and much other source material for his book, *Compagni di viaggio*, Consiglio Regionale de Piemonte/ANED, Franco Angeli, 1994. Both his lists are now published in Italo Tibaldi, 'Primo Levi e i suoi "compagni di viaggio"' in *Primo Levi: testimone e scrittore di storia*, Giuntina, 1999, pp. 160–231.

p. 239

¶ 'Silvio, by contrast . . .'   Author interviews with SO, and letter from him, 17 December 1999; also letter from Ada Ortona, 22 December 1999. And: Anello Poma and Gianni Perona, *La Resistenza nel Biellese*, Istituto Storico della Resistenza in Piemonte, Guanda, 1972, p. 82; *Il movimento di liberazione nel Biellese*, Centro Storico della Resistenza nel Biellese, 1957, p. 1.

¶ 'Silvio had been . . .'   Author interviews with and letter from SO; Poma and Perona, *La Resistenza*, pp. 54, 203.

¶ 'Alberto and Bianca . . .' and next two ¶¶   Author interviews with AS and BGS.

p. 240

¶ 'Together, Sandro . . .' See Chapter 4 above, page 144. For Alberto's career in Giustizia e Libertà: Gay Rochat, *La Resistenza*, p. 78, and *Le formazioni GL nella Resistenza*, Istituto Nazionale per la storia del movimento di liberazione in Italia, Franco Angeli, 1985, ed. Giovanni De Luna, pp. 401–2 (Zona Valli di Susa). See also e.g. Carlo Mussa and Giorgio Rolli, 'I partigiani della Val Pellice', *Nuovi Quaderni di G & L*, No. 5–6, January–August 1945, p. 179.

¶ 'Primo's two oldest . . .' Author interviews with Leo Gallico and GCD.

¶ 'And what was happening . . .' Author interviews with Carla Maestro and Renata Gaddini.

p. 241

¶ 'Luciana's family . . .' and next ¶ Author interviews with Luciana Nissim, and Guadagni portrait, p. 16; Davide Nissim, 'L'Aiuto agli Israeliti nel Biellese', document held in CDEC, p. 90. See also Nicco, p. 30.

¶ 'The Val D'Aosta . . .' Nicco, p. 8, and in 'Aspetti e problemi della Resistenza Valdostana al suo escordio', talk given at Aosta, April 1988, p. 3; R. Levi, *Ricordi*, p. 53; PL, 'Il faraone'; author interviews with Carla Maestro and letter from SO, 17 December 1999.

p. 242

'but because . . .' Della Torre, *Messaggio*, p. 89.

¶ 'Primo could not accept . . .' PL letter to Paolo Momigliano, 26 June 1980, published in *La Stampa*, 17 April 1987, and in Pesaro debate, 5 May 1986, p. 19; author interviews with AP and GB, with Paolo Momigliano, Director of the Istituto Storico della Resistenza, Aosta, and with Franco Motta of Aosta.

¶ 'His hesitation ended . . .' 'Il faraone'; *PT*, p. 131.

¶ 'Guido Bachi . . .' and next three ¶¶ Author interviews with GB and AP.

p. 243

¶ ' "Aldo" was . . .' and next two ¶¶ Author interviews with AP; Nicco, p. 26.

¶ 'At some point . . .' Author interviews with GB and AP; Nicco, p. 26; PL documents at CDEC: 'CDEC, Sezione Italiana' and Ministero dell'assistenza post-bellica, Commissione regionale di Piemonte per la qualifica di partigiano (application for certification as a partisan).

p. 244

¶ 'It was now . . .' In his partisan documents at CDEC Primo rounds the date up to 1 October; at Pesaro, for instance, he said that he became a partisan in November. Carnazzi, the Fascist head of Aosta province, says in his report to the Tribunale Speciale that the Amay group was formed at the end of October or beginning of November. (Documents held by the Istituto Storico Della Resistenza in Aosta and the Tribunale of Aosta. I thank Paolo Momigliano for helping me to obtain these documents, and both him and Roberto Nicco for sending me photocopies of these and other documents concerning the partisan groups of the Val d'Ayas.)

¶ 'The extra confusion . . .' '1943–1983: La memoria, i giorni, le parole', *Notizie della Regione Piemonte*, Speciale Resistenza, p. 24.

¶ 'But groups . . .'   Nicco, pp. 23–9; 'Breve cenno sulla lotta di liberazione ad Arnaz', Comitato di Liberazione Nazionale, Alta Italia, 112 Brigata d'assalto Garibaldi 'Aosta', by 'Riccardino', Comandante of the Brigade, Arnaz, 13 January 1946; *Lo Partisan*, Aosta, 22 February 1946, p. 2; *Le formazioni Matteotti nella lotta di liberazione*, ed. Marco Brunazzi and Agostino Conti, L'Arciere, Cuneo, 1986, pp. 51–2.

¶ 'The Arcésaz group . . .' and next ¶   Cesare Levreri, *I ribelli di Casale in Val d'Ayas*, in Rivista dell'amministrazione provinciale, *La Provincia di Alessandria*, Anno XXVII, No. 1, January–March 1980, pp. 21–7, on p. 22; Favretto, *Casale partigiana*, pp. 12–13; Nicco, pp. 26, 29–30; *Lo Partisan*, p. 2; author interviews with GB and AP.

p. 245

¶ 'At just about . . .'   Author interviews with GB; Nicco, p. 19. Information on Aurelio Peccei from *Dieci anni del Circolo della Stampa di Torino*, p. 81, and Mario Giovana, *La Resistenza in Piemonte*, 1962, p. 29.

¶ 'At the same time . . .' and next ¶   Author interviews with GB and AP. Carnazzi's report to the Tribunale Speciale, 7 March 1944, p. 2, says that there were fifteen men at Frumy.

p. 246

¶ ' "It was typical . . .'   Author interviews with AP.

¶ 'But even Aldo . . .'   *Conversations*, p. 8; *Echi*, pp. 68 and 242; 'Gold', *PT*, p. 130 and *ITIAM*, p. 19 ('friends little more experienced than myself'); author interviews with AP.

p. 247

'We went on foot . . .'   *Echi*, p. 242 (from interview with Massimo Mila on *Bric a Brac*, RAI 3, 29 November 1983).

p. 248

¶ 'Women were very rarely . . .'   The first official account of the band after the war was in GB's application for partisan qualification for 'the autonomous band of Ayas', 29 October 1946 (Luciana Nissim appears on p. 4). Author interviews with AP.

¶ 'In ten or twelve days . . .'   Author interviews with GB and AP.

¶ 'It is unlikely . . .'   Author interviews with Luciana Nissim.

'No one who saw her . . .'   *Donne piemontesi*, p. 87.

¶ 'This anonymous . . .'   My reasons are, e.g., that the account is written by a 'compagno di prigionia', i.e. a male fellow-prisoner, and that PL filled in Vanda's partisan details along with his own. But most of all my reasons are stylistic. The portrait has PL's power and concision, and the image of strength which is not 'natural', but 'the fruit of a resolution constantly renewed', is one he used elsewhere, e.g. about Leonardo De Benedetti.

'Vanda was . . .'   *Donne piemontesi*, p. 87.

p. 249

¶ 'The first warning . . .' and next four ¶¶   Author interviews with Guido Bonfiglioli.

p. 250

¶ 'The second warning . . .' Author interviews with EGT, and EGT, 'Primo Levi: Parcours', p. 6.

¶ 'Was Amay . . .' Author interviews with AP.

¶ 'But Amay . . .' Author interviews with SO and letter, 17 December 1999, and with EGT.

p. 251

¶ 'Some of this . . .' Author interviews with Guido Bonfiglioli and BGS, BGS in Blakeway. Ester Valabrega also agreed that bad luck was the main factor. On the other hand, Giorgio Bocca, who was a distinguished partisan in the Langhe, agrees with EGT and SO that the Col di Joux was a bad choice; and it seems that this was among the things PL said himself, on the rare occasions that he spoke at any length about his partisan time (author interviews with Adolfo Arri of SIVA). In any case, I think that my conclusion that PL's harsh judgement of his partisan group was excessive still stands. Both Paolo Momigliano (in 'L'esperienza della Resistenza nella vita e nell'opera di Primo Levi', in *Primo Levi: testamone e scrittore di storia*, p. 72) and Nicco (p. 34) agree.

¶ 'It was now . . .' Author interviews with GB and AP.

¶ 'There was – especially . . .', next ¶, quotation and following ¶ Gianni Oliva, 'La repressione della delinquenza', in Fiorio, *Resistenza e liberazione nella provincia di Torino*, pp. 93–6.

p. 252

¶ 'In the Amay band . . .' and next four ¶¶ Author interviews with GB and AP; Nicco, p. 32; Carnazzi report, 7 March 1944, p. 2.

p. 253

'amongst us . . .' *PT*, p. 132.

¶ 'I do not believe . . .' On Primo spending his weeks as a partisan near despair: GB remembers that he suffered visibly.

¶ 'It was really . . .' Nicco, p. 31; *Lo Partisan*, p. 2. PL always said this: see e.g. *ITIAM*, p. 19, and Vincenti, p. 44.

¶ 'Towards the end . . .' to end of section This account of the betrayal of the Arcésaz and Amay bands by the spies Cagni, De Ceglie and Bianchi has been pieced together from the Tribunale of Aosta documents of interrogations, depositions and hearings between 1946 and 1949. They are in sum: Carnazzi's report to the Tribunale Speciale of 7 March 1944 and letter to Dolfin, Secretary to the Duce, 11 January 1944; depositions by members of the Amay band (Luciana Nissim, AP and PL) and by Marie Varisellaz in 1946; interrogations of and depositions by members of the Arcésaz band (e.g. Edoardo De Vasi, Giuseppe Anglesio and Giuseppe Barbesino), and of/by various local people, e.g. Serafino Court, the then Mayor of Brusson, in 1944 and 1946; depositions by GB (1945) and AP (1944 and 1945); depositions by Cagni ('Redi'), De Ceglie ('Meoli') and Bianchi ('Cerri') between 1946 and 1949; and trial records, 21 June 1945, 5 March 1946, 4 May 1946. Also: Nicco, pp. 31–3; Levreri, pp. 22–3, 27; and author interviews with GB and AP.

p. 255

¶ 'Amay had no warning . . .' Author interviews with Luciana Nissim, and Luciana Nissim in Giacomoni, *La Repubblica*, 16 February 1997; *ITIAM*, p. 19; author interviews with AP.

† *Le formazioni Matteotti nella lotta di liberazione*, pp. 90–91; 'Divisione Italo Rossi' in *Il contribuito socialista nella Resistenza in Piemonte, 1943–1945*, ed. Domenico Zucàro, Edizioni Il Grido del Popolo, Turin, 1955, p. 17; and 'Italo Rossi' in ibid., p. 53. Primo gave this to CDEC as the name of his and Vanda's brigade.

p. 256

¶ 'Fifty militiamen . . .' Author interviews with AP, GB, and Luciana Nissim, and Luciana Nissim in Guadagni portrait; 'Gold', *PT* p. 131. When PL gives the number of militiamen as 300 in 'Gold', he is including those who went to Arcésaz.

¶ 'Ferro . . .' Author interviews with AP and GB; Nicco, p. 33; 'Gold', *PT*, p. 131. PL calls Ferro 'Fossa' in 'Gold'.

¶ 'Four prisoners . . .' and next two ¶¶ Carnazzi, letter to Dolfin, Secretary to the Duce, 11 January 1944; 'Gold', *PT*, p. 131; author interviews with AP and GB.

¶ 'He did two things . . .' 'Gold'; *Conversations*, p. 7; Vincenti, p. 45; PL interviews with Giuseppe Mayda, 'Il poeta triste dei Lager', *Resistenza*, G. & L. monthly magazine, Anno XVII, No. 5, May 1963, p. 5, BBC *Bookmark*, and Kleiner, 1986 (the last in *Conversazioni e interviste*).

p. 257

¶ 'The militiamen . . .' 'Gold'; Paolo Spriano, 'L'avventura di Primo Levi', *Unità*, 14 July 1963, p. 8; author interviews with GB; Guadagni portrait of Luciana Nissim, p. 16.

¶ 'The five . . .' 'Gold'; 'Fine del Marinese', *Il Ponte*, August–September 1949, pp. 1170–73 (in *Opere I*, p. 1109).

¶ 'Meanwhile . . .' Author interviews with Luciana Nissim, and Guadagni portrait.

¶ 'In Aosta . . .' Author interviews with GB and Luciana Nissim.

¶ 'For the men . . .' 'Gold'; author interviews with GB. On the later behaviour of Cagni: case documents and depositions by De Vasi, Barbesino and Court.

★ Quotation from 'Fine del Marinese'.

p. 258

¶ 'It is this move . . .' and next ¶ Author interviews with AP, GB, and Luciana Nissim; *Conversations*, pp. 8–9; Herzer, *The Italian Refuge*, p. 103; 'Gold', *PT*, p. 134. Carnazzi's report to the Tribunale Speciale confirms that GB was known to be a Jew (p. 3).

¶ 'It's almost certainly . . .' Author interviews with Luciana Nissim and GB; PL's deposition for the trial of Friedrich Bosshammer, 1971, published in *La Stampa*, 25 April 2001.

¶ 'Why *did* he make it . . .' 'Gold', *PT*, p. 134; *ITIAM*, pp. 19–20; *Conversations*, pp. 7–8; Kleiner interview, 1986; *La tregua* preface, 1965; and Vincenti, p. 45 all give the 'practical' reason of avoiding certain death at the hands of the Tribunale Speciale. *Conversations* (p. 8) and 'Itinerario' also give pride (*Opere II*, p. 1163), and e.g. 'La deportazione degli ebrei', in *Quaderni del Centro Studi sulla deportazione e l'internamento*, No. 4, 1967 (in *Opere II*, p. 1217) adds 'stupidly'. See also e.g. PL interviews with Oreste del Buono, in *Europeo*, 5 July 1982, pp. 82–5, Biagi, *1935 e dintorni*, p. 88, and Rudolf (*VM*, pp. 24–5); and letter to *Commentary*, February 1986.

p. 259

¶ 'Immediately after . . .'   Author interviews with Carla Maestro and Luciana Nissim.

¶ 'Luciana's family . . .' and next ¶   Author interviews with Luciana Nissim, and Guadagni portrait, p. 16; Davide Nissim, 'L'Aiuto agli Isrealiti nel Biellese', pp. 90–91. Don Péaquin also sheltered a family of Yugoslav Jews. He had to defy his bishop and parishioners to do so, and ended the war having to take refuge with the partisans (Susan Zuccotti in Herzer, *The Italian Refuge*, p. 270). It is worth noting here the courage of many of the lower clergy, like Don Péaquin and Don Giuseppe Annichini in this book, despite the lack of a lead, or worse, from their superiors – right up, of course, to the Pope. See most recently Susan Zuccotti, *Under His Very Windows: The Vatican and the Holocaust in Italy*, Yale, 2001.

¶ 'Three months after . . .' and next three ¶¶   Della Torre, *Messaggio*, pp. 14–17.

p. 260

¶ 'Luckily . . .'   Della Torre, *Messaggio*, pp. 14–17, plus author interviews with SO, and SO in Guadagni, 'Primo Levi'.

¶ ' "Gold" . . .' and next three ¶¶   'Gold'; *Conversations*, p. 8.

Chapter 8: Fossoli: February 1944

p. 262

¶ 'On or about . . .'   Paolo Momigliano, in 'L'esperienza della Resistenza', says that Primo's stay in Aosta lasted until 20 January (*Primo Levi: testimone e scrittore di storia*, p. 73). But they arrived in Fossoli on 27 January (see 'Primo Levi racconta al magistrato di Berlino gli orrori di Auschwitz', *La Stampa*, 4 May 1971), and saw one sunset on their journey (see *Echi*, p. 160): presumably, therefore, they left the day before.

¶ 'The next day . . .'   Author interviews with Luciana Nissim.

¶ 'Fossoli is . . .'   *Museo*, pp. 21–35; Luciano Casali, 'La deportazione dall'Italia: Fossoli di Carpi', in *Spostamenti di popolazione e deportazioni in Europa 1939–1945*, Capelli Editore, 1987 (papers delivered at a conference in Carpi, October 1985), p. 384.

p. 263

¶ 'On 30 November . . .'   De Felice, p. 448; Casali, 'La deportazione', pp. 382, 386; *Museo*, p. 22; Giuseppe Mayda, *Ebrei sotto Salò*, Feltrinelli, 1978, p. 184; Liliana Picciotto Fargion in Herzer, *The Italian Refuge*, p. 130. (PL said there were 100–200 Jews in Fossoli when they arrived (deposition, *La Stampa*, 25 April

2001) or – evidently as a mean – 150 (Vincenti, p. 45); Casali says there were 198 by early January (Casali, 'La deportazione', p. 386).)

¶ 'All along . . .' Picciotto Fargion in Herzer, *The Italian Refuge*, pp. 136, 302; Giuseppe Mayda, 'La deportazione degli ebrei italiani' in *Il dovere di testimoniare*, papers delivered at a conference in Turin, 28–9 October 1983, p. 43; PL, deposition, *La Stampa*, 25 April 2001; De Felice, pp. 447, 451; Casali, 'La deportazione', p. 386; Carpi, p. 296.

¶ 'But at the time . . .' De Felice, pp. 464–5; Mayda, *Ebrei sotto Salò*, pp. 187, 189; Vanda Maestro, first letter from Fossoli, 4 February 1944. I thank Carla Maestro for showing me Vanda's letters from Fossoli. GCD says that when the family heard that Primo had been sent to Fossoli, they were relieved.

¶ 'It was largely . . .' The story of the Jews who returned to prison comes from De Felice, p. 464.

p. 264

¶ 'Three weeks after . . .' Author interviews with Silvio Barabas.

¶ 'Throughout their journey . . .' and next ¶ Silvio Barabas, 'Fossoli (February 16–22 [1944]): Recollections'. I thank Silvio Barabas for composing and sending me these 'Recollections', and for all his other memories of Fossoli and of Auschwitz.

¶ In fact . . .' Primo noticed the first SS on 20 February, but noted that others had reported them several days earlier (deposition, *La Stampa*, 25 April 2001).

¶ 'For earlier arrivals . . .' Mayda, *Ebrei sotto Salò*, p. 184; *Museo*, p. 21; Casali, 'La deportazione', p. 394; Barabas, 'Recollections'; *Conversations*, p. 9.

¶ 'But Fossoli . . .' Barabas, 'Recollections'; LDB and Vanda Maestro letters from Fossoli; author letters from Aldo Moscati; PL, deposition, *La Stampa*, 25 April 2001; PL in interviews with Risa Sodi ('A Last Talk', *Present Tense*, May/June 1988, p. 43) and Kleiner; *Conversations*, p. 9; author interviews with Luciana Nissim; *ITIAM*, p. 80. I thank Elio Vitale for giving me copies of Leonardo's letters.

p. 265

¶ 'While Primo . . .' Barabas, 'Recollections'; Vanda Maestro first letter, 4 February; *Museo*, p. 26; Renzo Bacino, *Fossoli*, Comune di Carpi, 1961, p. 38; Enea Fergnani, *Un uomo e tre numeri*, Speroni Editore, Milan, 1945, pp. 113, 115; PL in Risa Sodi interview, *Present Tense*, p. 43.

¶ 'This "Italian" . . .' Barabas, 'Recollections'.

★ Casali, 'La deportazione', p. 387. Since there were also the basic rations of rice and pasta, and there was no forced labour, this was more than adequate.

p. 266

¶ 'What would young . . .' and next ¶ Author interviews with Luciana Nissim.

pp. 266–8

Franco Information on Franco Sacerdoti from author interviews with Alda and Pino Sacerdoti (Turin), Ulda Sacerdoti (Padua), Luciana Nissim, and letter from Wanda Sacerdoti to Alda, answering author's questions, 26 January 1994. (Pino Sacerdoti is Franco's younger brother; Ulda is the widow of his elder brother Fulvio, and Wanda the widow of his eldest brother Enrico.) For Franco's arrest in Lanzo: Italo Tibaldi, list of *sommersi* from Primo's transport in *Primo Levi: testimone*, p. 190; also Liliana Picciotto Fargion, *Il libro della memoria*, Mursia, 1991. I thank the Sacerdoti family for their help and friendship.

p. 269

¶ 'Vanda's first feeling . . .'   Vanda's letters from Fossoli, 4, 15 and 17 February 1944; GCD in Rosenfeld TV.

¶ 'Primo didn't . . .'   *Museo*, pp. 24–5; PL in Risa Sodi interview, *Present Tense*, p. 43.

¶ 'Vanda's relief . . .' and next ¶   Vanda's letters from Fossoli 15, 17 and 2? February (probably 21 February, since they were told they were about to leave on that day (*ITIAM*, p. 20)).

p. 270

¶ 'Probably Nella . . .'   Author interviews with Carla Maestro.

¶ 'And during . . .'   Author interviews with Luciana Nissim; Gisella.

¶ 'Alberto Dalla Volta . . .'   Author interviews with Paolo Dalla Volta and Luciana Nissim; Silvio Barabas, 'Recollections' and letter to the author 10 February 1995.

¶ 'Primo's friends . . .' and next ¶   PL, 'Small Causes', *Moments of Reprieve*, Abacus, 1987, pp. 38 and 112; *ITIAM*, p. 161.

p. 271

¶ 'They *were* alike . . .'   Author interviews with Paolo Dalla Volta. 'Ideal symbiont' is from *ITIAM*, p. 143.

p. 272

¶ 'Alberto was also . . .' to end of section on Alberto, p. 274   Author interviews with Paolo Dalla Volta; Massimo Tedeschi, interview with Paolo Dalla Volta, 'L'Olocausto in casa mia', *Bresciaoggi*, 14 August 1996, p. 10 and 'Ebrei, l'onta dimenticata', *Bresciaoggi*, 10 August 1996, p. 8. Also Liliana Picciotto Fargion, 'La deportazione degli ebrei dall'Italia' in *Spostamenti di popolazione e deportazioni in Europa*, pp. 300–301, and Mayda, 'La deportazione', in *Il dovere di testimoniare*, p. 44.

p. 274

¶ 'About Leonardo . . .'   PL, 'Ricordo di un uomo buono', *La Stampa*, 21 October 1983 (in *Opere II*, p. 1194).

¶ 'In 1944 . . .'   On Leonardo's extraordinary sweetness and kindness: all author interviews about LDB, e.g. with Ferrucio Maruffi, Giuliana Tedeschi, Carla Ovazza Debenedetti, Franco Levi, Sion Segre Amar, Anna Maria Bruzzone, as well as with all members of his family, and with his housekeeper Anna Piersanti.

¶ 'If Leonardo . . .'   Author interviews with Franco Levi, Anna Piersanti, Elio and Marlene Vitale; PL, 'Ricordo di un uomo buono'.

¶ 'In fact Primo . . .'   PL, 'Ricordo di un uomo buono'; *ITIAM*, p. 63.

¶ 'Leonardo was . . .' and rest of section on LDB, to p. 279   Author interviews with Leonardo's family and friends: Alessandro De Benedetti, Emma De Benedetti, Carla Ovazza Debenedetti, Simone Fubini, Sandra Hirsch, Franco Levi, Mario Levi, Ferruccio Maruffi, Elsa Muggia, Ernesto Muggia, Anna Piersanti, Alberto Vita, Elena Vita Finzi, Paola and Gisella Vita Finzi, Elio and Marlene Vitale, Anna and Stuart Woolf. And: LDB, interview with ANED, 1982; letters from LDB's patients to his family on his death; LDB letter from Katowice, 7 March 1945; Tibaldi list of survivors from Primo's transport, in *Primo Levi: testimone*, p. 160. On Jolanda's work for ADEI: 'L'ADEI nell'immediato dopo-guerra', *Il Portavoce*, No. 5, November/December 1944. On DELASEM: De Felice, pp. 427–8 and 430–31.

p. 279

¶ 'At first . . .'   LDB letters from Fossoli, 16 January, 24 January and 5 February 1944, and reports of later letters from Signor Alocco (Beniamino Debenedetti's secretary) to the family. Information about the escape plan made for the De Benedettis by Giorgio Jarach from Simone Fubini.

¶ 'Around 15 February . . .'   For the takeover of Fossoli by the Germans, officially on 15 March but actually a month before: *Museo*, p. 23; Mayda, *Ebrei sotto Salò*, p. 186; PL in *La Stampa*, 25 April 2001 and Kleiner interview; LDB in 'Torinesi scampati alle camere a gas depongono contro il Vice di Eichmann' (deposition in the trial of Friedrich Bosshammer), *Gazzetta del Popolo*, 1 May 1971. For the rest of the ¶: Barabas, 'Recollections'. The *capo campo* was almost certainly Guido Melli from Modena (PL to Melli's daughters, 10 May 1975, in *Primo Levi: la dignità dell'uomo*, Citadella Editrice, 1996, p. 21). Melli, who was forty-eight in 1944, died in Auschwitz in May (Tibaldi's lists, *Primo Levi: testimone*, p. 185).

¶ 'They were right . . .'   See *Museo*, p. 24; Mayda, *Ebrei sotto Salò*, p. 186; Picciotto Fargion in *Spostamenti*, p. 308; Carmine Lops, 'L'Organizzazione del campo [Fossoli]' in *Albori della Nuova Europa*, Vol. II, Part II, Chapter 2, Fossoli-Auschwitz, p. 259; Barabas, 'Recollections'; *ITIAM*, p. 20; PL, deposition, *La Stampa*, 25 April 2001. There was actually a previous train to leave Fossoli before PL's, which was therefore the second, not the first: 141 people were sent on 19 February to Bergen-Belsen. (See *Museo*, p. 27; Mayda, *Ebrei sotto Salò*, p. 192; and Tibaldi, in *Primo Levi: testimone*, p. 155, who says 146.)

p. 280

¶ 'This was the moment . . .'   Signor Alocco letter to the Debenedetti family, 10 March 1944; Barabas, 'Recollections'.

¶ ' "Only a few . . .', 'and washed their children . . .' and 'That night . . .'   *ITIAM*, pp. 20–22; PL in radio interview with Alberto Gozzi, 1985. Aldo Moscati confirms the accuracy of PL's account of the last night at Fossoli (letters to the author).

¶ 'There was a last . . .'   Author interviews with Luciana Nissim.

p. 281

¶ 'Primo reports . . .'   *ITIAM*, pp. 7–8, 21. The word 'nefanda' is not translated in the English version, which reads only 'lustfully intoxicated for the last time'.

¶ 'But what, then . . .'   Author interviews with Gisella.

¶ 'Vanda was . . .'   Author interviews with Luciana Nissim and with Gisella.

Chapter 9: *Auschwitz: 22 February 1944 – 27 January 1945*

p. 282

¶ 'There are some days . . .' and next ¶   *ITIAM*, p. 22; *D. & S.*, pp. 70, 92. PL noted in his deposition against Bosshammer (*La Stampa*, 25 April 2001) that the first roll-call was held on the 21st. On Vanda's attempt to commit suicide: author interviews with Luciana Nissim, Carla Maestro, GCD, Gisella.

¶ 'We know . . .'   On PL's knowing little: *ITIAM*, p. 23; deposition, *La Stampa*, 25 April 2001; interviews with Risa Sodi, 1988, p. 43, Ian Thomson, *PN Review*, 1987, p. 15, in *VM*, p. 35, and Daniele Toaff, 'Ritorno ad Auschwitz', *Sorgente di vita*, RAI 2 TV, 25 April 1983, in *VM*, p. 210; letter to Rosanna Benzi in *Gli Altri*, 1979. On LDB: his first ANED questionnaire, 1965. On Luciana Nissim: *Donne*, p. 20; on Silvio Barabas: author interviews. For rest of ¶: *ITIAM*, p. 22; Barabas, 'Recollections'.

p. 283

¶ 'Primo's was . . .'   Deposition, *La Stampa*, 25 April 2001.

¶ 'At the station . . .'   *ITIAM*, p. 22; *D. & S.*, pp. 70, 85–6; deposition, *La Stampa*, 25 April 2001; *Donne*, p. 19; author interviews with Silvio Barabas; Dini & Jesurum, p. 38. In his deposition against Bosshammer, PL estimated that his bus had left Fossoli at about ten, that the train had been loaded by about two, and that they left at about six.

¶ 'Amid the chaos . . .'   Picciotto Fargion in *Spostamenti*, p. 310; author interviews with Luciana Nissim and Paolo Dalla Volta; *Donne*, p. 19; LDB, ANED interview, 1982, p. 6; PL in *D. & S.*, p. 88; *La Stampa*, 4 May 1971, and *ITIAM*, pp. 22–3.

p. 284

¶ 'Almost always . . .'   *D. & S.*, pp. 85–8; *Donne*, p. 19; *Rapporto*, pp. 535–44.

¶ 'You had been . . .'   As previous 91, and: *D. & S.*, pp. 60, 88; *Echi*, p. 179; *ITIAM*, p. 24.

¶ 'The mothers . . .' and next five ¶¶   *D. & S.*, pp. 60, 86–9; *Echi*, p. 179; *ITIAM*, pp. 20, 24; PL deposition, *La Stampa*, 25 April 2001; *Donne*, pp. 19–21; LDB, ANED interview, 1982, p. 6; author interviews with Luciana Nissim; Vincenti, p. 46.

p. 285

'*Cara Bianca* . . .'   Dini & Jesurum, p. 40.

¶ 'At midday . . .' and next ¶   *ITIAM*, p. 23, *Donne*, p. 21.

p. 286

¶ 'All Jews . . .' and next ¶   *D. & S.*, p. 96; Picciotto Fargion, *Il libro della memoria*, pp. 46–7; Italo Tibaldi in *Primo Levi: testimone*, p. 156; Mayda, *Ebrei sotto Salò*, p. 192; *Rapporto*, p. 37; PL in *La Stampa*, 4 May 1971, and in Angelo d'Orsi taped interview. PL even claimed no knowledge of deaths in his car on deposition, under oath, against Bosshammer (*La Stampa*, 25 April 2001).

¶ 'The man's name' and next two ¶¶   Angelo d'Orsi, 'Un poeta nella bufera: il dramma di un ebreo fascista cuneese', offprint kindly given me by Angelo d'Orsi;

author interviews with Angelo D'Orsi and Fabio Levi. For Arturo Foà's dying before the arrival at Auschwitz, see 'Un poeta nella bufera', Note 38, *D. & S.*, p. 26, and *Primo Levi: testimone*, p. 174.

p. 287

¶ 'Neither this . . .' *D. & S.*, p. 110: the role of partisan was one which 'was not mine'.

¶ 'During those four . . .' and next ¶ *ITIAM*, pp. 23, 25; *Donne*, p. 57 ('povera piccola Vanda, che aveva sempre saputo che sarebbe morta': 'poor little Vanda, who had always known she would die').

¶ 'The train . . .' and next ¶ LDB, ANED questionnaire, 1965, and interview, 1982, p. 5; *Donne*, pp. 22–3; *ITIAM*, pp. 24–5; Waitz, extract kindly given me by Hermann Langbein, p. 469; *Echi*, p. 179 ('Ritorno ad Auschwitz'); Aldo Moscati, in *La speranza tradita, Antologia della deportazione politica toscana 1943–1945*, Pacini Editore, Pisa, 1992, p. 138; *Rapporto*, p. 38.

¶ 'No one understands . . .' and next ¶ PL, ANED interview, 1983, *VM*, p. 222; *Donne*, p. 23; author interviews with Luciana Nissim; Waitz, p. 470.

¶ 'Among them, Primo . . .' *ITIAM*, p. 26; Gisella Vita Finzi, *Bollettino della comunità ebraica di Milano*, December 1989, p. 15; Giorgina Arian Levi, 'Emilia Levi', *Unità*, offprint kindly given me by Giorgina Arian Levi, date unrecorded.

p. 289

¶ 'It was the same . . .' and next four ¶¶ *ITIAM*, pp. 24–6; *Echi*, pp. 179–80 ('Ritorno ad Auschwitz'); Tibaldi list of *sommersi* from Primo's transport, in *Primo Levi: testimone*, p. 182; 'Itinerario', *Opere II*, p. 1217; Myriam Anissimov, *Primo Levi ou la tragédie d'un optimiste*, Lattès, Paris, 1996, p. 165; *D. & S.*, p. 35.

¶ 'Once they were . . .' and next four ¶¶ *ITIAM*, p. 63; author interviews with Paolo Dalla Volta; Paolo Dalla Volta in *Bresciaoggi*, 14 August 1996; PL, ANED interview, 1983, *VM*, p. 220; author interviews with Paul Steinberg; *D. & S.*, pp. 19–21.

p. 290

¶ 'The Italian transports . . .' *D. & S.*, pp. 85–6; Waitz, p. 469; author interviews with JS.

¶ 'It was incomprehensible . . .' and next five ¶¶ *ITIAM*, pp. 26–33; Waitz, pp. 471–5; Dante, *Inferno*, Canto III; *Rapporto*, p. 38; Moscati in *La speranza tradita*, p. 138; Barabas, 'Recollections'; *Echi*, p. 180 ('Ritorno ad Auschwitz'); *D. & S.*, pp. 106–7; PL in interviews with Stefano Jesurum, *Essere Ebrei in Italia*, Longanesi, 1987, p. 101, and Silvia Ciairano, private taped interview, 19 November 1975; Tibaldi lists of Primo's transport in *Primo Levi: testimone*.

p. 292

'*Per me si va . . .*' Dante, *Inferno*, Canto III.

¶ 'Luciana is not . . .' and next four ¶¶ *Donne*, pp. 22, 24–7, 29–31; *ITIAM*, p. 28; *Echi*, p. 179 ('Ritorno ad Auschwitz'); *Rapporto*, p. 39.

¶ 'The worst . . .' and next ¶ *ITIAM*, p. 32; *D. & S.*, pp. 24, 95, 101.

p. 293

¶ 'In the first few . . .' and next three ¶¶ *ITIAM*, pp. 31–3, 42; Moscati in *La speranza tradita*, pp. 61–2; *D. & S.*, pp. 89–91; Waitz, p. 488; *Echi*, p. 179 ('Ritorno ad Auschwitz').

p. 294

¶ 'The next day . . .' and next ¶   *ITIAM*, p. 35.

¶ 'For the Italians . . .'   *D. & S.*, pp. 70, 72, 74; PL in interviews with Greer, p. 16, and Ernesto Olivero, *Progetto* Nos. 8–9, August–September 1980, p. 5; *Echi*, p. 182; Mayda, *Ebrei sotto Salò*, p. 192.

p. 295

¶ 'There is always . . .' and next four ¶¶   *D. & S.*, pp. 71–2, 23–5, 63, 106, 108, 115; PL, ANED interview, *VM*, pp. 220, 225; *ITIAM*, pp. 43, 34, 63; *Donne*, pp. 31–2; *Echi*, p. 187; Waitz, p. 486; author interviews with Edith Bruck; PL in interview with Giorgio De Rienzo, *Famiglia cristiana*, 20 July 1975, p. 42.

p. 296

¶ 'It very nearly . . .'   PL, ANED interview, *VM*, pp. 220. For the first days being the worst, see also: PL in interviews with Olivero, pp. 4–5, and Greer, *VM*, p. 4; *D. & S.*, pp. 25, 79; Waitz, p. 468; and Lazzaro Levi's Diary, *Il Koncentrations [sic] Lager*, in CDEC, p. 3.

¶ 'How did he survive . . .' and next two ¶¶   PL in ANED interview, 1983, pp. 3–4 and *Ateneo*, p. 12 (BBC *Bookmark* interview); *ITIAM*, pp. 63, 143, 145; *MR*, pp. 94 (Alberto), 36–7, 53 (Schlome, Chaim); *D. & S.*, p. 63.

p. 297

¶ 'Reznik was . . .'   On Reznik: *ITIAM*, p. 71; Myriam Anissimov, 'Maurice Reznik: Dans le même Block à Auschwitz', *Les Nouveaux Cahiers*, No. 114, Autumn 1993, p. 48 (and translated in *La Stampa*, 31 October 1993). On Schlome and Chaim: *ITIAM*, pp. 37, 53. Quotation 'on the way down' from author interviews with Paul Steinberg.

¶ 'But of course . . .' and next four ¶¶   *ITIAM*, pp. 71, 73–5; *D. & S.*, pp. 93–4; Anissimov, 'Maurice Reznik', pp. 48–9.

★ Anissimov, 'Maurice Reznik', p. 48.

p. 298

¶ 'But he was . . .' and next two ¶¶   *D. & S.*, pp. 63, 106–7, 109; PL in interview with Enrico Boeri, *VM*, p. 69.

¶ 'That had always . . .' and next two ¶¶   *D. & S.*, pp. 75, 107–8; PL in Pesaro debate, 1986, p. 14; *ITIAM*, pp. 39–40, 43, 45, 51; Waitz, p. 474; Lazzaro Levi, Diary, p. 3. For learning German in the camp, see also Greer, *VM*, p. 4. Primo knew some German even before Auschwitz, not only from his chemical studies, but from a Czech Jew he met in Milan in 1942–3 (Dini & Jesurum, pp. 126–7).

p. 300

¶ 'To understand . . .' and next ¶   *MR*, p. 99; *ITIAM*, pp. 15, 42; *D. & S.*, pp. 6, 63; PL, Preface to *La vita offesa*, ed. Anna Bravo and Daniele Jalla, Franco Angeli, Milan, 1987 (in *Opere II*, p. 1347). For Waitz, see his essay as cited; for Ella Lingens Reiner, see her *Prisoners of Fear*, 1948; for Robert, see *D. & S.*, p. 63.

¶ 'Most people . . .' and next ¶   Author interviews with JS; *ITIAM*, pp. 15, 93, 182; *Conversations*, p. 13; *D. & S.*, pp. 27, 74; PL, 'Eclissi dei profeti', *Opere II*, p. 854.

'Thousands . . .'   *ITIAM*, p. 93.

p. 301

¶ 'It may be . . .'   See e.g. Greer, *VM*, p. 4, and Roth, *VM*, p. 17, in which PL speaks of his intense need to understand in Auschwitz. For its perhaps going back to the very first night: see e.g. PL, letter to Heinz Riedt, 13 May 1960, in which PL says that his book is an answer to the SS man who laughed at the truss, as well as to Alex, Pannwitz and those who hanged the Last One (the SS man is left out in *D. & S.*, p. 143). His observer's instinct went back even further, to the very instant of his arrival: he had tried to count the number of women chosen for work, and had got the number right – twenty-nine (see his deposition against Bosshammer, *La Stampa*, 25 April 2001).

¶ 'Whether it was . . .', quotation following, and next ¶   'Itinerario', p. 1218; Vincenti, p. 54; PL in Roth, *VM*, p. 17, and in the Pesaro debate, 1986, p. 9; *MR*, pp. 9, 11, 88; PL, 'Un "giallo" del Lager', *Opere II*, p. 911. (The quotation is from Roth.)

¶ 'It is hard . . .' and next ¶   Author interviews with JS. For PL's rejection of the idea of being chosen, see e.g. *D. & S.*, p. 62, and Chapter 11 below. For his saying that no book is worth a life: see Bocca.

¶ 'Deliberately . . .'   Author interviews with JS, and JS in *Il presente del passato*, 1988, p. 25. For PL's already writing in Auschwitz: *La tregua*, p. 381; *Echi*, p. 93; PL, ANED interview, *VM*, p. 225; Vincenti, p. 54; and e.g. PL interview with Marina Verna, 'Primo Levi, la chimica della parola', in 1982, locus alas unrecorded.

¶ 'His task . . .'   *D. & S.*, pp. 63, 117; *Echi*, p. 186; *MR*, p. 11; author interviews with Edith Bruck, Lydia Rolfi and Giuliana Tedeschi; PL in Pesaro debate, 1986, pp. 8–9 and in ANED interview, *VM*, p. 234. On his scientific interest in Auschwitz, see also A. Alvarez, introduction to *Primo Levi*, BBC TV, 1996; and on PL as anthropologist, EGT, 'Primo Levi: Parcours' and Roth.

¶ 'Primo's camp . . .'   Waitz, p. 472; *D. & S.*, p. 94; Langbein, *Menschen in Auschwitz*, p. 506; *ITIAM*, pp. 78–9; *Rapporto*, p. 38; PL in 'Ritorno ad Auschwitz' interview; JS, 'L'homme face à l'univers concentrationnaire', talk delivered at Colmar, 1 April 1985, p. 7 (kindly given me by JS); *Conversations*, 29.

p. 303

¶ 'Among the foreign . . .' and next two ¶¶   *ITIAM*, pp. 31, 37–8, 78; Waitz, p. 486; *MR*, p. 39; *Conversations*, p. 62; *Rapporto*, pp. 38–9; author interviews with JS; LDB, ANED interview, 1982, p. 7; Lazzaro Levi, Diary, p. 3; *D. & S.*, pp. 93–4.

¶ 'Primo dedicated . . .' and next ¶   ITIAM, Ch. 5, 'Our Nights'; *D. & S.*, pp. 1–2; *Rapporto*, p. 39; Lazzaro Levi, Diary, p. 5.

p. 304

¶ 'And behind . . .' and next two ¶¶   *ITIAM*, pp. 44–5, 69–70; *D. & S.*, pp. 91–3; PL, *Moments of Reprieve*, p. 57; Lazzaro Levi, Diary, p. 4; Waitz, pp. 487–8.

¶ 'When the counting . . .' and next two ¶¶   *ITIAM*, pp. 36, 41–2, 96, 107, 116; *D. & S.*, pp. 45, 91–2; PL in radio interview 'The Little Theatre of Memory', in *VM*, p. 50; PL, *MR*, p. 57; Waitz, pp. 479, 485–7; *Rapporto*, p. 40; PL in German TV interview, 1989; *Echi*, p. 181. For three months being the maximum survival period, see: *ITIAM*, p. 96; PL, 'La resistenza nei Lager', *Quaderni del Centro Studi sulla deportazione e l'internamento*, No. 3, 1966, in *Opere I*, p. 1146, and 'La deportazione degli ebrei' in the same *Quaderni*, No. 4, 1967, in *Opere I*, p. 1163; *Conversations*, p. 31. Also e.g. in Langbein, *Menschen in Auschwitz*; Ruth Weidenreich, *Un medico nel campo di Auschwitz*, Istituto Storico della Resistenza in Toscana, Florence 1960, p. 20, and author interviews with Paul Steinberg.

p. 306
¶ 'But of course . . .' and next¶   Waitz, pp. 474, 492; *Rapporto*, pp. 39–42; *ITIAM*, pp. 40–41, 70; *D. & S.*, pp. 72, 107; *Echi*, pp. 181–2 ('Ritorno ad Auschwitz'); JS, Colmar talk, p. 3.
¶ ' "Dying was easy . . .'   *Echi*, pp. 184–5; *ITIAM*, pp. 39, 95–6; Waitz, pp. 489, 491; JS, Colmar talk, p. 12; PL, ANED interview, *VM*, pp. 221–2.

p. 307
¶ 'No one really . . .'   *ITIAM*, pp. 48–9, 94, 96; *D. & S.*, p. 77; Waitz, p. 490. Hermann Langbein says in *Menschen in Auschwitz* that there was a total of 405,000 slaves in the Nazi Lagers.
¶ 'Selections took place . . .'   *Rapporto*, p. 45; Waitz, p. 493; Lazzaro Levi, Diary, p. 6; *Conversations*, p. 62; *Donne*, p. 41; Giuliana Tedeschi, *There is a Place on Earth*, translated by Tim Parks, Lime Tree, 1993, p. 21; JS, Colmar talk, p. 8. For PL writing *ITIAM* 'backwards', with the October selection one of the earlier chapters: e.g. *Echi*, p. 94, and author interviews with Vanna Rava.

p. 308
¶ 'If you managed . . .' and next two ¶¶   Waitz, p. 488; *ITIAM*, pp. 15, 40; *Conversations*, p. 30; Langbein, *Menschen in Auschwitz*; *Rapporto*, p. 43; *D. & S.*, p. 31. The quotation '*It was my good fortune . . .*' is on p. 15.
¶ 'For the first few . . .' and next three ¶¶   *ITIAM*, pp. 44, 101–4; Lazzaro Levi, Diary, pp. 3–4; PL, letter to Hermann Langbein, 19 April 1961; PL in Pesaro debate, 1986, p. 14; *MR*, p. 60; *D. & S.*, pp. 110–11. Both Silvio Barabas and Paul Steinberg confirm the accuracy of Primo's portrait of Elias. Paul Steinberg also confirms the strangling event, and dates it to soon after PL's arrival (Paul Steinberg, *Speak You Also*, Allen Lane, The Penguin Press, 2000, p. 46).

p. 309
'Then he gripped . . .'   *D. & S.*, p. 111.
¶ 'The washroom . . .'   *ITIAM*, pp. 46–7; PL letter to Anna Yona, 25 October 1973; Tibaldi list of *sommersi* from Primo's transport, *Primo Levi: testimone*, p. 176. (Here Glucksmann's name appears without an 's', but this was a typographical error. The name had an 's' in Tibaldi's original list, in PL's list for the deposition against Bosshammer (*Primo Levi: testimone*, p. 232), and in PL's letter to Anna Yona.)

p. 310
'We are slaves . . .' and next ¶   *ITIAM*, p. 47.
¶ 'Now came' and next two ¶¶   Author interviews with JS; *ITIAM*, pp. 48, 61, 127, 129, 139; LDB, ANED interview, 1982, p. 33; author interviews with

Liana Millu. Though PL says the Italians stopped meeting very soon (*ITIAM*, p. 43), Aldo Moscati says that a few did continue to meet, including LDB, PL and himself. The quotation from Maurice Reznik comes from Anissimov, 'Maurice Reznik', p. 48.

p. 311

¶ 'Leonardo was even . . .' and next two ¶¶   PL, 'Ricordo di un uomo buono'; LDB, ANED interview, 1982, pp. 7, 12; LDB, letter from Katowice, 24 February 1945; author interviews with Leonardo's family and with Aldo Moscati.

p. 312

¶ 'Leonardo himself . . .' and next two ¶¶   LDB, ANED interview, 1982, pp. 7–8, 16–17, 29, 32; LDB, 'Denuncio Mengele' (in LDB papers, Library of the Jewish Community of Turin); author interviews with Alessandro Debenedetti, Carla Ovazza Debenedetti, Emma Debenedetti; Waitz, p. 494; Langbein, *Menschen in Auschwitz*; *Rapporto*, p. 45; LDB letters from Katowice, 24 February and 29 April 1945.

¶ 'That was why . . .'   LDB, letter to Aldo Moscati, 2 October 1945; LDB, ANED interview, 1982, pp. 8–9, 15, 17; PL 'Ricordo di un uomo buono'; author interviews with Elio and Marlene Vitale; LDB, letter from Katowice, 7 March 1945; *ITIAM*, p. 119.

p. 313

Section on Franco Sacerdoti from: Waitz, p. 475; author interviews with Luciana Nissim, Alda Sacerdoti, Ulda Sacerdoti; letter to Alda Sacerdoti from Wanda Sacerdoti, 26 January 1994. Silvio Barabas remembers little now of what he told the Sacerdotis just after the war.

p. 313–15

Section on Luciana and Vanda from: *Donne*, pp. 32–55; author interviews with Luciana Nissim and Carla Maestro; 'Vanda Maestro' in *Donne piemontesi nella lotta di liberazione*; Tedeschi, *There is a Place on Earth*, pp. 3, 20–22. Waitz, p. 484, and *Rapporto*, p. 45 confirm that there was always a delay between the selections and gassing.

p. 315

¶ 'It was as well . . .'   Gobetti, *Diario partigiano*, pp. 114–15, 128; author interviews with EGT; CDEC documents on Franco Momigliano.

¶ 'By the end . . .'   *ITIAM*, p. 55.

¶ 'For days . . .' and next three ¶¶   *ITIAM*, pp. 48–51, 55–9, 62.

p. 316

¶ 'Understanding . . .'   *ITIAM*, pp. 50, 57, 61, 148, 158, 163; *D. & S.*, p. 56.

p. 317

¶ 'The other great . . .' and next three ¶¶   *ITIAM*, pp. 62–3, 77–9.

¶ 'From the beginning . . .'   Author interviews with Paolo Dalla Volta and Silvio Barabas.

p. 318

¶¶ 'He may also . . .' and 'The meaning . . .'   Author interviews with Paolo Dalla Volta and Silvio Barabas; Paolo Dalla Volta in *Bresciaoggi*, 14 August 1996. On Guido Dalla Volta's death in a selection: PL letter to JS, 23 March 1946; *D. & S.*, pp. 19–21; PL in interviews with Leonardo Vergani in *Corriere della Sera*, 20 May 1979, and Mario Viglino in April 1978 (private interview held in the Library of the Jewish Community of Turin), p. 26. Tibaldi gives Guido Dalla Volta's date of death as 15.11.44; but since he gives Alberto's as 'after 5.5.44', it is likely that he (or someone) confused the two Dalla Voltas. (See *Primo Levi: testimone*, pp. 171–2.)

p. 319

Lorenzo

¶ 'On 7 June . . .' and next four ¶¶   Dini & Jesurum, p. 80; *ITIAM*, pp. 79–80, 122; *MR*, pp. 150–54. For civilian workers being sent into Auschwitz as punishment, see also Waitz, p. 475n., and LDB, ANED interview, 1982, p. 14.

p. 320

¶ 'Lorenzo also gave . . .'   *ITIAM*, p. 125; *MR*, pp. 155–6; author interviews with Secondo Perone.

¶ 'Primo and Alberto . . .'   *ITIAM*, p. 126; *MR*, pp. 152, 155, 159; PL in *Midstream*, April 1986, p. 27; author interviews with Secondo Perone and Dr Menardi of the Castello degli Acaja Library, Fossano; also letter from JS to Yad Vashem about Lorenzo, 14 January 1998.

¶ 'Only after his return . . .' and next five ¶¶   *MR*, pp. 151, 152, 156; *D. & S.*, p. 98; PL in Roth; author interviews with Secondo Perone, Giuseppe Perone, Emma Bard, Don Carlo Lenta of Fossano, Dr Menardi, and Beppe Manfredi of Fossano. On I. G. Farben's factories at Blechhammer, Heydebreck and Auschwitz: Hans Deichmann, 'Letter to a Friend', 11 July 1977, p. 8, in dossier of material on I. G. Farben by Hans Deichmann kindly given me by Giorgio Vaccarino.

p. 322

¶ 'The Italian workers' camp . . .'   Hans Deichmann, 'Letter to a Friend', pp. 10–11, and Appendix to Giorgio Vaccarino, 'Nuove fonti sull'imperialismo nazista: La I. G. Farben e "il nuovo ordine"', *Italia contemporanea*, No. 169, December 1987; PL in 'La deportazione degli ebrei', 1997, p. 64, and in *Midstream*, April 1986, p. 27.

¶ 'One day in late June . . .' and next four ¶¶   *MR*, pp. 29–33; *D. & S.*, pp. 81–2.

p. 323

Lorenzo's first letter to BGS (actually a postcard): photograph from 'Il bestiale fascismo è vinto!', 'The beast of Fascism is beaten!', Exhibition on the Resistance, Milan, April–June 1975; negative and transcription of text both held at CDEC, Milan.

¶ '"I believe . . ."' and following quotation   *ITIAM*, pp. 127–8.

p. 324

¶ 'Some time in June or July . . .'   *ITIAM* suggests June (see p. 111, 'been here . . . three months', and p. 117, 'a clear June sky'), and so does *MR* (p. 28). However, PL said July in his interview with Silvia and Giovanni Tesio, 1986; and in his letter to PL of 12 February 1965, Mendi [Rabbi Menachem Chaim (Emil) Davidowicz] says that the date of formation of the Chemical Kommando was 20 July.

¶ 'On the day . . .' and next three ¶¶   *ITIAM*, pp. 107–110, 116, 137–8, 142,

144; *MR*, pp. 27, 50; PL's list of Kommando 98 (Chemical Kommando) members, sent to JS, 31 July 1961; JS, Colmar talk, p. 5, and author interviews; letter from Mendi to PL, 1965; *D. & S.*, p. 60; *Rapporto*, p. 43.

p. 325

¶ 'Nonetheless it was . . .' *MR*, p. 57; *ITIAM*, p. 154; PL's list of Kommando 98 members. According to PL's list, the chemists in the Kommando – apart from himself, Alfred Fisch ('Alfred L.' – see 346 and Note on p. 782), Brackier and Kandel – included Alfred Rosenfeld, a chemical engineer, Paul Sómogyi (who would die in the Infectious Ward during the 'Ten Days'), and Bela Fischer, a distinguished Hungarian biochemist who had worked on Vitamin C before the war. Apart from JS, the pharmacists included Bandi (Endre Szanto), Joulty, Wolf and Kraus. Iss Clausner was a physicist, Leon Treistmann (almost certainly 'Rappoport', see p. 347 and Note on p. 782) a doctor, Cardos an engineer, Arnold Silberlust a mathematician, and Gerhard Goldbaum a sound engineer. Istvan Balla was a chemistry student like Alberto; Paul Steinberg and Silvio Barabas had both planned to study chemistry. Mendi was no scientist at all, but a rabbi, and a brave and clever man who spoke seven languages, as PL wrote (*ITIAM*, p. 110); he got into the Chemical Kommando, and survived. Tischler was one of two Polish *tischlers* (carpenters); there was also a Dutch one.

p. 326

¶ 'When the day . . .' and next five ¶¶ *ITIAM*, pp. 109–114; *MR*, p. 89. 'that poor brute . . .' *ITIAM*, p. 114.

¶ 'Primo always said . . .' From the Preface to *ITIAM* onwards; see p. 15.

¶ 'By this time . . .' *ITIAM*, p. 115; JS in Colmar talk and author interviews; JS in interview with Susan Tarrow, *Forum Italicum*, Vol. 28, No. 1, Spring 1994, p. 3.

★ He admitted it, e.g., to Greer in 1985, and to Silvia and Giovanni Tesio in 1986.

p. 328

¶ 'The Kommando . . .' *ITIAM*, pp. 116–17; author interviews with JS; JS in Colmar talk and Tarrow interview; author interviews with Silvio Barabas; Mendi letter to PL, 1965.

p. 329

¶ 'He had arrived . . .' and next six ¶¶ JS in author interviews, Colmar talk, Tarrow interview and *Il presente del passato*; also in Blakeway and Rosenfeld TV. For the date of Pierre Samuel's transfer to Jawischowitz, see Martin Gilbert, *The Holocaust*, Guild Publishing, 1986, p. 425. Gilbert mentions only the notorious Jawischowitz mines, but there was also a quarry, and it was to this that Pierrot was sent. For JS's passion for maths: both Mendi and Silvio Barabas remembered this clearly. For the return to reality being difficult, see *ITIAM*, *passim* (e.g. pp. 49–50, 61, 120, 148, 177), and JS in Tarrow interview. For a week between PL's and JS's two meetings, see *ITIAM*, p. 116. 'The Canto of Ulysses' is the single most anthologized piece of Holocaust literature, according to Alberto Cavaglion (*Belfagor*, No. 31, July 1994, p. 476).

p. 330

¶ 'Every day . . .' and next two ¶¶ *ITIAM*, pp. 115–18; author interviews with

JS and Silvio Barabas; Primo's list of Kommando 98 members; JS in *Il presente del passato* and Tarrow interview.

p. 331

¶ 'Ulysses' voice . . .' and next two ¶¶   Dante, *Inferno*, Canto XXVI.

p. 332

'*Considerate* . . .'   Dante, *Inferno*, Canto XXVI, lines 118–20.

¶¶ ' 'Pikolo begs me . . .', 'Primo held . . .' and 'But he could not . . .'   *ITIAM*, pp. 119–21.

'Three times . . .'   Dante, *Inferno*, Canto XXVI, lines 139–41.

'*Infin* . . .'   Dante, *Inferno*, Canto XXVI, line 142.

¶ 'Today Jean . . .' and next two ¶¶   Author interviews with JS; and JS in *Il presente del passato* and Blakeway. See also *D. & S.*, p. 112: 'Dante did not interest him, but I did.' The quotation '*The characters in these pages* . . .' is on p. 127 of *ITIAM*.

p. 333

¶ 'Dante had reinvented . . .' and next two ¶¶   See PL letter to Heinz Riedt, undated reply to Riedt's of 3 March 1960: 'Questo poeta, che altrove appare un astratto teorico della teologia, . . . in questi versi è invece pieno di ammirazione e di amore per il suo Ulisse, eroe e peccatore a un tempo': i.e. Dante, the Christian theologian, in Canto XXVI is full of love and admiration for Ulysses, hero and sinner at the same time. The quotation from Croce is in Dante's *Inferno*, translation and comment by John D. Sinclair, Oxford University Press, New York, 1961, p. 331. I have drawn on Sinclair's commentary on Canto XXVI for this section. For Primo telling JS many times that he meant to record and report Auschwitz to the world: author interviews with JS and JS interview with Tarrow, p. 5.

p. 334

¶ 'In August . . .'   PL dates Jup's arrival to August in the list of Kommando 98 members. For rest of ¶: *ITIAM*, pp. 122, 143; PL, 'Un "giallo" del Lager', *Opere II*, p. 909; author interviews with JS, and JS in Colmar talk and Rosenfeld TV; Mendi letter to Primo, 1965.

p. 335

¶ 'The wider situation . . .'   *ITIAM*, pp. 123–4; PL, 'Buco nero di Auschwitz', *La Stampa*, 22 January 1987, in *Opere II*, p. 1321; *MR*, p. 86.

¶ 'Despite all this . . .'   *MR*, pp. 19, 22, 93–4; *ITIAM*, pp. 122, 139, 144, 151, 161; JS in Tarrow interview; author interviews with JS, Silvio Barabas, and Paolo Dalla Volta. *Re* Lonzana: see *MR* on 'Valerio'. In the original typescript PL had written 'Lonzana'; and there was a Lonzana in his transport: Cesare Formiggini Lonzana, b. 1897, d. after April 1944, 'in luogo ignoto', place unknown (Tibaldi in *Primo Levi: testimone*, p. 183).

¶ 'Silvio had squeezed . . .' and next ¶   Author interviews with Silvio Barabas. About Silvio's survival on the *Bunasuppe* alone, Hermann Langbein said: 'I cannot rule it out.'

★ Quotation from 'Last Christmas of the War', *MR*, p. 86.

p. 336

¶ 'His wealth also . . .'   Author interviews with JS, and JS in Colmar talk; PL in Pesaro debate, 1986, and in Risa Sodi, 'Interview with Primo Levi', *Partisan Review*, 1987, p. 360, in *Conversazioni e interviste*, p. 230; *ITIAM*, p. 148; *MR*, 'Lilith'.

p. 337

¶ 'Together with Alberto . . .'   *ITIAM*, pp. 333–5; JS interviews with author and Colmar talk.

¶ 'In August . . .'   Lorenzo's second card, dated 20 August 1944, in CDEC.

¶ 'Soon after . . .'   *MR*, 'A Disciple'.

p. 338

¶ 'Luciana was still . . .' and next four ¶¶   Author interviews with Luciana Nissim; *Donne*, pp. 48, 55–6; author interviews with Giuliana Giuliana Tedeschi, and Giuliana Tedeschi, *There is a Place on Earth*, p. 129.

p. 339

¶ ' "We fought . . .' and next two ¶¶   *ITIAM*, pp. 129, 142; *D. & S.*, pp. 134–7; 'La resistenza nei Lager', 1966, in *Opere I*, p. 1146.

¶ 'By the end . . .'   Gilbert, *The Holocaust*, pp. 718, 722, 735; *D. & S.*, p. 41.

¶ 'What happened . . .'   Carmine Lops, 'L'Organizzazione del campo [Fossoli]', p. 267; Gilbert, *The Holocaust*, pp. 744–7; Langbein in *Il presente del passato*, p. 66; *D. & S.*, pp. 41–2; PL, 'La resistenza nei Lager'; *Rapporto*, p. 45.

p. 340

¶ 'Nonetheless . . .' and next ¶   *ITIAM*, pp. 154–5; Eugenio Ravenna (from PL's transport), deposition 6 December 1946 (CDEC); LDB, ANED interview, 1982, p. 12; author interviews with JS.

¶ 'Primo made this . . .' and next ¶   Langbein in *Il presente del passato*, p. 65; *ITIAM*, p. 155. On PL refusing to judge anyone, including the 'crows of the crematorium', see *D. & S.*, pp. 42–3.

'Because we too . . .'   *ITIAM*, p. 156.

¶ 'By late October . . .' and next three ¶¶   'La resistenza nei Lager'; *ITIAM*, pp. 130–34, 142–3; *Rapporto*, p. 45; Waitz, p. 494. For 250 bodies in the room, see PL, 'Un lager alle porte d'Italia', *La Stampa*, 19 January 1979, *Opere I*, p. 1257.

p. 341

¶ 'Like everyone else . . .' and next two ¶¶   *ITIAM*, pp. 134–5; Greer, *VM*, pp. 5–6; PL, ANED interview, *VM*, p. 242. The quotation 'saved by my trade' comes from Greer; PL said, 'We were all *Untermenschen* down there' to David Mendel. Primo's dissent from Jean Améry is in *D. & S.*, Ch. 6.

'. . . A prayer . . .'   *D. & S.*, p. 118.

p. 342

¶ 'This is a peak moment . . .'   'But not very brave' is from Silvia Ciairano, private interview, 1975.

p. 343

¶ 'This may explain . . .'   *ITIAM*, p. 235.

'Kuhn is . . .'   *ITIAM*, pp. 135–6.

¶ 'Is this the same . . .'   Primo never changed his mind about Kuhn. See e.g.

Ateneo, p. 11 (BBC *Bookmark*), and Pesaro debate, 1986, p. 13. For his having given up on the Nazis, see *D. & S.*, p. 23.

¶ 'The last selection . . .' and next ¶ *Donne*, p. 57; Tedeschi, *There is a Place on Earth*, pp. 138–9; author interviews with Luciana Nissim, Giuliana Tedeschi, Carla Maestro, and Edoardo Gridelli; *The Truce*, p. 206; *Donne piemontesi*, p. 88; Primo's information on Vanda's CDEC form. Gilbert (*The Holocaust*, p. 767) says that 31 October was the last day the gas chambers functioned in Auschwitz.

p. 344

¶ 'On 1 November . . .' and next two ¶¶ Lorenzo's third letter from Auschwitz for Primo, dated 1 November 1944, CDEC; *MR*, pp. 92–5.

p. 345

¶ 'The Chemical Kommando . . .' *ITIAM*, p. 144.

¶ 'We have already . . .' Author interviews with Paul Steinberg.

‡ Palptil Brackier was a Pole from Belgium, Jean Kandel a Romanian living in France (from PL's list of Kommando 98 members).

p. 346

¶ 'Already now . . .' Quotation 'a very few superior individuals . . .' is from *ITIAM*, p. 98. Rest of ¶: *D. & S.*, pp. 60–61, 63.

¶ 'Another is . . .' PL identifies 'Alfred L.' as Alfred Fisch in his list of Kommando 98 members; and JS confirmed it in a letter to me, 14 January 1998. Primo's story of Fisch is in *ITIAM*, pp. 99–101. The detail that the job of Technical Head was created for him is in a letter from PL to Heinz Riedt, 28 November 1959.

¶ 'Fisch was not insane . . .' For the identification of 'Rappoport' with Leon Treistmann: on his list of Kommando 98 members PL notes that Treistmann is a Pole who has been practising medicine in Italy, and who speaks Italian well: just like 'Rappoport'. There is also the name 'Leon', and the fact that Treistmann was on PL's transport. Many of PL's Italian contacts (e.g. 'Steinlauf') were people he'd already met on the transport.

p. 347

¶ 'Rappoport . . .' *MR*, 'Rappoport's Testament'. Fisch as 'joyless': *ITIAM*, p. 101.

¶ ' "Henri's real name . . .' and next ¶ Steinberg, *Speak You Also*. The description of Steinberg ('He was young and attractive') is from *ITIAM*, pp. 104–5.

★ Quotation '*how vain is the myth* . . .': ITIAM, p. 99.

p. 348

¶ 'He did not often talk . . .' Author interviews with Paul Steinberg; PL in RAI TV interview, 'Il mestiere di raccontare', broadcast 25 May and 3 June 1974.

¶ 'Like everyone . . .' and next two ¶¶ *ITIAM*, pp. 104–6; author interviews with Paul Steinberg; Steinberg, *Speak You Also*.

¶ 'All this Primo records . . .' On PL's suspicion that Steinberg used his body as well as his mind: see letter to Heinz Riedt, 28 November 1959, in which PL replies to Riedt's hesitation over translating 'Sodoma's San Sebastian', since it carries a homosexual implication: '*Traduca pure*', 'Go ahead and translate it.' Quotations from *ITIAM*, p. 106.

¶ 'It is a harsh verdict . . .' and next ¶ Steinberg, *Speak You Also*; author interviews with Paul Steinberg and JS. For PL's later attitudes to the grey zone, see e.g. *D. & S.*, p. 33.

¶ 'Perhaps, too . . .'   'an instrument in ["Henri" 's] hands'   *ITIAM*, p. 106. 'I felt penetrated . . .'   Pesaro debate, 1986, p. 22.

¶ 'Even in Auschwitz . . .'   On Steinberg's dismissing PL from his mind: author interviews with Paul Steinberg; on his retaining his charm and calculation, letter to the author from Robert Francès, 26 January 1998. Paul Steinberg has since died (in December 1999). In *Speak You Also* Steinberg remembers being in the same laboratory as PL, but this is certainly wrong. From his descriptions it is clear that he was in the Styrene laboratory with Fisch.

p. 350

¶ 'By November . . .' and next ¶   *ITIAM*, pp. 142–3; *Rapporto*, p. 39.

¶ 'And then it happened . . .' and next two ¶¶   *ITIAM*, pp. 144–7; *PT*, p. 214.

p. 351

¶ 'The work was . . .' and next two ¶¶   *PT*, pp. 214, 222; Biagi, *1935 e dintorni*, 1982; *MR*, pp. 88–90, 110–14; *ITIAM*, pp. 141–54; author interviews with Silvio Barabas.

p. 352

¶ 'With the Germans . . .'   *PT*, p. 214. For Meyer's arrival in November, Anissimov, *Primo Levi*, p. 296, from Meyer's first letter to PL, 2 March 1967. For 'No one could be so ignorant unless he chose to be': see Hans Deichmann in Appendix to Vaccarino, 'Nuove fonti', p. 98, who confirms it.

¶ 'Then there was . . .'   *ITIAM*, pp. 109, 146–7; *D. & S.*, pp. 138–9; Anissimov, *Primo Levi*, 303.

p. 353

¶ 'Finally . . .' and next ¶   *ITIAM*, p. 149; *MR*, pp. 90–92.

p. 354

¶ 'At the end of December . . .' and next ¶   *MR*, pp. 156–7 and PL in *Midstream*, April 1986, p. 27.

¶ 'A week or so . . .' and next five ¶¶   *MR*, pp. 110–14.

p. 355

11–16 January   *ITIAM*, pp. 157–8, 172, 175; *The Truce*, p. 393; PL letter to JS, 23 March 1946; Anissimov, *Primo Levi*, p. 321; author interviews with Charles Conreau.

p. 357

16 January: Samuelidis   *ITIAM*, pp. 158–61; PL to JS, 23 March 1946; author interviews with Charles Conreau.

p. 358

17 January: Alberto   *ITIAM*, p. 161; author interviews with Charles Conreau.

pp. 358–60

18 January: The March

¶ 'The prisoners . . .'   Author interviews with JS; Maurice Reznik, 'La marche de la mort des déportés', *Le Monde Juif*, No. 77, January–March 1985, French text by Henri Bulawko, Centre de Documentation Juive Contemporaine, Paris; Gilbert, *The Holocaust*, p. 771; Anissimov, *Primo Levi*, p. 319.

¶ 'They joined . . .'   *ITIAM*, p. 161; Gilbert, *The Holocaust*, p. 775; JS in author interviews, Tarrow interview and Colmar talk; Maurice Goldstein in *Il presente del passato*, p. 92; Reznik, 'La marche de la mort'; Lazzaro Levi, Diary, p. 7; author interviews with Silvio Barabas; Silvio Barabas letter to PL, 20 December 1945 (CDEC).

¶ 'But Alberto and Franco . . .' and next five ¶¶   Author interviews with Silvio Barabas; JS, Colmar talk and Tarrow interview; Reznik, 'La marche de la mort'; Lazzaro Levi, Diary; Mendi letter to PL, 1965; *ITIAM*, p. 160; PL to JS, 23 March 1946; Gilbert, *The Holocaust*, p. 774; Silvio Barabas letter to PL, 20 December 1945.

¶ 'Whichever version . . .'   PL to Emma Dalla Volta, 26 December 1945; *ITIAM*, p. 161.

pp. 360–61

18–19 January: '*Remorques*'   Author interviews with Aldo Moscati; *Rapporto*, p. 46; *ITIAM*, pp. 162–3; PL to Jean, 23 March 1946; Anissimov, *Primo Levi*, p. 319; LDB, ANED interview, 1982, p. 21; *Roots*, pp. 101–17.

p. 361

¶ 'No one will ever know . . .'   *MR*, p. 114; LDB, ANED interview, 1982, p. 33; Gilbert, *The Holocaust*, p. 773; Langbein, *Menschen in Auschwitz*; Anissimov, *Primo Levi*, pp. 319, 391, 397–8.

¶ 'The most likely . . .'   *ITIAM*, pp. 164, 187; Anissimov, *Primo Levi*, p. 324; General Petrenko, Commander of the Soviet forces which liberated Auschwitz, at the commemorations for the fiftieth anniversary of the liberation, London, 29 January 1995.

pp. 361–4

20 January: Heat, 21 January: Light and *22 January: Soup and Speeches*   *ITIAM*, pp. 164–71; author interviews with Charles Conreau; Charles Conreau in Blakeway; PL to JS, 23 March 1946; Greer, *VM*, p. 7.

pp. 364–5

23 January: The Finest Hour   PL map of Monowitz, held by JS; *ITIAM*, pp. 171–2, 243–4; author interviews with Charles Conreau; PL to JS, 23 March 1946; PL in interviews with Greer, *VM*, p. 7, and Risa Sodi, *Partisan Review*, p. 361 (in *Conversazioni e interviste*, pp. 232–3). On Raffaele Grassini: Tibaldi list of *sommersi* from PL's transport, in *Primo Levi: testimone*, p. 176. Grassini died on 24 February 1945 at Auschwitz, the only one of PL's transport to die after liberation in this way, as far as he knew (according to his list of the fates of seventy-five members of his transport, prepared to accompany his deposition against Bosshammer in 1971, in *Primo Levi: testimone*, p. 232. PL used the annotation 'm' for 'malattia' (illness), 's' for 'selezione' (selection) and 't' for 'trasporto' (transport, i.e. the death march); Grassini is the only 'l', for 'liberazione' (liberation).) On Lello: author interviews with Lello Perugia; *ITIAM*, pp. 60, 172–5, 244; PL in interview with Graziella Granà, *VM*, p. 150. I thank Graziella Granà for giving me the unpublished part of this interview.

pp. 365–7

24 January: 'On est dehors', 25 January: Sómogyi, 26 January: Charles, 27 January:

Burial   ITIAM, pp. 173–9; *The Truce*, pp. 187, 393; author interviews with
Charles Conreau, and Charles Conreau in Blakeway; PL to JS, 23 March 1946;
Langbein, *Menschen in Auschwitz*; PL in Risa Sodi interview, *Partisan Review*,
Conversazioni e interviste, pp. 232–3.

Chapter 10: *The Truce: 27 January – 19 October 1945*

p. 368

¶ 'Liberation . . .'   LDB, ANED interview, 1982, p. 24.

¶ 'It should . . .'   *The Truce*, p. 188; *D. & S.*, pp. 52–3, 56; author interviews with
Lello Perugia.

p. 369

¶ 'Again . . .' and next two ¶¶   Author interviews with JS; *D. & S.*, pp. 52, 58–9;
INNW, p. 234; *The Truce*, pp. 187–91.

¶ 'Now came . . .' and next ¶   *The Truce*, pp. 191–2; LDB, ANED interview,
1982, pp. 24–5; *D. & S.*, p. 57.

¶ 'For Primo . . .'   Typescript of *The Truce* in Einaudi Archive, Chapter 'Il greco',
p. 1.

¶ 'For three days . . .' and next ¶   *The Truce*, pp. 192–6; author interviews with
Charles Conreau, and Charles Conreau in Blakeway.

pp. 370–73

'*Hurbinek's Word*'   Vincenti, p. 52; *The Truce*, pp. 196–203, 207.

p. 373

¶ 'Love and death . . .' and next two ¶¶   *The Truce*, pp. 205–6.

'I did not suffer . . .'   Giovanni Tesio, 'Tutta l'odissea in un guaderno', *La Stampa*,
Speciale La tregua, 9 February 1997, p. 3.

pp. 374–9

'*The Greek*'   *The Truce*, Ch. 3, 'The Greek'.

Also:

p. 374

On the Jews of Salonika in Auschwitz, *ITIAM*, pp. 34, 85; *The Truce*, p. 213;
Rudolf, *VM*, p. 25.

p. 376

On PL's wanting to write a whole book about the Greek: PL in Mayda, 'Il poeta
triste del Lager', p. 5. On Alberto Dalla Volta's dedication to freedom, *ITIAM*,
p. 145.

p. 379

On the Greek giving PL a pair of trousers, see also Rudolf, *VM*, p. 26. On PL's
trying to trace him after the war: PL told Rudolf that there were 'at least thirty'
Leon Levis in Salonika (*VM*, p. 26), but this was one of his exaggerations for
effect. He told Gisella that there were seven.

pp. 379–80

The Messenger   *The Truce*, pp. 226–7. The episode of 'Daniele' throwing bread to
German prisoners is on pp. 291–2. The identification of 'Daniele' as Luciano

Mariani is proven by two points: (1) In the original typescript of *The Truce* in the Einaudi Archive, Ch. 8 ('Southwards'), PL had begun by writing 'Luciano', and only later changed the name to 'Daniele' (e.g. on pp. 85, 91, 99); (2) Luciano Mariani lost all eighteen members of his family deported with him, like 'Daniele' (LDB, letter to Hermann Langbein, 26 February 1960 and to *La Stampa*, 2 September 1967; though Tibaldi counts only seven (*Primo Levi: testimone*, p. 157).

pp. 380–85

Katowice   *The Truce*, Ch. 4, 'Katowice'; author interviews with Lello Perugia; and Corrado Saralvo, *Più morti più spazio, tempo di Auschwitz*, Baldini & Castoldi, 1969, Chs. 'Il lager di Katowice' and 'Promozione a "pirivoc"'. It is Saralvo who calls 'Riva' 'Rovi', and he uses real names throughout (e.g. Egorov's). Lello Perugia also remembers 'Colonel Rovi'.

Also:

p. 381

For the companions PL found at Katowice, see also PL, letter to BGS from Katowice, 6 June 1945 (CDEC); LDB, letter to Aldo Moscati, 20 October 1945 (kindly given me by Aldo Moscati); Saralvo, *Più morti più spazio*, p. 230; and Tibaldi list, *Primo Levi: testimone*, pp. 160–63.

pp. 382–3

LDB's story: LDB, ANED interview, 1982, p. 25; LDB letters to his family from Katowice, 24 February, 7 March, 6 April, 28 April and 29 April 1945, and to Aldo Moscati, 20 October 1945; PL, 'Ricordo di un uomo buono'.

p. 383

Quotations 'these . . . dear dear Russians' and 'extremely intelligent and willing' both from LDB's letter of 28 April 1945. For everyone ending up in the Bogucice surgery: PL, 'Leonardo De Benedetti', *Ha Keillah*, December 1983, in *Opere II*, p. 1197.

★ For name changes in *The Truce*, pp. 43 and 66 of original typescript.

p. 384

For Galina being seventeen or eighteen: PL starts with seventeen in his typescript (p. 67), then changes to eighteen. On PL falling deeper and deeper in love: see also *The Truce*, p. 359. For Galina's being like Gabriella Garda, see *PT*, p. 114.

p. 385

¶ 'Who was Galina? . . .'   For the description of PL at Katowice: PL to Bianca, 6 June 1945; Bice Azzali, *Unità*, c. 11 April 1987.

pp. 385–94

'*Cesare*'   *The Truce*, Ch. 5, 'Cesare', and Ch. 6, 'Victory Day'; author interviews with Lello Perugia.

Also:

p. 385

¶ 'Cesare and the Greek . . .'   PL in interviews with Mario Viglino, April 1978, and Giorgina Arian Levi, *Ha Keillah*, April 1978. Lello let PL's stories stand until 'Per questo Primo si è ucciso', an interview with Luciano Tas in *Shalom*, No. 5,

April 1988. For Lello's saying he does not want to challenge PL: author interviews with Lello Perugia, and e.g. to Tas in *Shalom*, p. 24. For Primo's making Cesare a twin to himself: see *MR*, pp. 140, 144; and e.g. pp. 392 (their exchanging identities) and 414 (both being counterfeiters) below.

pp. 386–9

Cesare's story from author interviews with Lello Perugia, and Lello Perugia curriculum vitae, Auschwitz memories and other personal documents, kindly given me by Lello Perugia; Lello Perugia interviews with Tas, with Stefano Jesurum in *Essere Ebrei in Italia*, pp. 91–4, and with Gabriella Mecucci in *Unità*, 3 September 1992, p. 17; Robert Katz, *Sabato nero*, Rizzoli, translation of *Black Sabbath: A Journey Through a Crime Against Humanity*, Toronto, 1969, pp. 92–3; De Felice, pp. 466–7; Susan Zuccotti, *The Italians and the Holocaust*, Peter Halban, London, 1987, Ch. 6, 'Rome, 1943: The October Roundup'; Italo Tibaldi, *Compagni di viaggio*, Transport 56, pp. 77–8. On Buna-Monowitz being better than Birkenau: LDB, ANED interview, 1982, p. 6; author interviews with Giuliana Tedeschi.

p. 389

¶ 'Now, this real Cesare . . .'   On the literariness of *The Truce*, see e.g. PL in *Echi*, p. 95, and in Lucarini and Roth. The quotations are from PL's letter to Lello Perugia on sending him *The Truce*, 10 June 1963.

p. 390

¶ 'Lello did judge . . .'   On Lello's suppressed anger against PL for his portraits of him in *The Truce* and 'Cesare's Last Adventure': author interviews with Lello Perugia; Jesurum interview, pp. 91, 94; author interviews with Stuart Woolf, and his letter to me of 21 September 1994.

¶ 'How did Primo betray . . .'   On Lello's organizing: Guadagni, 'Primo Levi', *Unità*, 21 February 1993.

p. 391

¶ 'Strictly speaking . . .'   The description of the entrance to the Bogucice camp, with its *propusk* arrangements and its Mongolian guard, is confirmed by Saralvo, *Più morti più spazio*, pp. 232, 246.

¶ 'This happened . . .'   Piero Frassica, in 'Primo Levi: eroe, antieroe o alter ego', in S. Salvatore, p. 30, also notes the significance of this switch of identities with an *alter ego*. Altogether this essay is rich and acute on the theme of PL's doubles/opposites/twins.

p. 392

¶ 'It worked like this . . .' and next ¶   The identification of 'Giacomantonio': author interviews with Lello Perugia, and Tibaldi, *Compagni di viaggio*, Transport 56 list. Author interviews with Lello Perugia confirmed this account of Primo's, like most of them, as true. (Where Lello and PL disagree, I make it clear.)

p. 394

¶ 'On one of these wild . . .'   That the other nationalities had already left by the Victory Day celebration is confirmed by Saralvo, *Più morti più spazio*, p. 349, and by LDB in his letter to his family from Katowice, 28 April 1945.

pp. 395–8

The End of Katowice   *The Truce*, Ch. 6, 'Victory Day', Ch. 7, 'The Dreamers' and

Ch. 8, 'Southwards'; and Saralvo, *Più morti più spazio*, p. 349; LDB, letters to his family from Katowice, 28 April and 11 May 1945, and to Aldo Moscati, 20 October 1945; PL to Bianca from Katowice, 6 June 1945; author interviews with Lello Perugia.

Also:

p. 396

For no one believed that the post was working: see e.g. Saralvo, *Più morti più spazio*, p. 233, and PL, 'The Tommy Gun under the Bed': even the Polish military command in Italy had difficulty contacting Poland (*Opere II*, p. 918). For PL could have been happy: see LDB to Aldo Moscati, 20 October 1945, and PL to Bianca, 6 June 1945.

pp. 396–7

For the story of Cravero, see also 'The Tommy Gun under the Bed'.

p. 398

LDB's testimonial is among his papers at the Library of the Jewish Community, Turin.

pp. 398–400

To Zhmerinka   *The Truce*, Ch. 8, 'Southwards'; and PL to Bianca, 6 June 1945; Saralvo, *Più morti più spazio*, Ch. 'In viaggio per Odessa'; author interviews with Lello Perugia; LDB to Aldo Moscati, 20 October 1945; Dr Einhorn's Red Cross report on LDB, in LDB's papers at the Library of the Jewish Community of Turin.

p. 398

★ Saralvo, *Più morti, più spazio*, pp. 240, 264; PL to Bianca, 6 June 1945; author interviews with Emma Pacifici.

pp. 400–403

The Wrong Way   *The Truce*, Ch. 9, 'Northwards' and Ch. 10, 'The Little Hen'; author interviews with Lello Perugia, and Saralvo, *Più morti più spazio*, Chs. 'In viaggio per Odessa', 'Il passaggio della Beresina' and 'Il campo di Sluzck'; *Echi*, p. 262; PL in interview with Carlo Paladini at Pesaro, 5 May 1986; Preface to *La tregua* schools edn, 1965, p. 8; Vincenti, p. 53.

Also:

p. 402

¶ 'There were six . . .'   Quotation 'the past that suits him best' from 'Uranium', *PT*, p. 199. The best candidate for 'Mr Unverdorben' is a fifty-six-year-old *triestino* called Moise Canarutto; his friend was probably Emilio Ziffer (author interviews with Lello Perugia; Tibaldi list of transport, p. 56; and PL's typescript of *La tregua*, in which he called the two *triestini* 'Guzzeri' and 'Zimmer'. 'Zimmer' is close to 'Ziffer', which leaves Canarutto for 'Guzzeri').

pp. 403–9

Starye Dorogi   *The Truce*, Ch. 11, 'Old Roads', Ch. 12, 'The Wood and the Path', Ch. 13, 'Holidays', and Ch. 14, 'The Theatre'; author interviews with Lello Perugia; and LDB to Aldo Moscati, 20 October 1945; Saralvo, *Più morti più spazio*, Ch. 'Amore nel Lager'; Lello Perugia interviews with Tas and Mecucci; 'Cesare's Last Adventure' in *MR*, p. 139.

Also:

p. 404

¶ 'This is a description . . .'   Luciano Mariani may have been one of those who tried to escape from Starye Dorogi, and may even have succeeded: he returned separately, and before PL and LDB (author interviews with Alberto Vita, and his note to me about Mariani, undated). Alternatively, Mariani may have left the train from Starye Dorogi early, like Lello: PL has 'Daniele' still with them on departure (p. 354).

p. 407

¶ 'Well, Primo may . . .'   On PL knowing Lello would mind: his letters to Lello, 10 June 1963 (about *The Truce*), and 11 September 1980 (about 'Cesare's Last Adventure'), both kindly given me by Lello Perugia. Also, e.g., *Echi*, pp. 19–20, and PL, interview with Graziella Granà, *VM*, p. 150.

pp. 409–16

'*Thirty-five Days*'   *The Truce*, Ch. 15, 'From Starye Dorogi to Iasi', Ch. 16, 'From Iasi to the Line', and Ch. 17, 'The Awakening' (for leaving date of 15 September, see pp. 316, 352); author interviews with Lello Perugia; and 'Itinerario', *Opere II*, p. 1221; Saralvo, *Più morti più spazio*, Ch. 'Sulla via di ritorno; LDB to Aldo Moscati, 20 October 1945; 'Cesare's Last Adventure', *MR*; Lello Perugia interviews with Tas and Mecucci; Lello Perugia documents (Luigi Dominici letter, RAF ticket), reproduced in Tas interview and given to me by Lello Perugia; PL's letter to Lello about 'Cesare's Last Adventure', 11 September 1980; Vincenti, p. 53. The information about £16 in 1945 comes from the Office of National Statistics, which lists £1 in 1945 as worth £23.78 in November 2001.

p. 416

19 October 1945   *The Truce*, pp. 379–80; author interviews with Lello Perugia. Date 19 October 1945 confirmed by LDB's letter to Aldo Moscati, 20 October 1945, and by his ANED 1982 interview, p. 26. And: PL to Rosselli students, *La Stampa*, 25 May 1979; *Echi*, p. 160; LDB, ANED interview, 1982, pp. 26–7; PL to JS, 23 March 1946; PL, 'My House', *OPT*, p. 1; PL in interviews with Marco Barberis, *Avanti*, 19 October 1971 and Gianni Milani, *Piemonte VIP*, March 1986; author interviews with BGS, GCD, Jole Segre, Silvio and Ada Ortona, Giorgio Luzzati, Anna Cases, Nereo Pezza, Vanna Rava; also Jole Segre and PL in BBC *Bookmark*, BGS in Blakeway and in Guadagni, *Unità*, 21 February 1993, and GCD in Rosenfeld TV.

Chapter 11: Levi Uomo: 1945–7

p. 419

¶ 'Many years later . . .'   Author interviews with Anna Maria Levi Bassan.

¶ 'All his life . . .'   *Conversations*, pp. 66–7; Viglino interview, 1978; *Mondoperaio*, in *VM*. For both PL and Italy being full of hope: PL's letter to Heinz Riedt, 31 January 1960; PL, 'Un passato che credevamo non dovesse tornare più', *Corriere della Sera*, 8 May 1974, in *Opere I*, p. 1184; PL in interviews with *Mondoperaio*,

1984 (in *VM*) and *Progetto*, 1980. Quotations from *La tregua* schools edn 1965 and *Echi*, p. 215 (interview with Giovanni Pacchioni, *Il Globo*, 13–14 June 1982).

p. 420

¶ 'Of course it did not . . .'   *The Truce*, p. 379; author interviews with GCD, Cesare Cases, and Cesare Cases in Blakeway; PL in Pesaro debate, p. 22.

¶ 'He was, he would say . . .'   *Opere II*, p. 1544 (PL to Mladen Machiedo, his Croatian translator, 22 June 1970); PL in BBC *Bookmark*, Paladini, 1986, Lucarini, 1983; *ITIAM*, p. 151. For grieving over his companions, especially Vanda: PL in interview with Giulio Goria, *Paese Sera*, 3 May 1982; author interviews with Gisella.

¶ 'And for all . . .'   *Conversations*, pp. 41–3; PL interviews with Olivero, *Progetto*, 1980, Grassano, 1979, *VM*, p. 129, Milva Spadi, *Westdeutscher Rundfunk*, September 1986 (in *La Terra*, No. 1, February 1995, pp. 78-83, and in *Conversazioni e interviste*).

p. 421

¶ 'His need . . .'   Vincenti, p. 54; Gabriella Poli, 'La memoria come impegno e come lotta', in *Primo Levi: testimone e scrittore di storia*, ed. Rosa Brambilla and Giuseppe Cacciatore, cittadella editrice, 1995, pp. 24–5; author interviews with Giosanna Abarella Sciaccaluga.

¶ 'And he noticed . . .'   Others who experienced not being listened to: author interviews with Giuliana Tedeschi, Lidia Rolfi, and Mario Rigoni Stern. PL being listened to: e.g. *Conversations*, p. 67; PL in interviews with *TG Dossier*, 1979, Silvia and Giovanni Tesio, 1986, and in 'Itinerario'; for Anna Maria listening, author interviews with Mario Rigoni Stern.

¶ 'He must have wanted . . .'   He had certainly contacted both Lorenzo and the Dalla Voltas by 3 November, two weeks after his return, which is the date of Lorenzo's letter to Emma Dalla Volta. As already noted, Paolo Dalla Volta says that PL came to ask them about Alberto even before he went home: but this is almost certainly a distorted memory, together with that of PL's being 'skeletally thin'.

pp. 421–5

Lorenzo   'Lorenzo's Return' in *MR*; author interviews with Lorenzo's family – Secondo Perone, Giuseppe Perone and Emma Bard – and with Dr Menardi of the Fossano library and Don Lenta of Fossano; copies of Lorenzo's documents, kindly given me by Emma Bard (his passport, *Libretto di Lavoro* (work record), Auschwitz payment receipts and evacuation camp paper); Carlo Lenta in *La Fedeltà*, 3 February 1982; birth certificate Lorenzo Perone, Atto No. 429, Parte 1, Anno 1904, Città di Fossano; Lorenzo Perone death certificate, Atto No. 24, Parte II, Serie B, Anno 1952, date 30 April 1952; PL in interviews with Alvin Rosenfeld in *Midstream*, 1986, pp. 27–8, with Gabriel Motola in *European Judaism*, Vol. 21, No. 2, 1988 Conference issue, pp. 44–5, and with Mario Viglino, 1978, p. 27. On TB still being a stigma in 1950s Piedmont, author interviews with Lidia Rolfi.

pp. 425–9

Alberto   PL to Bianca, 6 June 1945 from Katowice, to JS, 23 March 1946, and to Emma Dalla Volta, 26 December 1945; *ITIAM*, pp. 63, 108–10, 144–5, 161,

172; 'Cerium', *PT*; author interviews with Paolo Dalla Volta; Paolo Dalla Volta
in *Bresciaoggi*, 14 August 1996, 'Ebrei, l'onta dimenticata' in *Bresciaoggi*, 10 August
1996, 'Appunti prigionieri' ('Prisoner Notes'), signed by Emma Dalla Volta, 14
December 1954, and Lorenzo Perone letter to Emma Dalla Volta, 3 November
1945, all kindly given me by Paolo Dalla Volta; *D. & S.*, pp. 20–21; PL interviews
with Giovanni De Luna in *Lotta Continua*, 10 November 198(2?) and Viglino,
1978; PL typescripts of *ITIAM*, kindly given me by Anna Yona, and De Silva
edition of *ITIAM*, kindly lent me by Vittorio Segre; author interviews with JS,
and JS letter to Yad Vashem, 14 January 1998.

p. 430

¶ 'And what about . . .'   Author interviews with JS.

Leonardo: LDB to Aldo Moscati, 20 October 1945; LDB, ANED interview,
1982, p. 27; author interviews with Alessandro Debenedetti, Carla Ovazza
Debenedetti, Mario Levi, Simone Fubini; LDB will, dated 14 May 1945, in
LDB's papers at the Jewish Library, Turin.

¶ 'Lello, as we know . . .'   Author interviews with Lello Perugia, Lello Perugia
documents; Afterword to *ITIAM/The Truce*, p. 393; *MR*, p. 140.

p. 431

¶ 'Of the Chemical Kommando . . .'   Silvio Barabas to PL, 20 December 1945;
PL to JS, 23 March 1946 and 31 July 1961; Steinberg, *Speak You Also*, p. 52. PL
also recorded those fates he knew of the members of his transport: Diena and
Flesch died of disease; Lonzana ('Valerio' of 'Rappoport's Testament') was
selected; Treistmann ('Rappoport' himself), Glücksmann ('Steinlauf') and *Ingegnere* Aldo Levi, father of Emilia and Italo, died on the evacuation march (PL's
list of seventy-five members of his transport, prepared for the deposition against
Bosshammer, in *Primo Levi: testimone*, p. 232).

¶ 'Primo also tried . . .'   PL in interview with Pier Maria Paoletti, *Il Giorno*, 7
August 1963 (in *VM*, pp. 81–2); Afterword to *ITIAM/The Truce*, p. 394;
'Vanadium', *PT*, p. 219.

¶ 'Finally, the French . . .'   Steinberg, *Speak You Also*; review of *Speak You Also*
by Martin Arnold, *New York Times*, 19 October 2000.

p. 432

¶ 'Charles . . .'   Afterword to *ITIAM/The Truce*, p. 393; PL in interview with
Risa Sodi, *Conversazioni e interviste*, p. 232; author interviews with Charles
Conreau and JS; Charles Conreau letter to the author, 6 February 2000.

¶ 'In early March . . .' and next four ¶¶   Afterword to *ITIAM/The Truce*, p. 393;
JS, 'Primo Levi: A Companion, a Friend, a Witness', paper delivered to Confer-
ence on PL, Philadelphia, 1997, p. 7, 'Littérature, science et savoir à Auschwitz',
delivered at PL Conference 'Le double lien', 18–19 November 1999, Strasbourg,
both kindly given me by JS; author interviews with JS and his interview with
Susan Tarrow; JS talk at Colmar, 1985; PL to JS, 23 March 1946 and July 1947.
Quotation 'rare moments of reprieve . . .' is from PL, 'La lingua dei chimici II',
Opere II, p. 746, translated as 'The Language of Chemists II' in *OPT*, p. 106.

p. 434

¶ 'But Luciana did . . .' and next four ¶¶   Author interviews with Luciana Nissim, and portrait by Guadagni, 1997. On Franco Momigliano: Franco Momigliano documents in CDEC; Gobetti, *Diario partigiano*, pp. 125, 128, 137, 273.

p. 435

¶ 'Bianca Morpurgo . . .' and next ¶ Testimony of Sofia Schafranov, doctor in Birkenau and Ravensbrück, in Alberto Cavaliere, *I campi della morte in Germania*, Sonzogni, Milan, 1945, pp. 10, 22–3, 26–8, 35, 51–2, 80; Tedeschi, *There is a Place on Earth*, pp. 207, 210; author interviews with Edoardo Gridelli, Liana Millu; PL letters to Hermann Langbein, April 1972; Tibaldi lists of survivors for *Compagni di viaggio*.

¶ 'In March . . .' and next seven ¶¶ Author interviews with AP, GB, EGT, and GCD.

p. 437

¶ 'And the spies . . .' and next two ¶¶ Deposition of Marie Varisellaz; trial documents, 1946–9; Ginsborg, *A History*, p. 92.

¶ 'Ada Della Torre . . .' and next three ¶¶ Della Torre, *Messaggio*, pp. 14, 116–17; Guadagni, *Unità*, 21 February 1993; Gobetti, *Diario partigiano*; author interviews with SO, BGS, GCD, Gabriella Garda Aliverti, Emilio Jona, Luisa Accati and Giovanni Levi, Anna Cases; SO in Blakeway; SO, 'Primo Levi: La ragione, la vita, la responsibilità collettiva' in *Ha Keillah*, 3 June 1997.

p. 438

¶ 'The last Primo had heard . . .' and next seven ¶¶ Author interviews with EGT, Carla Maestro, Luciana Nissim; EGT, 'La Resistenza a Cogne', 1997, 'L'Esate di Cogne' and 'Esodo 1944', unpublished essays kindly given me by EGT; 'Sulle note di Polvere di Stelle', *Bollettino della Comunità Israelitica di Milano*; Guadagni, 'Prima del grande buio', p. 54.

p. 439

¶ 'Bianca and Alberto . . .' and next five ¶¶ Gobetti, *Diario partigiano*, pp. 187, 288–300, 326–7, 348–9, 361, 363, 369; *L'Anno di Ada*, Centro Studi Piero Gobetti, 1998, p. 2; author interviews with Giorgio Diena and Franca Mussa.

p. 441

If This is a Man

¶ 'From the start . . .' *ITIAM*, pp. 15–16; *PT*, 152–3; PL in interviews with: Silori, 1963; Claudio Toscani, *Il Ragguaglio Librario*, No. 3, March 1972, pp. 88–90; Viglino, 1978, and Filippo Ivaldi, *La Stampa*, 2 May 1978; Grassano, 1979; Olivero, 1980; Monticelli, 1981; Lucarini, 1983; BBC *Bookmark*, 1985; Nico Orengo, *Tuttolibri*, *La Stampa*, 1 June 1985; Enrico Lombardi, *Radio Svizzera Italiana*, 3 June 1985; Paladini, Roth and Rudolf, 1986; Risa Sodi, 1987. Also: *Echi*, pp. 45, 92–5; *Conversations*, pp. 42, 43, 61; 'Itinerario'.

¶ 'Almost from the start . . .' 'Questions by Silori', *Settimo giorno*, 19 October 1963.

¶ 'As *Se questo* . . .' Cavaglion 1993, pp. 9, 38; Tesio in S. Salvatore, p. 261, and *Piemonte letterario*, pp. 173–96, 'Su alcune varianti di Se questo è un uomo'; author interviews with EGT; Primo to JS, 23 March 1946; JS in Tarrow interview, p. 6.

p. 442

¶ 'But we know . . .' Vincenti, p. 54; author interviews with JS; JS in Tarrow interview, p. 5, in Blakeway, and in *Il presente del passato*, p. 25; PL in Roth and in 'Itinerario', pp. 1217–18. 'Just written for family and friends' is in *Conversations*, p. 43.

¶ 'And in fact he had begun . . .' Cavaglion 1993, pp. 38–41; Introduction to *Rapporto, Opere I*, pp. 1339–60.

p. 443

¶ 'The *Report on the Health* . . .' Cavaglion (*Primo Levi*, p. 38) and Belpoliti (*Opere I*, p. 1379) both note the scientific cast of the *Rapporto*. For modelling *ITIAM* on the weekly factory lab report, see e.g. *Echi*, p. 97; and PL interviews with Milani, 1986, p. 19, Roth, *VM*, p. 18, and Giorgio Martellini, *Il Gazzettino*, 12 June 1984. For this being only half serious, see PL interview with Piero Bianucci, *Tuttolibri, La Stampa*, 26 October 1985.

¶ 'After his first . . .' See e.g. PL in Enrico Lombardi interview 1985: 'I had tested the stories verbally, telling them aloud, and they had acquired . . . a narrative form.'

¶ 'This is the part . . .' For PL's surprise, author interviews with Giosanna Albarello Sciaccaluga. For doing this for weeks, as well as PL interviews already listed (e.g. Grassano, Rudolf, Paladini, Sodi 1987, and Vincenti, p. 58): author interviews with e.g. GCD, Gabriella Garda Aliverti, Anna Cases, Nico Dallaporta, and Leo Gallico. For each episode being told many times before being written, see e.g. *Echi*, p. 45, Lombardi, p. 38, Lucarini, p. 3.

¶ 'He began to write . . .' Tesio, Introduction to *Se questo è un uomo* schools edn, 1997, p. xxxi (November date). Rest of description from interviews already cited, especially *Mondoperaio*, Lombardini, Ivaldi. Unless and until Lucia Levi releases the original exercise book manuscript, or Giovanni Tesio releases his notes, it is impossible to date the exact order of composition of the chapters of *ITIAM*. Several of Anna Yona's typescripts are dated, but these may be the dates of final typing rather than of original composition: e.g. 'The Story of Ten Days', which PL always said he wrote first, is dated February 1946. For falling into depression: apart from PL's guarded public admissions, e.g. in *PT*, p. 151, and in several interviews (e.g. to Giorgio De Rienzo in July 1975: 'mesi durissimi', 'very difficult months'): author interviews with Gisella and with Giuliana Tedeschi.

¶ 'It must have been now . . .' It is impossible to date Nico Dallaporta's visit exactly. PL only says '1946' (*D. & S.*, p. 62); Nico Dallaporta remembers only that he went to see PL 'as soon as possible' ('Mon amitié avec Primo Levi', talk given at Paris conference on PL, 1999). For the rest of the ¶: Pesaro debate, p. 13; *D. & S.*, p. 62; *Conversations*, p. 68.

p. 444

¶ 'Poetry played . . .' See *Echi*, pp. 90–91, and e.g. PL interview with Alberto Gozzi, 1985, p. 8. On two main periods of poetry: e.g. interview with Giulio Nascimbeni, 1984 (in *Conversazioni e interviste*), and with Raffaella Manzini and Brunetto Salvarini in *QOL*, No. 4, September–October 1986, p. 7. On PL's saying he didn't know why: e.g. in the cover copy for *Ad ora incerta*, Garzanti, 1984 (in *Opere II*, p. 517); and to *QOL*. He suggested the unpredictability of the

Muse (e.g. to *QOL*), or the incompatibility with factory work (e.g. to Lombardi, 1985, p. 44).

¶ 'The dates tell . . .' and following poems   *CP*, pp. 5–15.

★ Author interviews with Giorgio Vaccarino. Quotations are from the poem 'Singing'.

p. 446

'*I know what it means . . .*'   Italics mine.

¶ 'For the first time . . .'   Author interviews with Gisella and Giuliana Tedeschi. There are fateful traces of this in *ITIAM*, as readers have often noted: in 'The Story of Ten Days', p. 166, where Primo says that 'to fall ill of diphtheria in those conditions was more surely fatal than jumping off a third floor' ('fourth floor', in the English, is a mistranslation. See *Opere I*, p. 156).

¶ 'If his solitude . . .'   Quotations from *PT*, p. 151.

¶ 'It was a sudden, total reversal . . .' and following quotation   *PT*, p. 153.

'Because you weren't there . . .'   From '11 February 1946', *CP*, p. 16.

¶ 'Not only was he . . .'   *PT*, p. 153. In the original typescript of 'Chromium' Primo had written that his writing was 'a noble labour' – which is what he really felt, but was too modest to say.

¶ 'We can be almost . . .'   We know from Primo's poem that the meeting with Lucia was on 11 February 1946; and he typed 'The Canto of Ulysses' on the 14th (Anna Yona typescripts; see also *Opere I*, p. 1378). Marco Belpoliti speculates (*Opere I*, p. 1400) that the date of this typescript was the date of original composition (and that the same is true of all the dated chapters, four in all). But until we see the original manuscript(s), this must remain speculation.

p. 447

¶ 'The trance . . .'   PL interviews as before, e.g. *Mondoperaio*, Lombardi, Ivaldi, Sodi. Dates are from the Anna Yona typescripts. For finishing in December: Tesio, *Se questo è un uomo*, 1997, p. xxxii, and Marco Belpoliti in *Opere I*, p. 1381. (Despite Primo's dating the composition from December 1945 to January 1947: see *Opere I*, p. 169.)

¶ '"Of course I wanted . . .'   PL in interview with Vanna Nocerino, *L'Ospite*, 1979, offprint kindly given me by Vanna Nocerino Bigogno, pp. 17–18. On Leonardo and Anna Maria encouraging him: author interviews with Alessandro Galante Garrone, Mario Rigoni Stern, Anna and Clara Bovero. On the others: author interviews with EGT, GCD, Giorgio Diena, Vanna Rava, Giorgio Vaccarino, Rita Levi Montalcini. On sending the book to several publishers: PL said 'a number', and 'three or four', in e.g. the Afterword to *ITIAM/The Truce*, p. 381, and to the Tesios and to Paladini in 1986. See also *Echi*, p. 94 and Belpoliti 1998, p. 150. On Einaudi being his first choice: Vincenti, p. 55. On his delivering it to Einaudi personally: Dini & Jesurum, p. 168.

¶ 'He was lucky . . .'   PL called the rejection of *ITIAM* by Einaudi his second failure in an interview with Marina Verna, *Gazzetta del popolo*, 6 September 1982.

¶ 'The others didn't matter . . .'   On PL's never forgetting the blow of rejection by Einaudi, and especially by Natalia Ginzburg: e.g. David Mendel, 'On Primo

Levi's *If This is a Man'*, p. 2 (kindly given me by David Mendel); Ferdinando Camon in *La Stampa*, 23 December 1996, and author interviews with him; PL interviews with Mario Viglino, 1978, p. 28, and Paladini, 1986, p. 48; author interviews with Edith Bruck, Rita Levi Montalcini, Alessandro Galante Garrone.

¶ 'At first it seemed . . .'   Nico Orengo, *La Stampa*, 1 June 1985 and 12 June 1987; *Panorama*, 28 June 1987; Giulio Einaudi, 'Primo Levi and his Publisher', talk delivered at Primo Levi Conference, Princeton, 30 April–2 May 1989 (trans. Susan Ezdinli and Guido Mascagni), p. 15; Severino Cesari, *Colloquio con Giulio Einaudi*, Theoria, 1991, p. 174; PL in Paladini interview, 1986, and *Conversations*, p. 51.

p. 448

¶ 'Being Primo . . .'   Cavaglion 1993, p. 5; PL in Paladini interview; Afterword to *ITIAM/The Truce*, p. 381. And see PL in *L'eco dell'educazione ebraica*, April 1955: 'Dei Lager, oggi, è indelicato parlare' (*Opere I*, p. 1113); Vincenti, p. 55; *Conversations*, p. 51.

¶ 'Natalia herself . . .'   Natalia Ginzburg in Orengo, *Tuttolibri*, 1987, and *Panorama*, 1987; G. Luti (ed.), 'Il Novecento', Vol. XI/2 of *Storia letteraria d'Italia*, Casa Editrice Dr Francesco Vallardi, 1993, p. 1297; Cavaglion 1993, p. 8; author interviews with Anna Bravo, Alessandro Galante Garrone and Oscar Mazzoleni.

¶ 'How did a reader . . .'   Author interviews with Oscar Mazzoleni, Ernesto Ferrero, and Guido Lopez; and see PL in Paladini interview, p. 148. Quotations from Natalia Ginzburg are in *Trovare Torino*, p. 42. For Natalia Ginzburg thinking of returning to Rome: Natalia Ginzburg to Giulio Einaudi, 22 February 1947, Einaudi Archive. She did return to Rome, in 1952 (*Trovare Torino*, p. 23).

p. 449

¶ 'But the answer . . .'   Author interviews with Giulio Bollati; Natalia Ginzburg to Sergio Antonelli about his *Il campo 29*, 9 July 1948, in Einaudi Archive.

¶ 'The 1947 typescript . . .'   Gabriella Poli also notes the growth in characters as a main difference between the 1947 and 1958 versions of *ITIAM* (*Echi*, p. 212). The quotation 'to the house of the dead' is from *ITIAM*, p. 37.

¶ 'Alessandro Galante Garrone . . .' and next two ¶¶   Author interviews with Alessandro Galante Garrone, Ernesto Ferrero, Edith Bruck, Maria Vittoria Malvano, and Oscar Mazzoleni; *Opere I*, p. lxxxiii; Oscar Mazzoleni, 'Antonicelli e la De Silva: l'editore d'avanguardia' in *Il coraggio delle parole*, Fondazione Franco Antonicelli, Belforte Editore Libraio, p. 147; Renzo Zorzi, 'Insieme alla "De Silva" e oltre', in *Franco Antonicelli, 'dell'impegno culturale'*, Provincia di Pavia, Assessorato ai servizi sociali, educativi e culturali; Mario Fubini, 'Il mestiere del letterato', in *Scritti su Franco Antonicelli*, Centro Studi Piero Gobetti, 1975 (also includes essays by Norberto Bobbio, Alessandro Galante Garrone, Guido Quazza and Natalino Sapegno); Norberto Bobbio, *Franco Antonicelli: Ricordi e testimonianze*, Bollati Boringhieri, and *30 anni*, pp. 118–20; *L'amico del popolo*, Anno III, No. 12, 29 March 1947. I thank Oscar Mazzoleni for helping me with material and ideas for this period.

p. 450

¶ 'That was how . . .'   See Tesio, Introduction to *Se questo è un uomo*, 1997, p. xxxi, who also notes the two stages of writing.

¶ 'To start with . . .'   *Storia degli uomini senza nome* is in papers held by JS; *Sul fondo* is in *L'Amico del popolo*. For PL's choice of *I sommersi e i salvati*, see e.g. his interviews with Giorgio Calcagno, *La Stampa*, 26 July 1986; Andrea Libertori, *Unità*, 25 September 1986; Garibba, April 1979 (reprinted in *Karnenu*, Anno XV, No. 3, March–April 1988, pp. 2–5). PL always said (e.g. in the interviews cited above) that the idea for the title was Antonicelli's. The suggestion that Zorzi proposed it is in Zorzi, 'Insieme alla "De Silva"', p. 64. PL expresses his regret at losing his Dantean title in e.g. Libertori, but his gratitude to Antonicelli in e.g. *Echi*, p. 48.

p. 451

¶ 'He too had been . . .'   Author interviews with Anna Yona. See also *Opere I*, pp. 1378, 1391.

¶ 'First and foremost . . .' and next five ¶¶   The comparisons and conclusions are mine. The quotations on pp. 452–3 are from *ITIAM*, pp. 120, 112 and 109 respectively.

p. 453

'My book is at the printers . . .'   PL to JS, July 1947.

pp. 453–4

Lucia   Cavaglion, *La scuola ebraica*, pp. 20, 31, 41–2, 56, 66–7; author interviews with GCD, Rita Levi Montalcini, Paola and Luisa Accati, Stuart and Anna Woolf, Emma Vita Levi, David Mendel, Gabriella Garda Aliverti, Giorgio Diena, Dario and Miranda Treves, Anna Cases, Alberto Piazza, Enzo Levi, Maria Vittoria Malvano, Sandra Weisz, Vanna Rava, and Anna and Clara Bovero; PL in Paladini interview 1986. The joke about Italian Jews being 'Jews of the Italian religion' was made by an Israeli ambassador to Italy and told to me by Angelo Pezzana, whom I thank for it.

p. 455

¶ 'There was only . . .'   Dini & Jesurum, pp. 48 and 73; author interviews with Anna Cases, Vittorio Satta, JS, and Ester Valabrega; PL to JS, 23 March 1946, 24 April 1946, July 1947; *Opere II*, p. 1544; original typescript of 'Nitrogen' in Einaudi Archive, in which PL had written that lack of money was '*un douleur sans pareille*'.

¶ 'At last, however . . .' and next seven ¶¶   *Opere I*, p. 1377 and *Opere II*, p. 1544; PL to JS, 23 March 1946; *CP*, p. 12; *PT*, pp. 151, 153; author interviews with Luciano Colombo; Luciano Colombo letter to *Il Giornale*, 15 April 1987; PL in Pesaro debate, p. 20. The quotation about Cesare on p. 457 is from *ITIAM*, p. 252.

p. 457

¶ 'So far, Dr Colombo's . . .' and next ¶   PL in interviews with Risa Sodi, *Partisan Review*, 1987 (*Conversazioni e interviste*, pp. 224–5), Paladini, p. 148, and Silvia and Giovanni Tesio, 1986; *PT*, p. 156; author interviews with Luciano Colombo, and Luciano Colombo letter to *Il Giornale*. Quotations are from the Sodi interview.

p. 458

¶ 'On 21 January . . .' and next ¶   *PT*, p. 157; PL, 'Il segreto del ragno', *La Stampa*, 9 November 1986, in *Opere II*, p. 1305; Dini & Jesurum, p. 73; PL to JS, 23 March 1946; 'Tantalio', *Opere II*, p. 137; author interviews with Luciano Colombo.

¶ 'In 1946, however . . .'   *PT*, p. 152; author interviews with Luciano Colombo, Vittorio Satta and Marcello Franceschi.

p. 459

¶ 'A few months before . . .' and next three ¶¶   *DL*, Ch. 5. Dr Colombo remembers this problem.

¶ 'For *The Periodic Table* . . .' and next six ¶¶   *PT*, pp. 150–59; author interviews with Luciano Colombo.

p. 461

¶ 'Why did he tell it . . .'   Quotation from *PT*, p. 154.

¶ 'That is also, I think . . .'   Quotations: *DL*, Ch. 5. For rest of ¶: 'Il segreto del ragno', *Opere II*, p. 1307; 'La sfida della molecula', *Opere II*, p. 167.

p. 462

¶ 'By the time he came . . .'   The original typescript of 'Chromium' is dated 18 November 1973; quotations from *PT*, pp. 158–9.

¶ 'Primo had done extremely well . . .' and next ¶   *Opere I*, p. 1386; *PT*, p. 188; author interviews with AS.

★ Author interviews with Luciano Colombo.

p. 463

¶ 'In *The Periodic Table* . . .' and next three ¶¶, including two quotations   *PT*, pp. 188–9; author interviews with Luciano Colombo; PL, 'Il testamento del vice capolaboratorio', dated June 1947, copy kindly given me by Luciano Colombo; Luciano Colombo, 'Ricordo di Primo Levi' in *Pitture e Vernici*, No. 4, April 1996, pp. 52–3 (PL's poem is printed in full on p. 53; as also in Montedison *Progetto Cultura*, Anno 2, No. 6, May 1987, p. 6).

pp. 464–8

The Truce

¶ 'Except for rare lapses . . .'   Author interviews with AS, BGS, Giorgio Vaccarino; *PT*, p. 185.

¶ 'This was the adventure . . .'   *PT*, p. 170; author interviews with AS, Francesco Cordero, Anna Cases, and BGS.

¶ 'It was not only Alberto . . .'   Author interviews with BGS, Anna Cases, Ada Ortona, Vanna Mariotti Grasso. Quotations are from *PT*, pp. 185–6.

¶ 'More than just the Salmonis' . . .' and next twelve ¶¶   'Tin', 'Arsenic' and 'Nitrogen', *PT*; 'Il segreto del ragno'; author interviews with Giorgio Vaccarino, GCD, EGT. 'Arsenic': typescript dated 10 August 1973.

pp. 467–8

★ Ponzio, *Chimica ganica*, p. 294.

¶¶ 'But in the end . . .' and 'Alberto accepted . . .'   *PT*, pp. 183, 189–90; author interviews with Giorgio Vaccarino, Francesco Cordero, BGS

p. 468

¶ 'That was in December . . .'   Marriage certificate PL–Lucia Morpurgo, Atto No. 84, Ufficio 2, Parte 1, Anno 1947, date 8 September 1947; author interviews with GCD, Leo Gallico; *PT*, p. 182.

¶ 'And then a month later . . .'   *ITIAM*, De Silva edition: 'Finito di stampare 11 ottobre 1947' at the back; Cavaglion 1993, p. 5.

¶ 'He was, he admitted . . .'   PL interview with Vanna Nocerino, 1979.

p. 469

If This is a Writer

¶ 'If it had not been . . .'   For PL's repeating that he would not have written without Auschwitz: e.g. RAI TV interview 'Il mestiere di raccontare', 1974; *Venerdí letterari* talk at Teatro Carignano, Turin, 19 November 1976, in *Echi*, pp. 92–105, on pp. 92–3 (the whole talk reprinted in *Opere I*, pp. 1202–7); Vanna Nocerino interview 1979; *Mondoperaio* (in *VM*); Sodi interview 1987 (in *Conversazioni e interviste*).

¶ 'And now the way . . .'   De Silva flyer; Cavaglion, 1993, p. 4 (for the De Silva series).

¶ 'The reviews started . . .'   Cavaglion 1993, pp. 57–8; Ferrero, Introduction to *Primo Levi: I racconti*, p. viii.

¶ 'Especially since . . .'   Information on Cajumi from Cavaglion 1993, p. 57n., and Bobbio, *30 anni*, p. 66. Cajumi's review is in Cavaglion 1993, pp. 59–61, and in Ferrero, *Antologia*, pp. 303–5.

¶ 'At least four others . . .'   Aldo Garosci, *La Stampa*, 26 November 1947 and *L'Italia socialista*, 27 December 1947; Umberto Olobardi, *Il Ponte*, March 1948, pp. 281–3; Cesare Cases, 'Levi racconta l'assurdo', *Bollettino della Comunità Israelitica di Milano*, May–June 1948, quoted in Ferrero, *Antologia*, p. 308, and reprinted in Cesare Cases, *Patrie lettere*, Einaudi, 1987; Italo Calvino, *Unità*, 6 May 1948, quoted in Ferrero, *Antologia*, pp. 306–7.

p. 470

¶ 'The other half . . .'   See e.g. PL interviews with Lucarini, 1983, and Milani, 1986, for Primo's joy at Cajumi's review.

¶ 'But what all of him wanted . . .'   Ferrero, 'Primo Levi scrittore', p. 182; author interviews with Maria Vittoria Malvano, Alessandro Galante Garrone, Oscar Mazzoleni; PL interview with Paladini, 1986, p. 149; *Opere I*, p. 1386.

¶ 'Primo was philosophical . . .'   Cavaglion 1993, pp. 5 and 57; Afterword to *ITIAM/The Truce*, p. 381; *Echi*, p. 94; PL in Paladini interview, p. 149, and in 'Itinerario'; author interviews with Anna Yona. For PL's claims to have achieved his goals and stopped writing: e.g. in interviews with Viglino, 1978, p. 29; Boeri, 1983, and *Mondoperaio*, p. 155; Edoardo Segantini, *Unità*, 1 May 1984; Paladini, 1986, p. 149; and see *Echi*, pp. 17, 61. The quotation 'solitary book' is from 'Itinerario'.

p. 471

¶ 'The truth slipped out . . .'   *PT*, p. 183; *D. & S.*, p. 137; and see PL interview with Ian Thomson, *PN Review*, 1987 (*VM*, p. 34): 'If I'd had an immediate success with *If This is a Man*, I would probably have given up my career as a chemist.'

¶ 'He was right . . .'   Quotations from *Echi*, p. 224 and *Mondoperaio*, *VM*, p. 162. Several people disagree with me, however, and think PL would have become a full-time writer immediately if *ITIAM* had been a success: e.g. Ernesto Ferrero, Edith Bruck (author interviews).

¶ 'And even this . . .'   PL to JS, 23 March 1946; PL in interviews with Lucarini in 1983 and Milani in 1986. For starting *The Truce* in 1947 and 48: Vincenti, p. 58; Paladini interview, p. 154; *Opere I*, pp. 1418–19. That he gave up *The Truce* because discouraged by the failure of *ITIAM* I deduce from the fact that he began it again in earnest after the success of *ITIAM* in 1958: see interviews with Roth, Paladini and Lucarini, and with Guido Gerosa, *Il Giorno*, 24 November 1981.

¶ 'There was one last lie . . .' and next ¶   For picking up *The Truce* regularly through the 1950s, see e.g.: PL to Heinz Riedt, 28 November 1959 (he tries every Sunday, but there is no time); the typescript of Ch. 3, 'Il greco', in the Einaudi Archive, which is dated July 1954 – March 1961. The other dates are taken from the relevant typescripts. See also *Opere I*, pp. 1419 and 1459: 'L'ultimo della classe', the story of Ferrari in Ch. 7, 'The Dreamers', was published in *Stampa Sera* on 19–20 December 1959. For writing all the additions to *ITIAM* in 1955–7: Cavaglion 1993, p. 8. On the stories: For 'I mnemagoghi' being told at university and written in 1946, author interviews with BGS, Giovanni Tesio, *Piemonte letterario*, pp. 164, 169, and author interviews with Giovanni Tesio; on the others Vincenti, p. 58, and *Opere I*, pp. 1430, 1432, 1437, 1447. For publishing at least another nine stories between 1949 and 1961: In 1949 he published 'Fine del marinese' and 'Turno di notte' (which became 'Sulphur' in *PT*); in 1952 he wrote 'The Sleeping Beauty in the Fridge'; in 1959 he published 'Capaneo' (which became 'Rappoport's Testament'); and between May 1960 and August 1961 he published three of the stories of *Storie naturali* ('Il versificatore', 'Censura in Bitinia' and 'Quaestio di Centauris'), plus 'A Disciple' and 'La carne dell'orso', which became 'Iron' in *PT*. I say 'at least nine' because he could also have written others he published later. (*Opere I*, pp. 1429–30, 1432–3, 1438, 1447, 1458; Tesio *Piemonte letterario*, p. 169). Primo admitted to several interviewers that he had written stories very early: e.g. to the *Venerdí letterari* audience (*Echi*, p. 95) he said he had written stories before *The Truce* (most of the stories of *Storie naturali*, he'd said to the *Corriere della Sera*, 24 July 1972); to Viglino in 1978 (p. 23) and to Bona Alterocca in *La Stampa*, 16 February 1978, he said he'd written 'I mnemagoghi' before *ITIAM*; to Claudio Toscani in 1972 he said he'd written stories since 1946.

DANCING

The quotation from Calvino on p. 473 comes from Giancarlo Borri, *Le divine impurità*, Luisè Editore, Rimini, 1992, p. 50.

Quotations on p. 475 from 'Phosphorus', *PT*, p. 126, and 'Tin', *PT*, p. 190.

This chapter is based on author interviews with and letters from Luciana Nissim, Gabriella Garda Aliverti, and Gisella.

Chapter 12: Levi Uomo II: 1948–63

p. 476

¶ 'It is not possible . . .'   Vincenti, p. 55.

¶ 'For their first few months . . .'   Author interviews with GCD; Anissimov, *Primo Levi*, p. 421; Dini & Jesurum, p. 73. Lucia taught literature (author interviews with Silvia Di Chio, Dario and Miranda Treves).

¶ 'From the start . . .' and next two ¶¶   Birth certificate Lisa Lorenza Levi, Atto No. 2867, Ufficio 2, Parte 1, Serie A, Anno 1948, date 31 October 1948; birth certificate Renzo Cesare Levi, Atto No. 2651, Ufficio 2, Parte 1, Serie A, Anno 1957, date 2 July 1957; author interviews with GCD, Gabriella Garda Aliverti, Erica Scroppo Newbury, Luciana and Paola Accati, and Giacomo Cherio.

p. 477

¶ 'His thoughts . . .'   PL in interviews with Filippo Ivaldi, *La Stampa*, 1978, Milva Spadi, 1986, pp. 82–3 (in *Conversazioni e interviste*, pp. 256–7), Alvin Rosenfeld in *Midstream*, 1986, p. 27; PL, ANED interview, *VM*, pp. 229, 232; Dini & Jesurum, p. 51; author interviews with Erica Scroppo Newbury.

p. 478

¶ 'And this is a story . . .'   PL in interview with Edith Bruck, *Il Messaggero*, 9 January 1976, p. 3 (in *VM*, pp. 263–4), Alberto Gozzi, RAI, 1985, p. 7, and Risa Sodi in *Present Tense*, 1988, p. 45; Erica Scroppo Newbury, 'Primo Levi, Personal Reflections', talk given to the Edinburgh Jewish Literary Society on 21 February 1993, and published in the Literary Society magazine for that period, pp. 22–4; PL, ANED interview *VM*, pp. 232–3); author interviews with Luciana Accati and Erica Scroppo Newbury. Lisa is a biologist, Renzo a physicist.

¶ 'In 1948 . . .' and next two ¶¶   Ginsborg, *A History*, Ch. 3, 'The Postwar Settlement, 1945–1948', pp. 72–120; Foa, *Il cavallo e la torre*, pp. 168–70; Alberto Papuzzi, 'Noi, vecchi ragazzi del partito d'azione', *La Stampa*, 13 July 1971; author interviews with Vittorio Satta, Marcello Franceschi, Renato Portesi, and Redento Selvestrel. For Primo's job at SIVA starting in February 1948: *Ordine dei Chimici* records; and e.g. 'Primo Levi', *Millelibri*, No. 52, April 1992, p. 45 and Boeri interview, *VM*, p. 65.

p. 479

¶ 'The new job . . .'   *Opere I*, p. lxxxv; author interviews with Luciana and Paola Accati.

¶ 'Federico Accati . . .' and next ¶   Author interviews with Luciana Accati, Paola Accati, Luisa Accati and Giovanni Levi; SIVA documents kindly given me by Paola Accati (the founding document of SIVA, *Costituzione della Società Industriale Vernici Affini – SIVA – di Federico Accati (& CO.?), Società in nome collettivo*, 10 February 1945, and registration documents with Turin commercial and legal bodies, 13 February and 6 March 1945); author interviews with Redento and Egisto Selvestrel. For the use of copper wire and its place in the post-war industrial boom: *DL*, Ch. 5; author interviews with Felice Malgaroli.

p. 480

¶ 'In 1948 SIVA . . .' and next ¶   Author interviews with Gianna Balzaretti Caccia, Redento and Egisto Selvestrel, and Nerina Freschi; SIVA employment registers, copies kindly given me by Renato Portesi. The registers (and my interviews) show that Piero Selvestrel began at SIVA in 1946 or 47, and that Egisto worked there from 1948 to 1979, and Redento from 1949 to 1987.

¶ 'Apart from space . . .' and next three ¶   Author interviews with Gianna Balzaretti, Egisto Selvestrel and Redento Selvestrel.

p. 481

¶ 'The resin they developed . . .' and next two ¶¶   Author interviews with Gianna Balzaretti, Felice Malgaroli, Francesco Cordero, Paola Accati, Luciana Accati, Renato Portesi, Keith Barnes, and Beppe Salvador; PL in transcript of Roberto Di Caro interview, 1987; PL, 'Tantalio', in *Opere II*, p. 137; AS in Guadagni, *Unità*, 21 February 1993. For a list of SIVA's resins, and for PL returning to the lab as often as possible, see Renato Portesi, 'Primo Levi: un chimico, un impiantista . . . un uomo', *Chimica & Industria*, May 2001.

pp. 482–4

Federico Accati: author interviews with Luciana Accati, Paola Accati, Luisa Accati and Giovanni Levi, Egisto Selvestrel, Renzo Groff, Renato Portesi, Orsola Azzario Ferrero, Franca Tambini, Adolfo Arri, and Gisella.

p. 484

¶ 'Very soon Accati . . .' and next ¶   Author interviews with Luisa Accati and Giovanni Levi, Paola Accati, and Luciana Accati; PL in interviews with Mayda, 1963, Ernesto Ferrero, *Terra Nostra*, 12 September 1963, 'Very Important Piemontesi' radio, 1981, Milva Spadi, 1986; RAI interview on the Liberation, 25 January 1975; *Conversations*, pp. 38–40.

p. 485

¶ 'But there was Primo Levi . . .' and next ¶   PL stopped going to Germany on business in the 1970s (Milva Spadi interview, p. 80, *Conversazioni e interviste*, p. 249). For rest of ¶: PL in interviews with Spadi, with 'G.L.L.' in *Bollettino della Comunità Israelitica di Milano*, 1965, in RAI interview on the Liberation, 1975, in 'Very Important Piemontesi', 1981, and with Calcagno, *La Stampa*, 26 July 1986 (*VM*, pp. 111–12); author interviews with Orsola Azzario Ferrero, Egisto Selvestrel, Adolfo Arri, Renato Portesi, and GCD; PL, ANED interview, *VM*, pp. 244–5; *Conversations*, pp. 37–9; *D. & S.*, pp. 28, 138, 143.

p. 486

¶ 'In 1954 Gabriella . . .' and next three ¶¶   Author interviews with Gabriella Poli, and Gabriella Poli in Blakeway; Gabriella Poli, 'La memoria come impegno e come lotta', in *Primo Levi: testimone e scrittove di storia*, 1995, p. 26.

p. 487

¶ 'In 1950 Dr Gianotti . . .'   SIVA registers; author interviews with Paola Accati, Egisto Selvestrel, and Redento Selvestrel. It is unclear exactly which year SIVA moved to Settimo: Redento Selvestrel says 1953, Renato Portesi thinks 1954, and a publicity brochure Redento showed me said 1955. But as Redento is quite certain, and was there, 1953 seems most likely.

¶ 'A house was still . . .' and next ¶   Author interviews with Renato Portesi, Egisto Selvestrel, and Anna Marchesio; SICME–SIVA–SCET brochure (not Redento's, but a more recent one, kindly given me by Paola Accati).

p. 488

¶ 'Despite his office . . .'   Author interviews with Paola Accati, Renato Portesi, and Franca Tambini; publicity brochure.

¶ 'This was Primo . . .'   *Echi*, pp. 61, 83; PL in TG 1 interview, 19 September 1985, and in 'Con la chiave della scienza', *La Stampa*, 20 September 1985, on the death of Calvino (*Opere II*, p. 1274), in Roth, in Regge, and in transcript of Di Caro interview; author interviews with Paola Accati, Egisto and Redento Selvestrel, Renato Portesi, Felice Malgaroli, Adolfo Arri, Franca Tambini, and Carmela Franchi.

p. 489

¶ 'On the other hand . . .'   Roth, *VM*, p. 18 and Di Caro transcript; author interviews with Paola Accati, Michael Tinker, Renato Portesi, Gianna Balzaretti, and Francesco Cordero; PL to Heinz Riedt, 28 November 1959; SIVA registers; SIVA lab books, kindly shown me by Renato Portesi.

p. 490

¶ 'In 1949 a young Tuscan . . .' and next four ¶¶   Author interviews with Marcello Franceschi and Guido Fubini.

p. 491

¶ ' "Argon" . . .'   See note to p. 471, Chapter 11, for dating of early stories. 'Fine del marinese' is in *Opere I*, p. 1109; 'I mnemagoghi' is in *Opere I*, p. 401, and translated as 'The Mnemagogues' in *TSD*, p. 11.

p. 492

¶ 'In 1950 to 52 . . .'   'Capaneo' was published in 1959, 'A Disciple' in 1961 (*Opere II*, p. 1532). 'A Disciple' was originally part of *The Truce*, and in *The Truce* exercise book (see Tesio, *La Stampa*, 9 February 1997, and *Opere I*, p. 1423).

¶ 'For there is one piece . . .'   See *Opere I*, p. 1437.

¶ ' "The Sleeping Beauty . . .'   *Opere I*, p. 477 and *TSD*, p. 55.

★ Author interviews with Gianna Balzaretti.

p. 493

¶ 'This is the first . . .'   For PL's stories being called science fiction: see e.g. Fadini interview, 1966, in *VM*, p. 84. PL rejected the term (see also e.g. *Echi*, p. 34). For PL thinking science our only hope, the only solution to its own problems: see e.g. his Preface to L. Caglioti, *I due volti della chimica*, 1979, in *Opere I*, p. 1312;

Venerdí letterari talk, 1976, in *Echi*, pp. 10–11 and 99–100; and cover copy for *Vizio di forma*, in *Opere I*, pp. 1442–3.

¶ 'He published the first . . .'   Publication date of 'Angelica Farfalla' in *Il Mondo*: 14 August 1962 (*Opere I*, p. 1439). Once again, until PL's papers are released we cannot know how close to their publication dates his stories were written. 'Angelica Farfalla' is in *Opere I*, p. 434, and translated as 'Angelic Butterfly' in *TSD*, p. 19.

p. 494

¶ 'This story is . . .'   For PL's identification of the connection between his Lager writing and his scientific fables, see e.g. *Echi*, p. 36 and *Opere I*, p. 435 (cover copy for *Storie naturali*, by Calvino, quoting a letter from PL).

¶ '"Versamina" . . .'   Date of first publication 8 August 1965, in *Il Giorno*; in *Opere I*, p. 467, translated as 'Versamina' in *TSD*, p. 45.

p. 495

¶ 'This is so startling . . .'   On PL's suggesting his stories were not important: see e.g. *'racconti scherzi'*, joke stories, on the cover of *Storie naturali* (*Opere I*, p. 1434), and *Echi*, p. 39 (from interview with Gabriella D'Angeli in *Famiglia cristiana*, 27 November 1966: 'Ho scritto le mie *Storie* per divertimento': 'I wrote my *Stories* for entertainment'). On other dark and pessimistic stories: e.g. 'Verso occidente', 'Vilmy', 'Knall', all in *Lilit*, 'Stabile/Instabile' in *Altrui mestiere*.

¶ *'Pain cannot be taken away . . .'*   The story of the psychiatrist and the good man comes from PL to Aldo Moscati, 1 March 1979. The psychiatrist was Silvano Arieti, the good man Giuseppe Pardo, President of the Jewish Community of Pisa. PL's own fears were of animals, especially insects: author interviews with e.g. Signora Mariotti, Vanna Grosso Mariotti, Nicoletta Neri, Mario Rigoni Stern (on Primo's fear of his bees). And see 'Paura dei ragni', *Opere II*, p. 755, translated as 'Fear of Spiders' in *OPT*, p. 141.

p. 496

¶ '"Retirement Fund" . . .'   'L'Ordine a buon mercato' was not published before *Storie naturali*. 'Alcune applicazioni del Mimete' was first published on 15 August 1964, 'La misura della bellezza' on 6 January 1965, 'Pieno impiego' on 27 February 1966 (*Opere I*, p. 1439). 'Retirement Fund' was also not previously published. (All are translated in *TSD*.) Marco Belpoliti also thinks that the NATCA stories were written as well as published last (*Opere I*, p. 1440).

p. 497

¶ 'Gilberto has managed . . .'   For some reason, the English translation says that Gilberto arrives at the narrator's office two months later: it is one month in the original.

¶ 'This is, in fact . . .'   Author interviews with SO and Francesco Cordero.

p. 498

¶ 'With Simpson heading for death . . .'   'The Sixth Day' is the story PL first thought of in 1946. The typescript is dated 22 December 1957 (*Opere I*, p. 1432).

p. 499

¶ 'The remaining four stories . . .'   'Il versificatore' was first published on 17

May 1960; 'Cladonia rapida' was not published before. Quotation 'universe of metaphors' from 'Romanzi dettati dai grilli', *Opere II*, p. 690 (translated as 'Novels Dictated by Crickets', *OPT*). The plant and tree stories include 'Disfilassi' and 'L'anima e gli ingegneri', in *Lilit*, and 'Ammutinamento' in *Vizio*; the man and animal stories are 'Vilmy' and 'Il fabbro di se stesso' in *Vizio*, 'Figli del vento' and 'Le sorelle della palude' in *Lilit*, 'La grande mutazione', 'Ranocchi sulla luna', and 'Nozze della formica' in *Stories and Essays*, and the late 'interviews' in 'Zoo immaginario' (with a gull, a mole, a giraffe, a spider and an *E. coli* bacterium); the man and animal essays are 'Romanzi dettati dai grilli', 'Domum servavit', 'Inventare un animale', 'Il salto della pulce', 'Le farfalle', 'Paura dei ragni', 'Gli scarabei', 'Il mondo invisibile' and 'Bisogno di paura', all in *Altrui mestiere*; the plant and animal poems are 'Wooden Heart', 'Agave', 'Autobiography', 'Dark Band', 'Arachne', 'Old Mole', 'Pearl Oyster', 'The Snail' and 'The Elephant'. Other explorers of this universe of metaphors are e.g. Calvino, Queneau, Borges.

¶ 'The first of these . . .'   'L'amico dell'uomo' was in *The Truce* notebook (Tesio, *La Stampa*, 9 February 1997, and *Opere I*, p. 1431).

p. 500

¶ 'And it is an allegory . . .'   Quotations from 'Decodificazione', *Lilit*, published 1981 (in *Opere II*, p. 185). On no one being more aware than PL of the difficulty of his enterprise of clarity: I owe this point to Giovanni Levi. The friend who remembers PL's great effort to be understood is Renato Portesi.

p. 501

¶ 'All Primo Levi's . . .'   Other stories on the themes of crossing barriers, of cross-fertilization, hybridization and mutation are e.g.: 'Disfilassi' and 'I figli del vento' in *Lilit*, neither of which has been translated into English; and 'La grande mutazione' and 'Il passa-muri' in *Stories and Essays*, written in 1983 and 1986 respectively, and both in *TMM* ('The Great Mutation' and 'Through the Walls'). These stories will be discussed in Ch. 15.

¶ 'The story is . . .'   Quotations from 'Zinc' and 'Argon', *PT*, pp. 35 and 9.

p. 502

¶ 'Primo would write . . .'   The two stories about *panspermiae* are 'Disfilassi' and 'I figli del vento'.

¶ 'Meanwhile, Primo . . .'   *Opere I*, pp. 1386–7 and lxxxv; author interviews with Oscar Mazzoleni and Giorgio Anglesio. PL's and Giorgio Anglesio's translation of *Advanced Organic Chemistry* was published in 1955 (*Edizioni Einaudi negli anni 1933–1993*, Piccola Biblioteca Einaudi, 1993, pp. 286–7).

p. 503

¶ 'Primo seems . . .'   *Echi*, p. 94; Tesio, Afterword ('Per approfondire') to *Se questo è un uomo*, 1997, p. 205.

¶ 'It was the tenth anniversary . . .'   PL, 'Deportati. Anniversario' in *Torino*, XXXI, No. 4, April 1955, special issue for the tenth anniversary of the Liberation; and in *L'eco dell'educazione ebraica*, special issue for the tenth anniversary of the Liberation, April 1955, p. 4, in *Opere I*, p. 1113; Vincenti, p. 56; PL in interviews with *Mondoperaio*, *VM*, pp. 164–5, and Paladini, 1986, pp. 149–50, and in 'Itinerario'; author interviews with Luciano Foa; *Opere I*, p. 1387.

¶ 'But in 1955 . . .'   Giulio Einaudi, 'Primo Levi and his Publisher', p. 2, and Cesari, *Colloquio con Giulio Einaudi*, p. 174; PL letters in Einaudi Archive; Ernesto Ferrero in *Speciale La tregua*, *La Stampa*, 9 February 1997, p. 2; *Opere I*, pp. 1387–8.

¶ 'Einaudi was . . .'   Giulio Einaudi, 'Primo Levi and his Publisher', p. 3; *Opere I*, pp. 1390–91; PL in Paladini interview, 149–50.

pp. 504–6

Changes to *ITIAM*: the comparisons and analyses of the changes from the 1947 to the 1958 editions of *ITIAM* are mine, though e.g. Gabriella Poli (*Echi*, p. 212) and Marco Belpoliti (*Opere I*, p. 1400) make similar judgements and findings.

p. 507

¶ 'From the moment . . .'   Franco Antonicelli, *La Stampa*, 31 May 1958, Piero Caleffi, *Avanti*, 8 July 1958, A. Seroni, *Unità*, 11 July 1958, B. Finzi, *Il Mondo*, 29 July 1958, and e.g. Giulio Goria, *Il Paese*, 16 July 1958 and Mario Spinella, *Il Contemporaneo*, October 1960 (all in Ferrero, *Antologia*, pp. 308–13); *Opere I*, pp. 1389–90 for selling out all 2,000 copies printed by the end of 1958.

¶ 'Two years before . . .' and next three ¶¶   Stuart Woolf, 'Primo Levi e il mondo anglosassone', in *Il presente del passato*, pp. 197–202; and author interviews with Stuart Woolf. See also *Opere II*, pp. 1590–1.

p. 508

¶ 'After a complicated journey . . .'   Ernesto Ferrero's chronology in the original *Opere* (I, p. xlviii) says that both the UK and the US editions came out in 1959, and Marco Belpoliti repeats this (*Opere II*, pp. 1590–91). Stuart Woolf (in *Il presente del passato*, p. 199) dates the UK edition to 1960, and the *TLS* review appeared on 15 April 1960. I thank Annie Lee for helping me to confirm the early English-language publishing history of *ITIAM*. For *ITIAM* falling into oblivion in America, see Alexander Stille, 'Primo Levi negli Stati Uniti', in *Presente del passato*, pp. 203–11, on p. 204.

¶ 'Primo resigned himself . . .'   *D. & S.*, pp. 137–8.

¶ 'He did not know . . .'   Author interviews with Heinz Riedt, and Riedt in Blakeway; *D. & S.*, pp. 139–41; PL letters in Einaudi Archive; PL in Paladini interview, p. 152; Calcagno, *La Stampa*, 15 April 1987; *Opere II*, pp. 1591–2; Alberto Papuzzi, interview with Heinz Riedt, *La Stampa*, 1 April 1995, and article on him, *La Stampa*, 4 January 1997.

p. 509

¶ 'Primo's response . . .'   PL to Heinz Riedt, 22 August 1959, quoted in Calcagno, 15 April 1987. I do not have a copy of this letter, nor of several others (all from Riedt to PL); of others I have only one or two pages, when there are clearly more. These copies were in the possession of Hans Engert of the Goethe Institute of Turin, and were kindly given me by Jutta Pabst.

¶ 'Eagerly they set out . . .' and next ¶   Levi–Riedt correspondence (twenty letters, between August 1959 and June 1960); *D. & S.*, pp. 141–2; *Opere II*, p. 1591; author interviews with and letters from Heinz Riedt.

¶ 'Once again the wait . . .'   Vincenti, p. 57; PL interviews with Mayda, 1963, Ferrero, 1963, and Garibba, 1979; Wolfgang Helbich review, *Die Zeit*, 29 February 1962, Heribert F. Bauer review, *Der Illustrierter Monatschrift*, May 1962, and Heinz Beckmann review, *Der Rheinische Merkur*, 1 December 1961; author interviews with Heinz Riedt.

p. 510

'. . . I am sure . . .'   PL to Heinz Riedt, 13 May 1960, published in *D. & S.*, p. 143.

¶ 'In the first few years . . .'   *Echi*, p. 13; *Conversations*, p. 36; 'G.L.L.', *Bollettino della Comunità Israelitica di Milano*; *D. & S.*, pp. 144, 149; Garibba interview, 1979.

¶ 'And about the letters . . .'   Vincenti, p. 57; Paolo Spriano, 'L'avventura di Primo Levi', *Unità*, 14 July 1963; PL in interview with Mayda, 1963, Garibba, 1979, and Paladini, 1986, p. 153; *Conversations*, p. 36; *D. & S.*, pp. 144–9; author interviews with Heinz Riedt, and Alfredo Venturi, 'Primo Levi riveduto e corretto in Germania', *La Stampa*, 14 January 1989.

p. 511

¶ 'I don't know . . .'   Heinz Riedt to PL, 8 June 1960; *D. & S.*, p. 159; Bernhard Schlink, *The Reader*, trans. Carol Brown Janeway, Phoenix, 1998, pp. 150 and 154.

¶ 'Three more translations . . .' and next ¶   *Echi*, p. 16; *Opere II*, p. 1592; Ernesto Ferrero, *La Stampa*, 9 February 1997; JS in Tarrow interview; PL letter of 4 November 1966 in Einaudi Archive; PL to Charles Conreau, 1 January 1985, kindly given me by Charles Conreau.

p. 512

¶ 'When he was nineteen . . .'   *Mondoperaio*, *VM*, pp. 164–5.

¶ 'In the normal . . .'   Author interviews with GCD. The Teatro Gobetti has now reopened (2000), after many decades of closure.

¶ 'He continued . . .'   Author interviews with GCD and Vanna Rava; *Mondoperaio* (*VM*, pp. 164–5) and Paladini (pp. 149–50) interviews.

¶ 'After the Einaudi . . .'   *Echi*, p. 94; Ferruccio Maruffi, Lidia Rolfi and Giuliana Tedeschi in *Il presente del passato*, pp. 213, 214, 222, 224, 231, and Lidia Rolfi in S. Salvatore, p. 56; author interviews with Alberto Cavaglion and Frida Malan.

p. 513

¶ 'From 1960 on . . .'   *Echi*, pp. 49–50, 94–5; Paladini interview, p. 154; author interviews with Mario Rigoni Stern; Maruffi and Rolfi in *Il presente del passato*, pp. 213 and 224 respectively. Primo's 'third career' became especially busy after the publication of the schools edition of *The Truce* in 1965, and of the schools edition of *ITIAM* in 1973 (*Echi*, p. 49).

¶ 'The first example . . .'   Roth, *VM*, p. 19; PL to Heinz Riedt, 28 November 1959.

p. 514

¶ 'Two years later . . .'   PL in interviews with e.g.: Ivaldi (1978), Guido Gerosa, *Il Giorno* (1981), Lucarini (1983), Segantini, *Unità* (1984), *Mondoperaio* (1984),

Roth (1986), Paladini (1986); Italo Calvino to PL, 22 November 1961, in *I libri degli altri, Lettere 1947–1981*, ed. Giovanni Tesio, Einaudi, 1991, pp. 382–3; author interviews with Alessandro Galante Garrone; Alessandro Galante Garrone, 'Il Grido di Primo Levi', *La Stampa*, 28 September 1961, and *Nuova Antologia*, July–September 1987, and Alessandro Galante Garrone in *La Stampa*, *Speciale La Tregua*, 9 February 1997.

¶ 'In fact . . .'   Typescripts of *The Truce* in Einaudi Archive; *Opere I*, p. 1419; Tesio, *La Stampa*, 9 February 1997; *The Truce*, p. 378. (There are a few insignificant differences in dating between myself, Tesio and Belpoliti; I base mine on the Einaudi typescripts.)

p. 515

¶ 'He took the typescript . . .'   *Opere I*, p. 1420 gives the contract date. I deduce from this that PL must have taken the book to Einaudi as soon as it was done, since Ch. 17 was only finished in November.

¶ 'Something else . . .'   Typescripts in Einaudi Archive; *Opere I*, pp. 1420–21.

'A high wind . . .'   *The Truce*, p. 208.

¶ 'It was like . . .'   Italicized quotation from *The Truce*, p. 379.

p. 516

¶ '*The Truce* was . . .'   Ernesto Ferrero, Introduction to *Primo Levi: I racconti*, Einaudi, 1996, p. ix; Mario Baudino, *La Stampa*, 9 February 1997. For Primo's saying that *The Truce* was his first literary book, see e.g. Roth, *VM*, p. 19 and *Echi*, p. 95.

¶ 'That was even before . . .'   On PL bearing his success badly, e.g. author interviews with Ferruccio Maruffi.

¶ 'That began with *La tregua* . . .'   Author interviews with GCD.

CORSO RE UMBERTO 75

p. 517

¶ 'Once he told . . .'   Interviews with Goria, 1982, Lucarini, 1983; author interviews with Claudio Cavallini.

Poem: '12 July 1980', *CP*, p. 42.

pp. 518–19

On Pirandello: Gaspare Giudice, *Luigi Pirandello*, UTET, 1963; translated and abridged by Alastair Hamilton as *Pirandello: A Biography*, OUP, 1975.

Quotation from 'L'uscita del vedovo', *Opere di Luigi Pirandello*, Arnaldo Mondadori, 1956, Vol. 1, pp. 42–21. Author's translation.

p. 520

Quotation from *INNW*, Abacus, 1987, p. 92.

p. 525

★ *Opere I*, p. 1419.

p. 526

¶ 'I say that no one . . .'   Quotation from *ITIAM* is from p. 61.

p. 527

¶ 'On all these levels . . .'   Quotation 'for chronological reasons' is from the Pesaro debate, p. 20. Alberto Cavaglion's suggestion is in *Primo Levi e Se questo è un uomo*, p. 14.

For the rest of the chapter: for reasons of discretion, I cannot name my interview sources.

Chapter 13: Centaur: 1963–75

p. 529

¶ '*La tregua* . . .'   *Opere I*, pp. 1423–4; *Echi*, p. 24.

¶ 'The reviews . . .' and next ¶   Franco Antonicelli, *La Stampa*, 20 March 1963 (part quoted in Ferrero, *Antologia*, pp. 313–14); Paolo Milano, *L'Espresso*, 21 April 1963 (wholly quoted in Ferrero, *Antologia*, pp. 315–18); Lorenzo Gigli, *Gazzetta del Popolo*, 24 April 1963; Gian Carlo Ferretti, *Unità*, 15 May 1963; Giansiro Ferrata, *Rinascita*, 6 July 1963; Carlo Bo, *Corriere della Sera*, 8 September 1963 (these summarized in Ferrero, *Antologia*, pp. 315–21); also Giorgio Calcagno, *La Stampa*, 9 February 1997, for a summary of the reviews, including Walter Pedullà, *Avanti*, 8 September 1963; author interviews with Alberto Cavaglion. All reviews cited are in the Einaudi Archive.

p. 530

¶ 'The pattern . . .'   Giancarlo Vigorelli, *Tempo*, 13 July 1963; Maria Bellonci, *Io e il Premio Strega*, Oscar Mondadori, 1987, p. 68; *Echi*, p. 15; author interviews with Alberto Cavaglion, Giulio Bollati, Giorgio Calcagno, Cesare Cases, and Alberto Sinigaglia.

¶ 'So began Primo's . . .'   Alfredo Chiesa, 'Interviste con gli scrittori: Primo Levi', *Paese Sera*, 12 July 1963.

p. 531

¶ 'On the evening . . .'   *Echi*, p. 15.

¶ 'But his first . . .'   *Echi*, p. 16; e.g. Vigorelli in *Tempo*; *Unità*, 4 July 1963; *Vita*, 11 July 1963; P. M. Paoletti in *Il Giorno*, 7 July 1963 (in *VM*); Belpoliti 1998, p. 12.

¶ 'The Campiello . . .' and next ¶   *Il Gazzettino*, 25 July 1982; *Vita*, 12 September 1963; *Lo Specchio*, 15 September 1963; *Corriere d'Informazione*, 4 September 1963; Paoletti, *Il Giorno*, 7 August 1963; *Giornale del mattino*, Florence, 17 September 1963.

¶ 'This time there was no question . . .'   Giancarlo Meloni, *La Notte*, 19 September 1963.

p. 532

¶ 'Despite its democratic ideals . . .' and next ¶   *Il Gazzettino*, Venice, 4 September 1963; *Il Gazzettino*, 25 July 1982; *Gazzetta Padana*, 5 September 1963; *Il Tempo*, 5 September 1963; *La Notte*, 19 September 1963.

¶ 'Then he went home . . .'   On PL worrying over *The Truce*: author interviews with Giorgio and Floriana Diena. On the success of *The Truce* as a turning point:

Il Gazzettino, 25 July 1982. Rest of ¶: PL interview with Enzo Fabiani, *Gente*, 20 September 1963.

p. 533

¶ 'But the reality . . .'   On PL finding praise impossible: Gabriella Poli, 'Primo Levi, comunicatore schivo', talk delivered to PL Round Table, Turin, 3 June 1993, copy kindly given me by Gabriella Poli, p. 2.

¶ 'The image . . .'   'Il sesto giorno', *Opere I*, p. 529, translated as 'The Sixth Day' in the collection of the same name, p. 90; 'Disfilassi', *Opere II*, p. 93; Fadini interview, 1966, in *VM*; Gabriella Poli, *Echi*, p. 215 and 'Comunicatore schivo', p. 1; Paolo Terni radio interview; Regge, p. 59; PL, Preface to *Altrui mestiere*, *Opere II*, p. 631; Ferrero interview, 1963; *The Wrench*, p. 52.

p. 534

¶ 'After his return . . .'   Papuzzi, *VM*, p. 62; author interviews with Silvio and Ada Ortona, Norberto and Valeria Bobbio, BGS, Carla Gobetti, Nicoletta Neri, Guido Bollati, and Alberto Papuzzi.

¶ 'Once he had settled . . .'   Author interviews with GCD and Gisella; PL interviews with Marina Verna (1982), Giulio Nascimbeni (1984), Roth (1986), Thomson (1987).

p. 536

¶ 'Apart from learning . . .'   Author interviews with GCD; 'Comunicatore schivo', p. 2; Graziella Granà, unpublished part of 1981 interview, p. 2; 'Very Important Piemontesi' interview, pp. 2–3; Ferrero interview, 1963; author interviews with Lorenzo Mondo and Giovanni Tesio.

¶ 'The only exception . . .'   Author interviews with Ferruccio Maruffi, Anna and Stuart Woolf, and Carla Ovazza Debenedetti.

¶ 'By now Leonardo . . .' and next three ¶¶   Author interviews with Alessandro Debenedetti, Simone Fubini, Paola and Gisella Vita Finzi, Elena Vita Finzi, Emma Debenedetti, Sandra Hirsch, Franco Levi, Mario Levi, Anna Piersanti, and Ferruccio Maruffi; 'Ricordo di un uomo buono'.

p. 538

¶ 'He had another . . .'   Author interviews with AS, Bruno Salmoni, Francesco Cordero, Franca Tambini, Ester Valabrega, GCD, and Gianna Balzaretti; PL to Emma Vita Levi, 5 July 1984.

¶ 'His two other . . .' and next two ¶¶   Author interviews with Luciana and Paola Accati, Alberto Piazza, Leo Gallico, EGT, BGS, GCD, Guido Bonfiglioli, Maria Vittoria Malvano, and Giorgio Diena.

p. 540

¶ 'In 1963 . . .'   Author interviews with SO, Emilio Jona, Anna Cases; SO in Blakeway; SO in *Ha Keillah*, June 1997.

¶ 'Ada did not see . . .'   Author interviews with Anna Cases, Gabriella Garda Aliverti, Jole Segre, Carla Vernaschi Fischer, and Anna Yona.

¶ 'And what about . . .'   SO in *Ha Keillah*, 1997; author interviews with Silvia Di Chio and BGS; PL, 'Psicofante', *Opere I*, p. 681 ('Psychophant', *The Sixth Day*, p. 174).

★ All the *Vizio di forma* stories were written between 1968 and 1970: see Vincenti, p. 112 and *Opere I*, p. 1440.

p. 541

¶ 'He could hardly . . .'   BGS, talk given at memorial service, 21 May 1987; author interviews with BGS, Guido Bonfiglioli, Giorgio Vaccarino, and Sandra Weisz.

¶ 'Despite this . . .'   Silvio Ortona in *Ha Keillah*, 1997; author interviews with Silvia Di Chio.

p. 542

¶ 'This group . . .' and next ¶   Author interviews with Alberto Cavaglion, Norberto and Valeria Bobbio, Gino and Cesarina Sacerdote, Nicoletta Neri, Elda Mancini, Silvia Di Chio, and Renato Portesi.

★ PL, *The Wrench*, p. 110.

p. 543

¶ 'These, then . . .'   Dini & Jesurum, p. 183; author interviews with Renato Portesi, EGT, Giulio Bollati, Giorgio Calcagno, and Alberto Papuzzi.

¶ 'The first was . . .' and next five ¶¶   Author interviews with Mario Rigoni Stern; Dini & Jesurum, Ch. 8, 'Un amico' and Ch. 9, 'Caro Mario' (PL letters to Mario Rigoni Stern, 21 September 1962 and 28 July 1984); author interviews with Norberto Bobbio and Stuart Woolf; PL interview with Paola Valabrega, 1981, *VM*, p. 143.

p. 545

¶ 'In the same year . . .' and next two ¶¶   Author interviews with Nuto Revelli; Nuto Revelli, *La guerra dei poveri*, Einaudi, 1962, pp. 14–15, 379, 382; Nuto Revelli in *Il presente del passato*, pp. 17–18; Dini & Jesurum, p. 193; author interviews with Bartolo Mascarello, Clara and Anna Bovero, Giulio Bollati, Giorgio Calcagno, and Alberto Papuzzi.

p. 547

¶ 'Already in the writing . . .'   *Echi*, pp. 39–40; *Opere I*, pp. 1434–5.

¶ 'He was not wrong . . .' and next ¶   PL interview, *Il Giorno*, 12 October 1966; and see e.g. Giorgio Chiesura, *Devozione*, Mondadori, 1990, pp. 149, 151, 213; Vincenti, p. 59; Dini & Jesurum, p. 164; *Opere I*, p. 1435; Belpoliti 1998, p. 12; author interviews with Roberto Cerati and Maria Vittoria Malvano.

¶ 'That was not the end . . .'   *Opere I*, pp. 1434–5; Dini & Jesurum, p. 164; Tesio, *Piemonte letterario*, p. 63.

¶ 'It didn't work . . .' and next ¶   Paolo Milano, *L'Espresso*, 9 October 1966 (in Ferrero, *Antologia*, pp. 322–30); Giuliano Gramigna, *Corriere della Sera*, 22 October 1966; Ferdinando Viria, *La voce repubblicana*, 31 October 1966; Adriana Martinelli, *Tempo presente*, April 1967; Vittorio Spinazzela, *Vie Nuove*, 20 October 1966; *Gli Shocks*, March 1967, p. 167; 'Didimo' (Rinaldo De Benedetti), *La Stampa*, 5 October 1966; Calcagno, *Il nostro tempo*, 13 November 1966; Claudio Marabini, *Il Resto di Carlino*, 10 October 1966; Lorenzo Mondo, *Gazzetta del popolo*, 12 October 1966; *La Provincia*, Cremona, 15 January 1967; *Il Ragguaglio Librario*, March 1967; and see Ferrero, *Antologia*, pp. 322–4.

p. 548

¶ 'On the whole . . .' *Echi*, p. 40; *Il Piccolo*, Trieste, 15 January 1967; *quaderni piacentini*, No. 29, 1967, p. 15; Cesare Cases's reply, printed in full in Ferrero, *Antologia*, pp. 324–9, and in Cases, *Patrie lettere*; Mondo and Marabini as above; Walter Pedullà, *Avanti*, 16 December 1966; *Il Giorno* interview, 12 October 1966.

★ Paolo Milano review, and e.g. *Il Giorno*, 12 October 1966 interview.

p. 549

¶ 'In fact, something unusual . . .' Vincenti, pp. 59–60, 112; Tesio, *Piemonte letterario*, p. 166; *Opere I*, pp. 1441, 1446; PL in interviews with Paoletti (1963), Fabiani (1963), Chiesa (1963), Ferrero (1963) and Fadini (1966).

¶ 'And the others? . . .' *Echi*, p. 49; Vincenti, pp. 60–61; Dini & Jesurum, p. 144; Stampa Archive records of PL contributions; author interviews with Giuliana Tedeschi, Keith Barnes, Pieralberto Marché; *Opere I*, p. lxxxix. For PL's Lager writings in the mid to late 60s, e.g.: 'La resistenza nei Lager' and 'La deportazione degli ebrei', 1966 and 1967; Preface to Yitzhak Katzenelson, *Il canto del popolo ebraico massacrato*, 1966 and to Leon Poliakoff, *Auschwitz*, 1968.

p. 550

¶ 'The first reason . . .' and next ¶ Author interviews with Renzo Groff and Maurillio Tambini; Fabiani interview, 1963; Regge, p. 63; *The Wrench*, p. 147; author interviews with Norberto Bobbio, Giorgio Bandini, Massimo Scaglione; *Echi*, p. 50. PL did not get on well with several of the SICME technicians (author interviews with Felice Malgaroli), or with Dr Gilardi, a bonhomous but lazy chemist colleague at SIVA (author interviews with Paola Accati, Francesco Cordero, Orsola Azzario Ferrero, Michael Tinker, and Egisto Selvestrel).

¶ 'First, for instance . . .' and next three ¶¶ SIVA registers; author interviews with Francesco Cordero, Renato Portesi, Paola Accati, Renzo Groff, Giuseppe Plateroti, and Keith Barnes. As well as Renato Portesi, Felice Malgaroli was a sympathetic and acute observer of PL's intense effort to communicate. See also Ferdinando Camon, article for *Le Monde* and *La Nación*, a copy of which he kindly gave me: 'Levi aveva il terrore di non essere capito', 'Levi was terrified of not being understood.' On PL's liking James Joyce, see also e.g. *Roots*, *Echi* p. 110, and Grassano, *VM*, p. 125.

p. 552

¶ 'There were, finally . . .' SIVA registers; author interviews with Francesco Cordero.

¶ 'The last friend . . .' and next three ¶¶ SIVA registers; author interviews with Orsola Azzario Ferrero. Paola Accati confirms that PL was very fond of Orsolina.

p. 553

¶ 'In truth, Primo . . .' and next four ¶¶ Author interviews with Silvio Ami, Paola Accati, Orsola Azzario Ferrero, Renzo Groff, Keith Barnes, and Michael Tinker.

p. 555

¶ 'He liked to keep . . .' Author interviews with Egisto Selvestrel, Carmela Franchi, Adolfo Arri, and Paola Accati; Felice Malgaroli, 'Un modo di essere uomo', *Mensile dei metalmeccanici*, April 1992.

¶ 'And then there were . . .'   PL in interviews with Dina Luce, RAI radio, 4 October 1982 (in *Conversazioni e interviste*), and Bocca; see also *Echi*, pp. 232–3.

¶ 'We already know . . .' and next ¶   As well as 'The Force of Amber' and 'Stable/ Unstable': author interviews with Orsola Azzario Ferrero, Egisto and Redento Selvestrel, and Renato Portesi.

† See Renato Portesi, 'Primo Levi: un chimico, un impiantista . . . un uomo', *Chimica e industria*, May 2001, p. 4.

p. 556

¶ 'One happened . . .'   Author interviews with Paola Accati, Egisto and Redento Selvestrel, and Adolfo Arri.

¶ 'In 1967, however . . .' and next ¶   Author interviews with Renato Portesi and Egisto Selvestrel; PL in Boeri interview, 1983, *VM*, p. 66, and in *The Wrench*, pp. 15, 21–2, 27–8. On PL's being good in emergencies: author interviews with Renato Portesi, Orsola Azzari Ferrero, and Adolfo Arri and Portesi in *Chimica e industria*, p. 4.

¶ 'Later, in *The Double Bond* . . .'   Boeri interview, *VM*, p. 66. I date the incident to the early 70s because PL's Russian trips, made to sort out this problem, were in those years (author interview with Silvio Ami; and see PL to Charles Conreau, 22 June 1972, and to Hety Schmitt Maass, 28 December 1972).

¶ 'In fact, what the disguise . . .' and next three ¶¶   *DL*, Ch. 5.

p. 558

¶ 'The second reason . . .'   Vincenti, pp. 59–60.

¶ 'In fact, he had always . . .'   Belpoliti 1998, pp. 126–7, 166; *Opere I*, p. 1432; Luca Scarlini, 'Teatro', in *Riga*, No. 13, *Primo Levi*, ed. Marco Belpoliti, Marcos y Marcos, 1997; PL, Introduction to the play version of *ITIAM*, *Quaderni del Teatro Stabile di Torino*, No. 8, 1966, pp. 39–43 (on pp. 41–2); *Echi*, p. 26.

p. 559

¶ 'The mid-60s was a time . . .'   Information about the *nouvelle vague* from Edgar Reitz. Rest of ¶: Vincenti, p. 58, author interviews with Eva Erber.

¶ 'They recorded its scenes . . .'   Author interviews with Giorgio Bandini and Pieralberto Marché; Marché in Introduction to *ITIAM* play as above, p. 45; *Opere I*, p. 1408; *Echi*, p. 27; author interviews with Eva Erber. Eva Erber, wife of the RAI doctor Bruno Erber, was not an actress, as Scarlini and Belpoliti say, but a native German speaker recruited for the radio *ITIAM*. In 1978 she would organize the foreign speakers for the radio version of *The Truce*.

p. 560

¶ 'Primo was fascinated . . .' and next ¶   PL in play *ITIAM*, p. 46; *Opere I*, p. 1408; author interviews with Giorgio Bandini and Eva Erber; Marché in Introduction to play *ITIAM*, p. 46; *Echi*, pp. 26, 34; Belpoliti 1998, p. 128; *Riga*, p. 489.

¶ 'Success encouraged . . .' and next ¶   *Echi*, pp. 34, 113–14; Guido Davico Bonino in *Il presente del passato*, p. 141, and in *Piemonte Vivo*, No. 3, 1991, 'Primo Levi, Torino, Il Teatro', pp. 57–63; author interviews with Massimo Scaglione; Belpoliti 1998, pp. 126–7, 171; *Riga*, p. 489; PL in Bona Alterocca interview, *La Stampa*, 16 February 1977. On PL's pleasure in film-makers' interest in *The Truce*: author interviews with GCD and Renato Portesi.

★ *Echi*, pp. 113, 119–20; Belpoliti 1998, p. 171; author interviews with Massimo Scaglione; and Guido Davico Bonino in *Piemonte Vivo*, p. 63 and *Presente del passato*, p. 146.

p. 561

¶ 'In fact, he had hesitated . . .' and next two ¶¶ Vincenti, p. 112; author interviews with Pieralberto Marché; Marché in Introduction to play *ITIAM*, pp. 46–8; PL in play *ITIAM*, pp. 42–3; Gabriella Poli in 'Comunicatore schivo', pp. 3, 7 and in *Echi*, pp. 42–7; PL undated letter to Gianfranco De Bosio, kindly given me by Pieralberto Marché; Nuccio Messina, 'Vivere per far rivivere', *La Discussione* (Rome), 4 May 1987 (Messina was production manager for the play of *ITIAM*).

p. 562

¶ 'The rehearsals . . .' Author interviews with Pieralberto Marché and Gianfranco De Bosio; PL letter to De Bosio as above; *Independent on Sunday*, 3 November 1996, p. 15, and *La Stampa*, 8 November 1996 (on the Florence flood); *Echi*, p. 42.

p. 563

¶ 'In the end . . .' PL's letter to De Bosio; author interviews with Marché, De Bosio, Gabriella Garda Aliverti, and Guido Davico Bonino; *Echi*, pp. 42, 45, 47; Davico Bonino in *Piemonte Vivo*, pp. 60, 62.

¶ 'Audiences continued . . .' Author interviews with Marché; Belpoliti 1998, p. 167; PL to Charles Conreau, 22 June 1972; *Echi*, p. 47; Davico Bonino, *Piemonte Vivo*, p. 62. The best review was in an American expatriate paper, *The Daily American*, 31 December 1966. Other less favourable reviews were, e.g.: *La Stampa*, 20 November 1966; *Corriere della Sera*, 20 November 1966; *Vie Nuove*, 1 December 1966; *Epoca*, 4 December 1966; *Corriere di Novara*, 15 December 1966; *Gazzetta del Jonio*, 20 December 1966; *Eco di Biella*, 5 January 1967 (all in the Archive of the Teatro Stabile, Turin).

¶ 'Primo's and Marché's . . .' Author interviews with Pieralberto Marché; *La Stampa Sera*, 28–9 November 1966; PL to Charles Conreau, 22 June 1972; Belpoliti 1998, p. 167. On PL's not wanting to profit from the deaths of his companions: author interviews with Ferruccio Maruffi. Ferruccio recalls that whenever PL had a success with a Lager story he went into crisis.

p. 564

¶ 'That was effectively . . .' *Riga*, p. 498; *Echi*, pp. 119–20; author interviews with Massimo Scaglione and Gianfranco De Bosio.

¶ 'There was one more reason . . .' and next seven ¶¶ Author interviews with Lilith. The quotations on pp. 565 and 566 are from 'Lilith' and 'Landing', *Collected Poems*, pp. 26 and 25.

p. 566

¶ '*Vizio di forma* . . .' PL, Introduction to *Vizio di forma*, 1987 (*Opere I*, p. 571); reviews of *Vizio di forma*: *Il Messaggero*, 22 May 1971; *Famiglia cristiana*, 25 April 1971; *Studi Cattolici*, 5 July 1971; *Oggi*, 31 May 1971; *Messaggero Veneto*, 7 May 1971 (these were the good ones); *Il Nostro Tempo*, 18 April 1971; *Corriere d'informazione*, 27 April 1971; *Il Giorno*, 7 July 1971; *Corriere della Sera* (Carlo Bo), 4 April 1971; *Paese Sera* (Daniele del Giudice), 16 April 1971; *Rinascita* (Mario Spinelli), 4 June 1971; *Avanti* (Giuseppe Bonaviri), 30 May 1971; *Il Secolo XIX*

(Eugenio Buonaccorsi), 7 May 1971; *L'Espresso* (Paolo Milano), 25 April 1971; *La Stampa* (Enzo Siciliani), 7 May 1971.

p. 567

¶ 'He was right . . .'   PL to Anna Yona, 7 September 1971 ('un libro scomodo . . . disincantato e disilluso': 'an uncomfortable book . . . disenchanted and disillusioned'). On his trying to deny this for reasons of social duty: see cover copy for *Vizio di forma*, almost certainly by PL himself (*Opere I*, p. 1442), and PL in interview with Lamberti, *L'Adige*, 11 May 1971, in *VM*. PL says to Lamberti that many readers thought his book 'desperate'. For *Studi Cattolici* reference, see Note to previous ¶. For rest of ¶: author interviews with Fiora Vincenti and Mario Miccinesi; Vincenti, pp. 113, 162–3; *Uomini e libri*, Anno XIII, No. 63, March–April 1977.

p. 568

¶ 'The story that . . .'   e.g. Calcagno in *Il Nostro Tempo*, 18 April 1971; *Famiglia cristiana*, 25 April 1971; *Oggi*, 31 May 1971; also Vincenti, pp. 115–16, Cases in *Tre narratori*, p. 102, and Andrea Libertori in *Unità*, 25 September 1986. 'Westward' is in *TSD*, p. 126.

¶ ' "I wrote that story . . ." '   PL to Andrea Libertori, in *Unità*, 1986.

p. 569

¶ 'In "Excellent is the Water" . . .'   Calcagno in *Il Nostro Tempo* picked this story as one of the best.

p. 571

¶ 'This is not only . . .'   Vincenti also focuses on 'Vilmy', for similar reasons (Vincenti, pp. 121–2). For PL's still feeling fear as well as desire for women: author conversations with Lilith (though she did not say so in so many words: see the next chapter, *Lilith*, and the chapter *The Double Bond*, p. 652).

p. 572

¶ 'On the cover . . .' and following quotation   *Opere I*, pp. 1442–3.

¶ ' "An old man . . ." '   Foa, *Il cavallo e la torre*, p. 341.

¶ 'But this is only . . .'   For Primo's working life being almost all frustration, see Note to p. 575 below. For his response to the violence of the 70s, see e.g. *Echi*, p. 125: these 'tempi tragici . . . lo angosciavano', 'these tragic times drove him to despair'; and e.g. PL, 'Perché non ritornino le SS', *La Stampa*, 20 April 1978 (in *Opere I*, p. 1236): 'la violenza che oggi respiriamo attorno a noi', 'the violence which we breathe in all around us today'.

¶ 'The 1970s were . . .'   Ginsborg, *A History*, Ch. 9, 'The Era of Collective Action, 1968–73', pp. 298–347; Maria Cecilia Rivoira, *Il Cogidas di Torino*, degree thesis 1992/3, kindly given me by Cogidas, Turin.

p. 573

¶ 'Violence had already started . . .'   Ginsborg, *A History*, pp. 333–4; Rivoira, *Il Cogidas de Torino*, p. 59; PL to 'Dear Friend' (Hety Schmitt Maass), 23 December 1972. The left's suspicions have proven accurate: see *London Review of Books*, 8 March 2001, p. 37.

¶ 'And it was happening . . .'   Rivoira, *Il Cogidas di Torino*, p. 61; *Sisifo II*, magazine of the Istituto Gramsci Piemontese, September 1987, '14 anni d'impegno del

Cogidas di Torino', pp. 29–30; *Una Regione contro il terrorismo, 1969–1978, dati e chronache,* Consiglio Regionale del Piemonte, 1979, p. 22; *L'Indagine sull'attività neofascista in Piemonte,* in the monthly *Notizie del consiglio regionale del Piemonte,* Anno IV, Special Supplement to No. 4, April 1975, pp. 47, 92–4, 113, 126.

¶ 'Nothing could have . . .' Renzo would have been in *liceo* from 1968 to 1975. Fabrizio Salmoni's arrest is reported in *Indagine,* p. 76 (it was on 10 November 1972). The son of a friend who was injured was Daniele Panzieri, son of Pucci Panzieri, widow of Raniero (*Indagine,* p. 100). For police inactivity, an undated Cogidas report kindly given me by Cogidas; and author interviews with Elda Mancini.

★ Ginsborg, *A History,* pp. 327–8.

p. 574

¶ 'Something had already . . .' *Sisifo II,* p. 29; Rivoira, *Il Cogidas de Torino,* p. 63. Other founding members of Cogidas, Turin, were e.g. Clara and Anna Bovero, Ester Valabrega, AS, Pucci Panzieri, Lia Corinaldi, Elda Mancini, Marisa Quazza (wife of the historian Guido Quazza), Ferdinando Mazzinghi, and Carlo Ottino, an active antifascist teacher at the Liceo Alfieri (Rivoira).

¶ 'For the next year . . .' and next ¶ Report signed by Lucia Levi, PL and PL for Ada Ortona (i.e. Ada Della Torre), 29 May 1973, kindly given me by Cogidas; *Indagine,* p. 93.

¶ 'We know how . . .' *Indagine.*

p. 575

¶ 'By the 1970s . . .' PL to Anna Yona, 7 September 1971; *Intervista Aziendale,* a radio play based on an idea by PL – the factory system turns workers into bees (*Opere I,* p. 1461); SIVA registers; PL to 'Dear Friend', 23 December 1972; author interviews with Egisto Selvestrel, Maurillio Tambini, and Michael Tinker.

¶ 'Finally, in the autumn . . .' Ginsborg, *A History,* Ch. 10, 'Crisis, Compromise and the *Anni di Piombo,* 1973–80', especially pp. 351–2, 'Economic Crisis'.

¶ 'And then it got worse . . .' and next two ¶¶ Author interviews with Paola Accati, Luisa Accati, Egisto Selvestrel, Michael Tinker, and the Downsizer, who for obvious reasons shall remain unnamed. The SIVA registers give PL's date of resignation as 30 November 1974.

p. 576

¶ 'Of course, being Primo . . .' and next ¶ PL in Boeri interview; PL to Hermann Langbein, 10 February 1974, to Anna Yona, 9 March 1975, to Emma Vita Levi, 5 July 1984, and to Edith Weisz, 6 February 1985; *Opere I,* p. xc; Gad Lerner, RAI TV programme on PL, 1997; author interviews with Paola Accati, Michael Tinker, Egisto Selvestrel, and Adolfo Arri.

★ SIVA registers and *Echi,* p. 123.

p. 577

¶ 'The truth is . . .' Author interviews with Egisto Selvestrel, Michael Tinker, Paola Accati, Renato Portesi, and Carmela Franchi; Regge, pp. 62–3; Roth, *VM,* pp. 18–19.

¶ 'When he had made . . .' On PL's depression of summer 1971: PL to LDB, 13 August 1971, PL to Anna Yona, 7 September 1971, and author interviews with

Gisella. It is also from Gisella that I know he did not count this one among his major depressions.

¶ 'In August 1971 . . .'   PL to LDB, 13 August 1971.

★ Author interviews with Egisto and Redento Selvestrel, Paola Accati, and the Downsizer.

p. 578

¶ 'In late 1972 . . .'   PL to 'Dear Friend', 23 December 1972, and to Hermann Langbein, 10 February 1974; author interviews with Keith Barnes.

¶ 'He must have realized . . .' and next ¶   Letter to the author from Renata Gaddini, 28 June 1994. The psychiatrist requested anonymity.

¶ 'It had been in his mind . . .'   Fabiani interview, 1963; also e.g. Spriano, Chiesa and Ferrero article and interviews of 1963.

p. 579

¶ 'He had certainly begun . . .'   For 'Carbon', see Note to p. 583 below; for the other line of chemical stories (i.e. *DL*), see *Echi*, pp. 124–5. Quotation 'They are my worst [stories] . . .' comes from the Fadini interview, 1966, *VM*, p. 85.

¶ 'But that was in the middle . . .'   *Opere I*, pp. 1446–8; original typescripts of *PT* in Einaudi Archive. We know that 'Lead' and 'Mercury' were written before the war, 'Titanium' in 1947, 'Sulphur' around 1950, the original of 'Iron' ('La carne dell'orso') in 1961, 'Hydrogen' in 1968 and 'Carbon' (perhaps finally) between 1968 and 1970. The Einaudi typescripts showed that the other chapters of *PT* were typed (or finished typing) on the following dates: 'Tin', 16 April 1972; 'Zinc', 3 December 1972; 'Potassium', 4 February 1973; 'Nickel', 1 May 1973; 'Gold', 26 May 1973; 'Argon' (rewrite), 24 June 1973; 'Lead' (rewrite), 30 September 1973; 'Chromium', 18 November 1973; 'Mercury' (rewrite), 6 January 1974; 'Iron' (final version), 15 April 1974; 'Phosphorus', 1 May 1974; 'Uranium', 30 June 1974; 'Nitrogen', 5–7/8 August 1974; 'Silver', 14–19 August 1974; and 'Vanadium', 15 September 1974.

¶ 'We have explored . . .'   'Uranium', 'Silver', 'Vanadium', 'Carbon': *PT*, pp. 191 to end.

¶ ' "Silver" picks up . . .'   'Sfida della molecula' is in *Opere II*, p. 162 (untranslated); 'Riprodurre I miracoli' is in *Opere II*, p. 966, translated as 'Reproducing Miracles' in *TMM*, p. 135; 'Pipetta di guerra' is in *Opere II*, p. 886, translated as 'Small Causes' in *MR*, p. 107.

p. 581

Secretly, PL did occasionally admit he'd written fiction elsewhere in *PT*: see e.g. *Echi*, p. 73, to Professor Bàrberi Squarotti (but he only admits to 'Lead' and 'Mercury'). For rest of ¶: author interviews with Tullio Regge (also Regge, p. xv and in *Presente del passato*, p. 163, but in these places he did not remember that PL's answer had been 'Vanadium').

¶ 'In fact, the person . . .'   PL in ANED interview, *VM*, p. 243; author interviews with Hermann Langbein; *D. & S.*, pp. 158, 160, 163; PL to Dr Ferdinand Meyer, 12 March 1967, kindly given me by Hermann Langbein. Although this correspondence is not otherwise available, JS possesses copies of it. Respecting a promise given to Meyer's family, he did not allow me to read it, but only to note its dates. It consists of six letters, plus the death announcement: Ferdinand Meyer to PL, 2 March 1967, and PL's reply of 12 March; Meyer to PL, 5 April 1967 (the long letter, eight pages in all) and PL's reply of 13 May; Meyer to PL, 29 June 1967; and Meyer's daughter to PL, 18 December 1967, telling him of Meyer's death, and enclosing the death announcement.

¶ 'There are other . . .' *PT*, pp. 222–3.

★ *Opere I*, p. 657.

p. 582

¶ 'Now, we do not have . . .' See also *Echi*, p. 192: Meyer's letter was 'vago', 'neboloso', vague and misty.

¶ 'Did he harden . . .' Quotation 'my opponent distracts me . . .' is from *PT*, p. 218. On PL's never forgiving an unrepentant enemy, see e.g. *Echi*, p. 102; his letter to *La Stampa*, 1 September 1967; his interview with Dina Luce, 1982 (in *Conversazioni e interviste*, p. 38); his contribution to Simon Wiesenthal, *The Sunflower*, 1969; in the Pesaro debate, p. 9; and in BBC *Bookmark*, published in *Ateneo*, pp. 9–13 (on p. 13).

¶ 'But Meyer . . .' PL in Pesaro debate, p. 9 and in BBC *Bookmark*; author interviews with Anna Yona.

★ Hermann Langbein, *Menschen in Auschwitz*, pp. 510–11. See also Ferdinand Meyer to Langbein, 27 June 1967, in which he expresses his gratitude for their recent meeting (copy kindly given me by Hermann Langbein).

p. 583

¶ 'Its own age . . .' PL's different accounts of 'Carbon': *Echi*, p. 85 and BBC *Bookmark* (Aosta); *PT, p. 128 (Milan); Tesio, Piemonte letterario*, p. 149, and in interviews with the author (*liceo*); author interviews with JS (Auschwitz). The date mentioned in 'Carbon' itself (*PT*, p. 231) is 1960. PL calls 'Carbon' his first literary dream in 'Carbon' itself (*PT*, p. 225), and said that it was the first story of an element he wrote in BBC *Bookmark* (*Ateneo*, p. 10).

¶ 'So many ideas . . .' In the Pesaro debate (p. 15) PL called the movement in the brain at the end of 'Carbon' a dance as well. The Jewish population of Italy is *c.* 40,000 out of *c.* 58 million.

p. 584

¶ ' "Carbon" itself . . .' For PL uniting his two halves in *PT*, see the interview with Luigi Angelino in *Il Monferrato*, 12 July 1975: 'Ho realizzato il vecchio sogno di riunire le due culture esistenti in me': 'I have realized the old dream of uniting the two cultures that exist in me.'

LILITH

p. 585

'La ragazza del libro', *Opere II*, p. 175, untranslated.

p. 588

'La valle di Guerrino', *Opere II*, p. 168, untranslated.

The rest of this chapter is from conversations with Lilith.

Chapter 14: Writer: 1975–85

p. 591

¶ 'They were his worst . . .'   Fadini interview, 1966, *VM*, p. 85.

¶ 'There wasn't a paper . . .'   Lorenzo Mondo, *La Stampa*, 24 May 1975; Natalia Ginzburg, *Corriere della Sera*, 25 May 1975; Roberto Vacca, *Nazione*, 22 June 1975. For Natalia Ginzburg's review pleasing PL, see *Echi*, p. 183; for Carlo Bo backing him for the Viareggio, see *Corriere della Sera*, 12 July 1975. *Il Ragguaglio Librario* review was by Claudio Toscani, *Rinascita* by Professor Leone De Castris. Guido Lopez's review was in *Uomini e libri*, June/July 1975. All reviews are in the Einaudi Archive, and summarized in Ferrero, *Antologia*, pp. 334–9.

p. 592

¶ 'In July . . .'   *Corriere della Sera*, 12 July 1975; *Il Tempo*, 12 July 1975; *Unità*, 13 September 1975; Belpoliti 1998, p. 160; *Opere I*, p. 1451; Gabriella Poli in *Echi*, pp. 25, 59, 70, 72, 74, 77, and in 'Comunicatore schivo', p. 2.

¶ '*The Periodic Table* . . .'   *Echi*, pp. 72–3, 92; Stille, 'Primo Levi negli Stati Uniti', p. 206; Greer, biographical introduction omitted from *VM*; Belpoliti 1998, p. 159.

¶ 'A few years . . .'   Regge, p. 63; author interviews with Lorenzo Mondo; Belpoliti 1998, pp. 15, 159.

p. 593

¶ 'The reception . . .'   PL interview with Gabriella Poli, *Tuttolibri*, *La Stampa*, 4 December 1976, quoted in *Echi*, pp. 124–5; author interviews with Gianna Balzaretti.

¶ 'He had begun . . .'   *Opere I*, p. 1445; *PT*, p. 157; author interviews with Gabriella Poli.

¶ 'So Primo began . . .'   *Echi*, p. 125; Belpoliti 1998, p. 42; *Opere I*, p. 1453; PL, 'Meditato con malizia', *La Stampa*, 13 March 1972; author interviews with Claudio Cavallini.

p. 594

¶ 'For the next . . .'   *Echi*, p. 125; Boeri interview, *VM*, p. 68; Grassano, *VM*, p. 133.

¶ 'At the same time . . .'   Author interviews with Lorenzo Mondo; PL, 'Trent'anni dopo, per non dimenticare', *La Stampa*, 9 February 1975, in *Opere I*, p. 1190 (under the title 'Così fu Auschwitz'); *Stampa* Archive records of PL contributions.

p. 595

¶ 'Would he have written . . .'   Author interviews with Lorenzo Mondo, Alberto Sinigaglia, and Gabriella Poli; Gabriella Poli in Blakeway.

¶ 'He was still . . .'   *Echi*, p. 76; *D. & S.*, pp. 166–7; PL, ANED interview, *VM*, p. 230; transcript of Di Caro interview; interviews with Giorgio Manzini, *Paese Sera*, 11 December 1978 and Silvia Giacomoni, *La Repubblica*, 24 January 1979.

¶ 'By now he was . . .'   Author interviews with Cogidas members, Elda Mancini, Carla Ovazza Debenedetti, and Marisa Quazza; Minutes of the Consiglio D'Azeglio, 2 April 1975 – 9 September 1976 (the period of PL's presidency), kindly given me by the school; Rivoira, *Il Cogidas de Torino*, pp. 13, 14, 138.

p. 596

¶ 'In the first few sessions . . .'   Minutes of the Consiglio D'Azeglio; author interviews with Giorgio Calcagno and Elda Mancini.

¶ 'And then there was SIVA . . .'   *Echi*, p. 76; *Opere II*, pp. 1584–5; *Le edizioni Einaudi negli anni 1933–1993*, p. 287.

¶ 'Some time ago . . .'   PL to Luciano Foa, 22 August 1975, quoted in *Opere II*, p. 1584; PL Preface to Jacques Presser, *La notte dei Girondini*, 1976, in *Opere I*, pp. 1208–11, on p. 1208; *Echi*, p. 74.

¶ '*La notte dei Girondini* . . .'   *Opere I*, p. 1467; author interviews with BGS; PL, Preface to Presser. He already used the term 'grey zone' in 1975 (see e.g. *Echi*, p. 75).

p. 597

¶ 'He made himself . . .'   *Echi*, p. 75 and author interviews with Gabriella Poli.

¶ 'So far only his close friends . . .'   *Echi*, p. 87; *Opere II*, pp. 1544, 1548; author interviews with SO. SO kindly showed me his copy of PL's privately circulated poems.

¶ 'Over the next five years . . .'   Belpoliti 1998, p. 123; Tesio, *Piemonte letterario*, pp. 221–2; PL to Einaudi, 29 March 1975, in Einaudi Archive.

p. 598

¶ 'There can be no stronger . . .'   Tesio, *Piemonte letterario*, pp. 199–200 and interviews with the author; Gabriella Poli, *Echi*, p. 87; Ruth Feldman, 'Remembering Primo Levi', 1990, p. 3 (talk kindly given me by Ruth Feldman), and 'Primo Levi's Poetry', in *Reason and Light: Essays on Primo Levi*, ed. Susan Tarrow, Cornell University, 1990, pp. 142–7, on p. 144. PL's 1945–6 poems about Auschwitz were 'Buna', 'Singing', '25 February 1944', 'Shemà', 'Reveille', 'Sunset at Fossoli' and possibly 'Ostjuden'; the other dark poems of the period were 'The Crow's Song', 'Monday', 'After R. M. Rilke' and 'The Glacier'. The two on Auschwitz between 1949 and 1974 were 'Waiting' and 'For Adolf Eichmann'. The quotations are from *CP*, pp. 29 and 30.

¶ 'Many of these . . .'   'To write is to bare oneself to the world' is from 'To a Young Reader', *OPT*, p. 206; poetry catching him 'in flagrante' is from *Echi*, pp. 90–91 striking him like 'a rash', 'an infection' is from Grassano, *VM*, p. 132. To Lucarini in 1983 he said poems struck him 'like meteors'.

¶ 'In fact he said so . . .'   Mario Macagno, *Cucire un motore*, Edizioni Leone & Griffa, 1992, p. 143, and interviews with the author.

¶ 'In September 1977 . . .'   *Echi*, p. 123n.; author interviews with Gabriella Poli and Keith Barnes.

¶ 'Nineteen-seventy-eight began well . . .'   *Echi*, pp. 113–14, 118.

¶ 'But it was not . . .'   Author interviews with Gisella; also with Giovanni Tesio and Sidney Calvi.

p. 600

¶ 'The first reason . . .'   *Una Regione contro il terrorismo*, pp. 13, 22, 31, 37, 54, 61, 78, 100, 126; Ginsborg, *A History*, pp. 362, 379, 384; Rivoira, *Il Cogidas de Torino*, p. 125.

¶ 'Casalegno . . .' and next two ¶¶   *Una Regione*, pp. 102, 118, 122–8, 160, 163,

173, 215–16, 226, 231; Ginsborg, *A History*, pp. 384–6; author interviews with Sergio Valvassori and Anna Yona.

p. 601

¶ 'First of all . . .'   Author interviews with Paola Accati, Felice Malgaroli, Fiora Vincenti and Mario Miccinesi, and Giorgio Colombo.

¶ 'With the end of SIVA . . .' and next ¶   Author interviews with and letters from Gabriella Garda Aliverti; 'Breve sogno', *La Stampa*, 24 June 1976, in *Opere I*, p. 200 (untranslated).

p. 602

¶ 'The first was to do . . .'   Birth certificate Ester Luzzati [Rina], Atto No. 1790, Ufficio 2, Parte 1, Anno 1895, shows her birth date as 28 June 1895. Rest of ¶: PL to Anna Yona, 29 March 1975 and to Hermann Langbein, 10 April 1976; author interviews with GCD.

¶ 'For a while this . . .'   Author interviews with Gisella; also with Anna Cases, Cesare Cases, Massimo Scaglione, and Bruno Salmoni; PL to Anna Yona, 5 May 1981 and to Emma Vita Levi, 5 July 1984.

¶ 'About this last . . .'   Author interviews with (e.g.) Giorgina Arian Levi and Anna Vitale (Jewish Community), Piero Bianucci (*La Stampa*), Guido Davico Bonino (Einaudi), Sidney Calvi (Chemistry class), Jutta Pabst (Goethe Institute), not to speak of Einaudi (e.g. Agnese Incisa). For PL's post-1978 depressions being triggered by his mother's decline: like all information about his depressions, this comes from Gisella. For his relationship to his mother as pathological: all the psychiatrists/psychoanalysts I spoke to agreed, e.g. Renata Gaddini, Franca Mussa; also family and friends, e.g. Anna Yona and Carla Gobetti. For Lucia's level of care as pathological: this is very widely agreed, but for reasons of discretion I shall give no individual sources.

p. 603

¶ 'In November . . .'   *L'Express*, 28 October – 4 November 1978, quoted in Deborah Lipstadt, *Denying the Holocaust*, Plume, 1994, p. 11.

¶ 'In December . . .' and next ¶   PL, 'Un Lager alle porte d'Italia', *La Stampa*, 19 January 1979, *Opere I*, p. 1253; Lipstadt, *Denying*, pp. 50, 65, 103; David Irving's *Hitler's War* was published in 1977.

¶ 'Primo replied . . .'   PL, 'Ma noi c'eravamo' ('But We Were There'), *Corriere della Sera*, 3 January 1979, *Opere II*, p. 1251; 'Chi vuole l'odio antisemita' ('Who Wants Antisemitic Hatred?'), *La Stampa*, 13 March 1979, *Opere II*, p. 1260; *Ha Tikwa*, Rome, March–April 1979, interview with Giorgio Segre (in *VM*). Also later: e.g. 'Cercatori di menzogne per negare l'Olocausto', *La Stampa*, 26 November 1980, *Opere II*, p. 1332, and 'Non sarebbe la sole autrice del diario?', *La Stampa*, 7 October 1980, *Opere II*, p. 1330. PL also said to Grassano in their 1979 interview that Faurisson was mad (typescript p. 2, omitted from *VM*).

p. 604

¶ 'He did not mean . . .'   On PL's inability to read Holocaust deniers: Norberto Bobbio in *Il presente del passato*, p. 14; and author interviews with Gisella and with Cesare Cases. On the great shock for PL of Holocaust denial: author interviews with GCD. Quotation 'ugly enterprise' from PL, Preface to *La Vita offesa*, Franco Angeli, 1992, in *Opere II*, p. 1347.

¶ 'It was not only . . .'   Anton Kaes, *Hitler to Heimat*, Harvard University Press, 1989, pp. 28–35; PL, 'Perché non ritornino gli olocausti di ieri', *La Stampa*, 29 June 1979, in *Opere I*, p. 1268 (dated to 20 May), 'Olocausto? Come un western romanzato', *La Stampa*, 25 May 1979, and 'Un Olocausto che pesa ancora sulla coscienza del mondo', *La Stampa*, 20 May 1979.

¶ 'For several years . . .'   Author interviews with Floriana Diena, Alberto Papuzzi, Carla Vernaschi Fischer, Anna Savoini, and Giosanna Albarello Sciaccaluga; PL in Giacomoni interview, 1979; *Echi*, pp. 198, 201; PL, 'Chi vuole l'odio antisemita', *Opere II*, p. 1260.

★ Kaes, *Hitler to Heimat*, p. 30.

p. 605

¶ 'By the end of that time . . .'   PL, ANED interview, *VM*, p. 230; author interview with Enrico Grosso; Belpoliti 1998, p. 53; Gabriella Poli in Blakeway; PL in 'Primo Levi a Acqui quella sera', *Nuova Antologia*, July–September 1987, p. 209 (here PL says 140 schools).

¶ 'At the time it seemed . . .'   Eleven Holocaust articles in the first half of 1979: *Opere I*, p. 1466 and *Opere II*, p. 1563. The *Lilit* stories in 1979 and 1980 were 'Lilith', *La Stampa*, 10 June 1979, 'A Disciple', 2 December 1979 and 'Cesare's Return', 7 September 1980. On *D. & S.*'s being a surprise: *Opere II*, p. 1566; and see Calcagno's question in *La Stampa*, 26 July 1986: 'Perché Primo Levi, dopo essere passato per tante altre esperienze, anche letterarie, ha voluto riprendere quel tema?': 'Why did Primo Levi want to return to that theme, after so many other experiences, including literary ones?'

¶ 'But the truth was . . .'   The gestation of 'Carbon' was perhaps as long as thirty years, from *liceo* to the 60s; that of *INNW* around fifteen years, from the mid-60s to the early 80s. For *D. & S.*'s going back to 1975 and the translation of Presser, see PL to Anna Yona, 9 March 1975 (he's already thinking of writing the story of Chaim Rumkowski); interviews with A. Colombo, 1987, quoted in *Opere II*, p. 1564, and with Giorgina Arian Levi, *Ha Keillah*, April 1978 and April 1979. For the renewal of the idea in 1979, see many 1979 interviews, e.g. with Giacomoni, with F. Colombo in *Eco di Bergamo*, 9 October 1979, and in *L'Informatore librario*, August–September 1979, quoted in *Opere II*, p. 1565. For the 1980 date, see *Opere II*, p. 1564, and the dates on the Einaudi typescripts of 'The Memory of the Offence' (5/80 and 30.01.81). For the anguish of writing *D. & S.*: *Echi*, p. 209, and Gabriella Poli in Blakeway; also author interviews with Anna Yona, and Giovanni Tesio in Blakeway. For its slow progress until 1985: *Opere II*, p. 1565, quoting Enrico Arosio interview, *Vogue* Italia, no. 426, September 1985. The 1982 text was 'Il difficile cammino della verità', *Opere I*, p. 1173. The end date of January 1986 comes from the bottom of the typescript of the Conclusion: 3 January 1986.

p. 606

¶ 'It would cost him . . .'   I owe the point that it would cost PL some of his literary reputation to Norberto Bobbio.

¶ 'At the end of 1976 . . .'   PL interview with Gabriella Poli, 'Lo scrittore è al suo secondo *Sistema periodico*', *La Stampa*, 4 December 1976; PL, 'Meditato con malizia', *La Stampa*, 13 March 1977.

¶ 'What had happened? . . .'   PL on the origins of Faussone: interviews with Manzini, *Paese Sera*, 11 December 1978, Francesco Poli, *Il quotidiano dei lavoratori*, 20 February 1979, and in Di Caro transcript, 1987; *Echi*, pp. 124, 129, 132. On the origins of the first story: author interviews with Giovanna Galante Garrone; PL interviews with Giacomoni, 1979, and with Enrico Deaglio, *Lotta Continua*, 30 December 1978; *Echi*, pp. 127, 129; *Opere I*, p. 1455.

* The evidence for a cut chapter is: in the Einaudi typescripts there is no Ch. 2, with 'La zona grigia' numbered 3; and Primo referred to nine chapters in a letter to Hermann Langbein, 28 March 1986.

p. 607

¶ 'Primo was still locked . . .'   Author interviews with Giovanna Galante Garrone; PL interviews with Francesco Poli and Giorgina Arian Levi as above. The dates of the chapters of *The Wrench* are: Ch. 1, not dated but published in *La Stampa*, 13 March 1977; Ch. 11, 1 April 1977; Ch. 3, 22 July 1977; Ch. 4, 19 September 1977; Ch. 5, 3 November 1977; Ch. 6, 24 November 1977; Ch. 7, 13 December 1977; Ch. 9, 29 December 1977; Ch. 10, 2 May 1978; Ch. 13, 22 May 1978; Ch. 8, 1.6.78–19.6.78; Ch. 12. 24/6; Ch. 14, 13.7–8.8.78; Ch. 2, 23.8–29.8.78 (all from the Einaudi typescripts, the last four as written).

¶ 'That was (with a few . . .'   PL in interviews with Giacomoni, Grassano, Francesco Poli; author interviews with Felice Malgaroli, Egisto Selvestrel, and Elena Deangeli; *Echi*, pp. 126–7; Belpoliti 1998, p. 43; typescript of *The Wrench* (thanks to G.L. and L.N.).

¶ 'That is what he always . . .'   See Note at the end of *The Wrench*; and e.g. interviews with Giorgio De Rienzo, 1978 and 1979, quoted in *Echi*, p. 127; *Echi*, p. 124. For Primo's saying in private that there was one model: author interviews with Alberto Papuzzi, Oreste Molina. For PL's naming Felice Malgaroli: Francesco Poli interview, and Giovanni De Luna, 'No, caro Bocca', *Italia Oggi*, 13 April 1987, p. 11.

p. 608

¶ 'Why did Primo . . .' and next ten ¶¶   Author interviews with Renzo Groff, Felice Malgaroli, and Paola Accati. For the story of the 'real' Faussone, see PL in Boeri interview, *VM*, pp. 66–7, and in transcript of Di Caro interview (p. 5), where he says that the young man's name was Carlo.

p. 610

¶ 'So that was how . . .'   For *The Wrench* having been easy to write: Grassano, *VM*, p. 133; author interviews with Carla Vernaschi Fischer. The tower disaster in Ch. 2, 'Cloistered', had been in the first chapter of the first version of *The Double Bond* (*Echi*, p. 127).

p. 611

¶ 'And who can blame . . .'   On *The Wrench* as PL's happiest book: author interviews with e.g. Lorenzo Mondo, Elena Deangeli (the Einaudi editor who worked on it), and Carla Vernaschi Fischer, who met PL through his Aunt Jole.

On the Russians not changing: PL to Charles Conreau, 22 June 1976. PL's Russian stories, when they're not in *The Wrench*, come from Silvio Ami, who heard them from Tullia, and from Pieralberto Marché, who heard them from PL.

¶ 'On a deeper level . . .' PL in Giorgina Arian Levi interview, 1979; *Echi*, pp. 127, 152–3, 161, 215.

p. 612

¶ 'And *La chiave* . . .' That *The Wrench* is about writing is also noted by Giovanni Tesio (in Blakeway) and Piero Bianucci, in *Gazzetta del popolo*, 21 December 1978; that it is about story-telling is a point I owe to Robert Gordon. That it is about PL's move from chemistry to writing is a point made in *Echi*, p. 132.

¶ 'Finally, *La chiave* . . .' About work, *Echi*, p. 150; about a new hero, *Echi*, p. 127; about language, *Echi*, pp. 155–6. The quotation 'a book that had never been written before' comes from Carla Vernaschi Fischer. *La parlata italo-tecno-piemontese* comes from 'La coppia conica' in *La Stampa*, 12 June 1977 (it was cut from the book).

¶ 'This new language . . .' Gianluigi Beccaria in Preface to the schools edition of *La chiave a stella*, Einaudi, 1983, p. x. The points about this language come from the Preface; and from author interviews with Carla Vernaschi Fischer, whom I thank for her help. See also Giovanni Tesio, 'Libertino Faussone in cerca del suo lettore ideale', in *Primo Levi: La dignità dell'uomo*, pp. 136–9.

p. 613

¶ 'The Turinese . . .' *The Wrench* is Carla Vernaschi Fischer's favourite, and Guido Davico Bonino's; also one of SO's. On other Italians getting about 70 per cent: Francesco Poli interview, quoted in *Echi*, p. 156.

¶ 'Primo had thought . . .' Typescript of *The Wrench* in Einaudi Archive; *Echi*, pp. 122, 137; *Opere I*, p. 1454.

¶ 'It was published . . .' Belpoliti 1998, p. 53. The first review was Lorenzo Mondo, *La Stampa*, 8 December 1978. The stinker was in *Corriere dell'informazione*, 6 January 1979. Others mentioned: Giovanni Raboni, *Tuttolibri*, 23 December 1978; Giorgio De Rienzo, *La Stampa*, 29 December 1978; Enrico Deaglio, *Lotta Continua*, 30 December 1978; Geno Pampaloni, *Il Giornale Nuovo*, 14 January 1979; Mario Lunetta, *Il Messaggero*, 10 February 1979; Paolo Milano, *Espresso*, 21 January 1979; Alberto Asor Rosa, *Unità*, 24 June 1979; summarized in Ferrero, *Antologia*, 339–47.

¶ 'Primo collected . . .' *Echi*, p. 162, Di Caro interview (transcript, p. 13); Belpoliti 1998, p. 13; Ferrero, *Antologia*, p. 339; *The Wrench*, pp. 79–80; Stefano Reggiani, *La Stampa*, 24 September 1982; letter from Tommaso Ciaula to *Lotta Continua*; *Echi*, pp. 137–8, 145 and author interviews with Gabriella Poli.

p. 614

¶ 'Slowly the controversy . . .' Raboni, *Tuttolibri*, 23 December 1978; Claudio Toscani, *Brescia Oggi*, 4 February 1979; Roberto Vacca, *Tuttolibri*, 10 February 1979; Corrado Stajano, *Il Messaggero*, 11 December 1978; *Echi*, pp. 163–6; Diana Aphel, *Il Tempo*, 6 July 1979.

p. 615

¶ 'After the controversy . . .' *Opere I*, pp. 1453, 1457; *Echi*, p. 210; author interviews with Giorgina Arian Levi, Giancarlo Borri, Giorgio Calcagno, and Gisella.

¶ 'But 1979 . . .'   Author conversations with Gisella; *Echi*, p. 209. 'Toward the Valley', *CP*, p. 38.

¶ 'In June . . .'   'Annunciation', *CP*, p. 37; 'La fuggitiva', *La Stampa*, 6 July 1979, in *Opere II*, p. 121; Tesio, *Piemonte letterario*, p. 200; author interviews with Gisella.

¶ 'In late December . . .'   'In una notte', *La Stampa*, 22 December 1979, in *Opere I*, p. 1289 (untranslated).

p. 616

¶ 'This is, once again . . .'   Author conversations with Gisella.

¶ 'In his last decade . . .'   *Echi*, pp. 266, 269–70.

¶ 'I have already . . .'   *Echi*, p. 263; PL in TG 2 'Studio aperta' interview, 17 May 1982; Alfredo Cattabiani interview, *Il Tempo*, 21 January 1979. Note about dating: Anna Savoini thought that her Goethe years with PL were 1979–82, with Hans Engert's death occurring only months after their 'abandonment' of him for another teacher. But the contemporary interviews show that PL began his Goethe course in 1978, making the three years 1978–81. (Unfortunately the Goethe Institute has no registers, which would have settled the question immediately.) I follow the contemporary record; also because it is a more or less universal trick of memory to move events close to landmark ones, especially when they are traumatic.

¶ 'Many survivors . . .'   *Echi*, p. 197; Cattabiani interview.

¶ 'This was a very Primo . . .'   'Tornare a scuola', *Opere II*, p. 655, translated as 'Going Back to School' in *OPT*, p. 170.

p. 617

¶ 'In fact, his German . . .'   Author interviews with Hermann Langbein, Jutta Pabst, Anna Savoini, and Cesare Cases.

¶ 'This teacher . . .'   Author interviews with BGS, Anna Savoini, Jutta Pabst; PL's first letter to Heinz Riedt, quoted in Calcagno, *La Stampa*, 18 April 1987; *La Stampa*, 25 November 1981.

¶ 'Its ending . . .'   'Tornare a scuola'; author interviews with Anna Savoini; *La Stampa*, 25 November 1981.

p. 618

¶ 'Primo hadn't . . .'   Author interviews with Anna Savoini, BGS; *La Stampa*, 25 November 1981.

¶ 'Primo was deeply . . .'   Author interviews with Anna Savoini, Gisella, and Jutta Pabst.

¶ '"After thirty-five . . .'   PL, 'Scrivere un romanzo', *Opere II*, p. 774, translated as 'Writing a Novel', *OPT*, p. 116; author interviews with BGS, who thought that PL felt if he was ever going to write a novel, he had better start.

¶ 'It was an aspect . . .'   *Echi*, pp. 252–3, 255; *Opere II*, p. 1538.

p. 619

¶ 'But this made him . . .'   Author interviews with Elena Vita Finzi, and Paola and Gisella Vita Finzi; and see PL's Note at the end of *INNW*, p. 279.

¶ 'Emilio had told . . .'   *Opere II*, p. 1538; and see interview with *Il Giorno*, 12

October 1966 (quoted in *Echi*, pp. 37–8), in which PL already has the idea for *INNW*; *Echi*, p. 254.

¶ 'He rang Emilio . . .' *Echi*, pp. 209, 254, 267–8; author interviews with Elena Vita Finzi and Giorgio Vaccarino; and see Primo's Note, *INNW*, pp. 280–81.

p. 620

¶ 'He didn't stop . . .' *Echi*, pp. 257–8; Primo's Note, *INNW*; author interviews with Vittorio Foa, who remembers Primo's delight at finding the Kaganovich diary.

¶ 'About the writing . . .' *Echi*, pp. 265–6, 269; PL, 'Writing a Novel'; author interviews with Gabriella Poli, and Gabriella Poli in Blakeway.

¶ 'His newest . . .' *Echi*, pp. 157, 258, 262, 265, 270–71; *Opere II*, p. 1540; *INNW* typescript in Einaudi Archive, p. 1; PL, 'Writing a Novel'.

p. 621

¶ 'So he always . . .' Author interviews with Alberto Papuzzi, Oreste Molina, Gabriella Poli, BGS; *Opere II*, p. 1539; Guadagni in *Unità*, 1993; typescript of *INNW*; PL, 'Writing a Novel'.

¶ 'In the summer . . .' *Opere II*, pp. 1576–7; *Echi*, pp. 246–7; Belpoliti 1998, p. 142; PL interview with Giovanni Tesio in *Nuovasocietà*, 11 July 1981, pp. 48–9.

p. 622

¶ 'Without the company . . .' Italo Calvino, *La Repubblica*, 11 June 1981, printed in full as Afterword to *Roots*, pp. 221–4; Lorenzo Mondo, *La Stampa*, 3 July 1981; Giulio Nascimbeni, *Corriere della Sera Illustrata*, 16 May 1981; Claudio Marabini, *Il Resto di Carlino*, 23 May 1981; Geno Pampaloni, *Il Giornale Nuovo*, 23 November 1981; Piero Bianucci, *Gazzetta del popolo*, 21 May 1981; Mario Lunetta, *Il Messaggero*, 10 June 1981. The only negative review was from Giorgio De Rienzo, *Famiglia cristiana*, 9 August 1981.

¶ '*Radici*, then . . .' On PL's enjoying writing *Roots*, and remaining fond of it, author interviews with Guido Davico Bonino and *Echi*, p. 247, respectively. On PL's theme of self-creation, see e.g. his introduction to Conrad in *Roots*, and 'Il fabbro di se stesso' in *Opere I*, p. 702 ('His Own Blacksmith' in *The Sixth Day*); also, on survivalism and inventiveness, 'Gli stregoni' in *Opere II*, p. 151, and 'Trenta ore sul *Castoro sei*' in *Opere II*, p. 704; on autodidacts, the Preface to *Altrui mestiere* and 'Le parole fossili'; and 'Roulette dei batteri' and 'Gli scacchisti irritabili' on individual minds (*Opere II*, pp. 631, 819, 950, 763). The quotation is from the Tesio interview of 11 July 1981, as above.

¶ 'The reason . . .' *Echi*, p. 247; Preface to *Roots*, p. 5.

¶ '"I have never . . .' *Opere II*, pp. 1576–8; Preface to *Roots*, p. 5; *Echi*, p. 215.

p. 623

¶ 'Despite the critics' . . .' 'Tradurre Kafka', *Opere II*, p. 939. PL did not manage to hide his dark side from his more acute critics, however; especially Giovanni Tesio (see his 1997 Introduction to *Se questo*); and on the stories, Vincenti (pp. 113, 120–21) and Carlo Sgorlon, *Il Gazzettino*, 13 December 1981: 'in Levi c'è una malattia segreta, che per fortuna solo raramente viene in primo piano; ossia il fatto di sentire l'universo come un'immensa macchina inutile' ('There is a secret illness in Levi, which fortunately takes centre stage only rarely: feeling the universe to be a huge and useless machine').

¶ 'As Calvino . . .'   Calvino review in *La Repubblica* (see also Tesio on *Roots*, in the 1997 *Se questo*, pp. xx–xxi); *Roots*, p. 214. See also PL's admission of the deep pessimism of *Roots* to Tesio, in *Nuovasocietà*, 18 June 1983.

¶ 'Nineteen-eighty-one . . .'   Belpoliti 1998, p. 14; *Echi*, p. 209; *Stampa* Archive records of PL contributions. Belpoliti says that *Lilit* was published in October (*Opere II*, p. 1535); Ferrero's original chronology says November (*Opere I*, p. lvi). I follow Ferrero, especially as the reviews only began in mid-November.

¶ '*Lilit* was divided . . .'   For critics' connection of *Lilit* to *The Wrench* and *PT*, see e.g. Giorgio De Rienzo in *Famiglia cristiana*, 27 December 1981, and Piero Bianucci in *Il Nostro Tempo*, 28 December 1981.

p. 624

¶ '*Lilit* was by far . . .'   Marabini, *Il Resto di Carlino*, 22 February 1982; Bo, *Corriere della Sera*, 27 December 1981; Bàrberi Squarotti, *La Stampa*, 5 December 1981.

¶ 'Nonetheless, the other stories . . .'   Reviews of *Lilit* in Einaudi Archive. PL published two books in 1981, and had a book about him published (Grassano's *Primo Levi*), so that his presence on the literary scene was very prominent this year. (Pampaloni makes this point in *Il Giornale Nuovo*, 23 November 1981.)

p. 625

¶ 'In late December . . .'   Typescripts in Einaudi Archive (the changes are mainly to Ch. 3, and dated between 24 December and 9 January); *Opere II*, p. 1542; Guido Lopez, *Shalom*, No. 2, February 1982, dateline 18 February.

¶ '*Se non ora* . . .'   Calcagno, *Tuttolibri*, 12 June 1982; *Echi*, p. 266; author interviews with Giorgio Vaccarino and Agnese Incisa.

¶ 'Yes, emphatically . . .'   Author interviews with Giorgio Vaccarino (on PL's keeping his reviews in folders). The closest reviews to stinkers were Giuseppe Bonura in *Avvenire*, 5 September 1982 and (again) Giorgio De Rienzo in *Famiglia cristiana*, 15 August 1982, but they were mild. The others were: Francesco Cosatello, *Il Sole 24 Ore*, 6 June 1982; Paola Cacìanti, *Avanti*, 8 September 1982; Pampaloni, *Il Giornale Nuovo*, 29 June 1982; Marabini, *Il Resto di Carlino*, 25 May 1982; Mondo, *La Stampa*, 19 May 1982; Gino Nogara, *Il Messaggero Lunedí*, 10 May 1982; Massimo Romano, *Avvenire*, 19 August 1982; Sgorlon, *Il Gazzettino*, 3 June 1982; Vacca, *Il Giorno*, 18 May 1982. Rest of ¶: PL in interviews with Stefano Jesurum, *Oggi*, 14 July 1982 and Oreste Del Buono, *Europeo*, 5 July 1982; *Il Giornale di Sicilia*, 26 June 1982 (on the Viareggio); on PL's winning the Campiello: *Il Giornale*, 5 September 1982, *Il Gazzettino*, 31 August 1982, *Il Tempo*, 3 September 1982; *Opere II*, p. 1542; Belpoliti 1998, p. 144; and Maria Pia Bonanate, *Madre*, 15 November 1982.

¶ 'And yet . . . This time . . .'   Sgorlon, Marabini, Pampaloni, Romano reviews as above; Claudio Magris, *Corriere della Sera*, 13 June 1982; G. Petrocchi, *Il Gazzettino*, 31 August 1982; R. Luperini, *Gazzetto del Mezzogiorno*, 27 May 1982; Paolo Spriano, *Unità*, 20 April 1982; G. Spagnoletti, *Il Tempo*, 25 June 1982; *Panorama*, 14 June 1982. Cesare Cases remembers the reviews for *INNW* as poor overall.

p. 626

¶ 'None of this . . .'   Marabini as above; PL in interview with Oreste Del Buono as above; Cacìanti as above.

¶ 'If he had ever . . .'   Interview with Jesurum as above; PL, 'Writing a Novel', p. 119.

¶ 'In fact, his risk-taking . . .'   See Mondo's review: 'Lo apriamo con l'apprensione che si trova davanti a pagine che sembrerebbero appartenere a un genere trapassato (il romanzo storico?), ma siamo subito catturati dalla loro vitalità e freschezza': 'We open the book a little worried that we may find ourselves faced with pages that belong to an outdated genre (the historical novel?), but instantly we are captivated by their vitality and freshness.'

p. 627

¶ 'His pure happiness . . .'   Author interviews with AS, Gabriella Garda Aliverti, BGS, Anna Yona, Cesare Cases, Norberto Bobbio, Vittorio Foa, Oreste Molina, Agnese Incisa.

¶ 'And then, still in June . . .'   *Echi*, pp. 176–8, 184 ('Return to Auschwitz'); Primo in interviews with Nascimbeni, *Corriere della Sera*, 28 October 1984, Thomson, *PN Review*, 1987, and Giacomoni, *Unità*, 26 April 1982; and 'Return to Auschwitz' transcript on the Internet, p. 13.

¶ 'The other thing . . .'   Israel invaded South Lebanon on 6 June 1982 (Paul Johnson, *A History of the Jews*, Weidenfeld & Nicolson, 1987, p. 580). The open letter was in *La Repubblica*, 16 June 1982. See also PL, *La Stampa*, 24 June, and in *Oggi* interview with Jesurum.

p. 628

¶ 'He returned . . .' and next ¶   Author interviews with Alberto Cavaglion and Stefano Levi Della Torre; reviews by Pampaloni as above, Gentiloni in *Il Manifesto*, 29 June 1982, and Forcella in *Il Messaggero*, 4 July 1982; PL in interviews with Monticelli, *Epoca*, 12 September 1982 and Pansa, *La Repubblica*, 24 September 1982 (latter in *VM*).

¶ 'He had been divided . . .'   Edith Bruck, *Il Messaggero*, 9 January 1976 *VM*, pp. 262–3); F. Diwan, *Corriere medico*, 3–4 September 1982; *Panorama*, 5 July 1982; author interviews with Renato Portesi, GCD, Giuliana Tedeschi; PL, 'Chi ha coraggio a Gerusalemme', *La Stampa*, 24 June 1982 (in *Opere II*, p. 1171), and interviews with *Panorama*, Pansa and Jesurum as above, and with Alberto Stabile, *La Repubblica*, 27/8 June 1982.

¶ 'In fact he had already . . .'   Aldo Zargani, fax to the author, 27 June 1995; author interviews with Sion Segre Amar; *PT*, p. 218.

p. 629

¶ 'He was more famous . . .'   'Chi ha coraggio a Gerusalemme'; PL interviews as above.

¶ 'He had family . . .'   *Echi*, p. 293; author interviews with Sion Segre Amar, Elio and Marlene Vitale; Andrea Baglino, *Corriere della Sera*, 7 July 1982; *Echi*, p. 310.

¶ 'And then, in September . . .'   The events of Sabra and Chatila happened on 16 September 1982 (Johnson, *A History*, p. 580); *Echi*, p. 296; Pansa interview, *VM*.

¶ 'That was his last word . . .'   Pansa interview, *VM*, pp. 285–6.

* PL, *La Repubblica*, 11 February 1983, and in Gad Lerner interview, *Espresso*, 30 September 1984 (the latter in *VM*). PL's interviews on Israel over the years are quoted by Gabriella Poli in *Echi*, pp. 293–305.

p. 630

¶ 'He had to . . .'   See e.g. Zargani fax: the reactions of the right 'letteralmente sconvolsero Primo Levi', 'literally overwhelmed Primo Levi'.

¶ 'The book was Kafka's *Trial* . . .'   See all PL's interviews on Kafka, e.g.: Luciano Genta, *Tuttolibri*, 9 April 1983; Fabrizio Dentice, *Espresso*, 24 April 1983; Oreste Del Buono, *La Stampa*, 28 April 1983; Federico De Melis, *Il Manifesto*, 5 May 1983 (in *VM*); Laura Mancinelli, *Il Secolo XIX*, 7 July 1983; Giuseppe Bernardi, *Il Giornale*, 22 May 1983; Franco Pappalardo, *Gazzetta del popolo*, 12 June 1983; Giovanni Tesio, *Nuovasocietà*, 18 June 1983; *L'Opinione*, 5 July 1983; and *Opere II*, p. 1586. The information about 7,500 *lire* in 1983 comes from ISTAT, which lists the annual index of inflation from 1983 to November 2001 as (approximately – I've rounded it up) 2.35.

¶ 'On the other hand . . .'   PL in De Melis interview and several others in 1983, in *Mondoperaio*, 1984, p. 155 (paragraph omitted in *VM*) in Kleiner interview 1986; his Note to his translation of *The Trial*, Einaudi, 1983, p. 254; his 'Tradurre Kafka'; his interview with Aurelio Andreoli, *Paese Sera*, 21 August 1981 (in *Conversazioni e interviste*).

p. 631

¶ 'With hindsight . . .'   Author interviews with Gisella; PL interviews with De Melis, Genta, Tesio, Pappalardo, and *L'Opinione*.

¶ 'By May he was . . .'   *Echi*, pp. 306, 310; PL interviews with Mancinelli, De Melis, Genta, Kleiner, and *L'Opinione*; his Note to *The Trial*; author interviews with Gisella.

¶ 'In his last year or two . . .'   PL interview with Greer (she interviewed him in Turin, but published the result in England); interview with *Mondoperaio*, *VM*, p. 164.

¶ 'Any one of these . . .'   Author interviews with Gisella; author's letter from Renata Gaddini, 28 June 1994; author interviews with Simone Fubini; PL in *Mondoperaio*, *VM*, p. 164.

p. 632

Poem '*Alla Musa*', written 25 August 1982, published in *La Stampa*, 5 September 1982, in *Opere II*, p. 605. A copy of the poem including the date of composition kindly given me by Gisella. Italics mine.

¶ 'The pit of this grave depression . . .'   'Stabile/Instabile', *La Stampa*, 10 November 1982; 'Vecchio io?', *Stampa Sera*, 15 November 1982 (in *VM*).

¶ 'After that, with the help . . .'   *Echi*, pp. 310–11; *Opere II*, p. 1588.

¶ 'At last, in May . . .'   *Echi*, pp. 246, 312; author interviews with Gisella.

p. 633

¶ 'That summer . . .'   *Echi*, p. 311; Daniela Dawan interview, *Bollettino della Comunità Israelitica di Milano*, June 1986, p. 4; author interviews with Giorgio Vaccarino.

¶ 'He was not yet . . .' and †, next page   *Opere II*, p. 1588; *Echi*, p. 312; Anissimov,

Primo Levi, p. 558; PL in Rudolf and BBC *Bookmark*; Pesaro debate, 1986, pp. 10–11; author interviews with Elie Wiesel.

p. 634

¶ 'The second half . . .'   Author interviews with Hermann Langbein. Hety Schmitt Maass died on 1 August 1983.

¶ 'Leonardo was only . . .' and next three ¶¶   LDB, ANED interview, 1982, p. 27; PL, 'Ricordo di un uomo buono', and 'Leonardo De Benedetti', in *Ha Keillah*, No. 2, 1983 (in *Opere II*, pp. 1194 and 1197); PL letter to Bice Azzali about LDB, 18 March 1981; author interviews with Paola and Gisella Vita Finzi, Mario Levi, Emma Debenedetti, Sandra Hirsch, Anna Piersanti, and Ferruccio Maruffi.

p. 636

¶ 'Nineteen-eighty-four . . .'   Dark poems after *L'Osteria di Brema*: 'Toward a Valley', 5 September 1979, *CP*, p. 38; 'Dark Band', 13 August 1980, *CP*, p. 43; 'Voices', 10 February 1981, *CP*, p. 46; 'Arachne', 29 October 1981, *CP*, p. 49. Pre 1982–3 depression poems already discussed: 'Laid Up', 27 June 1982, *CP*, p. 53; 'Old Mole', 22 September 1982, *CP*, p. 54; 'A Bridge', 25 November 1982, *CP*, p. 55; 'Alla Musa', 25 August 1982, uncollected; 'Pliny', 27 May 1978, *CP*, p. 33; author interviews with Clara and Anna Bovero.

'Le pratiche inevase', 'Unfinished Business': *CP*, p. 47.

¶ 'For "*In fondo*" . . .'   Giovanni Tesio in S. Salvatore, p. 262, and in interviews with the author.

'*Un topo*', 'A Mouse': *CP*, p. 57.

¶ 'In the twinning . . .'   Author interviews with Giovanni Tesio.

p. 637

¶ 'That must be . . .'   *Echi*, p. 311; PL in interviews with *QOL* (1986), Lombardi (1985), Nascimbeni (1984). PL covered up completely to Rudolf in 1985, e.g., saying that his second 'wave' of poetry, after *INNW*, was 'perhaps connected to a new flow of vitality in me' (*VM*, p. 28).

¶ 'Not all the poems . . .'   'A Profession', *CP*, p. 62, 'Flight', *CP*, p. 63, 'The Survivor', *CP*, p. 64, 'The Elephant', *CP*, p. 65, 'Agave', *CP*, p. 59, 'Pearl Oyster', *CP*, p. 60, 'The Snail', *CP*, p. 61, 'Wooden Heart', *CP*, p. 39.

★ *Stampa* Archive records.

p. 638

'Chess', *CP*, p. 69, 'Chess II', *CP*, p. 70, 'Il Decatleta', *Opere II*, p. 607, 'Polvere', *Opere II*, p. 609, 'Una Valle', *Opere II*, p. 610, 'Agenda', *Opere II*, p. 612 ('Memorandum Book', *CP*, pp. 71–2), 'Carichi pendenti', *Opere II*, p. 614.

p. 639

¶ 'His family . . .'   Tesio, S. Salvatore, p. 262. PL also told Gisella that his family was unhappy with 'Le pratiche inevase'.

¶ '*L'Osteria di Brema* . . .'   *Opere II*, p. 1549.

¶ 'The reason was . . .'   Author interviews with Oreste Molina, Agnese Incisa, and Giovanni Tesio; Cesari, *Colloquio con Giulio Einaudi*, p. 164; PL to Emma Vita Levi, 5 July 1984.

¶ 'In the circumstances . . .'   *Echi*, pp. 314–15.

¶ 'Apart from a few . . .'   Giovanni Raboni, *La Stampa*, 17 November 1984; Giulio Nascimbeni, *Corriere della Sera*, 28 October 1984; Giovanni Tesio, *La Stampa*, 17 November 1984; Claudio Marabini, *Il Resto di Carlino*, 5 June 1985; *La Stampa*, 26 July 1985; *Opere II*, p. 1550. On PL's wanting ordinary readers even more in poetry than in prose: author interviews with Giovanni Tesio. He told Nascimbeni that more people wrote to him about his poetry than about his prose; and *Ad ora incerta* sold well for a book of poetry (*Opere II*, p. 1550).

p. 640

¶ 'Despite Einaudi . . .'   *Echi*, pp. 314, 318.

¶ 'It happened in November . . .' and next ¶   Stille, 'Primo Levi negli Stati Uniti' in *Presente del passato*, pp. 203–4; John Gross, *New York Times*, 29 November 1984; account of Ascherson and West in *Il Mattino*, 17 March 1984; Alvin Rosenfeld, *New York Times Book Review*, 23 December 1984. On Saul Bellow: *Echi*, p. 322; *Il Mattino* as above; Ernesto Ferrero in *La Stampa*, 9 February 1997, p. 2.

¶ 'This was the moment . . .'   *Echi*, p. 323; Walter Clemons, *Newsweek*, 6 May 1985; Bocca (quoted in *Echi*, p. 325).

p. 641

¶ 'As soon as he was restored . . .'   Belpoliti 1998, p. 15; PL, Preface to Höss, *Opere II*, p. 1276.

¶ 'At the same time . . .'   *Opere II*, pp. 1557, 1560; Belpoliti 1998, p. 24.

¶ 'Despite Primo's . . .'   Belpoliti 1998, p. 59; Giulia Massari, *Il Giornale*, 31 March 1985.

★ James Atlas, 'The Survivor's Suicide', *Vanity Fair* 51, No. 1, January 1988; Stille in *Presente del passato*, pp. 205–6; author interviews with Saul Bellow, Arturo Colombo, Bonnie Fetterman, and Irene Williams.

p. 642

¶ '*Altrui mestiere* . . .'   PL, Preface to *Altrui mestiere*, *Opere II*, p. 631; other quotation from 'Domum servavit', *Opere II*, p. 698 (in *OPT*, p. 156).

¶ 'Everything strong . . .'   Quotations from 'Gli scarabei', *Opere II*, pp. 793 and 792 ('Beetles', in *Other People's Trades*, pp. 18 and 16).

¶ 'Yet even in *Altrui mestiere* . . .' and next ¶   *Opere II*, p. 1559.

p. 643

¶ 'The invitation . . .'   Author interviews with Irene Williams and BGS.

¶ 'His mother . . .'   Author interviews with Amir Eshel; PL interview with Risa Sodi, *Endpapers*, 1988, p. 45; PL to Ruth Feldman, 3 February 1983; author interviews with Elda Mancini.

p. 644

¶ 'If he couldn't . . .'   PL letters to Charles Conreau, 1 January 1985, Ruth Feldman, 12 January and 6 February 1985, and Edith Weisz, 6 February 1985; PL interview with Sodi, 1988, p. 45; Agnese Incisa in Atlas, 'The Survivor's Suicide', p. 82; author interviews with Giorgio Colombo, Gretchen Getty, GCD, and Amir Eshel.

¶ 'America was . . .'   Schedule for US trip kindly given me by Anna Yona, and PL to Anna Yona, 16 February 1985; PL in interviews with Sodi, 1988, and

Greer, 1985; *Echi*, pp. 251, 253, 323; author interviews with Arthur Samuelson, Irene Williams, Edith Weisz, Ruth Feldman, and Anna Yona. PL's talk was the English translation of 'Itinerario'.

¶ 'As for Primo . . .'   On his fame coming too late: e.g. his letter to Anna Yona, 16 February 1985, and author interviews with Nereo Pezza. On rest of ¶: author interviews with Giorgio Colombo, Arthur Samuelson, and Irene Williams; PL, 'Tra le vette di Manhattan', *Opere II*, p. 954; Irene Williams letter to Ester Fein, 25 November 1991, kindly given me by Irene Williams.

p. 645

¶ 'Above all, however . . .'   PL interviews with Gad Lerner, *Espresso*, 30 September 1984 (in *VM*), Sodi, 1987 (in *Conversazioni e interviste*) and Greer, 1985 (in *VM*); author interviews with Irene Williams and Germaine Greer; Ernesto Ferrero in *La Stampa*, 9 February 1997, p. 2; author interviews with Ruth Feldman.

¶ 'And then there were . . .'   PL, 'Cena in piedi', *La Stampa*, 22 January 1977, *Opere I*, p. 1212; 'Tra le vette di Manhattan'; *New York Times* article on Kenneth B. Smilen awards, 3 May 1985; author interviews with Anna Yona, Irene Williams, Arthur Samuelson, and Giorgio Colombo.

¶ 'His US adventure . . .'   Author interviews with EGT, Anna Yona, Bonnie Fetterman, and Arthur Samuelson; PL interview with Sodi, 1988, p. 45.

p. 646

¶ 'The truth was . . .'   On PL's unhappiness away from his mother: author interviews with Irene Williams and Bonnie Fetterman; author interviews with Edith Weisz.

¶ 'Back home . . .'   'Aeroporto', *Opere II*, p. 619, untranslated.

p. 647

¶ 'International fame . . .'   PL interviews with Bocca, 13 June 1985; Lombardi, Radio Svizzera Italiana, 3 June 1985; BBC *Bookmark*, filmed summer 1985; *Opere II*, pp. 1560, 1597; author interview with Arthur Samuelson; Atlas, 'The Survivor's Suicide', p. 81; *Echi*, p. 328.

¶ 'Calvino wrote . . .'   Italo Calvino to PL, 10 August 1985, quoted in Manuela Bertone, *S. Salvatore*, p. 236; PL, 'Con la chiave della scienza', *La Stampa*, 20 September 1985, in *Opere II*, p. 1274; PL, 'La Cosmogonia di Queneau', *Opere II*, p. 766; PL, 'Calvino, Queneau e le scienze', *Opere II*, p. 1344 (quoted in *Echi*, pp. 329–31).

¶ 'This time . . .' and next ¶   Italo Calvino to PL, 10 August 1985; PL, 'Con la chiave della scienza'; Italo Calvino to Vanni Scheiwiller, 23 August 1985, quoted in Bertone, *S. Salvatore*, p. 237; *Echi*, p. 329.

p. 648

¶ ' "Reading Primo Levi" . . .'   Fernanda Eberstadt, 'Reading Primo Levi', *Commentary*, October 1985, pp. 41–7.

¶ 'Primo put on a brave face . . .'   PL to Anna Yona, 15 December 1985; PL interview with *VM*, p. 38, 1987; author interviews with Arthur Samuelson, Irene Williams, and Gisella; letters Raymond Rosenthal, Alan Viterbi and PL to *Commentary*, February 1986 (PL's written November 1985).

p. 649

¶ 'In October . . .'   Author interviews with JS, and JS in Philadelphia talk, 1997, p. 9.

p. 650

¶ 'Primo finished . . .'   D. & S. typescripts in the Einaudi Archives; *Echi*, p. 328; author interviews with Pierluigi Olivetti.

THE DOUBLE BOND

This chapter from conversations with and letters from Gabriella Garda Aliverti, Lilith, and Gisella.

p. 654

The interview with Dina Luce appears in *Conversazioni e interviste*; this exchange is on p. 43. See also e.g. PL in Greer, *VM*, p. 9; 'I'm very afraid both of my own suffering and the suffering of others.' The information on Primo's catching the verruca at the swimming-pool comes from Alberto Papuzzi; that on Primo's fearing it was cancer from JS.

p. 655

'I am a talker . . .': *Conversations*, p. 47.

★ *Conversations*, p. 63; author interviews with Ferdinando Camon.

p. 656

PL on communication is from 'Dello serivere oscuro', *Opere II*, p. 676, translated as 'On Obscure Writing', in *OPT*. Gabriella Poli's 'to communicate experiences' is from her *Communicatore Schivo*, p. 5. PL's 'That is why . . . I am bound to her for life', is from *Conversations*, p. 66.

Chapter 15: The Drowned and the Saved: 1986

p. 657

¶ 'At last, in early January . . .'   *Echi*, p. 331.

¶ 'Primo's relief . . .'   For D. & S. leaving him weary: e.g. *Echi*, pp. 331, 334; author interviews with JS.

p. 658

¶ 'People often asked . . .' and next two ¶¶   Author interviews with Anna and Stuart Woolf; *Echi*, p. 331; author interviews with Gabriella Poli and Gisella. In the end the Montedison magazine, *Progetto Cultura*, published PL's Duco poem, 'Il testamento del vice capolaboratorio', together with a remembrance of him, in the issue after his death (Anno 2, No. 6, May 1987, last page).

¶ 'He began . . .' and next four ¶¶   DL, Ch. (or Letter) 1.

p. 659

¶ 'This was a delightful start . . .'   Author interviews with Lilith, Gisella, SO, Gabriella Poli, Ernesto Ferrero, BGS, and AS. For showing everything first to

Lucia: Vincenti, p. 55, Dini & Jesurum, p. 184, *Panorama*, 26 April 1987, and author conversations with Gisella.

¶ 'For this first letter . . .'   For PL's remaining in control to the end, see e.g. Norberto Bobbio in Atlas, 'The Survivor's Suicide', p. 82. For his seizing the high moments: Gisella.

p. 660

¶ 'Ada – his sister-substitute . . .'   Author interviews with Anna Cases, Silvio and Ada Ortona, Gabriella Garda Aliverti, and Gisella. Ada died in July.

¶ 'In mid-January . . .'   PL to Emma Vita Levi, 13 January 1985.

¶ 'Twice – probably . . .'   Author interviews with Pierluigi Olivetti.

p. 661

¶ 'The last glimpse . . .' and next ¶   PL, ANED interview, *VM*, pp. 230–31; PL interviews with Alberto Gozzi, 1985, F. G. Colombo, *Sabato*, December 1984, Bocca, 1985; PL to Mario Macagno, 25 October 1985. The quotation is from the interview with Milani, *Piemonte VIP*, March 1986 (quoted in *Echi*, p. 332).

¶ 'It was much the same . . .'   Sodi interview, 1988, p. 45; author interviews with Giorgio Colombo, Luigi Meneghello, and Agnese Incisa.

¶ 'He gave only two talks . . .'   Interviews with Tim Radford, 'Lifeline from Auschwitz', *Guardian*, 17 April 1986, and Rudolf, *VM*; author interviews with Giorgio Colombo, Luigi Meneghello and Paola Accati; Stuart Woolf, 'Primo Levi e il mondo anglosassone', as before; Roth (quoted in *Echi*, p. 268); PL, 'Bella come una fiore', *Opere II*, p. 986.

p. 662

¶ 'Although this visit . . .'   Author interviews with Philip Roth and Claire Bloom.

¶ 'He told the story . . .' and next two ¶¶   PL, 'Un "giallo" del Lager', *Opere II*, p. 909, translated as 'A Mystery in the Lager' in *TMM*, p. 66; author interviews with JS and Giorgio Colombo.

p. 664

¶ 'He returned . . .'   *Echi*, pp. 331–2; Pesaro debate; Sodi interview, 1988, p. 45. For foreign interviews: e.g. Sodi, Kleiner, Spadi interviews, all in summer 1986.

¶ 'Then, at the end . . .'   *Opere II*, p. 1569 ('mid-year'); the first reviews appeared in early June.

¶ 'This gravest . . .'   For PL's intentions, see contemporary interviews, e.g. with Daniela Dawan, *Bollettino della Comunità Israelitica di Milano*, June 1986, and Francesco Mannoni, *Unione Sarda*, 28 July.

¶ 'All of these . . .'   *D. & S.*, pp. 23, 97, 169–70.

p. 665

¶ 'It was dangerous . . .'   For Primo's knowing it was dangerous, see Dawan interview: 'mi pareva che andasse detto, a costo, a rischio di suscitare polemiche, che forse ci saranno': 'It seemed to me it had to be said, at the cost, at the risk of giving rise to polemics, which will perhaps occur.' Quotation from *D. & S.*, p. 26.

¶ 'Thankfully, neither danger . . .'   Author interviews with Bruno Vasari, and Bruno Vasari in Blakeway; *D. & S.*, pp. 28–9, 36–7, 41–3.

¶ 'The other danger . . .' and following quotation   *D. & S.*, pp. 12–13, 32–3. See also PL, 'Film e svastiche', *La Stampa*, 12 February 1977, in *Opere I*, p. 1217, and in interview with Giacomoni, January 1979.

p. 666

¶ 'The reviews . . .'   Cesare Cases, *L'Indice*, July 1986 (English version in October; reprinted in *Patrie lettere*); Pier Vincenzo Mengaldo, *Nuova Venezia*, 12 June 1986; Lorenzo Mondo, *La Stampa*, 14 July 1986; Giovanni Raboni, *Unità*, 3 September 1986; Filippo Gentiloni, *Il Manifesto*, 12 June 1986; Paolo Campostrini, *Alto Adige*, 17 July 1986; Sergio Quinzio, *L'Espresso*, 7 July 1986; *Quaderni del Centro Studi della Deportazione e dell'Internamento*, 1986–1990, p. 139; *D. & S.*, pp. 61, 110, 127–8, 138, 144, 149. (All summarized in Ferrero, *Antologia*, pp. 378–84.)

¶ 'As for the Germans . . .'   *D. & S.*, pp. 4, 150.

¶ 'The gravest of Primo Levi's books . . .'   *D. & S.*, p. 9. For PL's replies to this question over the years, see e.g. Mayda interview 1963, *Echi*, pp. 204–5 and 342 (quoting him in 1979, 1983 and 1986), 'Return to Auschwitz', 1982, *VM*, pp. 215–16, and *Conversations*, p. 50 for the answer no, it will not return, at least to Europe. But it could, and we must be vigilant: e.g. PL, *La Stampa*, 18 July 1959, Mayda interview 1963 again, *Avanti* interview, 19 October 1971, 'Difficile cammino della verità', 1982, and Preface to *La vita offesa*, 1986.

p. 667

¶ 'He had not really . . .'   See Calcagno interview, 26 July 1976; *D. & S.*, p. 63.

¶ 'I think it is the truth . . .'   Stefano Levi Della Torre quotation is from 'Eredità di Primo Levi', *Rassegna Mensile d'Israele*, Vol. LVI, Nos. 2–3, May–December 1989, p. 195.

p. 668

¶ 'That darkness . . .'   Stille, *New York Times Book Review*, 5 July 1987; Peter Porter, *Guardian*, 15 April 1988; Vivienne Joffe, *Jewish Book News*, July 1988; Rhett Waldman, *Jerusalem Post*, August 1988; Peter Gilbert, *Jerusalem Quarterly*, Winter 1988–9; Cynthia Ozick, 'Primo Levi's Suicide Note', in *Metaphor and Memory*, Knopf, 1989; BGS in Rosenfeld TV; Cases, Mondo and *Quaderni* reviews as above.

¶ 'This was testimony . . .'   On PL's reluctance to present *D. & S.*: *Echi*, p. 334.

¶ 'The furthest . . .'   Marina Morpurgo, *Unità*, 14 June 1986, and Pier Luigi Gandini, *La Repubblica*, 14 June 1986.

¶ 'Very likely . . .'   PL to Ruth Feldman, 1 October 1986; author interviews with Jolanda Gasperi.

¶ 'She did not die . . .'   Rina's nurse's deposition to the police, 11 May 1987, says that she started in August. On Rina's being paralysed on her left side: David Mendel, 'Autobiography in Primo Levi', p. 2. Rest of description: author interviews with Philip Roth and Gisella.

p. 669

¶ 'Amir finished . . .'   Author interviews with Amir Eshel, GCD, Philip Roth, Raffaella Pagani, Gisella, Ruth Feldman, and Massimo Scaglione; Atlas, 'The Survivor's Suicide', p. 83; Ruth Feldman, 'Remembering Primo Levi', p. 4.

¶ 'Primo was hugely . . .'   Author interviews with Gisella, Renato Portesi, and Paola Accati.

¶ 'The couple came . . .' and next four ¶¶   *Echi*, p. 337; Roth; Furio Colombo, *La Stampa*, 26 February 1989; author interviews with Philip Roth, Claire Bloom, and Paola Accati.

p. 671

¶ 'Out of this happy visit . . .' and ★   Roth; author interviews with Philip Roth. The information that PL liked the Roth interview very much comes from Roberto Di Caro.

p. 672

¶ 'By the end . . .'   Philip Roth, *Patrimony*, Simon & Schuster, 1991, p. 211; author interviews with Philip Roth and Claire Bloom.

¶¶ 'The reprieve . . .' and 'Only his doctors . . .'   Author interviews with Gisella and SO. Information on PL's doctor stopping his sleeping-pills comes from friends of the doctor.

¶ 'He was still himself . . .' and next five ¶¶   *DL*, Ch. 2.

p. 674

¶ 'Primo showed . . .'   Author interviews with Lilith, Gisella, SO, and Gabriella Poli.

p. 675

¶ 'And there was also . . .'   Roth in *Conversazioni e interviste*, p. 91, and quoted in *Echi*, p. 268 (paragraph omitted in English language versions); author interviews with Anna and Stuart Woolf, Gino and Cesarina Sacerdote, BGS, and Norberto Bobbio. In December PL summed up the reasons for his depression to Gisella: his mother's illness, and his desire that she die; the end of his American success; his inability to feel any desire; and his unhappiness with *Il doppio legame*.

¶ 'It was the same as in 1982 . . .' and next ¶   Author conversations with Gisella.

p. 676

¶ 'Then in mid-October . . .'   BGS in Blakeway; *DL*, Ch. 3.

¶ 'I have already suggested . . .'   *Re* PL's fearing to reveal his secret weakness to his public: in 1981, for example, he had said to Gisella: 'Non voglio perdere l'immagine che il lettore ha di me', 'I don't want to lose the image my readers have of me'.

¶ 'We have already looked . . .'   *DL*, Ch. 3.

p. 677

¶ 'He had stripped . . .'   Author interviews with Gisella, Lilith, Ernesto Ferrero and Gabriella Poli; *Echi*, p. 338.

¶ 'Writing this . . .'   Arturo Colombo, 'Primo Levi a Acqui, quella sera', *Nuova Antologia*, 1987; author interviews with Vittorio Foa.

¶ 'The prize was . . .'   Colombo, 'Primo Levi a Acqui', pp. 207–8; Piero Bianucci, *Stampa Sera*, 20 October 1986, p. 10; Guadagni in *Unità*, 1993; author interviews with Vittorio Foa.

p. 678

¶ 'By the end of October . . .' and next thirteen ¶¶   *DL*, Ch. 4; author conversations with Lilith and Gisella.

p. 680

¶ 'Primo had probably . . .'   Author conversations with Lilith and Gisella.

¶ 'Still he managed . . .'   *Echi*, p. 338; *Storia vissuta*, Franco Angeli, 1988; *La vita offesa*, Franco Angeli, 1986 (see p. 46 for PL advising the editors). The quotation 'ugly enterprise' is from p. 7 of his Preface.

¶ 'In his speech . . .' and next ¶   *Echi*, pp. 340–41; *Opere II*, p. 1575. The Afterword to *ITIAM* we have today is a slightly expanded version of the original 1976 one, translated by Ruth Feldman.

p. 681

¶ 'He went on writing . . .'   'A Mystery in the Lager' and 'Bella come una fiore'; 'Forza maggiore', *Opere II*, p. 906, translated as 'Force Majeure' in *TMM*, p. 62; 'The Fly', *Opere II*, p. 626; author interviews with JS. Ennio Mariotti died in December 1982.

¶ 'Like "Force Majeure" . . .'   'Scacco al tempo', *Opere II*, p. 913; 'Covare il cobra', *Opere II*, p. 990, translated as 'Hatching the Cobra', *TMM*, p. 172. For PL's theme of a Hippocratic Oath for scientists in his last year, see *Echi*, p. 338, *Uomini e libri*, No. 112, 1987 (in *VM*), and 'Focus' TV interview, 22 December 1986 (quoted in *Echi*, pp. 343–4).

¶ 'Even afterwards . . .'   'Il mitra sotto il letto', 'The Tommy Gun under the Bed'; *Racconti e saggi* (*Stories and Essays*), La Stampa, 1988, publishing details at the back; Introduction to *Racconti e saggi*, *Opere II*, p. 833.

p. 682

¶ 'By late November . . .'   'Il dromedario', 24 November 1986, *Opere II*, p. 627. 'My realm . . .'   Italics mine.

¶ 'Then, at the very end . . .'   *DL*, Ch. 5, dated 29 November – 4 December 1986, and author conversations with Gisella.

p. 682

¶ 'In "A Bottle of Sunshine" . . .' and next ¶   'A Bottle of Sunshine', *OPT*, pp. 19–23.

p. 683

¶ 'This is not the first . . .'   Quotation from *PT*, pp. 140–41.

p. 684

¶ 'When he returns . . .' and next six ¶¶   *DL*, Ch. 5.

p. 685

¶ 'It didn't help . . .'   Author conversations with Lilith.

¶ 'Chapter 6 . . .'   *DL*, Ch. 6.

¶ 'This too is a subject . . .' and next ¶   PL, 'L'Assimetria e la vita', *Prometeo*, Anno 2, No. 7, September 1984, pp. 62–7. I thank Bice Fubini Garrone for finding a copy for me. It is now in *Opere II*, p. 1231.

p. 686

¶ 'Now, in the sixth . . .' and next four ¶¶   *DL*, Ch. 6.

★ I thank Adam Smith for this explanation.

p. 687

¶ '*And yet* . . .'   For PL's dreading television: Gabriella Poli, 'Comunicatore schivo', p. 2.

¶ 'The easiest interview . . .'   Author interview with Mario Miccinesi; *Uomini e libri*, Anno XXIII, No. 112, January–February 1987, p. 13 (in *VM*). Roberto Di Caro's interview was published after PL's death.

¶ 'The television interview . . .' and quotation following   TG2 'Focus', eds. Ennio Mastrostefano and Paolo Meucci, 22 December 1986, quoted in *Echi*, pp. 341–5.

¶ 'The interviewer was . . .' and next six ¶¶   Author interviews with Roberto Di Caro; Roberto Di Caro, 'La fatica di scrivere', *L'Espresso*, 26 April 1987, pp. 30–33, and 'Il necessario e il superfluo, Primo Levi e l'economia della narrazione', *Piemonte Vivo*, Vol. 21, No. 1, 1987, pp. 53–7; and the complete transcript of the taped interview, kindly given me by Roberto Di Caro. This is an important interview, extensively quoted in *Echi*, pp. 347–52, and published in *Conversazioni e interviste*.

p. 689

¶ 'At Christmas . . .'   *Echi*, p. 318; Agnese Incisa in Atlas, 'The Survivor's Suicide', p. 82.

¶ 'Giovanni Tesio . . .' and next ¶   Author interviews with Giovanni Tesio, and Tesio in S. Salvatore, p. 264.

¶ 'He wrote a poem . . .' and poem following   *Echi*, p. 352; 'Almanacco', 2 January 1987, *Opere II*, p. 628, my translation.

p. 690

¶ 'One of Primo Levi's . . .'   See all the factory disaster stories in *The Wrench*, *The Double Bond* and *Altrui mestiere*.

¶ 'That ironic pattern . . .'   PL to Hermann Langbein, 28 March 1986; Belpoliti 1998, p. 16. PL worked on his Collected Works (the *Opere*, 1987): see Giulio Nascimbeni, *Corriere della Sera*, 8 February 1988 and Ernesto Ferrero in *Panorama*, 26 April 1987. On fame coming too late: e.g. Di Caro transcript, p. 17; PL to Anna Yona, 15 December 1985; author interviews with Philip Roth and Nereo Pezza. Many people make the point that he died just as he was becoming world-famous: e.g. Gabriel Motola in *European Judaism*, 1988, as before, p. 42, and Carlo Fruttero in *La Repubblica*, 13 April 1987; and, in conversation with me, Ernesto Ferrero and Edith Bruck.

p. 691

¶ 'He often put his fears . . .'   'Auschwitz, città tranquilla', *Opere II*, p. 873; *Conversations*, p. 26; Hermann Langbein, *Menschen in Auschwitz*, p. 511. PL also identified 'Mertens' as Heidebroek to Camon (author interviews with Ferdinando Camon).

¶ 'In 1941 Heidebroek . . .'   'Auschwitz, città tranquilla'; *Conversations*, pp. 26–7. Heidebroek's wife's story was also told to Langbein (see *Menschen in Auschwitz*, pp. 515–16). She had been with the wife of another German functionary, Frau Faust, who, so far from giving the woman bread, had called the police.

¶ 'Years later . . .' and next ¶   *Menschen in Auschwitz*, p. 511; 'Auschwitz, città tranquilla'; *Conversations*, p. 27.

p. 692

¶ 'In 1977, on the eve . . .' and next ¶   'La bestia nel tempio', *La Stampa*, 6 August 1977, in *Opere II*, p. 87, untranslated.

p. 693

¶ 'Then there are two . . .' and next two ¶¶   'Il servo', *Opere I*, p. 710, translated as 'The Servant' in *TSD*, p. 203.

¶ 'And then there is . . .' and next two ¶¶   'Tantalio', *Opere II*, p. 136, untranslated.

p. 694

¶ 'Primo had never . . .'   On there being no other Micheles in PL's stories: the closest – interestingly – is the protagonist of 'Force Majeure', who is called 'M'.

¶ 'It goes back . . .'   'Disfilassi', *Opere II*, p. 93, untranslated; 'La grande mutazione', *Opere II*, p. 868, translated as 'The Great Mutation' in *TMM*, p. 17.

p. 695

¶ 'This longing . . .'   'Lavoro creativo', *Opere I*, p. 671, untranslated.

¶ 'When the writer . . .'   'Nel parco', *Opere I*, p. 671, untranslated.

¶ 'Now, in the spring . . .' and next five ¶¶   'Il passa-muri', *Opere II*, p. 898, translated as 'Through the Walls', *TMM*, p. 52.

THE DOUBLE BIND: 1987

p. 697

¶ 'In the summer . . .' and next two ¶¶   Author interviews with David Mendel; David Mendel, 'Autobiography in Primo Levi', talk delivered at the Italian Cultural Institute, London, 4 April 1995, p. 2; David Mendel, 'Requiem for a Quiet Man of Courage', *Sunday Telegraph*, 6 September 1991. The quotation 'a rather serious depression' is from PL's letter of 7 February to Mendel, which is quoted in both essays. I thank David Mendel for all his help, and especially for giving me copies of four of PL's letters.

p. 698

¶ 'The depression . . .'   PL to David Mendel, 14 February and 20 February 1987.

¶ 'This was . . .'   On the other hand, it was true that his dose of Parmodalin had been doubled in January, and then stopped, because of prostate complications (author conversations with Gisella).

¶ 'Parmodalin . . .'   Information from Jeremy Mack, as credited; also from a contemporary article on depression in *Newsweek*, 4 May 1987, pp. 42–8.

¶ 'In January . . .'   Information on Nicolin from Gisella. Rest of ¶: PL to David Mendel, 14 February 1987; Giovanni Tesio in S. Salvatore, pp. 264–5, 267, in Valeria Gandus and Gian Paolo Rossetti, 'Finalmente fuori dal Lager', *Panorama*, 26 April 1987, pp. 58–61, and in author interviews.

★ Mendel, 'Autobiography in Primo Levi', p. 3.

p. 699

¶ 'On the 16th . . .'   *Echi*, pp. 352–3; Michele Prisco, 'La coscienza del dolore', *Il Mattino*, Napoli, 12 April 1987; Maurice Goldstein in *Il presente del passato*, pp. 92–3; Vittorio Giuntella in *Il presente del passato*, pp. 79–80, and in *La conferenza di Wannsee*, Franco Angeli, 1988, p. 37; author conversations with Gisella.

¶ 'The very next day . . .'   'Partigia', *Opere II*, p. 561, translated as 'Partisan', *CP*,

p. 48; Mirna Cicioni, *Primo Levi, Bridges of Knowledge*, Berg, Washington DC, 1995, pp. 153, 168; *Echi*, p. 353; PL, 'Buco nero di Auschwitz', *La Stampa*, 22 January 1987, *Opere II*, p. 1321.

p. 700

¶ 'On the 26th . . .' and next ¶ Tesio in S. Salvatore, pp. 265, 268, in *Panorama*, 26 April 1987, and in author interviews.

p. 701

¶ 'With friends . . .' Author interviews with Clara Moschino and Eugenio Bolley; PL, Introduction to *Vizio di forma*, *Opere I*, p. 571, dated January 1987.

¶ 'He could not write . . .' On 'Argilla di Adamo' having been written some time before: *Echi*, p. 353. It is in *Opere II*, p. 1328.

¶ 'A week before . . .' 'Buck dei lupi', *La Stampa*, 11 January 1987, *Opere II*, p. 1317.

p. 702

¶ 'In January . . .' 'Naso contro naso, un incontro d'amore nel buio', in 'Zoo immaginario, le storie naturali di Primo Levi', in *Airone*, January 1987, p. 168; in *Opere II*, p. 1325. The others were: 'In diretto dal nostro intestino: l'Escherichia coli', February 1987, p. 160, in *Opere II*, p. 1332; 'Il gabbiano di Chivasso', March 1987, p. 174, in *Opere II*, p. 1335; 'La giraffa', April 1987, p. 206, in *Opere II*, p. 1338; and 'Amori sulla tela', *La Stampa*, 26 April 1987, and *Airone*, May 1987, p. 179, in *Opere II*, p. 1341. They are translated in *TMM* as 'Five Intimate Interviews', starting p. 28. The dates of composition (or typing, as usual) are given here, on p. 46: 'The Mole' and 'E. coli', 17 November 1986; 'The Gull', 14 January 1987; 'The Giraffe', 1 February 1987; and the last one, 26 February 1987. *TMM* was first published by Schocken Books in the US, who must have taken the dates from PL's typescripts. (Marco Belpoliti dates 'E. coli' to 7 December, but agrees about the others.)

¶ 'The idea went back . . .' 'Nozze della formica', *La Stampa*, 20 April 1986, *Opere II*, p. 902, translated as 'The Ant's Wedding' in *TMM*, p. 57.

p. 703

¶ 'In fact this began . . .' 'Le fans dei spot di Delta cep', published in *L'Astronomia*, No. 54, April 1986, in *Opere II*, p. 1297. PL sent this letter to Piero Bianucci after appearing on his television programme *Voyage inside the Atom*; Bianucci dated this to 1985 in *Corriere della Sera*, 9 August 1986, but to January 1986 in conversation with me.

p. 704

¶ ' "Old Mole" . . .' 'Old Mole', 22 September 1982, *CP*, p. 54 (*Opere II*, p. 566).

¶ 'For the third interview . . .' 'The Gulls of Settimo', 9 April 1979, *CP*, p. 36 (*Opere II*, p. 551).

p. 705

¶ 'By now it was . . .' PL letters to Ruth Feldman, 19 February 1987, and David Mendel, 20 February 1987.

¶ 'The last interview . . .' and next ¶ 'Amori sulla tela', *Opere II*, p. 1341, translated as 'The Spider', *TMM*, pp. 39–42; 'Arachne', 29 October 1981, *CP*, p. 49 (*Opere II*, p. 562); 'Romanzi dettati dai grilli', 'Novels Dictated by Crickets', as before.

p. 706

¶ 'On 8 February . . .' Tesio in S. Salvatore, p. 268.

¶ 'By now Primo . . .' On the foot problem and the shingles: author interviews with Giovanni Tesio, and Anissimov, *Primo Levi*, p. 599; EGT and Ferdinando Camon also remember the foot trouble at the end (author interviews). Rest of ¶: PL to David Mendel, 7 February 1987, quoted in 'Autobiography in Primo Levi', p. 3; Tesio in 'Schiacciato dal fantasma dei Lager', *Corriere della Sera*, 12 April 1987, p. 3 and *Il Giornale*, 13 April 1987.

★ Anissimov, *Primo Levi*, p. 599; author interviews with Giovanni Tesio.

p. 707

¶ 'At the end . . .' Tesio in S. Salvatore, p. 265, and in contemporary articles, e.g. in: *Corriere della Sera*, 12 April 1987, *La Repubblica*, 12 April 1987, *Il Giornale*, 13 April 1987, *Gente*, 24 April 1987 ('Auschwitz ha ucciso Primo Levi 40 anni dopo', by Giorgio Lazzarini, pp. 11–13 and 175), *Panorama* as before; also in Atlas, 'The Survivor's Suicide', p. 84. It is not clear exactly when PL knew he would have to be operated on. Dr Roberto Pattono says that there was only a short time between the diagnosis and the operation in mid-March (author interviews), and Gisella remembers that it was decided urgently. Perhaps because it was the ultimate trauma for him, PL put off telling people as long as possible: he did not even tell Gisella until a week before, and Bianca, it seems, even later (author conversations with Gisella). Very likely, therefore, it was some time after their 8 February session that PL told Tesio as well.

¶ 'Something else . . .' Tesio in S. Salvatore, p. 265 and author interviews.

¶ 'In February . . .' PL to David Mendel, 14 February 1987; author conversations with Gisella (on PL's giving up driving).

¶ 'On the 19th . . .' and next ¶ PL to Ruth Feldman, 19 February 1987, copy kindly given me by Ruth Feldman, together with the rest of her correspondence with PL; PL to David Mendel, 14 February 1987; author interviews with Ruth Feldman. Ruth Feldman spoke often about her terrible last letter from PL (e.g. in 'Remembering Primo Levi', p. 4); and wrote a poem, or part of a poem, about it: 'A Gray Day in Treviso', published in *Birthmark*, Jewish Writers Chapbook Series No. 9, 1993, pp. 5–6, of which the last verse is: 'I am remembering Primo Levi's last letter,/ that reached me a month before his death./ He was living through a period worse/ than Auschwitz, he wrote, partly because/ he was no longer young and resilient./ He signed it "*de profundis.*"/ Despite our wishful thinking,/ survivors only appear to have survived.'

p. 708

¶ 'In the autumn . . .' Author interviews with AS and BGS; PL to David Mendel, 14 February 1987; Roberto Vacca in *La Nazione*, 12 April 1987.

¶ 'He saw Giorgio . . .' Information on Giorgio Lattes and Livio Norzi from Gisella; author interviews with Pierluigi Olivetti and Alfredo Fedele.

¶ 'Up to around . . .' *Echi*, pp. 353–4; Ernesto Ferrero in *Panorama*, 26 April 1987, in *La Stampa*, 13/14 April, and in author interviews; author interviews with Agnese Incisa.

p. 709

¶ 'In the last months . . .'   Author interviews with Ernesto Ferrero and Agnese Incisa.

¶ 'Then he began . . .'   Einaudians in *Corriere della Sera*, 12 April 1987; author interviews with Ernesto Ferrero, Giorgina Arian Levi, and Felice Malgaroli.

¶ 'He had been . . .'   PL to David Mendel, 20 February 1987; author interviews with Dr Pattono and Gisella. For the period between diagnosis and operation, see Notes to page 707. Atlas also confirms that PL was taken off antidepressants for his operation ('The Survivor's Suicide', p. 84); his informant was Anna Maria's husband, Julian Zimet (author interview with James Atlas).

¶ 'The last time . . .'   Author interviews with Agnese Incisa.

¶ 'After that he did not . . .'   *Echi*, pp. 353–4; PL to David Mendel, 16 November 1986; PL to Greg Gatenby, Director of the Harbourfront Festival, Toronto, Canada, 1 March 1987, a copy kindly sent me by Greg Gatenby; Cicioni, *Primo Levi*, p. 170; 'Tre parole di sgomento', by Dany Aperio Bella, in *Il Messaggero*, 12 April 1987, and author interviews with Mario Rigoni Stern (on the Leopoli Commission); author conversations with Gisella.

★ Author interviews with Agnese Incisa and Gisella.

p. 710

¶ 'I don't know . . .' and next two ¶¶   Author interviews with Luciana Nissim.

¶ 'Primo went . . .' and next ¶   Author conversations with Gisella and with the analyst.

¶ 'There were two . . .'   Bruno Vasari to Hermann Langbein, 4 September 1987; author interviews with Vittorio Foa.

¶ 'Such moments apart . . .'   Author interviews with all the friends, e.g. Luciana Nissim, Giovanni Tesio.

p. 711

¶ 'He hardly ate . . .' and next ¶   Author conversations with Lilith and Gisella.

¶ 'He went into the San Giovanni . . .'   For dates, Gisella and Dr Pattono. Information on the operation from Gisella, AS, and Alberto Piazza, who would not tell me, but did tell a friend (letter to the author from Jonathan Galassi, 19 July 1996, for which I thank him).

¶ 'In the recovery room . . .'   Dr Pattono in *Panorama*, 26 April 1987, in Atlas, 'The Survivor's Suicide', p. 94, and in author interviews; author interviews with Philip Roth.

¶ 'He stayed . . .'   Author interviews with Dr Pattono; Plinio Pinna Pintor in Andrea Libertori, *Unità*, 13 April 1987.

¶ 'Pinna Pintor . . .'   Information that PL hoped the operation would cure his depression from Gisella.

¶ 'Still, the operation . . .'   That the doctors had suspected cancer is confirmed by Alberto Piazza (Jonathan Galassi to the author, 19 July 1996). That PL did not have cancer: Piazza, in ibid.; and author interviews with GCD, Elena Vita Finzi, Luciana Accati; also most of the contemporary newspaper reports state or imply it: e.g. *Il Secolo XIX*, 12 April 1987 (quoting Giulio Einaudi), *La Repubblica*, 12/13 April 1987, *Il Manifesto*, 12/13 April 1987, *La Stampa*, 13 April 1987.

p. 712

¶ 'He came home . . .' and next ¶   Author conversations with Gisella and with Paola Accati; Anissimov, *Primo Levi*, pp. 610 and 619–20.

¶ 'Many friends . . .'   Mario Rigoni Stern in *La Nazione*, 12 April 1987; Paolo Spriano in *Unità*, 12 April 1987; Ernesto Ferrero in *Corriere della Sera*, 12 April 1987, *La Repubblica*, 12/13 April 1987, *Panorama*, 26 April 1987; Rita Levi Montalcini in 'Primo', *Annuario* of the Fondazione Schlesinger, 1993, pp. 41–5, on p. 45; author interviews with EGT and Giorgio Vaccarino.

¶ 'Bruno Vasari . . .'   Bruno Vasari to Hermann Langbein, 4 September 1987; Francesco Rosi in *Corriere della Sera*, 12 April 1987, *La Stampa*, 13 April 1987, and also in *La Repubblica*, 21 December 1996.

p. 713

¶ 'When Edith Bruck . . .'   Edith Bruck in *Echi*, pp. 354–5, and in author interviews; Edith Bruck, *Lettera alla madre*, Garzanti. 1988, p. 71.

¶ 'Alessandro Galante Garrone . . .'   Anissimov, *Primo Levi*, p. 610.

¶ 'He hardly went out . . .'   Author interviews with BGS, Paola Accati, and Gisella; Maria Celeste Crucillà, 'Ora è nel vento con loro', *Oggi*, 29 April 1987, pp. 11–13, especially p. 11; Edith Bruck, *Lettera alla madre*, p. 71, and author interviews with Edith Bruck.

¶ 'And yet: no one . . .'   Norberto Bobbio in *Panorama*, 26 April 1987, p. 59; author interviews with Amir Eshel; PL, 'Dello scrivere oscuro', *Opere II*, p. 679, 'On Obscure Writing', *OPT*, p. 161; PL to Greg Gatenby, 1 March 1987; PL to Jeanne Wikler, 8 April 1987, kindly shown me by JS.

p. 714

¶ 'There were several . . .'   Liana Millu in S. Salvatore, pp. 62–3, and in author interviews.

¶ 'That was before . . .'   Author interviews with Agnese Incisa.

p. 715

¶ 'The truth is . . .'   Tesio in S. Salvatore, p. 265 (meeting AS at Corso Re Umberto 75); author conversations with Gisella (Bianca coming to the hospital); Anissimov, *Primo Levi*, pp. 609 and 613.

¶ 'A few days later . . .' and next two ¶¶   Author interviews with BGS, Gabriella Poli, and Gisella; Anissimov, *Primo Levi*, p. 615; BGS in Blakeway, in *Panorama*, 26 April 1987, p. 60, and in Guadagni, *Unità*, 1993.

¶ 'He did not come out . . .'   Author interviews with Eva Erber.

¶ 'April the 8th . . .'   PL to Jeanne Wikler, 8 April 1987; contemporary newspaper reports, e.g. *La Repubblica*, 12/13 April 1987, *La Stampa*, 13 April 1987, *Unità*, 13 April 1987; Ferdinando Camon in *Il Giorno*, 28 April 1987 and in author interviews.

p. 716

¶ 'Ever since . . .'   Ferdinando Camon, *Il Giorno* and author interviews as above; PL to Camon, 8 April 1987, copy kindly given me by Ferdinando Camon.

¶ 'This letter . . .' and next ¶   Ferdinando Camon as above; Camon, 'Incontri e dialoghi con Primo Levi', article written for *Le Monde* and *La Nación* (from which the quotation 'It is impossible to think . . .' is taken); Camon in Maurizio Assalto, 'Toaff: Primo Levi mi annunciò il suicidio', *La Stampa*, 12 April 1997; Camon to the author, 14 June 1995. One of those who, following Camon, take it as a matter of fact that Primo posted his letter to Camon on Saturday morning is Diego Gambetta, in 'Gli ultimi momenti di Primo Levi', *Belfagor*, 31 May 1999, pp. 325–9, translated as 'Primo Levi's Last Moments', in *Boston Review*, Summer 1999, pp. 25–9 (in abridged version in *New York Times*, 7 August 1999), and in Giorgio Calcagno, 'Primo Levi, se questo è un suicidio', *La Stampa*, 25 May 1999: see e.g. *Boston Review*, p. 28.

¶ 'On the same day . . .'   Giulio Einaudi, 'Primo Levi and his Publisher', p. 22, in *Panorama*, 26 April 1987, p. 58, and in Atlas, 'The Survivor's Suicide', p. 94; Cicioni, *Primo Levi*, p. 170.

★ Author interviews with Ferdinando Camon; *Opere II*, p. 1598.

p. 717

¶ 'Giulio Einaudi knew . . .'   Einaudi, 'Primo Levi and his Publisher', p. 22; and contemporary newspaper reports quoting Einaudi, e.g.: *Il Mattino*, 12 April 1987, *La Repubblica*, 12/13 April 1987, *La Stampa*, 13 April 1987, *Corriere della Sera*, 13 April 1987, *Unità*, 13 April 1987.

¶ 'That evening . . .'   Anissimov, *Primo Levi*, p. 614; author interviews with Mario Macagno.

¶ 'He phoned Elie Wiesel . . .'   Author interviews with Elie Wiesel and Eugenio Bolley.

¶ 'That night he also spoke . . .'   Author conversations with Gisella.

¶ 'On Thursday . . .'   Ernesto Ferrero in *Corriere della Sera*, 12 April 1987, *La Repubblica*, 12/13 April 1987, *Stampa Sera*, 13 April 1987. ('Perhaps I am getting better' is in *La Repubblica*.)

p. 718

¶ 'He may have made . . .' and next ¶   Rabbi Toaff in Maurizio Assalto, 'Toaff: Primo Levi mi annunciò il suicidio', *La Stampa*, 12 April 1997; Calcagno, 'Primo Levi, se questo è un suicidio', *La Stampa*, 25 May 1999. The private conversation was with Ernesto Ferrero (author interviews with Ernesto Ferrero). Diego Gambetta dismisses Rabbi Toaff's claim in his essay (see e.g. *Boston Review*, p. 28). It is Gambetta who first pointed out, correctly, that the rabbi could not have answered the phone on Saturday; but his deductions from this are faulty.

¶ 'On Friday Primo . . .'   Author interviews with Dario and Miranda Treves, Leo Gallico, and GCD; GCD in Rosenfeld TV; Anissimov, *Primo Levi*, p. 619.

¶ 'We know of two . . .'   Rita Levi Montalcini in *La Stampa*, 13 April 1997, and reported by Gambetta, *Boston Review*, p. 28; Giovanni Tesio, in author interviews and contemporary reports, e.g.: *Il Giornale d'Italia* (Rome), 13 April 1987, *Gente*, 24 April 1987, *Panorama*, 26 April 1987. Since Rita Levi Montalcini did not report her last conversation this way at the time (and indeed implied in 'Primo', written in 1992, that she had heard anguish in his voice the night before), I was initially inclined to put this down to the 'beautification' of memory, in PL's phrase. Given Tesio's account, however, which has never varied, it may well be true. On the photographer coming on Sunday: PL had accepted other appointments too. Rita Levi Montalcini said that a German journalist who was interviewing her on Saturday was due to see PL the next day (*Panorama*, 3 May 1987); and Camon says that a *La Stampa* journalist was coming to see PL on Monday (in Assalto, *La Stampa*, 12 April 1997). I have already (perhaps unfairly) doubted the reliability of both; but Germaine Greer met a pair of journalists in Holland who also had an appointment with PL for shortly after 11 April (author interview with Germaine Greer). Once again, therefore, their evidence should stand. Everyone deduces from all these plans – including the one with Tesio – that Primo cannot have committed suicide; but they only show that he cannot have planned to commit suicide. Tesio himself agrees: their conversation on Friday was, he says, 'the last burst of energy' (author interviews with Giovanni Tesio).

p. 719

¶ 'And then it happened . . .'   Police Report, Commissario San Secondo, filed at 3 p.m., 11 April 1987, signed Il Dirigente Dott. Carretta, and Police Report, Questura San Secondo, filed 15 May 1987, signed Dr E. Carretta, both to the Procura della Repubblica, Turin; handwritten report from the Servizio Sanitario Nazionale (the National Ambulance Service), signature illegible, date 11 April 1987; depositions of Jolanda Gasperi, 30 April 1987, and the nurse, 11 May 1987; all documents held by the Procura della Repubblica, Turin. (Rina's nurse resisted every effort to be interviewed; I therefore withhold her name, in order to protect her privacy.)

¶ 'Reporters arrived . . .'   Author interviews with Giuseppe Di Chio, Bruno Salmoni, GCD; *Il Giornale*, 13 April 1987, and *Avvenire*, 13 April 1987; David Mendel, 'Autobiography in Primo Levi', p. 2; author interviews with Alessandro Galante Garrone and Nuto Revelli.

¶ 'Euge, in Milan . . .'   Author interviews with EGT, and EGT in Rosenfeld TV; author interviews with Eva Erber and with Emma and Amir Eshel.

¶ 'The autopsy . . .'   Autopsy Report in Procura della Repubblica documents: dated 13 April 1987, stating that the body was brought in at approximately 11.45; author conversations with Gisella. In fact PL was buried seventy-two hours after his death, rather than twenty-four.

p. 720

¶ ' "Suicide is . . .' and ★   Primo to Agnese Incisa, 14 October 1980, enclosing a dozen pages of notes from the *Shulkhàn Aruch* (the note about suicide is on p. 7); author interview with Elena Artom. All the contemporary reports of the funeral note that ceremonies are forbidden during Passover (e.g. *La Stampa*, 14 April 1987, *Corriere della Sera*, 14 April 1987). That the family wanted a minimal funeral was reported e.g. by *Il Centro* (Pescara), 14 April 1987.

¶ 'The family . . .' and next ¶   The family wanting the funeral to be private, e.g. *Avvenire*, 14 April 1987, *L'Unione Sarda*, 14 April 1987, *Il Centro*, 14 April 1987; accounts of the funeral in e.g. *La Stampa*, 13 April and 14 April 1987, *La Repubblica*, 14 April 1987, *Corriere della Sera*, 14 April 1987, *Avvenire*, 14 April 1987, *Il Centro*, 14 April 1987, *Corriere Mercantile* (Genova), 14 April 1987, *L'Unione Sarda*, 14 April 1987.

p. 721

¶ 'That evening . . .' *La Stampa*, 14 April 1987, *Il Centro*, 14 April 1987, *Avvenire*, 14 April 1987, *Il Giornale*, 14 April 1987.

¶ 'The papers . . .' e.g. *Corriere della Sera*, 12 April 1987, *La Nazione*, 12 April 1987, *Unità*, 12 April 1987, *Il Giornale*, 12 April 1987, *Il Resto di Carlino*, 12 April 1987, *Il Piccolo*, 12 April 1987, *Il Secolo XIX*, 12 April 1987, *Stampa Sera*, 13 April 1987, *La Stampa*, 14 April 1987, *Il Nostro Tempo*, 19 April 1987. Arpino was quoted in *Stampa Sera*, Firpo in *Il Giornale*, Camon in *Il Mattino di Padova*, 12 April 1987.

¶ 'Over the next days . . .' Author interviews with Elena Vita Finzi, Mario Liboi, and Frida Malan; and with Elie Wiesel, Nuto Revelli and Alessandro Galante Garrone.

¶ 'The next idea . . .' Rita Levi Montalcini, 'Primo Levi non si è suicidato', *Unità*, 25 April 1987, p. 7, and 'Non si è suicidato', *Panorama*, 3 May 1987, pp. 62–3.

p. 722

¶ 'This line was taken . . .' David Mendel, *Sunday Telegraph*, 8 September 1991, and 'Autobiography in Primo Levi', as before.

¶ 'The first person . . .' Author interviews with Roberto Di Caro.

¶ 'To the other person . . .' and next two ¶¶ Author interviews with Raffaella Pagani.

★ Measured by Diego Gambetta's father, as reported in Gambetta articles.

p. 723

¶ 'Apart from his family . . .' Letter to the author, July 1995, from Anna Yona, to whom Renzo and his friend recounted this event; also letter to the author, 18 November 1995, from Ruth Feldman, reporting the same story.

¶ 'At around half past nine . . .' and next two ¶¶ Sisto Capra, in *Il Mattino di Padova*, 12 April 1987, and *Il Centro* (Pescara), 12 April 1987; author interviews with Jolanda Gasperi, and Jolanda Gasperi in all contemporary reports.

p. 724

¶ 'Renzo telephoned Lisa . . .' Author interviews with Jolanda Gasperi; *La Stampa*, 13 April 1987; *Avvenire*, 14 April 1987; *Oggi*, 29 April 1987; Sisto Capra in the two papers as above. The other observer's identity must remain undisclosed.

¶ 'It was said . . .' e.g. *Corriere della Sera*, 14 April 1987, and e.g. Gambetta, *Boston Review*, p. 27. PL's will is handwritten on his headed paper, dated 28 August 1975, registered 3 June 1987, No. 31590, and listed as No. 250 in the Wills of 1987; also deposition of Giovanni Re, Notaio (Notary), describing the will and enclosing it, all in the Ufficio Successione della Pretura di Torino.

¶ 'It was reported . . .' Many contemporary newspaper reports, e.g. *La Stampa*, *La Repubblica*, *Corriere della Sera*, as above; author interviews with Jolanda Gasperi and Hermann Langbein. *Re* PL's keeping his worst suffering from Lucia: he told Gisella as late as January that he was not telling Lucia the true depth of his depression.

¶ 'From the start . . .' Led by Rita Levi Montalcini, in *Unità* and *Panorama* as above; *ITIAM*, p. 166 (correcting the error of 'fourth' floor for 'third'); 15

metres: see e.g. *Il Giorno*, 28 April 1987, p. 7. On chemicals: Rita Levi Montalcini and David Mendel as above.

p. 725

¶ 'But Rita Levi Montalcini . . .' In *Unità*, 25 April 1987 (and see e.g. *La Repubblica*, 12 April 1987, which describes the stairwell as 'un stretto pertugio', 'a narrow opening'); Gambetta, *Boston Review*, p. 26.

¶ 'And there is one other point . . .' Nurse's deposition, 11 May 1987.

¶ 'Despite all this . . .' Author interviews with the psychoanalyst; contemporary newspaper reports and author interviews with Luciana Accati (on Lucia); author interviews with Edith Bruck (on Anna Maria), GCD, BGS, AS, EGT, Silvio and Ada Ortona, Lilith, and Gisella.

p. 726

¶ 'That is: those who knew him . . .' Author conversations with Gabriella Garda Aliverti (on the chemistry class).

¶ 'No one wants . . .' Jeremy Mack, 'Primo Levi: His Last Days', University of Pennsylvania Conference paper as before, p. 3 (copy kindly given me by Jeremy Mack); Edith Bruck, *Lettera alla madre*, p. 34; Clive James, 'Last Will and Testament', *New Yorker*, 23 May 1988; *New Yorker*, 'Talk of the Town' (Elizabeth Macklin), 11 May 1987, p. 32.

¶ 'In any case . . .' 'Auschwitz killed him 40 years later' is the headline in *Gente*, 24 April 1987; see also e.g. *Corriere della Sera*, 'Schiacciato dal fantasma dei Lager', 'Crushed by the ghost of the Lagers'. The majority of headlines suggested this line. Renzo Levi was quoted in *Panorama*, 26 April 1987. Elie Weisel said it in *Il Messaggero*, 12 April 1987, Bettelheim in *Europeo*, 28 April 1987, and Maurice Goldstein in *Il presente del passato*, p. 83. Natalia Ginzburg said it in *La Repubblica*, 12/13, and in a letter to Iris Origo, 12(?) April 1987, kindly given me by Iris Origo's biographer, Caroline Moorehead. Marabini said it in *Il Resto di Carlino*, and Sgorlon in *Il Piccolo*, both 12 April 1987.

¶ 'But to the best . . .' BGS in Tarrow, *Reason and Light*, pp. 12–13, in Blakeway, and to the author; David Mendel in *Sunday Telegraph* and 'Autobiography in Primo Levi'; author interviews with all the friends named (apart from Vittorio Daneo, whom I did not see, but whose exchanges with PL were described to me by Alfredo Fedele). That 'the poison of Auschwitz no longer ran in his veins' comes from *Echi*, p. 333, quoting an interview with Lucia Borgia on RAI 3, 3 February 1985.

p. 727

¶ 'The central, painful . . .' That depression and suicide were in him from the start was said to me by e.g. PL's analyst friends, Luciana Nissim and Franca Mussa, by Giuliana Tedeschi, and by Gisella.

¶ 'In the pit . . .' Author conversations with Gisella. On Dr Gozzi, see Rita Levi Montalcini in *Unità*, 25 April 1987, who reports him as saying: 'Levi era depresso e preoccupato negli ultimi tempi. Ma non mi ha parlato di farla finita': 'Levi was depressed and worried towards the end. But he didn't talk to me about ending it all.' On BGS, and on the psychoanalyst: author interviews.

¶ 'He told Gisella . . .' and next ¶ Author conversations with Gisella and with AS.

p. 728

¶ 'Because this time . . .'   Author conversations with Gisella. On Primo's fear of illness, pain, ageing and so on: as well as Gisella, author interviews with JS, GCD, Luciana Accati, Alberto Papuzzi, Francesco Ciafaloni; and PL interviews with Dina Luce, 1982, Boeri, 1983, and Greer, 1985. On his dislike of injections, see 'Il mondo invisibile', *Opere II*, p. 800 ('The Invisible World', *OPT*, p. 47); on his having to have them now, Rina's nurse's deposition (she gave him one daily).

¶ 'His loss of memory . . .'   On his sense of having failed as a 'real' writer, because of *INNW*: author interviews with BGS, Norberto Bobbio, Gino Sacerdote, and Gisella.

¶ 'The strongest bind . . .'   Quotation from Norberto Bobbio is in *Panorama*, 26 April 1987, p. 59. On Primo's relationship to his mother as abnormal (all author interviews, unless otherwise specified): the psychoanalysts Renata Gaddini, Luciana Nissim and Franca Mussa, and Jeremy Mack in 'Primo Levi: His Last Days', pp. 12–13; PL's biographer Gabriella Poli; amongst his family, Anna Yona; amongst his friends, Luciana Accati, Elie Wiesel, Philip Roth, and BGS in *Panorama*, 26 April 1987, p. 59; amongst his more distant friends and acquaintances, Anna Savoini, Raffaella Pagani, Erica Scroppo Newbury, and David Mendel in 'Autobiography in Primo Levi', p. 9.

p. 729

¶ 'At the end . . .'   Giulio Einaudi in *Il Secolo XIX*, 12 April 1987; Einaudians: e.g. Agnese Incisa in author interviews, Lorenzo Fazio in *Panorama*, 26 April 1987, p. 59; Francesco Quaglia in e.g. *Corriere della Sera*, 12 April 1987, *La Repubblica*, 12/13 April 1987, *La Stampa*, 13 April 1987; Rabbi Toaff and BGS as above; author conversations with Gisella; nurse's deposition.

¶ 'The trouble was . . .'   Author interviews with Ferruccio Maruffi, Franca Mussa, Ernesto Ferrero, Massimo Scaglione, GCD; Lorenzo Fazio in *Panorama* as above. Primo told Gisella too that he wanted his mother to die. 'Io mi sento in lotta con mia madre,' he told her, 'a volte vedo la mia vita contro la sua e questo mi consuma e mi lacera': 'I feel at war with my mother; sometimes it seems that it is my life or hers, and this consumes and torments me.'

¶ 'It could not be . . .'   Death Certificate Ester Luzzati, Atto No. 700. Ufficio 1, Parte 1, Anno 1991, date 21 December 1991. On her being told Primo had had a heart attack: *La Stampa*, 13 April 1987, *Corriere della Sera*, 13 April 1987, *Oggi*, 29 April 1987, p. 11, and author interviews with GCD and Jolanda Gasperi. GCD told me that Rina did not believe it, and always asked people what had happened.

¶ 'After the first shock . . .'   Author conversations with Gisella, and with Alberto and Bruno Salmoni.

p. 730

¶ 'Then he was ill . . .'   Author conversations with Gisella.

¶ 'It was clear . . .'   For Lucia's dedication being extreme: author interviews with PL's doctor friends, Bruno Salmoni and Amir Eshel; with his analyst friends Luciana Nissim and Franca Mussa; and with e.g. Luciana Accati, Giuliana Tedeschi, Francesco Ciafaloni, and Anna Vitale. For understanding the other side: Gisella; and some of these, e.g. Luciana Nissim, Franca Mussa, and Giuliana Tedeschi.

¶ 'It was a beautiful, sunny day . . .'   Author interviews with Ernesto Ferrero and Agnese Incisa; and Andrea Liberatori, 'La morte di Primo Levi', in *Unità*, 12 April 1987.

¶ 'Perhaps it happened . . .'   PL to David Mendel, 14 February 1987.

¶ 'He went to the phone . . .'   Author interviews with Felice Malgaroli; nurse's deposition.

Bibliography

A. Books

Books by Primo Levi

IN ENGLISH

If This is a Man & The Truce, Abacus paperback, 1987 (and 1991)
Survival in Auschwitz, tr. Stuart Woolf, Simon & Schuster, 1996
The Reawakening, tr. Stuart Woolf, Simon & Schuster, 1996
The Periodic Table, tr. Raymond Rosenthal, Schocken, 1995
The Monkey's Wrench, tr. Ruth Feldman, Viking Penguin, 1995
If Not Now, When?, tr. William Weaver, Viking Penguin, 1995
Moments of Reprieve, tr. Ruth Feldman, Viking Penguin, 1995
Collected Poems: Primo Levi, tr. Ruth Feldman and Brian Swann, Faber & Faber, 1988
The Drowned and the Saved, tr. Raymond Rosenthal, Summit, 1988
Other People's Trades, tr. Raymond Rosenthal, Summit, 1989
The Sixth Day and Other Stories, tr. Raymond Rosenthal, Summit, 1990
The Mirror Maker: Stories and Essays, tr. Raymond Rosenthal, Schocken, 1990
The Search for Roots, trans. and with an Introduction by Peter Forbes, and with an Afterword by Italo Calvino, Allen Lane, The Penguin Press, 2001
Beyond Survival [translation of 'Itinerario di uno scrittore ebreo', 1982], trans. Gail Soffer, Prooftexts 4, Johns Hopkins University Press, 1984

IN ITALIAN

Opere [Collected Works] I & II, ed. Marco Belpoliti, Nuova Universale Einaudi 225* and 225**, Giulio Einaudi Editore, 1997
Original *Opere*, in three volumes, ed. Ernesto Ferrero, Einaudi, 1987
Se questo è un uomo [*If This is a Man*], play version, in *I quaderni del Teatro Stabile della città di Torino*, No. 8, Edizioni del Teatro Stabile di Torino, 1986

Books on Primo Levi

BIOGRAPHIES *(in chronological order)*

Vincenti, Fiora, *Invito alla lettura di Primo Levi*, Mursia, 1973
Poli, Gabriella, and Calcagno, Giorgio, *Echi di una voce perduta*, Mursia, 1992
Dini, Massimo, and Jesurum, Stefano, *Primo Levi: le opere e i giorni*, Rizzoli, 1992
Anissimov, Miryam, *Primo Levi, ou la tragédie d'un optimiste*, J. C. Lattès, Paris, 1996, in English as *Primo Levi: Tragedy of an Optimist*, trans. Steve Cox, Aurum Press, 1998

ALSO

Amsallem, Daniela, *Au miroir de son œuvre: Primo Levi, le témoin, l'écrivain, le chimiste*, Editions Cosmogone, Lyons, 2001

Belpoliti, Marco, *Primo Levi*, Arnaldo Mondadori, 1998

—— (ed.), *Primo Levi, Conversazioni e interviste 1963–1987*, Einaudi, 1997, trans. as *The Voice of Memory*, ed. Marco Belpoliti and Robert Gordon, trans. Robert Gordon, Polity Press in association with Blackwell Publishers Ltd, 2001

—— (ed.), 'Primo Levi', *Riga 13*, Marcos e Marcos, 1997

Borri, Giancarlo, *Le divine impurità*, Luisè Editore, Rimini, 1992

Camon, Ferdinando, *Conversations with Primo Levi*, trans. John Shepley, Marlboro Press, Marlboro, Vermont, 1989

Cavaglion, Alberto, *Primo Levi e Se questo è un uomo*, Loescher Editore, 1993

Cerati, Roberto, *et al.*, *Le edizioni Einaudi negli anni 1933–1993*, Piccola Biblioteca Einaudi, 1993

Cicioni, Mirna, *Primo Levi: Bridges of Knowledge*, Berg, Washington, DC, 1995

Ferrero, Ernesto (ed.), *Primo Levi: un antologia della critica*, Piccola Biblioteca Einaudi, 1997

—— (ed.), *Primo Levi: I racconti*, Einaudi, 1996

Gordon, Robert, *Primo Levi's Ordinary Virtues*, OUP, 2001

Grassano, Giuseppe, *Primo Levi*, La Nuova Italia, 1981

Lopez, Guido, *Se non lui, chi*, Centro di cultura ebraica della comunità israelitica di Roma, 1987

Regge, Tullio, and Levi, Primo, *Dialogo*, Princeton University Press, 1989

Rudolf, Anthony, *At an Uncertain Hour: Primo Levi's War against Oblivion*, Menard Press, 1990

Terstal, Susanna, *Primo Levi, Scritti sparsi*, 1993 (degree thesis)

Tesio, Giovanni, *Piemonte letterario dell'otto-novecento*, Bulzoni, 1991 (includes 'Primo Levi', 'Su alcune giunte e varianti di Se questo è un uomo', 'Premesse su Primo Levi poeta', and 'Primo Levi tra ordine e chaos')

—— (ed.), *Se questo è un uomo*, Einaudi, 1997, schools edition (includes Introduction and Afterword by Tesio)

CONFERENCES ON PRIMO LEVI *(in chronological order)*

Primo Levi: Il presente del passato, ed. Alberto Cavaglion, Franco Angeli, 1991 (conference held in Turin, 28–29 March 1988)

Primo Levi as Witness, ed. Piero Frassica, Casalini Libri, 1990 (conference held at Princeton University, 30 April–2 May 1989)

Primo Levi: Memoria e invenzione, ed. Giovanna Ioli, Edizioni della Biennale 'Piemonte e Letteratura', San Salvatore Monferrato, 1995 (conference held at San Salvatore Monferrato, 26–28 September 1991)

Primo Levi: La dignità dell'uomo, ed. Rosa Brambilla and Giuseppe Cacciatore, cittadella editrice, 1995 (conference held in Assisi, 20–23 November 1994)

Primo Levi: testimone e scrittore di storia, ed. Paolo Momigliano Levi and Rosanna Gorris, Giuntina, 1999 (conference held in St Vincent, Aosta, 15–16 October 1997

Al di qua del bene e del male, ed. Enrico Mattioda, Franco Angeli, 2000 (conference held in Turin, 15–16 December 1999)

On history

OF BENE VAGIENNA

Gli Amici di Bene, *Bene Vagienna: storia di una città*
—— *Notizie storiche sulla città di Bene*

OF TURIN

Bobbio, Norberto, *30 anni di storia della cultura a Torino*, Società Piemontese CRT, 1977
D'Orsi, Angelo, *Torino*, Laterza, 1987
Martellini, Giorgio, *Ritratto di città con persone*, G.C.C., Inner Wheel Club, Turin, 1986

OF ITALY

Ginsborg, Paul, *A History of Contemporary Italy, Society and Politics, 1943–1988*, Penguin, 1990

OF JEWS IN PIEDMONT

Cavaglion, Alberto, *La scuola ebraica a Torino, 1938–1943*, Pluriversa, 1993
Levi, Primo, *et al.*, *Ebrei a Torino, Ricerche per il Centenario della Sinagoga, 1884–1984*, Allemandi, Turin, 1984
Momigliano, Arnaldo, *Pagine ebraiche*, Einaudi, 1987
Ortona, Silvio, *Ortona, Della Torre, Casale Monferrato, ecc.*, unpublished monograph, May 1993

On Primo Levi's school

Annuario dell'anno scolastico 1967–68, Liceo-Ginnasio Statale 'M. D'Azeglio', Torino, Vincenzo Bona, Turin, 1968
Arici, Azelia, *Scritti e conferenze, 1939–1976*, Edizioni EDA, Turin, 1979
D'Amico, Nicola, *Eravamo compagni di banco*, Sugar Co Edizioni, 1987
Lajolo, Davide, *Pavese: Il vizio assurdo*, Rizzoli, 1984

On university

Ponzio, Giacomo, *Preparazioni, reazioni ed esperienze di Chimica Organica per l'anno academico 1939–40*, Litografia Felice Gili, Turin, 1940

On Milan, 1942–3

Della Torre, Ada, *Messaggio speciale*, Editori Riuniti, Biblioteca Giovani, 1979
Gentili Tedeschi, Eugenio, *I giochi della paura*, Le Chateau Edizioni, Aosta, 1999

On the Resistance

ANPI, Comitato provinciale di Torino, *25 April: La Resistenza in Piemonte*, Orma, 1946

Brunazzi, Marco, and Conti, Agostino (eds.), *Le formazioni Matteotti nella lotta di liberazione*, L'Arciere, Cuneo, 1986

Centro Storico della Resistenza nel Biellese, *Il Movimento di liberazione nel Biellese*, 1957

Centro Studi Piero Gobetti, *L'Anno di Ada*, 1998

Commissione Femminile dell'ANPI provinciale di Torino, *Donne piemontesi nella lotta di liberazione*, 1953

Della Torre, Ada, *Messaggio speciale*, as above

De Luna, Giovanni (ed.), *Le formazioni GL nella Resistenza*, Istituzione nazionale per la storia del movimento di liberazione in Italia, Franco Angeli, 1985

—— (ed.), *Un'amicizia partigiana, Lettere 1943–1945* [letters of Giorgio Agosti and Livio Bianco], Albert Meynier, 1990

—— (ed.), *Torino in guerra, 1940–1945*, catalogue to exhibition, Mole Antonelliana, Turin, 5 April–28 May, 1995

Favretto, Sergio, *Casale partigiana, 1943–1945*, Libertas Club, Casale Monferrato, 1977

Fiorio, Michele, *Resistenza e liberazione nella provincia di Torino, 1943–45*, Gribaudi Editore, 1993

Gay Rochat, Donatella, *La Resistenza nelle valle Valdesi*, Claudiana, Turin, 1969

Giovana, Mario, *La Resistenza in Piemonte*, 1962

Gobetti, Ada, *Diario partigiano*, Einaudi, 1956

Istituto Storico della Resistenza, Cuneo, *La guerra di liberazione 1943–45: I caduti in provincia di Cuneo*, 1989

Nicco, Roberto, *La Resistenza in Valle D'Aosta*, Istituto Storico della Resistenza in Valle D'Aosta, Musumeci Editore, 1990

Notizario Gielle, Anno II, No. 45, April–May 1948

Poma, Anello, and Perona, Gianni, *La Resistenza nel Biellese*, Istituto Storico della Resistenza in Piemonte, Guanda, 1972

Prearo, Antonio, *Terra ribelle*, Silvestrelli, 1948

Zucàro, Domenico (ed.), *Il contribuito socialista nella Resistenza in Piemonte*, Edizioni Il Grido del Popolo, Turin, 1955

On the war period

De Felice, Renzo, *Storia degli ebrei sotto il fascismo*, Einaudi, 1961 and 1993

Gilbert, Martin, *The Holocaust*, Guild Publishing, 1986

Herzer, Ivo (ed.), *The Italian Refuge*, The Catholic University of America Press, Washington, DC, 1989

Katz, Robert, *Black Sabbath: A Journey through a Crime Against Humanity*, Toronto, 1969

Mayda, Giuseppe, *Ebrei sotto Salò*, Feltrinelli, 1978

Stille, Alexander, *Benevolence and Betrayal*, Cape, 1992
Yona, Davide, and Foa, Anna, *Noi due*, Il Mulino, 1997
Zucotti, Susan, *The Italians and the Holocaust*, Peter Halban, 1987
—— *Under His Very Windows: The Vatican and the Holocaust in Italy*, Yale, 2001

On Fossoli

Bacino, Renzo, *Fossoli*, Comune di Carpi, 1961
Fergnani, Enea, *Un'uomo e tre numeri*, Speroni Editore, 1945
Gibertoni, Roberta, and Melodi, Annalisa, *Fossoli, il Museo Monumento al Deportato a Carpi*, Guide Artistiche Electa, 1997

On deportation and Auschwitz

Bravo, Anna, and Jalla, Daniele (eds.), *La vita offesa*, Franco Angeli, 1987
Cavaliere, Alberto, *I campi della morte in Germania*, Sonzogni, 1945
Cereja, F., and Mantelli, B. (eds.), *La deportazione nei campi di sterminio nazisti*, Franco Angeli, 1986
Langbein, Hermann, *Menschen in Auschwitz*, Europaverlag, Vienna, 1972 and 1987
Levi, Lazzaro, *Il Konzentrations Lager*, 1945, unpublished diary (held in CDEC)
Lingens Reiner, Ella, *Prisoners of Fear*, Gollancz, 1948
Nissim, Luciana, and Lewinska, Pelagia, *Donne contro il mostro*, Vincenzo Ramelli Editore, Turin, 1946
Picciotto Fargion, Liliana, *Il libro della memoria*, Mursia, 1991
Saralvo, Corrado, *Più morti più spazio, tempo di Auschwitz*, Baldini & Castoldi, 1969
Steinberg, Paul, *Speak You Also*, trans. Linda Coverdale with Bill Ford, Allen Lane, The Penguin Press, 2000
Tedeschi, Giuliana, *There is a Place on Earth*, trans. Tim Parks, Lime Tree, 1993
Tibaldi, Italo, *Compagni di viaggio*, Franco Angeli, 1994
Weidenreich, Ruth, *Un medico nel campo di Auschwitz*, Istituto Storico della Resistenza in Toscana, Florence, 1960

CONFERENCES ON DEPORTATION *(in chronological order)*
Il dovere di testimoniare, Franco Angeli, 1984 (conference held in Turin, 28–9 October 1983)
Spostamenti di popolazione e deportazioni in Europa, 1939–45, Capelli Editore, 1987 (conference held in Carpi, 1985)
Storia vissuta, Franco Angeli, 1988 (conference held in Turin, 21–22 November 1986)
La conferenza di Wannsee, Franco Angeli, 1988 (Round Table held in Turin, 1987)
Il ritorno dai lager, ed. A. Cavaglion, Franco Angeli, 1993 (conference held in Turin, 23 November 1991)

On Franco Antonicelli and De Silva

Bobbio, Norberto, *Franco Antonicelli: Ricordi e testimonianze*, Bollati Boringhieri
Centro Studi Piero Gobetti, *Scritti su Franco Antonicelli*, 1975

On Einaudi

Cesari, Severino, *Colloquio con Giulio Einaudi*, Theoria, 1991

On the 'anni di piombo'

Consiglio regionale del Piemonte, *Una Regione contro il terrorismo, 1969–1978*, 1979
Rivoira, Maria Cecila, *La partecipazione dei genitori al rinnovamento della scuola: il Cogidas di Torino* (unpublished degree thesis, academic year 1992–3)

On negationism and revisionism

Kaes, Anton, *From Hitler to Heimat*, Harvard University Press, 1989
Lipstadt, Deborah, *Denying the Holocaust*, Plume, 1994

Other selected books

Accati, Luisa, *Il matrimonio di Raffaele Albanese*, Anabasi, 1994
Améry, Jean, *At the Mind's Limits*, trans. Sidney Rosenfeld and Stella R. Rosenfeld, Indiana University Press, 1980
Bellonci, Maria, *Io e il Premio Strega*, Oscar Mondadori, 1987
Berardi, Roberto, *Un Balilla negli Anni Trenta*, L'Arciere, Cuneo, 1994
Biagi, Enzo, *1935 e dintorni*, Milan, 1982
Bruck, Edith, *Lettera alla madre*, Garzanti, 1988
Calvino, Italo, *I libri degli altri, Lettere 1947–1981*, ed. Giovanni Tesio, Einaudi, 1991
Cases, Cesare, *Patrie lettere*, Einaudi, 1987 (contains 'Levi racconta l'assurdo' [1948], 'Difesa di "un" cretino' [1967] and 'Levi ripensa l'assurdo' [1986])
Cavaglion, Alberto (ed.), *Moralità armata: studi su Emanuele Artom (1915–1944)*, Collana dell'Istituto Storico della Resistenza in Piemonte, Franco Angeli, 1993
Chiesura, Giorgio, *Devozione*, Mondadori, 1990
Circolo della Stampa, *Dieci anni del premio del Circolo della Stampa*, 3 December 1990
—— *Premio del Circolo della Stampa*, 1984–5
—— *Premio del Circolo della Stampa*, 1993–4
Feldman, Ruth, *Birthmark*, Jewish Writers Chapbook Series No. 9, Cross-Cultural Communications, Merrick, New York, 1993 (contains 'A Gray Day in Treviso')
Foa, Vittorio, *Il cavallo e la torre*, Einaudi, 1991
Giudice, Gaspare, *Luigi Pirandello*, UTET, Turin, 1963, trans. and abridged by Alastair Hamilton as *Pirandello: A Biography*, Oxford University Press, 1975
Holroyd, Michael, *Works on Paper*, Little, Brown, 2002
Johnson, Paul, *A History of the Jews*, Weidenfeld & Nicolson, 1987

Levi, Paolo, *Il filo della memoria*, Rizzoli, 1984
Levi, Riccardo, *Ricordi politici di un ingegnere*, Vangelista, 1981
Levi Montalcini, Rita, *L'Elogio dell'imperfezione*, Garzanti, 1990
—— *Senz'olio contro vento*, Baldini & Castoldi, 1996
Macagno, Mario, *Cucire un motore*, Leone & Griffa, 1992
Pirandello, Luigi, *Opere*, Arnaldo Mondadori, 1956
Revelli, Nuto, *La guerra dei poveri*, Einaudi, 1953 and 1990
Rigoni Stern, Mario, *Il sergente nella neve*, Einaudi, 1962 and 1993
Roth, Philip, *Patrimony*, Simon & Schuster, 1991
Schlink, Bernhard, *The Reader*, trans. Carol Brown Janeway, Phoenix, 1998
Sinclair, John D., *Dante, The Divine Comedy*: Vol. 1, *Inferno*, trans. and comment by John D. Sinclair, Oxford University Press, New York, 1961
Wiesenthal, Simon, *The Sunflower*, 1969

B. Interviews, articles, talks, etc.

For reasons of space, I have not included any reviews of Primo Levi's books, or any newspaper articles more than fifty years old. Only the main interview on Primo Levi's translation of Kafka is included, and only the main articles on his death.

The key interviews are in *Conversazioni e Interviste* and its English translation, *The Voice of Memory*. I give the *Voice of Memory* title, except where the interview appears only in the Italian original:

Balbi, Rosanna, '*If Not Now, When?*', 1982
Boeri, Enrico, 'Chemistry', 1983
Bruck, Edith, 'Jewish, Up to a Point', 1976
Caccamo De Luca, Rita, and Olagnero, Manuela, 'Primo Levi', 1984
Calcagno, Giorgio, '*The Drowned and the Saved*', 1986
De Melis, Federico, 'An Assault Called Franz Kafka', 1983
De Rienzo, Giorgio, and Gagliano, Ernesto, '*The Periodic Table*', 1975
Di Caro, Roberto, 'The Essential and the Superfluous', 1987
Fadini, Edoardo, 'Science Fiction I: *Storie naturali* (1966–1971)', 1966
Giacomoni, Silvia, '*The Wrench*', 1979
Grassano, Giuseppe, 'A Conversation with Primo Levi', 1979
Greer, Germaine, 'Germaine Greer Talks to Primo Levi', 1985
Grieco, Giuseppe, 'God and I', 1983
Kleiner, Barbara, 'Ritratto della dignità e della sua mancanza negli uomini', 1986
Lamberti, Luca, 'Science Fiction II: *Vizio di forma* (1971)', 1971
Luce, Dina, 'Il suono e la mente', 1982
Nascimbeni, Giulio, 'Levi: l'ora incerta della poesia', 1984
Pansa, Giacomo, 'Primo Levi: Begin Should Go', 1982
Paoletti, Pier Maria, '*The Truce*', 1963
Papuzzi, Alberto, 'Mountaineering', 1984
Roth, Philip, 'A Man Saved by his Skills', 1986

Rudolf, Anthony, 'Primo Levi in London', 1986
Segre, Giorgio, 'Intervista a Primo Levi', 1979
Sodi, Risa, 'Un intervista a Primo Levi', 1987
Spadi, Milva, 'Capire e far capire', 1986
Tesio, Giovanni, 'Turin', 1980
—— 'Credo che il mio destino profondo sia la spaccatura', 1981
'The Little Theatre of Memory', RAI radio, 1982
Thomson, Ian, 'Primo Levi in Conversation', 1987
Toaff, Daniele, and Ascarelli, Emanuele, 'Return to Auschwitz', 1982
Valabrega, Paola, 'Interview for a Dissertation', 1981
Vigevani, Marco, 'Words, Memory, Hope', 1984

Other selected interviews, articles and talks

Alterocca, Bona, 'Fantascienza in TV con Primo Levi', *La Stampa*, 16 February 1977
Amendola, Anna, and Belardelli, Giorgio, 'Il mestiere di raccontare', 20–23 April and 3 June 1974, RAI Canale 1
Amsallem, Daniela, 'Primo Levi, juif de retour', *Les Nouveaux Cahiers*, No. 114, Autumn 1993
Angelino, Luigi, 'Primo Levi a Casale', *Il Monferrato*, 12 July 1975
Arian Levi, Giorgina, ' "La tregua" alla radio', *Ha Keillah*, April 1978
—— 'L'antieroe di Primo Levi', *Ha Keillah*, April 1979
Arosio, Enrico, 'Primo Levi', *Vogue* Italia, No. 426, September 1985
Baglino, Andrea, interview in *Corriere della Sera*, 7 July 1982
Bailey, Paul, Introduction to *If This is a Man/The Truce*, Abacus paperback, 1987
—— Introduction to *The Drowned and the Saved*, Michael Joseph, 1988, and Abacus paperback, 1991
Barberis, Marco, interview in *Avanti*, 19 October 1971
Baudino, Mario, in *Speciale La Tregua*, *La Stampa*, 9 February 1997
Bianucci, Piero, interviews in *Tuttolibri*, *La Stampa*, 26 October 1985 and in *Stampa Sera*, 20 October 1986
Bocca, Giorgio, 'Conversazione con Primo Levi', 'Prima pagina', RAI Canale 5, 13 January 1985
Bonura, Giuseppe, 'La parola come lavoro', *Avvenire*, 9 February 1984
Calcagno, Giorgio, interview in *La Stampa*, 12 June 1982
—— in *Speciale La Tregua*, *La Stampa*, 9 February 1997
Cases, Cesare, 'Ricordo di Primo Levi', in *Tre narratori*, ed. Gianfranco Folena, Liviana Editrice
Cattabiani, Alfredo, in *Il Tempo*, 21 January 1979
Cavaglion, Alberto, 'Senza scomodare Augusto Monti e Giorgio Pasquali', *Belfagor*, 31 July 1994
Chiesa, Alfredo, interview in *Paese Sera*, 12 July 1963
Ciairano, Silvia, private taped interview, 19 November 1975
Colombo, Arturo, 'Primo Levi a Acqui, quella sera', *Nuova Antologia*, July–September 1987

Colombo, Gian Franco, 'Il Primo poeta', *Il Sabato*, December 1984

Dallaporta, Nico, 'Mon amitié avec Primo Levi', unpublished talk given at Primo Levi conference, Paris, 1999

D'Angeli, Gabriella, 'Il sonno della ragione genera mostri', in *Famiglia cristiana*, 27 November 1966

Davico Bonino, Guido, 'Primo Levi, Torino, il teatro', *Piemonte vivo*, No. 3, 1991

Dawan, Daniela, interview in *Bollettino della Comunità Israelitica di Milano*, June 1986

Deaglio, Enrico, interview in *Lotta Continua*, 30 December 1978

Del Buono, Oreste, 'Questo ebreo me lo sono inventato', *L'Europeo*, 5 July 1982

De Luna, Giovanni, interview in *Lotta Continua*, 10 November 198[2?]

—— 'No, caro Bocca', *Italia oggi*, 13 April 1987

De Rienzo, Giorgio, 'In un alambicco quanta poesia', *Famiglia cristiana*, 20 July 1975

Di Caro, Roberto, unpublished transcript of 'Il necessario e il superfluo'/'La fatica di scrivere', 1987

D'Orsi, Angelo, private taped interview, 1983/5

Eberstadt, Fernanda, 'Reading Primo Levi', *Commentary*, October 1985

Fabiani, Enzo, 'Un tatuaggio rivela il dramma dello scrittore', *Gente*, No. 38, 20 September 1963

Feldman, Ruth, 'Remembering Primo Levi', unpublished talk, 1990

—— 'Primo Levi's Poetry: Darkness and Light', in Susan R. Tarrow (ed.), *Reason and Light: Essays on Primo Levi*, Center for International Studies, Cornell University, 1990

Ferrero, Ernesto, 'Intervista a Primo Levi', *Terra nostra*, 12 September 1963

—— 'Primo Levi scrittore', in *Notizario dell'Istituto Storico della Resistenza in Cuneo e provincia*, No. 32, December 1985

—— 'Bellow, passaporto per il successo', in *Speciale La Tregua, La Stampa*, 9 February 1997

Frassica, Pietro, 'Primo Levi: eroe, antieroe o *alter ego*?' in *Primo Levi: Memoria e invenzione*, ed. Giovanna Ioli, Edizione della Biennale 'Piemonte e Letteratura', 1995

Galante Garrone, Alessandro, 'Il grido di Primo Levi', *La Stampa*, 28 September 1968 and *Nuova Antologia*, July–September 1987

—— in *Speciale La Tregua, La Stampa*, 9 February 1997

Garibba, Nicola, 'Primo Levi il testimone', *Karnenu*, Anno XV, No. 3, March–April 1988 (from April 1979)

Gentili Tedeschi, Eugenio, 'La Resistenza ha cominciato in Via Roma', *Ha Keillah*, No. 3, February 1978

—— 'Primo Levi, parcours de la laïcité à la Résistance', talk given at Primo Levi conference, Paris, 1999

Gerosa, Guido, 'Parole di un libro in cambio di Santa Lucia', *Il Giorno*, 24 November 1981

G.L.L., 'Serata con Primo Levi', *Bollettino della Comunità Israelitica di Milano*, date unknown

Goria, Giulio, 'Sono diventato ebreo quasi per forza', *Paese Sera*, 3 May 1982

Gozzi, Alberto, 'Conversazione con Primo Levi', 'Lo specchio del cielo', RAI, 13 January 1985

Granà, Graziella, 'Incontro con Primo Levi', *Controcampo*, Anno VIII, No. 6, June 1981, translated as 'Encounter with Primo Levi' in *The Voice of Memory*
—— unpublished part of above interview

Grassano, Giuseppe, complete typescript of 'Conversazione con Primo Levi', 1979

Guadagni, Annamaria, 'Primo Levi', *Unità, Cultura*, 21 February 1993

Guidetti Serra, Bianca, unpublished memorial talk, 21 May 1987

Hughes, H. Stuart, 'Two Captives Called Levi', in *Prisoners of Hope*, Harvard University Press, 1983

Ivaldi, Filippo, 'Se questa è vita!', *La Stampa*, 2 May 1978

Jesurum, Stefano, 'Primo Levi', in *Essere ebrei in Italia*, Longanesi, 1987
—— 'Si è offuscata la luce', *Oggi*, 14 July 1982

Leo Club, Cuneo, 'Incontro con Primo Levi', November 1975 (transcript)

Lerner, Gad, 'Torinesissimo Primo Levi', *La Stampa*, 7 February 1997

Levi Della Torre, Stefano, 'Eredità di Primo Levi', in *Rassegna Mensile d'Israele*, Vol. XVI, Nos. 2–3, May–December 1989
—— 'Il bene e il male alla prova di Auschwitz', *Ha Keillah*, April 1997

Levi Montalcini, Rita, 'Primo', in *L'Annuario della Fondazione Schlesinger*, 1993

Liberatori, Andrea, 'Primo Levi: "La mia America, i miei anni in fabbrica"', *Unità*, 25 September 1986

Lombardi, Enrico, 'Primo Levi: Conversazione con Enrico Lombardi', Radio Svizzera Italia, 3 June 1985 (transcript)

Lopez, Guido, in *Shalom* No. 2, February 1982

Lucarini, Paola, 'Intervista a Primo Levi', *Firme nostre*, Anno XXV, No. 100, September–December 1983

Luti, G., in 'Il novecento', Vol. XI/2 of *Storia letteraria d'Italia*, Casa Editrice Dr Francesco Vallardi, 1993

Malgaroli, Felice, 'Primo Levi: un modo di essere uomo', in *Mensile dei metalmeccanici*, April 1992

Mancinelli, Laura, 'Cosí ho inventato Gedale', *Unità*, 8 July 1982
—— 'Un "curioso" della vita (con amore)', *Il Secolo XIX*, 23 April 1985

Manzini, Giorgio, 'Elogio del libero lavoro', *Paese Sera*, 11 December 1978

Manzini, Raffaella, and Salvarani, Brunetto, 'Essere ebrei senze religione, intervista a Primo Levi', *QOL*, No. 4, September–October 1986

Martellini, Giorgio, 'Io sono un centauro', *Il Gazzettino*, 12 June 1984

Mayda, Giuseppe, 'Il poeta triste del Lager', *Resistenza*, Anno XVII, No. 5, May 1963

Mendel, David, 'Autobiography in Primo Levi', unpublished talk given at the Italian Cultural Institute, London, 4 April 1995
—— 'On Primo Levi's *If This is a Man*', unpublished essay

Messina, Nuccio, 'Vivere per far rivivere', *La Discussione*, 4 May 1987

Miccinesi, Mario, interviews with Primo Levi in *Uomini e libri*, No. 18, 1969, No. 63, March–April 1977, No. 72, January–February 1979, No. 91, November–December 1982, and No. 112, January–February 1987 (last one in *The Voice of Memory*)

Milani, Gianni, 'Al chimico va stretta la memoria del lager', *Piemonte VIP*, Anno III, No. 3, March 1986

Montedison *Progetto Cultura*, Anno 2, No. 6, May 1987

Monticelli, Gabriella, 'Quel treno da Badenheim', *Epoca*, 10 October 1981

—— 'Dov'è finita la terra promessa?', *Epoca*, 17 September 1982

Motola, Gabriel, 'Primo Levi: His Life and Death', *European Judaism*, Vol. 21, No. 2, 1988, Conference Issue

Newbury, Erica Scroppo, 'Primo Levi, Personal Reflections', in the journal of the Edinburgh Jewish Literary Society, February 1993

Nocerino, Vanna, 'Primo Levi', unsourced offprint, probably 1979

Olivero, Ernesto, 'Dialogando con Primo Levi', *Progetto*, August–September 1980

Orengo, Nico, 'Come ho pubblicato il mio primo libro', *Tuttolibri*, *La Stampa*, 1 June 1985

—— 'Natalia Ginzburg: nessuno "censurò" Primo Levi', *Tuttolibri*, *La Stampa*, 12 June 1987

Ortona, Silvio, 'Primo Levi: un ebreo giusto', *Ha Keillah*, April 1987

—— 'Primo Levi: la ragione, la vita, la responsabilità collettiva', *Ha Keillah*, 3 June 1997

Pacchioni, Giovanni, 'Segrete avventure di eroi involontari', *Il Globo*, 13 June 1982

Paladini, Carlo, 'A colloquio con Primo Levi', *Lavoro, criminalità, alienazione mentale*, ed. P. Sorcinelli, Il Lavoro Editoriale, 1987

Papuzzi, Alberto, 'Huxley, la violinista e il sibarita', *La Stampa*, 24 July 1994

—— 'Noi, vecchi ragazzi del partito d'azione', *La Stampa*, 13 July 1991

'Pesaro: il dibattito', 5 May 1986 (transcript)

Pivano, Fernanda, 'Il mio compagno Levi ed io', *Corriere della Sera*, 18 April 1987

—— 'Quella misteriosa bocciatura in italiano', *Elle*, No. 7, July 1994

Poli, Francesco, 'Tino Faussone, la storia di un operaio specializzato', *Quotidiano dei lavoratori*, 28 February 1979

Poli, Gabriella, 'Primo Levi, l'alfabeto della chimica', *Tuttolibri*, *La Stampa*, 4 December 1976

—— 'Primo Levi, communicatore schivo', unpublished talk given at Round Table, Turin, 3 June 1993

—— *La Stampa*, 13 July 1971

—— 'La memoria come impegno e come lotta', in *Primo Levi: testimone e scrittore di storia*, citadella editore, 1995

Portesi, Renato, 'Primo Levi: un chimico, un impiantista . . . un uomo', *Chimica & Industria*, May 2001

Radford, Tim, 'Lifeline from Auschwitz', *Guardian*, 17 April 1986

Rosenfeld, Alvin, 'Primo Levi: Questions and Answers at Indiana University', *Midstream*, April 1986

Ross, Peter, 'Primo Levi Revisited', unpublished talk delivered to University of the Third Age, London, 1998

Samuel, Jean, 'Primo Levi: A Companion, a Friend, a Witness', unpublished talk given at Primo Levi conference, University of Pennsylvania, 1997

Segantini, Edoardo, 'Un muro ben fatto, ecco la felicità', *Unità*, 1 May 1984

Serri, Mirella, in *Speciale La Tregua*, *La Stampa*, 9 February 1997

Silori, 'Le domande di Silori: a Primo Levi', *Settimo Giorno*, 19 October 1963

Sodi, Risa, 'Primo Levi: A Last Talk', *Present Tense*, Vol. 15, No. 4, May–June 1988

Spriano, Paolo, 'L'avventura di Primo Levi', *Unità*, 14 July 1963

Tarrow, Susan, Introduction to *Reason and Light: Essays on Primo Levi*, ed. Susan R. Tarrow, Center for International Studies, Cornell University, 1990

Terni, Paolo, 'Pomeriggio musicale', RAI radio, 13–17 February 1984

Tesio, Giovanni, 'Nego di essere un gran lettore di classici e di romanzi', *Nuova società*, 11 July 1981

—— interview in *Nuovasocietà*, 18 June 1983

—— 'A proposito di una biografica mancata', in *Primo Levi: Memoria e invenzione*, ed. Giovanna Ioli, Edizione della Biennale 'Piemonte e Letteratura', 1995

—— 'Tutta l'odissea in un quaderno', *Speciale La Tregua*, *La Stampa*, 9 February 1997

—— and Tesio, Silvia, private taped interview, January 1986

Toscani, Claudio, 'Incontro con Primo Levi', *Ragguaglio librario*, March 1972

Unione Culturale di Torino, 'Incontro con Primo Levi', 4 June 1975 (transcript)

Vacca, Roberto, 'Un western dalla Russia a Milano', *Il Giorno*, 18 May 1982

Vergani, Leonardo, 'Parla Primo Levi, il numero 174517', *Corriere della Sera*, 20 May 1979

Verna, Marina, 'Primo Levi, la chimica della parola', source uncertain, 1982

—— interview in *Gazzetta del popolo*, 6 September 1982

'Very Important Piemontesi', RAI radio, 21 May 1981

Viglino, Mario, private interview for school thesis, April 1978

Woolf, Stuart, 'Primo Levi: Drowning and Surviving', *Jewish Quarterly*, Vol. 34, No. 127, 1987

—— 'Primo Levi e il mondo anglosassone', in *Il presente del passato*, ed. Alberto Cavaglion, Franco Angeli, 1991

—— 'Primo Levi's Sense of History', *Journal of Modern Italian Studies*, Vol. 3, No. 3, 1998

On Turin

Torino come eravamo, Supplement to *La Stampa*, 20 January 1978

Trovare Torino, Supplement to *La Stampa*, 3 November 1987

'Torino e dintorni', in *Tuttocittà*, Turin guide, 1991

On Jews in Piedmont and Italy

Arnaldi, Roberto, 'Immagini di un passato ebraico nel Monregalese', in *I quaderni de 'La Ghisleriana'*, 1982

Colombo, Dino, 'Il ghetto di Mondovì', in *Rassegna Mensile d'Israele*, April 1968

Diena, Paola, 'Il Giudeo-Piemontese', degree thesis, University of Turin, 1979–80

Foa, Salvatore, 'Ebrei a Torino', *Lunario Israelitico 5962*, F. Servi, Turin, 1932

Jesurum, Stefano, 'Comunità Italia', in *Gli Speciali della Sette*, undated, 1995

On university

Borello, Enzo, *et al.* in *L'Ateneo, Notizario dell'Università degli Studi di Torino*, Anno XIII, No. 3, May/June 1997

Marino, Gianlorenzo, 'Primo Levi, chimico e scrittore', *CNS (La Chimica nella Scuola)*, No. 4, September–October 1993

On mountaineering

Mila, Massimo, 'Alpinismo come cultura', *Il Ponte*, Nos. 8–9, 1947

On Balangero

Articles in *La Stampa*, 1 and 3 October 1995

On Milan, 1942–3

Guadagni, Annamaria, 'Prima del grande buio', in *Unità, Diario della settimana*, 2–7 April 1997

Ortona, Silvio, 'Disgrazia (Monte)', unpublished essay, 28 June 1983

On the Resistance

Campiglio, Mario, in *Bollettino Storico per la provincia di Novara*, Anno LXXXV, No. 1, 1994, pp. 20–21

Gentili Tedeschi, Eugenio, 'La Resistenza a Cogne', unpublished essay, June 1997

—— 'L'Estate di Cogne', unpublished essay

—— 'Esodo 1944', unpublished essay

—— 'Sulle note di Polvere di Stelle', *Bollettino della Comunità Ebraica*, undated offprint

Levreri, Cesare, 'I ribelli di Casale in Val d'Ayas', in *La Provincia di Alessandria, Rivista dell'amministrazione provinciale*, Anno XXVII, No. 1, January–March 1980, pp. 21-7

Momigliano, Paolo, 'L'Esperienza della Resistenza nella vita e nell'opera di Primo Levi', in *Primo Levi: testimone e scrittore di storia*, Giuntina, 1999

Mussa, Carlo, and Rolli, Giorgio, 'I partigiani della Val Pellice', *Nuovi quaderni di G & L*, Nos. 5–6, January–August 1945

Nicco, Roberto, 'Aspetti e problemi della Resistenza Valdostana al suo esordio', paper delivered at Resistance conference, Aosta, 1988

Toscano, Aldo, in *Bollettino storico per la provincia di Novara*, Anno LXXXIV, No. 1, 1993, pp. 9–12

'1943–1983: La memoria, i giorni, le parole', *Notizie della Regione Piemonte, Speciale Resistanza*, 1983

On Fossoli

Barabas, Silvio, 'Fossoli (February 16–22 [1944]): Recollections', unpublished essay, 1995

Levi, Primo, Deposition for the trial of Friedrich Bosshammer, 1971, in *La Stampa*, 25 April 2001

Lops, Carmine, 'L'Organizzazione del campo [Fossoli]', in *Albori della Nuova Europa*, Vol. II, Part II, Ch. 2, 'Fossoli–Auschwitz'

On deportation and Auschwitz

ANED interviews with Primo Levi (27 January 1983), Leonardo De Benedetti (30 September 1982) and Gianni Aliberti (12 and 14 May 1982). All held by ANED, Turin; Primo Levi's published in *Rassegna Mensile d'Israele*, Nos. 2–3, May–December 1987 and in *The Voice of Memory*; Leonardo's held among his papers at the Jewish Library, Turin

Anissimov, Miryam, 'Maurice Reznik: dans le même Block à Auschwitz', in *Les Nouveaux Cahiers*, No. 114, Autumn 1993

Arian Levi, Giorgina, 'Emilia Levi', in *Unità*, date unrecorded

Carpi, Daniele, 'The Development of Fascist Antisemitism in Italy', in Gutman and Rothkirscher (eds.), *The Catastrophe of European Jewry*, Yad Vashem, 1976

D'Orsi, Angelo, 'Poeta nella bufera: il dramma di un ebreo fascista cuneese', offprint, source unrecorded

Moscati, Aldo, in *La speranza tradita, Antologia della deportazione politica toscana, 1943–1945*, Pacini Editore, Pisa, 1992

Nissim, Davide, 'L'Aiuto agli Israeliti nel Biellese', document held by CDEC, Milan

Reznik, Maurice, 'La marche de la mort des déportés', French text by Henri Bulawko, in *Le Monde Juif*, No. 77, January–March 1985, held by the Centre de Documentation Juive Contemporaine, Paris

Samuel, Jean, 'L'homme face à l'univers concentrationnaire', unpublished talk given at Colmar, 1 April 1985

—— interview with Susan Tarrow, in *Forum Italicum*, Vol. 28, No. 1, Spring 1994

—— 'Littérature, science et savoir à Auschwitz', unpublished talk given at Primo Levi conference, Strasbourg, 1999

Tibaldi, Italo, 'Primo Levi e i suoi "compagni di viaggio": ricostruzione del trasporto da fossoli ad Auschwitz', in *Primo Levi: testimone e scrittore di storia*, Giuntina, 1999

Vaccarino, Giorgio, 'Nuove fonte sull'imperialismo nazista: la I G Farben e "il nuovo ordine"', in *Italia contemporanea*, No. 169, December 1987

Vita Finzi, Gisella, 'I Levi: una famiglia amica scomparsa nel nulla', in *Bollettino della comunità israelitica di Milano*, December 1989

Waitz, Robert, 'Auschwitz III (Monowitz)', in 'De l'Université aux Camps de Concentration, Témoignages Strasbourgeois', in *Les Belles Lettres*, 1947

On Franco Antonicelli and De Silva

Mazzoleni, Oscar, 'Antonicelli e la De Silva: l'editore d'avanguardia', in *Il coraggio della parola*, ed. E. Mannari, Fondazione Franco Antonicelli, Belforte Editore Libraio, 1996

Zorzi, Renzo, 'Insieme alla "De Silva" e oltre', in *Franco Antonicelli, 'dell'impegno culturale'*, Provincia di Pavia, Assessorato ai servizi sociali, educativi e culturali

On Duco Avigliana

Colombo, Luciano, 'Ricordo di Primo Levi', in *Pitture e vernici*, No. 4, April 1996

—— letter to *Il Giornale*, 15 April 1987

On Einaudi

Einaudi, Giulio, 'Primo Levi e la casa editrice Einaudi', in *Primo Levi as Witness*, ed. Piero Frassica, Casalini libri, 1990 (Princeton conference, 1989); English translation (in typescript) by Susan Ezdinli and Guido Mascagni

On others

ON EMANUELE ARTOM

Ha Tikwa, Rome, November 1960

Treves, Benvenuta, 'Emanuele Artom (1915–1944)', *Eco dell'educazione ebraica*, No. 7, April 1955

ON ALBERTO DALLA VOLTA

Tedeschi, Massimo, 'Ebrei, l'onta dimenticata', *Bresciaoggi*, 10 August 1996

—— 'L'Olocausto bussò a casa mia' (interview with Paolo Dalla Volta), *Bresciaoggi*, 14 August 1996

ON HANS ENGERT

La Stampa, 25 November 1981

ON BIANCA GUIDETTI SERRA

Guidetti Serra, Bianca, 'Minima personalia', *Belfagor*, 31 July 1971

ON LUCIANA NISSIM

Guadagni, Annamaria, 'Luciana Nissim: La memoria del bene', in *Unità, Diario della settimana*, 26 February–4 March 1997

ON LORENZO PERONE

Lenta, Carlo, in *La Fedeltà*, 3 February 1982

ON LELLO PERUGIA

Jesurum, Stefano, 'Lello Perugia', in *Essere ebrei in Italia*, Longanesi, 1987
Mecucci, Gabriella, in *Unità*, 3 September 1992
Tas, Luciano, 'Per questo Primo si è suicidato', *Shalom*, No. 5, April 1988

ON HEINZ RIEDT

Calcagno, Giorgio, in *La Stampa*, 15 April 1987
Papuzzi, Alberto, interview with Heinz Riedt, *La Stampa*, 1 April 1995
—— article on Heinz Riedt, *La Stampa*, 4 January 1997
Venturi, Alfredo, 'Primo Levi riveduto e corretto in Germania', *La Stampa*, 14 January 1989

On the *'anni di piombo'*

'14 anni d'impegno del Cogidas di Torino', in *Sisifo II*, September 1987 (review of the Istituto Gramsci Piemontese, Turin)
'L'Indagine sull'attività neofascista in Piemonte', in *Notizie del Consiglio Regionale del Piemonte*, Anno IV, No. 4, April 1975, Special Supplement

On Primo Levi's death

Assalto, Maurizio, 'Toaff: Primo Levi mi annunciò il suicidio', in *La Stampa*, 12 April 1997
Atlas, James, 'The Survivor's Suicide', in *Vanity Fair*, 51, No. 1, January 1988
Calcagno, Giorgio, 'Se questo è un suicidio', *La Stampa*, 25 May 1999
Camon, Ferdinando, in *Il Giorno*, 25 April 1987
—— 'Incontri e dialoghi con Primo Levi', undated offprint for *Le Monde* and *La Nación*
Crucillà, Maria Celeste, 'Ora è nel vento con loro', *Oggi*, 29 April 1987
Gambetta, Diego, 'Gli ultimi momenti di Primo Levi', in *Belfagor*, 31 May 1999, trans. as 'Primo Levi's Last Moments', in *Boston Review*, Summer 1999
Gandus, Valeria, and Rossetti, Gian Paolo, 'Finalmente fuori dal Lager', in *Panorama*, 26 April 1987
James, Clive, 'Last Will and Testament', *New Yorker*, 23 May 1988
Lazzarini, Giorgio, 'Auschwitz ha ucciso Primo Levi 40 anni dopo', in *Gente*, 24 April 1987
Levi Montalcini, Rita, 'Primo Levi non si è suicidato', in *Unità*, 25 April 1987
—— 'Non si è suicidato', in *Panorama*, 3 May 1987
Liberatori, Andrea, in *Unità*, 13 April 1987
Mack, Jeremy, 'Primo Levi: His Last Days', unpublished paper delivered at Primo Levi conference, University of Pennsylvania, 1997
Macklin, Elizabeth, 'Talk of the Town', *New Yorker*, 11 May 1987
Mendel, David, 'Requiem for a Quiet Man of Courage', in *Sunday Telegraph*, 6 September 1991
Ozick, Cynthia, 'Primo Levi's Suicide Note', in *Metaphor and Memory*, Knopf, 1989

Stille, Alexander, 'Primo Levi: Reconciling the Man and the Writer', in *New York Times Book Review*, 5 July 1987

Styron, William, 'Why Primo Levi Need Not Have Died', *New York Times*, 19 December 1988

Thomson, Ian, 'Death of a Survivor', in *Sunday Times Books*, 30 April 1987

C. Television programmes

ITALIAN *(in chronological order)*

RAI, 'Interview on the Liberation', 25 January 1975

TG (Telegiornale) 'Dossier' interview, 1979

TG2, 'Studio aperto' interview, 17 May 1982

Toaff, Daniele, 'Ritorno ad Auschwitz', *Sorgente di vita*, RAI 2, 25 April 1983, translated as 'Return to Auschwitz' in *The Voice of Memory*, and transcript in English on the Internet

TG1 interview, 19 September 1985

TG2, 'Focus' interview, 22 December 1986

Lerner, Gad, 'Primo Levi', RAI, April 1997

NON-ITALIAN *(in chronological order)*

Primo Levi, *Bookmark*, BBC2, 1985 (repeated, with a new introduction by A. Alvarez, in '25 Great Writers', 1996)

Primo Levi by Netty Rosenfeld, VPRO (Holland), 1988

Zu ungeweiser stunde ['At an uncertain hour'] by Nina Fischer, Deutsche Rundfunk (Germany), 1989

The Memory of the Offence by Denys Blakeway, BBC2, 1992

Index